W9-AFJ-747

HOCKEY HALL OF FAME

# BOOK

## OF

# PLAYERS

# A FIREFLY BOOK

Published by Firefly Books Ltd. 2018
Copyright © 2018 Firefly Books Ltd.
Text copyright © 2018 Hockey Hall of Fame
Photographs © as listed on page 4

All rights reserved. No part of this publication may be reproduced, stored in a retrieval system, or transmitted in any form or by any means, electronic, mechanical, photocopying, recording or otherwise, without the prior written permission of the Publisher.

FIRST PRINTING

Library of Congress Control Number: 2018943204

Library and Archives Canada Cataloguing in Publication
    Hockey Hall of Fame book of players / edited by Steve Cameron.—3rd edition.

Includes index.
"Hockey Hall of Fame".
ISBN 978-0-228-10137-6 (softcover)

    1. Hockey players--History--Miscellanea.  2. Hockey players--Pictorial works.
3. Hockey--History--Miscellanea.  4. Hockey Hall of Fame--Collectibles--Pictorial works.
I. Cameron, Steve, 1981-, editor  II. Hockey Hall of Fame

GV847.H635 2018                    796.962'64                    C2018-902763-0

Published in the United States by
Firefly Books (U.S.) Inc.
P.O. Box 1338, Ellicott Station
Buffalo, New York 14205

Published in Canada by
Firefly Books Ltd.
50 Staples Avenue, Unit 1
Richmond Hill, Ontario L4B 0A7

Cover and interior design: Gareth Lind, Lind Design
Research for the first edition: James Duplacey and Eric Zweig
Additional research and writing for the third edition: Eric Zweig

Printed in China

We acknowledge the financial support of the Government of Canada.

# HOCKEY HALL OF FAME

# BOOK OF PLAYERS

Edited by Steve Cameron · Third Edition

FIREFLY BOOKS

# Hockey League Abbreviations

AAHL Alberta Amateur Hockey League
AHA Amateur Hockey Association
AHAC Amateur Hockey Association of Canada
AHL American Hockey League
Al-Cup Allan Cup
ANDHL Alberta National Defense Hockey League
APHL Alberta Professional Hockey League
ASHL Alberta Senior Hockey League
BCHL British Columbia Hockey League
BCBHL British Columbia Boundary Hockey League
Big-4 Big-4 Hockey League
CAHL Canadian Amateur Hockey League
Can-Am Canadian-American Hockey League
Can-Pro Canadian Professional Hockey League
CCSHL Central Canada Senior Hockey League
CHA Canadian Hockey Association
CHL Central Hockey League
CIHU Canadian Intercollegiate Hockey Union
CJHL Central Junior A Hockey League
COWHL Central Ontario Women's Hockey League
EAHL Eastern Amateur Hockey League
ECAC Eastern College Athletic Conference
ECAHA Eastern Canada Amateur Hockey Association
ECHA Eastern Canada Hockey Association

ECJHL Edmonton City Junior League
EHL Eastern Hockey League
EPHL Eastern Professional Hockey League
Exhib Exhibition Games
FAHL Federal Amateur Hockey League
High-NH High School – New Hampshire
IAHL International-American Hockey League
IHL International Pro Hockey League (1903–1907)
IHL International Hockey League (1945–2001 and 2007–10)
IPAHU Inter-Provincial Amateur Hockey Union
Ivy Ivy League Collegiate Hockey Division
M-Cup Memorial Cup
MCHL Montreal City Hockey League
MCJHL Montreal City Junior Hockey League
MHL Manitoba Hockey League
MHL-Pro Manitoba Professional Hockey League
MHL-Sr. Manitoba Senior Hockey League
MIHA Maritime Intermediate Hockey Association
MJHL Manitoba Junior Hockey League
MNWHA Manitoba Northwest Hockey Association
MNWHA-Int. Manitoba Northwest Intermediate Hockey Association
MPHL Maritime Professional Hockey League
MTBHL Manitoba-Thunder Bay Hockey League
Nat-Team National Team
NBHL Nickel Belt Hockey League

NHA National Hockey Association
NHL National Hockey League
NOHA Northern Ontario Hockey Association
NOHL New Ontario Hockey League
NOJHL Northern Ontario Junior Hockey League
NWHL North West Hockey League
NWHL National Women's Hockey League
OCAA Ontario Colleges Athletic Association
OCHL Ottawa City Hockey League
OCJHL Ottawa City Junior Hockey League
OHA Ontario Hockey Association
OHA-Int Ontario Intermediate Hockey Association
OHA-Jr. Ontario Junior Hockey Association
OHA-Sr. Ontario Senior Hockey Association
OMJHL Ontario Major Junior Hockey League
OPHL Ontario Professional Hockey League
OWHA Ontario Women's Hockey Association
Pacific Rim Pacific Rim Championships
PCHA Pacific Coast Hockey Association
PCHL Pacific Coast Hockey League
QJHL Quebec Junior Hockey League
QMJHL Quebec Major Junior Hockey League
QSHL Quebec Senior Hockey League

QSSF Quebec Student Sports Federation
Sask-Pro Saskatchewan Professional Hockey League
SSHL Saskatchewan Senior Hockey League
St-Cup Stanley Cup Challenge Series
TBJHL Thunder Bay Junior Hockey League
TPHL Temiskaming Professional Hockey League
TBSHL Thunder Bay Senior Hockey League
TMHL Toronto Mercantile Hockey League
UOVHL Upper Ottawa Valley Hockey League
USAHA United States Amateur Hockey Association
USHL United States Hockey League
WCAHA Western Canada Amateur Hockey Association
WCHL Western Canada Hockey League
WCJHL Western Canada Junior Hockey League
WCSHL West Coast Senior Hockey League
WHA World Hockey Association
WHL Western Hockey League
West-P Western Playoffs
WOHA Western Ontario Hockey Association
WPHL Western Pennsylvania Hockey League
W-S World Series of Hockey
WSrHL Winnipeg Senior Hockey League
WWC Women's World Championships

## Photo Credits

All photographs © Hockey Hall of Fame unless otherwise noted.

**Hockey Hall of Fame**
Graphic Artists 17 36, 37, 47, 77, 86, 108, 109, 115, 127, 160, 190, 199, 255, 258, 272, 282, 283, 286, 289, 302, 304, 331, 336, 362, 363, 365, 368; Paul Bereswill 6, 88, 97, 100, 102, 125, 129, 159, 168, 175, 178, 187, 202, 203, 205, 228, 240, 257, 268, 273, 279, 340, 356; Michael Burns Sr. 213; DiMaggio-Kalish 42; HHOF 20, 28, 30 34, 35, 38, 44, 52, 54, 55, 58, 59, 70, 71, 73, 74, 80, 81, 92, 94, 103, 104, 105, 106, 119, 121, 122, 123, 134, 135, 136, 137, 143, 148, 152, 157, 161, 162, 163, 170, 171, 176, 180, 182, 183, 191, 198, 209, 210, 216, 217, 222, 223, 224, 231, 234, 235, 236, 239, 244, 245, 246, 247,

248, 249, 259, 260, 267, 275, 276, 284, 294, 298, 301, 306, 308, 313, 316, 319, 334, 342, 343, 344, 346, 347, 349, 361, 366, 377, 369, 372, 374, 376, 377, 378, 379, 380, 381, 382, 384, 385, 386, 387; Imperial Oil–Turofsky 14, 15, 16, 18, 19, 21, 24, 39, 45, 46, 49, 50, 51, 53, 60, 64, 65, 68, 69, 72, 78, 79, 84, 107, 113, 140, 150, 155, 169, 172, 173, 179, 184, 185, 188, 189, 192, 193, 206, 212, 221, 227, 229, 230, 233, 237, 238, 242, 243, 250, 251, 254, 261, 273, 285, 287, 290, 291, 293, 295, 296, 299, 305, 311, 321, 322, 323, 328, 329, 335, 337, 338, 352, 354, 355, 358, 359; Fred Keenan 281; David Klutho 196; Doug MacLellan 56, 111, 124, 132, 138, 146, 164, 207, 330, 333; Matthew Manor 25, 83, 99, 117, 252, 269, 307, 327, 353, 388–89; Mecca 13, 141, 174, 350; O-Pee-Chee 11, 118, 153, 186, 256, 264, 277, 324, 332; Portnoy 26, 29, 82, 85, 87, 139, 149, 158, 200, 204, 232, 266, 280, 288, 330, 351, 360, 364;

Frank Prazak 9B, 21, 23, 48, 62, 76, 110, 126, 142, 147, 181, 194, 201, 265, 297, 309, 320, 326, 339, 348; Chris Relke 90, 177, 208, 215; James Rice 40, 63, 112, 120, 130, 151, 154, 274, 312, 318, 325, 345, 383; Andre Ringuette 8B, 300; Hal Roth 27, 43, 75, 95, 101, 131, 195, 253, 303; Dave Sandford 8T, 9T, 12, 32, 33, 41, 57, 61, 89, 91, 93, 96, 98, 114, 128, 133, 144, 145, 156, 165, 197, 211, 214, 220, 225, 226, 241, 270, 271, 272, 278, 292, 317, 341, 357; Le Studio du Hockey 22

Cover (L-R): Top: Bereswill, Graphic Artists; Middle: Le Studio du Hockey, Imperial–Oil Turofsky; Bottom: Portnoy, Bereswill, HHOF, Imperial–Oil Turofsky.
Back Cover: Frank Prazak

**Other Sources**
373: © G.G. Bain/Shorpy Inc.
375: Wikimedia commons

Wayne Gretzky during his most prodigious years in Edmonton. His arrival in the NHL changed the game of hockey forever.

# Introduction

**H**ockey is a spellbinding game to witness. It is rough-and-tumble and skilled and beautiful all at once. Watching elite hockey is like looking into a fire—the continuous flow of the action rarely stops long enough for the viewer to look away. The goalies, defensemen, forwards, referees, coaches and spectators—all the moving parts of the game—blend into a seamless wave of defensive stands and offensive opportunities.

But, as in every other sport, there are a few who break away from the pack, demand to be noticed and completely master the game. Because hockey is a team sport that requires cooperation and selfless play, a single player who can take over the game is the rare exception, and when they appear, they invariably grab the spotlight. Those few dominant players, like magicians, make what every other player toils to accomplish during the push and pull of the game look easy.

The very best of the best, the players who break the mold and stand out from all the rest, are honored with induction into the Hockey Hall of Fame. Of the thousands of people who have played the sport at an elite level, these are the chosen few who, through their sublime skill and their immeasurable character, leadership and drive, have managed to rise above the rest. They are the ambassadors of hockey.

Among them are virtuosos whose novel approach to the game forever changed how it is played. There are the great leaders who pushed their teams to even greater successes, and there are the consistently great performers who found a way, night in and night out—on poor teams and on great ones—to raise the bar for themselves and everyone else.

All of the players in the Hockey Hall of Fame exemplify what it takes to be great. Some have played in All-Star games, others have won individual awards and others have won championships—and for many of the men and women presented here, they have done it all. But the greatest contribution these players have made to the sport might simply be that their on-ice exploits captured our imaginations. The men and women in the following pages have become our heroes and heroines, and as a result they have spawned generation after generation of new hockey fans and, subsequently, hockey stars, each one a little different from the rest.

Please enjoy this collection of the best of the best—the players of the Hockey Hall of Fame.

—Steve Cameron, editor

# Class of 2018

## 30

# Martin Brodeur 2018

**NO. RETIRED BY NEW JERSEY**

**New Jersey Devils**
**St. Louis Blues**

Played 21 NHL seasons
from 1993–2004,
2005–2015

### AWARDS
Calder Memorial
Trophy (1994)

Vezina Trophy (2003,
2004, 2007, 2008)

William M. Jennings
Trophy (1997, 1998,
2003, 2004, 2010)

Stanley Cup (1994–95,
1999–2000, 2002–03)

### ALL-STAR SELECTIONS
All-Rookie Team (1994)

First All-Star Team
Goaltender (2003,
2004, 2007)

Second All-Star Team
Goaltender (1997,
1998, 2006, 2008)

### INTERNATIONAL AWARDS
Gold Medal: Winter
Olympics (2002, 2010)

World Cup (2004)

Silver Medal: World
Championships
(1996, 2005)

## 16

RIGHT WING

# Jayna Hefford 2018

**Brampton Thunder**
**Canadian National Team**
**Mississauga Chiefs**
**Toronto Varsity Blues**

Played 18 elite amateur
seasons from 1996–2014

### INTERNATIONAL AWARDS
Gold Medal: Winter
Olympics (2002,
2006, 2010, 2014)

Silver Medal: Winter
Olympics (1998)

Gold Medal: World
Championships (1997,
1999, 2000, 2001,
2004, 2007, 2012)

Silver Medal: World
Championships (2005,
2008, 2009, 2011, 2013)

# Class of 2018

## 2018 Martin St-Louis

**26**

First All-Star Team Right Wing (2004)
Second All-Star Team Right Wing (2007, 2010, 2011, 2013)

**INTERNATIONAL AWARDS**
Gold Medal: Winter Olympics (2014)
World Cup (2004)
Silver Medal: World Championships (2008, 2009)

NO. RETIRED BY TAMPA BAY

Calgary Flames
New York Rangers
Tampa Bay Lightning

Played 16 NHL seasons from 1998–2004, 2005–2015

**AWARDS**
Art Ross Trophy (2004, 2013)
Hart Memorial Trophy (2004)
Ted Lindsay Award* (2004)
Lady Byng Memorial Trophy (2010, 2011, 2013)
Stanley Cup (2003–04)
* Known as the Lester B. Pearson Award from 1971 to 2009

---

**LEFT WING**

**15**

## 2018 Alexander Yakushev

**INTERNATIONAL AWARDS**
Summit Series (1974)
Gold Medal: Winter Olympics (1972, 1976)
Gold Medal: World Championships (1967, 1969, 1970, 1973, 1974, 1975, 1979)
Silver Medal: World Championships (1972, 1976)
Bronze Medal: World Championships (1977)

ALTERNATES
**11**

Kapfenberger SV
Spartak Moscow

Played 20 seasons of European elite hockey from 1963–1983

| | | | | | |
|---|---|---|---|---|---|
| AVE NDREYCHUK | BILL BARBER | DOUG BENTLEY | TOE BLAKE | JOHN BUCYK | ROY CONACHER |
| UN OOK | RUSTY CRAWFORD | ALEX DELVECCHIO | CY DENNENY | DICK DUFF | WOODY DUMART |
| OB GAINEY | JIMMY GARDNER | CLARK GILLIES | MOOSE GOHEEN | MICHEL GOULET | DANIELLE GOYETTE |
| GEORGE HAY | SYD HOWE | BOBBY HULL | BUSHER JACKSON | AURÈLE JOLIAT | PAUL KARIYA |
| VALERI KHARLAMOV | HERBIE LEWIS | TED LINDSAY | FRANK MAHOVLICH | DICKIE MOORE | BERT OLMSTEAD |

# LEFT WING

Dave Andreychuk 12
Bill Barber 13
Doug Bentley 14
Toe Blake 15
John Bucyk 17
Roy Conacher 18
Bun Cook 19
Rusty Crawford 20
Alex Delvecchio 21
Cy Denneny 22
Dick Duff 23
Woody Dumart 24
Bob Gainey 26
Jimmy Gardner 28
Clark Gillies 29
Moose Goheen 30
Michel Goulet 31
Danielle Goyette 32
George Hay 34
Syd Howe 35
Bobby Hull 36
Busher Jackson 38

Aurèle Joliat 40
Paul Kariya 41
Valeri Kharlamov 42
Herbie Lewis 44
Ted Lindsay 45
Frank Mahovlich 47
Dickie Moore 49
Bert Olmstead 50
Lynn Patrick 51
Tommy Phillips 52
Bob Pulford 53
George Richardson 54
Gordon Roberts 55
← *Luc Robitaille* 56
Blair Russel 58
Fred Scanlan 59
Sweeney Schriner 60
Brendan Shanahan 60
Steve Shutt 62
Babe Siebert 63
Harry E. Watson 64
Harry P. Watson 65

# 25

# Dave Andreychuk 2017

## 14 · 23 · 29
## 38 · 52

Boston Bruins
Buffalo Sabres
Colorado Avalanche
New Jersey Devils
Tampa Bay Lightning
Toronto Maple Leafs

Shoots: Right

Height: 6'-4"

Weight: 220 lbs.

Born: September 29, 1963: Hamilton, Ontario

Drafted by the Buffalo Sabres 16th overall in 1982

Played 23 NHL seasons from 1982–2004, 2005–06

Stats: See Page 390

"It started in junior. I realized [that the front of the net is] where my bread and butter was going to be. Not a lot of pretty goals, to be honest. Not sure if [I ever scored] a highlight-reel goal."

**AWARDS**

Stanley Cup (2003–04)

**INTERNATIONAL AWARDS**

Bronze Medal: World Championships (1986)

- Ranks 14th in NHL history through the 2017–18 season with 640 goals; Ranks first all-time with 274 power-play goals.

- Led the NHL with 28 power-play goals in 1991–92 and with 32 power-play goals in 1992–93, which is the second-highest single season total in NHL history behind Tim Kerr's 34 in 1985–86

- Was never voted to a First or Second All-Star Team but finished third in voting at left wing in 1992–93 and 1993–94

- Represented Buffalo in the NHL All-Star Game in 1990 and Toronto in 1994

- His 53 goals for Toronto in 1993–94 represent the second-highest single season total in franchise history, while his 368 goals in 837 games for Buffalo rank him third on the Sabres' all-time list behind Gilbert Perreault (512) and Rick Martin (382)

- Was captain of the Tampa Bay Lightning from 2002–03 through 2005–06

- Played 22 seasons before winning the Stanley Cup with the Lightning in 2003–04, equaling an NHL mark with Ray Bourque for the longest career before winning a championship

- Earned a bronze medal with Team Canada at the 1983 World Junior Championships during the same season in which he made his NHL debut

# 1990 Bill Barber

# 7

> "You have to have a passion to play hockey and you have to express that passion for the people who come to watch you when you're playing."

NO. RETIRED BY
PHILADELPHIA

**Philadelphia Flyers**

Shoots: Left

Height: 6'

Weight: 195 lbs.

Born: July 11, 1952;
Callander, Ontario

Drafted by the
Philadelphia Flyers
seventh overall in 1972

Played 12 NHL seasons
from 1972–84

Stats: See page 390

- Shares NHL record (with Wayne Presley) for most short-handed goals in single playoff series (3), accomplished in 1980

- Shares NHL record for most short-handed goals in single playoff season (3), accomplished in 1980

- Holds Philadelphia Flyers team records for career goals (420) and regular season points by a left winger (883)

- Played amateur hockey with North Bay Trappers (1967–69); Kitchener Rangers (1969–72)

- Played minor pro hockey with Richmond Robins (1972–73)

- Led NHL in short-handed goals (6) in 1978–79; led NHL in shots on goal (380) in 1975–76

- Played in NHL All-Star Game (1975, 1976, 1978, 1980, 1981, 1982)

- Led World Hockey Championships in goals (8) in 1982

- World Championships First All-Star Team Left Wing (1982)

- Coached Hershey Bears (1984–85, 1995–96); coached Philadelphia Phantoms (1996–2000)

- Coached Calder Cup–winning Philadelphia Phantoms (1998)

- Served as assistant coach of Philadelphia Flyers (1985–88)

- Served as Philadelphia Flyers Director of Pro Scouting (1988–95)

- Coached Philadelphia Flyers (2000–02)

**AWARDS**

Jack Adams Award (2001)

Stanley Cup (1973–74, 1974–75)

**ALL-STAR SELECTIONS**

First All-Star Team
Left Wing (1976)

Second All-Star Team
Left Wing (1979, 1981)

**INTERNATIONAL AWARDS**

Canada Cup (1976)

Bronze Medal: World
Championships (1982)

# 7

# Doug Bentley 1964

ALTERNATES

## 14 · 19 · 6

**Chicago Black Hawks
New York Rangers**

Alternate Position: C

Shoots: Left

Height: 5'-8"

Weight: 145 lbs.

Born: September 3, 1916:
Delisle, Saskatchewan

Died:
November 24, 1972:
Saskatoon,
Saskatchewan

Played 13 NHL seasons
from 1939–44,
1945–52, 1953–54

Stats: See page 391

"I thought about quitting, but you know, I've never liked the word quit."

**AWARDS**

NHL Scoring
Leader (1943)

**ALL-STAR
SELECTIONS**

First All-Star Team Left
Wing (1943, 1944, 1947)

Second All-Star Team
Center (1949)

- Played amateur hockey with Delisle Tigers (1932–33); Saskatoon Wesleys (1933–34); Regina Victorias (1934–35); Moose Jaw Millers (1935–38); Drumheller Miners (1938–39)

- Led Southern Saskatchewan Senior League in assists (19) and points (37) in 1936–37; led S-SSHL in playoff assists (8) and points (14) in 1936–37

- Led ASHL in playoff goals (7) in 1938–39

- ASHL First All-Star Team Left Wing (1938–39)

- Member of the Chicago's famed Pony Line with brother Max Bentley and Bill Mosienko

- Member of the NHL's first all-brother line with Max and Reggie during the 1942–43 season

- Led NHL in goals in 1942–43 (33) and 1943–44 (38)

- Led NHL in assists in 1947–48 (37) and 1948–49 (43)

- Missed entire 1944–45 season after being given permission to stay home and tend to family farm by Canadian Armed Forces officials, September 1944

- Played in NHL All-Star Game (1947, 1948, 1949, 1950, 1951)

- Served as captain of Chicago Black Hawks (1942–44)

- Traded to N.Y. Rangers by Chicago for cash, June 30, 1953

- Served as Player/Coach with Saskatoon Quakers (1951–56)

# Toe Blake

1966

**6**

ALTERNATES

**16 · 21 · 8**

**Montreal Canadiens
Montreal Maroons**

Shoots: Left

Height: 5'-10"

Weight: 165 lbs.

Born: August 21, 1912:
Victoria Mines, Ontario

Died: May 17, 1995:
Montreal, Quebec

Played 14 NHL seasons
from 1934–48

Stats: See page 391

"Toe Blake hated to lose so much that he made us the same way."

— Defenseman J.C. Trembley on Blake as a coach

- Played amateur hockey with Cochrane Dunlops (1929–30); Sudbury Cub Wolves (1930–32); Sudbury CIL (1930–31); Sudbury Wolves (1930–31); Falconbridge Falcons (1931–32); Hamilton Tigers (1932–35)

- Played minor pro hockey with Providence Reds (1935–36); Buffalo Bisons (1948–49); Valleyfield Braves (1949–51)

- Led NOJHL in goals (5) in 1931–32; led NBHL in goals (8) in 1931–32

- Led NHL in points (47) in 1938–39; led NHL playoffs in assists (11) and points (18) in 1943–44; led NHL playoffs in goals (7) in 1945–46; led NHL playoffs in assists (7) in 1946–47

- Finished among NHL top-5 in goals in 1938–39 (24); 1944–45 (29) and 1945–46 (29)

- Member of Montreal Canadiens' famed Punch Line with Maurice Richard and Elmer Lach

- Served as captain of Montreal Canadiens (1940–47, 1947–48)

- Scored Stanley Cup–winning overtime goal in Montreal's 5–4 victory over Chicago Black Hawks, April 13, 1944; scored Stanley Cup–winning goal in Montreal's 6–3 victory over Boston Bruins, April 9, 1946

- Coached Houston Huskies to USHL championship (1947–48); coached Valleyfield Braves to Alexander Cup championship (1950–51); coached Montreal Canadiens to Stanley Cup championship (1955–60, 1964–65, 1965–66, 1967–68)

- Ranks second in Stanley Cup championships won by a coach (8)

AWARDS

NHL Scoring Leader (1939)

Hart Memorial Trophy (1939)

Lady Byng Memorial Trophy (1946)

Stanley Cup (1934–35, 1943–44, 1945–46)

ALL-STAR SELECTIONS

First All-Star Team Left Wing (1939, 1940, 1945)

Second All-Star Team Left Wing (1938, 1946)

Blake continued on page 16

**15**

# A Great Player Becomes a Legendary Coach

**Toe Blake talks with Maurice Richard and Jean Béliveau in the mid-1950s.**

Hector "Toe" Blake—all-star left winger, key component of the Punch Line and once the NHL's most valuable player—was hobbled by a Bill Juzda hit late in the third period of a game against the New York Rangers on January 10, 1948. Blake was carted from the ice, and it was later revealed that his awkward fall into the boards broke the fibula and fractured the tibia in his right ankle. The injuries forced him to miss the remainder of the season. Blake, 35 at the time, finished out the year as coach of the Houston Huskies in the United States Hockey League and was offered the chance to coach Montreal's American Hockey League affiliate in Buffalo the following season. He accepted, forever stepping away from life as an NHL player. Thus began his second hockey career, one that arguably eclipsed his first.

After coaching the Buffalo Bisons, Blake coached Valleyfield of the Quebec Senior Hockey League from 1949–50 until 1954–55. That summer, general manager Frank Selke invited Blake to coach the Canadiens. Selke needed someone who could handle the mercurial Maurice Richard. Blake fit the bill perfectly—he was bilingual, had coaching and playing experience and was a friend and former teammate of Richard's. It was a perfect match.

The Canadiens captured the Stanley Cup in each of Blake's first five seasons as coach. So strong were his teams, in fact, that the NHL, in an attempt to quell Montreal's dominance, altered a rule before the 1956–57 season. Previous to this, players receiving two-minute minor penalties would serve the entirety of their penalty, and scoring multiple goals on a power play was permitted—a staple of the Montreal attack. Because of this, the rule was changed to allow the penalized player to return to the ice should the opposition score a goal.

On May 11, 1968, having just won his 11th Stanley Cup (three as a player and eight as a coach), Blake stated the he'd had enough, claiming "the pressure is too much." In 914 regular season games, the Canadiens under Blake had won 500 contests, tied 159 and lost 255. In 119 playoff games, Blake-led charges went 82-37.

# 1981 John Bucyk

**9**

"I played physical but clean hockey. Most people think that the only reason a player wins the Lady Byng is because he is gentlemanly, but I had the ability to play physical and not draw penalties. I contributed offensively and stayed out of the penalty box."

NO. RETIRED BY BOSTON

ALTERNATE
**20**

Boston Bruins
Detroit Red Wings

Shoots: Left
Height: 6'
Weight: 215 lbs.
Born: May 12, 1935: Edmonton, Alberta
Played 23 NHL seasons from 1955–78
Stats: See page 391

- Holds record as oldest NHL player to score 50 goals in regular season, established in 1970–71
- Holds Boston Bruins team record for career goals (545)
- Holds Boston Bruins team record for consecutive games played (418), accomplihed 1969–75
- Played amateur hockey with Edmonton Maple Leafs (1949–52); Edmonton Oil Kings (1951–54)
- Played minor pro hockey with Edmonton Flyers (1953–56)
- Named WHL Rookie of the Year (1955)
- Traded to Boston by Detroit with cash for Terry Sawchuk, June 10, 1957

- Registered 1,000th career NHL point in Boston's 8–3 victory over Detroit Red Wings, November 9, 1972; recorded 500th career NHL goal in Boston's 3–2 victory over St. Louis Blues, October 30, 1975
- Served as captain of Boston Bruins (1966–67, 1973–77)
- Member of Boston Bruins' famed Uke Line with Vic Stasiuk and Bronco Horvath
- Played in NHL All-Star Game (1955, 1963, 1964, 1965, 1968, 1970, 1971)
- Led NHL in shooting percentage in 1970–71 (22.7%), 1972–73 (23.8%) and 1973–74 (22.3%)

AWARDS
Lady Byng Memorial Trophy (1971, 1974)
Lester Patrick Trophy (1977)
Stanley Cup (1969–70, 1971–72)

ALL-STAR SELECTIONS
First All-Star Team Left Wing (1971)
Second All-Star Team Left Wing (1968)

# 9

## LEFT WING

# Roy Conacher 1998

ALTERNATES

## 11 · 8

Boston Bruins
Chicago Black Hawks
Detroit Red Wings

Shoots: Left

Height: 6'-2"

Weight: 175 lbs.

Born: October 5, 1916:
Toronto, Ontario

Died: December 29, 1984:
Victoria, British Columbia

Played 11 NHL seasons
from 1938–42, 1945–52

Stats: See page 392

"He was a man self-effacing, who believed that merit should speak for itself. My father became, at least for one season, certainly the best in the world at what he did. He was driven to that pinnacle by a deeply-rooted motivation — a desire for perfection."

— Roy Conacher's son, speaking at his father's posthumous induction into the Hockey Hall of Fame

AWARDS
Art Ross Trophy (1949)
Stanley Cup (1938–39, 1940–41)

ALL-STAR
SELECTIONS
First All-Star Team
Left Wing (1949)

- First rookie in NHL history in lead league in goals (1938–39)

- Played amateur hockey with West Toronto Nationals (1933–36); Toronto Dominions (1936–37); Kirkland Lake Wright-Hargreaves (1937–38)

- Led OHA-Jr. in goals (12) in 1935–36

- Signed as a free agent by Boston, October 23, 1938

- Member of Memorial Cup–winning West Toronto Nationals (1935–36); recorded 8 goals and 13 points in Memorial Cup playoffs

- Played with Saskatoon RCAF (1942–43); Dartmouth RCAF (1943–45); Millward RCAF (1944–45) during World War II

- Led Halifax City League in goals (9) in 1943–44

- Traded to Detroit by Boston for Joe Carveth, June 25, 1946

- Led NHL in goals (26) in 1938–39; led NHL in points (68) in 1948–49

- Finished second in NHL goals in 1940–41 (24), 1941–42 (24), 1946–47 (30) and 1948–49 (26)

- Scored Stanley Cup–winning goal in Boston's 3–1 victory over Toronto Maple Leafs, April 16, 1939

- Brother of Hall of Fame member Charlie Conacher, who played in NHL with Toronto, N.Y. Americans and Detroit from 1929–41; brother of Hall of Fame member Lionel Conacher, who played in NHL with Pittsburgh Pirates, N.Y. Americans, Montreal Maroons and Chicago from 1925–37

- Coached Midland Greenshirts (1953–54)

# 1995 Bun Cook

# 6

ALTERNATES:

# 5 · 8 · 10

**Boston Bruins**
**New York Rangers**
**Saskatoon Crescents**

Shoots: Left

Height: 5'-11"

Weight: 180 lbs.

Born: September 18,
1903; Kingston, Ontario

Died: March 19, 1988;
Kingston, Ontario

Played 13 professional
seasons from 1924–37

Stats: See page 392

"Although we didn't
get paid much, it
was a lot of fun. We
played with intensity.
All in all, hockey has
been real good to me."

- Played amateur hockey with Sault Ste. Marie Greyhounds (1921–24)

- Earned nickname "Bun" when a journalist noted that he was "quick as a bunny"

- Signed as a free agent by Saskatoon Crescents (WCHL), September 20, 1924

- Traded to N.Y. Rangers by Saskatoon (WHL) for cash, October 18, 1926

- Assisted on first goal in N.Y. Rangers' franchise history in N.Y. Rangers' 1–0 victory over Montreal Maroons, November 16, 1926

- Starred for the N.Y. Rangers with brother Bill Cook at right wing and Frank Boucher at center on what is considered one of the NHL's first great forward lines

- Line scored every goal for the N.Y. Rangers in the Stanley Cup final against Montreal Maroons in 1928

- Traded to Boston by N.Y. Rangers for cash, September 10, 1936

- IAHL First All-Star Team Coach (1939, 1940)

- AHL First All-Star Team Coach (1941, 1942, 1944, 1945)

- Coached Providence Reds (1937–43); coached Cleveland Barons (1943–56); coached Sault Ste. Marie Greyhounds (1956–57)

- Won Calder Cup (AHL Championship) as coach (1938, 1940, 1945, 1948, 1953, 1954)

- Credited with helping pioneer the drop pass and the slap shot

**AWARDS**
Stanley Cup
(1927–28, 1932–33)

**ALL-STAR SELECTIONS**
Second All-Star Team
Left Wing (1931)

## LEFT WING

# 8 Rusty Crawford 1962

ALTERNATE:
## 5

Calgary Tigers
Ottawa Senators
Quebec Bulldogs
Prince Albert Mintos
Saskatoon Crescents
Saskatoon Hoo-Hoos
Saskatoon Sheiks
Saskatoon Wholesalers
Saskatoon/
Moose Jaw Crescents
Toronto Arenas
Vancouver Maroons

Shoots: Left

Height: 5'-11"

Weight: 165 lbs.

Born: November 7, 1885:
Cardinal, Ontario

Died: December 19,
1971: Prince Albert,
Saskatchewan

Played 16 professional
and elite amateur
seasons from 1910–26

Stats: See page 393

AWARDS
Stanley Cup
(1912–13, 1917–18)

"Rusty Crawford played a hard effective game while he was on, showing lots of speed and aggressiveness."
— *Quebec Daily Telegraph*, January 19, 1913

- Played amateur hockey with Montreal Montagnards (1907–08); Newington Ontarios (1908–09); Prince Albert Mintos (1909–11); Saskatoon Hoo Hoos (1911–12); Saskatoon Wholesalers (1911–12); Prince Albert Mintos (1930–31)

- Sask-Pro First All-Star Team Left Wing (1912)

- Played minor pro hockey with Minneapolis Millers (1926–30)

- Both his Prince Albert (1911) and Saskatoon (1912) teams challenged for the Stanley Cup, but were eliminated from competition before facing the defending champions

- Signed as a free agent by Quebec Bulldogs, December 12, 1912

- Renowned for his speed and longevity, he played competitive hockey until the age of 45

- Quebec Bulldogs were already Stanley Cup champions when he signed with them and helped them defend their title in 1912–13

- Signed as a free agent by Toronto, February 9, 1918; signed as a free agent by Ottawa, December 2, 1918

- Signed as a free agent by Saskatoon (WCHL), November 12, 1921; traded to Calgary (WCHL) by Saskatoon (WCHL) for cash, February 10, 1923; traded to Vancouver (WHL) by Calgary (WHL) for Fern Headley, November 3, 1925

# Alex Delvecchio

**1977**

**10**

NO. RETIRED BY DETROIT

ALTERNATES

**17 · 15**

"When I first came up ... You always played to win at home. And if you thought you could get away with a tie on the road, you were glad to get it."

**Detroit Red Wings**

Alternate Position: C

Shoots: Left

Height: 6'

Weight: 195 lbs.

Born: December 4, 1932: Fort William, Ontario

Played 24 NHL seasons from 1950–74

Stats: See page 393

- Played amateur hockey with Fort William Hurricane-Rangers (1946–50); Port Arthur West End Bruins (1948–49); Oshawa Generals (1950–51)
- Led TBJHL in penalty minutes (53) in 1948–49; led TBJHL in assists (20) in 1949–50; led OHA-Jr. in assists (62) in 1950–51
- Served as captain of Detroit Red Wings (1962–74)
- Holds Detroit team record for consecutive games played (548), established from 1956–64
- Ranks 14th in NHL career games played (1,550)
- Led NHL in short-handed goals (4) in 1965–66
- Finished among NHL top-5 in points in 1952–53 (59) and 1964–65 (67)

- Finished among NHL top-5 in assists in 1952–53 (43), 1961–62 (43), 1964–65 (42), 1967–68 (48) and 1968–69 (58)
- Number retired by Detroit on November 10, 1991
- Played in NHL All-Star Game (1953, 1954, 1955, 1956, 1957, 1958, 1959, 1961, 1962, 1963, 1964, 1965, 1967)
- Nicknamed "Fats" because of his full, round face
- Registered 1,000th career NHL point in Detroit's 6–3 victory over L.A. Kings, February 16, 1969
- Coached Detroit Red Wings (1973–75, 1975–76, 1976–77)
- One of six Hall of Famers (with Sid Abel, Doug Bentley, Dit Clapper, Neil Colville and Mark Messier) to be selected as an NHL All-Star at two different positions

**AWARDS**

Lady Byng Memorial Trophy (1959, 1966, 1969)

Lester Patrick Trophy (1974)

Stanley Cup (1951–52, 1953–54, 1954–55)

**ALL-STAR SELECTIONS**

Second All-Star Team Center (1953)

Second All-Star Team Left Wing (1959)

# 5 Cy Denneny 1959

ALTERNATES

## 6 · 10 · 16

Boston Bruins
Ottawa Senators
Toronto Blueshirts
Toronto Shamrocks

Shoots: Left
Height: 5'-7"
Weight: 168 lbs.
Born: December 23, 1891:
Farrow's Point, Ontario
Died: September 9,
1970: Ottawa, Ontario
Played 15 professional
seasons from 1914–29
Stats: See page 394

"When I was a rookie, a lad had to earn his berth on a pro club the hard way. They slammed me down at every opportunity and really gave me the business. But, after that, I was on my way."

AWARDS
NHL Scoring
Leader (1924)
Stanley Cup (1919–1920,
1920–21, 1922–23,
1926–27, 1928–29)

- Held NHL record for career goals (247) and career points (336); goals record surpassed by Howie Morenz in 1933–34; points record surpassed by Morenz in 1931–32

- Played amateur hockey with Cornwall Internationals (1910–12); Russell Athletics (1912–13); Cobalt O'Brien Mines (1913–14); Russell H.C. (1914–15)

- One of the first players to experiment with a curved stick, using hot water to shape and bend the blade

- Nicknamed "The Cornwall Colt" because of his tremendous speed and feisty manner

- Assistant coach for Boston Bruins upon winning their first Stanley Cup in franchise history (1929)

- Served as NHL on-ice official (1929–31)

- Led NHL in goals (22) and points (24) in 1923–24; led NHL in assists in 1917–18 (10) and 1924–25 (14)

- Fifth player in NHL history to score six goals in a single game in Ottawa Senators' 12–5 victory over Hamilton Tigers, March 7, 1921

- Scored Stanley Cup–winning goal in Ottawa's 3–1 victory over Boston Bruins, April 13, 1927

- Coached Ottawa Senators (1932–33)

- Brother of Corb Denneny, who played in NHL with Toronto Arenas, Toronto St. Pats, Hamilton Tigers and Chicago from 1917–28

- Denneny brothers combined to score 473 goals in pro hockey, the top total by a brother duo in the pre-World War II era

# 2006 Dick Duff

# 9

> "The thing that I always kept to myself was that when the best players were playing for the best prize [the Stanley Cup], I could compete with them all. When the end of the year was coming around, they wanted me there for the playoffs ... I just wanted to be good at the end when it counted."

**ALTERNATES**

## 17 · 20 · 8
## 7 · 24

Buffalo Sabres
Los Angeles Kings
Montreal Canadiens
New York Rangers
Toronto Maple Leafs

Shoots: Left

Height: 5'-9"

Weight: 166 lbs.

Born: February 18, 1936: Kirkland Lake, Ontario

Played 18 NHL seasons from 1954–72

Stats: See page 394

- Holds NHL record for scoring fastest two goals (1:08) from the start of a playoff game, accomplished in Toronto's 4–2 victory over Detroit, April 9, 1963

- Played amateur hockey with St. Michael's Buzzers (1952–53); St. Michael's Majors (1952–55)

- One of only six players in NHL history (with Red Kelly, Frank Mahovlich, Bryan Trottier, Patrick Roy and Larry Murphy) to win two or more Stanley Cup championships with two- or-more teams

- Played in NHL All-Star Game (1956, 1957, 1958, 1962, 1963, 1965, 1967)

- Scored Stanley Cup–winning goal in Toronto's 2–1 victory over Chicago Black Hawks, April 22, 1962

- Traded to N.Y. Rangers by Toronto with Bob Nevin, Rod Seiling, Arnie Brown, and Bill Collins for Andy Bathgate and Don McKenney, February 22, 1964

- Traded to Montreal by N.Y. Rangers with Dave McComb for Bill Hicke and the loan of Jean-Guy Morissette for remainder of 1964–65 season, December 22, 1964

- Led NHL in game-winning goals (8) in 1967–68; led NHL in shooting percentage (22.5%) in 1967–68

- Coached Toronto Maple Leafs (1979–80)

- Served as assistant coach of Toronto Maple Leafs (1979–81)

**AWARDS**

Stanley Cup (1961–62, 1962–63, 1964–65, 1965–66, 1967–68, 1968–69)

23

# 14

# Woody Dumart 1992

**ALTERNATE**
## 10

**Boston Bruins**

Shoots: Left

Height: 6'

Weight: 190 lbs.

Born: December 23,
1916: Berlin, Ontario

Died: October 20,
2001: Needham,
Massachusetts

Played 16 NHL seasons
from 1935–42, 1945–54

Stats: See page 395

> "He used to kid me a lot that I couldn't see out of my left eye because, of course, Woody was on the left side."
>
> — Milt Schmidt, on his Kraut Line teammate

**AWARDS**
Stanley Cup
(1938–39, 1940–41)

**ALL-STAR
SELECTIONS**
Second All-Star Team
Left Wing (1940,
1941, 1947)

- Played amateur hockey with Kitchener Empires (1933–34); Kitchener Greenshirts (1934–35)

- Led OHA-Jr. playoffs in assists (3) in 1933–34

- Led OHA-Jr. in points (28) in 1934–35

- Played with Ottawa RCAF (1941–43) and Millward RCAF (1942–43) during World War II

- Member of the Allan Cup–winning Ottawa RCAF Flyers (1942), scoring 14 goals in 13 Allan Cup playoff games

- Signed as a free agent by Boston Bruins, October 9, 1935

- Played in NHL All-Star Game (1947, 1948)

- Member of Boston's famed Kraut Line with Milt Schmidt and Bobby Bauer

- Providence Reds coach Albert "Battleship" Leduc originally labeled the Bruins' trio "The Sauerkraut Line" in reference to their German ancestry

- Renowned for his checking and defensive ability, he "shadowed" Gordie Howe during the Boston-Detroit semi-finals in 1953 and held the scoring champion to two goals as Boston won the series

- Nicknamed "Porky"

- Finished second in NHL goals (22) in 1939–40; finished second in NHL points (43) in 1939–40

- Played with AHL's Providence Reds (1954–55) after retiring from NHL

Commemorative 25th-anniversary sweater worn by Bruins forward Woody Dumart during the 1948–49 NHL season.

# 23

## LEFT WING

## Bob Gainey <small>1992</small>

NO. RETIRED BY MONTREAL

**Montreal Canadiens**

Shoots: Left

Height: 6'-2"

Weight: 200 lbs.

Born: December 13, 1953; Peterborough, Ontario

Drafted by the Montreal Canadiens eighth overall in 1973

Played 16 NHL seasons from 1973–89

Stats: See page 395

"One of the aspects of the [Frank Selke Trophy] I've always appreciated the most was that it was named after Mr. Selke. He really was strong in his belief that style of player needs to be recognized."

—Bob Gainey, on recognition for defensive forwards

**AWARDS**

Frank J. Selke Trophy (1978, 1979, 1980, 1981)

Conn Smythe Trophy (1979)

Stanley Cup (1975–76, 1976–77, 1977–78, 1978–79, 1985–86)

**INTERNATIONAL AWARDS**

Canada Cup (1976)

Bronze Medal: World Championships (1982, 1983)

- Played amateur hockey with Peterborough TPT's (1970–73)
- Played minor pro hockey with Nova Scotia Voyageurs (1973–74)
- Served as player/coach of Epinal Squirrels (France II) in 1989–90
- Inaugural winner of Frank J. Selke Trophy for NHL's top defensive forward
- Played in NHL All-Star Game (1977, 1978, 1980, 1981)
- Finished even or better in plus/minus rating in 14 of 16 NHL seasons
- Served as captain of Montreal Canadiens (1981–89)
- Coached Minnesota North Stars/ Dallas Stars (1990–95, 1995–96)
- Coached Minnesota North Stars to Clarence Campbell Conference championship (1990–91)
- Served as general manager of Dallas Stars (1992–2001, 2001–02)
- Coached Montreal Canadiens (2005–06, 2008–09)
- Served as general manager of Montreal Canadiens (2003–10)
- Won Stanley Cup as general manager of Dallas Stars (1998–99)
- No. 23 jersey retired by Montreal Canadiens, February 23, 2008

# Home Away from Home

When Bob Gainey decided to retire from the NHL in 1989, there wasn't much he hadn't accomplished. During his 16-year career, all spent with the Montreal Canadiens, he won the Selke Trophy as the league's best defensive forward four times, won four Stanley Cups during the dynastic 1970s, earned the Conn Smythe Trophy during the 1979 playoffs, captained Montreal to a Stanley Cup in 1986 and starred for Canada in the 1976 and 1981 Canada Cup tournaments, where his checking and skating prompted Soviet coach Viktor Tikhonov to call him the best all-around player in the world.

"I was ready to move on from my playing career, but like a lot of players I wasn't sure if I could just quit," Gainey says of his NHL retirement.

Where he ended his on-ice career was far from the beaten path for a world-class player, as he chose to become the player-coach of the Epinal Squirrels of the National 1B Division of the French hockey league.

"Epinal had contacted me several times by old-fashioned mail. We went over there on a family holiday in the summer… and decided to stay for a year."

A local savings and loan company sponsored the Squirrels. Their logo was meant to convey the idea of "squirreling money away," and advertising was everywhere on the team uniform and around the arena. When Gainey arrived, the club was thinking of folding or relocating, but his star power righted the franchise. Today the team is named Gaymo

**Bob Gainey wore this jersey in 1989–90 as the player/coach of the Epinal Squirrels of the National 1B Division in the French Hockey League.**

d'Epinal and has played in France's top division since 2003.

As in his days in Montreal, Gainey focused on a team game as opposed to individual exploits: "I'd distribute the puck, try to raise the ability of the players and have some fun," Gainey said.

The coaching experience whetted Gainey's appetite, and he returned to the NHL to coach, taking the Minnesota North Stars to the Stanley Cup final in 1991. He left coaching in 1995 to concentrate on managing the Dallas Stars, the new home of the relocated Minnesota franchise, and four years later he was the first general manager of a sun-belt team to win the Stanley Cup.

**27**

# 7

# Jimmy Gardner 1962

ALTERNATE

9

Calumet Miners
Montreal AAA
Montreal Canadiens
Montreal Shamrocks
Montreal Wanderers
New Westminster
Royals
Pittsburgh
Professionals

Shoots: Left
Height: 5'-9"
Weight: 180 lbs.

Born: May 21, 1881:
Montreal, Quebec

Died: November 6, 1940:
Montreal, Quebec

Played 15 elite amateur
and professional
seasons from 1900–15

Stats: See page 396

"It is not often that in hockey's history can be found a player who figured on more than one 'great' championship team. Jimmy Gardner, is however, a notable example."

— D.A.L. MacDonald,
*Montreal Gazette*,
January 16, 1934

AWARDS
Stanley Cup (1901–02,
1902–03, 1909–10)

ALL-STAR
SELECTIONS
IHL Second All-Star
Team Left Wing (1905)

- Played amateur hockey with Montreal AAA (1899–1903); Montreal AAA-2 (1900–02)

- Member of CAHL intermediate champions Montreal AAA-2 (1900, 1901)

- Led Stanley Cup playoffs in penalty minutes in 1901–02 (12) and 1908–09 (13)

- Led ECAHA in penalty minutes (42) in 1907–08; led NHA in penalty minutes (67) in 1909–10

- Learned to play hockey growing up in Montreal with future Hall of Fame member Dickie Boon

- Member of IHL-champion Calumet Miners (1905)

- Member of the Stanley Cup–winning Montreal Amateur Athletic Association team that became known as the "Little Men of Iron" (1902)

- Served as player/coach with Montreal Canadiens (1913–14, 1914–15)

- Served as on-ice official in WCHL (1923–24)

- Coached Hamilton Tigers (1924–25); coached Providence Reds (1928–31); coached Chicoutimi Carabins (1931–32); coached Sherbrooke Red Raiders (1937–38); coached Verdun Maple Leafs (1939–40)

# 2002 Clark Gillies

**9**

"When we got beat by Edmonton for that fifth Cup, it really took a lot of the heart and soul out of me. It took me a while to even want to play the game again."

NO. RETIRED BY
NEW YORK ISLANDERS

**ALTERNATES**

**39 · 90**

Buffalo Sabres
New York Islanders

Shoots: Left

Height: 6'-3"

Weight: 215 lbs.

Born: April 7, 1954: Moose Jaw, Saskatchewan

Drafted by the New York Islanders fourth overall in 1974

Played 14 NHL seasons with from 1974–88

Stats: See page 396

- Played amateur hockey with Moose Jaw Canucks (1969–71); Regina Pats (1971–74)
- Member of the Memorial Cup–winning Regina Pats (1974), registering four points in three games during tournament
- WCJHL First All-Star Team Left Wing (1974)
- Played in NHL All-Star Game (1978)
- Captain of N.Y. Islanders (1976–79)
- Member of the N.Y. Islanders' Long Island Lighting Company line with Billy Harris and Bryan Trottier
- Recorded three consecutive game-winning goals against Buffalo Sabres in 1977 quarterfinals to tie NHL record
- Scored 93 power-play and 44 game-winning goals in 14-year career

- Member of Team NHL that played Soviet Union in 1979 Challenge Cup; member of Team Canada in 1981 Canada Cup tournament
- Nicknamed "Jethro" by New York Islanders teammates because of his resemblance to the character on the *Beverly Hillbillies* TV show
- Claimed by Buffalo from N.Y. Islanders in waiver draft, October 6, 1986
- Uncle of Colton Gillies, who played in the NHL from 2008 to 2013 with the Minnesota Wild and Columbus Blue Jackets
- Played three seasons of minor-league baseball as a first baseman and outfielder in the Houston Astros organization (1970–72)
- Inducted into Saskatchewan Sports Hall of Fame (2000)

**AWARDS**

Stanley Cup (1979–80, 1980–81, 1981–82, 1982–83)

**ALL-STAR SELECTIONS**

First All-Star Team Left Wing (1978, 1979)

# 3

# Moose Goheen 1952

**Buffalo Majors
St. Paul Saints**

Shoots: Left

Height: 6'

Weight: 220 lbs.

Born: February 8, 1894;
White Bear Lake,
Minnesota

Died: November 13, 1979;
Maplewood, Minnesota

Played 16 elite amateur
and professional
seasons from 1914–32

Stats: See page 396

"He had terrific speed
and fight. I coined
the term, 'Moose.'
He had a chest like
a house and huge
strong legs, with
thighs as big as
[teammate] Emmy
Garrett's waist. No
man ever trained
more."

— Tony Conroy,
teammate on the
St. Paul AC

**INTERNATIONAL
AWARDS**

Silver Medal: Winter
Olympics (1920)

- Played amateur hockey with St. Paul Athletic Club (1914–22); St. Paul Saints (1922–26); White Bear Lakers (1916–17)

- Served with the U.S. Army signal corps during World War I (1917–19)

- Graduate of Valparaiso (Indiana) University

- Scored seven goals in four games for the United States at the 1920 Olympics

- Turned down offer to join Boston Bruins in 1928 to remain at home and continue off-ice career with Northern States Power Company

- Second American-born and trained player to be elected to Hockey Hall of Fame (after Hobey Baker)

- Inducted into Minnesota Sports Hall of Fame (1958)

- Inducted into the United States Hockey Hall of Fame (1973)

- Member of MacNaughton Cup (U.S. amateur) champion St. Paul AC (1916, 1920). St. Paul defeated American Soo three games to none to win the 1916 championship and shared the 1920 title with Canadian Soo after both teams completed the season with identical 9–3 records

- He is credited with being the first player to score using a slap shot. In a February 1924 edition of the New York Times, the account of a game between St. Paul and Boston reported that St. Paul won the game 1–0 thanks to a "slap shot" by the legendary Moose Goheen

# 1998 Michel Goulet

# 16

> "It was a dream come true. I really enjoyed the city and the fans in Quebec City. For me, to start my NHL career there in Quebec City was the best. I knew there was something good there, and during my 10 years we did pretty well."

NO. RETIRED BY QUEBEC

**ALTERNATE**

## 9

Birmingham Bulls
Chicago Blackhawks
Quebec Nordiques

Shoots: Left

Height: 6'-1"

Weight: 195 lbs.

Born: April 21, 1960; Peribonka, Quebec

Drafted by the Quebec Nordiques 20th overall in 1979

Played 16 WHA and NHL seasons from 1978–94

Stats: See page 397

- Played amateur hockey with Mistasinni Majors (1976–77); Quebec Remparts (1976–78)

- QMJHL Second All-Star Team Left Wing (1978)

- Holds Quebec Nordiques/Colorado Avalanche team record for regular season plus/minus (plus-62), established in 1983–84

- Holds Quebec Nordiques/Colorado Avalanche record for goals in regular season (57), established in 1982–83

- Played in NHL All-Star Game (1983, 1984, 1985, 1986, 1988)

- Made professional debut as an underage free agent in the World Hockey Association with the Birmingham Bulls in 1978

- One of six teenage players on Birmingham Bulls team, who were collectively known as the "Baby Bulls"

- Led NHL in short-handed goals (6) in 1981–82; led NHL in game-winning goals (16) in 1983–84

- Finished second in NHL power-play goals in 1984–85 (17), 1985–86 (28) and 1987–88 (29)

- Registered nine points in 10 games at 1983 World Hockey Championships in West Germany

- Traded to Chicago by Quebec with Greg Millen and Quebec's sixth-round choice (Kevin St. Jacques) in 1991 Entry Draft for Mario Doyon, Everett Sanipass and Dan Vincelette, March 5, 1990

- Suffered career-ending head injury in game vs. Montreal, March 16, 1994

**ALL-STAR SELECTIONS**

First All-Star Team Left Wing (1984, 1986, 1987)

Second All-Star Team Left Wing (1983, 1988)

**INTERNATIONAL AWARDS**

Canada Cup (1984, 1987)

Bronze Medal: World Championships (1983)

# 15

# Danielle Goyette 2017

Calgary Oval X-Treme
Canadian National Team

Shoots: Left

Height: 5'-6"

Weight: 145 lbs.

Born: January 30, 1966

Saint-Nazaire, Quebec

Played 16 elite amateur
seasons from 1991–2007

Stats: See Page 397

"I just played with read and react. I didn't know systems. All the players on the national team didn't want to play with me because I didn't know all the Xs and Os.... I didn't grow up with coaches teaching me how to play the game. I'd just watch on TV and try to [imitate] what I saw the game before."

INTERNATIONAL
AWARDS

Gold Medal: Winter
Olympics (2002, 2006)

Silver Medal: Winter
Olympics (1998)

Gold Medal: World
Championships (1992,
1994, 1997, 1999, 2000,
2001, 2004, 2007)

Silver Medal: World
Championships (2005)

- Is one of the most prolific scorers in the history of women's hockey, collecting 114 goals and 105 assists for 219 points in 172 games with Team Canada

- Led the Women's World Championships with 10 points (three goals, seven assists) in five games in her tournament debut in 1992 and led with nine goals in five games in 1994

- Was the top goal-scorer with eight goals in six games when women's hockey made its Olympic debut in Nagano in 1998

- Led the Olympics with seven assists and 10 points in five games at Salt Lake City in 2002

- Carried the flag for Canada in the opening ceremonies at the 2006 Winter Olympics in Torino

- Was named MVP at the 2003 Esso Women's National Championships after leading Team Alberta to the Abby Hoffman Cup

- Was named head coach of the women's hockey team at the University of Calgary shortly after her retirement as a player in 2007 and won a national championship in 2010–11

- Was an assistant coach with Team Canada for gold medal victories at the 2012 Women's World Championships and the 2014 Winter Olympics

# Hockey as a Second Language

The tiny town of Saint-Nazaire, Quebec, lies some three hours by car north of Quebec City near Lac Saint-Jean. While not far from the town of Saguenay (formerly Chicoutimi) with a population approaching 150,000 people, Saint-Nazaire was home to about 800 people when Danielle Goyette was growing up. According to recent census data, 98.9 percent of the population lists French as their first language. None list English. Goyette spoke almost no English when she joined the Canadian National Women's Team at the age of 25 in 1991. It was a lonely experience for her, since few of her new teammates spoke French.

**Danielle Goyette shows off an Olympic gold medal following Team Canada's 3–2 win over the United States at the 2002 Games.**

Goyette began skating at the age of four, but had no team to play hockey with until she was 15. As the second youngest of eight children in her family, when her older sisters would go out with friends on Saturday night, Goyette would have the TV to herself and watch the Montreal Canadiens. When she was alone on the ice, she would try to mimic the moves she had seen on TV. Goyette was an excellent athlete. She was a top junior tennis player and a member of the Under-21 National Fastball Team, but hockey was her passion. "Being from a big family," she has said, "I think the sport allowed me to be outside of all the people yelling at each other, the kids fighting in the house. For me, the sport allowed me to be me, to be myself on the ice."

Still speaking little English, Goyette moved to Calgary at the age of 30 in 1996 to be where the women's high-performance hockey program was centered. This allowed her to concentrate more on fitness and training, while also learning to improve her English. Hayley Wickenheiser played with Goyette on the National Team and later for her at the University of Calgary. "I think she's a living example of 'no excuses,'" Wickenheiser told Amalie Benjamin of NHL.com in 2017. "[She's] someone who moved across the country, didn't speak a word of English, worked a part-time job, went after her dream, and didn't complain about it."

# 5 George Hay 1958

ALTERNATES

## 4 · 7 · 8

Chicago Black Hawks
Detroit Cougars
Detroit Falcons
Detroit Red Wings
Portland Rosebuds
Regina Capitals

Shoots: Left

Height: 5'-10"

Weight: 155 lbs.

Born: January 10, 1898;
Listowel, Ontario

Died: July 13, 1975;
Stratford, Ontario

Played 12 professional
seasons from
1921–31, 1932–34

Stats: See page 397

"I've seen a lot of good ones, but none who had more stuff than George. He was one of the easiest players to handle I ever had, always in condition, always on the job, always willing to play any position. He never got into any trouble on the ice and was rarely sent to the penalty box."

— Jack Adams

ALL-STAR
SELECTIONS

WCHL First All-Star
Team Left Wing
(1922, 1923, 1924)

WHL First All-Star Team
Left Wing (1926)

- Played amateur hockey with the Winnipeg Strathconas (1914–15); Winnipeg Monarchs (1915–17); Regina Victorias (1919–21)

- Signed as a free agent by Regina Capitals (WCHL), December 1, 1921

- Rights transferred to Portland (WHL) after Regina (WCHL) franchise relocated, September 1, 1925; rights transferred to Chicago after NHL club purchased Portland (WHL) franchise, May 15, 1926

- Scored first goal in history of Chicago Black Hawks franchise in 4–1 victory over Toronto St. Pats, November 17, 1926

- Traded to Detroit Cougars by Chicago with Percy Traub for $15,000, April 11, 1927

- Named to "Unofficial" NHL First All-Star Team Left Wing (1928)

- Finished second to New York Rangers center Frank Boucher in voting for the Lady Byng Trophy (1928)

- Scored first playoff goal in Detroit franchise history in 3–1 loss to Toronto St. Pats, March 20, 1929

- Served as captain of Detroit Falcons (1930–31)

- Served as player/coach of Detroit Olympics (1931–32) and didn't play in the NHL for the entire season

- Coached London Tecumsehs (1935–36); coached Listowel Intermediates (1938–39)

- Served as flight lieutenant and instructor with the Royal Canadian Air Force during World War II

# 1965 Syd Howe

**8**

ALTERNATES

**15 · 11**

**Detroit Red Wings**
**Ottawa Senators**
**Philadelphia Quakers**
**St. Louis Eagles**
**Toronto Maple Leafs**

Alternate Position: C

Shoots: Left

Height: 5'-9"

Weight: 165 lbs.

Born: September 28, 1911; Ottawa, Ontario

Died: May 20, 1976; Ottawa, Ontario

Played 17 NHL seasons from 1929–46

Stats: See page 398

*"I'll never forget the night Detroit fans gave me toward the end of my career. I got a lot of gifts, including a piano. You know how it is when they give you a night. It usually turns out that team gets beat and you can't come close to scoring. I was a lot luckier. We beat the Black Hawks, 2–0 and I scored both goals."*

- Played amateur hockey with Glebe Collegiate (1925–26); Landsdowne Park Juveniles (1925–26); Ottawa Gunners (1927–28); Ottawa Rideaus (1928–30)

- Became sixth player — and first in hockey's modern era — to score six goals in a single game in Detroit's 12–2 victory over N.Y. Rangers, February 3, 1944

- Held NHL record for scoring fastest playoff overtime goal (25 seconds), accomplished in Detroit's 2–1 victory over N.Y. Americans, March 19, 1940; surpassed by Ted Irvine (19 seconds), April 2, 1969

- Finished second in NHL points in 1934–35 (47) and 1940–41 (44)

- Played in NHL All-Star Game (1939)

- Held NHL record for career regular season points (529); surpassed by Bill Cowley

- Signed as a free agent by Ottawa, January 16, 1930

- Claimed by Toronto from Ottawa for 1931–32 season in Dispersal Draft, September 26, 1931

- Transferred to St. Louis after Ottawa franchise relocated, September 22, 1934; traded to Detroit by St. Louis with Ralph Bowman for Teddy Graham and $50,000, February 11, 1935

- On the ice when Mud Bruneteau scored in the sixth overtime period to give Detroit a 1–0 win over Montreal Maroons in longest game in NHL history

**AWARDS**
Stanley Cup (1935–36, 1936–37, 1942–43)

**ALL-STAR SELECTIONS**
Second All-Star Team Center (1945)

# 9

# Bobby Hull 1983

NO. RETIRED BY CHICAGO
& WINNIPEG

ALTERNATE
16

Chicago Black Hawks
Hartford Whalers
Winnipeg Jets

Shoots: Left

Height: 5'-10"

Weight: 195 lbs.

Born: January 3, 1939;
Point Anne, Ontario

Played 23 NHL and WHA
seasons from 1957–80

Stats: See page 398

"All I've done all my life is just tried to better the game for our players and for those people watching."

**AWARDS**

Art Ross Trophy
(1960, 1962, 1966)

Hart Memorial Trophy
(1965, 1966)

Lady Byng Memorial
Trophy (1965)

Stanley Cup (1960–61)

**ALL-STAR
SELECTIONS**

First All-Star Team Left
Wing (1960, 1962, 1964,
1965, 1966, 1967, 1968,
1969, 1970, 1972)

Second All-Star Team
Left Wing (1963, 1971)

**INTERNATIONAL
AWARDS**

Canada Cup (1976)

- First player in NHL history to record more than 50 goals in a season, March 12, 1966

- Held NHL record for goals in regular season (58); surpassed by Phil Esposito, March 11, 1971

- Only Hall of Fame member to play in all seven seasons of WHA's existence

- Played amateur hockey with Galt Black Hawks (1953–54); Hespeler Shamrocks (1953–54); Woodstock Warriors (1954–55); St. Catharines Teepees (1955–57)

- Led NHL in power-play goals in 1965–66 (22) and 1968–69 (20); led NHL in game-winning goals in 1968–69 (11) and 1969–70 (8)

- Led NHL in goals seven times (1959–60, 1961–62, 1963–64, 1965–66, 1966–67, 1967–68, 1968–69); led NHL in short-handed goals (4) in 1963–64

- Led NHL playoffs in goals in 1961–62 (8), 1962–63 (8), 1964–65 (10); led WHA in goals (77) in 1974–75

- Named WHA Most Valuable Player (1973, 1974); WHA First All-Star Team Left Wing (1973, 1974, 1975); WHA Second All-Star Team Left Wing (1976, 1977); member of WHA-champion Winnipeg Jets (1976, 1977, 1978)

- Played for Team Canada in 1974 Summit Series and led series in goals (7) and points (9)

- Came out of retirement to play for N.Y. Rangers in the DN-Cup Tournament in Sweden (1981)

- Brother of Dennis Hull, who played in NHL with Chicago and Detroit from 1964–78; father of Hall of Fame member Brett Hull, who played in NHL with Calgary, St. Louis, Dallas, Detroit and Phoenix from 1985–2006

- Registered 1,000th career NHL point in Chicago's 5–2 victory over Minnesota North Stars, December 13, 1970; recorded 500th career goal in Chicago's 4–2 victory over NHL Rangers, February 21, 1970

# Game Changer

You could say Bobby Hull, "The Golden Jet," was tailor-made for stardom. With his multi-watt smile and lighthearted demeanor, Hull combined his powerful physique and great skating ability with a wicked shot and a nose for the net in order to break scoring records and change the shape of the professional game.

Hull's skill and charisma were on prominent display in his third season, 1959–60, when he truly put himself on the map. That campaign he scored a league-high 39 goals and 81 points, earning himself the Art Ross Trophy and a place on the NHL's First All-Star Team. More importantly, Hull helped resurrect the fortunes of a struggling franchise. Prior to his arrival in 1957, Chicago had missed the play-offs 10 out of the previous 11 seasons. Starting in 1958–59, Hull's Chicago squads made the playoffs for 10 consecutive years, winning the Stanley Cup in 1960–61 and ending the club's 23-year Stanley Cup drought.

His time in Chicago was a golden era for the Black Hawks, as Hull set NHL single-season scoring marks in 1965–66 (54 goals) and again in 1968–69 (58 goals). Chicago is also where Hull (along with teammate Stan Mikita) created the single biggest stick advancement hockey had ever seen: the curved blade. Hull would soak the blade of a stick and then wedge it underneath a door and keep it there until the wood dried with the blade bent. The result saw pucks fly like no one had ever seen and changed hockey forever.

Hull changed the game again—and ruffled

**Bobby Hull, fresh from leaving the NHL for the Winnipeg Jets and the World Hockey Association.**

more than a few feathers—when he signed with the Winnipeg Jets of the upstart rival World Hockey Association in 1972.

His defection from the NHL not only helped establish the WHA, but it paved the way for higher player salaries in the old league. He was also integral to the successful infusion of European talent into North American hockey, playing on a high-scoring line with Swedish superstars Anders Hedberg and Ulf Nilsson. The trio set numerous scoring records while blending the finest aspects of the game—from both sides of the Atlantic.

Following the NHL/WHA merger in 1979, Hull was traded to the Hartford Whalers 18 games into the 1979–80 NHL season, where he ended his career playing alongside Gordie Howe. He retired with 1,170 NHL points in 1,063 NHL regular-season games—and a legacy as one of hockey's biggest stars.

# 11

# Busher Jackson 1971

ALTERNATES
## 18 · 17

Boston Bruins
New York Americans
Toronto Maple Leafs

Alternate Position: D
Shoots: Left
Height: 5'-11"
Weight: 195 lbs.
Born: January 19, 1911:
Toronto, Ontario
Died: June 25, 1966:
Toronto, Ontario
Played 15 NHL seasons
from 1929–44
Stats: See page 399

"[Maple Leafs trainer Tim] Daly asked me to carry the sticks for him. I told him I wasn't a stick boy, I was a hockey player. So he said I was nothing but a fresh busher [a term for someone who had just been called up from the minors] and the name stuck."

—Harvey Jackson on his nickname, "Busher"

**AWARDS**
NHL Scoring Leader (1932)
Stanley Cup (1931–32)
**ALL-STAR SELECTIONS**
First All-Star Team
Left Wing (1932, 1934, 1935, 1937)
Second All-Star Team
Left Wing (1933)

- First NHL player to score four goals in a single period in Toronto's 5–2 victory over St. Louis Eagles, November 20, 1934

- Played amateur hockey with Humberside Collegiate (1925–27) and Toronto Marlboros (1927–29)

- Led OHA-Jr. league in playoff goals (7) and points (9) in 1928–29

- Member of Memorial Cup–winning Toronto Marlboros who defeated the Ottawa Shamrocks and Elmwood (Manitoba) Millionaires in 1929. Jackson scored 15 goals and registered 10 assists in 13 games during the Memorial Cup playoffs

- Signed as a free agent by Toronto Maple Leafs, December 6, 1929

- Member of Toronto's famed Kid Line with Joe Primeau and Charlie Conacher

- Played in NHL All-Star Game (1934, 1937, 1939)

- Led NHL in points (53) in 1931–32

- Youngest player to lead NHL in scoring (21 years, 3 months) until Wayne Gretzky (aged 20 years, 3 months) won scoring title in 1980–81

- Traded to N.Y. Americans by Toronto with Buzz Boll, Doc Romnes, Jimmy Fowler and Murray Armstrong for Sweeney Schriner, May 18, 1939; traded to Boston by N.Y. Americans for $7,500, January 4, 1942

- Played the occasional shift as a defenseman in his final season with the Boston Bruins

# The Kid is Alright

Harvey "Busher" Jackson was a flashy member of the Kid Line, the Toronto Maple Leafs trio that dominated the National Hockey League in the 1930s. Along with big Charlie Conacher and the slick-passing Joe Primeau, Jackson established himself as a star on the left wing with his flair and wicked backhand.

Jackson signed with the Maple Leafs in 1929, joining his Toronto Marlboros teammate Conacher, who'd turned pro just a few games before him. At 18, Jackson was the youngest player in the league, but he was brash and confident. He earned his nickname when he refused to help trainer Tim Daly carry sticks—a rookie duty—because he insisted that carrying sticks wasn't the job of an NHLer. For his retort, Daly called him "nothing but a fresh busher!" The nickname stuck with him for the rest of his life.

**Busher Jackson during the Kid Line era in Toronto.**

The Kid Line wasn't formed until the middle of the 1929–30 season, when Joe Primeau, whose NHL career was off to an unremarkable start, was placed between the hard-shooting Conacher and the speedy Jackson. The line caught fire almost immediately, and the three players were consistently among the league's scoring leaders over the next five years.

Jackson was a great rusher, with good size and an uncanny knack for finding the back of the net. He was famous for his backhand, which was lethal as he darted across the ice from the left side. In 1931–32, the Kid Line was at its peak, with Jackson leading the league in scoring (53 points), Primeau leading the league in assists (37) and Conacher leading the league in goals (34). The trio led the Leafs to their first Stanley Cup since 1921–22, when they were known as the St. Patricks.

After Primeau retired in 1936, Busher played on a line with his brother, Art Jackson, for one season before joining Syl Apps and Gord Drillon on another high-scoring Leafs unit. When Busher's output sagged in 1938–39, he was traded to the New York Americans for Sweeney Schriner. He played two years with the Americans and then three more with the Boston Bruins—even spending some time on the blue line—before retiring in 1944.

# 4 Aurèle Joliat 1947

**Montreal Canadiens**

Shoots: Left

Height: 5'-7"

Weight: 136 lbs.

Born: August 29, 1901:
Ottawa, Ontario

Died: June 2, 1986:
Ottawa, Ontario

Played 16 NHL seasons
from 1922–38

Stats: See page 399

"One night [Eddie Shore] dislocated my shoulder and they carried me off in a lot of pain. Then I look around and Shore is leading a fancy rush. Forget the sore shoulder. I leaped over the boards and intercepted the big bugger. Hit him with a flyin' tackle. Hit him so hard he was out cold on the ice. He had it comin' I'd say."

**AWARDS**

Hart Memorial
Trophy (1934)

Stanley Cup (1923–24,
1929–30, 1930–31)

**ALL-STAR
SELECTIONS**

First All-Star Team
Left Wing (1931)

Second All-Star
Team Left Wing
(1932, 1934, 1935)

- Ranks second among Montreal Canadiens left wingers in career goals (269)

- Finished among NHL top-5 in goals in 1923–24 (15), 1924–25 (30), 1927–28 (28) and 1933–34 (21)

- Finished among NHL top-5 in assists in 1925–26 (9), 1927–28 (11), 1930–31 (22) and 1931–32 (24)

- Finished among NHL top-5 in points in 1923–24 (21), 1924–25 (42), 1925–26 (26) and 1927–28 (39)

- Known as both "The Little Giant" and "The Mighty Atom"

- Played amateur hockey with Ottawa New Edinburghs (1916–17, 1918–20); Ottawa Aberdeens (1917–18); Iroquois Falls Flyers (1920–21)

- Played football with Regina Boat Club in 1922, where he was first noticed by officials of the Saskatoon Sheiks hockey club

- Signed as a free agent by Saskatoon Sheiks (WCHL), September 1, 1922

- Rights traded to Montreal Canadiens by Saskatoon Sheiks (WCHL) with $3,500 for Newsy Lalonde, September 18, 1922

- Played in NHL All-Star Game (1934, 1937)

- Older brother, Homer, was killed in action in France during World War I

- Played in a benefit All-Star game in 1982 at the age of 80 and scored a hat-trick as the NHL Oldstars defeated his Ottawa Old-Pros 18–12

# 2017 Paul Kariya

**9**

> "Paul Kariya's career was marked by his speed, his shot, his discipline and his leadership. Paul was a dynamic, determined and distinguished NHL player — and an outstanding competitor."
>
> — NHL Commissioner Gary Bettman

Colorado Avalanche
Mighty Ducks of Anaheim
Nashville Predators
St. Louis Blues

Shoots: Left

Height: 5'-10"

Weight: 185 lbs.

Born: October 16, 1974; Vancouver, British Columbia

Drafted by the Mighty Ducks of Anaheim 4th overall in 1993

Played 15 NHL seasons from 1994–2004, 2005–2010

Stats: See Page 399

- Won back-to-back MVP awards in the British Columbia Hockey League with the Penticton Panthers in 1990–91 and 1991–92 and was named the Canadian Junior A Player of the Year in 1991–92

- Won NCAA championship with University of Maine in 1992–93 and became the first freshman to win the Hobey Baker Award as the NCAA's top player

- Represented Canada at the World Junior Championships for the second straight season in 1993 and won a gold medal; joined Canadian national team in 1993–94

- Was the first draft pick in Ducks franchise history in 1993; entered the NHL in 1994–95 and finishing third in voting for the Calder Trophy behind Peter Forsberg and Jim Carey

- Established career highs with 50 goals and 108 points playing with Teemu Selanne in Anaheim in 1995–96

- Finished third in NHL scoring (44 goals, 55 assists, 99 points) behind Mario Lemieux and Selanne in 1996–97; finished second in voting for the Hart Trophy as NHL MVP behind Dominik Hasek

- Was Ducks captain from 1996–97 to 2002–03, leading the team to the Stanley Cup Final in 2003

- Set single-season scoring records for the Nashville Predators with 54 assists and 85 points in 2005–06

- Concussion symptoms brought a premature end to his career after sitting out the 2010–11 season.

**AWARDS**

Lady Byng Memorial Trophy (1996, 1997)

**ALL-STAR SELECTIONS**

All-Rookie Team (1995)

First All-Star Team Left Wing (1996, 1997, 1999)

Second All-Star Team Left Wing (2000, 2003)

**INTERNATIONAL AWARDS**

Gold Medal: Winter Olympics (2002)

Silver Medal: Winter Olympics (1994)

Gold Medal: World Championships (1994)

Silver Medal: World Championships (1996)

# 17

## LEFT WING
# Valeri Kharlamov 2005

**CSKA Moscow**

Shoots: Left

Height: 5'-8"

Weight: 165 lbs.

Born: January 14, 1948;
Moscow, Union of Soviet
Socialist Republics

Died: August 27, 1981;
Moscow, Union of Soviet
Socialist Republics

Played 14 seasons of
Russian elite amateur
hockey from 1967–81

Stats: See page 400

"His talents were
God-given and he
could do practically
everything — a
smart play, a tricky
pass, a precise
shot. Everything
he did looked so
easy, so elegant. His
execution of hockey
was aesthetic and he
amazed millions."

— Vladislav Tretiak

**INTERNATIONAL
AWARDS**

Summit Series (1974)

Challenge Cup (1979)

Gold Medal: Winter
Olympics (1972, 1976)

Silver Medal: Winter
Olympics (1980)

Gold Medal: World
Championships (1969,
1970, 1971, 1973, 1974,
1975, 1978, 1979)

Silver Medal: World
Championships
(1972, 1976)

Bronze Medal: World
Championships (1977)

- One of only two European-born and trained players (with Vladislav Tretiak) without NHL experience to be inducted into Hockey Hall of Fame
- Renowned for his performance during the 1972 Summit Series where he recorded three goals and seven points in seven games
- Played amateur hockey with Zvezda Chebarkul (1967–68); CSKA Moscow (1967–81)
- Led USSR Elite League in goals (40) in 1970–71
- Led USSR Elite League in points (42) in 1971–72
- Named USSR League Most Valuable Player (1972, 1973)
- USSR First All-Star Team Left Wing (1971, 1972, 1973, 1974, 1975, 1976, 1978)

- Named World Championships Best Forward (1976)
- World Championships First All-Star Team Left Wing (1972, 1973, 1975, 1976)
- Inducted into the International Ice Hockey Federation (IIHF) Hall of Fame (1998)
- Legacy honored by the Kharlamov Trophy, awarded to the best Russian NHL player as voted by Russian NHL players
- Died in an automobile accident on highway that connects St. Petersburg and Moscow, August 27, 1981
- At point of accident (kilometer marker #73) there is a memorial stone bearing the inscription: "The star of Russian hockey fell here."

# The King of Russian Hockey

**H**e was already a major star in the Soviet Union, but on Monday, September 2, 1972, during the second period of the first game of the legendary Summit Series, a dynamic left winger shocked Canadian hockey fans: that winger was 24-year-old Valeri Kharlamov.

Moscow's Central Red Army powerhouse had already challenged the ill-informed assumptions Canadians held about the weaknesses of the Russian hockey system after skating with Canada to a 2–2 tie in the first period. But it was Kharlamov who shattered those assumptions as he scored the only two goals of the second period, propelling the Soviets to a numbing 7–3 victory. In the process, Kharlamov earned himself the game's Most Valuable Player award as well as the sudden, nervous respect of hockey fans from the Atlantic to the Pacific.

Strong, fast and with a blistering shot and featherlike touch, Kharlamov was a multi-tooled player whose game epitomized the Soviet system, which emphasized puck control, skating into passing lanes and cycling the puck in all areas of the ice. He had already won a gold medal at the 1972 Olympics and scored 140 goals in 155 Russian League games when he and his unknown teammates arrived in Canada for their September to remember.

With the USSR up in the Summit Series 3-1-1, the turning point was undoubtedly a slash by Bobby Clarke that fractured Kharlamov's ankle during Game 6 in Moscow. Kharlamov couldn't play the next game and was obviously still not himself in Game 8; the Canadians took the series 4-3-1.

Neutralizing Kharlamov became a necessary tactic to beat a Soviet team in the 1970s. When the Central Red Army played

**Valeri Kharlamov wore this jersey in his final season of hockey, 1980–81, before his death in a car accident during the summer of 1981.**

the Philadelphia Flyers during the 1975–76 Super Series, he was knocked out by a booming check from the Flyers' Ed Van Impe, prompting a temporary walk-off by the Red Army team.

Kharlamov continued to star both domestically and internationally, and in total he won 11 USSR championships and eight world championships with the Central Sports Club of the Army Moscow (CSKA Moscow). But in August 1981 he and his wife, Irina, were killed in a car crash on the highway between St. Petersburg and Moscow, leaving two young children, including five-year-old Alexander, who became an NHL first-round draft choice in 1994.

# 4 Herbie Lewis 1989

ALTERNATES
## 9 · 7

Detroit Cougars
Detroit Falcons
Detroit Red Wings

Shoots: Left
Height: 5'-9"
Weight: 163 lbs.
Born: April 17, 1906;
Calgary, Alberta
Died: January 20, 1991;
Indianapolis, Indiana
Played 11 NHL seasons
from 1928–39
Stats: See page 400

"[He] was a sportsman of the highest type. I defy baseball or football or boxing or any other sport to produce an individual who can eclipse Herbie Lewis as a perfect model of what an athlete should stand for."

— Jack Adams

- Nicknamed "The Duke of Duluth"

- Played amateur hockey with Calgary Hustlers (1921–22), Calgary Canadians (1922–24) and Duluth Hornets (1924–28)

- Led Calgary Junior League in goals (17) and points (24) in 1922–23

- Signed as a free agent by Duluth Hornets (CHL), November 4, 1926

- Led CHL in assists (11) and points (28) in 1925–26

- CHL First All-Star Team Left Wing (1926)

- Claimed by Detroit Cougars from Duluth Hornets (AHA) in Inter-League Draft, May 14, 1928

- Led NHL playoffs in goals in 1933–34 (6) and 1936–37 (4)

- Played in NHL All-Star Game (1934)

- Played for all three teams in the history of the Detroit franchise: Cougars (1928–30), Falcons (1930–32) and Red Wings (1932–39)

- Served as captain of Detroit Red Wings (1933–34)

- Held Detroit franchise record for career goals (147); surpassed by Syd Howe during 1943–44 season

- Coached Indianapolis Capitols (1939–43)

- Was alleged to have been the NHL's highest-paid player in 1935 when he received a salary of $8,000

- Times have changed — the Indianapolis Capitols held a "Herbie Lewis Night" on January 10, 1940 and presented Lewis with a picnic basket and two hams

# 1966 Ted Lindsay

**7**

NO. RETIRED BY DETROIT
**ALTERNATES**
## 14 · 15

> "I don't know how I got [my] nickname and tough guy persona because I'm such a nice person. I guess I got rough because I hated to lose. It took me some time to learn the art of losing graciously."
>
> — Lindsay on his nickname, "Terrible Ted"

Chicago Black Hawks
Detroit Red Wings

Shoots: Left

Height: 5'-8"

Weight: 163 lbs.

Born: July 29, 1925;
Renfrew, Ontario

Played 17 NHL seasons
from 1944–60, 1964–65

Stats: See page 400

- Played amateur hockey with Kirkland Lake Lakers (1942–43); St. Michael's Majors (1943–44); Oshawa Generals (1943–44)
- Signed as a free agent by the Detroit Red Wings, October 18, 1944
- Led NHL in goals (33) in 1947–48; led NHL in assists in 1949–50 (55) and 1956–57 (55); led NHL in penalty minutes (184) in 1958–59
- Nicknamed "Terrible Ted" and "Scarface" because of scrappy, chippy play that contributed to more than 400 stitches to his face
- Attempted to organize the first NHL Players Association in 1957, an activity that led to his trade to the last-place Chicago Black Hawks

- Member of Detroit's famed Production Line with Sid Abel and Gordie Howe
- Traded to Chicago by Detroit with Glenn Hall for Johnny Wilson, Forbes Kennedy, Hank Bassen and Bill Preston, July 23, 1957; rights traded to Detroit by Chicago for cash, October 14, 1964
- Played in 11 consecutive NHL All-Star Games (1947–57)
- Ended four-year retirement in 1964–65 to rejoin the Detroit Red Wings and at age 39 ranked second in penalty minutes (173)
- Served as general manager of Detroit Red Wings (1976–80); coached Detroit Red Wings (1979–80, 1980–81)
- Served as general manager of Kansas City Red Wings (1977–79)

**AWARDS**
Art Ross Trophy (1950)
Lester Patrick Trophy (2008)
Stanley Cup (1949–50, 1951–52, 1953–54, 1954–55)

**ALL-STAR SELECTIONS**
First All-Star Team Left Wing (1948, 1950, 1951, 1952, 1953, 1954, 1956, 1957)
Second All-Star Team Left Wing (1949)

Lindsay continued on page 46

**45**

# Trailblazer

**Ted Lindsay, known sometimes as "Terrible Ted," gets the attention of the Toronto Maple Leafs with his stick work during the early 1950s.**

When Ted Lindsay made his NHL debut on October 29, 1944, he made league history as the first son of an original NHLer to skate in the league. His father, Bert Lindsay, had donned the pads for the Montreal Wanderers and the Toronto Arenas during the NHL's first two seasons.

Ted Lindsay was signed to his first pro contract only 11 days before his 1944 debut, but it wasn't easy for Detroit's Jack Adams to get him to commit. Even as a teenager, Lindsay was a tough negotiator, threatening to go back to junior hockey if the terms weren't to his liking. He also proved to be as tough on the ice as anyone who ever played the game, and within a few seasons, Lindsay was starring alongside Sid Abel and Gordie Howe.

Lindsay led the NHL with 33 goals in 1947–48 and with 55 assists and 78 points in 1949–50. With the Production Line humming, Detroit dominated the NHL during the late 1940s through the mid-1950s, finishing first seven times between 1948–49 and 1954–55 and winning the Stanley Cup four times (1949–50, 1951–52, 1953–54 and 1954–55). Lindsay was captain for those final two Cups, but he had already launched a Stanley Cup tradition in 1950 by scooping up Lord Stanley's mug and skating around the ice with it.

"When they presented the Cup, I just went over and picked it up," Lindsay said. "I wanted the fans to see what we were playing for."

Lindsay enjoyed his best statistical season with the Wings during the 1956–57 campaign, leading the NHL with 55 assists while collecting 85 points, but it was his work behind the scenes that really made headlines.

Lindsay had launched a crusade to form the first NHL Players' Association.

His goal was to give the players a voice and to allow them to negotiate contracts fairly. He convinced top players such as Gus Mortson of the Chicago Black Hawks, Bill Gadsby of the New York Rangers, Jim Thomson of the Toronto Maple Leafs and Montreal Canadiens star Doug Harvey that there was merit in forming a players' association. From his own pocket, Lindsay hired the same New York lawyers who had helped baseball players negotiate their first collective agreement. The owners of the six NHL teams saw his plan as a threat to their monopoly and scuttled the players' association.

Slowly, the owners turned the players against the idea of forming an association, and in February 1957 the NHLPA certification bid was defeated. As a form of punishment in the summer of 1957, Lindsay was dealt to the lowly Black Hawks, who hadn't won a playoff series since 1944. His dream had been sidelined, but he remained undeterred, and his efforts paved the way for the eventual establishment of the NHL Players' Association in 1967.

# 1981 Frank Mahovlich

# 27

NO. RETIRED BY TORONTO

**ALTERNATES**

# 26 · 11

Birmingham Bulls
Detroit Red Wings
Montreal Canadiens
Toronto Maple Leafs
Toronto Toros

"Detroit just opened everything up. It was like a piano had been lifted off my back. I finally felt like playing."

— Frank Mahovlich, commenting on his trade to Detroit

Shoots: Left

Height: 6'

Weight: 205 lbs.

Born: January 10, 1938; Timmins, Ontario

Played 22 NHL and WHA seasons from 1956–78

Stats: See page 401

- Played amateur hockey with St. Michael's Majors (1953–57)
- Led OHA-Jr. in goals (52) in 1956–57
- Led NHL playoffs in assists (11) in 1963–64; led NHL playoffs in goals (14) and points (27) in 1970–71
- Finished second in NHL in goals in 1960–61 (48), 1961–62 (33), 1965–66 (32) and 1968–69 (49)
- Played in NHL All-Star Game (1959, 1960, 1961, 1962, 1963, 1964, 1965, 1967, 1968, 1969, 1970, 1971, 1972, 1973, 1974)
- Known as "The Big M" for his lanky frame and long, flowing skating style
- One of only six players in NHL history (with Dick Duff, Red Kelly, Bryan Trottier, Patrick Roy and Larry Murphy) to win two or more Stanley Cup championships with two or more teams
- Member of the all-WHA Team Canada '74 that played eight game summit series against the Soviet Union

- Registered 1,000th career NHL point in Montreal's 7–6 loss to Philadelphia Flyers, February 17, 1973
- Recorded 500th career NHL goal in Montreal's 3–2 victory over Vancouver Canucks, March 21, 1973
- Traded to Detroit by Toronto with Pete Stemkowski, Garry Unger and the rights to Carl Brewer for Norm Ullman, Paul Henderson, Floyd Smith and Doug Barrie, March 3, 1968
- Traded to Montreal by Detroit for Guy Charron, Bill Collins and Mickey Redmond, January 13, 1971
- Brother of Peter Mahovlich, who played in the NHL with Detroit, Montreal and Pittsburgh from 1965–81
- Trade to Detroit was considered to be the biggest trade of the entire decade
- First former NHL player to be appointed to the Canadian Senate (1998)

**AWARDS**

Calder Memorial Trophy (1958)

Stanley Cup (1961–62, 1962–63, 1963–64, 1966–67, 1970–71, 1972–73)

**ALL-STAR SELECTIONS**

First All-Star Team Left Wing (1961, 1963, 1973)

Second All-Star Team Left Wing (1962, 1964, 1965, 1966, 1969, 1970)

**INTERNATIONAL AWARDS**

Summit Series (1972)

Mahovlich continued on page 48

**47**

# The Big M

**Frank Mahovlich skates as the assistant captain for the Montreal Canadiens in the early 1970s.**

Frank Mahovlich, "the Big M," cannot be defined by a moment or a year but rather by his career as a whole. He never scored 50 goals in a season, though he came close with Toronto in 1960–61 (48) and with Detroit in 1968–69 (49). He never had 100 points in a year, and, amazingly, after winning the Calder Trophy in 1957–58, he never won another individual award in the NHL. But he did break the 500-goal and 1,000-point plateaus, and he won win six Stanley Cups.

Mahovlich's legacy is that of a talented and classy winger, a large man with the skills and hands of a pure scorer. But he is also remem- bered as a frustrating athlete: When things went well, he looked like a star without trying; when times were tough, he looked as though he didn't care. In Toronto he had battles with coach Punch Imlach that diminished his love for the game, and he responded to the coach's berating by not reacting to it. He admitted later that they didn't speak for five years, and Mahovlich was hospital- ized in 1964, suffering from acute tension and depression. He returned to the team but struggled on the ice, his goal production dropping to 18 in 1966–67, the year of his final Cup victory with Toronto.

The Leafs decided to trade the big winger to the Detroit Red Wings in 1968. Free from all the pressure and conflict in Toronto, Mahovlich experi- enced a rebirth. He was put on a line with Gordie Howe and Alex Delvecchio and had his best goal-scoring year in his first full season with the team, 49 goals in 1968–69.

Montreal's Sam Pollock acquired Mahovlich to play alongside Jean Béliveau in 1971. The Habs won two Stanley Cups in the next three years, and in 1971 the Big M led all scorers with 14 goals and 27 points in the postseason. He left the NHL in 1974, played a few years in the WHA and then came back to attend the Red Wings' training camp briefly in the fall of 1979. Deep down Mahovlich knew it was time to hang up his skates—and he did so on his own terms.

# 1974 Dickie Moore

# 12

> "When Toe [Blake] became coach, I was elated. He kept me on the team. I was lucky to have a guy who believed in me. You're only as good as how somebody can lift you up to the heights where he thinks you can play."

NO. RETIRED BY MONTREAL

**ALTERNATE**

# 16

**Montreal Canadiens**
**St. Louis Blues**
**Toronto Maple Leafs**

Shoots: Left

Height: 5'-10"

Weight: 168 lbs.

Born: January 6, 1931; Montreal, Quebec

Died: December 19, 2015; Montreal, Quebec

Played 14 NHL seasons from 1951–63, 1964–65, 1967–68

Stats: See page 401

- Shares NHL record for most points (4) in one playoff period, accomplished in Montreal's 8–1 victory over Boston, March 25, 1954

- Played amateur hockey with Montreal Jr. Royals (1947–50); Montreal Jr. Canadiens (1949–51); Montreal Royals (1951–52, 1953–54)

- QJHL First All-Star Team Left Wing (1951); QJHL Second All-Star Team Left Wing (1950)

- Member of Memorial Cup–winning Montreal Jr. Royals (1949) and Montreal Jr. Canadiens (1950)

- Led QJHL playoffs in assists (13) and penalty minutes (51); led Memorial Cup playoffs in penalty minutes (41)

- Scored Stanley Cup–winning goal in Montreal's 5–1 victory over Boston Bruins, April 16, 1957

- Established NHL record for points in regular season (96) in 1958–59

- Won his first NHL scoring title in 1957–58 finishing the season while playing with a broken wrist; he wore a specially designed cast to protect his injury

- Played only 13 games in 1953–54 season recovering from a collarbone injury suffered in game vs. Boston, October 10, 1953

- Led NHL in goals (36) and points (84) in 1957–58; led NHL in assists (55) and points (96) in 1958–59

- Played in NHL All-Star Game (1953, 1956, 1957, 1958, 1959, 1960)

**AWARDS**

Art Ross Trophy (1958, 1959)

Stanley Cup (1952–53, 1955–56, 1956–57, 1957–58, 1958–59, 1959–60)

**ALL-STAR SELECTIONS**

First All-Star Team Left Wing (1958, 1959)

Second All-Star Team Left Wing (1961)

# 15

### LEFT WING

# Bert Olmstead 1985

**ALTERNATES**

## 16 · 14 · 19

Chicago Black Hawks
Montreal Canadiens
Toronto Maple Leafs

Shoots: Left

Height: 6'-1"

Weight: 180 lbs.

Born: September 4, 1926:
Sceptre, Saskatchewan

Died: November 16, 2015:
High River, Alberta

Played 14 NHL seasons
from 1948–62

Stats: See page 402

"I'm a hockey man
through and through.
I have a lot of love
for the game and for
what it means."

**AWARDS**

Stanley Cup (1952–53,
1955–56, 1956–57,
1957–58, 1961–62)

**ALL-STAR
SELECTIONS**

Second All-Star Team
Left Wing (1953, 1956)

- Held NHL record for assists in regular season (56); surpassed by Jean Béliveau (58) in 1960–61

- Shared NHL record (with Maurice Richard) for most points in a regular season game (8); surpassed by Darryl Sittler (10), February 7, 1976

- Played amateur hockey with Moose Jaw Canucks (1944–46)

- Played minor pro hockey with Kansas City Pla-Mors (1946–49); Milwaukee Seagulls (1950–51)

- Played in NHL All-Star Game (1953, 1956, 1957, 1959)

- Led NHL in assists in 1954–55 (48) and 1955–56 (56); led NHL in playoff assists (10) in 1955–56

- Finished among NHL top-5 in points in 1953–54 (52) and 1955–56 (70)

- Traded to Detroit by Chicago with Vic Stasiuk for Lee Fogolin and Steve Black, December 2, 1950; traded to Montreal by Detroit for Leo Gravelle, December 19, 1950

- Claimed by Toronto from Montreal in Intra-League Draft, June 3, 1958

- Renowned for skills as a ferocious, antagonistic checker — an early version of today's power forward

- Served as player/assistant coach with Toronto (1958–59)

- Coached (WHL) Vancouver Canucks (1965–67)

- Served as coach and general manager of Oakland Seals (1967–68)

# 1980 Lynn Patrick

**9**

"I was never judged on my merit as a hockey player. The fans felt the only reason I made the Rangers was because my dad Lester was the big man."

— Lynn Patrick, on accusations of nepotism

**New York Rangers**

Alternate Position: C
Shoots: Left
Height: 6'-1"
Weight: 192 lbs.
Born: February 3, 1912:
Victoria, British Columbia
Died: January 26, 1980:
St. Louis, Missouri
Played 10 NHL seasons
from 1934–43, 1945–46
Stats: See page 402

- Played amateur hockey with Montreal Royals (1933–34)
- Played basketball with Vancouver Blue Ribbons, Dominion of Canada champions (1933)
- Played basketball with Montreal Nationales (1934)
- Played football with the Montreal Football Club (1934)
- Signed as a free agent by N.Y. Rangers, November 4, 1934
- Led NHL in goals (32) in 1941–42
- Finished second in NHL points in 1941–42 (55); tied for third in points in 1940–41 (44)
- Coached New Haven Ramblers (1946–48); coached Los Angeles Blades (1965–66)

- Coached N.Y. Rangers (1948–50); coached Boston Bruins (1950–55)
- Coached St. Louis Blues (1967–68, 1974–75, 1975–76)
- Served as general manager of Boston Bruins (1954–64); served as general manager of St. Louis Blues (1967–68, 1971–72)
- Brother of Muzz Patrick, who played in the NHL with N.Y. Rangers from 1937–46
- Father of Craig Patrick, who played in the NHL with California, St. Louis, Kansas City and Washington from 1971–79
- Son of Lester Patrick, nephew of Frank Patrick, founding fathers of professional hockey on the west coast of North America

**AWARDS**
Lester Patrick Trophy (1989)
Stanley Cup (1939–40)

**ALL-STAR SELECTIONS**
First All-Star Team
Left Wing (1942)
Second All-Star Team
Left Wing (1943)

# Tommy Phillips 1945

Edmonton
Professionals
Kenora Thistles
Montreal AAA
Ottawa Senators
Rat Portage Thistles
Toronto Marlboros
Vancouver Millionaires

Shoots: Right

Height: 5'-9"

Weight: 168 lbs.

Born: May 22, 1883:
Rat Portage, Ontario

Died: November 30,
1923: Toronto, Ontario

Played 8 elite amateur
and professional
seasons from
1901–09, 1911–12

Stats: See page 403

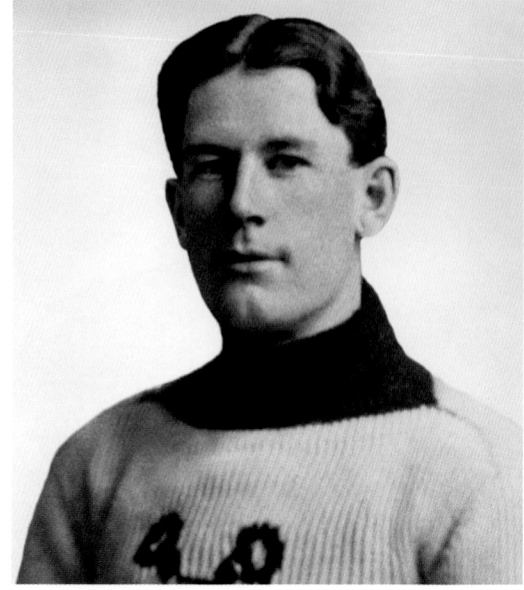

"He is the best in the game; that's what I think of him. Let me tell you that Tom Phillips is very, very far from all in."

—Lester Patrick to the *Ottawa Citizen*, December 22, 1909

**AWARDS**
Stanley Cup
(1902–03, 1906–07)

- Considered by many to be the greatest player of his era
- Starred on local school and junior teams in Rat Portage (Kenora) with future Hall of Famers Si Griffis, Tommy Hooper and Billy McGimisie
- Attended McGill University while playing for the Stanley Cup–winning Montreal Amateur Athletic Association (1902–03)
- Attended business school in Toronto while with the Ontario Senior–champion Toronto Marlboros (1903–04)
- Served as captain/playing coach of the Kenora Thistles from 1905–07
- Member of Manitoba champion–Rat Portage Thistles (1904–05); member of Stanley Cup–winning Kenora Thistles (1906–07)
- MHL-Pro First All-Star Team Left Wing (1907)

- Led Manitoba Pro League in goals (18) in 1906–07; led Stanley Cup playoffs in goals (9) and penalty minutes (16) in 1906–07
- Scored all four goals in Kenora's 4–2 victory over Montreal Wanderers in Game 1 of 1907 Stanley Cup playoffs, January 17, 1907
- Scored three goals in Kenora's 8–6 victory over Montreal Wanderers in Game 2 of 1907 Stanley Cup playoffs, January 21, 1907
- ECAHA First All-Star Team Left Wing (1908)
- Retired and worked in lumber business in Vancouver (1909–11), but returned to play in the PCHA in 1911–12
- Served as PCHA on-ice official (1912–15)

# 1991 Bob Pulford

**20**

"My story is this:
A Canadian kid who
can play the game
well is the luckiest
kid in the world.
There is no limit."

Los Angeles Kings
Toronto Maple Leafs

Shoots: Left

Height: 5'-11"

Weight: 188 lbs.

Born: March 31, 1936;
Newton Robinson,
Ontario

Played 16 NHL seasons
from 1956–72

Stats: See page 403

- Played amateur hockey with Weston Dukes (1953–54); Toronto Marlboros (1953–56)
- Member of Memorial Cup–winning Toronto Marlboros (1955, 1956)
- Led Memorial Cup playoffs in goals (16) and points (24) in 1955–56
- Led NHL in playoff assists (10) in 1966–67
- Led NHL in short-handed goals (4) in 1963–64
- Awarded assist on Bobby Baun's game-winning overtime goal in Toronto's 4–3 victory over Detroit Red Wings in Game 6 of the 1964 Stanley Cup final even though he wasn't on the ice at the time, April 23, 1964

- Played in NHL All-Star Game (1960, 1962, 1963, 1964, 1968)
- Served as president of the NHL Players' Association (1967–72)
- Traded to L.A. Kings by Toronto for Garry Monahan and Brian Murphy, September 3, 1970
- Served as captain of Los Angeles Kings (1971–73)
- Coached Los Angeles Kings (1972–77)
- Coached Chicago Blackhawks (1977–79, 1981–82, 1984–85, 1985–87, 1999–2000)
- Served as general manager of Chicago Blackhawks (1977–89, 1992–93, 1993–97, 1999–2000, 2003–04, 2004–05)

**AWARDS**
Jack Adams Award (1975)
Stanley Cup (1961–62, 1962–63, 1963–64, 1966–67)

**53**

# 14

### LEFT WING

# George Richardson 1950

Kingston 14th Regiment
Kingston Frontenacs
Queen's University

Shoots: Right

Height: Unknown

Weight: Unknown

Born: September 14,
1886: Kingston, Ontario

Died: February 9,
1916: Killed in action,
Bailleul, France

Played nine elite
amateur seasons from
1902–10, 1911–12

Stats: See page 403

"A hero in sport and war. Those who recall his play will remember how he seemed to start instantaneously at full speed in one stroke."

— *Toronto Telegram* tribute, 1921

- Was a member of a prominent and wealthy family in Kingston, Ontario
- Renowned as a clean and gentlemanly player who was a fine puckhandler and prolific scorer
- Member of Queen's University club that defeated Princeton and Yale to win the 1903 intercollegiate title of America
- Member of Canadian University champion Queen's Golden Gaels (1903–04, 1905–06)
- Member of Ontario Hockey Association senior champion Kingston's 14th Regiment (1907–08)
- Scored seven goals in Kingston's 9–7 victory over Stratford that clinched 1908 OHA senior title
- Led OHA-Sr. playoffs in goals in 1907–08 (18) and 1908–09 (13)
- Led OHA-Sr. in goals (8) in 1908–09
- Served on the executive of the Kingston Frontenacs team that captured OHA junior championship in 1910–11
- Served as captain in the Canadian Army with the 14th P.W.O. Rifles when he was killed in action in World War I
- Legacy honored by Richardson Stadium, erected on the campus of Queen's University in his name (1920)
- Awarded La legion d'honneur Croix de Guerre by France, March 10, 1916

# 1971 Gordon Roberts

**6**

ALTERNATES

**8 · 7**

Ottawa Emmetts
Ottawa Seconds
Ottawa Senators
Montreal Wanderers
Seattle Metropolitans
Vancouver Millionaires

Shoots: Left

Height: 5'-11"

Weight: 180 lbs.

Born: September 5, 1891: Ottawa, Ontario

Died: September 2, 1966: Oakland, California

Played 11 elite amateur and professional seasons from 1908–18, 1919–20

Stats: See page 404

"Gordon Roberts ... was the real sensation of the night ... Roberts checked Millar to a standstill, and in addition notched no less than four of the Ottawa goals — a phenomenal performance for a youngster."

— *Ottawa Citizen*, January 19, 1910, recapping the Senators' 8–4 win over Edmonton in a Stanley Cup game

- Played amateur hockey with Stratford HC (1906–07); Ottawa Emmetts (1908–09); Ottawa Seconds (1909–10)

- Led Ottawa City Senior League in goals (19) in 1908–09

- Played with Montreal Wanderers while studying medicine at McGill University

- Obtained medical degree from McGill University (1916)

- Finished among league leaders in NHA scoring every season from 1911–12 to 1915–16

- Finished second in NHA goals in 1913–14 (31) and 1914–15 (29)

- Signed as a free agent by Seattle Metropolitans, December 25, 1917

- Led PCHA in goals (43) in 1916–17

- Retired to operate medical practice (1918)

- Signed as a free agent by Vancouver Millionaires, December 12, 1919

- Attracted interest from the NHL's Senators while in Ottawa in 1922 doing post-graduate work in medicine but decided against making another comeback

AWARDS
Stanley Cup (1909–10)

ALL-STAR SELECTIONS
NHA First All-Star Team Left Wing (1914)

PCHA First All-Star Team Left Wing (1917)

# 20

# Luc Robitaille 2009

NO. RETIRED BY
LOS ANGELES

**Detroit Red Wings**
**Los Angeles Kings**
**New York Rangers**
**Pittsburgh Penguins**

Shoots: Left

Height: 6'-1"

Weight: 215 lbs.

Born: February 17, 1966;
Montreal, Quebec

Drafted by the Los
Angeles Kings 171st
overall in 1984

Played 19 NHL seasons
from 1986–2004,
2005–06

Stats: See page 4 04

> "As a hockey player, you play for the team and for your teammates. You never play for yourself or think about yourself. This is not tennis, where you're alone on the court. Hockey is a team game."

**AWARDS**
Calder Memorial
Trophy (1987)

Stanley Cup (2001–02)

**ALL-STAR SELECTIONS**
All-Rookie Team (1987)

First All-Star Team
Left Wing (1988, 1989,
1990, 1991, 1993)

Second All-Star
Team Left Wing
(1987, 1992, 2001)

**INTERNATIONAL AWARDS**
Canada Cup (1991)

Gold Medal: World
Championships (1994)

- Holds NHL record for career goals (668) and points (1,394) by a left wing
- Holds NHL record for points (125) by a left wing in regular season, established in 1992–93
- Holds L.A. Kings' team record for points by a rookie (84), established in 1986–87
- Ranks fifth in NHL career power-play goals (247)
- Played amateur hockey with Bourassa Angevins (1982–83); Hull Olympiques (1983–86)
- Led QMJHL in assists (123) and points (191) in 1985–86; led QMJHL playoffs in points (44) in 1985–86
- Named CHL Player of the Year (1986); led Memorial Cup Tournament in goals (8) in 1985–86

- QMJHL First All-Star Team Left Wing (1986); QMJHL Second All-Star Team Left Wing (1985)
- Played in NHL All-Star Game (1988, 1989, 1990, 1991, 1992, 1993, 1999, 2001)
- Led NHL in shooting percentage (24.8%) in 1989–90
- Finished among NHL top-5 in points in 1987–88 (111) and 1991–92 (107)
- Finished among NHL top-5 in goals in 1987–88 (53) and 1992–93 (63)
- Finished among NHL top-5 in power-play goals in 1986–87 (18), 1989–90 (20), 1991–92 (26), 1992–93 (24), 1993–94 (24), 1999-2000 (13)

# Long-shot Lefty

**D**rafted as a late-round long shot, 171st overall by the Los Angeles Kings in 1984, Luc Robitaille seemed unlikely to have a future in the NHL. The Montreal native had only tallied 85 points in 70 games with the Hull Olympiques of the Quebec Major Junior Hockey League the year he was drafted—great totals, but a drop in the bucket in a league where the 10th best scorer totaled 120 points. But Robitaille improved to 148 points his next season and a staggering 191 points the season after that.

Called up to the Kings for the 1986–87 season, his hot hand continued as he scored 45 goals and 39 assists for 84 points, earning a selection to the NHL's Second All-Star Team and the Calder Trophy as the league's top rookie.

**Luc Robitaille during his second stint with the Los Angeles Kings (1997–98 to 2000–01).**

The sharp-shooting left winger scored more than 40 goals in each of his first eight NHL seasons, including three seasons with 50 or more goals and a career-best 63 goals in 1992–93. That season, Robitaille set NHL records for most goals and most points (125) in a season by a left winger. (Alex Ovechkin bettered his goal total by two in 2007–08.) The Kings ended up losing to the Montreal Canadiens in the 1992–93 Stanley Cup final, and Robitallie's prodigious production with the Kings began to decline.

Still nearly a point-per-game player, Robitaille bounced from Pittsburgh to New York then back to Los Angeles and then to Detroit, where he hoped to win a Stanley Cup: "When I went to Detroit, I knew I was there to win, but the adjustment for me was going from playing 20 minutes a game to 13 or 14," he said. "It took me a good four or five months to understand and accept it."

He ended up scoring 30 goals and 20 assists for 50 points, helping the Wings take the Presidents' Trophy and their 10th Stanley Cup.

Robitaille returned for a third stint with Los Angeles in 2003–04, and on March 13, 2004, he scored his 650th career goal. Four days later, he played his 1,000th game as a member of the Kings, and on January 19, 2006, he scored a hat trick to tie and then surpass Marcel Dionne's franchise record of 550 goals.

Robitaille's improbable NHL career concluded with 668 goals, 726 assists and 1,394 points, setting NHL records for left wingers in both goals and points.

# Blair Russel 1965

**Montreal Victorias**

Shoots: Left

Height: Unknown

Weight: Unknown

Born: September 17, 1880;
Montreal, Quebec

Died: December 7, 1961;
Montreal, Quebec

Played 11 elite amateur
and professional
seasons from 1899–1910

Stats: See page 405

"He was probably the most useful member of the club [Montreal Victorias] for he was a tireless skater, a great back checker and a fine scorer in his own right."

— *Montreal Gazette*,
April 14, 1934

- Played as an amateur throughout his career, like Montreal Victorias teammate and future Hall of Fame member Russell (Dubbie) Bowie

- Renowned for his two-way play, he was an aggressive defender and productive forward

- Scored seven goals in a game on January 2, 1904 and also had a six-goal game and a five-goal game during his career

- Refused all offers to become professional with the Montreal Wanderers when the Eastern Canada Amateur Hockey Association became fully professional after the 1907–08 season

- ECAHA First All-Star Team Left Wing (1907)

- Scored four goals in Montreal Victorias' 13–5 loss to Ottawa, February 16, 1907; scored four goals in Montreal Victorias' 13–8 victory over Montreal AAA, February 27, 1907

- Served as president of both the Montreal Victorias and the Inter-Provincial Amateur Hockey Union (1908–09)

- Played amateur hockey with Montreal Jr. Victorias (1894–99); Montreal Royal-Queen (1897–99)

# Fred Scanlan

**1965**

Montreal Shamrocks
Winnipeg Victorias

Shoots: Unknown

Height: Unknown

Weight: Unknown

Born: May 5, 1877:
Montreal, Quebec

Died: November 5, 1950:
San Francisco, California

Played six elite amateur
seasons from 1897–1903

Stats: See page 405

"'Frindy' has always had the reputation of being one of the best forwards in the Dominion. He is a fast skater and a splendid stickhandler."

— *Montreal Gazette*, December 19, 1901

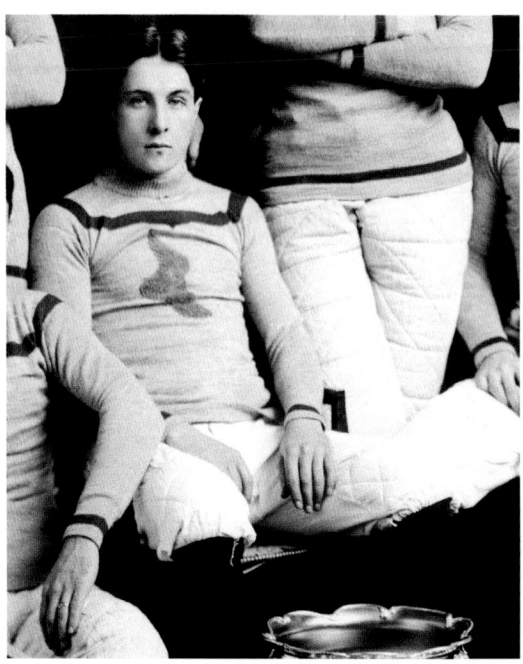

- Renowned for his skating speed and skill as a puckhandler who was considered one of the top forwards in Canada

- Member of Montreal Shamrocks' outstanding forward line with future Hall of Fame members Harry Trihey and Arthur Farrell

- Member of Stanley Cup–winning Montreal Shamrocks team that defeated Queen's University (March, 1899), Winnipeg (February, 1900) and Halifax (March, 1900) to win and retain championship

- Employment opportunity with the Canadian Northern Railway brought him to Winnipeg, where he joined the Victorias hockey team

- Member of Stanley Cup–winning Winnipeg Victorias team that defeated Toronto Wellingtons 5–3 and 5–3 to capture championship, January 29–31, 1901

- Moved to San Francisco in the fall of 1903 and survived the 1906 earthquake

- Died in San Francisco on November 5, 1950 and buried in family plot at Notre Dame des Neiges Cemetery in Montreal on November 11, 1950

**AWARDS**
Stanley Cup (1898–99, 1899–1900, 1901–02)

# 11

# Sweeney Schriner 1962

**ALTERNATE**

**14**

New York Americans
Toronto Maple Leafs

Shoots: Left

Height: 6'

Weight: 185 lbs.

Born: November 30,
1911: Saratov, Russian
Federation

Died: July 4, 1990:
Calgary, Alberta

Played 11 NHL seasons
from 1934–43, 1944–46

Stats: See page 405

"He was the best left winger I ever saw. That includes everybody: Frank Mahovlich, Busher Jackson, Bobby Hull, everybody."

—Conn Smythe

**AWARDS**

Calder Memorial Trophy (1935)

NHL Scoring Leader (1936, 1937)

Stanley Cup (1941–42, 1944–45)

**ALL-STAR SELECTIONS**

First All-Star Team Left Wing (1936, 1941)

Second All-Star Team Left Wing (1937)

- Nicknamed "Sweeney" because of his devotion to a semi-pro baseball player named Bill Sweeney

- Played amateur hockey with Calgary North Hill (1925–28), Calgary Canadians (1928–31) and Calgary Bronks (1931–33)

- Led ASHL in goals (19) and points (22) in 1931–32; goals (22) and points (26) in 1932–33

- Played in NHL All-Star Game (1937)

- Traded to Toronto by N.Y. Americans for Busher Jackson, Buzz Boll, Doc Romnes, Jimmy Fowler and Murray Armstrong, May 18, 1939

- Finished among NHL top-5 in goals in 1935–36 (19), 1936–37 (21), 1937–38 (21) and 1940–41 (24)

- Finished among NHL top-5 in assists in 1935–36 (26), 1936–37 (25) and 1938–39 (32)

- Finished among NHL top-5 in points in 1935–36 (45), 1936–37 (46) and 1938–39 (45)

- Coached Lethbridge Maple Leafs (1946–48); Crow's Nest Pass Coalers (1951–52)

- Played with Regina Capitals (1948–49) and helped team advance to the Allan Cup final

- WCSHL Second All-Star Team Left Wing (1949)

- His legacy is honored by the Dave "Sweeney" Schriner Trophy, which is awarded to the top scorer in the Canada West Universities Athletic Association

# 2013 Brendan Shanahan

*"At every level I have tried to learn and my key to success was having people around me that helped me improve my game."*

## ALTERNATES
## 11 · 18
## 19 · 94

**Detroit Red Wings**
**Hartford Whalers**
**New Jersey Devils**
**New York Rangers**
**St. Louis Blues**

Shoots: Right

Height: 6'-3"

Weight: 220 lbs.

Born: January 23, 1969; Mimico, Ontario

Drafted by the New Jersey Devils second overall in 1987

Played 21 NHL seasons from 1987–2004, 2005–09

Stats: See page 405

- Played amateur hockey with the Mississauga Reps (1984–85), Dixie Beehives (1984–85) and London Knights (1985–87)

- Holds St. Louis Blues single-season record for points (102) and goals (52) by a left wing (1993–94)

- Holds St. Louis Blues playoff record for fastest hat trick (4:16), May 13, 1995

- Led NHL in shorthanded goals (7) and shots on goal (397) in 1993–94; led NHL in power-play goals (20) and shots on goal (82) in 1997 playoffs

- Led St. Louis Blues in game-winning goals for three consecutive seasons (1992–93 to 1994–95)

- Led the Detroit Red Wings in goals for four consecutive seasons (1996–97 to 1999–2000)

- Ranks second in NHL career goals by a left wing (656); ranks third in NHL career assists by a left wing (698 — tied with Dave Andreychuk) and third in career points by a left wing (1,354)

- Tied for third in NHL career 20–goal seasons (19); tied for 10th in NHL career overtime goals (12)

- Played in NHL All-Star Game (1994, 1996, 1997, 1998, 1999, 2000, 2002, 2007)

- Became president of Toronto Maple Leafs on April 11, 2014, after almost three years in the NHL's Department of Player Safety

**AWARDS**

King Clancy Award (2003)

Stanley Cup (1996–97, 1997–98, 2001–02)

**ALL-STAR SELECTIONS**

First All-Star Team Left Wing (1994, 2000)

Second All-Star Team Left Wing (2002)

**INTERNATIONAL AWARDS**

Canada Cup (1991)

Gold Medal: Winter Olympics (2002)

Gold Medal: World Championships (1994)

# 22

# Steve Shutt 1993

ALTERNATE

## 11

Montreal Canadiens
Los Angeles Kings

Shoots: Left

Height: 5'-11"

Weight: 185 lbs.

Born: July 1, 1952:
Toronto, Quebec

Drafted by the Montreal
Canadiens fourth
overall in 1972

Played 13 NHL seasons
from 1972–85

Stats: See page 406

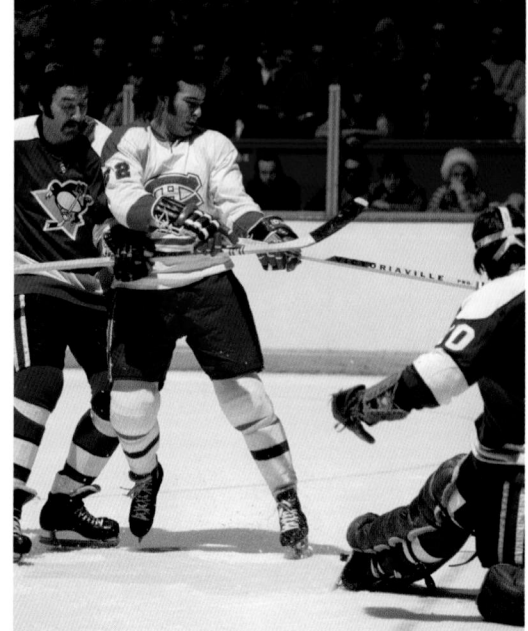

"When you're playing, you don't worry about being in the Hall of Fame. When they come up and say, 'Hey, you've been inducted,' it was a thrill for everybody. You're being acknowledged by your peers and the people within the industry, and that's impressive ... That, more than anything, gave me the greatest satisfaction."

**AWARDS**

Stanley Cup (1972–73, 1975–76, 1976–77, 1977–78, 1978–79)

**ALL-STAR SELECTIONS**

First All-Star Team Left Wing (1977)

Second All-Star Team Left Wing (1978, 1980)

**INTERNATIONAL AWARDS**

Canada Cup (1976)

- Played amateur hockey with North York Rangers (1968–69); Toronto Marlboros (1968–72)
- Led OHA-Jr. in goals (63) in 1971–72
- OHA-Jr. First Team All-Star Left Wing (1972); OHA-Jr. Second Team All-Star Left Wing (1971)
- Holds Montreal Canadiens team record for career goals (408) and points (776) by a left wing
- Shares Montreal Canadiens team record (with Guy Lafleur) for goals in regular season (60), accomplished in 1976–77
- Held NHL record for most goals by a left wing in regular season (60); surpassed by Luc Robitaille in 1992–93

- Led NHL in goals (60) in 1976–77; led NHL in even-strength goals (52) in 1976–77
- Led NHL in game-winning goals (9) in 1976–77
- Played in NHL All-Star Game (1976, 1978, 1981)
- Traded to L.A. Kings by Montreal for future considerations, November 19, 1984
- Claimed on waivers by Montreal from L.A. Kings, June 18, 1985
- Nicknamed "Bullet" because of his powerful shot

# Babe Siebert

*1964*

# 6

> "When I was put on defense and began having 40 and 45 minutes of play each game, I was alright again. That was all there was to it. I hadn't lost what ability I had — I just wasn't getting the opportunity to use it."
>
> — Babe Siebert, reflecting on his "amazing" comeback

**ALTERNATES**

## 12 · 4 · 1

**Boston Bruins**
**Montreal Canadiens**
**Montreal Maroons**
**New York Rangers**

Alternate Position: D

Shoots: Left

Height: 5'-10"

Weight: 182 lbs.

Born: January 14, 1904; Plattsville, Ontario

Died: August 25, 1939; Zurich, Ontario

Played 14 NHL seasons from 1925–39

Stats: See page 407

- Played amateur hockey with Zurich Intermediates (1920–21); Exeter Hawks (1921–22); Kitchener Greenshirts (1922–23); Kitchener Twin Cities (1923–24); Niagara Falls Cataracts (1925–26)

- Signed as a free agent by Montreal Maroons, March 16, 1925

- Member of Montreal Maroons famed S Line with Hooley Smith and Nels Stewart

- Moved back to defense when he joined the Boston Bruins and earned three All-Star team berths as a defenseman

- Played in NHL All-Star Game (1937)

- Served as captain of Montreal Canadiens (1936–39)

- Named head coach of the Montreal Canadiens (June 9, 1939)

- Traded to N.Y. Rangers by Montreal Maroons for cash, July 2, 1932; traded to Boston by N.Y. Rangers for Vic Ripley and Roy Burmeister, December 18, 1933; traded to Montreal by Boston with Roger Jenkins for Leroy Goldsworthy, Sammy McManus and $10,000, September 10, 1936.

- Drowned while swimming with family on Lake Huron, near Zurich, Ontario (August 25, 1939)

- Third NHL Memorial All-Star Game was played in his honor. The Babe Siebert Memorial Game was held at the Montreal Forum on Sunday, October 29, 1939

- The All-Stars defeated the Montreal Canadiens 5–2 in the Siebert Memorial Game that raised $15,000 for Siebert's widow and two young daughters

**AWARDS**

Hart Memorial Trophy (1937)

Stanley Cup (1925–26, 1932–33)

**ALL-STAR SELECTIONS**

First All-Star Team Defense (1936, 1937, 1938)

# Harry E. Watson 1962

Parkdale Canoe Club
Toronto Aura Lee
Toronto Dentals
Toronto Granites
Toronto Marlboros
Toronto Nationals

Shoots: Left

Height: Unknown

Weight: 165 lbs.

Born: July 14, 1898:
St. John's, Newfoundland

Died: September 11,
1957: London, Ontario

Played 13 elite
amateur seasons
from 1916–17, 1918–28,
1929–30, 1931–32

Stats: See page 407

"Savoie, the Swiss goalkeeper, was peppered with bullet-like shots throughout the three periods today. On coming off the ice he said with a grim smile he would about as soon face a machine gun as a hot one off Watson, Munro or McCaffrey."

— *Toronto Daily Star*, January 30, 1924, on Canada's 33–0 Olympic victory over Switzerland in which Watson scored 12 goals

**INTERNATIONAL AWARDS**

Gold Medal: Winter Olympics (1924)

- Played amateur hockey with Whitby Athletics (1913–14); Toronto St. Andrews (1914–15); Toronto Aura Lee (1915–17)
- OHA-Jr. First All-Star Team Left Wing (1915)
- Led OHA-Sr. in goals in 1916–17 (18) and 1922–23 (21)
- Named OHA-Sr. Most Valuable Player (1922, 1923)
- OHA-Sr. First All-Star Team Left Wing (1922, 1923); OHA-Sr. Second All-Star Team Left Wing (1920)
- Led OHA-Sr. playoffs in goals in 1921–22 (5), 1922–23 (3)
- Member of Allan Cup–winning Toronto Granites (1922, 1923); led Allan Cup playoffs in goals (11) and points (15) in 1922–23

- Led Winter Olympics in goals (36) and points (50) in 1924
- Served as a fighter pilot with the Royal Flying Corps during World War I
- Member of OHA-Sr.-champion Toronto Granites (1919–20, 1921–22, 1922–23)
- Turned down offer of $30,000 to turn professional and play with the NHL's Montreal Maroons in 1925
- Coached Toronto National "Sea Fleas" (1930–32); coached Toronto City Hall (1931–32)
- Guided the Toronto National "Sea Fleas" to the Allan Cup championship in 1932 but retired before the team earned a silver medal at the 1933 World Championships

# 1994 **Harry P. Watson**

**4**

> "He was a larger man than many players of our era, very strong, and a solid bodychecker. He was a clean player who did not have to resort to fouls because of his skill level."
>
> — Bill Ezinicki, Watson's teammate with the Maple Leafs from 1946–50

**ALTERNATES**

**5 · 17
18 · 19**

**Brooklyn Americans
Chicago Black Hawks
Detroit Red Wings
Toronto Maple Leafs**

Shoots: Left

Height: 6'-1"

Weight: 207 lbs.

Born: May 6, 1923: Saskatoon, Saskatchewan

Died: November 19, 2002: Toronto, Ontario

Played 14 NHL seasons from 1941–43, 1945–57

Stats: See page 407

- Played amateur hockey with Saskatoon Wesleys (1934–38); Saskatoon Chiefs (1938–40); Saskatoon Dodgers (1939–40); Saskatoon Quakers (1940–41)

- Signed as a free agent by Brooklyn Americans, October 10, 1941

- Made NHL debut in 1–0 loss to Chicago Black Hawks, November 6, 1941

- Played with Montreal RCAF, Saskatoon Navy and Winnipeg RCAF during World War II

- Rights transferred to Detroit from Brooklyn in Special Dispersal Draft October 9, 1942; traded to Toronto by Detroit for Billy Taylor, September 21, 1946

- Finished second in NHL goals in 1948–49 (26)

- Assisted on Bill Barilko's Stanley Cup–winning goal in Game 5 of the 1951 Stanley Cup final against Montreal goaltender Gerry McNeil, April 2, 1951

- Scored Stanley Cup–winning goal in Toronto's 7–2 victory over Detroit Red Wings, April 14, 1948

- Played the entire 1948–49 season without registering a single minute in penalties and received only 150 minutes in penalties in 809 NHL games

- Traded to Chicago by Toronto for cash, December 10, 1954

- Nicknamed "Whipper" because of his resemblance to famous wrestler "Whipper" Billy Watson

- Played in NHL All-Star Game (1947, 1948, 1949, 1951, 1952, 1953, 1955)

**AWARDS**

Stanley Cup (1942–43, 1946–47, 1947–48, 1948–49, 1950–51)

**65**

| | JACK ADAMS | SYL APPS | DAN BAIN | MARTY BARRY | JEAN BÉLIVEAU |
|---|---|---|---|---|---|
| ...X ...NTLEY | FRANK BOUCHER | BILLY BURCH | BOBBY CLARKE | BILL COWLEY | MARCEL DIONNE |
| ...HIL ...POSITO | SERGEI FEDOROV | BERNIE FEDERKO | PETER FORSBERG | FRANK FOYSTON | RON FRANCIS |
| ...RANK ...REDRICKSON | DOUG GILMOUR | CAMMI GRANATO | WAYNE GRETZKY | DALE HAWERCHUK | DICK IRVIN |
| ...NGELA JAMES | DUKE KEATS | TED KENNEDY | DAVE KEON | ELMER LACH | PAT LAFONTAINE |

# CENTRE

# 12

## Sid Abel 1969

NO. RETIRED BY DETROIT

ALTERNATE

**20**

**Chicago Black Hawks
Detroit Red Wings**

Alternate Position: LW

Shoots: Left

Height: 5'-11"

Weight: 170 lbs.

Born: February 22, 1918:
Melville, Saskatchewan

Died: February 7,
2000: Farmington
Hills, Michigan

Played 14 NHL seasons
from 1938–43, 1945–54

Stats: See page 408

"I kept telling my wife Gloria to pinch me. I felt sure I was going to wake up and find that I'd been having a wonderful dream."
— Sid Abel, on winning the Hart Trophy

**AWARDS**

Hart Memorial
Trophy (1949)

Stanley Cup (1942–43,
1949–50, 1951–52)

**ALL-STAR
SELECTIONS**

First All-Star Team
Center (1949, 1950)

Second All-Star Team
Center (1951)

Second All-Star Team
Left Wing (1942)

- Played amateur hockey with Melville Millionaires (1936–37); Saskatoon Wesleys (1936–37); Flin Flon Bombers (1937–38)
- Led NHL in goals (28) in 1948–49
- Finished among NHL top-5 in assists in 1941–42 (31), 1947–48 (30), 1948–49 (26), 1949–50 (35), 1950–51 (38) and 1951–52 (36)
- Finished among NHL top-5 in points in 1941–42 (49), 1948–49 (54), 1949–50 (69) and 1950–51 (61)
- One of only six Hall of Fame members (with Doug Bentley, Dit Clapper, Neil Colville, Mark Messier and Alex Delvecchio) to be selected as an NHL All-Star at two different positions (Left Wing and Center)

- Nicknamed "Boot Nose" after Rocket Richard punched him in the nose and broke it
- Played in NHL All-Star Game (1949, 1950, 1951)
- Member of Detroit's famed Production Line with Ted Lindsay and Gordie Howe
- Traded to Chicago by Detroit for cash, July 22, 1952
- Served as player/coach of Chicago Black Hawks (1952–54)
- Coached Detroit Red Wings (1958–68, 1969–70) and St. Louis Blues (1971–72)
- Served as general manager of Detroit Red Wings (1962–71), St. Louis Blues (1972–73) and Kansas City Scouts (1974–76)

# Abel-bodied

They may call Gordie Howe "Mr. Hockey," but for the 33 years, between 1938 and 1971, another hockey giant loomed large in Detroit's collective hockey conscious. As an All-Star player, then coach and then general manager, Sid Abel was one of the most recognizable figures in Detroit's sporting scene. Howe may have the moniker, but there are few men who have done more with one franchise than Abel did with the Detroit Red Wings.

On the ice, Abel was an accomplished playmaking center and team leader who served as the club's captain from the tender age of 24. He also missed two full seasons to fight in World War II. Shortly after his return he was put on a unit with Howe and Ted Lindsay, and the prodigious Production Line was born. Abel snared the Hart Trophy as league MVP in 1949, when he was 30, and he was a key factor in three Red Wings Cup victories, his biggest contribution coming in the 1949–50 final. That series against the New York Rangers saw Abel—without Howe in the lineup due to injury—pace all scorers, with five goals and two assists for seven points in seven games.

A two-year stint with the Chicago Black Hawks at the end of his playing career allowed Abel to try his hand at being a player/coach. He scored only nine points but, more importantly, realized that he truly enjoyed instructing players. He retired from hockey in 1953–54 but returned partway through the 1957–58 season as Red Wings coach. Under Abel's guidance, the Red Wings reached the

**Coach Sid Abel stands between Gordie Howe and Pete Goegan during the 1959–60 playoffs.**

Stanley Cup final four times (1961, 1963, 1964 and 1966) but were victims to the upstart Black Hawks and the mid-dynasty Toronto Maple Leafs and Montreal Canadiens.

Abel added the responsibilities of general manager to his portfolio in 1962–63, a post he held until 1971. One of the major transactions he oversaw was the blockbuster trade that brought Frank Mahovlich to Detroit and sent Norm Ullman to Toronto in March 1968. While still holding the position of Detroit general manager, Abel was elected to the Hockey Hall of Fame as a player in 1969.

**69**

### CENTER

# Jack Adams 1959

**ALTERNATES**

## 9 · 4 · 11 · 8

Ottawa Senators
Toronto Arenas
Toronto St. Patricks
Vancouver Millionaires

Shoots: Right

Height: 5'-9"

Weight: 175 lbs.

Born: June 14, 1894;
Fort William, Ontario

Died: May 1, 1968;
Detroit, Michigan

Played 10 professional
seasons from 1917–27

Stats: See page 408

"No one ever shook the jolly out of Jack and got away with it. Life with Jack was like that. You either laughed with him or snarled with him or forfeited your right to his company."

— *Montreal Gazette* tribute

- Signed as a free agent by Toronto Arenas, February 9, 1918

- Traded to Vancouver Millionaires (PCHA) by Toronto Arenas for cash, December 7, 1919

- Led PCHA in penalty minutes (60) in 1920–21; led PCHA in goals (26) and points (30) in 1922–23

- Lost in the Stanley Cup final in each of his last two seasons with Vancouver against teams he would play for later in his career — the Ottawa Senators and Toronto St. Pats

- Traded to Toronto St. Pats by Vancouver Millionaires (PCHA) for the rights to Corb Denneny, December 18, 1922

- Led NHL in penalty minutes (66) in 1922–23

- Served as general manager for 35-straight years (1927–62) managing the Detroit Cougars, Detroit Falcons and Detroit Red Wings

- Coached for 20-straight years (1927–47): Detroit Cougars, Detroit Falcons and Detroit Red Wings

- Founded the Central Professional Hockey League and served as the league's first president (1963–68)

**AWARDS**

Lester Patrick
Trophy (1966)

Stanley Cup
(1917–18, 1926–27)

**ALL-STAR
SELECTIONS**

PCHA First All-Star Team
Center (1921, 1922)

First All-Star Team
Coach (1937, 1943)

Second All-Star Team
Coach (1945)

- Only person in NHL history to have his name engraved on the Stanley Cup as a player (1918, 1927), coach (1936, 1937, 1943) and general manager (1936, 1937, 1943, 1950, 1952, 1954, 1955)

- Nicknamed "Jolly Jack"

- Played amateur hockey with Fort William Collegiate (1909–10); Fort William YMCA (1910–12); Fort William CYMA (1912–14); Fort William Maple Leafs (1914–17); Calumet Miners (1915–16); Peterborough 247th (1916–17); Sarnia Sailors (1917–18)

- Led TBSHL in goals (11) and points (11) in 1912–13, goals (33) and points (33) in 1913–14 and goals (16) and points (16) in 1914–15

- Led OIHA in goals (19) and points (22) in 1916–17

# Jack Adams, the Player

Jack Adams, the Hall of Fame player turned executive, is best known today for his off-ice talents, as the trophy annually given to the NHL's best coach is named in his honor. But before his long tenure orchestrating the Detroit Red Wings of the 1930s, 40s and 50s, he was a highly sought-after player.

Adams was playing senior hockey in Calumet, Michigan, in 1915 as a 19-year-old in the Northern Michigan Senior Hockey League when he was referred to by a journalist as a "bobcat on blades." It was a rough league and Adams had to learn to fight in order to survive—his toughness became a calling card throughout his entire hockey life.

The young star turned pro with the Toronto Arenas of the newly formed National Hockey League during the 1917–18 season. He played eight games and two playoff contests with the Arenas, helping them win the Stanley Cup. Two years later he was lured to the Vancouver Millionaires in the Pacific Coast Hockey Association (PCHA) after receiving a desperate telegram from team owner Frank Patrick. "Our team in very bad shape," it read, "Skinner has twisted knee cartilage and Duncan with shoulder ligaments both out of game for month or more. I would greatly appreciate if you would make a big effort to come and help us out…"

Adams played three seasons in Vancouver, winning the PCHA scoring championship in his third, but the Millionaires never did win the Stanley Cup with Adams. Twice the team represented the PCHA in the Stanley Cup

**Jack Adams as a member of the 1917–18 Toronto Arenas.**

final, and twice they faltered, losing a pair of five-games sets, first against Ottawa in 1921 and then against Toronto in 1922.

Adams intended to quit hockey in 1923, but a lucrative offer from the Toronto St. Pats took him back to Ontario for the 1922–23 season. He finished third in scoring that year and stayed three more seasons with the club before being sold to the Ottawa Senators. With Adams, the Senators finished first in the league in 1926–27 and defeated the Boston Bruins to win the Stanley Cup. It would be Adams' last year as a player; he was 31 years old. He began coaching the very next season with the Detroit Cougars, who later became the Detroit Red Wings, and a second legend was born.

# 10

## CENTER

# Syl Apps 1961

NO. RETIRED BY TORONTO

**Toronto Maple Leafs**

Shoots: Left

Height: 6'

Weight: 185 lbs.

Born: January 18, 1915:
Paris, Ontario

Died: December 24, 1998:
Kingston, Ontario

Played 10 NHL seasons
from 1936–43, 1945–48

Stats: See page 408

"[Apps] was getting $6,000 for the season and he came to me and said, 'Conn, I'm making more than I deserve. I want to give you this check.' Well, I almost died of heart failure. Of course, I refused his check. I felt that anyone who thought in such terms was bound to square off what he thought was a debt the following season."

—Conn Smythe, on Apps trying to return money after missing half a season with an injury

AWARDS

Calder Memorial
Trophy (1937)

Lady Byng Memorial
Trophy (1942)

Stanley Cup (1941–42,
1946–47, 1947–48)

**ALL-STAR
SELECTIONS**

First All-Star Team
Center (1939, 1942)

Second All-Star Team
Center (1938, 1941, 1943)

- Played amateur hockey with Paris Greens (1930–31); McMaster University (1931–35); Hamilton Tigers (1935–36); Toronto Dominions (1935–36)

- Led OHA-Sr. in points (38) in 1935–36, led OHA-Sr. in playoff assists (7) and points (19) in 1935–36

- Won gold medal in pole vault representing Canada at 1934 British Empire Games in London, England; placed sixth at the 1936 Summer Olympics

- Led NHL in assists in 1936–37 (29) and 1937–38 (29)

- Finished second in NHL regular season points in 1936–37 (45), 1937–38 (50); tied for third in points in 1940–41 (44)

- Played in NHL All-Star Game (1947)

- Served as captain of Toronto Maple Leafs (1940–43, 1945–48)

- Played for Toronto Army Daggers (1943–44) and Ottawa All-Stars (1944–45) during World War II

- Father of Syl Apps Jr. who played in NHL with N.Y. Rangers, Pittsburgh and L.A. Kings from 1970–80

- Grandfather of Gillian Apps, member of the gold medal–winning Canadian women's hockey team at 2006, 2010 and 2014 Winter Olympics

- Legacy honored by Canada Post, who issued a 47-cent stamp featuring his profile

- Member of Legislative Assembly of Ontario representing Kingston (1963–67); member of Legislative Assembly of Ontario representing Kingston and the Islands (1967–77)

# 1949 Dan Bain

> "Those were the days of real athletes. When we passed, the puck never left the ice and if the wingman wasn't there to get it, it was because he had a broken leg."
>
> — Dan Bain, on the hockey of his era

**Winnipeg Victorias**

Shoots: Right

Height: 6'

Weight: 185 lbs.

Born: February 14, 1874; Belleville, Ontario

Died: August 15, 1962; Winnipeg, Manitoba

Played eight elite amateur seasons from 1894–1902

Stats: See page 408

- Helped Winnipeg Victorias win seven consecutive Manitoba Provincial Championships, from 1895 to 1902
- Led Manitoba Northwest League in goals (10) in 1895–96; led MNWHA in goals (7) and points (8) in 1896–97; led MNWHA in goals (11) and points (12) in 1898–99
- Scored Stanley Cup–winning goal in Winnipeg's 2–0 victory over Montreal Victorias, February 14, 1896
- First player to score a Stanley Cup–winning goal in overtime in Winnipeg's 2–1 victory over Montreal Shamrocks, January 31, 1901

- Won Campbell Trophy as Winnipeg gymnastic champion (1891)
- Won Carruthers' Cup Cycling Championship (1984–96)
- Won Canadian trapshooting championship (1903)
- Named Canada's Top Athlete of the Half-Century (1900)
- Served as captain of Winnipeg Victorias (1898–1901)
- Inducted into Canada's Sports Hall of Fame (1971)
- Inducted into Manitoba Sports Hall of Fame (1981)

**AWARDS**

Stanley Cup (1895–96, 1900–01, 1901–02)

# **7** Marty Barry 1965

**ALTERNATES**
## 8 · 10 · 14
## 11 · 9

Boston Bruins
Detroit Red Wings
Montreal Canadiens
New York Americans

Shoots: Left

Height: 5'-11"

Weight: 175 lbs.

Born: December 8, 1904;
Quebec City, Quebec

Died: August 20, 1969;
Halifax, Nova Scotia

Played 12 NHL seasons
from 1927–28, 1929–40

Stats: See page 409

"The rink seemed like it was miles long along about 10 minutes to 2 o'clock in the morning. Players of both teams were praying for somebody to score before we all fell from exhaustion."

— Marty Barry, on the NHL's longest overtime game, March 24, 1936

**AWARDS**

Lady Byng Memorial Trophy (1937)

Stanley Cup (1935–36, 1936–37)

**ALL-STAR SELECTIONS**

First All-Star Team Center (1937)

- Played amateur hockey with Montreal St-Ann's (1924–25); Montreal St-Anthony (1924–26); Montreal Bell Telephone (1926–27)

- Led Can-Am in goals (19) and points (29) in 1928–29

- Nicknamed "Goal-A-Game Barry"

- Finished among NHL top-5 in goals in 1932–33 (24), 1933–34 (27) and 1935–36 (21)

- Finished among NHL top-5 in assists in 1936–37 (27) and 1938–39 (28)

- Finished among NHL top-5 in points in 1933–34 (39), 1935–36 (40), 1936–37 (44) and 1938–39 (41)

- Led NHL playoffs in goals (4), assists (7) and points (11) in 1936–37

- Missed only two games in his first 10 NHL seasons

- Scored Stanley Cup–winning goal in Detroit's 3–0 victory over N.Y. Rangers, April 15, 1937

- Inducted into Detroit Red Wings' Hall of Fame (1944)

- Described in an article by Detroit Times' writer Bob Murphy as a player who "possesses that faculty of mechanical perfection"

- Played in NHL All-Star Game (1937)

- Served as player/coach of Minneapolis Millers (1940–41)

- Coached Minneapolis Millers (1941–42)

- Coached Halifax St. Mary's Saints (1947–52); coached St. Mary's Crescents (1947–49)

# Forgotten Iron Man

**M**arty Barry was a technically skilled iron man who missed only two games in his first 10 full NHL seasons, finishing among the NHL's top-five scorers four times, and he tied with Harvey "Busher" Jackson for most points in the 1930s. Yet he is seldom given the attention of other 1930s luminaries, like Eddie Shore and Howie Morenz.

But Barry certainly left his mark: He scored the winning goal in the Detroit Red Wings' second Stanley Cup victory, played in the longest game in NHL history, led all playoff scorers in 1930 and 1937 and played in two of the invitational matches (one of them being Morenz's memorial game) that set the stage for the NHL's official All-Star Game.

According to Barry's daughter Barbara Cormier, the moment that transformed her father's career—which was going well in Boston—happened when Boston's general manager, Art Ross, acquired Cooney Weiland of the Detroit Red Wings. "Art Ross, really wanted to get Cooney Weiland. He and Jack Adams [manager] of the Red Wings were talking, and Adams said he could have Weiland if the Bruins gave dad to the Red Wings. That's how the deal was made, just talking. And Adams said later, 'Art Ross just gave me the Stanley Cup.' … And [Detroit] did win it that year, for the first time, and they won it again the next year too."

That made the Red Wings the first American-based team to win back-to-back Stanley Cups. Barry centered a potent line, with Herbie Lewis and Larry Aurie on the flanks, and in 1936–37 he became the first Red Wing to win the Lady Byng Trophy for gentlemanly conduct.

In November 1939 Barry signed with the

**Marty Barry wore this Detroit jersey during one of his four seasons with the club. In 1942 — two years after his retirement — Barry wore this All-Star jersey in the "Victory All-Star Game"; on a team of retired NHLers, Barry played against the Boston Bruins to raise funds for U.S. Army relief.**

Montreal Canadiens, for whom he played his last NHL season. In 1940–41 he suited up for the Minneapolis Millers of the American Hockey Association then retired as a player to try his hand at coaching. Under his tutelage the Halifax St. Mary's juniors reached the eastern Canada final, one step short of the Memorial Cup, in 1947.

Barry gained a place in the Red Wings Hall of Fame in 1944 and the Hockey Hall of Fame in 1965.

# 4

CENTER

## Jean Béliveau 1972

NO. RETIRED BY MONTREAL

ALTERNATES

## 12 · 17 · 20

**Montreal Canadiens**

Shoots: Left

Height: 6'-3"

Weight: 205 lbs.

Born: August 31, 1931: Trois Rivières, Quebec

Died: December 2, 2014: Montreal, Quebec

Played 20 NHL seasons from 1950–51, 1952–71

Stats: See page 409

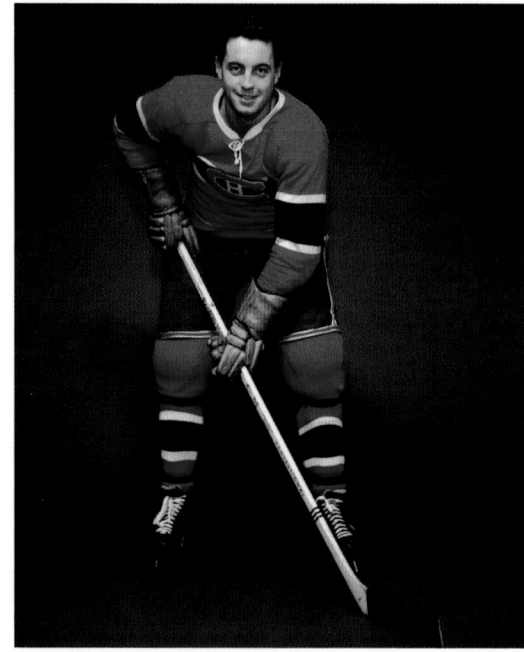

"Ever since I was a boy, I dreamt of two things: one, to wear the sweater of the Montreal Canadiens, and two, to win the Stanley Cup."

**AWARDS**

Art Ross Trophy (1956)

Conn Smythe Trophy (1965)

Hart Memorial Trophy (1956, 1964)

Stanley Cup (1955–56, 1956–57, 1957–58, 1958–59, 1959–60, 1964–65, 1965–66, 1967–68, 1968–69, 1970–71)

**ALL-STAR SELECTIONS**

First All-Star Team Center (1955, 1956, 1957, 1959, 1960, 1961)

Second All-Star Team Center (1958, 1964, 1966, 1969)

- Holds NHL record for fastest Stanley Cup–winning goal (14 seconds) in Montreal's 4–0 victory over Chicago Black Hawks, April 14, 1965

- First winner of Conn Smythe Trophy as NHL playoff MVP (1965)

- Played amateur hockey with Victoriaville Tigers (1947–49); Quebec Citadelles (1949–51)

- Named QJHL Rookie of the Year (1949); QMHL First All-Star Team Center (1951, 1953)

- Led QJHL in goals (48) in 1948–49; led QJHL playoffs in goals (22) and points (31) in 1949–50; led QJHL in goals (63) and points (124) in 1950–51; led QJHL playoffs in goals (12), assists (14) and points (26) in 1950–51

- Led NHL in goals in 1955–56 (47) and 1958–59 (45)

- Led NHL in assists in 1960–61 (58) and 1965–66 (48)

- Led NHL in points (88) in 1955–56

- Played in NHL All-Star Game (1953, 1954, 1955, 1956, 1957, 1958, 1959, 1960, 1963, 1964, 1965, 1968, 1969)

- Registered 1,000th career NHL point in Montreal's 5–2 loss to Detroit Red Wings, March 3, 1968; recorded 500th career NHL goal in Montreal's 6–2 victory over Minnesota North Stars, February 11, 1971

- Nicknamed "Le Gros Bill" after a character in Quebec folklore

- Served as captain of Montreal Canadiens (1961–71)

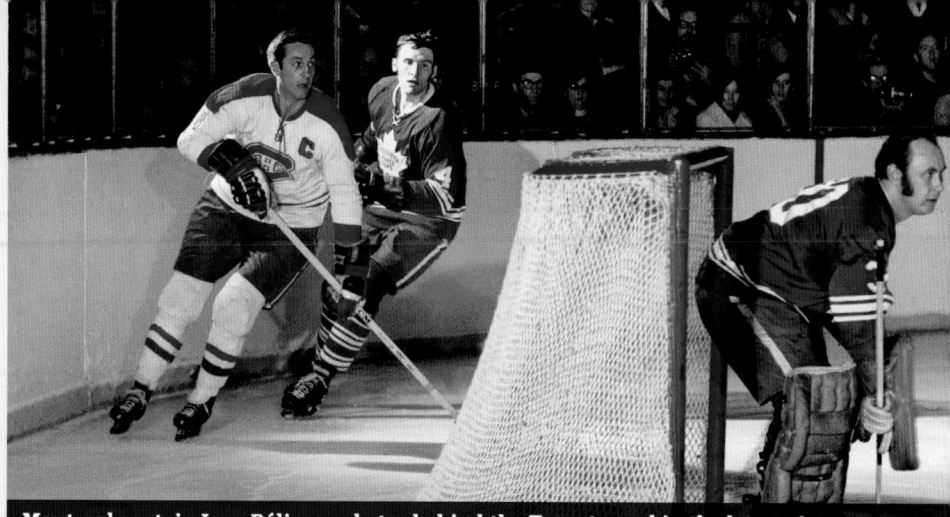

**Montreal captain Jean Béliveau skates behind the Toronto goal in the late 1960s.**

# Le Gros Bill

Perhaps no other player in hockey's history embodies integrity and defines ability better than Jean Béliveau, "Le Gros Bill." A gentleman off ice and a competitor on it, he commanded respect and engendered awe. Tall and strong, he quickly proved himself physically, with a couple of one-sided fights and impressive goals, and then never had to prove himself again. A graceful skater with a fluid stride, he played with a tenacity that belied—or, perhaps, confirmed—his gentleman's reputation.

Yet Béliveau holds no single NHL record. His 507 career goals—an elite total—are not a record. Ditto for his 1,219 points and 1,125 games played. His 176 career playoff points are no longer tops, and even his amazing 10 Stanley Cups were surpassed by teammate Henri Richard. And yet, Béliveau still rates among a handful of legends as one of the greatest to ever play the game.

As the captain of the Montreal Canadiens, Béliveau led by example and followed his own code: "A captain has three roles on the team. "One, is during a game, when the fans and referees are watching him. Two, is his role between management and the players—to be available to the players at all times, whether it's for hockey reasons or personal reasons. And three, a captain must represent his team and city well." With this code, Béliveau set the gold standard for sports captains, especially hockey.

Of all his feats, Béliveau, like many others before and since, cherished his first Stanley Cup victory most of all: "In 1956, we finally won the Cup. Ever since I was a boy, I dreamt of two things: one, to wear the sweater of the Montreal Canadiens, and two, to win the Stanley Cup. In 1954 and 1955, we lost to Detroit. We came so close, but we never won. Then, finally, in 1956, we won."

The 1955–56 season was Béliveau's fifth with the club and third as a roster regular. The Canadiens' Cup win that season ended a Detroit dynasty that had seen the team win three Cups in six years; it also started the greatest dynasty in hockey's history, as Béliveau and the Habs rolled to five consecutive Stanley Cup victories.

# 7 Max Bentley 1966

**ALTERNATES:**
## 5 · 18 · 22

**Chicago Black Hawks
New York Rangers
Toronto Maple Leafs**

Shoots: Left

Height: 5'-10"

Weight: 155 lbs.

Born: March 1, 1920;
Delisle, Saskatchewan

Died: January 19,
1984; Saskatoon,
Saskatchewan

Played 12 NHL seasons
from 1940–43, 1945–54

Stats: See page 410

"He was the best, a dipsy-doodler who could really skate and was tremendous with the puck."

— Vic Lynn, teammate

**AWARDS**

NHL Scoring Leader
(1946, 1947)

Lady Byng Memorial
Trophy (1943)

Hart Memorial
Trophy (1946)

Stanley Cup (1947–48,
1948–49, 1950–51)

**ALL-STAR
SELECTIONS**

First All-Star Team
Center (1946)

Second All-Star Team
Center (1947)

- Shares NHL record for most goals in a single period (4), accomplished in Chicago's 10–1 victory over N.Y. Rangers, January 28, 1943

- Nicknamed "The Dipsy-Doodle Dandy from Delisle"

- Played amateur hockey with Rosetown Red Wings (1935–37); Drumheller Miners (1937–39); Saskatoon Quakers (1939–40)

- Played with Victoria Navy, San Diego Skyhawks and Calgary Currie Army during World War II (1942–45)

- Led ASHL in points (43) in 1936–37; led ASHL in playoff goals (7) and points (8) in 1936–37

- Led SSHL in goals (37) in 1939–40

- Led ANDHL in goals (18), points (31) and penalty minutes (26) in 1942–43

- Played in NHL All-Star Game (1947, 1948, 1949, 1951)

- Led NHL in points in 1945–46 (61) and 1946–47 (72)

- Finished second in NHL assists in 1942–43 (44), 1945–46 (30) and 1946–47 (43)

- Finished among NHL top-5 in goals in 1945–46 (31), 1946–47 (29) and 1947–48 (26)

- Traded to Toronto by Chicago with Cy Thomas for Gus Bodnar, Bud Poile, Gaye Stewart, Ernie Dickens and Bob Goldham, November 2, 1947

- Brother of Doug Bentley, who played in NHL with Chicago and N.Y. Rangers from 1939–54; brother of Reggie Bentley, who played in NHL with Chicago in 1942–43

# The Dipsy-Doodle Dandy from Delisle

**M**ax Bentley was the youngest of six hockey-playing brothers from Delisle, Saskatchewan, two of whom, Reg and Doug, also played in the NHL. The brothers were all small by NHL standards, and they were taught early on that "If they can't hit you, they can't hurt you." In response, Max developed the extraordinary puckhandling skills that made him famous in the NHL as the "Dipsy-Doodle Dandy from Delisle" and allowed him to evade physical play.

Bentley's first real shot at the NHL came with the Chicago Black Hawks in 1940, at the urging of his brother Doug, who had cracked the Hawks' lineup in 1939. Max Bentley started poorly, but he got a toehold of NHL respectability in his second season, as he earned 30 points in 39 games. He exploded in his third season, tallying 70 points in 47 games and winning the Lady Byng Memorial Trophy as the league's most gentlemanly player.

Just as he was becoming an elite NHLer, Bentley put his career aside and enlisted with the Canadian Armed Forces. While serving his country he played hockey with the Currie Barracks team of Calgary to stay sharp. Bentley rejoined the NHL after the war effort, leading the league in scoring his first two seasons back (1945–46 and 1946–47) as well as being named the league's Most Valuable Player in 1945–46.

On November 2, 1947, needing help throughout their lineup, the Hawks traded Bentley and prospect Cy Thomas to the Toronto Maple Leafs for five players. The

**Max Bentley (right) stands with his older brother Doug (left) after Max was traded in 1947.**

trade captivated Torontonians, and Bentley's puckhandling prowess dazzled the Maple Leafs faithful; Toronto is where the centerman earned his famous nickname.

More famous than the trade and nickname, however, is what became of the Leafs after Bentley's arrival. Toronto had won their first Stanley Cup since 1942 the year before Bentley arrived, and with Bentley they repeated as Cup champions. Then the Leafs won it again the following season to make it three in a row (an NHL first), with Bentley filling in ably for the retired Syl Apps. In 1950 Detroit extinguished the Leafs' hopes for a fourth consecutive Cup, but Toronto rose to the challenge one more time, snaring the Cup from Montreal in 1951. Max Bentley would play three more distinguished seasons, his final with his brother Doug in New York in 1953–54.

# 7 Frank Boucher 1958

**ALTERNATES**

**8 · 17**

Ottawa Senators
New York Rangers
Vancouver Maroons

Shoots: Left
Height: 5'-9"
Weight: 185 lbs.
Born: October 7, 1901:
Ottawa, Ontario
Died: December 12,
1977: Ottawa, Ontario
Played 18 professional
seasons from
1921–38, 1943–44
Stats: See page 410

"My thought was that hockey had become a see-saw affair. Defending teams were jammed in their own end for minutes because they couldn't pass their way out against the new five-man attack."

— Frank Boucher, commenting on his idea to introduce the red line to hockey

**AWARDS**

Lady Byng Memorial Trophy (1928, 1929, 1930, 1931, 1933, 1934, 1935)

Lester Patrick Trophy (1993)

Stanley Cup (1927–28, 1932–33)

**ALL-STAR SELECTIONS**

PCHA First All-Star Team Center (1923, 1924)

WCHL First All-Star Team Center (1925)

First All-Star Team Center (1933, 1934, 1935)

Second All-Star Team Center (1931)

First All-Star Team Coach (1942)

Second All-Star Team Coach (1940)

- Held NHL record for career assists (264), surpassed by Bill Cowley in 1943–44
- Played amateur hockey with Ottawa New Edinburghs (1916–19); Ottawa Munitions (1917–18); Lethbridge Vets (1919–20)
- Nicknamed "Raffles" after the gentlemanly thief in E.W. Hornung's books because of his ability to steal the puck from opposing players and overall clean play
- Signed as a free agent by Ottawa Senators, December 6, 1921; traded to Vancouver Maroons (PCHA) by Ottawa for cash, September 19, 1922
- Renowned for his ability to draw opposition players toward him and deftly pass to his linemates and is credited with perfecting the drop pass

- Starred for the N.Y. Rangers with brothers Bill Cook at right wing and Bun Cook at left wing on what is considered one of the NHL's first great forward lines
- Assisted on the first goal scored in the history of the N.Y. Rangers franchise in Rangers' 1–0 victory over Montreal Maroons, November 16, 1926
- Scored Stanley Cup–winning goal in N.Y. Rangers' 2–1 victory over Montreal Maroons, April 14, 1928
- Played in NHL All-Star Game (1937)
- Led NHL playoffs in goals (7) and points (10) in 1927–28
- Led NHL in assists in 1928–29 (16), 1929–30 (36) and 1932–33 (28)
- Coached N.Y. Rovers (1938–39); coached N.Y. Rangers (1939–49, 1953–54)

# 1974 Billy Burch

# 5

**ALTERNATES**
## 4 · 9 · 6
## 12 · 8

Boston Bruins
Chicago Black Hawks
Hamilton Tigers
New York Americans

Alternate Position: LW

Shoots: Left

Height: 6'

Weight: 200 lbs.

Born: November 20, 1900: Yonkers, New York

Died: November 30, 1950: Toronto, Ontario

Played 11 NHL seasons from 1922–33

Stats: See page 410

> "He broke in and played in the days when the going was rough and a player had to be good to stick. If you didn't make it, there was no going back to the amateur ranks. Billy turned pro and never looked back. He was a major leaguer all the way."
>
> —Tommy Shields, *Montreal Gazette* columnist

- First United States-born player to become a star in the NHL

- Born in Yonkers—but trained in Toronto— he was still promoted by N.Y. Americans management as "the Babe Ruth of hockey" to arouse hockey interest in New York

- Played amateur hockey with Toronto (Parkdale) Canoe Club Paddlers (1919–20); Toronto Aura Lee (1920–22)

- Member of Memorial Cup–winning Toronto Canoe Club (1920)

- Led Memorial Cup playoffs in goals (42), assists (12) and points (54)

- Led OHA-Jr. in assists (10) and points (23) in 1921–22

- Played quarterback for Toronto Central YMCA, Canadian Junior Football Champions (1920)

- Played lacrosse with Toronto Maitlands

- Served as captain of N.Y. Americans (1925–32)

- Scored first goal in history of N.Y. Americans franchise in 2–1 victory over Pittsburgh Pirates, December 2, 1925

- Member of Hamilton Tigers team that refused to participate in 1925 playoffs without extra pay—often considered to be the first players strike in NHL history

- Transferred to N.Y. Americans after NHL club purchased Hamilton franchise, September 25, 1925

- Traded to Boston by N.Y. Americans for cash, April 13, 1932; traded to Chicago by Boston for Vic Ripley, January 17, 1933

**AWARDS**

Hart Memorial Trophy (1925)

Lady Byng Memorial Trophy (1927)

# 16 Bobby Clarke 1987

NO. RETIRED BY
PHILADELPHIA

ALTERNATE
## 36

Philadelphia Flyers

Shoots: Left

Height: 5'-10"

Weight: 176 lbs.

Born: August 13, 1949;
Flin Flon, Manitoba

Drafted by the
Philadelphia Flyers
17th overall in 1969

Played 15 NHL seasons
from 1969–84

Stats: See page 410

"We take the shortest route to the puck and arrive in ill humor."
— Bobby Clarke, talking about the Broad Street Bullies

AWARDS

Bill Masterton Memorial
Trophy (1972)

Hart Memorial Trophy
(1973, 1975, 1976)

Ted Lindsay Award* (1973)

Frank J. Selke Trophy (1983)

Lester Patrick Trophy (1980)

Stanley Cup
(1974–75, 1975–76)

ALL-STAR
SELECTIONS

First All-Star Team
Center (1975, 1976)

Second All-Star Team
Center (1973, 1974)

INTERNATIONAL
AWARDS

Summit Series (1972)

Canada Cup (1976)

Bronze Medal: World
Championships (1982)

*Known as the Lester
B. Pearson Award
from 1971 to 2009

- First player from an expansion-era team (post-1967) to win Hart Trophy as NHL MVP (1973)

- Played amateur hockey with Flin Flon Midget Bombers (1965–66); Flin Flon Bombers (1965–69)

- Led MJHL in goals (71), assists (112) and points (183) in 1966–67

- Led WCJHL in assists (117) and points (168) in 1967–68, assists (86) and points (137) in 1968–69

- Led WCJHL playoffs in assists (16) and points (25) in 1968–69; named WCJHL MVP in 1968–69

- Overlooked by many NHL teams in Amateur Draft because he suffered from juvenile diabetes

- Led NHL in assists in 1974–75 (89) and 1975–76 (89)

- Led NHL in plus/minus (plus-83) in 1975–76

- Led NHL in short-handed goals in 1973–74 (5) and 1976–77 (6)

- Finished among NHL top-5 in points in 1972–73 (104), 1973–74 (87) and 1975–76 (119)

- Registered 1,000th career NHL point in Philadelphia's 5–3 victory over Boston Bruins, March 19, 1981

- Served as captain of Philadelphia Flyers (1972–79, 1982–84)

- Served as general manager of Philadelphia Flyers (1985–90, 1994–2006), Florida Panthers (1993–94) and Minnesota North Stars (1990–92)

Bobby Clarke wore this jersey while playing for the Flin Flon Bombers of the Western Canadian Junior Hockey League (WCJHL) during the 1968–69 season. Clarke's Bombers won the WCJHL championship that year.

# 10

# Bill Cowley 1968

ALTERNATES:

## 17 · 15

Boston Bruins
St. Louis Eagles

Shoots: Left

Height: 5'-10"

Weight: 165 lbs.

Born: June 12, 1912:
Bristol, Quebec

Died: December 31,
1993: Ottawa, Ontario

Played 13 NHL seasons
from 1934–47

Stats: See page 411

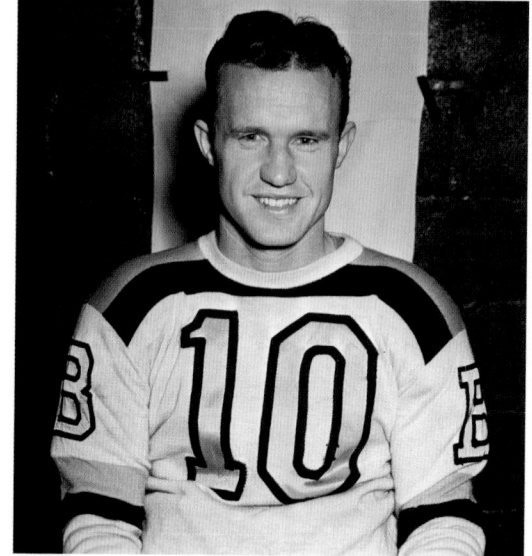

> "Two points a game over an 80-game schedule, that would be amazing. I never thought I'd see the day when a player would do that. I always thought that would be impossible."
>
> — Bill Cowley, commenting on Wayne Gretzky breaking his point-per-game record

**AWARDS**

NHL Scoring
Leader (1941)

Hart Memorial
Trophy (1941, 1943)

Stanley Cup
(1938–39, 1940–41)

**ALL-STAR
SELECTIONS**

First All-Star Team Center
(1938, 1941, 1943, 1944)

Second All-Star Team
Center (1945)

- Held NHL record for highest points-per-game average (1.97) in regular season (71 points in 36 games in 1943–44); surpassed by Wayne Gretzky in 1980–81 (2.05)

- Held NHL record for career points in the regular season (549); surpassed by Elmer Lach, February 23, 1952

- Held NHL record for career assists in the regular season (354); surpassed by Elmer Lach in 1951–52

- Set NHL record for assists in the regular season in 1940–41 (47); surpassed by Clint Smith in 1943–44

- Played amateur hockey with Ottawa Glebe Collegiate (1929–30); Ottawa Primrose (1930–31); Ottawa Shamrocks (1931–33); Halifax Wolverines (1933–34)

- One of only two players (with Wayne Gretzky) to record more assists than next leading scorer had points (1940–41)

- Led Ottawa City Junior League in playoff goals (4) in 1930–31; led OCJHL in playoff goals (4), assists (4) and points (8) in 1931–32

- Led Maritime Senior League in goals (25), assists (25) and points (50) in 1933–34

- Led NHL in assists in 1938–39 (34), 1940–41 (47) and 1942–43 (47); led NHL in points (64) in 1940–41

- Led NHL playoffs in points (14) in 1938–39

- Coached Ottawa Army (1947–48); coached Vancouver Canucks (1948–49)

- Only Hall of Fame member to have started his NHL career with the St. Louis Eagles

# 1992 Marcel Dionne

> "People ask if I regret not winning a Stanley Cup, but winning the series against the Soviet Union was the best. It was the greatest experience of my hockey career."

**NO. RETIRED BY LOS ANGELES**

**ALTERNATES:**

**5 · 12**

**Detroit Red Wings**
**Los Angeles Kings**
**New York Rangers**

Shoots: Right

Height: 5'-9"

Weight: 190 lbs.

Born: August 3, 1951;
Drummondville, Quebec

Drafted by the Detroit Red Wings second overall in 1971

Played 18 NHL seasons from 1971–89

Stats: See page 411

**AWARDS**

Lady Byng Memorial Trophy (1975, 1977)

Ted Lindsay Award*
(1979, 1980)

Art Ross Trophy (1980)

Lester Patrick Trophy (2006)

**ALL-STAR SELECTIONS**

First All-Star Team Center (1977, 1980)

Second All-Star Team Center (1979, 1981)

**INTERNATIONAL AWARDS**

Bronze Medal: World Championships (1978, 1983, 1986)

Canada Cup (1976)

*Known as the Lester B. Pearson Award from 1971 to 2009

- Ranks fifth in NHL career goals (731) and sixth in NHL career points (1,771)

- Ranks eighth in NHL career power-play goals (234) through 2017–18; ranks third in NHL career shots on goal (5,366)

- Played amateur hockey with Montreal Laurentides (1966–67); Drummondville Rangers (1967–68); St. Catharines Black Hawks (1968–71)

- Led QJHL in playoff goals (14) in 1967–68; led OHA-Jr. in goals (55), assists (77) and points (132) in 1969–70; led OHA-Jr. in points (143) in 1970–71; led OHA-Jr. in playoff goals (25), assists (26) and points (55) in 1970–71

- OHA-Jr. Second All-Star Team Center (1970); OHA-Jr. First All-Star Team Center (1971)

- Played in NHL All-Star Game (1975, 1975, 1977, 1978, 1980, 1981, 1983, 1985)

- Led NHL in points (137) in 1979–80; led NHL in short-handed goals (10) in 1974–75

- Led NHL in shots on goal in 1976–77 (378), 1978–79 (362), 1979–80 (348) and 1980–81 (342)

- Finished among NHL top-5 in goals in 1974–75 (47), 1976–77 (53), 1978–79 (59), 1979–80 (53), 1980–81 (58), 1982–83 (56)

- Finished among NHL top-5 in power-play goals in 1976–77 (14), 1978–79 (19), 1979–80 (17), 1980–81 (23), 1984–85 (16) and 1987–88 (22)

# 7

CENTER

# Phil Esposito 1984

NO. RETIRED BY BOSTON

**ALTERNATES:**

# 77 · 12

Boston Bruins
Chicago Black Hawks
New York Rangers

Shoots: Left

Height: 6'-1"

Weight: 205 lbs.

Born: February 20, 1942:
Sault Ste. Marie, Ontario

Played 18 NHL seasons
from 1963–81

Stats: See page 412

**AWARDS**

Art Ross Trophy (1969,
1971, 1972, 1973, 1974)

Hart Memorial
Trophy (1969, 1974)

Ted Lindsay Award*
(1971, 1974)

Lester Patrick
Trophy (1978)

Stanley Cup
(1969–70, 1971–72)

**ALL-STAR
SELECTIONS**

First All-Star Team
Center (1969, 1970,
1971, 1972, 1973, 1974)

Second All-Star Team
Center (1968, 1975)

**INTERNATIONAL
AWARDS**

Summit Series (1972)

Canada Cup (1976)

*Known as the Lester
B. Pearson Award
from 1971 to 2009

> "I was a lucky guy.
> There is nothing
> better than good
> teammates. I don't
> care what anybody
> says, you can't do it
> alone. It takes a good
> team for you to be a
> good player."

- Holds NHL record for shots on goal in a single season (550), established in 1970–71

- Held NHL record for goals in regular season (76); surpassed by Wayne Gretzky (92), February 24, 1982; held NHL record for points in regular season (152); surpassed by Wayne Gretzky (164) in 1980–81

- Ranks third in NHL career game-winning goals (118); ranks fifth in NHL career power-play goals (246); ranks fifth in NHL career goals (717); ranks tenth in NHL career points (1,590)

- Played in NHL All-Star Game (1969, 1970, 1971, 1972, 1973, 1974, 1975, 1977, 1978, 1980)

- Led NHL in short-handed goals (5) in 1972–73; led NHL in game-winning goals in 1970–71 (16), 1971–72 (16) and 1972–73 (11); led NHL in shots on goal in 1970–71 (550), 1971–72 (426), 1972–73 (411) and 1973–74 (393)

- Registered 700th career NHL goal in N.Y. Rangers' 6–3 victory over Washington Capitals, February 2, 1980

- Served as captain of N.Y. Rangers (1975–78); coached N.Y. Rangers (1986–87, 1988–89)

- Served as general manager of N.Y. Rangers (1986–89); served as general manager of Tampa Bay Lightning (1992–98)

- Brother of Hall of Fame member Tony Esposito, who played in NHL with Montreal and Chicago from 1968–84

**86**

# Bold Moves

For Phil Esposito, a trade to Bobby Orr's Boston Bruins in 1967 was just the ticket to change his career, going from rising star in Chicago to superstar in Beantown. Although he sometimes lined up with Bobby Hull in Chicago, Esposito really found his groove with Orr, Wayne Cashman and Ken Hodge. With those four powering the offense and Gerry Cheevers manning the net, the early 1970s Bruins became a powerhouse team, winning two Stanley Cups in three years.

Esposito and Orr were A-list celebrities in Boston, and Espo held the NHL's scoring record—76 goals in a single season, in 1970–71—until he was surpassed by Wayne Gretzky. Espo and Orr took home many NHL awards during their time together, with Esposito winning the Art Ross Trophy five times, the Hart Trophy twice, the Lester B. Pearson Award (known since 2010 as the Ted Lindsay Award) twice and the Lester Patrick Trophy once.

While a member of the Boston Bruins, Esposito scored 40 or more goals in seven straight seasons and 50 or more in five straight seasons. In his 76-goal season, he also recorded an amazing 76 assists for a then-league record of 152 points. What's more, over his 19-year career he was an eight-time All-Star and represented Canada in the 1972 Summit Series, the 1976 Canada Cup and the 1977 World Championship, winning both the Summit Series and the Canada Cup.

Esposito's career began to wind down after he was traded to the New York Rangers in

**Phil Esposito skates with the New York Rangers in the late 1970s. He stayed with the club post-retirement as coach and, later, as general manager.**

1975. He was still a point-per-game player, but the gaudy statistics he had become known for were a thing of the past. But New York provided other opportunities, and he became one of the Rangers' assistant coaches after he retired from playing in 1981—a move that saw him ultimately end up in management with the club. That experience led to his most important off-ice achievement and what Esposito calls his "greatest accomplishment in hockey": bringing the NHL to Florida. In 1992 the NHL debuted the Tampa Bay Lightning; Esposito remained the general manager of the team until 1998.

On the ice or off, not many players have had as big an impact on the game as Phil Esposito.

# 24

# Bernie Federko 2002

NO. RETIRED BY ST. LOUIS

ALTERNATE:

## 42

**Detroit Red Wings
St. Louis Blues**

Shoots: Left

Height: 6'

Weight: 178 lbs.

Born: May 12, 1956; Foam Lake, Saskatchewan

Drafted by the St. Louis Blues seventh overall in 1976

Played 14 NHL seasons from 1976–90

Stats: See page 412

"I was given the opportunity by Emile Francis to be the nucleus of the Blues. I just always felt it was my job to be consistent and that they were relying on me to make sure we were going to compete all of the time."

- Holds St. Louis Blues team records for career seasons (13), games played (927), assists (721) and points (1,073)

- Ranks 11th in NHL career assists-per-game (0.76)

- Played amateur hockey with Foam Lake Flyers (1972–73); Saskatoon Blades (1973–76)

- Led WHL in assists (115) and points (187) in 1975–76; led WHL playoffs in goals (15) in 1974–75; led WHL playoffs in assists (27) and points (45) in 1975–76

- Named WHL Player of the Year (1976); WHL First All-Star team Center (1976)

- Played minor pro hockey with Kansas City Blues (1976–77)

- Nicknamed "The Magician" because of his wizardry behind the net

- Named CHL Rookie of the Year (1977); CHL Second All-Star Team Center (1977)

- First player in NHL history to record at least 50 assists in 10 consecutive seasons

- Played in NHL All-Star Game (1980, 1981)

- Led NHL playoffs in points (21) in 1985–86

- Served as captain of St. Louis Blues (1988–89)

- Registered 1,000th career NHL point in St. Louis' 5–3 loss to Hartford Whalers, March 18, 1988

- Traded to Detroit by St. Louis Blues with Tony McKegney for Adam Oates and Paul MacLean, June 15, 1989

# 91

## 2015 Sergei Fedorov

> "I have always played hockey because I loved it, not because I wanted to win awards."

Columbus Blue Jackets
Detroit Red Wings
Mighty Ducks of Anaheim
Washington Capitals

Shoots: Left

Height: 6'-1"

Weight: 200 lbs.

Born: December 13, 1969; Pskov, USSR

Drafted by the Detroit Red Wings 74th overall in 1989

Played 18 NHL seasons from 1990–2004, 2005–09

Stats: See page 413

### AWARDS

Hart Memorial Trophy (1994)

Frank J. Selke Trophy (1994, 1996)

Ted Lindsay Award* (1994)

Stanley Cup (1996–97, 1997–98, 2001–02)

### ALL-STAR SELECTIONS

All-Rookie Team (1991)

First All-Star Team Center (1994)

### INTERNATIONAL AWARDS

Silver Medal: Winter Olympics (1998)

Bronze Medal: Winter Olympics (2002)

Gold Medal: World Championships (1989, 1990, 2008)

Silver Medal: World Championships (2010)

*Known as the Lester B. Pearson Award from 1971 to 2009

- Represented the Soviet Union at the World Junior Championships in 1987, 1988 and 1989; he won silver in 1988 and was named to the tournament All-Star Team

- In 1989 he played on a line with future Hall of Famer Pavel Bure and Alexander Mogilny at the 1989 World Junior Championships where they won gold; he also won gold that year with the Soviet team at the World Championships

- Defected from the Soviet national team while playing at the 1990 Goodwill Games in Portland, Oregon

- Is the only player to win the Hart Trophy as league MVP and the Frank J. Selke Trophy as best defensive forward in the same season (1993–94)

- His second-place finish in the NHL scoring race in 1993–94 (120 points) is the highest finish for any player who has won the Selke Trophy

- Scored 30-plus goals 10 times in his career, including a career-high 56 in 1993–94

- Centered the Red Wings' "Russian Five" unit with Vyacheslav Kozlov on left wing, Igor Larionov on right wing, and Vladimir Konstantinov and Slava Fetisov on defense

- Became the first Russian-born player to reach the 1,000-point plateau in the NHL while with Anaheim on February 4, 2004

- Played in NHL All-Star Game (1992, 1994, 1996, 2001, 2002, 2003)

Fedorov continued on page 90

**89**

# Stalwart Sergei

**Sergei Fedorov talks with fellow Red Wing and Russian native Viacheslav Fetisov during a game against the Vancouver Canucks.**

E ven if he hadn't become a Hall of Famer, a case would still have been made that Sergei Fedorov was one of the most influential players of the 1990s.

Fedorov was part of a new wave of young Russian stars playing alongside Pavel Bure and Alexander Mogilny. All three helped the Soviet Union win gold medals at both the World Junior Championship and the World Championships in 1989 before Mogilny defected. Bure and Fedorov helped the Soviets repeat as World Champions in 1990, but that summer Fedorov—who had been drafted by the Detroit Red Wings in 1989—also defected. Fedorov wasn't looking for political asylum; in fact he spoke openly of his desire to return to his homeland in the future, and would actually play for the Soviets again as shortly as the 1991 Canada Cup. Fedorov just wished to play in the NHL and his high-profile defection led the way towards a transfer system that would soon allow Bure and several Soviet veterans to play in the NHL.

Fedorov was an immediate success in Detroit. As a rookie in 1990–91, he had 31 goals and 48 assists and finished second behind Ed Belfour in voting for the Calder Trophy. A year later, Fedorov had 32 goals and 54 assists, and his strong two-way play saw him finish second behind Guy Carbonneau in voting for the Frank J. Selke Trophy as the NHL's best defensive forward. In 1993–94, Fedorov finished with 120 points for second in the scoring race behind Wayne Gretzky's 130 points. This effort earned him the Hart Trophy, the Selke Trophy and First All-Star Team honors. A year later, Detroit reached the Stanley Cup final for the first time since 1965–66. The Red Wings lost that year, but Fedorov would win the Cup with Detroit in 1997, 1998 and 2002.

Signed as a free agent by the Mighty Ducks of Anaheim prior to the 2003–04 season, Fedorov later played for the Columbus Blue Jackets and the Washington Capitals before returning to Russia in 2009–10, where he played for three more years. Retiring in 2012, Fedorov became the general manager of CSKA Moscow, the former Red Army hockey team where his career had begun.

# 2014 Peter Forsberg

## 21

NO. RETIRED BY COLORADO

**Colorado Avalanche**
**Nashville Predators**
**Philadelphia Flyers**
**Quebec Nordiques**

Shoots: Left

Height: 6'

Weight: 205 lbs.

Born: July 20, 1973:
Ornskoldsvik, Sweden

Drafted by the Quebec
Nordiques sixth
overall in 1991

Played 14 NHL seasons
from 1994–2004,
2005–08, 2010–11

Stats: See page 414

"He could beat you with skill or he could beat you with power. He loved the challenge of going head to head physically with the biggest guys in the league."
— Rob Blake

- Traded on June 30, 1992, to the Quebec Nordiques by the Philadelphia Flyers with Steve Duchesne, Kerry Huffman, Mike Ricci, Ron Hextall, Philadelphia's first-round choice in the 1993 Entry Draft, $15 million and futures considerations for Eric Lindros

- Was named MVP of the Swedish Hockey League with MODO in 1993 and 1994 at the ages of 19 and 20 His gold-medal-winning goal at the 1994 Winter Olympics was commemorated on a Swedish postage stamp

- Helped lead Quebec to a division title in his NHL rookie season of 1994–95 and helped lead the franchise to the Stanley Cup the following season in its first year in Colorado

- Had a career–high 86 assists and 116 points in 1995–96 to finish fifth in NHL scoring

- Led the NHL with 77 assists and 106 points in 2002–03

- Led the NHL in playoff scoring with 27 points in 20 games in 2001–02 despite Colorado being eliminated in the Western Conference Final

- Served as captain of Philadelphia Flyers (2006–07)

- Ranks fourth all-time in the NHL in assists-per-game average (.898) and eighth all-time in points-per-game average (1.250)

- Won a silver medal at the World Junior Championships in 1992 and 1993; he set tournament scoring records with 24 assists and 31 points (in seven games) in 1993

**AWARDS**

Calder Memorial
Trophy (1995)

Art Ross Trophy (2003)

Hart Memorial
Trophy (2003)

Stanley Cup (1995–96,
2000–01)

**ALL-STAR
SELECTIONS**

All-Rookie Team (1995)

First All-Star Team Center
(1998, 1999, 2003)

**INTERNATIONAL
AWARDS**

Gold Medal: Winter
Olympics (1994, 2006)

Gold Medal: World
Championships
(1992, 1998)

Silver Medal: World
Championships
(1993, 2003, 2004)

## CENTER

# 4 Frank Foyston 1958

ALTERNATES:
## 10 · 5 · 9

Detroit Cougars
Seattle Metropolitans
Toronto Blueshirts
Victoria Cougars

Alternate Position: RW

Shoots: Left

Height: 5'-9"

Weight: 158 lbs.

Born: February 2, 1891:
Minesing, Ontario

Died: January 19, 1966:
Seattle, Washington

Played 16 professional
seasons from 1912–28

Stats: See page 414

"You missed one of the all-time greats if you never saw Frank Foyston perform with a hockey stick. He wielded it like [conductor] Fritz Kreisler his bow, Willie Mays his bat and Arnold Palmer his two-iron."

—Eulogy in the *Seattle Post-Intelligencer*

**AWARDS**

Stanley Cup (1913–14,
1916–17, 1924–25)

**ALL-STAR
SELECTIONS**

PCHA First All-Star
Team Center (1917, 1918,
1920, 1921, 1923, 1924)

PCHA Second All-Star
Team Center (1919, 1922)

- Played amateur hockey with Barrie Athletic Club (1908–11); Toronto Eatons (1911–12)

- OHA-Jr. First All-Star Team Center (1909)

- Led OHA-Sr. playoffs in goals (5) in 1911–12

- One of several Toronto players lured to the Pacific Coast Hockey Association when the Seattle Metropolitans were added to the league in 1915–16

- Led PCHA playoffs in goals (3) in 1918–19

- Led Stanley Cup playoffs in goals (9) and points (10) in 1918–19; goals (6) and points (7) in 1919–20

- Led PCHA in goals in 1919–20 (26) and 1920–21 (26)

- Named PCHA Most Valuable Player (1917)

- Ranked third in the PCHA with a career-high 36 goals in 1916–17

- Member of Stanley Cup–winning Seattle Metropolitans—first American-based team to win the Stanley Cup (1916–17)

- Member of PCHA champion Seattle Metropolitans (1917, 1919, 1920)

- Member of WHL champion Victoria Cougars (1925, 1926)

- Member of Stanley Cup–winning Victoria Cougars—last non-NHL club to win the Stanley Cup (1924–25)

- Served as player/coach of Detroit Olympics (1927–28, 1928–30)

- Coached Bronx Tigers (1931–32); coached Seattle Seahawks (1934–36)

# 2007 Ron Francis

**10**

"As a kid growing up in the little city of Sault Ste. Marie, Ontario, I dreamed of one day playing in the NHL, but never did I expect it to be as much fun as it turned out to be."

NO. RETIRED BY
CAROLINA/HARTFORD

**ALTERNATES:**

**9 · 4 · 21**

Carolina Hurricanes
Hartford Whalers
Pittsburgh Penguins
Toronto Maple Leafs

Shoots: Left

Height: 6'-3"

Weight: 200 lbs.

Born: March 1, 1963;
Sault Ste. Marie, Ontario

Drafted by the Hartford Whalers fourth overall in 1981

Played 23 NHL seasons from 1981–2004

Stats: See page 415

- Shares NHL record (with Gordie Howe) for most consecutive seasons with at least 50 points (22)
- Holds Hartford/Carolina team records for career games (1,186), seasons (16), goals (382), assists (793) and points (1,175)
- Holds Hartford/Carolina team records for career playoff assists (25)
- Ranks fifth in NHL career points (1,798); ranks second in NHL career assists (1,249)
- Played amateur hockey with Sault Ste. Marie Legionnaires (1979–80); Sault Ste. Marie Greyhounds (1980–82)
- Served as captain of Hartford Whalers (1984–85, 1985–91); served as captain of Pittsburgh Penguins (1994–95, 1997–98)

- Led NHL in assists in 1994–95 (48) and 1995–96 (92)
- Led NHL in plus/minus (plus-30) in 1994–95
- Nicknamed "Ronnie Franchise"
- Served as captain of Carolina Hurricanes (1999–2004)
- Only player in NHL history to captain two separate franchises (Hartford/Carolina and Pittsburgh) on two separate occasions
- Played in NHL All-Star Game (1983, 1985, 1990, 1996)
- Registered 1,000th career NHL point in Pittsburgh's 7–3 loss to Quebec Nordiques, October 28, 1993; recorded 500th career goal in Carolina's 6–3 loss to Boston Bruins, January 2, 2002

**AWARDS**

Frank J. Selke Trophy (1995)

Lady Byng Memorial Trophy (1995, 1998, 2002)

King Clancy Memorial Trophy (2002)

Stanley Cup (1990–91, 1991–92)

**INTERNATIONAL AWARDS**

Silver Medal: World Championship (1985)

# 5

# Frank Fredrickson 1958

**ALTERNATES:**

## 4 · 10
## 7 · 17

Boston Bruins
Detroit Cougars
Detroit Falcons
Pittsburgh Pirates
Victoria Aristocrats
Victoria Cougars

Shoots: Left

Height: 5'-11"

Weight: 180 lbs.

Born: June 11, 1895:
Winnipeg, Manitoba

Died: May 28, 1979:
Vancouver,
British Columbia

Played 11 professional
seasons from 1920–31

Stats: See page 415

**AWARDS**
Stanley Cup (1924–25)

**ALL-STAR
SELECTIONS**
PCHA First All-Star
Team Center (1921,
1922, 1923, 1924)

WHL First All-Star
Team Center (1926)

**INTERNATIONAL
AWARDS**
Gold Medal:
Winter Olympics (1920)

"My best outlet was hockey. I got my first pair of skates when I was five and had a great time learning to play. In 1914 I enrolled at the University of Manitoba, took liberal arts courses, and a year later was named captain of the hockey team."

- Played amateur hockey with Winnipeg Falcons (1913–16, 1919–20); Winnipeg 223rd Battalion (1916–17)

- Studied Law and Liberal Arts at the University of Manitoba before enlisting in the armed forces

- Led Manitoba Senior league in goals (13) and points (16) in 1915–16, goals (17) and points (20) in 1916–17, goals (23) and points (28) in 1919–20

- Captained the Winnipeg Falcons team that represented Canada and captured the gold medal at the 1920 Olympics, where hockey was played in a spring sports festival.

- Signed as a free agent by Victoria Aristocrats (PCHA), December 23, 1920

- Led PCHA in goals (39), assists (16) and points (55) in 1922–23

- Rights transferred to Detroit after NHL club purchased Victoria (WHL) franchise, May 15, 1926

- Traded to Boston by Detroit with Harry Meeking for Duke Keats and Archie Briden, January 7, 1927

- Traded to Pittsburgh by Boston for Mickey MacKay and $12,000, December 21, 1928

- Coached Pittsburgh Pirates (1929–30)

- Coached Princeton University (1933–35); coached Sea Island Flyers (1940–45); coached University of British Columbia (1945–50)

- Inducted into UBC Sports Hall of Fame (1983); inducted into Manitoba Sports Hall of Fame (1980); inducted into Canadian Olympic Hall of Fame (2006)

- Noted for his skills as a violinist, he also served on the Vancouver City Council

Frank Fredrickson wore this jersey in 1924–25 for the Victoria Cougars of the Western Canada Hockey League. The Cougars were the last non-NHL team to win the Stanley Cup.

# 93

# Doug Gilmour 2011

NO. RETIRED BY TORONTO

**ALTERNATES:**

## 9 · 18 · 39

Buffalo Sabres
Calgary Flames
Chicago Blackhawks
Montreal Canadiens
New Jersey Devils
St. Louis Blues
Toronto Maple Leafs

Shoots: Left

Height: 5'-11"

Weight: 175 lbs.

Born: June 25, 1963;
Kingston, Ontario

Drafted by the
St. Louis Blues 134th
overall in 1982

Played 20 NHL seasons
from 1983–2003

Stats: See page 416

> "He's not a big man,
> but he's got the heart
> of a lion. You can
> see it in his eyes. It's
> like he's saying, 'I'm
> going to go out and
> win this game. Who's
> with me?'"
>
> — Ken Baumgartner
> on Doug Gilmour

**AWARDS**

Stanley Cup (1988–89)

Frank J. Selke Trophy
(1993)

**INTERNATIONAL
AWARDS**

Canada Cup (1987)

- Played amateur hockey with Kingston Voyageurs (1979–80); Belleville Bulls (1979–80); Cornwall Royals (1980–83)
- OHL First All-Star Team Center (1983)
- Member of Memorial Cup–winning Cornwall Royals (1981)
- Led OHL in assists (107) and points (177) in 1982–83; named OHL Most Valuable Player (1982–83)
- Holds Toronto Maple Leafs team record for assists (95) and points (127) in one season, accomplished in 1992–93; holds Toronto Maple Leafs team record for career playoff assists (60) and points (77)
- Ranks sixth in NHL career playoff assists (128); ranks eighth in NHL career playoff points (188) through 2017–18

- Played in two NHL All-Star Games (1993, 1994)
- Led the NHL in playoff points (21) and shorthanded playoff goals (2) in 1985–86; led the NHL in playoff assists (25) and playoff plus/minus (plus-16) in 1992–93
- Registered 1,000th NHL career point in Toronto's 6–1 victory over Edmonton, December 23, 1995
- Traded to Calgary by St. Louis with Mark Hunter, Steve Bozek and Michael Dark for Mike Bullard, Craig Coxe and Tim Corkery, September 6, 1988; traded to Toronto by Calgary with Jamie Macoun, Ric Nattress, Kent Manderville and Rick Wamsley for Gary Leeman, Alexander Godynyuk, Jeff Reese, Michel Petit, Craig Berube, January 2, 1992

# Killer Instinct

Doug Gilmour's small size—generously listed at 5-foot-11 and 177 pounds during his NHL career—was always considered a weakness. It didn't matter that he was a two-time Memorial Cup champion or that he led the Ontario Hockey League in scoring in 1982–83, with 177 points.

But like many small players before him, Gilmour, drafted 134th overall by the St. Louis Blues in 1982, used the criticism of his size to galvanize his play. By the end of his first season he had already earned the nickname "Killer," which defined his intensity and his relentless checking, qualities that endeared him to thousands of blue-collar hockey fans. It is with this style of play, and his ability to elevate his game during the playoffs, that Gilmour left his most indelible mark on the game.

In his third season, 1985–86, Killer posted 21 points in 19 playoff games during the Blues' run to the conference final. He followed that up with 105 regular-season points in 1986–87, and after one more go in St. Louis he was traded to the Calgary Flames in 1988. Gilmour continued his strong play in Calgary, adding 22 points in 22 playoff games, including the Cup-winning goal as the Flames defeated the Montreal Canadiens for the Stanley Cup in 1988–89.

However, Gilmour's relationship with the Flames became increasingly acrimonious, leading Calgary to make Gilmour the centerpiece of a 10-player blockbuster deal with the Toronto Maple Leafs in 1992; still the largest trade in NHL history.

**Doug Gilmour carries the Stanley Cup during postgame celebrations in 1989.**

Gilmour was a star for the Leafs, playing the best hockey of his career in the Blue and White. He set a franchise record with 127 points in his first full season with Toronto, 1992–93. That season he was voted second to Mario Lemieux as the league's Most Valuable Player, and he won the Selke Trophy as the NHL's top defensive forward.

Playoff success, though, was never to come to Gilmour in Toronto. He did pace the Leafs to back-to-back conference final appearances, scoring 63 points in 39 playoff games over those two postseasons, but Toronto could never break through to the Stanley Cup final.

Killer went on to play in New Jersey, Buffalo, Chicago and Montreal before returning to the Leafs and retiring after a knee injury late in the 2003 season.

**97**

# 21

# Cammi Granato 2010

B.C. Breakers
Concordia Stingers
Providence College
U.S. National Team
Vancouver Griffins

Alternate Position: RW

Shoots: Right

Height: 5'-7"

Weight: 140 lbs.

Born: March 25, 1971:
Downers Grove, Illinois

Played 16 elite
amateur seasons
from 1989–2005

Stats: See page 416

"As a kid I was
an equal. I never
thought of myself
any different.
I wanted to be a
Chicago Blackhawk
exactly like my
brothers."

— Cammi Granato,
commenting on
her childhood
ambitions

AWARDS
Lester Patrick
Trophy (2007)

INTERNATIONAL
AWARDS
Gold Medal: Winter
Olympics (1998)
Silver Medal: Winter
Olympics (2002)
Gold Medal: World
Championships (2005)
Silver Medal: World
Championships (1990,
1992, 1994, 1997, 1999,
2000, 2001, 2004)

- Played amateur hockey with Providence College Friars (1989–93); U.S. National Women's Team (1990–2005); Concordia University Stingers (1995–97); Vancouver Griffins (2002–03); B.C. Breakers (2004–05)

- Holds Providence College records for single-season goals (48), assists (43) and points (84)

- Holds Providence College records for career goals (139) and points (256)

- Named ECAC Women's Player of the Year (1991, 1992, 1993); named U.S.A. Women's Player of the Year (1996)

- Inducted into International Ice Hockey Hall of Fame (2008); inducted into U.S. Hockey Hall of Fame (2008)

- IIHF All-Tournament Team (1992, 1997, 2002); named IIHF Best Forward (1992); named IIHF All-Tournament Player (1997)

- Served as captain of U.S. Women's Olympic Team (1998); was U.S. flag bearer during the Winter Olympics' closing ceremony

- Invited to the New York Islanders' training camp in 1997 but turned down the offer because she was worried about getting hurt

- Became second women (after Sherry Ross) in NHL history to work as a broadcaster when hired by the L.A. Kings as a radio color commentator in 1998

# Can-do Cammi

Dreams do come true, but sometimes they aren't exactly as imagined.

After realizing she would probably never get to play in the NHL, Catherine "Cammi" Granato took a break from playing hockey during her last two years of high school. She was crushed that her brothers were able to chase their dreams and that she could not.

Growing up near Chicago with five older siblings—four brothers, including future NHLer Tony, and a sister—Granato took playing hockey with the boys for granted, until bodychecking became prevalent and the boys' increasing size and strength began to take its toll.

But a new hockey dream presented itself when Granato was offered a scholarship to hockey powerhouse Providence College in 1989, just as women's hockey was taking its fledgling steps into international play.

**Cammi Granato delivers her 2010 Hockey Hall of Fame induction speech.**

She was Freshman Player of the Year and eventually led the Friars to the Eastern College Athletic Conference championships in 1992 and 1993. In her four-year college career, Granato scored 135 goals and 110 assists in just 93 games.

Granato was an easy choice for the U.S. national team, and she became its longest-serving member—participating in every World Championship from the first-ever Women's Worlds in 1990 through to 2005.

Blessed with extraordinary leadership skills, Granato became the most recognized female hockey player in the U.S., and she was a deeply trusted spokesperson and role model for the women's game.

Her biggest on-ice achievement was captaining the U.S. Olympic team for the 1998 games—the first ever to feature women's hockey. Granato scored the American's first goal of the tournament and led the U.S. to an upset gold-medal win over world-champion Canada. Her American side narrowly missed repeating as Olympic champions in 2002, earning a silver medal, and after a controversial decision to leave her off the 2006 Olympic roster, she retired.

Not long after, she was enshrined as a member of both the U.S. Hockey Hall of Fame and the International Hockey Hall of Fame, with the ultimate recognition of the Hockey Hall of Fame coming in 2010, making yet another unlikely dream come true.

# 99

## CENTER

# Wayne Gretzky 1999

NO. RETIRED BY EDMONTON,
LOS ANGELES & THE NHL

Edmonton Oilers
Los Angeles Kings
New York Rangers
St. Louis Blues

Shoots: Left

Height: 6'

Weight: 185 lbs.

Born: January 26, 1961;
Brantford, Ontario

Played 21 WHA and NHL
seasons from 1978–99

Stats: See page 417

"A good hockey player plays where the puck is. A great hockey player plays where the puck is going to be."

AWARDS

Hart Memorial Trophy
(1980–87, 1989)

Art Ross Trophy (1981–87,
1990, 1991, 1994)

Lady Byng Memorial Trophy
(1980, 1991, 1992, 1994, 1999)

Conn Smythe Trophy
(1985, 1988)

Ted Lindsay Award* (1982,
1983, 1984, 1985, 1987)

Lester Patrick Trophy (1994)

Stanley Cup (1983–84,
1984–85, 1986–87, 1987–88)

ALL-STAR
SELECTIONS

First All-Star Team
Center (1981–87, 1991)

Second All-Star Team
Center (1980, 1988–90,
1994, 1997, 1998)

INTERNATIONAL
AWARDS

Canada Cup
(1984, 1987, 1991)

*Known as the Lester
B. Pearson Award
from 1971 to 2009

- At time of retirement in 1999, held 40 regular season NHL records, 15 playoff records and six All-Star Game records

- Only player in NHL history to have his number (99) retired by the league

- Holds NHL records for career goals (894), short-handed goals (73), assists (1,963) and points (2,857); holds NHL records for single-season goals (92), assists (163) and points (212); holds NHL records for career playoff goals (122), assists (260) and points (382)

- Shares NHL record (with Brett Hull) for career playoff game-winning goals (24)

- OMJHL Second All-Star Team Center (1978); WHA Second All-Star Team Center (1979); named OHA-B Rookie of the Year (1979); named WHA Rookie of the Year (1979)

- Served as general manager of gold medal–winning Team Canada at 2002 Winter Olympic Games in Salt Lake City, Utah

- Registered 1,000th career NHL point in Edmonton's 7–4 victory over L.A. Kings, December 19, 1984; registered 2,000th career NHL point in L.A. Kings' 6–2 loss to Winnipeg Jets, October 26, 1990; surpassed Gordie Howe with 802nd career NHL goal in L.A. Kings' 6–3 loss to Vancouver Canucks, March 23, 1994

- Traded to Los Angeles by Edmonton with Mike Krushelnyski and Marty McSorley for Jimmy Carson, Martin Gelinas, Los Angeles' first round choices in 1989 (later traded to New Jersey; New Jersey selected Jason Miller), 1991 (Martin Rucinsky) and 1993 (Nick Stajduhar) and cash, August 9, 1988

- Recorded 378 goals and 120 assists in 85 games as a 10-year-old with the Brantford Nadrofsky Steelers

- Played amateur hockey with Vaughan Nationals (1975–76); Seneca Nationals (1976–77); Peterborough Petes (1976–77); Sault Ste. Marie Greyhounds (1977–78)

# Great at Eight

Even the tallest tree in the forest was once a sapling. And like all the others, Wayne Gretzky—who grew to become "The Great One," achieved 61 separate NHL records, won eight straight Hart Trophies as league MVP and put the game on his back and carried it into several Sun Belt markets—had to start somewhere. That somewhere was the Brantford Minor Hockey Association.

When Gretzky started playing organized hockey as a six-year-old in 1967, he was four years younger than many of his teammates and opponents—the lowest age classification in Brantford hockey was the 10-year-old atom league. The standard-issue atom sweater was far too big for a player of Gretzky's age, so to gain greater freedom of movement he began tucking the right side of his sweater into his hockey pants. It was a habit he maintained throughout his extraordinary 20-year NHL career, and it became one of the enduring symbols of his inimitable style.

His almost equally famous father, Walter Gretzky, had his son on skates long before he was six, and the backyard rink he built was where Wayne, his sister and three brothers could play as long as they wanted. That rink became known as the Wally Coliseum, and once Wayne began lighting up the NHL it spawned an entire cottage industry in Canada.

Gretzky first gained national attention as an eight-year-old with Brantford's Nadrofsky Steelers, when he recorded 167 points. Two years later, as a 10-year-old, he toppled that number with 378 goals and 139 assists for 517 points. He played his only full season of major junior hockey with the Ontario Hockey League's Sault Ste. Marie Greyhounds at the age of 16 in 1977–78, and he finished

**Wayne Gretzky wore this jersey as a youth while making national headlines with Brantford Ontario's Nadrofsky Steelers.**

second in league scoring. He also had to change from his customary No. 9 (in honor of Gordie Howe) to a new number because team veteran Brian Gualazzi had squatter's rights to Gretzky's preferred digit. He settled on No. 99, and ultimately made it his, so much so that the NHL retired the number league-wide, ensuring there would be no imitators.

Gretzky, like Muhammad Ali, Michael Jordan and Babe Ruth, came to transcend his sport, and he made No. 99 a symbol of excellence worldwide. Perhaps it was no accident that No. 99 retired in 1999 and was inducted into the Hall of Fame that same year. The date of that induction, November 22, also happens to be the same date of the informal founding of the NHL. Kismet.

# 10

# Dale Hawerchuk 2001

NO. RETIRED BY ARIZONA

**Buffalo Sabres**
**Philadelphia Flyers**
**St. Louis Blues**
**Winnipeg Jets**

Shoots: Left

Height: 5'-11"

Weight: 190 lbs.

Born: April 4, 1963;
Toronto, Ontario

Drafted by the Winnipeg
Jets first overall in 1981

Played 16 NHL seasons
from 1981–97

Stats: See page 418

"We won [the 1987 Canada Cup] because we jelled into a very good team. Each man did whatever the coaches asked him to do and every player on the roster was very important in the whole picture of the team."

**AWARDS**
Calder Memorial
Trophy (1982)

**ALL-STAR SELECTIONS**
Second All-Star Team
Center (1985)

**INTERNATIONAL AWARDS**
Canada Cup (1987, 1991)
Bronze Medal: World
Championships
(1982, 1986)
Silver Medal: World
Championships (1989)

- Held NHL record as youngest player to register 100-point season (1981–82); surpassed by Sidney Crosby in 2005–06

- Played amateur hockey with Oshawa Legionnaires (1978–79); Cornwall Royals (1979–81)

- Led QMJHL in goals (81), assists (102) and points (183) in 1980–81; led QMJHL playoffs in goals (20), assists (25) and points (45) in 1979–80

- Member of Memorial Cup–winning Cornwall Royals (1980, 1981)

- Led Memorial Cup tournament in goals (8) and points (12) in 1981

- Memorial Cup All-Star Team (1980, 1981)

- Named Memorial Cup Most Valuable Player (1981); named Memorial Cup Most Sportsmanlike Player (1980)

- QMJHL First All-Star Team Center (1981); CMJHL Player of the Year (1981)

- Scored a goal and recorded two assists in third game of the 1987 Canada Cup final series against the Soviet Union

- Inducted into the Arizona Coyotes' Ring of Honor (2007)

- Played in NHL All-Star Game (1982, 1985, 1986, 1988, 1997)

- Served as captain of Winnipeg Jets (1984–89)

# 1958 Dick Irvin

**3**

> "Sometimes I think hockey players would be better off if there were no coaches. Kids today are over-coached. They don't develop a style of their own and most of them look alike out there on the ice."

**ALTERNATE**

**6**

Chicago Black Hawks
Portland Rosebuds
Regina Capitals
Regina Victorias
Winnipeg Ypres

Shoots: Left

Height: 5'-9"

Weight: 162 lbs.

Born: July 19, 1892;
Hamilton, Ontario

Died: May 16, 1957;
Montreal, Quebec

Played 12 elite amateur and professional seasons from 1916–18, 1919–29

Stats: See page 418

- Ranks seventh in all-time NHL games coached (1,449); ranks seventh in all-time wins by an NHL coach (691)

- Played amateur hockey with Winnipeg Strathconas-Jr. (1909–11); Winnipeg Strathconas-Sr. (1912–14); Winnipeg Monarchs (1911–16); Winnipeg Ypres (1917–18); Regina Victorias (1919–21)

- Led Western Senior League in goals (16) in 1911–12; led Manitoba Intermediate League in goals (32) in 1912–13

- Member of Allan Cup–winning Winnipeg Monarchs (1915); led all Allan Cup competitors in goals (17) and points (20) as Winnipeg defeated Fort William, Edmonton and Melville to win the Canadian Senior Hockey Championship

- Led Manitoba Senior League in goals (23) and points (24) in 1913–14; goals (23) and points (26) in 1914–15; goals (17) and points (20) in 1915–16; goals (29) and points (37) in 1917–18

- Led Southern Saskatchewan Senior League in goals (32) and points (36) in 1919–20; led WCHL in goals (31) in 1925–26

- Served as first captain of the Chicago Black Hawks (1926–29)

- Led NHL in assists (18) in 1926–27

- Coached Toronto Maple Leafs (1931–40); Montreal Canadiens (1940–55); Chicago Black Hawks (1928–29, 1930–31, 1955–56)

- Inducted into Manitoba Sports Hall of Fame (1963)

**ALL-STAR SELECTIONS**

PCHA Second All-Star Team Center (1917)

WCHL First All-Star Team Center (1924)

WCHL Second All-Star Team Center (1922)

WHL Second All-Star Team Center (1926)

NHL First All-Star Team Coach (1944, 1945, 1946)

NHL Second All-Star Team Coach (1931, 1932, 1933, 1934, 1935, 1941)

# CENTER

# 8 Angela James 2010

NO. RETIRED BY
SENECA COLLEGE

Canadian National
Team
Newtonbrook Panthers
North York/
Beatrice Aeros
Seneca College
Toronto Aeros
Toronto Red Wings

Alternate Position: D

Shoots: Right

Height: 5'-5"

Weight: 147 lbs.

Born: December 22,
1964: Toronto, Ontario

Played 18 elite
amateur seasons
from 1982–2000

Stats: See page 418

"She could do it all. She had end-to-end speed, she had finesse as a stick handler and her slap shot was harder and more accurate than any female player I have ever seen. She was a pure goal scorer like Mike Bossy and aggressive like Mark Messier. In her prime, she was referred to as the 'Wayne Gretzky of Women's Hockey.'"

—Robin Brown,
CBC commentator

INTERNATIONAL
AWARDS

Gold Medal: World
Championships (1990,
1992, 1994, 1997)

- Holds Team Canada record for most goals in a single World Hockey Championship tournament (11), established in 1990

- OCAA First All-Star Team Defense (1984, 1985); named OCAA Women's Hockey MVP (1983, 1984, 1985)

- Inducted into Ontario Colleges Athletic Association (OCAA) Hall of Fame (2005); inducted into Black Hockey and Sports Hall of Fame (2006); inducted into International Ice Hockey Hall of Fame (2008); inducted into Canada's Sports Hall of Fame (2009)

- IIHF All-Tournament All-Star Team (1990, 1992)

- Named Best Forward at 1994 IIHF World Championships

- Registered 33 goals and 21 assists in 50 games during nine-year career with Canadian National Women's Team

- Member of National Women's Champion Toronto Aeros (1991, 1993)

- COWHL First All-Star Team Center (1991, 1992, 1993); named COWHL MVP (1991); named NWHL MVP (1999)

- Legacy is honored with the Angela James Bowl, awarded to the top scorer in the Canadian Women's Hockey League

- Member of 12 medal-winning teams at Canadian National Women's Championships

- Named MVP of Canadian National Women's Championships eight times

# A Career for the Ages

"When I was a young kid, I didn't think hockey was just for boys. I thought everyone played hockey," said Angela James, who, along with American Cammi Granato, in 2010 became one of the first two women inducted into the Hockey Hall of Fame. "That's what we did as kids. I would play on the outdoor arenas until the lights would go out or shoot tennis balls against the walls until I couldn't see any more."

In the early 1970s James played boys' hockey in the Toronto neighborhood of Flemingdon Park, and she later joined the Ontario Women's Hockey Association (OWHA), where she led her teams to numerous league and provincial championships. James' style has been described as a combination of the aggressiveness of Mark Messier and the pure goal-scoring talent of Mike Bossy, and in the OWHA she led the league in scoring for eight seasons and was the most valuable player in six.

**Angela James with the Beatrice Aeros in the late 1990s.**

In 1990 James was selected to join Canada's team at the inaugural Women's World Championship, held in Ottawa. She led the Canadian side to the gold medal and scored 11 goals in five games. Canada and James repeated as champions in 1992, 1994 and 1997. In 1996 and 1999, James led Canada to the gold medal at the Three Nations Cup.

In a highly controversial decision, James was excluded from Team Canada's Olympic squad for the 1998 games, the first time women's hockey was played in the Olympics. The hockey world was stunned—from 1987 until that point, James had been Canada's greatest scoring threat. She retired in 2000, after one last season in the National Women's Hockey League, recording 44 points in 27 games for North York's Beatrice Aeros.

The greatness of James' career was recognized swiftly and often, as she was humbled with inductions into the Ontario Colleges Athletic Association Hall of Fame (2005), the Black Ice Hockey and Sports Hall of Fame (2006), the International Ice Hockey Federation Hall of Fame (2008) and Canada's Sports Hall of Fame (2009). She was also recognized in 2008 with a trophy named in her honor: the Angela James Bowl, awarded annually to the leading scorer in the Canadian Women's Hockey League. The Flemingdon Park Arena, where she earned her lumps as a youth, was renamed Angela James Arena in 2009.

**105**

# 5

# Duke Keats 1958

**ALTERNATES**

**3 · 8 · 4**

Boston Bruins
Chicago Black Hawks
Detroit Cougars
Edmonton Eskimos
Toronto Blueshirts

Shoots: Right

Height: 5'-11"

Weight: 195 lbs.

Born: March 21, 1895;
Montreal, Quebec

Died: January 16, 1972;
Victoria, British Columbia

Played 12 elite amateur
and professional
seasons from
1915–17, 1919–29

Stats: See page 419

"You would have thought he had a nail in the end of his stick, the way he could carry that puck around. He was that good."

— Lloyd McIntyre, Duke Keats' teammate with the Edmonton Eskimos

**ALL-STAR SELECTIONS**

WCHL First All-Star Team Center (1922, 1923, 1924, 1925)

WHL First All-Star Team Center (1926)

- Nicknamed "The Iron Duke"

- Played amateur hockey with Cobalt McKinley Mines (1912–13); Cobalt O'Brien Mines (1913–14); North Bay Trappers (1913–14); Haileybury Hawks (1914–15); Edmonton Eskimos (1919–21)

- Became so angered by the poor performance of goaltender Billy Nicholson while playing for the Toronto Blueshirts of the NHA during the 1916–17 season, he strapped on the pads and took over in net himself for the next period

- Reinstated as an amateur and signed as a free agent by Edmonton Eskimos (Big-4), December, 1919

- Led Big-4 in goals (18), assists (14) and points (32) in 1919–20; led Big-4 in goals (23) and points (29) in 1920–21

- Signed as free agent by Edmonton Eskimos (WCHL), November 4, 1921

- Led WCHL in goals (31), assists (24) and points (55) in 1921–22

- Traded to Boston by Edmonton Eskimos (WHL) for cash, September 4, 1926; traded to Detroit by Boston with Archie Briden for Frank Fredrickson and Harry Meeking, January 7, 1927

- Scored the first hat trick in Detroit franchise history in 7–1 victory over Pittsburgh Pirates, March 10, 1927

- Traded to Chicago by Detroit for Gord Fraser and $5,000, December 16, 1927

- Traded to Tulsa Oilers (AHA) by Chicago for cash, November 28, 1928

- Led AHA in goals (22) and points (33) in 1928–29

# Ted Kennedy

**1966**

**9**

> "I never had much speed, certainly not in the way Syl Apps or Max Bentley or Milt Schmidt, the great centers, did. So I compensated by using my wingers. To be able to pass reasonably well made up for my lack of speed."

NO. RETIRED BY TORONTO

**ALTERNATE**

**10**

Toronto Maple Leafs

Shoots: Right

Height: 5'-10"

Weight: 170 lbs.

Born: December 12, 1925;
Humberstone, Ontario

Died: August 14, 2009;
Port Colbourne, Ontario

Played 14 NHL seasons
from 1942–55, 1956–57

Stats: See page 419

- Played amateur hockey with Port Colbourne Sailors (1942–43)

- Rights traded to Toronto by Montreal for the rights to Frank Eddolls, September 10, 1943

- Scored Stanley Cup–winning goal in Toronto's 2–1 victory over Montreal Canadiens, April 19, 1947

- Leafs fan John Arnott, sitting high up in the stands, often shouted "C'mon Teeder" during a quiet moment at home games to rally the team. The rally cry continued to be heard at Maple Leaf Gardens until the building closed in 1999

- In 1953, Conn Smythe created the J.P. Bickell Trophy for the most valuable Maple Leaf because Kennedy hadn't won a league award up to that point

- Played in NHL All-Star Game (1947, 1948, 1949, 1950, 1951, 1954)

- Finished among NHL top-5 in goals in 1944–45 (29) and 1946–47 (28)

- Finished among NHL top-5 in assists in 1946–47 (32), 1950–51 (43) and 1954–55 (42)

- Finished among NHL top-5 in points in 1944–45 (54), 1946–47 (60) and 1950–51 (61)

- Led NHL in assists (43) in 1950–51

- Served as captain of Toronto Maple Leafs (1948–55)

- Led NHL playoffs in goals (7) in 1944–45; led NHL playoffs in goals (8) and points (14) in 1947–48; led NHL playoffs in assists (6) in 1948–49

**AWARDS**

Hart Memorial Trophy (1955)

Stanley Cup (1944–45, 1945–46, 1946–47, 1947–48, 1948–49, 1950–51)

**ALL-STAR SELECTIONS**

Second All-Star Team Center (1950, 1951, 1954)

**107**

# 14 Dave Keon 1986

CENTER

NO. RETIRED BY TORONTO

Hartford Whalers
Indianapolis Racers
Minnesota
Fighting Saints
New England Whalers
Toronto Maple Leafs

Shoots: Left

Height: 5'-9"

Weight: 165 lbs.

Born: March 22, 1940:
Noranda, Quebec

Played 22 NHL and WHA
seasons from 1960–82

Stats: See page 419

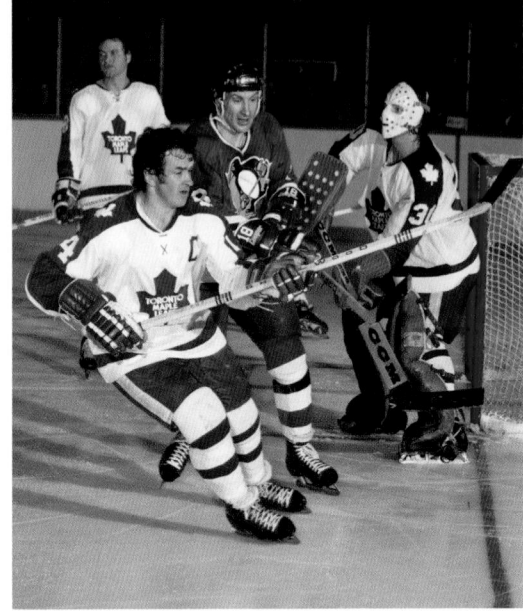

"Most kids today slap the puck. The backhand takes time to learn. It's not something you do naturally. But it is an effective shot."

— Dave Keon touting the importance of shooting backhand, something he was particularly adept at

AWARDS

Calder Memorial
Trophy (1961)

Lady Byng Memorial
Trophy (1962, 1963)

Conn Smythe
Trophy (1967)

Stanley Cup (1961–62,
1962–63, 1963–64,
1966–67)

ALL-STAR
SELECTIONS

Second All-Star Team
Center (1962, 1971)

- Shares NHL record for most short-handed goals (2) in a single playoff game, accomplished in Toronto's 3–1 victory over Detroit Red Wings, April 18, 1963

- Played amateur hockey with St. Michael's Buzzers (1956–57); St. Michael's Majors (1956–59); Kitchener-Waterloo Dutchmen (1959–60); Sudbury Wolves (1959–60)

- Won OHA-Jr. B Rookie of the Year Award (1957)

- Played in NHL All-Star Game (1962, 1963, 1964, 1967, 1968, 1970, 1971, 1973)

- Won Paul Deneau Trophy (WHA Most Gentlemanly Player) in 1977 and 1978

- Led NHL in shorthanded goals in 1968–69 (6) and 1970–71 (8)

- Nicknamed "Mister Perpetual Motion" by legendary hockey announcer Foster Hewitt

- An excellent penalty killer and checker, he scored the majority of his goals with the backhand

- Only member of the Maple Leafs to win the Conn Smythe Trophy as playoff MVP

- Served as captain of Toronto Maple Leafs (1969–75)

- Number nine jersey retired by Mississauga (St. Michael's) Majors, December 14, 2008

- Scored 67 power-play goals and 65 game-winning goals during his NHL career

- Received the only five minute major of his entire career for fighting with Boston's Gregg Sheppard in final game of 1973–74 season

# Two-Way Ace

**D**ave Keon played the game the way that Toronto Maple Leafs coach Punch Imlach preached: hard-nosed, strong two-way hockey. It wasn't the flashiest style, but Keon excelled at it.

He could be a dazzling offensive player, using bursts of speed and deft moves around the net; he also had what was widely considered to be one of the best backhands in the game—a deceptive, often powerful shot that flummoxed opposing goaltenders. Keon used his agility as a pesky penalty-killer, covering a large portion of the ice and turning shorthanded situations into scoring chances for his own team. He set a league record for most goals while killing penalties, with eight in the 1970–71 season. "If you play the game the way you're supposed to," Keon said, "the opportunities will present themselves and the goals will come."

His checking prowess can be traced to his days as a teenager playing for St. Michael's College in the Leafs farm system. Coaches Bob Goldham and Father David Bauer instilled in him the importance of defensive hockey—the game without the puck. That training helped prime him as the best two-way center in the NHL.

He won the Calder Trophy as the top rookie in 1960–61 and the Lady Byng Trophy twice, in 1962 and 1963, as the NHL's most gentlemanly player. He quickly became, along with Red Kelly and Bob Pulford, a key part of Toronto's four Stanley Cup triumphs in the 1960s. Keon was the playoff MVP in 1967, the last year the Maple Leafs won the Stanley Cup.

**Dave Keon examines the Conn Smythe Trophy as the winner for the 1967 playoffs.**

However, Keon's leadership and productivity over his 15 years with the Leafs were all forgotten in the summer of 1975, at least by Harold Ballard, the cantankerous and headstrong owner of the team. Ballard, determined to rebuild the Leafs with youth, chose not to resign Keon, who bolted for the rival World Hockey Association. Keon's relationship with the Leafs remained fractious for decades.

Very quietly in the summer of 1982, Keon ended his 22-year professional career. He informed Hartford Whalers director of hockey operations Larry Pleau of his decision and then declined to have a press conference, preferring to end his career without formality. He left the game the same way he had played it, selflessly and with a great deal of grace.

**109**

# 16

## CENTER

# Elmer Lach 1966

NO. RETIRED BY MONTREAL

ALTERNATES
**14 · 10**

**Montreal Canadiens**

Shoots: Left
Height: 5'-10"
Weight: 165 lbs.

Born: January 22, 1918:
Nokomis, Saskatchewan

Died: April 4, 2015:
Kirkland, Quebec

Played 14 NHL seasons
from 1940–54

Stats: See page 420

> "I would say scoring the winning goal when we beat Boston in overtime to end the series in 1953. It doesn't get any better than that!"
>
> —Elmer Lach on his most unforgettable moment

**AWARDS**

NHL Scoring
Leader (1945)

Art Ross Trophy (1948)

Hart Memorial
Trophy (1945)

Stanley Cup (1943–44,
1945–46, 1952–53)

**ALL-STAR
SELECTIONS**

First All-Star Team
Center (1945, 1948, 1952)

Second All-Star Team
Center (1944, 1946)

- Held NHL record for career points (610); surpassed by Maurice Richard, December 12, 1953

- Played amateur hockey with Regina Abbots (1935–36); Weyburn Beavers (1936–38); Moose Jaw Millers (1938–40)

- SSHL First All-Star Team Center (1940)

- Centered Montreal's famed Punch Line with Toe Blake and Maurice "Rocket" Richard

- Nicknamed "Elegant Elmer" and the "Nokomis Flash"

- Solid two-way player with offensive flair, excellent speed and superb puck-handling skills

- Played in NHL All-Star Game (1948, 1952, 1953)

- Led NHL in points in 1944–45 (80) and 1947–48 (61); led NHL in assists in 1944–45 (54); 1945–46 (34) and 1951–52 (50)

- Led NHL playoffs in assists (11) in 1943–44; led NHL playoffs in assists (12) and points (17) in 1945–46

- Inaugural recipient of Art Ross Trophy for leading NHL in points (1948)

- Scored Stanley Cup–winning overtime goal in Montreal's 1–0 victory over Boston Bruins, April 16, 1953

- Had his number retired along with Butch Bouchard's on December 4, 2009, to coincide with the Canadiens' 100th anniversary

- Coached Montreal Jr. Canadiens (1954–55); coached Montreal Royals (1955–57)

# 2003 Pat LaFontaine

**16**

> "That was a special feeling to win that Game 7 and be a part of some history as far as the National Hockey League. I look at that goal and it was really a stepping stone in my career."
>
> — Pat LaFontaine on scoring the winning goal in the "Easter Epic," which remains the longest game in Islander history

**NO. RETIRED BY BUFFALO**

Buffalo Sabres
New York Islanders
New York Rangers

Shoots: Right

Height: 5'-10"

Weight: 182 lbs.

Born: February 22, 1965; St. Louis, Missouri

Drafted by the New York Islanders third overall in 1983

Played 15 NHL seasons from 1983–98

Stats: See page 420

- Holds NHL record for most points in regular season by a U.S.-born player (148), established 1992–93
- Holds NHL record for fastest two goals from start of a playoff period (35 seconds), established in N.Y. Islanders' 5–2 loss to Edmonton Oilers, May 19, 1984
- Holds Buffalo Sabres' record for points in regular season (148), established 1992–93
- Played amateur hockey with Detroit Compuware (1981–82); Verdun Juniors (1982–83); USA National Team (1983–84)
- Led QMJHL in goals (104), assists (130) and points (234) in 1982–83; led QMJHL playoffs in assists (24) and points (35) in 1982–83

- QMJHL First Team All-Star Center (1983)
- Named QMJHL MVP (1983); named QMJHL Playoff MVP (1983); named Canadian Junior Player of the Year (1983)
- Played in NHL All-Star Game (1988, 1989, 1990, 1991, 1993)
- Scored "Easter Epic" goal in fourth overtime period of N.Y. Islanders' 3–2 victory over Washington Capitals in Game 7 of 1987 Patrick Division Semifinals
- Registered 1,000th career NHL point in N.Y. Rangers' 4–3 loss to Philadelphia Flyers, January 22, 1998
- Suffered career-ending head injury in game vs. Ottawa, March 16, 1998

**AWARDS**
Bill Masterton Memorial Trophy (1995)

**ALL-STAR SELECTIONS**
Second All-Star Team Center (1993)

**INTERNATIONAL AWARDS**
World Cup (1996)

111

# CENTER

# 4

# Newsy Lalonde 1950

ALTERNATE

## 11

Canadian Soo
Haileybury Hockey Club
Les Canadiens
(Montreal)
Montreal Canadiens
New York Americans
Portage la Prairie
Renfrew Hockey Club
Saskatoon Crescents
Saskatoon Sheiks
Toronto Professionals
Vancouver Millionaires

Shoots: Right

Height: 5'-9"

Weight: 168 lbs.

Born: October 31, 1888:
Cornwall, Ontario

Died: November 21, 1971:
Montreal, Quebec

Played 21 professional
seasons from 1906–27

Stats: See page 421

AWARDS

NHL Scoring Leader
(1919, 1921)

Stanley Cup (1915–16)

ALL-STAR
SELECTIONS

OPHL First All-Star
Team Center (1908)

PCHA First All-Star
Team Center (1912)

NHA First All-Star
Team Center (1914)

WCHL First All-Star
Team Center (1924)

"As I got more experience, I got less and less nervous and really began to enjoy professional hockey. The money was good and I was able to make extra cash playing professional lacrosse. I played in Vancouver and got $6,000 for 12 games."

- Shares NHL record for most goals in a single playoff game (5), accomplished in Montreal's 6–3 victory over Ottawa Senators, March 1, 1919

- Scored first goal in Montreal Canadiens franchise history in 7–6 victory over Cobalt Creamery Kings, January 5, 1910

- Earned nickname "Newsy" working in a local newsprint plant as a youth

- Played amateur hockey with Cornwall Victorias (1903–05); Cornwall HC (1904–05); Woodstock HC (1905–06)

- Led Ontario Professional League in goals (32) in 1907–08; led NHA in goals (38) in 1909–10; led PCHA in goals (27) in 1911–12; led NHA in goals (28) in 1915–16; led NHL in goals (23), assists (10) and points (33) in 1918–19; led NHL in points (43) in 1920–21

- Traded to Saskatoon (WCHL) by Montreal Canadiens for rights to Aurele Joliat and $3,500, September 18, 1922

- Led WCHL in goals (30) in 1922–23

- Coached Montreal Canadiens (1915–21, 1932–35); coached N.Y. Americans (1926–27); coached Ottawa Senators (1929–31)

- Named Lacrosse Athlete of the Half Century (1950)

- Inducted into Canadian Lacrosse Hall of Fame (1965); inducted into Canadian Sports Hall of Fame (1965)

# 1993 Edgar Laprade

**10**

> "I was taught early on that you can't score from the penalty box."

**New York Rangers**

Shoots: Right

Height: 5'-8"

Weight: 160 lbs.

Born: October 10, 1919; Port Arthur, Ontario

Died: April 28, 2014; Thunder Bay, Ontario

Played 10 NHL seasons from 1945–55

Stats: See page 421

- Nicknamed "Beaver" because of his work ethic and defensive abilities
- Played amateur hockey with Port Arthur Juniors (1935–37); Port Arthur Bearcats (1938–43)
- Member of the Allan Cup–winning Port Arthur Bearcats (1939); led Allan Cup playoffs in goals (22) and points (26)
- Led TBJHL in goals (19) and points (33) in 1936–37; goals (23) and points (34) in 1937–38
- Led TBSHL in goals (31) and points (40) in 1938–39; led TBSHL in goals (20); led TBSHL in goals (26), assists (21) and points (47) in 1940–41; led TBSHL in assists (23) and points (41) in 1941–42

- Delayed starting his NHL career to serve in the Canadian Armed Forces during World War II
- Signed with N.Y. Rangers instead of Montreal Canadiens because they gave him a $5,000 bonus to pay for the mortgage on his house
- Third player (with Gus Bodnar and Gaye Stewart) in four years from the Port Arthur/Fort William area to win the Calder Trophy
- Distinguished himself as a solid two-way player who was adept at poke checking
- Played in NHL All-Star Game (1947, 1948, 1949, 1950)
- Recorded two or fewer penalty minutes in six of his 10 NHL seasons

**AWARDS**

Calder Memorial Trophy (1946)

Lady Byng Memorial Trophy (1950)

# 8

# Igor Larionov 2008

**ALTERNATES**

## 18 · 7

CSKA Moscow
Detroit Red Wings
Florida Panthers
New Jersey Devils
San Jose Sharks
Vancouver Canucks

Shoots: Left

Height: 5'-9"

Weight: 170 lbs.

Born: December 3, 1960: Voskresensk, Union of Soviet Socialist Republics

Drafted by the Vancouver Canucks 214th overall in 1985

Played 14 NHL seasons from 1989–92, 1993–2004

Stats: See page 421

"I was quoted in the media and expressing myself quite openly that the day would come where I would play in the NHL, but I wasn't sure when. It took us a while to get the doors open for many of us to come to the National Hockey League."

— Igor Larionov on his openly challenging the Soviet government to let hockey players leave the country to play in the NHL

**AWARDS**

Stanley Cup (1996–97, 1997–98, 2001–02)

**INTERNATIONAL AWARDS**

Canada Cup (1981)

Gold Medal: Winter Olympics (1994, 1998)

Bronze Medal: Winter Olympics (2002)

Gold Medal: World Championships (1982, 1983, 1986, 1990)

Silver Medal: World Championships (1987)

Bronze Medal: World Championships (1985)

- Played amateur hockey with Khimik Voskresensk (1977–81); CSKA Moscow (1981–89)

- USSR First All-Star Team Center (1983, 1986, 1987, 1988)

- Named USSR Player of the Year (1988)

- Member of the Soviet Union's famed K-L-M Line with Vladimir Krutov and Sergei Makarov

- Played European pro hockey with HC Luongo (1992–93); Sierre Tigers (2004–05); Brunflo IK (2005–06)

- Nicknamed "The Professor" because of his scholarly approach to the game

- Claimed by San Jose from Vancouver in Waiver Draft, October 4, 1992

- Played in NHL All-Star Game (1998)

- Became oldest player (41 years, seven months) in NHL history to score a game-winning goal in the Stanley Cup final in Detroit's 3–2 overtime victory over Carolina Hurricanes, June 8, 2002

- Traded to Detroit by San Jose for Ray Sheppard, October 24, 1995; signed as a free agent by Florida, July 1, 2000

- Traded to Detroit by Florida for Yan Golubovsky, December 28, 2000; signed as a free agent by New Jersey, September 10, 2003

- Officially announced retirement, April 20, 2004

- Known as the "Russian Wayne Gretzky" in the Soviet Union

# 1984 Jacques Lemaire

**25**

> "With Montreal, there was a certain way to play the game that other teams didn't know. It came from being with winners. As a youngster, I played on good teams that didn't win, but I went to Montreal and right away, won two Stanley Cups in my first two seasons. It was those other guys who showed me how to win."

**Montreal Canadiens**

Shoots: Left

Height: 5'-10"

Weight: 180 lbs.

Born: September 7, 1945: LaSalle, Quebec

Played 12 NHL seasons from 1967–79

Stats: See page 422

- Played amateur hockey with Lachine Maroons (1962–63); Montreal Jr. Canadiens (1963–66)
- Led QJHL in points (104) in 1962–63
- Played minor pro hockey with Quebec Aces (1964–65); Houston Apollos (1966–67)
- First person in NHL history to play 100 playoff games and coach 100 playoff games
- Scored Stanley Cup–winning overtime goal in Montreal's 2–1 victory over Boston, May 14, 1977; scored Stanley Cup–winning goal in Montreal's 4–1 victory over N.Y. Rangers, May 21, 1979
- One of only five players (with Jack Darragh, Henri Richard, Mike Bossy and Jean Béliveau) to score two Cup-winning goals

- Played in NHL All-Star Game (1970, 1973)
- Runner-up to Boston Bruins Derek Sanderson in voting for rookie of the year in 1967–68
- Member of Montreal's famed Donut Line with Steve Shutt and Guy Lafleur
- Served as player/coach with HC Sierre (1979–81)
- Served as assistant coach of Plattsburgh State University Cardinals (1981–82)
- Coached Montreal Canadiens (1983–85); coached New Jersey Devils (1993–98, 2009–10); coached Minnesota Wild (2000–09)
- Coached Stanley Cup–winning New Jersey Devils (1995)

**AWARDS**

Jack Adams Award (1994, 2003)

Stanley Cup (1967–68, 1968–69, 1970–71, 1972–73, 1975–76, 1976–77, 1977–78, 1978–79)

**115**

# 66

# Mario Lemieux 1997

NO. RETIRED BY PITTSBURGH

**Pittsburgh Penguins**

Shoots: Right

Height: 6'-4"

Weight: 230 lbs.

Born: October 5, 1965;
Montreal, Quebec

Drafted by the
Pittsburgh Penguins
first overall in 1984

Played 17 NHL seasons
from 1984–94, 1995–97,
2000–04, 2005–06

Stats: See page 423

### AWARDS

Calder Memorial
Trophy (1985)

Ted Lindsay Award* (1986,
1988, 1993, 1996)

Art Ross Trophy (1988, 1989,
1992, 1993, 1996, 1997)

Hart Memorial Trophy
(1988, 1993, 1996)

Conn Smythe Trophy
(1991, 1992)

Bill Masterton Memorial
Trophy (1993)

Lester Patrick
Trophy (2000)

Stanley Cup
(1990–91, 1991–92)

### ALL-STAR
### SELECTIONS

First All-Star Team
Center (1988, 1989,
1993, 1996, 1997)

Second All-Star Team Center
(1986, 1987, 1992, 2001)

### INTERNATIONAL
### AWARDS

Canada Cup (1987)

Silver Medal: World
Championships (1985)

Gold Medal: Winter
Olympics (2002)

*Known as the Lester B. Pearson
Award from 1971 to 2009

"All I can say to young players is enjoy every moment of it. Just enjoy every moment. Your career goes by very quickly."

○ Ranks 10th in NHL career goals (690); 11th in NHL career assists (1,033); eighth in NHL career points (1,723)

○ Holds NHL record for short-handed goals in regular season (13), accomplished in 1988–89

○ Shares NHL record for goals (5) and points (8) in a single playoff game and goals in a single playoff period (4), all accomplished in Pittsburgh's 10–7 victory over Philadelphia Flyers, April 25, 1989

○ Played amateur hockey with Montreal Hurricane (1979–80); Montreal-Concordia (1980–81); Laval Voisins (1981–84)

○ Led QMJHL in goals (133), assists (149) and points (282) in 1983–84; led QMJHL playoffs in goals (29), assists (23) and points (52) in 1983–84

○ QMJHL First All-Star Team Center (1984); QMJHL Second All-Star Team Center (1983); CHL Player of the Year (1984)

○ Led NHL in short-handed goals in 1987–88 (10), 1988–89 (13) and 1995–96 (8); led NHL in power-play goals in 1988–89 (31) and 1995–96 (31)

○ Only player in NHL history to score five goals in five different ways (even-strength goal, a power-play goal, a shorthanded goal, a penalty-shot goal and an empty-net goal) in a single game, December 31, 1988

○ One of only three players (with Gordie Howe and Guy Lafleur) to play in NHL after being inducted into the Hall of Fame

○ Registered 1,000th career NHL point in Pittsburgh's 4–3 loss to Detroit Red Wings, March 24, 1992; recorded 500th career NHL goal in Pittsburgh's 7–5 victory over N.Y. Islanders, October 26, 1992

# Unreal

The Pittsburgh Penguins' Mario Lemieux made the things he did on the ice look so easy that he was sometimes maligned for not working hard enough. At 6-foot-4 and 230 pounds, Lemieux was as big, or bigger, than many power forwards in the NHL, yet he had the skill, grace and talent of smaller, sleeker stars like Wayne Gretzky and Guy Lafleur.

Make no mistake, Lemieux was working hard, but his movements were like an optical illusion. His great balance, long strides and extended reach allowed him to cover the same amount of space while moving less. As a result, it sometimes looked like he was moving in slow motion, and he often caught defenders flat-footed and goalies gazing.

In his first NHL shift, Lemieux stole the puck from Boston's star defenseman Ray Bourque and moved in and beat goalie Pete Peeters with his first NHL shot. In his home debut in Pittsburgh, he got an assist, again in his first shift, and won his first fight as well. He kept up the scoring pace that first year (1984–85) and became just the third rookie in league history to record 100 or more points.

On December 31, 1988, Lemieux put on what many have called the greatest individual scoring performance in NHL history. He tabulated five goals in a game in five different ways: even strength, power play, shorthanded, penalty shot and empty net. No one had done it before, and no one has done it since. He went on to finish the 1988–89 season with 85 goals and 199 points to lead the league for the second consecutive season.

Lemieux and his Pittsburgh Penguins won

Mario Lemieux scored the 1987 Canada Cup–winning goal while wearing this jersey. His goal, scored with 1:26 left in regulation, was his 11th in nine games and is one of Canada's most celebrated hockey moments.

consecutive Cups in 1991 and 1992, but afterward Lemieux received the news that he was suffering from Hodgkin's lymphoma. He missed two months midway through the 1992–93 season before returning to lead the league in scoring. He sat out 62 games in 1993–94 and the entire 1994–95 season because of health problems relating to his cancer and chronic back pain.

Lemieux returned to play 70 games in 1995–96, leading the league in total points and winning both the Hart Trophy as league MVP and the Lester B. Pearson Award (known since 2010 as the Ted Lindsay Award) as the league MVP as voted by the players.

He retired after the 1997 season and was immediately inducted into the Hall of Fame. In 2000 Lemieux became one of three players to resume their career after being inducted into the Hall of Fame. He played parts of five more seasons and captained the Canadian squad that captured gold at the 2002 Salt Lake City Olympics.

# 88

### CENTER

# Eric Lindros 2016

No. Retired by
Philadelphia

Dallas Stars
New York Rangers
Philadelphia Flyers
Toronto Maple Leafs

Shoots: Right

Height: 6'-4"

Weight: 240 lbs.

Born: February 28, 1973
London, Ontario

Drafted by the
Quebec Nordiques
1st overall in 1991

Played 14 NHL seasons
from 1992–2004,
2005–2007

Stats: See Page 423

"It's not necessarily
the amount of
time you spend at
practice that counts;
it's what you put into
the practice."

**AWARDS**

Hart Memorial
Trophy (1995)

Ted Lindsay
Award* (1995)

**ALL-STAR
SELECTIONS**

All-Rookie Team (1993)

First All-Star Team
Center (1995)

Second All-Star Team
Center (1996)

**INTERNATIONAL
AWARDS**

Canada Cup (1991)

Gold Medal: Winter
Olympics (2002)

Silver Medal: Winter
Olympics (1992)

*Known as the Lester
B. Pearson Award
from 1971 to 2009

- Won the 1990 Memorial Cup with the Oshawa Generals; led the OHL with 71 goals and 149 points in 1990–91, winning league MVP and being named the Canadian Hockey League Player of the Year

- Played for Canada as a 16-year-old at the 1990 World Junior Championship and won a gold medal; also won gold in 1991

- Refused to report to the Quebec Nordiques after advising the team not to select him in the 1991 NHL Draft; joined the Canadian national team and represented Canada at the 1991 Canada Cup, the 1992 World Junior Championship and the 1992 Winter Olympics

- Was awarded to Philadelphia by an arbitrator after Quebec worked out trades for his rights with both the Flyers and the New York Rangers at the 1992 NHL Draft

- Tied Jaromir Jagr for the NHL scoring lead with 70 points in 46 games during the lockout-shortened 1994–95 season (Did not win the Art Ross Trophy because Jagr had 32 goals to his 29)

- Established career highs with 47 goals, 68 assists and 115 points in 1995–96; finished third in voting for the Hart Trophy behind Mario Lemieux and Mark Messier

- Served as captain of the Flyers from 1994–95 to 1999–2000; was captain of Team Canada at the 1998 Nagano Olympics

- Played in the NHL All-Star Game six times (1994, 1996–2000)

- Concussions and other injuries began to hamper him in 1997–98 and he missed the entire 2000–01 season; retired in 2007 at the age of 34

# 1952 Mickey MacKay

**9**

> "He was perhaps the greatest center we ever had on the coast. MacKay was a great crowd pleaser. He was clean, splendidly courageous, a happy player with a stylish way of going. He was one of those who helped make pro hockey a great game. He was outstanding in every way."
>
> — Lester Patrick

**ALTERNATES**

**5 · 3 · 6**
**7 · 12**

Boston Bruins
Calgary Columbus Club
Chicago Black Hawks
Pittsburgh Pirates
Vancouver Maroons
Vancouver Millionaires

Shoots: Left

Height: 5'-9"

Weight: 162 lbs.

Born: May 21, 1894;
Chelsey, Ontario

Died: May 21, 1940;
Ymir, British Columbia

Played 16 elite amateur and professional seasons from 1914–30

Stats: See page 424

- Nicknamed "The Wee Scot"
- Played amateur hockey with Chelsey ACC (1910–12); Edmonton Dominions (1912–13); Grand Forks AC (1913–14)
- Led ASHL in playoff goals (8) in 1912–13; led BCBHL in goals (15) and points (15) in 1913–14
- Led PCHA in goals in 1914–15 (33), 1923–24 (21) and 1924–25 (27); led PCHA in assists (12) in 1921–22; led PCHA in goals in 1923–24 (21) and 1924–25 (27)
- Led PCHA playoffs in goals (2) and points (3) in 1916–17; led Stanley Cup tournament in points (10) in 1917–18; led PCHA playoffs in assists (3) in 1920–21
- Signed as a free agent by Vancouver Millionaires (PCHA), November 3, 1914

- Scored four goals and registered six points in the Vancouver Millionaires' Stanley Cup victory over the Ottawa Senators in March 1915
- Traded to Chicago by Vancouver (WHL) for cash, October 4, 1926; traded to Pittsburgh by Chicago for cash, September 1928; traded to Boston by Pittsburgh with a reported $12,000 for Frank Fredrickson, December 21, 1928
- Scored 250 goals in 459 professional games between 1914 and 1930
- Inducted into British Columbia Sports Hall of Fame (1989); inducted into British Columbia Hockey Hall of Fame (2001)

**AWARDS**
Stanley Cup
(1914–15, 1928–29)

**ALL-STAR SELECTIONS**
PCHA First All-Star Team Center (1915, 1917, 1919, 1922, 1923)

PCHA Second All-Star Team Center (1916, 1918, 1921)

WCHL First All-Star Team Center (1925)

WHL First All-Star Team Center (1926)

# CENTER

# 4

# Joe Malone 1950

**ALTERNATES**

# 7 · 11 · 9

Hamilton Tigers
Montreal Canadiens
Quebec Bulldogs
Waterloo Colts

Alternate Position: LW

Shoots: Left

Height: 5'-10"

Weight: 150 lbs.

Born: February 28, 1890;
Quebec City, Quebec

Died: May 15, 1969;
Montreal, Quebec

Played 15 professional
seasons from 1909–24

Stats: See page 424

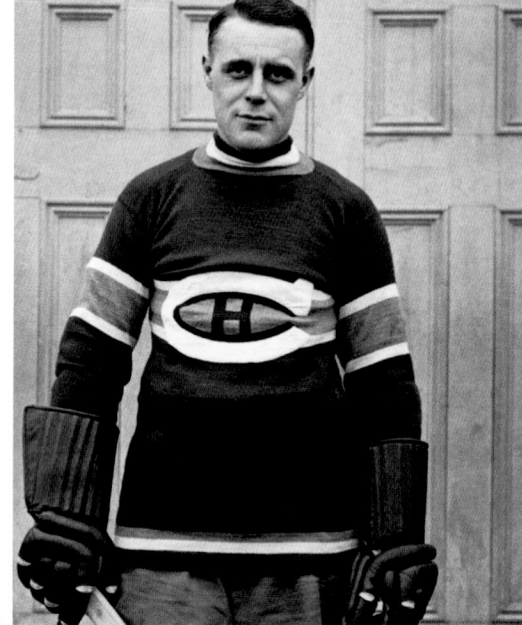

"In my day, there was no trophy, no bonus, no prize of any kind for leading the league [in points]. They didn't even count assists. Now the winner gets a fine cup and $1,000. That's more money than I ever made in a season."

**AWARDS**

NHL Scoring Leader
(1918, 1920)

Stanley Cup: (1911–12,
1912–13, 1923–24)

- Holds NHL record for goals in a single game (7), established in Quebec's 10–6 victory over Toronto Arenas, January 31, 1920

- Held NHL record for most goals in regular season (44) from 1917–18 to 1944–45; surpassed by Maurice Richard (50), February 25, 1945

- Held NHL record for most points in regular season (49) from 1919–20 to 1927–28; surpassed by Howie Morenz (59) in 1927–28

- Only player in NHL history to score six or more goals in a single game twice (seven goals against Toronto, January 31, 1920; six goals against Ottawa, March 10, 1920)

- Led NHA in goals (43) in 1912–13; goals (41) and points (49) in 1916–17

- Led NHL in goals (44) and points (48) in 1917–18; goals (39) and points (49) in 1919–20

- Nicknamed "The Phantom" for his ability to find openings and "invisibly" weave through opposition defenses

- Played amateur hockey with Quebec Crescents (1907–08); Quebec Bulldogs (1908–10)

- Scored nine goals for Quebec Bulldogs in 14–3 Stanley Cup playoff win over Sydney Millionaires on March 8, 1913

- Served as captain of the Quebec Bulldogs (1910–17)

- Scored five goals in Montreal Canadiens' NHL debut in 7–4 win over the Ottawa Senators, December 19, 1917

# Better Than His NHL Best

Joe Malone's scoring exploits of a century ago have made him the best-known star from the NHL's early years. In an era of rough and rowdy hockey, Malone stood out for his sportsmanship, but it was his scoring prowess that has made him a legend. Malone scored 44 goals in just 20 games for the Montreal Canadiens in the NHL's first season of 1917–18, and his seven goals in a single game for the Quebec Bulldogs on January 31, 1920, is a mark that has never been beaten.

Malone enjoyed a breakout year with the Bulldogs of the National Hockey Association back in 1911–12. He scored a team-leading 21 goals in 18 games that season as Quebec claimed the Stanley Cup for the first time. Malone and the Bulldogs were even more dominant in 1912–13 when he led the NHA with 43 goals in a 20-game season to lead Quebec to a 16–4–0 record.

The Bulldogs also boasted future Hall of Famers in flashy scorer Tommy Smith (who helped Malone power the offense with 39 goals of his own that season), tough-as-nails defenseman Joe Hall and goalie Paddy Moran. Still, Malone was the team's biggest star as he proved with the best single-game performance of his career in a lopsided win over the Sydney Millionaires in a Stanley Cup challenge on March 8, 1913.

Despite playing with a bad cold, Malone scored his first goal of the night just 1:30 into the first period. It was 4–2 Quebec after one with Malone scoring his second of the game

**Joe Malone in the early 1920s during his time with the short-lived Hamilton Tigers team.**

late in the period. Quebec set a much faster pace after intermission and Malone scored his third of the night at 2:30 of the second frame, with Smith and Malone again finding the net in the next 30 seconds. Malone scored three more times before the period ended, and then scored two more in the first six minutes of the third. That gave him nine on the night and put Quebec ahead 13–2 en route to a 14–3 victory. Malone sat out the second game, but the Bulldogs still scored an easy 6–2 win to clinch the Stanley Cup.

# Frank McGee 1945

**Ottawa Aberdeens
Ottawa Seconds
Ottawa Silver Seven**

Shoots: Right

Height: 5'-6"

Weight: 150 lbs.

Born: November 4, 1878: Ottawa, Ontario

Died: September 16, 1916: Killed in action, Courcelette, France

Played seven elite amateur seasons from 1899–1906

Stats: See page 424

"He was even better than they say he was. He had everything — speed, stick-handling, scoring ability and was a punishing checker. He was strongly built but beautifully proportioned and he had an almost animal rhythm."

— Hockey Hall of Fame builder Frank Patrick

**AWARDS**

Stanley Cup (1902–03, 1903–04, 1904–05, 1905–06)

- Played amateur hockey with Ottawa Secords (1899–00); Ottawa Aberdeens (1900–02)

- Holds Stanley Cup playoff record for goals in a single game (14), established in Ottawa's 23–2 victory over Dawson City Nuggets, January 16, 1905

- Known as "One Eyed Frank McGee" after losing sight in left eye when struck by a puck in game against Hawkesbury, March 21, 1900

- Shared FAHL goals scoring lead (17) with future Hall of Fame member Jack Marshall (1904–05)

- Scored Stanley Cup–winning goal in Ottawa's 5–4 victory over Rat Portage Thistles while playing with a broken wrist, March 11, 1905

- Finished third in the ECAHA scoring (28 goals) behind teammate Harry Smith (brother of Hall of Fame members Alf and Tommy Smith) and future Hall of Fame member Dubbie Bowie in 1905–06

- Scored eight goals versus the Montreal Wanderers in an ECAHA league game on March 3, 1906

- Member of prominent Ottawa family — his father (John Joseph McGee) was Clerk of the Privy Council (Canada's highest-ranking civil servant) and his uncle (Thomas D'Arcy McGee) was a "Father of Confederation" who was assassinated in 1868

- Killed in combat while serving in the Canadian Army during World War I

# 1962 Billy McGimsie

> "My ambition when I started was to play on a winning Stanley Cup team, and I had three cracks at it."

**Kenora Thistles**
**Rat Portage Thistles**

Shoots: Left

Height: 5'-8"

Weight: 145 lbs.

Born: June 7, 1880: Woodsville, Ontario

Died: October 28, 1968: Calgary, Alberta

Played six elite amateur seasons from 1901–07

Stats: See page 424

- Family moved to Rat Portage (Kenora) when he was one year old and he grew up to star on local school and junior teams with future Hall of Fame members Tommy Phillips, Si Griffis and Tom Hooper

- Member of Manitoba champion Rat Portage Thistles (1902–03)

- Member of Rat Portage Thistles that lost Stanley Cup challenge to Ottawa "Silver Seven" (1902–03, 1904–05)

- Led the Manitoba and North West Hockey League in goals (28) in 1904–05

- Member of Manitoba champion Kenora Thistles (1905–06)

- Finished third in scoring (21 goals) in the Manitoba Hockey League (1905–06)

- Scored goal in Kenora's 8–6 victory over the Montreal Wanderers that helped clinch Stanley Cup championship, January 21, 1907

- Suffered dislocated shoulder during an exhibition game in Ottawa following Kenora's Stanley Cup victory and never played again

- Coached Fort Williams Forts (1910–11)

**AWARDS**

Stanley Cup (1906–07)

# 11

# Mark Messier 2007

NO. RETIRED BY EDMONTON
& NEW YORK RANGERS

**Cincinnati Stingers
Edmonton Oilers
Indianapolis Racers
New York Rangers
Vancouver Canucks**

Alternate Position: LW

Shoots: Left

Height: 6'-1"

Weight: 210 lbs.

Born: January 18, 1961;
Edmonton, Alberta

Drafted by the Edmonton
Oilers 48th overall in 1979

Played 26 WHA and NHL
seasons from 1978–2004

Stats: See page 425

### AWARDS

Conn Smythe Trophy (1984)

Hart Memorial Trophy
(1990, 1992)

Ted Lindsay Award*
(1990, 1992)

Lester Patrick
Trophy (2009)

Stanley Cup (1983–84,
1984–85, 1986–87, 1987–88,
1989–90, 1993–94)

### ALL-STAR SELECTIONS

First NHL All-Star Team
Left Wing (1982, 1983)

First NHL All-Star Team
Center (1990, 1992)

Second NHL All-Star
Team Left Wing (1984)

### INTERNATIONAL AWARDS

Canada Cup
(1984, 1987, 1991)

Silver Medal: World
Championships (1989)

*Known as the Lester
B. Pearson Award
from 1971 to 2009

"I had the people and support from the president all the way down to the manager and coaches that shared in my belief, and together, we were part of something that hadn't been done in 54 years. It was an amazing time for us all."

— Mark Messier, on winning the Cup with the Rangers

- First player to serve as captain on two different Stanley Cup–winning teams (Edmonton, 1990 and N.Y. Rangers, 1994)

- One of only six Hall of Fame members (with Sid Abel, Doug Bentley, Dit Clapper, Neil Colville and Alex Delvecchio) to be selected as an NHL All-Star at two different positions

- Played amateur hockey with Spruce Grove Mets (1976–77); St. Albert Saints (1977–79); Portland Winter Hawks (1977–78)

- Ranks third in NHL career points (1,887); ranks second in NHL career short-handed goals (63)

- Ranks third in NHL career assists (1,193); ranks eighth in NHL career goals (694)

- Registered 1,000th career NHL point in Edmonton's 5–3 victory over Pittsburgh Penguins, January 13, 1991; recorded 500th career NHL goal in N.Y. Rangers' 4–2 victory over Calgary Flames, November 6, 1995

- Played in NHL All-Star Game (1982, 1983, 1984, 1986, 1988, 1989, 1990, 1991, 1992, 1994, 1996, 1997, 1998, 2000, 2004)

- Renowned for guaranteeing a win by the New York Rangers over the New Jersey Devils in Game 6 of the 1994 Eastern Conference final

- Legacy honored by the NHL with the creation of the Mark Messier Leadership Award in 2005

- Scored Stanley Cup–winning goal in N.Y. Rangers' 3–2 victory over Vancouver Canucks, June 14, 1994

# Consummate Captain

Everyone assumed the Edmonton Oilers' dynasty would perish with The Trade, but someone forgot to tell Mark Messier. Wayne Gretzky's move from the Oilers to the Los Angeles Kings in 1988—after four Cups in his previous five seasons with Edmonton—seemed to doom the Oilers. But Messier, who had replaced his close friend Gretzky as the Oilers' captain, had other ideas. Two years after the trade that broke Canada's collective heart, Messier and his teammates willed the Cup back to the NHL's northernmost franchise.

A hometown boy, Messier wore the Oilers' C like an extra layer of skin. He prided himself on playing a complete game. Like Gordie Howe before him, he could skate, score, puckhandle, pass, hit and fight. And he could set an example for his teammates and usually make them follow it.

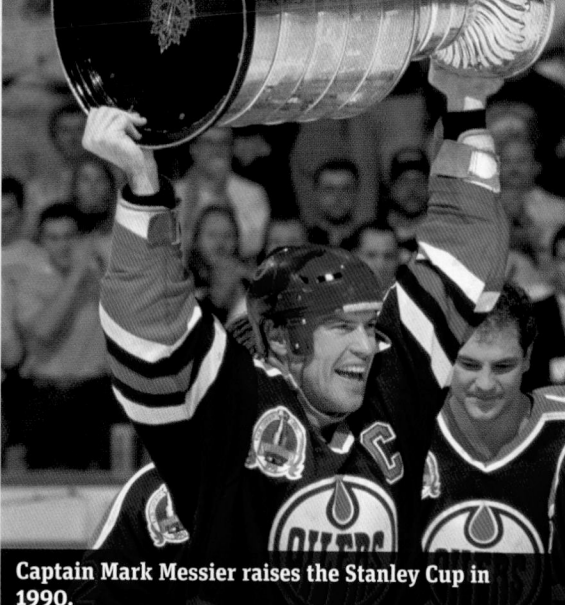

**Captain Mark Messier raises the Stanley Cup in 1990.**

"In team sport it's important to have a leader and to have a leader who's consistent in his behavior and can get outside himself—even when things aren't going well for him personally—so he can have a feel for the rest of the players around him," said Messier, adding, "Actions really depict that, and players will look up to those players in tough, crucial situations."

Messier's actions always spoke louder than his words, even when he spoke louder than anyone else, as he did when he guaranteed to the press that his New York Rangers would win Game 6 of the 1994 Eastern Conference final; he went on to score a third period hat trick to make certain it happened. He didn't make any such promise to Edmonton fans in 1990, but when the Oilers fell behind two games to one to the Blackhawks in the Western Conference final, Messier scored twice and assisted on the other two goals in a 4–2 victory in Game 4 in Chicago. Rescued and awed by their leader, the Oilers lost only one more game on their way to the 1990 Stanley Cup title.

The 1990 Cup win capped a career year for Messier, as he recorded 129 points in his second season as captain. Messier would wear the captain's C for every team he played on for the rest of his career, and in 1994 he led the Rangers to the Stanley Cup, becoming the only player to have captained two different franchises to Cup titles.

# 21

## CENTER

# Stan Mikita 1983

NO. RETIRED BY CHICAGO

**Chicago Black Hawks**

Alternate Position: RW

Shoots: Right

Height: 5'-9"

Weight: 169 lbs.

Born: May 20, 1940:
Sokolce, Czechoslovakia

Played 22 NHL seasons
from 1959–80

Stats: See page 425

"One year, I must have had five or more [misconducts]. That's 50 minutes right there! So, I said, 'Keep your mouth shut. Don't change your style of play but don't take those lazy penalties and let's see what happens.' The next season, in the first 20 games, I only had one penalty. It was unbelievable!"

**AWARDS**

Art Ross Trophy (1964, 1965, 1967, 1968)

Hart Memorial Trophy (1967, 1968)

Lady Byng Memorial Trophy (1967, 1968)

Stanley Cup (1960–61)

Lester Patrick Trophy (1976)

**ALL-STAR SELECTIONS**

First All-Star Team Center (1962, 1963, 1964, 1966, 1967, 1968)

Second All-Star Team Center (1965, 1970)

**INTERNATIONAL AWARDS**

Summit Series (1972)

- Played amateur hockey with St. Catharines Tee Pees (1956–59)
- Led OHA-Jr. in assists (59) and points (97)
- First player in NHL history to win three individual awards in the same season (1967, 1968)
- Holds Chicago Blackhawks' team records for seasons (22), games (1,394), assists (926), and career points (1,467)
- Ranks 14th in career NHL points (1,467)
- Renowned for making dramatic change in style of play from aggressive agitator to pacifist point producer
- Led NHL in points in 1963–64 (89), 1964–65 (87), 1966–67 (97) and 1967–68 (87)

- Led NHL playoffs in goals (6) in 1960–61; led NHL playoffs in assists (15) and points (1961–62); led NHL playoffs in penalty minutes (53) in 1964–65
- Led NHL in power-play goals (14) in 1963–64; led NHL in game-winning goals in 1967–68 (8) and 1969–70 (8)
- Led NHL in assists in 1964–65 (59), 1965–66 (48) and 1966–67 (62)
- Finished second in NHL goals in 1963–64 (39), 1966–67 (35) and 1967–68 (40)
- Played in NHL All-Star Game (1964, 1967, 1968, 1969, 1971, 1972, 1973, 1974, 1975)
- First Czechoslovakian-born player to be inducted into the Hall of Fame

# Stan's the Man

Stan Mikita hadn't ever skated—or even seen an NHL game—when, at nine years old, his friend Archie Maybe convinced him to lie about his age and sign up for the local St. Catharines youth hockey league.

Born Stanislaus Guoth on May 20, 1940, in Sokolce, Czechoslovakia (present-day Slovakia), the young lad moved to St. Catharines, Ontario and was adopted by his aunt and uncle, the Mikitas. He was eight years old and didn't speak English. After some time in school Stan picked up enough English to get by, and before he knew it, he and Archie were lining up to play hockey against boys two years their senior.

Mikita was a natural athlete, and it didn't take long for him to translate his soccer sensibilities into an understanding of hockey. By the time he was 13 he was already on the fast track, as his rights were claimed by the St. Catharines TeePees organization, the junior affiliate of the Chicago Black Hawks.

From there a star was born, and Mikita joined the long-struggling Hawks as an 18-year-old junior sensation, suiting up for the 1958–59 season. Chicago won the Stanley Cup in 1960–61, and Mikita, Bobby Hull and Glenn Hall formed a nucleus that kept the Hawks competitive for the rest of the Original Six era.

Mikita would go on to reach great personal heights in the years following the Hawks' 1961 Cup win. His most astounding transformation was from an ornery, aggressive player who averaged 114 penalty minutes per season (over

**Stan Mikita hones one of his "banana blade" sticks during the mid-1960s.**

his first six seasons) into a multiple Lady Byng Trophy–winner as the league's most gentlemanly player. In 1966–67, Mikita's eighth season, he cut his penalty minutes to 12 and was awarded the Lady Byng for the first time. Moreover, that season he also became the first player to be awarded three major trophies in a single season, snagging the Art Ross Trophy (most points) and the Hart Trophy (NHL MVP) in addition to the Lady Byng. Just to show it wasn't a fluke, he repeated the trifecta the next season.

Mikita retired in 1979–80 after playing 21 exceptional seasons, all with the Black Hawks. Although he didn't win another championship, the consistency he provided to Chicago was enough to transform a once moribund franchise into a contender.

# 9 Mike Modano 2014

NO. RETIRED BY DALLAS

**Dallas Stars**
**Detroit Red Wings**
**Minnesota North Stars**

Shoots: Right

Height: 6'-3"

Weight: 205 lbs.

Born: June 7, 1970:
Livonia, Michigan

Drafted by the
Minnesota North Stars
first overall in 1988

Played 21 NHL
seasons from
1989–2004, 2005–11

Stats: See page 426

> "I want to be out there on the ice when the game is on the line. I want to be the one who decides the game."

**AWARDS**

Stanley Cup (1998–99)

**ALL-STAR SELECTIONS**

All-Rookie Team (1990)

Second All-Star Team
Center (2000)

**INTERNATIONAL AWARDS**

Silver Medal: Winter
Olympics (2002)

World Cup (1996)

- Leads all American-born NHL players with 561 career goals and 1,374 points in the regular season, as well as 146 points in the playoffs

- Finished among the NHL's top-10 scorers in 1999–2000, 2001–02 and 2002–03

- Scored a career-high 50 goals in 1993–94 during the Dallas Stars' inaugural season following a career-high 60 assists the previous year in his last Minnesota season

- Led the Stars in regular-season goal scoring six times, assists eight times, and points 11 times

- Served as captain of Dallas Stars (2003–06)

- Played in NHL All-Star Game (1993, 1998, 1999, 2000, 2003, 2004, 2009)

- Holds Dallas Stars team records in nearly every category, including games played (1,459), goals (557), assists (802), points (1,359), game-winning goals (92), power-play goals (156), short-handed goals (29), playoff games (174), playoff goals (56), playoff assists (87) and playoff points (143)

- Was runner-up to Sergei Makarov for the Calder Trophy as rookie of the year in 1989–90

- Was inducted into the U.S. Hockey Hall of Fame in 2012

- Represented the United States at the World Junior Championships (1988, 1989), World Championships (1990, 1993, 2005), Canada Cup (1991), World Cup (1996, 2004) and Winter Olympics (1998, 2002, 2006)

# The Stars Align

**M**ike Modano was the second American-born player to be selected first overall in the NHL Entry Draft when he was picked by the Minnesota North Stars in 1988. Five years earlier, the North Stars had made Brian Lawton the first American number-one pick. Lawton didn't pan out, but Modano went on to become the leading American-born scorer in NHL history.

A high-scoring midget hockey player in his native Michigan, Modano left home for Prince Albert, Saskatchewan, in 1986 and played three years of junior hockey with the Prince Albert Raiders of the Western Hockey League. He cracked the top 10 in scoring with 127 points in 65 games in 1987–88, finishing behind future NHL stars Joe Sakic, Theo Fleury and Mark Recchi. He missed 25 games with a broken wrist the following season but still had 105 points in just 41 games. He also made his NHL debut that year, playing two playoff games with the North Stars, and was in the NHL to stay by 1989–90. His 75 points with Minnesota that season ranked second in rookie scoring behind former Soviet star Sergei Makarov, who was 31 years old. Modano was just 19, and after Makarov beat him out to win the Calder Trophy, the NHL changed the rules of eligibility to say that no player could be named the rookie of the year if he was more than 26 years old.

Modano helped the North Stars reach the Stanley Cup Final in 1990–91, and was then the team's leading scorer the next two seasons. In 1993–94, the North Stars left Minnesota

Mike Modano playing against the Pittsburgh Penguins during one of his four years in Minnesota before the team moved to Dallas.

and became the Dallas Stars. Modano helped win over fans in the new city by scoring 50 goals that year. By 1996–97, Dallas was an NHL powerhouse and the Stars won the Stanley Cup in 1999. Modano led the team in playoff scoring despite suffering a broken wrist in game two of the final against the Buffalo Sabres. Always a gifted offensive player, Modano had developed into a solid defensive player as well. He was a finalist for the Selke Trophy as the NHL's best defensive forward in 2000–01.

Despite spending his final NHL season with the Detroit Red Wings in 2010–11, Modano signed a one-day contract with Dallas in the offseason so that he could end his 21-year career as a Star.

CENTER

# 7 Howie Morenz 1945

NO. RETIRED BY MONTREAL

ALTERNATES

## 3 · 6 · 12

Chicago Black Hawks
Montreal Canadiens
New York Rangers

Shoots: Left

Height: 5'-9"

Weight: 165 lbs.

Born: September 21, 1902: Mitchell, Ontario

Died: March 8, 1937: Montreal, Quebec

Played 14 NHL seasons from 1923–37

Stats: See page 427

"The old spirit is back. There was something missing inside when I was away the last two seasons. I got it back when I came back with the Canadiens. I'm giving the fans everything I've got. The end may be in sight but the heart is still sound."

AWARDS

NHL Scoring Leader (1928, 1931)

Hart Memorial Trophy (1928, 1931, 1932)

Stanley Cup (1923–24, 1929–30, 1930–31)

ALL-STAR SELECTIONS

First All-Star Team Center (1931, 1932)

Second All-Star Team Center (1933)

- ○ Nicknamed the "Stratford Streak," "Canadiens Comet" and "Mitchell Meteor" because of his tremendous speed and agility with the puck

- ○ Named the top hockey player of the first half of the 20th century by Canadian Press

- ○ First player to have his number retired by the Montreal Canadiens (1937)

- ○ Played amateur hockey with Stratford Midgets (1919–22); Stratford Indians (1921–23)

- ○ Led OHA-Jr. in assists (12) and points (31) in 1920–21; led OHA-Jr. in playoff goals (38), assists (18) and points (56) in 1919–20

- ○ Led OHA-Jr. in playoff goals (17), assists (4) and points (21) in 1921–22; led OHA-Sr. in playoff goals (15), assists (8) and points (23) in 1921–22

- ○ Led NHL in points in 1927–28 (51) and 1930–31 (51); led NHL in assists (18) in 1927–28; led NHL in goals (33) in 1927–28

- ○ Scored Stanley Cup–winning goal in Montreal Canadiens' 3–0 victory over Calgary Tigers, March 25, 1924

- ○ Played in NHL All-Star Game (1934)

- ○ Traded to Chicago by Montreal Canadiens with Lorne Chabot and Marty Burke for Leroy Goldsworthy, Lionel Conacher and Roger Jenkins, October 3, 1934

- ○ Traded to N.Y. Rangers by Chicago for Glenn Brydson, January 26, 1936; traded to Montreal Canadiens by N.Y. Rangers for cash, September 1, 1936

- ○ Suffered career-ending leg injury in game against Chicago, January 28, 1937

# A Memorial for Morenz

I t was impossible to believe, and the communal sense of loss was overwhelming. Howie Morenz, the NHL's first universally recognized megastar, was dead. Officially, he succumbed to complications from a broken leg he had suffered in a game five weeks earlier, on January 28, 1937, when Earl Siebert crashed into him and snapped his leg in four places. According to bereaved teammate Aurèle Joliat, Morenz actually died of a broken heart because he could no longer play the game he loved so much.

Morenz, the maestro of the end-to-end rush, was the fastest skater most fans had ever seen, for which he earned his "Stratford Streak" moniker. He was twice an NHL scoring champion and three times a league Most Valuable Player, and he led the Canadiens to three Stanley Cups. When he died at just 34 years of age he was in his second stint with the Habs and in his 14th NHL season.

He was so popular that 50,000 people came to view his body as it lay in state at center ice in the Montreal Forum. His famous No. 7 became the first Canadiens sweater to be retired, and in 1950 the Canadian Press named Morenz the best hockey player of the first half of the 20th century.

At the start of the 1937–38 season, a benefit game for Morenz's family was arranged. It was played between a combined Montreal Canadiens/Montreal Maroons All-Star squad versus the NHL All-Stars. Lionel Conacher came out of retirement to play for the Montreal side, as did Maroons coach Francis "King" Clancy. Joliat and Johnny Gagnon, Morenz's last linemates, also played for the Montreal team, as did Hector "Toe" Blake, who had started his NHL career as a Maroon.

The game, played on November 2, 1937,

These sweaters were worn by the Montreal Canadiens-Maroons split squad (red) and the NHL All-Stars (white) for the Howie Morenz Memorial Game. The game raised $20,000 for the Morenz family.

was a high-spirited evening, with Blake registering an assist on Montreal's second goal and the Detroit Red Wings' Marty Barry scoring the eventual winner in a 6–5 NHL All-Star victory. The emotional highlight of the night was Morenz's 11-year-old son skating with his father's former teammates in the warm-up. Howie Jr. grew up to be a good junior and senior player in Montreal.

The Morenz Memorial Game added to the All-Star appetite created by the Ace Bailey Benefit Game three years before, eventually leading to the first NHL All-Star Game 10 years later.

# 25

# Joe Nieuwendyk 2011

Calgary Flames
Dallas Stars
Florida Panthers
New Jersey Devils
Toronto Maple Leafs

Shoots: Left
Height: 6'-2"
Weight: 205 lbs.

Born: September 10, 1966: Oshawa, Ontario

Drafted by the Calgary Flames 27th overall in 1985

Played 20 seasons from 1987–2004, 2005–06

Stats: See page 427

"I'm just one player on [the] team. You can only do so much. The big thing is to focus on your own job and make sure you do the best you can."

**AWARDS**
Calder Memorial Trophy (1988)
Dodge Ram Tough Award (1988)
King Clancy Memorial Trophy (1995)
Conn Smythe Trophy (1999)
Stanley Cup (1988–89, 1998–99, 2002–03)

**ALL-STAR SELECTIONS**
All-Rookie Team (1988)

**INTERNATIONAL AWARDS**
Gold Medal: Winter Olympics (2002)

- Played amateur hockey with Pickering Panthers (1983–84), Cornell University (1984–87), Canadian National Team (1986–87)

- Selected to ECAC First All-Star Team (1986, 1987) and NCAA East First All-American (1986, 1987)

- Holds Calgary Flames team records for points by a rookie (92) and goals by a rookie (51), accomplished in 1987–88; holds Calgary Flames team record for regular-season power-play goals (31), established in 1987–88

- Holds Minnesota North Stars/Dallas Stars team record for fastest goal to start a regular-season game (7 seconds), accomplished in Dallas' 5–1 victory over Detroit, November 13, 1998

- Played in NHL All-Star Game (1988, 1989, 1990, 1994)

- One of 10 players in NHL history to win Stanley Cup with three different teams (Calgary, Dallas, New Jersey)

- Led NHL in regular-season power-play goals (31) in 1987–88; led NHL in regular-season game-winning goals (11) in 1988–89; led NHL in playoff goals (11) in 1998–99; led NHL in playoff game-winning goals (6) in 1998–99

- Recorded 500th NHL career goal in New Jersey's 2–1 victory over Carolina, January 17, 2003; registered 1,000th NHL career point in New Jersey's 4–3 victory over Pittsburgh, February 23, 2003

- Member of Minto Cup–champion Whitby Warriors lacrosse team (1984, 1985); named Most Valuable Player of Minto Cup tournament (1984)

- Served as captain of Calgary Flames (1991–95); named general manager of Dallas Stars (2009)

# Joe Champion

Joe Nieuwendyk scored a lot of goals in the NHL—564 regular-season tallies to be exact—and like many NHLers, he honed a lot of what goes into scoring goals (hand-eye coordination, strong wrists and good aim) by playing lacrosse. Nieuwendyk was such a good lacrosse player that he led his Whitby Warriors to back-to-back Minto Cup championships in 1984 and 1985. In 1984 he led all players with 22 Minto Cup series points and was an easy choice for tournament MVP.

Fresh off his second Minto Cup title, Nieuwendyk made the move to New York State and Cornell University. It wasn't the most surefire way to the NHL, but Nieuwendyk, scouted by Cornell while playing Junior B, starred for the Ivy League school's hockey team and was twice named to the East Coast Athletic Conference's First All-Star Team (in 1986 and 1987). He was also selected as an All-American both years.

Drafted by the Calgary Flames in 1985, he appeared in a handful of games in 1986–87 and then caught on with the club in 1987-88 and became the second NHL player, after Mike Bossy, to score 50 goals in his rookie season. Nieuwendyk was named the NHL's top rookie, and the next year he helped the Flames to their first-ever Stanley Cup.

With Calgary dumping salaries in the mid-1990s, Nieuwendyk was moved out to

**Joe Nieuwendyk skates during the 1999–2000 playoffs.**

the Dallas Stars in 1995. The Stars weren't competitive that season, but from 1996–97 to his last full season with the club, 2000–01, the Stars made the postseason every year, appearing in the conference final and the Stanley Cup final twice, winning the top prize in 1998–99. Nieuwendyk was named the MVP of the playoffs that year, in large part because of his six game-winning goals.

Nieuwendyk won a third Cup with the New Jersey Devils in 2002–03, becoming just one of 10 players to win the Stanley Cup with three different franchises. He added an Olympic gold medal to his collection at the 2002 Winter Olympics, and he can safely claim to be the world's only Stanley Cup, Minto Cup and Olympic champion.

**133**

# 6

# Frank Nighbor 1947

ALTERNATE

7

Ottawa Senators
Toronto Blueshirts
Toronto Maple Leafs
Vancouver Millionaires

Shoots: Right
Height: 5'-9"
Weight: 160 lbs.
Born: January 26, 1893:
Pembroke, Ontario
Died: April 13, 1966:
Pembroke, Ontario
Played 18 professional
seasons from 1912–30
Stats: See page 428

"They hand out a
$1,000 check with
the Byng award today,
but I wouldn't trade
this for $10,000."

—Frank Nighbor,
commenting on
the trophy he was
given by Lady Byng
in 1925

AWARDS
Hart Memorial
Trophy (1924)
Lady Byng Memorial
Trophy (1925, 1926)
Stanley Cup (1914–15,
1919–20, 1920–21,
1922–23, 1926–27)

ALL-STAR
SELECTIONS
PCHA First All-Star
Team Center (1915)

- First player to win the Hart Trophy and the Lady Byng Trophy
- Nicknamed "The Pembroke Peach" because of his sweet and smooth style of play
- Played amateur hockey with Pembroke Debators (1910–11)
- Made professional debut with the Port Arthur Bearcats of the Northern Ontario Hockey League in 1911
- Scored six goals in Toronto Blueshirts' 10–3 victory over Montreal Wanderers, February 15, 1913
- Member of Stanley Cup–winning Vancouver Millionaires in 1914–15
- Re-signed by Vancouver (PCHA), October 22, 1915 but jumped contract to sign with Ottawa (NHA), November 12, 1915

- Led NHA in goals (41) and points (51) in 1916–17
- Led NHL in assists (16) in 1919–20; led NHL in assists (14) in 1925–26
- Finished among NHL top-5 in goals in 1918–19 (19), 1919–20 (26) and 1920–21 (19)
- Finished among NHL top-5 in assists in 1918–19 (9), 1919–20 (16), 1920–21 (10), 1923–24 (6) and 1925–26 (14)
- Finished among NHL top-5 in points in 1918–19 (28), 1919–20 (42) and 1920–21 (29)
- Noted for being a master of the sweep check, a common defensive maneuver now but an innovative and pioneering move during Nighbor's playing days

# Last of the 60-Minute Players

rank Nighbor possessed a skill set of seemingly opposing traits. He was fast and energetic, but he was also among the last of the "60-minute players," who never really left the ice. He was a prolific goal-scorer, but he was also known for his defensive prowess as professional hockey's first expert at the sweep check. For a gifted scorer he took a lot of penalties, but he was also considered the most gentlemanly player of his era.

In fact, in 1925, when Evelyn Byng—the Viscountess Byng of Vimy and wife of Canada's then governor-general—decided to donate a trophy to the NHL that was to be awarded to the player exhibiting the most sportsmanship, gentlemanly conduct and skill, she chose Nighbor as the first winner (Nighbor won the trophy again the next season). Nighbor had added to his firsts in 1924, when he was named the inaugural winner of the Hart Trophy, which was initiated by the fledgling NHL to honor its Most Valuable Player.

Nighbor grew up in Pembroke, Ontario, and joined the Toronto Blueshirts of the National Hockey Association (NHA) as a 19-year-old and scored 25 times in 17 games, including six times in one night against the powerful Montreal Wanderers. Lured west to the Pacific Coast Hockey Association, Nighbor played for the Vancouver Millionaires on a line with Frederick "Cyclone" Taylor and averaged better than a goal a game. When Vancouver won the 1915 Stanley Cup over the Ottawa Senators, Nighbor scored four times in three games.

The following year he returned home to play for the Senators, who were on the verge of becoming the game's dominant team. Nighbor and Joe Malone, of the Quebec

**Frank Nighbor as a member of the Ottawa Senators.**

Bulldogs, each scored 41 goals in just 19 NHA games in the 1916–17 season.

Two years after helping found the NHL in 1917, the Senators started a run of three Stanley Cups in four seasons, a mark that wouldn't be matched until the late 1940s, by the Toronto Maple Leafs. Nighbor won another Cup with Ottawa in 1927, bringing his total to five, and he retired in 1930.

## CENTER

# 4 Reg Noble 1962

ALTERNATES
**3 · 12 · 15
7 · 11 · 6**

Detroit Cougars
Detroit Falcons
Detroit Red Wings
Montreal Canadiens
Montreal Maroons
Toronto Arenas
Toronto Blueshirts
Toronto St. Patricks

Alternate Position: D

Shoots: Left

Height: 5'-8"

Weight: 180 lbs.

Born: June 23, 1896:
Collingwood, Ontario

Died: January 19, 1962:
Alliston, Ontario

Played 17 professional
seasons from 1916–33

Stats: See page 428

AWARDS
Stanley Cup (1917–18,
1921–22, 1925–26)

"He had an iron constitution and my players told me that every time they came in bodily contact with him, they were jarred from head to heels. He gave back with interest anything anybody was able to hand out."

—Frank Selke

- Played amateur hockey with Collingwood ACC (1912–15); St. Michael's College (1915–16); Toronto Riversides (1915–16)

- OHA-Jr. First All-Star Team Center (1915)

- Led NHL in assists (10) in 1917–18; led NHL in penalty minutes (79) in 1923–24

- Finished among NHL top-5 in goals in 1917–18 (29), 1919–20 (24) and 1920–21 (19)

- Finished among NHL top-5 in assists in 1917–18 (10), 1922–23 (11) and 1925–26 (9)

- Served as captain of the Toronto St. Patricks (1920–22) and Detroit Cougars (1927–30)

- Suffered a fractured skull when clipped by the stick of Ottawa's Hooley Smith in a 1925–26 game, but was back in the Maroons lineup after missing just four games

- Played for all three teams in the history of the Detroit franchise — Cougars (1927–30), Falcons (1930–32) and Red Wings (1932–33)

- Last player from inaugural NHL season of 1917–18 to be an active player in the league

- Worked as an NHL referee (1937–39)

- His niece, Gayle Noble, is a member of the McGill University Sports Hall of Fame for her contributions to the school in the sport of soccer

# 1988 Buddy O'Connor

**10**

ALTERNATES
**5 · 21**

"I never met a finer person than Buddy. We played hockey together as kids and over the many years of association, he was always a gentleman and devoted family man."

— Pete Morin, former linemate

**Montreal Canadiens New York Rangers**

Shoots: Right

Height: 5'-8"

Weight: 142 lbs.

Born: June 21, 1916; Montreal, Quebec

Died: August 24, 1977; Montreal, Quebec

Played 10 NHL seasons from 1941–51

Stats: See page 429

- First player to win Hart Trophy and Lady Byng Trophy in the same year (1948)
- Named Canadian Athlete of the Year (1948)
- Played amateur hockey with Montreal Crane Juniors (1933–34); Montreal Jr. Royals (1934–35); Montreal Sr. Royals (1934–42)
- Led Montreal Junior League in goals (15) and points (22) in 1934–35
- Led Quebec Senior League in assists (23) and points (36) in 1938–39
- Led Quebec Senior League in assists in 1936–37 (17) and 1940–41 (38)
- Member of Allan Cup–winning Montreal Royals in 1939; registered 10 goals and 10 assists in Allan Cup playoffs
- QSHL First All-Star Team Center (1937, 1941)

- Member of Razzle Dazzle Line with Pete Morin and Gerry Heffernan. During the 1941–42 season, the entire line was promoted from the Quebec Senior League and brought up to play with the Canadiens
- Finished among NHL top-5 in assists in 1942–43 (43), 1943–44 (42) and 1947–48 (36)
- Collected 210 points (78 goals and 132 assists) in 168 regular season games with the Royals and 98 points (42 goals and 56 assists) in 71 playoff games
- Traded to N.Y. Rangers by Montreal with Frank Eddolls for Hal Laycoe, Joe Bell and George Robertson, August 19, 1947
- AHL Second All-Star Team Center (1952)
- Served as player/coach of Cincinnati Mohawks (1952–53)

**AWARDS**

Lady Byng Memorial Trophy (1948)

Hart Memorial Trophy (1948)

Stanley Cup (1943–44, 1945–46)

**ALL-STAR SELECTIONS**

Second All-Star Team Center (1948)

# 12

# Adam Oates 2012

ALTERNATES
## 34 · 21 · 77

Boston Bruins
Detroit Red Wings
Edmonton Oilers
Mighty Ducks of
Anaheim
Philadelphia Flyers
St. Louis Blues
Washington Capitals

Shoots: Right

Height: 5'-11"

Weight: 190 lbs.

Born: August 27, 1962;
Weston, Ontario

Played 19 seasons
from 1985–2004

Stats: see page 429

"The game didn't come naturally to me. I was more analytical. Some guys, the game came so easy, they were fantastic and they can't explain necessarily how they did what they did."

ALL-STAR
SELECTIONS

Second All-Star Team
Center (1991)

- Played amateur hockey with the Port Credit Titans (1979–80), Markham Waxers (1979–82), R.P.I. Engineers (1982–85)

- Selected to ECAC First All-Star Team (1985) and ECAC Second All-Star Team (1984)

- Selected to NCAA East First All-American Team (1984, 1985) and NCAA Championship All-Tournament Team (1985)

- Member of NCAA Division I Champion R.P.I. Engineers (1985)

- Holds the St. Louis Blues team record for assists in one season (90), established in 1990–91

- Ranks seventh in NHL career assists (1,079)

- Led NHL in assists in 1992–93 (97), 2000–01 (69) and 2001–02 (64)

- Led NHL in game-winning goals in 1992–93 (11)

- Led St. Louis Blues in assists for three consecutive seasons (1990–92)

- Led Boston Bruins in assists and points for four consecutive seasons (1993–96)

- Led Washington Capitals in assists for five consecutive seasons (1998–2002)

- Played in NHL All-Star Game (1991, 1992, 1993, 1994, 1997)

- Served as captain of Washington Capitals (1999–2000); served as assistant coach of Tampa Bay Lightning (2009–10); served as assistant coach of New Jersey Devils (2010–12); served as head coach of Washington Capitals (2012)

# 1990 Gilbert Perreault

**11**

> "In my first seasons, [general manager/coach Punch] Imlach told me to go for goals and not worry about checking. That really helped me get my confidence. The first few years I was there, it was loose. I was rushing the puck a lot. We had style."

**NO. RETIRED BY BUFFALO**

**Buffalo Sabres**

Shoots: Right

Height: 6'-1"

Weight: 180 lbs.

Born: November 13, 1950: Victoriaville, Quebec

Drafted by the Buffalo Sabres first overall in 1970

Played 17 NHL seasons from 1970–87

Stats: See page 429

---

- Holds Buffalo team records for career games (1,191), goals (512), assists (814) and points (1,326)

- Holds Buffalo team record for points in a single game (7), accomplished in Buffalo's 9–5 victory over Oakland, February 1, 1976

- Played amateur hockey with Thetford Mines Canadiens (1966–67); Montreal Jr. Canadiens (1967–70)

- Member of Memorial Cup–winning Montreal Jr. Canadiens (1969, 1970)

- Led Memorial Cup playoffs in goals (17), assists (21) and points (38) in 1970

- OHA-Jr. First All-Star Team Center (1969, 1970); named OHA-Jr. MVP (1969–70)

- Member of Buffalo's famed French Connection Line with Rick Martin and Rene Robert

- Led NHL in game-winning goals (9) in 1976–77

- Finished among NHL top-5 in points in 1975–76 (113), 1976–77 (95) and 1979–80 (106); finished among NHL top-5 in assists in 1972–73 (60), 1975–76 (69) and 1979–80 (66)

- Registered 1,000th career NHL point in Buffalo's 5–4 victory over Montreal Canadiens, April 3, 1982; recorded 500th career NHL goal in Buffalo's 4–3 victory over New Jersey, March 9, 1986

- Member of Team NHL that played Soviet Union in 1979 Challenge Cup Series

- Member of Team Canada in 1981 Canada Cup Tournament — Canada finished second to the Soviet Union

- Served as captain of Buffalo Sabres (1980–86)

**AWARDS**

Calder Memorial Trophy (1971)

Lady Byng Memorial Trophy (1973)

**ALL-STAR SELECTIONS**

Second All-Star Team Center (1975, 1976)

**INTERNATIONAL AWARDS**

Summit Series (1972)

Canada Cup (1976)

**139**

# 10

CENTER

# Joe Primeau 1963

ALTERNATES
## 12 · 15
Toronto Maple Leafs

Shoots: Left

Height: 5'-11"

Weight: 153 lbs.

Born: January 29, 1906;
Lindsay, Ontario

Died: May 14, 1989;
Toronto, Ontario

Played nine NHL
seasons from 1927–36

Stats: See page 430

"Times have certainly changed in hockey since the antics of our Leaf team on the late 1920s and early 1930s. A 70-game schedule would have provided just that much more time to cook up gags."

AWARDS
Lady Byng Memorial
Trophy (1932)
Stanley Cup (1931–32)
ALL-STAR
SELECTIONS
Second All-Star Team
Center (1934)

- Nicknamed "Gentleman Joe" because of his classy and calm demeanor on the ice

- Played amateur hockey with St. Michael's Majors (1923–24); Toronto St. Mary's (1924–26); Toronto Marlboros (1925–26)

- Member of Toronto Maple Leafs' famed Kid Line with Charlie Conacher and Busher Jackson

- Led OHA-Jr. goals (15) and points (17) in 1925–26

- Made professional debut with the Toronto Ravinas of the Canadian-Professional Hockey League (1927–28)

- Led NHL in assists in 1930–31 (32), 1931–32 (37) and 1933–34 (32)

- Finished among NHL top-5 in points in 1931–32 (50) and 1933–34 (46)

- Played in NHL All-Star Game (1934)

- Retired at age 30 to operate a concrete business that eventually expanded to include five plants across the country

- Coached West Toronto Juniors (1932–33); coached Upper Canada College Blues (1938–43); St. Michael's Majors (1943–48); Toronto Marlboros (1948–50); Toronto Maple Leafs (1950–52)

- Coached Toronto St. Michael's Majors to Memorial Cup championship (1944–45)

- Coached Toronto Marlboro seniors to Allan Cup championship (1949–50)

- Coached Toronto Maple Leafs to Stanley Cup championship (1950–51)

- Only man to coach teams to the Allan, Memorial and Stanley Cup championships

# Jean Ratelle

**1985**

"Management in New York put a lot of pressure on me. They wanted me to play a more aggressive brand of hockey, but that just wasn't the way I played the game."

**NO. RETIRED BY NEW YORK RANGERS**

**ALTERNATES**

**10 · 14**

**Boston Bruins**
**New York Rangers**

Shoots: Left

Height: 6'-1"

Weight: 180 lbs.

Born: October 3, 1940;
Lac St-Jean, Quebec

Played 21 NHL seasons
from 1960–81

Stats: See page 430

- Played amateur hockey with Guelph Biltmores (1958–61)
- Led OHA-Jr. in assists (61) in 1960–61
- OHA-Jr. Second All-Star Team Center (1961)
- Played minor pro hockey with Trois-Rivieres Lions (1959–60)
- Member of N.Y. Rangers' famed GAG (Goal-a-Game) Line with Rod Gilbert and Vic Hadfield
- Played in NHL All-Star Game (1970, 1971, 1972, 1973, 1980)
- Led NHL in shooting percentage (25.1%) in 1971–72; led NHL in even strength goals (40) in 1971–72
- Renowned for sportsmanship and smooth style that was often compared to Montreal's Jean Béliveau

- Finished among NHL top-5 in points in 1967–68 (78) and 1971–72 (109); finished among NHL top-5 in assists in 1967–68 (46), 1971–72 (63) and 1975–76 (69)
- Considered quitting hockey to play professional baseball in the Milwaukee Braves organization
- First member of the N.Y. Rangers to register 100 points in a season (1971–72)
- Traded to Boston by N.Y. Rangers with Brad Park and Joe Zanussi for Phil Esposito and Carol Vadnais, November 7, 1975
- Registered 1,000th career NHL point in Boston's 7–4 victory over Toronto Maple Leafs, April 3, 1977

**AWARDS**

Bill Masterton Memorial Trophy (1971)

Lady Byng Memorial Trophy (1972, 1976)

Ted Lindsay Award* (1972)

**ALL-STAR SELECTIONS**

Second All-Star Team Center (1972)

**INTERNATIONAL AWARDS**

Summit Series (1972)

*Known as the Lester B. Pearson Award from 1971 to 2009

# 16

CENTER

# Henri Richard 1979

NO. RETIRED BY MONTREAL

**Montreal Canadiens**

Shoots: Right

Height: 5'-7"

Weight: 160 lbs.

Born: February 29, 1936:
Montreal, Quebec

Played 20 NHL seasons
from 1955–75

Stats: See page 431

"There were a lot
of people who told
me that playing
with Maurice was
going to add a lot of
pressure but I never
felt any pressure.
I never thought about
my brother Maurice
being a big star. It
was normal for me."

**AWARDS**

Bill Masterton Memorial
Trophy (1974)

Stanley Cup (1955–56,
1956–57, 1957–58,
1958–59, 1959–60,
1964–65, 1965–66,
1967–68, 1968–69,
1970–71, 1972–73)

**ALL-STAR
SELECTIONS**

First All-Star Team
Center (1958)

Second All-Star Team
Center (1959, 1961, 1963)

- Holds NHL record for most Stanley Cup championships won by a player (11)

- Shares record (with Boston Celtics' Bill Russell) for most championships won by a professional athlete (11)

- Nicknamed "The Pocket Rocket"

- Played amateur hockey with Montreal Nationale (1951–52); Joliette Cyclones (1951–52); St. Laurent Castors (1951–52); Montreal Jr. Canadiens (1952–54); Montreal Royals (1952–53)

- Led QJHL in goals (53), assists (56) and points (109) in 1953–54; led QJHL in goals (33) and points (66) in 1954–55

- Played in NHL All-Star Game (1956, 1957, 1958, 1959, 1960, 1961, 1963, 1965, 1967, 1974)

- Led NHL in assists in 1957–58 (52) and 1962–63 (50)

- Served as captain of Montreal Canadiens (1971–75)

- Scored Stanley Cup–winning overtime goal in Montreal's 3–2 victory over Detroit, May 5, 1966; scored Stanley Cup–winning goal in Montreal's 3–2 victory over Chicago, May 18, 1971

- Registered 1,000th career NHL point in Montreal's 2–2 tie with Buffalo Sabres, December 20, 1973

- Brother of Hall of Fame member Maurice "Rocket" Richard, who played in the NHL with Montreal from 1942–60

- Renowned for his skills as a passer and excellent two-way player, he was featured on the cover of *Sports Illustrated* on April 2, 1973

# "Pocket Rocket" Becomes "Mr. Stanley Cup"

It didn't take long for Henri Richard to go from living in a huge shadow to casting one of his own. When he joined his older brother Maurice "Rocket" Richard on the Montreal Canadiens in the fall of 1955 as a 19-year-old, there were widespread assumptions that he made the team as a pacifier to the franchise legend; Maurice even admitted he likely would have retired earlier had it not been for the chance to play with Henri. Even Elmer Lach, the Rocket's all-star linemate, had said the younger Richard would never be an NHL player, despite coaching him during a superlative junior career.

**A young Henri Richard and older Maurice share a moment in the late 1950s.**

But the "Pocket Rocket," as Henri Richard was known, boasted excellent credentials, having won the Quebec junior scoring title the two previous years, and though short and slight, he was a crafty puckhandler and play-maker. Henri scored big goals, forechecked like he was possessed and could acquit himself well in a fight. In 1960, his older brother's last hurrah, Henri led all playoff scorers with 12 points, helping the Canadiens become the first NHL franchise to win five straight championships.

Richard was a Stanley Cup winner each of his first five years in the NHL, and before he retired he hoisted the Cup 11 times—the most championships won by any professional team athlete. (Bill Russell of the NBA's Boston Celtics shares this record.) He led the league in assists twice, and he scored two Stanley

Cup–winning goals, one in 1966 and the other in 1971.

That 1970–71 season was a tumultuous one for Montreal. After missing the playoffs in 1970 for the first time in 22 years, and the only time in Richard's career, the Canadiens rebounded to make the playoffs and upset the heavily favored Boston Bruins in the first round. They went on to win the Cup in seven games over the Chicago Black Hawks. Down by two goals in Game 7, Richard, benched by coach Al MacNeil earlier in the series, scored twice in the comeback, including the winner. He later said that Cup win, his 10th, "was the best because we were such underdogs it wasn't funny."

Richard assumed the Canadiens' captaincy in 1971–72, as Jean Béliveau retired, and he led the team to his final Cup in 1972–73.

# 19

# Joe Sakic 2012

NO. RETIRED BY COLORADO

ALTERNATE

## 88

**Colorado Avalanche
Quebec Nordiques**

Shoots: Left

Height: 5'-11"

Weight: 195 lbs.

Born: July 7, 1969; Burnaby,
British Columbia

Drafted by the Quebec
Nordiques 15th
overall in 1987

Played 20 seasons from
1988–2004, 2005–09

Stats: see page 432

**AWARDS**

Conn Smythe Trophy (1996)

Hart Memorial Trophy (2001)

Lady Byng Memorial
Trophy (2001)

Ted Lindsay Award* (2001)

Bud Light Plus/Minus
Award (2001)

NHL Foundation
Award (2007)

Stanley Cup
(1995–96, 2000–01)

**ALL-STAR
SELECTIONS**

First All-Star Team Center
(2001, 2002, 2004)

**INTERNATIONAL
AWARDS**

World Cup (2004)

Gold Medal: Winter
Olympics (2002)

Gold Medal: World
Championships (1994)

Silver Medal: World
Championships (1991)

*Known as the Lester
B. Pearson Award
from 1971 to 2009

"It's an honour [to
be named captain],
but it's also a big
responsibility. As
captain, you're sort
of the mediator
between the
coaching staff and
the players."

- Played amateur hockey with the Burnaby BC Selects (1985–86); Lethbridge Broncos (1985–86); Swift Current Broncos (1986–88); Canadian National Team (1986–87)

- Holds NHL record for career overtime playoff points (14) and for career overtime playoff goals (8)

- Named CHL Player of the Year (1988); named WHL Rookie of the Year (1987); named WHL Player of the Year (1987, 1988); named to WHL East First All-Star Team (1988); named to WHL East Second All-Star Team (1987)

- Led NHL in playoff goals (18), playoff points (34), playoff power-play goals (6), playoff game–winning goals (6) and playoff shots on goal (98) in 1995–96

- Holds Quebec Nordiques/Colorado Avalanche team records for career goals (625), career assists (1,016), career points (1,641), career game-winning goals (86), career power-play goals (205), career shorthanded goals (32) and career game-tying goals (13)

- Holds Quebec Nordiques/Colorado Avalanche team records for career playoff points (188), career playoff games (172), career playoff goals (84), career playoff power-play goals (27), career playoff game–winning goals (19), career playoff shorthanded goals (4), career playoff assists (104)

- Played in NHL All-Star Game (1990, 1991, 1992, 1993, 1994, 1996, 1998, 2000, 2001, 2002, 2004, 2007)

# World Class

The 1995–96 season was a good time to get on the bandwagon in Denver. The Quebec Nordiques had migrated to the Rockies and become the Colorado Avalanche. That season the franchise won its first Stanley Cup, which was hugged and hoisted by their lead-by-example captain Joe Sakic, who was also named playoff MVP.

Sakic had grown steadily into the role of exemplary leader during his seven seasons in Quebec—the franchise's final years in the NHL. Taken 15th overall with the Nordiques' *second* pick in the first round of the 1987 draft, Sakic requested to stay with his junior club, the Swift Current Broncos, for the 1987–88 season so he could hone his game for the NHL. In the process, he scored 160 points and was named Canada's major junior Hockey Player of the Year. Patterning his game after Wayne Gretzky's creative style, Sakic became a 100-point scorer in his sophomore NHL season and reached that mark twice more as a Nordique, averaging 1.2 points per game during his Quebec career.

The Nordiques made Sakic their captain in 1992–93, and he led the club to their first playoff berth in six years and to the greatest single-season turnaround in NHL history at the time (plus-52 points). He continued to wear the C until he retired with Colorado in 2009, having scored 625 goals and 1,641 points.

Winning the first Stanley Cup in Nordiques/Avalanche franchise history is the middle jewel in Sakic's drought-ending crown. In 1994 he helped Canada end its

**Joe Sakic raises the Cup with teammate Ray Bourque.**

World Championship drought with its first men's win in 33 years, scoring seven points in eight games. Then in 2002 he had four points in the gold-medal game in Salt Lake City, Utah, and was named the tournament's Most Valuable Player as Canada ended its Olympic drought by winning its first Olympic title in 50 years. A gold medal at the 1988 World Junior Hockey Championship and the 2004 World Cup completed Sakic's international trophy case.

But for all his success, Sakic may be most fondly remembered for one moment: After being presented the Stanley Cup in 2001 (his second), he—without hoisting or celebrating—immediately passed it to his Avalanche teammate Ray Bourque, who had waited 22-years to hoist the trophy. Bourque immediately retired after the championship.

Joe Sakic: classy captain and world-class player.

# 18

# Denis Savard 2000

NO. RETIRED BY CHICAGO

**ALTERNATE:**

# 9

Chicago Blackhawks
Montreal Canadiens
Tampa Bay Lightning

Shoots: Right

Height: 5'-10"

Weight: 175 lbs.

Born: February 4, 1961;
Pointe Gatineau, Quebec

Drafted by the Chicago
Black Hawks third
overall in 1980

Played 17 NHL seasons
from 1980–97

Stats: See page 432

**AWARDS**
Stanley Cup (1992–93)

**ALL-STAR
SELECTIONS**
Second All-Star Team
Center (1983)

"I've learned that it doesn't matter how many goals you get or how many points. One-on-one doesn't win the Cup, and that's what you play for."

- Shares NHL record (with Claude Provost) for fastest goal from the start of a period (4 seconds), established in third period of Chicago's 4–2 victory over Hartford Whalers, January 12, 1986

- Holds Chicago Blackhawks' team record for assists (87) and points (131) in regular season

- Shares Chicago Blackhawks' team record for points (29) in one playoff season, established in 1984–85

- Played amateur hockey with Montreal Juniors (1977–80)

- QMJHL Rookie of the Year (with Normand Rochefort) in 1977–78

- QMJHL First All-Star Team Center (1980); QMJHL Third All-Star Team Center (1977)

- Named QMJHL MVP (1979–80)

- Led QMJHL in assists (112) in 1978–79

- Played in NHL All-Star Game (1982, 1983, 1984, 1986, 1988, 1991, 1996)

- Member of the Les Trois Denis Line with Denis Cyr and Denis Tremblay on the Montreal Juniors. All three players shared the same birthday and all were born in the same hospital

- Served as co-captain (with Dirk Graham) of Chicago Blackhawks (1988–89)

- Registered 1,000th career NHL point in Chicago's 6–4 loss to St. Louis Blues, March 11, 1990

- Traded to Montreal by Chicago for Chris Chelios and Montreal's second round choice (Michael Pomichter) in 1991 Entry Draft, June 29, 1990

- Broke his foot in the third round of the 1993 playoffs and spent the rest of the playoffs serving as an assistant to coach Montreal coach Jacques Demers

- Coached Chicago Blackhawks (2006–09)

# 1961 Milt Schmidt

**15**

> "I was 18 years of age when I signed my contract and started playing with the Boston Bruins in 1936–37. Two years later, in 1938–39, we won the Stanley Cup. It was the greatest charge I ever got out of playing hockey."

**NO. RETIRED BY BOSTON**

**Boston Bruins**

Alternate Position: D

Shoots: Left

Height: 6'

Weight: 185 lbs.

Born: March 5, 1918: Kitchener, Ontario

Died: January 4, 2017: Needham, Massachusetts

Played 16 NHL seasons from 1936–42, 1945–55

Stats: See page 433

- Played amateur hockey with Kitchener Empires (1933–34); Kitchener Greenshirts (1934–36); Ottawa RCAF Flyers (1941–42)
- Led OHA-Jr. playoffs in goals (4) and points (5) in 1935–36
- Member of Allan Cup–winning Ottawa RCAF Flyers (1941–42); recorded 6 goals and 16 assists in 13 games in Allan Cup playoffs
- Member of Boston's famed Kraut Line with Bobby Bauer and Woody Dumart
- Entire line finished 1–2–3 in scoring (Schmidt, Dumart, Bauer) in 1939–40, first time in NHL history three teammates accomplished that feat
- Led NHL in assists (30) and points (52) in 1939–40; led NHL playoffs in points (11) in 1940–41

- Finished among NHL top-5 in points in 1939–40 (52), 1946–47 (62) and 1950–51 (61)
- Played in NHL All-Star Game (1947, 1948, 1951, 1952)
- Served as captain of Boston Bruins (1951–54)
- Officially announced retirement, December 25, 1954 and named coach of Boston Bruins
- Coached Boston Bruins (1954–55, 1955–61, 1962–63, 1963–66)
- Served as general manager of Boston Bruins (1967–72)
- Coached Washington Capitals (1974–76)
- Served as general manager of Washington Capitals (1974–76)

**AWARDS**

NHL Scoring Leader (1940)

Hart Memorial Trophy (1951)

Lester Patrick Trophy (1996)

Stanley Cup (1938–39, 1940–41)

**ALL-STAR SELECTIONS**

First All-Star Team Center (1940, 1947, 1951)

Second All-Star Team Center (1952)

# Oliver Seibert 1961

**Berlin Hockey Club
Canadian Soo
Guelph OAC**

Shoots: Unknown

Height: Unknown

Weight: 180 lbs.

Born: March 18, 1881:
Berlin, Ontario

Died: May 15, 1944:
Kitchener, Ontario

Played six elite amateur
and professional
seasons from 1899–1905

Stats: See page 433

"Oliver Seibert of the old 'Flying Dutchmen' brought hockey fame many years ago to Kitchener."

— *Ottawa Citizen*,
March 30, 1932,
in a story about
Oliver Seibert's
son — future Hall of
Famer Earl Seibert

- Renowned as being among the first Canadian players to skate on artificial ice as a member of the Berlin Rangers in an exhibition game in St. Louis

- Father of Hall of Fame member Earl Seibert, who played in NHL with N.Y. Rangers, Detroit and Chicago from 1931–46

- First father-and-son team to be inducted into the Hall of Fame in the player category

- Member of prominent sports family in Berlin (now Kitchener), Ontario, where he once played on the All-Seibert Team with brothers Edward, Nelson, Clarence, Bert and Shannon

- Father "Butch" Seibert was reputed to have beaten a horse in a one-mile race on the frozen Grand River

- Began his career as a goaltender before moving to forward

- Played five games as a goaltender for the Berlin Pros posting a 2-2-1 record with a 6.72 goals-against average in 1906–07

- Member of Western Ontario Hockey champion Berlin Rangers (1899–00, 1900–01, 1901–02, 1903–04)

- Led WOHA in goals (17) in 1901–02

- Signed as a free agent by Canadian Soo, January 31, 1905

- Suffered broken leg in the first game of the season with the Canadian Soo team in the professional International Hockey League in 1904–05

# Darryl Sittler

**1989**

**27**

**ALTERNATE**

**9**

"In the 80s, when Wayne Gretzky and Mario Lemieux were breaking all kinds of records, I thought one of those guys would break it. But now the game has changed so much. You hardly see five- or six-goal games between two teams, let alone one player."

— Darryl Sittler, on the longevity of his 10-point record

Detroit Red Wings
Philadelphia Flyers
Toronto Maple Leafs

Shoots: Left

Height: 6'

Weight: 190 lbs.

Born: September 18, 1950: Kitchener, Ontario

Drafted by the Toronto Maple Leafs eighth overall in 1970

Played 15 NHL seasons from 1970–85

Stats: See page 433

- Holds NHL record for points in a single game (10), established in Toronto's 11–4 victory over Boston, February 7, 1976

- Shares NHL record for goals in a single playoff game (5), established in Toronto's 8–5 victory over Philadelphia, April 22, 1976

- Played amateur hockey with Elmira Sugar Kings (1966–67); London Nationals/Knights (1967–68); London Knights (1968–70)

- OHA-Jr. Second Team All-Star Center (1969)

- Scored Canada Cup–winning overtime goal in Canada's 5–4 victory over Czechoslovakia, September 15, 1976

- Led NHL in shots on goal (311) in 1977–78

- Served as captain of Toronto Maple Leafs (1975–81)

- Son Ryan was drafted seventh overall by Philadelphia Flyers in 1992 Entry Draft

- Canada Cup All-Star Team (1976)

- Played in NHL All-Star Game (1975, 1978, 1980, 1983)

- Registered 1,000th career NHL point in Philadelphia's 5–2 victory over Calgary Flames, January 20, 1983

- Traded to Philadelphia by Toronto for the rights to Rich Costello, Hartford's second round choice (previously acquired, Toronto selected Peter Ihnacak) in 1982 Entry Draft and future considerations (Ken Strong, May, 1982), January 20, 1982

**ALL-STAR SELECTIONS**
Second All-Star Team Center (1978)

**INTERNATIONAL AWARDS**
Canada Cup (1976)
Bronze Medal: World Championships (1982, 1983)

# 10

# Clint Smith 1991

**ALTERNATES**
**3 · 14 · 20**

**Chicago Black Hawks**
**New York Rangers**

Shoots: Left

Height: 5'-8"

Weight: 165 lbs.

Born: December 12, 1913:
Assiniboia, Saskatchewan

Died: May 19, 2009:
Vancouver,
British Columbia

Played 11 NHL seasons
from 1936–47

Stats: See page 434

"I can't explain the feeling of winning the Stanley Cup. It's the ultimate. It's something you always strive for — just to get into the Stanley Cup Final. And then when you win — it's something you always remember."

**AWARDS**

Lady Byng Memorial
Trophy (1939, 1944)

Stanley Cup (1939–40)

- Shares NHL record for most goals in a period (4), established in third period of Chicago Black Hawks' 6–4 win over Montreal Canadiens, March 4, 1945

- Held NHL record for assists (49) in regular season in 1943–44; surpassed by Elmer Lach (54) in 1944–45

- Credited with scoring first empty-net goal in NHL history in Chicago Black Hawks' 6–4 win over Boston on November 11, 1943

- Played amateur hockey with Saskatoon Wesleys (1930–32); Saskatoon Crescents (1932–34); Saskatoon Indians (1932–33); Vancouver Lions (1933–36)

- Led NHL in assists (49) in 1943–44

- Led Northern Saskatchewan Junior League in goals (5) and points (6) in 1931–32; led Northern Saskatchewan Senior League in goals (19) in 1931–32

- Led North West Hockey League in goals (25) in 1933–34; led NWHL in assists (22) and points (44) in 1934–35; led NWHL in assists (32) and points (53) in 1935–36

- Finished among NHL top-5 in goals in 1938–39 (21) and 1945–46 (26)

- Finished among NHL top-5 in points in 1938–39 (41), 1943–44 (72), 1944–45 (54) and 1945–46 (50)

- Won Herman Paterson Cup as USHL MVP (1948)

- Was the longest surviving member of the 1940 Stanley Cup champion N.Y. Rangers

# 1972 Hooley Smith

> "There was a popular cartoon in the papers when I was a kid called Happy Hooligan. One day, my dad called me Hooligan, then he shortened it to Hooley and the name stuck. I mean, what kid would want to go through life with a tag like Reginald?"

**ALTERNATES:**

## 17 · 5 · 6

Boston Bruins
Montreal Maroons
New York Americans
Ottawa Senators

Alternate Positions: RW/D

Shoots: Right

Height: 5'-10"

Weight: 155 lbs.

Born: January 7, 1903: Toronto, Ontario

Died: August 24, 1963: Montreal, Quebec

Played 17 NHL seasons from 1924–41

Stats: See page 434

- Played amateur hockey with Toronto (Parkdale) Canoe Club (1920–21); Toronto Granites (1921–24)

- Member of Allan Cup–champion Toronto Granites (1922, 1923)

- As a member of the Toronto Granites, he represented Canada at the 1924 Olympic Games, registering a tournament-high 16 assists as Canada captured the gold medal

- Made NHL debut in Ottawa Senators' 5–3 loss to Hamilton Tigers, November 30, 1924

- Renowned for his skills as an oarsman, amateur boxer and rugby player, he also played football with the Toronto Argonauts and Balmy Beach

- Member of Montreal Maroons' famed S Line with Babe Siebert and Nels Stewart

- A physically dominant player who played with a "bitter edge," Smith was renowned for his defensive skills and was an expert at utilizing the "hook" check to sweep the puck off opposing players sticks

- Played in NHL All-Star Game (1934)

- Finished among NHL top-5 in assists in 1924–25 (14), 1925–26 (9) and 1931–32 (33)

- Finished among NHL top-5 in points in 1932–33 (41) and 1935–36 (38)

- Played partial seasons on defense as a member of the N.Y. Americans

**AWARDS**

Stanley Cup (1926–27, 1934–35)

**ALL-STAR SELECTIONS**

First All-Star Team Center (1936)

Second All-Star Team Center (1932)

**INTERNATIONAL AWARDS**

Gold Medal: Winter Olympics (1924)

# 7

### CENTER

# Tommy Smith 1973

Brantford Redmen
Brantford Professionals
Galt Professionals
Haileybury Hockey Club
Moncton Victorias
Montreal Canadiens
Ottawa Silver Seven
Ottawa Vics
Quebec Bulldogs
Pittsburgh Lyceum
Pittsburgh
Professionals
Toronto Shamrocks

Alternate Position: RW

Shoots: Left

Height: 5'-6"

Weight: 150 lbs.

Born: September 27, 1885: Ottawa, Ontario

Died: August 1, 1966: Ottawa, Ontario

Played 13 elite amateur and professional seasons from 1905–17, 1919–20

Stats: See page 434

### AWARDS
Stanley Cup
(1905–06, 1912–13)

"Tommy Smith ... is known by nearly all those who attend the games as 'Snake,' and the name fits him like a new glove for when he secures the puck one might as well try to catch and hold a reptile as he."

—*Pittsburgh Press,* March 6, 1907

- Led FAHL in goals (12) in 1905–06
- FAHL First Team All-Star Center (1906)
- Scored eight goals in a single game against Brockville, February 23, 1906
- Led OPHL in goals (40) in 1908–09
- OPHL First Team All-Star Center (1909)
- Played in unsuccessful Stanley Cup challenges with Galt Pros in 1911 and Moncton Victorias in 1912
- Signed as a free agent by Quebec Bulldogs, December 1, 1912
- Led NHA in goals (39) and points (45) in 1913–14; goals (40) and points (44) in 1914–15
- Scored at least one goal in 10 consecutive games (1912–13)

- Tied NHA single game record with nine goals in Quebec's 12–6 victory over Montreal Wanderers, January 21, 1914
- One of seven hockey-playing brothers (George, Alf, Dan, Jack, Harry and Willie) from Ottawa who formed their own "All-Smith" team
- Member of Stanley Cup–winning Quebec Bulldogs (1912–13)
- Member of NHA champion Montreal Canadiens team that lost Stanley Cup Final to Seattle Metropolitans (1916–17)
- Returned briefly as a player in 1919–20 when Quebec Bulldogs entered the NHL but retired permanently after the season

# 1998 Peter Stastny

# 26

"The small ice made for a more physical game ... But I never minded. I could take a hit and keep the puck.... I liked the small ice."

— Peter Stastny on the difference between NHL and International rink sizes

**NO. RETIRED BY QUEBEC & COLORADO**

**ALTERNATE**

## 29

**New Jersey Devils**
**Quebec Nordiques**
**St. Louis Blues**

Shoots: Left

Height: 6'-1"

Weight: 200 lbs.

Born: September 18, 1956: Bratislava, Czechoslovkia

Played 15 NHL seasons from 1980–95

Stats: See page 435

---

- Shares NHL record (with Anton Stastny) for points in a regular season road game (8), established in Quebec's 11–7 victory over Washington Capitals, February 22, 1981

- Shares NHL record (with Joe Juneau) for assists in regular season by a rookie (70), established in 1980–81

- First player in NHL history to record 100 points in rookie season (109), established in 1980–81

- First European-born and trained player in NHL history to register 1,000 career points

- Ranked second (behind Wayne Gretzky) for most points from 1979–80 to 1988–89 (986)

- Played amateur hockey with Slovan Bratislava (1974–80)

- Named Czechoslovakian Player of the Year (1980)

- Signed as a free agent by Quebec, August 26, 1980

- Finished among NHL top-5 in points in 1981–82 (139), 1982–83 (124), 1983–84 (119) and 1987–88 (111)

- Named Best Forward at World-B Championships (1995); World-B Championships All-Star Team Center (1995)

- Brothers Anton and Marian Stastny and sons Yan and Paul Statsny all played in the NHL.

- Elected Member of European Parliament, representing the Slovak Democratic and Christian Union Party (2005)

**AWARDS**

Calder Memorial Trophy (1981)

**INTERNATIONAL AWARDS**

Gold Medal: World Championships (1976, 1977)

Silver Medal: World Championships (1978, 1979)

CENTER

# 5 Nels Stewart 1952

**ALTERNATES:**
## 7 · 6 · 19

**Boston Bruins**
**Montreal Maroons**
**New York Americans**

Shoots: Left

Height: 6'-1"

Weight: 195 lbs.

Born: December 29, 1899; Montreal, Quebec

Died: August 21, 1957; Wasaga Beach, Ontario

Played 15 NHL seasons from 1925–40

Stats: See page 435

"He was terrific in front of the net, a big strong fellow who had moves like a cat. Stewart never seemed to be paying any attention to where the puck was and, if you were checking him, he'd even hold a little conversation with you. But the minute he'd see the puck coming his way he'd bump you, take the puck and go off and score."

—Hall of Fame referee Cooper Smeaton

**AWARDS**

NHL Scoring Leader (1926)

Hart Memorial Trophy (1926, 1930)

Stanley Cup (1925–26)

- Held NHL record for career goals (324) from 1939–40 until 1952; surpassed by Maurice Richard, November 8, 1952

- Held NHL record for career points (515) from 1939–40 until 1945; surpassed by Syd Howe. March 8, 1945

- Shares NHL record (with Deron Quint of the Winnipeg Jets) for fastest two goals (four seconds) in a game, January 3, 1931

- Played amateur hockey with Toronto (Parkdale) Canoe Club Seniors (1919–20); Cleveland Indians (1920–24); Cleveland Blues (1924–25)

- Earned the nickname "Old Poison" because of his deadly accurate shot; also known as "Big Sam" during his NHL career

- Played in NHL All-Star Game (1934)

- Led USAHA in goals in 1920–21 (23), 1922–23 (22) and 1924–25 (21); led USAHA in goals (21) and points (28) in 1923–24

- Led NHL in goals (34) and points (42) in 1925–26; led NHL in penalty minutes (129) in 1926–27; led NHL in goals (23) in 1936–37

- Member of the Montreal Maroons' famous S Line with Babe Siebert and Hooley Smith

- Finished among NHL top-5 in goals in eight different seasons (1925–26, 1928–29 to 1930–31, 1933–34 to 1936–37)

- Finished among NHL top-5 in points in 1925–26 (42), 1927–28 (34), 1928–29 (29) and 1933–34 (39)

154

# Old Poison

**N**els Stewart was one of the most truculent and feared players in the NHL, but he was also one of the most offensively talented; between 1940 and 1952 he was the NHL's all-time goal-scoring leader.

Known as "Old Poison," Stewart had a terrifying shot and was deadly around the net. At 6-foot-1 and nearly 200 pounds, he wasn't a great skater, but he used physical intimidation as an effective weapon. When Stewart won the NHL scoring title and was named the league's Most Valuable Player as a rookie with the Montreal Maroons in 1925–26, his 121 penalty minutes were nearly double what any other top-10 scorer incurred that year. But his 34 goals represented 37 percent of the Maroons' offense and stood as a rookie record for 45 years. In that year's playoffs, Stewart scored six of Montreal's 10 goals as the second-year franchise won the Stanley Cup over the Victoria Cougars.

Beginning in 1929–30, Stewart was the pivot between his boyhood friend Hooley Smith and Babe Siebert on the legendary S Line, on which he scored 39 goals to help win his second Hart Trophy as league MVP that year.

On January 3, 1931, Stewart set an NHL record by scoring two goals in four seconds against the Boston Bruins. This feat was unmatched until December 1995, when Deron Quint of the Winnipeg Jets produced two similarly quick goals. The S Line was broken up when Stewart was traded to Boston prior to the 1932–33 season. In 1934 Stewart was

**Nels Stewart during his retirement.**

selected to be one of the NHL All-Stars who faced off against the Toronto Maple Leafs in the historic Ace Bailey Benefit Game.

Stewart finished his career with the New York Americans, and in 1936–37, his second season with the club, he led the NHL in goals 11 years after he led the NHL in goals in his rookie season. When he retired in 1940, his 324 goals stood as an NHL record until Maurice "Rocket" Richard blew by it 12 years later.

# 13

# Mats Sundin 2012

NO. RETIRED BY TORONTO

**Quebec Nordiques**
**Toronto Maple Leafs**
**Vancouver Canucks**

Shoots: Right

Height: 6'-5"

Weight: 230 lbs.

Born: February 13, 1971:
Bromma, Sweden

Drafted by the
Quebec Nordiques
first overall in 1989

Played 18 seasons from
1990–2004, 2005–09

Stats: see page 436

"I was [privileged] to play my entire career in Canada, where hockey really matters. Having my hobby and love for a sport become my livelihood really allowed me to live my dream."

**AWARDS**
Mark Messier
Leadership Award (2008)

**ALL-STAR**
**SELECTIONS**
Second All-Star Team
Center (2002, 2004)

**INTERNATIONAL**
**AWARDS**
Gold Medal: Winter
Olympics (2006)
Gold Medal: World
Championships
(1991, 1992, 1998)
Silver Medal: World
Championships (2003)
Bronze Medal: World
Championships
(1994, 2001)

- Played amateur hockey with Nacka IK (1988–89)

- Holds Toronto Maple Leafs team records for career goals (420), career points (987), career game-winning goals (79), career power-play goals (124), career overtime goals (14), 20-goal seasons (13), 30-goal seasons (10) and overtime goals in one season (4); career goals in shootout (10)

- Shares Quebec Nordiques/Colorado Avalanche team record for goals in a regular-season game (5), established in Quebec's 10–4 win over Hartford, March 5, 1992

- Ranks among NHL career leaders in regular-season overtime goals (15) and points (28)

- Tied for fourth in NHL career 20-goal seasons (17); tied for fourth in NHL career 30-goal seasons (13)

- Played in NHL All-Star Game (1996, 1997, 1998, 1999, 2000, 2001, 2002, 2004)

- Recorded 500th NHL career goal in Toronto's 5–4 win over Calgary, October 14, 2006; registered 1,000th NHL career point in Toronto's 3–2 victory over Edmonton, March 10, 2003

- First European-born and European-trained player to be taken first overall in NHL Entry Draft (1989)

# 1950 **Harry Trihey**

*"In Canada, Farrell and Trihey are considered two of the best forwards that have ever played hockey."*

— *New York Times*, March 17, 1899

**Montreal Orioles
Montreal Shamrocks**

Shoots: Unknown

Height: Unknown

Weight: Unknown

Born: December 25, 1877: Montreal, Quebec

Died: December 9, 1942: Montreal, Quebec

Played six elite amateur seasons from 1895–1901

Stats: see page 436

- Member of forward line with the Montreal Shamrocks that included future Hall of Fame members Art Farrell and Fred Scanlan

- Renowned for helping introduce teamwork and strategy to the game of hockey

- Served as captain of Montreal Shamrocks (1898–1901)

- Member of Stanley Cup–winning Montreal Shamrocks (1898–99, 1899–00)

- Led CAHL in goals in 1898–99 (19) and 1899–00 (17)

- Scored CAHL-record 10 goals in Montreal Shamrocks' 13–4 victory over Quebec, February 4, 1899

- Scored 12 goals in five Stanley Cup games during the 1899–00 season

- Scored three goals in Montreal Shamrocks' 6–2 victory over Queen's University in team's first successful Stanley Cup defense, March 14, 1899

- Injuries limited his effectiveness in 1900–01 when the Shamrocks lost Stanley Cup challenge to the Winnipeg Victorias

- Retired due to injuries in 1901 but remained active in hockey as a referee, executive with the CAHL and advisor to the Montreal Wanderers

- Operated a successful law practice in Montreal

- Served as lieutenant-colonel with the 199th Battalion Irish Canadian Rangers during World War I

**AWARDS**
Stanley Cup
(1898–99, 1899–1900)

# 19

# Bryan Trottier 1997

**NO. RETIRED BY
NEW YORK ISLANDERS**

**New York Islanders
Pittsburgh Penguins**

Shoots: Left

Height: 5'-11"

Weight: 195 lbs.

Born: July 17, 1956;
Val Marie, Saskatchewan

Drafted by the New
York Islanders 22nd
overall in 1974

Played 18 NHL seasons
from 1975–92, 1993–94

Stats: See page 436

"When I was holding the Cup, I could feel all the names. My senses peaked. I could hear everyone. The crowd was incredible, one continuous roar."

## AWARDS

Calder Memorial
Trophy (1976)

Art Ross Trophy (1979)

Hart Memorial
Trophy (1979)

Conn Smythe
Trophy (1980)

King Clancy Memorial
Trophy (1989)

Stanley Cup
(1979–80, 1980–81,
1981–82, 1982–83,
1990–91, 1991–92)

## ALL-STAR
SELECTIONS

First NHL All-Star Team
Center (1978, 1979)

Second NHL All-Star
Team Center (1982, 1984)

- Holds NHL record for most points in a regular season period (6), established in N.Y. Islanders' 9–4 victory over N.Y. Rangers, December 23, 1978

- Holds NHL record for longest consecutive point-scoring streak in playoffs (27 games), established from 1980 through 1982; holds NHL record for longest consecutive point-scoring streak in one playoff season (18 games), established in 1981

- Holds N.Y. Islanders' team records for career games (1,123), assists (853), points (1,353), regular season assists (87), points in a regular season game (6) and points by a rookie (95)

- Played amateur hockey with Humboldt Broncos (1971–72); Swift Current Broncos (1972–74); Lethbridge Broncos (1974–75)

- Led WCJHL in assists (98) in 1974–75; WCJHL First All-Star Team Center (1975)

- One of only six players in NHL history (with Dick Duff, Red Kelly, Frank Mahovlich, Patrick Roy and Larry Murphy) to win two or more Stanley Cup championships with two or more teams

- Played for Team USA at 1984 Canada Cup tournament

- Led NHL in points (134) in 1978–79; led NHL in assists in 1977–78 (77) and 1978–79 (87); led NHL in plus/minus (plus-76) in 1978–79

- Registered 1,000th career NHL point in N.Y. Islanders' 4–4 tie with Minnesota North Stars, January 29, 1985; recorded 500th career NHL goal in N.Y. Islanders' 4–2 loss to Calgary Flames, February 13, 1990

- Coached N.Y. Rangers (2002–03); served as assistant coach of Colorado Avalanche (1998–2002)

- Brother of Rocky Trottier, who played in NHL with New Jersey Devils from 1983–85

# Consummate Cup Winner

When Bryan Trottier retired in 1994, he did so as the NHL's sixth-highest scorer, having put up 1,425 points in 1,279 games. He now sits 17th on the NHL's all-time list, but in 1974—the year he was drafted—there was concern among the NHL's top brass that players of his caliber might not end up on any of the NHL's stat sheets.

Trottier was selected 22nd overall by the New York Islanders in the 1974 NHL Amateur Draft. That year the NHL, fearing that the rival World Hockey Association (WHA) would poach the top talent, held their draft early and in secret, by teleconference. The previous year, the WHA had surprised the NHL by allowing their member clubs to draft "underage" players (those younger than 19). As a result, the 1974 NHL Amateur Draft became the first in which the NHL permitted the selection of underage players. Trottier was 18 when he was drafted, the eighth underaged player taken that year.

Trottier joined the Islanders for the 1975–76 season. In his second game he had a hat trick and five points. After 11 games, he had 20 points. Trottier finished the year with rookie records in assists (63) and points (95), and he was an easy choice for the Calder Trophy as the top newcomer.

With the addition of future–Hall of Famer Mike Bossy on the wing in 1977, Trottier and fellow 1974 draftee Clarke Gilles formed one of the most dominant trios in hockey. Dubbed the Long Island Lighting Company—for the way they powered the offense and triggered the goal light—the troika came to define the

**Bryan Trottier holds the Prince of Wales Trophy in 1991. His Pittsburgh Penguins would go on to win the Stanley Cup.**

dynastic Islanders teams of the early 1980s.

In 1980 the Islanders won their first Stanley Cup. Trottier was the star of the show, leading all playoff scorers with 29 points and earning the Conn Smythe Trophy as the most outstanding postseason performer. It was just the year previous that he had won the Art Ross Trophy as the league's leading scorer and the Hart Trophy as the league's MVP. Then Wayne Gretzky entered the league and stole the show. But while Gretzky was winning individual awards, Trottier and his Islanders continued winning Cups, three more in succession, to be precise.

Trottier ended his career in Pittsburgh. No longer the offensive leader, he was called upon to add veteran savvy to a team that boasted both Mario Lemieux and Jaromir Jagr. Trottier was essential to Pittsburgh's Cup victories in 1991 and 1992.

**159**

# 7

# Norm Ullman 1982

**ALTERNATES**

## 9 · 16

**Detroit Red Wings**
**Edmonton Oilers**
**Toronto Maple Leafs**

Shoots: Left

Height: 5'-10"

Weight: 175 lbs.

Born: December 26,
1935: Provost, Alberta

Played 22 NHL and WHA
seasons from 1955–77

Stats: See page 437

"It's the biggest accolade you can get to be honored as one of the best in the game. All of a sudden you sit back and say, 'My God, I'm in the Hockey Hall of Fame!' It is a great honor and really caps off a career for a player."

**ALL-STAR**
**SELECTIONS**

First All-Star Team
Center (1965)

Second All-Star Team
Center (1967)

- Played amateur hockey with Edmonton Oil Kings (1951–54)
- Led WCJHL in assists (47) and points (76) in 1952–53; led WCJHL in goals (56) and points (101) in 1953–54; led WCJHL playoffs in assists (26) and points (37) in 1953–54
- Led Memorial Cup playoffs in assists (18) and points (30) in 1953–54
- Played minor pro hockey with Edmonton Flyers (1953–55)
- Led NHL in goals (42) in 1964–65
- Led NHL playoffs in assists (12) and points (16) in 1962–63; led NHL playoffs in goals (6) and points (15) in 1965–66
- Led NHL in game-winning goals (10) in 1964–65; led NHL in even-strength goals (32) in 1964–65

- Played in NHL All-Star Game (1955, 1960, 1961, 1962, 1963, 1964,1965, 1967, 1968, 1969, 1974)
- Registered 1,000th career NHL point in Toronto's 5–3 loss to N.Y. Rangers, October 16, 1971
- Involved in one of the biggest transactions in NHL history when he was traded to Toronto by Detroit with Floyd Smith, Paul Henderson and Doug Barrie for Frank Mahovlich, Pete Stemkowski, Garry Unger and the rights to Carl Brewer, March 3, 1968
- One of the founding members of the NHL Players Association (1967)
- Selected by Edmonton (WHA) in 1972 General Player Draft, February 12, 1972

# 1960 Jack Walker 7

"The type of player who plays the puck and not the man. Like [Frank] Nighbor, he is a poke-check expert ... and a credit to the game. Hockey owes much to players like Jack Walker."

— *Ottawa Citizen,*
May 3, 1927

**ALTERNATE**
**6**

Detroit Cougars
Moncton Victorias
Port Arthur Lake City
Seattle Metropolitans
Toronto Blueshirts
Victoria Cougars

Shoots: Left

Height: 5'-8"

Weight: 153 lbs.

Born: November 28, 1888;
Silver Mountain, Ontario

Died: February 16, 1950;
Seattle, Washington

Played 18 elite amateur
and professional
seasons from 1910–28

Stats: See page 438

- Played amateur hockey with Port Arthur East Greys (1905–07); Port Arthur Lake City (1907–12)

- Credited with inventing the hook and sweep check that enabled him to become one of the best defensive forwards of his era

- Associated with hockey for more than 30 years, but spent all but two years of his playing career in leagues that either predated or rivaled the NHL

- Won Stanley Cup championship three times with three different teams from three different leagues (Toronto Blueshirts, NHA; Seattle Metropolitans, PCHA; Victoria Cougars, WCHL)

- Jumped contract with Toronto (NHA) to sign with Seattle (PCHA), November 12, 1915

- Led NHA in assists (16) in 1913–14

- Member of Stanley Cup–winning Seattle Metropolitans (1916–17); first U.S.-based team to win the Stanley Cup

- Traded to Detroit by Victoria (WHL) for cash, May 15, 1926

- Member of Stanley Cup–winning Victoria Cougars (1924–25) — last non-NHL club to win the Stanley Cup

- Led WCHL playoffs in goals (4) in 1924–25; led Stanley Cup playoffs in goals (4) and points (6) in 1924–25

- Played minor pro hockey with Seattle Eskimos (1928–31); Hollywood Stars (1931–32); Oakland Sheiks (1932–33)

- Led PCHL in assists in 1929–30 (11) and 1930–31 (13)

**AWARDS**
Stanley Cup (1913–14, 1916–17, 1924–25)

**ALL-STAR SELECTIONS**
PCHA First All-Star Team Center (1921, 1922, 1923)

PCHA Second All-Star Team Center (1917, 1919, 1920)

**161**

# Marty Walsh 1962

Canadian Soo
Kingston A.C.
Ottawa Senators
Queen's University

Shoots: Left
Height: 5'-7"
Weight: 155 lbs.
Born: October 16, 1884;
Ottawa, Ontario
Died: March 27, 1915;
Muskoka, Ontario
Played 10 elite amateur
and professional
seasons from 1902–12
Stats: See page 438

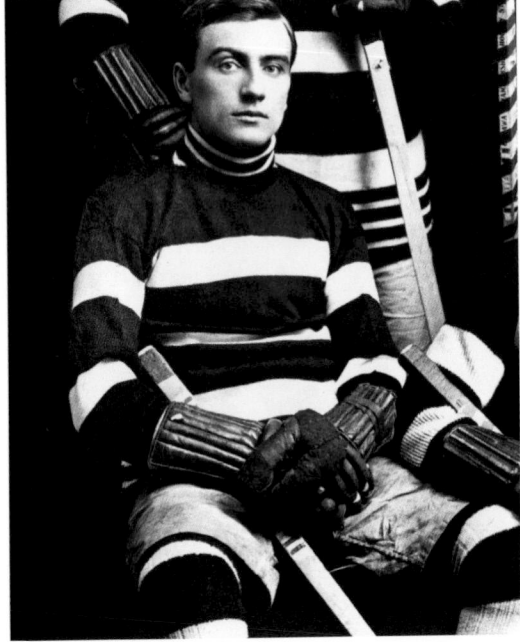

"One of the best hockey players Kingston ever produced and a player who was a distinct credit to the game. He ... was admired for his straightforward, upright qualities as well as for his great skill as a player."

— *The Toronto Daily Star*, March 29, 1915

AWARDS
Stanley Cup (1908–09,
1909–10, 1910–11)

- Member of Canadian University champion Queen's University (1903–04, 1905–06)
- Led Canadian University League in goals (9) and penalty minutes (30) in 1903–04
- Led Canadian University League in goals (15) in 1905–06
- Signed as a free agent by Canadian Soo Algonquins, December 4, 1906
- Signed as a free agent by Ottawa Senators, December 3, 1907
- ECAHA First All-Star Team Center (1908); ECHA First All-Star Team Center (1909)
- Member of Stanley Cup–winning Ottawa Senators (1908–09, 1909–10, 1910–11)

- Led ECHA in goals (42) in 1908–09; finished second in ECAHA in goals (27) in 1907–08
- Scored six goals in Ottawa's 12–3 Stanley Cup series victory over Galt, January 5, 1910
- Scored 10 goals in Ottawa's 14–4 Stanley Cup series victory over Port Arthur, March 16, 1911—the second-highest total in Stanley Cup history behind Frank McGee's 14 goals against Dawson City in 1905
- Coached Edmonton Sr. Eskimos (1913–14)
- Led NHA in goals in 1910–11 (35); led Stanley Cup playoffs in goals in 1910–11 (13)

# 1971 Cooney Weiland

"I definitely believe there is a place for bodychecking in the game of hockey, but I'd just like to see it out in the open. So long as a player is checked in the open, he has room to elude his opponent."

**ALTERNATE**

**14**

**Boston Bruins**
**Detroit Red Wings**
**Ottawa Senators**

Shoots: Left

Height: 5'-7"

Weight: 150 lbs.

Born: November 5, 1904;
Edmondville, Ontario

Died: July 3, 1985;
Boston, Massachusetts

Played 11 NHL seasons
from 1928–39

Stats: See page 438

- Held NHL record for points (73) in regular season (1929–30). Record tied by Doug Bentley in 1942–43 and surpassed by Herb Cain (82) in 1943–44

- Played amateur hockey with Seaforth Highlanders (1918–22); Owen Sound Greys (1922–24); Minneapolis Rockets (1924–25)

- Led OHA-Jr. in goals (33) and points (38) in 1923–24

- Member of the Memorial Cup–winning Owen Sound Greys (1924); led Memorial Cup playoffs in goals (37) and points (46) in 1923–24

- Led AHA in goals (21) in 1927–28; led AHA playoffs in goals (4) and points (5) in 1926–27; led AHA playoffs in assists (2) and points (4) in 1927–28

- Led NHL in goals (43) and points (73) in 1929–30; finished among top-5 in goals in 1930–31 (25)

- Coached Boston Bruins (1939–41), Hershey Bears (1941–45) and New Haven Nighthawks (1945–46)

- Coached Boston Bruins to Stanley Cup championship (1941)

- AHL First All-Star Team Coach (1943)

- Won Spencer Penrose Coach of the Year Award as NCAA Coach of the Year (1955, 1971)

- Coached Harvard University (1950–71) to four berths in the NCAA finals, eight Ivy League titles, two ECAC championships, and five Beanpot Trophy tournament victories

- Awarded Hobey Baker Legend of College Hockey Award (2006)

**AWARDS**

NHL Scoring
Leader (1930)

Stanley Cup (1928–29,
1938–39)

Lester Patrick
Trophy (1972)

**ALL-STAR
SELECTIONS**

Second All-Star Team
Center (1935)

First All-Star Team
Coach (1941)

# 19

# Steve Yzerman 2009

NO. RETIRED BY DETROIT

**Detroit Red Wings**

Shoots: Right

Height: 5'-11"

Weight: 185 lbs.

Born: May 9, 1965; Cranbrook, British Columbia

Drafted by the Detroit Red Wings fourth overall in 1983

Played 22 NHL seasons from 1983–2004, 2005–06

Stats: See page 439

### AWARDS

Ted Lindsay Award* (1989)

Conn Smythe Trophy (1998)

Frank J. Selke Trophy (2000)

Bill Masterton Memorial Trophy (2003)

Lester Patrick Trophy (2006)

Stanley Cup (1996–97, 1997–98, 2001–02)

### ALL-STAR SELECTIONS

All-Rookie Team (1984)

First All-Star Team Center (2000)

### INTERNATIONAL AWARDS

Canada Cup (1984)

Gold Medal: Winter Olympics (2002)

Silver Medal: World Championships (1985)

Silver Medal: World Championships (1989)

*Known as the Lester B. Pearson Award from 1971 to 2009

"When you're on the ice, you have very little time, you see very little, and everything happens really quick."

- Played amateur hockey with Nepean Raiders (1980–81); Peterborough Petes (1981–83)

- Led CJHL in assists (54) in 1980–81

- Holds Detroit Red Wings team records for goals (65), assists (90) and points (155) in regular season, established in 1988–89; holds Detroit Red Wings team record for points by a rookie in the regular season (87), established in 1983–84

- Ranks third in NHL career short-handed goals (50); ranks seventh in NHL career points (1,755)

- Ranks eighth in NHL career assists (1,063); ranks ninth in NHL career goals (692)

- Led NHL in short-handed goals in 1989–90 (7), 1991–92 (8) and 1992–93 (7)

- Led NHL in shots on goal (388) in 1988–89; led NHL in even-strength goals (45) in 1988–89

- Served as captain of Detroit Red Wings (1986–2006)

- Registered 1,000th career NHL point in Detroit's 10–7 loss to Buffalo Sabres, February 24, 1993; recorded 500th career NHL goal in Detroit's 3–2 victory over Colorado Avalanche, January 17, 1996

- Played in NHL All-Star Game (1984, 1988, 1989, 1990, 1991, 1992, 1993, 1997, 2000)

- Served as general manager for gold medal–winning Team Canada at 2010 and 2014 Winter Olympics

- Named general manager of Tampa Bay Lightning in 2010–11

# Stevie Wonder

Steve Yzerman was a young, slick center when he entered the NHL, but his team, the Detroit Red Wings, was old, tired and struggling. Things didn't really change during his early years. But through it all Yzerman dedicated himself to improving his all-around game and restoring the franchise's luster. His work ethic was legendary, and he became one of the league's most respected leaders (and the longest-serving captain in NHL history), finally leading the Wings to the Stanley Cup in 1997, after 42 years of futility.

**Steve Yzerman talks strategy with Russian superstar Sergei Fedorov.**

The year before the 1983 NHL Entry Draft, the Detroit Red Wings were bought by Mike Ilitch, who entrusted general manager Jim Devellano with the job of rebuilding the failing franchise. The Red Wings had the fourth overall pick, and Devellano's first choice was Pat LaFontaine, a hometown boy who would surely revive the interest of the Detroit fans. But LaFontaine was picked third, and Devellano selected Yzerman to be the cornerstone of the new Wings.

Still only 18, Yzerman immediately established himself as an impact player with the Red Wings. In his first year, 1983–84, he set Detroit records for goals by a rookie, with 39, and for points, with 87. Named Red Wings captain as a 21-year-old in 1986 (then the youngest player ever to earn that honor), Yzerman took the role seriously. Between 1988 and 1993, he never failed to top 100 points, and five times he scored 50 or more goals. He won the Lester B. Pearson Award (known since 2010 as the Ted Lindsay Award) in 1988–89.

Yzerman's first trip to a Stanley Cup final ended in a sweep at the hands of the New Jersey Devils in the lockout-shortened 1994–95 season. The 1995–96 season would end with defeat in the conference final, but in 1996–97 everything came together for the hard-working captain as Detroit swept the Philadelphia Flyers for the Stanley Cup.

The next season the Red Wings repeated as Cup champions, and Yzerman's name was engraved on another award: the Conn Smythe Trophy. Yzerman led all players in playoff scoring with 24 points, and he was an effective checker that Detroit coach Scotty Bowman could use in all situations.

Injuries caught up with Yzerman, but there would be one more Cup victory, in 2001–02, and a few more valiant efforts before the centerman hung up his skates for good after the 2005–06 season.

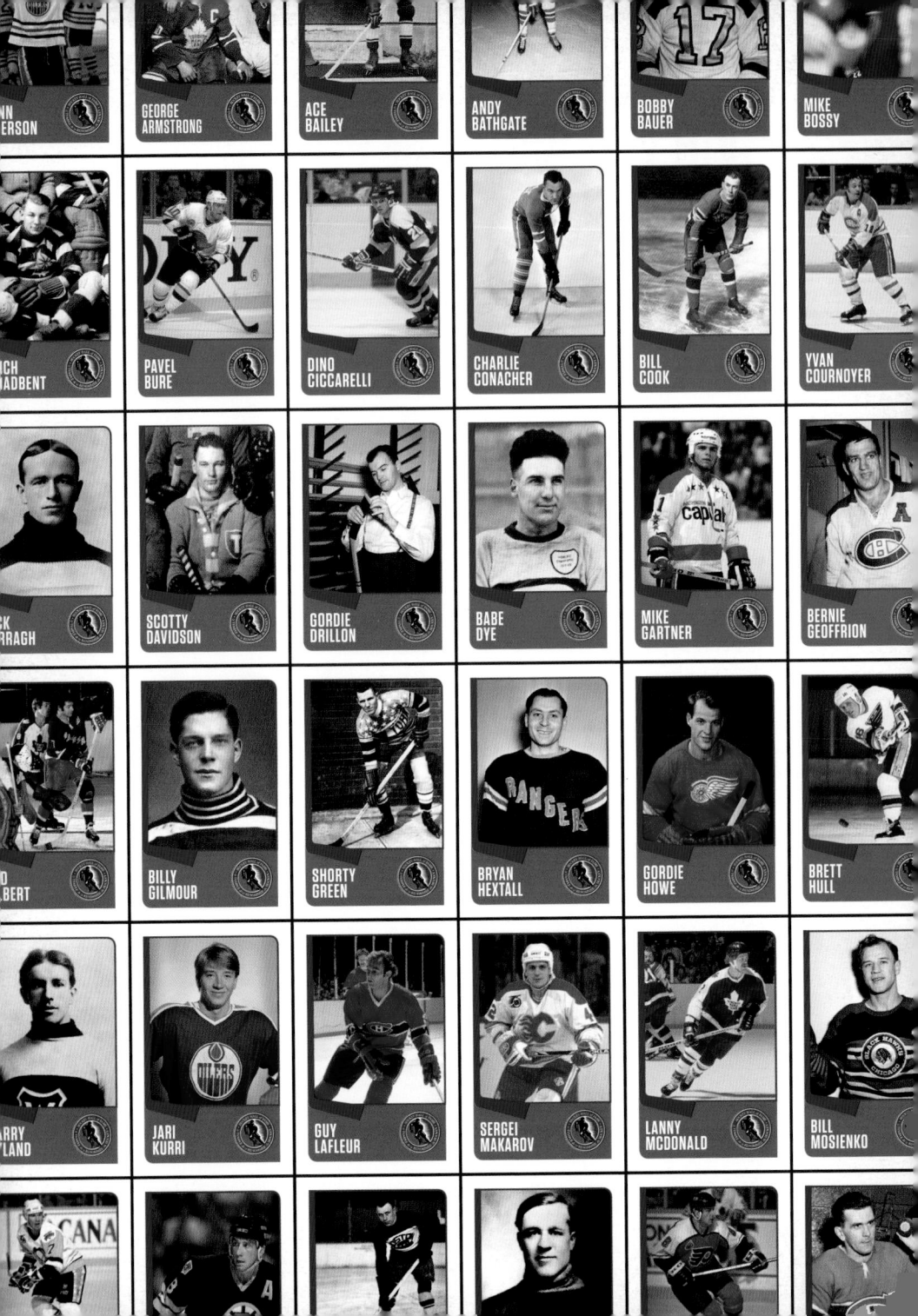

ERSON

GEORGE
ARMSTRONG

ACE
BAILEY

ANDY
BATHGATE

BOBBY
BAUER

MIKE
BOSSY

CH
ADBENT

PAVEL
BURE

DINO
CICCARELLI

CHARLIE
CONACHER

BILL
COOK

YVAN
COURNOYER

K
RRAGH

SCOTTY
DAVIDSON

GORDIE
DRILLON

BABE
DYE

MIKE
GARTNER

BERNIE
GEOFFRION

D
BERT

BILLY
GILMOUR

SHORTY
GREEN

BRYAN
HEXTALL

GORDIE
HOWE

BRETT
HULL

RRY
LAND

JARI
KURRI

GUY
LAFLEUR

SERGEI
MAKAROV

LANNY
MCDONALD

BILL
MOSIENKO

# RIGHT WING

## RIGHT WING

# 9 Glenn Anderson 2008

NO. RETIRED BY EDMONTON

ALTERNATES:
## 36 · 10

Edmonton Oilers
New York Rangers
St. Louis Blues
Toronto Maple Leafs

Shoots: Left

Height: 6'-1"

Weight: 190 lbs.

Born: October 2, 1960:
Vancouver,
British Columbia

Drafted by the
Edmonton Oilers 69th
overall in 1979

Played 16 NHL seasons
from 1980–96

Stats: See page 440

"The bond between the guys was very special. There was a closeness between us, the likes I have not seen on any other team I've played for."

— Glenn Anderson, on the team unity of the Edmonton Oilers

AWARDS
Stanley Cup (1983–84,
1984–85, 1986–87,
1987–88, 1989–90,
1993–94)

INTERNATIONAL
AWARDS
Canada Cup (1984, 1987)

- Shares NHL record for points in a single playoff period (4), established in Edmonton's 7–4 victory over Winnipeg Jets, April 6, 1988

- Played amateur hockey with Bellingham Blazers (1977–78); New Westminster Bruins (1977–78); Seattle Breakers (1978–80); University of Denver (1978–79); Canadian National Team (1979–80); Canadian Olympic Team (1979–80)

- Ranks fourth in NHL career playoff points (214)

- Tied for third in NHL career playoff overtime goals (5)

- Led NHL in game-winning goals (9) in 1985–86

- Scored 151 power-play goals, 85 game-winning goals and 13 shorthanded goals in 15-season career

- Played in NHL All-Star Game (1984, 1985, 1986, 1988)

- Finished among NHL top-5 in goals in 1983–84 (54) and 1985–86 (54)

- Registered 1,000th career NHL point in Toronto's 8–1 victory over Vancouver Canucks, February 22, 1993

- Played for Canada in 1980 Olympics, registering four points in six games

- Attempted to play for Canada in the 1994 Winter Olympics because he had negotiated that clause into his contract, but NHL Commissioner Gary Bettman vetoed it

- Played European pro hockey with Augsburger Panther (1995–96); HC Bolzano (1996–97) and HC La Chaux-de-Fonds (1996–97)

**168**

# 10

## 1975 George Armstrong

"When that goal went in, they all could relax. The fans could let the air out. Before that, it was still nip and tuck. More people remember that than the guy [Jim Pappin] who scored the winning goal, for crying out loud."

—George Armstrong, commenting on the empty-net goal that sealed the Leafs' 1967 Stanley Cup win

NO. RETIRED BY TORONTO

**ALTERNATES:**
## 15 · 20 · 8

**Toronto Maple Leafs**

Shoots: Right

Height: 6'-1"

Weight: 204 lbs.

Born: July 6, 1930; Skead, Ontario

Played 21 NHL seasons from 1949–50, 1951–71

Stats: See page 440

- Holds Toronto Maple Leafs team record for career seasons (21) and games played (1,187)

- Holds Toronto Maple Leafs team record for career assists (417) and points (713) by a right wing

- Nicknamed "Chief" because of his Native heritage. Also known as "Chief-Shoot-The-Puck"

- Played amateur hockey with Copper Cliff Redmen (1946–47); Prince Albert Blackhawks (1946–47); Stratford Kroehlers (1947–48); Toronto Jr. Marlboros (1948–50); Toronto Sr. Marlboros (1948–50)

- Led OHA-Jr. in assists (43) and points (73) in 1947–48; led OHA-Jr. playoffs in goals (7), assists (10) and points (17) in 1948–49

- Led OHA-Jr. in goals (64) in 1949–50

- Member of Allan Cup–winning Toronto Sr. Marlboros (1950)

- Scored final goal of the Original Six era in Toronto's 3–1 victory over Montreal, May 2, 1967

- Played in NHL All-Star Game (1956, 1957, 1959, 1962, 1963, 1964, 1968)

- Served as captain of the Toronto Maple Leafs (1957–69)

- Coached Toronto Marlboros (1972–77); won Memorial Cup as coach of the Toronto Marlboros (1973, 1975)

- Served as scout with Quebec Nordiques (1978–87)

- Coached Toronto Maple Leafs (1988–89)

**AWARDS**

Stanley Cup (1961–62, 1962–63, 1963–64, 1966–67)

**169**

RIGHT WING

# 6

# Ace Bailey 1975

NO. RETIRED BY TORONTO

ALTERNATE:

## 12

Toronto Maple Leafs
Toronto St. Patricks

Shoots: Right

Height: 5'-10"

Weight: 160 lbs.

Born: July 3, 1903;
Bracebridge, Ontario

Died: April 7, 1992;
Toronto, Ontario

Played eight NHL
seasons from 1926–34

Stats: See page 441

"I hold no grudge. I see Eddie often when he comes up to Toronto for the games. It was just one of those things that happens."

— Ace Bailey, on the incident that ended his career

AWARDS

NHL Scoring
Leader (1929)

Stanley Cup (1931–32)

- Played amateur hockey with Bracebridge Bird Mill (1918–22); Toronto St. Mary's (1922–24); Peterborough Petes (1924–25); Peterborough Seniors (1925–26)

- Signed as a free agent by Toronto St. Pats, November 3, 1926

- Led NHL in goals (22) and points (32) in 1928–29; led NHL playoffs in assists (2) and points (3) in 1928–29

- Scored Stanley Cup–winning goal in Toronto's 6–4 victory over N.Y. Rangers, April 9, 1932

- Suffered career-ending head injury in game vs. Boston, December 12, 1933, when knocked down from behind by Bruins defenseman Eddie Shore

- First NHL All-Star Game held in his honor with the proceeds ($20,909) going to Bailey and his family, February 14, 1934

- In show of good sportsmanship, Bailey participated in a ceremonial handshake with Eddie Shore at center ice before the start of the Bailey Benefit Game

- Coached Toronto Dominions (1934–35)

- Coached University of Toronto Varsity Blues (1935–40, 1945–49)

- Worked as timekeeper at Maple Leaf Gardens (1938–84)

- Allowed his retired No. 6 to be worn by Maple Leafs' winger Ron Ellis from 1968–81 because he respected the way Ellis played the game

**170**

# An All-Star Game Born of Tragedy

On December 12, 1933, with the Toronto Maple Leafs visiting the Boston Bruins, a case of mistaken identity changed Ace Bailey's life forever.

Boston favorite Eddie Shore was "having a very frustrating night," explained Red Horner. "He was playing a great game but it wasn't getting him or the Bruins anywhere."

Then, in the second period, Horner laid a wicked hip-check on Shore. Wanting to exact revenge, Shore got up and skated wildly toward Bailey, "He thought that Bailey was me," remembered Horner. "He charged into Bailey on an angle from the side and flipped him in the air, just like a rag doll. Bailey landed on his head just a few feet from where I was standing."

With Bailey convulsing on the ice, Horner coldcocked Shore, knocking him unconscious and leaving him with a 3-inch gash on his head. But Bailey's injury was far more serious: a cerebral hemorrhage. Death seemed imminent.

Dr. Donald Munro performed two operations to relieve the pressure on Bailey's brain; with a pulse of 160 and a temperature over 106°F, doctors were measuring Bailey's life expectancy in minutes. However, by the following morning he was showing sufficient recovery to give medical staff hope, and by Christmas he was expected to live.

NHL president Frank Calder suspended Eddie Shore indefinitely (later 16 games, one-third of the season) and Red Horner until January 1, 1934. Shore was not permitted to visit Bailey in the hospital, but when Boston's

MAR-6-1934

**Ace Bailey and Eddie Shore shake hands on March 6, 1934.**

manager Art Ross visited the Leafs' star, Bailey absolved Shore of any willful wrongdoing.

Bailey was never able to play hockey again. The Boston Bruins set aside almost $8,000 in gate receipts from a contest with the Montreal Maroons for Bailey. The NHL—based on an idea originally proposed by *Ottawa Journal* sports editor Walter Gilhooley—staged the first-ever All-Star Game on February 14, 1934; all the proceeds went to Bailey's family. Prior to the game, Bailey presented the All-Stars with their jerseys. As Shore and Bailey met, silence fell over the crowd. Bailey extended his hand to the Bruins star and the audience roared its approval. The paid attendance at Maple Leaf Gardens that night raised $20,909 for Bailey, and the tribute game set the model for future All-Star contests.

# 9

## RIGHT WING

# Andy Bathgate 1978

NO. RETIRED BY
NEW YORK RANGERS

ALTERNATES:
## 21 · 14 · 16

Detroit Red Wings
New York Rangers
Pittsburgh Penguins
Toronto Maple Leafs
Vancouver Blazers

Shoots: Right

Height: 6'

Weight: 180 lbs.

Born: August 28, 1932:
Winnipeg, Manitoba

Died: February 26, 2016:
Brampton, Ontario

Played 18 NHL and WHA
seasons from 1952–68,
1970–71, 1974–75

Stats: See page 441

"I couldn't run over people. I had to maneuver around them."

### AWARDS
Hart Memorial
Trophy (1959)

Stanley Cup (1963–64)

### ALL-STAR
### SELECTIONS
First All-Star Team Right
Wing (1959, 1962)

Second All-Star Team
Right Wing (1958, 1963)

- Played amateur hockey with Winnipeg Excelciors (1943–44); Winnipeg Rangers (1946–48); Winnipeg Black Hawks (1948–49); Guelph Biltmores (1949–53)

- Member of Memorial Cup–winning Guelph Biltmores (1952)

- Tied (with Bobby Hull) for NHL lead in points (84) in 1961–62; led NHL in assists in 1961–62 (56) and 1963–64 (58)

- Finished among NHL top-5 in goals in 1958–59 (40) and 1962–63 (35)

- Served as captain of N.Y. Rangers (1961–64)

- Scored first goal in history of Pittsburgh Penguins franchise in 2–1 loss to Montreal Canadiens, October 11, 1967

- Played in NHL All-Star Game (1957, 1958, 1959, 1960, 1961, 1962, 1963, 1964)

- Scored Stanley Cup–winning goal in Toronto's 4–0 victory over Detroit Red Wings, April 25, 1964

- Member of Calder Cup–winning Cleveland Barons (1954); member of WHL champion Vancouver Canucks (1969, 1970)

- Named WHL playoffs MVP (1970); WHL First All-Star Team Right Wing (1970)

- Inducted into Manitoba Hockey Hall of Fame (1985); inducted into Manitoba Sports Hall of Fame (1993)

- Served as player/coach with HC Sierre (1971–73)

- Coached WHL's Vancouver Canucks (1969–70); coached WHA's Vancouver Blazers (1973–74)

# Bobby Bauer

**1996**

"There was no better person than Bobby. [He] gave everything he had. He was the brains of the line, always thinking, and a very clever playmaker."

— Woody Dumart, Kraut Line teammate

**Boston Bruins**

Shoots: Right

Height: 5'-6"

Weight: 155 lbs.

Born: February 16, 1915; Waterloo, Ontario

Died: September 16, 1964; Kitchener, Ontario

Played nine NHL seasons from 1936–42, 1945–47, 1951–52

Stats: See page 442

- Played amateur hockey with St. Michael's Buzzers (1930–31); St. Michael's Majors (1931–34); Toronto British Consols (1934–35); Kitchener Greenshirts (1934–35); Kitchener-Waterloo Dutchmen (1947–50, 1951–52)
- Played minor pro with Boston Cubs (1935–36); Providence Reds (1936–37)
- Member of Boston's famed Kraut Line with Milt Schmidt and Woody Dumart
- Scored Stanley Cup–winning goal in Boston's 3–1 victory over Detroit Red Wings, April 12, 1941
- Member of Allan Cup–winning Ottawa RCAF Flyers (1941–42)

- Came out of retirement to play one game with Boston when the team honored the Kraut Line and scored a goal and assisted on Milt Schmidt's 200th career goal, March 18, 1952
- Coached Guelph Biltmores (1947–48)
- Served as coach, general manager and/or president of Kitchener-Waterloo Dutchmen (1952–64)
- Coached Allan Cup–winning Kitchener-Waterloo Dutchmen (1952–53, 1955–56)
- Coached Kitchener-Waterloo Dutchmen team that represented Canada at 1956 and 1960 Winter Olympic Games
- Brother of Father David Bauer, founder and first coach of the Canadian National Team program

**AWARDS**

Lady Byng Memorial Trophy (1940, 1941, 1947)

Stanley Cup (1938–39, 1940–41)

**ALL-STAR SELECTIONS**

Second All-Star Team Right Wing (1939, 1940, 1941, 1947)

# 22

# Mike Bossy 1991

NO. RETIRED BY
NEW YORK ISLANDERS

New York Islanders

Shoots: Right

Height: 6'

Weight: 186 lbs.

Born: January 22, 1957;
Montreal, Quebec

Drafted by the New
York Islanders 15th
overall in 1977

Played 10 NHL seasons
from 1977–87

Stats: See page 442

"I think a quick release is more important than aiming the puck. I always figured it was harder for a goalie to stop what he wasn't expecting than for me to look for a particular hole. Besides, in the NHL you almost never get the chance to pick a particular spot."

**AWARDS**

Calder Memorial
Trophy (1978)

Conn Smythe
Trophy (1982)

Lady Byng Memorial
Trophy (1983, 1984, 1986)

Stanley Cup
(1979–80, 1980–81,
1981–82, 1982–83)

**ALL-STAR
SELECTIONS**

First All-Star Team
Right Wing (1981, 1982,
1983, 1984, 1986)

Second All-Star
Team Right Wing
(1978, 1979, 1985)

**INTERNATIONAL
AWARDS**

Canada Cup (1984)

- First NHL rookie to score 50 goals in the regular season (1977–78)
- Became second player in NHL history (with Maurice Richard) to score 50 goals in 50 games in N.Y. Islanders' 7–4 victory over Quebec Nordiques, January 24, 1981
- Holds NHL record for most game-winning goals in a single playoff series (4), established in 1983
- Shares NHL record (with Cam Neely) for most power-play goals in a single playoff season (9), established in 1981
- Shares NHL record (with Wayne Gretzky) for most 50 or more goal seasons (9); shares NHL record (with Wayne Gretzky) for most 60 or more goal seasons (5)
- Played amateur hockey with Montreal-Bourassa Canadiens (1972–73); Laval Nationale (1972–77)

- Led QMJHL in goals (84) in 1974–75
- Scored Stanley Cup–winning goal in N.Y. Islanders' 3–1 victory over Vancouver Canucks, May 16, 1982
- Scored Stanley Cup–winning goal in N.Y. Islanders' 4–2 victory over Edmonton Oilers, May 17, 1983
- Played in NHL All-Star Game (1978, 1980–86)
- Led NHL in game-winning goals in 1980–81 (10) and 1985–86 (9); led NHL in power-play goals in 1977–78 (25), 1978–79 (27) and 1980–81 (28)
- Registered 1,000th career NHL point in N.Y. Islanders' 7-5 victory over Washington Capitals, January 24, 1986; recorded 500th career NHL goal in N.Y. Islanders' 7-5 victory over Boston Bruins, January 2, 1986

# Goals over Goons

Only a sniper of Mike Bossy's unparalleled accuracy would consider 38 goals a failure. But Bossy's goal-scoring standards were so high that when chronic back troubles limited him to 63 games and 38 goals in the 1986–87 season, he knew he should retire.

No one would have considered his retirement a possibility six years earlier, in 1981–82. That year Bossy—who surpassed the 50-goal mark in every season but his shortened 1986–87 campaign—broke the 60-goal barrier for the third time and set the scoring record for right wingers, with 147 points.

It was only four years earlier, in 1977–78, that Bossy had made his NHL debut. Islanders head coach Al Arbour had assembled what would go on to become the New York Islanders' most prolific line ever, with center Bryan Trottier and massive left winger Clark Gillies. The Bossy-Trottier-Gillies trio, known as the Long Island Lighting Company, skated their way right into NHL history, as Bossy became the first NHL rookie ever to score more than 50 goals in a season, finishing with 53. Bossy would later whip a perfect pass from Trottier past Quebec Nordiques goalie Ron Grahame in 1981 to become the first player since Maurice "Rocket" Richard (in 1945) to score 50 goals in 50 games.

Thirty-two percent of Bossy's 573 goals came with the Islanders enjoying a manpower advantage. That success, in turn, made other teams less aggressive, for fear of taking penalties, creating another advantage for

**Mike Bossy poses with pucks after scoring his 50th goal in the 50th game of the 1981 season.**

the Islanders. Many Islander fans, however, argued that New York's opponents weren't penalized nearly enough for the manner in which they tried to neutralize Bossy's ability to score—his career-ending back problems the legacy of that abuse.

Bossy became the first major star of the modern era to criticize the violence in NHL hockey, warning that it was subjecting the game to public ridicule in the United States. And all through his career, he played the game the way he wanted others to play it, averaging only 21 penalty minutes a season and winning three Lady Byng Memorial Trophies—all while being one of the most feared shooters in the history of the NHL.

# 4 Punch Broadbent 1962

**ALTERNATES**

**9 · 6 · 7 · 8**

Montreal Maroons
Ottawa Senators
New York Americans

Shoots: Right
Height: 5'-7"
Weight: 183 lbs.
Born: July 13, 1892;
Ottawa, Ontario
Died: March 5, 1971;
Ottawa, Ontario
Played 14 professional
seasons from
1912–15, 1918–29
Stats: See page 442

"It's an unfortunate thing, but Punch might have left an even greater record if it hadn't been for the war. He lost four of his best seasons in his career because of service in World War One, and it was tribute to his ability that he came back and still did so well in hockey."

— Sportswriter
Baz O'Meara

**AWARDS**

NHL Scoring
Leader (1922)
Stanley Cup (1919–20,
1920–21, 1922–23,
1925–26)

- Holds NHL record for most consecutive regular season games with at least one goal (16), established from December 24, 1921 to February 15, 1922

- Played amateur hockey with Ottawa Emmetts (1908–09); Ottawa Seconds (1909–10); Ottawa Cliffsides (1909–11); Hull Volants (1909–10); Ottawa New Edinburghs (1911–12)

- Served in the Canadian CEF during World War I and earned Military Medal for heroism in combat

- Renowned for his ability to dance around or skate over an opponent, he was considered to be one of the first true power-forwards in the game

- Nicknamed "Punch" because he had a knockout scoring punch and a knack for scoring at clutch times

- Nicknamed "Old Elbows" because he used his elbows to intimidate opposition players

- Led NHL in goals (31) and points (45) in 1921–22

- Scored Stanley Cup–winning goal in Ottawa's 1–0 victory over Edmonton Eskimos, March 23, 1923

- Traded to Montreal Maroons by Ottawa with Clint Benedict for cash, October 20, 1924; traded to Ottawa by Montreal Maroons with $22,500 for Hooley Smith, October 7, 1927; traded to N.Y. Americans by Ottawa for cash, October 15, 1928

- Coached Ottawa Rideaus (1931–35)

# 2012 **Pavel Bure**

**10**

NO. RETIRED BY VANCOUVER

**ALTERNATES**
**9 · 96**

Florida Panthers
New York Rangers
Vancouver Canucks

Shoots: Left

Height: 5'-10"

Weight: 190 lbs.

Born: March 31, 1971:
Moscow, Union of Soviet
Socialist Republics

Drafted by the
Vancouver Canucks
113th overall in 1989

Played 12 NHL seasons
from 1991–2003

Stats: see page 443

"When I look at the
net, I don't see a
goalie. I see scoring
chances."

- Played amateur hockey with CSKA Moscow (1987–91); played European professional hockey with Spartak Moscow (1994–95) and EV Landshut (1994–95)

- Holds NHL record for scoring the highest percentage of a team's total regular-season goals (29.5%), established with the Florida Panthers in 2000–01

- Holds Vancouver Canucks single-season records for goals (60), points by a right wing (110), shots on goal (407), playoff goals (16) and playoff points (31), established in 1993–94

- Played in NHL All-Star Game (1993, 1994, 1997, 1998, 2000, 2001)

- Holds Florida Panthers single-season records for goals (59), points (94), game-winning goals (14) and shots on goal (384), established in 1999–2000

- Led the NHL in goals in 1993–94 (60), 1999–2000 (58); 2000–01 (59); led NHL in power-play goals in 1993–94 (25); led NHL in shorthanded goals in 1992–93 (7) and 1997–98 (6); led NHL in game-winning goals in 1999–2000 (14)

- Only Calder Trophy–winner not selected to NHL All-Rookie Team (1992)

- Inducted into International Ice Hockey Federation Hall of Fame (2012); first Vancouver Canuck inducted into the Hockey Hall of Fame (2012)

- Served as captain of Florida Panthers (2001–02)

- Brother of Valeri Bure, who played in the NHL with Montreal, Florida, Calgary, St. Louis and Dallas (1995–2004)

**AWARDS**

Calder Memorial
Trophy (1992)

Maurice Richard
Trophy (2000, 2001)

**ALL-STAR
SELECTIONS**

First All-Star Team
Right Wing (1994)

Second All-Star Team
Right Wing (2000, 2001)

**INTERNATIONAL
AWARDS**

Gold Medal: World
Championships (1990)

Silver Medal: Winter
Olympics (1998)

Bronze Medal: World
Championships (1991)

Bronze Medal: Winter
Olympics (2002)

# 20

# Dino Ciccarelli 2010

ALTERNATE
## 22

Detroit Red Wings
Florida Panthers
Minnesota North Stars
Tampa Bay Lightning
Washington Capitals

Shoots: Right
Height: 5'-10"
Weight: 185 lbs.
Born: February 8, 1960:
Sarnia, Ontario
Played 19 NHL seasons
from 1980–99
Stats: See page 443

"In our sport, you only get to celebrate the ultimate when you win the Cup. You don't celebrate winning a division or a conference, so that leaves a lot of people out of celebrating an accomplishment. That's why this is so special."

—Dino Ciccarelli, commenting on his Hall of Fame induction

### INTERNATIONAL AWARDS

Bronze Medal: World Championships (1982)

- Holds NHL record for goals by a rookie in a single playoff year (14), established in 1980–81

- Shares NHL record (with Ville Leino and Jake Guentzel) for points by a rookie in a single playoff year (21)

- Played amateur hockey with Sarnia Army Vets (1974–75); Sarnia Bees (1975–76); London Knights (1976–80)

- Played minor pro hockey with Oklahoma City Stars (1979–81)

- OMJHL Second All-Star Team Right Wing (1978)

- Suffered serious leg injury in 1978–79 season and was not selected in the annual NHL Amateur Draft

- Played in NHL All-Star Game (1982, 1983, 1989, 1997)

- Finished among NHL top-10 in goals (55), power-play goals (20) and points (106) in 1981–82; goals (52), power-play goals (22) and points (103) in 1986–87

- Finished among NHL top-10 in game-winning goals in 1988–89 (8), 1991–92 (7) and 1992–93 (10)

- Registered 1,000th career NHL point in Detroit's 5–1 victory over Calgary Flames, March 9, 1994; recorded 500th career NHL goal in Detroit's 6–3 victory over L.A. Kings, January 8, 1994

- Renowned for his ability to stand in the slot, deflect shots from the point and battle for rebounds

- Inducted into National Italian Sports Hall of Fame (2000)

- No. 8 jersey retired by OHL's London Knights (2002)

# 1961 **Charlie Conacher**

> "I never had a finer friend in Toronto than Charlie. He was my protection as a Maple Leaf ... He didn't go looking for trouble, but if it came along, he would clear it up."
>
> — King Clancy, commenting on his teammate

**NO. RETIRED BY TORONTO**

**ALTERNATES:**

## 17 · 6 · 4

Toronto Maple Leafs
Detroit Red Wings
New York Americans

Shoots: Right

Height: 6'-1"

Weight: 195 lbs.

Born: December 9, 1909: Toronto, Ontario

Died: December 30, 1967: Toronto, Ontario

Played 12 NHL seasons from 1929–41

Stats: See page 444

- Holds NHL record for fastest game-winning goal (7 seconds), established in Toronto's 6–0 victory over Boston, February 6, 1932
- One of three Conacher brothers (along with Roy and Lionel) to be inducted into the Hockey Hall of Fame
- Nicknamed "The Big Bomber" because of his explosive shot
- Played amateur hockey with North Toronto Juniors (1926–27); North Toronto Seniors (1926–27); Toronto Marlboros (1927–29)
- Led OHA-Jr. in goals (18) and points (21) in 1928–29; led Memorial Cup playoffs in goals (28) and points (36) in 1929
- Led NHL in goals in 1930–31 (31), 1931–32 (34), 1933–34 (32), 1934–35 (36) and 1935–36 (23)

- Signed as a free agent by Toronto, October 7, 1929
- First player in Toronto Maple Leaf history to score five goals in one game in 11–3 victory over N.Y. Americans, January 19, 1932
- Played in NHL All-Star Game (1934, 1937)
- Coached Chicago Black Hawks (1947–48)
- His legacy is remembered through the Charlie Conacher Research Fund for cancer
- Inducted into Canada's Sports Hall of Fame (1975)
- NHL presented an award in his name from 1968 to 1984 to the player best exhibiting outstanding humanitarian and public service contributions

**AWARDS**

NHL Scoring Leader (1934, 1935)

Stanley Cup (1931–32)

**ALL-STAR SELECTIONS**

First All-Star Team Right Wing (1934, 1935, 1936)

Second All-Star Team Right Wing (1931, 1932)

# 5

# Bill Cook 1952

New York Rangers
Saskatoon Crescents
Saskatoon Sheiks

Shoots: Right

Height: 5'-10"

Weight: 170 lbs.

Born: October 8, 1895;
Brantford, Ontario

Died: May 5, 1986;
Kingston, Ontario

Played 15 professional
seasons from 1922–37

Stats: See page 444

"Bill's cry was the most amazing half-grunt, half-moan, half-yell that I ever heard. He'd let this weird sound out of him, meaning that he was in the clear. And he'd say in these skull-sessions of ours, 'When I yell, I want the puck then, don't look up to see where I am. Just put it there and I'll be there.'"

— Frank Boucher, commenting on his teammate

AWARDS

NHL Scoring Leader
(1927, 1933)

Stanley Cup
(1927–28, 1932–33)

ALL-STAR
SELECTIONS

First All-Star Team Right
Wing (1931, 1932, 1933)

Second All-Star Team
Right Wing (1934)

WCHL First All-Star Team
Right Wing (1924, 1925)

WHL First All-Star Team
Right Wing (1926)

- Second oldest player in NHL history (37 years, 5 months) to win scoring title (1932–33); surpassed by Martin St. Louis (37 years, 10 months) in 2012–13.

- Played amateur hockey with Kingston Frontenacs (1913–15, 1919–20); Sault Ste. Marie Greyhounds (1920–22)

- Led OHA-Sr. in goals (12) and points (19) in 1919–20; led AAHA in goals (20) and points (28) in 1921–22

- Led WCHL in goals (26), assists (14) and points (40) in 1923–24; led WHL in goals (31) and points (44) in 1925–26; led WHL playoffs in goals (2) in 1925–26

- Starred for the N.Y. Rangers with brother Bun Cook at left wing and Frank Boucher at center on what is considered one of the NHL's first great forward lines

- Served as captain of N.Y. Rangers (1926–37)

- Scored first goal in history of N.Y. Rangers franchise in 1–0 victory over Montreal Maroons, November 16, 1926

- Scored Stanley Cup–winning goal in N.Y. Rangers' 1–0 victory over Toronto Maple Leafs, April 13, 1933

- Led NHL in goals in 1926–27 (33) and 1932–33 (28); led NHL in points in 1926–27 (37) and 1932–33 (50)

- Coached Cleveland Barons to AHL championship (1938–39, 1940–41); coached Minneapolis Millers to USHL championship (1949–50)

# 1982 Yvan Cournoyer

"People think we exaggerate when we say it was like a war out there but that's exactly what it was. It was more than just a series of eight hockey games. It was a clash of different ideals and ways of life. It was an amazing experience and something I'll never forget."

— Yvan Cournoyer, on the Summit Series of 1972

**NO. RETIRED BY MONTREAL**

ALTERNATE

## 25

**Montreal Canadiens**

Shoots: Left

Height: 5'-7"

Weight: 178 lbs.

Born: November 22, 1943; Drummondville, Quebec

Played 16 NHL seasons from 1963–79

Stats: See page 444

- Played amateur hockey with Lachine Maroons (1960–61); Montreal Jr. Canadiens (1961–64)
- Led OHA-Jr. in goals (63) in 1963–64; led OHA-Jr. playoffs in goals (19) in 1963–64
- Played minor pro hockey with Quebec Aces (1964–65)
- Nicknamed "The Roadrunner" because of his outstanding speed
- Ranks fourth in Montreal Canadiens career regular season goals (428); ranks sixth in Montreal Canadiens career regular season assists (435) and ranks third in Montreal Canadiens career playoff goals (64)
- Played in NHL All-Star Game (1967, 1971, 1972, 1973, 1974, 1978)
- Led NHL in power-play goals (20) in 1966–67
- Led NHL in game-winning goals in 1966–67 (7) and 1975–76 (12)
- Finished second in NHL shooting percentage in 1971–72 (22.6%) and finished fourth in 1973–74 (21.4%)
- Scored Stanley Cup–winning goal in Montreal's 6–4 victory over Chicago Black Hawks, May 10, 1973
- Served as captain of Montreal Canadiens (1975–79)
- Coached Montreal Roadrunners (named after him) of the Roller Hockey International League (1994–95)
- Served as assistant coach of Montreal Canadiens (1996–97)

AWARDS

Conn Smythe Trophy (1973)

Stanley Cup (1964–65, 1965–66, 1967–68, 1968–69, 1970–71, 1972–73, 1975–76, 1976–77, 1977–78, 1978–79)

ALL-STAR SELECTIONS

Second All-Star Team Right Wing (1969, 1971, 1972, 1973)

INTERNATIONAL AWARDS

Summit Series (1972)

**181**

# 7

# Jack Darragh 1962

**ALTERNATE**
# 5

Ottawa Senators

Shoots: Right

Height: 5'-10"

Weight: 168 lbs.

Born: December 4, 1890: Ottawa, Ontario

Died: June 25, 1924: Ottawa, Ontario

Played 13 professional seasons from 1910–21, 1922–24

Stats: See page 445

"I have always wanted to make good on the Ottawa team and now, feeling in my prime, I thought it all out and decided to jump the amateur ranks. I believe what I have done, under the circumstances, was just and fair."

**AWARDS**
Stanley Cup (1910–11, 1919–20, 1920–21, 1922–23)

**ALL-STAR SELECTIONS**
NHA First All-Star Team Right Wing (1914)

- Played amateur hockey with Ottawa Stewartons (1908–11); Ottawa Cliffsides (1909–10); Fort Coulonge Bankers (1909–10)

- Scored a goal in professional debut against Georges Vezina in Ottawa's 5–3 victory over Montreal Canadiens in NHA's season opener, December 31, 1910

- Scored game-winning goal in all three of the Ottawa Senators' wins in the 1919–20 Stanley Cup series against Seattle

- Scored Stanley Cup–winning goal in Ottawa's 6–1 victory over Seattle, April 1, 1920; scored Stanley Cup–winning goal in Ottawa's 2–1 victory over Vancouver, April 4, 1921

- One of only two players (with Mike Bossy) to score Stanley Cup–winning goal in back-to-back seasons

- Led NHL in assists (14) in 1920–21

- Renowned for his backhand shot, blistering speed and clever puckhandling skills

- Surprisingly retired following 1920–21 season and coached Ottawa Gunners (1921–22) during his year away from the game

- Worked for Ottawa Dairy Company while he was playing for the Senators

- Died of a ruptured appendix following the 1923–24 season, June 25, 1924

- Brother of Harold Darragh, who played in the NHL with Pittsburgh, Philadelphia, Boston and Toronto from 1925–32

# 1950 Scotty Davidson

**3**

"Young players of the caliber of Davidson are the making of the game, and play much better hockey than the old-timers, who have nothing but their reputations of years gone by to travel on."

*— Toronto Daily Star,*
November 13, 1912

Calgary Athletics
Kingston 14th Regiment
Kingston Frontenacs
Toronto Blueshirts
Toronto Tecumsehs

Shoots: Right

Height: 6'-1"

Weight: 195 lbs.

Born: March 6, 1891: Kingston, Ontario

Died: June 16, 1915: Killed in action, Belgium

Played six professional and elite amateur seasons from 1908–14

Stats: See page 445

- Led OHA-Sr. in goals (8) in 1908–09
- Led NHA playoffs in penalty minutes (11) in 1913–14
- Had a brief but brilliant hockey career before losing his life in World War I
- Learned the game in his hometown of Kingston under the coaching of James T. Sutherland, who often is called "The Father of Hockey"
- Member of Ontario Junior–champion Kingston Frontenacs (1910, 1911)
- Ranked among NHA top-10 in goals in 1912–13 (19) and 1913–14 (23)

- Ranked second in NHA assists (13) in 1913–14
- Served as captain of Stanley Cup–winning Toronto Blueshirts (1913–14)
- First professional hockey player to enlist in the Canadian Army following the outbreak of World War I
- Legacy commemorated on the Vimy Memorial
- Selected as Right Wing on *Maclean's Magazine* All-Time All-Star Team (1925)

**AWARDS**
Stanley Cup (1913–14)

# 12

# Gordie Drillon 1975

**ALTERNATE**

**21**

Montreal Canadiens
Toronto Maple Leafs

Shoots: Right

Height: 6'-2"

Weight: 178 lbs.

Born: October 23, 1913: Moncton, New Brunswick

Died: September 23, 1985: Saint John, New Brunswick

Played seven NHL seasons from 1936–43

Stats: See page 445

> "I spent ten years playing in the slot before anyone invented a name for it."

**AWARDS**

NHL Scoring Leader (1938)

Lady Byng Memorial Trophy (1938)

Stanley Cup (1941–42)

**ALL-STAR SELECTIONS**

First All-Star Team Right Wing (1938, 1939)

Second All-Star Team Right Wing (1942)

○ First New Brunswick native to be inducted into Hockey Hall of Fame

○ Played amateur hockey with Moncton Athletics (1930–31); Moncton Wheelers (1931–32); Moncton Hawks (1932–33); Toronto Young Rangers (1933–34); Toronto Lions (1934–36); Toronto Dominions (1933–35); Saint John Beavers (1949–50)

○ Led Moncton City Junior League in goals (15) and points (19) in 1930–31; led Moncton Commercial League playoffs in goals (13) and points (17) in 1932–33

○ Played minor pro hockey with Pittsburgh Yellowjackets (1935–36); Syracuse Stars (1936–37)

○ Last member of the Toronto Maple Leafs to win NHL scoring title (1937–38)

○ Played in NHL All-Star Game (1939)

○ Led NHL in goals (26) and points (52) in 1937–38

○ Led NHL playoffs in goals in 1937–38 (7) and 1938–39 (7)

○ Played with Toronto Army Daggers (1943–44); Valleyfield Braves (1944–45); Dartmouth RCAF (1944–45); Halifax Army (1945–46) during World War II

○ Renowned for being one of the "star" players benched by coach Hap Day during Toronto's historic comeback in 1942 Stanley Cup final against Detroit

○ Traded to Montreal Canadiens by Toronto for cash, October 4, 1942

○ Inducted into New Brunswick Sports Hall of Fame (1970); inducted into Canada's Sport Hall of Fame (1989)

# 1970 Babe Dye

**6**

ALTERNATES
**4 · 7 · 9
14**

Chicago Black Hawks
Hamilton Tigers
New York Americans
Toronto Maple Leafs
Toronto St. Patricks

Shoots: Right

Height: 5'-8"

Weight: 150 lbs.

Born: May 13, 1897;
Hamilton, Ontario

Died: January 3, 1962;
Chicago, Illinois

Played 11 NHL seasons
from 1919–29, 1930–31

Stats: See page 445

> "I think I could do even better today with these long schedules. I could always fire a puck and I knew where it was going. I could skate when I had to. The big difference, as I see it, is the crowds are bigger and the boys are getting a lot more money then we ever did."
> — Babe Dye, 1961

- Holds NHL record for most goals in a Stanley Cup final series (9), established in Toronto St. Pats' five-game series victory over Vancouver Millionaires in 1922

- Played amateur hockey with Toronto Aura Lee (1916–17); Toronto De LaSalle (1917–18); Toronto Sr. St. Pats (1918–19)

- Led OHA-Jr. in goals (31) in 1916–17

- Led OHA-Sr. in points (14) in 1918–19; OHA-Sr. Second All-Star Team Right Wing (1919)

- Signed as a free agent by Toronto St. Pats, December 15, 1919

- Led NHL in goals in 1920–21 (35), 1922–23 (27) and 1924–25 (38)

- Led NHL in points in 1922–23 (40) and 1924–25 (46)

- Nicknamed "Babe" by his teammates because of his love of baseball

- Played professional baseball with Toronto Maple Leafs, Buffalo Bisons and Baltimore Orioles in the International League; turned down the opportunity to play baseball with the Philadelphia Athletics in 1923

- Traded to Chicago Black Hawks by Toronto for $15,000, October 18, 1926; traded to N.Y. Americans by Chicago for $15,000, October 17, 1928; traded to New Haven (Can-Am) by N.Y. Americans for George Massecar, November 13, 1929

- Coached St. Louis Flyers (1930–31)

- Coached Chicago Shamrocks (1931–32)

- Served as minor league and NHL on-ice official (1933–43)

AWARDS
NHL Scoring Leader
(1923, 1925)
Stanley Cup (1921–22)

**185**

# 11

# Mike Gartner 2001

**ALTERNATE:**
# 22

Cincinnati Stingers
Minnesota North Stars
New York Rangers
Phoenix Coyotes
Toronto Maple Leafs
Washington Capitals

Shoots: Right

Height: 6'

Weight: 187 lbs.

Born: October 29, 1959;
Ottawa, Ontario

Drafted by the
Washington Capitals
fourth overall in 1979

Played 20 WHA and NHL
seasons from 1978–98

Stats: See page 446

"When I went there, hockey was in no way the number one sport. In fact, it wasn't number two, three or four either! Yet, it was a great experience for me."

—Mike Gartner, on playing for the Washington Capitals

**INTERNATIONAL AWARDS**

Canada Cup (1984, 1987)

Bronze Medal: World Championships (1982, 1983)

- Holds NHL record for most seasons with at least 30 goals (17)

- Shares NHL record (with Jaromir Jagr) for most consecutive seasons with at least 30 goals (15)

- Holds Washington Capitals team record for consecutive games with at least one point (17), established in 1980–81

- Ranks seventh in NHL career regular season goals (708)

- Ranks sixth in NHL career shots on goal (5,090); tied (with Jagr) for 11th in NHL career power-play goals (217); ranks 22nd in NHL career game-winning goals (90)

- Only player in NHL history to record 500th goal, 500th assist, 1,000th point and play in his 1,000th game in the same season (1991–92)

- Played amateur hockey with Barrie Co-Op (1974–75); Mississauga Reps (1974–75); Toronto Young Nationals (1975–76); St. Catharines Black Hawks (1975–76); Niagara Falls Flyers (1976–78)

- OMJHL First All-Star Team Right Wing (1978)

- Played in NHL All-Star Game (1981, 1985, 1986, 1988, 1990, 1993, 1996)

- Served as president of NHL Players' Association (1996–98)

- Scored final goal in Chicago Stadium history in Toronto's 1–0 victory over Chicago Blackhawks, April 28, 1994

# Consistency Is the Key

I f you could attribute the adjective "consistent" to one player in the Hall of Fame, Mike Gartner would be a good choice. Always blessed with blazing speed, Gartner went on to record seventeen 30-goal seasons in his 19 years in the NHL—more than any other player. He scored the first goal in the Phoenix Coyotes' history and the last goal at Chicago Stadium. He became the fifth NHLer to surpass 700 goals, and he is the only NHLer to record his 500th goal, 500th assist, 1,000th point and 1,000th game in the same season.

But for all of his consistent greatness, Gartner never took home a single NHL award, end of season All-Star nomination or the Stanley Cup. Drafted by the lowly Washington Capitals in 1979 after spending his first pro year alongside Mark Messier with the Cincinnati Stingers of the World Hockey Association, Gartner rarely suited up for teams that had much playoff luck. His best chance at a Stanley Cup run in his 15 playoff appearances was with the 1993–94 Toronto Maple Leafs, but, for the second consecutive year, the Leafs lost in the conference final. As for individual awards, Gartner's career was one of many to be star-crossed with Wayne Gretzky—not to mention fellow right wingers Mike Bossy, Jari Kurri and Brett Hull.

But Gartner's success was evident to those playing with and against him. He was a coveted offensive weapon who was acquired by several teams looking to take the next step. And he was always willing to suit up for his country, representing Canada eight times in international competition.

**Mike Gartner speeds down the ice with the New York Rangers in the early 1990s.**

His first international experience whetted his appetite, as he and his midget Barrie Co-ops team won the 1975 Wrigley National Midget Hockey Tournament, along with the right to represent the country in a tournament in the Soviet Union. Next Gartner won a bronze medal at the 1978 World Junior Championship.

But for all his international stops, the highlight of his career was the 1987 Canada Cup, where—alongside luminaries like Wayne Gretzky, Mario Lemieux, Ray Bourque and Paul Coffey—Gartner's speed and skill were required to play a solid two-way game and to keep pace with the smooth-skating European clubs.

As Gartner said, "To say I was part of the best hockey team in the world at that time was, and is, a point of pride for me."

**187**

# 5

# Bernie Geoffrion 1972

NO. RETIRED BY MONTREAL

**Montreal Canadiens**
**New York Rangers**

Shoots: Right
Height: 5'-9"
Weight: 166 lbs.

Born: February 16, 1931;
Montreal, Quebec

Died: March 11, 2006;
Atlanta, Georgia

Played 16 NHL seasons
from 1950–64, 1966–68

Stats: See page 446

"Look, the Montreal Canadiens were very good to me, but I was very good to them too. There are things I wish could have been different but I have no regrets ... I got to play hockey for my favorite team."

**AWARDS**

Calder Memorial
Trophy (1952)

Art Ross Trophy
(1955, 1961)

Hart Memorial
Trophy (1961)

Stanley Cup (1952–53,
1955–56, 1956–57,
1957–58, 1958–59,
1959–60)

**ALL-STAR
SELECTIONS**

First All-Star Team
Right Wing (1961)

Second All-Star Team
Right Wing (1955, 1960)

- Nicknamed "Boom Boom" because of the sound his stick blade made when it struck the puck and the sound his shot made when it missed the net and struck the boards

- Played amateur hockey with Montreal–St. Louis College (1945–46); Montreal Concordia Civics (1946–47); Montreal Nationale (1947–51); Montreal Royals (1948–50); Laval Nationale (1949–50)

- Led QJHL in goals (52) and points (86) in 1949–50

- QJHL First All-Star Team Right Wing (1949, 1950, 1951)

- Signed as a free agent by Montreal, February 14, 1951

- Second player in NHL history to score 50 goals in the regular season (1960–61)

- Led NHL in goals (38) and points (75) in 1954–55, goals (50) and points (95) in 1960–61

- Led NHL playoffs in goals (6) in 1952–53; led NHL playoffs in goals (11) and points (18) in 1956–57; led NHL playoffs in assists (10) and points (12) in 1959–60

- Claimed on waivers by N.Y. Rangers from Montreal, June 9, 1966

- Coached Quebec Aces (1964–66)

- Coached N.Y. Rangers (1968–69); coached Atlanta Flames (1972–75); coached Montreal Canadiens (1979–80)

- Son-in-law of Hall of Fame member Howie Morenz, father of Danny Geoffrion and grandfather of Blake Geoffrion—the only four-generation family in NHL history

# The Slap Shot Personified

t is not uncommon for athletes to have nick-names, but for an athlete to have a name so perfect that it immediately calls to mind their aura and greatness, that is rare. Sports fans the world over know "Sweetness," "The Bambino," "The Great One" and "The Golden Bear," and, many fans also know "Boom Boom."

That's the nickname Bernie Geoffrion went by from the late 1940s, when the *Montreal Star*'s Charlie Boire asked Geoffrion, then a young sensation with the Laval Nationale of the Quebec Junior Hockey League, if he could apply the moniker. At the time Geoffrion was pioneering the use of the slap shot, something he said he invented as a child. Boire's use of the nickname was in homage to Geoffrion's novel and powerful shot, the idea being that "Boom" was the sound of the puck leaving Geoffrion's stick, and the second "Boom" was the sound of the puck hitting the boards, thus "Boom Boom."

After 18 impressive games in 1950–51, Geoffrion put the NHL on notice in his official rookie season of 1951–52. He played 67 games during that campaign and led the Canadiens with 30 goals. For his efforts he was named the Rookie of the Year. In 1954–55 he led the NHL in goal scoring, with 38, and was the Art Ross Trophy recipient with 75 points.

With Geoffrion a key part of the lineup, the Canadiens proceeded to win an

**Ab McDonald, Ralph Backstrom and Bernie Geoffrion celebrate after Game 4 of the 1959 Stanley Cup final. Montreal won the Cup in five games.**

unprecedented five consecutive Stanley Cups (1955–56 to 1959–60). Boom Boom averaged 1.38 points per game over those five playoff runs, and twice (1956–57 and 1959–60) he was the top scorer in the playoffs. Although the Canadiens didn't make it six in a row, Boom Boom played well enough in 1960–61 to win the Art Ross Trophy and the Hart Trophy as the league's MVP; that season he also became the second player in NHL history to score 50 goals in a single season.

Curiously, Boom Boom left the NHL in 1964 to coach the minor pro Quebec Aces—the idea being he would one day coach the Canadiens. But when plans changed, Geoffrion came out of retirement and played two more seasons with the New York Rangers. It wasn't a fairy-tale ending, but it was on his terms, and for that Boom Boom was happy.

**189**

# 7 Rod Gilbert 1982

NO. RETIRED BY
NEW YORK RANGERS

**ALTERNATE:**
**16**

New York Rangers

Shoots: Right

Height: 5'-9"

Weight: 180 lbs.

Born: July 1, 1941;
Montreal, Quebec

Played 18 NHL seasons
from 1960–78

Stats: See page 447

"I would have loved to have played on a Stanley Cup winner; that's for sure. But I had my share of thrills and, in a lot of ways, I was very lucky guy considering my dream of making the NHL and being able to do what I did with all those back problems."

**AWARDS**

Bill Masterton Memorial Trophy (1976)

**ALL-STAR SELECTIONS**

First All-Star Team Right Wing (1972)

Second All-Star Team Right Wing (1968)

**INTERNATIONAL AWARDS**

Summit Series (1972)

- Held NHL record for most shots on goal in a single game (16); surpassed by Ray Bourque (19), March 21, 1991

- Holds N.Y. Rangers team records for career seasons (18), goals (406) and points (1,021)

- Played amateur hockey with Guelph Biltmores (1957–60); Guelph Royals (1960–61)

- Led OHA-Jr. in goals (54) and points (103) in 1960–61

- OHA-Jr. First All-Star Team Right Wing (1961)

- Played minor pro hockey with Trois-Rivières Lions (1959–60); Kitchener-Waterloo Beavers (1961–62)

- Member of N.Y. Rangers' famed GAG (Goal-a-Game) Line with Jean Ratelle and Vic Hadfield

- Registered 1,000th career NHL point in N.Y. Rangers' 5–2 loss to N.Y. Islanders, February 19, 1977

- First player in N.Y. Rangers history to have his number retired, October 14, 1979

- Recorded one goal and four points in 1972 Summit Series, including key assist on Bill White's tying goal in second period of Game 8

- Hampered by back troubles most of his career, he underwent delicate spinal fusion surgery in 1961 and again in 1965

- Officially announced retirement, December 6, 1977

# Billy Gilmour 1962

"Billy Gilmour is easily the finest stickhandler on the Ottawa professional squad."

— *Ottawa Citizen*, December 24, 1908

McGill Redmen
Montreal Victorias
Ottawa Senators
Ottawa Silver Seven

Shoots: Unknown

Height: Unknown

Weight: Unknown

Born: March 21, 1885: Ottawa, Ontario

Died: March 13, 1959: Montreal, Quebec

Played eight elite amateur and professional seasons from 1902–09, 1915–16

Stats: See page 447

- Played amateur hockey with Ottawa Aberdeens (1900–02)
- Member of prominent Ottawa family that featured brothers Dave and Suddy Gilmour, who also played for Ottawa's famed "Silver Seven"
- Played as an amateur throughout the majority of his career
- Member of Stanley Cup–winning Ottawa "Silver Seven" while playing hockey and studying engineering at McGill University (1902–03, 1903–04, 1904–05)
- MCHL First All-Star Team Right Wing (1907); ECAHA First All-Star Team Right Wing (1908); ECHA First All-Star Team Right Wing (1909)

- Led ECHA in penalty minutes (74) in 1908–09
- Did not play hockey after 1908–09 until making brief comeback during the 1915–16 season
- Signed as a free agent by Ottawa Senators, January 15, 1916
- Scored final goal of his career against future Hockey Hall of Fame member Georges Vezina in Ottawa's 5–2 victory over Montreal Canadiens, January 15, 1916
- Enlisted in Canadian Army for service in World War I (1916)

**AWARDS**

Stanley Cup (1902–03, 1903–04, 1904–05, 1908–09)

**191**

# 8

# Shorty Green 1962

ALTERNATES:

## 16 · 6

**Hamilton Tigers
New York Americans
Sudbury Wolves**

Shoots: Right

Height: 5'-10"

Weight: 152 lbs.

Born: July 17, 1896;
Sudbury, Ontario

Died: April 19, 1960;
Sudbury, Ontario

Played nine elite
amateur and NHL
seasons from 1918–27

Stats: See page 448

"Professional hockey is a money-making affair. The promoters are in the game for what they can make out of it and the players wouldn't be in the game if they didn't look at matters in the same light."

- Played amateur hockey with Sudbury All-Stars (1914–16); Hamilton 227th (1916–17); Hamilton Tigers (1918–19); Sudbury Wolves (1919–23)

- Led OHA-Sr. in playoff goals (5) and points (8) in 1918–19; led Northern Ontario Hockey Association in goals (23) and points (27) in 1919–20

- Served overseas in World War I and was injured in a gas attack, prompting his return to Canada in December of 1918

- Member of Allan Cup–winning Hamilton Tigers (1919), scoring three goals in Hamilton's 7–6 two-game, total-goal series win over the Winnipeg Selkirks

- Captain of the Hamilton Tigers when the team went on strike before the playoffs to protest not receiving extra pay for post-season play. The entire team was suspended by NHL president Frank Calder and the franchise was relocated to New York and renamed the Americans before the start of the 1925–26 season

- Scored first goal in history of Madison Square Garden in N.Y. Americans 3–1 loss to the Montreal Canadiens, December 15, 1925

- Suffered a career-ending kidney injury in game against N.Y. Rangers, February 28, 1928. Green had his kidney removed and was administered the last rites before recovering

- Brother of Redvers "Red" Green, who played in NHL with Hamilton, N.Y. Americans, Boston and Detroit Cougars from 1923–29

# 1969 Bryan Hextall

# 12

> "He was the hardest bodychecking forward I had seen in more than forty years of watching hockey."
>
> —Herb Goren, *N.Y. Sun* reporter

**ALTERNATES**

**19 · 15**

**New York Rangers**

Shoots: Left

Height: 5'-10"

Weight: 180 lbs.

Born: July 31, 1913: Grenfell, Saskatchewan

Died: July 25, 1984: Portage la Prairie, Manitoba

Played 11 NHL seasons from 1936–44, 1945–48

Stats: See page 448

- Played amateur hockey with Winnipeg Monarchs (1931–32); Portage Terriers (1932–34); Vancouver Lions (1933–36); St. Catharines Saints (1944–45); Poplar Point Memorials (1949–52, 1953–54)

- Led MJHL in assists (8) and points (18) in 1932–33

- Played minor pro hockey with Philadelphia Ramblers (1936–37); Cleveland Barons (1948–49); Washington Lions (1948–49)

- Led NWHL in goals (29) in 1935–36; led IAHL in goals (27) in 1936–37

- Led NHL in goals in 1939–40 (24) and 1940–41 (26); led NHL in points (56) in 1941–42

- Scored Stanley Cup–winning overtime goal in N.Y. Rangers' 3–2 victory over Toronto Maple Leafs, April 13, 1940

- Renowned for great speed, puckhandling ability and toughness

- Coached Saint Boniface Canadiens (1952–53); served as player/coach of Minnedosa Jets (1954–56)

- Father of Bryan Hextall Jr., who played in NHL with N.Y. Rangers, Pittsburgh, Atlanta Flames, Detroit and Minnesota North Stars from 1962–63, 1970–76

- Father of Dennis Hextall, who played in NHL with N.Y. Rangers, L.A. Kings, California, Minnesota North Stars, Detroit and Washington from 1967–80

- Grandfather of Ron Hextall, who played in NHL with Philadelphia, Quebec and N.Y. Islanders from 1986–99

**AWARDS**

NHL Scoring Leader (1942)

Stanley Cup (1939–40)

**ALL-STAR SELECTIONS**

First All-Star Team Right Wing (1940, 1941, 1942)

Second All-Star Team Right Wing (1943)

# 9

## RIGHT WING

# Gordie Howe 1972

NO. RETIRED BY DETROIT
ALTERNATE:

## 17

Detroit Red Wings
Hartford Whalers
Houston Aeros
New England Whalers

Shoots: Right

Height: 6'

Weight: 205 lbs.

Born: March 31, 1928:
Floral, Saskatchewan

Died: June 10, 2016:
Sylvania, Ohio

Played 32 NHL and
WHA seasons from
1946–1971, 1973–1980

Stats: See page 448

### AWARDS

Art Ross Trophy
(1951, 1952, 1953,
1954, 1957, 1963)

Hart Memorial Trophy
(1952, 1953, 1957,
1958, 1960, 1963)

Lester Patrick
Trophy (1967)

Stanley Cup
(1949–50, 1951–52,
1953–54, 1954–55)

### ALL-STAR SELECTIONS

First All-Star Team
Right Wing (1951,
1952, 1953, 1954, 1957,
1958, 1960, 1963, 1966,
1968, 1969, 1970)

Second All-Star Team
Right Wing (1949, 1950,
1956, 1959, 1961, 1962,
1964, 1965, 1967)

"You've got to love
what you're doing.
If you love it, you
can overcome any
handicap or the
soreness or all the
aches and pains, and
continue to play for a
long, long time."

- Played amateur hockey with
  Saskatoon Jr. Lions (1943–44); Galt
  Red Wings (1944–45)

- USHL Second All-Star Team Right
  Wing (1946)

- Scored first NHL goal in first NHL
  game in Detroit's 3–3 tie with Toronto
  Maple Leafs, October 16, 1946

- Scored Stanley Cup–winning goal in
  Detroit's 3–1 victory over Montreal
  Canadiens, April 14, 1955

- Holds NHL record for seasons played
  (26) from 1946–1971, 1979–80; holds
  NHL record for career games played
  (1,767)

- Holds NHL record for goals (801)
  by a right wing, trailing only Wayne
  Gretzky on the all-time list

- Ranks fourth all time in the NHL in
  points (1,850) and ranks ninth in
  assists (1,049)

- Registered 2,000th professional point
  in Houston Aeros' 8–0 victory over
  Winnipeg Jets, March 27, 1975

- Named WHA Most Valuable Player
  (1974); WHA First All-Star Team Right
  Wing (1974, 1975)

- Played on a line with sons Mark and
  Marty in an NHL game in Hartford's
  4–4 tie with Detroit Red Wings, March
  12, 1980

- Brother of Vic Howe, who played in
  NHL with N.Y. Rangers from 1950–54

- Signed a one-game contract with
  IHL's Detroit Vipers and played a
  single shift to become hockey's first
  six decade player, October 3, 1997

# The Second Career

As the only man to play big-league hockey in five different decades, Gordie Howe—a.k.a. "Mr. Hockey"—built a massive memory bank of exceptional moments.

"But the day I first stepped on the ice professionally with the boys had to be the biggest thrill," Howe recalled in a 1977 interview, adding, "There is no way I can possibly relate to people how it felt."

The chance to play for the Houston Aeros alongside Marty and Mark, his two eldest sons, in the World Hockey Association's (WHA) second season of 1973–74 pulled Howe out of a two-year retirement, which seemed premature even at the age of 43.

Two years before retiring he had scored 103 points with the NHL's Detroit Red Wings, but recurring wrist problems had forced him to move from the ice to the team's front office in 1971. His career in Detroit saw him win four Stanley Cups, six Hart Trophies and six Art Ross Trophies, and he posted a phenomenal run of 20 straight seasons in which he finished no lower than fifth in NHL scoring.

Howe was almost universally regarded as the best to have ever played the game, but he felt that he was being underused and underappreciated by the Wings after his retirement. So when the chance came to play with 19-year-old Marty and 18-year-old Mark, he jumped at it.

"How many [players], when they go on a road trip, get to take half their family with them?" Howe would later recall with great enjoyment.

Howe underwent wrist surgery in order to play with the Aeros, and the team immediately became one of the league's flagship franchises. Houston won their only two Avco

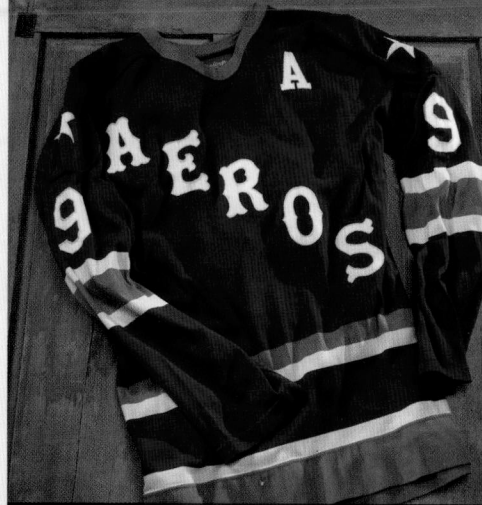

**Gordie Howe wore this Houston Aeros jersey when he came out of retirement in 1973 to play with his sons Mark and Marty in the World Hockey Association.**

Cups as WHA champions in the trio's first two seasons with the team. The family patriarch registered 31 goals and 100 points his first year in Texas, winning the Gary L. Davidson Award as the league's Most Valuable Player. The next season the award was renamed in his honor. Mark, meanwhile, was the Rookie of the Year.

Howe had 369 points in four years with Houston before the family moved to the New England Whalers in 1977–78 for the final two years of the WHA. After the Whalers were included in the WHA's 1979 merger with the NHL, Howe, now 51, played his final NHL season, scoring 15 goals and 41 points nine years after he had originally retired from the league.

# 16

# Brett Hull 2009

NO. RETIRED BY ST. LOUIS

**ALTERNATES:**

## 17 · 22
## 9 · 15

Calgary Flames
Dallas Stars
Detroit Red Wings
Phoenix Coyotes
St. Louis Blues

Shoots: Right

Height: 5'-11"

Weight: 203 lbs.

Born: August 9, 1964;
Belleville, Ontario

Drafted by the
Calgary Flames 117th
overall in 1984

Played 20 NHL seasons
from 1985–2004,
2005–06

Stats: See page 449

**AWARDS**

Lady Byng Memorial
Trophy (1990)

Hart Memorial
Trophy (1991)

Ted Lindsay Award*
(1991)

Stanley Cup
(1998–99, 2001–02)

**ALL-STAR
SELECTIONS**

First All-Star Team Right
Wing (1990, 1991, 1992)

**INTERNATIONAL
AWARDS**

World Cup (1996)

Silver Medal: Winter
Olympics (2002)

*Known as the Lester
B. Pearson Award
from 1971 to 2009

"The game almost picked me.
I didn't pick the game."

- Holds NHL record for career playoff power-play goals (38); holds NHL record for goals in a single season by right wing (86), established in 1990–91

- Shares NHL record (with Wayne Gretzky) for career playoff game-winning goals (24)

- Holds St. Louis Blues team record for career goals (527); holds St. Louis Blues team record for goals (86) and points (131) in a single season

- Ranks fourth in NHL career goals (741); second in NHL career power-play goals (265); tied for fourth in NHL career game-winning goals (110); ranks ninth in NHL career shots on goal (4,876)

- Scored Stanley Cup–winning overtime goal in Dallas' 2–1 victory over Buffalo Sabres, June 19, 1999

- Played amateur hockey with North Shore Winter Club (1981–82); Penticton Knights (1982–84); University of Minnesota-Duluth (1984–86)

- Played minor pro hockey with Moncton Golden Flames (1986–87); AHL First All-Star Team Right Wing (1987); named AHL Rookie of the Year (1987)

- Became fifth player in NHL history (with Maurice Richard, Mike Bossy, Wayne Gretzky and Mario Lemieux) to score 50 goals in 50 or fewer games, January 25, 1991

- Led NHL in goals in 1989–90 (72); 1990–91 (86) and 1991–92 (70); led NHL in power-play goals in 1989–90 (27), 1990–91 (29) and 1993–94 (25)

- Led NHL in game-winning goals in 1989–90 (12), 1990–91 (11) and 1998–99 (11); led NHL in shots-on-goal in 1989–90 (385), 1990–91 (389) and 1991–92 (408)

# Like Father, Like Son

**W**ith heredity on his side, Brett Hull was born to score goals. But the Calgary Flames—who drafted him 117th overall in 1984 and shuttled him between the minors and the NHL during his brief tenure with the team—had trouble seeing his innate brilliance. They traded the 23-year-old "Golden Brett" to the St. Louis Blues in March 1988.

Hull wore sweater No. 16 with St. Louis—the same number his famous father, Bobby "The Golden Jet," had worn during his first four seasons with the Chicago Black Hawks—and made it synonymous with the Hull name once again.

In his first full season with the Blues, Hull scored 41 goals. The next fall, center Adam Oates arrived in St. Louis from the Detroit Red Wings, and the pair became prolific. Oates' creativity in getting Hull the puck resulted in the Golden Brett notching 72 goals, making him the first player to record 50 or more goal seasons in the National Collegiate Athletic Association (52, with the University of Minnesota-Duluth in 1986), the American Hockey League (50, with the Moncton Golden Flames in 1987) and the NHL. Hull also won the Lady Byng Memorial Trophy that season.

In 1990–91 Oates had 90 assists and Hull scored 86 goals, the third-highest total ever recorded and the single-season record for goals by a right winger. He won the Hart Memorial Trophy as the league's Most Valuable Player, and his 131 points set a Blues franchise record that still stands. And even though Oates was traded late in the 1991–92

**Brett Hull, known as his father was for a wicked shot, unloads during the 1999–2000 Stanley Cup final.**

season, Hull still scored 70 times. It was his third straight season with 70 or more goals and the second straight year that he scored his first 50 goals within his first 50 games, making him the only player other than Wayne Gretzky to do so in back-to-back years.

In Hull's 11 seasons in St. Louis, the Blues never advanced past the conference semifinals, and in 1998–99 he signed with the Dallas Stars and scored what many consider to be the most controversial Stanley Cup–winning goal ever. It came against the Buffalo Sabres' Dominik Hasek in the third overtime of Game 6 of the final and gave the Stars their first Stanley Cup championship. Hull would win one more Cup with Detroit in 2002, and he retired in 2005 as the third-highest scorer in NHL history.

# 4 Harry Hyland 1962

ALTERNATES:

## 7 · 9

Montreal Shamrocks
Montreal Wanderers
New Westminster
Royals
Ottawa Senators

Shoots: Right

Height: 5'-6"

Weight: 156 lbs.

Born: January 2, 1889:
Montreal, Quebec

Died: August 8, 1969:
Montreal, Quebec

Played 10 professional
seasons from 1908–18

Stats: See page 449

"A fast skater and a powerful accurate shot, Hyland was a high scorer and dominant figure with [the Montreal Wanderers]."

— *Montreal Gazette,*
August 9, 1969

AWARDS
Stanley Cup (1909–10)

ALL-STAR
SELECTIONS
PCHA First All-Star Team
Right Wing (1912)

- Played amateur hockey with Montreal Shamrocks (1906–09)

- Led Montreal Shamrocks in goals (19) as an ECHA rookie (1908–09)

- Scored two goals in professional debut in Montreal Wanderers' 9–8 victory over Quebec Bulldogs, January 2, 1909

- Led Montreal Wanderers in goals (24) in 1909–10

- Signed as a free agent by New Westminster, November 12, 1911

- Finished second in PCHA in goals (26) in 1911–12

- Won national championship in lacrosse with New Westminster Salmonbellies (1912)

- Scored eight goals in Montreal Wanderers' 10–6 victory over Quebec Bulldogs, January 25, 1913

- Coached Montreal Shamrocks (1913–14) while engaged in contract dispute with Montreal Wanderers

- Scored five goals in Montreal Wanderers' 10–9 victory over Toronto Arenas on the first night in NHL history, December 19, 1917

- Claimed by Ottawa Senators in NHL Dispersal Draft after Montreal Wanderers club folded, January 4, 1918

# Jari Kurri

2001

# 17

NO. RETIRED BY EDMONTON

**Colorado Avalanche**
**Edmonton Oilers**
**Los Angeles Kings**
**Mighty Ducks**
**of Anaheim**
**New York Rangers**

Shoots: Right

Height: 6'

Weight: 194 lbs.

Born: May 18, 1960:
Helsinki, Finland

Drafted by the
Edmonton Oilers 69th
overall in 1980

Played 17 NHL seasons
from 1980–90, 1991–98

Stats: See page 450

"It took me a year to get to know the league, the systems and just being away from the old country, my parents and friends. It's not just the hockey that's different but a whole different lifestyle."

— Jari Kurri, on adjusting to the NHL

- First European-born and trained player in NHL history to record 500 career goals, October 17, 1992

- Shares NHL record (with Reggie Leach) for goals in a single playoff year (19), established in 1984–85

- Ranks fourth in NHL goals (601) and assists (797) by a European-trained player; ranks third in NHL points (1,398) by a European-trained player

- Ranks sixth in NHL short handed goals (39)

- Played amateur hockey with Jokerit Helsinki-Jr. (1974–80)

- Scored Stanley Cup–winning goal in Edmonton's 3–1 victory over Philadelphia Flyers, May 31, 1987

- Played in NHL All-Star Game (1983, 1985, 1986, 1988, 1989, 1990, 1993, 1998)

- World Championships All-Star Team (1991, 1994)

- Played with Milano Devils (Italy) in 1990–91

- Led NHL in game-winning goals in 1984–85 (13) and 1985–86 (9); led NHL in goals (68) in 1985–86; led NHL in shooting percentage (28.8%) in 1985–86; finished second in NHL goals (71) in 1984–85; finished second in NHL points in 1984–85 (135) and 1986–87 (108); finished second in NHL plus/minus (plus-76) in 1986–87

- Played for Team Finland in 1980 Olympics, 1981 Canada Cup Tournament, 1982 World Championships, 1989 World Championships, 1991 Canada Cup Tournament, 1991 World Championships, 1994 World Championships, 1997 World Cup and 1998 Olympics

**AWARDS**
Lady Byng Memorial
Trophy (1985)
Stanley Cup (1983–84,
1984–85, 1986–87,
1987–88, 1989–90)

**ALL-STAR
SELECTIONS**
First All-Star Team Right
Wing (1985, 1987)
Second All-Star
Team Right Wing
(1984, 1986, 1989)

**INTERNATIONAL
AWARDS**
Silver Medal: World
Championships (1994 )
Bronze Medal: Winter
Olympics (1998)

**199**

## RIGHT WING

# 10 Guy Lafleur 1988

NO. RETIRED BY MONTREAL

**Montreal Canadiens**
**New York Rangers**
**Quebec Nordiques**

Shoots: Right

Height: 6'

Weight: 185 lbs.

Born: September 20, 1951: Thurso, Quebec

Drafted by the Montreal Canadiens first overall in 1971

Played 17 NHL seasons from 1971–85, 1988–91

Stats: See page 450

> "Go ahead, work hard and never be afraid to try something. Even if you don't make it, at least you can say you tried."

**AWARDS**

Art Ross Trophy (1976, 1977, 1978)

Conn Smythe Trophy (1977)

Hart Memorial Trophy (1977, 1978)

Ted Lindsay Award* (1976, 1977, 1978)

Stanley Cup (1972–73, 1975–76, 1976–77, 1977–78, 1978–79)

**ALL-STAR SELECTIONS**

First All-Star Team Right Wing (1975, 1976, 1977, 1978, 1979, 1980)

**INTERNATIONAL AWARDS**

Canada Cup (1976)

*Known as the Lester B. Pearson Award from 1971 to 2009

○ First player in NHL history to score at least 50 goals and register at least 100 points in six consecutive seasons (1974–80)

○ Holds Montreal Canadiens' team record for career assists (728) and points (1,246); holds Montreal Canadiens' team record for points in regular season (136), established in 1976–77; shares Montreal Canadiens' team record (with Steve Shutt) for goals in regular season (60), established in 1977–78

○ Played amateur hockey with Quebec Aces (1966–69); Quebec Remparts (1969–71)

○ Member of Memorial Cup–winning Quebec Remparts (1971); led Memorial Cup playoffs in goals (9) and points (14) in 1971

○ Led QMJHL in assists (103) in 1969–70; led QMJHL playoffs in goals (25) and points (43) in 1969–70

○ Led NHL in goals (60) in 1977–78; led NHL in assists (80) in 1976–77; led NHL in points in 1975–76 (125), 1976–77 (136) and 1977–78 (132); led NHL in plus/minus (+73) in 1977–78

○ Led QMJHL in assists (130) and points (209) in 1970–71; led QMJHL playoffs in goals (22), assists (21) and points (43) in 1970–71

○ QMJHL First All-Star Team Right Wing (1970, 1971)

○ Led NHL in game-winning goals in 1974–75 (11), 1975–76 (12), 1977–78 (12) and 1978–79 (12)

○ One of only three players (with Gordie Howe and Mario Lemieux) to play in the NHL after being inducted into the Hall of Fame

○ Played in NHL All-Star Game (1975, 1976, 1977, 1978, 1980, 1991)

○ Scored Stanley Cup–winning goal in Montreal's 5–3 victory over Philadelphia Flyers, May 16, 1976

# Last in a Long Line

The Montreal Canadiens' legacy was seemingly built on a string of star players: Howie Morenz was Montreal's first superstar, and he was followed ably by Maurice Richard, who was then succeeded by Jean Béliveau—Hall of Famers all. But who would follow Béliveau?

Montreal didn't have a surefire answer, but general manager Sam Pollock had designs on nabbing Quebec junior sensation Guy Lafleur in the 1971 draft.

**Guy Lafleur and Steve Shutt salute fans during Montreal's 1976 Stanley Cup parade.**

It started in 1970, when Pollock sent Montreal's first-round draft pick to the Oakland Seals (which ended up being the 10th overall selection, Chris Oddleifson) along with minor-pro player Ernie Hicke (whose brother, 20-goal man Bill Hicke, played for the Seals) in exchange for François Lacombe and a first-round draft choice in 1971. The Seals' consistently poor play essentially assured Montreal of having one of the earliest picks in the draft. But as the 1970–71 season went on, the Los Angeles Kings looked like they would supplant Oakland as the NHL's worst team. Pollock then sent center Ralph Backstrom to the Kings for two perennial minor leaguers. That acquisition sparked LA to a strong stretch drive, leaving the Seals in last place.

With the first pick in the 1971 draft, Montreal happily plucked Lafleur and tabbed him as their heir apparent.

The transition wasn't immediate, but in his fourth year, 1974–75, Lafleur exploded with 119 points, 55 more than his previous best. He earned both the Art Ross Trophy and the Lester B. Pearson Award (known since 2010 as the Ted Lindsay Award) the next three seasons

(1975–76 to 1977–78) and the Hart Trophy in 1976–77 and again in 1977–78, and he was named to the NHL's First All-Star Team six straight seasons (1974–75 to 1979–80). During his 14 seasons in Montreal, Lafleur reached the 60-goal mark once, bettered the 50-goal mark six times and scored more than 20 goals 13 times. With Lafleur at his peak, the Canadiens won the Stanley Cup in 1973, 1976, 1977, 1978 and 1979; in 1977 he was named playoff MVP.

But during the 1984–85 season, Lafleur's productivity declined drastically as he clashed with new coach and former teammate Jacques Lemaire. Clearly disgruntled, 19 games into the 1984–85 season Lafleur retired.

But he still had something left to give, and in 1988–89 he made an NHL comeback, playing parts of three seasons with the New York Rangers and the Quebec Nordiques. He scored sparingly but enjoyed the game and retired fully satisfied in 1991. As for Montreal, it is fair to say no player has been able to pick up the torch from Lafleur.

# 24

# Sergei Makarov 2016

ALTERNATES:
## 42

Calgary Flames
CSKA Moscow
Dallas Stars
San Jose Sharks

Shoots: Left

Height: 5'-11"

Weight: 185 lbs.

Born: June 19, 1958

Chelyabinsk, Union
of Soviet Socialist
Republics

Drafted by the
Calgary Flames 231st
overall in 1983

Played 7 NHL seasons
from 1989–1995,
1996–97

Stats: See Page 451

"We opened a new era in hockey to the NHL. We were old already in hockey, like 30, when we got to the NHL, but we opened the way for young guys to make it easy for them to get in the NHL."

— Sergei Makarov, on the first wave of Russians to play in the NHL

AWARDS

Calder Memorial
Trophy (1990)

ALL-STAR
SELECTIONS

All-Rookie Team (1990)

INTERNATIONAL
AWARDS

Challenge Cup (1979)

Canada Cup (1981)

Gold Medal: Winter
Olympics (1984, 1988)

Silver Medal: Winter
Olympics (1980)

Gold Medal: World
Championships (1978,
1979, 1981, 1982, 1983,
1986, 1989, 1990)

Silver Medal: World
Championships (1987)

Bronze Medal: World
Championships (1985, 1991)

- Starred on the famous Soviet KLM Line with Vladimir Krutov and Igor Larionov

- In 11 seasons with CSKA Moscow (Central Red Army) from 1978–79 through 1988–89, he won 11 Soviet league championships, led the league in scoring nine times, led the league in goals three times, won the Soviet Player of the Year Award three times, and was named to the Soviet League All-Star Team ten times

- Represented the Soviet national team at 11 World Championships, three Olympic Games, three Canada Cup tournaments, the 1979 Challenge Cup and the 1987 Rendez-Vous tournament; also won gold medals at the World Junior Championships in 1977 and 1978

- Became one of the first Soviet stars permitted to play in the NHL when he joined the Calgary Flames in 1989–90; played the full NHL schedule of 80 games and led all rookies with 62 assists and 86 points

- Won the Calder Trophy in 1990, but because of his age (31) and years of experience in the Soviet Union, the NHL changed the rules about eligibility for the Calder to say that a player had to be under 26

- Re-teamed with Igor Larionov with the San Jose Sharks in 1993–94 and equaled his NHL high (first set with Calgary in 1990–91) with 30 goals

- Was inducted into the International Ice Hockey Federation Hall of Fame in 2001

# The Russian Gretzky

When this great Russian superstar was inducted into the Hockey Hall of Fame in 2016, *Toronto Star* hockey writer Kevin McGran asked the question, "Was Sergei Makarov the greatest hockey player ever?" That's asking a lot… but Makarov was always compared favorably to the very best of his era.

"He was referred to as the Russian Gretzky," said Cliff Fletcher, who drafted Makarov as general manager of the Calgary Flames back in 1983. "Unfortunately he didn't come to the NHL until he was approaching the twilight of his career, but it was amazing what he could do with that puck."

Gary Roberts was a teammate of Makarov in Calgary from 1989 to 1993. A star in his own right and now a leader in hockey training and fitness, Roberts says of Makarov: "People would always say to me, 'Who's the toughest guy in the NHL to get the puck away from?' and I'd answer, 'Jaromir Jagr.' But the other guy was Sergei. Sergei wasn't a tall guy… but he'd play keep-away with us in practice and you couldn't lift his stick up because he was built like a fire hydrant. He protected the puck as well as anyone in the NHL ever has."

During a hugely high-scoring era, Makarov put up decent numbers in his five full NHL seasons—especially considering he was in his 30s and at the tail end of an already spectacular career. However, it is his numbers in the Soviet Union that were truly remarkable. Playing with his KLM linemates

**Sergei Makarov of the Soviet Union digs for a loose puck behind NHL All-Star Grant Fuhr during Game 1 of Rendez-vous '87.**

Vladimir Krutov and Igor Larionov, and often with defensemen Slava Fetisov and Alexei Kasatonov on the five-man Green Unit, Makarov was the offensive go-to guy for both CSKA Moscow in Russian league play and for the Soviet National Team at international events. In 11 seasons with CSKA Moscow, Makarov led the league in scoring nine times. In 13 seasons in the Russian league he had 322 goals and 388 assists for 710 points in just 519 games. In 101 games at the World Championships, Makarov had 56 goals and 67 assists for 123 points. In 22 games at the Olympics had had 11 goals and 17 assists for 28 points. Gretzky-like production, indeed.

## RIGHT WING

# 9 Lanny McDonald 1992

NO. RETIRED BY CALGARY

ALTERNATE:

# 7

Calgary Flames
Colorado Rockies
Toronto Maple Leafs

Shoots: Right

Height: 6'

Weight: 185 lbs.

Born: February 16,
1953: Hanna, Alberta

Drafted by the Toronto
Maple Leafs fourth
overall in 1973

Played 16 NHL seasons
from 1973–89

Stats: See page 451

"My Mom and Dad drove me into Hanna to play hockey. It was so much fun playing the game that not only my father had played, but that my older brother played as well. It was a great way to grow up."

**AWARDS**

Bill Masterton Memorial
Trophy (1983)

King Clancy Memorial
Trophy (1988)

Stanley Cup (1988–89)

**ALL-STAR
SELECTIONS**

Second All-Star Team
Right Wing (1977, 1983)

**INTERNATIONAL
AWARDS**

Canada Cup (1976)

- Played amateur hockey with Lethbridge Sugar Kings (1969–71); Calgary Centennials (1970–71); Medicine Hat Tigers (1971–73)

- Named AJHL Most Valuable Player (1971); AJHL Second All-Star Team Right Wing (1971)

- Led WCJHL in playoff goals (18) in 1972–73; WJCHL First All-Star Team Right Wing (1973)

- Holds Calgary Flames' team record for goals in regular season (66), established in 1982–83

- Played in NHL All-Star Game (1977, 1978, 1983, 1984)

- Led NHL in power-play goals (16) in 1976–77; led NHL in even strength goals (49) in 1982–83

- Scored series-winning overtime goal in Game 7 of Toronto's 2–1 victory over N.Y. Islanders, April 21, 1978

- Finished among NHL top-5 in goals in 1976–77 (46), 1977–78 (47) and 1982–83 (66); finished among NHL top-5 in shots on goal in 1978–79 (314) and 1979–80 (334); finished among NHL top-5 in short handed goals in 1975–76 (3) and 1976–77 (4)

- His distinctive mustache is considered iconic

- His middle name (King) is a tribute to Maple Leaf great King Clancy; inaugural winner of NHL's King Clancy Memorial Trophy (1988)

- Became chairman of Hockey Hall of Fame on March 25, 2015

# Forever a Flame

When Lanny McDonald was traded to the Calgary Flames by the Colorado Rockies in November 1981, he gave the Flames their first real Albertan identity since moving from Atlanta to the Stampede City the previous year.

McDonald, an Alberta boy, had been a star with the Toronto Maple Leafs throughout the 1970s, playing on a powerful line with his best friend, Darryl Sittler. McDonald's overtime goal in Game 7 of the Stanley Cup quarterfinal (scored while he had a broken nose and wrist) lifted the Leafs to an upset of the New York Islanders in the 1978 playoffs; he also drew an assist on

Lanny McDonald hoists the Stanley Cup in 1989.

an overtime goal from Sittler to win the 1976 Canada Cup.

But a feud between Sittler and Leafs general manager George "Punch" Imlach led to the dismissal of McDonald by way of a trade to the lowly Colorado Rockies in late 1979. Imlach's power play, intended to stifle his captain's dissention, prompted Toronto fans to protest outside of Maple Leaf Gardens.

McDonald performed well in Colorado, but it wasn't enough to save the moribund franchise. With a fresh start with a new team that was in a new market, McDonald surged as the star in Calgary. His 66 goals in 1982–83 obliterated the Flames' franchise record as well as his personal best. The club stitched a C onto his No. 9 sweater in 1983, and three years later the Flames made their first Stanley Cup final, losing the 1985–86 title to the Montreal Canadiens.

In the final month of the 1988–89 season, the captain recorded his 1,000th point (March 7 versus the Winnipeg Jets) and scored his 500th goal (March 21 versus the New York Islanders). In the playoffs the Flames narrowly escaped a hard-fought series with the Vancouver Canucks and went on to defeat the Los Angeles Kings and Chicago Blackhawks to again challenge Montreal for the Cup. Although McDonald had been a scratch for Games 3, 4 and 5, coach Terry Crisp dressed him for the Cup-clinching Game 6. McDonald retired after the season, but not before scoring his last NHL goal in the 4–2 Game 6 victory and, as captain, hoisting his and the Flames' only Stanley Cup.

"Winning the Cup for the team in my own backyard, scoring a goal in the last game, winning it in Montreal where they had never lost the Cup on home ice," McDonald marveled, "I don't think it gets any better than that."

# 8

# Bill Mosienko 1965

**Chicago Black Hawks**

Shoots: Right

Height: 5'-8"

Weight: 160 lbs.

Born: November 2, 1921:
Winnipeg, Manitoba

Died: July 9, 1994:
Winnipeg, Manitoba

Played 14 NHL seasons
from 1941–55

Stats: See page 452

"It was quite an accomplishment, I hope [the record] stays. After I scored the third goal, Jim Peters skated up to me and told me to keep the puck because I had set a new record. I was very happy and proud. It was like being on cloud nine."

– Bill Mosienko,
reflecting on
his 3 goals in 21
seconds record

**AWARDS**

Lady Byng Memorial
Trophy (1945)

**ALL-STAR
SELECTIONS**

Second All-Star Team
Right Wing (1945, 1946)

- Scored his first two NHL goals in 21 seconds in Chicago's 4–3 loss to N.Y. Rangers on February 8, 1942

- Holds NHL record for scoring fastest three goals (21 seconds) in a single game, established in Chicago's 7–6 victory over N.Y. Rangers, March 23, 1952

- Played amateur hockey with Winnipeg Sherburn-Juvenile (1938–39) and Winnipeg Monarchs (1939–40)

- Made professional debut with Kansas City Americans (1940–41)

- Right winger on the Pony Line with Max and Doug Bentley

- Played in NHL All-Star Game (1947, 1949, 1950, 1952, 1953)

- Finished among NHL top-5 in goals in 1944–45 (28) and 1951–52 (31)

- Finished among NHL top-5 in points in 1944–45 (54) and 1945 (48)

- WHL Prairie First All-Star Team (1957–59)

- Member of WHL champion Winnipeg Warriors (1956); member of Edinburgh Trophy (top minor professional team in Canada) champion Winnipeg Warriors (1956)

- Led WHL in playoff assists (12) in 1956; led Edinburgh Trophy series in goals (6) in 1956

- Coached WHL's Winnipeg Warriors (1959–61)

- Named Manitoba's Athlete of the Year (1957); inducted into Manitoba Sports Hall of Fame (1980); selected to Manitoba's All-Century First All-Star Team

# 2000 Joseph Mullen

# 7

ALTERNATE:
## 11

**Boston Bruins**
**Calgary Flames**
**Pittsburgh Penguins**
**St. Louis Blues**

Shoots: Right

Height: 5'-9"

Weight: 180 lbs.

Born: February 26, 1957:
New York, New York

Played 17 NHL seasons
from 1979–80, 1981–97

Stats: See page 452

"I could look out my window and see Madison Square Garden, which was half a block up the street from me. We had a schoolyard right across the street from us where we played roller hockey. So, the combination of all that gave me my love for the game."

- First American-born- and-trained player to record 500 goals and 1,000 points
- Played amateur hockey with New York 14 Precinct (1971–72); New York Westsiders (1971–75); Boston College Eagles (1975–79)
- Led NYJHL in goals (110) and points (182) in 1974–75; led NYJHL playoffs in goals (27) and points (37) in 1974–75
- ECAC First All-Star Team Right Wing (1978, 1979); NCAA East First All-American Team (1978, 1979)
- Named CHL Rookie of the Year (1980); named CHL Most Valuable Player (1981); CHL Second All-Star Team Right Wing (1980); CHL First All-Star Team Right Wing (1981)

- Led CHL in playoff goals (9) in 1979–80; led CHL in points (117) in 1980–81
- Played in NHL All-Star Game (1989, 1990, 1994)
- Led NHL playoffs in goals in 1985–86 (12) and 1988–89 (16)
- Nicknamed "Slippery Rock Joe" by Pittsburgh Penguins' broadcaster Mike Lange for his agility and toughness on the ice
- Grew up in the Hell's Kitchen area of New York, where he and younger brother Brian learned to play hockey on roller skates
- Brother of Brian Mullen, who played in NHL with Winnipeg, N.Y. Rangers, San Jose and N.Y. Islanders from 1982–93

**AWARDS**
Lady Byng Memorial Trophy (1987, 1989)

Lester Patrick Trophy (1995)

Stanley Cup (1988–89, 1990–91, 1991–92)

**ALL-STAR SELECTIONS**
First NHL All-Star Team Right Wing (1989)

# 8

# Cam Neely 2005

NO. RETIRED BY BOSTON

ALTERNATE:

## 21

Boston Bruins
Vancouver Canucks

Shoots: Right

Height: 6'-1"

Weight: 218 lbs.

Born: June 6, 1965;
Comox, British Columbia

Drafted by the
Vancouver Canucks
ninth overall in 1983

Played 13 NHL seasons
from 1983–96

Stats: See page 452

> "It meant as much to me to give a big hit as it did to score a big goal. And to leave a mark for being that kind of player is special to me."

AWARDS
Bill Masterton Memorial
Trophy (1994)

ALL-STAR
SELECTIONS
Second All-Star Team
Right Wing (1988,
1990, 1991, 1994)

- Holds Boston Bruins team record for career playoff goals (55) and career playoff power-play goals (24)

- Holds Boston Bruins team record for goals in regular season by a right wing (55), established in 1988–89

- Played amateur hockey with Ridge Meadows Lightning (1981–82); Portland Winter Hawks (1982–84)

- Member of Memorial Cup–winning Portland Winter Hawks (1983); led Memorial Cup tournament in goals (5) in 1983

- Traded to Boston by Vancouver with Vancouver's first round choice (Glen Wesley) in 1987 Entry Draft for Barry Pederson, June 6, 1986

- Led NHL in power-play goals (16) in 1994–95

- Led NHL in shooting percentage (27%) in 1993–94

- Played in NHL All-Star Game (1988, 1989, 1990, 1991, 1996)

- Led NHL in game-winning goals in 1989–90 (12) and 1993–94 (13)

- Only second player (with Phil Esposito) in Boston team history to record back-to-back 50-goal seasons

- Developed a condition called myositis ossificans, which causes abnormal bone formation within deep muscle tissue, forcing his premature retirement

- Made cameo appearances in the movies *Dumb and Dumber*, *Me, Myself and Irene*, and *Stuck on You*

- Became president of the Bruins in June 2010

# 1967 Harry Oliver

# 9

> "When I was a kid, there was no organized hockey. We just went out and played, sometimes on an outdoor rink, but mostly on the river."

ALTERNATES:

# 8 · 10 · 7 6

**Boston Bruins**
**Calgary Tigers**
**New York Americans**

Shoots: Right

Height: 5'-8"

Weight: 155 lbs.

Born: October 26, 1898: Selkirk, Manitoba

Died June 16, 1985: Winnipeg, Manitoba

Played 16 professional seasons from 1921–37

Stats: See page 453

- Played amateur hockey with Selkirk Jr. Fishermen (1915–18); Selkirk Sr. Fishermen (1918–20); Calgary Canadians (1920–21)

- Led WCHL in assists (13) and points (33) in 1924–25

- Inducted in Manitoba Hockey Hall of Fame (1985)

- Nicknamed "Pee-Wee" because of his diminutive size

- Signed as a free agent by Calgary Tigers (WCHL), December 22, 1921

- Traded to Boston by Calgary Tigers (WHL) for cash, September 4, 1926; traded to N.Y. Americans by Boston for cash, November 2, 1934

- Played on a line with scoring ace Frank Fredrickson and Perk Galbraith in Boston

- Scored the opening goal and set up the Stanley Cup–winning goal in Boston's 2–1 victory over the N.Y. Rangers, March 26, 1929

- Played on a line with Art Chapman and Lorne Carr as a member of the N.Y. Americans

- Renowned for his gentlemanly conduct on the ice and impeccable decorum outside of the rink

AWARDS

Stanley Cup (1928–29)

ALL-STAR SELECTIONS

WCHL Second Team All-Star Right Wing (1923, 1924, 1925)

# 5

# Didier Pitre 1962

ALTERNATE:

## 10

American Soo Indians
Les Canadiens
(Montreal)
Montreal Canadiens
Montreal Nationals
Montreal Shamrocks
Renfrew Creamery
Kings
Vancouver Millionaires

Alternate Positions: D/R

Shoots: Right

Height: 5'-11"

Weight: 185 lbs.

Born: September 1, 1883;
Valleyfield, Quebec

Died: July 29, 1934; Sault
Ste. Marie, Michigan

Played 19 professional
seasons from 1904–23

Stats: See page 453

"Pitre earns every cent he gets. He would play until he dropped of sheer exhaustion. I consider him one of the greatest athletes in the country."

— George Kennedy,
Montreal Canadiens
manager, 1917

**AWARDS**

Stanley Cup (1915–16)

**ALL-STAR
SELECTIONS**

IHL First All-Star Team
Right Wing (1906, 1907)

NHA First All-Star Team
Right Wing (1917)

○ Nicknamed "Cannonball" because of his rambunctious and explosive style of play and the sound his shot made when it crashed into the end boards. Also known as "Bullet Shot," "Old Folks" and "Pit"

○ Played amateur hockey with Montreal Nationals (1903–05)

○ First player signed by Jack Laviolette for the new Montreal Canadiens franchise in 1909

○ Led IHL in goals (41) and points (41) in 1905–06

○ Led NHA in assists (15) and points (39) in 1915–16

○ Played 12 seasons of professional lacrosse with the Montreal Nationals

○ One of the fastest skaters of his time, it was said that he could skate as fast backward as he could forward

○ Led NHA in playoff scoring with four goals in five games, including a hat trick against the Pacific Coast Hockey Association's Portland Rosebuds in helping the Montreal Canadiens win the first Stanley Cup in franchise history. The winner's share for winning the Cup in 1916 was $238

○ He was embroiled in numerous contract controversies between professional leagues from coast to coast because of his tendency to jump from league to league

# 2017 Mark Recchi

**8**

"I did what I could on the ice and if it was good enough, it was good enough. I had a wonderful career. I had wonderful teammates."

ALTERNATES:
## 28 · 11 · 18

Atlanta Thrashers
Boston Bruins
Carolina Hurricanes
Montreal Canadiens
Philadelphia Flyers
Pittsburgh Penguins
Tampa Bay Lightning

Shoots: Left

Height: 5'-10"

Weight: 195 lbs.

Born: February 1, 1978: Kamloops, British Columbia

Drafted by the Pittsburgh Penguins 67th overall in 1988

Played 22 NHL seasons from 1988–2004, 2005–2011

Stats: See Page 454

- Is one of only 10 NHL players to win the Stanley Cup with three different teams and one of only eight to win it in three different decades
- Became the oldest player (43) ever to score in a Stanley Cup Final in 2011
- Ranks fifth all-time in the NHL in games played (1,652) and 12th in points (1,533)
- Led the Stanley Cup-champion Pittsburgh Penguins in goals (40), assists (73) and points (113) in 1990–91
- Established career highs with 53 goals and 123 points for the Philadelphia Flyers in 1992–93

- Led the NHL with 63 assists in 1999–2000 and also finished among the top 10 in assists in 1990–91 (73), 1993–94 (67) and 2003–04 (49)
- Finished among the top 10 in points in 1990–91 (113), 1992–93 (123), 1993–94 (107) and 1999-00 (91).
- Played in the NHL All-Star Game seven times (1991, 1993, 1994, 1997–2000); was MVP of the 1997 All-Star Game
- Played for Team Canada at the 1990 and 1993 World Championships in addition to his 1997 gold medal win, and at the 1998 Winter Olympics
- Won the World Junior Championships with Team Canada in 1988

**AWARDS**
Stanley Cup (1990–91, 2005–06, 2010–11)

**ALL-STAR SELECTIONS**
Second All-Star Team Right Wing (1992)

**INTERNATIONAL AWARDS**
Gold Medal: World Championships (1997)

# 9 Maurice Richard 1961

NO. RETIRED BY MONTREAL

ALTERNATE:
## 15

**Montreal Canadiens**

Shoots: Left

Height: 5'-10"

Weight: 170 lbs.

Born: August 4, 1921:
Montreal, Quebec

Died: May 27, 2000:
Montreal, Quebec

Played 18 NHL seasons
from 1942–1960

Stats: See page 455

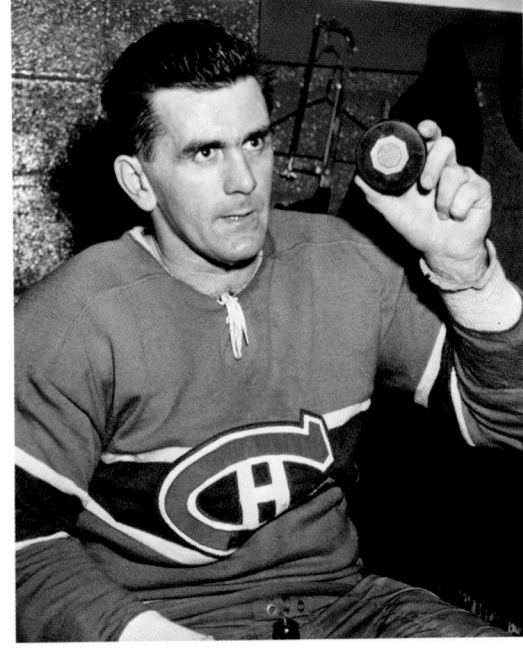

"His dark eyes glowed
like embers as he
bore down on the
opposing goaltender."

— Jack Adams

**AWARDS**

Hart Memorial
Trophy (1947)

Stanley Cup (1943–44,
1945–46, 1952–53,
1955–56, 1956–57,
1957–58, 1958–59,
1959–60)

**ALL-STAR
SELECTIONS**

First All-Star Team
Right Wing (1945,
1946, 1947, 1948, 1949,
1950, 1955, 1956)

Second All-Star Team
Right Wing (1944, 1951,
1952, 1953, 1954, 1957)

- Became first player in NHL history to record 500 career NHL goals in Montreal's 3–1 victory over Chicago Black Hawks, October 19, 1957

- First NHL player to score 50 goals in regular season (1944–45)

- Held NHL record for goals in regular season (50); surpassed by Bobby Hull, March 12, 1966

- Held NHL record for most career regular season goals (544); surpassed by Gordie Howe, November 10, 1963

- Held NHL record for most career regular season points (966); surpassed by Gordie Howe, January 16, 1960

- Shares NHL record for most goals in a single playoff game (5), established in Montreal's 5–1 victory over Toronto Maple Leafs, March 23, 1944

- Held NHL record for career playoff overtime goals (6); surpassed by Joe Sakic, April 24, 2006

- Shares NHL record for most overtime goals in a single playoff season (3), established in 1951

- Played amateur hockey with Verdun Maple Leafs (1938–40); Montreal Paquette Midgets (1938–39); Montreal Sr. Canadiens (1940–42)

- Served as captain of Montreal Canadiens (1956–60)

- Played in 13 consecutive NHL All-Star Games (1947–59)

- Legacy honored by NHL with the creation of the Maurice "Rocket" Richard Trophy, given to the goal-scoring leader during the regular season

# The Rocket's Red Glare

Maurice "Rocket" Richard started out with a different nickname, but the fire in his eyes—a flame that intensified as he approached the net—never, ever changed.

The Rocket's original nickname was "*Le Comet*," but when Montreal Canadiens' center Ray Getliffe remarked that Richard "went in like a rocket" toward the goal, a sportswriter—the *Montreal Star*'s Baz O'Meara and the *Montreal Gazette*'s Dink Carroll are usually given credit—took that observation and made the nickname Richard's forever.

The Canadiens' Jacques Plante said it was the best moniker ever hung on an athlete and liked to quote "The Star-Spangled Banner" line "the rocket's red glare" in reference to Richard's burning eyes.

**Maurice Richard beats Toronto's Harry Lumley during the 1953–54 season.**

It was between 1943–44 and 1944–45 that Richard's legend began to take root. In the opening round of the 1943–44 playoffs he scored all five of Montreal's goals in a Game 2 win against the Toronto Maple Leafs. That season he joined Hector "Toe" Blake and Elmer Lach to form the legendary Punch Line, which in 1944–45 combined for a then-record 220 points. On December 28, 1944, Richard again had five goals (as well as three assists) in a game against the Detroit Red Wings despite having moved his young family into a new home that day. By the end of that 1944–45 season, Richard had become the first NHL player to score 50 goals in a season, doing it in 50 games.

Richard prevailed over several serious injuries, and his determination and tenacity allowed him to become the first NHLer to reach the 500-goal plateau. He played with anger and muscle, and his temper once led him to strike an official, which in turn led to his famous 1955 suspension, which barred him from playing throughout the entire playoffs. The suspension precipitated the infamous St. Patrick's Day riots in Montreal, and Richard himself had to release a public plea to angered fans to stop rioting. His battles with league president Clarence Campbell are often cited as the true seeds of Quebec's Quiet Revolution.

He was so important to Quebec history and culture that at 1996's official closing of the Montreal Forum, the crowd chanted his name for 16 emotional minutes; his provincial funeral in May 2000 was the first ever accorded to a Canadian athlete.

# 8

# Teemu Selanne 2017

NO. RETIRED BY ANAHEIM

**ALTERNATE:**

## 13

Anaheim Ducks
Colorado Avalanche
Mighty Ducks of
Anaheim
San Jose Sharks

Shoots: Right

Height: 6'

Weight: 208 lbs.

Born: July 3, 1970:
Helsinki, Finland

Drafted by the Winnipeg
Jets 10th overall in 1988

Played 21 NHL seasons
from 1992–2004,
2005–2014

Stats: See Page 455

**AWARDS**

Calder Memorial
Trophy (1993)

Maurice Richard
Trophy (1999)

Bill Masterton Memorial
Trophy (2006)

Stanley Cup (2006–07)

**ALL-STAR
SELECTIONS**

First All-Star Team Right
Wing (1993, 1997)

Second All-Star Team
Right Wing (1998, 1999)

**INTERNATIONAL
AWARDS**

Silver Medal: Winter
Olympics (2006)

Bronze Medal: Winter
Olympics (1998, 2010, 2014)

Silver Medal: World
Championships (1999)

Bronze Medal: World
Championships (2008)

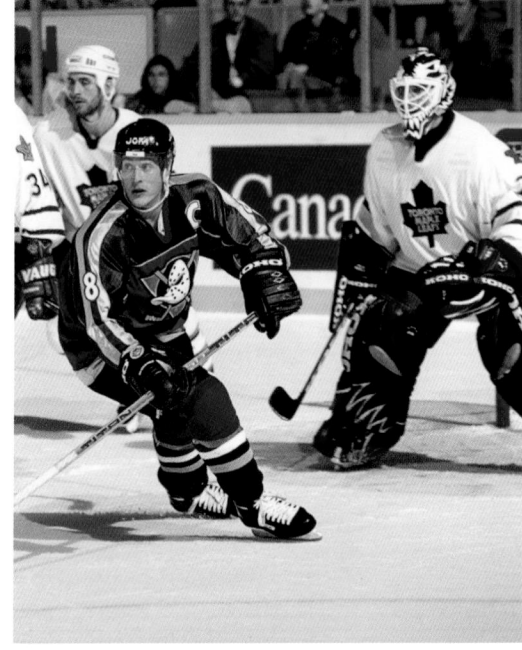

"You keep shooting.
You hope it goes in,
and you smile."

- Shattered Mike Bossy's previous rookie record of 53 goals and shared the NHL lead with Alexander Mogilny with 76 goals in 1992–93; also established a rookie record with 132 points

- Finished second in the NHL behind Keith Tkachuk with 51 goals in 1996–97; was second behind Mario Lemieux with 109 points

- Tied Peter Bondra for the NHL lead in goals in 1997–98 (52); led the NHL in 1998–99 (47)

- Became the oldest player in NHL history (36) to top 45 goals with 48 for Anaheim in 2006–07 and led the Ducks to the Stanley Cup

- Became the oldest player in NHL history to play all 82 games in a season at the age of 41 in 2011–12

- Ranks 11th in NHL history with 684 goals; trails only Jaromir Jagr (766) among players trained in Europe

- Finished among the top 10 in the NHL in goals six times in his career and among the top 10 in points seven times; played in 10 NHL All-Star Games

- Represented Finland at the European Junior Championships in 1988, at the World Junior Championships in 1989, at the World Championships five times, at the Canada Cup in 1991, and at the World Cup of Hockey in 1997 and 2004

- Represented Finland at the Winter Olympics six times; was named best forward in 2006 and Olympic MVP in 2014

- Was named the Finnish ice hockey player of the year a record nine times

# The Finnish Flash
# Sets Rookie Records

"My goal was to play in the top league in Finland," said Teemu Selanne in his Hockey Hall of Fame induction speech in 2017, "and my dream was playing [for] the national team. My fantasy was the NHL. The NHL felt like too far. I didn't believe I was going to ever make it, but all those things happened very, very fast."

Not too fast. Not at first. But then, very fast indeed!

The original Winnipeg Jets selected Selanne tenth overall in the 1988 NHL Draft, but he remained in Finland for four more years, completing his mandatory military service and starring with Jokerit in his hometown of Helsinki. Selanne led the Finnish league with 39 goals in 44 games in 1991–92, but there was nothing to suggest the explosion of goals that was to come when he finally entered the NHL with the Jets in 1992–93.

Selanne's first regular-season game was played in Winnipeg on October 6, 1992. He had two assists in a 4–1 victory over Detroit. He scored his first goal two nights later in a 4–3 loss to the Sharks in San Jose… and he just kept on scoring. Selanne had 11 goals in 12 games in October, had 30 goals in 38 games by January 2, and reached 40 goals in 52 games by the end of that month. Selanne tied Dale Hawerchuk's Jets rookie record with his 45th goal on February 14, but then slumped through three games before netting No. 46.

**Teemu Selanne skates against the Vancouver Canucks during his record-breaking rookie campaign of 1992–93.**

After scoring again in his next game, Selanne netted a season-high four goals in a 7–6 win over the Minnesota North Stars on February 28 to reach 51. He scored 15 seconds into his next game against the Quebec Nordiques on March 2, and then tied Mike Bossy's rookie record with his 53rd at 16:59 of the second period. Selanne then passed Bossy with his hat trick goal at 9:26 of the third. He added 22 more goals over Winnipeg's final 20 games to finish up with 76 goals and 132 points and establish rookie records not likely to be broken any time soon.

"It was unbelievable," Selanne has said of his debut season. "The whole year was like a dream."

# Alf Smith 1962

Kenora Thistles
Ottawa Capitals
Ottawa Hockey Club
Ottawa Senators
Ottawa Silver Seven
Pittsburgh Bankers
Pittsburgh Duquesne
Pittsburgh PAC

Shoots: Right

Height: 5'-7"

Weight: 165 lbs.

Born: June 3, 1873:
Ottawa, Ontario

Died: August 21, 1953:
Ottawa, Ontario

Played 12 elite amateur
and professional
seasons from 1894–97,
1899–1900, 1901–09

Stats: See page 456

"That was the way
Alf Smith played,
all-out and to win. He
made allowances for
inability, but he had
no time or patience
for the athlete who
did not give his best."
— *Ottawa Citizen*,
August 24, 1953

**AWARDS**
Stanley Cup
(1903–04, 1904–05,
1905–06, 1906–07)

- Played amateur hockey with Ottawa HC (1894–99); Ottawa Capitals (1899–1901)

- Renowned for his all-round athletic ability, he played quarterback with Ottawa Rough Rider football club and lacrosse with Ottawa Capitals

- Led AHAC in goals (12) in 1896–97

- Led WPHL in assists (9) and points (20) in 1901–02

- WPHL First All-Star Team Right Wing (1902)

- FAHL Second All-Star Team Right Wing (1905)

- ECAHA Second All-Star Team Right Wing (1907)

- Signed as a free agent by Kenora Thistles, March, 1907

- Served as player/coach of Stanley Cup–winning Ottawa "Silver Seven" team that won and retained championship on eight separate occasions between 1903 and 1906

- Member of Stanley Cup–winning Kenora Thistles team that defeated Brandon Wheat Kings in March, 1907 before losing to Montreal Wanderers

- Coached Renfrew Creamery Kings (1908); coached Pittsburgh Duquesne (1908–09); coached Ottawa Cliffsides (1910–11)

- Coached Montreal Canadiens (1912–13); coached Ottawa Senators (1918–19); coached N.Y. Americans (1925–26)

- Brother of Hall of Fame member Tommy Smith, who played 15 seasons of elite amateur and professional hockey

# 1962 **Barney Stanley**

# 14

> "It is a great source of pleasure to me to have you write as you did about my hockey career and as you say I did have some terrific teammates. I enjoy reading [Charles Coleman's] *The Trail of the Stanley Cup* and relive many moments tabulated therein."
>
> — Barney Stanley, in a letter to a fan

**ALTERNATES:**

# 3 · 4 · 6
# 7 · 8

Calgary Tigers
Chicago Black Hawks
Edmonton Eskimos
Regina Capitals
Vancouver Millionaires
Winnipeg Maroons

Shoots: Left

Height: 6'

Weight: 175 lbs.

Born: January 1, 1893:
Paisley, Ontario

Died: May 16, 1971:
Edmonton, Alberta

Played 14 elite amateur and professional seasons from 1914–28

Stats: See page 456

**AWARDS**

Stanley Cup (1914–15)

**ALL-STAR SELECTIONS**

PCHA Second All-Star Team Right Wing (1918)

WCHL First All-Star Team Right Wing (1922, 1923)

- Played amateur hockey with Edmonton Maritmers (1911–12); Edmonton Dominions (1912–14); Edmonton Albertans (1914–15)

- Signed as free agent by Vancouver Millionaires (PCHA), February, 1915

- Scored five goals and recorded six points in the 1915 Stanley Cup championship series against Ottawa Senators

- Led PCHA in assists (18) in 1916–17

- Signed as a free agent by Calgary Tigers (WCHL), November 30, 1921; traded to Regina Capitals (WCHL) by Calgary Tigers (WCHL) for cash, November 13, 1922

- Signed as a free agent by Chicago Black Hawks and appointed coach, April 4, 1927; coached Chicago Black Hawks (1927–28)

- Signed as a free agent by Edmonton Eskimos (WCHL), November 7, 1924; named playing coach of Winnipeg Maroons (AHA) after resigning position with Edmonton Eskimos (AHA), October 28, 1926

- Coached Edmonton Eskimos (1925–26); coached Winnipeg Maroons (1926–27); coached Edmonton Poolers (1929–31)

- Father of Don Stanley, who won a gold medal at the IIHF World Championships as a member of the Edmonton Mercurys in 1950; uncle of Hall of Fame member Allan Stanley, who won four Stanley Cup championships with the Toronto Maple Leafs in the 1960s

- Scored 171 goals in 320 professional games between 1915 and 1929

- Designed a hockey helmet and presented it at an NHL Board of Governors meeting after Chicago Black Hawk captain Dick Irvin suffered a fractured skull in a game during the 1927–28 season. There was no interest in his creation

**217**

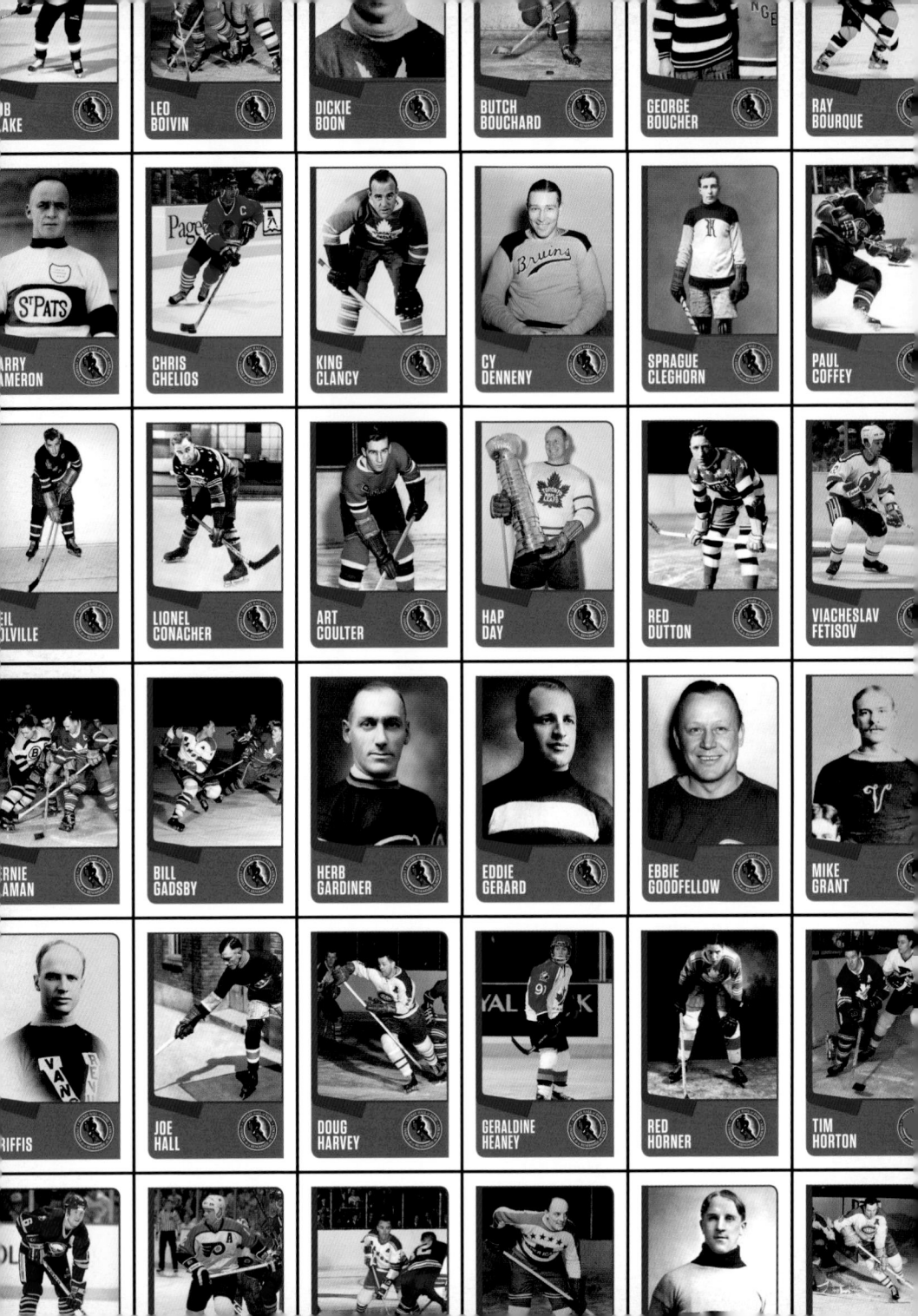

B
AKE

LEO
BOIVIN

DICKIE
BOON

BUTCH
BOUCHARD

GEORGE
BOUCHER

RAY
BOURQUE

RRY
MERON

CHRIS
CHELIOS

KING
CLANCY

CY
DENNENY

SPRAGUE
CLEGHORN

PAUL
COFFEY

EIL
LVILLE

LIONEL
CONACHER

ART
COULTER

HAP
DAY

RED
DUTTON

VIACHESLAV
FETISOV

ERNIE
AMAN

BILL
GADSBY

HERB
GARDINER

EDDIE
GERARD

EBBIE
GOODFELLOW

MIKE
GRANT

IFFIS

JOE
HALL

DOUG
HARVEY

GERALDINE
HEANEY

RED
HORNER

TIM
HORTON

# DEFENSE

Rob Blake  220
Leo Boivin  221
Dickie Boon  222
Butch Bouchard  223
George Boucher  224
Ray Bourque  225
Harry Cameron  227
Chris Chelios  228
King Clancy  229
Dit Clapper  230
Sprague Cleghorn  231
Paul Coffey  232
Neil Colville  233
Lionel Conacher  234
Art Coulter  236
Hap Day  237

Red Dutton  239
Viacheslav Fetisov  240
Fernie Flaman  242
Bill Gadsby  243
Herb Gardiner  244
Eddie Gerard  245
Ebbie Goodfellow  246
Mike Grant  247
Si Griffis  248
Joe Hall  249
Doug Harvey  250
Geraldine Heaney  252
Red Horner  254
Tim Horton  255
Phil Housley  256
Mark Howe  257
Harry Howell  258
Ching Johnson  259
Ernie Johnson  260
Tom Johnson  261
Red Kelly  262
Rod Langway  264
Jacques Laperriere  265
Guy Lapointe  266
Jack Laviolette  267
Brian Leetch  268
Nicklas Lidstrom  270
Al MacInnis  272
Sylvio Mantha  274

Jack Marshall  275
George McNamara  276
Larry Murphy  277
Scott Niedermayer  278
Bobby Orr  280
Brad Park  282
Lester Patrick  284
Pierre Pilote  286
Denis Potvin  288
Babe Pratt  290
Chris Pronger  292
Marcel Pronovost  293
Harvey Pulford  294
Bill Quackenbush  295
Kenny Reardon  296
Larry Robinson  297
Art Ross  298
Angela Ruggiero  300
Jack Ruttan  301
← *Borje Salming*  302
Serge Savard  304
Earl Seibert  305
Eddie Shore  306
Joe Simpson  308
Allan Stanley  309
Scott Stevens  310
Jack Stewart  311
Hod Stuart  312
Phat Wilson  313

## DEFENSE

# 4

# Rob Blake 2014

NO. RETIRED BY
LOS ANGELES

Colorado Avalanche
Los Angeles Kings
San Jose Sharks

Shoots: Right

Height: 6'-4"

Weight: 227 lbs.

Born: December 10,
1969: Simcoe, Ontario

Drafted by the Los
Angeles Kings 70th
overall in 1988

Played 20 NHL
seasons from
1989–2004, 2005–10

Stats: See page 457

> "His slapshot made guys back off. When he was with us on the power play, we definitely got a little more room out there."
>
> — Colorado Avalanche teammate Joe Sakic

## AWARDS

James Norris Memorial Trophy (1998)

Stanley Cup (2000–01)

### ALL-STAR SELECTIONS

All-Rookie Team (1991)

First All-Star Team Defense (1998)

Second All-Star Team Defense (2000, 2001, 2002)

### INTERNATIONAL AWARDS

Gold Medal: Winter Olympics (2002)

Gold Medal: World Championships (1994, 1997)

Silver Medal: World Championships (1991)

- Succeeded Wayne Gretzky as captain of the Los Angeles Kings late in 1995–96, serving through 2000–01 and again in 2007–08

- Also served as captain of the San Jose Sharks in 2009–10

- Helped the Kings reach the Stanley Cup final for the first time in franchise history in 1993

- A six-time winner of the Kings' Most Outstanding Defenseman Award (1990–91 to 1993–94, 1997–98 and 1999–2000) and two-time winner of the team's Most Valuable Player Award (1997–98 and 1999–2000)

- Is the Kings' all-time leader in games played (805), goals (161), assists (333) and points (494) by a defenseman

- Played in NHL All-Star Game (1994, 1999, 2000, 2001, 2002, 2003, 2004)

- Was named Best Defenseman at the 1997 World Championships and 1998 Winter Olympics

- Played three seasons at Bowling Green University, earning CCHA and NCAA West First All-Star Team honors, as well as the award for Best Offensive Defenseman in the CCHA in his final season (1989–90)

# 1986 Leo Boivin

**20**

> "My dream was to win the Stanley Cup, but I never did win it. It's just the way it goes."

ALTERNATES:
**19 · 2 · 5
4 · 18**

**Boston Bruins
Detroit Red Wings
Minnesota North Stars
Pittsburgh Penguins
Toronto Maple Leafs**

Shoots: Left

Height: 5'-8"

Weight: 183 lbs.

Born: August 2, 1932; Prescott, Ontario

Played 19 NHL seasons from 1951–70

Stats: See page 457

- Played amateur hockey with Inkerman Rockets (1948–49); Port Arthur West End Bruins (1949–51)

- Served as captain of Boston Bruins (1963–66)

- Played in NHL All-Star Game (1961, 1962, 1964)

- Traded to Toronto by Boston with Fernie Flaman, Ken Smith and Phil Maloney for Bill Ezinicki and Vic Lynn, November 16, 1950

- Traded to Boston by Toronto for Joe Klukay, November 9, 1954

- Traded to Detroit by Boston with Dean Prentice for Gary Doak, Ron Murphy, Bill Lesuk and future considerations (Steve Atkinson, June 6, 1966), February 16, 1966

- Claimed by Pittsburgh from Detroit in Expansion Draft, June 6, 1967

- Traded to Minnesota by Pittsburgh for Duane Rupp, January 24, 1969

- Served as scout for Minnesota North Stars (1970–72)

- Coached Ottawa 67's (1972–74)

- Served as scout and assistant coach of St. Louis Blues (1974–76, 1978–84)

- Coached St. Louis Blues (1975–76, 1977–78)

- Renowned for his stay-at-home, hard-rock hitting style

- One of several Hall of Fame players who never won a Stanley Cup

# Dickie Boon 1952

Montreal AAA
Montreal Wanderers

Shoots: Right
Height: 5'-5"
Weight: 130 lbs
Born: January 10, 1878:
Belleville, Ontario
Died: May 3, 1961:
Montreal, Quebec
Played six elite amateur
seasons from 1899–1905
Stats: See page 458

"Last year, Dickie was named to the Hockey Hall of Fame, a popular salute by those who remembered him, to a 'Little Man of Iron' who weighed only 115 pounds when he was the game's composite Rocket Richard and Gordie Howe."

—Vern DeGeer,
*Montreal Gazette*,
January 10, 1953

**AWARDS**
Stanley Cup
(1901–02, 1902–03)

- Renowned for his ability to use the poke check to steal pucks from rival players

- Won Junior Amateur Speedskating championship in 1892

- Began playing organized hockey as a 16-year-old in 1894

- Starred on defense for the 1902 Montreal Amateur Athletic Association team that defeated the Winnipeg Victorias in a thrilling three-game series for the Stanley Cup and earned the nickname "Little Men of Iron" for the tenacious way they hung on for a 2–1 victory in the final game

- One of several Montreal AAA stars recruited to join the Montreal Wanderers when the team was formed in 1903–04

- Served as player/manager of Montreal Wanderers (1903–04, 1904–05)

- Manager of Stanley Cup–winning Montreal Wanderers (1905–06, 1906–07, 1907–08, 1909–10)

- Coached Montreal Wanderers (1906–16)

# 1966 Butch Bouchard

# 3

**ALTERNATE:**

# 17

"I was a determined, enthusiastic, young fellow. That's what you need to make a success in life. You work hard, you're enthusiastic, and very disciplined at your game."

**Montreal Canadiens**

Shoots: Right

Height: 6'-2"

Weight: 205 lbs.

Born: September 4, 1919: Montreal, Quebec

Died: April 14, 2012: Longueuil, Quebec

Played 15 NHL seasons from 1941–56

Stats: See page 458

- Played amateur hockey with Verdun Jr. Maple Leafs (1937–39); Verdun Sr. Maple Leafs (1939–40); Montreal Sr. Canadiens (1940–41)

- Played minor pro hockey with AHL's Providence Reds (1940–41)

- Nicknamed "Butch" by a junior teammate who said his last name was similar to the English word butcher

- Served as captain of Montreal Canadiens (1948–56)

- Played in NHL All-Star Game (1947, 1948, 1950, 1951, 1952, 1953)

- Combined with Doug Harvey, the preeminent rushing defenseman of his time, to form one of the top backline pairs in the history of the game

- Renowned for his size, physical play and defensive domination

- Served as president of the Montreal Royals AAA baseball club when the Royals won the Governors' Cup as champions of the International League (1958)

- Served as Municipal Council member for the city of Longueil (1960–62)

- Served as president of Montreal Metropolitan Junior "A" Hockey League (1968)

- Received the National Order of Quebec Chevalier (2008)

- Received the Order of Canada (2009)

- Father of Pierre Bouchard, who played in NHL with Montreal and Washington from 1970 to 1982

**AWARDS**

Stanley Cup (1943–44, 1945–46, 1952–53, 1955–56)

**ALL-STAR SELECTIONS**

First All-Star Team Defense (1945, 1946, 1947)

Second All-Star Team Defense (1944)

# 3

# George Boucher 1960

**ALTERNATES:**

# 9 · 4 · 12
# 15

Chicago Black Hawks
Montreal Maroons
Ottawa Senators

Alternate Position: LW

Shoots: Left

Height: 5'-9"

Weight: 169 lbs.

Born: August 17, 1895
Ottawa, Ontario

Died: October 17, 1960:
Ottawa, Ontario

Played: 17 professional
seasons from 1915–32

Stats: See page 458

> "He is what I know to be an honest player and an honest sportsman. He lifted us off the floor and carried us through the playoffs."
>
> —Dave MacKell, Ottawa Senators president

**AWARDS**

Stanley Cup
(1919–20, 1920–21, 1922–23, 1926–27)

- Played amateur hockey with Ottawa New Edinburghs (1913–15); Ottawa Royal Canadians (1914–15); Montreal La Casquette (1915–16)

- Played running back with Ottawa Rough Riders football club (1913–15)

- Began professional career as a forward with Senators but switched to defense in his third season

- Second in NHL in assists (9) and third in points (22) in 1923–24; second in NHL in penalty minutes (90) in 1924–25

- Coached Montreal Maroons (1930–31); coached Ottawa Senators (1933–34); coached St. Louis Eagles (1934–35)

- Coached Boston Cubs (1932–33)

- Coached Springfield Indians (1936–1938); coached Noranda Eagles (1938–39); coached Quebec Beavers (1939–40); coached Ottawa Senators (1946–49)

- Coached Allan Cup–winning Ottawa Senators (1949)

- Coached Boston Bruins (1949–50)

- Helped assemble and coach Ottawa RCAF team that represented Canada at the 1948 Winter Olympic Games and captured the gold medal

- Renowned for his skills as a puckhandler and puck rusher

- Brother of Bobby Boucher, who played in NHL with Montreal Canadiens in 1923–24; brother of Billy Boucher, who played in NHL with Montreal Canadiens, N.Y. Americans and Boston from 1921–28

- Brother of Hall of Fame member Frank Boucher

# **Ray Bourque** 2004

# 77

> "I loved what I did and I enjoyed the game. I had a passion for it. I think that is what kept me going."

**NO. RETIRED BY BOSTON & COLORADO**

**ALTERNATE:**

**7**

**Boston Bruins**
**Colorado Avalanche**

Shoots: Left

Height: 5'-11"

Weight: 219 lbs.

Born: December 28, 1960: Montreal, Quebec

Drafted by the Boston Bruins eighth overall in 1979

Played 22 NHL seasons from 1979–2001

Stats: See page 459

**AWARDS**

Calder Memorial Trophy (1980)

James Norris Memorial Trophy (1987, 1988, 1990, 1991, 1994)

King Clancy Trophy (1992)

Lester Patrick Trophy (2003)

Stanley Cup (2000–01)

**ALL-STAR SELECTIONS**

First All-Star Team Defense (1980, 1982, 1984, 1985, 1987, 1988, 1990, 1991, 1992, 1993, 1994, 1996, 2001)

Second All-Star Team Defense (1981, 1983, 1986, 1989, 1995, 1999)

**INTERNATIONAL AWARDS**

Canada Cup (1984, 1987)

- Holds NHL records for career points by a defenseman (1,579), career goals by a defenseman (410), career assists by a defenseman (1,169), career playoff assists by a defenseman (139)

- Holds NHL record for most career shots on goal (6,209)

- Holds Boston Bruins team records for career games (1,518), assists (1,111) and points (1,506); holds Boston Bruins team record for career goals (395) by a defenseman

- Ranks fourth in NHL career assists (1,169); ranks 10th in NHL career games (1,612); ranks 11th in NHL career points (1,579)

- Led NHL in shots on goal in 1983–84 (343), 1986–87 (334) and 1994–95 (210)

- Played amateur hockey with Trois-Rivières Draveurs (1976–77); Sorel Eperviers (1976–77); Verdun Eperviers (1977–79)

- QMJHL First All-Star Team Defense (1978, 1979); named QMJHL Defenseman of the Year (1979)

- Played in NHL All-Star Game (1981–86, 1988–94, 1996–01)

- Served as co-captain of Boston Bruins (1985–88); served as captain of Boston Bruins (1988–2000)

- Registered 1,000th career NHL point in Boston's 5–5 tie with Washington Capitals, February 29, 1992

- Officially announced retirement on June 26, 2001, two weeks after finally winning the Stanley Cup

Bourque continued on page 226

# Going out on Top

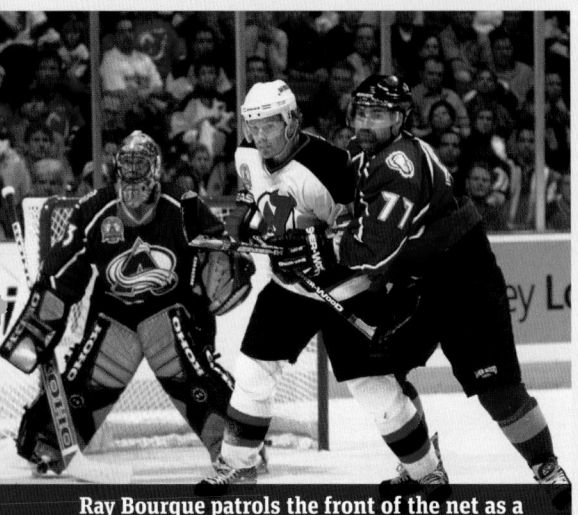

**Ray Bourque patrols the front of the net as a member of the Colorado Avalanche.**

On June 9, 2001, Joe Sakic's Colorado Avalanche beat the New Jersey Devils 3–1 in the seventh game of the Stanley Cup final. But when the Colorado captain accepted the Cup from NHL commissioner Gary Bettman, he ignored the NHL's traditional rhythm and neither hoisted the Cup nor skated it around the arena. Instead, he passed it over to his assistant captain so he could perform those happy rituals. And 22 seasons, 214 playoff games and 1,612 regular-season games after he had entered the NHL, Raymond Bourque was finally holding the Stanley Cup in his talented hands.

Sakic's unselfish move underscored the esteem the entire hockey world held for Bourque, who was an uncommonly complete player with spectacular offensive skills and the most accurate shot in hockey. Originally a centerman, Bourque was switched to defense while still in his youth, but the skills he learned up front helped him to become the NHL career record-holder for goals, assists and points by a defenseman.

The Cup win brought joy to Colorado and even—perhaps especially—to Boston, where Bourque had played for the Bruins for 21 years including 15 as captain, the longest tenure in the franchise's history. He started his career in Boston wearing No. 7, the number made famous in Beantown by none other than the legendary Phil Esposito. During the 1987 Boston Garden ceremony to honor Esposito, Bourque peeled off his sweater to reveal his new No. 77 so that Esposito's famous No. 7 could be retired.

Bourque had endeared himself to Bruins' fans long before that, scoring a goal in his first NHL game, in 1979, and later being named Rookie of the Year. Bourque went on to win five Norris Trophies as the league's top defenseman while in Boston, but the closest he came to the Stanley Cup were losses to the Edmonton Oilers in the 1988 and 1990 finals.

Knowing his chances to win a Cup were coming to a close and that Boston was a long shot, he accepted a trade as a necessary evil. Game 7 of the Stanley Cup final was Bourque's last in uniform and he went out on top, not only with his team but also as an individual. Twenty-two years after he had become the first rookie position player to be selected to the First All-Star Team, he was named a First All-Star again and was runner-up for the Norris Trophy. His No. 77 has been retired by both Colorado and Boston.

# 1962 Harry Cameron

*"Ornery? You bet. Mean? At times. But he was the best when he was at his best."*
— Charlie Querrie

**ALTERNATE:**
**15**

Montreal Canadiens
Montreal Wanderers
Ottawa Senators
Saskatoon Crescents
Toronto Arenas
Toronto Blueshirts
Toronto St. Patricks

Shoots: Right

Height: 5'-10"

Weight: 155 lbs.

Born: February 6, 1890:
Pembroke, Ontario

Died: October 20, 1953:
Vancouver,
British Columbia

Played 14 professional
seasons from 1912–26

Stats: See page 459

- First NHL defenseman to score four goals in a single game twice — in Toronto's 7–5 victory over Montreal Canadiens, December 26, 1917, and Montreal Canadiens' 16–3 victory over Quebec, March 3, 1920

- One of three natives of Pembroke, Ontario (with Frank Nighbor and Hugh Lehman), to be inducted into the Hall of Fame

- Played amateur hockey with Pembroke Debaters (1908–11); Port Arthur Lake City (1911–12)

- Led UOVHL in goals (9) and points (10) in 1910–11; led UOVHL playoffs in assists (4) and points (8) in 1910–11

- Led NHL in assists in 1917–18 (10) and 1921–22 (17)

- Renowned for developing hockey's first curved shot with a straight blade

- One of the original rushing defensemen in the history of the game, noted for end-to-end rushes

- Was believed to be the first player in NHL history to record a goal, assist and fight in the same game, later called the Gordie Howe hat trick, in Toronto's 6–3 loss to Ottawa, December 22, 1920, but the NHL no longer credits him with an assist in that game

- Played minor pro with Saskatoon Sheiks (1926–27), Minneapolis Millers (1927–28), St. Louis Flyers (1928–31) and Saskatoon Crescents (1932–33) after retiring as an NHL player

- Coached Saskatoon Standards (1934–36); coached Saskatoon Quakers (1936–37)

**AWARDS**
Stanley Cup: (1913–14, 1917–18, 1921–22)

**ALL-STAR SELECTIONS**
NHA First All-Star Team Defense (1914)

# DEFENSE

# 24 Chris Chelios 2013

ALTERNATE:
7

Atlanta Thrashers
Chicago Blackhawks
Detroit Red Wings
Montreal Canadiens

Shoots: Right

Height: 6'

Weight: 191 lbs.

Born: January 25, 1962:
Chicago, Illinois

Drafted by the
Montreal Canadiens
40th overall in 1981

Played 26 NHL
seasons from
1983–2004, 2005–10

Stats: See page 460

"There's no reason in the world I should have made the NHL. I always said I'd last until the tank was empty — and I did."

AWARDS
James Norris Memorial
Trophy (1989, 1993, 1996)

Bud Light Plus/Minus
Award (2002)

Mark Messier
Leadership Award (2007)

Stanley Cup (1985–86,
2001–02, 2007–08)

ALL-STAR
SELECTIONS
All-Rookie Team (1985)

First All-Star Team
Defense (1989, 1993,
1995, 1996, 2002)

Second All-Star Team
Defense (1991, 1997)

INTERNATIONAL
AWARDS
World Cup (1996)

Silver Medal: 2002
Winter Olympics

- Holds NHL record for most years in the playoffs (24); holds NHL record for most playoff games (266); holds NHL record for most regular-season games by a defenseman and by an American-born player (1,651)

- Shares (with Gordie Howe) NHL career record for most seasons played (26)

- Played amateur hockey with the Moose Jaw Canucks (1979–81) and the University of Wisconsin (1981–83)

- Selected to WCHA Second All-Star Team (1983) and NCAA Championship All-Tournament Team (1983)

- Holds Montreal Canadiens team records for assists by a rookie (55) and points by a rookie defenseman (64), established in 1984–85

- Holds Chicago Blackhawks single-season team record for assists by a defenseman (58), established in 1992–93 and repeated in 1995–96

- Holds Chicago Blackhawks single-season team record for playoff goals (6) and playoff points (21) by a defenseman, established in 1992

- Ranks second in NHL for assists by a rookie defenseman (55), established in 1984–85; ranks fourth in NHL for regular-season and playoff games (1,917); ranks sixth in NHL for regular-season games (1,651)

- Played in NHL All-Star Game (1985, 1990, 1991, 1992, 1993, 1994, 1996, 1997, 1998, 2000 and 2002)

- One of only two players in hockey history (the other is Mats Sundin) to be selected to Canada Cup (1991) and World Cup (1996) All-Star Teams

- Served as captain of Montreal Canadiens (1989–90) and Chicago Blackhawks (1995–1999)

# 1958 King Clancy

**7**

NO. RETIRED BY TORONTO

ALTERNATE:

**9**

Ottawa Senators
Toronto Maple Leafs

Shoots: Left

Height: 5'-7"

Weight: 155 lbs.

Born: February 25,
1902: Ottawa, Ontario

Died: November 8,
1986: Toronto, Ontario

Played 16 NHL seasons
from 1921–37

Stats: See page 461

"Everybody says I have a gift for the gab and I suppose it's true that I never take a backseat to anyone when it comes to conversation. In fact, a sportswriter once described me as '135 pounds of muscle and conversation.'"

- Played amateur hockey with Ottawa Sandy Hill (1916–17); Ottawa St. Joseph's (1916–17); Ottawa Munitions (1917–18); Ottawa College (1917–18); Ottawa St. Brigands (1918–21)

- Nicknamed "King" because that was his father's nickname

- First defenseman in NHL to score on a penalty shot, established in Toronto's 6–2 victory over Chicago Black Hawks, November 14, 1936

- Only player in NHL history to supposedly play all four positions (defense, forward, rover and goaltender) in a single Stanley Cup playoff game in Ottawa's 1–0 victory over Edmonton Eskimos, March 31, 1923

- Played in NHL All-Star Game (1934, 1937)

- Toronto Maple Leafs owner Conn Smythe used the winnings from the money he bet on one of his horses, Rare Jewel, a 200–1 shot, to buy Clancy from Ottawa for $35,000 plus players Eric Pettinger and Art Smith

- Coached Montreal Maroons (1937–38); coached Cincinnati Mohawks (1949–51); coached Pittsburgh Hornets (1951–53); coached Toronto Maple Leafs (1953–56)

- Served as NHL and AHL official (1938–49)

- Substituted for Punch Imlach as Toronto coach (February 18 to March 11, 1967); substituted for John McLellan as Toronto coach (February 23 to March 22, 1972)

**AWARDS**

Stanley Cup (1922–23, 1926–27, 1931–32)

**ALL-STAR SELECTIONS**

First All-Star Team
Defense (1931, 1934)

Second All-Star Team
Defense (1932, 1933)

# 5 Dit Clapper 1947

NO. RETIRED BY BOSTON

ALTERNATES:

**12 · 3**

**Boston Bruins**

Alternate Position: RW

Shoots: Right

Height: 6'-2"

Weight: 195 lbs.

Born: February 9, 1907;
Newmarket, Ontario

Died: January 21, 1978;
Peterborough, Ontario

Played 20 NHL seasons
from 1927–47

Stats: See page 461

> "Clapper diagnosed the plays like a great infielder in baseball. He put himself where the puck had to come."
>
> —Tiny Thompson, Boston goaltender

**AWARDS**

Stanley Cup (1928–29, 1938–39, 1940–41)

**ALL-STAR SELECTIONS**

First All-Star Team Defense (1939, 1940, 1941)

Second All-Star Team Right Wing (1931, 1935)

Second All-Star Team Defense (1944)

- First player in NHL history to be named to the NHL All-Star Team at two different positions—right wing and defense

- First player in NHL history to play 20 seasons

- One of his given names is Victor, but because of a childhood lisp, his name became Dit

- Played amateur hockey with Toronto (Parkdale) Canoe Club (1925–26) and Boston Tigers (1926–27)

- Traded to Boston Bruins by Boston Tigers (Can-Am) for cash, October 25, 1927

- Played nine seasons on right wing and 11 seasons on defense

- Member of Boston's famed Dynamite Line with Dutch Gainor and Cooney Weiland

- Played in NHL All-Star Game (1937, 1939)

- Well-liked by players and fans throughout the NHL because of the tough way he played the game and his class and character off the ice

- Served as captain of Boston Bruins (1932–38, 1939–47)

- Coached Boston Bruins (1945–49)

- Coached Buffalo Bisons (1959–60)

- Elected to Hockey Hall of Fame immediately after his retirement

- Grandfather of Greg Theberge, who played in NHL with Washington from 1979–84

# 1958 Sprague Cleghorn

# 3

ALTERNATES:

## 2·1

"He typified the old-time, driving hockey player, of which there are too few in the game today."
— Frank Selke

Boston Bruins
Montreal Canadiens
Montreal Wanderers
Ottawa Senators
Renfrew Hockey Club
Toronto St. Patricks

Shoots: Left

Height: 5'-10"

Weight: 190 lbs.

Born: March 11, 1890: Montreal, Quebec

Died: July 12, 1956: Montreal, Quebec

Played 17 professional seasons from 1910–17, 1918–28

Stats: See page 461

- Played amateur hockey with Montreal Canadian Rubber (1908–09); New York Wanderers (1909–10)
- Nicknamed "Peg"
- Renowned for his questionable on ice antics, it was noted that he played the game with "vigilante vigor"
- Missed entire 1917–18 season recovering from broken leg suffered in off-ice accident
- Served as captain of Boston Bruins (1925–27); served as player/assistant coach of Boston Bruins (1927–28)
- Led NHL in penalty minutes (80) in 1921–22
- Signed as a free agent by Ottawa Senators after securing his release from Toronto St. Pats and allowed to play in Stanley Cup playoffs, March 15, 1921

- Rights transferred to Hamilton by NHL, April 6, 1921; traded to Montreal Canadiens by Hamilton for Harry Mummery and Amos Arbour, November 26, 1921; traded to Boston by Montreal Canadiens for $5,000, November 8, 1925
- Served as player/coach of Newark Bulldogs (1928–29)
- Coached Providence Reds (1930–31)
- Coached Montreal Maroons (1931–32)
- Coached Verdun Maple Leafs (1932–34); coached Edmonton Eskimos (1934–35); coached Pittsburgh Shamrocks (1935–36); coached Cornwall Cougars (1946–47)
- Brother of Odie Cleghorn, who played in NHL with Montreal Canadiens and Pittsburgh Pirates from 1917–28

AWARDS
Stanley Cup (1919–20, 1920–21, 1923–24)

# Paul Coffey

**7** DEFENSE

**Paul Coffey** 2004

NO. RETIRED BY EDMONTON

**ALTERNATES:**

**77 · 74**

Boston Bruins
Carolina Hurricanes
Chicago Blackhawks
Detroit Red Wings
Edmonton Oilers
Hartford Whalers
Los Angeles Kings
Pittsburgh Penguins
Philadelphia Flyers

Shoots: Left

Height: 6'

Weight: 205 lbs.

Born: June 1, 1961;
Weston, Ontario

Drafted by the
Edmonton Oilers sixth
overall in 1980

Played 21 NHL seasons
from 1980–2001

Stats: See page 462

**AWARDS**
James Norris Memorial
Trophy (1985, 1986, 1995)

Stanley Cup
(1983–84, 1984–85,
1986–87, 1990–91)

**ALL-STAR
SELECTIONS**
First All-Star Team
Defense (1985,
1986, 1989, 1995)

Second All-Star
Team Defense (1982,
1983, 1984, 1990)

**INTERNATIONAL
AWARDS**
Canada Cup
(1984, 1987, 1991)

"We were very lucky to have a general manager at that time, and he ended up being our coach, who allowed us to be ourselves; who allowed us to express ourselves whether it was on or off the ice. We had a simple set of rules: be on time, don't embarrass the coach and work hard, and we tried to do that."

— Paul Coffey, on his Edmonton Oiler days

- ○ Holds NHL record for goals in a single season by a defenseman (48), established in 1985–86; holds NHL record for career playoff goals (59) and career playoff points (196) by a defenseman

- ○ Holds Edmonton Oilers team records for career goals (209), assists (460), points (669) and career playoff points (103) by a defenseman; holds Edmonton Oilers' team records for points in a single season by a defenseman (138)

- ○ Holds two of the top five spots for points in a single-season by a Red Wings defenseman (77 and 74)

- ○ Ranks sixth in NHL career assists (1,135); ranks 13th in NHL career points (1,531)

- ○ Holds Pittsburgh Penguins team records for career goals (108), assists (332) and points (440) by a defenseman; holds Pittsburgh Penguins team records for goals (30), assists (83) and points (113) in a single season by a defenseman

- ○ Played amateur hockey with North York Rangers (1977–78); Kingston Canadians (1977–78); Sault Ste. Marie Greyhounds (1978–80); Kitchener Rangers (1979–80)

- ○ OMJHL Second All-Star Team Defense (1980)

- ○ Led NHL in short-handed goals (9) in 1985–86

- ○ Played in NHL All-Star game (1982, 1983, 1984, 1985, 1986, 1988, 1989, 1990, 1991, 1992, 1993, 1994, 1996, 1997)

# 1967 Neil Colville

**6**

> "A neat puck manipulator, a smart ice general, the gray-thatched center has given local customers more thrills per game than any other member of the hockey cast."
>
> — *Ottawa Citizen*

**New York Rangers**

Alternate Position: C

Shoots: Right

Height: 5'-11"

Weight: 175 lbs.

Born: August 4, 1914: Edmonton, Alberta

Died: December 26, 1987: Richmond, British Columbia

Played 12 NHL seasons from 1935–42, 1944–49

Stats: See page 462

- Played amateur hockey with Edmonton Ebarcos (1929–30); Edmonton Canadians (1930–31); Edmonton Poolers (1931–33); Edmonton Athletic Club (1933–34); N.Y.-Hamilton Crescents (1934–35)

- Led Edmonton City Junior League in goals (14) and points (18) in 1933–34; led ECJHL playoffs in goals (4), assists (2) and points (6) in 1933–34

- Led EAHL in goals (24) and points (35) in 1934–35; led EAHL playoffs in goals (8) in 1934–35

- EAHL First All-Star Team Center (1935)

- One of six Hall of Fame members (with Sid Abel, Doug Bentley, Dit Clapper, Alex Delvecchio and Mark Messier) to be selected as NHL All-Star at two different positions

- Played in NHL All-Star Game (1939, 1948)

- Member of N.Y. Rangers' famed Bread Line with brother Mac Colville and Alex Shibicky

- Member of Allan Cup–winning Ottawa Commandos (1942–43)

- Led QSHL in assists (32) in 1942–43; led QSHL playoffs in goals (11), assists (7) and points (18) in 1942–43

- Led Allan Cup playoffs in goals (14), assists (14) and points (28) in 1942–43

- Served as captain of N.Y. Rangers (1945–49)

- Switched from center to defense after returning to NHL from World War II

- Coached N.Y. Rangers (1950–52)

**AWARDS**

Stanley Cup (1939–40)

**ALL-STAR SELECTIONS**

Second All-Star Team Center (1939, 1940)

Second All-Star Team Defense (1948)

# 3

DEFENSE

# Lionel Conacher 1994

ALTERNATES:
## 2 · 15

Chicago Black Hawks
Montreal Maroons
Pittsburgh Pirates
New York Americans

Shoots: Left
Height: 6'-2"
Weight: 195 lbs.
Born: May 24, 1900:
Toronto, Ontario
Died: May 26, 1954:
Ottawa, Ontario
Played 12 NHL seasons
from 1925–37
Stats: See page 463

"The cost to the professional athlete of his success is most invariably overlooked when he is exposed to the glamour created by roaring crowds, breezy headlines and over-enthusiastic ballyhoo. But is the climb worthwhile? Sometimes I wonder, especially after contemplating [my injuries]."

AWARDS
Stanley Cup
(1933–34, 1934–35)

ALL-STAR
SELECTIONS
First All-Star Team
Defense (1934)
Second All-Star Team
Defense (1933, 1937)

- Played amateur hockey with Toronto Century Rovers (1916–17); Toronto Aura Lee (1917–19, 1920–22); Toronto (Parkdale) Canoe Club (1919–20); North Toronto Intermediates (1922–23); Pittsburgh Yellowjackets (1923–25)

- Member of Memorial Cup–winning Toronto Canoe Club (1919–20)

- Member of USAHA champion Pittsburgh Yellowjackets (1923–24, 1924–25)

- Named Canada's Athlete of the Half-Century (1950)

- Played professional football, lacrosse and baseball during his time in the NHL

- Won Grey Cup (Canadian Football championship) as a member of the Toronto Argonauts (1921)

- Won Canadian amateur light heavyweight boxing championship (1921)

- Inducted into Canadian Lacrosse Hall of Fame (1965); inducted into Canadian Football Hall of Fame (1963); inducted into Canada's Sports Hall of Fame (1955)

- Nicknamed "Big Train" because of his endless energy and stamina

- Served as Liberal Member of Provincial Parliament (MPP) for the Toronto riding of Bracondale (1937–43); served as Liberal Member of Federal Parliament in the Toronto riding of Trinity (1949–54)

- Brothers Roy and Charlie, son Brian and nephew Pete all played in the NHL

# The Big Train

**Lionel Conacher in the early 1930s, demonstrating his football skills.**

It's hard to imagine anyone having the time to accomplish what Lionel Conacher did, let alone the skill to accomplish it.

Conacher was named by the Canadian Press as Canada's athlete of the first half of the 20th century in 1950, having starred on teams that won the Grey Cup (football), the Stanley Cup, the Memorial Cup and the U.S. Amateur Hockey Association championship. He also wrestled professionally, fought Jack Dempsey in an amateur boxing match and was the runaway scoring leader in the first-ever indoor professional lacrosse league. Conacher was an early inductee into Canada's Sports Hall of Fame, its Football Hall of Fame and its Lacrosse Hall of Fame, and the award the Canadian Press bestows upon the Canadian male athlete of the year is named after him. Brothers Charlie and Roy Conacher are also in the Hockey Hall of Fame (inducted 1961 and 1998, respectively).

"My father's sports career was achieved in an era that will never be repeated," said Lionel's son Brian, who played for the Toronto Maple Leafs' last Stanley Cup–championship team in 1967. "The seasons were more defined. There were times he played two different sports in the same day, but generally the seasons didn't overlap much. And the players are far more specialized in all sports today."

Known as "The Big Train," Conacher was a large, determined athlete. He didn't begin skating until he was 16, but he knew that pro hockey afforded him his best chance at making good money and he reached the NHL with the Pittsburgh Pirates at the age of 25. He was never the best skater or the biggest point producer, but he was a formidable force on the blue line.

Conacher was traded to the New York Americans in 1926. He spent five seasons there before being sold to the Montreal Maroons, where he spent six of his last seven seasons in two three-year stints. Sandwiched in between was the 1933–34 season, when he helped the Chicago Black Hawks win their first Stanley Cup championship. Conacher was then sent back to the Maroons in a three-team deal that landed Montreal Canadiens superstar Howie Morenz in Chicago. He won a second straight Stanley Cup in 1934–35 and retired after the 1936–37 despite making the NHL's Second All-Star Team and finishing as runner-up for the Hart Trophy.

After leaving sports Conacher entered politics, holding posts in both the Ontario provincial and the Canadian federal governments. An athlete to his last day, Conacher died unexpectedly on a sports field in 1954 just two days after his 54th birthday. The Big Train was playing in the annual softball game between the members of Parliament and the press corps on the lawn of Parliament Hill. He smacked a pitch into the outfield and legged out a triple before collapsing at third base. Twenty minutes later, the great Lionel Conacher was pronounced dead of a heart attack. There will never be another multi-sport athlete like him.

# 2

# Art Coulter 1974

**ALTERNATES:**

## 17 · 21 · 18

**Chicago Black Hawks
New York Rangers**

Shoots: Right

Height: 5'-11"

Weight: 185 lbs.

Born: May 31, 1909:
Winnipeg, Manitoba

Died: October 14, 2000:
Mobile, Alabama

Played 11 NHL seasons
from 1931–42

Stats: See page 463

"Art Coulter was our best player. He was a leader ... he could really carry the puck. But he had to head-man the puck. That's the way we played."

—Clint Smith, Art Coulter's teammate on the 1940 Rangers

**AWARDS**
Stanley Cup
(1933–1934, 1939–1940)

**ALL-STAR
SELECTIONS**
Second All-Star
Team Defense (1935,
1938, 1939, 1940)

- Nicknamed "The Trapper" because of his love of fishing and hunting
- Played amateur hockey with Winnipeg Pilgrims (1925–27)
- Played minor pro with Philadelphia Arrows (1929–32)
- Led Can-Am in penalty minutes (109) in 1930–31
- Traded to Chicago by Philadelphia Arrows (Can-Am) for cash and the loan of Frank Ingram, February, 1932
- Traded to N.Y. Rangers by Chicago for Earl Seibert, January 15, 1936
- Led NHL in penalty minutes (90) in 1937–38; finished second in NHL penalty minutes (68) in 1939–40

- Served as captain of the N.Y. Rangers (1937–42)
- Joined U.S. Navy and played with Coast Guard Clippers during World War II
- Member of the American Amateur champion Coast Guard Cutters (1943, 1944)
- Inducted into Manitoba Hockey Hall of Fame (1985)
- Inducted into Manitoba Sports Hall of Fame (2009)
- Operated a hardware store in Miami, Florida, after retiring from the NHL
- Brother of Tom Coulter, who played in the NHL with Chicago Black Hawks in 1933–34

1961 # Hap Day

"Fame is fleeting, no matter how many Cups you've won. I remember once I saw Reg Bentley, brother of Max and Doug, at a hockey game. I said, 'Hi ya, Reg.' He looked at me kind of puzzled. I said, 'Happy Day.' 'Oh,' he said, 'Same to you.'"

NO. RETIRED BY TORONTO

New York Americans
Toronto Maple Leafs
Toronto St. Patricks

Alternate Position: LW

Shoots: Left

Height: 5'-11"

Weight: 175 lbs.

Born: June 14, 1901;
Owen Sound, Ontario

Died: February 17, 1990;
Toronto, Ontario

Played 14 NHL seasons
from 1924–38

Stats: See page 463

- Only member of the Toronto Maple Leafs to serve as captain, coach and general manager
- Played amateur hockey with Collingwood Seniors (1921–22); Hamilton Tigers (1922–24)
- OHA-Sr. First All-Star Team Defense (1923)
- Played in NHL All-Star Game (1934, 1937)
- Nicknamed "Happy"—later shortened to "Hap"—because of his cheery disposition
- Graduated with a degree in pharmacy from the University of Toronto
- Signed by Toronto St. Pats owner Charlie Querrie for salary of $5,000 and the promise he wouldn't miss too many classes

- Played left wing on a line with future Hall of Famers Jack Adams and Babe Dye before switching to defense in his fourth season
- Owned a drugstore during his playing days that was located inside Maple Leaf Gardens
- Served as captain of Toronto Maple Leafs (1927–37)
- Coached Toronto Maple Leafs (1940–50); coached Toronto Maple Leafs to Stanley Cup championship (1942, 1945, 1947, 1948, 1949)
- Served as general manager of Toronto Maple Leafs (1957–58)
- Scored first Stanley Cup Final goal in Toronto Maple Leafs franchise history, April 15, 1932

**AWARDS**
Stanley Cup (1931–32)

Day continued on page 238

**237**

# Company Man

**Hap Day celebrates as Toronto wins the 1949 Stanley Cup.**

Clarence Day's perpetually cheery demeanor earned him the nickname "Happy," which was later shortened to "Hap." Hap was nothing if not committed. He loved hockey so much that as a youth it is said he routinely walked 5 miles with his gear to play games in Port McNicholl, Ontario.

As a vaunted amateur, he insisted that he would only turn pro if he could continue his pharmaceutical studies at the University of Toronto. Even as a professional, he maintained a pharmacy inside Maple Leaf Gardens (it eventually became Dick Dowling's Grill). He remained loyal to the Leafs for nearly his entire hockey life, more than 30 years.

Charlie Querrie, owner of the Toronto St. Pats, and Bert Corbeau, the team's star player, are the two who finally convinced Day to turn pro, after having seen him play at U of T. The 23-year-old made his debut on December 13, 1924, as a left wing, and his linemates were none other than future Hall of Famers Jack Adams and Babe Dye. He wound up scoring 10 goals and 27 points in 26 games in his rookie season, but, as a sure skater, Day was shifted to defense. He spent the rest of his career at the point.

With a new owner in Conn Smythe, the team was renamed the Maple Leafs, and Day became the new club's first captain; it was a post he held with pride for 10 seasons, through to 1936–37. Smythe and the Leafs moved into their new home, Maple Leaf Gardens, during the 1931–32 season, and that spring Day led the team to the Stanley Cup. It was the only one he would win as a player, but after his retirement and a couple of years refereeing, Day returned to the Leafs franchise as coach in 1940. He led the club to five Cup victories—three of those wins coming successively, making the Leafs the first NHL team to achieve the feat.

The Leafs appointed Day as an assistant to general manager Conn Smythe in 1950, and despite the title, Day in fact ran the team. He picked up a Stanley Cup in his new role in 1951 and was appointed general manager in 1954. Day was elected to the Hockey Hall of Fame in 1961.

# 1958 Red Dutton

**2**

> "I wasn't a good hockey player, but I was a good competitor."

**ALTERNATES:**
**3 · 8**

Calgary Tigers
Montreal Maroons
New York Americans

Shoots: Right

Height: 6'

Weight: 185 lbs.

Born: July 23, 1897:
Russell, Manitoba

Died: March 15, 1987:
Calgary, Alberta

Played 15 professional
seasons from 1921–36

Stats: See page 463

- Played amateur hockey with Winnipeg St. John's (1914–15); Winnipeg Winnipegs (1919–20); Calgary Canadians (1920–21)

- Served in World War I with the Princess Patricia's Light Infantry (1915–19); was severely wounded during the Battle of Vimy Ridge, April 11, 1917

- Led Big-4 in penalty minutes (38) in 1920–21

- Led WCHL in penalty minutes in 1921–22 (73) and 1923–24 (54)

- Played in NHL All-Star Game (1934)

- Traded to N.Y. Americans by Montreal Maroons with Mike Neville, Hap Emms and Frank Carson for $35,000, May 14, 1930

- Led NHL in penalty minutes in 1928–29 (141) and 1931–32 (111)

- Real name is Norman Alexander Dutton, but he was commonly known as "Mervyn"

- Served as a Trustee of the Stanley Cup (1950–87)

- Served as second president of the National Hockey League (1943–46)

- Coached N.Y. Americans (1934–40)

- Served as general manager of N.Y. Americans (1940–42)

- Performed the official face-off prior to Calgary Flames' first home game on October 9, 1980

**AWARDS**
Lester Patrick Trophy (1993)

**ALL-STAR SELECTIONS**
WCHL First All-Star Team
Defense (1922, 1923)

Second All-Star Team
Coach (1939)

# 2 Viacheslav Fetisov 2001

CSKA Moscow
Detroit Red Wings
New Jersey Devils

Shoots: Left

Height: 6'-1"

Weight: 220 lbs.

Born: April 20, 1958;
Moscow, Union of Soviet
Socialist Republics

Drafted by the Montreal
Canadiens 201st
overall in 1978

Drafted by the New
Jersey Devils 150th
overall in 1983 (re-entry)

Played nine NHL seasons
from 1989–98

Stats: See page 464

> "I was the first Soviet to sign a direct contract with the NHL, and I'm proud to say that not only hockey players followed me. The door opened for people in every profession."

**AWARDS**

Stanley Cup
(1996–97, 1997–98)

**INTERNATIONAL AWARDS**

Canada Cup (1981)

Gold Medal: Winter
Olympics (1984, 1988)

Silver Medal: Winter
Olympics (1980)

Gold Medal: World
Championships
(1978, 1981, 1982, 1983,
1986, 1989, 1990)

Silver Medal: World
Championships (1987)

Bronze Medal: World
Championships
(1977, 1985, 1991)

- Shares New Jersey Devils team record (with Tom Kurvers and Bruce Driver) for points in a regular season game by a defenseman (5), March 29, 1990
- Played amateur hockey with CSKA Moscow (1974–89)
- Named USSR Player of Year (1986); USSR First All-Star Team Defense (1984, 1985, 1986, 1987, 1988)
- Won Golden Stick Award (European Player of Year) in 1984, 1986 and 1990
- Canada Cup First All-Star Team Defense (1987)
- Named World Championships Most Valuable Player (1989); named World Championships Best Defenseman (1985, 1986, 1989)
- Played in NHL All-Star Game (1997, 1998)
- Won USSR Pravda Trophy (most points by a defenseman) in 1984, 1986, 1987, 1988
- World Championships First All-Star Team Defense (1985, 1986, 1987, 1989, 1990, 1991)
- Among a group of eight Soviet players who were allowed to play in the NHL in 1989 on the provision they continue to play internationally for the Soviet Union
- Served as assistant coach with New Jersey (1998–2002)
- Received IOC Olympic Order (2000); inducted into IIHF Hall of Fame (2005)
- Coached bronze medal–winning Team Russia at 2002 Winter Olympic Games in Salt Lake City, Utah

# A True Trailblazer

**V**iacheslav "Slava" Fetisov, captain of both the powerful Moscow Red Army and the Union of Soviet Socialist Republics' national team, risked his hockey career and future lifestyle in the late 1980s by openly challenging his communist government and eventually blazing the trail, for himself and many Russians after him, to play in the NHL.

Fetisov and longtime blue-line partner Alexei Kasatonov—along with the legendary "KLM Line" of Igor Larionov, Vladimir Krutov and Sergei Makarov—formed the USSR's "Big Five" or "Green Unit." Together they were the centerpiece of most of the Soviet Union's seven world and two Olympic championships won during Fetisov's career.

In 1978 the Montreal Canadiens played a long shot and selected Fetisov with the 201st pick of the 1978 NHL draft. They didn't expect him to ever play in North America—and neither did the New Jersey Devils, who chose him 150th overall when he was re-entered into the draft in 1983.

But Fetisov was determined to gain freedom from the Soviet authorities. He had spoken openly against the heavy-handed Soviet hockey regime and had been threatened by the authorities with criminal charges and banishment to one of the USSR's hockey outposts. When national team leaders announced that Fetisov would not be eligible for the 1989 World Championship, his teammates rallied behind him and said they would not play without their captain. In effect, they threatened a players' strike.

Because of his untouchable national

**Viacheslav Fetisov (far left) celebrates with (from left, clockwise) Dimtri Mironov, Slava Kozlov, Igor Larionov and Vladimir Konstantinov.**

stature—and with the reforms of the Glasnost policy coloring the larger political picture—the government eventually allowed Fetisov to become one of the first Soviet citizens to receive a visa to work in the West. He and seven other veterans were permitted to play in the NHL, with the proviso that they would return to play for the national team.

Although he was 31 years old when he first suited up for New Jersey, Fetisov contributed eight goals and 42 points in the 1989–90 season. Traded to the Detroit Red Wings late in the 1994–95 season, he helped them win back-to-back Stanley Cups in 1996–97 and 1997–98 before retiring as one of only four players to win the Stanley Cup, a World Championship, an Olympic championship, the Canada/World Cup and a World Junior Championship.

Fetisov's entire, difficult journey came full circle when he took the Stanley Cup home in 1997, the first time the NHL's top trophy had ever been to Russia.

# 14

# Fernie Flaman 1990

**ALTERNATES:**

**10 · 12 · 15**
**4 · 3 · 6**

Boston Bruins
Toronto Maple Leafs

Shoots: Right

Height: 5'-10"

Weight: 190 lbs.

Born: January 25, 1927:
Dysart, Saskatchewan

Died: June 22, 2012:
Westwood,
Massachusetts

Played 17 NHL seasons
from 1944–61

Stats: See page 464

"Fernie was the toughest guy out there. Strong on his skates. I tell you, he didn't lose too many."

—NHL official Art Skov

**AWARDS**
Stanley Cup (1950–51)

**ALL-STAR SELECTIONS**
Second All-Star Team Defense (1955, 1957, 1958)

- Played amateur hockey with Regina Abbots (1942–43)

- Played first regular-season game for Boston at age 18 and became a full-time player late in his third year

- Considered the toughest defenseman of his era, he was noted for his body-checking and shot-blocking

- Traded to Toronto by Boston with Ken Smith, Phil Maloney and Leo Boivin for Bill Ezinicki and Vic Lynn, November 16, 1950

- Traded to Boston by Toronto for Dave Creighton, July 20, 1954

- Served as captain of Boston Bruins (1956–61)

- Led NHL in penalty minutes (150) in 1954–55

- One of the founders of the first NHL Players Association in 1958

- Served as player/coach/general manager of Rhode Island/Providence Reds (1961–65)

- Coached Los Angeles Blades (1966–67)

- Served as coach/general manager of the Fort Worth Red Wings (1967–69)

- Served as scout for Boston Bruins (1969–70)

- Coached Northeastern University Huskies (1970–89); coached Northeastern University to Hockey East championship (1989)

- Named ECAC and NCAA Division I Coach of the Year (1982)

# 1970 Bill Gadsby

**4**

ALTERNATE:

**16**

Chicago Black Hawks
Detroit Red Wings
New York Rangers

Shoots: Left

Height: 6'

Weight: 180 lbs.

Born: August 8, 1927:
Calgary, Alberta

Died: March 20, 2016:
Farmington Hills,
Michigan

Played 20 NHL seasons
from 1946–66

Stats: See page 464

"When the Red Wings acquired me at age 34 in 1961, [Boston Bruins' great] Eddie Shore said, 'He will play three to five more years. He is virtually indestructible.' That kind of praise means plenty to me because it meant that I never cheated on my effort."

- Held NHL record for regular season assists by a defenseman (46); surpassed by Bobby Orr (87) in 1969–70

- Held NHL record for career games played by a defenseman (1,248); surpassed by Harry Howell in 1969–70

- First NHL defenseman to record 500 regular-season career points (1961–62)

- First NHL player to play at least 300 games with three different teams (Chicago, New York, Detroit)

- Played amateur hockey with Calgary Grills (1943–44); Edmonton Canadiens (1944–46)

- Led Memorial Cup playoffs in goals (12) in 1945–46

- Led NHL playoffs in penalty minutes (36) in 1962–63

- Played in NHL All-Star Game (1953, 1954, 1956, 1957, 1958, 1959, 1960, 1965)

- Signed as a free agent by Chicago Black Hawks, July 14, 1946

- Traded to N.Y. Rangers by Chicago with Pete Conacher for Allan Stanley, Nick Mickoski and Rich Lamoureux, November 23, 1954; traded to Detroit Red Wings by N.Y. Rangers for Les Hunt, June 12, 1961

- Finished among NHL top-10 in assists in 1955–56 (42), 1956–57 (37) and 1958–59 (46)

- Coached Detroit Red Wings (1968–69, 1969–70)

**ALL-STAR SELECTIONS**
First All-Star Team Defense (1956, 1958, 1959)
Second All-Star Team Defense (1953, 1954, 1957, 1965)

# DEFENSE

# 2 Herb Gardiner 1958

ALTERNATES:
**1 · 3**

Calgary Tigers
Chicago Black Hawks
Montreal Canadiens

Shoots: Left
Height: 5'-10"
Weight: 190 lbs.
Born: May 8, 1891:
Winnipeg, Manitoba
Died: January 11,
1972: Philadelphia,
Pennsylvania
Played eight
professional seasons
from 1921–29
Stats: See page 465

"Herb Gardiner is a wonderful story, beginning with the fabled reports that, as a 35-year-old rookie, he played every second of all 48 Canadiens games that 1926–27 season to win the Hart Trophy as the NHL's most valuable player."

— Sportswriter Dave Stubbs, *Montreal Gazette*

**AWARDS**
Hart Memorial
Trophy (1927)

**ALL-STAR
SELECTIONS**
WCHL First All-Star Team
Defense (1923, 1925)

- First non-goaltender in NHL history to wear No. 1 (1926–28); first Montreal Canadiens player to wear No. 1 after Georges Vezina

- First defenseman to win Hart Trophy as NHL MVP

- One of three players (with Wayne Gretzky and Nels Stewart) to win Hart Trophy in their first NHL season

- Played amateur hockey with Winnipeg Merchants Bank (1906–08); Winnipeg Victorias (1908–10); Winnipeg Northern Crowns (1910); Calgary Monarchs (1914–15); Calgary Rotarians (1918–19); Calgary Wanderers (1919–21)

- Named to the "Unofficial" NHL Second All-Star Team Defense (1927)

- Member of WCHL champion Calgary Tigers team that lost Stanley Cup challenge series to the Montreal Canadiens two games to none in 1924. Calgary had defeated the Regina Capitals four goals to two in the two-game, total-goal series to win the WCHL title

- Loaned to Chicago by Montreal Canadiens and named playing coach of Black Hawks, August 27, 1928; recalled by Montreal Canadiens from Chicago, February 12, 1929

- Coached Philadelphia Arrows (1929–36), coached Philadelphia Ramblers (1936–40)

- Quit hockey at age 18 to work for the CPR as a surveyor. After serving three years with the Canadian Army, Gardiner rejoined the CPR while playing with the Calgary Tigers in the WCHL

# 1945 Eddie Gerard

**8**

> "He has an unblemished career in sports. He was never a publicity seeker but will live long in the memory of every person who had the pleasure of his acquaintance. He was a man."
>
> — Gerard Obituary, *Ottawa Citizen*

Ottawa Senators
Toronto St. Patricks

Alternate Position: LW

Shoots: Left

Height: 5'-9"

Weight: 168 lbs.

Born: February 22, 1890: Ottawa, Ontario

Died: August 7, 1937: Ottawa, Ontario

Played 10 professional seasons from 1913–23

Stats: See page 465

- Played amateur hockey with Ottawa Seconds (1907–10); Ottawa New Edinburghs (1910–14)
- Led IPAHU in goals (16) in 1912–13
- Signed as a free agent by Ottawa Senators, November 20, 1913
- Began career in Ottawa playing on a forward line with Jack Darragh and Skene Ronan, then switched to defense three years later
- Served as captain of Ottawa Senators (1919–23)
- Served as player/coach of Ottawa Senators (1917–18)
- Loaned to Toronto St. Pats by Ottawa for fourth game of Stanley Cup final between Toronto and Vancouver on emergency injury basis, March 25, 1922

- Top 5 in the NHL in assists in 1921–22 (11) and 1922–23 (11)
- Coached Montreal Maroons (1924–29, 1932–34); coached N.Y. Americans (1930–32); coached St. Louis Eagles (1934–35)
- Coach of Stanley Cup–winning Montreal Maroons (1926)
- Retired following the 1922–23 season because of a growth in throat that limited his breathing, an ailment that ultimately caused his early death
- Played half-back for the Ottawa Rough Riders Football Club (1909–13)
- Inducted into Ottawa Sports Hall of Fame (1968)

**AWARDS**

Stanley Cup (1919–20, 1920–21, 1921–22, 1922–23)

# 5

# Ebbie Goodfellow 1963

ALTERNATE:

10

Detroit Cougars
Detroit Falcons
Detroit Red Wings

Alternate Position: C
Shoots: Left
Height: 6'
Weight: 175 lbs.
Born: April 9, 1906;
Ottawa, Ontario
Died: September 10,
1985; Sarasota, Florida
Played 14 NHL seasons
from 1929–43
Stats: See page 465

"Playing forward and defense, I saw both sides of the action. Forward seemed a better position because a man can make more mistakes there and not be criticized as much for it. When you're back on defense and someone skates past you, then you're the goat."

**AWARDS**
Hart Memorial
Trophy (1940)
Stanley Cup (1935–36,
1936–37, 1942–43)

**ALL-STAR
SELECTIONS**
First All-Star Team
Defense (1937, 1940)
Second All-Star Team
Defense (1936)

- Played amateur hockey with Ottawa Montagnards (1926–28)
- Member of the Ottawa City–champion Ottawa Montagnards, leading all playoff scorers in goals (4) and points (5) in 1928
- Made professional debut with Detroit Olympics (1928–29)
- Led Can-Pro League in goals (26) and points (34) in 1928–29
- Held Detroit franchise record for points as a rookie (34) in 1929–30; surpassed by Steve Wojciechowski (39) in 1944–45
- Played center before becoming an All-Star defenseman after the 1934–35 season
- Finished second (48 points) to Howie Morenz in NHL scoring race (1930–31); finished among NHL top-5 in goals (25) in 1930–31
- Scored series-winning goal in Detroit's 1–0 victory over the Toronto Maple Leafs in the fifth and deciding game of semi-final series, March 30, 1934
- Served as captain of Detroit Red Wings (1934–35, 1938–41)
- Served as player/assistant coach of Detroit Red Wings (1941–42)
- Coached St. Louis Flyers (1946–50); coached Chicago Black Hawks (1950–52)
- Inducted in Ottawa Sports Hall of Fame (1968)

# 1950 Mike Grant

> "Mike Grant ... has the rare qualities that make him at once a good player and a good captain."
>
> — *The Metropolitan*, Montreal, April 13, 1895

Montreal Maples
Montreal Shamrocks
Montreal Victorias

Shoots: Unknown

Height: Unknown

Weight: Unknown

Born: November 27, 1873: Montreal, Quebec

Died: August 20, 1955: St. Lambert, Quebec

Played nine elite amateur seasons from 1893–1902

Stats: See page 466

- Renowned as the first rushing defenseman in hockey history
- Champion speedskater in his youth, he also played lacrosse growing up in Montreal
- Member of Montreal City Junior champion Montreal Jr. Crystals (1890–91); member of Montreal City Intermediate champion Montreal Crystals (1891–92, 1892–93)
- Served as captain of Stanley Cup–winning Montreal Victorias (1894–95, December 1896, 1897)
- After losing a challenge to the Winnipeg Victorias in February of 1896, the Montreal "Vics" quickly won back their title and defended it successfully into the 1898–99 season

- Famously served as a referee during the 1905 Stanley Cup series between Ottawa and the Rat Portage Thistles, wearing a hard hat on his head during a rough series played on soft ice
- After retiring, he gave demonstrations and organized hockey exhibitions in the United States
- Joined Montreal Shamrocks as emergency replacement for Frank Tansey and played in Stanley Cup challenge series against Winnipeg Victorias, January 1901

**AWARDS**

Stanley Cup (1894–95, 1895–96, 1896–97, 1897–98, 1898–99)

# 6

## DEFENSE

# Si Griffis 1950

ALTERNATE:

## 5

Kenora Thistles
Rat Portage Thistles
Vancouver Millionaires

Alternate Position: R

Shoots: Left

Height: 6'-1"

Weight: 195 lbs.

Born: September 22, 1883: Onega, Kansas

Died: July 9, 1950: Vancouver, British Columbia

Played 13 elite amateur and professional seasons from 1902–07, 1911–19

Stats: See page 466

"Of the visitors, Griffis is probably the star at rover. He is a big fellow and a rattling good stickhandler and his rushes are a continual feature of the game."

— *Manitoba Free Press*, March 10, 1904

AWARDS
Stanley Cup
(1906–07, 1914–15)

- Born in Kansas, he was raised in St. Catharines and Rat Portage (Kenora), Ontario

- Renowned as one of the fastest skaters of his era and one of the game's largest players

- Starred on local school and amateur teams in Rat Portage (Kenora) with future Hall of Fame members Tommy Phillips, Tom Hooper and Billy McGimisie

- Member of MNWHA champion Rat Portage Thistles (1902–03, 1904–05)

- Challenged for Stanley Cup with Rat Portage in 1903 and 1905 but lost to the Ottawa "Silver Seven" on both occasions

- Member of MHL champion Kenora Thistles (1905–06)

- Member of Stanley Cup–winning Kenora Thistles team that defeated Montreal Wanderers in January of 1907

- Signed as a free agent by Vancouver Millionaires, November 6, 1911

- Served as captain of PCHA champion Vancouver Millionaires but was unable to play in the Stanley Cup series against Ottawa Senators due to a broken leg (1914–15)

- Returned to play two more full seasons and parts of two others before retiring in 1919

# 1961 Joe Hall

**3**

> "Well, I'm one of those fellows able to take care of himself if anybody starts anything. But I don't think I am as bad as I am painted."
>
> — Joe Hall, on his reputation

Brandon Elks
Edmonton Professionals
Montreal AAA
Montreal Canadiens
Montreal Shamrocks
Montreal Wanderers
Portage Lakes
Winnipeg Maple Leafs
Winnipeg Rowing Club

Shoots: Right

Height: 5'-10"

Weight: 175 lbs.

Born: May 3, 1881:
Milwich, England

Died: April 5, 1919:
Seattle, Washington

Played 17 elite amateur and professional seasons from 1902–19

Stats: See page 466

- Moved to Canada at age of two and was raised in Winnipeg

- Played forward early in his career but later became a star defenseman

- Played amateur hockey with Brandon HC (1900–03); Winnipeg Rowing Club (1903–04); Brandon Wheat Cities (1904–05)

- Member of Manitoba Intermediate champion Brandon Hockey Club (1901–02)

- Led IHL in penalty minutes (98) in 1905–06; member of IHL champion Portage Lakes (1905–06)

- Nicknamed "Bad Joe" or simply "The Bad Man" because of his temper, though teammates would later say his tough guy reputation was overrated

- Member of Stanley Cup–winning Kenora Thistles team that defeated Montreal Wanderers in January of 1907 although he did not see action in the series

- Member of Stanley Cup–winning Quebec Bulldogs (1911–12, 1912–13); named Quebec Bulldogs' Most Popular Player by fans (1913–14)

- Joined the Montreal Canadiens for the inaugural NHL season of 1917–18 and helped them win the NHL championship in 1918–19

- Died in a Seattle hospital from complications brought on by influenza during 1919 Stanley Cup final, leading to cancellation of the competition

**AWARDS**

Stanley Cup (1906–07, 1911–12, 1912–13)

**ALL-STAR SELECTIONS**

IHL First All-Star Team Defense (1906)

# 2 Doug Harvey 1973

NO. RETIRED BY MONTREAL

ALTERNATES:

## 5 · 6 · 17

Detroit Red Wings
Montreal Canadiens
New York Rangers
St. Louis Blues

Shoots: Left

Height: 5'-11"

Weight: 187 lbs.

Born: December 19, 1924; Montreal, Quebec

Died: December 26, 1989; Montreal, Quebec

Played 19 NHL seasons from 1947–64, 1966–67, 1968–69

Stats: See page 467

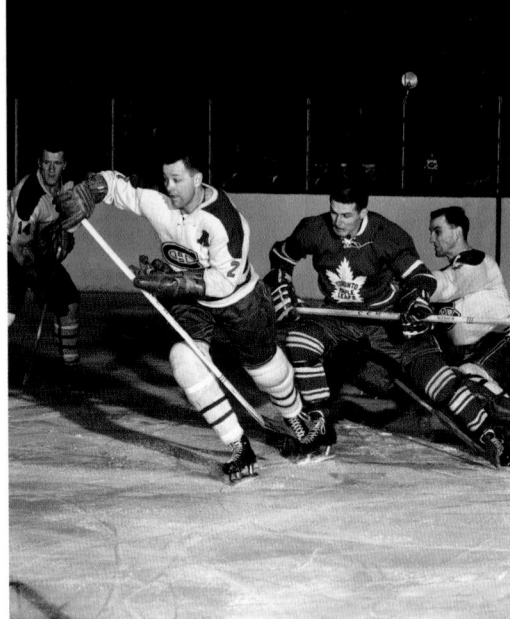

"I'm not throwing any pucks away. I'm trying to do what's best for the team. That's why I take my time and make the play."

—Doug Harvey, describing his puck-moving style that changed the way the game is played

**AWARDS**

James Norris Memorial Trophy (1955, 1956, 1957, 1958, 1960, 1961, 1962)

Stanley Cup (1952–53, 1955–56, 1956–57, 1957–58, 1958–59, 1959–60)

**ALL-STAR SELECTIONS**

First All-Star Team Defense (1952, 1953, 1954, 1955, 1956, 1957, 1958, 1960, 1961, 1962)

Second All-Star Team Defense (1959)

- Played amateur hockey with Montreal Navy (1942–45); Montreal Jr. Royals (1942–45); Montreal Royals (1942–45)

- Played in NHL All-Star Game (1951, 1952, 1953, 1954, 1955, 1956, 1957, 1958, 1959, 1960, 1961, 1962, 1969)

- Originated the spin-a-rama move to avoid checking defenders later popularized by Canadiens' defenseman Serge Savard

- Served as captain of Montreal Canadiens (1960–61)

- Traded to N.Y. Rangers by Montreal for Lou Fontinato, June 13, 1961

- Player/coach of the N.Y. Rangers (1961–62)

- Signed as a free agent by Quebec Aces, November 26, 1963

- AHL Second All-Star Team Defense (1964)

- Played minor pro hockey with St. Paul Rangers (1963–64); Quebec Aces (1963–65); Baltimore Clippers (1966–67); Pittsburgh Hornets (1966–67); Kansas City Blues (1967–68)

- Signed as a free agent by Detroit and assigned to AHL's Pittsburgh Hornets, January 6, 1967

- Played two games for the Detroit Red Wings in the 1966–67 season when called up from the team's AHL affiliate in Pittsburgh

- Signed as a free agent by St. Louis and named playing coach of Kansas City Blues, June 1, 1967

- Coached Laval Saints (1969–70); coached Houston Aeros (1973–75)

# The Game Changer

**D**oug Harvey was a multi-sport athlete who excelled at football and baseball, but it was on the blue line of the Montreal Canadiens from 1947–48 to 1960–61 that he left his most indelible mark. Without Harvey, there may never have been a Bobby Orr.

Harvey's biggest contribution to the game was as its original "offensive defenseman." He was the first of his era to carry the puck from his zone instead of dumping it away. For Harvey, puck control translated into game control: if he had the puck, the other team didn't, and if he had the puck, he could dictate the pace of the game, slowing it down or speeding it up.

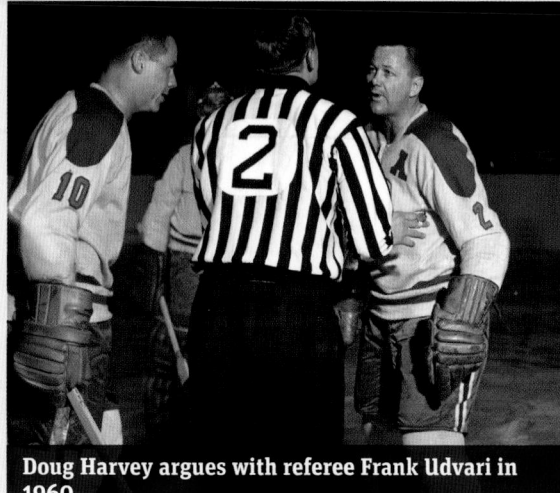

**Doug Harvey argues with referee Frank Udvari in 1960.**

In the Original Six era, teams didn't carry as many players as they do today on their active roster. By slowing the game down, Harvey not only gave his forwards a chance to set up, he also gave them an opportunity to catch their breath. When he sped things up, he would either rush the puck for a surprise offensive chance or dish the puck to an open teammate when he drew extra coverage.

It took a while for the players and coaches to understand what Harvey was doing, but once they did, Havey's puckhandling prowess became an essential part of Montreal's attack. He quarterbacked Montreal's power play with sure-handedness and creativity, and the effectiveness of the power play led the league to adapt the rule book so that a penalized player was returned to the ice if his team was scored on. Previously a player had to serve his entire two-minute penalty, no matter how many goals were scored.

Harvey's leadership from the blue line led the Canadiens to six Stanley Cups, five of them consecutive. His novel approach also won him individual honors, as he took home the Norris Trophy as the league's top defenseman a then-record seven times (Bobby Orr, the next great offensive defenseman, surpassed Harvey with his eighth Norris in 1974–75).

Harvey was also a leader off the ice, helping Ted Lindsay attempt to form the first players' union in 1957. The owners squashed the players' efforts, and Harvey, like many of those involved, felt he was being punished for his participation in the union when he was traded to the New York Rangers in 1961.

It was in New York that he won his seventh Norris Trophy. He went on to play, mentor and coach in the minor leagues before returning to play in the NHL briefly with Detroit and St. Louis.

# 91

## DEFENSE

# Geraldine Heaney 2013

NO. RETIRED BY
TORONTO AEROS

Canadian National
Team
North York Beatrice
Aeros
Seneca College
Toronto Aeros

Shoots: Right
Height: 5'-8"
Weight: 141 lbs.

Born: October 1, 1967:
Belfast, Northern Ireland,
United Kingdom

Played 13 years for Team
Canada from 1990–2002

Stats: See page 468

### AWARDS

Directorate Award (Best
Defender), Women's World
Hockey Championships
(1992, 1994)

Best Defender, Pacific
Rim Women's Hockey
Championship (1996)

Most Valuable Player, Esso
Women's Nationals (1992)

Best Defender, Esso
Women's Nationals
(1993, 1997, 1999, 2001)

OWHA Best Defender
(1988, 1992, 1993)

### ALL-STAR
SELECTIONS

Women's World
Championship Media All-
Star Team, Defense (1992)

### INTERNATIONAL
AWARDS

Gold Medal: Winter
Olympics (2002)

Gold Medal: Women's World
Hockey Championships
(1990, 1992, 1994, 1997,
1999, 2000, 2001)

Silver Medal: Winter
Olympics (1998)

"As a child growing up you watch it on TV and it was a male game when I played. Going down to the Hall of Fame many times, you would never see any females, so you really didn't think, 'Could this ever happen?' I'm so glad that it has."

○ Member of OCAA-champion Seneca College Scouts (1987), OCAA First All-Star Team (1996–87) and OCAA All-Tournament Team (1987)

○ Member of NWHL-champion Toronto Beatrice Aeros (2000, 2001, 2002)

○ Played 18 seasons with the Toronto Aeros and was a member of six provincial-championship teams

○ Played in every Canadian Esso Women's National senior hockey championship from 1987 to 2001

○ Only female hockey player to be a member of the gold medal–winning team in each of the first seven Women's World Hockey Championships (1990–2001)

○ Scored game-winning goal in Team Canada's 5–2 victory over the United States in the first Women's World Hockey Championship, March 25, 1990

○ Inducted into International Ice Hockey Hall of Fame (2008)

○ Won gold medal with Team Canada at Women's World Roller Hockey Championship in Springe, Germany (1992); won silver medal with Team Canada at Women's World Roller Hockey Championship in Algarve, Portugal (1994)

○ Switched from defense to right wing in final year with the Toronto Aeros (2002)

○ Served as coach of the University of Waterloo Warriors (2005–2011)

○ Holds Team Canada record for career goals (27), assists (66) and points (93) by a defender

○ Holds Team Canada record for career games (35), goals (8), assists (28) and points (36) by a defender in the Women's World Hockey Championships

○ Shares Team Canada record for most goals by a defender (3), established in 1999; most assists by a defender (6), established in 1990 and repeated 1999; and most points by a defender (8), established in 1990, in a single Women's World Hockey Championship tournament

○ Inducted into Ontario Collegiate Athletic Association (OCAA) Hall of Fame (2003); named a member of the OCAA All-Millennium Team (2003)

Geraldine Heaney wore this jersey in her last National Women's Hockey League season, 2003–04. She retired a national champion after scoring the championship-deciding goal in overtime.

# 2

## DEFENSE

# Red Horner 1965

ALTERNATES:
## 11 · 15

**Toronto Maple Leafs**

Shoots: Right

Height: 6'

Weight: 190 lbs.

Born: May 28, 1909;
Lynden, Ontario

Died: April 27, 2005;
Toronto, Ontario

Played 12 NHL seasons
from 1928–40

Stats: See page 468

"I asked Mrs. Selke if she thought her husband would mind if I came down and tried out for the Marlboro Juniors ... Twenty or thirty young fellas were trying to make the team ... At the first of the season back in those days, they had the SPA — the Sportsmen's Patriotic Association. If you lost a game, you were out."

**AWARDS**
Stanley Cup (1931–32)

- Held NHL record in 1935–36 for penalty minutes in regular season (167); surpassed by N.Y. Rangers' Lou Fontinato, who registered 206 penalty minutes in 1955–56

- Played amateur hockey with Toronto Marlboros (1926–28) and Solway Mills Bankers (1926–28)

- Registered seven goals and 12 points in 1928 Memorial Cup playoffs with Toronto Jr. Marlboros

- Signed as a free agent by Toronto, December 22, 1929 and made his NHL debut that evening in a 3–2 loss to Pittsburgh Pirates. Horner had played a junior game for the Toronto Marlboros the night before and a commercial game with Solway Mills that afternoon

- Replaced penalized goaltender Lorne Chabot in net for the Maple Leafs in a 6–2 loss to Boston on March 15, 1932. Horner allowed one goal in the one minute he "pinch hit" for Chabot

- Led the league in penalty minutes seven times in eight seasons (1932–37; 1938–1940)

- Played in NHL All-Star Game (1934, 1937)

- Served as captain of Toronto Maple Leafs (1938–40)

- Worked for two seasons as a NHL linesman and later owned and operated the Canada Coal Company

- At the time of his death in 2005, he was the oldest living NHL player and oldest living member of the Hockey Hall of Fame

# 1977 Tim Horton

> "Horton's the hardest body-checker I've ever come up against. He's as strong as an ox and hits with terrific force."
>
> — John Ferguson

NO. RETIRED BY TORONTO

## 2

NO. RETIRED BY BUFFALO

**ALTERNATES:**

## 16 · 20 · 26

Buffalo Sabres
New York Rangers
Pittsburgh Penguins
Toronto Maple Leafs

Shoots: Right

Height: 5'-10"

Weight: 180 lbs.

Born: January 12, 1930:
Cochrane, Ontario

Died: February 21, 1974:
St. Catharines, Ontario

Played 24 NHL seasons
from 1949–50, 1951–74

Stats: See page 469

- Held NHL record for games played by a defenseman (1,445); surpassed by Larry Murphy in 1998–99
- Better known today throughout Canada and the United States for chain of restaurants that bear his name
- Played amateur hockey with Cooper Cliff Redmen (1946–47); St. Michael's Majors (1947–49); Toronto Swansea Sentinals (1947–48)
- Led OHA-Jr. in penalty minutes (137) in 1947–48
- AHL First All-Star Team Defense (1951–52)
- Nicknamed "Mister Magoo" because of his poor eyesight and "Superman" because of his strength

- Renowned for his "Tim Horton Bear Hug," a ploy he would use instead of engaging in fisticuffs
- Led all NHL defensemen in game-winning goals (7) in 1963–64
- Played in NHL All-Star Game (1954, 1961, 1962, 1963, 1964, 1968, 1969)
- Regarded as one of the toughest, strongest and most durable defensive defensemen in NHL history
- Traded to N.Y. Rangers by Toronto for future considerations (Denis Dupere), March 3, 1970
- Claimed by Pittsburgh from N.Y. Rangers in Intra-League Draft, June 8, 1971; claimed by Buffalo from Pittsburgh in Intra-League Draft, June 5, 1972

**AWARDS**

Stanley Cup (1961–62, 1962–63, 1963–64, 1966–67)

**ALL-STAR SELECTIONS**

First All-Star Team Defense (1964, 1968, 1969)

Second All-Star Team Defense (1954, 1963, 1967)

# 6

# Phil Housley 2015

ALTERNATE:
## 96

Buffalo Sabres
Calgary Flames
Chicago Blackhawks
New Jersey Devils
St. Louis Blues
Toronto Maple Leaf
Washington Capitals
Winnipeg Jets

Shoots: Left

Height: 5'-10"

Weight: 185 lbs.

Born: March 9, 1964:
St. Paul, Minnesota

Drafted by the
Buffalo Sabres sixth
overall in 1982

Played 21 NHL seasons
from 1982–2003

Stats: see page 469

"I always looked at it as an opportunity if somebody traded for me. My attitude was always another challenge."

ALL-STAR
SELECTIONS

All-Rookie Team (1983)

Second All-Star Team
Defenseman (1992)

INTERNATIONAL
AWARDS

Silver Medal: Winter
Olympics (2002)

World Cup (1996)

- Scored 118 goals as a bantam eighth-grader before going on to star at South St. Paul High School, where he represented the United States at both the World Junior Championships and the World Championships in 1981–82

- Entered the NHL directly out of high school as an 18-year-old with the Buffalo Sabres in 1982–83 and finished second in voting for the Calder Trophy as rookie of the year behind Steve Larmer

- Played in NHL All-Star Game (1984, 1989, 1990, 1991, 1992, 1993, 2000)

- Scored a career-high 31 goals for Buffalo in his second NHL season (1983–84) and had a career high 79 assists and 97 points for Winnipeg (1992–93)

- Ranks fourth all-time in goals by a defenseman (338), fifth in assists (894) and fourth in points (1,232)

- On November 8, 1997, he became the second American-born player in NHL history (first defenseman) to reach 1,000 points and held the NHL record for career points (1,232) by an American-born player until it was broken by Mike Modano on November 7, 2007

- Represented the United States at the World Championships in 1982, 1986, 1989, 2000, 2001 and 2003, as well as at the 1984 and 1987 Canada Cup tournaments

- Was elected to the U.S. Hockey Hall of Fame in 2004 and the IIHF Hall of Fame in 2012

# 2011 **Mark Howe** **2**

> "When I first came to Philadelphia back in 1982, it was as if I was born to be a Flyer. The orange and black began to flow through my veins and instantly consumed my heart. The memories of playing for the Flyers will be a part of me forever."

NO. RETIRED BY PHILADELPHIA

ALTERNATES:

## 4 · 5

Detroit Red Wings
Hartford Whalers
Houston Aeros
New England Whalers
Philadelphia Flyers

Shoots: Left

Height: 5'-11"

Weight: 185 lbs.

Born: May 28, 1955; Detroit, Michigan

Drafted by the Boston Bruins 25th overall in 1974

Played 22 WHA and NHL seasons from 1973–95

Stats: see page 470

- Played amateur hockey with Detroit Junior Red Wings (1970–72); United States Olympic Team (1971–72); Toronto Marlboros (1972–73)

- Selected to OJHL First All-Star Team (1971)

- Member of Memorial Cup–winning Toronto Marlboros (1973); named Memorial Cup Most Valuable Player (1973); member of WHA Champion Houston Aeros (1974, 1975)

- Named WHA Rookie of the Year (1974); WHA Second All-Star Team Defense (1974); WHA First All-Star Team Defense (1979); ranks eighth in WHA career points (504)

- Holds Philadelphia Flyers team records for points (82), goals (24) and plus/minus (plus-87) by a defenseman in one season, established in 1985–86

- Holds Philadelphia Flyers team records for career goals (138), career assists (342) and career points (480) by a defenseman; holds Philadelphia Flyers team records for career playoff assists (45) and career playoff points (53) by a defenseman

- Holds Hartford Whalers/Carolina Hurricanes team record for assists by a defenseman (56) in one season, established in 1979–80

- Led NHL in regular-season plus/minus (plus-87) in 1985–86

- Played in NHL All-Star Game (1981, 1983, 1986, 1988)

- Finished second in NHL shorthanded goals in 1982–83 (5) and 1985–86 (7)

- Son of Hall of Famer Gorddie Howe

AWARDS

Emery Edge Award (1986)

ALL-STAR SELECTIONS

First All-Star Team Defense (1983, 1986, 1987)

INTERNATIONAL AWARDS

Silver Medal: Winter Olympics (1972)

# 3

## DEFENSE

# Harry Howell 1979

ALTERNATE:

## 5

Calgary Cowboys
California Golden Seals
Los Angeles Kings
New York Rangers
N.Y. Golden Blades/
New Jersey Knights
Oakland Seals
San Diego Mariners

Shoots: Left

Height: 6'-1"

Weight: 195 lbs.

Born: December 28,
1932: Hamilton, Ontario

Played 25 NHL and WHA
seasons from 1952–76

Stats: See page 471

"We played mostly road hockey, and if someone was fortunate enough to have a rink in their backyard, that's where we headed. That was it until I was seven or eight years old."

AWARDS
James Norris Memorial
Trophy (1967)

ALL-STAR
SELECTIONS
First All-Star Team
Defense (1967)

- Holds N.Y. Rangers team record for career games played (1,160)
- Played amateur hockey with Guelph Biltmores (1949–52)
- Member of Memorial Cup–winning Guelph Biltmores (1952); recorded five goals and 10 points in 1952 Memorial Cup playoffs
- Nicknamed "Harry the Horse" because of his work ethic and the fact he missed only 20 games in his first 16 NHL seasons
- Scored first NHL goal in first NHL game on first NHL shot in N.Y. Rangers' 4–3 loss to Toronto, October 18, 1952
- Last player to win the Norris Trophy before Bobby Orr—who won the award for the next eight seasons

- Played in NHL All-Star Game (1954, 1963, 1964, 1965, 1967, 1968, 1970)
- Served as captain of N.Y. Rangers (1955–57)
- Never won the Stanley Cup as a player, but did win as a scout with the Edmonton Oilers in 1990
- Underwent spinal fusion surgery in 1969 and recovered to play another seven professional seasons in the NHL and WHA
- Coached N.Y. Golden Blades/Jersey Knights (1973–74); coached San Diego Mariners (1974–75)
- Coached Minnesota North Stars (1978–79); coached Team Canada (1978)

# 1958 Ching Johnson 3

**18**

New York Americans
New York Rangers

Shoots: Left

Height: 5'-11"

Weight: 210 lbs.

Born: December 7, 1897;
Winnipeg, Manitoba

Died: June 16, 1979;
Silver Spring, Maryland

Played 12 NHL seasons
from 1926–38

Stats: See page 471

"Ching Johnson's grin is as wide as ever ... He played with such buoyant zest that he was the idol of the galleries and he played with such consummate skill that he has won a niche in hockey's Hall of Fame."

— Arthur Daly,
*New York Times*,
on Johnson's induction into the Hockey Hall of Fame

- Given name was Ivan; earned nickname because of his talents as a cook

- Played amateur hockey with Winnipeg Monarchs (1918–20); Eveleth Rangers (1920–23); Minneapolis Millers (1923–24, 1925–26); Minneapolis Rockets (1924–25)

- USAHA First All-Star Team Defense (1924); CHL First All-Star Team Defense (1926); AHA First All-Star Team Defense (1939)

- Signed as a free agent by N.Y. Rangers, September 2, 1926

- Finished second to Howie Morenz in voting for the Hart Trophy (1931–32)

- Played in NHL All-Star Game (1934)

- Coached Washington Lions (1941–43); coached Hollywood Wolves (1943–44)

- Served as player/coach of Minneapolis Millers (1938); served as player/coach of Marquette Ironmen (1940–41)

- Worked as a AHL and EHL linesman (1944–45)

- Also known as "Ivan the Terrible" around the league because of his rugged style and bruising body checks.

- Led N.Y. Rangers team in penalty minutes in eight of his 11 seasons he played with New York

- Led NHL in playoff penalty minutes in 1928 (46) and 1932 (24)

- Inducted into Manitoba Hockey Hall of Fame (1985)

- Inducted into Manitoba Sports Hall of Fame (2004)

**AWARDS**
Stanley Cup
(1927–28, 1932–33)

**ALL-STAR SELECTIONS**
First All-Star Team
Defense (1932, 1933)

Second All-Star Team
Defense (1931, 1934)

# 3

### DEFENSE

# Ernie Johnson 1952

Montreal AAA
Montreal Wanderers
New Westminster
Royals
Portland Rosebuds
Victoria Aristocrats
Victoria Cougars

Alternate Position: LW

Shoots: Left

Height: 5'-11"

Weight: 185 lbs.

Born: February 26, 1886:
Montreal, Quebec

Died: March 24,
1963: White Rock,
British Columbia

Played 19 elite amateur
and professional
seasons from 1903–22

Stats: See page 472

"I don't pay much attention to rules. There is only one rule that I really know — there is the puck and there's the net. Just put the puck in the net."

AWARDS

Stanley Cup
(1905–06, 1906–07,
1907–08, 1909–10)

ALL-STAR
SELECTIONS

PCHA First All-Star Team
Defense (1912, 1913, 1915,
1916, 1917, 1918, 1919, 1921)

- Played amateur hockey with Montreal St. Lawrence (1902–03)

- Started his career as a winger with the Montreal Wanderers; switched to defense when he joined the PCHA

- ECAHA Second All-Star Team Left Wing (1907); ECHA Second All-Star Team Left Wing (1908)

- Teamed with Frank "Pud" Glass with the Montreal Wanderers and the pair were inseparable on and off the ice. Known as "The Hockey Twins," they were fined early and often for their "behavior" off the ice

- Scored four goals in Stanley Cup playoff game against Ottawa Vics, January 13, 1908; scored four goals in Stanley Cup playoff game against Winnipeg Maple Leafs, March 12, 1908

- Earned the nickname "Moose" because of his incredibly long reach

- In the days long before stick regulations and rules, he was noted for using the longest stick ever in hockey, measuring 99 inches in length

- Member of the Montreal Wanderers team that successfully defended the Stanley Cup seven times against Ottawa "Silver Seven," New Glasgow, Edmonton, Ottawa Victorias, Winnipeg, Toronto and Berlin

- Notorious for signing and then rejecting contracts, he jumped, re-jumped and jumped back between the Montreal Wanderers and New Westminster Royals three times in less than a year

# Tom Johnson

**1970**

# 10

**ALTERNATE:**

## 22

**Boston Bruins**
**Montreal Canadiens**

Shoots: Left

Height: 6'

Weight: 180 lbs.

Born: February 18, 1928:
Baldur, Manitoba

Died: November 21, 2007:
Falmouth, Massachusetts

Played 16 NHL seasons
from 1947–48, 1950–65

Stats: See page 472

"I was classified as a defensive defenseman. I stayed back and minded the store. With the high powered scoring teams I was with, I just had to get them the puck and let them do the rest."

- Played amateur hockey with Winnipeg Monarchs (1946–47); Montreal Royals (1947–48)
- Signed as a free agent by Montreal, April 30, 1947
- Played in NHL All-Star Game (1952, 1953, 1956, 1957, 1958, 1959, 1960)
- Inducted into Manitoba Hockey Hall of Fame (1985)
- Inducted into Manitoba Sports Hall of Fame (1993)
- Coached Boston Bruins (1971–73)
- Coached Boston Bruins to Stanley Cup championship (1971–72)

- Renowned for his abilities as a penalty killer and skill at stripping the puck from opposing players and feeding a perfect pass to teammates
- Nicknamed "Tomcat" because he was always on the prowl when he was on the ice
- Claimed by Boston Bruins from Montreal in Waiver Draft, June 4, 1963
- Suffered career-ending leg injury in game vs. Chicago, February 28, 1965
- Served as assistant general manager (1970–71, 1973–79) and vice-president of the Boston Bruins (1979–99)

**AWARDS**

James Norris Memorial Trophy (1959)

Stanley Cup (1952–53, 1955–56, 1956–57, 1957–58, 1958–59, 1959–60)

**ALL-STAR SELECTIONS**

First All-Star Team Defense (1959)

Second All-Star Team Defense (1956)

## DEFENSE

# 4 Red Kelly 1969

NO. RETIRED BY TORONTO

**ALTERNATE:**

## 20

**Detroit Red Wings
Toronto Maple Leafs**

Alternate Position: C

Shoots: Left

Height: 5'-11"

Weight: 180 lbs.

Born: July 9, 1927;
Simcoe, Ontario

Played 20 NHL seasons
from 1947–67

Stats: See page 473

"[Coach] Joe Primeau taught me you don't win games in the penalty box. You've got to stay on the ice. Players would try to get you off the ice sometimes but you're more valuable to a team when you're on the ice."

**NHL AWARDS**

Lady Byng Memorial
Trophy (1951, 1953,
1954, 1961)

James Norris Memorial
Trophy (1954)

Stanley Cup
(1949–50, 1951–52,
1953–54, 1954–55,
1961–62, 1962–63,
1963–64, 1966–67)

**ALL-STAR
SELECTIONS**

First All-Star Team
Defense (1951, 1952,
1953, 1954, 1955, 1957)

Second All-Star Team
Defense (1950, 1956)

- Only player in NHL history to win Lady Byng Memorial Trophy as both a defenseman and a forward

- One of only six players in NHL history (with Dick Duff, Frank Mahovlich, Bryan Trottier, Patrick Roy and Larry Murphy) to win two or more Stanley Cup championships with two or more teams

- Played amateur hockey with St. Michael's Midgets (1943–44); St. Michael's Buzzers (1944–45); St. Michael's Majors (1944–47)

- Member of Memorial Cup–winning St. Michael's Majors (1946–47)

- Played in NHL All-Star Game (1950, 1951, 1952, 1953, 1954, 1955, 1956, 1957, 1958, 1960, 1962, 1963)

- Converted to center from defense when acquired by Toronto from Detroit, February 10, 1960

- Rights traded to L.A. Kings by Toronto on condition he would coach and not play, June 8, 1967

- One of only 10 players to be inducted into Hockey Hall of Fame without having to serve three-year waiting period

- Coached L.A. Kings (1967–69); Pittsburgh Penguins (1969–73); Toronto Maple Leafs (1973–77)

- Served in House of Commons as Liberal Member of Parliament for York West (1962–65)

- Received the Member of the Order of Canada (2005)

# Shut 'Em Down

Red Kelly's long career can be summed up with a single word: versatile. From being a rock-solid defenseman with the Detroit Red Wings from 1947–48 to 1959–60 to his transformation into a tight-checking two-way center with the Toronto Maple Leafs from 1959–60 to 1966–67, Kelly carved out a Hall of Fame career as a shutdown performer.

He did, however, have an offensive upside too. Through 12 and a half seasons as a Detroit defenseman, Kelly averaged just under 40 points per campaign. His role was two-fold: shut down the opposition's best and quarterback the play, providing an offensive punch and a sure pass to his all-star forwards, like Gordie Howe and Ted Lindsay.

Despite the position change, in Toronto his responsibilities were very similar. Coach Punch Imlach wanted him to shut down the opposition's best center and to provide secondary scoring for a Leafs club that needed contributions from all hands. Over his seven and a half seasons in Toronto he averaged nearly 50 points per season—including his only 70-point campaign (1960–61).

In Detroit, Kelly had been part of four Stanley Cup championships and was chosen for the NHL's First All-Star Team six times and to the Second Team twice. He was the inaugural winner of the Norris Trophy, as the league's premier defenseman in 1954, and he also played tough but clean, earning three Lady Byng wins while in the Motor City. So he was stunned when he learned he was traded from the Red Wings to the New York Rangers

**Toronto captain George Armstrong and Detroit captain Red Kelly at a center ice ceremony.**

in February of 1960. Rather than report, Kelly retired, only to be talked out of it less than a week later by the Leafs.

Imlach was bolstering his roster with hard-nosed, proven veterans, and Kelly fit the bill. Whether he could play center as well as he had defense was yet to be seen. But Kelly proved the skeptics wrong, winning another Lady Byng Trophy in Toronto in 1960–61. With the reformed blue-liner playing tough minutes at center against some of the league's best talent, the Leafs won four Stanley Cups, bringing Kelly's total to eight.

He shut down his shutdown career after the Leafs' last Cup win in 1967 and moved into the coaching ranks, where for 10 years he plied yet another new trade.

# 5 Rod Langway 2002

NO. RETIRED BY
WASHINGTON

ALTERNATE:
17

Birmingham Bulls
Montreal Canadiens
Washington Capitals

Shoots: Left
Height: 6'-3"
Weight: 218 lbs.
Born: May 3, 1957:
Maag, Taiwan
Drafted by the
Montreal Canadiens
36th overall in 1977
Played 16 WHA and NHL
seasons from 1977–93
Stats: See page 473

"It was a case that it was simply my time. If I had stayed in Montreal, I would have been the same kind of player, but I wouldn't have received the accolades of winning the Norris Trophy because I would have been put into different situations."

—Rod Langway, on being traded to Washington

**AWARDS**

James Norris Memorial Trophy (1983, 1984)

Stanley Cup (1978–79)

**ALL-STAR SELECTIONS**

First All-Star Team Defense (1983, 1984)

Second All-Star Team Defense (1985)

- Played amateur hockey with Randolph Rockets (1972–75); University of New Hampshire (1975–77)

- Played football, baseball and hockey at Randolph High School (1972–75)

- Played minor pro hockey with Hampton Gulls (1977–78)

- Played linebacker in football and defense in hockey at University of New Hampshire (1975–77)

- Nicknamed "The Secretary of Defense" during his career in Washington

- Traded to Washington by Montreal with Doug Jarvis, Craig Laughlin and Brian Engblom for Ryan Walter and Rick Green, September 9, 1982

- Played in NHL All-Star Game (1981, 1982, 1983, 1984, 1985, 1986)

- Played with Team U.S.A. in 1981, 1984 and 1987 Canada Cup Tournament

- Named to the Canada Cup First All-Star Team Defense (1984)

- Only player in NHL history to be born in Taiwan

- Served as assistant coach with Richmond Renegades (1993–94, 1996–97, 2000–01)

- Served as assistant coach with Providence Bruins (1997–98)

- Served as player/coach with Richmond Renegades (1994–95); San Francisco Spiders (1995–96)

- Coached Richmond Renegades (2003–04)

- Number retired by Washington, November 26, 1997

# 1987 Jacques Laperriere

**2**

ALTERNATE:

**26**

**Montreal Canadiens**

Shoots: Left

Height: 6'-2"

Weight: 190 lbs.

Born: November 22, 1941: Rouyn, Quebec

Played 12 NHL seasons from 1962–74

Stats: See page 474

"You cover the area you're responsible for. You don't get caught out of position. You gain control of the puck. You pass it to somebody or else you carry it over the blueline and then pass it to somebody else."

- Played amateur hockey with St. Laurent Jets (1957–58); Hull-Ottawa Jr. Canadiens (1958–62); Brockville Canadiens (1959–60)

- Played minor pro hockey with Hull-Ottawa Canadiens (1959–63)

- EPHL Second All-Star Team Defense (1963)

- Played on six Stanley Cup–winning teams in 12 seasons as a player and won two more Stanley Cup championships (1986, 1993) in 16 seasons as an assistant coach with Montreal Canadiens

- Played in NHL All-Star Game (1964, 1965, 1967, 1968, 1970)

- Named to the NHL Second All-Star Team as a rookie

- A tall and mobile defenseman who broke up plays with his long reach, he possessed an excellent low, hard drive from the point

- Only player other than Bobby Orr to lead the NHL in plus/minus between 1970–75 (plus-77 in 1972–73)

- Father of Dan Laperriere, who played in the NHL with St. Louis and Ottawa from 1993–96

- Coached Montreal Red, White and Blue (1975–76); coached Montreal Juniors (1976–77)

- Served as assistant coach with Montreal Canadiens (1981–97); Boston Bruins (1997–2000); N.Y. Islanders (2001–03); New Jersey Devils (2003–08)

**AWARDS**

Calder Memorial Trophy (1964)

James Norris Memorial Trophy (1966)

Stanley Cup (1964–65, 1965–66, 1967–68, 1968–69, 1970–71, 1972–73)

**ALL-STAR SELECTIONS**

First All-Star Team Defense (1965, 1966)

Second All-Star Team Defense (1964, 1970)

# 5

# Guy Lapointe 1993

**ALTERNATES:**
## 17 · 4 · 27

**Boston Bruins**
**Montreal Canadiens**
**St. Louis Blues**

Shoots: Left
Height: 6'
Weight: 205 lbs.
Born: March 18, 1948;
Montreal, Quebec
Played 16 NHL seasons
from 1968–84
Stats: See page 474

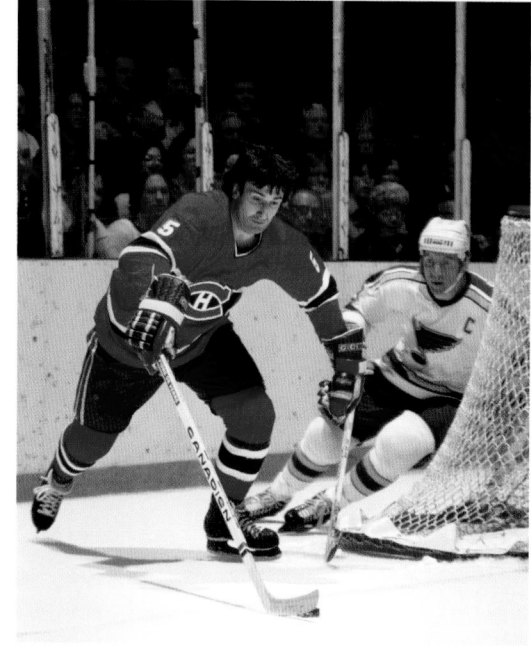

> "I was a kid who grew up in Montreal about a half hour away from the Forum. You don't even think that one day you're going to play for the Montreal Canadiens."

**AWARDS**
Stanley Cup
(1970–71, 1972–73,
1975–76, 1976–77,
1977–78, 1978–79)

**ALL-STAR
SELECTIONS**
First All-Star Team
Defense (1973)
Second All-Star
Team Defense
(1975, 1976, 1977)

**INTERNATIONAL
AWARDS**
Summit Series (1972)
Canada Cup (1976)

- Shares Montreal Canadiens team record (with Larry Robinson) for all-time playoff goals by a defenseman (25)

- Holds Montreal Canadiens team record for goals by a defenseman in regular season (28), established in 1974–75

- Holds Montreal Canadiens team record for goals by a rookie defenseman (15), established in 1970–71

- Played amateur hockey with Verdun Maple Leafs (1965–67); Montreal Jr. Canadiens (1967–68)

- Played in All-Star Game (1973, 1975, 1976, 1977)

- Became only fifth NHL defenseman to score 20 or more goals in regular season (1974–75)

- Member of Team NHL that played Soviet Union in 1979 Challenge Cup

- Member of Montreal's Big Three on defense with Serge Savard and Larry Robinson

- Runner-up up to Bobby Orr in voting for the 1972–73 Norris Trophy

- Was awarded Dit Clapper's retired jersey No. 5 when he joined Boston, but switched after Clapper family protested

- Coached Longueuil Chevaliers (1985–86)

**DEFENSE**

# 1962 Jack Laviolette

# 3

> "I do not wish to discuss my personal merit as a player. The public is the judge of that. But I know that every time I put on a uniform to play hockey … I put my whole heart, courage and desire to win into the game."

**ALTERNATES:**

# 6 · 7 · 2

**Michigan Soo Indians**
**Montreal Canadiens**
**Montreal Nationals**
**Montreal Shamrocks**

Alternate Position: RW

Shoots: Right

Height: 5'-11"

Weight: 170 lbs.

Born: July 17, 1879: Belleville, Ontario

Died: January 9, 1960: Montreal, Quebec

Played 14 professional seasons from 1904–18

Stats: See page 475

- Starred in both hockey and lacrosse and also was renowned as an automobile racer
- Played amateur hockey with Montreal Bell Telephone (1902–03); Montreal Nationals (1903–04)
- Signed as a free agent by Michigan Soo, November, 1904
- Signed as a free agent by Montreal Shamrocks, December 15, 1907
- Helped form, organize and manage the Montreal Canadiens in their inaugural season (1909–10)
- Replaced goaltender Pat Larochelle in net for the final five minutes of overtime in Montreal Canadiens' 5–4 victory over Montreal Shamrocks, March 11, 1910

- Served as first captain of Montreal Canadiens (1909–10)
- Nicknamed "The Speed Merchant" because of his legendary speed — a skill that prompted sportswriters to dub his Montreal Canadiens teammates "The Flying Frenchmen"
- Member of Stanley Cup–winning Montreal Canadiens (1915–16)
- Career came to an end when his right leg had to be amputated below the knee following an automobile accident, May 1, 1918

**AWARDS**
Stanley Cup (1915–16)

**ALL-STAR SELECTIONS**
IHL First All-Star Team
Right Wing (1905, 1907)

# 2 Brian Leetch 2009

NO. RETIRED BY
NEW YORK RANGERS

ALTERNATE:
22

Boston Bruins
New York Rangers
Toronto Maple Leafs

Shoots: Left

Height: 6'

Weight: 185 lbs.

Born: March 3, 1968:
Corpus Christi, Texas

Drafted by the New York Rangers ninth overall in 1986

Played 18 NHL seasons from 1987–2004, 2005–06

Stats: See page 475

**AWARDS**

Calder Memorial Trophy (1989)

James Norris Memorial Trophy (1992, 1997)

Conn Smythe Trophy (1994)

Lester Patrick Trophy (2007)

Stanley Cup (1993–94)

**ALL-STAR SELECTIONS**

All-Rookie Team (1989)

First All-Star Team Defense (1989, 1992, 1997)

Second All-Star Team Defense (1991, 1994, 1996)

**INTERNATIONAL AWARDS**

World Cup (1996)

"I was proud to be a Ranger for my entire career, and I wanted to be here when things got turned around. So I was disappointed and still am."

—Brian Leetch, on being traded to Toronto in 2004

- Holds N.Y. Rangers team record for assists in regular season (80), established in 1991–92

- Holds N.Y. Rangers team records for career goals (240), assists (741) and points (981) by a defenseman

- One of only five defensemen (with Bobby Orr, Paul Coffey, Al MacInnis and Denis Potvin) in NHL history to record more than 100 points in a season

- Last NHL defenseman to register 100 points in regular season (1991–92)

- First American-born and trained player to win the Conn Smythe Trophy (1994)

- Played amateur hockey with Cheshire High Rams (1983–84); Avon Old Farms (1984–86); Boston College (1986–87); U.S.A. National Team (1987–88)

- Hockey East First All-Star Team Defense (1987); NCAA East First All-American Team Defense (1987)

- Led NHL playoffs in assists (23) and points (34) in 1993–94

- Played in NHL All-Star Game (1990, 1991, 1992, 1994, 1996, 1997, 1998, 2000, 2001)

- Finished among NHL top-10 in assists in 1990–91 (72), 1991–92 (80), 1995–96 (70), 1996–97 (58) and 2000–01 (58)

- Signed as a free agent by Boston, August 3, 2005

- Registered 1,000th career NHL point in Boston's 4–3 loss to Montreal Canadiens, October 18, 2005

- Inducted into Avon Old Farms Hall of Fame (2004)

# American Made

**B**rian Leetch had favorite players, but he didn't have any role models, so he became one. "I grew up in Connecticut, and no one was going to the NHL from there," recalled Leetch, who along with Craig Janney became the only two bona fide NHLers of their era to come from that state. "There was no one to show us the way. I didn't have a thought of the NHL when I was playing town hockey and high school. It was a far-off dream... The only thing that seemed realistic was maybe the Olympics."

After leading his hometown Cheshire Rams to a state championship and some further seasoning at Avon Old Farms School, an all-boys prep school in Avon, Connecticut, Leetch was drafted ninth overall in 1986 by the New York Rangers. From there he enrolled at Boston College, where, like his father before him, he became an All-Star defenseman. After a year at Boston College and another with the United States Olympic team—where he skated in the 1988 Calgary Olympics—Leetch joined the Rangers and got off to a prophetic start, notching an assist in his first game: a February 29, 1988, contest against the St. Louis Blues that New York won 5–2.

In 1988–89, which was his official rookie season after having only played 17 games in 1987–88, he scored 23 goals, setting a record for rookie defensemen, and won the Calder Memorial Trophy. In his brilliant 16 seasons with the Rangers, he won two Norris Trophies (1992 and 1997) and became the first American defenseman with a 100-point season

Brian Leetch wore these heavily reinforced skates from 1989 through to 1995. During that span, Leetch won a Norris Trophy (1992) and a Conn Smythe Trophy (1994) as his New York Rangers won the Stanley Cup in 1994 for the first time in 54 years.

(1991–92) and the first American to win the Conn Smythe Trophy, which he earned when the Rangers won the 1994 Stanley Cup, their first in 54 years. That playoff run saw Leetch lead the Rangers in scoring, with 11 goals and 23 assists for 34 points.

Leetch then captained the American side to a World Cup victory in 1996, and he was an integral part of the silver medal–winning team at the 2002 Salt Lake Olympics. On April 18, 1999, he was the scoring end of a Wayne Gretzky play that ended up being the "Great One's" last NHL point. In all Leetch tallied 1,028 points in 1,205 games, the seventh highest total of any American-born NHLer.

## DEFENSE

# 5 Nicklas Lidstrom 2015

**NO. RETIRED BY DETROIT**

Detroit Red Wings

Shoots: Left

Height: 6'-1"

Weight: 190 lbs.

Born: April 28, 1970; Vasteras, Sweden

Drafted by the Detroit Red Wings 53rd overall in 1989

Played 20 NHL seasons from 1991–2004, 2005–12

Stats: See page 476

**AWARDS**

James Norris Memorial Trophy (2001, 2002, 2003, 2006, 2007, 2008, 2011)

Conn Smythe Trophy (2002)

Stanley Cup (1996–97, 1997–98, 2001–02, 2007–08)

**ALL-STAR SELECTIONS**

All-Rookie Team (1992)

First All-Star Team Defenseman (1998, 1999, 2000, 2001, 2002, 2003, 2006, 2007, 2008, 2011)

Second All-Star Team Defenseman (2009, 2010)

**INTERNATIONAL AWARDS**

Gold Medal: Winter Olympics (2006)

Gold Medal: World Championships (1991)

"We had some great players, and we had a great coach in Scotty Bowman, but we had a lot of fun along the way, too. We won lots, and had a lot of fun doing it."

- Competed for Sweden in the European Junior Championships (1988), World Junior Championships (1990), World Championships (1991) and Canada Cup (1991) before joining the NHL

- Finished second behind Pavel Bure in voting for the Calder Trophy as rookie of the year in 1991–92

- His seven Norris Trophy wins are tied with Doug Harvey for second behind Bobby Orr's eight; he also finished second in voting for the trophy behind Rob Blake in 1998, Al MacInnis in 1999 and Chris Pronger in 2000

- Led all NHL defensemen in scoring in 1997–98, 1999–2000, 2005–06 and 2007–08

- Established career highs of 20 goals in 1999–2000, and 64 assists and 80 points in 2005–06

- Among NHL defensemen, he ranks sixth all-time in assists (878) and points (1,142), and ninth in goals (264)

- With the exception of the 2004–05 lockout season, he participated in the playoffs for 20 consecutive seasons, an NHL record he shares with Larry Robinson; his 263 career playoff games rank second all-time behind Chris Chelios (266)

- In 2002 he became the first European player to win the Conn Smythe Trophy as playoff MVP; in 2008 he was the first to captain a Stanley Cup championship team

- Served as captain of Red Wings for the final six seasons of his career (2006–12)

- Played in NHL All-Star Game (1996, 1998, 1999, 2000, 2001, 2002, 2003, 2004, 2007, 2008, 2011)

- Member of the Triple Gold Club for winning the Stanley Cup, an Olympic gold medal and a World Championship gold medal

- Represented Sweden at the World Cup in 1996 and 2004, and at the Olympics in 1998, 2002, 2006 and 2010

- Was inducted into the IIHF Hall of Fame in 2014

# Hockeytown For Life

Any conversation about the greatest defensemen in NHL history would be incomplete without the inclusion of Nicklas Lidstrom. Few players at any position have been as consistently excellent over a long period of time as Lidstrom. "During my career," said Lidstrom at the time of the announcement of his induction into the Hockey Hall of Fame, "I was always focused on the next game or the next season… I took a lot of pride in being dedicated to the game, so it means a great deal to me to be recognized by those who know the game best."

Lidstrom played 20 seasons in the NHL, all with the Detroit Red Wings. Physically strong and fundamentally smart, Lidstrom annually ranked among the leaders in time on ice and in scoring by defensemen. He used good positioning to defend in his own end, and rarely took penalties, finishing second in voting for the Lady Byng Trophy five times in his career—a rare feat for a defenseman since the award usually goes to a forward. Lidstrom never missed more than six games in a year until his final season of 2011–12, when he missed 12 games at the age of 41. Over the last 14 years of his career, Lidstrom was a First Team All-Star 10 times and a Second Team All-Star twice. He never finished lower than sixth in voting for the Norris Trophy during those 14 years, and won it on seven occasions. That tied him with Doug Harvey for second in Norris wins, just one behind Bobby Orr's eight.

As a rookie in 1991–92, Lidstrom finished

**Nicklas Lidstrom hoists the Stanley Cup in 1998 after the Red Wings defeated the Capitals in four games.**

second behind Pavel Bure in voting for the Calder Trophy. He was runner-up for the Norris Trophy behind Rob Blake, Al MacInnis and Chris Pronger for three straight seasons before winning it for the first time in 2000–01, and then won it again five times over the next six years. His final Norris victory came in 2010–11, after his 19th NHL season. Lidstrom won the Stanley Cup in 1997 and 1998, and became the first European player to win the Conn Smythe Trophy as playoff MVP when Detroit won the Cup again in 2002. He succeeded Steve Yzerman as Red Wings captain in 2006–07, and after being named the best European-trained player in NHL history by *The Hockey News* in 2007, he became the first European player to lead his team to the Stanley Cup in 2008.

# 2

## DEFENSE
# Al MacInnis 2007

NO. RETIRED BY ST. LOUIS

ALTERNATES:
## 11 · 22

Calgary Flames
St. Louis Blues

Shoots: Right
Height: 6'-2"
Weight: 204 lbs.

Born: July 11, 1963:
Inverness, Nova Scotia

Drafted by the
Calgary Flames 15th
overall in 1981

Played 23 NHL seasons
from 1981–2004

Stats: See page 477

"I can remember spending hours just shooting pucks off a sheet of plywood against my Dad's barn. I was just doing it to pass the time, never thinking it would end up the way it did [that I'd] and be known for the slap shot."

AWARDS
Conn Smythe
Trophy (1989)
James Norris Memorial
Trophy (1999)
Stanley Cup (1988–89)

ALL-STAR
SELECTIONS
First All-Star Team (1990,
1991, 1999, 2003)
Second All-Star Team
(1987, 1989, 1994)

INTERNATIONAL
AWARDS
Canada Cup (1991)
Gold Medal: Winter
Olympics (2002)

- Holds NHL record for most consecutive playoff games with at least one point by a defenseman (19), established from 1989–90
- Holds Calgary Flames team records for career assists (609), career playoff points (102), career playoff assists (77) and single playoff season points (31)
- Holds St. Louis Blues record for career points by a defenseman (450)
- First defenseman to lead NHL playoffs outright in points (31) in 1988–89
- Ranks fifth in NHL career shots on goal (5,157); ranks third in NHL career points by a defenseman (1,274)

- One of only five defensemen (with Bobby Orr, Paul Coffey, Brian Leetch and Denis Potvin) in NHL history to record more than 100 points in a season
- Played amateur hockey with Cole Harbour Wings (1978–79); Regina Blues (1979–80); Kitchener Rangers (1980–83)
- OHL First All-Star team Defense (1982, 1983)
- Won Hardest Shot Competition at the NHL All-Star Game (1991, 1992, 1997, 1998, 1999, 2000, 2003)
- Played minor pro hockey with Colorado Flames (1983–84)
- Played in NHL All-Star Game (1985, 1988, 1990, 1991, 1992, 1994, 1996, 1997, 1998, 1999, 2000, 2003)

# The Shot

I t isn't really fair to boil down a Hall of Fame career to one attribute, but some attributes are too overwhelming to ignore. For Al MacInnis, the first Nova Scotian to be inducted into the Hockey Hall of Fame, that attribute was his shot.

Sure MacInnis was a tough two-way defender who finished his career with a plus/minus of plus-371, the 16th best total *ever* posted. And yes, he is one of only five defensemen in NHL history to score more than 100 points in a season, which he did with the Calgary Flames in 1990–91. He was also a seven-time All-Star, but really, his shot...

MacInnis was drafted by Calgary 15th overall in 1981 and made his NHL debut with the Flames during the 1981–82 season. He played a handful of games for Calgary between 1981–82 and 1982–83, and after spending the early part of the 1983–84 season with the Central Hockey League's Colorado Flames, MacInnis got another chance to crack Calgary's blue line. On January 17, 1984, while playing for Calgary in a game against St. Louis, MacInnis wound up and fired a shot from outside the blue line that caught Blues netminder Mike Liut flush on the mask, splitting it. Liut fell to the ice as the puck dribbled over the goal line. No one took MacInnis' shot for granted after that. In total he played 51 games and scored 11 goals and 34 assists that season.

MacInnis honed his famous shot as a bored kid pounding pucks off a sheet of plywood against his dad's barn. He ended up winning the NHL All-Star Game's hardest shot

**Al MacInnis hoists the Stanley Cup in 1989.**

competition seven times.

After his blistering rookie season, MacInnis spent 10 more seasons in Calgary and was an integral part of the Flames' Stanley Cup championship in 1989. He collected seven goals and 24 assists in 22 games, making him the first defenseman to lead the playoffs in scoring, and he was named the MVP of the playoffs. Traded to St. Louis in 1994, MacInnis continued to dominate, his work culminating in a Norris Trophy win in 1999 as the league's top defenseman.

He finished his career after 23 NHL seasons ranked third in goals (340), assists (934) and points (1,274) by a defenseman. It is safe to say his shot was a major reason why.

**273**

# 2

# Sylvio Mantha 1960

ALTERNATE:

# 8

Boston Bruins
Montreal Canadiens

Shoots: Right

Height: 5'-10"

Weight: 178 lbs.

Born: April 14, 1902:
Montreal, Quebec

Died: August 7, 1974:
Montreal, Quebec

Played 14 NHL seasons
from 1923–37

Stats: See page 477

"I think I can relate to players because I've been through the process. I've been sent down to the minors, I've been put on waivers, I've been claimed on waivers, I've been traded, I've played for different coaches and had to learn different styles."

— Sylvio Mantha, commenting on his qualifications as coach

AWARDS

Stanley Cup (1923–24,
1929–30, 1930–31)

ALL-STAR
SELECTIONS

Second All-Star Team
Defense (1931, 1932)

- Played amateur hockey with the Notre Dame de Grace (1918–19), Verdun HC (1919–20); Montreal Imperial Tobacco (1920–21); Montreal Northern Electric (1921–22); Montreal Nationales (1922–23)

- Signed as free agent by Montreal Canadiens, December 3, 1923

- Member of the Stanley Cup–winning Montreal Canadiens team that "forgot" the Stanley Cup on the side of the street while changing a flat tire on the team car following a victory reception at the University of Montreal, April 3, 1924

- Scored first goal in history of Boston Garden in Montreal Canadiens' 1–0 victory over Boston Bruins, November 20, 1928

- Missed only 12 games in 13 full NHL seasons

- Signed as free agent by Boston, February 11, 1937

- Worked as a linesman and referee for the AHL and NHL

- Coached Montreal Canadiens (1935–36)

- Coached Montreal Concordias (1938–39); Laval Nationales (1943–45); Verdun Maple Leafs (1945–47) and St. Jerome Eagles (1947–48)

- After retirement, operated dairy businesses in Ontario and Quebec. Elected member of the Canadian Commodity Exchange in June of 1938

# 1965 Jack Marshall

**8**

ALTERNATES:
**3 · 7**

Montreal AAA
Montreal Shamrocks
Montreal Wanderers
Ottawa Montagnards
Toronto Blueshirts
Winnipeg Victorias

Alternate Position: C

Shoots: Right

Height: 5'-9"

Weight: 160 lbs.

Born: March 14, 1877: Saint-Vallier, Quebec

Died: August 7, 1965: Montreal, Quebec

Played 16 elite amateur and professional seasons from 1900–05, 1906–17

Stats: See page 478

"I knew the boys could do it and they played with every ounce that was in them. It was a rough, hard-checking contest from start to finish, but we were always going strong and I was sure that we would make it three straight."

— Jack Marshall, on Toronto's 1914 Stanley Cup victory

- Only player in hockey history to win the Stanley Cup with four different franchises (Winnipeg, Montreal AAA, Montreal Wanderers, Toronto Blueshirts)

- Played amateur hockey with Montreal Pointe Charles (1894–98)

- Was an all-around athlete who also starred at basketball, football, soccer, baseball, lacrosse and bowling

- Born in Quebec and raised in Montreal, he first came to prominence in hockey in Winnipeg

- Member of Stanley Cup–winning Winnipeg Victorias team that defeated Montreal Shamrocks in January of 1901

- Scored Stanley Cup–winning goal in Montreal AAA's 2–1 victory over Winnipeg Victorias, March 17, 1903

- Led FAHL in goals in 1903–04 (11) and 1904–05 (17)

- Won Stanley Cup as forward with the Montreal Wanderers (1906–07)

- Won Stanley Cup as a defenseman with the Montreal Wanderers (1909–10) and played defense for the rest of his career

- Served as player/coach of Stanley Cup–winning Toronto Blueshirts (1913–14)

- Retired to serve as NHA referee (1916–17)

- Coached Montreal AAA (1919–23); coached Montreal British Consols (1924–25)

- Played exhibition season with Toronto Pros in 1905–06

**AWARDS**
Stanley Cup
(1900–01, 1901–02, 1902–03, 1906–07, 1909–10, 1913–14)

# 3

# George McNamara 1958

ALTERNATE:

## 4

Canadian Soo
Halifax Crescents
Montreal Shamrocks
Toronto 228th Battalion
Toronto Blueshirts
Toronto Ontarios
Toronto Shamrocks
Toronto Tecumsehs
Waterloo Colts

Shoots: Left

Height: 6'-1"

Weight: 220 lbs.

Born: August 26, 1886;
Penetanguishene,
Ontario

Died: March 10, 1952;
Miami, Florida

Played 10 professional
seasons from
1906–09, 1910–17

Stats: See page 478

"The McNamara brothers checked well … In the second period, George McNamara got away for one of his rushes. He bore well in past the Wanderers' defense and scored the winning goal."

— *Toronto World*,
February 10, 1913

AWARDS

Stanley Cup (1913–14)

- Played amateur hockey with Sault Ste. Marie Monarchs (1904–06)

- Renowned as a rugged, hard-checking defenseman who was often paired with brother Howard throughout his hockey career

- The McNamara Brothers were known as "The Dynamite Twins" despite being born three years apart

- A third brother—Harold—was often teamed with the "Twins"

- Signed as a free agent by Toronto Tecumsehs, December 12, 1912; traded to Toronto Blueshirts by Toronto Ontarios for cash, January 12, 1914

- Member of Stanley Cup–winning Toronto Blueshirts (1913–14)

- Enlisted in the Canadian army during Word War I and played with the 228th Battalion team that began the 1916–17 season playing in the NHA before being sent overseas

- Credited with naming Sault Ste. Marie team the "Greyhounds" because a "greyhound is much faster than a wolf" in reference to local rivals, the Sudbury Wolves

- Coached Sault Ste. Marie Greyhounds (1920–26)

- Coached Allan Cup–winning Sault Ste. Marie Greyhounds (1924)

- Coached Detroit Greyhounds (1926–27)

- Served on Ontario Athletic Commission (1941–45)

# 2004 Larry Murphy

# 55

> "Once you get your hands on the Stanley Cup, it gets so much tougher to lose, and you ache to get at it again."

**ALTERNATES:**
## 8 · 5

**Detroit Red Wings**
**Los Angeles Kings**
**Minnesota North Stars**
**Pittsburgh Penguins**
**Toronto Maple Leafs**
**Washington Capitals**

Shoots: Right

Height: 6'-2"

Weight: 210 lbs.

Born: March 8, 1961; Scarborough, Ontario

Drafted by the Los Angeles Kings fourth overall in 1980

Played 21 NHL seasons from 1980–2001

Stats: See page 478

- Holds NHL record for points by a rookie defenseman (76), established in 1980–81

- Holds NHL record for assists by a defenseman in Stanley Cup final (9), established in 1990–91

- Holds Washington Capitals' record for assists (60) and points (81) by a defenseman in regular season, established in 1986–87

- Played on four Stanley Cup–winning teams in the 1990s, the most of any NHL player in that decade

- One of only six players in NHL history (with Red Kelly, Frank Mahovlich, Bryan Trottier, Patrick Roy and Dick Duff) to win two or more Stanley Cup championships with two or more teams

- Ranks ninth in NHL career games played (1,615)

- Ranks fourth in NHL career assists by a defenseman (929)

- Ranks fifth in NHL career points by a defenseman (1,217)

- Played amateur hockey with Don Mills Flyers (1977–78); Toronto Red Wings (1977–78); Peterborough Petes (1978–80)

- Member of Memorial Cup–winning Peterborough Petes (1979); led Memorial Cup playoffs in assists (6) in 1979–80

- OMJHL First All-Star Team Defense (1980); Named OMJHL Outstanding Defenseman (1980)

- Played in NHL All-Star Game (1994, 1996, 1999)

**AWARDS**
Stanley Cup (1990–91, 1991–92, 1996–97, 1997–98)

**ALL-STAR SELECTIONS**
Second All-Star Team Defenseman (1987, 1993, 1995)

**INTERNATIONAL AWARDS**
Canada Cup (1987, 1991)

Silver Medal: World Championships (1985)

# 27

# Scott Niedermayer 2013

NO. RETIRED BY
NEW JERSEY

Anaheim Ducks
Mighty Ducks of
Anaheim
New Jersey Devils

Shoots: Left

Height: 6'-1"

Weight: 194 lbs.

Born: August 31, 1973:
Edmonton, Alberta

Drafted by the New
Jersey Devils third
overall in 1991

Played 18 NHL
seasons from
1991–2004, 2005–10

Stats: See page 479

**AWARDS**

James Norris Memorial
Trophy (2004)

Conn Smythe
Trophy (2007)

Stanley Cup (1994–95,
1999–2000, 2002–03,
2006–07)

**ALL-STAR
SELECTIONS**

All-Rookie Team (1993)

First All-Star Team
Defense (2004,
2006, 2007)

Second All-Star Team
Defense (1998)

**INTERNATIONAL
AWARDS**

Gold Medal: Winter
Olympics (2002, 2010)

Gold Medal: World
Championship (2004)

World Cup (2004)

"It's special. You can only dream of passing [the Stanley Cup] to your brother. To be able to do that is definitely a highlight of my career."

- Set record for most NHL career regular-season overtime goals by a defenseman (13); set NHL record for most regular-season overtime goals by a defenseman in a single season (4) in 2001–02 (tied by Shayne Gostisbehere in 2015–16)

- Only player in hockey history to win Memorial Cup, Stanley Cup, World Cup, World Championship, World Junior Hockey Championship and Olympic Gold Medal

- Played amateur hockey with Cranbrook Blazers (1988–89) and Kamloops Blazers (1989–92)

- Member of Memorial Cup–winning Kamloops Blazers (1992)

- Holds New Jersey Devils team record for most assists in a single playoff season (16), established in 2002–03

- WHL West First All-Star Team (1991, 1992); Canadian Major Junior Scholastic Player of the Year (1991); Memorial Cup All-Star Team Defense (1992); Stafford Smythe Memorial Trophy (Memorial Cup MVP; 1992)

- Holds New Jersey Devils team career records for goals (112), assists (364), points (476), power-play goals (51), power-play points (189), playoff assists (47) and playoff points (64) by a defenseman

- Holds Anaheim Ducks team career records for most points (264), assists (204), power-play goals (39), power-play assists (106), power-play points (145), shorthanded assists (8), shorthanded points (8), game-winning goals (13) and overtime goals (5) by a defenseman

# Winning

**W**inning is the thing. It always has been. But the elements that make one person a winner and another merely a gifted athlete are incredibly subjective and one of the great mysteries of sport.

Yet it is safe to say, unequivocally, that Scott Niedermayer is a winner. It is more than just his being on good teams or his fortunate timing. In fact, Niedermayer is such a winner that he is the only player in history to win a Memorial Cup, a World Junior Championship, a World Championship, the World Cup, an Olympic gold medal and the Stanley Cup. (And his teams have won Olympic gold twice and four Stanley Cups.)

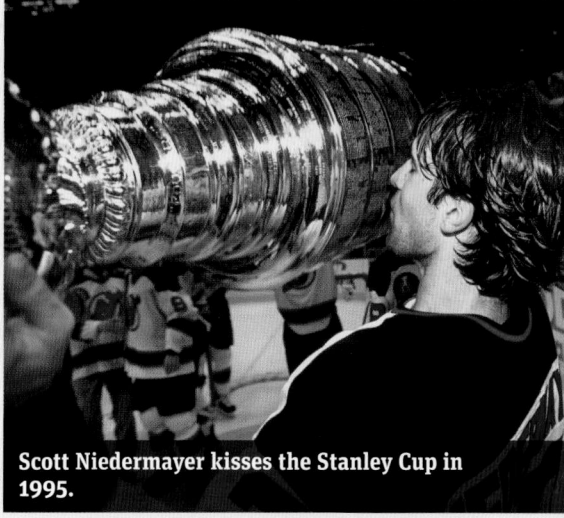

**Scott Niedermayer kisses the Stanley Cup in 1995.**

Taken third overall in the 1991 draft— an event largely famous for the Quebec Nordiques selecting Eric Lindros first overall and his subsequent refusal to sign with the team—Niedermayer often existed in the shadow of Lindros and other NHL up-and-comers.

At that point Niedermayer had already won a World Junior Championship (alongside Lindros), but his game didn't garner the raucous headlines of others. Niedermayer was a gifted passer and a great skater with a knack for knowing where the play was headed. He was a student of the game, and over his career he eschewed greater personal point totals in favor of responsible team play, resulting in greater team success. His contributions were sometimes hard to see for the casual observer, but those in the know often considered Niedermayer to be the best player on the ice.

And he didn't leave the NHL without a couple of individual accolades. He won the Norris Trophy as defenseman of the year in 2004 and the Conn Smythe Trophy as the playoff MVP in 2007.

Niedermayer's team-first game was defined by his play in the important moments, like during the 2010 Olympic gold-medal game. Niedermayer took the second most shifts on the team, and was called upon in the most demanding situations. And of course, it was Niedermayer's pass that started the sequence of events that led to Sidney Crosby's Olympic-winning goal.

Whether you call it heart or leadership or a winning attitude, Niedermayer has it in spades. But he also possesses a greater quality, the selflessness that is needed to truly excel in team sports. His balancing act between this selflessness and the need for individual gratification may be Niedermayer's greatest skill.

# 4 Bobby Orr 1979

NO. RETIRED BY BOSTON

**Boston Bruins**
**Chicago Black Hawks**

Shoots: Left

Height: 6'

Weight: 197 lbs.

Born: March 20, 1948:
Parry Sound, Ontario

Played 12 NHL seasons
from 1966–77, 1978–79

Stats: See page 480

### AWARDS

Calder Memorial
Trophy (1967)

James Norris Memorial
Trophy (1968, 1969,
1970, 1971, 1972,
1973, 1974, 1975)

Art Ross Trophy
(1970, 1975)

Conn Smythe Trophy
(1970, 1972)

Hart Memorial Trophy
(1970, 1971, 1972)

Ted Lindsay Award*
(1975)

Lester Patrick
Trophy (1979)

Stanley Cup
(1969–70, 1971–72)

### ALL-STAR SELECTIONS

First All-Star Team
Defense (1968, 1969,
1970, 1971, 1972,
1973, 1974, 1975)

Second All-Star Team
Defense (1967)

### INTERNATIONAL AWARDS

Canada Cup (1976)

*Known as the Lester
B. Pearson Award
from 1971 to 2009

"I never thought
there could be such
a day. This is what
every kid dreams of,
scoring the winning
goal in a Stanley Cup
overtime final. Wow!
I can't find words to
express what I feel."

— Bobby Orr, on
his famous 1970
overtime goal

- Only defenseman in NHL history to win league scoring title (1970, 1975)
- First defenseman in NHL history to record 100 points in regular season (1969–70)
- First player in NHL history to win Conn Smythe Trophy twice (1970, 1972)
- Holds NHL record for regular season assists (102) and points (139) by a defenseman, established in 1970–71
- Holds NHL record for plus/minus rating in regular season (plus-124), established in 1970–71
- Shares NHL record for assists in a regular season game by a defenseman (6), January 1, 1973
- Played in NHL All-Star Game (1968, 1969, 1970, 1971, 1972, 1973, 1975)

- Played amateur hockey with Oshawa Generals (1962–66)
- Scored Stanley Cup–winning overtime goal in Boston's 4–3 victory over St. Louis Blues, May 10, 1970
- Led NHL in assists in 1969–70 (87), 1970–71 (102), 1971–72 (80), 1973–74 (90) and 1974–75 (89); led NHL playoffs in assists (19) and points (24) in 1971–72; led NHL in shots on goal in 1969–70 (413) and 1974–75 (384)
- Led Canada Cup Tournament in points (9) in 1976; named Canada Cup MVP (1976)
- Burdened by knee injuries through the majority of career; missed 1972 Summit Series and entire 1977–78 season recovering from off-season surgery

# Beantown's Best

Rare is the athlete who has the innate ability to completely transform their chosen profession. Bobby Orr is one such athlete.

The Boston Bruins knew Orr was special, and they went out of their way to acquire the rights to the wunderkind from Parry Sound, Ontario, sponsoring the teams he played on all the way up until he reached the NHL.

By 1966–67, Orr was an 18-year-old who was regularly turning the heads of NHL players, executives and fans. He played 61 games that season, recorded 41 points and was named Rookie of the Year. It was his style of play, however, that really garnered headlines. Orr was an end-to-end virtuoso, capable of starting a rush from behind his own goal line that wound through the entire team and finished with the puck in the back of the opposition's net. His offensive forays drew double and triple coverage, and the odd-numbered matchups always ensured he had a teammate open for a pass. He back-checked hard and used his great skating to keep players to the outside, making the shots easier for his goalies to handle. Quite simply, Orr was the first to play defense offensively.

With the addition of Phil Esposito in 1967–68, the Bruins really took off. In the six-team league, Boston players had won only eight NHL individual trophies over a 25-year span (1942–43 to 1966–67). But the Bruins of the Orr-Esposito era (1967–68 to 1974–75) won 28 awards, with Orr hauling in 15: three Hart Trophies, two Art Ross Trophies, eight Norris Trophies and two Conn Smythe Trophies.

**Bobby Orr sails through the air after scoring the 1970 Stanley Cup winner.**

The duo also helped lead Boston to a pair of Stanley Cups (1970 and 1972), the first erasing a 29-year Cup drought for the Bruins. Among hockey's most recognizable images is the photograph of Orr in mid-flight, after being tripped by St. Louis Blues defenseman Noel Picard, moments after scoring the overtime goal that gave the Bruins that drought-ending Cup.

Orr was the first defenseman to lead the NHL in scoring and the first player at any position to record 100 assists in one season. He set the single-season league record for plus/minus with a plus-124 rating, and he set the single-season points record for defensemen with 139.

He was, however, vulnerable, and his knees gave way long before his drive did. His last memorable moment came with Team Canada at the 1976 Canada Cup, where he was named tournament MVP.

# 2 DEFENSE

# Brad Park 1988

ALTERNATE:
## 22

Boston Bruins
Detroit Red Wings
New York Rangers

Shoots: Left

Height: 6'

Weight: 200 lbs.

Born: July 6, 1948:
Toronto, Ontario

Drafted by the New
York Rangers second
overall in 1966

Played 17 NHL seasons
from 1968–85

Stats: See page 480

"I never thought I'd get to a thousand games and quite a few other people didn't think I would either. There was just no indication how much hockey was left in my knees. Even though there was a lot of damage done to my knees, they held together remarkably well through the years."

AWARDS
Bill Masterton Memorial
Trophy (1984)

ALL-STAR
SELECTIONS
First All-Star Team
Defense (1970, 1972,
1974, 1976, 1978)

Second All-Star Team
Defense (1971, 1973)

INTERNATIONAL
AWARDS
Summit Series (1972)

- Held NHL record for career points by a defenseman (896); surpassed by Denis Potvin in 1986–87

- Held NHL record for consecutive years appearing in the playoffs (17); surpassed by Larry Robinson in 1989–90

- Played amateur hockey with Scarborough Lions (1959–63); Eglington Aces (1963–65); Toronto Westclairs (1965–66); Toronto Marlboros (1965–68)

- OHA-Jr. Second All-Star Team Defense (1968)

- Member of Memorial Cup–winning Toronto Marlboros (1967)

- First defenseman in N.Y. Rangers history to record a hat trick in N.Y. Rangers' 6–1 victory over Pittsburgh Penguins, December 12, 1971

- One of only seven players to play every game in 1972 Canada–Soviet Union Summit Series

- Named Player of the Game (with Paul Henderson) in Game 8 of 1972 Summit Series

- Played in nine consecutive NHL All-Star Games from 1970–78

- Finished among NHL top-10 in assists in 1973–74 (57), 1976–77 (55) and 1977–78 (57)

- Finished as runner-up in Norris Trophy voting six times

- Named N.Y. Rangers MVP after leading team in scoring with 82 points in 1973–74

- Coached Detroit Red Wings (1985–86)

# Second Place Ain't So Bad

Through 17 NHL seasons, Brad Park exemplified blue line excellence. From his time on Broadway with the New York Rangers to his tour with the Don Cherry's "Lunch Pail Gang" in Boston to his last seasons in Detroit, he was heralded as one of the best defensemen in the league.

But, Park's best years coincided with the best years of the game-changing Bobby Orr. And Orr wasn't just any star, he was

**Brad Park skates as a Boston Bruin in the mid-1970s.**

universally recognized as the best player to ever lace up a pair of skates. It wasn't until Wayne Gretzky came on the scene that another player challenged that notion.

As for Brad Park, he was often considered the second-best defenseman in the league. In fact, from 1969 to 1985 only seven players laid claim to the Norris Trophy as the NHL's premier defenseman. Bobby Orr was the recipient of the Norris in each of the first seven seasons Park played in the NHL, and Park was voted runner-up in four of those seasons (1970, 1971, 1972 and 1974). Park was also voted second to Denis Potvin in 1976 and again in 1978—a banner year for Park. That season he finished with a plus-69 rating and scored 22 goals and added 57 assists for 79 points; it was his best offensive output since 1974, when he finished 10th in league scoring.

Park was traded from New York to Boston in 1975, three years after he and the Rangers lost the Stanley Cup to Orr and the Bruins. In 1976–77 and 1977–78, Park's Bruins advanced to the Stanley Cup final. But another great force was in Park's way: the Montreal Canadiens. Twice the Canadiens foiled the Bruins' bid for the Cup, leaving the talented defender without an NHL championship.

Park did earn some plaudits, snagging seven All-Star nominations (five of them on the First Team), and he was a key defensive cog on the 1972 Canadian Summit Series team. He was one of seven players to play in all eight games, recording one goal and four assists over the series, and in the series clincher he was named along with Paul Henderson as Canada's co-players of the game.

Brad Park kept good company.

**283**

# DEFENSE

# 2 Lester Patrick 1947

ALTERNATES:
## 3 · 16

Brandon Hockey Club
Montreal Wanderers
Nelson HC
New York Rangers
Renfrew Hockey Club
Seattle Metropolitans
Spokane Canaries
Victoria Aristocrats
Victoria Cougars
Westmount Hockey Club

Alternate Position: R

Shoots: Left

Height: 6'-1"

Weight: 180 lbs.

Born: December 31, 1883;
Drummondville, Quebec

Died: June 1, 1960;
Victoria, BC

Played 22 elite amateur
and professional
seasons from 1903–22,
1925–27, 1927–28

Stats: See page 481

"Without doubt, Lester Patrick had something on every one of the remaining players. The big fellow is in a class without opposition as a defenseman … Patrick at point would make any second-rate team look formidable."

—Malcolm Brice,
*Ottawa Free Press*,
December 1908

**AWARDS**

Stanley Cup (1905–06,
1906–07, 1927–28)

**ALL-STAR
SELECTIONS**

PCHA First All-Star
Team Defense (1913,
1915, 1916, 1917)

PCHA Second All-Star
Team Defense
(1918, 1920)

First All-Star Team
Coach (1931, 1932, 1933,
1934, 1935, 1936, 1938)

- Brother of Hall of Fame member Frank Patrick (inducted as a builder), who played 19 elite amateur and professional seasons from 1901–24

- Father of Hall of Fame member Lynn Patrick, who played in NHL with N.Y. Rangers from 1934–46; father of Muzz Patrick, who played in NHL with N.Y. Rangers from 1937–46

- Learned to play hockey in Montreal but came to prominence with Brandon, Manitoba, team that lost Stanley Cup challenge to the Ottawa "Silver Seven" in March of 1904

- Played with future Hall of Fame members Frank Patrick, Cyclone Taylor, Newsy Lalonde and Fred Whitcroft on the Renfrew Millionaires of the National Hockey Association in 1909–10

- Scored final two goals in 12–10 two-game, total-goal series that clinched Montreal Wanderers' Stanley Cup victory over Ottawa in March of 1906

- Helped form and launch Pacific Coast Hockey Association in 1911–12 with brother Frank Patrick

- Served as player, coach, general manager and owner of Victoria Aristocrats and Victoria Cougars (1911–16, 1918–26)

- Coached Stanley Cup–winning Victoria Cougars—last non-NHL team to win the Stanley Cup in 1924–25

- Coached N.Y. Rangers (1926–39); served as general manager of N.Y. Rangers (1926–45)

- Replaced an injured Lorne Chabot in goal during N.Y. Rangers' 2–1 victory over Montreal Maroons, April 7, 1928

# Pioneer Man

Lester Patrick was an all-star defenseman with an offensive upside who won three Stanley Cups over his 22-year playing career, which spanned eight different leagues—both amateur and professional—in hockey's formative years.

He scored the clinching goal of the 1906 Stanley Cup and famously donned the pads to replace the injured Lorne Chabot in the New York Rangers net for a 2–1 overtime victory in Game 2 of the 1928 final, but Patrick's on-ice heroics are but a small part of his hockey legacy.

Together with his brother Frank, Lester used the money from the sale of his family's British Columbia lumber business to create a league to rival the National Hockey Association (NHA). The Pacific Coast Hockey Association (PCHA) was born in 1911 with three teams: the Victoria Aristocrats, the New Westminster Royals and the Vancouver Millionaires. Lester played, coached, managed and owned the Aristocrats, while Frank did the same with the Millionaires. The Patricks built new arenas in each city and introduced artificial ice to western Canada.

The PCHA lured a number of stars from the competing NHA, including Newsy Lalonde and Cyclone Taylor, and became a significant force, so much so, that beginning in 1913–14, the Stanley Cup championship was decided by a series between the champions of the PCHA and NHA. That first Stanley Cup match saw the Aristocrats lose three games to none against the Toronto Blueshirts.

The Patricks introduced many innovations to the PCHA that have since permeated the

**Lester Patrick consults with New York Rangers coach Frank Boucher in 1941.**

National Hockey League, such as numbered sweaters, blue lines, penalty shots, assists on goals, changing players on the fly, using three lines and allowing goaltenders to leave their feet to make a stop.

The PCHA merged with the Western Canada Hockey League in 1924, but by 1926 the 10-team NHL had control of the Stanley Cup. Patrick was brought to New York to assume the roles of coach and general manager of the newly formed Rangers. Tagged "the classiest team in hockey," the Rangers won the Stanley Cup in 1928, only their second year in existence, and they won it again in 1933 and 1940.

Patrick continued to coach the Rangers until 1939, when he chose to focus strictly on his duties as general manager, a position he remained in until 1946, when he retired from the NHL.

Today Patrick is remembered with the Lester Patrick Award, which the NHL instituted in 1966 to honor contributions to hockey in the United States.

# 3

# Pierre Pilote 1975

NO. RETIRED BY CHICAGO

ALTERNATES:

## 21 · 2

**Chicago Black Hawks
Toronto Maple Leafs**

Shoots: Left
Height: 5'-10"
Weight: 178 lbs.
Born: December 11, 1931:
Kenogami, Quebec
Played 14 NHL seasons
from 1955–69
Stats: See page 481

"I always believed that if I had the puck, the other team didn't have it. My first instinct was always playing forward. I'm what you call 'Mr. Xerox' — I copy. If it's good for you, it's mine. My hero was Doug Harvey. I picked up tricks from him and from other guys and that's how I learned."

**AWARDS**

James Norris Trophy
(1963, 1964, 1965)
Stanley Cup (1960–61)

**ALL-STAR
SELECTIONS**

First All-Star Team
Defense (1963, 1964,
1965, 1966, 1967)
Second All-Star
Team Defense
(1960, 1961, 1962)

○ Held NHL record for regular season points by a defenseman (59); surpassed by Bobby Orr (68) in 1968–69

○ Played amateur hockey with St. Catharines Tee Pees (1950–52)

○ Led OHA-Jr. in penalty minutes (230) in 1950–51; led OHA-Jr. playoffs in penalty minutes (50) in 1951–52

○ Played minor pro hockey with Buffalo Bisons (1951–56)

○ Played 376 consecutive NHL games from 1956–61

○ Led NHL in penalty minutes (169) in 1960–61; led NHL playoffs in assists (12) and points (15) in 1960–61

○ Served as captain of Chicago Black Hawks (1961–68)

○ Played in NHL All-Star Game (1960, 1961, 1962, 1963, 1964, 1965, 1966, 1967, 1968)

○ Finished among NHL top-5 in assists in 1963–64 (46), 1964–65 (45) and 1966–67 (46)

○ Traded to Toronto by Chicago for Jim Pappin, May 23, 1968

○ Number 3 jersey retired by Chicago Blackhawks, November 12, 2008

○ Legacy honored by Canada Post, who issued a stamp featuring his image in 2005

○ Renowned as a tough, physical hitter and pinpoint passer

# Chicago's Great Fortune

Pierre Pilote didn't crack an NHL roster until he was 24—a late start compared to most superstars, until you consider that Pilote didn't begin seriously playing hockey until he was 17. His childhood dream was to play major league baseball, but once he strapped on skates and started playing industrial league men's hockey, he knew the game was for him.

A hard-checking, aggressive player with pinpoint accurate passing, Pilote started as a centerman. When he was told that the local Junior B team in Niagara Falls, Ontario, was in need of defensemen, he made the switch and made the club the next season. From there Pilote signed on to play for the St. Catharines Teepees, a club that then belonged to the Buffalo Bisons of the American Hockey League (AHL). Shortly thereafter, the Chicago Black Hawks bought the Bisons and all of their holdings to serve as their farm system. Pilote split the 1955–56 season between the AHL Bisons and the NHL Black Hawks, and he became a permanent member of the Black Hawks the next season.

Buying the Bisons was an astute move, as it gave the Black Hawks the rights to not only Pilote but to Elmer Vasko, Bobby Hull and Stan Mikita to name a few, and all were integral to the Hawks' future success.

In the 14 seasons between the beginnings of the Original Six era and Pilote joining the team in 1955–56, Chicago had made the playoffs only three times and had finished dead last seven times. But the ill fortune of the Hawks reversed quickly with their

**NHL president Clarence Campbell presents an award to Pierre Pilote at the 1962 All-Star Game.**

new charges, and by 1958–59, Chicago had climbed into contention, making the playoffs for the first time in six years. The Hawks made the playoffs the next 10 seasons that Pilote was in the lineup, winning the Cup in 1961.

Pilote was named captain in 1961 and held the post until he left Chicago in 1968. Despite his rugged style of play, Pilote suited up for 376 consecutive games before a shoulder injury ended the streak during the 1961–62 season. From 1959–60 through 1966–67, Pilote was voted a First or Second Team All-Star, and he was a three-time recipient of the Norris Trophy as the NHL's best defenseman (1963 to 1965). His 59 points (14 goals and 45 assists) in 1964–65 was an NHL record for defensemen in the pre-expansion era.

# 5 Denis Potvin 1991

NO. RETIRED BY
NEW YORK ISLANDERS

**New York Islanders**

Shoots: Left

Height: 6'

Weight: 205 lbs.

Born: October 29, 1953;
Ottawa, Ontario

Drafted by the New
York Islanders first
overall in 1973

Played 15 NHL seasons
from 1973–88

Stats: See page 481

"Often I'm asked which Cup I fancy the most and I often reply by saying, 'It's like having four children. Which one do you love the most?' All are totally different but the first one is always very special because it is the first one."

**AWARDS**

Calder Memorial
Trophy (1974)

James Norris Memorial
Trophy (1976, 1978, 1979)

Stanley Cup
(1979–80, 1980–81,
1981–82, 1982–83)

**ALL-STAR
SELECTIONS**

First All-Star Team
Defense (1975, 1976,
1978, 1979, 1981)

Second All-Star Team
Defense (1977, 1984)

**INTERNATIONAL
AWARDS**

Canada Cup (1976)

Bronze Medal: World
Championships (1986)

- Holds NHL record most power-play goals by a defenseman (3) in single playoff game, established in N.Y. Islanders' 6–3 victory over Edmonton, April 17, 1981

- Holds nine N.Y. Islander team records for scoring by a defenseman

- Ranks fifth in career NHL goals by an defenseman (310); ranks seventh in career NHL points by a defenseman (1,052)

- Played amateur hockey with Ottawa 67's (1968–73)

- OMJHL First All-Star Team Defense (1971, 1972, 1973)

- First NHL defenseman to register 1,000 career points, reaching the milestone in N.Y. Islanders' 6–6 tie with Buffalo Sabres, April 4, 1987

- Second defenseman (after Bobby Orr) in NHL history to record 30 goals in a season (1977–78) and register 100 points in a season (1978–79)

- Played in NHL All-Star Game (1974, 1975, 1976, 1977, 1978, 1981,1983,1984,1988)

- Served as captain of N.Y. Islanders (1979–87)

- Brother of Jean Potvin, who played in NHL with L.A. Kings, Philadelphia, N.Y. Islanders, Cleveland Barons and Minnesota North Stars from 1970–81

- Served as color commentator for Florida Panthers television broadcasts (1993–2009)

- Inducted into Canada's Sports Hall of Fame (2001)

# Rock Steady

**D**enis Potvin was the rock that Long Island hockey built itself upon. Drafted first overall by the New York Islanders in 1973, the franchise's second season, Potvin quickly became one of the most dominant defenders in the NHL. He announced his arrival with a Calder Trophy win as the league's top rookie, having collected 54 points in 77 games for a team that finished with a miserable 19-41-18 record.

Pound for pound one of the best hitters in the NHL, Potvin played a sound defensive game and was a spark plug for the Islanders vaunted offense, which included Mike Bossy, Bryan Trottier and Clarke Gillies. He collected three Norris Trophies as the league's best defenseman and became the second defenseman in NHL history to record single-season marks of 30 goals and 100 points. Over his 15-year career, all spent on Long Island, he averaged 0.99 points per game.

**Denis Potvin circles the Islanders' net in the early 1970s.**

Born and raised in Ottawa, Ontario, Potvin spent his entire amateur hockey career in his hometown, leaving home to play only after he was drafted to the NHL in 1973. Potvin had carved a five-year career in the Ontario Major Junior A loop with the Ottawa 67's, first playing with the club as a 15-year-old. He recorded 329 points over 254 games with the 67's.

His 15 seasons with the Islanders were memorable. He was handed the captaincy from Gillies in 1979, after four semifinal losses over five years, and that season Potvin led his troops to the franchise's first Stanley Cup. The much-hyped Islanders had struggled in the regular season, with Potvin sidelined with a broken thumb. But upon his return—and with the addition of Ken Morrow from the U.S. "Miracle on Ice" Olympic team and two-way center Butch Goring from the LA Kings—the Islanders went undefeated in their last 12 games of the season. The club marched through the playoffs, losing only four games in their first three series before beating the NHL's regular-season champion, the Philadelphia Flyers, in six games for the Cup.

Potvin and the Islanders went on to win the Cup three more times in succession, becoming only the second franchise to win four or more consecutive Stanley Cups (Montreal had done it twice before: five straight from 1956 to 1960 and four straight from 1976 to 1979).

# 2

### DEFENSE

# Babe Pratt 1966

**ALTERNATES:**
## 11 · 21 · 12

Boston Bruins
New York Rangers
Toronto Maple Leafs

Shoots: Left
Height: 6'-3"
Weight: 212 lbs.

Born: January 7, 1916:
Stony Mountain,
Manitoba

Died: December 16, 1988:
Vancouver,
British Columbia

Played 12 NHL seasons
from 1935–47

Stats: See page 482

"It was a different kind of game then. Today, they stress board-checking and checking from behind, both unheard of when we played. We'd hit a man standing right up and now the players don't seem to want to take that kind of check. The only check they want is on the first and fifteenth of the month."

**AWARDS**

Hart Memorial
Trophy (1944)

Stanley Cup
(1939–40, 1944–45)

**ALL-STAR
SELECTIONS**

First All-Star Team
Defense (1944)

Second All-Star Team
Defense (1945)

- Held NHL record for regular season assists (41) and points (58) by a defenseman; assists record surpassed by Bill Gadsby (42) in 1954–55; points record surpassed by Pierre Pilote (59) in 1964–65

- Played amateur hockey with Elmwood Millionaires (1932–33); Kenora Thistles (1933–35); Brandon Wheat Kings (1933–35)

- Led MJHL in assists (23) and points (42) in 1934–35

- Nicknamed "Babe" at age of 10 because of his love for baseball and the obvious connection to Babe Ruth

- Member of Can-Am champion Philadelphia Ramblers (1936)

- Scored Stanley Cup–winning goal in Toronto's 2–1 victory over Detroit Red Wings, April 22, 1945

- Suspended by NHL president Red Dutton for gambling violations, January 29, 1946; suspension lifted, February 15, 1946

- Traded to Boston by Toronto for the rights to Eric Pogue and cash, June 19, 1946

- Played minor pro hockey with New Westminster Royals (1948–51); Tacoma Rockets (1951–52)

- PCHL North First All-Star Team Defense (1949, 1950); PCHL First All-Star Team Defense (1951)

- Served as player/coach of New Westminster Royals (1949–51, 1951–52)

- Coached New Westminster Royals (1952–53)

# Babe's the Name

W alter "Babe" Pratt was such a big baseball fan as a child that the nickname "Babe" stuck with him all his life. It helped that he grew to become an affable fellow with a larger-than-life sense of humor and a physique to match. At 6-foot-3 and 212 pounds, Pratt was no pushover, and those who rushed his side of the ice certainly felt his presence.

Babe turned professional in 1935–36, having been signed by the New York Rangers, with whom he played 17 games that season. Learning from veteran defenders Ching Johnson, Art Coulter and Ott Heller, Pratt progressed steadily, and by 1939–40, he and Heller were the league's best defensive pairing. In 48 games that season the duo allowed only 17 goals against, and their play was instrumental in the Rangers' Stanley Cup win. Pratt had 28 points in 1941–42 as the Rangers won the regular-season championship, but they could not find the touch in the playoffs.

Midway through the 1942–43 season, Pratt was traded to the Toronto Maple Leafs for Hank Goldup and Red Garrett. Pratt had his best seasons with the Maple Leafs. In 1943–44 he led all defensemen with 58 points in 50 games—the best total ever by a defender to that point and a mark that would stay in the books for 21 seasons. Pierre Pilote broke the record with 59 points, but he had played in 18 more games than Pratt. In 1944 Pratt was awarded the Hart Trophy as the league's Most Valuable Player, an award rarely given to defensemen. He was also selected to the

**Babe Pratt gets his portrait taken as a Toronto Maple Leaf in the 1940s.**

league's First All-Star Team. He was a Second Team All-Star in 1944–45, and that season's playoffs saw Pratt score the biggest goal of his career: the Game 7 winner over the Detroit Red Wings for the Stanley Cup.

Traded to Boston for the 1946–47 campaign, Pratt recorded his lowest offensive output since his rookie season. He retired after that year but continued to play hockey in the Pacific Coast Hockey League (PCHL), where he was the league's Most Valuable Player in the North Division in 1948-49 and 1949-50. In the PCHL Pratt was a high-scoring defender with the 1950 league-champion New Westminster Royals, in his adopted province of British Columbia, and he coached the club from 1949–51.

# 44

# Chris Pronger 2015

**ALTERNATES:**
## 25 · 20

Anaheim Ducks
Arizona Coyotes
Edmonton Oilers
Hartford Whalers
Philadelphia Flyers
St. Louis Blues

Shoots: Left

Height: 6'-6"

Weight: 220 lbs.

Born: October 10, 1974:
Dryden, Ontario

Drafted by the Hartford
Whalers second
overall in 1993

Played 18 NHL seasons
from 1994–2004,
2005–12

Stats: See page 482

"Chris is one of the smartest guys in hockey I know. He has a real grasp of the game and a real understanding of his position and everybody else's position on the ice."

— Paul Holmgren on Chris Pronger

**AWARDS**

Bud Ice Plus-Minus (1998)

Bud Light Plus-Minus (2000)

Hart Trophy (2000)

Norris Trophy (2000)

Stanley Cup (2006–07)

**ALL-STAR SELECTIONS**

All-Rookie Team (1994)

First All-Star Team Defenseman (2000)

Second All-Star Team Defenseman (1998, 2004, 2007)

**INTERNATIONAL AWARDS**

Gold Medal: Winter Olympics (2002, 2010)

Gold Medal: World Championships (1997)

- Won the World Junior Championship with Team Canada in 1993 and earned the Max Kaminsky Trophy (OHL's Top Defenseman), as well as OHL First-Team All-Star, CHL First-Team All-Star and CHL Top Defenseman honors as a member of the Peterborough Petes in 1992–93

- Selected second behind Alexandre Daigle in the 1993 NHL Entry Draft

- Was traded from Hartford to St. Louis before the 1994–95 season for fellow future Hall of Famer Brendan Shanahan

- Served as captain of St. Louis Blues (1997–2002), Anaheim Ducks (2007–08) and Philadelphia Flyers (2011–12)

- Played in NHL All-Star Game (1999, 2000, 2002, 2004, 2008)

- In the 1999–2000 season, he became the first defenseman to win the Hart Trophy as NHL MVP since Bobby Orr in 1971–72

- Became the first player in NHL history to score a goal on a penalty shot in the Stanley Cup Final (2006)

- Teamed with Scott Niedermayer on the Anaheim Ducks' defense in 2006–07 and helped the franchise win its first-ever Stanley Cup

- Helped the Philadelphia Flyers reach the Stanley Cup final in 2010; suffered a career-ending injury with the Flyers in 2011–12

- Represented Canada at the Olympics in 1998, 2002, 2006 and 2010 and is a member of the Triple Gold Club for winning the Stanley Cup, an Olympic gold medal and a World Championship gold medal

# 1978 Marcel Pronovost

# 3

"Making a dangerous play on the ice didn't make me any more nervous than crossing the street might make someone else. He doesn't worry about getting hit by a car and I don't worry about getting hurt on the ice. If I did, I'd probably go crazy."

**ALTERNATES:**
## 18 · 23 · 22

**Detroit Red Wings**
**Toronto Maple Leafs**

Shoots: Left

Height: 6'

Weight: 190 lbs.

Born: June 15, 1930:
Lac-de-Tortue, Quebec

Died: April 26, 2015:
Windsor, Ontario

Played 20 NHL seasons
from 1950–70

Stats: See page 483

- Played amateur hockey with Windsor Spitfires (1947–49); Detroit Auto Club (1947–48)
- Played left wing and center for Windsor Spitfires (1947–48)
- Named USHL Rookie of the Year (1950)
- USHL First All-Star Team Defense (1950); AHL Second All-Star Team Defense (1951)
- Played in NHL All-Star Game (1950, 1954, 1955, 1957, 1958, 1959, 1960, 1961, 1963, 1965, 1968)
- Traded to Toronto by Detroit with Aut Erickson, Larry Jeffrey, Eddie Joyal and Lowell MacDonald for Billy Harris, Gary Jarrett and Andy Bathgate, May 20, 1965
- Coached Tulsa Oilers (1969–72)

- Coached Chicago Cougars (1972–73)
- Coached Hull Festivals (1975–77, 1979–80)
- Coached Buffalo Sabres (1977–79)
- Coached Windsor Spitfires (1981–83)
- Brother of Jean Pronovost, who played in NHL with Pittsburgh, Washington and Atlanta from 1968–82
- Brother of goaltender Claude Pronovost, who played in NHL with Boston (1955–56) and Montreal (1958–59)
- Served as scout with New Jersey Devils (1989–2009)
- No. 4 jersey honored by Windsor Spitfires (2005)

**AWARDS**

Stanley Cup (1949–50, 1951–52, 1953–54, 1954–55, 1966–67)

**ALL-STAR SELECTIONS**

First All-Star Team Defense (1960, 1961)

Second All-Star Team Defense (1958, 1959)

# Harvey Pulford 1945

Ottawa Aberdeens
Ottawa Hockey Club
Ottawa Senators
Ottawa Silver Seven

Shoots: Unknown

Height: 6'

Weight: 180 lbs.

Born: April 22, 1875:
Toronto, Ontario

Died: October 31, 1940:
Ottawa, Ontario

Played 15 elite
amateur seasons
from 1893–1908

Stats: See page 484

"Without Pulford, the team would be sorely handicapped. His all-around knowledge of the game, capability as a stick-handler, great defense work and aggressiveness on the attack have proved him the backbone of the team."

— *The Pittsburgh Press*, December 31, 1906

AWARDS
Stanley Cup (1902–03,
1903–04, 1904–05,
1905–06)

- Renowned as a versatile athlete who was named All-Around Sports Champion while attending Ottawa's Model School

- Starred in football, lacrosse, boxing, paddling and rowing

- Served as captain of Ottawa "Silver Seven" (1900–05)

- Member of Stanley Cup–winning Ottawa "Silver Seven" (1902–03, 1903–04, 1904–05, 1905–06)

- ECAHA Second All-Star Team Defense (1907, 1908)

- Led Stanley Cup playoffs in penalty minutes (24) in 1905–06

- Renowned as a solid checker and effective rusher who could consistently carry the puck out of danger in his own end

- Helped Ottawa successfully defend the Stanley Cup in eight consecutive challenge matches—more than any other championship team during his era

- Member of Canadian football champion Ottawa Rough Riders (1898, 1899, 1900)

- Member of Ottawa Capitals lacrosse club (1897–1900)

- Won numerous national and international championships with the Ottawa Rowing Club from 1905–12 and competed in the English Henley Regatta

- Served as NHA (1912–17) and NHL (1917–18) on-ice official

# **11**

## 1976 **Bill Quackenbush**

"I wasn't a body-checker. I was a poke checker, I had to play a certain style. I found that if I did a lot of body checking, I got tired very easily. I was on the ice an awful lot because I didn't get penalties."

**ALTERNATES:**
# **3 · 16 · 15**

**Boston Bruins**
**Detroit Red Wings**

Shoots: Left

Height: 5'-11"

Weight: 190 lbs.

Born: March 2, 1922:
Toronto, Ontario

Died: September 12,
1999: Newtown,
Pennsylvania

Played 14 NHL seasons
from 1942–56

Stats: See page 484

---

- First defenseman to win the Lady Byng Trophy

- Played amateur hockey with Toronto Western High (1939–40); Toronto Native Sons (1940–41); Toronto Campbell's (1940–41); Brantford Lions (1941–42); Toronto Tip Top Tailors (1941–42)

- Played the entire 1948–49 season (and a total of 131 consecutive games over three seasons including playoffs) without recording a single penalty; record finally broken when he was penalized for tripping Chicago's Jim Conacher in a 5–1 loss to the Black Hawks on January 26, 1950

- Finished among top-10 in scoring by NHL defensemen 11 times in 14 NHL seasons

- Recorded only 95 minutes in penalties in 775 NHL games

- Played in eight consecutive NHL All-Star Games from 1947 to 1954

- Coached Princeton University Tigers (1967–73). Led team to their best season since 1936 in 1967–68 when the team compiled a 13–10–1 record, won the ECAC Christmas tournament championship and earned a berth in the ECAC playoffs

- Coached Princeton University Women's Hockey Team (1978–85); coached Princeton University Golf Team (1969–85)

- Brother of Max Quackenbush, who played in the NHL with the Boston Bruins and Chicago Black Hawks from 1950–52

**AWARDS**

Lady Byng Memorial
Trophy (1949)

**ALL-STAR SELECTIONS**

First All-Star Team
Defense (1948,
1949, 1951)

Second All-Star Team
Defense (1947, 1953)

# 17

DEFENSE

# Kenny Reardon 1966

ALTERNATE:

4

Montreal Canadiens

Shoots: Left

Height: 5'-10"

Weight: 180 lbs.

Born: April 1, 1921:
Winnipeg, Manitoba

Died: March 15, 2008:
Saint-Sauveur, Quebec

Played seven
NHL seasons from
1940–42, 1945–50

Stats: See page 484

"When I was playing it was hard to stay in the league if you were the least bit shy. Some could, but if they weren't fighters, they had to be able to take [the punishment]."

AWARDS
Stanley Cup (1945–46)
ALL-STAR
SELECTIONS
First All-Star Team
Defense (1947, 1950)
Second All-Star
Team Defense
(1946, 1948, 1949)

- Played amateur hockey with Blue River Rebels (1937–38); Edmonton Athletic Club (1938–40)

- Nicknamed "Beans" because he was "full of it" on the ice

- Made NHL debut in 1–1 tie against Boston Bruins, November 3, 1940. It was the first time Reardon had ever skated in the Montreal Forum

- Played in NHL All-Star Game (1947, 1948, 1949)

- Awarded Field Marshall Montgomery Certificate of Merit for bravery in battle during World War II

- Member of Allan Cup–winning Ottawa Commandos (1943); Ottawa defeated the Ottawa RCAF Flyers and Victoria Army to win the title

- Managed Cincinnati Mohawks to five consecutive IHL championships (1952–57); during that time, the club lost only five games in the five championship finals they played

- Coached Kitchener-Waterloo Jr. Greenshirts (1954–55)

- In his capacity as Eastern Canada scout, he helped sign and develop future Montreal Canadiens stars such as Ralph Backstrom, Terry Harper, Dave Balon, Bill Hicke, and Red Berenson

- Brother of Terry Reardon, who played in NHL with Boston Bruins and Montreal Canadiens from 1939–47

- Served as scout, assistant general manager and Vice-president in Montreal Canadiens organization from 1950 to 1966

# 1995 Larry Robinson

# 19

> "Speed only means you might be able to catch somebody, but if you don't have any mobility you're going to stick out like a sore thumb."

NO. RETIRED BY MONTREAL

**Los Angeles Kings**
**Montreal Canadiens**

Shoots: Left

Height: 6'-4"

Weight: 225 lbs.

Born: June 2, 1951;
Winchester, Ontario

Drafted by the
Montreal Canadiens
20th overall in 1971

Played 20 NHL seasons
from 1972–92

Stats: See page 484

- Shares NHL record with Nicklas Lidstrom for most consecutive years appearing in the playoffs (20)

- Holds Montreal Canadiens' team record for career games played (1,202), goals (197), assists (686) and points (883) by a defenseman

- Holds Montreal Canadiens' team record for assists (66) and points (85) by a defenseman in regular season

- Played amateur hockey with Hull Castors (1968–69); Brockville Braves (1969–70); Kitchener Rangers (1970–71); played minor pro with Nova Scotia Voyageurs (1971–73)

- Scored 22 goals as a left winger and center with OJHL's Brockville Braves

- Led NHL in plus/minus (plus-120) in 1976–77, second highest regular season plus/minus rating in NHL history

- Played in NHL All-Star Game (1974, 1976, 1977, 1978, 1980, 1982, 1986, 1988, 1989, 1992)

- Nicknamed "Big Bird" because his height and gangly posture resembled the character on *Sesame Street* TV show

- Member of Montreal's famed defensive trio with Serge Savard and Guy Lapointe collectively known as "Les Trois Gros" (The Big Three)

- Signed as a free agent by Los Angeles, July 26, 1989

- Served as assistant coach of New Jersey Devils (1993–95)

- Coached Los Angeles Kings (1995–99); coached New Jersey Devils (1999–2000, 2000–01, 2001–02, 2005–06)

- Brother of Moe Robinson, who played in the NHL with Montreal in 1979–80

**AWARDS**

James Norris Memorial Trophy (1977, 1980)

Conn Smythe Trophy (1978)

Stanley Cup (1972–73, 1975–76, 1976–77, 1977–78, 1978–79, 1985–86)

**ALL-STAR SELECTIONS**

First Team All-Star Team Defense (1977, 1979, 1980)

Second All-Star Team Defense (1978, 1981, 1986)

**INTERNATIONAL AWARDS**

Canada Cup (1976, 1984)

# 4

## DEFENSE

## Art Ross 1949

ALTERNATE:

## 2

All-Montreal
Brandon Elks
Cobalt Silver Kings
Haileybury Comets
Kenora Thistles
Montreal Wanderers
Ottawa Senators
Pembroke Lumber Kings
Westmount Hockey Club

Shoots: Left

Height: 5'-11"

Weight: 190 lbs.

Born: January 13, 1886:
Naughton, Ontario

Died: August 5, 1964:
Boston, Massachusetts

Played 14 elite amateur
and professional
seasons from 1904–18

Stats: See page 485

"Hockey isn't a gentle pastime — not as it is played by the big teams. If it were, people wouldn't go to see it ... With the possible exception of football ... hockey is the most strenuous game I know."

— Art Ross (who also played football), 1910

AWARDS

Lester Patrick
Trophy (1984)

Stanley Cup
(1906–07, 1907–08)

ALL-STAR
SELECTIONS

First All-Star Team
Coach (1939)

Second All-Star Team
Coach (1938, 1943)

- Renowned as a top defensemen, went on to become a pivotal coach, manager, inventor and strategist throughout a lifetime of service to hockey

- First came to prominence as an athlete playing hockey and football in Montreal suburb of Westmount; became a hockey star playing in Brandon, Manitoba 1905–07

- Loaned to the Kenora Thistles and became a member of Stanley Cup–winning team (January 1907)

- MHL-Pro First All-Star Team Defense (1907)

- Member of Stanley Cup–winning Montreal Wanderers (1907–08)

- ECAHA First All-Star Team Defense (1908)

- Served as player/coach with Montreal Wanderers (1913–14; 1917–18)

- Playing career ended when the Montreal Wanderers withdrew from league during inaugural NHL season of 1917–18

- Coached Hamilton Tigers (1922–23); coached Boston Bruins (1924–34, 1936–39, 1941–45)

- Served as general manager of Boston Bruins (1924–54)

- Responsible for improving the design of the puck and goal nets used in the NHL

- Donated Art Ross Trophy to league, which has gone to the NHL's leading scorer since 1947–48

# More Than a Name on a Trophy

I n his foreword to the 2015 biography, *Art Ross: The Hockey Legend Who Built the Bruins*, Ron MacLean of *Hockey Night in Canada* wrote that Ross was "the kind of man who could not only buy a violin and play it, he could build the violin…. He knew how hockey should look. And he knew what a hockey player should look like." Along with brothers Frank and Lester Patrick, whom he'd known since childhood when they all lived in the Montreal suburb of Westmount, Ross did more than almost anyone to modernize the game of hockey.

Ross spent most of his playing career in the National Hockey Association with the Montreal Wanderers. He also ran a sporting goods business in Montreal, where he created and sold his own line of hockey equipment. Always a tinkerer, shortly after his playing career ended in 1918, Ross improved the design of the hockey puck by beveling the edges. The NHL replaced the Spalding puck with Ross' design for the 1918–19 season and would later adopted the Art Ross Puck as its official puck from 1940 until 1968. The NHL also introduced the Art Ross Net for the 1927–28 season, which featured a new design to better trap pucks within the mesh and cut down on disputed goals. The NHL, and virtually everyone else who played hockey, used Ross' net design through the 1983–84 season.

In addition to his puck and net, Ross was instrumental in adopting rules that allowed goalies to drop to the ice to make saves, and he helped bring in rules that opened up the

**Boston Bruins head coach Art Ross in 1941.**

NHL game to forward passing. Still, even though he was also the coach and/or general manager of the Boston Bruins from the team's inception in 1924–25 through the 1953–54 season, Ross is best known for the trophy he donated, along with his sons Arthur and John, to honor the NHL's top scorer. Ross had originally planned to donate a trophy in 1941 that would have let players vote for the NHL MVP (much like the Ted Lindsay Award today). It's unclear why that trophy was never put to use, but the Art Ross Trophy for scoring was accepted by the NHL governors in 1948 and has been awarded in every season that's been played since.

# 4 Angela Ruggiero 2015

Boston Blades
Harvard University
Crimson
Minnesota Whitecaps
Montreal Axion
Tulsa Oilers
U.S. National Team

Shoots: Right
Height: 5'-9"
Weight: 190 lbs.
Born: January 3, 1980;
Panorama City, California
Played 15 elite amateur
seasons from 1996–2011
Stats: See page 485

## AWARDS

NCAA All-American First
Team (2000, 2004)
NCAA All-American Second
Team (1999, 2003)
Harvard MVP (2000,
2003, 2004)
Ivy League Player of
the Year (2004)
Patty Klezmer Memorial
Trophy (2004)
Directorate Award (Top
Defenseman) Winter
Olympics (2002, 2006)
Directorate Award (Top
Defenseman) World
Championships (2001,
2004, 2005, 2008)
United States Olympic
Committee Player of
the Year (2003)

## INTERNATIONAL AWARDS

Gold Medal: Winter
Olympics (1998)
Silver Medal: Winter
Olympics (2002, 2010)
Bronze Medal: Winter
Olympics (2006)
Gold Medal: World
Championships (2005,
2008, 2009, 2011)
Silver Medal: World
Championships (1997, 1999,
2000, 2001, 2004, 2007)

"I wanted to play for the L.A. Kings. I showed up to a career day in the second grade with my hockey gear on. I knew I wanted to play. I just didn't know where it would take me."

- Made Team USA for the first time at age 15 in 1996

- Was the youngest member of the U.S. Olympic team that won the first gold medal for women's hockey at the 1998 Nagano Winter Games

- Scored the tournament-winning goal in a shootout at the 2005 World Championships

- Voted the USA's Women's Player of the Year in 2003 and 2004, and was ranked the #1 female hockey player in the world by The Hockey News in 2003

- Was the first female non-goalie to play professional men's hockey in North America, suiting up for the Tulsa Oilers of the Central Hockey League (along with her brother Bill) in 2004–05

- Was elected as a member of the International Olympic Committee Athletes' Commission and the United States Olympics Committee's Board of Directors in 2010

- Holds the record as the all-time leader in games played for Team USA's women's hockey team (256); she has 208 points in those games (67 goals and 141 assists)

- Her 253 points (96 goals and 157 assists) in four seasons ranks sixth all-time at Harvard and first among defensemen

- Won the 1999 NCAA championship with Harvard and won the Western Women's Hockey League championship with the Minnesota Whitecaps in 2009

# 1962 Jack Ruttan

"Jack Ruttan enjoyed a long and illustrious career in hockey, both as a player and coach, all of it in amateur ranks. His stature in Winnipeg ... was such that he became an example for younger players."

—Thumbnail sketch from early Hockey Hall of Fame yearbook

St. John's College
University of Manitoba
U. of Manitoba Varsity
Winnipeg Somme
Winnipeg Winnipegs

Shoots: Unknown

Height: Unknown

Weight: Unknown

Born: April 5, 1889; Winnipeg, Manitoba

Died: January 7, 1973; Winnipeg, Manitoba

Played nine elite amateur seasons from 1905–13, 1917–18

Stats: See page 486

- Played amateur hockey with Armstrong Point (1905–06); Winnipeg Rustlers (1906–07); Winnipeg St. John's (1905–08)

- Legendary figure in Winnipeg hockey during a time when the city was one of the most important hockey centers in Canada

- Member of Winnipeg Juvenile champion Armstrong Point (1905–06) and Winnipeg Rustlers (1906–07)

- Member of Manitoba University hockey champion St. John's College (1907–08)

- Member of Winnipeg Senior champion University of Manitoba (1909–10)

- Member of Allan Cup–winning Winnipeg Winnipegs (1912–13)

- Served as a captain in Canadian Army during World War I and ran the Military Hockey League in Winnipeg

- Coached University of Manitoba (1923–24)

- Active in hockey as a referee and coach in Winnipeg for many years after the War

- Inducted into Manitoba Hockey Hall of Fame (1985)

# 21

# Borje Salming 1996

NO. RETIRED BY TORONTO

Detroit Red Wings
Toronto Maple Leafs

Shoots: Left
Height: 6'-1"
Weight: 193 lbs.
Born: April 17, 1951:
Kiruna, Sweden
Played 17 NHL seasons
from 1973–90
Stats: See page 486

"Borje was a once-in-a-lifetime find. Here is a player you can mention in the same sentence with Bobby Orr, Brad Park and Larry Robinson when you're talking about the great defensemen of the modern era."

— Gerry McNamara, Toronto scout

**ALL-STAR SELECTIONS**

First All-Star Team Defense (1977)

Second All-Star Team Defense (1975, 1976, 1978, 1979, 1980)

**INTERNATIONAL AWARDS**

Bronze Medal: World Championships (1972)

Silver Medal: World Championships (1973)

- First Swedish-born and trained player to earn an NHL All-Star berth
- First Swedish-born and trained player to be inducted into Hockey Hall of Fame
- Holds Toronto Maple Leafs team record for career assists (620)
- Holds Toronto Maple Leafs team records for career goals (148), assists (620) and points (768) by a defenseman
- Holds Toronto Maple Leafs team record for assists in regular season by a defenseman (66), established in 1976–77
- Played amateur hockey with Brynäs Gävle (1970–73)

- Discovered by Maple Leaf scout Gerry McNamara (along with winger Inge Hammarstrom) during a holiday tournament in Sweden
- Signed as a free agent by Toronto, May 12, 1973
- Played in NHL All-Star Game (1976, 1977, 1978)
- Renowned as one of the first European-born players to make an impact on the North American game and helping open the NHL door to players born and trained in Europe
- Signed as a free agent by Detroit, June 12, 1989
- Played in Sweden with AIK Solna (1990–93) after retiring from the NHL

# Coming to Canada

The hockey world was rapidly shrinking in the 1970s. The 1972 Summit Series illustrated that Canada's best players weren't light-years ahead of their European counterparts, and the upstart World Hockey Association created a need for more quality hockey players.

NHL teams had been dabbling with European talent since the Original Six era, but the players that had been invited to NHL training camps weren't ready for the big league. That all changed in 1973, when the Toronto Maple Leafs brought over a pair of Swedish stars: forward Inge Hammarstrom and defenseman Borje Salming. Hammarstrom played six seasons in the NHL, recording respectable, but not overwhelming, totals, but Salming—he was the real deal.

Born on April 17, 1951, in Kiruna, Sweden's northernmost city, Salming loved hockey and idolized his older brother, Stig, who taught him how to play the game.

They both advanced rapidly through Kiruna's hockey ranks, and Borje followed his brother south to play in the Swedish Elite League with Brynäs, a team located just outside of Stockholm in Gävle. Brynäs won the league championship in 1971 and in 72.

At the time, the Swedish National Team had summoned Borje to man their defense, and he participated in two exhibition matches against Team Canada. The Canadians, in the midst of the Canada-USSR Summit Series, followed their four Canadian games with two exhibition matches in Sweden before heading off to Moscow to conclude the series. The exhibition games solidified Team Canada prior to the resumption of the benchmark series, and Salming gained the confidence to play with the best players in the world.

**Borje Salming wore this Brynäs IF Gävle jersey before playing in the NHL.**

Three months later, Maple Leafs' scout Gerry McNamara discovered Salming.

Salming and Hammarstrom debuted in the NHL on October 10, 1973. The jitters turned out to be the easy part; both players faced a barrage of abuse at the hands of opponents. But the pair stood up to the challenges and slights and over time earned respect with their well-rounded games.

Salming never did win the Stanley Cup, but he remained in the NHL for 16 more seasons, being named to the First All-Star Team once and the Second All-Star Team five times. He tallied at least 50 points in a season seven times in his career and only once fell short of 20. His biggest legacy, however, is becoming the first European-trained player to play regularly in the NHL, his success opening the door for many others.

# 18

# Serge Savard 1986

NO. RETIRED BY MONTREAL

**ALTERNATE:**
## 24

Montreal Canadiens
Winnipeg Jets

Shoots: Left

Height: 6'-3"

Weight: 210 lbs.

Born: January 22, 1946;
Montreal, Quebec

Played 17 NHL seasons
from 1966–83

Stats: See page 487

"Your goal when you're a kid is to make the National Hockey League. Your second goal after is to win the Stanley Cup. Having your number retired? That's something that's never even in your dreams as an athlete."

**AWARDS**

Conn Smythe
Trophy (1969)

Bill Masterton Memorial
Trophy (1979)

Stanley Cup (1967–68,
1968–69, 1970–71,
1972–73, 1975–76,
1976–77, 1977–78,
1978–79)

**ALL-STAR
SELECTIONS**

Second All-Star Team
Defense (1979)

**INTERNATIONAL
AWARDS**

Summit Series (1972)

Canada Cup (1976)

- Played amateur hockey with Montreal Jr. Canadiens (1963–66)

- OHA-Jr. Second All-Star Team Defense (1966)

- Played minor pro hockey with Omaha Knights (1964–65)

- CPHL Second All-Star Team Defense (1967)

- Nicknamed "The Senator" and "Minister of Defense"

- Renowned for the "Savardian Spinnerama" — a 360-degree maneuver used to avoid opposing checkers

- Key component in Team Canada's 1972 Summit Series victory; the team won every game that Savard played in

- Served as captain of Montreal Canadiens (1979–81)

- Served as general manager of Montreal Canadiens (1983–96), winning the Stanley Cup in this role in 1986 and 1993

- Played in NHL All-Star Game (1970, 1973, 1977, 1978)

- Missed remainder of 1970–71 season and majority of 1971–72 season recovering from leg injury suffered in game vs. Toronto, January 30, 1971.

- Claimed by Winnipeg Jets from Montreal in Waiver Draft, October 5, 1981

- Member of Montreal's "Big Three" on defense with Guy Lapointe and Larry Robinson

# 17

# 1963 Earl Seibert

**ALTERNATES:**
## 2 · 21

**Chicago Black Hawks
Detroit Red Wings
New York Rangers**

Shoots: Right

Height: 6'-2"

Weight: 198 lbs.

Born: December 7,
1910: Berlin, Ontario

Died: May 20, 1990:
Agawam,
Massachusetts

Played 15 NHL seasons
from 1931–46

Stats: See page 487

"Let's put it this way,
no one wanted any
part of 'Si' in a fight.
Even Eddie Shore and
Red Horner steered
clear of him, and
Shore and Horner
were considered the
toughest guys in the
league at the time."

— Ching Johnson

- Played amateur hockey with Kitchener Greenshirts (1927–29)

- Along with father Oliver Seibert, became first father-son duo to be honored as members of the Hockey Hall of Fame. The elder Seibert played for the Western Ontario Senior champion Berlin HC

- Can-Am First All-Star Team Defense (1931)

- Scored five goals and added two assists in 10 playoff games to help the Black Hawks upset the Toronto Maple Leafs and win the Stanley Cup in 1938. He scored only eight goals in 48 regular season games during the 1937–38 season

- A pugnacious, hard-hitting defender, it was Seibert who upended Howie Morenz in a game on January 28, 1937, causing the Montreal Canadiens star to slide feet first into the end boards. Seibert fell on top of Morenz' leg, breaking it in four places. Morenz would never play again, and six weeks later he died of complications from the injury

- Played in NHL All-Star Game (1939)

- Served as captain of Chicago Black Hawks (1940–42)

- Coached Indianapolis Capitols (1945–46); coached Springfield Indians (1946–51)

**AWARDS**
Stanley Cup (1932–33, 1937–38)

**ALL-STAR
SELECTIONS**
First All-Star Team
Defense (1935,
1942, 1943, 1944)

Second All-Star Team
Defense (1936, 1937,
1938, 1939, 1940, 1941)

**305**

# 2 Eddie Shore 1947

NO. RETIRED BY BOSTON

Boston Bruins
Edmonton Eskimos
New York Americans
Regina Capitals

Shoots: Right

Height: 5'-11"

Weight: 190 lbs.

Born: November 25, 1902: Fort Qu'Appelle, Saskatchewan

Died: March 16, 1985: Springfield, Massachusetts

Played 16 professional seasons from 1924–40

Stats: See page 487

"I'm not sorry about anything I've done."

**AWARDS**

Hart Memorial Trophy (1933, 1935, 1936, 1938)

Stanley Cup (1928–29, 1938–39)

Lester Patrick Trophy (1970)

**ALL-STAR SELECTIONS**

WHL First All-Star Team Defense (1925)

First All-Star Team Defense (1931, 1932, 1933, 1935, 1936, 1938, 1939)

Second All-Star Team Defense (1934)

- First player to win the Hart Trophy as NHL MVP four times; only defenseman to win the Hart Trophy as NHL MVP four times

- Nicknamed "The Edmonton Express"

- Played amateur hockey with Melville Millionaires (1923–24)

- Led NHL in penalty minutes (165) in 1927–28

- Finished among NHL top-10 in assists in 1930–31 (16), 1932–33 (27) and 1934–35 (26); finished among NHL top-10 in points in 1928–29 (19) and 1932–33 (35)

- Renowned as the toughest and dirtiest player of his era

- When Shore owned and managed the AHL's Springfield Indians, his players went on strike in December of 1966 to protest his "constant harassment" and the suspensions of four Springfield players. The strike was settled with the help of lawyer Allan Eagleson, who later helped form the NHLPA

- Played in NHL All-Star Game (1934, 1937, 1939)

- Coached Springfield Indians (1941–42, 1953–55), coached Buffalo Bisons (1942–43), coached Fort Worth Rangers (1945–46), coached Oakland Oaks (1949–50)

- Managed Calder Cup–winning (AHL championship) Springfield Indians (1960, 1961, 1962)

# Truculent

Eddie Shore was a polarizing figure until the day he died. He was the preeminent defender of his day, being named to the NHL's First All-Star Team seven times in an era with no other individual distinction for defensemen. He also won the Hart Trophy as the league's Most Valuable Player four times—the first player to achieve the feat—a remarkable accomplishment for anyone, especially a defenseman as the Hart is synonymous with offense.

**Eddie Shore began wearing a helmet in the mid-1930s, after the injury he gave Ace Bailey in 1933 made him realize the dangers of head trauma. This is one of Shore's helmets from that time.**

But Shore also had a reputation as an indiscriminate bruiser. In his 15 seasons he was among the top-ten NHL penalty-minute earners nine times, and in 1927–28 he finished first with 165 minutes in just 43 games. He harangued officials, injured players and almost killed Ace Bailey—though the incident softened him and his penalty totals decreased significantly afterward.

But despite his wickedness, Shore was the face of the NHL as it went through the Depression. His talent and antics allowed the fans to cheer and jeer. He was to hockey what Babe Ruth was to baseball.

And then there was Eddie Shore the hockey coach and executive. Shore purchased the minor-pro Springfield Indians in 1939, and many have called his tenure tyrannical. He treated his players with contempt, withholding pay for little or no reason, forcing them to clean the arena after games and practices, and suspending them at whim. He administered his own medical and chiropractic services that often did more damage than good, and he was cheap.

But he won. With Shore at the helm the Indians won the American Hockey League (AHL) title four times—three in succession from 1960 to 1962 and another one in 1975. Shore was a hockey savant of sorts, making his players dance to improve balance, which he considered the key building block of fitness—long before core workouts were de rigueur. His players did strike in 1966, however, and this strike was the catalyst for players to form unions in both the AHL and the NHL.

But there are others who pay Shore a debt of gratitude for his unusual ways, like Kent Douglas, a Springfield alumnus who became an NHL Rookie of the Year. According to Douglas, "Studying with Shore was like getting your doctorate in hockey science. He taught me things about the game that nobody else ever mentioned."

While Shore's reputation as an eccentric may often dominate the public's consciousness, he is also a bona fide NHL legend.

# 2

### DEFENSE

# Joe Simpson 1962

ALTERNATE:

# 4

Edmonton Eskimos
New York Americans

Shoots: Right
Height: 5'-10"
Weight: 175 lbs.
Born: August 13, 1893;
Selkirk, Manitoba
Died: December 25, 1973;
Coral Gables, Florida
Played 10 professional
seasons from 1921–31
Stats: see page 488

"Simpson was a great skater, a defenseman whose end-to-end rushes wowed fans wherever he went. The nickname 'Bullet Joe' was well deserved and his fame well understood by everyone who watched him play the game at another level than most."

—Canadian Sports Hall of Fame

ALL-STAR
SELECTIONS
WCHL First All-Star
Team Defense
(1922, 1923, 1925)
WCHL Second All-Star
Team Defense (1924)

- Played amateur hockey with the Winnipeg Strathconas (1912-13); Selkirk Fishermen (1913–14); Winnipeg Victorias (1914–15); Winnipeg 61st Battalion (1915–16)

- Nicknamed "Bullet Joe" because of his blinding speed and in reference to the wounds he suffered during World War I

- Member of Allan Cup–winning Winnipeg 61st Battalion team that defeated the Regina Capitals 13–3 in the two game total goal series in 1916. Simpson had four goals and two assists in five playoff games

- During World War I, he served with the 43rd Cameron Highlanders in a battalion commanded by Major Winston Churchill

- Twice wounded in the war—at the Battle of the Somme and Amiens—he was awarded the Military Medal for Valor

- Signed as a free agent by Edmonton Eskimos (WCHL), November 4, 1921

- Big-4 First All-Star team Defense (1921)

- Established WCHL record for goals (21) and points (33) by a defenseman (1921–22)

- Established WCHL record for assists (14) by a defenseman (1922–23)

- Coached N.Y. Americans (1931–34); New Haven Eagles (1934–36); Minneapolis Millers (1936–38); Miami Clippers (1938–39)

# 1981 Allan Stanley

# 26

ALTERNATES:

**8 · 4 · 10 6**

**Boston Bruins
Chicago Black Hawks
New York Rangers
Philadelphia Flyers
Toronto Maple Leafs**

Shoots: Left

Height: 6'-1"

Weight: 170 lbs.

Born: March 1, 1926; Timmins, Ontario

Played 21 NHL seasons from 1948–69

Stats: see page 488

"I was just a kid, but I remember asking my uncle Barney what hockey players drink between periods to make them play hockey better. He said, 'We usually drink tea with honey,' so I drank tea and honey for years after that. It seems to have helped."

- Played amateur hockey with Holman Pluggers (1939–43); Boston Olympics (1943–44, 1945–46, 1947–48); Porcupine Combines (1944–45); Port Arthur Navy (1944–45)

- Member of the Ontario Juvenile champion Holman Pluggers (1942–43, 1943–44)

- Played minor pro hockey with Providence Reds (1947–49); Vancouver Canucks (1953–54)

- Played in NHL All-Star Game (1955, 1957, 1960, 1962, 1963, 1967, 1968)

- Awarded the J.P. Bickell Trophy by the Toronto Maple Leafs' board of directors for outstanding achievement on and off the ice (1965, 1966)

- Booed out of New York and considered too old to play in Boston, his career was rejuvenated in Toronto

- Led all NHL defensemen in goals (10) in 1959–60

- Nicknamed "Snowshoes" because of plodding skating style

- Traded to N.Y. Rangers by Providence (AHL) for Eddie Kullman, Moe Morris, cash and future considerations (Buck Davies, June 1949), December 9, 1948

- Traded to Boston by Chicago for cash, October 8, 1956; traded to Toronto by Boston for Jim Morrison, October 8, 1958

- Claimed by Philadelphia (Quebec-AHL) from Toronto in Reverse Draft, June 13, 1968

- Nephew of Hall of Fame member Barney Stanley, who played 11 professional seasons from 1914–19 and 1921–28

**AWARDS**
Stanley Cup (1961–62, 1962–63, 1963–64, 1966–67)

**ALL-STAR SELECTIONS**
Second All-Star Team Defense (1960, 1961, 1966)

## DEFENSE

# 4

# Scott Stevens 2007

NO. RETIRED BY
NEW JERSEY

ALTERNATES:

3 · 2

New Jersey Devils
St. Louis Blues
Washington Capitals

Shoots: Left

Height: 6'-2"

Weight: 215 lbs.

Born: April 1, 1964:
Kitchener, Ontario

Drafted by the
Washington Capitals
fifth overall in 1982

Played 22 NHL seasons
from 1982–2004

Stats: see page 489

"I'm a firm believer that a big hit could change momentum in a game, just like a big goal could. I'm proud of [my reputation]."

AWARDS

Conn Smythe
Trophy (2000)

Stanley Cup (1994–95,
1999–2000, 2002–03)

ALL-STAR
SELECTIONS

All-Rookie Team (1983)

First Team All-Star Team
Defense (1988, 1994)

Second All-Star
Team Defense
(1992, 1997, 2001)

INTERNATIONAL
AWARDS

Bronze Medal: World
Championships (1983)

Silver Medal: World
Championships
(1985, 1989)

- Played amateur hockey with Kitchener Ranger B's (1980–81); Kitchener Rangers (1980–82)

- Member of Memorial Cup–winning Kitchener Rangers (1982)

- Ranks second in career NHL games played by a defenseman (1,635) and eighth all time.

- Played in NHL All-Star Game (1985, 1989, 1991. 1992, 1993, 1994, 1996, 1997, 1998, 1999, 2000, 2001, 2003)

- Led NHL in plus/minus (plus-53) in 1993–94

- Served as captain of New Jersey Devils (1992–2003)

- Finished among NHL top-5 in power-play goals (16) in 1984–85

- Renowned for his devastating open-ice body-checks

- Scored first NHL goal in first NHL game on first NHL shot in Washington's 5–4 victory over N.Y. Rangers, October 6, 1982

- Signed as a free agent by St. Louis, July 16, 1990

- Transferred to New Jersey from St. Louis as compensation for St. Louis' signing of free agent Brendan Shanahan, September 3, 1991

- Officially announced his retirement, September 6, 2005

- Brother of Mike Stevens, who played in NHL with Vancouver, Toronto, N.Y. Islanders and Boston from 1984–90

# 1964 Jack Stewart

2

ALTERNATE:

19

**Chicago Black Hawks
Detroit Red Wings**

Shoots: Left

Height: 5'-10"

Weight: 190 lbs.

Born: May 6, 1917: Pilot Mound, Manitoba

Died: May 26, 1983: Detroit, Michigan

Played 12 NHL seasons from 1938–43, 1945–52

Stats: See page 489

> "I bodychecked some fellow one night and when he woke up the next day in the hospital he asked who'd hit him with a blackjack."
>
> — Black Jack Stewart, on how he got his moniker

- Nicknamed "Black Jack" because of his bruising body checks, he was known as the hardest-hitting defenseman in the NHL during his career

- Known for using the heaviest stick in the league. When asked how he could shoot with a stick so heavy, he replied, "I don't use it for shooting, I use it for breaking arms."

- Played amateur hockey with Portage Terriers (1935–37)

- Played with Montreal RCAF and Winnipeg RCAF during World War II

- Led NHL in penalty minutes (73) in 1945–46

- Played in NHL All-Star Game (1947, 1948, 1949, 1950)

- Served as captain of the Chicago Black Hawks (1950–52)

- Served as player/coach with Chatham Maroons (1953–54)

- Traded to Chicago by Detroit with Harry Lumley in a nine player deal on July 13, 1950. It was the largest trade in NHL history until Calgary-Toronto 10-player trade in January of 1992

- Coached Kitchener-Waterloo Dutchmen (1955–56); Windsor Bulldogs (1957–59); Sault Ste-Marie Greyhounds (1959–60); Pittsburgh Hornets (1962–63)

- Inducted into Manitoba Sports Hall of Fame (1997)

- Selected to Manitoba's All-Century First All-Star Team (1999)

**ALL-STAR SELECTIONS**

First All-Star Team Defense (1943, 1948, 1949)

Second All-Star Team Defense (1946, 1947)

# Hod Stuart 1945

Calumet Miners
Montreal Wanderers
Ottawa Hockey Club
Quebec Bulldogs
Pittsburgh Bankers
Pittsburgh
Professionals
Portage Lakes

Shoots: Unknown

Height: 6'

Weight: 190 lbs.

Born: February 20,
1879; Ottawa, Ontario

Died: June 23, 1907:
Belleville, Ontario

Played nine elite amateur
and professional seasons
from 1898–1907

Stats: see page 490

"We won the Cup in the most gentlemanly manner we could and I am glad to see that Montrealers appreciate it. We will do our best to keep the Cup in our possession."

—Hod Stuart to the crowd outside Montreal's Savoy hotel before a dinner to honor the Wanderers' 1907 Stanley Cup victory in Kenora

**AWARDS**

Stanley Cup (1906–07)

**ALL-STAR SELECTIONS**

WPHL First All-Star
Team Defense (1903)

IHL First All-Star Team
Defense (1905, 1906)

ECAHA First All-Star
Team Defense (1907)

- Brother of Hall of Fame member Bruce Stuart, who played 13 elite amateur and professional seasons from 1898–1911

- Member of WPHL champion Calumet Miners (1903); member of United States Pro champion Portage Lakes (1904)

- Served as player/coach of IHL champion Calumet Miners (1905)

- Renowned as one of the best defensemen in hockey during his career

- Signed as a free agent by Pittsburgh Pros, December 3, 1906

- Jumped contract with Pittsburgh to sign as a free agent with Montreal Wanderers, January 3, 1907

- Member of Stanley Cup–winning Montreal Wanderers team that defeated Kenora Thistles, March 23–25, 1907

- Died three months after Stanley Cup victory when he broke his neck in a diving accident while swimming near Belleville, Ontario

- Hod Stuart Memorial All-Star Game between Montreal Wanderers and NHA All-Stars was played to raise funds for his wife and two children, January 2, 1908. Wanderers won game 10–7

- Seven future Hall of Fame members (Riley Hern, Art Ross, Ernie Russell, Moose Johnson, Percy LeSueur, Jack Marshall and Frank Patrick) played in the game

# 1962 **Phat Wilson** 5

"A brilliant defenseman remembered for his rink-long rushes, he won several scoring titles throughout his career.... Given the fact that he was 30 years of age when he captained the Seniors to their first Allan Cup title in 1926, his accomplishments on the ice were that much more impressive."

— Northwestern Ontario Sports Hall of Fame

Iroquois Falls Flyers
Port Arthur 141st Battalion
Port Arthur Columbus Club
Port Arthur Hockey Club
Port Arthur Ports
Port Arthur Shuniahs
Port Arthur War Vets

Shoots: Left

Height: Unknown

Weight: Unknown

Born: December 29, 1895: Port Arthur, Ontario

Died: July 26, 1970: Thunder Bay, Ontario

Played 16 elite amateur seasons from 1915–17, 1918–32

Stats: See page 490

- Renowned for his skills as a baseball player in his youth and became a top baseball organizer in the Port Arthur (Thunder Bay) area

- Didn't learn to skate until he joined a local church league team in 1914

- Played amateur hockey throughout his career despite several offers to turn professional

- Considered one of the greatest amateur players of all time and one of the finest defensemen of his era

- Inducted into Northwestern Ontario Sports Hall of Fame (1982)

- Led MTBHL in assists (9) in 1928–29; led TSBHL in assists in 1929–30 (8); led TSBHL in assists (8) and points (17) in 1930–31

- Member of Allan Cup–winning Port Arthur Hockey Club (1925, 1926, 1929)

- Coached Port Arthur Ports (1932–42)

- Served as coach and general manager of numerous Port Arthur senior teams in the 1930s and 40s and was a co-founder of a local girls hockey league

| LFOUR | CLINT BENEDICT | JOHNNY BOWER | FRANK BRIMSEK | TURK BRODA | GERRY CHEEVERS |

| EX NNELL | KEN DRYDEN | BILL DURNAN | TONY ESPOSITO | GRANT FUHR | CHUCK GARDINER |

| DIE ACOMIN | GEORGE HAINSWORTH | GLENN HALL | DOMINIK HASEK | RILEY HERN | HAP HOLMES |

| USE TTON | HUGH LEHMAN | PERCY LESUEUR | HARRY LUMLEY | PADDY MORAN | BERNIE PARENT |

| CQUES ANTE | CHUCK RAYNER | PATRICK ROY | TERRY SAWCHUK | BILLY SMITH | TINY THOMPSON |

# GOALIE

# GOALIE

# 20

# Ed Belfour 2011

ALTERNATES:

## 30 · 31

Chicago Blackhawks
Dallas Stars
Florida Panthers
San Jose Sharks
Toronto Maple Leafs

Catches: Left

Height: 5'-11"

Weight: 202 lbs.

Born: April 21, 1965:
Carman, Manitoba

Played 17 NHL seasons
from 1988–89,
1990–2004, 2005–07

Stats: See page 491

"[The eagle] is a strong figure representing individuality, leadership, confidence, and outstanding vision. Its hunting and aggression are characteristics I admire, so when I was thinking of what I wanted on my mask, the eagle was a natural choice."

AWARDS

Calder Memorial
Trophy (1991)

Vezina Trophy
(1991, 1993)

William M. Jennings
Trophy (1991, 1993,
1995, 1999)

Stanley Cup (1998–99)

ALL-STAR
SELECTIONS

All-Rookie Team (1991)

First All-Star Team
Goaltender (1991, 1993)

Second All-Star Team
Goaltender (1995)

INTERNATIONAL
AWARDS

Canada Cup (1991)

Gold Medal: Winter
Olympics (2002)

o Played amateur hockey with Winkler Flyers (1983–86); University of North Dakota (1986–87); Canadian National Team (1989–90); played European professional hockey with Leksands IF (2007–08)

o Named MJHL Top Goaltender (1986); named IHL Rookie of the Year (1988)

o Selected to WCHA First All-Star Team (1987) and NCAA Championship All-Tournament Team (1987)

o Signed as a free agent by Chicago, September 25, 1987; signed as a free agent by Dallas, July 2, 1997; signed as a free agent by Toronto, July 2, 2002

o Holds Chicago Blackhawks team record for regular-season wins (43), established in 1990–91

o Holds Minnesota North Stars/Dallas Stars team playoff records for career games by a goalie (73), career wins (44) and career shutouts (8)

o Ranks third in NHL career wins (484); ranks fifth in NHL career games by a goalie (963); ranks third in NHL career playoff games by a goalie (161); tied for fourth in NHL career playoff wins (88)

o Led NHL in wins (43) in 1990–91; led NHL in goals-against average in 1990–91 (2.47) and 1997–98 (1.88)

o Led NHL in shutouts in 1991–92 (5), 1992–93 (7), 1993–94 (7) and 1994–95 (5)

o Played in NHL All-Star Game (1992, 1993, 1996, 1998, 1999)

# Prickly Perfection

E d Belfour was a volatile goalie whose prickly personality and stellar play harkened back to Billy Smith, another Hall of Fame legend.

Stylistically, Belfour and Smith were a couple of generations apart, but both were technical masters at the poke check and the two-pad stack—and both were willing to unfurl their bodies and throw themselves toward pucks that many thought were unstoppable. For "Eddie the Eagle" it was this never-say-die attitude, and his constant drive toward perfection, that endeared him to his teammates and made up for his otherwise gruff facade.

Known for his intense personality, Belfour was legendary among his teammates for being extremely particular about his gear, especially his skates, which he trusted to no one but himself to sharpen.

He carried his intensity onto the ice, where he collected 380 career penalty minutes, just 109 less than the tyrannical Smith and well over 100 minutes more than most of his contemporaries. This could be seen as a liability, but Belfour's play stood above his indiscretions.

He arrived in the NHL as a late bloomer. In the 1990–91 season, Belfour was a well-seasoned 25-year-old rookie who started 74 of the Chicago Blackhawks' 80 games, posting a record of 43-19-7. His 43 wins were the best in the NHL that season and the third-highest win count of all time (43 wins is now the sixth highest total). He won the Calder Trophy as Rookie of the Year and the Vezina

**Ed Belfour performs during a shutout in Game 5 of the 2000 Stanley Cup Final.**

as the league's best goalie and was a nominee for the Hart Trophy as the NHL's MVP.

The next season Belfour led the Blackhawks to the Stanley Cup final. Mario Lemieux and the Pittsburgh Penguins proved to be too much for the talented Hawks, but, despite the loss, Belfour posted the best goals-against average of the playoffs. The next season he won the Vezina for a second time.

The 1991–92 playoff loss stayed with Belfour until the 1998–99 season, when he backstopped his new team, the Dallas Stars, to Stanley Cup victory. In the final he outdueled six-time Vezina champ Dominik Hasek by putting up a 1.26 goals-against average to Hasek's 1.68 over the six games played.

Belfour finished his career with 963 regular-season games played and 484 wins, good for the third highest total of all time.

# 1 GOALIE

# Clint Benedict 1965

**ALTERNATE:**

# 9

Montreal Maroons
Ottawa Senators

Catches: Left

Height: Unknown

Weight: Unknown

Born: September 26,
1882: Ottawa, Ontario

Died: November 12,
1976: Ottawa, Ontario

Played 18 professional
seasons from 1912–30

Stats: See page 491

"[Benedict] devised an elaborate series of ruses to allow him to get to his knees — ruses that other goaltenders began copying. One routine allegedly saw him dropping to his knees to give thanks to God — a play that gave rise among outraged Toronto fans to the nickname 'Praying Bennie.'"

— Douglas Hunter,
*A Breed Apart*

**AWARDS**

Stanley Cup: (1920–21,
1922–23, 1925–26)

- First NHL goaltender to win the Stanley Cup with two different teams: Ottawa Senators (1920–21, 1922–23), and Montreal Maroons (1925–26)

- First NHL goaltender to wear mask in a NHL game during Montreal Maroons' 3–3 tie with N.Y. Americans, February 20, 1930. Wore his mask for five games until he was injured again

- First NHL goaltender to record three consecutive shutouts in a single playoff season (1926)

- First NHL goaltender to record four shutouts in a single playoff season (1926)

- Nicknamed "Praying Bennie" because he was the first goaltender to fall to his knees to make a save

- Played amateur hockey with Ottawa Stewartons (1909–10), Ottawa New Edinburghs (1910–12) and Windsor Bulldogs (1930–31)

- Led NHL in wins in 1918–19 (12), 1919–20 (19), 1920–21 (14), 1921–22 (14), 1922–23 (14) and 1923–24 (15)

- Led NHL in shutouts in 1917–18 (1), 1918–19 (2), 1919–20 (5), 1920–21 (2), 1921–22 (2), 1922–23 (4), 1923–24 (3)

- Led NHL in goals-against average in 1918–19 (2.85), 1919–20 (2.66), 1920–21 (3.08), 1921–22 (3.34), 1922–23 (2.18) and 1926–27 (1.42)

- His habit of "accidentally" falling to the ice to make a save or smother loose pucks is often credited for changing the rule early in the first NHL season that said goaltenders had to stand up at all times

# Creative Puck-Stopping

Clint Benedict is mostly remembered for being the first NHL netminder to don a facemask, which he did during the 1929–30 season after taking a shot to the nose from Montreal Canadiens superstar Howie Morenz, but the true legacy of "Praying Benny" lies a little closer to the ice than does his injured proboscis.

Goaltenders weren't permitted to drop to stop shots when Benedict first made his name as a stalwart keeper, but that didn't keep him from trying. With a stack of elaborate excuses, Benedict would often pretend to be knocked over during the play, and angry Toronto fans gave him his Praying Benny nickname for reportedly kneeling on the ice to "thank the heavens."

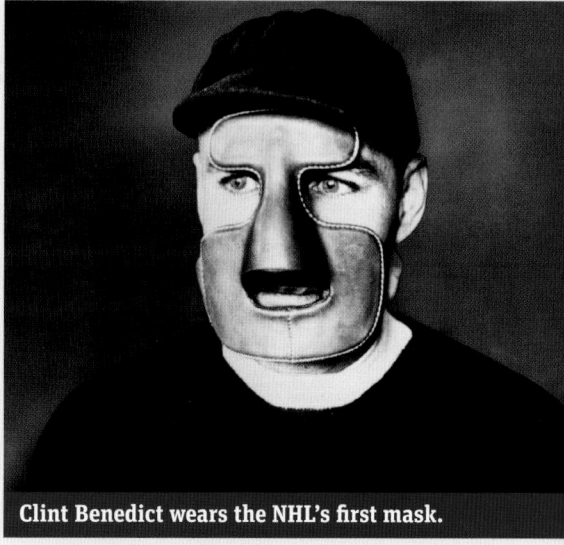

**Clint Benedict wears the NHL's first mask.**

"You had to do something," said Benedict. "Quite a few of the players could put a curving drop on a shot, and the equipment wasn't exactly the greatest in those days."

The NHL changed its rules for puck stopping early in its inaugural season of 1917–18. With the new rule in place, Benedict took to the ice at will.

An Ottawa native, Benedict got an early start in the game and showed steady and rapid improvement. At age 15 he moved into senior hockey and at 20 joined the Ottawa Senators of the National Hockey Association (the forerunner of the NHL). In 1915 the Senators lost the Stanley Cup final to the Vancouver Millionaires, but Benedict stuck with the Ottawa club through the formation of the NHL and the club's Stanley Cup victories in 1920, 1921 and 1923. Sold to the NHL's new entry, the Montreal Maroons, on October 20, 1924, he led his new club to a Stanley Cup victory in the 1925–26 season with four playoff shutouts and a sterling 1.00 goals-against average—the first goalie to backstop two different Cup-winning NHL teams.

In 1919–20 Benedict's 2.66 goals-against average was more than two goals less than the league average, a difference that has never been bettered. In six of seven NHL seasons with Ottawa, he led the league in wins and had the lowest goals-against average in five of those campaigns. He also posted the NHL's lowest goals-against average with the Maroons in 1926–27.

Benedict retired from the league with 57 NHL career shutouts and played one final pro season (1930–31) with the Windsor Bulldogs in the International Hockey League before retiring for good.

# Johnny Bower 1976

NO. RETIRED BY TORONTO
**New York Rangers**
**Toronto Maple Leafs**

Catches: Left

Height: 5'-11"

Weight: 189 lbs.

Born: November 8, 1924: Prince Albert, Saskatchewan

Died: December 26, 2017: Toronto, Ontario

Played 15 NHL seasons from 1953–55, 1956–57, 1958–70

Stats: See page 492

"When you played in the American league, you just had to be patient, wait your turn for a rebuilding team. A lot of good goalies came out of our league, too."

**AWARDS**
Vezina Trophy (1961, 1965)

Stanley Cup (1961–62, 1962–63, 1963–64, 1966–67)

**ALL-STAR SELECTIONS**
First All-Star Team Goaltender (1961)

- Holds AHL record for career shutouts (45); holds AHL record for career wins (359)

- Played amateur hockey with Prince Albert Warhawks (1943–44); Prince Albert Blackhawks (1944–45); Laura Beavers (1944–45)

- Played minor pro hockey with Providence Reds (1945–46); Cleveland Barons (1945–53); Vancouver Canucks (1954–55)

- Led AHL in wins in 1949–50 (38), 1950–51 (44), 1952–53 (40) and 1955–56 (45); led AHL in shutouts in 1949–50 (5) and 1952–53 (6); led AHL in goals-against average in 1956–57 (2.37) and 1957–58 (2.17)

- Led WHL in shutouts (7) and goals-against average (2.71) in 1954–55

- AHL First All-Star Team Goaltender (1952, 1953, 1956, 1957, 1958); AHL Second All-Star Team Goaltender (1952)

- Named AHL Most Valuable Player (1956, 1957, 1958); named WHL Top Goaltender (1954–55)

- Led NHL in wins (33) in 1960–61; led NHL in goals-against average in 1963–64 (2.11), 1964–65 (2.38) and 1965–66 (2.26)

- Played in NHL All-Star Game (1961, 1962, 1963, 1964)

- Nicknamed "China Wall" because of his age when he became an NHL regular

- Legally changed his name to John Bower from John Kiszkan in his second year of professional hockey

# The Old Battle Ax

With NHL roster spots at a premium during the six-team era, scores of gifted hockey players were resigned to having rewarding careers in the minor leagues. Some were good enough to play in the NHL, and many waited for the call that never came. In the early 1950s, that seemed to be the fate of Johnny Bower.

Bower rode the bus with the Cleveland Barons from 1945–46 until he got his first chance in the NHL in 1953, when the New York Rangers swung a deal for his services. And just like that, after eight American Hockey League (AHL) seasons, Bower broke through. He played every Ranger game on the schedule that year, even though incumbent goalie Gump Worsley had been the NHL's Rookie of the Year the previous season. Much to Bower's surprise, he found himself back in the minors the following campaign, and Worsley got his NHL job back. After his demotion, Bower was named the AHL's MVP three of the four years he remained in the Rangers system, but he played only seven games as a call-up over that span.

Fortune turned Bower's way after a particularly strong playoff series in 1958 against the Springfield Indians. Punch Imlach, who ran the Indians, was hired by the Toronto Maple Leafs that year, and signed Bower after Toronto had drafted him. Although initially reluctant to join the Leafs, Bower was persuaded to report to training camp and quickly established himself as a number-one NHL goalie, winning the Vezina Trophy in

**Johnny Bower dives to poke the puck away from Claude Laforge in 1958.**

1961 and three consecutive Stanley Cups, from 1962 to 1964.

Bower made his name by fearlessly putting his body in harm's way—playing without a mask and diving face-first to wield his patented poke check, a move he perfected after learning it from Rangers goalie Chuck Rayner. Bower's lined and scarred face led many to suspect he was even older than his reported age, and Bower was intentionally vague about dates.

In 1965 Bower split duties with Terry Sawchuk. The pair shared the Vezina Trophy that year and performed admirably two years later, in 1967, as the aging Leafs surprised the Montreal Canadiens for the last Cup victory of the Original Six era.

After playing what could be considered two full careers, Bower retired in 1970 at the age of 45, the oldest goalie ever to play in the NHL—and he may have had a few more starts left in him then.

# 1

# Frank Brimsek 1966

**ALTERNATES:**

## 10 · 17

**Boston Bruins**
**Chicago Black Hawks**

Catches: Left

Height: 5'-9"

Weight: 170 lbs.

Born: September 26, 1913: Eveleth, Minnesota

Died: November 11, 1998: Virginia, Minnesota

Played 10 NHL seasons from 1938–43, 1945–50

Stats: See page 492

"The kid had the fastest hands I ever saw — like lightning."

— Art Ross

**AWARDS**

Calder Memorial Trophy (1939)

Vezina Trophy (1939, 1942)

Stanley Cup (1938–39, 1940–41)

**ALL-STAR SELECTIONS**

First All-Star Team Goaltender (1939, 1942)

Second All-Star Team Goaltender (1940, 1941, 1943, 1946, 1947, 1948)

- Played amateur hockey with Eveleth Rangers (1934–35); Pittsburgh Yellowjackets (1934–37)

- Renowned for using his stick to knock opposition players off their feet if they skated too close to his crease

- First goaltender to win the Calder Trophy and Vezina Trophy in the same season

- Earned the nickname "Mr. Zero" by recording six shutouts in his first seven NHL games after being given the starter's job by the Boston Bruins in 1938–39

- Led EAHL in wins (20) and shutouts (8) in 1935–36; led IAHL in goals-against average (1.75) and playoff wins (5) in 1937–38

- EAHL First All-Star Team (1936); IAHL First All-Star Team Goaltender (1938)

- Signed as free agent by Boston Bruins and assigned to IAHL's Providence Reds, October 27, 1937

- Led NHL in wins in 1938–39 (33) and 1939–40 (31)

- Led NHL in shutouts in 1938–39 (10) and 1940–41 (6); led NHL in goals-against average in 1938–39 (1.56) and 1941–42 (2.35)

- Led NHL in playoff wins (8) and goals-against average (1.25) in 1938–39; playoff wins (8), shutouts (1) and goals-against average (2.04) in 1940–41

- Played for U.S. Coast Guard Cutters (1943–44) during World War II

- Played in NHL All-Star Game (1947, 1948)

- Inducted in U.S.A. Hockey Hall of Fame (1973)

**322**

# 1967 Turk Broda

"The bonus money for winning wasn't much but I always needed it. Or maybe I was just too dumb to know the situation was serious."

— Broda, on his reputation as a "money" goalie

NO. RETIRED BY TORONTO

ALTERNATE:

**19**

**Toronto Maple Leafs**

Catches: Left

Height: 5'-9"

Weight: 180 lbs.

Born: May 15, 1914: Brandon, Manitoba

Died: October 17, 1972: Toronto, Ontario

Played 14 NHL seasons from 1936–43, 1945–52

Stats: See page 493

- Holds Toronto Maple Leafs team goaltending records for career games (629), wins (304) and shutouts (61)

- Holds Toronto Maple Leafs team goaltending records for career playoff games (101), playoff wins (60) and playoff shutouts (13)

- First goaltender in NHL history to play 100 playoff games, March 27, 1952

- Played amateur hockey with Brandon Native Sons (1932–33); Winnipeg Monarchs (1933–34); Detroit Farm Crest (1934–35); Detroit Olympics (1935–36)

- Led IHL in wins (26) and goals-against average (2.10) in 1935–36; led IHL playoffs in wins (6), shutouts (1) and goals-against average (1.32)

- Traded to Toronto Maple Leafs by Detroit Olympics for $8,000 on May 6, 1936

- Played in NHL All-Star Game (1947, 1948, 1949, 1950)

- Led NHL in wins in 1940–41 (28) and 1947–48 (32)

- Led NHL in shutouts in 1941–42 (6) and 1949–50 (9)

- Led NHL in goals-against average in 1940–41 (2.00) and 1947–48 (2.38)

- Nicknamed "Turk" because his freckles resembled the surface of a turkey egg

- Renowned for his comedic wit and ability to play his best in the playoffs when "the real money" was on the line

- Inducted into Manitoba Hockey Hall of Fame (1967); inducted into Manitoba Sports Hall of Fame (1985)

- Coached Ottawa Senators (1953–54); Toronto Jr. Marlboros (1954–60, 1961–63); Charlotte Checkers (1963–64); Newmarket Huskies (1964–66); Moncton Beavers (1968–69); Quebec Aces (1969–70); London Nationals (1970–71)

- Coached Memorial Cup–winning Toronto Marlboros (1955, 1956)

**AWARDS**

Vezina Trophy (1941, 1948)

Stanley Cup (1941–42, 1946–47, 1947–48, 1948–49, 1950–51)

**ALL-STAR SELECTIONS**

First All-Star Team Goaltender (1941, 1948)

Second All-Star Team Goaltender (1942)

# 30

# Gerry Cheevers 1985

**ALTERNATES:**

# 31 · 1

Boston Bruins
Cleveland Crusaders
Toronto Maple Leafs

Catches: Left

Height: 5'-11"

Weight: 180 lbs.

Born: December 7, 1940;
St. Catharines, Ontario

Played 17 NHL and WHA
seasons from 1961–80

Stats: See page 493

"If you see a white
mask today, it stands
out. I hated white.
It reminded me of
purity, which was
not the case the way
I played goal."

**AWARDS**

Stanley Cup
(1969–70, 1971–72)

**ALL-STAR
SELECTIONS**

WHA First All-Star Team
Goaltender (1973)

WHA Second All-Star
Team Goaltender
(1974, 1975)

- Holds NHL record for longest undefeated streak (32 games) by a goaltender in regular season, established in 1971–72

- Played amateur hockey with St. Michael's Majors (1956–60)

- Renowned for his signature "stitch" mask that featured painted black replications of the stitches he would have had without wearing a mask

- Led OHA-Jr. in shutouts (5) and goals-against average (3.08); led OHA-Jr. playoffs in shutouts (1) and goals-against average (2.60) in 1960–61

- Played eight games as left winger for St. Michael's Majors during 1960–61 season

- AHL First All-Star Team Goaltender (1965)

- Played in NHL All-Star Game (1969)

- Led NHL playoffs in shutouts (3) in 1968–69

- Finished third in NHL wins in 1967–68 (21) and 1968–69 (27)

- Led WHA in shutouts in 1972–73 (5), 1973–74 (4) and 1974–75 (4); led WHA in goals-against average (2.84) in 1972–73

- Won Ben Haskins Trophy (Top WHA Goaltender) in 1973

- Member of Team Canada '74 that played eight game summit series against the Soviet Union

- Member of Team NHL in 1979 Challenge Cup Series between NHL All-Stars and Soviet Union

- Coached Boston Bruins (1980–85)

# 1958 **Alex Connell**

**1**

"He's a little man, as fast as a flash and as cool-headed as Georges Vezina of the Canadiens."

— Tommy Gorman, general manager of the Ottawa Senators, on signing Connell to a professional contract

Detroit Falcons
Montreal Maroons
New York Americans
Ottawa Senators

Catches: Left

Height: 5'-9"

Weight: 150 lbs.

Born: February 8, 1900; Ottawa, Ontario

Died: May 10, 1958; Ottawa, Ontario

Played 12 NHL seasons from 1924–35, 1936–37

Stats: See page 494

- Holds NHL record for longest shutout sequence by a goaltender in the regular season (460:49), established from January 31, 1928, to February 18, 1928

- Only goaltender in NHL history to record 15 shutouts in regular season twice, 1925–26 (15) and 1927–28 (15)

- Tied for sixth in NHL career shutouts (81)

- Played amateur hockey with Kingston Ponies (1916–17); Kingston Frontenacs (1917–19); Ottawa Cliffsides (1919–20); Ottawa St. Brigands (1920–21, 1922–24); Ottawa Gunners (1921–22)

- Led NHL in wins in 1925–26 (24) and 1926–27 (30)

- Led NHL in goals-against average (1.12) in 1925–26

- Led NHL in shutouts in 1924–25 (7), 1925–26 (15), 1927–28 (15) and 1934–35 (9)

- Nicknamed "The Ottawa Fireman" because he was the secretary of the Ottawa Fire Department in the off-season

- Loaned to N.Y. Americans by Ottawa to replace injured Roy Worters in N.Y. Americans' 3–2 victory over Ottawa, March 15, 1934

- Played lacrosse with Ottawa Shamrocks and helped team win the Eastern Canada championship twice

- Coached St. Patrick's College Irish (1938–49); coached Ottawa Senators (1949–50)

- Elected to Ottawa Sports Hall of Fame (1968)

**AWARDS**
Stanley Cup (1926–27, 1934–35)

# 29

## GOALIE

# Ken Dryden 1983

NO. RETIRED BY MONTREAL

**Montreal Canadiens**

Catches: Left

Height: 6'-4"

Weight: 205 lbs.

Born: August 8, 1947; Hamilton, Ontario

Drafted by the Boston Bruins 14th overall in 1964

Played eight NHL seasons from 1970–72, 1973–79

Stats: See page 494

"I think it took me so long to want to be part of the team because I was afraid of a team. Afraid of always having to do what a team does; afraid of losing my own right to be different. When I realized I could be part of a team, and still be different, I could then be less different. Then I realized I wasn't very different at all."

### AWARDS

Conn Smythe Trophy (1971)

Calder Memorial Trophy (1972)

Vezina Trophy (1973, 1976, 1977, 1978, 1979)

Stanley Cup (1970–71, 1972–73, 1975–76, 1976–77, 1977–78, 1978–79)

### ALL-STAR SELECTIONS

First All-Star Team Goaltender (1973, 1976, 1977, 1978, 1979)

Second All-Star Team Goaltender (1972)

### INTERNATIONAL AWARDS

Summit Series (1972)

- Only player in NHL history to win a major award (Conn Smythe Trophy) before winning the Calder Trophy as top rookie (1971)

- Played amateur hockey with Humber Valley Packers (1963–64); Etobicoke Indians (1964–65); Cornell University Big Red (1966–69); Canadian National Team (1969–70)

- NCAA All-Tournament Team (1967); NCAA All-America First Team (1966–67, 1967–68, 1968–69)

- Rights traded to Montreal by Boston Bruins with Alex Campbell for Guy Allen and Paul Reid, June 28, 1964

- Sat out the entire 1973–74 season because of a contract dispute and spent the year articling at a Toronto law firm

- Played in NHL All-Star Game (1972, 1975, 1976, 1977, 1978)

- Led NHL in wins in 1971–72 (39), 1972–73 (33), 1975–76 (42) and 1976–77 (41)

- Led NHL in shutouts in 1972–73 (6), 1975–76 (8), 1976–77 (10) and 1978–79 (5); led NHL in goals-against average in 1972–73 (2.26), 1975–76 (2.03), 1977–78 (2.05) and 1978–79 (2.30)

- Wrote *The Game*, considered to be the most definitive book ever written about hockey

- Served as president of the Toronto Maple Leafs (1997–2004)

- Served as Ontario Youth Commissioner (1984–86); elected as Liberal Member of Parliament for York Centre (2004, 2006)

# Master of the Game

Ken Dryden was a spectacular force in the Montreal Canadiens net for eight seasons, and his early retirement was almost as surprising as his NHL debut.

Called up for six games at the end of the 1970–71 NHL season, Dryden performed better than expected, winning all six contests and allowing only nine goals in total. Yet it was still a shocking decision when the Habs decided to play their rookie, as opposed to starter Rogie Vachon, against the powerhouse Boston Bruins in the 1971 playoffs.

Dryden, however, lead a Montreal upset of the Bruins on the way to a seven-game victory over the heavily favored Chicago Black Hawks in the Stanley Cup final. For his efforts he was named the playoff MVP.

Dryden was never a typical hockey player, and his unconventional choices and career reflect the Renaissance man he became. His first irregular choice was to spend his development years attending Cornell University instead of the proven minor-pro system. He sat out his freshman season but was an All-American the next three campaigns while getting a history degree as a step to becoming a lawyer. He then continued his studies over the 1969–70 season while playing for Canada's national team. When the team was disbanded, Dryden finally stepped into

**Ken Dryden wore this pretzel-style mask during his time at Cornell University and as a rookie with Montreal.**

Montreal's farm system, where his performance led to his famous NHL debut.

The talented puck-stopper dispelled any notion of a sophomore jinx when he won the 1972 Calder Trophy. Dryden then played for Canada in the 1972 Summit Series the following September, and he earned his first Vezina Trophy in 1973 while backstopping Montreal to another Cup victory over Chicago.

Disenchanted with his contract and the Canadiens' refusal to renegotiate it, Dryden joined a law firm as an articling student and sat out the 1973–74 season, during which the Habs faltered. Dryden got the new contract he wanted.

From the 1975–76 season up until the end of his career in 1979, Dryden performed impeccably. He won the Vezina Trophy four more times and posted a goals-against average of 2.30 or better each year. Montreal won four consecutive Stanley Cups, giving Dryden six rings in eight seasons.

Although physically sound enough to continue playing, Dryden quit after the 1978–79 season to pursue other interests. He penned *The Game* (one of hockey's most insightful books), and several other books, spent time broadcasting and even served as an executive with the Toronto Maple Leafs. In 2004 he entered the political arena, serving as a Toronto member of Parliament and a Liberal cabinet minister.

# 1

# Bill Durnan 1964

**Montreal Canadiens**

Catches: Right/Left

Height: 6'

Weight: 190 lbs.

Born: January 22, 1916:
Toronto, Ontario

Died: October 31, 1972:
Toronto, Ontario

Played seven NHL
seasons from 1943–50

Stats: See page 495

"He's the best goaler
in 20 years in the
National Hockey
League because
he has the most
competitive spirit
and is the least
temperamental and
he's the greatest of
all goalers under fire."

—Dick Irvin Sr.,
Montreal coach

**AWARDS**

Vezina Trophy
(1944, 1945, 1946,
1947, 1949, 1950)

Stanley Cup
(1943–44, 1945–46)

**ALL-STAR
SELECTIONS**

First All-Star Team
Goaltender (1944, 1945,
1946, 1947, 1949, 1950)

- Last goaltender to captain a team
  (1947–48) until Roberto Luongo
  (2008–10); only ambidextrous
  goaltender in NHL history

- Played amateur hockey with North
  Toronto Juniors (1931–32); Sudbury
  Cub Wolves (1932–33); Toronto
  British Consols (1933–34); Toronto
  McColl-Frontenacs (1934–35); Toronto
  Dominions (1935–36); Kirkland Lake
  Blue Devils (1936–40); Montreal
  Royals (1940–43)

- Led North Bay Junior League in
  shutouts (2) and goals-against
  average (1.00) in 1932–33

- TMHL First All-Star Team Goaltender
  (1934); NOHA First All-Star Team
  Goaltender (1937)

- Led NOHA in wins (8) and goals-
  against average (2.66) in 1937–38;
  led NOHA in wins (7), shutouts (3)
  and goals-against average (1.00) in
  1938–39

- Member of Allan Cup–winning
  Kirkland Lake Blue Devils (1939–40)

- Led QSHL in wins (21), playoff wins
  (6) and playoff shutouts (1) in 1940–41

- Played in NHL All-Star Game (1947,
  1948, 1949)

- Led NHL in wins in 1943–44 (38),
  1944–45 (38), 1945–46 (24) and
  1946–47 (34)

- Led NHL in shutouts in 1945–46 (4)
  and 1948–49 (10)

- Led NHL in goals-against average
  in 1943–44 (2.18), 1944–45 (2.42),
  1945–46 (2.60), 1946–47 (2.30),
  1948–49 (2.10) and 1949–50 (2.20)

# The Ambidextrous Goalie

**B**ill Durnan was a man of principle and pride—and a unique quirk never seen before or since—and all of these qualities greatly influenced his Hall of Fame career.

Initially signed by the Toronto Maple Leafs and invited to their camp in 1936 at the age of 20, Durnan was jilted when the Leafs rescinded their offer upon learning he had injured his knee. The experience caused him to lose his enthusiasm for the pro game, and he contemplated retiring from hockey completely. He then spent four seasons with the Kirkland Lake Blue Devils, winning the 1940 Allan Cup, senior amateur hockey's top prize.

The Montreal Canadiens came calling three years later, after scouting him with the Montreal Royals of the Quebec senior league. Still smarting from his Toronto experience and wary of the pressures of the pro game, Durnan drove a hard bargain, maintaining he was content to make less playing amateur hockey in return for less stress. General manager Tommy Gorman eventually got his man, and Durnan was a Hab for the 1943–44 season.

Excellent at cutting off his angles, Durnan was a strong fundamental goalie, but his finest trick to dumfound shooters was his ambidexterity. Durnan wore specially fingered gloves that each had a pocket like a trapper and a padded back like a blocker, allowing him to hold his stick and catch the puck with either hand. Over his seven NHL seasons,

**Bill Durnan is one of the few goalies to be named team captain.**

Durnan confounded shooters enough to win the Vezina Trophy six times as well as earn six First All-Star Team berths; he also backstopped the Habs to Stanley Cup victories in 1943–44 and again in 1945–46.

A serious and constantly vocal player, Durnan was handed the captain's C in 1948, and his frequent forays to discuss game matters with the referee led the league to bar goaltenders from executing the captain's duties on the ice.

Durnan's play continued to be stellar, but Montreal was faltering and the stress was getting to the puck-stopper. After failing to make the playoffs in 1947–48 he contemplated quitting, but the Canadiens talked him out of it—temporarily.

Despite numbers well within his career average in 1949–50, Durnan felt his play was weakening. When Montreal fell behind three games to none in the semifinals in 1950, Durnan abruptly quit—feeling it was better to not play at all then to play poorly, and he never played another game.

# 35
# Tony Esposito 1988

NO. RETIRED BY CHICAGO

ALTERNATES:

# 29 · 1

Chicago Black Hawks
Montreal Canadiens

Catches: Right

Height: 5'-11"

Weight: 185 lbs.

Born: April 23, 1943:
Sault Ste. Marie, Ontario

Played 16 NHL seasons
from 1968–84

Stats: See page 495

"I wanted something different. I wanted something to make me stand out and for people to notice."

— Tony Esposito, on his decision to wear number 35 in Chicago

**AWARDS**

Calder Memorial
Trophy (1970)

Vezina Trophy
(1970, 1972, 1974)

Stanley Cup (1968–69)

**ALL-STAR
SELECTIONS**

First All-Star Team
Goaltender (1970,
1972, 1980)

Second All-Star Team
Goaltender (1973, 1974)

**INTERNATIONAL
AWARDS**

Summit Series (1972)

- Ranks eighth in career NHL games played by a goaltender (886); ranks ninth in career NHL wins (423); tied for ninth in career NHL shutouts (76)

- First NHL rookie to win Vezina Trophy since Bill Durnan (1944)

- Played amateur hockey with Sault Ste. Marie Greyhounds (1962–63); Michigan Tech University Huskies (1963–67)

- NCAA West First All-American Team Goaltender (1965, 1966, 1967); NCAA Championship All-Tournament Team Goaltender (1965)

- Played minor pro hockey with Vancouver Canucks (1967–68)

- Claimed by Chicago from Montreal in Intra-League Draft, June 11, 1969

- Played in NHL All-Star Game (1970, 1971, 1972, 1973, 1974, 1980)

- Led NHL in wins in 1969–70 (38) and 1970–71 (35); led NHL in shutouts in 1969–70 (15), 1971–72 (9) and 1979–80 (6); led NHL in goals-against average (1.77) in 1971–72

- Acquired American citizenship and played for Team U.S.A. in 1981 Canada Cup tournament

- Renowned for revolutionizing NHL goaltending with his unique legs-open "butterfly" style

- Brother of Hall of Fame member Phil Esposito, who played in NHL with Chicago, Boston and N.Y. Rangers from 1963–81

- Served as general manager of Pittsburgh Penguins (1988–89, 1989)

# Tony O

As one half of the most colorful brother act in NHL history, Tony "O" Esposito was as sensational in keeping pucks out of the net as his older brother Phil was at putting them in. When Phil was playing for the Chicago Black Hawks in the mid-1960s, Tony, an All-American at Michigan Tech, was getting an NHL apprenticeship from Phil's teammate Glenn Hall. At the time, no one knew how well Hall's paying it forward would work out for the Hawks.

Esposito came to refine Hall's butterfly style with an even wider stance, enabling him to peek through screens and quickly drop to the ice to cover the lower part of the net. He also worked to refine his equipment, adding an elastic mesh web between his pant legs—a device that was quickly banned (he instead widened his pant legs by adding foam)—as well as adding a cheater to his catching glove. The glove enhancement effectively made the cuff of the glove as wide as the mitt on top, which became a prototype for the modern catcher. He designed a protective neckpiece in 1971, and he tinkered with an early mask design in 1974–75, adding a wire cage over the eyeholes of his mask and a fiberglass extension to protect the top of his head.

The Montreal Canadiens first signed Esposito in 1967, but confusing his unorthodox style as a fundamental flaw, they left him unprotected in the 1969 Intra-League Draft. Chicago happily picked up his rights, needing a goalie to fill the void left by the recently departed Hall. Aged 26, Esposito was

**Tony Esposito makes a save against Toronto.**

still officially a rookie in 1969–70, when he won the Calder Trophy, the Vezina Trophy, and a First All-Star Team berth. He played 63 games, and his 15 shutouts remain the modern single-season NHL record.

Tony O won the Vezina Trophy two more times and backstopped the Hawks to the 1971 and 1973 Stanley Cup final, losing both to his former team. In fact, Esposito's only Cup win was as a member of the Canadiens, sitting on the bench as a backup in 1969.

At age 41 Esposito, the oldest player in the league, hung up his pads after the 1983–84 season. Despite not winning a Cup in Chicago, his teams never failed to make the playoffs, and his 76 career regular-season shutouts were the seventh-highest total at the time of his retirement; at the conclusion of the 2017–18 season he remained tied at ninth spot.

# 31
## GOALIE
# Grant Fuhr 2003

NO. RETIRED BY EDMONTON

ALTERNATE:

1

Buffalo Sabres
Calgary Flames
Edmonton Oilers
Los Angeles Kings
St. Louis Blues
Toronto Maple Leafs

Catches: Right

Height: 5'-10"

Weight: 201 lbs.

Born: September 28,
1962: Spruce Grove,
Alberta

Drafted by the
Edmonton Oilers
eighth overall in 1981

Played 19 NHL seasons
from 1981 – 2000

Stats: See page 495

"It was a great honor as a kid to get drafted to the National Hockey League, but for me it was kind of a bonus. I got drafted to my hometown."

AWARDS

Vezina Trophy (1988)

William M. Jennings
Trophy (1994)

Stanley Cup (1983–84,
1984–85, 1986–87,
1987–88, 1989–90)

ALL-STAR
SELECTIONS

First All-Star Team
Goaltender (1988)

Second All-Star Team
Goaltender (1982)

INTERNATIONAL
AWARDS

Canada Cup (1984, 1987)

Bronze Medal: World
Championships (1988)

- Holds NHL record for most games played by a goaltender in regular season (79) and most consecutive starts by a goaltender in regular season (76), established in 1995–96

- Holds NHL record for assists (14) and points (14) by a goaltender in regular season, established in 1983–84

- Shares NHL record for most wins in a single playoff season (16), established in 1987–88

- Ranks third in all-time NHL playoff wins (92)

- Ranks 12th in NHL career wins (403)

- Ranks eighth in NHL career shots against (24,371)

- Played amateur hockey with Sherwood Park Crusaders (1978–79); Victoria Cougars (1979–81)

- Named WHL Rookie of the Year (1980); Named WHL Top Goaltender (1981)

- WHL First All-Star Team Goaltender (1980, 1981)

- Led WHL in wins (48), shutouts (4) and goals-against average (2.78) in 1980–81; led WHL playoffs in wins (12), shutouts (1) and goals-against average (3.00)

- Played in NHL All-Star Game (1982, 1984, 1985, 1986, 1988, 1989)

- Led NHL in wins in 1983–84 (30) and 1987–88 (40); led NHL in shutouts (4) in 1987–88

**332**

# A Style All His Own

I n the era of stand-up goalies, Grant Fuhr was an acrobatic marvel.

Born in Spruce Grove, Alberta, just outside the city of Edmonton, Fuhr had the good fortune to be coached as a peewee by Hall of Famer Glenn Hall, whose farm was only 5 miles away. Hall was legendary for his unique style of play—a precursor of the modern butterfly style—and Fuhr incorporated Hall's move, crouching low to the ice in order to take away the bottom of the net with quick leg saves, into his own routine.

**Grant Fuhr does the splits in Toronto in 1991–92.**

But that is where the comparisons between Fuhr and Hall end, as Fuhr had a style all his own: jabbing kick saves, spearing glove saves and impossible acrobatic recoveries.

He was "a natural," recalled Ron Low, a former Oiler goalie and coach, adding, "Yet he had no style. Or, rather, his style was all styles. He would come out 15 feet to challenge the shot on one offensive rush. The next time he would be back in his crease. He could read the game so well. He anticipated the game. Grant was just… different. Different from anyone I'd ever seen."

Drafted eighth overall by the Edmonton Oilers in the 1981 NHL Entry Draft, Fuhr played 48 games for the 1981–82 Oilers, posting a 28–5–14 record. Those totals were good enough for him to earn a berth on the Second All-Star Team. Before the decade was out, he had earned five Stanley Cup rings with the star-laden but predominantly offensive-minded Edmonton club.

The 1987–88 campaign was undoubtedly Fuhr's finest. He was a workhorse, guiding Canada to victory in the preseason Canada Cup tournament then setting an NHL regular-season record by starting 75 games. Fuhr made the First All-Star Team, earned the Vezina Trophy and helped the Oilers to the final Cup of the Gretzky dynasty.

As the Oilers unloaded talent, Fuhr was traded to Toronto, and from there he bounced to Buffalo, Los Angeles, St. Louis and Calgary, mentoring younger goaltenders while also getting in some quality playing time. In St. Louis he set an NHL record with 79 starts—76 in succession—in 1995–96. In Calgary in 1999–2000, he notched his 400th career victory, becoming only the sixth NHL goalie to hit that milestone. Fuhr was inducted into the Hockey Hall of Fame in his first year of eligibility, 2003.

**333**

# 1 Chuck Gardiner 1945

**Chicago Black Hawks**

Catches: Right

Height: 5'-9"

Weight: 176 lbs.

Born: December 31, 1904;
Edinburgh, Scotland

Died: June 13, 1934;
Winnipeg, Manitoba

Played seven NHL
seasons from 1927–34

Stats: See page 496

"Chuck was always a cheery soul and a real inspiration to the team in front of him. He was a sportsman from his head to his heels as well as one of the greatest goalkeepers the game has ever produced."

—Frank Calder,
NHL president

**AWARDS**

Vezina Trophy
(1932, 1934)

Stanley Cup (1933–34)

**ALL-STAR
SELECTIONS**

First All-Star Team
Goaltender (1931,
1932, 1934)

Second All-Star Team
Goaltender (1933)

- Played amateur hockey with Winnipeg Assiniboia (1919–21); Winnipeg Tigers (1921–24); Selkirk Fisherman (1924–25)

- Made professional debut with American Hockey Association's Winnipeg Maroons (1926–27)

- First right-handed catching goaltender to win the Vezina Trophy

- Named captain of the Black Hawks in November of 1933, he is the only NHL goaltender to captain his team to a Stanley Cup victory

- Played in All-Star Game (1934)

- Led NHL in shutouts in 1930–31 (12); 1933–34 (10); led NHL in goals-against average in 1931–32 (1.85)

- A renowned vocalist who gave numerous radio recitals, he was also noted for his skills as a trapshooter

- After backstopping Black Hawks to the 1934 Stanley Cup championship, he was carried through Chicago's downtown Loop in a wheelbarrow

- Died of a brain hemorrhage only two months after leading the Chicago Black Hawks to the franchise's first Stanley Cup championship, June 13, 1934

- Inducted into Manitoba Sports Hall of Fame (1989)

- In September of 2009, four teams—the Toronto Marlies, Hamilton Bulldogs, Edinburgh Capitals and Belfast Giants—participated in the Gardiner Cup Tournament in Scotland, dedicated to his memory

# Chicago's Tragic Hero

Chuck Gardiner played in every game from his first game in the autumn of 1927, when he joined the lowly Chicago Black Hawks, to the Hawks' Stanley Cup victory in the spring of 1934, missing just two full periods of action in all that time. Along the way, he distinguished himself as one of the game's legendary netminders.

Born in Scotland in 1904, at age seven Gardiner immigrated with his family to Winnipeg. He rose through the local hockey ranks, eventually turning pro with the Winnipeg Maroons in 1925. His success at the minor-pro level was noted by the newly formed NHL team in Chicago, who bought his contract and put him between the pipes for the Black Hawks' second season, in 1927–28. The team was bad, but Gardiner was a standout. After winning only 13 games over two seasons, the Hawks made the playoffs in 1929–30, but everything really started to come together the following season.

Gardiner made the NHL's inaugural All-Star Team in 1930–31, leading the league with a personal-best 12 shutouts. He posted a 1.73 goals-against average, good for second in the league, and backstopped his club all the way to the Stanley Cup final. Despite his sparkling 1.32 playoff average, the Hawks failed to score in the deciding fifth game, and the Montreal Canadiens triumphed.

Gardiner won his first Vezina Trophy in 1931–32, a feat he replicated two seasons later. He repeated as First All-Star Team goalie, made the Second Team in 1932–33, and made the First Team again the following

**Chuck Gardiner poses as an NHL All-Star before the Ace Bailey Benefit Game in 1934.**

season. Gardiner also received the honor of being named Black Hawks team captain in 1933–34, in what turned out to be his final campaign. On February 14, 1934, he played in the NHL's first All-Star Game, a benefit for injured Toronto player Ace Bailey.

After leading the league in the regular season with 10 shutouts, Gardiner capped an excellent year with a shutout in double overtime in the deciding fourth game of the playoffs. Chicago had its first Stanley Cup victory. Sadly, Gardiner died shortly after the Hawk's Cup win. He suffered a brain hemorrhage in the days following the victory and died two months later. Chicago played the next season without a team captain.

**335**

# 1

# Eddie Giacomin 1987

NO. RETIRED BY
NEW YORK RANGERS

ALTERNATE:

31

Detroit Red Wings
New York Rangers

Catches: Left

Height: 5'-11"

Weight: 180 lbs.

Born: June 6, 1939;
Sudbury, Ontario

Played 13 NHL seasons
from 1965–78

Stats: See page 496

"I really loved being a Ranger and being in New York. I guess it showed. It's hard for me even today to sign Detroit Red Wings' hockey cards. It isn't natural because I never felt like I was a Red Wing."

AWARDS
Vezina Trophy (1971)

ALL-STAR
SELECTIONS

First All-Star Team
Goaltender (1967, 1971)

Second All-Star
Team Goaltender
(1968, 1969, 1970)

- Nicknamed "Fast Eddie" because of his penchant for leaving the net to reach loose pucks before incoming forwards

- Played amateur hockey with Commack Comets (1957–58); Sudbury Bell Telephone (1958–59); Clinton Comets (1958-60); N.Y. Rovers (1959–61); Washington Presidents (1958–59)

- Suffered serious burns as a teenager but he recovered and played in an industrial men's league in Sudbury and a senior team in the Nickel Belt League

- Traded to N.Y. Rangers by Providence Reds (AHL) for Marcel Paille, Aldo Guidolin, Sandy McGregor and Jim Mikol, May 18, 1965

- Led NHL in wins in 1966–67 (30), 1967–68 (36) and 1968–69 (38)

- Led NHL in shutouts in 1966–67 (9), 1967–68 (8) and 1970–71 (8)

- Played in NHL All-Star Game (1967, 1968, 1969, 1970, 1971, 1973)

- Started wearing a mask in the 1970–71 season, even though he had been critical of it the year before saying it would hurt his style because he liked to shoot the puck

- Claimed on waivers by Detroit from N.Y. Rangers, October 31, 1975

- Served as N.Y. Rangers' goaltending coach (1986–89)

# 1961 George Hainsworth

**1**

> "I'm sorry I can't put on a show like some of the other goaltenders. I can't look excited because I'm not. I can't shout at other players because that's not my style. I can't dive on easy shots and make them look hard. I guess all I can do is stop pucks."

**ALTERNATES:**

**12 · 17**

Montreal Canadiens
Saskatoon Crescents
Toronto Maple Leafs

Catches: Left

Height: 5'-6"

Weight: 150 lbs.

Born: June 26, 1895;
Toronto, Ontario

Died: October 9, 1950;
Gravenhurst, Ontario

Played 14 professional
seasons from 1923–37

Stats: See page 497

- Holds NHL record for shutouts in regular season (22), established in 1928–29

- Holds NHL record for consecutive shutout minutes in a single playoff season (270:08) established in 1930

- Shares NHL record for shutouts in a single calendar month (6), established in February of 1929; record tied by Dominik Hasek in December of 1997

- Ranks third in career NHL shutouts (94)

- Ranks second in professional career shutouts (104) with 94 NHL shutouts and 10 WCHL/WHL shutouts

- Led OHA-Sr. in wins in 1912–13 (3), 1913–14 (7), 1914–15 (5), 1915–16 (8), 1917–18 (9) and 1919–20 (6)

- Led OHA-Sr. in shutouts in 1915–16 (1), 1919–20 (1), 1920–21 (3) and 1921–22 (1)

- Played amateur hockey with Berlin Mavericks (1910–11); Berlin Union Jacks (1911–12); Berlin City Seniors (1913–16); Toronto Kew Beach (1916–17); Kitchener Greenshirts (1918–23)

- Led OHA-Sr. in goals-against average in 1913–14 (1.57), 1914–15 (1.80), 1917–18 (3.44) and 1919–20 (2.00)

- Led WCHL in shutouts (4) in 1923–24

- Led NHL in wins in 1927–28 (26), 1931–32 (25), 1933–34 (26) and 1934–35 (30); led NHL in shutouts in 1926–27 (14) and 1928–29 (22)

- Played in NHL All-Star Game (1934)

**AWARDS**
Vezina Trophy (1927, 1928, 1929)

Stanley Cup (1929–30, 1930–31)

**ALL-STAR SELECTIONS**
WHL First All-Star Team Goaltender (1926)

# 1

# Glenn Hall 1975

NO. RETIRED BY CHICAGO

**ALTERNATE:**

# 22

Chicago Black Hawks
Detroit Red Wings
St. Louis Blues

Catches: Left

Height: 5'-11"

Weight: 180 lbs.

Born: October 3, 1931:
Humboldt, Saskatchewan

Played 18 NHL seasons
from 1952–53, 1954–71

Stats: See page 497

"Our first priority was staying alive.
Our second was stopping the puck."

—Glenn Hall, on the reality of playing goal without a mask

**AWARDS**

Calder Memorial
Trophy (1956)

Conn Smythe
Trophy (1968)

Vezina Trophy
(1963, 1967, 1969)

Stanley Cup (1960–61)

**ALL-STAR
SELECTIONS**

First All-Star Team
Goaltender (1957,
1958, 1960, 1963,
1964, 1966, 1969)

Second All-Star Team
Goaltender (1956,
1961, 1962, 1967)

- Nicknamed "Mr. Goalie"

- Holds NHL record for consecutive games played by a goaltender (502), established from 1955–62

- Ranks fourth in NHL career shutouts (84)

- Played amateur hockey with Humboldt Indians (1947–49); Windsor Spitfires (1949–51)

- Led OHA-Jr. in shutouts (6) in 1950–51

- Played minor pro with Indianapolis Capitols (1951–52); Edmonton Flyers (1952–55)

- Led WHL in wins (38) in 1954–55; led WHL in playoff wins (10) in 1952–53

- WHL First All-Star Team Goaltender (1954–55); WHL Second All-Star Team Goaltender (1952–53)

- Led NHL in wins in 1956–57 (38), 1962–63 (30), 1963–64 (34) and 1965–66 (34)

- Led NHL in goals-against average (2.38) in 1966–67

- Led NHL in shutouts in 1955–56 (12), 1959–60 (6), 1960–61 (6), 1961–62 (9), 1962–63 (5) and 1968–69 (8)

- Played in NHL All-Star Game (1955, 1956, 1957, 1958, 1960, 1961, 1962, 1963, 1964, 1965, 1967, 1968, 1969)

- Traded to Chicago by Detroit with Ted Lindsay for Johnny Wilson, Forbes Kennedy, Bill Preston and Hank Bassen, July 23, 1957

- Claimed by St. Louis from Chicago in Expansion Draft, June 6, 1967

- Second player from losing team (after Roger Crozier in 1966) to be awarded Conn Smythe Trophy

Glenn Hall shows off his butterfly style against Montreal.

# Mr. Goalie

Glenn "Mr. Goalie" Hall earned his nickname for his consistently sterling play over more than 1,000 games, including an "iron man" record that will likely stand the test of time. Beginning with the first game of the 1955–56 season, Hall played nearly every minute of every game until a back injury forced him out of action on November 7, 1962. His streak ended at 502 regular-season games (551 including playoffs)—all without a mask, and there was nothing cautious about his play, either.

Hall pioneered the "butterfly" style of goaltending. He discovered that crouching and keeping his legs spread below his knees allowed him to go down quickly while his legs covered the bottom of the net and his erect body covered the top. Hall's innovative method was ridiculed by many, who saw it as "flopping" and contrary to the accepted stand-up style. Of course, Hall's method was the opposite of flopping, as it was a calculated move—albeit one that put his unprotected face into harm's way.

He entered the Detroit Red Wings' farm system in 1951 and eventually supplanted goaltending legend Terry Sawchuk for the

1955–56 NHL season; Hall was named Rookie of the Year with a league-leading 12 shutouts. He made the First All-Star Team the following season, yet it was his last in Detroit, as he was dealt with Ted Lindsay to the lowly Chicago Black Hawks as punishment for supporting Lindsay's attempt at forming a players' union.

Hall didn't miss a beat—or a game—with the move to the Windy City, and the Hawks were immeasurably improved by the addition of other "rebels" from various teams as well as their own prospects, like Bobby Hull and Stan Mikita. In 1961 Hall and company claimed the team's first Stanley Cup victory since 1938, and before the decade was out Hall thrice got his name on the Vezina Trophy (twice while in Chicago).

Hall finished his career with the St. Louis Blues, who wisely chose the 35-year-old as their first pick in the 1967 Expansion Draft. He backstopped the Blues to three consecutive Stanley Cup final and earned the 1968 Conn Smythe Trophy as the playoffs' Most Valuable Player, but his St Louis teams didn't muster a single win in their three finals. Hall retired in 1971 with 84 career shutouts; he remains fourth on the career-shutout list.

# 39

# Dominik Hasek 2014

NO. RETIRED BY BUFFALO

ALTERNATES:
## 34 · 31

Buffalo Sabres
Chicago Blackhawks
Detroit Red Wings
Ottawa Senators

Catches: Left
Height: 6'-1"
Weight: 180 lbs.
Born: January 29, 1965;
Pardubice, Czechoslovakia
Drafted by the Chicago
Blackhawks 199th
overall in 1983
Played 16 NHL seasons
from 1990–2002,
2003–04, 2005–08
Stats: See page 498

AWARDS
Hart Memorial Trophy
(1997, 1998)
Ted Lindsay Award*
(1997, 1998)
Vezina Trophy (1994, 1995,
1997, 1998, 1999, 2001)
William M. Jennings Trophy
(1994, 2001, 2008)
Stanley Cup (2001–02,
2007–08)

ALL-STAR
SELECTIONS
All-Rookie Team (1992)
First All-Star Team
Goaltender (1994, 1995,
1997, 1998, 1999, 2001)

INTERNATIONAL
AWARDS
Gold Medal: Winter
Olympics (1998)
Bronze Medal: Winter
Olympics (2006)
Silver Medal: World
Championships (1983)
Bronze Medal: World
Championships
(1987, 1989, 1990)
*Known as the Lester
B. Pearson Award
from 1971 to 2009

"They say I am unorthodox, I flop around the ice like some kind of fish. I say, who cares as long as I stop the puck?"

- Known as "The Dominator"

- In 1997 he became the first goalie since Jacques Plante in 1962 to win the Hart Trophy as NHL MVP; in 1998 he became the first goalie to win it twice

- His six Vezina Trophy wins trail only Plante's seven and are the most since the rules were changed to make the Vezina Trophy a voted award rather than statistical

- Led the NHL in goals-against average in 1993–94 and 1994–95; in shutouts in 1993–94, 1994–95, 1997–98 and 2000–01; and in save percentage for six straight seasons from 1993–94 to 1998–99

- His career-best 13 shutouts in 1997–98 are the most in the NHL since Tony Esposito had 15 in 1969–70

- Led the NHL with a career-high 41 wins for Detroit in 2001–02

- His 1.95 goals-against average in 1993–94 was the first below 2.00 since Bernie Parent's 1.89 in 1973–74

- Had a career-best 1.87 goals-against average and .937 save percentage in 1998–99, and helped the Buffalo Sabres reach the Stanley Cup final

- Played in NHL All-Star Game (1996, 1997, 1998, 1999, 2001, 2002)

- Became the first goalie in Sabres history to have his number retired (2014–15)

- Was named Best Goaltender at the 1998 Olympic Winter Games in Nagano

- Was inducted into the IIHF Hall of Fame in 2015

# The Dominator

I t was little more than a long shot when the Chicago Blackhawks selected Dominik Hasek with the 199th pick in the 1983 NHL Entry Draft. Players from Communist countries were often reluctant to enter the NHL, and were frequently prevented from doing so, regardless of what they wanted.

Hasek remained in Czechoslovakia, starring with his hometown Pardubice club until 1990 before finally coming to North America. He spent the majority of the next two seasons with the Indianapolis Ice, leading the American Hockey League in shutouts and goals-against average in 1990–91, but saw limited action in Chicago behind Blackhawks star Ed Belfour. During the summer of 1992, Hasek was traded to the Buffalo Sabres for goalie Stephane Beauregard and a draft choice (Chicago later used it to select Eric Daze). Hasek played backup to another future Hall of Famer with the Sabres until an injury to Grant Fuhr during the 1992–93 season finally gave him a starting job. Hasek never looked back.

Though he was a highly intelligent player with a strong competitive spirit, Hasek was best known for his unorthodox goaltending style. Incredibly fit, and so flexible that a MasterCard commercial jokingly referred to him "having a slinky for a spine," Hasek flopped to the ice on almost every shot to cover the bottom of the net. Rolling and flailing in his crease, he made saves that seemed impossible, occasionally dropping his stick so that he could cover the puck with either hand.

In nine seasons with the Sabres through

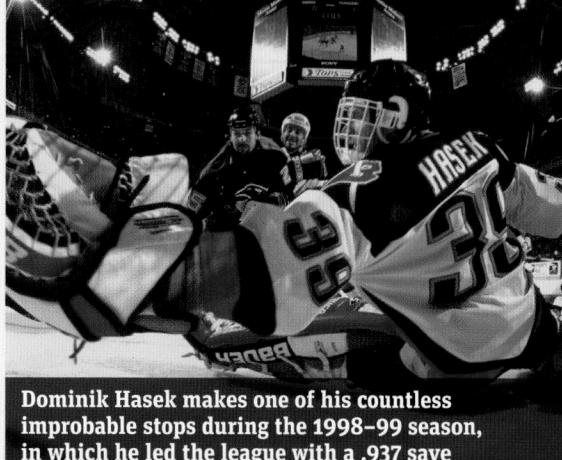

**Dominik Hasek makes one of his countless improbable stops during the 1998–99 season, in which he led the league with a .937 save percentage.**

2000–01, Hasek won the Vezina Trophy six times, was selected as a First-Team All-Star six times and won the William M. Jennings Trophy two times. He also became the first (and to date, only) goaltender to win the Hart Trophy as NHL MVP twice (1996–97 and 1997–98). Already a star in his homeland, Hasek solidified that status by leading the Czech Republic to an Olympic gold medal in 1998 and was named the Czech Hockey Player of the 20th Century that year.

Hasek led Buffalo to the Stanley Cup final in 1999, but it took a trade to the Detroit Red Wings in the summer of 2001 before he finally won the Cup in 2002. Hasek retired after that season, but returned to the NHL in 2003–04, playing for both Detroit and the Ottawa Senators before retiring again in 2008. He ended up playing two more seasons in Europe before officially hanging up his skates in 2011 at the age of 46.

# Riley Hern 1962

Montreal Wanderers
Pittsburgh Keystones
Portage Lakes

Catches: Left

Height: 5'-9"

Weight: 170 lbs.

Born: December 5, 1880;
St. Marys, Ontario

Died: June 24, 1929;
Montreal, Quebec

Played 10 elite amateur
and professional
seasons from 1901–11

Stats: See page 499

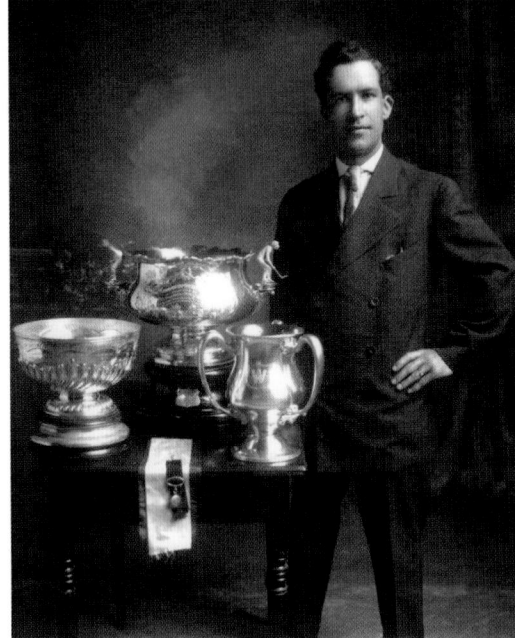

"Hern was without a doubt one of the greatest drawing cards hockey has ever known, and the success of the Wanderers in winning the world's championship [three] times during his [five] years on the team is adequate evidence of his ability."

— *Montreal Gazette*,
June 25, 1929

**AWARDS**

Stanley Cup (1906–07, 1907–08, 1909–10)

**ALL-STAR SELECTIONS**

IHL First All-Star Team Goaltender (1905)

- Played amateur hockey with Stratford HC (1898–01)
- Played as both a goaltender and forward with Stratford (1900–01)
- Member of Western Pennyslvania Hockey League champion Pittsburgh Keystones (1901–02)
- Member of IHL champion with Portage Lakes (1903–04, 1905–06)
- WPHL First All-Star Team Goaltender (1902)
- Led WPHL in wins (14) in 1901–02
- Led IHL in shutouts (2) and goals-against average (3.54) in 1904–05
- ECAHA First All-Star Team Goaltender (1907)

- ECHA First All-Star Team Goaltender (1909)
- Led ECAHA in wins in 1906–07 (10) and 1907–08 (8); led Stanley Cup playoff in wins (5) in 1907–08
- Led NHA in wins (11) in 1909–10
- Retired after the 1910–11 season but remained in the game as a goal judge and referee
- Made his permanent home in Montreal after joining the Wanderers and was prominent in many sporting clubs and business organizations there for the rest of his life

# 1972 Hap Holmes

Detroit Cougars
Seattle Metropolitans
Toronto Arenas
Toronto Blueshirts
Victoria Cougars

Catches: Left

Height: 5'-10"

Weight: 170 lbs.

Born: February 21, 1888:
Aurora, Ontario

Died: June 27, 1941: Fort
Lauderdale, Florida

Played 16 professional
seasons from 1912–28

Stats: See page 499

"Jack Marshall of the Torontos thinks a lot of Harry Holmes as a goaltender and says that with coaching he will be as good as any net guardian in the NHA."

— *Toronto World*,
January 7, 1913

- Played amateur hockey with Toronto Young Torontos (1907–08); Toronto (Parkdale) Canoe Club (1908–11); Toronto Tecumsehs (1911–12)

- Starred in all five (NHA, NHL, WCHL, WHL, PCHA) of professional hockey's top leagues during his career

- Led NHA in wins (13) in 1913–14

- Led PCHA in wins in 1916–17 (16), 1921–22 (12), 1922–23 (15) and 1923–24 (14)

- Led PCHA in shutouts in 1916–17 (2), 1919–20 (4), 1923–24 (2) and 1924–25 (3)

- Appeared in the Stanley Cup final seven times, winning with four teams (Toronto Blueshirts, Toronto Arenas, Seattle, Victoria) in four different leagues (NHA, NHL, PCHA, WHL)

- Member of Stanley Cup–winning Victoria Cougars—last non-NHL club to win the Stanley Cup (1924–25)

- Signed as a free agent by Victoria (WCHL), November 7, 1924; rights transferred to Detroit after NHL club purchased Victoria (WHL) franchise, May 26, 1926

- Coached Cleveland Indians (1929–35); coached Cleveland Falcons (1935–36)

- Legacy honored by the American Hockey League with the Harry "Hap" Holmes Memorial Trophy, presented annually to the league's top goaltender

**AWARDS**
Stanley Cup (1913–14, 1916–17, 1917–18, 1924–25)

**ALL-STAR SELECTIONS**
PCHA Second All-Star Team Goaltender (1916, 1917, 1919, 1920, 1922, 1923)

WHL First All-Star Team Goaltender (1925)

# Bouse Hutton 1962

Ottawa Hockey Club
Ottawa Senators
Ottawa Silver Seven

Catches: Left

Height: Unknown

Weight: Unknown

Born: October 24, 1877;
Ottawa, Ontario

Died: October 27, 1962;
Ottawa, Ontario

Played seven elite
amateur seasons from
1898–1904, 1908–09

Stats: See page 500

"No one wants to hear about the Silver Seven days. There was nothing exciting about the old days. People want to read about today's stars."

—Bouse Hutton, on the fleeting nature of fame

**AWARDS**

Stanley Cup
(1902–03, 1903–04)

- Posted much lower goals-against averages than many contemporaries, despite playing in an era when goalies wore little protection and had to remain standing when making saves

- Won national championships in three sports: lacrosse, football and hockey

- Played fullback with Ottawa Rough Riders football club

- Played goal with the Ottawa Capitals lacrosse club (1901–10)

- Made debut in senior hockey in 1898–99 but also led his Ottawa intermediate team to the Canadian Amateur Hockey League championship that season

- Member of CAHL champion Ottawa Hockey Club (1900–01)

- Earned shutout in Ottawa "Silver Seven" 8–0 victory over Montreal Victorias that clinched Ottawa's first Stanley Cup title, March 10, 1903

- Led CAHL in wins (6) in 1902–03

- Led Stanley Cup playoffs in wins (6) in 1903–04

- Signed professional contract to play lacrosse after winning his Stanley Cup title in 1903–04, which made him ineligible to play amateur hockey in Canada

- Continued to play lacrosse and coach hockey before returning to play hockey with Ottawa Senators in 1908–09

- Led FAHL in shutouts (1) in 1908–09

# 1

## 1958 Hugh Lehman

> "Lehman played hard and worked hard and life had been good to him ... Few players can match his nomadic exploits and, quite possibly, there never has been a goalkeeper who can match his ironman career."
>
> — *Canadian Press* obituary, April 13, 1961

**ALTERNATE:**

# 15

Berlin Professionals
Canadian Soo
Chicago Black Hawks
Galt Professionals
New Westminster
Royals Pembroke
Lumber Kings
Vancouver Maroons
Vancouver Millionaires

Catches: Left

Height: 5'-8"

Weight: 168 lbs.

Born: October 27, 1885:
Pembroke, Ontario

Died: April 8, 1961:
Toronto, Ontario

Played 22 professional
seasons from 1906–28

Stats: See page 500

- Holds PCHA career records for games played by a goaltender (262), wins (142), losses (118) and shutouts (17)

- Only one of two goaltenders (with Percy LeSueur) to challenge for Stanley Cup with two different teams in same season (1909–10)

- Played amateur hockey with Pembroke HC (1902–06)

- Led UOVHL in wins (8), shutouts (1) and goals-against average (1.67) in 1905–06; led UOVHL playoffs in shutouts (1) in 1905–06

- Loaned to Galt Pro team that lost Stanley Cup challenge to Ottawa Senators in January of 1909

- Member of OPHL champion Berlin Dutchmen (1909–10)

- Led OPHL in wins (17) in 1909–10

- Led PCHA in wins in 1911–12 (9), 1914–15 (13), 1918–19 (12), 1921–22 (12), 1922–23 (16)

- Led PCHA in goals-against average in 1911–12 (5.07), 1913–14 (4.87), 1914–15 (4.08), 1917–18 (3.05), 1922–23 (2.33) and 1923–24 (2.60)

- Led PCHA in shutouts in 1914–15 (1), 1917–18 (1), 1920–21 (3), 1921–22 (4) and 1922–23 (5)

- Member of PCHA champion New Westminster Royals (1911–12)

- Member of PCHA champion Vancouver Millionaires (1914–15, 1917–18, 1920–21, 1921–22); member of PCHA champion Vancouver Maroons (1922–23, 1923–24)

- Coached Chicago Black Hawks (1927–28)

**AWARDS**

Stanley Cup (1914–15)

**ALL-STAR SELECTIONS**

OPHL First All-Star Team
Goaltender (1910)

PCHA First All-Star
Team Goaltender
(1912, 1914, 1915, 1916,
1918, 1919, 1920, 1921,
1922, 1923, 1924)

# 1

# Percy LeSueur 1961

Ottawa Senators
Smiths Falls Seniors
Toronto Blueshirts
Toronto Shamrocks

Catches: Left

Height: 5'-7"

Weight: 150 lbs.

Born: November 21, 1881:
Quebec City, Quebec

Died: January 27, 1962:
Hamilton, Ontario

Played 13 elite amateur
and professional
seasons from 1903–16

Stats: See page 501

"LeSueur was so effective and so capable that it appeared easy. From the top of his head to his toes he was bombarded with drives. He saw most of them when they started and never winked an eye."

— *New York Times*, March 21, 1911, on opening game of $1,000 grudge match between Montreal Wanderers and St. Nicholas Rink

**AWARDS**

Stanley Cup (1908–09, 1909–10, 1910–11)

- One of only two goaltenders (with Hugh Lehman) to challenge for Stanley Cup with two different teams (Smiths Falls and Ottawa) in same season (1905–06)

- Career in hockey spanned 50 years as a player, coach, manager, columnist and broadcaster

- Began career as a right winger in his hometown of Quebec City, but became a goalie while playing in Smiths Falls, Ontario

- Attracted attention of Ottawa "Silver Seven" team when they defeated Smith Falls in Stanley Cup challenge series in March of 1906

- Selected as NHA All-Star goaltender in the Hod Stuart Memorial Game, first "Major League" All-Star game in hockey history, January 2, 1908

- Led ECHA in wins (10) in 1908–09

- Member of Stanley Cup–winning Ottawa Senators team that successfully defended title twice in January of 1910

- Served as captain of Ottawa Senators (1910–11)

- Led NHA in wins (13) in 1910–11

- Nicknamed "Peerless Percy" by *Ottawa Free Press* sportswriter Malcolm Brice

- Playing career ended in 1916 when he volunteered for the Canadian Army in World War I

- Coached Guelph Intermediates to Ontario Hockey Association Intermediate championship (1920–21)

- Coached Hamilton Tigers (1923–24)

# Peerless Percy

A student of hockey, Percy LeSueur made numerous contributions to the game. In 1909 he penned an influential handbook, *How to Play Hockey*. In 1912 he designed the first net with a crossbar and webbing to trap rising shots. When he returned from military service after World War I, he did some refereeing and then coached at the amateur, minor pro and NHL level. He managed hockey teams and arenas (including the famous Detroit Olympia when it first opened). As a Hamilton Spectator hockey columnist, he introduced the "shots on goal" statistic to game summaries. LeSueur was also a popular "Hot Stove League" commentator in the early radio broadcasts of Hockey Night in Canada. But playing hockey was definitely the highlight of his multi-faceted career.

Originally a right winger, LeSueur donned the rudimentary goalie equipment for his Smiths Falls senior team when the club's regular goaltender suddenly took ill. He never looked back.

In March 1906, Smiths Falls earned the right to challenge the Ottawa "Silver Seven" for the Stanley Cup. Although his team lost, LeSueur impressed the Stanley Cup champs. When Ottawa was hammered 9–1 by the Montreal Wanderers in Game 1 of another Cup challenge six days later, they called on LeSueur to help them out. With the ink barely dry on his contract, LeSueur started Game 2, and though Ottawa fell short in the two game total point series, LeSueur had a new home.

"Peerless Percy" spent the following eight

**Percy LeSueur is seated immediately to the left of the Stanley Cup in this 1909 photo.**

seasons in the Ottawa goal. He backstopped the Ottawa Senators (formerly the Silver Seven) to Stanley Cup victories in 1908–09, 1909–10 and 1910–11, also acting as the team's captain for the last challenge. LeSueur remained team captain for his last three seasons in Ottawa, before being traded to the Toronto Shamrocks for the 1914–15 campaign. He played one last National Hockey Association season for the Toronto Blueshirts the following year, and then he enlisted during World War I, serving overseas with the 48th Highlanders. His return to the game as a referee, coach and commentator sealed his path to the Hall of Fame.

GOALIE

# Harry Lumley 1980

Boston Bruins
Chicago Black Hawks
Detroit Red Wings
New York Rangers
Toronto Maple Leafs

Catches: Left

Height: 6'

Weight: 195 lbs.

Born: November 11, 1926:
Owen Sound, Ontario

Died: September 13,
1998: London, Ontario

Played 16 NHL seasons
from 1943–56, 1957–60

Stats: See page 501

"It started when I was a rookie. I was pretty rosy-cheeked and people noticed it. The thing was, if I was playing a good game, the fans would call me Apple Cheeks. But if I was bad on any given night, they'd call me Redneck."

— Harry Lumley,
on his crimson
nickname

**AWARDS**
Vezina Trophy (1954)
Stanley Cup (1949–50)

**ALL-STAR SELECTIONS**
First All-Star Team
Goaltender (1954, 1955)

- Played junior hockey with Barrie Colts (1942–43)

- Is the youngest goalie ever to play in the NHL, making his debut for Detroit on December 19, 1943 at age 17.

- Loaned to N.Y. Rangers by Detroit to replace injured Ken McAuley, December 23, 1943. Lumley played the third period and didn't allow a goal as the Red Wings defeated the Rangers 5–3

- Recorded league-leading eight wins, three shutouts and 1.86 goals-against average in backstopping Detroit to the Stanley Cup championship in 1950 playoffs. Despite those impressive statistics, he was traded to Chicago to make room in Detroit for Terry Sawchuk

- Led NHL in shutouts in 1947–48 (7); 1952–53 (10) and 1953–54 (13)

- Led NHL in goals-against average in 1953–54 (1.86) and 1954–55 (1.91)

- Played in NHL All-Star Game (1951, 1954, 1955)

- Traded to Chicago by Detroit with Jack Stewart, Al Dewsbury, Pete Babando and Don Morrison for Metro Prystai, Gaye Stewart, Bob Goldham and Jim Henry, July 13, 1950. Trade was largest in NHL history until Calgary and Toronto exchanged ten players — including Doug Gilmour — on January 2, 1992

- AHL Second All-Star Team Goaltender (1957)

- Played with the Kingston Frontenacs and Winnipeg Warriors (1960–61) after NHL career ended

# 1958 Paddy Moran

**1**

> "Paddy stopped them from all angles, and his brilliant work put heart into the players in front of him and sent them after Wanderers in a style that threatened to take the champions off their feet."
>
> — *Montreal Gazette*, January 18, 1909

All-Montreal
Haileybury Comets
Quebec Athletics
Quebec Bulldogs

Catches: Left

Height: 5'-11"

Weight: 180 lbs.

Born: March 11, 1877; Quebec City, Quebec

Died: January 24, 1966; Quebec City, Quebec

Played 16 elite amateur and professional seasons from 1901–17

Stats: See page 502

- Played majority of career with Quebec Bulldogs in era when goaltenders were required to remain standing at all times, retiring a year before the formation of the NHL

- Played amateur hockey with Quebec Dominions (1898–99); Quebec Crescents (1899–01); Quebec Athletics (1901–05)

- Member of Canadian Intermediate champion Quebec Crescents (1900–01)

- Led CAHL in wins in 1903–04 (5) and 1904–05 (7)

- ECAHA First All-Star Team Goaltender (1908)

- Signed as a free agent by Haileybury HC, January 16, 1910, from All-Montreal.

- Rejoined Quebec club when team was admitted to the NHA (1910–11)

- Member of Stanley Cup–winning Quebec Bulldogs (1911–12, 1912–13)

- Led NHA in wins in 1911–12 (10) and 1912–13 (16); led NHA in shutouts in 1912–13 (1) and 1913–14 (1)

- Selected to play on NHA All-Star Team in a postseason series against PCHA All-Stars in March of 1913

- Renowned as a clutch goaltender who was difficult to beat in important games

**AWARDS**

Stanley Cup
(1911–12, 1912–13)

# 1

# Bernie Parent 1984

NO. RETIRED BY
PHILADELPHIA

ALTERNATE:
## 30

Boston Bruins
Philadelphia Blazers
Philadelphia Flyers
Toronto Maple Leafs

Catches: Left
Height: 5'-10"
Weight: 180 lbs.
Born: April 3, 1945;
Montreal, Quebec
Played 14 NHL and WHA
seasons from 1965–79
Stats: See page 502

"You don't have to be crazy to be a goalie, but it helps."

AWARDS
Conn Smythe Trophy
winner (1974, 1975)
Vezina Trophy
(1974, 1975)
Stanley Cup
(1973–74, 1974–75)
ALL-STAR
SELECTIONS
First All-Star Team
Goaltender (1974, 1975)

- Held NHL record for wins in regular season (47); surpassed by Martin Brodeur (48) in 2006–07

- First player to win Conn Smythe Trophy in back-to-back seasons

- Holds Philadelphia Flyers team records for career shutouts (50) and single season shutouts (12)

- Played amateur hockey with Rosemount Raiders (1962–63); Niagara Falls Flyers (1963–65)

- Led OHA-Jr. in goals-against average in 1963–64 (2.86) and 1964–65 (2.58); led OHA-Jr. playoffs in wins (6) and goals-against average (1.86) in 1964–65

- Member of Memorial Cup–winning Niagara Falls Flyers (1964–65); led Memorial Cup playoffs in wins (10) and goals-against average (1.63)

- OHA-Jr. First All-Star Team Goaltender (1965); OHA-Jr. Second All-Star Team Goaltender (1964)

- Played minor pro hockey with Oklahoma City Blazers (1965–67); led CPHL in shutouts (4) in 1966–67

- Played in NHL All-Star Game (1969, 1970, 1974, 1975, 1977)

- Led NHL in goals-against average in 1973–74 (1.89) and 1974–75 (2.04)

- Led NHL in shutouts in 1973–74 (12), 1974–75 (12) and 1977–78 (7); led NHL in wins in 1973–74 (47) and 1974–75 (44)

- Suffered career-ending eye injury in game vs. N.Y. Rangers, February 17, 1979

# Philadelphia's Savior

"**O**nly the Lord saves more than Bernie Parent" was a popular refrain in Philadelphia in the early 1970s. But Parent's puck-stopping wasn't always so divine.

The future Hall of Famer broke into the NHL straight out of junior hockey in 1965, landing in Boston for the final two years of the Original Six era and compiling an unimpressive record of 16-32-5. He bounced from Boston to the Philadelphia Flyers and then to the Toronto Maple Leafs in a 1971 trade that seemed heaven sent.

As a child growing up in Montreal in the 1950s, Parent had idolized the Canadiens' star netminder, Jacques Plante. Plante, by the time of Parent's trade, was a 42-year-old veteran and had joined the Leafs earlier that season, and he helped Parent take a more systematic approach to goaltending.

"There was no one in the world quite like Plante," noted Parent. "I learned more from him in two years with the Leafs than I did in all my other hockey days."

With Plante's tutelage and more NHL experience, Parent was emerging as a top NHL talent when he jumped ship and suited up for the World Hockey Association's Philadelphia Blazers for the 1972–73 season. Disenchanted with having to face an excessive barrage of pucks and paychecks that sometimes bounced, Parent worked a deal to rejoin the Flyers, and he immediately fashioned back-to-back Stanley Cup–winning seasons.

In 1973–74 Parent set an NHL record with 47 wins and earned a league-best and career-high dozen shutouts while compiling a

**Bernie Parent makes a save as a Toronto Maple Leaf in the early 1970s.**

1.89 goals-against average. He won the Vezina Trophy (in a tie with Chicago's Tony Esposito) and was selected to the First All-Star Team, and in the playoffs he led the Flyers past the Boston Bruins for the Stanley Cup. Parent won the Conn Smythe Trophy as playoff MVP. He was named to the First All-Star Team and won the Vezina and the Conn Smythe again in 1974–75 and hoisted the Cup after the Flyers vanquished the Buffalo Sabres in six. In both Cup wins Parent notched shutouts in the deciding game.

On February 17, 1979, during a goalmouth scramble, an errant stick hit Parent in his right eye, and he was forced to retire with permanent damage to his depth perception and his ability to focus. Later, as Philadelphia's goaltending coach, Parent helped Pelle Lindbergh to a Vezina Trophy–winning season in 1984–85 and Ron Hextall to the same in 1986–87.

# 1 Jacques Plante 1978

NO. RETIRED BY MONTREAL

**ALTERNATES:**

**31 · 30**

Boston Bruins
Edmonton Oilers
Montreal Canadiens
New York Rangers
St. Louis Blues
Toronto Maple Leafs

Catches: Left

Height: 6'

Weight: 175 lbs.

Born: January 17, 1929; Shawinigan Falls, Quebec

Died: February 27, 1986; Geneva, Switzerland

Played 19 NHL and WHA seasons from 1952–65, 1968–73, 1974–75

Stats: See page 503

"Hockey is an art. It requires speed, precision, and strength like other sports, but it also demands an extraordinary intelligence to develop a logical sequence of movements, a technique which is smooth, graceful and in rhythm with the rest of the game."

**AWARDS**

Vezina Trophy (1956, 1957, 1958, 1959, 1960, 1962, 1969)

Hart Memorial Trophy (1962)

Stanley Cup (1952–53, 1955–56, 1956–57, 1957–58, 1958–59, 1959–60)

**ALL-STAR SELECTIONS**

First All-Star Team Goaltender (1956, 1959, 1962)

Second All-Star Team Goaltender (1957, 1958, 1960, 1971)

○ First goaltender to regularly wear a facemask after he was struck by a shot in game against N.Y. Rangers, November 1, 1959

○ Won record seven Vezina Trophies, including five in a row during the seasons when the Montreal Canadiens won five consecutive Stanley Cups

○ Ranks seventh in NHL career wins (437)

○ Ranks fifth in NHL career shutouts (82)

○ Played amateur hockey with Shawinigan Cataracts (1946–47); Quebec Citadelle (1947–48); Montreal Jr. Canadiens (1947–48); Montreal Sr. Royals (1949–50)

○ Led QJHL in wins (35) in 1948–49; QJHL First All-Star Team Goaltender (1948, 1949)

○ Played in NHL All-Star Game (1956, 1957, 1958, 1959, 1960, 1962, 1969, 1970)

○ Led NHL in wins in 1955–56 (42), 1957–58 (34), 1958–59 (38), 1959–60 (40), 1961–62 (42)

○ Led NHL in shutouts in 1956–57 (9), 1957–58 (9), 1958–59 (9) and 1962–63 (5)

○ Renowned for pioneering the art of stopping the puck behind the net for defensemen and signaling teammates on icing calls

○ Coached Quebec Nordiques (WHA) (1973–74)

# The Face of Goaltending

Jacques Plante was a game changer. He was a Hart Trophy winner, a seven-time All-Star, a seven-time Vezina winner and a six-time Stanley Cup champion. However, today he is best known as the first NHL goalie to regularly wear a mask. He started wearing one in practice in 1956, but he never wore one in a game until November 1, 1959, after Andy Bathgate ripped his nose open with a backhand shot. His actions, and his refusal to bow to the notion that masks projected cowardice, changed the face of goaltending forever.

**Jacques Plante wore this mask when he returned to action after needing stitches to close a wound left by an Andy Bathgate shot on November 1, 1959.**

the Montreal zone and sustain pressure.

But Plante was not without his eccentricities. Most were harmless, such as knitting his own hats and undershirts, but others were deemed harmful to team camaraderie, such as staying in a different hotel than his teammates because he felt the air was better for his asthma.

In the end Plante eventually wore out his welcome in Montreal, and he was traded to the New York Rangers in 1963. He retired in 1965 to take care of his ailing wife, but he was lured

Nicknamed "Jake the Snake" for his quick reflexes, Plante perfected a stand-up style of goaltending while playing for the Montreal Canadiens. He emphasized positional play, cutting down the angles and staying square to the shooter. He also changed the game with the way he interacted with the puck. Like Chuck Rayner before him, Plante would sometimes act as a third defenseman, coming out far from his net to play the puck—passing it to an open player or clearing the zone himself. He was the first to stop the puck from ringing the boards behind the net on a shoot-in, and his puck-play made it very difficult for opposing teams to gain entry to

out of retirement by the St. Louis Blues three years later. There he shared goaltending duties with the great Glenn Hall, and the veteran tandem took the Blues to the 1969 and 1970 Stanley Cup final. His final NHL duty of consequence was tutoring up-and-coming goaltender Bernie Parent, with whom he platooned in Toronto during the 1970–71 and 1971–72 seasons.

Plante retired in 1975 after a season with the World Hockey Association's Edmonton Oilers. He was 46—his longevity attained by his style and his mask, and his legacy maintained by all modern goalies, who can thank Jake the Snake for their smile.

# 1

# Chuck Rayner 1973

Brooklyn Americans
New York Americans
New York Rangers

Catches: Left

Height: 5'-11"

Weight: 190 lbs.

Born: August 11, 1920: Sutherland, Saskatchewan

Died: October 6, 2002: Langley, British Columbia

Played 10 NHL seasons from 1940–42, 1945–53

Stats: See page 503

"I stopped a shot and the puck bounced straight out. I skated out to get clear, found myself alone and went the rest of the way. When I got about 15 feet from the other goal, I shot and scored."

— Chuck Rayner, describing his infamous goal

AWARDS

Hart Memorial Trophy (1950)

ALL-STAR SELECTIONS

Second All-Star Team Goaltender (1949, 1950, 1951)

- Was part of a unique "platoon" goaltending tandem during the 1945–46 season. N.Y. Rangers coach Frank Boucher played Rayner and Sugar Jim Henry in alternate games and sometimes would switch them from shift to shift like regular skaters

- First goaltender since Roy Worters (1929) to be awarded the Hart Trophy as NHL MVP

- Played amateur hockey with Saskatoon Wesleys (1936–37); Kenora Thistles (1937–40); Nelson Maple Leafs (1954–56); played minor pro with Springfield Indians (1940–42); New Haven Ramblers (1947–48); Saskatoon Quakers (1953–54)

- Led Manitoba Junior League in wins (15) and shutouts (1) in 1939–40

- Led AHL in shutouts (6) and goals-against average (2.29) in 1940–41; AHL Second All-Star Team Goaltender (1941)

- Played with Victoria Navy and Halifax RCAF during World War II

- While playing for a touring Royal Canadian Armed Forces All-Star team in Halifax during World War II, Rayner became the first goaltender to skate the length of the ice and score a goal

- Led NHL in shutouts (5) in 1946–47

- Played in All-Star Game (1949, 1950, 1951)

- Used as an extra forward during the last minute and a half of a February 1, 1947 game against Montreal

- Coached Edmonton Flyers (1962–63)

# Hard-Luck Chuck

T here are many players in the Hockey Hall of Fame who have never won a Stanley Cup, but there are none quite like Chuck Rayner. Over his 10-year NHL career, Rayner backstopped a slew of weak teams and never once posted a winning season total. The closest he came was a 28-30-11 record with the New York Rangers in the 1949–50 season.

Rayner got his professional start with the Springfield Indians of the American Hockey League in 1940–41, where he earned a Second Team All-Star selection. More importantly, he received instruction from legendary defenseman and new team owner Eddie Shore. Shore's "creative" but notorious coaching methods and parsimonious ways generally made enemies of his students, but Rayner acknowledged him as the greatest goaltending coach he ever had.

At Shore's insistence, Rayner participated in every skating drill with his teammates and fired pucks until he couldn't move from fatigue. This training helped Rayner develop outstanding skating and shooting abilities, which became hallmarks of his own innovative style.

Rayner enlisted in the Canadian Navy after having played 48 games over two NHL seasons (1940–41 and 1941–42) with the New York/Brooklyn Americans franchise, and when the war ended in 1945, he signed with the New York Rangers.

Although the Rangers had fallen into the league cellar during the later years of WWII, Rayner often brought the crowd to its feet with his unprecedented roaming from the crease,

**Chuck Rayner gets a hook on a Toronto player.**

and his poke check became a signature move. He surprised many attacking forwards when he dove headfirst to knock the puck away, and playing the puck became a way of life for Rayner on his weak Rangers teams. He fielded the puck, fired passes to his teammates and even made rink-long rushes attempting to score.

The 1949–50 season saw the Rangers finish fourth in the league, and Rayner guided New York to a surprisingly successful playoff run, losing the Cup to the Detroit Red Wings in the second overtime period of the seventh game. Rayner was named the league's Most Valuable Player in 1950, the second goalie, after Roy "Shrimp" Worters, to be named as such, and one of only six to receive the honor to date.

The Rangers didn't qualify for the playoffs again during Rayner's tenure, and he concluded his career in the Western International Hockey League in 1955–56.

# 33

# Patrick Roy 2006

NO. RETIRED BY
MONTREAL & COLORADO

**Colorado Avalanche**
**Montreal Canadiens**

Catches: Left

Height: 6'-2"

Weight: 185 lbs.

Born: October 5, 1965;
Quebec City, Quebec

Drafted by the
Montreal Canadiens
51st overall in 1984

Played 19 NHL seasons
from 1984–2003

Stats: See page 504

"I can't hear what
Jeremy says,
because I've got
my two Stanley Cup
rings plugging my
ears."

— Patrick Roy,
responding to
negative comments
made by Chicago's
Jeremy Roenick
during 1996
playoffs

## AWARDS

Vezina Trophy (1989,
1990, 1992)

Conn Smythe Trophy
(1986, 1993, 2001)

William M. Jennings
Trophy (1987, 1988,
1989, 1992, 2002)

Stanley Cup (1985–86,
1992–93, 1995–96,
2000–01)

## ALL-STAR
## SELECTIONS

All-Rookie Team (1986)

First All-Star Team
Goaltender (1989,
1990, 1992, 2002)

Second All-Star Team
Goaltender (1988, 1991)

- Only player to win three Conn Smythe trophies (1986, 1993, 2001)
- Only player to win Conn Smythe Trophy with two different teams (Montreal, Colorado)
- Second player (after Ken Dryden, later accomplished by Cam Ward) to win Conn Smythe Trophy and Stanley Cup as a rookie (1986)
- Holds NHL records for most playoff games played by a goaltender (247), most playoff wins (151)
- Led NHL in wins in 1989–90 (31) and 1996–97 (38)
- Ranks second in NHL career wins (551); ranks second in NHL career games played by a goaltender (1,029)

- Played amateur hockey with Ste. Foy Gouvernors (1981–82); Granby Bisons (1982–85)
- Played in NHL All-Star Game (1988, 1990, 1991, 1992, 1993, 1994, 1997, 1998, 2001, 2002, 2003)
- Led NHL in shutouts in 1991–92 (5), 1993–94 (7) and 2001–02 (9)
- Led NHL in goals-against average in 1988–89 (2.47), 1991–92 (2.36) and 2001–02 (1.94); led NHL in save percentage in 1987–88 (.900), 1988–89 (.908), 1989–90 (.912) and 1991–92 (.914)
- Named coach and general manager of Quebec Remparts (2005)
- Was coach and vice president of hockey operations of the Colorado Avalanche in 2013–2016

# Saint Patrick

Many athletes have divine status bestowed on them by fans or critics, but few are like "Saint Patrick," actually inspiring disciples. And if Saint Patrick's followers accept him as the spiritual leader of modern NHL goaltending, then the religion they all follow is most certainly the "Butterfly."

Patrick Roy is the goalie they call Saint Patrick. Plucked from the junior ranks after barely any seasoning in the minors, Roy performed his first miracle when, as a rookie, he led the unlikely 1985–86 Montreal Canadiens to the Stanley Cup. It was a performance that harkened back to another Habs rookie-turned-goaltending-great, Ken Dryden. And just like Dryden, Roy was awarded the Conn Smythe as the playoff MVP.

With the Cup win, Roy's legion of followers congregated, and the butterfly technique began its rise to prominence. Goaltending coach François Allaire had used Roy to workshop the new technique during their time together in Montreal. Allaire rightly figured that a prone goalie was out of the play and that goalies needed a way to be both up and down at the same time. Fashioning his new technique first after Glenn Hall's and then Tony Esposito's, Allaire took the wide-legged stance and movements of those goaltenders and tweaked them so that when Roy dropped to his knees his feet didn't fall behind him, but rather to the sides, as he lay each pad like a wall perpendicular to the shooter. With his knees held closely together and his feet out to either side, Roy could cover the bottom of the net while his erect upper

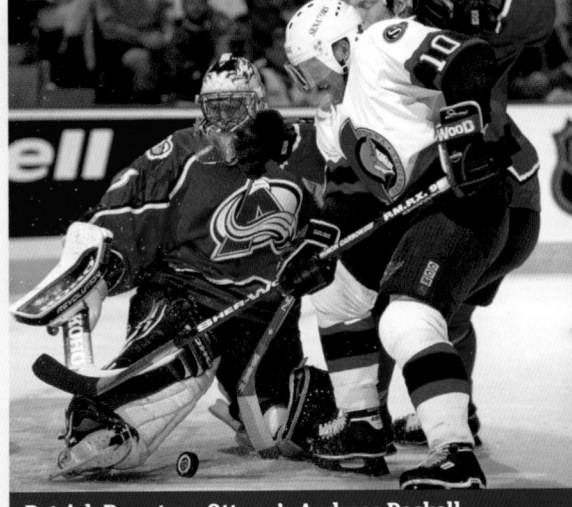

**Patrick Roy stops Ottawa's Andreas Dackell.**

half and ready gloves covered the top half. It worked extraordinarily well. Many goalies in the province of Quebec followed suit, and soon it became an international style.

With the butterfly, Roy was a six-time All-Star and won the Vezina Trophy as the league's top netminder three times. In 1993 he again took a long-shot Canadiens team to the Stanley Cup (and again was named playoff MVP).

But for all his divine powers, Saint Patrick was dealt midway through the 1995–96 campaign after a disagreement with Montreal's management. Sent to the Colorado Avalanche, Roy won a third Cup that spring and another in 2001, when he also won his record-setting third Conn Smythe Trophy. He retired while still in top form after the 2002–03 season and currently sits second all-time in both games played and wins.

GOALIE

# 1 Terry Sawchuk 1971

NO. RETIRED BY DETROIT

**ALTERNATES:**

## 30 · 24
## 29

Boston Bruins
Detroit Red Wings
Los Angeles Kings
New York Rangers
Toronto Maple Leafs

Catches: Left

Height: 5'-11"

Weight: 195 lbs.

Born:
December 28, 1929:
Winnipeg, Manitoba

Died: May 31, 1970: New
York City, New York

Played 21 NHL seasons
from 1949–70

Stats: See page 504

"I don't think people understood the suffering he went through. He shouldn't have been an athlete. He was a freak of nature and was driven by two things — fear and adrenaline."

— Jerry Sawchuk,
Terry's son

**AWARDS**

Calder Memorial
Trophy (1951)

Vezina Trophy (1952,
1953, 1955, 1965)

Lester Patrick
Trophy (1971)

Stanley Cup (1951–52,
1953–54, 1954–55,
1966–67)

**ALL-STAR
SELECTIONS**

First All-Star Team
Goaltender (1951,
1952, 1953)

Second All-Star Team
Goaltender (1954,
1955, 1959, 1963)

- Ranks second in NHL career shutouts (103)

- Ranks sixth in NHL career games played by a goaltender (971)

- Ranks sixth in NHL career wins (445)

- Played amateur hockey with Winnipeg Rangers (1945–46); Galt Red Wings (1946–47); Windsor Spitfires (1947–48); Windsor Hettche (1947–48)

- Named USHL Rookie of the Year (1948); named AHL Rookie of the Year (1949)

- Played in NHL All-Star Game (1950, 1951, 1952, 1953, 1954, 1955, 1956, 1959, 1963, 1964, 1968)

- Led NHL in shutouts in 1950–51 (11), 1951–52 (12) and 1954–55 (12)

- Led NHL in wins in 1950–51 (44), 1951–52 (44), 1952–53 (32), 1953–54 (35) and 1954–55 (40)

- Won all eight playoff games he played in 1951–52, recording four shutouts and goals-against average of 0.62

- Claimed by Toronto from Detroit in the 1964 Intra-League Draft and won the Vezina Trophy with Johnny Bower in 1964–65

- Died on May 31, 1970 of heart failure following two operations that were the result of a wrestling match with teammate Ron Stewart on April 29

- Elected into the Hall of Fame in 1971 without having to wait the minimum three-year period

- Inducted into Manitoba Sports Hall of Fame (1982); inducted into Canada's Sports Hall of Fame (1975)

# A Goalie's Goalie

Goalies, it is said, have always been a different breed. They've been labeled as eccentrics, kooks and nut-bars. Basically, until very recently, many thought that in order to succeed in goal you had to loosen your grip on your sanity. This assertion is almost as old as hockey itself, and while no one goalie is responsible for originating it, many have perpetuated it. During the Original Six era, one goalie seemed to personify all the goaltending stereotypes perfectly, and that goalie was Terry Sawchuk.

His was a glorious career that ended tragically and was filled with the dangerous hallmarks of the goaltending trade. He was edgy (some might say neurotic) and quick tempered. He suffered nervous breakdowns and often played through injury. Most of all though, he played a crouching style that put his unprotected face in harm's way, leading directly to many concussions and facial contusions. Some estimate he had over 350 stiches in his face to close the wounds left by pucks and sticks.

But for all his tendencies, Sawchuk was a stellar net-minder, always giving his team a chance to win. He held the NHL shutout record, with 103 blanked games, for nearly 40 years, until Martin Brodeur surpassed him in 2009. He won the Calder Trophy as the Rookie of the Year and was a seven-time All Star. Four times he won the Vezina Trophy, and four times he backstopped teams to the Stanley Cup. He was at his best playing for the Detroit Red Wings through the 1950s and 60s—his indelible mark on that city being his three Cup wins in four years on

**Terry Sawchuk dives headfirst to make a dangerous and daring save in 1960.**

Motown teams that featured Gordie Howe and Ted Lindsay. But he is also remembered fondly in Toronto, where his stellar relief of Johnny Bower helped claim the Maple Leafs' improbable 1967 Cup.

After that triumph, Sawchuk was picked in the NHL's Expansion Draft by Los Angeles, where he played the 1967–68 campaign. However, at 38, his age was beginning to show. He bounced back to Detroit for 13 games the following season and concluded his career with the New York Rangers in 1969–70, appearing in only eight games. Sadly, shortly after the end of the season, he and teammate Ron Stewart got in an altercation that hospitalized Sawchuk. He had two operations to repair damaged organs, but ultimately died of heart failure. The usual waiting period was waived, and Sawchuk was entered into the Hall of Fame, posthumously, in 1971.

# 31

# Billy Smith 1993

NO. RETIRED BY
NEW YORK ISLANDERS

ALTERNATE:

## 29

Los Angeles Kings
New York Islanders

Catches: Left

Height: 5'-10"

Weight: 185 lbs.

Born: December 12,
1950: Perth, Ontario

Drafted by the Los
Angeles Kings 59th
overall in 1970

Played 18 NHL seasons
from 1971–89

Stats: See page 505

"I knew as soon as it went in, I was the last guy to touch the puck. It's pretty exciting but unfortunately the way we've been playing took all the excitement out of it."

—Billy Smith, on his goal

**AWARDS**

Vezina Trophy (1982)

Conn Smythe Trophy (1983)

William M. Jennings Trophy (1983)

Stanley Cup (1979–80, 1980–81, 1981–82, 1982–83)

**ALL-STAR SELECTIONS**

First All-Star Team Goaltender (1982)

- First NHL goaltender to be credited with scoring a goal in Colorado Rockies' 7–4 victory over N.Y. Islanders, November 28, 1979

- Held NHL record for career playoff wins (88); surpassed by Patrick Roy in 1996–97

- Played amateur hockey with Smiths Falls Bears (1968–69); Hull Castors (1968–69); Cornwall Royals (1969–70)

- Played minor pro hockey with Springfield Kings (1970–72)

- Led AHL in shutouts (4) in 1971–72; led AHL in playoff wins (11), shutouts (1) and goals-against average (2.56) in 1970–71

- Played in NHL All-Star Game (1978)

- Led NHL in wins (32) in 1981–82

- Led NHL in playoff wins for five straight years (1980–84); led NHL playoffs in shutouts (1) and goals-against average (1.93) in 1978–79; shutouts (1) and goals-against average (2.51) in 1981–82; shutouts (2) and goals-against average (2.69) in 1982–83

- Nicknamed "Battlin' Billy" and "Hatchet Man" because of his active stick work and refusal to back down from physical play

- Served as assistant coach of N.Y. Islanders (1989–93); served as assistant coach of Florida Panthers (1999–2001)

- Brother of Gord Smith, who played in NHL with Washington and Winnipeg from 1974–80

# Tiny Thompson

**1**

**1959**

"Never make a move until the man with the puck makes his. There's no room for guesswork in goaltending."

**Boston Bruins
Detroit Red Wings**

Catches: Left

Height: 5'-10"

Weight: 160 lbs.

Born: May 31, 1905; Sandon, British Columbia

Died: February 9, 1981; Calgary, Alberta

Played 12 NHL seasons from 1928–40

Stats: See page 506

- Tied for sixth in all-time NHL career shutouts (81)
- First goaltender to win Vezina Trophy four times
- Earned nickname ironically as a teenager because he was the tallest player on his youth team
- Played amateur hockey with Calgary Monarchs (1919–20); Calgary Alberta Grain (1920–21); Belleville Colts (1921–22); Belleville Bulldogs (1922–24); Duluth Hornets (1924–25)
- Led NHL in shutouts in 1931–32 (9); 1932–33 (11); 1935–36 (10); 1936–37 (6)
- Played in NHL All-Star Game (1937)
- Recorded 1–0 shutout victory over the Pittsburgh Pirates in his NHL debut, November 15, 1928
- Led NHL in wins in 1928–29 (26); 1929–30 (38); 1930–31 (28); 1932–33 (25); 1937–38 (30)

- Led NHL in goals-against average in 1929–30 (2.19); 1932–33 (1.76); 1935–36 (1.68); 1937–38 (1.80)
- First goaltender to be awarded an assist for actually passing the puck to a teammate. In a game during the 1935–36 season, he passed the puck to Babe Siebert who skated down the ice and scored
- Wore the same goal pads from the beginning of his professional career in Duluth until he retired in 1940
- Played with Calgary RCAF Mustangs during World War II
- Coached Buffalo Bisons (AHL 1940–42); coached Calgary RCAF Mustangs (1942–43)
- Together with Paul Thompson became second brother duo in league history (along with Lionel and Charlie Conacher in 1933–34) to be named to NHL First All-Star Team in the same season (1937–38)

**AWARDS**

Vezina Trophy (1930, 1933, 1936, 1938)

Stanley Cup (1928–29)

**ALL-STAR SELECTIONS**

First All-Star Team Goaltender (1936, 1938)

Second All-Star Team Goaltender (1931, 1935)

# 20

GOALIE

# Vladislav Tretiak 1989

**CSKA Moscow**

Catches: Left

Height: 6'-1"

Weight: 202 lbs.

Born: April 25, 1952:
Dmitrov, Union of Soviet
Socialist Republics

Drafted by the Montreal
Canadiens 143rd
overall in 1983

Played 16 seasons of
Russian elite amateur
hockey with Moscow
CSKA from 1968–84

Stats: See page 506

"I would have loved to play in the [Montreal] Forum. I was hoping to one day play in the NHL. I would have liked to do it even for just one season. Unfortunately, it didn't work out that way. I regret not having the chance."

**INTERNATIONAL AWARDS**

Summit Series (1974)

Challenge Cup (1979)

Canada Cup (1981)

Gold Medal: World
Championships
(1970, 1971, 1973,
1974, 1975, 1978, 1979,
1981, 1982, 1983)

Silver Medal: World
Championships
(1972, 1977)

Gold Medal: Winter
Olympics (1972,
1976, 1984)

Silver Medal: Winter
Olympics (1980)

- Only male athlete in Olympic hockey history to win three gold medals (1972, 1976, 1984) and one silver medal (1980)

- First European-born player without NHL experience and first Russian-born and trained player to be inducted into Hockey Hall of Fame

- USSR First All-Star Team Goaltender (1971, 1972, 1973, 1974, 1975, 1976, 1977, 1978, 1979, 1980, 1981, 1982, 1983)

- Named USSR Elite League MVP (1974, 1975, 1976, 1981, 1983)

- Named World Championships Best Goaltender (1974, 1979, 1981, 1983)

- Canada Cup First All-Star Team Goaltender (1981)

- World Championships First All-Star Team Goaltender (1975, 1979, 1983)

- Named Best Russian Hockey Player of 20th century by the IIHF and Russian Hockey Federation (2000)

- Named Goalkeeper of the Century on the IIHF Centennial All-Star Team (2008)

- Won Golden Stick Award (European Player of Year) in 1981, 1982 and 1984

- Served as Chicago Blackhawks goaltending consultant (1990–92, 2000–04)

- Served as Chicago Blackhawks goaltending coach (1992–2000)

- Montreal Canadiens' general manager Serge Savard traveled to Soviet Union in 1984 but failed to secure permission from Soviet authorities for Tretiak to leave Russia and play in the NHL

# Greatness Across the Pond

**V**ladislav Tretiak was first observed in North America as the "weak link" of the Soviet squad that was to face Team Canada in the 1972 Summit Series.

That series was the first time Canada's best players, all NHLers, played against the powerhouse Soviets, who had long dominated international hockey. Canadian scouts had dismissed the 20-year-old Tretiak based on a match they had seen between the Soviet National Team and the Red Army club in which Tretiak allowed nine goals. As it turned out, his mind was on other things: he was getting married the next morning.

**Vladislav Tretiak stops Stan Mikita in 1972.**

Anticipating a brutal routing of the young netminder, NHLer Jacques Plante, perhaps the most analytical goaltending expert of the day, took pity on Tretiak and gave him tips on how to stop Canada's best shooters. By the conclusion of the eight-game match, Canada's series-clinching hero, Paul Henderson, was likening Tretiak to the great Terry Sawchuk—and no one scoffed.

Tretiak was first tutored by the legendary Soviet coach Anatoly Tarasov as a 15-year-old in 1967, when he filled in as a fourth goaltender with the Central Red Army team. He got his first Olympic experience in 1972, where he collected his first Olympic gold medal. Before he was done, he had won three Olympic gold medals and one silver and backstopped the Soviets to 10 World Championships and nine European titles. He guided the Red Army team to 13 league titles while capturing MVP honors five times. He was awarded the Order of Lenin for his service to his country in 1978 and won the coveted Golden Hockey Stick as the outstanding European player in 1981, 1982 and 1984.

In a performance that many still hail as the greatest goaltending spectacle of all time, Tretiak held the powerhouse Montreal Canadiens to a 3–3 draw on New Year's Eve of 1975, despite having his team badly outplayed and outshot 38–13. Eight years later, the Montreal Canadiens made Tretiak their surprising seventh-round choice in the 1983 Entry Draft. Despite Tretiak's interest, Soviet officials never did consent to his playing in the NHL.

Tretiak retired from active play on a high note in 1984, after shutting out Czechoslovakia 2–0 to win Olympic gold in Sarajevo. Some say his retirement was in protest of the authorities denying him his chance to play in the NHL; he was only 31.

# 30

GOALIE

# Rogie Vachon 2016

**NO. RETIRED BY
LOS ANGELES**

**ALTERNATES**

## 1 · 29 · 40

Boston Bruins
Detroit Red Wings
Los Angeles Kings
Montreal Canadiens

Catches: Left

Height: 5'-10"

Weight: 170 lbs.

Born: September 8, 1945:
Palmarolle, Quebec

Played 16 NHL seasons
from 1966–1982

Stats: See Page 507

"On most nights, when we would win close games, 3–1 or 2–1 ... it was usually him who bailed us out and made big stops. He would keep the ship afloat and we'd finally understand that we'd better get going.... He taught us how to win."

—Former Los Angeles teammate Bob Berry

**AWARDS**

Vezina Trophy (1968)

Stanley Cup (1967–68, 1968–69, 1970–71)

**ALL-STAR SELECTIONS**

Second All-Star Team Goaltender (1975, 1977)

**INTERNATIONAL AWARDS**

Canada Cup (1976)

- Full name is Rogatien Rosaire Vachon

- After making his NHL debut with Montreal in 1966–67 he shared the Vezina Trophy with Gump Worsley in 1967–68

- Was the Canadiens number-one goaltender in 1969–70 and 1970–71, but lost the starting job to Ken Dryden and was traded to Los Angeles on November 4, 1971

- Was Kings' team MVP four consecutive seasons starting with 1972–73; was runner-up for the Vezina Trophy behind Bernie Parent in 1974–75

- Played every game for Canada at the inaugural Canada Cup in 1976, going 6–1–0 with a 1.39 goals-against average and two shutouts and was named to the tournament All-Star Team

- Set Kings franchise records for most career games by a goaltender (389), most career wins (171), most career shutouts (32), lowest single-season goals-against average (2.24), and most shutouts in a season (8) although all have been surpassed by Jonathan Quick

- Became general manger of the Kings in 1983–84 and served in the role through 1991–92; also served three short stints as interim coach

- On February 14, 1985, his number 30 became the first number retired by the Los Angeles Kings

# Put on a Happy Face

**A**fter a solid debut season as a 1967 NHL expansion team, the Los Angeles Kings struggled over the next few years. Even the acquisition of Rogie Vachon early in the 1971–72 season didn't help much at first – mostly because the team in front of him wasn't nearly as talented as he was. The Kings finally seemed to put all the pieces together during the 1974–75 season, when they would finish fourth in the NHL's overall standings with 105 points on a record of 42–17–21 during an 80-game season. Vachon had 27 of those wins (27–14–13) and posted a 2.24 goals-against average as he and partner Gary Edwards finished second behind Bernie Parent of the Stanley Cup champion Philadelphia Flyers for the Vezina Trophy.

"When Vachon first joined the Kings" wrote legendary Los Angeles Times sports columnist Jim Murray midway through the 1974–75 season, "there were nights when he thought it was raining pucks. Now, there are nights when he doesn't even need [his] stick. Which is why Rogie is that rarity in the NHL—a smiling goalie."

Was Murray alluding to Vachon's signature goalie mask; a piece of vintage fibreglass known to aficionados as the "smiley" mask? Although not as iconic as Gerry Cheevers' "stitch" mask, or Doug Favell's Flyers Orange Halloween paint job of the same era, the smile-shaped mouth hole on Vachon's mask always made it look like he was having fun no

**Rogie Vachon plays the puck at Maple Leaf Gardens wearing an early version of his smiley mask.**

matter how tough the night.

"It was a mask-maker in Ottawa," Vachon recalled when asked how the smile came about. "The mask needed an opening for the mouth anyway, and I was a happy guy when I played goal, so I wanted a smile. In fact, I wanted to see if I could have a cigar sticking out, but we decided to go with the smile!

"Sometimes, when I let in a goal, it was strange because it looked like I was still happy about it, but I was always happy playing goal, and I was happy out in L.A., so I decided to put on a smile. After all these years, the fans still remember it."

# 1

# Georges Vezina 1945

Montreal Canadiens

Catches: Left

Height: 5'-6"

Weight: 185 lbs.

Born: January 21, 1887; Chicoutimi, Quebec

Died: March 27, 1926; Chicoutimi, Quebec

Played 16 professional seasons from 1910–26

Stats: See page 507

"He stood upright in the net and scarcely ever left his feet; he simply played all his shots in a standing position. Vezina was a pale, narrow-featured fellow, almost frail looking, yet remarkably good with his stick. He'd pick off more shots with it than he did with his glove."

— Frank Boucher, Hall of Fame player

**AWARDS**

Stanley Cup (1915–16, 1923–24)

**ALL-STAR SELECTIONS**

NHA First All-Star Team Goaltender (1914)

- Nicknamed "The Chicoutimi Cucumber" because of his poise and cool demeanor in the nets

- Played amateur hockey with Chicoutimi Sagueneens (1909–10)

- Signed by Montreal Canadiens after he shutout the Canadiens in an exhibition game while playing with a Chicoutimi intermediate team on February 17, 1910

- Never missed a single regular season or playoff game from the time he joined the Montreal Canadiens in 1910–11 until he became ill during a game on November 25, 1925

- Led NHA in wins (13), goals-against average (3.14) and shutouts (1) in 1913–14; led NHA in wins (16) in 1915–16

- Led NHL in wins (12), shutouts (1) and goals-against average (3.93) in 1917–18; led NHL in shutouts (3) and goals-against average (1.97) in 1923–24; led NHL in goals-against average (1.81) in 1924–25

- Recorded first shutout in NHL history with 9–0 victory over the Toronto Arenas on February 18, 1918

- First goaltender to be awarded an assist when Canadiens teammate Newsy Lalonde took a rebound that Vezina stopped, skated up ice and scored in Montreal's 6–3 victory over Toronto Arenas, December 28, 1918

- The ownership of the Canadiens donated the Vezina Trophy — awarded to the league's top goaltender — to the NHL in his honor

# Cool Under Fire

Georges Vezina's name was immortalized when the NHL began presenting its top goaltending award in his memory the year after his death. A key figure in the early history of the Montreal Canadiens, Vezina's life was steeped in both tragedy and glory. In 1909–10, starring for his hometown Chicoutimi Sagueneens, Vezina shut out the Montreal Canadiens in an exhibition match. The Canadiens, a new team in their first season in the National Hockey Association (NHA), were duly impressed and signed the man, who became known as the "Chicoutimi Cucumber" for his calm demeanor, for the 1910–11 campaign.

Vezina then began an epic run with the Canadiens, playing a remarkable 367 consecutive games—including 39 playoff contests—over 16 seasons. He led the Canadiens to their first Stanley Cup as they claimed the 1915–16 NHA league title and defeated the first-ever American Cup challenger, the Portland Rosebuds. The Canadiens would vie for the Cup two more times over the next three seasons, each time battling the Seattle Metropolitans, who got the best of Vezina and the Canadiens in 1916–17. In 1918–19 Vezina backstopped the Canadiens to a series tie with the Metropolitans, but the Cup was never claimed, as five players on the

**Georges Vezina's 1910–11 rookie card. In it he is wearing a Canadiens sweater worn for only that season.**

Canadiens fell ill with the Spanish influenza and the series was never completed.

Vezina didn't taste Stanley Cup action again until 1924. After leading the NHL with a 1.97 goals-against average and three shutouts, he won six consecutive games, beating the Ottawa Senators 2–0 in the best-of-three NHL final, defeating the Vancouver Maroons 2–0 in a best-of-three Stanley Cup semifinal and the Calgary Tigers 2–0 in the best-of-three final to win his second Stanley Cup.

In 1924–25 his goals-against average again led the NHL, and he again delivered Montreal to the Stanley Cup final. However, the Canadiens lost to the Victoria Cougars, and Vezina's career was almost over.

In the second period of Montreal's 1925–26 home opener, Vezina collapsed on the ice, coughing up blood. He was rushed to hospital and never played another game. He died later that spring of tuberculosis, and the Montreal ownership immediately established the Vezina Trophy for the league's top goalie. Until 1981–82, the award went to the goaltender(s) with the lowest goals-against average. Since then, it has gone to "the goaltender adjudged to be the best at his position," selected by the league's general managers.

**367**

# 1

# Gump Worsley 1980

**ALTERNATE:**

## 30

Minnesota North Stars
Montreal Canadiens
New York Rangers

Catches: Left

Height: 5'-7"

Weight: 180 lbs.

Born: May 14, 1929:
Montreal, Quebec

Died: January 26, 2007:
St-Hyacinthe, Quebec

Played 21 NHL seasons
from 1952–53, 1954–74

Stats: See page 508

"The only job worse [than goaltending] is javelin catcher at a track-and-field meet."

**AWARDS**

Calder Memorial
Trophy (1953)

Vezina Trophy
(1966, 1968)

Stanley Cup (1964–65,
1965–66, 1967–68,
1968–69)

**ALL-STAR
SELECTIONS**

First All-Star Team
Goaltender (1968)

Second All-Star Team
Goaltender (1966)

- Nicknamed "Gump" as a youngster because his hair "style" was similar to comic book character Andy Gump

- Played amateur hockey with Verdun Cyclones (1946–49); N.Y. Rovers (1948–50)

- QJHL Second All-Star Team Goaltender (1949)

- Led EAHL in shutouts (7) in 1949–50; led EAHL in playoff wins (8), shutouts (1) and goals-against average (2.25)

- EAHL First All-Star Team Goaltender (1950); USHL First All-Star Team Goaltender (1951); WHL First All-Star Team Goaltender (1954)

- PCHL Second All-Star Team Goaltender (1952); AHL Second All-Star Team Goaltender (1964)

- Played minor pro with New Haven Ramblers (1949–50); St. Paul Saints (1950–51); Saskatoon Quakers (1951–1953); Edmonton Flyers (1952–53); Vancouver Canucks (1953–54); Quebec Aces (1963–65)

- Led USHL in shutouts (3) and goals-against average (2.82) in 1950–51; led WHL in wins (39) and goals-against average (2.40) in 1953–54

- Named USHL Rookie of the Year (1951)

- Named USHL Top Goaltender (1951); named WHL Top Goaltender (1954); named WHL MVP (1954)

- Led NHL in goals-against average (1.98) in 1967–68; finished second in NHL shutouts (6) in 1967–68

- Last Hall of Fame goaltender to play in the NHL without wearing a mask

- Only Calder Trophy winner not to play a single NHL game in the season after winning the award

- When asked one time by a reporter which team gave him the most trouble during his days in New York, he replied with the unforgettable line, "The Rangers."

- Played in NHL All-Star game (1961, 1962, 1965, 1972)

# Roy Worters

1969

"He was called the
Mighty Mite and I
think he was the first
goalie to adopt the
style of steering the
puck into the corners
[with his blocker]."

— Toe Blake

Montreal Canadiens
New York Americans
Pittsburgh Pirates

Catches: Left

Height: 5'-3"

Weight: 135 lbs.

Born: October 19, 1900:
Toronto, Ontario

Died: November 7, 1957:
Toronto, Ontario

Played 12 NHL seasons
from 1925–37

Stats: See page 508

- Nicknamed "Shrimp" because of his diminutive (5'-3") height. He was the shortest goaltender to ever play in the NHL

- Played amateur hockey with Toronto (Parkdale) Canoe Club Paddlers (1918–20); Porcupine Miners (1920–22); Toronto Argonauts (1922–23); Pittsburgh Yellow Jackets (1923–25)

- Member of Memorial Cup–winning Toronto Canoe Club Paddlers (1920)

- Member of the two-time USAHA champion Pittsburgh Yellow Jackets (1924, 1925)

- Led USAHA in wins (15), shutouts (7) and goals-against average (1.23) in 1923–24; led USAHA in playoff wins (9), shutouts (5) and goals-against average (0.86) in 1924

- Led USAHA in wins (25), shutouts (17) and goals-against average (0.81) in 1924–25; led USAHA playoffs in wins (6) and goals-against average (1.20) in 1925

- Stopped 70 shots in 3–1 loss to the New York Americans on December 26, 1926. The Pirates and Americans combined for 141 shots in the game, which is still a NHL record

- First goaltender to win the Hart Trophy (1929) as the league's most valuable player

- Loaned to Montreal by N.Y. Americans to replace injured George Hainsworth, February 27, 1930 (Montreal 6, Toronto 2)

- Led NHL in goals-against average in 1930–31 (1.61)

**AWARDS**

Hart Memorial
Trophy (1929)

Vezina Trophy (1931)

**ALL-STAR
SELECTIONS**

Second All-Star Team
Goaltender (1932, 1934)

**369**

HOBEY
BAKER

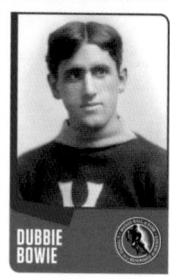

DUBBIE
BOWIE

GRAHAM
DRINKWATER

TOMMY
DUNDERDALE

ARTHUR
FARRELL

TOM
HOOPER

FRED
MAXWELL

FRANK
RANKIN

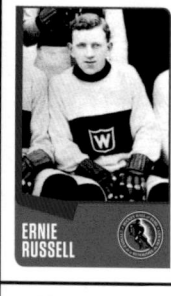

ERNIE
RUSSELL

BRUCE
STUART

CYCLONE
TAYLOR

HARRY
WESTWICK

FRED
WHITCROFT

# ROVER

# Hobey Baker 1945

New York St. Nicholas
Princeton University
Tigers
St. Paul's School

Shoots: Right

Height: 5'-9"

Weight: 160 lbs.

Born: January 15,
1892: Wissahickon,
Pennsylvania

Died: December 21,
1918: Toul, France

Played 10 elite amateur
seasons from 1906–16

Stats: See page 509

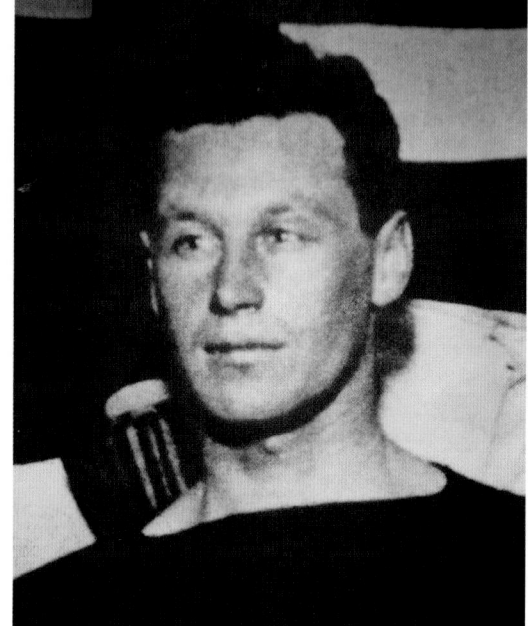

"Baker is the greatest hockey player ever developed in the United States. Canadian experts maintain if he took up the game professionally he might rank as the greatest player in the world."

— *Ottawa Citizen*,
June 16, 1916

**AWARDS**
Lester Patrick
Trophy (1987)

- Inaugural member of the Hockey Hall of Fame (1945)

- Inaugural member of the United States Hockey Hall of Fame (1973)

- Inducted into College Football Hall of Fame (1975)

- Legacy honored with The Hobey Baker Award, presented annually to the outstanding player in NCAA men's hockey since its introduction in 1981

- Players at St. Paul's Prep School compete for an award known simply as "Hobey's Stick"

- Member of the Ivy League champion Princeton University Tigers (1912, 1914)

- Served as captain of Princeton University Tigers in both football and hockey

- Hockey arena at Princeton University is named in his honor

- AAHL First All-Star Team Rover (1915, 1916)

- Led AAHL in goals (17) in 1914–15

- Served in U.S. Air Force during World War I and was awarded Croix de Guerre by the government of France for his service

- Died in an airplane crash while conducting a test flight after the completion of the war

# America's Best

Hobart "Hobey" Baker was arguably the first hockey legend born in the United States. Accomplished as he was, he is mostly remembered for his passionate conviction that hockey should be played with the utmost sportsmanship, in addition to skill, to preserve the game's integrity. Despite many professional offers, he maintained his amateur status, enjoying the game for the love of playing it. He was also known for his postgame visits to the opposition's dressing room to congratulate each team member on a fine effort.

**Hobey Baker as a member of the Princeton Tigers football team in 1913.**

Born in Wissahickon, Pennsylvania, in 1892, Baker spent two years at St. Paul's School in Concord, New Hampshire, from 1908 to 1910. It was there that he first crafted a reputation for being a tremendous and versatile athlete as well as a gentleman in competition. Baker vowed to take his skating and puckhandling ability to the highest level in order to compensate for his lack of size.

By the time he entered Princeton University in 1910, Baker was an extremely well-rounded sportsman. The budding star led the Tigers through an undefeated season in 1911–12, which culminated in an intercollegiate championship. As a rover, he was given the freedom to improvise and display his immense ability all over the ice. Baker became well-known for his end-to-end rushes and unheard of level of stamina, which enabled him to dominate an entire game. He was such a one-man show at times that the Princeton squad came to be known as "Baker and Six Other Players."

Baker left college on a high note by captaining the Tigers to another collegiate title in his senior year, 1913–14. He also served as captain of the school's varsity football team, for which he received accolades equal to those he earned while starring on the ice. Throughout his entire college program, he matched his athletic achievements with exemplary scholastic results.

Following his graduation, Baker suited up for the St. Nicholas amateur team in New York City, where each player was required to pay his own way to participate. He left the game during World War I and distinguished himself as a pilot. He was awarded the Croix de Guerre for his superior conduct under fire. Tragically, Baker lost his life as a result of a post-war flying accident in Toul, France.

Today Baker is remembered with the Hobey Baker Memorial Award, which is presented annually to the outstanding collegiate hockey player in the United States, as well as the Hobey Baker Stick, which is awarded at his old prep school in Concord. The Princeton Tigers have also named their hockey arena after him.

# Dubbie Bowie 1947

**Montreal Victorias**

Alternate Position: C

Shoots: Unknown

Height: 5'-5"

Weight: 122 lbs.

Born: August 24, 1879;
Montreal, Quebec

Died: April 8, 1959;
Montreal, Quebec

Played 12 elite amateur
seasons from 1898–1910

Stats: See page 509

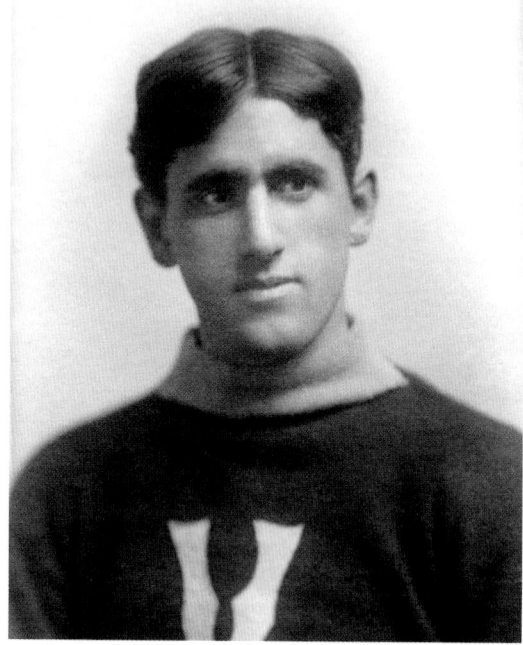

"I am an amateur, was an amateur, and will die an amateur. I played for fun."

—Dubbie Bowie, who refused all offers to play for money during his career

**AWARDS**

Stanley Cup (1898–99)

- Played amateur hockey with Montreal St. John's (1892–93); Montreal Tucker's Academy (1893–95); Montreal Comets (1894–97)

- Averaged nearly three goals per game during the course of his career, a statistic matched only by Frank McGee as the greatest scorer of his era

- ECAHA First All-Star Team Rover (1905, 1909)

- ECAHA Second All-Star Team Rover (1907)

- Led CAHL in goals in 1900–01 (24), 1902–03 (22), 1903–04 (27) and 1904–05 (27)

- Led ECAHA in goals (31) in 1907–08

- Scored eight goals in Montreal Victorias' 16–5 victory over Montreal Shamrocks, January 16, 1907

- Scored seven goals in a game twice in his career and had six goals in a game on five occasions

- Despite his individual prowess, he only won the Stanley Cup as a rookie when the Montreal Victorias successfully defended a midseason challenge from Winnipeg in February 1899

- Though he played in an era when professionalism first came to hockey, he refused to give up his amateur status, once turning down an offer of $1,000 (a huge amount of money at the time) to play just two games

- Served as a referee in the National Hockey Association during the 1910s

# Playing for Fun, not Profit

**N**o players in hockey history have ever scored goals at the same amazing rate as Frank McGee of the Ottawa Silver Seven and Russell "Dubbie" Bowie of the Montreal Victorias in the early years of the 20th century. Both averaged nearly three goals per game, but the difference is that Frank McGee played only four seasons at the game's highest level, while Bowie maintained his pace for nearly 12 years.

Though many fans of his era regarded Dubbie Bowie as the game's greatest player (for his part, he told D.A.L. McDonald of the Montreal Gazette in 1934 that McGee was the greatest individual star he ever competed against), Bowie likely isn't as famous as McGee is today because he never had the same level of Stanley Cup success. Bowie won the Cup only once, as an 18-year-old rookie in a midseason challenge in 1898–99 at the very end of the Victorias' early dynasty. His best chance at another championship may have come when the Montreal Wanderers tried to obtain him for their Stanley Cup defense in January of 1907 against a challenge from the Kenora Thistles. But that transaction never materialized.

Reports claimed that the Wanderers offered Bowie $1,000 to play for them in the best-of-three series against Kenora. (This may also be where the stories that he was offered a grand piano to join the Wanderers come from. Those cannot be confirmed.) Bowie, however, admitted to accepting a check for $325

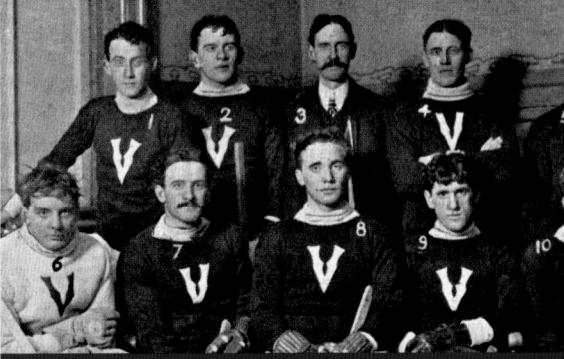

Dubbie Bowie, placed bottom row, second from the right (No. 9), is pictured with the Montreal Victorias circa 1905.

from the Wanderers, but said that his main motivation wasn't money—it was never money for the avowed amateur—but to help keep the Stanley Cup in his hometown of Montreal.

In the end, Bowie decided not to play for the Wanderers and returned the money the following morning. Even without having spent a cent of the $325 and having returned the check, the Amateur Athletic Federation of Canada was asked to investigate whether or not the brief transaction was enough to violate Bowie's amateur standing. After a thorough examination it was determined that Bowie would still be allowed to compete as an amateur.

The proud, lifelong amateur gave up playing top-level hockey in 1908 in order to protect his amateur status. Professional teams would continue to pursue Bowie until a broken collarbone ended his career in 1910.

# Graham Drinkwater 1950

**Montreal Victorias**

Shoots: Right

Height: 5'-11"

Weight: 165 lbs.

Born: February 22, 1875; Montreal, Quebec

Died: September 26, 1946: Montreal, Quebec

Played six elite amateur seasons from 1892–93, 1894–99

Stats: See page 509

"Bob MacDougall, Graham Drinkwater and Norman Rankin formed the astonishing forward line which delighted the Vic's admirers ... Drinkwater and MacDougall are dead sure shots."

— Montreal's *Metropolitan* newspaper, April 13, 1895

**AWARDS**

Stanley Cup (1894–95, 1895–96, 1896–97, 1897–98, 1898–99)

- Renowned as a smooth skater and slick puckhandler who could play forward or defense with equal skill
- Played football at McGill University
- Won a junior hockey championship with the Montreal Amateur Athletic Association in 1892–93, the same year he made his senior debut with the Montreal Victorias
- Member of Stanley Cup–winning Montreal Victorias team that was awarded championship after winning Amateur Hockey Association league title, March, 1895
- After losing a Stanley Cup challenge to the Winnipeg Victorias in February of 1896, he scored a goal in the rematch won 6–5 by the Montreal Victorias in December of 1896
- Scored career-high 10 goals during Montreal Victorias' perfect 8–0 season in 1897–98 which resulted in another Stanley Cup championship
- Served as captain of Montreal Victorias (1898–99)
- Helped Montreal Victorias successfully defend Stanley Cup title against Winnipeg Victorias before losing their league title (and the Cup) to the Montreal Shamrocks (1898–99)
- Served as an original trustee for the Allan Cup, donated in 1908 to recognize Canada's amateur hockey champion

# Tommy Dunderdale

**1974**

**8**

ALTERNATES:

**4 · 5**

Edmonton Eskimos
Quebec Bulldogs
Strathcona-Alberta
Montreal Shamrocks
Portland Rosebuds
Saskatoon Crescents
Victoria Aristocrats
Victoria Cougars
Winnipeg Maple Leafs
Winnipeg Shamrocks
Winnipeg Strathconas

Alternate Position: C

Shoots: Right

Height: 5'-8"

Weight: 160 lbs.

Born: May 6, 1887:
Benella, Australia

Died: December 15, 1960:
Winnipeg, Manitoba

Played 18 professional
seasons from 1906–24

Stats: See page 509

> "More excitement
> was caused over
> the arrival of Tommy
> Dunderdale, who will
> play this season at
> Victoria, than any
> other player from
> the east to go west
> this winter."
>
> — *Toronto World*,
> December 25, 1911

- Holds PCHA record for career goals (198)
- Holds PCHA record for penalty minutes in a single season (141) in 1916–17
- Holds PCHA record for game-winning goals in a single season (6) in 1913–14
- Holds PCHA record for most consecutive games with at least one goal (15), established in 1913–14
- Played amateur hockey with Winnipeg Ramblers (1905–06)
- Led Manitoba Pro League in penalty minutes (44) in 1906–07
- Led MHL-Pro in assists (7) and points (24) in 1908–09

- Led PCHA in goals in 1912–13 (24), 1913–14 (24) and 1919–20 (26)
- Led PCHA in points in 1912–13 (29) and 1919–20 (33); led PCHA in penalty minutes in 1916–17 (141), 1917–18 (57) and 1921–22 (37)
- Born in Australia, he came to Canada in 1894 and was raised in Ottawa
- Scored goals in 15 straight games in 1913–14 and tied Cyclone Taylor for the league lead with 24 goals
- Member of PCHA champion Victoria Aristocrats (1913, 1914)
- Member of PCHA champion Portland Rosebuds (1916)

**ALL-STAR SELECTIONS**

PCHA First All-Star Team Center (1912, 1913, 1914, 1915, 1920, 1921)

# Arthur Farrell 1965

**Berlin Hockey Club**
**Montreal Shamrocks**

Alternate Position:
Forward

Shoots: Unknown

Height: Unknown

Weight: Unknown

Born: February 8, 1877:
Montreal, Quebec

Died: February 7, 1909:
Montreal, Quebec

Played five elite amateur
seasons from 1896–1901

Stats: See page 509

"A team should feel
that it can defeat any
seven that opposes it.
... A team that goes on
the ice thinking that
defeat is probable is
already beaten."

—Art Farrell, in
*Hockey: Canada's
Royal Winter Game*

**AWARDS**
Stanley Cup
(1898–99, 1899–1900)

- Played school hockey with Montreal St. Mary's College (1893–96)
- Wrote what is believed to be the first book about hockey in Canada—*Hockey: Canada's Royal Winter Game* (1899)
- Wrote books about hockey for the Spalding Sports Series in the early 1900s
- Member of Montreal Shamrocks team that also featured future Hall of Fame members Harry Trihey and Fred Scanlan
- One of the men responsible for moving the focus of hockey from individual play to a team-oriented game

- Credited with scoring five goals in a game versus the Quebec Bulldogs on January 19, 1901
- Scored 33 goals in 25 league games for the Shamrocks over four seasons
- Scored two goals in a 6–2 victory over Queen's University in a one-game Stanley Cup challenge on March 14, 1899, and had 10 goals in five games during two sets of challenges in 1900, including a pair of four-goal games
- Went into business with his father after retiring from hockey and died of tuberculosis at age 32

# 1962 Tom Hooper

> "He was born in Rat Portage, learned the game there and has been a mainstay of the team for several years. He is considered the cleverest all-round performer on the team. Though on the forward line, he can play any position with equal efficiency and played [defense] for two seasons."
>
> — *Montreal Gazette*, March 7, 1905

Kenora Thistles
Montreal AAA
Montreal Wanderers
Pembroke Lumber Kings
Rat Portage Thistles

Shoots: Right

Height: 5'-10"

Weight: 175 lbs.

Born: November 24, 1883; Rat Portage, Ontario

Died: March 23, 1960; Vancouver, British Columbia

Played seven elite amateur and professional seasons from 1901–08

Stats: See page 510

- Starred on local school and junior teams in Rat Portage (Kenora) with future Hall of Fame members Tommy Phillips, Si Griffis and Billy McGimisie

- Member of Manitoba Northwest champion Rat Portage Thistles (1902–03)

- Lost Stanley Cup challenge to the Ottawa "Silver Seven" (1902–03, 1904–05)

- Member of Manitoba Senior league champion Kenora Thistles (1905–06)

- Member of Stanley Cup–winning Kenora Thistles team that defeated Montreal Wanderers in January of 1907

- Scored three goals in Kenora Thistles' Stanley Cup–clinching 8–6 victory over Montreal Wanderers, January 21, 1907

- Injured and unable to play when the Thistles lost a Stanley Cup rematch to the Wanderers in March of 1907

- Member of Stanley Cup–winning Montreal Wanderers team that defeated Ottawa, Toronto, Winnipeg and Edmonton (1907–08)

**AWARDS**

Stanley Cup
(1906–07, 1907–08)

# Fred Maxwell 1962

Winnipeg Monarchs
Winnipeg Winnipegs

Shoots: Unknown

Height: Unknown

Weight: 135 lbs.

Born: May 19, 1890;
Winnipeg, Manitoba

Died: September 11, 1975;
Winnipeg, Manitoba

Played six elite amateur
seasons from 1909–15

Stats: See page 510

"Although Bert Andrews played a mighty fine game last night, our old friend Steamer Maxwell gave an exhibition of back-checking and all-around skating which was a treat to witness. Steamer ... has made a name for himself that even the mighty Bert will have to travel to equal."

—*Manitoba Free Press*, February 13, 1914

- Earned nickname "Steamer" because of his tremendous speed

- Offered $1,500 to turn pro with the Toronto Blueshirts of the National Hockey Association in 1913 and $1,800 to join the PCHA in 1914 but preferred to remain in Winnipeg as an amateur

- Member of Manitoba champion Winnipeg Monarchs (1913–14, 1914–15)

- Member of Allan Cup–winning Winnipeg Monarchs (1914–15) that defeated the Melville Millionaires 7–6 in two-game, total-goal series

- MHL-Sr. Second All-Star Team Rover (1911)

- Coached Allan Cup–winning Winnipeg Falcons (1919–20) that represented Canada at Spring Sports Festival during 1920 Antwerp (Summer) Olympics

- Coached Elmwood Millionaires (1929–31); coached Winnipeg Winnipegs (1932–33)

- Coached Winnipeg Monarchs to gold medal victory at 1935 World Championships in Davos, Switzerland

- Continued to coach at both the amateur and professional levels and won several more Manitoba championships in the 1920s and 1930s

- Served as a referee during Memorial Cup and Allan Cup playoffs in the west and in exhibition games for the top professional leagues

- Won eight Winnipeg City League baseball championships between 1908 and 1923 as a player, manager and general manager with the Arena Baseball Club

# 1961 **Frank Rankin**

"The professionals
have offered him
twenty-five hundred
dollars, but he
refuses to make
the jump. His work
in mid-ice this year
has been positively
sensational."

— *Lethbridge Daily
Herald*, reporting
on the Toronto
hockey scene,
January 11, 1913

Stratford Hockey Club
Toronto Eaton's
Toronto St. Michael's

Shoots: Right

Height: 5'-5"

Weight: 145 lbs.

Born: April 1, 1891:
Stratford, Ontario

Died: July 23, 1932:
Stratford, Ontario

Played 10 elite amateur
seasons from 1904–14

Stats: See page 510

- Member of prominent sports family from Stratford, Ontario

- Member of Ontario Junior champion Stratford Hockey Club (1907, 1908, 1909)

- Member of Ontario Senior champion Toronto Eatons (1910–11, 1911–12)

- Led St. Michael's to the OHA senior finals in 1912–13 and 1913–14

- OHA-Sr. First All-Star Team Rover (1910, 1911, 1913)

- OHA-Sr. Second All-Star Team Rover (1912, 1914, 1915)

- Led OHA-Sr. in goals (15) in 1910–11; led OHA-Sr. playoffs in goals (4) in 1910–11

- Led OHA-Sr. in goals (22) in 1912–13

- Served in the Canadian Armed Forces during World War I

- Coached Toronto Granites to gold medal finish at first Winter Olympic Games in Chamonix, France (1924)

# 4 Ernie Russell 1965

Montreal AAA
Montreal Wanderers

Alternate Position: C

Shoots: Right

Height: 5'-6"

Weight: 160 lbs.

Born: October 21, 1883;
Montreal, Quebec

Died: February 23, 1963:
Montreal, Quebec

Played nine elite
amateur and
professional seasons
from 1904–08, 1909–14

Stats: See page 510

"[Jimmy] Gardner, an all-time great himself, picked Ernie Russell, Russell Bowie, Frank McGee and Art Farrell as among the best he ever saw. He rated Georges Vezina the greatest goaltender and Cyclone Taylor the fastest skater of them all."

—*Montreal Gazette*, November 7, 1940

**AWARDS**

Stanley Cup
(1905–06, 1906–07,
1907–08, 1909–10)

- Starred in both football and hockey while growing up in Montreal
- Served as captain of Sterling Athletics, Canadian Junior hockey champions (1903)
- Served as captain of Montreal Amateur Athletic Association, Canadian Junior football champions (1904)
- Member of Stanley Cup–winning Montreal Wanderers (1907)
- Member of Canadian Senior Football champion Montreal AAA (1907)
- Played his first year of senior hockey with the Montreal AAA in 1904–05 before joining the Wanderers
- Led the Eastern Canada Amateur Hockey Association in goals (43) in 1906–07

- ECAHA First All-Star Team Rover (1907); ECHA Second All-Star Team Center (1908)
- Scored eight goals in Montreal Wanderers' 18–5 victory over Montreal Shamrocks, February 19, 1907
- Scored eight goals in Montreal Wanderers' 16–5 victory over Montreal Shamrocks, March 6, 1907
- Scored at least three goals in five straight games in 1906–07
- Did not play 1908–09 season because of dispute over his amateur status
- Scored a goal in 10 straight games during the 1911–12 season

# 1961 **Bruce Stuart**

"Give us a couple of good, square officials and we will beat the champions with two or three goals to spare."

— Bruce Stuart of the Ottawa Senators, before a key game against the Wanderers in Montreal on February 6, 1909. (The Senators won the game 9–8, then later wrapped up the Stanley Cup with an 8–3 win in Ottawa.)

Montreal Wanderers
Ottawa Hockey Club
Ottawa Senators
Pittsburgh Victorias
Portage Lakes
Quebec Bulldogs

Alternate Position: C

Shoots: Right

Height: 6'-2"

Weight: 180 lbs.

Born: November 30, 1881: Ottawa, Ontario

Died: October 28, 1961: Ottawa, Ontario

Played 13 elite amateur and professional seasons from 1898–1911

Stats: See page 511

- Brother of Hall of Fame member Hod Stuart, who played nine elite amateur and professional seasons between 1898 and 1907

- Among the first Canadians to play professionally when he signed with Pittsburgh Victorias (1902)

- Led WPHL in goals (16) and points (22) in 1902–03

- WPHL First All-Star Team Center (1903)

- Capable of playing any forward position, he was renowned for his skills as a rover during the seven-man era

- Member of IHL champion Portage Lakes (1903–04, 1905–06, 1906–07)

- Signed as a free agent by Montreal Wanderers, December 10, 1907

- Member of Stanley Cup–winning Montreal Wanderers team that defeated Ottawa (January, 1908); Winnipeg (March, 1908); Toronto (March, 1908); Edmonton (December, 1908)

- ECHA First All-Star Team Rover (1909)

- Served as captain of Stanley Cup–winning Ottawa Senators (1909–10)

- Coached Ottawa Stewartons (1912–13)

**AWARDS**

Stanley Cup
(1907–08, 1908–09, 1909–10, 1910–11)

**ALL-STAR SELECTIONS**

IHL First All-Star Team Center (1906)

IHL Second All-Star Team Center (1905)

# 4 Cyclone Taylor 1947

Ottawa Senators
Pittsburgh
Professionals
Portage Lakes
Portage la Prairie
Renfrew Hockey Club
Vancouver Millionaires

Alternate Position: D

Shoots: Left

Height: 5'-8"

Weight: 165 lbs.

Born: June 23, 1884:
Tara, Ontario

Died: June 9, 1979:
Vancouver,
British Columbia

Played 17 professional
seasons from
1905–21, 1922–23

Stats: See page 511

"I don't think I'd like to play the game now. I was used to going on at the start of the game and playing to the finish. I think any man between the ages of 18 and 35 who can't play 60 minutes of hockey — well, he just doesn't want to play, that's all."

**AWARDS**

Stanley Cup
(1908–09, 1914–15)

**ALL-STAR
SELECTIONS**

IHL First All-Star
Team Rover (1907)

PCHA First All-Star
Team Rover (1913,
1914, 1915, 1918)

- Holds PCHA record for career assists (104)

- Given name was Frederick; earned nickname "Cyclone" for his matchless speed as a skater and the furious rushes he led during his time with the Ottawa Senators

- Member of IHL champion Portage Lakes (1905–06, 1906–07)

- Played mainly as a forward until moving back to defense with the Ottawa Senators in 1907–08 and helped them win the Stanley Cup the following season; played forward again after moving to the PCHA in 1912–13

- ECAHA First All-Star Team Defense (1908)

- Signed as a free agent by Vancouver Millionaires, November 20, 1912

- Member of Stanley Cup–winning Vancouver Millionaires (1914–15); led Stanley Cup playoffs in goals (8) in 1914–15

- Set a PCHA record with six goals in game against Victoria, February 1, 1916

- Led PCHA in goals in 1913–14 (24), 1917–18 (32) and 1918–19 (23)

- Recorded 16 hat tricks and seven four-goal games during PCHA career

- Served as president of PCHL (1936–39)

- Legacy honored by Cyclone Taylor Cup — the championship trophy awarded to British Columbia's top Junior B hockey club

# Star Attraction

Frederick Wellington "Cyclone" Taylor was one of hockey's first superstars. Born in the village of Tara, Ontario, Taylor grew up in nearby Listowel. He helped the Listowel Juniors reach the Ontario Hockey Association (OHA) finals in 1904, but after being forced to sit out the 1904–05 OHA season, he jumped at the chance to play for the Portage la Prairie team of the Manitoba Senior Hockey League for the 1905–06 season. He was then signed by Houghton, Michigan's Portage Lakers franchise of the International Professional Hockey League (IHL) midway through the schedule. Based in northern Michigan, the IHL was the first openly professional loop in North America. Taylor helped Houghton win league titles in both 1905–06 and 1906–07.

**The 1908–09 Stanley Cup–champion Ottawa Senators. Cyclone Taylor is located in the top row, immediately to the right of the center oval. Taylor was the star attraction of the Ottawa club.**

In 1907–08, Taylor joined the Ottawa Senators of the Eastern Canada Amateur Hockey Association (ECAHA). It was there that he made a name for himself as an explosive rushing defenseman. The Ottawa press dubbed him "Cyclone" after a cartoonist with the Ottawa Journal depicted one of his whirlwind rushes, complete with Taylor wrapped in a cyclone. His excellent play helped Ottawa win the Stanley Cup in 1909, but in a transaction that caused a stir across Canada, Taylor was signed by the Renfrew Millionaires, who were preparing to join the newly founded National Hockey Association (NHA) in 1909–10. His salary was reputed to be $5,250 that season (equivalent to more than $110,000 in 2018).

Renfrew disbanded after the 1910–11 season, and when Taylor couldn't reach a satisfactory agreement to stay in the NHA in 1911–12, the Vancouver Millionaires of the Pacific Coast Hockey Association (PCHA) signed him for the 1912–13 season. Team manager Frank Patrick moved Cyclone to the forward position, and he thrived as a rover and at center. Taylor led the PCHA in points four times in five seasons from 1913–14 through 1918–19 and helped Vancouver win the Stanley Cup in 1915. He would remain in Vancouver, active in his community, until his death in 1979.

Cyclone Tayor was elected into the Hockey Hall of Fame in 1947, and was given the honor of turning the sod for the construction of the Hockey Hall of Fame building that opened in 1961. He is also a member of Canada's Sports Hall of Fame and the British Columbia Sports Hall of Fame.

**385**

# Harry Westwick 1962

Kenora Thistles
Ottawa Capitals
Ottawa Hockey Club
Ottawa Silver Seven
Ottawa Senators

Shoots: Unknown

Height: Unknown

Weight: Unknown

Born: April 22, 1876:
Ottawa, Ontario

Died: April 3, 1957:
Ottawa, Ontario

Played 14 elite amateur
and professional
seasons from
1894–98, 1899–1909

Stats: See page 511

"No one was killed, but there was hardly one of the 14 players at the end of the match who couldn't show some bruise or cut."

— Harry Westwick, recalling a particularly rough game between Ottawa's "Silver Seven" and the Montreal Wanderers

**AWARDS**

Stanley Cup (1902–03,
1903–04, 1904–05,
1905–06, 1906–07)

- Earned nickname "Rat" because of his small stature, aggressive nature and elusive style

- Member of World Lacrosse Champion Ottawa Capitals (1900)

- Began career as a goaltender before switching to rover and averaged a goal a game over the course of his career

- FAHL Second All-Star Team Rover (1905)

- Recorded career-best 24 goals in 13 regular-season and Stanley Cup challenge games during 1904–05 season

- Member of Stanley Cup–winning Ottawa "Silver Seven" (1902–03, 1903–04, 1904–05, 1905–06)

- Helped Ottawa capture Stanley Cup title for three straight seasons from 1902–03 to 1904–05 and defend it successfully in two challenges during the 1905–06 season

- Signed as a free agent by Kenora Thistles in March of 1907

- Member of Stanley Cup–winning Kenora Thistles team that defeated Brandon 8–6 and 6–1 in best-of-three series, March 17–18, 1907 but then lost to Montreal Wanderers

- Inducted into Ottawa Sports Hall of Fame (1968)

# 1962 **Fred Whitcroft**

Edmonton
Professionals
Kenora Thistles
Midland Hockey Club
Peterborough Colts
Renfrew Hockey Club

Shoots: Right

Height: 5'-10"

Weight: 165 lbs.

Born: December 20,
1882: Milford, Ireland

Died: August 9, 1931:
Edmonton, Alberta

Played eight elite
amateur and
professional seasons
from 1902–10

Stats: See page 511

"Whitcroft, on top of having to manage the team, played up to the top of his form. … His reputation had suffered some [but] he made a new name for himself…. His handling of the team on the ice and his own individual work as a member of the team, places him in the front rank of hockey players anywhere."

*— Edmonton Bulletin*,
January 12, 1909

- Family came to Canada before his first birthday and settled in Port Perry, Ontario; later moved to Peterborough
- Played amateur hockey with Peterborough Jr. Colts (1899–1902); Midland HC (1904–05); Peterborough Colts (1902–04, 1905–07)
- Member of Ontario Hockey Association Junior champion Peterborough Jr. Colts (1901)
- Served as captain of OHA Intermediate champion Peterborough Colts (1906)
- Led MHL-Pro League playoffs in goals (5) in 1906–07
- Member of Stanley Cup–winning Kenora Thistles team that defeated Brandon 8–6 and 6–1 to retain Stanley Cup title, March 17–18, 1907 but then lost to Montreal Wanderers

- Signed as a free agent by Edmonton, December 22, 1907
- Led Alberta Pro League in goals (35), assists (7) and points (42) in 1907–08
- APHL First All-Star Team Rover (1908)
- Led Edmonton to unsuccessful Stanley Cup challenges in December of 1908 versus the Montreal Wanderers and January of 1910 versus Ottawa Senators
- Played with future Hall of Fame members Frank and Lester Patrick, Cyclone Taylor and Newsy Lalonde in Renfrew
- Returned to Edmonton in 1910 to coach, operate local arena and scout for Lester and Frank Patrick in the Pacific Coast Hockey Association

**AWARDS**
Stanley Cup (1906–07)

Mail this cop

| SCORE COMPTÉ | 1 | DATE | May 1st–1955 | DOU APT. 16, 2 MO |

| SCORE COMPTÉ | 2 | PLACE ENDROIT | Montreal Forum |

| ME TEAM – CLUB RECEVEUR PLAYER – JOUEUR | 2 MINUTES | INFRACTION | TIME TEMPS | 2 MINUTE |
|---|---|---|---|---|
| PERREAULT | | 1ST | | HANNIGA |
| TALBOT | 3 ZENIUK | "C" | 2.36 | |
| MIRANDE | 3 LEGER | INT. | 3.06 | |
| DUBE | S HODGSON | "C" | 6.21 | S TALBU |
| KACHUR | S F. PERREAULT | H.S. | 11.21 | |
| ROSSE | | 2ND | | |
| EGER | S TURNER | INT. | 5.05 | |
| ODGSON | E STANKIEWICZ | H.S | 5.05 | |
| RNER | S TURNER | "H" | 8.05 | |
| RODEN | E ZENIUK | HP | 11.11 | |
| OVOST | S TURNER | HK | 11.28 | |
| AULNIERS | E BUCYK | "CC" | 16.3 | |

| | 5 MINUTES | INFRACTION | TIME TEM |
|---|---|---|---|
| ENIS | | | |
| LKNER | | | |
| RREAULT | | | |
| RNEY | | | |
| OWIE | | | |
| | | | |
| ENEAD | | | |

| Y R | ASSISTED BY — ASSISTÉ PAR | TIME TEMPS | SCORED BY COMPTÉ PAR | ASSISTE |
|---|---|---|---|---|
| | 2ND | | | |
| K | ALLEN – HORVATH | 9.13 | S DUR | |

TEAM TOTALS

NA
OFFICI
NOTE: PT

# STATISTICS

ediately followin...
to:

. HARNEY
MPTON AVENUE
. 28, P.Q.

INFRAC...

GRUNING ... 19
H. LA ROSE ... 21
THOMPSON ... 32
SANTICCI ... 33
HUSHACK ... 34
...EN P ... 44
... ... 47
... 55
... 71

1st
2nd SHOTS
3rd

NAL HOCKEY LEAGUE
...PORT OF MATCH
BE SENT TO LEAGUE OFFICE IMMEDIATELY.

VS

FINLAND

DATE: SEP 1...

RINK

VISITING CLUB:

...ANADA

GOAL

... M KIPRUSOFF

...TONEN

# Dave Andreychuk  Profile: See page 12

## REGULAR SEASON

| SEASON | AGE | TEAM | LG | GP | G | A | PTS | +/- | PIM | ESG | PPG | SHG | GWG | SOG | S% |
|---|---|---|---|---|---|---|---|---|---|---|---|---|---|---|---|
| 1982-83 | 19 | Buffalo Sabres | NHL | 43 | 14 | 23 | 37 | 4 | 16 | 11 | 3 | 0 | 1 | 65 | 21.5 |
| 1983-84 | 20 | Buffalo Sabres | NHL | 78 | 38 | 40 | 80 | 20 | 40 | 28 | 10 | 0 | 7 | 179 | 21.2 |
| 1984-85 | 21 | Buffalo Sabres | NHL | 64 | 31 | 30 | 61 | -5 | 54 | 17 | 14 | 0 | 2 | 153 | 20.3 |
| 1985-86 | 22 | Buffalo Sabres | NHL | 80 | 36 | 51 | 87 | 3 | 61 | 24 | 12 | 0 | 3 | 226 | 15.9 |
| 1986-87 | 23 | Buffalo Sabres | NHL | 77 | 25 | 48 | 73 | -1 | 44 | 12 | 13 | 0 | 2 | 254 | 9.8 |
| 1987-88 | 24 | Buffalo Sabres | NHL | 80 | 30 | 48 | 78 | 1 | 112 | 15 | 15 | 0 | 5 | 253 | 11.9 |
| 1988-89 | 25 | Buffalo Sabres | NHL | 56 | 28 | 24 | 52 | 0 | 40 | 21 | 7 | 0 | 3 | 145 | 19.3 |
| 1989-90 | 26 | Buffalo Sabres | NHL | 73 | 40 | 42 | 82 | 6 | 42 | 22 | 18 | 0 | 3 | 206 | 19.4 |
| 1990-91 | 27 | Buffalo Sabres | NHL | 80 | 36 | 33 | 69 | 11 | 32 | 23 | 13 | 0 | 4 | 234 | 15.4 |
| 1991-92 | 28 | Buffalo Sabres | NHL | 80 | 41 | 50 | 91 | -9 | 71 | 13 | 28 | 0 | 2 | 337 | 12.2 |
| 1992-93 | 29 | Buffalo Sabres | NHL | 52 | 29 | 32 | 61 | -8 | 48 | 9 | 20 | 0 | 2 | 171 | 17.0 |
| 1992-93 | 29 | Toronto Maple Leafs | NHL | 31 | 25 | 13 | 38 | 12 | 8 | 13 | 12 | 0 | 2 | 139 | 18.0 |
| 1993-94 | 30 | Toronto Maple Leafs | NHL | 83 | 53 | 46 | 99 | 22 | 98 | 27 | 21 | 5 | 8 | 333 | 15.9 |
| 1994-95 | 31 | Toronto Maple Leafs | NHL | 48 | 22 | 16 | 38 | -7 | 34 | 14 | 8 | 0 | 2 | 168 | 13.1 |
| 1995-96 | 32 | Toronto Maple Leafs | NHL | 61 | 20 | 24 | 44 | -11 | 54 | 6 | 12 | 2 | 3 | 200 | 10.0 |
| 1995-96 | 32 | New Jersey Devils | NHL | 15 | 8 | 5 | 13 | 2 | 10 | 6 | 2 | 0 | 0 | 41 | 19.5 |
| 1996-97 | 33 | New Jersey Devils | NHL | 82 | 27 | 34 | 61 | 38 | 48 | 22 | 4 | 1 | 2 | 233 | 11.6 |
| 1997-98 | 34 | New Jersey Devils | NHL | 75 | 14 | 34 | 48 | 19 | 26 | 10 | 4 | 0 | 2 | 180 | 7.8 |
| 1998-99 | 35 | New Jersey Devils | NHL | 52 | 15 | 13 | 28 | 1 | 20 | 11 | 4 | 0 | 3 | 110 | 13.6 |
| 1999-00 | 36 | Boston Bruins | NHL | 63 | 19 | 14 | 33 | -11 | 28 | 12 | 7 | 0 | 2 | 192 | 9.9 |
| 1999-00 | 36 | Colorado Avalanche | NHL | 14 | 1 | 2 | 3 | -9 | 2 | 0 | 1 | 0 | 1 | 41 | 2.4 |
| 2000-01 | 37 | Buffalo Sabres | NHL | 74 | 20 | 13 | 33 | 0 | 32 | 12 | 8 | 0 | 4 | 119 | 16.8 |
| 2001-02 | 38 | Tampa Bay Lightning | NHL | 82 | 21 | 17 | 38 | -12 | 109 | 11 | 9 | 1 | 5 | 161 | 13.0 |
| 2002-03 | 39 | Tampa Bay Lightning | NHL | 72 | 20 | 14 | 34 | -12 | 34 | 5 | 15 | 0 | 3 | 170 | 11.8 |
| 2003-04 | 40 | Tampa Bay Lightning | NHL | 82 | 21 | 18 | 39 | -9 | 42 | 11 | 10 | 0 | 5 | 165 | 12.7 |
| 2005-06 | 42 | Tampa Bay Lightning | NHL | 42 | 6 | 12 | 18 | -13 | 16 | 1 | 4 | 1 | 1 | 81 | 7.4 |
| NHL Career — 23 Seasons | | | | 1639 | 640 | 698 | 1338 | 32 | 1121 | 356 | 274 | 10 | 77 | 4556 | 14.0 |

## PLAYOFFS

| SEASON | AGE | TEAM | LG | GP | G | A | PTS | +/- | PIM | ESG | PPG | SHG | GWG | SOG | S% |
|---|---|---|---|---|---|---|---|---|---|---|---|---|---|---|---|
| 1982-83 | 19 | Buffalo Sabres | NHL | 4 | 1 | 0 | 1 | -2 | 4 | 1 | 0 | 0 | 0 | 3 | 33.3 |
| 1983-84 | 20 | Buffalo Sabres | NHL | 2 | 0 | 1 | 1 | -2 | 2 | 0 | 0 | 0 | 0 | 5 | 0.0 |
| 1984-85 | 21 | Buffalo Sabres | NHL | 5 | 4 | 3 | 7 | 4 | 4 | 4 | 0 | 0 | 2 | 12 | 33.3 |
| 1987-88 | 24 | Buffalo Sabres | NHL | 6 | 2 | 4 | 6 | -2 | 0 | 1 | 1 | 0 | 0 | 15 | 13.3 |
| 1988-89 | 25 | Buffalo Sabres | NHL | 5 | 0 | 3 | 3 | 0 | 0 | 0 | 0 | 0 | 0 | 15 | 0.0 |
| 1989-90 | 26 | Buffalo Sabres | NHL | 6 | 2 | 5 | 7 | 2 | 2 | 1 | 1 | 0 | 0 | 20 | 10.0 |
| 1990-91 | 27 | Buffalo Sabres | NHL | 6 | 2 | 2 | 4 | -2 | 8 | 1 | 1 | 0 | 0 | 21 | 9.5 |
| 1991-92 | 28 | Buffalo Sabres | NHL | 7 | 1 | 3 | 4 | 0 | 12 | 1 | 0 | 0 | 0 | 27 | 3.7 |
| 1992-93 | 29 | Toronto Maple Leafs | NHL | 21 | 12 | 7 | 19 | 6 | 35 | 8 | 4 | 0 | 3 | 72 | 16.7 |
| 1993-94 | 30 | Toronto Maple Leafs | NHL | 18 | 5 | 5 | 10 | -3 | 16 | 1 | 3 | 1 | 0 | 50 | 10.0 |
| 1994-95 | 31 | Toronto Maple Leafs | NHL | 7 | 3 | 2 | 5 | 3 | 25 | 1 | 2 | 0 | 0 | 19 | 15.8 |
| 1996-97 | 33 | New Jersey Devils | NHL | 1 | 0 | 0 | 0 | 0 | 0 | 0 | 0 | 0 | 0 | 5 | 0.0 |
| 1997-98 | 34 | New Jersey Devils | NHL | 6 | 1 | 0 | 1 | -2 | 4 | 0 | 1 | 0 | 0 | 17 | 5.9 |
| 1998-99 | 35 | New Jersey Devils | NHL | 4 | 2 | 0 | 2 | 0 | 4 | 2 | 0 | 0 | 0 | 7 | 28.6 |
| 1999-00 | 36 | Colorado Avalanche | NHL | 17 | 3 | 2 | 5 | -3 | 18 | 1 | 2 | 0 | 0 | 38 | 7.9 |
| 2000-01 | 37 | Buffalo Sabres | NHL | 13 | 1 | 2 | 3 | 0 | 4 | 0 | 1 | 0 | 0 | 17 | 5.9 |
| 2002-03 | 39 | Tampa Bay Lightning | NHL | 11 | 3 | 3 | 6 | -1 | 10 | 2 | 1 | 0 | 1 | 25 | 12.0 |
| 2003-04 | 40 | Tampa Bay Lightning | NHL | 23 | 1 | 13 | 14 | -2 | 14 | 1 | 0 | 0 | 0 | 30 | 3.3 |
| NHL Career — 18 Seasons | | | | 162 | 43 | 55 | 98 | -4 | 162 | 25 | 17 | 1 | 6 | 398 | 10.8 |

# Bill Barber  Profile: See page 13

## REGULAR SEASON

| SEASON | AGE | TEAM | LG | GP | G | A | PTS | +/- | PIM | ESG | PPG | SHG | GWG | SOG | S% |
|---|---|---|---|---|---|---|---|---|---|---|---|---|---|---|---|
| 1972-73 | 20 | Philadelphia Flyers | NHL | 69 | 30 | 34 | 64 | 11 | 46 | 23 | 7 | 0 | 2 | 214 | 14.0 |
| 1973-74 | 21 | Philadelphia Flyers | NHL | 75 | 34 | 35 | 69 | 33 | 54 | 23 | 9 | 2 | 5 | 290 | 11.7 |
| 1974-75 | 22 | Philadelphia Flyers | NHL | 79 | 34 | 37 | 71 | 45 | 66 | 21 | 8 | 5 | 4 | 275 | 12.5 |
| 1975-76 | 23 | Philadelphia Flyers | NHL | 80 | 50 | 62 | 112 | 74 | 104 | 31 | 15 | 4 | 10 | 380 | 13.2 |
| 1976-77 | 24 | Philadelphia Flyers | NHL | 73 | 20 | 35 | 55 | 32 | 62 | 17 | 3 | 0 | 3 | 243 | 8.2 |
| 1977-78 | 25 | Philadelphia Flyers | NHL | 80 | 41 | 31 | 72 | 31 | 34 | 29 | 8 | 4 | 9 | 262 | 15.6 |
| 1978-79 | 26 | Philadelphia Flyers | NHL | 79 | 34 | 46 | 80 | 20 | 22 | 18 | 10 | 6 | 4 | 258 | 13.2 |
| 1979-80 | 27 | Philadelphia Flyers | NHL | 79 | 40 | 32 | 72 | 38 | 17 | 31 | 7 | 2 | 7 | 265 | 15.1 |
| 1980-81 | 28 | Philadelphia Flyers | NHL | 80 | 43 | 42 | 85 | 6 | 69 | 25 | 16 | 2 | 2 | 292 | 14.7 |
| 1981-82 | 29 | Philadelphia Flyers | NHL | 80 | 45 | 44 | 89 | 2 | 85 | 28 | 13 | 4 | 6 | 350 | 12.9 |
| 1982-83 | 30 | Philadelphia Flyers | NHL | 66 | 27 | 33 | 60 | 16 | 28 | 20 | 5 | 2 | 1 | 214 | 12.6 |
| 1983-84 | 31 | Philadelphia Flyers | NHL | 63 | 22 | 32 | 54 | 4 | 36 | 19 | 3 | 0 | 1 | 204 | 10.8 |
| NHL Career — 12 Seasons | | | | 903 | 420 | 463 | 883 | 312 | 623 | 285 | 104 | 31 | 54 | 3246 | 12.9 |

## Bill Barber (continued)

**PLAYOFFS**

| SEASON | AGE | TEAM | LG | GP | G | A | PTS | +/- | PIM | ESG | PPG | SHG | GWG | SOG | S% |
|---|---|---|---|---|---|---|---|---|---|---|---|---|---|---|---|
| 1972–73 | 20 | Philadelphia Flyers | NHL | 11 | 3 | 2 | 5 | -2 | 22 | 3 | 0 | 0 | 0 | 29 | 10.3 |
| 1973–74 | 21 | Philadelphia Flyers | NHL | 17 | 3 | 6 | 9 | 2 | 18 | 3 | 0 | 0 | 1 | 51 | 5.9 |
| 1974–75 | 22 | Philadelphia Flyers | NHL | 17 | 6 | 9 | 15 | 6 | 8 | 6 | 0 | 0 | 0 | 55 | 10.9 |
| 1975–76 | 23 | Philadelphia Flyers | NHL | 16 | 6 | 7 | 13 | 9 | 18 | 3 | 3 | 0 | 0 | 66 | 9.1 |
| 1976–77 | 24 | Philadelphia Flyers | NHL | 10 | 1 | 4 | 5 | -1 | 2 | 1 | 0 | 0 | 0 | 38 | 2.6 |
| 1977–78 | 25 | Philadelphia Flyers | NHL | 12 | 6 | 3 | 9 | -2 | 2 | 5 | 1 | 0 | 0 | 43 | 14.0 |
| 1978–79 | 26 | Philadelphia Flyers | NHL | 8 | 3 | 4 | 7 | -1 | 8 | 3 | 0 | 0 | 0 | 36 | 8.3 |
| 1979–80 | 27 | Philadelphia Flyers | NHL | 19 | 12 | 9 | 21 | 10 | 23 | 8 | 1 | 3 | 4 | 74 | 16.2 |
| 1980–81 | 28 | Philadelphia Flyers | NHL | 12 | 11 | 5 | 16 | 7 | 0 | 7 | 3 | 1 | 1 | 53 | 20.8 |
| 1981–82 | 29 | Philadelphia Flyers | NHL | 4 | 1 | 5 | 6 | 1 | 4 | 0 | 0 | 1 | 0 | 16 | 6.3 |
| 1982–83 | 30 | Philadelphia Flyers | NHL | 3 | 1 | 1 | 2 | -4 | 2 | 0 | 1 | 0 | 0 | 6 | 16.7 |
| NHL Career — 11 Seasons | | | | 129 | 53 | 55 | 108 | 25 | 107 | 39 | 9 | 5 | 6 | 467 | 11.3 |

## Doug Bentley   Profile: See page 14

**REGULAR SEASON**

| SEASON | AGE | TEAM | LG | GP | G | A | PTS | PIM |
|---|---|---|---|---|---|---|---|---|
| 1939–40 | 23 | Chicago Black Hawks | NHL | 39 | 12 | 7 | 19 | 12 |
| 1940–41 | 24 | Chicago Black Hawks | NHL | 47 | 8 | 20 | 28 | 12 |
| 1941–42 | 25 | Chicago Black Hawks | NHL | 38 | 12 | 14 | 26 | 11 |
| 1942–43 | 26 | Chicago Black Hawks | NHL | 50 | 33 | 40 | 73 | 18 |
| 1943–44 | 27 | Chicago Black Hawks | NHL | 50 | 38 | 39 | 77 | 22 |
| 1945–46 | 29 | Chicago Black Hawks | NHL | 36 | 19 | 21 | 40 | 16 |
| 1946–47 | 30 | Chicago Black Hawks | NHL | 52 | 21 | 34 | 55 | 18 |
| 1947–48 | 31 | Chicago Black Hawks | NHL | 60 | 20 | 37 | 57 | 16 |
| 1948–49 | 32 | Chicago Black Hawks | NHL | 58 | 23 | 43 | 66 | 38 |
| 1949–50 | 33 | Chicago Black Hawks | NHL | 63 | 20 | 33 | 53 | 28 |
| 1950–51 | 34 | Chicago Black Hawks | NHL | 44 | 9 | 23 | 32 | 20 |
| 1951–52 | 35 | Chicago Black Hawks | NHL | 8 | 2 | 3 | 5 | 4 |
| 1953–54 | 37 | New York Rangers | NHL | 20 | 2 | 10 | 12 | 2 |
| NHL Career — 13 Seasons | | | | 565 | 219 | 324 | 543 | 217 |

**PLAYOFFS**

| SEASON | AGE | TEAM | LG | GP | G | A | PTS | PIM |
|---|---|---|---|---|---|---|---|---|
| 1939–40 | 23 | Chicago Black Hawks | NHL | 2 | 0 | 0 | 0 | 0 |
| 1940–41 | 24 | Chicago Black Hawks | NHL | 5 | 1 | 1 | 2 | 4 |
| 1941–42 | 25 | Chicago Black Hawks | NHL | 3 | 0 | 1 | 1 | 4 |
| 1943–44 | 27 | Chicago Black Hawks | NHL | 9 | 8 | 4 | 12 | 4 |
| 1945–46 | 29 | Chicago Black Hawks | NHL | 4 | 0 | 2 | 2 | 0 |
| NHL Career — 5 Seasons | | | | 23 | 9 | 8 | 17 | 12 |

## Toe Blake   Profile: See page 15

**REGULAR SEASON**

| SEASON | AGE | TEAM | LG | GP | G | A | PTS | PIM |
|---|---|---|---|---|---|---|---|---|
| 1934–35 | 22 | Montreal Maroons | NHL | 8 | 0 | 0 | 0 | 0 |
| 1935–36 | 23 | Montreal Canadiens | NHL | 11 | 1 | 2 | 3 | 38 |
| 1936–37 | 24 | Montreal Canadiens | NHL | 43 | 10 | 12 | 22 | 12 |
| 1937–38 | 25 | Montreal Canadiens | NHL | 43 | 17 | 16 | 33 | 33 |
| 1938–39 | 26 | Montreal Canadiens | NHL | 48 | 24 | 23 | 47 | 10 |
| 1939–40 | 27 | Montreal Canadiens | NHL | 48 | 17 | 21 | 38 | 48 |
| 1940–41 | 28 | Montreal Canadiens | NHL | 48 | 12 | 20 | 32 | 19 |
| 1941–42 | 29 | Montreal Canadiens | NHL | 48 | 17 | 28 | 45 | 39 |
| 1942–43 | 30 | Montreal Canadiens | NHL | 48 | 23 | 36 | 59 | 26 |
| 1943–44 | 31 | Montreal Canadiens | NHL | 41 | 26 | 33 | 59 | 10 |
| 1944–45 | 32 | Montreal Canadiens | NHL | 49 | 29 | 38 | 67 | 35 |
| 1945–46 | 33 | Montreal Canadiens | NHL | 50 | 29 | 21 | 50 | 2 |
| 1946–47 | 34 | Montreal Canadiens | NHL | 60 | 21 | 29 | 50 | 6 |
| 1947–48 | 35 | Montreal Canadiens | NHL | 32 | 9 | 15 | 24 | 4 |
| NHL Career — 14 Seasons | | | | 577 | 235 | 294 | 529 | 282 |

**PLAYOFFS**

| SEASON | AGE | TEAM | LG | GP | G | A | PTS | PIM |
|---|---|---|---|---|---|---|---|---|
| 1934–35 | 22 | Montreal Maroons | NHL | 1 | 0 | 0 | 0 | 0 |
| 1936–37 | 24 | Montreal Canadiens | NHL | 5 | 1 | 0 | 1 | 0 |
| 1937–38 | 25 | Montreal Canadiens | NHL | 3 | 3 | 1 | 4 | 2 |
| 1938–39 | 26 | Montreal Canadiens | NHL | 3 | 1 | 1 | 2 | 2 |
| 1940–41 | 28 | Montreal Canadiens | NHL | 3 | 0 | 3 | 3 | 5 |
| 1941–42 | 29 | Montreal Canadiens | NHL | 3 | 0 | 3 | 3 | 2 |
| 1942–43 | 30 | Montreal Canadiens | NHL | 5 | 4 | 3 | 7 | 0 |
| 1943–44 | 31 | Montreal Canadiens | NHL | 9 | 7 | 11 | 18 | 2 |
| 1944–45 | 32 | Montreal Canadiens | NHL | 6 | 0 | 2 | 2 | 5 |
| 1945–46 | 33 | Montreal Canadiens | NHL | 9 | 7 | 6 | 13 | 5 |
| 1946–47 | 34 | Montreal Canadiens | NHL | 11 | 2 | 7 | 9 | 0 |
| NHL Career — 11 Seasons | | | | 58 | 25 | 37 | 62 | 23 |

## John Bucyk   Profile: See page 17

**REGULAR SEASON**

| SEASON | AGE | TEAM | LG | GP | G | A | PTS | +/- | PIM | ESG | PPG | SHG | GWG | SOG | S% |
|---|---|---|---|---|---|---|---|---|---|---|---|---|---|---|---|
| 1955–56 | 20 | Detroit Red Wings | NHL | 38 | 1 | 8 | 9 | | 18 | 0 | 1 | 0 | 1 | | |
| 1956–57 | 21 | Detroit Red Wings | NHL | 66 | 10 | 11 | 21 | | 39 | 9 | 1 | 0 | 3 | | |
| 1957–58 | 22 | Boston Bruins | NHL | 68 | 21 | 31 | 52 | | 57 | 20 | 1 | 0 | 4 | | |
| 1958–59 | 23 | Boston Bruins | NHL | 69 | 24 | 36 | 60 | | 36 | 22 | 2 | 0 | 6 | | |
| 1959–60 | 24 | Boston Bruins | NHL | 56 | 16 | 36 | 52 | -14 | 26 | 11 | 5 | 0 | 1 | 149 | 10.7 |
| 1960–61 | 25 | Boston Bruins | NHL | 70 | 19 | 20 | 39 | -31 | 48 | 15 | 3 | 1 | 3 | 173 | 11.0 |
| 1961–62 | 26 | Boston Bruins | NHL | 67 | 20 | 40 | 60 | -43 | 32 | 14 | 6 | 0 | 2 | 202 | 10.0 |
| 1962–63 | 27 | Boston Bruins | NHL | 69 | 27 | 39 | 66 | -22 | 36 | 22 | 4 | 1 | 3 | 162 | 16.7 |
| 1963–64 | 28 | Boston Bruins | NHL | 62 | 18 | 36 | 54 | -12 | 36 | 17 | 1 | 0 | 2 | 142 | 12.7 |
| 1964–65 | 29 | Boston Bruins | NHL | 68 | 26 | 29 | 55 | -25 | 24 | 19 | 7 | 0 | 2 | 196 | 13.3 |
| 1965–66 | 30 | Boston Bruins | NHL | 63 | 27 | 30 | 57 | -1 | 12 | 24 | 3 | 0 | 5 | 186 | 14.5 |
| 1966–67 | 31 | Boston Bruins | NHL | 59 | 18 | 30 | 48 | -5 | 12 | 13 | 4 | 1 | 1 | 250 | 12.0 |
| 1967–68 | 32 | Boston Bruins | NHL | 72 | 30 | 39 | 69 | 18 | 8 | 23 | 6 | 1 | 4 | 175 | 17.1 |

### John Bucyk (continued)

**REGULAR SEASON**

| SEASON | AGE | TEAM | LG | GP | G | A | PTS | +/- | PIM | ESG | PPG | SHG | GWG | SOG | S% |
|---|---|---|---|---|---|---|---|---|---|---|---|---|---|---|---|
| 1968-69 | 33 | Boston Bruins | NHL | 70 | 24 | 42 | 66 | -4 | 18 | 13 | 11 | 0 | 3 | 192 | 12.5 |
| 1969-70 | 34 | Boston Bruins | NHL | 76 | 31 | 38 | 69 | 19 | 13 | 17 | 14 | 0 | 6 | 190 | 16.3 |
| 1970-71 | 35 | Boston Bruins | NHL | 78 | 51 | 65 | 116 | 37 | 8 | 29 | 22 | 0 | 5 | 225 | 22.7 |
| 1971-72 | 36 | Boston Bruins | NHL | 78 | 32 | 51 | 83 | 15 | 4 | 19 | 13 | 0 | 7 | 174 | 18.4 |
| 1972-73 | 37 | Boston Bruins | NHL | 78 | 40 | 53 | 93 | 17 | 12 | 30 | 10 | 0 | 10 | 168 | 23.8 |
| 1973-74 | 38 | Boston Bruins | NHL | 76 | 31 | 44 | 75 | 13 | 8 | 19 | 12 | 0 | 9 | 139 | 22.3 |
| 1974-75 | 39 | Boston Bruins | NHL | 78 | 29 | 52 | 81 | 11 | 10 | 20 | 9 | 0 | 4 | 167 | 17.4 |
| 1975-76 | 40 | Boston Bruins | NHL | 77 | 36 | 47 | 83 | 22 | 20 | 23 | 13 | 0 | 9 | 151 | 23.8 |
| 1976-77 | 41 | Boston Bruins | NHL | 49 | 20 | 23 | 43 | -1 | 12 | 14 | 6 | 0 | 2 | 98 | 20.4 |
| 1977-78 | 42 | Boston Bruins | NHL | 53 | 5 | 13 | 18 | -1 | 4 | 0 | 5 | 0 | 0 | 48 | 10.4 |
| NHL Career—23 Seasons | | | | 1540 | 556 | 813 | 1369 | -7 | 493 | 393 | 159 | 4 | 92 | 3087 | 16.2 |

**PLAYOFFS**

| SEASON | AGE | TEAM | LG | GP | G | A | PTS | +/- | PIM | ESG | PPG | SHG | GWG | SOG | S% |
|---|---|---|---|---|---|---|---|---|---|---|---|---|---|---|---|
| 1955-56 | 20 | Detroit Red Wings | NHL | 10 | 1 | 1 | 2 | | 8 | 1 | 0 | 0 | 0 | 0 | |
| 1956-57 | 21 | Detroit Red Wings | NHL | 5 | 0 | 1 | 1 | | 0 | 0 | 0 | 0 | 0 | | |
| 1957-58 | 22 | Boston Bruins | NHL | 12 | 0 | 4 | 4 | | 16 | 0 | 0 | 0 | 0 | | |
| 1958-59 | 23 | Boston Bruins | NHL | 7 | 2 | 4 | 6 | | 6 | 2 | 0 | 0 | 0 | | |
| 1967-68 | 32 | Boston Bruins | NHL | 3 | 0 | 2 | 2 | -4 | 0 | 0 | 0 | 0 | 0 | 0 | |
| 1968-69 | 33 | Boston Bruins | NHL | 10 | 5 | 6 | 11 | 5 | 0 | 3 | 2 | 0 | 1 | 33 | 15.2 |
| 1969-70 | 34 | Boston Bruins | NHL | 14 | 11 | 8 | 19 | 13 | 2 | 7 | 4 | 0 | 1 | 49 | 22.5 |
| 1970-71 | 35 | Boston Bruins | NHL | 7 | 2 | 5 | 7 | 4 | 0 | 2 | 0 | 0 | 0 | 11 | 18.2 |
| 1971-72 | 36 | Boston Bruins | NHL | 15 | 9 | 11 | 20 | 6 | 6 | 4 | 5 | 0 | 0 | 43 | 20.9 |
| 1972-73 | 37 | Boston Bruins | NHL | 5 | 0 | 3 | 3 | -3 | 0 | 0 | 0 | 0 | 0 | 7 | 0.0 |
| 1973-74 | 38 | Boston Bruins | NHL | 16 | 8 | 10 | 18 | 10 | 4 | 5 | 3 | 0 | 1 | 43 | 18.6 |
| 1974-75 | 39 | Boston Bruins | NHL | 3 | 1 | 0 | 1 | -2 | 0 | 1 | 0 | 0 | 0 | 10 | 10.0 |
| 1975-76 | 40 | Boston Bruins | NHL | 12 | 2 | 7 | 9 | 0 | 0 | 0 | 2 | 0 | 0 | 14 | 14.3 |
| 1976-77 | 41 | Boston Bruins | NHL | 5 | 0 | 0 | 0 | 0 | 0 | 0 | 0 | 0 | 0 | 1 | 0.0 |
| NHL Career—14 Seasons | | | | 124 | 41 | 62 | 103 | 29 | 42 | 25 | 16 | 0 | 3 | 211 | 18.0 |

## Roy Conacher   Profile: See page 18

**REGULAR SEASON**

| SEASON | AGE | TEAM | LG | GP | G | A | PTS | PIM |
|---|---|---|---|---|---|---|---|---|
| 1938-39 | 22 | Boston Bruins | NHL | 47 | 26 | 11 | 37 | 12 |
| 1939-40 | 23 | Boston Bruins | NHL | 31 | 18 | 12 | 30 | 9 |
| 1940-41 | 24 | Boston Bruins | NHL | 41 | 24 | 15 | 39 | 7 |
| 1941-42 | 25 | Boston Bruins | NHL | 43 | 24 | 13 | 37 | 12 |
| 1945-46 | 29 | Boston Bruins | NHL | 4 | 2 | 1 | 3 | 0 |
| 1946-47 | 30 | Detroit Red Wings | NHL | 60 | 30 | 24 | 54 | 6 |
| 1947-48 | 31 | Chicago Black Hawks | NHL | 52 | 22 | 27 | 49 | 4 |
| 1948-49 | 32 | Chicago Black Hawks | NHL | 60 | 26 | 42 | 68 | 8 |
| 1949-50 | 33 | Chicago Black Hawks | NHL | 70 | 25 | 31 | 56 | 16 |
| 1950-51 | 34 | Chicago Black Hawks | NHL | 70 | 26 | 24 | 50 | 14 |
| 1951-52 | 35 | Chicago Black Hawks | NHL | 12 | 3 | 1 | 4 | 0 |
| NHL Career—11 Seasons | | | | 490 | 226 | 201 | 427 | 88 |

**PLAYOFFS**

| SEASON | AGE | TEAM | LG | GP | G | A | PTS | PIM |
|---|---|---|---|---|---|---|---|---|
| 1938-39 | 22 | Boston Bruins | NHL | 12 | 6 | 5 | 11 | 12 |
| 1939-40 | 23 | Boston Bruins | NHL | 6 | 2 | 1 | 3 | 0 |
| 1940-41 | 24 | Boston Bruins | NHL | 11 | 1 | 5 | 6 | 4 |
| 1941-42 | 25 | Boston Bruins | NHL | 5 | 2 | 1 | 3 | 0 |
| 1945-46 | 29 | Boston Bruins | NHL | 3 | 0 | 0 | 0 | 0 |
| 1946-47 | 30 | Detroit Red Wings | NHL | 5 | 4 | 4 | 8 | 2 |
| NHL Career—6 Seasons | | | | 42 | 15 | 16 | 31 | 18 |

## Bun Cook   Profile: See page 19

**REGULAR SEASON**

| SEASON | AGE | TEAM | LG | GP | G | A | PTS | PIM |
|---|---|---|---|---|---|---|---|---|
| 1924-25 | 21 | Saskatoon Crescents | WCHL | 28 | 17 | 4 | 21 | 44 |
| 1925-26 | 22 | Saskatoon Crescents | WHL | 30 | 8 | 4 | 12 | 22 |
| 1926-27 | 23 | New York Rangers | NHL | 44 | 14 | 11 | 25 | 42 |
| 1927-28 | 24 | New York Rangers | NHL | 44 | 14 | 14 | 28 | 45 |
| 1928-29 | 25 | New York Rangers | NHL | 43 | 13 | 5 | 18 | 74 |
| 1929-30 | 26 | New York Rangers | NHL | 43 | 24 | 18 | 42 | 59 |
| 1930-31 | 27 | New York Rangers | NHL | 44 | 18 | 17 | 35 | 72 |
| 1931-32 | 28 | New York Rangers | NHL | 45 | 14 | 20 | 34 | 47 |
| 1932-33 | 29 | New York Rangers | NHL | 48 | 22 | 15 | 37 | 35 |
| 1933-34 | 30 | New York Rangers | NHL | 48 | 18 | 15 | 33 | 36 |
| 1934-35 | 31 | New York Rangers | NHL | 48 | 13 | 21 | 34 | 26 |
| 1935-36 | 32 | New York Rangers | NHL | 26 | 4 | 5 | 9 | 12 |
| 1936-37 | 33 | Boston Bruins | NHL | 44 | 4 | 5 | 9 | 8 |
| Career—13 Seasons | | | | 535 | 183 | 154 | 337 | 524 |

**PLAYOFFS**

| SEASON | AGE | TEAM | LG | GP | G | A | PTS | PIM |
|---|---|---|---|---|---|---|---|---|
| 1924-25 | 21 | Saskatoon Crescents | WCHL | 2 | 0 | 1 | 1 | 0 |
| 1925-26 | 22 | Saskatoon Crescents | WHL | 2 | 0 | 0 | 0 | 0 |
| 1926-27 | 23 | New York Rangers | NHL | 2 | 0 | 0 | 0 | 6 |
| 1927-28 | 24 | New York Rangers | NHL | 9 | 2 | 1 | 3 | 10 |
| 1928-29 | 25 | New York Rangers | NHL | 6 | 1 | 0 | 1 | 12 |
| 1929-30 | 26 | New York Rangers | NHL | 4 | 2 | 0 | 2 | 2 |
| 1930-31 | 27 | New York Rangers | NHL | 4 | 0 | 0 | 0 | 11 |
| 1931-32 | 28 | New York Rangers | NHL | 7 | 6 | 2 | 8 | 12 |
| 1932-33 | 29 | New York Rangers | NHL | 8 | 2 | 0 | 2 | 4 |
| 1933-34 | 30 | New York Rangers | NHL | 2 | 0 | 0 | 0 | 2 |
| 1934-35 | 31 | New York Rangers | NHL | 4 | 2 | 0 | 2 | 0 |
| Career—11 Seasons | | | | 50 | 15 | 4 | 19 | 59 |

# Rusty Crawford   Profile: See page 20

**REGULAR SEASON**

| SEASON | AGE | TEAM | LG | GP | G | A | PTS | PIM |
|---|---|---|---|---|---|---|---|---|
| 1910–11 | 25 | Prince Albert Mintos | Sask-Pro | 7 | 26 | 0 | 26 | |
| 1911–12 | 26 | Saskatoon Hoo-Hoos | Sask-Pro | 7 | 7 | 0 | 7 | |
| 1911–12 | 26 | Saskatoon Wholesalers | Sask-Pro | 1 | 2 | 0 | 2 | |
| 1912–13 | 27 | Quebec Bulldogs | NHA | 19 | 4 | 0 | 4 | 29 |
| 1913–14 | 28 | Quebec Bulldogs | NHA | 19 | 15 | 10 | 25 | 14 |
| 1914–15 | 29 | Quebec Bulldogs | NHA | 20 | 18 | 8 | 26 | 30 |
| 1915–16 | 30 | Quebec Bulldogs | NHA | 22 | 18 | 5 | 23 | 54 |
| 1916–17 | 31 | Quebec Bulldogs | NHA | 19 | 11 | 9 | 20 | 77 |
| 1917–18 | 32 | Ottawa Senators | NHL | 13 | 2 | 2 | 4 | 15 |
| 1917–18 | 32 | Toronto Arenas | NHL | 7 | 1 | 2 | 3 | 51 |
| 1918–19 | 33 | Toronto Arenas | NHL | 18 | 7 | 4 | 11 | 49 |
| 1919–20 | 34 | Saskatoon Crescents | SSHL | 12 | 3 | 3 | 6 | 14 |
| 1920–21 | 35 | Saskatoon Crescents | SSHL | 14 | 11 | 7 | 18 | 12 |
| 1921–22 | 36 | Saskatoon/Moose Jaw | WCHL | 24 | 8 | 8 | 16 | 29 |
| 1922–23 | 37 | Saskatoon Sheiks | WCHL | 19 | 7 | 6 | 13 | 10 |
| 1922–23 | 37 | Calgary Tigers | WCHL | 11 | 3 | 1 | 4 | 7 |
| 1923–24 | 38 | Calgary Tigers | WCHL | 26 | 4 | 4 | 8 | 21 |
| 1924–25 | 39 | Calgary Tigers | WCHL | 27 | 12 | 2 | 14 | 27 |
| 1925–26 | 40 | Vancouver Maroons | WHL | 14 | 0 | 0 | 0 | 8 |
| Career – 16 Seasons | | | | 299 | 159 | 71 | 230 | 447 |

**PLAYOFFS**

| SEASON | AGE | TEAM | LG | GP | G | A | PTS | PIM |
|---|---|---|---|---|---|---|---|---|
| 1910–11 | 25 | Prince Albert Mintos | Sask-Pro | 4 | 4 | 0 | 4 | 26 |
| 1911–12 | 26 | Saskatoon Wholesalers | Sask-Pro | 2 | 2 | 0 | 2 | 12 |
| 1912–13 | 27 | Quebec Bulldogs | St-Cup | 1 | 0 | 0 | 0 | 0 |
| 1917–18 | 32 | Toronto Arenas | NHL | 2 | 2 | 1 | 3 | 9 |
| 1920–21 | 35 | Saskatoon Crescents | SSHL | 4 | 2 | 2 | 4 | 4 |
| 1923–24 | 38 | Calgary Tigers | St-Cup | 2 | 0 | 0 | 0 | 0 |
| 1923–24 | 38 | Calgary Tigers | WCHL | 2 | 1 | 0 | 1 | 2 |
| 1923–24 | 38 | Calgary Tigers | West-P | 3 | 0 | 1 | 1 | 4 |
| 1924–25 | 39 | Calgary Tigers | WCHL | 2 | 0 | 0 | 0 | 4 |
| Career – 7 Seasons | | | | 22 | 11 | 4 | 152 | 61 |

# Alex Delvecchio   Profile: See page 21

**REGULAR SEASON**

| SEASON | AGE | TEAM | LG | GP | G | A | PTS | +/- | PIM | ESG | PPG | SHG | GWG | SOG | S% |
|---|---|---|---|---|---|---|---|---|---|---|---|---|---|---|---|
| 1950–51 | 18 | Detroit Red Wings | NHL | 1 | 0 | 0 | 0 | | 0 | 0 | 0 | 0 | 0 | | |
| 1951–52 | 19 | Detroit Red Wings | NHL | 65 | 15 | 22 | 37 | | 22 | 14 | 1 | 0 | 6 | | |
| 1952–53 | 20 | Detroit Red Wings | NHL | 70 | 16 | 43 | 59 | | 28 | 13 | 3 | 0 | 1 | | |
| 1953–54 | 21 | Detroit Red Wings | NHL | 69 | 11 | 18 | 29 | | 34 | 9 | 2 | 0 | 2 | | |
| 1954–55 | 22 | Detroit Red Wings | NHL | 70 | 17 | 31 | 48 | | 37 | 14 | 3 | 0 | 3 | | |
| 1955–56 | 23 | Detroit Red Wings | NHL | 70 | 25 | 26 | 51 | | 24 | 17 | 8 | 0 | 7 | | |
| 1956–57 | 24 | Detroit Red Wings | NHL | 48 | 16 | 25 | 41 | | 8 | 10 | 6 | 0 | 4 | | |
| 1957–58 | 25 | Detroit Red Wings | NHL | 70 | 21 | 38 | 59 | | 22 | 16 | 1 | 4 | 4 | | |
| 1958–59 | 26 | Detroit Red Wings | NHL | 70 | 19 | 35 | 54 | | 6 | 12 | 5 | 2 | 3 | | |
| 1959–60 | 27 | Detroit Red Wings | NHL | 70 | 19 | 28 | 47 | -26 | 8 | 13 | 5 | 1 | 3 | 261 | 7.3 |
| 1960–61 | 28 | Detroit Red Wings | NHL | 70 | 27 | 35 | 62 | 0 | 26 | 20 | 5 | 2 | 3 | 268 | 10.1 |
| 1961–62 | 29 | Detroit Red Wings | NHL | 70 | 26 | 43 | 69 | 4 | 18 | 20 | 5 | 1 | 1 | 291 | 8.9 |
| 1962–63 | 30 | Detroit Red Wings | NHL | 70 | 20 | 44 | 64 | 16 | 8 | 16 | 4 | 0 | 4 | 274 | 7.3 |
| 1963–64 | 31 | Detroit Red Wings | NHL | 70 | 23 | 30 | 53 | -12 | 11 | 17 | 6 | 0 | 2 | 229 | 10.0 |
| 1964–65 | 32 | Detroit Red Wings | NHL | 68 | 25 | 42 | 67 | 10 | 16 | 19 | 6 | 0 | 7 | 259 | 9.7 |
| 1965–66 | 33 | Detroit Red Wings | NHL | 70 | 31 | 38 | 69 | 19 | 16 | 18 | 9 | 4 | 6 | 238 | 13.0 |
| 1966–67 | 34 | Detroit Red Wings | NHL | 70 | 17 | 38 | 55 | -18 | 10 | 12 | 4 | 1 | 2 | 225 | 7.6 |
| 1967–68 | 35 | Detroit Red Wings | NHL | 74 | 22 | 48 | 70 | 7 | 14 | 19 | 3 | 0 | 2 | 212 | 10.4 |
| 1968–69 | 36 | Detroit Red Wings | NHL | 72 | 25 | 58 | 83 | 42 | 8 | 18 | 7 | 0 | 2 | 221 | 11.3 |
| 1969–70 | 37 | Detroit Red Wings | NHL | 73 | 21 | 47 | 68 | 26 | 24 | 17 | 4 | 0 | 3 | 218 | 9.6 |
| 1970–71 | 38 | Detroit Red Wings | NHL | 77 | 21 | 34 | 55 | -20 | 6 | 15 | 6 | 0 | 2 | 171 | 12.3 |
| 1971–72 | 39 | Detroit Red Wings | NHL | 75 | 20 | 45 | 65 | -17 | 22 | 11 | 9 | 0 | 5 | 123 | 16.3 |
| 1972–73 | 40 | Detroit Red Wings | NHL | 77 | 18 | 53 | 71 | 6 | 13 | 10 | 8 | 0 | 3 | 130 | 13.8 |
| 1973–74 | 41 | Detroit Red Wings | NHL | 11 | 1 | 4 | 5 | -13 | 2 | 0 | 1 | 0 | 0 | 9 | 11.1 |
| NHL Career – 24 Seasons | | | | 1550 | 456 | 825 | 1281 | 24 | 383 | 330 | 111 | 15 | 75 | 3129 | 10.1 |

**PLAYOFFS**

| SEASON | AGE | TEAM | LG | GP | G | A | PTS | +/- | PIM | ESG | PPG | SHG | GWG | SOG | S% |
|---|---|---|---|---|---|---|---|---|---|---|---|---|---|---|---|
| 1951–52 | 19 | Detroit Red Wings | NHL | 8 | 0 | 3 | 3 | | 4 | 0 | 0 | 0 | 0 | | |
| 1952–53 | 20 | Detroit Red Wings | NHL | 6 | 2 | 4 | 6 | | 2 | 2 | 0 | 0 | 0 | | |
| 1953–54 | 21 | Detroit Red Wings | NHL | 12 | 2 | 7 | 9 | | 7 | 1 | 1 | 0 | 0 | | |
| 1954–55 | 22 | Detroit Red Wings | NHL | 11 | 7 | 8 | 15 | | 2 | 4 | 3 | 0 | 1 | | |
| 1955–56 | 23 | Detroit Red Wings | NHL | 10 | 7 | 3 | 10 | | 2 | 4 | 3 | 0 | 2 | | |
| 1956–57 | 24 | Detroit Red Wings | NHL | 5 | 3 | 2 | 5 | | 2 | 1 | 2 | 0 | 0 | | |
| 1957–58 | 25 | Detroit Red Wings | NHL | 4 | 0 | 1 | 1 | | 0 | 0 | 0 | 0 | 0 | | |
| 1959–60 | 27 | Detroit Red Wings | NHL | 6 | 2 | 6 | 8 | 2 | 0 | 2 | 0 | 0 | 0 | 20 | 10.0 |
| 1960–61 | 28 | Detroit Red Wings | NHL | 11 | 4 | 5 | 9 | 5 | 0 | 2 | 2 | 0 | 1 | 30 | 13.3 |
| 1962–63 | 30 | Detroit Red Wings | NHL | 11 | 3 | 6 | 9 | 0 | 2 | 3 | 0 | 0 | 0 | 48 | 6.3 |
| 1963–64 | 31 | Detroit Red Wings | NHL | 14 | 3 | 8 | 11 | -5 | 0 | 3 | 0 | 0 | 2 | 60 | 5.0 |
| 1964–65 | 32 | Detroit Red Wings | NHL | 7 | 2 | 3 | 5 | -4 | 4 | 0 | 2 | 0 | 0 | 27 | 7.4 |
| 1965–66 | 33 | Detroit Red Wings | NHL | 12 | 0 | 11 | 11 | 3 | 4 | 0 | 0 | 0 | 0 | 31 | 0.0 |
| 1969–70 | 37 | Detroit Red Wings | NHL | 4 | 0 | 2 | 2 | -4 | 0 | 0 | 0 | 0 | 0 | 11 | 0.0 |
| NHL Career – 14 Seasons | | | | 121 | 35 | 69 | 104 | -3 | 29 | 22 | 13 | 0 | 6 | 227 | 6.2 |

# Cy Denneny  Profile: See page 22

### REGULAR SEASON

| SEASON | AGE | TEAM | LG | GP | G | A | PTS | PIM |
|---|---|---|---|---|---|---|---|---|
| 1914–15 | 23 | Toronto Shamrocks | NHA | 8 | 6 | 0 | 6 | 43 |
| 1915–16 | 24 | Toronto Blueshirts | NHA | 24 | 24 | 4 | 28 | 57 |
| 1916–17 | 25 | Ottawa Senators | NHA | 10 | 3 | 0 | 3 | 17 |
| 1917–18 | 26 | Ottawa Senators | NHL | 21 | 36 | 10 | 46 | 80 |
| 1918–19 | 27 | Ottawa Senators | NHL | 18 | 18 | 6 | 24 | 55 |
| 1919–20 | 28 | Ottawa Senators | NHL | 24 | 16 | 6 | 22 | 31 |
| 1920–21 | 29 | Ottawa Senators | NHL | 24 | 34 | 7 | 41 | 10 |
| 1921–22 | 30 | Ottawa Senators | NHL | 22 | 28 | 12 | 40 | 20 |
| 1922–23 | 31 | Ottawa Senators | NHL | 24 | 21 | 12 | 33 | 28 |
| 1923–24 | 32 | Ottawa Senators | NHL | 22 | 22 | 2 | 24 | 10 |
| 1924–25 | 33 | Ottawa Senators | NHL | 29 | 27 | 14 | 41 | 16 |
| 1925–26 | 34 | Ottawa Senators | NHL | 36 | 24 | 12 | 36 | 18 |
| 1926–27 | 35 | Ottawa Senators | NHL | 42 | 17 | 6 | 23 | 14 |
| 1927–28 | 36 | Ottawa Senators | NHL | 44 | 3 | 0 | 3 | 12 |
| 1928–29 | 37 | Boston Bruins | NHL | 23 | 1 | 2 | 3 | 2 |
| Career—15 Seasons | | | | 371 | 280 | 93 | 373 | 413 |

### PLAYOFFS

| SEASON | AGE | TEAM | LG | GP | G | A | PTS | PIM |
|---|---|---|---|---|---|---|---|---|
| 1916–17 | 25 | Ottawa Senators | NHA | 2 | 1 | 0 | 1 | 8 |
| 1918–19 | 27 | Ottawa Senators | NHL | 5 | 3 | 2 | 5 | 6 |
| 1919–20 | 28 | Ottawa Senators | St-Cup | 5 | 0 | 2 | 2 | 2 |
| 1920–21 | 29 | Ottawa Senators | NHL | 2 | 2 | 0 | 2 | 5 |
| 1920–21 | 29 | Ottawa Senators | St-Cup | 5 | 2 | 2 | 4 | 12 |
| 1921–22 | 30 | Ottawa Senators | NHL | 2 | 2 | 0 | 2 | 4 |
| 1922–23 | 31 | Ottawa Senators | NHL | 2 | 2 | 0 | 2 | 2 |
| 1922–23 | 31 | Ottawa Senators | St-Cup | 6 | 1 | 2 | 3 | 10 |
| 1923–24 | 32 | Ottawa Senators | NHL | 2 | 2 | 0 | 2 | 2 |
| 1925–26 | 34 | Ottawa Senators | NHL | 2 | 0 | 0 | 0 | 0 |
| 1926–27 | 35 | Ottawa Senators | NHL | 6 | 5 | 0 | 5 | 0 |
| 1927–28 | 36 | Ottawa Senators | NHL | 2 | 0 | 0 | 0 | 0 |
| 1928–29 | 37 | Boston Bruins | NHL | 2 | 0 | 0 | 0 | 0 |
| Career—11 Seasons | | | | 43 | 20 | 8 | 28 | 51 |

# Dick Duff  Profile: See page 23

### REGULAR SEASON

| SEASON | AGE | TEAM | LG | GP | G | A | PTS | +/- | PIM | ESG | PPG | SHG | GWG | SOG | S% |
|---|---|---|---|---|---|---|---|---|---|---|---|---|---|---|---|
| 1954–55 | 18 | Toronto Maple Leafs | NHL | 3 | 0 | 0 | 0 | | 2 | 0 | 0 | 0 | 0 | | |
| 1955–56 | 19 | Toronto Maple Leafs | NHL | 69 | 18 | 19 | 37 | | 74 | 11 | 7 | 0 | 3 | | |
| 1956–57 | 20 | Toronto Maple Leafs | NHL | 70 | 26 | 14 | 40 | | 48 | 17 | 9 | 0 | 3 | | |
| 1957–58 | 21 | Toronto Maple Leafs | NHL | 65 | 26 | 23 | 49 | | 79 | 22 | 3 | 1 | 1 | | |
| 1958–59 | 22 | Toronto Maple Leafs | NHL | 69 | 29 | 24 | 53 | | 71 | 24 | 4 | 1 | 5 | | |
| 1959–60 | 23 | Toronto Maple Leafs | NHL | 67 | 19 | 22 | 41 | 5 | 53 | 15 | 4 | 0 | 2 | 180 | 10.6 |
| 1960–61 | 24 | Toronto Maple Leafs | NHL | 67 | 16 | 17 | 33 | 14 | 54 | 14 | 2 | 0 | 2 | 160 | 10.0 |
| 1961–62 | 25 | Toronto Maple Leafs | NHL | 51 | 17 | 20 | 37 | 32 | 37 | 15 | 2 | 0 | 2 | 144 | 11.8 |
| 1962–63 | 26 | Toronto Maple Leafs | NHL | 69 | 16 | 19 | 35 | -7 | 56 | 14 | 2 | 0 | 2 | 202 | 7.9 |
| 1963–64 | 27 | Toronto Maple Leafs | NHL | 52 | 7 | 10 | 17 | -12 | 59 | 5 | 2 | 0 | 0 | 95 | 7.4 |
| 1963–64 | 27 | New York Rangers | NHL | 14 | 4 | 4 | 8 | -7 | 2 | 2 | 2 | 0 | 0 | 40 | 10.0 |
| 1964–65 | 28 | New York Rangers | NHL | 29 | 3 | 9 | 12 | -11 | 20 | 2 | 1 | 0 | 0 | 47 | 13.6 |
| 1964–65 | 28 | Montreal Canadiens | NHL | 40 | 9 | 7 | 16 | -2 | 16 | 9 | 0 | 0 | 3 | 66 | 6.4 |
| 1965–66 | 29 | Montreal Canadiens | NHL | 63 | 21 | 24 | 45 | 2 | 80 | 16 | 5 | 0 | 2 | 156 | 13.5 |
| 1966–67 | 30 | Montreal Canadiens | NHL | 51 | 12 | 11 | 23 | -7 | 23 | 9 | 3 | 0 | 2 | 98 | 12.2 |
| 1967–68 | 31 | Montreal Canadiens | NHL | 66 | 25 | 21 | 46 | 5 | 21 | 19 | 6 | 0 | 8 | 111 | 22.5 |
| 1968–69 | 32 | Montreal Canadiens | NHL | 68 | 19 | 21 | 40 | -14 | 24 | 14 | 5 | 0 | 2 | 138 | 13.8 |
| 1969–70 | 33 | Montreal Canadiens | NHL | 17 | 1 | 1 | 2 | -7 | 4 | 1 | 0 | 0 | 0 | 21 | 4.8 |
| 1969–70 | 33 | Los Angeles Kings | NHL | 32 | 5 | 8 | 13 | -15 | 8 | 5 | 0 | 0 | 0 | 37 | 13.5 |
| 1970–71 | 34 | Los Angeles Kings | NHL | 7 | 1 | 0 | 1 | -2 | 0 | 1 | 0 | 0 | 0 | 4 | 25.0 |
| 1970–71 | 34 | Buffalo Sabres | NHL | 53 | 7 | 13 | 20 | -18 | 12 | 7 | 0 | 0 | 1 | 67 | 10.5 |
| 1971–72 | 35 | Buffalo Sabres | NHL | 8 | 2 | 2 | 4 | -2 | 0 | 2 | 0 | 0 | 0 | 5 | 40.0 |
| NHL Career—18 Seasons | | | | 1030 | 283 | 289 | 572 | -46 | 743 | 224 | 57 | 2 | 38 | 1571 | 11.7 |

### PLAYOFFS

| SEASON | AGE | TEAM | LG | GP | G | A | PTS | +/- | PIM | ESG | PPG | SHG | GWG | SOG | S% |
|---|---|---|---|---|---|---|---|---|---|---|---|---|---|---|---|
| 1955–56 | 19 | Toronto Maple Leafs | NHL | 5 | 1 | 4 | 5 | | 2 | 0 | 1 | 0 | 0 | | |
| 1958–59 | 22 | Toronto Maple Leafs | NHL | 12 | 4 | 3 | 7 | | 8 | 3 | 0 | 1 | 2 | | |
| 1959–60 | 23 | Toronto Maple Leafs | NHL | 10 | 2 | 4 | 6 | 0 | 6 | 2 | 0 | 0 | 0 | 21 | 9.5 |
| 1960–61 | 24 | Toronto Maple Leafs | NHL | 5 | 0 | 1 | 1 | -1 | 2 | 0 | 0 | 0 | 0 | 7 | 0.0 |
| 1961–62 | 25 | Toronto Maple Leafs | NHL | 12 | 3 | 10 | 13 | 6 | 20 | 1 | 2 | 0 | 1 | 51 | 5.9 |
| 1962–63 | 26 | Toronto Maple Leafs | NHL | 10 | 4 | 1 | 5 | 8 | 2 | 4 | 0 | 0 | 1 | 25 | 16.0 |
| 1964–65 | 28 | Montreal Canadiens | NHL | 13 | 3 | 6 | 9 | -3 | 17 | 1 | 2 | 0 | 0 | 25 | 12.0 |
| 1965–66 | 29 | Montreal Canadiens | NHL | 10 | 2 | 5 | 7 | 0 | 2 | 1 | 1 | 0 | 0 | 19 | 10.5 |
| 1966–67 | 30 | Montreal Canadiens | NHL | 10 | 2 | 3 | 5 | 1 | 4 | 1 | 1 | 0 | 0 | 9 | 22.2 |
| 1967–68 | 31 | Montreal Canadiens | NHL | 13 | 3 | 4 | 7 | 7 | 4 | 3 | 0 | 0 | 1 | 25 | 12.0 |
| 1968–69 | 32 | Montreal Canadiens | NHL | 14 | 6 | 8 | 14 | 8 | 11 | 3 | 3 | 0 | 1 | 30 | 20.0 |
| NHL Career—11 Seasons | | | | 114 | 30 | 49 | 79 | 26 | 78 | 19 | 10 | 1 | 6 | 187 | 11.8 |

## Woody Dumart  Profile: See page 24

**REGULAR SEASON**

| SEASON | AGE | TEAM | LG | GP | G | A | PTS | PIM |
|---|---|---|---|---|---|---|---|---|
| 1935–36 | 19 | Boston Bruins | NHL | 1 | 0 | 0 | 0 | 0 |
| 1936–37 | 20 | Boston Bruins | NHL | 17 | 4 | 4 | 8 | 2 |
| 1937–38 | 21 | Boston Bruins | NHL | 48 | 13 | 14 | 27 | 6 |
| 1938–39 | 22 | Boston Bruins | NHL | 46 | 14 | 15 | 29 | 2 |
| 1939–40 | 23 | Boston Bruins | NHL | 48 | 22 | 21 | 43 | 16 |
| 1940–41 | 24 | Boston Bruins | NHL | 42 | 18 | 16 | 34 | 2 |
| 1941–42 | 25 | Boston Bruins | NHL | 35 | 14 | 15 | 29 | 8 |
| 1945–46 | 29 | Boston Bruins | NHL | 50 | 22 | 12 | 34 | 2 |
| 1946–47 | 30 | Boston Bruins | NHL | 60 | 24 | 28 | 52 | 12 |
| 1947–48 | 31 | Boston Bruins | NHL | 59 | 21 | 16 | 37 | 14 |
| 1948–49 | 32 | Boston Bruins | NHL | 59 | 11 | 12 | 23 | 6 |
| 1949–50 | 33 | Boston Bruins | NHL | 69 | 14 | 25 | 39 | 14 |
| 1950–51 | 34 | Boston Bruins | NHL | 70 | 20 | 21 | 41 | 7 |
| 1951–52 | 35 | Boston Bruins | NHL | 39 | 5 | 8 | 13 | 0 |
| 1952–53 | 36 | Boston Bruins | NHL | 62 | 5 | 9 | 14 | 2 |
| 1953–54 | 37 | Boston Bruins | NHL | 69 | 4 | 3 | 7 | 6 |
| NHL Career — 16 Seasons | | | | 774 | 211 | 219 | 430 | 99 |

**PLAYOFFS**

| SEASON | AGE | TEAM | LG | GP | G | A | PTS | PIM |
|---|---|---|---|---|---|---|---|---|
| 1936–37 | 20 | Boston Bruins | NHL | 3 | 0 | 0 | 0 | 0 |
| 1937–38 | 21 | Boston Bruins | NHL | 3 | 0 | 0 | 0 | 0 |
| 1938–39 | 22 | Boston Bruins | NHL | 12 | 1 | 3 | 4 | 6 |
| 1939–40 | 23 | Boston Bruins | NHL | 6 | 1 | 0 | 1 | 0 |
| 1940–41 | 24 | Boston Bruins | NHL | 11 | 1 | 3 | 4 | 9 |
| 1945–46 | 29 | Boston Bruins | NHL | 10 | 4 | 3 | 7 | 0 |
| 1946–47 | 30 | Boston Bruins | NHL | 5 | 1 | 1 | 2 | 8 |
| 1947–48 | 31 | Boston Bruins | NHL | 5 | 0 | 0 | 0 | 0 |
| 1948–49 | 32 | Boston Bruins | NHL | 5 | 3 | 0 | 3 | 0 |
| 1950–51 | 34 | Boston Bruins | NHL | 6 | 1 | 2 | 3 | 0 |
| 1951–52 | 35 | Boston Bruins | NHL | 7 | 0 | 1 | 1 | 0 |
| 1952–53 | 36 | Boston Bruins | NHL | 11 | 0 | 2 | 2 | 0 |
| 1953–54 | 37 | Boston Bruins | NHL | 4 | 0 | 0 | 0 | 0 |
| NHL Career — 13 Seasons | | | | 88 | 12 | 15 | 27 | 23 |

## Bob Gainey  Profile: See page 26

**REGULAR SEASON**

| SEASON | AGE | TEAM | LG | GP | G | A | PTS | +/- | PIM | ESG | PPG | SHG | GWG | SOG | S% |
|---|---|---|---|---|---|---|---|---|---|---|---|---|---|---|---|
| 1973–74 | 20 | Montreal Canadiens | NHL | 66 | 3 | 7 | 10 | -9 | 34 | 3 | 0 | 0 | 0 | 55 | 5.5 |
| 1974–75 | 21 | Montreal Canadiens | NHL | 80 | 17 | 20 | 37 | 25 | 49 | 16 | 1 | 0 | 2 | 132 | 12.9 |
| 1975–76 | 22 | Montreal Canadiens | NHL | 78 | 15 | 13 | 28 | 20 | 57 | 12 | 1 | 2 | 1 | 155 | 9.7 |
| 1976–77 | 23 | Montreal Canadiens | NHL | 80 | 14 | 19 | 33 | 31 | 41 | 13 | 0 | 1 | 3 | 143 | 9.8 |
| 1977–78 | 24 | Montreal Canadiens | NHL | 66 | 15 | 16 | 31 | 11 | 57 | 13 | 0 | 2 | 1 | 140 | 10.7 |
| 1978–79 | 25 | Montreal Canadiens | NHL | 79 | 20 | 18 | 38 | 12 | 44 | 18 | 1 | 1 | 1 | 153 | 13.1 |
| 1979–80 | 26 | Montreal Canadiens | NHL | 64 | 14 | 19 | 33 | -1 | 32 | 9 | 4 | 1 | 3 | 153 | 9.2 |
| 1980–81 | 27 | Montreal Canadiens | NHL | 78 | 23 | 24 | 47 | 13 | 36 | 15 | 5 | 3 | 3 | 181 | 12.7 |
| 1981–82 | 28 | Montreal Canadiens | NHL | 79 | 21 | 24 | 45 | 36 | 24 | 17 | 1 | 3 | 1 | 172 | 12.2 |
| 1982–83 | 29 | Montreal Canadiens | NHL | 80 | 12 | 18 | 30 | 6 | 43 | 11 | 0 | 1 | 3 | 149 | 8.1 |
| 1983–84 | 30 | Montreal Canadiens | NHL | 77 | 17 | 22 | 39 | 11 | 41 | 17 | 0 | 0 | 3 | 125 | 13.6 |
| 1984–85 | 31 | Montreal Canadiens | NHL | 79 | 19 | 13 | 32 | 14 | 40 | 16 | 0 | 3 | 3 | 164 | 11.6 |
| 1985–86 | 32 | Montreal Canadiens | NHL | 80 | 20 | 23 | 43 | 11 | 20 | 18 | 0 | 2 | 4 | 133 | 15.0 |
| 1986–87 | 33 | Montreal Canadiens | NHL | 47 | 8 | 8 | 16 | 0 | 19 | 7 | 0 | 1 | 3 | 73 | 11.0 |
| 1987–88 | 34 | Montreal Canadiens | NHL | 78 | 11 | 11 | 22 | 8 | 14 | 11 | 0 | 0 | 1 | 101 | 10.9 |
| 1988–89 | 35 | Montreal Canadiens | NHL | 49 | 10 | 7 | 17 | 13 | 34 | 9 | 1 | 0 | 2 | 65 | 15.4 |
| NHL Career — 16 Seasons | | | | 1160 | 239 | 262 | 501 | 201 | 585 | 205 | 14 | 20 | 34 | 2094 | 11.4 |

**PLAYOFFS**

| SEASON | AGE | TEAM | LG | GP | G | A | PTS | +/- | PIM | ESG | PPG | SHG | GWG | SOG | S% |
|---|---|---|---|---|---|---|---|---|---|---|---|---|---|---|---|
| 1973–74 | 20 | Montreal Canadiens | NHL | 6 | 0 | 0 | 0 | -1 | 6 | 0 | 0 | 0 | 0 | 5 | 0.0 |
| 1974–75 | 21 | Montreal Canadiens | NHL | 11 | 2 | 4 | 6 | 7 | 4 | 2 | 0 | 0 | 1 | 21 | 9.5 |
| 1975–76 | 22 | Montreal Canadiens | NHL | 13 | 1 | 3 | 4 | 4 | 20 | 1 | 0 | 0 | 0 | 34 | 2.9 |
| 1976–77 | 23 | Montreal Canadiens | NHL | 14 | 4 | 1 | 5 | 2 | 25 | 3 | 0 | 1 | 1 | 28 | 14.3 |
| 1977–78 | 24 | Montreal Canadiens | NHL | 15 | 2 | 7 | 9 | 4 | 14 | 1 | 0 | 1 | 0 | 45 | 4.4 |
| 1978–79 | 25 | Montreal Canadiens | NHL | 16 | 6 | 10 | 16 | 4 | 10 | 6 | 0 | 0 | 1 | 38 | 15.8 |
| 1979–80 | 26 | Montreal Canadiens | NHL | 10 | 1 | 1 | 2 | 2 | 4 | 1 | 0 | 0 | 1 | 23 | 4.4 |
| 1980–81 | 27 | Montreal Canadiens | NHL | 3 | 0 | 0 | 0 | -5 | 2 | 0 | 0 | 0 | 0 | 9 | 0.0 |
| 1981–82 | 28 | Montreal Canadiens | NHL | 5 | 0 | 1 | 1 | -1 | 8 | 0 | 0 | 0 | 0 | 10 | 0.0 |
| 1982–83 | 29 | Montreal Canadiens | NHL | 3 | 0 | 0 | 0 | -2 | 4 | 0 | 0 | 0 | 0 | 2 | 0.0 |
| 1983–84 | 30 | Montreal Canadiens | NHL | 15 | 1 | 5 | 6 | 6 | 9 | 1 | 0 | 0 | 0 | 10 | 10.0 |
| 1984–85 | 31 | Montreal Canadiens | NHL | 12 | 1 | 3 | 4 | -7 | 13 | 1 | 0 | 0 | 0 | 15 | 6.7 |
| 1985–86 | 32 | Montreal Canadiens | NHL | 20 | 5 | 5 | 10 | 3 | 12 | 4 | 0 | 1 | 3 | 36 | 13.9 |
| 1986–87 | 33 | Montreal Canadiens | NHL | 17 | 1 | 3 | 4 | -7 | 6 | 1 | 0 | 0 | 0 | 26 | 3.9 |
| 1987–88 | 34 | Montreal Canadiens | NHL | 6 | 0 | 1 | 1 | -4 | 6 | 0 | 0 | 0 | 0 | 5 | 0.0 |
| 1988–89 | 35 | Montreal Canadiens | NHL | 16 | 1 | 4 | 5 | 0 | 8 | 1 | 0 | 0 | 0 | 14 | 7.1 |
| NHL Career — 16 Seasons | | | | 182 | 25 | 48 | 73 | 5 | 151 | 22 | 0 | 3 | 7 | 106 | 7.8 |

# Jimmy Gardner  Profile: See page 28

**REGULAR SEASON**

| SEASON | AGE | TEAM | LG | GP | G | A | PTS | PIM |
|---|---|---|---|---|---|---|---|---|
| 1900-01 | 19 | Montreal AAA | CAHL | 1 | 0 | 0 | 0 | 0 |
| 1901-02 | 20 | Montreal AAA | CAHL | 8 | 1 | 0 | 1 | 16 |
| 1902-03 | 21 | Montreal AAA | CAHL | 3 | 3 | 0 | 3 | 9 |
| 1903-04 | 22 | Montreal Wanderers | FAHL | 6 | 5 | 0 | 5 | 12 |
| 1904-05 | 23 | Calumet Miners | IHL | 23 | 16 | 0 | 16 | 33 |
| 1905-06 | 24 | Calumet Miners | IHL | 19 | 3 | 0 | 3 | 30 |
| 1906-07 | 25 | Pittsburgh Professionals | IHL | 20 | 10 | 8 | 18 | 61 |
| 1907-08 | 26 | Montreal Shamrocks | ECAHA | 10 | 7 | 0 | 7 | 42 |
| 1908-09 | 27 | Montreal Wanderers | ECHA | 12 | 11 | 0 | 11 | 61 |
| 1909-10 | 28 | Montreal Wanderers | NHA | 13 | 13 | 0 | 13 | 67 |
| 1910-11 | 29 | Montreal Wanderers | NHA | 14 | 5 | 0 | 5 | 35 |
| 1911-12 | 30 | New Westminster Royals | PCHA | 15 | 8 | 0 | 8 | 50 |
| 1912-13 | 31 | New Westminster Royals | PCHA | 13 | 3 | 4 | 7 | 21 |

**REGULAR SEASON**

| SEASON | AGE | TEAM | LG | GP | G | A | PTS | PIM |
|---|---|---|---|---|---|---|---|---|
| 1913-14 | 32 | Montreal Canadiens | NHA | 15 | 10 | 9 | 19 | 12 |
| 1914-15 | 33 | Montreal Canadiens | NHA | 2 | 0 | 0 | 0 | 0 |
| Career – 15 Seasons | | | | 174 | 95 | 21 | 116 | 452 |

**PLAYOFFS**

| SEASON | AGE | TEAM | LG | GP | G | A | PTS | PIM |
|---|---|---|---|---|---|---|---|---|
| 1901-02 | 20 | Montreal AAA | St-Cup | 3 | 0 | 0 | 0 | 12 |
| 1902-03 | 21 | Montreal AAA | St-Cup | 2 | 1 | 0 | 1 | 6 |
| 1903-04 | 22 | Montreal Wanderers | St-Cup | 1 | 1 | 0 | 1 | 0 |
| 1908-09 | 27 | Montreal Wanderers | NHA | 2 | 0 | 0 | 0 | 13 |
| 1909-10 | 28 | Montreal Wanderers | NHA | 1 | 3 | 0 | 3 | 9 |
| 1909-10 | 28 | Montreal Wanderers | St-Cup | 1 | 0 | 0 | 0 | 6 |
| Career – 5 Seasons | | | | 10 | 5 | 0 | 5 | 46 |

# Clark Gillies  Profile: See page 29

**REGULAR SEASON**

| SEASON | AGE | TEAM | LG | GP | G | A | PTS | +/- | PIM | ESG | PPG | SHG | GWG | SOG | S% |
|---|---|---|---|---|---|---|---|---|---|---|---|---|---|---|---|
| 1974-75 | 20 | New York Islanders | NHL | 80 | 25 | 22 | 47 | -4 | 66 | 17 | 8 | 0 | 4 | 165 | 15.2 |
| 1975-76 | 21 | New York Islanders | NHL | 80 | 34 | 27 | 61 | 20 | 96 | 19 | 15 | 0 | 6 | 210 | 16.2 |
| 1976-77 | 22 | New York Islanders | NHL | 70 | 33 | 22 | 55 | 18 | 93 | 21 | 12 | 0 | 5 | 215 | 15.4 |
| 1977-78 | 23 | New York Islanders | NHL | 80 | 35 | 50 | 85 | 49 | 76 | 26 | 9 | 0 | 2 | 277 | 12.6 |
| 1978-79 | 24 | New York Islanders | NHL | 75 | 35 | 56 | 91 | 57 | 68 | 24 | 11 | 0 | 5 | 210 | 16.7 |
| 1979-80 | 25 | New York Islanders | NHL | 73 | 19 | 35 | 54 | 29 | 49 | 12 | 7 | 0 | 5 | 175 | 10.9 |
| 1980-81 | 26 | New York Islanders | NHL | 80 | 33 | 45 | 78 | 27 | 99 | 24 | 9 | 0 | 3 | 188 | 17.6 |
| 1981-82 | 27 | New York Islanders | NHL | 79 | 38 | 39 | 77 | 39 | 75 | 30 | 8 | 0 | 5 | 200 | 19.0 |
| 1982-83 | 28 | New York Islanders | NHL | 70 | 21 | 20 | 41 | 10 | 76 | 17 | 4 | 0 | 2 | 148 | 14.2 |
| 1983-84 | 29 | New York Islanders | NHL | 76 | 12 | 16 | 28 | 6 | 65 | 9 | 3 | 0 | 2 | 137 | 8.8 |
| 1984-85 | 30 | New York Islanders | NHL | 54 | 15 | 17 | 32 | 1 | 73 | 10 | 5 | 0 | 2 | 125 | 12.0 |
| 1985-86 | 31 | New York Islanders | NHL | 55 | 4 | 10 | 14 | -8 | 55 | 3 | 1 | 0 | 0 | 74 | 5.4 |
| 1986-87 | 32 | Buffalo Sabres | NHL | 61 | 10 | 17 | 27 | 0 | 83 | 9 | 1 | 0 | 2 | 106 | 9.4 |
| 1987-88 | 33 | Buffalo Sabres | NHL | 25 | 5 | 2 | 7 | 1 | 51 | 5 | 0 | 0 | 1 | 23 | 21.7 |
| NHL Career – 14 Seasons | | | | 958 | 319 | 378 | 697 | 245 | 1025 | 226 | 93 | 0 | 44 | 2253 | 14.2 |

**PLAYOFFS**

| SEASON | AGE | TEAM | LG | GP | G | A | PTS | +/- | PIM | ESG | PPG | SHG | GWG | SOG | S% |
|---|---|---|---|---|---|---|---|---|---|---|---|---|---|---|---|
| 1974-75 | 20 | New York Islanders | NHL | 17 | 4 | 2 | 6 | -2 | 36 | 4 | 0 | 0 | 2 | 29 | 13.8 |
| 1975-76 | 21 | New York Islanders | NHL | 13 | 2 | 4 | 6 | -1 | 16 | 2 | 0 | 0 | 1 | 27 | 7.4 |
| 1976-77 | 22 | New York Islanders | NHL | 12 | 4 | 4 | 8 | 5 | 15 | 4 | 0 | 0 | 4 | 34 | 11.8 |
| 1977-78 | 23 | New York Islanders | NHL | 7 | 2 | 0 | 2 | 1 | 15 | 1 | 1 | 0 | 0 | 21 | 9.5 |
| 1978-79 | 24 | New York Islanders | NHL | 10 | 1 | 2 | 3 | 2 | 11 | 1 | 0 | 0 | 0 | 20 | 5.0 |
| 1979-80 | 25 | New York Islanders | NHL | 21 | 6 | 10 | 16 | 6 | 63 | 5 | 1 | 0 | 2 | 41 | 14.6 |
| 1980-81 | 26 | New York Islanders | NHL | 18 | 6 | 9 | 15 | 7 | 28 | 3 | 3 | 0 | 0 | 50 | 12.0 |
| 1981-82 | 27 | New York Islanders | NHL | 19 | 8 | 6 | 14 | 5 | 34 | 4 | 4 | 0 | 3 | 51 | 15.7 |
| 1982-83 | 28 | New York Islanders | NHL | 8 | 0 | 2 | 2 | -2 | 10 | 0 | 0 | 0 | 0 | 8 | 0.0 |
| 1983-84 | 29 | New York Islanders | NHL | 21 | 12 | 7 | 19 | 2 | 19 | 9 | 3 | 0 | 0 | 41 | 29.3 |
| 1984-85 | 30 | New York Islanders | NHL | 10 | 1 | 0 | 1 | 0 | 9 | 1 | 0 | 0 | 0 | 13 | 7.7 |
| 1985-86 | 31 | New York Islanders | NHL | 3 | 1 | 0 | 1 | -2 | 6 | 1 | 0 | 0 | 0 | 7 | 14.3 |
| 1987-88 | 33 | Buffalo Sabres | NHL | 5 | 0 | 1 | 1 | -3 | 25 | 0 | 0 | 0 | 0 | 5 | 0.0 |
| NHL Career – 13 Seasons | | | | 164 | 47 | 47 | 94 | 18 | 287 | 35 | 12 | 0 | 12 | 347 | 13.5 |

# Moose Goheen  Profile: See page 30

**REGULAR SEASON**

| SEASON | AGE | TEAM | LG | GP | G | A | PTS | PIM |
|---|---|---|---|---|---|---|---|---|
| 1922-23 | 28 | St. Paul Saints | USAHA | 20 | 11 | 0 | 11 | |
| 1923-24 | 29 | St. Paul Saints | USAHA | 20 | 10 | 4 | 14 | |
| 1924-25 | 30 | St. Paul Saints | USAHA | 32 | 6 | 0 | 6 | |
| 1925-26 | 31 | St. Paul Saints | CHL | 36 | 13 | 10 | 23 | 87 |
| 1926-27 | 32 | St. Paul Saints | AHA | 27 | 2 | 7 | 9 | 40 |
| 1927-28 | 33 | St. Paul Saints | AHA | 39 | 19 | 5 | 24 | 96 |
| 1928-29 | 34 | St. Paul Saints | AHA | 28 | 7 | 4 | 11 | 39 |
| 1929-30 | 35 | St. Paul Saints | AHA | 35 | 9 | 6 | 15 | 47 |
| 1930-31 | 36 | Buffalo Majors | AHA | 2 | 0 | 0 | 0 | |
| 1931-32 | 37 | St. Paul Saints | CHL | 20 | 2 | 7 | 9 | 17 |
| Career – 10 Seasons | | | | 259 | 79 | 43 | 122 | 326 |

**PLAYOFFS**

| SEASON | AGE | TEAM | LG | GP | G | A | PTS | PIM |
|---|---|---|---|---|---|---|---|---|
| 1922-23 | 28 | St. Paul Saints | USAHA | 4 | 3 | 0 | 3 | |
| 1923-24 | 29 | St. Paul Saints | USAHA | 8 | 1 | 3 | 4 | |
| 1928-29 | 34 | St. Paul Saints | AHA | 8 | 2 | 0 | 2 | 20 |
| Career – 3 Seasons | | | | 20 | 6 | 3 | 9 | 20 |

## Michel Goulet  Profile: See page 31

**REGULAR SEASON**

| SEASON | AGE | TEAM | LG | GP | G | A | PTS | +/- | PIM | ESG | PPG | SHG | GWG | SOG | S% |
|--------|-----|------|----|----|----|----|-----|-----|-----|-----|-----|-----|-----|-----|-----|
| 1978–79 | 18 | Birmingham Bulls | WHA | 78 | 28 | 30 | 58 | 13 | 65 | 25 | 3 | 0 | | 146 | 19.2 |
| 1979–80 | 19 | Quebec Nordiques | NHL | 77 | 22 | 32 | 54 | -10 | 48 | 17 | 5 | 0 | 1 | 167 | 13.2 |
| 1980–81 | 20 | Quebec Nordiques | NHL | 76 | 32 | 39 | 71 | 0 | 45 | 27 | 3 | 2 | 3 | 265 | 12.1 |
| 1981–82 | 21 | Quebec Nordiques | NHL | 80 | 42 | 42 | 84 | 35 | 48 | 28 | 8 | 6 | 3 | 250 | 16.8 |
| 1982–83 | 22 | Quebec Nordiques | NHL | 80 | 57 | 48 | 105 | 30 | 51 | 43 | 10 | 4 | 4 | 256 | 22.3 |
| 1983–84 | 23 | Quebec Nordiques | NHL | 75 | 56 | 65 | 121 | 66 | 76 | 43 | 11 | 2 | 16 | 239 | 23.4 |
| 1984–85 | 24 | Quebec Nordiques | NHL | 69 | 55 | 40 | 95 | 10 | 55 | 38 | 17 | 0 | 5 | 260 | 21.2 |
| 1985–86 | 25 | Quebec Nordiques | NHL | 75 | 53 | 51 | 104 | 7 | 64 | 25 | 28 | 0 | 3 | 244 | 21.7 |
| 1986–87 | 26 | Quebec Nordiques | NHL | 75 | 49 | 47 | 96 | -10 | 61 | 32 | 17 | 0 | 6 | 276 | 17.8 |
| 1987–88 | 27 | Quebec Nordiques | NHL | 80 | 48 | 58 | 106 | -31 | 56 | 18 | 29 | 1 | 4 | 284 | 16.9 |
| 1988–89 | 28 | Quebec Nordiques | NHL | 69 | 26 | 38 | 64 | -20 | 67 | 15 | 11 | 0 | 2 | 162 | 16.0 |
| 1989–90 | 29 | Quebec Nordiques | NHL | 57 | 16 | 29 | 45 | -33 | 42 | 8 | 8 | 0 | 0 | 144 | 11.1 |
| 1989–90 | 29 | Chicago Blackhawks | NHL | 8 | 4 | 1 | 5 | 1 | 9 | 2 | 1 | 1 | 0 | 10 | 40.0 |
| 1990–91 | 30 | Chicago Blackhawks | NHL | 74 | 27 | 38 | 65 | 27 | 65 | 18 | 9 | 0 | 1 | 167 | 16.2 |
| 1991–92 | 31 | Chicago Blackhawks | NHL | 75 | 22 | 41 | 63 | 20 | 69 | 13 | 9 | 0 | 4 | 176 | 12.5 |
| 1992–93 | 32 | Chicago Blackhawks | NHL | 63 | 23 | 21 | 44 | 10 | 43 | 13 | 10 | 0 | 5 | 125 | 18.4 |
| 1993–94 | 33 | Chicago Blackhawks | NHL | 56 | 16 | 14 | 30 | 1 | 26 | 13 | 3 | 0 | 6 | 120 | 13.3 |
| Career — 16 Seasons | | | | 1167 | 576 | 635 | 1210 | 112 | 890 | 378 | 182 | 16 | 63 | 3291 | 17.5 |

**PLAYOFFS**

| SEASON | AGE | TEAM | LG | GP | G | A | PTS | +/- | PIM | ESG | PPG | SHG | GWG | SOG | S% |
|--------|-----|------|----|----|----|----|-----|-----|-----|-----|-----|-----|-----|-----|-----|
| 1980–81 | 20 | Quebec Nordiques | NHL | 4 | 3 | 4 | 7 | 1 | 7 | 3 | 0 | 0 | 1 | 16 | 18.8 |
| 1981–82 | 21 | Quebec Nordiques | NHL | 16 | 8 | 5 | 13 | -7 | 6 | 4 | 2 | 2 | 0 | 55 | 14.6 |
| 1982–83 | 22 | Quebec Nordiques | NHL | 4 | 0 | 0 | 0 | -2 | 6 | 0 | 0 | 0 | 0 | 10 | 0.0 |
| 1983–84 | 23 | Quebec Nordiques | NHL | 9 | 2 | 4 | 6 | 0 | 17 | 2 | 0 | 0 | 0 | 17 | 11.8 |
| 1984–85 | 24 | Quebec Nordiques | NHL | 17 | 11 | 10 | 21 | 0 | 17 | 4 | 7 | 0 | 0 | 51 | 21.6 |
| 1985–86 | 25 | Quebec Nordiques | NHL | 3 | 1 | 2 | 3 | -2 | 10 | 0 | 1 | 0 | 0 | 12 | 8.3 |
| 1986–87 | 26 | Quebec Nordiques | NHL | 13 | 9 | 5 | 14 | -2 | 35 | 5 | 4 | 0 | 1 | 40 | 22.5 |
| 1989–90 | 29 | Chicago Blackhawks | NHL | 14 | 2 | 4 | 6 | 2 | 6 | 2 | 0 | 0 | 0 | 18 | 11.1 |
| 1991–92 | 31 | Chicago Blackhawks | NHL | 9 | 3 | 4 | 7 | 4 | 6 | 3 | 0 | 0 | 1 | 19 | 15.8 |
| 1992–93 | 32 | Chicago Blackhawks | NHL | 3 | 0 | 1 | 1 | -1 | 0 | 0 | 0 | 0 | 0 | 1 | 0.0 |
| Career — 10 Seasons | | | | 92 | 39 | 39 | 78 | -7 | 110 | 23 | 14 | 2 | 3 | 239 | 16.3 |

## Danielle Goyette  Profile: See page 32

**REGULAR SEASON**

| SEASON | AGE | TEAM | LG | GP | G | A | PTS | +/- | PIM |
|--------|-----|------|----|----|----|----|-----|-----|-----|
| 1991–92 | 25 | Canadian National Team | | 5 | 3 | 7 | 10 | 2 | |
| 1993–94 | 27 | Canadian National Team | | 5 | 9 | 3 | 12 | 0 | 14 |
| 1996–97 | 30 | Canadian National Team | | 5 | 2 | 1 | 3 | 2 | |
| 1997–98 | 31 | Canadian National Team | | 6 | 8 | 1 | 9 | 10 | 10 |
| 1998–99 | 32 | Canadian National Team | | 5 | 3 | 2 | 5 | 2 | 5 |
| 1999–00 | 33 | Canadian National Team | | 5 | 6 | 1 | 7 | 0 | 9 |
| 2000–01 | 34 | Canadian National Team | | 5 | 4 | 5 | 9 | 0 | 8 |
| 2001–02 | 35 | Canadian National Team | | 5 | 3 | 7 | 10 | 0 | 7 |
| 2003–04 | 37 | Canadian National Team | | 5 | 2 | 5 | 7 | 6 | 7 |
| 2004–05 | 38 | Canadian National Team | | 5 | 2 | 2 | 4 | 4 | 9 |
| 2005–06 | 39 | Canadian National Team | | 5 | 4 | 2 | 6 | 6 | 4 |
| 2006–07 | 40 | Canadian National Team | | 5 | 6 | 5 | 11 | 0 | 10 |
| Career — 12 Seasons | | | | 61 | 52 | 41 | 93 | 32 | 83 |

## George Hay  Profile: See page 34

**REGULAR SEASON**

| SEASON | AGE | TEAM | LG | GP | G | A | PTS | PIM |
|--------|-----|------|----|----|----|----|-----|-----|
| 1921–22 | 24 | Regina Capitals | WCHL | 25 | 21 | 11 | 32 | 9 |
| 1922–23 | 25 | Regina Capitals | WCHL | 30 | 28 | 8 | 36 | 12 |
| 1923–24 | 26 | Regina Capitals | WCHL | 25 | 20 | 11 | 31 | 8 |
| 1924–25 | 27 | Regina Capitals | WCHL | 20 | 16 | 6 | 22 | 6 |
| 1925–26 | 28 | Portland Rosebuds | WHL | 30 | 19 | 12 | 31 | 4 |
| 1926–27 | 29 | Chicago Black Hawks | NHL | 35 | 14 | 10 | 24 | 12 |
| 1927–28 | 30 | Detroit Cougars | NHL | 42 | 22 | 13 | 35 | 22 |
| 1928–29 | 31 | Detroit Cougars | NHL | 41 | 11 | 8 | 19 | 14 |
| 1920–30 | 32 | Detroit Cougars | NHL | 44 | 18 | 15 | 33 | 8 |
| 1930–31 | 33 | Detroit Falcons | NHL | 44 | 8 | 10 | 18 | 22 |
| 1932–33 | 35 | Detroit Red Wings | NHL | 34 | 1 | 6 | 7 | 9 |
| Career — 11 Seasons | | | | 371 | 178 | 110 | 288 | 126 |

**PLAYOFFS**

| SEASON | AGE | TEAM | LG | GP | G | A | PTS | PIM |
|--------|-----|------|----|----|----|----|-----|-----|
| 1921–22 | 24 | Regina Capitals | WCHL | 4 | 0 | 0 | 0 | 4 |
| 1921–22 | 24 | Regina Capitals | West-P | 2 | 0 | 1 | 1 | 0 |
| 1922–23 | 25 | Regina Capitals | WCHL | 2 | 1 | 0 | 1 | 0 |
| 1923–24 | 26 | Regina Capitals | WCHL | 2 | 1 | 1 | 2 | 0 |
| 1926–27 | 29 | Chicago Black Hawks | NHL | 2 | 1 | 0 | 1 | 2 |
| 1928–29 | 31 | Detroit Cougars | NHL | 2 | 1 | 0 | 1 | 0 |
| 1932–33 | 35 | Detroit Red Wings | NHL | 4 | 0 | 1 | 1 | 0 |
| Career — 7 Seasons | | | | 18 | 4 | 3 | 7 | 6 |

# Syd Howe  Profile: See page 35

### REGULAR SEASON

| SEASON | AGE | TEAM | LG | GP | G | A | PTS | PIM |
|---|---|---|---|---|---|---|---|---|
| 1929–30 | 18 | Ottawa Senators | NHL | 12 | 1 | 1 | 2 | 0 |
| 1930–31 | 19 | Philadelphia Quakers | NHL | 44 | 9 | 11 | 20 | 22 |
| 1931–32 | 20 | Toronto Maple Leafs | NHL | 3 | 0 | 0 | 0 | 0 |
| 1932–33 | 21 | Ottawa Senators | NHL | 48 | 12 | 12 | 24 | 17 |
| 1933–34 | 22 | Ottawa Senators | NHL | 42 | 13 | 7 | 20 | 18 |
| 1934–35 | 23 | St. Louis Eagles | NHL | 36 | 14 | 13 | 27 | 23 |
| 1934–35 | 23 | Detroit Red Wings | NHL | 14 | 8 | 12 | 20 | 11 |
| 1935–36 | 24 | Detroit Red Wings | NHL | 48 | 16 | 14 | 30 | 26 |
| 1936–37 | 25 | Detroit Red Wings | NHL | 45 | 17 | 10 | 27 | 10 |
| 1937–38 | 26 | Detroit Red Wings | NHL | 48 | 8 | 19 | 27 | 14 |
| 1938–39 | 27 | Detroit Red Wings | NHL | 48 | 16 | 21 | 37 | 11 |
| 1939–40 | 28 | Detroit Red Wings | NHL | 46 | 14 | 23 | 37 | 17 |
| 1940–41 | 29 | Detroit Red Wings | NHL | 48 | 20 | 24 | 44 | 8 |
| 1941–42 | 30 | Detroit Red Wings | NHL | 48 | 16 | 19 | 35 | 6 |
| 1942–43 | 31 | Detroit Red Wings | NHL | 50 | 20 | 35 | 55 | 10 |
| 1943–44 | 32 | Detroit Red Wings | NHL | 46 | 32 | 28 | 60 | 6 |

### REGULAR SEASON

| SEASON | AGE | TEAM | LG | GP | G | A | PTS | PIM |
|---|---|---|---|---|---|---|---|---|
| 1944–45 | 33 | Detroit Red Wings | NHL | 48 | 17 | 36 | 53 | 6 |
| 1945–46 | 34 | Detroit Red Wings | NHL | 26 | 4 | 7 | 11 | 9 |
| NHL Career — 17 Seasons | | | | 700 | 237 | 292 | 529 | 214 |

### PLAYOFFS

| SEASON | AGE | TEAM | LG | GP | G | A | PTS | PIM |
|---|---|---|---|---|---|---|---|---|
| 1929–30 | 18 | Ottawa Senators | NHL | 2 | 0 | 0 | 0 | 0 |
| 1935–36 | 24 | Detroit Red Wings | NHL | 7 | 3 | 3 | 6 | 2 |
| 1936–37 | 25 | Detroit Red Wings | NHL | 10 | 2 | 5 | 7 | 0 |
| 1938–39 | 27 | Detroit Red Wings | NHL | 6 | 3 | 1 | 4 | 4 |
| 1939–40 | 28 | Detroit Red Wings | NHL | 5 | 2 | 2 | 4 | 2 |
| 1940–41 | 29 | Detroit Red Wings | NHL | 9 | 1 | 7 | 8 | 0 |
| 1941–42 | 30 | Detroit Red Wings | NHL | 12 | 3 | 5 | 8 | 0 |
| 1942–43 | 31 | Detroit Red Wings | NHL | 7 | 1 | 2 | 3 | 0 |
| 1943–44 | 32 | Detroit Red Wings | NHL | 5 | 2 | 2 | 4 | 0 |
| 1944–45 | 33 | Detroit Red Wings | NHL | 7 | 0 | 0 | 0 | 2 |
| NHL Career — 10 Seasons | | | | 70 | 17 | 27 | 44 | 10 |

# Bobby Hull  Profile: See page 36

### REGULAR SEASON

| SEASON | AGE | TEAM | LG | GP | G | A | PTS | +/- | PIM | ESG | PPG | SHG | GWG | SOG | S% |
|---|---|---|---|---|---|---|---|---|---|---|---|---|---|---|---|
| 1957–58 | 19 | Chicago Black Hawks | NHL | 70 | 13 | 34 | 47 | | 60 | 10 | 3 | 0 | 1 | | |
| 1958–59 | 20 | Chicago Black Hawks | NHL | 70 | 18 | 32 | 50 | | 52 | 15 | 2 | 1 | 5 | | |
| 1959–60 | 21 | Chicago Black Hawks | NHL | 70 | 39 | 42 | 81 | 27 | 68 | 33 | 6 | 0 | 8 | 319 | 12.2 |
| 1960–61 | 22 | Chicago Black Hawks | NHL | 67 | 31 | 25 | 56 | 5 | 43 | 26 | 5 | 0 | 5 | 309 | 10.0 |
| 1961–62 | 23 | Chicago Black Hawks | NHL | 70 | 50 | 34 | 84 | 10 | 35 | 41 | 9 | 0 | 7 | 375 | 13.3 |
| 1962–63 | 24 | Chicago Black Hawks | NHL | 65 | 31 | 31 | 62 | 0 | 27 | 23 | 8 | 0 | 7 | 305 | 10.2 |
| 1963–64 | 25 | Chicago Black Hawks | NHL | 70 | 43 | 44 | 87 | 14 | 48 | 27 | 12 | 4 | 5 | 408 | 10.5 |
| 1964–65 | 26 | Chicago Black Hawks | NHL | 61 | 39 | 32 | 71 | 23 | 32 | 27 | 10 | 2 | 5 | 368 | 10.6 |
| 1965–66 | 27 | Chicago Black Hawks | NHL | 65 | 54 | 43 | 97 | 19 | 66 | 31 | 22 | 1 | 7 | 351 | 15.4 |
| 1966–67 | 28 | Chicago Black Hawks | NHL | 66 | 52 | 28 | 80 | 28 | 52 | 32 | 18 | 2 | 3 | 320 | 16.3 |
| 1967–68 | 29 | Chicago Black Hawks | NHL | 71 | 44 | 31 | 75 | 13 | 39 | 34 | 8 | 2 | 6 | 367 | 12.0 |
| 1968–69 | 30 | Chicago Black Hawks | NHL | 74 | 58 | 49 | 107 | 12 | 48 | 36 | 20 | 2 | 11 | 414 | 14.0 |
| 1969–70 | 31 | Chicago Black Hawks | NHL | 61 | 38 | 29 | 67 | 20 | 8 | 26 | 10 | 2 | 8 | 289 | 13.1 |
| 1970–71 | 32 | Chicago Black Hawks | NHL | 78 | 44 | 52 | 96 | 35 | 32 | 33 | 11 | 0 | 11 | 378 | 11.6 |
| 1971–72 | 33 | Chicago Black Hawks | NHL | 78 | 50 | 43 | 93 | 53 | 24 | 39 | 8 | 3 | 9 | 337 | 14.9 |
| 1972–73 | 34 | Winnipeg Jets | WHA | 63 | 51 | 52 | 103 | | 37 | 35 | 14 | 2 | 7 | | |
| 1973–74 | 35 | Winnipeg Jets | WHA | 75 | 53 | 42 | 95 | | 38 | 43 | 9 | 1 | 9 | | |
| 1974–75 | 36 | Winnipeg Jets | WHA | 78 | 77 | 65 | 142 | 55 | 41 | 50 | 27 | 0 | | 556 | 13.8 |
| 1975–76 | 37 | Winnipeg Jets | WHA | 80 | 53 | 70 | 123 | 62 | 30 | 39 | 14 | 0 | 10 | 416 | 12.7 |
| 1976–77 | 38 | Winnipeg Jets | WHA | 34 | 21 | 32 | 53 | 16 | 14 | 14 | 7 | 0 | | 102 | 20.6 |
| 1977–78 | 39 | Winnipeg Jets | WHA | 77 | 46 | 71 | 117 | 55 | 23 | 36 | 10 | 0 | | 257 | 17.9 |
| 1978–79 | 40 | Winnipeg Jets | WHA | 4 | 2 | 3 | 5 | 1 | 0 | 1 | 1 | 0 | | 12 | 16.7 |
| 1979–80 | 41 | Winnipeg Jets | NHL | 18 | 4 | 6 | 10 | -7 | 0 | 3 | 1 | 0 | 0 | 25 | 16.0 |
| 1979–80 | 41 | Hartford Whalers | NHL | 9 | 2 | 5 | 7 | -3 | 0 | 1 | 1 | 0 | 0 | 13 | 15.4 |
| Career — 23 Seasons | | | | 1474 | 913 | 895 | 1808 | 438 | 817 | 655 | 236 | 22 | 91 | 5920 | 15.4 |

### PLAYOFFS

| SEASON | AGE | TEAM | LG | GP | G | A | PTS | +/- | PIM | ESG | PPG | SHG | GWG | SOG | S% |
|---|---|---|---|---|---|---|---|---|---|---|---|---|---|---|---|
| 1958–59 | 20 | Chicago Black Hawks | NHL | 6 | 1 | 1 | 2 | | 2 | 1 | 0 | 0 | 0 | | |
| 1959–60 | 21 | Chicago Black Hawks | NHL | 3 | 1 | 0 | 1 | -1 | 2 | 1 | 0 | 0 | 0 | 5 | 20.0 |
| 1960–61 | 22 | Chicago Black Hawks | NHL | 12 | 4 | 10 | 14 | 10 | 4 | 2 | 2 | 0 | 1 | 48 | 8.3 |
| 1961–62 | 23 | Chicago Black Hawks | NHL | 12 | 8 | 6 | 14 | -3 | 12 | 4 | 4 | 0 | 0 | 77 | 10.4 |
| 1962–63 | 24 | Chicago Black Hawks | NHL | 5 | 8 | 2 | 10 | -2 | 4 | 5 | 3 | 0 | 0 | 28 | 28.6 |
| 1963–64 | 25 | Chicago Black Hawks | NHL | 7 | 2 | 5 | 7 | 0 | 2 | 1 | 1 | 0 | 0 | 34 | 5.9 |
| 1964–65 | 26 | Chicago Black Hawks | NHL | 14 | 10 | 7 | 17 | 4 | 27 | 6 | 4 | 0 | 2 | 58 | 17.2 |
| 1965–66 | 27 | Chicago Black Hawks | NHL | 6 | 2 | 2 | 4 | -3 | 10 | 1 | 1 | 0 | 1 | 24 | 8.3 |
| 1966–67 | 28 | Chicago Black Hawks | NHL | 6 | 4 | 2 | 6 | 1 | 0 | 2 | 2 | 0 | 2 | 40 | 10.0 |
| 1967–68 | 29 | Chicago Black Hawks | NHL | 11 | 4 | 6 | 10 | 2 | 15 | 2 | 1 | 1 | 1 | 53 | 7.5 |
| 1969–70 | 31 | Chicago Black Hawks | NHL | 8 | 3 | 8 | 11 | 2 | 2 | 3 | 0 | 0 | 0 | 26 | 11.5 |
| 1970–71 | 32 | Chicago Black Hawks | NHL | 18 | 11 | 14 | 25 | 9 | 16 | 5 | 6 | 0 | 4 | 92 | 12.0 |
| 1971–72 | 33 | Chicago Black Hawks | NHL | 8 | 4 | 4 | 8 | 2 | 6 | 3 | 0 | 1 | 0 | 43 | 9.3 |
| 1972–73 | 34 | Winnipeg Jets | WHA | 14 | 9 | 16 | 25 | | 16 | 7 | 2 | 0 | 3 | | |
| 1973–74 | 35 | Winnipeg Jets | WHA | 4 | 1 | 1 | 2 | | 4 | | | 0 | 0 | | |
| 1975–76 | 36 | Winnipeg Jets | WHA | 13 | 12 | 8 | 20 | 15 | 4 | | | 0 | | | |
| 1976–77 | 37 | Winnipeg Jets | WHA | 20 | 13 | 9 | 22 | 6 | 2 | | | 0 | 2 | | |
| 1977–78 | 38 | Winnipeg Jets | WHA | 9 | 8 | 3 | 11 | 5 | 12 | | | 0 | 2 | | |
| 1979–80 | 41 | Hartford Whalers | NHL | 3 | 0 | 0 | 0 | -5 | 0 | 0 | 0 | 0 | 0 | 3 | 0.0 |
| Career — 19 Seasons | | | | 179 | 105 | 104 | 209 | 42 | 140 | 43 | 26 | 2 | 19 | 531 | 11.5 |

# Busher Jackson  Profile: See page 38

**REGULAR SEASON**

| SEASON | AGE | TEAM | LG | GP | G | A | PTS | PIM |
|---|---|---|---|---|---|---|---|---|
| 1929–30 | 19 | Toronto Maple Leafs | NHL | 31 | 12 | 6 | 18 | 31 |
| 1930–31 | 20 | Toronto Maple Leafs | NHL | 43 | 18 | 13 | 31 | 92 |
| 1931–32 | 21 | Toronto Maple Leafs | NHL | 48 | 28 | 25 | 53 | 63 |
| 1932–33 | 22 | Toronto Maple Leafs | NHL | 48 | 27 | 17 | 44 | 43 |
| 1933–34 | 23 | Toronto Maple Leafs | NHL | 38 | 20 | 18 | 38 | 38 |
| 1934–35 | 24 | Toronto Maple Leafs | NHL | 42 | 22 | 22 | 44 | 27 |
| 1935–36 | 25 | Toronto Maple Leafs | NHL | 47 | 11 | 11 | 22 | 19 |
| 1936–37 | 26 | Toronto Maple Leafs | NHL | 46 | 21 | 19 | 40 | 12 |
| 1937–38 | 27 | Toronto Maple Leafs | NHL | 48 | 17 | 17 | 34 | 18 |
| 1938–39 | 28 | Toronto Maple Leafs | NHL | 42 | 10 | 17 | 27 | 12 |
| 1939–40 | 29 | New York Americans | NHL | 43 | 12 | 8 | 20 | 10 |
| 1940–41 | 30 | New York Americans | NHL | 46 | 8 | 18 | 26 | 4 |
| 1941–42 | 31 | Boston Bruins | NHL | 26 | 5 | 7 | 12 | 18 |
| 1942–43 | 32 | Boston Bruins | NHL | 44 | 19 | 15 | 34 | 38 |
| 1943–44 | 33 | Boston Bruins | NHL | 42 | 11 | 21 | 32 | 25 |
| NHL Career — 15 Seasons | | | | 634 | 241 | 234 | 475 | 450 |

**PLAYOFFS**

| SEASON | AGE | TEAM | LG | GP | G | A | PTS | PIM |
|---|---|---|---|---|---|---|---|---|
| 1930–31 | 20 | Toronto Maple Leafs | NHL | 2 | 0 | 0 | 0 | 2 |
| 1931–32 | 21 | Toronto Maple Leafs | NHL | 7 | 5 | 2 | 7 | 13 |
| 1932–33 | 22 | Toronto Maple Leafs | NHL | 9 | 3 | 1 | 4 | 2 |
| 1933–34 | 23 | Toronto Maple Leafs | NHL | 5 | 1 | 0 | 1 | 8 |
| 1934–35 | 24 | Toronto Maple Leafs | NHL | 7 | 3 | 2 | 5 | 4 |
| 1935–36 | 25 | Toronto Maple Leafs | NHL | 9 | 3 | 2 | 5 | 4 |
| 1936–37 | 26 | Toronto Maple Leafs | NHL | 2 | 1 | 0 | 1 | 2 |
| 1937–38 | 27 | Toronto Maple Leafs | NHL | 6 | 1 | 0 | 1 | 8 |
| 1938–39 | 28 | Toronto Maple Leafs | NHL | 8 | 0 | 1 | 1 | 2 |
| 1939–40 | 29 | New York Americans | NHL | 3 | 0 | 1 | 1 | 2 |
| 1941–42 | 31 | Boston Bruins | NHL | 5 | 0 | 1 | 1 | 0 |
| 1942–43 | 32 | Boston Bruins | NHL | 9 | 1 | 2 | 3 | 10 |
| NHL Career — 12 Seasons | | | | 72 | 18 | 12 | 30 | 57 |

# Aurèle Joliat  Profile: See page 40

**REGULAR SEASON**

| SEASON | AGE | TEAM | LG | GP | G | A | PTS | PIM |
|---|---|---|---|---|---|---|---|---|
| 1922–23 | 21 | Montreal Canadiens | NHL | 24 | 13 | 10 | 23 | 31 |
| 1923–24 | 22 | Montreal Canadiens | NHL | 24 | 15 | 6 | 21 | 27 |
| 1924–25 | 23 | Montreal Canadiens | NHL | 25 | 30 | 12 | 42 | 81 |
| 1925–26 | 24 | Montreal Canadiens | NHL | 35 | 17 | 9 | 26 | 62 |
| 1926–27 | 25 | Montreal Canadiens | NHL | 43 | 14 | 4 | 18 | 79 |
| 1927–28 | 26 | Montreal Canadiens | NHL | 44 | 28 | 11 | 39 | 103 |
| 1928–29 | 27 | Montreal Canadiens | NHL | 44 | 12 | 5 | 17 | 59 |
| 1929–30 | 28 | Montreal Canadiens | NHL | 42 | 19 | 13 | 32 | 40 |
| 1930–31 | 29 | Montreal Canadiens | NHL | 43 | 13 | 22 | 35 | 73 |
| 1931–32 | 30 | Montreal Canadiens | NHL | 48 | 15 | 24 | 39 | 48 |
| 1932–33 | 31 | Montreal Canadiens | NHL | 48 | 17 | 21 | 38 | 53 |
| 1933–34 | 32 | Montreal Canadiens | NHL | 48 | 21 | 15 | 26 | 27 |
| 1934–35 | 33 | Montreal Canadiens | NHL | 48 | 17 | 12 | 29 | 18 |
| 1935–36 | 34 | Montreal Canadiens | NHL | 48 | 15 | 8 | 23 | 16 |
| 1936–37 | 35 | Montreal Canadiens | NHL | 47 | 17 | 15 | 32 | 30 |
| 1937–38 | 36 | Montreal Canadiens | NHL | 44 | 6 | 7 | 13 | 24 |
| Career — 16 Seasons | | | | 655 | 270 | 190 | 460 | 771 |

**PLAYOFFS**

| SEASON | AGE | TEAM | LG | GP | G | A | PTS | PIM |
|---|---|---|---|---|---|---|---|---|
| 1922–23 | 21 | Montreal Canadiens | NHL | 2 | 1 | 0 | 1 | 11 |
| 1923–24 | 22 | Montreal Canadiens | NHL | 2 | 1 | 0 | 1 | 2 |
| 1923–24 | 22 | Montreal Canadiens | St-Cup | 4 | 3 | 1 | 4 | 6 |
| 1924–25 | 23 | Montreal Canadiens | NHL | 1 | 0 | 0 | 0 | 5 |
| 1924–25 | 23 | Montreal Canadiens | St-Cup | 4 | 2 | 0 | 2 | 16 |
| 1926–27 | 25 | Montreal Canadiens | NHL | 4 | 1 | 0 | 1 | 10 |
| 1927–28 | 26 | Montreal Canadiens | NHL | 2 | 0 | 0 | 0 | 4 |
| 1928–29 | 27 | Montreal Canadiens | NHL | 3 | 1 | 1 | 2 | 10 |
| 1929–30 | 28 | Montreal Canadiens | NHL | 6 | 0 | 2 | 2 | 6 |
| 1930–31 | 29 | Montreal Canadiens | NHL | 10 | 0 | 4 | 4 | 12 |
| 1931–32 | 30 | Montreal Canadiens | NHL | 4 | 2 | 0 | 2 | 4 |
| 1932–33 | 31 | Montreal Canadiens | NHL | 2 | 2 | 1 | 3 | 2 |
| 1933–34 | 32 | Montreal Canadiens | NHL | 2 | 0 | 0 | 0 | 6 |
| 1934–35 | 33 | Montreal Canadiens | NHL | 2 | 1 | 0 | 1 | 0 |
| 1936–37 | 35 | Montreal Canadiens | NHL | 5 | 0 | 3 | 3 | 2 |
| Career — 13 Seasons | | | | 53 | 14 | 13 | 27 | 94 |

# Paul Kariya  Profile: See page 41

**REGULAR SEASON**

| SEASON | AGE | TEAM | LG | GP | G | A | PTS | +/- | PIM | ESG | PPG | SHG | GWG | SOG | S% |
|---|---|---|---|---|---|---|---|---|---|---|---|---|---|---|---|
| 1994–95 | 20 | Mighty Ducks of Anaheim | NHL | 47 | 18 | 21 | 39 | -17 | 4 | 10 | 7 | 1 | 3 | 134 | 13.4 |
| 1995–96 | 21 | Mighty Ducks of Anaheim | NHL | 82 | 50 | 58 | 108 | 9 | 20 | 27 | 20 | 3 | 9 | 349 | 14.3 |
| 1996–97 | 22 | Mighty Ducks of Anaheim | NHL | 69 | 44 | 55 | 99 | 36 | 6 | 26 | 15 | 3 | 10 | 340 | 12.9 |
| 1997–98 | 23 | Mighty Ducks of Anaheim | NHL | 22 | 17 | 14 | 31 | 12 | 23 | 14 | 3 | 0 | 2 | 103 | 16.5 |
| 1998–99 | 24 | Mighty Ducks of Anaheim | NHL | 82 | 39 | 62 | 101 | 17 | 40 | 26 | 11 | 2 | 4 | 429 | 9.1 |
| 1999–00 | 25 | Mighty Ducks of Anaheim | NHL | 74 | 42 | 44 | 86 | 22 | 24 | 28 | 11 | 3 | 3 | 324 | 13.0 |
| 2000–01 | 26 | Mighty Ducks of Anaheim | NHL | 66 | 33 | 34 | 67 | -9 | 20 | 12 | 18 | 3 | 3 | 230 | 14.3 |
| 2001–02 | 27 | Mighty Ducks of Anaheim | NHL | 82 | 32 | 25 | 57 | -15 | 28 | 21 | 11 | 0 | 8 | 289 | 11.1 |
| 2002–03 | 28 | Mighty Ducks of Anaheim | NHL | 82 | 25 | 56 | 81 | -3 | 48 | 13 | 11 | 1 | 2 | 257 | 9.7 |
| 2003–04 | 29 | Colorado Avalanche | NHL | 51 | 11 | 25 | 36 | -5 | 22 | 5 | 5 | 1 | 1 | 110 | 10.0 |
| 2005–06 | 31 | Nashville Predators | NHL | 82 | 31 | 54 | 85 | -6 | 40 | 17 | 14 | 0 | 3 | 245 | 12.7 |
| 2006–07 | 32 | Nashville Predators | NHL | 82 | 24 | 52 | 76 | 6 | 36 | 19 | 5 | 0 | 2 | 224 | 10.7 |
| 2007–08 | 33 | St. Louis Blues | NHL | 82 | 16 | 49 | 65 | -10 | 50 | 11 | 5 | 0 | 1 | 223 | 7.2 |
| 2008–09 | 34 | St. Louis Blues | NHL | 11 | 2 | 13 | 15 | 1 | 2 | 2 | 0 | 0 | 0 | 31 | 6.5 |
| 2009–10 | 35 | St. Louis Blues | NHL | 75 | 18 | 25 | 43 | -7 | 36 | 15 | 3 | 0 | 2 | 221 | 8.1 |
| NHL Career — 15 Seasons | | | | 989 | 402 | 587 | 989 | 31 | 399 | 246 | 139 | 17 | 53 | 3509 | 11.5 |

**PLAYOFFS**

| SEASON | AGE | TEAM | LG | GP | G | A | PTS | +/- | PIM | ESG | PPG | SHG | GWG | SOG | S% |
|---|---|---|---|---|---|---|---|---|---|---|---|---|---|---|---|
| 1996–97 | 22 | Mighty Ducks of Anaheim | NHL | 11 | 7 | 6 | 13 | -2 | 4 | 3 | 4 | 0 | 1 | 61 | 11.5 |
| 1998–99 | 24 | Mighty Ducks of Anaheim | NHL | 3 | 1 | 3 | 4 | 0 | 0 | 1 | 0 | 0 | 0 | 11 | 9.1 |
| 2002–03 | 28 | Mighty Ducks of Anaheim | NHL | 21 | 6 | 6 | 12 | 0 | 6 | 6 | 0 | 0 | 1 | 53 | 11.3 |
| 2003–04 | 29 | Colorado Avalanche | NHL | 1 | 0 | 1 | 1 | -1 | 0 | 0 | 0 | 0 | 0 | 2 | 0.0 |
| 2005–06 | 31 | Nashville Predators | NHL | 5 | 2 | 5 | 7 | 0 | 0 | 0 | 2 | 0 | 0 | 12 | 16.7 |
| 2006–07 | 32 | Nashville Predators | NHL | 5 | 0 | 2 | 2 | -4 | 2 | 0 | 0 | 0 | 0 | 10 | 0.0 |
| NHL Career — 6 Seasons | | | | 46 | 16 | 23 | 39 | -7 | 12 | 10 | 6 | 0 | 2 | 149 | 10.7 |

# Valeri Kharlamov   Profile: See page 42

## REGULAR SEASON

| SEASON | AGE | TEAM | LG | GP | G | A | PTS | PIM |
|--------|-----|------|-----|-----|-----|-----|-----|-----|
| 1967–68 | 20 | CSKA Moscow | USSR | 15 | 2 | 3 | 5 | 6 |
| 1968–69 | 21 | CSKA Moscow | USSR | 42 | 37 | 12 | 49 | 24 |
| 1969–70 | 22 | CSKA Moscow | USSR | 33 | 33 | 10 | 43 | 16 |
| 1970–71 | 23 | CSKA Moscow | USSR | 34 | 40 | 12 | 52 | 18 |
| 1971–72 | 24 | CSKA Moscow | USSR | 31 | 24 | 16 | 42 | 22 |
| 1972–73 | 25 | CSKA Moscow | USSR | 27 | 19 | 13 | 32 | 22 |
| 1973–74 | 26 | CSKA Moscow | USSR | 26 | 20 | 10 | 30 | 28 |
| 1974–75 | 27 | CSKA Moscow | USSR | 31 | 15 | 24 | 39 | 35 |
| 1975–76 | 28 | CSKA Moscow | USSR | 34 | 18 | 18 | 36 | 6 |
| 1976–77 | 29 | CSKA Moscow | USSR | 21 | 18 | 8 | 26 | 16 |
| 1977–78 | 30 | CSKA Moscow | USSR | 29 | 18 | 24 | 42 | 35 |
| 1978–79 | 31 | CSKA Moscow | USSR | 41 | 22 | 26 | 48 | 36 |
| 1979–80 | 32 | CSKA Moscow | USSR | 41 | 16 | 22 | 38 | 40 |
| 1980–81 | 33 | CSKA Moscow | USSR | 30 | 9 | 16 | 25 | 14 |
| Career — 14 Seasons | | | | 435 | 291 | 214 | 507 | 318 |

# Herbie Lewis   Profile: See page 44

## REGULAR SEASON

| SEASON | AGE | TEAM | LG | GP | G | A | PTS | PIM |
|--------|-----|------|-----|-----|-----|-----|-----|-----|
| 1928–29 | 22 | Detroit Cougars | NHL | 37 | 9 | 5 | 14 | 33 |
| 1929–30 | 23 | Detroit Cougars | NHL | 44 | 19 | 11 | 30 | 34 |
| 1930–31 | 24 | Detroit Falcons | NHL | 43 | 15 | 6 | 21 | 38 |
| 1931–32 | 25 | Detroit Falcons | NHL | 48 | 5 | 14 | 19 | 23 |
| 1932–33 | 26 | Detroit Red Wings | NHL | 48 | 20 | 14 | 34 | 20 |
| 1933–34 | 27 | Detroit Red Wings | NHL | 43 | 16 | 15 | 31 | 15 |
| 1934–35 | 28 | Detroit Red Wings | NHL | 47 | 16 | 27 | 43 | 26 |
| 1935–36 | 29 | Detroit Red Wings | NHL | 45 | 14 | 23 | 37 | 25 |
| 1936–37 | 30 | Detroit Red Wings | NHL | 45 | 14 | 18 | 32 | 14 |
| 1937–38 | 31 | Detroit Red Wings | NHL | 42 | 13 | 18 | 31 | 12 |
| 1938–39 | 32 | Detroit Red Wings | NHL | 42 | 6 | 10 | 16 | 8 |
| NHL Career — 11 Seasons | | | | 484 | 147 | 161 | 308 | 248 |

## PLAYOFFS

| SEASON | AGE | TEAM | LG | GP | G | A | PTS | PIM |
|--------|-----|------|-----|-----|-----|-----|-----|-----|
| 1931–32 | 25 | Detroit Falcons | NHL | 2 | 0 | 0 | 0 | 0 |
| 1932–33 | 26 | Detroit Red Wings | NHL | 4 | 1 | 0 | 1 | 0 |
| 1933–34 | 27 | Detroit Red Wings | NHL | 9 | 6 | 2 | 7 | 2 |
| 1935–36 | 29 | Detroit Red Wings | NHL | 7 | 2 | 3 | 5 | 0 |
| 1936–37 | 30 | Detroit Red Wings | NHL | 10 | 4 | 3 | 7 | 4 |
| 1938–39 | 32 | Detroit Red Wings | NHL | 6 | 1 | 2 | 3 | 0 |
| NHL Career — 6 Seasons | | | | 38 | 14 | 10 | 24 | 6 |

# Ted Lindsay   Profile: See page 45

## REGULAR SEASON

| SEASON | AGE | TEAM | LG | GP | G | A | PTS | PIM | ESG | PPG | SHG | GWG |
|--------|-----|------|-----|-----|-----|-----|-----|-----|-----|-----|-----|-----|
| 1944–45 | 19 | Detroit Red Wings | NHL | 45 | 17 | 6 | 23 | 43 | 15 | 2 | 0 | 5 |
| 1945–46 | 20 | Detroit Red Wings | NHL | 47 | 7 | 10 | 17 | 14 | 7 | 0 | 0 | 0 |
| 1946–47 | 21 | Detroit Red Wings | NHL | 59 | 27 | 15 | 42 | 57 | 21 | 5 | 1 | 4 |
| 1947–48 | 22 | Detroit Red Wings | NHL | 60 | 33 | 19 | 52 | 95 | 26 | 4 | 3 | 2 |
| 1948–49 | 23 | Detroit Red Wings | NHL | 50 | 26 | 28 | 54 | 97 | 19 | 6 | 1 | 4 |
| 1949–50 | 24 | Detroit Red Wings | NHL | 69 | 23 | 55 | 78 | 141 | 19 | 4 | 0 | 4 |
| 1950–51 | 25 | Detroit Red Wings | NHL | 67 | 24 | 35 | 59 | 110 | 21 | 2 | 1 | 5 |
| 1951–52 | 26 | Detroit Red Wings | NHL | 70 | 30 | 39 | 69 | 123 | 20 | 9 | 1 | 3 |
| 1952–53 | 27 | Detroit Red Wings | NHL | 70 | 32 | 39 | 71 | 111 | 23 | 9 | 0 | 3 |
| 1953–54 | 28 | Detroit Red Wings | NHL | 70 | 26 | 36 | 62 | 110 | 14 | 11 | 1 | 5 |
| 1954–55 | 29 | Detroit Red Wings | NHL | 49 | 19 | 19 | 38 | 85 | 12 | 7 | 0 | 8 |
| 1955–56 | 30 | Detroit Red Wings | NHL | 67 | 23 | 50 | 161 | 13 | 14 | 0 | 4 |
| 1956–57 | 32 | Detroit Red Wings | NHL | 70 | 30 | 55 | 85 | 103 | 23 | 6 | 1 | 4 |
| 1957–58 | 32 | Chicago Black Hawks | NHL | 68 | 15 | 24 | 39 | 110 | 10 | 5 | 0 | 3 |
| 1958–59 | 33 | Chicago Black Hawks | NHL | 70 | 22 | 36 | 58 | 184 | 14 | 8 | 0 | 2 |
| 1959–60 | 34 | Chicago Black Hawks | NHL | 68 | 7 | 19 | 26 | 91 | 7 | 0 | 0 | 1 |
| 1964–65 | 39 | Detroit Red Wings | NHL | 69 | 14 | 14 | 28 | 173 | 13 | 1 | 0 | 1 |
| NHL Career — 17 Seasons | | | | 1068 | 379 | 472 | 851 | 1808 | 277 | 93 | 9 | 58 |

## PLAYOFFS

| SEASON | AGE | TEAM | LG | GP | G | A | PTS | PIM | ESG | PPG | SHG | GWG |
|--------|-----|------|-----|-----|-----|-----|-----|-----|-----|-----|-----|-----|
| 1944–45 | 19 | Detroit Red Wings | NHL | 14 | 2 | 0 | 2 | 6 | 2 | 0 | 0 | 1 |
| 1945–46 | 20 | Detroit Red Wings | NHL | 5 | 0 | 1 | 1 | 4 | 0 | 0 | 0 | 0 |
| 1946–47 | 21 | Detroit Red Wings | NHL | 5 | 2 | 2 | 4 | 10 | 1 | 0 | 0 | 0 |
| 1947–48 | 22 | Detroit Red Wings | NHL | 10 | 3 | 1 | 4 | 6 | 3 | 0 | 0 | 0 |
| 1948–49 | 23 | Detroit Red Wings | NHL | 11 | 2 | 6 | 8 | 29 | 1 | 1 | 0 | 0 |
| 1949–50 | 24 | Detroit Red Wings | NHL | 13 | 4 | 4 | 8 | 16 | 4 | 0 | 0 | 0 |
| 1950–51 | 25 | Detroit Red Wings | NHL | 6 | 0 | 1 | 1 | 8 | 0 | 0 | 0 | 0 |
| 1951–52 | 26 | Detroit Red Wings | NHL | 8 | 5 | 2 | 7 | 8 | 2 | 3 | 0 | 1 |
| 1952–53 | 27 | Detroit Red Wings | NHL | 6 | 4 | 4 | 8 | 6 | 4 | 0 | 0 | 0 |
| 1953–54 | 28 | Detroit Red Wings | NHL | 12 | 4 | 4 | 8 | 14 | 2 | 2 | 0 | 1 |
| 1954–55 | 29 | Detroit Red Wings | NHL | 11 | 7 | 12 | 19 | 12 | 4 | 3 | 0 | 1 |
| 1955–56 | 30 | Detroit Red Wings | NHL | 10 | 6 | 3 | 9 | 22 | 6 | 0 | 0 | 3 |

## Ted Lindsay (continued)

**PLAYOFFS**

| SEASON | AGE | TEAM | LG | GP | G | A | PTS | PIM | ESG | PPG | SHG | GWG |
|--------|-----|------|-----|-----|-----|-----|-----|-----|-----|-----|-----|-----|
| 1956–57 | 31 | Detroit Red Wings | NHL | 5 | 2 | 4 | 6 | 8 | 2 | 0 | 0 | 0 |
| 1958–59 | 33 | Chicago Black Hawks | NHL | 6 | 2 | 4 | 6 | 13 | 1 | 1 | 0 | 0 |
| 1959–60 | 34 | Chicago Black Hawks | NHL | 4 | 1 | 1 | 2 | 0 | 1 | 0 | 0 | 0 |
| 1964–65 | 39 | Detroit Red Wings | NHL | 7 | 3 | 0 | 3 | 34 | 2 | 1 | 0 | 0 |
| NHL Career — 16 Seasons | | | | 133 | 47 | 49 | 96 | 192 | 35 | 12 | 0 | 7 |

## Frank Mahovlich Profile: See page 47

**REGULAR SEASON**

| SEASON | AGE | TEAM | LG | GP | G | A | PTS | +/– | PIM | ESG | PPG | SHG | GWG | SOG | S% |
|--------|-----|------|-----|-----|-----|-----|-----|-----|-----|-----|-----|-----|-----|-----|-----|
| 1956–57 | 19 | Toronto Maple Leafs | NHL | 3 | 1 | 0 | 1 | | 2 | 0 | 1 | 0 | 0 | | |
| 1957–58 | 20 | Toronto Maple Leafs | NHL | 67 | 20 | 16 | 36 | | 67 | 15 | 5 | 0 | 2 | | |
| 1958–59 | 21 | Toronto Maple Leafs | NHL | 63 | 22 | 27 | 49 | | 94 | 16 | 6 | 0 | 3 | | |
| 1959–60 | 22 | Toronto Maple Leafs | NHL | 70 | 18 | 21 | 39 | -2 | 61 | 15 | 3 | 0 | 2 | 200 | 9.0 |
| 1960–61 | 23 | Toronto Maple Leafs | NHL | 70 | 48 | 36 | 84 | 23 | 131 | 41 | 7 | 0 | 10 | 223 | 21.5 |
| 1961–62 | 24 | Toronto Maple Leafs | NHL | 70 | 33 | 38 | 71 | 31 | 87 | 32 | 1 | 0 | 9 | 236 | 14.0 |
| 1962–63 | 25 | Toronto Maple Leafs | NHL | 67 | 36 | 37 | 73 | 22 | 56 | 27 | 9 | 0 | 8 | 239 | 15.1 |
| 1963–64 | 26 | Toronto Maple Leafs | NHL | 70 | 26 | 29 | 55 | 8 | 66 | 20 | 6 | 0 | 4 | 205 | 12.7 |
| 1964–65 | 27 | Toronto Maple Leafs | NHL | 59 | 23 | 28 | 51 | 9 | 76 | 16 | 7 | 0 | 4 | 182 | 12.6 |
| 1965–66 | 28 | Toronto Maple Leafs | NHL | 68 | 32 | 24 | 56 | 3 | 68 | 22 | 10 | 0 | 6 | 245 | 13.1 |
| 1966–67 | 29 | Toronto Maple Leafs | NHL | 63 | 18 | 28 | 46 | 0 | 42 | 14 | 4 | 0 | 3 | 173 | 10.4 |
| 1967–68 | 30 | Toronto Maple Leafs | NHL | 50 | 19 | 17 | 36 | 1 | 30 | 17 | 2 | 0 | 4 | 151 | 12.6 |
| 1967–68 | 30 | Detroit Red Wings | NHL | 13 | 7 | 9 | 16 | 2 | 2 | 7 | 0 | 0 | 1 | 39 | 17.9 |
| 1968–69 | 31 | Detroit Red Wings | NHL | 76 | 49 | 29 | 78 | 44 | 38 | 42 | 7 | 0 | 5 | 293 | 16.7 |
| 1969–70 | 32 | Detroit Red Wings | NHL | 74 | 38 | 32 | 70 | 14 | 59 | 22 | 14 | 1 | 5 | 251 | 15.1 |
| 1970–71 | 33 | Detroit Red Wings | NHL | 35 | 14 | 18 | 32 | 4 | 30 | 7 | 6 | 1 | 2 | 104 | 13.5 |
| 1970–71 | 33 | Montreal Canadiens | NHL | 38 | 17 | 24 | 41 | 5 | 11 | 12 | 4 | 1 | 2 | 100 | 17.0 |
| 1971–72 | 34 | Montreal Canadiens | NHL | 76 | 43 | 53 | 96 | 42 | 36 | 25 | 14 | 4 | 4 | 261 | 16.5 |
| 1972–73 | 35 | Montreal Canadiens | NHL | 78 | 38 | 55 | 93 | 42 | 51 | 28 | 8 | 2 | 5 | 242 | 15.7 |
| 1973–74 | 36 | Montreal Canadiens | NHL | 71 | 31 | 49 | 80 | 16 | 47 | 21 | 8 | 2 | 3 | 221 | 14.0 |
| 1974–75 | 37 | Toronto Toros | WHA | 73 | 38 | 44 | 82 | 8 | 27 | 30 | 8 | 0 | | 268 | 14.2 |
| 1975–76 | 38 | Toronto Toros | WHA | 75 | 34 | 55 | 89 | -16 | 14 | 27 | 6 | 1 | 1 | 239 | 14.2 |
| 1976–77 | 39 | Birmingham Bulls | WHA | 17 | 3 | 20 | 23 | -1 | 12 | 1 | 2 | 0 | | 45 | 6.7 |
| 1977–78 | 40 | Birmingham Bulls | WHA | 72 | 14 | 24 | 38 | -5 | 22 | 8 | 6 | 0 | | 125 | 11.2 |
| Career — 22 Seasons | | | | 1418 | 622 | 713 | 1335 | 252 | 1129 | 466 | 144 | 12 | 83 | 4043 | 13.9 |

**PLAYOFFS**

| SEASON | AGE | TEAM | LG | GP | G | A | PTS | +/– | PIM | ESG | PPG | SHG | GWG | SOG | S% |
|--------|-----|------|-----|-----|-----|-----|-----|-----|-----|-----|-----|-----|-----|-----|-----|
| 1958–59 | 21 | Toronto Maple Leafs | NHL | 12 | 6 | 5 | 11 | | 18 | 4 | 1 | 1 | 1 | | |
| 1959–60 | 22 | Toronto Maple Leafs | NHL | 10 | 3 | 1 | 4 | -3 | 27 | 3 | 0 | 0 | 3 | 35 | 8.6 |
| 1960–61 | 23 | Toronto Maple Leafs | NHL | 5 | 1 | 1 | 2 | -3 | 6 | 1 | 0 | 0 | 0 | 10 | 10.0 |
| 1961–62 | 24 | Toronto Maple Leafs | NHL | 12 | 6 | 6 | 12 | -2 | 29 | 5 | 1 | 0 | 2 | 37 | 16.2 |
| 1962–63 | 25 | Toronto Maple Leafs | NHL | 9 | 0 | 2 | 2 | 1 | 8 | 0 | 0 | 0 | 0 | 19 | 0.0 |
| 1963–64 | 26 | Toronto Maple Leafs | NHL | 14 | 4 | 11 | 15 | 0 | 20 | 3 | 1 | 0 | 2 | 45 | 8.9 |
| 1964–65 | 27 | Toronto Maple Leafs | NHL | 6 | 0 | 3 | 3 | 1 | 9 | 0 | 0 | 0 | 0 | 7 | 14.3 |
| 1965–66 | 28 | Toronto Maple Leafs | NHL | 4 | 1 | 0 | 1 | -2 | 10 | 0 | 1 | 0 | 0 | 46 | 6.5 |
| 1966–67 | 29 | Toronto Maple Leafs | NHL | 12 | 3 | 7 | 10 | -4 | 8 | 0 | 3 | 0 | 1 | 5 | 0.0 |
| 1969–70 | 32 | Detroit Red Wings | NHL | 4 | 0 | 0 | 0 | -6 | 2 | 0 | 0 | 0 | 0 | 81 | 17.3 |
| 1970–71 | 33 | Montreal Canadiens | NHL | 20 | 14 | 13 | 27 | 2 | 18 | 11 | 3 | 0 | 0 | 13 | 23.1 |
| 1971–72 | 34 | Montreal Canadiens | NHL | 6 | 3 | 2 | 5 | -5 | 2 | 2 | 1 | 0 | 0 | 44 | 20.5 |
| 1972–73 | 35 | Montreal Canadiens | NHL | 17 | 9 | 14 | 23 | 0 | 6 | 8 | 1 | 0 | 0 | 16 | 6.3 |
| 1973–74 | 36 | Montreal Canadiens | NHL | 6 | 1 | 2 | 3 | -4 | 0 | 1 | 0 | 0 | 0 | | |
| 1974–75 | 37 | Toronto Toros | WHA | 6 | 3 | 0 | 3 | | 2 | | | | 0 | | |
| 1977–78 | 40 | Birmingham Bulls | WHA | 3 | 1 | 1 | 2 | 2 | 0 | | | | 0 | | |
| Career — 16 Seasons | | | | 146 | 55 | 68 | 123 | 123 | 165 | 38 | 12 | 1 | 9 | 373 | 12.1 |

## Dickie Moore Profile: See page 49

**REGULAR SEASON**

| SEASON | AGE | TEAM | LG | GP | G | A | PTS | +/– | PIM | ESG | PPG | SHG | GWG | SOG | S% |
|--------|-----|------|-----|-----|-----|-----|-----|-----|-----|-----|-----|-----|-----|-----|-----|
| 1951–52 | 21 | Montreal Canadiens | NHL | 33 | 18 | 15 | 33 | | 44 | 14 | 4 | 0 | 2 | | |
| 1952–53 | 22 | Montreal Canadiens | NHL | 18 | 2 | 6 | 8 | | 19 | 1 | 1 | 0 | 1 | | |
| 1953–54 | 23 | Montreal Canadiens | NHL | 13 | 1 | 4 | 5 | | 12 | 1 | 0 | 0 | 0 | | |
| 1954–55 | 24 | Montreal Canadiens | NHL | 67 | 16 | 20 | 36 | | 32 | 15 | 1 | 0 | 6 | | |
| 1955–56 | 25 | Montreal Canadiens | NHL | 70 | 11 | 38 | 49 | | 55 | 5 | 6 | 0 | 3 | | |
| 1956–57 | 26 | Montreal Canadiens | NHL | 70 | 29 | 29 | 58 | | 56 | 16 | 13 | 0 | 10 | | |
| 1957–58 | 27 | Montreal Canadiens | NHL | 70 | 36 | 48 | 84 | | 65 | 21 | 14 | 1 | 9 | | |
| 1958–59 | 28 | Montreal Canadiens | NHL | 70 | 41 | 55 | 96 | | 61 | 27 | 13 | 1 | 7 | | |
| 1959–60 | 29 | Montreal Canadiens | NHL | 62 | 22 | 42 | 64 | 27 | 54 | 12 | 10 | 0 | 2 | 176 | 12.5 |
| 1960–61 | 30 | Montreal Canadiens | NHL | 57 | 35 | 34 | 69 | 11 | 62 | 22 | 13 | 0 | 2 | 188 | 18.6 |

## Dickie Moore (continued)

### REGULAR SEASON

| SEASON | AGE | TEAM | LG | GP | G | A | PTS | +/- | PIM | ESG | PPG | SHG | GWG | SOG | S% |
|--------|-----|------|----|----|----|----|-----|-----|-----|-----|-----|-----|-----|-----|-----|
| 1961–62 | 31 | Montreal Canadiens | NHL | 57 | 19 | 22 | 41 | 25 | 52 | 17 | 2 | 0 | 4 | 153 | 12.4 |
| 1962–63 | 32 | Montreal Canadiens | NHL | 67 | 24 | 26 | 50 | 13 | 57 | 19 | 5 | 0 | 5 | 159 | 15.1 |
| 1964–65 | 34 | Toronto Maple Leafs | NHL | 38 | 2 | 4 | 6 | -5 | 68 | 2 | 0 | 0 | 0 | 30 | 6.7 |
| 1967–68 | 37 | St. Louis Blues | NHL | 27 | 5 | 3 | 8 | -8 | 9 | 4 | 1 | 0 | 0 | 37 | 13.5 |
| NHL Career – 14 Seasons | | | | 719 | 261 | 346 | 607 | 63 | 646 | 16 | 83 | 2 | 1 | 743 | 13.1 |

### PLAYOFFS

| SEASON | AGE | TEAM | LG | GP | G | A | PTS | +/- | PIM | ESG | PPG | SHG | GWG | SOG | S% |
|--------|-----|------|----|----|----|----|-----|-----|-----|-----|-----|-----|-----|-----|-----|
| 1951–52 | 21 | Montreal Canadiens | NHL | 11 | 1 | 1 | 2 | | 12 | 1 | 0 | 0 | 1 | | |
| 1952–53 | 22 | Montreal Canadiens | NHL | 12 | 3 | 2 | 5 | | 13 | 3 | 0 | 0 | 0 | | |
| 1953–54 | 23 | Montreal Canadiens | NHL | 11 | 5 | 8 | 13 | | 8 | 3 | 2 | 0 | 1 | | |
| 1954–55 | 24 | Montreal Canadiens | NHL | 12 | 1 | 5 | 6 | | 32 | 0 | 1 | 0 | 1 | | |
| 1955–56 | 25 | Montreal Canadiens | NHL | 10 | 3 | 6 | 9 | | 12 | 3 | 0 | 0 | 0 | | |
| 1956–57 | 26 | Montreal Canadiens | NHL | 10 | 3 | 7 | 10 | | 4 | 2 | 1 | 0 | 1 | | |
| 1957–58 | 27 | Montreal Canadiens | NHL | 10 | 4 | 7 | 11 | | 4 | 0 | 4 | 0 | 1 | | |
| 1958–59 | 28 | Montreal Canadiens | NHL | 11 | 5 | 12 | 17 | | 8 | 3 | 2 | 0 | 0 | | |
| 1959–60 | 29 | Montreal Canadiens | NHL | 8 | 6 | 4 | 10 | 6 | 4 | 3 | 3 | 0 | 0 | 34 | 17.6 |
| 1960–61 | 30 | Montreal Canadiens | NHL | 6 | 3 | 1 | 4 | 1 | 4 | 2 | 1 | 0 | 0 | 13 | 23.1 |
| 1961–62 | 31 | Montreal Canadiens | NHL | 6 | 4 | 2 | 6 | 4 | 8 | 2 | 2 | 0 | 0 | 26 | 15.4 |
| 1962–63 | 32 | Montreal Canadiens | NHL | 5 | 0 | 1 | 1 | 0 | 2 | 0 | 0 | 0 | 0 | 14 | 0.0 |
| 1964–65 | 34 | Toronto Maple Leafs | NHL | 5 | 1 | 1 | 2 | 2 | 6 | 1 | 0 | 0 | 0 | 4 | 25.0 |
| 1967–68 | 37 | St. Louis Blues | NHL | 18 | 7 | 7 | 14 | -1 | 15 | 5 | 2 | 0 | 1 | 53 | 13.2 |
| NHL Career – 14 Seasons | | | | 135 | 46 | 64 | 110 | 12 | 132 | 28 | 18 | 0 | 6 | 144 | 14.6 |

# Bert Olmstead   Profile: See page 50

### REGULAR SEASON

| SEASON | AGE | TEAM | LG | GP | G | A | PTS | PIM |
|--------|-----|------|----|----|----|----|-----|-----|
| 1948–49 | 22 | Chicago Black Hawks | NHL | 9 | 0 | 2 | 2 | 4 |
| 1949–50 | 23 | Chicago Black Hawks | NHL | 70 | 20 | 29 | 49 | 40 |
| 1950–51 | 24 | Chicago Black Hawks | NHL | 15 | 2 | 1 | 3 | 0 |
| 1950–51 | 24 | Montreal Canadiens | NHL | 39 | 16 | 22 | 38 | 50 |
| 1951–52 | 25 | Montreal Canadiens | NHL | 69 | 7 | 28 | 35 | 49 |
| 1952–53 | 26 | Montreal Canadiens | NHL | 69 | 17 | 28 | 45 | 83 |
| 1953–54 | 27 | Montreal Canadiens | NHL | 70 | 15 | 37 | 52 | 85 |
| 1954–55 | 28 | Montreal Canadiens | NHL | 70 | 10 | 48 | 58 | 103 |
| 1955–56 | 29 | Montreal Canadiens | NHL | 70 | 14 | 56 | 70 | 99 |
| 1956–57 | 30 | Montreal Canadiens | NHL | 64 | 15 | 33 | 48 | 74 |
| 1957–58 | 31 | Montreal Canadiens | NHL | 57 | 9 | 28 | 37 | 69 |
| 1958–59 | 32 | Toronto Maple Leafs | NHL | 70 | 10 | 31 | 41 | 74 |
| 1959–60 | 33 | Toronto Maple Leafs | NHL | 53 | 15 | 21 | 36 | 63 |
| 1960–61 | 34 | Toronto Maple Leafs | NHL | 67 | 18 | 34 | 52 | 84 |
| 1961–62 | 35 | Toronto Maple Leafs | NHL | 56 | 13 | 23 | 36 | 10 |
| NHL Career – 14 Seasons | | | | 848 | 181 | 421 | 602 | 887 |

### PLAYOFFS

| SEASON | AGE | TEAM | LG | GP | G | A | PTS | PIM |
|--------|-----|------|----|----|----|----|-----|-----|
| 1950–51 | 24 | Montreal Canadiens | NHL | 11 | 2 | 4 | 6 | 9 |
| 1951–52 | 25 | Montreal Canadiens | NHL | 11 | 0 | 1 | 1 | 4 |
| 1952–53 | 26 | Montreal Canadiens | NHL | 12 | 2 | 2 | 4 | 4 |
| 1953–54 | 27 | Montreal Canadiens | NHL | 11 | 0 | 1 | 1 | 19 |
| 1954–55 | 28 | Montreal Canadiens | NHL | 12 | 0 | 4 | 4 | 21 |
| 1955–56 | 29 | Montreal Canadiens | NHL | 10 | 4 | 10 | 14 | 8 |
| 1956–57 | 30 | Montreal Canadiens | NHL | 10 | 0 | 9 | 9 | 13 |
| 1957–58 | 31 | Montreal Canadiens | NHL | 9 | 0 | 3 | 3 | 0 |
| 1958–59 | 32 | Toronto Maple Leafs | NHL | 12 | 4 | 2 | 6 | 13 |
| 1959–60 | 33 | Toronto Maple Leafs | NHL | 10 | 3 | 4 | 7 | 0 |
| 1960–61 | 34 | Toronto Maple Leafs | NHL | 3 | 1 | 2 | 3 | 10 |
| 1961–62 | 35 | Toronto Maple Leafs | NHL | 4 | 0 | 1 | 1 | 0 |
| NHL Career – 12 Seasons | | | | 115 | 16 | 43 | 59 | 101 |

# Lynn Patrick   Profile: See page 51

### REGULAR SEASON

| SEASON | AGE | TEAM | LG | GP | G | A | PTS | PIM |
|--------|-----|------|----|----|----|----|-----|-----|
| 1934–35 | 22 | New York Rangers | NHL | 48 | 9 | 13 | 22 | 17 |
| 1935–36 | 23 | New York Rangers | NHL | 48 | 11 | 14 | 25 | 29 |
| 1936–37 | 24 | New York Rangers | NHL | 45 | 8 | 16 | 24 | 23 |
| 1937–38 | 25 | New York Rangers | NHL | 48 | 15 | 19 | 34 | 24 |
| 1938–39 | 26 | New York Rangers | NHL | 35 | 8 | 21 | 29 | 25 |
| 1939–40 | 27 | New York Rangers | NHL | 48 | 12 | 16 | 28 | 34 |
| 1940–41 | 28 | New York Rangers | NHL | 48 | 20 | 24 | 44 | 12 |
| 1941–42 | 29 | New York Rangers | NHL | 47 | 32 | 23 | 55 | 18 |
| 1942–43 | 30 | New York Rangers | NHL | 50 | 22 | 39 | 61 | 28 |
| 1945–46 | 33 | New York Rangers | NHL | 38 | 8 | 6 | 14 | 30 |
| NHL Career – 10 Seasons | | | | 455 | 145 | 191 | 336 | 240 |

### PLAYOFFS

| SEASON | AGE | TEAM | LG | GP | G | A | PTS | PIM |
|--------|-----|------|----|----|----|----|-----|-----|
| 1934–35 | 22 | New York Rangers | NHL | 4 | 2 | 2 | 4 | 0 |
| 1936–37 | 24 | New York Rangers | NHL | 9 | 3 | 0 | 3 | 2 |
| 1937–38 | 25 | New York Rangers | NHL | 3 | 0 | 1 | 1 | 0 |
| 1938–39 | 26 | New York Rangers | NHL | 7 | 1 | 1 | 2 | 0 |
| 1939–40 | 27 | New York Rangers | NHL | 12 | 2 | 2 | 4 | 4 |
| 1940–41 | 28 | New York Rangers | NHL | 3 | 1 | 0 | 1 | 14 |
| 1941–42 | 29 | New York Rangers | NHL | 6 | 1 | 0 | 1 | 0 |
| NHL Career – 7 Seasons | | | | 44 | 10 | 6 | 16 | 20 |

## Tommy Phillips   Profile: See page 52

**REGULAR SEASON**

| SEASON | AGE | TEAM | LG | GP | G | A | PTS | PIM |
|---|---|---|---|---|---|---|---|---|
| 1901–02 | 18 | Rat Portage Thistles | MNWHA-Int | 9 | 7 | 0 | 7 | 7 |
| 1902–03 | 19 | Montreal AAA | CAHL | 4 | 6 | 0 | 6 | |
| 1903–04 | 20 | Toronto Marlboros | OHA-Sr. | 4 | 5 | 0 | 5 | 21 |
| 1904–05 | 21 | Rat Portage Thistles | MHL | 8 | 26 | 0 | 26 | |
| 1905–06 | 22 | Kenora Thistles | MHL | 9 | 24 | 0 | 24 | |
| 1906–07 | 23 | Kenora Thistles | MHL-Pro | 6 | 18 | 0 | 18 | |
| 1907–08 | 24 | Ottawa Senators | ECAHA | 10 | 26 | 0 | 26 | 40 |
| 1908–09 | 25 | Edmonton Professionals | ECAHA | 1 | 0 | 2 | 2 | 3 |
| 1911–12 | 28 | Vancouver Millionaires | PCHA | 17 | 17 | 0 | 17 | 38 |
| Career — 8 Seasons | | | | 68 | 129 | 2 | 131 | 109 |

**PLAYOFFS**

| SEASON | AGE | TEAM | LG | GP | G | A | PTS | PIM |
|---|---|---|---|---|---|---|---|---|
| 1902–03 | 19 | Montreal AAA | St-Cup | 4 | 3 | 0 | 3 | |
| 1903–04 | 20 | Toronto Marlboros | OHA-Sr. | 2 | 6 | 6 | 12 | 9 |
| 1903–04 | 20 | Toronto Marlboros | St-Cup | 2 | 1 | 2 | 3 | 6 |
| 1904–05 | 21 | Rat Portage Thistles | St-Cup | 3 | 8 | 0 | 8 | |
| 1906–07 | 23 | Kenora Thistles | MHL-Pro | 2 | 4 | 0 | 4 | 9 |
| 1906–07 | 23 | Kenora Thistles | St-Cup | 4 | 9 | 0 | 9 | 16 |
| 1908–09 | 25 | Edmonton Professionals | St-Cup | 1 | 1 | 0 | 1 | 0 |
| Career — 5 Seasons | | | | 18 | 32 | 8 | 40 | 40 |

## Bob Pulford   Profile: See page 53

**REGULAR SEASON**

| SEASON | AGE | TEAM | LG | GP | G | A | PTS | +/- | PIM | ESG | PPG | SHG | GWG | SOG | S% |
|---|---|---|---|---|---|---|---|---|---|---|---|---|---|---|---|
| 1956–57 | 20 | Toronto Maple Leafs | NHL | 65 | 11 | 11 | 22 | | 32 | 7 | 4 | 0 | 0 | | |
| 1957–58 | 21 | Toronto Maple Leafs | NHL | 70 | 14 | 17 | 31 | | 48 | 11 | 3 | 0 | 1 | | |
| 1958–59 | 22 | Toronto Maple Leafs | NHL | 70 | 23 | 14 | 37 | | 55 | 15 | 3 | 5 | 5 | | |
| 1959–60 | 23 | Toronto Maple Leafs | NHL | 70 | 24 | 28 | 52 | 7 | 81 | 17 | 1 | 6 | 2 | 231 | 10.4 |
| 1960–61 | 24 | Toronto Maple Leafs | NHL | 40 | 11 | 18 | 29 | 3 | 41 | 11 | 0 | 0 | 2 | 114 | 9.6 |
| 1961–62 | 25 | Toronto Maple Leafs | NHL | 70 | 18 | 21 | 39 | -4 | 95 | 13 | 3 | 2 | 1 | 210 | 8.6 |
| 1962–63 | 26 | Toronto Maple Leafs | NHL | 70 | 19 | 25 | 44 | 10 | 49 | 17 | 2 | 0 | 3 | 231 | 8.2 |
| 1963–64 | 27 | Toronto Maple Leafs | NHL | 70 | 18 | 30 | 48 | 14 | 73 | 13 | 1 | 4 | 1 | 237 | 7.6 |
| 1964–65 | 28 | Toronto Maple Leafs | NHL | 65 | 19 | 20 | 39 | 10 | 46 | 14 | 1 | 4 | 4 | 175 | 10.9 |
| 1965–66 | 29 | Toronto Maple Leafs | NHL | 70 | 28 | 28 | 56 | 9 | 51 | 15 | 11 | 2 | 2 | 238 | 11.8 |
| 1966–67 | 30 | Toronto Maple Leafs | NHL | 67 | 17 | 28 | 45 | 10 | 28 | 15 | 1 | 1 | 1 | 195 | 8.7 |
| 1967–68 | 31 | Toronto Maple Leafs | NHL | 74 | 20 | 30 | 50 | -7 | 40 | 13 | 4 | 3 | 3 | 229 | 8.7 |
| 1968–69 | 32 | Toronto Maple Leafs | NHL | 72 | 11 | 23 | 34 | -9 | 22 | 7 | 3 | 1 | 1 | 180 | 6.1 |
| 1969–70 | 33 | Toronto Maple Leafs | NHL | 74 | 18 | 19 | 37 | -22 | 31 | 15 | 3 | 0 | 1 | 227 | 7.9 |
| 1970–71 | 34 | Los Angeles Kings | NHL | 59 | 17 | 26 | 43 | -13 | 53 | 10 | 6 | 1 | 2 | 170 | 10.0 |
| 1971–72 | 35 | Los Angeles Kings | NHL | 73 | 13 | 24 | 37 | -27 | 48 | 10 | 2 | 1 | 0 | 170 | 7.6 |
| NHL Career — 16 Seasons | | | | 1079 | 281 | 362 | 643 | -21 | 793 | 203 | 48 | 30 | 29 | 2607 | 8.9 |

**PLAYOFFS**

| SEASON | AGE | TEAM | LG | GP | G | A | PTS | +/- | PIM | ESG | PPG | SHG | GWG | SOG | S% |
|---|---|---|---|---|---|---|---|---|---|---|---|---|---|---|---|
| 1958–59 | 22 | Toronto Maple Leafs | NHL | 12 | 4 | 4 | 8 | | 8 | 2 | 1 | 1 | 0 | | |
| 1959–60 | 23 | Toronto Maple Leafs | NHL | 10 | 4 | 1 | 5 | -4 | 4 | 0 | 0 | 0 | | 29 | 13.8 |
| 1960–61 | 24 | Toronto Maple Leafs | NHL | 5 | 0 | 0 | 0 | -4 | 8 | 0 | 0 | 0 | | 7 | 0.0 |
| 1961–62 | 25 | Toronto Maple Leafs | NHL | 12 | 7 | 1 | 8 | 4 | 24 | 5 | 1 | 1 | 2 | 36 | 19.4 |
| 1962–63 | 26 | Toronto Maple Leafs | NHL | 10 | 2 | 5 | 7 | 4 | 14 | 2 | 0 | 0 | 0 | 31 | 6.5 |
| 1963–64 | 27 | Toronto Maple Leafs | NHL | 14 | 5 | 3 | 8 | 0 | 20 | 3 | 0 | 2 | 1 | 41 | 12.2 |
| 1964–65 | 28 | Toronto Maple Leafs | NHL | 6 | 1 | 1 | 2 | 2 | 16 | 1 | 0 | 0 | 0 | 9 | 11.1 |
| 2965–66 | 29 | Toronto Maple Leafs | NHL | 4 | 1 | 1 | 2 | -1 | 12 | 1 | 0 | 0 | 0 | 13 | 7.7 |
| 1966–67 | 30 | Toronto Maple Leafs | NHL | 12 | 1 | 10 | 11 | 3 | 12 | 1 | 0 | 0 | 1 | 48 | 2.1 |
| 1968–69 | 32 | Toronto Maple Leafs | NHL | 4 | 0 | 0 | 0 | -7 | 2 | 0 | 0 | 0 | 0 | 6 | 0.0 |
| NHL Career — 10 Seasons | | | | 89 | 25 | 26 | 51 | -3 | 126 | 19 | 2 | 4 | 4 | 220 | 9.5 |

## George Richardson   Profile: See page 54

**REGULAR SEASON**

| SEASON | AGE | TEAM | LG | GP | G | A | PTS | PIM |
|---|---|---|---|---|---|---|---|---|
| 1902–03 | 16 | Queen's University | CIHU | | | | | |
| 1903–04 | 17 | Queen's University | CIHU | 4 | 6 | 0 | 6 | 3 |
| 1904–05 | 18 | Queen's University | CIHU | 4 | 6 | 0 | 6 | 0 |
| 1905–06 | 19 | Queen's University | CIHU | 4 | 11 | 0 | 11 | 2 |
| 1906–07 | 20 | Kingston 14th Regiment | OHA-Sr. | 7 | 23 | 0 | 23 | 0 |
| 1907–08 | 21 | Kingston 14th Regiment | OHA-Sr. | 3 | 9 | 3 | 12 | 12 |
| 1908–09 | 22 | Kingston 14th Regiment | OHA-Sr. | 4 | 8 | 0 | 8 | 9 |
| Career — 7 Seasons | | | | 25 | 63 | 3 | 66 | 26 |

**PLAYOFFS**

| SEASON | AGE | TEAM | LG | GP | G | A | PTS | PIM |
|---|---|---|---|---|---|---|---|---|
| 1905–06 | 19 | Queen's University | St-Cup | 2 | 3 | 0 | 3 | 0 |
| 1906–07 | 20 | Kingston 14th Regiment | OHA-Sr. | 2 | 2 | 0 | 2 | 0 |
| 1907–08 | 21 | Kingston 14th Regiment | OHA-Sr. | 4 | 18 | 0 | 18 | 9 |
| 1908–09 | 22 | Kingston 14th Regiment | OHA-Sr. | 2 | 13 | 0 | 13 | 0 |
| 1909–10 | 23 | Kingston Frontenacs | Exhib. | 2 | 8 | 0 | 8 | 0 |
| 1911–12 | 25 | Kingston Frontenacs | OHA-Sr. | 1 | 1 | 0 | 1 | 0 |
| Career — 6 Seasons | | | | 13 | 45 | 0 | 45 | 9 |

## Gordon Roberts  Profile: See page 55

### REGULAR SEASON

| SEASON | AGE | TEAM | LG | GP | G | A | PTS | PIM |
|---|---|---|---|---|---|---|---|---|
| 1908–09 | 17 | Ottawa Emmetts | OCHL | 6 | 19 | 0 | 19 | 8 |
| 1909–10 | 18 | Ottawa Senators | CHA | 1 | 3 | 0 | 3 | 6 |
| 1909–10 | 18 | Ottawa Senators | NHA | 9 | 13 | 0 | 13 | 34 |
| 1909–10 | 18 | Ottawa Seconds | OCHL | 1 | 3 | 0 | 3 | 5 |
| 1910–11 | 19 | Montreal Wanderers | NHA | 4 | 1 | 0 | 1 | 3 |
| 1911–12 | 20 | Montreal Wanderers | NHA | 18 | 16 | 0 | 16 | 28 |
| 1912–13 | 21 | Montreal Wanderers | NHA | 16 | 16 | 0 | 16 | 22 |
| 1913–14 | 22 | Montreal Wanderers | NHA | 20 | 31 | 13 | 44 | 15 |
| 1914–15 | 23 | Montreal Wanderers | NHA | 19 | 29 | 5 | 34 | 74 |
| 1915–16 | 24 | Montreal Wanderers | NHA | 21 | 18 | 7 | 25 | 64 |
| 1916–17 | 25 | Vancouver Millionaires | PCHA | 23 | 43 | 10 | 53 | 42 |
| 1917–18 | 26 | Seattle Metropolitans | PCHA | 18 | 20 | 3 | 23 | 24 |
| 1919–20 | 28 | Vancouver Millionaires | PCHA | 22 | 16 | 3 | 19 | 13 |
| Career — 11 Seasons | | | | 178 | 228 | 41 | 269 | 338 |

### PLAYOFFS

| SEASON | AGE | TEAM | LG | GP | G | A | PTS | PIM |
|---|---|---|---|---|---|---|---|---|
| 1908–09 | 17 | Ottawa Emmetts | OCHL | 2 | 2 | 0 | 2 | 0 |
| 1909–10 | 18 | Ottawa Senators | St-Cup | 2 | 7 | 0 | 7 | 0 |
| 1914–15 | 23 | Montreal Wanderers | NHA | 2 | 0 | 0 | 0 | 15 |
| 1917–18 | 26 | Seattle Metropolitans | PCHA | 2 | 0 | 0 | 0 | 3 |
| 1919–20 | 28 | Vancouver Millionaires | PCHA | 2 | 1 | 0 | 1 | 0 |
| Career — 5 Seasons | | | | 10 | 10 | 0 | 10 | 18 |

## Luc Robitaille  Profile: See page 56

### REGULAR SEASON

| SEASON | AGE | TEAM | LG | GP | G | A | PTS | +/- | PIM | ESG | PPG | SHG | GWG | SOG | S% |
|---|---|---|---|---|---|---|---|---|---|---|---|---|---|---|---|
| 1986–87 | 20 | Los Angeles Kings | NHL | 79 | 45 | 39 | 84 | -19 | 28 | 27 | 18 | 0 | 3 | 199 | 22.6 |
| 1987–88 | 21 | Los Angeles Kings | NHL | 80 | 53 | 58 | 111 | -9 | 82 | 36 | 17 | 0 | 6 | 220 | 24.1 |
| 1988–89 | 22 | Los Angeles Kings | NHL | 78 | 46 | 52 | 98 | 5 | 65 | 36 | 10 | 0 | 4 | 237 | 19.4 |
| 1989–90 | 23 | Los Angeles Kings | NHL | 80 | 52 | 49 | 101 | 8 | 38 | 32 | 20 | 0 | 7 | 210 | 24.8 |
| 1990–91 | 24 | Los Angeles Kings | NHL | 76 | 45 | 46 | 91 | 28 | 68 | 34 | 11 | 0 | 5 | 229 | 19.7 |
| 1991–92 | 25 | Los Angeles Kings | NHL | 80 | 44 | 63 | 107 | -4 | 95 | 18 | 26 | 0 | 6 | 240 | 18.3 |
| 1992–93 | 26 | Los Angeles Kings | NHL | 84 | 63 | 62 | 125 | 18 | 100 | 37 | 24 | 2 | 8 | 265 | 23.8 |
| 1993–94 | 27 | Los Angeles Kings | NHL | 83 | 44 | 42 | 86 | -20 | 86 | 20 | 24 | 0 | 3 | 267 | 16.5 |
| 1994–95 | 28 | Pittsburgh Penguins | NHL | 46 | 23 | 19 | 42 | 10 | 37 | 18 | 5 | 0 | 3 | 109 | 21.1 |
| 1995–96 | 29 | New York Rangers | NHL | 77 | 23 | 46 | 69 | 13 | 80 | 12 | 11 | 0 | 4 | 223 | 10.3 |
| 1996–97 | 30 | New York Rangers | NHL | 69 | 24 | 24 | 48 | 16 | 48 | 19 | 5 | 0 | 4 | 200 | 12.0 |
| 1997–98 | 31 | Los Angeles Kings | NHL | 57 | 16 | 24 | 40 | 5 | 66 | 11 | 5 | 0 | 7 | 130 | 12.3 |
| 1998–99 | 32 | Los Angeles Kings | NHL | 82 | 39 | 35 | 74 | -1 | 54 | 28 | 11 | 0 | 7 | 292 | 13.4 |
| 1999–00 | 33 | Los Angeles Kings | NHL | 71 | 36 | 38 | 74 | 11 | 68 | 23 | 13 | 0 | 7 | 221 | 16.3 |
| 2000–01 | 34 | Los Angeles Kings | NHL | 82 | 37 | 51 | 88 | 10 | 66 | 20 | 16 | 1 | 4 | 235 | 15.7 |
| 2001–02 | 35 | Detroit Red Wings | NHL | 81 | 30 | 20 | 50 | -2 | 38 | 17 | 13 | 0 | 5 | 190 | 15.8 |
| 2002–03 | 36 | Detroit Red Wings | NHL | 81 | 11 | 20 | 31 | 4 | 50 | 8 | 3 | 0 | 0 | 148 | 7.4 |
| 2003–04 | 37 | Los Angeles Kings | NHL | 80 | 22 | 29 | 51 | 4 | 56 | 10 | 12 | 0 | 4 | 221 | 10.0 |
| 2005–06 | 39 | Los Angeles Kings | NHL | 65 | 15 | 9 | 24 | -6 | 52 | 12 | 3 | 0 | 2 | 125 | 12.0 |
| NHL Career — 19 Seasons | | | | 1431 | 668 | 726 | 1394 | 71 | 1177 | 418 | 247 | 3 | 89 | 3961 | 16.9 |

### PLAYOFFS

| SEASON | AGE | TEAM | LG | GP | G | A | PTS | +/- | PIM | ESG | PPG | SHG | GWG | SOG | S% |
|---|---|---|---|---|---|---|---|---|---|---|---|---|---|---|---|
| 1986–87 | 20 | Los Angeles Kings | NHL | 5 | 1 | 4 | 5 | -7 | 2 | 1 | 0 | 0 | 0 | 5 | 20.0 |
| 1987–88 | 21 | Los Angeles Kings | NHL | 5 | 2 | 5 | 7 | -8 | 18 | 0 | 2 | 0 | 1 | 6 | 33.3 |
| 1988–89 | 22 | Los Angeles Kings | NHL | 11 | 2 | 6 | 8 | 0 | 10 | 2 | 0 | 0 | 1 | 24 | 8.3 |
| 1989–90 | 23 | Los Angeles Kings | NHL | 10 | 5 | 5 | 10 | -5 | 12 | 4 | 1 | 0 | 1 | 28 | 17.9 |
| 1990–91 | 24 | Los Angeles Kings | NHL | 12 | 12 | 4 | 16 | -2 | 22 | 7 | 5 | 0 | 2 | 44 | 27.3 |
| 1991–92 | 25 | Los Angeles Kings | NHL | 6 | 3 | 4 | 7 | -1 | 12 | 2 | 1 | 0 | 1 | 28 | 10.7 |
| 1992–93 | 26 | Los Angeles Kings | NHL | 24 | 9 | 13 | 22 | -13 | 28 | 5 | 4 | 0 | 2 | 71 | 12.7 |
| 1994–95 | 28 | Pittsburgh Penguins | NHL | 12 | 7 | 4 | 11 | 5 | 26 | 7 | 0 | 0 | 2 | 33 | 21.2 |
| 1995–96 | 29 | New York Rangers | NHL | 11 | 1 | 5 | 6 | 1 | 8 | 1 | 0 | 0 | 0 | 36 | 2.8 |
| 1996–97 | 30 | New York Rangers | NHL | 15 | 4 | 7 | 11 | 7 | 4 | 4 | 0 | 0 | 0 | 43 | 9.3 |
| 1997–98 | 31 | Los Angeles Kings | NHL | 4 | 1 | 2 | 3 | 1 | 6 | 1 | 0 | 0 | 0 | 13 | 7.7 |
| 1999–00 | 33 | Los Angeles Kings | NHL | 4 | 2 | 2 | 4 | -1 | 6 | 2 | 0 | 0 | 0 | 8 | 25.0 |
| 2000–01 | 34 | Los Angeles Kings | NHL | 13 | 4 | 3 | 7 | 1 | 10 | 3 | 1 | 0 | 1 | 24 | 16.7 |
| 2001–02 | 35 | Detroit Red Wings | NHL | 23 | 4 | 5 | 9 | 4 | 10 | 3 | 1 | 0 | 1 | 43 | 9.3 |
| 2002–03 | 36 | Detroit Red Wings | NHL | 4 | 1 | 0 | 1 | 1 | 0 | 1 | 0 | 0 | 0 | 12 | 8.3 |
| NHL Career — 15 Seasons | | | | 159 | 58 | 69 | 127 | -17 | 174 | 43 | 15 | 0 | 12 | 418 | 13.9 |

## Blair Russel  Profile: See page 58

| REGULAR SEASON | | | | | | | | |
|---|---|---|---|---|---|---|---|---|
| SEASON | AGE | TEAM | LG | GP | G | A | PTS | PIM |
| 1899-00 | 19 | Montreal Victorias | CAHL | 7 | 9 | 0 | 9 | |
| 1900-01 | 20 | Montreal Victorias | CAHL | 8 | 8 | 0 | 8 | |
| 1901-02 | 21 | Montreal Victorias | CAHL | 8 | 9 | 0 | 9 | 3 |
| 1902-03 | 22 | Montreal Victorias | CAHL | 8 | 7 | 0 | 7 | 6 |
| 1903-04 | 23 | Montreal Victorias | CAHL | 8 | 17 | 0 | 17 | 15 |
| 1904-05 | 24 | Montreal Victorias | CAHL | 8 | 19 | 0 | 19 | 6 |
| 1905-06 | 25 | Montreal Victorias | ECAHA | 4 | 7 | 0 | 7 | 0 |
| 1906-07 | 26 | Montreal Victorias | ECAHA | 10 | 25 | 0 | 25 | 6 |

| REGULAR SEASON | | | | | | | | |
|---|---|---|---|---|---|---|---|---|
| SEASON | AGE | TEAM | LG | GP | G | A | PTS | PIM |
| 1907-08 | 27 | Montreal Victorias | ECAHA | 6 | 8 | 0 | 8 | 26 |
| 1908-09 | 28 | Montreal Victorias | IPAHU | 1 | 2 | 0 | 2 | 1 |
| 1909-10 | 29 | Montreal Victorias | IPAHU | 1 | 2 | 0 | 2 | 2 |
| Career—11 Seasons | | | | 69 | 113 | 0 | 113 | 65 |

| PLAYOFFS | | | | | | | | |
|---|---|---|---|---|---|---|---|---|
| SEASON | AGE | TEAM | LG | GP | G | A | PTS | PIM |
| 1902-03 | 22 | Montreal Victorias | St-Cup | 2 | 0 | 0 | 0 | 6 |
| Career—1 Season | | | | 2 | 0 | 0 | 0 | 6 |

## Fred Scanlan  Profile: See page 59

| REGULAR SEASON | | | | | | | |
|---|---|---|---|---|---|---|---|
| SEASON | AGE | TEAM | LG | GP | G | A | PTS |
| 1897-98 | 20 | Montreal Shamrocks | AHAC | 8 | 2 | 0 | 2 |
| 1889-99 | 21 | Montreal Shamrocks | CAHL | 8 | 4 | 0 | 4 |
| 1899-00 | 22 | Montreal Shamrocks | CAHL | 7 | 6 | 0 | 6 |
| 1900-01 | 23 | Montreal Shamrocks | CAHL | 8 | 5 | 0 | 5 |
| 1901-02 | 24 | Winnipeg Victorias | MNWHA | 3 | 5 | 0 | 5 |
| 1902-03 | 25 | Winnipeg Victorias | WSrHL | 6 | 6 | 2 | 8 |
| Career—6 Seasons | | | | 40 | 28 | 2 | 30 |

| PLAYOFFS | | | | | | | |
|---|---|---|---|---|---|---|---|
| SEASON | AGE | TEAM | LG | GP | G | A | PTS |
| 1898-99 | 21 | Montreal Shamrocks | St-Cup | 1 | 1 | 0 | 1 |
| 1899-00 | 22 | Montreal Shamrocks | St-Cup | 5 | 2 | 0 | 2 |
| 1900-01 | 23 | Montreal Shamrocks | St-Cup | 2 | 0 | 0 | 0 |
| 1901-02 | 24 | Winnipeg Victorias | St-Cup | 5 | 2 | 0 | 2 |
| 1902-03 | 25 | Winnipeg Victorias | St-Cup | 4 | 1 | 0 | 1 |
| Career—5 Seasons | | | | 17 | 6 | 0 | 6 |

## Sweeney Schriner  Profile: See page 60

| REGULAR SEASON | | | | | | | | |
|---|---|---|---|---|---|---|---|---|
| SEASON | AGE | TEAM | LG | GP | G | A | PTS | PIM |
| 1934-35 | 23 | New York Americans | NHL | 48 | 18 | 22 | 40 | 6 |
| 1935-36 | 24 | New York Americans | NHL | 48 | 19 | 26 | 45 | 8 |
| 1936-37 | 25 | New York Americans | NHL | 48 | 21 | 25 | 46 | 17 |
| 1937-38 | 26 | New York Americans | NHL | 48 | 21 | 17 | 38 | 22 |
| 1938-39 | 27 | New York Americans | NHL | 48 | 13 | 32 | 45 | 20 |
| 1939-40 | 28 | Toronto Maple Leafs | NHL | 39 | 11 | 15 | 26 | 10 |
| 1940-41 | 29 | Toronto Maple Leafs | NHL | 48 | 24 | 14 | 38 | 6 |
| 1941-42 | 30 | Toronto Maple Leafs | NHL | 47 | 20 | 16 | 36 | 21 |
| 1942-43 | 31 | Toronto Maple Leafs | NHL | 37 | 19 | 17 | 36 | 13 |
| 1944-45 | 33 | Toronto Maple Leafs | NHL | 26 | 22 | 15 | 37 | 10 |
| 1945-46 | 34 | Toronto Maple Leafs | NHL | 47 | 13 | 7 | 20 | 15 |
| NHL Career—11 Seasons | | | | 484 | 201 | 206 | 408 | 148 |

| PLAYOFFS | | | | | | | | |
|---|---|---|---|---|---|---|---|---|
| SEASON | AGE | TEAM | LG | GP | G | A | PTS | PIM |
| 1935-36 | 24 | New York Americans | NHL | 5 | 3 | 1 | 4 | 2 |
| 1937-38 | 26 | New York Americans | NHL | 6 | 1 | 0 | 1 | 0 |
| 1938-39 | 27 | New York Americans | NHL | 2 | 0 | 0 | 0 | 20 |
| 1939-40 | 28 | Toronto Maple Leafs | NHL | 9 | 1 | 3 | 4 | 4 |
| 1940-41 | 29 | Toronto Maple Leafs | NHL | 7 | 2 | 1 | 3 | 4 |
| 1941-42 | 30 | Toronto Maple Leafs | NHL | 13 | 6 | 3 | 9 | 10 |
| 1942-43 | 31 | Toronto Maple Leafs | NHL | 4 | 2 | 2 | 4 | 0 |
| 1944-45 | 33 | Toronto Maple Leafs | NHL | 13 | 3 | 1 | 4 | 4 |
| NHL Career—8 Seasons | | | | 59 | 18 | 11 | 29 | 44 |

## Brendan Shanahan  Profile: See page 61

| REGULAR SEASON | | | | | | | | | | | | | | | |
|---|---|---|---|---|---|---|---|---|---|---|---|---|---|---|---|
| SEASON | AGE | TEAM | LG | GP | G | A | PTS | +/- | PIM | ESG | PPG | SHG | GWG | SOG | S% |
| 1987-88 | 19 | New Jersey Devils | NHL | 65 | 7 | 19 | 26 | -20 | 131 | 5 | 2 | 0 | 2 | 72 | 9.7 |
| 1988-89 | 20 | New Jersey Devils | NHL | 68 | 22 | 28 | 50 | 2 | 115 | 13 | 9 | 0 | 0 | 152 | 14.5 |
| 1989-90 | 21 | New Jersey Devils | NHL | 73 | 30 | 42 | 72 | 15 | 137 | 22 | 8 | 0 | 5 | 196 | 15.3 |
| 1990-91 | 22 | New Jersey Devils | NHL | 75 | 29 | 37 | 66 | 4 | 141 | 22 | 7 | 0 | 2 | 195 | 14.9 |
| 1991-92 | 23 | St. Louis Blues | NHL | 80 | 33 | 36 | 69 | -3 | 171 | 20 | 13 | 0 | 2 | 215 | 15.3 |
| 1992-93 | 24 | St. Louis Blues | NHL | 71 | 51 | 43 | 94 | 10 | 174 | 33 | 18 | 0 | 8 | 232 | 22.0 |
| 1993-94 | 25 | St. Louis Blues | NHL | 81 | 52 | 50 | 102 | -9 | 211 | 30 | 15 | 7 | 8 | 397 | 13.1 |
| 1994-95 | 26 | St. Louis Blues | NHL | 45 | 20 | 21 | 41 | 7 | 136 | 12 | 6 | 2 | 6 | 153 | 13.1 |
| 1995-96 | 27 | Hartford Whalers | NHL | 74 | 44 | 34 | 78 | 2 | 125 | 25 | 17 | 2 | 6 | 280 | 15.7 |
| 1996-97 | 28 | Hartford Whalers | NHL | 2 | 1 | 0 | 1 | 1 | 0 | 0 | 0 | 1 | 0 | 13 | 7.7 |
| 1996-97 | 28 | Detroit Red Wings | NHL | 79 | 46 | 41 | 87 | 31 | 131 | 24 | 20 | 2 | 7 | 323 | 14.2 |
| 1997-98 | 29 | Detroit Red Wings | NHL | 75 | 28 | 29 | 57 | 6 | 154 | 12 | 15 | 1 | 9 | 266 | 10.5 |
| 1998-99 | 30 | Detroit Red Wings | NHL | 81 | 31 | 27 | 58 | 2 | 123 | 26 | 5 | 0 | 5 | 288 | 10.8 |
| 1999-00 | 31 | Detroit Red Wings | NHL | 78 | 41 | 37 | 78 | 24 | 105 | 27 | 13 | 1 | 9 | 283 | 14.5 |
| 2000-01 | 32 | Detroit Red Wings | NHL | 81 | 31 | 45 | 76 | 9 | 81 | 15 | 15 | 1 | 7 | 278 | 11.2 |
| 2001-02 | 33 | Detroit Red Wings | NHL | 80 | 37 | 38 | 75 | 23 | 118 | 22 | 12 | 3 | 7 | 277 | 13.4 |
| 2002-03 | 34 | Detroit Red Wings | NHL | 78 | 30 | 38 | 68 | 5 | 103 | 17 | 13 | 0 | 6 | 260 | 11.5 |
| 2003-04 | 35 | Detroit Red Wings | NHL | 82 | 25 | 28 | 53 | 15 | 117 | 17 | 8 | 0 | 7 | 280 | 8.9 |
| 2005-06 | 37 | Detroit Red Wings | NHL | 82 | 40 | 41 | 81 | 29 | 105 | 26 | 14 | 0 | 6 | 289 | 13.8 |
| 2006-07 | 38 | New York Rangers | NHL | 67 | 29 | 33 | 62 | 2 | 47 | 12 | 14 | 3 | 3 | 295 | 9.8 |
| 2007-08 | 39 | New York Rangers | NHL | 73 | 23 | 23 | 46 | -2 | 35 | 12 | 11 | 0 | 3 | 265 | 8.7 |
| 2008-09 | 40 | New Jersey Devils | NHL | 34 | 6 | 8 | 14 | -2 | 29 | 4 | 2 | 0 | 1 | 77 | 7.8 |
| NHL Career—21 Seasons | | | | 1524 | 656 | 698 | 1354 | 151 | 2489 | 396 | 237 | 23 | 109 | 5086 | 12.9 |

## Brendan Shanahan (continued)

### PLAYOFFS

| SEASON | AGE | TEAM | LG | GP | G | A | PTS | +/- | PIM | ESG | PPG | SHG | GWG | SOG | S% |
|---|---|---|---|---|---|---|---|---|---|---|---|---|---|---|---|
| 1987–88 | 19 | New Jersey Devils | NHL | 12 | 2 | 1 | 3 | 0 | 44 | 1 | 1 | 0 | 0 | 11 | 18.2 |
| 1989–90 | 21 | New Jersey Devils | NHL | 6 | 3 | 3 | 6 | 0 | 20 | 2 | 1 | 0 | 1 | 16 | 18.8 |
| 1990–91 | 22 | New Jersey Devils | NHL | 7 | 3 | 5 | 8 | 3 | 12 | 1 | 2 | 0 | 0 | 20 | 15.0 |
| 1991–92 | 23 | St. Louis Blues | NHL | 6 | 2 | 3 | 5 | 0 | 14 | 1 | 1 | 0 | 0 | 17 | 11.8 |
| 1992–93 | 24 | St. Louis Blues | NHL | 11 | 4 | 3 | 7 | 0 | 18 | 2 | 2 | 0 | 0 | 36 | 11.1 |
| 1993–94 | 25 | St. Louis Blues | NHL | 4 | 2 | 5 | 7 | 6 | 4 | 2 | 0 | 0 | 0 | 20 | 10.0 |
| 1994–95 | 26 | St. Louis Blues | NHL | 5 | 4 | 5 | 9 | 2 | 14 | 3 | 1 | 0 | 1 | 23 | 17.4 |
| 1996–97 | 28 | Detroit Red Wings | NHL | 20 | 9 | 8 | 17 | 8 | 43 | 7 | 2 | 0 | 2 | 82 | 11.0 |
| 1997–98 | 29 | Detroit Red Wings | NHL | 20 | 5 | 4 | 9 | 5 | 22 | 2 | 3 | 0 | 2 | 60 | 8.3 |
| 1998–99 | 30 | Detroit Red Wings | NHL | 10 | 3 | 7 | 10 | 2 | 6 | 2 | 1 | 0 | 1 | 31 | 9.7 |
| 1999–00 | 31 | Detroit Red Wings | NHL | 9 | 3 | 2 | 5 | 0 | 10 | 3 | 0 | 0 | 0 | 41 | 7.3 |
| 2000–01 | 32 | Detroit Red Wings | NHL | 2 | 2 | 2 | 4 | 3 | 0 | 2 | 0 | 0 | 1 | 12 | 16.7 |
| 2001–02 | 33 | Detroit Red Wings | NHL | 23 | 8 | 11 | 19 | 5 | 20 | 7 | 1 | 0 | 2 | 78 | 10.3 |
| 2002–03 | 34 | Detroit Red Wings | NHL | 4 | 1 | 1 | 2 | -1 | 4 | 0 | 1 | 0 | 0 | 17 | 5.9 |
| 2003–04 | 35 | Detroit Red Wings | NHL | 12 | 1 | 5 | 6 | 4 | 20 | 0 | 0 | 1 | 0 | 41 | 2.4 |
| 2005–06 | 37 | Detroit Red Wings | NHL | 6 | 1 | 1 | 2 | 0 | 6 | 1 | 0 | 0 | 0 | 21 | 4.8 |
| 2006–07 | 38 | New York Rangers | NHL | 10 | 5 | 2 | 7 | -5 | 12 | 2 | 3 | 0 | 2 | 41 | 12.2 |
| 2007–08 | 39 | New York Rangers | NHL | 10 | 1 | 4 | 5 | 0 | 8 | 1 | 0 | 0 | 0 | 30 | 3.3 |
| 2008–09 | 40 | New Jersey Devils | NHL | 7 | 1 | 2 | 3 | -1 | 2 | 1 | 0 | 0 | 0 | 25 | 4.0 |
| NHL Career — 19 Seasons | | | | 184 | 60 | 74 | 134 | 31 | 279 | 40 | 19 | 1 | 12 | 622 | 9.6 |

## Steve Shutt  Profile: See page 62

### REGULAR SEASON

| SEASON | AGE | TEAM | LG | GP | G | A | PTS | +/- | PIM | ESG | PPG | SHG | GWG | SOG | S% |
|---|---|---|---|---|---|---|---|---|---|---|---|---|---|---|---|
| 1972–73 | 20 | Montreal Canadiens | NHL | 50 | 8 | 8 | 16 | 5 | 24 | 7 | 1 | 0 | 2 | 55 | 14.6 |
| 1973–74 | 21 | Montreal Canadiens | NHL | 70 | 15 | 20 | 35 | 19 | 17 | 12 | 3 | 0 | 1 | 131 | 11.5 |
| 1974–75 | 22 | Montreal Canadiens | NHL | 77 | 30 | 35 | 65 | 40 | 40 | 27 | 3 | 0 | 5 | 165 | 18.2 |
| 1975–76 | 23 | Montreal Canadiens | NHL | 80 | 45 | 34 | 79 | 73 | 47 | 38 | 7 | 0 | 7 | 223 | 20.2 |
| 1976–77 | 24 | Montreal Canadiens | NHL | 80 | 60 | 45 | 105 | 89 | 28 | 52 | 8 | 0 | 9 | 293 | 20.5 |
| 1977–78 | 25 | Montreal Canadiens | NHL | 80 | 49 | 37 | 86 | 56 | 24 | 33 | 16 | 0 | 7 | 243 | 20.2 |
| 1978–79 | 26 | Montreal Canadiens | NHL | 72 | 37 | 40 | 77 | 38 | 31 | 27 | 10 | 0 | 6 | 190 | 19.5 |
| 1979–80 | 27 | Montreal Canadiens | NHL | 77 | 47 | 42 | 89 | 45 | 34 | 30 | 17 | 0 | 4 | 224 | 21.0 |
| 1980–81 | 28 | Montreal Canadiens | NHL | 77 | 35 | 38 | 73 | 30 | 51 | 28 | 7 | 0 | 3 | 232 | 15.1 |
| 1981–82 | 29 | Montreal Canadiens | NHL | 57 | 31 | 24 | 55 | 26 | 40 | 26 | 5 | 0 | 3 | 154 | 20.1 |
| 1982–83 | 30 | Montreal Canadiens | NHL | 78 | 35 | 22 | 57 | 9 | 26 | 27 | 8 | 0 | 0 | 203 | 17.3 |
| 1983–84 | 31 | Montreal Canadiens | NHL | 63 | 14 | 23 | 37 | -19 | 29 | 10 | 4 | 0 | 2 | 146 | 9.6 |
| 1984–85 | 32 | Montreal Canadiens | NHL | 10 | 2 | 0 | 2 | 2 | 9 | 1 | 1 | 0 | 0 | 17 | 11.8 |
| 1984–85 | 32 | Los Angeles Kings | NHL | 59 | 16 | 25 | 41 | -19 | 10 | 11 | 5 | 0 | 1 | 127 | 12.6 |
| NHL Career — 13 Seasons | | | | 930 | 424 | 393 | 817 | 394 | 410 | 329 | 95 | 0 | 50 | 2403 | 17.6 |

### PLAYOFFS

| SEASON | AGE | TEAM | LG | GP | G | A | PTS | +/- | PIM | ESG | PPG | SHG | GWG | SOG | S% |
|---|---|---|---|---|---|---|---|---|---|---|---|---|---|---|---|
| 1972–73 | 20 | Montreal Canadiens | NHL | 1 | 0 | 0 | 0 | -2 | 0 | 0 | 0 | 0 | 0 | 0 | |
| 1973–74 | 21 | Montreal Canadiens | NHL | 6 | 5 | 3 | 8 | 3 | 9 | 4 | 1 | 0 | 0 | 22 | 22.7 |
| 1974–75 | 22 | Montreal Canadiens | NHL | 9 | 1 | 6 | 7 | 2 | 4 | 1 | 0 | 0 | 0 | 10 | 10.0 |
| 1975–76 | 23 | Montreal Canadiens | NHL | 13 | 7 | 8 | 15 | 9 | 2 | 4 | 3 | 0 | 0 | 33 | 21.2 |
| 1976–77 | 24 | Montreal Canadiens | NHL | 14 | 8 | 10 | 18 | 18 | 2 | 6 | 2 | 0 | 3 | 39 | 20.5 |
| 1977–78 | 25 | Montreal Canadiens | NHL | 15 | 9 | 8 | 17 | 9 | 20 | 6 | 3 | 0 | 0 | 50 | 18.0 |
| 1978–79 | 26 | Montreal Canadiens | NHL | 11 | 4 | 7 | 11 | 7 | 6 | 3 | 1 | 0 | 0 | 44 | 9.1 |
| 1979–80 | 27 | Montreal Canadiens | NHL | 10 | 6 | 3 | 9 | -1 | 6 | 4 | 2 | 0 | 2 | 28 | 21.4 |
| 1980–81 | 28 | Montreal Canadiens | NHL | 3 | 2 | 1 | 3 | 1 | 4 | 2 | 0 | 0 | 0 | 12 | 16.7 |
| 1982–83 | 30 | Montreal Canadiens | NHL | 3 | 1 | 0 | 1 | -1 | 0 | 1 | 0 | 0 | 0 | 7 | 14.3 |
| 1983–84 | 31 | Montreal Canadiens | NHL | 11 | 7 | 2 | 9 | 5 | 8 | 5 | 2 | 0 | 0 | 26 | 26.9 |
| 1984–85 | 32 | Los Angeles Kings | NHL | 3 | 0 | 0 | 0 | -4 | 4 | 0 | 0 | 0 | 0 | 6 | 0.0 |
| NHL Career — 12 Seasons | | | | 99 | 50 | 48 | 98 | 46 | 65 | 36 | 14 | 0 | 5 | 277 | 18.1 |

# Babe Siebert  Profile: See page 63

**REGULAR SEASON**

| SEASON | AGE | TEAM | LG | GP | G | A | PTS | PIM |
|---|---|---|---|---|---|---|---|---|
| 1925–26 | 21 | Montreal Maroons | NHL | 35 | 16 | 7 | 23 | 110 |
| 1926–27 | 22 | Montreal Maroons | NHL | 42 | 5 | 3 | 8 | 118 |
| 1927–28 | 23 | Montreal Maroons | NHL | 39 | 8 | 9 | 17 | 119 |
| 1928–29 | 24 | Montreal Maroons | NHL | 40 | 3 | 5 | 8 | 54 |
| 1929–30 | 25 | Montreal Maroons | NHL | 41 | 14 | 19 | 33 | 94 |
| 1930–31 | 26 | Montreal Maroons | NHL | 43 | 16 | 12 | 28 | 78 |
| 1931–32 | 27 | Montreal Maroons | NHL | 48 | 21 | 18 | 39 | 66 |
| 1932–33 | 28 | New York Rangers | NHL | 43 | 9 | 10 | 19 | 38 |
| 1933–34 | 29 | New York Rangers | NHL | 13 | 0 | 1 | 1 | 16 |
| 1933–34 | 29 | Boston Bruins | NHL | 32 | 5 | 6 | 11 | 33 |
| 1934–35 | 30 | Boston Bruins | NHL | 48 | 6 | 18 | 24 | 80 |
| 1935–36 | 31 | Boston Bruins | NHL | 45 | 12 | 9 | 21 | 66 |
| 1936–37 | 32 | Montreal Canadiens | NHL | 44 | 8 | 20 | 28 | 38 |
| 1937–38 | 33 | Montreal Canadiens | NHL | 37 | 8 | 11 | 19 | 56 |
| 1938–39 | 34 | Montreal Canadiens | NHL | 44 | 9 | 6 | 15 | 36 |
| Career — 14 Seasons | | | | 592 | 140 | 154 | 294 | 1002 |

**PLAYOFFS**

| SEASON | AGE | TEAM | LG | GP | G | A | PTS | PIM |
|---|---|---|---|---|---|---|---|---|
| 1925–26 | 21 | Montreal Maroons | NHL | 4 | 1 | 0 | 1 | 4 |
| 1925–26 | 21 | Montreal Maroons | St-Cup | 4 | 1 | 2 | 3 | 2 |
| 1926–27 | 22 | Montreal Maroons | NHL | 2 | 1 | 0 | 1 | 2 |
| 1927–28 | 23 | Montreal Maroons | NHL | 9 | 2 | 1 | 3 | 26 |
| 1929–30 | 25 | Montreal Maroons | NHL | 3 | 0 | 0 | 0 | 0 |
| 1930–31 | 26 | Montreal Maroons | NHL | 2 | 0 | 0 | 0 | 6 |
| 1931–32 | 27 | Montreal Maroons | NHL | 4 | 0 | 1 | 1 | 4 |
| 1932–33 | 28 | New York Rangers | NHL | 8 | 1 | 0 | 1 | 12 |
| 1934–35 | 30 | Boston Bruins | NHL | 4 | 0 | 0 | 0 | 6 |
| 1935–36 | 31 | Boston Bruins | NHL | 2 | 0 | 1 | 1 | 0 |
| 1936–37 | 32 | Montreal Canadiens | NHL | 5 | 1 | 2 | 3 | 2 |
| 1937–38 | 33 | Montreal Canadiens | NHL | 3 | 1 | 1 | 2 | 0 |
| 1938–39 | 34 | Montreal Canadiens | NHL | 3 | 0 | 0 | 0 | 0 |
| Career — 12 Seasons | | | | 53 | 8 | 8 | 16 | 64 |

# Harry E. Watson  Profile: See page 64

**REGULAR SEASON**

| SEASON | AGE | TEAM | LG | GP | G | A | PTS | PIM |
|---|---|---|---|---|---|---|---|---|
| 1916–17 | 18 | Toronto Aura Lee | OHA-Sr. | 8 | 18 | 0 | 18 | |
| 1918–19 | 20 | Toronto Dentals | OHA-Sr. | | | | | |
| 1919–20 | 21 | Toronto Granites | OHA-Sr. | 8 | 17 | 4 | 21 | |
| 1920–21 | 22 | Toronto Granites | OHA-Sr. | 9 | 10 | 4 | 14 | |
| 1921–22 | 23 | Toronto Granites | OHA-St. | 10 | 18 | 4 | 22 | |
| 1922–23 | 24 | Toronto Granites | OHA-Sr. | 12 | 21 | 4 | 25 | |
| 1923–24 | 25 | Canada | Exhib. | 14 | 24 | 6 | 30 | |
| 1923–24 | 25 | Canada | Olympics | 5 | 36 | 14 | 50 | 2 |
| 1924–25 | 26 | Parkdale Canoe Club | OHA-Sr. | 6 | 6 | 2 | 8 | |
| 1925–26 | 27 | Parkdale Canoe Club | OHA-Sr. | 1 | 1 | 1 | 2 | |
| 1926–27 | 28 | Parkdale Canoe Club | OHA-Sr. | 1 | 2 | 0 | 2 | |
| 1927–28 | 29 | Toronto Marlboros | OHA-Sr. | 2 | 1 | 1 | 2 | 2 |
| 1929–30 | 31 | Toronto Nationals | OHA-Sr. | 1 | 0 | 0 | 0 | 0 |
| 1931–32 | 33 | Toronto Nationals | OHA-Sr. | 2 | 0 | 0 | 0 | 0 |
| Career — 13 Seasons | | | | 79 | 154 | 40 | 194 | 4 |

**PLAYOFFS**

| SEASON | AGE | TEAM | LG | GP | G | A | PTS | PIM |
|---|---|---|---|---|---|---|---|---|
| 1918–19 | 20 | Toronto Dentals | OHA-Sr. | 1 | 1 | 0 | 1 | |
| 1919–20 | 21 | Toronto Granites | Al-Cup | 2 | 1 | 0 | 1 | |
| 1919–20 | 21 | Toronto Granites | OHA-Sr. | 5 | 4 | 1 | 5 | |
| 1920–21 | 22 | Toronto Granites | OHA-Sr. | 2 | 2 | 0 | 2 | |
| 1921–22 | 23 | Toronto Granites | Al-Cup | 5 | 13 | 2 | 15 | |
| 1921–22 | 23 | Toronto Granites | OHA-Sr. | 2 | 5 | 0 | 5 | |
| 1922–23 | 24 | Toronto Granites | Al-Cup | 6 | 11 | 4 | 15 | 2 |
| 1922–23 | 24 | Toronto Granites | OHA-Sr. | 2 | 3 | 0 | 3 | 0 |
| 1925–26 | 27 | Parkdale Canoe Club | OHA-Sr. | 2 | 0 | 0 | 0 | |
| Career — 6 Seasons | | | | 27 | 40 | 7 | 47 | 2 |

# Harry P. Watson  Profile: See page 65

**REGULAR SEASON**

| SEASON | AGE | TEAM | LG | GP | G | A | PTS | PIM |
|---|---|---|---|---|---|---|---|---|
| 1941–42 | 18 | Brooklyn Americans | NHL | 47 | 10 | 8 | 18 | 6 |
| 1942–43 | 19 | Detroit Red Wings | NHL | 50 | 13 | 18 | 31 | 10 |
| 1945–46 | 22 | Detroit Red Wings | NHL | 44 | 14 | 10 | 24 | 4 |
| 1946–47 | 23 | Detroit Red Wings | NHL | 44 | 19 | 15 | 34 | 10 |
| 1947–48 | 24 | Toronto Maple Leafs | NHL | 57 | 21 | 20 | 41 | 16 |
| 1948–49 | 25 | Toronto Maple Leafs | NHL | 60 | 26 | 19 | 45 | 0 |
| 1949–50 | 26 | Toronto Maple Leafs | NHL | 60 | 19 | 16 | 35 | 11 |
| 1950–51 | 27 | Toronto Maple Leafs | NHL | 68 | 18 | 19 | 37 | 18 |
| 1951–52 | 28 | Toronto Maple Leafs | NHL | 70 | 22 | 17 | 39 | 18 |
| 1952–53 | 29 | Toronto Maple Leafs | NHL | 63 | 16 | 8 | 24 | 8 |
| 1953–54 | 30 | Toronto Maple Leafs | NHL | 70 | 21 | 7 | 28 | 30 |
| 1954–55 | 31 | Toronto Maple Leafs | NHL | 8 | 1 | 1 | 2 | 0 |
| 1954–55 | 31 | Chicago Black Hawks | NHL | 43 | 14 | 16 | 30 | 4 |
| 1955–56 | 32 | Chicago Black Hawks | NHL | 55 | 11 | 14 | 25 | 6 |
| 1956–57 | 33 | Chicago Black Hawks | NHL | 70 | 11 | 19 | 30 | 9 |
| NHL Career — 14 Seasons | | | | 809 | 236 | 207 | 443 | 150 |

**PLAYOFFS**

| SEASON | AGE | TEAM | LG | GP | G | A | PTS | PIM |
|---|---|---|---|---|---|---|---|---|
| 1942–43 | 19 | Detroit Red Wings | NHL | 7 | 0 | 0 | 0 | 0 |
| 1945–46 | 22 | Detroit Red Wings | NHL | 5 | 2 | 0 | 2 | 0 |
| 1946–47 | 23 | Toronto Maple Leafs | NHL | 11 | 3 | 2 | 5 | 6 |
| 1947–48 | 24 | Toronto Maple Leafs | NHL | 9 | 5 | 2 | 7 | 9 |
| 1948–49 | 25 | Toronto Maple Leafs | NHL | 9 | 4 | 2 | 6 | 2 |
| 1949–50 | 26 | Toronto Maple Leafs | NHL | 7 | 0 | 0 | 0 | 2 |
| 1950–51 | 27 | Toronto Maple Leafs | NHL | 5 | 1 | 2 | 3 | 4 |
| 1951–52 | 28 | Toronto Maple Leafs | NHL | 4 | 1 | 0 | 1 | 2 |
| 1953–54 | 30 | Toronto Maple Leafs | NHL | 5 | 0 | 1 | 1 | 2 |
| NHL Career — 9 Seasons | | | | 62 | 16 | 9 | 25 | 27 |

## Sid Abel — Profile: See page 68

**REGULAR SEASON**

| SEASON | AGE | TEAM | LG | GP | G | A | PTS | PIM |
|---|---|---|---|---|---|---|---|---|
| 1938–39 | 20 | Detroit Red Wings | NHL | 15 | 1 | 1 | 2 | 0 |
| 1939–40 | 21 | Detroit Red Wings | NHL | 24 | 1 | 5 | 6 | 4 |
| 1940–41 | 22 | Detroit Red Wings | NHL | 47 | 10 | 22 | 32 | 29 |
| 1941–42 | 23 | Detroit Red Wings | NHL | 48 | 18 | 31 | 49 | 45 |
| 1942–43 | 24 | Detroit Red Wings | NHL | 49 | 18 | 24 | 42 | 33 |
| 1945–46 | 27 | Detroit Red Wings | NHL | 7 | 0 | 3 | 3 | 0 |
| 1946–47 | 28 | Detroit Red Wings | NHL | 60 | 19 | 29 | 48 | 29 |
| 1947–48 | 29 | Detroit Red Wings | NHL | 60 | 14 | 30 | 44 | 69 |
| 1948–49 | 30 | Detroit Red Wings | NHL | 60 | 28 | 26 | 54 | 49 |
| 1949–50 | 31 | Detroit Red Wings | NHL | 69 | 34 | 35 | 69 | 46 |
| 1950–51 | 32 | Detroit Red Wings | NHL | 69 | 23 | 38 | 61 | 30 |
| 1951–52 | 33 | Detroit Red Wings | NHL | 62 | 17 | 36 | 53 | 32 |
| 1952–53 | 34 | Chicago Black Hawks | NHL | 39 | 5 | 4 | 9 | 6 |
| 1953–54 | 35 | Chicago Black Hawks | NHL | 3 | 0 | 0 | 0 | 4 |
| NHL Career — 14 Seasons | | | | 612 | 188 | 284 | 472 | 376 |

**PLAYOFFS**

| SEASON | AGE | TEAM | LG | GP | G | A | PTS | PIM |
|---|---|---|---|---|---|---|---|---|
| 1938–39 | 20 | Detroit Red Wings | NHL | 3 | 1 | 1 | 2 | 2 |
| 1939–40 | 21 | Detroit Red Wings | NHL | 5 | 0 | 3 | 3 | 21 |
| 1940–41 | 22 | Detroit Red Wings | NHL | 9 | 2 | 2 | 4 | 2 |
| 1941–42 | 23 | Detroit Red Wings | NHL | 12 | 4 | 2 | 6 | 8 |
| 1942–43 | 24 | Detroit Red Wings | NHL | 10 | 5 | 8 | 13 | 4 |
| 1945–46 | 27 | Detroit Red Wings | NHL | 3 | 0 | 0 | 0 | 0 |
| 1946–47 | 28 | Detroit Red Wings | NHL | 3 | 1 | 1 | 2 | 2 |
| 1947–48 | 29 | Detroit Red Wings | NHL | 10 | 0 | 3 | 3 | 16 |
| 1948–49 | 30 | Detroit Red Wings | NHL | 11 | 3 | 3 | 6 | 6 |
| 1949–50 | 31 | Detroit Red Wings | NHL | 14 | 6 | 2 | 8 | 6 |
| 1950–51 | 32 | Detroit Red Wings | NHL | 6 | 4 | 3 | 7 | 0 |
| 1951–52 | 33 | Detroit Red Wings | NHL | 7 | 2 | 2 | 4 | 12 |
| 1952–53 | 34 | Chicago Black Hawks | NHL | 1 | 0 | 0 | 0 | 0 |
| NHL Career — 13 Seasons | | | | 94 | 28 | 30 | 58 | 79 |

## Jack Adams — Profile: See page 70

**REGULAR SEASON**

| SEASON | AGE | TEAM | LG | GP | G | A | PTS | PIM |
|---|---|---|---|---|---|---|---|---|
| 1917–18 | 22 | Toronto Arenas | NHL | 8 | 0 | 0 | 0 | 31 |
| 1918–19 | 23 | Toronto Arenas | NHL | 17 | 3 | 3 | 6 | 47 |
| 1919–20 | 24 | Vancouver Millionaires | PCHA | 22 | 9 | 6 | 15 | 18 |
| 1920–21 | 25 | Vancouver Millionaires | PCHA | 24 | 17 | 12 | 29 | 60 |
| 1921–22 | 26 | Vancouver Millionaires | PCHA | 24 | 26 | 4 | 30 | 24 |
| 1922–23 | 27 | Toronto St. Patricks | NHL | 23 | 18 | 12 | 30 | 66 |
| 1923–24 | 28 | Toronto St. Patricks | NHL | 22 | 13 | 6 | 19 | 51 |
| 1924–25 | 29 | Toronto St. Patricks | NHL | 27 | 21 | 14 | 35 | 67 |
| 1925–26 | 30 | Toronto St. Patricks | NHL | 36 | 21 | 8 | 29 | 56 |
| 1926–27 | 31 | Ottawa Senators | NHL | 40 | 5 | 1 | 6 | 66 |
| Career — 10 Seasons | | | | 243 | 133 | 66 | 199 | 486 |

**PLAYOFFS**

| SEASON | AGE | TEAM | LG | GP | G | A | PTS | PIM |
|---|---|---|---|---|---|---|---|---|
| 1917–18 | 22 | Toronto Arenas | NHL | 2 | 1 | 0 | 1 | 9 |
| 1919–20 | 24 | Vancouver Millionaires | PCHA | 2 | 0 | 0 | 0 | 0 |
| 1920–21 | 25 | Vancouver Millionaires | PCHA | 2 | 3 | 0 | 3 | 0 |
| 1920–21 | 25 | Vancouver Millionaires | St-Cup | 5 | 2 | 1 | 3 | 6 |
| 1921–22 | 26 | Vancouver Millionaires | PCHA | 2 | 1 | 0 | 1 | 0 |
| 1921–22 | 26 | Vancouver Millionaires | St-Cup | 5 | 6 | 1 | 7 | 18 |
| 1921–22 | 26 | Vancouver Millionaires | West-P | 2 | 0 | 0 | 0 | 12 |
| 1924–25 | 29 | Toronto St. Patricks | NHL | 2 | 1 | 0 | 1 | 7 |
| 1926–27 | 31 | Ottawa Senators | NHL | 6 | 0 | 0 | 0 | 0 |
| Career — 6 Seasons | | | | 28 | 14 | 2 | 16 | 40 |

## Syl Apps — Profile: See page 72

**REGULAR SEASON**

| SEASON | AGE | TEAM | LG | GP | G | A | PTS | PIM |
|---|---|---|---|---|---|---|---|---|
| 1936–37 | 22 | Toronto Maple Leafs | NHL | 48 | 16 | 29 | 45 | 10 |
| 1937–38 | 23 | Toronto Maple Leafs | NHL | 47 | 21 | 29 | 50 | 9 |
| 1938–39 | 24 | Toronto Maple Leafs | NHL | 44 | 15 | 25 | 40 | 4 |
| 1939–40 | 25 | Toronto Maple Leafs | NHL | 27 | 13 | 17 | 30 | 5 |
| 1940–41 | 26 | Toronto Maple Leafs | NHL | 41 | 20 | 24 | 44 | 6 |
| 1941–42 | 27 | Toronto Maple Leafs | NHL | 38 | 18 | 23 | 41 | 0 |
| 1942–43 | 28 | Toronto Maple Leafs | NHL | 29 | 23 | 17 | 40 | 2 |
| 1945–46 | 31 | Toronto Maple Leafs | NHL | 40 | 24 | 16 | 40 | 2 |
| 1946–47 | 32 | Toronto Maple Leafs | NHL | 54 | 25 | 24 | 49 | 6 |
| 1947–48 | 33 | Toronto Maple Leafs | NHL | 55 | 26 | 27 | 53 | 12 |
| NHL Career — 10 Seasons | | | | 423 | 201 | 231 | 432 | 56 |

**PLAYOFFS**

| SEASON | AGE | TEAM | LG | GP | G | A | PTS | PIM |
|---|---|---|---|---|---|---|---|---|
| 1936–37 | 22 | Toronto Maple Leafs | NHL | 2 | 0 | 1 | 1 | 0 |
| 1937–38 | 23 | Toronto Maple Leafs | NHL | 7 | 1 | 4 | 5 | 0 |
| 1938–39 | 24 | Toronto Maple Leafs | NHL | 10 | 2 | 6 | 8 | 2 |
| 1939–40 | 25 | Toronto Maple Leafs | NHL | 10 | 5 | 2 | 7 | 2 |
| 1940–41 | 26 | Toronto Maple Leafs | NHL | 7 | 3 | 2 | 5 | 0 |
| 1941–42 | 27 | Toronto Maple Leafs | NHL | 13 | 5 | 8 | 13 | 2 |
| 1946–47 | 32 | Toronto Maple Leafs | NHL | 11 | 5 | 1 | 6 | 0 |
| 1947–48 | 33 | Toronto Maple Leafs | NHL | 9 | 4 | 4 | 8 | 0 |
| NHL Career — 8 Seasons | | | | 69 | 25 | 28 | 53 | 6 |

## Dan Bain — Profile: See page 73

**REGULAR SEASON**

| SEASON | AGE | TEAM | LG | GP | G | A | PTS |
|---|---|---|---|---|---|---|---|
| 1894–95 | 20 | Winnipeg Victorias | MNWHA | 3 | 9 | 0 | 12 |
| 1895–96 | 21 | Winnipeg Victorias | MNWHA | 5 | 10 | 3 | 13 |
| 1896–97 | 22 | Winnipeg Victorias | MNWHA | 5 | 9 | 1 | 10 |
| 1897–98 | 23 | Winnipeg Victorias | MNWHA | 5 | 13 | 1 | 16 |
| 1898–99 | 24 | Winnipeg Victorias | MNWHA | 3 | 10 | 1 | 11 |
| 1899–00 | 25 | Winnipeg Victorias | MNWHA | 2 | 9 | 1 | 14 |
| 1900–01 | 26 | Winnipeg Victorias | MNWHA | 3 | 2 | 1 | 3 |
| 1901–02 | 27 | Winnipeg Victorias | MNWHA | 1 | 3 | 0 | 3 |
| Career — 8 Seasons | | | | 27 | 65 | 17 | 82 |

**PLAYOFFS**

| SEASON | AGE | TEAM | LG | GP | G | A | PTS |
|---|---|---|---|---|---|---|---|
| 1895–96 | 21 | Winnipeg Victorias | St-Cup | 2 | 3 | 0 | 3 |
| 1898–99 | 24 | Winnipeg Victorias | St-Cup | 1 | 0 | 0 | 0 |
| 1899–00 | 25 | Winnipeg Victorias | St-Cup | 3 | 4 | 0 | 4 |
| 1900–01 | 26 | Winnipeg Victorias | St-Cup | 2 | 3 | 0 | 3 |
| 1901–02 | 27 | Winnipeg Victorias | St-Cup | 3 | 0 | 0 | 0 |
| Career — 5 Seasons | | | | 11 | 10 | 0 | 10 |

## Marty Barry  Profile: See page 74

### REGULAR SEASON

| SEASON | AGE | TEAM | LG | GP | G | A | PTS | PIM |
|---|---|---|---|---|---|---|---|---|
| 1927–28 | 22 | New York Americans | NHL | 7 | 1 | 0 | 1 | 2 |
| 1929–30 | 24 | Boston Bruins | NHL | 44 | 18 | 15 | 33 | 34 |
| 1930–31 | 25 | Boston Bruins | NHL | 44 | 20 | 11 | 31 | 26 |
| 1931–32 | 26 | Boston Bruins | NHL | 48 | 21 | 17 | 38 | 22 |
| 1932–33 | 27 | Boston Bruins | NHL | 47 | 24 | 13 | 37 | 40 |
| 1933–34 | 28 | Boston Bruins | NHL | 48 | 27 | 12 | 39 | 12 |
| 1934–35 | 29 | Boston Bruins | NHL | 48 | 19 | 21 | 40 | 33 |
| 1935–36 | 30 | Detroit Red Wings | NHL | 48 | 21 | 19 | 40 | 16 |
| 1936–37 | 31 | Detroit Red Wings | NHL | 47 | 17 | 27 | 44 | 6 |
| 1937–38 | 32 | Detroit Red Wings | NHL | 48 | 9 | 20 | 29 | 34 |
| 1938–39 | 33 | Detroit Red Wings | NHL | 48 | 13 | 28 | 41 | 4 |
| 1939–40 | 34 | Montreal Canadiens | NHL | 30 | 4 | 10 | 14 | 2 |
| Career — 12 Seasons | | | | 509 | 195 | 192 | 387 | 231 |

### PLAYOFFS

| SEASON | AGE | TEAM | LG | GP | G | A | PTS | PIM |
|---|---|---|---|---|---|---|---|---|
| 1928–29 | 23 | New Haven Eagles | Can-Am | 2 | 0 | 1 | 1 | 2 |
| 1929–30 | 24 | Boston Bruins | NHL | 6 | 3 | 3 | 6 | 12 |
| 1930–31 | 25 | Boston Bruins | NHL | 5 | 1 | 1 | 2 | 4 |
| 1932–33 | 27 | Boston Bruins | NHL | 5 | 2 | 2 | 4 | 6 |
| 1934–35 | 29 | Boston Bruins | NHL | 4 | 0 | 0 | 0 | 4 |
| 1935–36 | 30 | Detroit Red Wings | NHL | 7 | 2 | 4 | 6 | 6 |
| 1936–37 | 31 | Detroit Red Wings | NHL | 10 | 4 | 7 | 11 | 2 |
| 1938–39 | 33 | Detroit Red Wings | NHL | 6 | 3 | 1 | 4 | 0 |
| Career — 7 Seasons | | | | 43 | 15 | 18 | 33 | 34 |

## Jean Béliveau  Profile: See page 76

### REGULAR SEASON

| SEASON | AGE | TEAM | LG | GP | G | A | PTS | +/– | PIM | ESG | PPG | SHG | GWG | SOG | S% |
|---|---|---|---|---|---|---|---|---|---|---|---|---|---|---|---|
| 1950–51 | 19 | Montreal Canadiens | NHL | 2 | 1 | 1 | 2 | | 0 | 1 | 0 | 0 | 0 | | |
| 1952–53 | 21 | Montreal Canadiens | NHL | 3 | 5 | 0 | 5 | | 0 | 4 | 1 | 0 | 1 | | |
| 1953–54 | 22 | Montreal Canadiens | NHL | 44 | 13 | 21 | 34 | | 22 | 10 | 3 | 0 | 1 | | |
| 1954–55 | 23 | Montreal Canadiens | NHL | 70 | 37 | 36 | 73 | | 58 | 23 | 14 | 0 | 7 | | |
| 1955–56 | 24 | Montreal Canadiens | NHL | 70 | 47 | 41 | 88 | | 143 | 28 | 19 | 0 | 8 | | |
| 1956–57 | 25 | Montreal Canadiens | NHL | 69 | 33 | 51 | 84 | | 105 | 21 | 12 | 0 | 4 | | |
| 1957–58 | 26 | Montreal Canadiens | NHL | 55 | 27 | 32 | 59 | | 93 | 21 | 6 | 0 | 5 | | |
| 1958–59 | 27 | Montreal Canadiens | NHL | 64 | 45 | 46 | 91 | | 69 | 32 | 13 | 0 | 7 | | |
| 1959–60 | 28 | Montreal Canadiens | NHL | 60 | 34 | 40 | 74 | 20 | 57 | 22 | 12 | 0 | 10 | 285 | 11.9 |
| 1960–61 | 29 | Montreal Canadiens | NHL | 69 | 32 | 58 | 90 | 10 | 57 | 19 | 13 | 0 | 11 | 324 | 9.9 |
| 1961–62 | 30 | Montreal Canadiens | NHL | 43 | 18 | 23 | 41 | 10 | 36 | 10 | 8 | 0 | 4 | 149 | 12.1 |
| 1962–63 | 31 | Montreal Canadiens | NHL | 69 | 18 | 49 | 67 | 5 | 68 | 9 | 9 | 0 | 1 | 241 | 7.5 |
| 1963–64 | 32 | Montreal Canadiens | NHL | 68 | 28 | 50 | 78 | 9 | 42 | 15 | 13 | 0 | 2 | 228 | 12.3 |
| 1964–65 | 33 | Montreal Canadiens | NHL | 58 | 20 | 23 | 43 | -15 | 76 | 11 | 9 | 0 | 1 | 185 | 10.8 |
| 1965–66 | 34 | Montreal Canadiens | NHL | 67 | 29 | 48 | 77 | 10 | 50 | 16 | 13 | 0 | 8 | 267 | 10.9 |
| 1966–67 | 35 | Montreal Canadiens | NHL | 53 | 12 | 26 | 38 | 3 | 22 | 10 | 2 | 0 | 0 | 166 | 7.2 |
| 1967–68 | 36 | Montreal Canadiens | NHL | 59 | 31 | 37 | 68 | 25 | 28 | 22 | 9 | 0 | 3 | 206 | 15.0 |
| 1968–69 | 37 | Montreal Canadiens | NHL | 69 | 33 | 49 | 82 | 15 | 55 | 26 | 7 | 0 | 5 | 235 | 14.0 |
| 1969–70 | 38 | Montreal Canadiens | NHL | 63 | 19 | 30 | 49 | 1 | 10 | 16 | 3 | 0 | 1 | 169 | 11.2 |
| 1970–71 | 39 | Montreal Canadiens | NHL | 70 | 25 | 51 | 76 | 24 | 42 | 18 | 7 | 0 | 4 | 172 | 14.5 |
| NHL Career — 20 Seasons | | | | 1125 | 507 | 712 | 1219 | 117 | 1033 | 334 | 173 | 0 | 83 | 2627 | 11.4 |

### PLAYOFFS

| SEASON | AGE | TEAM | LG | GP | G | A | PTS | +/– | PIM | ESG | PPG | SHG | GWG | SOG | S% |
|---|---|---|---|---|---|---|---|---|---|---|---|---|---|---|---|
| 1953–54 | 22 | Montreal Canadiens | NHL | 10 | 2 | 8 | 10 | | 4 | 1 | 1 | 0 | 0 | | |
| 1954–55 | 23 | Montreal Canadiens | NHL | 12 | 6 | 7 | 13 | | 18 | 4 | 2 | 0 | 0 | | |
| 1955–56 | 24 | Montreal Canadiens | NHL | 10 | 12 | 7 | 19 | | 22 | 9 | 3 | 0 | 2 | | |
| 1956–57 | 25 | Montreal Canadiens | NHL | 10 | 6 | 6 | 12 | | 15 | 5 | 1 | 0 | 1 | | |
| 1957–58 | 26 | Montreal Canadiens | NHL | 10 | 4 | 8 | 12 | | 10 | 4 | 0 | 0 | 1 | | |
| 1958–59 | 27 | Montreal Canadiens | NHL | 3 | 1 | 4 | 5 | | 4 | 0 | 1 | 0 | 0 | | |
| 1959–60 | 28 | Montreal Canadiens | NHL | 8 | 5 | 2 | 7 | 7 | 6 | 5 | 0 | 0 | 3 | 34 | 14.7 |
| 1960–61 | 29 | Montreal Canadiens | NHL | 6 | 0 | 5 | 5 | 2 | 0 | 0 | 0 | 0 | 0 | 21 | 0.0 |
| 1961–62 | 30 | Montreal Canadiens | NHL | 6 | 2 | 1 | 3 | -3 | 4 | 0 | 2 | 0 | 1 | 14 | 14.3 |
| 1962–63 | 31 | Montreal Canadiens | NHL | 5 | 2 | 1 | 3 | -1 | 2 | 1 | 1 | 0 | 0 | 14 | 14.3 |
| 1963–64 | 32 | Montreal Canadiens | NHL | 5 | 2 | 0 | 2 | -2 | 18 | 1 | 1 | 0 | 0 | 8 | 25.0 |
| 1964–65 | 33 | Montreal Canadiens | NHL | 13 | 8 | 8 | 16 | -1 | 34 | 3 | 5 | 0 | 4 | 55 | 14.6 |
| 1965–66 | 34 | Montreal Canadiens | NHL | 10 | 5 | 5 | 10 | 4 | 6 | 4 | 1 | 0 | 1 | 37 | 13.5 |
| 1966–67 | 35 | Montreal Canadiens | NHL | 10 | 6 | 5 | 11 | 2 | 26 | 4 | 2 | 0 | 0 | 47 | 12.8 |
| 1967–68 | 36 | Montreal Canadiens | NHL | 10 | 7 | 4 | 11 | 4 | 6 | 4 | 3 | 0 | 1 | 41 | 17.1 |
| 1968–69 | 37 | Montreal Canadiens | NHL | 14 | 5 | 10 | 15 | 2 | 8 | 4 | 1 | 0 | 1 | 37 | 13.5 |
| 1970–71 | 39 | Montreal Canadiens | NHL | 20 | 6 | 16 | 22 | 13 | 28 | 4 | 2 | 0 | 0 | 57 | 10.5 |
| NHL Career — 17 Seasons | | | | 162 | 79 | 97 | 176 | 27 | 211 | 53 | 26 | 0 | 15 | 365 | 13.2 |

## Max Bentley — Profile: See page 78

### REGULAR SEASON

| SEASON | AGE | TEAM | LG | GP | G | A | PTS | PIM |
|---|---|---|---|---|---|---|---|---|
| 1940–41 | 20 | Chicago Black Hawks | NHL | 36 | 7 | 10 | 17 | 6 |
| 1941–42 | 21 | Chicago Black Hawks | NHL | 39 | 13 | 17 | 30 | 2 |
| 1942–43 | 22 | Chicago Black Hawks | NHL | 47 | 26 | 44 | 70 | 2 |
| 1945–46 | 25 | Chicago Black Hawks | NHL | 47 | 31 | 30 | 61 | 6 |
| 1946–47 | 26 | Chicago Black Hawks | NHL | 60 | 29 | 43 | 72 | 12 |
| 1947–48 | 27 | Chicago Black Hawks | NHL | 6 | 3 | 3 | 6 | 4 |
| 1947–48 | 27 | Toronto Maple Leafs | NHL | 53 | 23 | 25 | 48 | 10 |
| 1948–49 | 28 | Toronto Maple Leafs | NHL | 60 | 19 | 22 | 41 | 18 |
| 1949–50 | 29 | Toronto Maple Leafs | NHL | 69 | 23 | 18 | 41 | 12 |
| 1950–51 | 30 | Toronto Maple Leafs | NHL | 67 | 21 | 41 | 62 | 34 |
| 1951–52 | 31 | Toronto Maple Leafs | NHL | 69 | 24 | 17 | 41 | 40 |
| 1952–53 | 32 | Toronto Maple Leafs | NHL | 36 | 12 | 11 | 23 | 16 |
| 1953–54 | 33 | New York Rangers | NHL | 57 | 14 | 18 | 32 | 15 |
| NHL Career — 12 Seasons | | | | 646 | 245 | 299 | 544 | 177 |

### PLAYOFFS

| SEASON | AGE | TEAM | LG | GP | G | A | PTS | PIM |
|---|---|---|---|---|---|---|---|---|
| 1940–41 | 20 | Chicago Black Hawks | NHL | 4 | 1 | 3 | 4 | 2 |
| 1941–42 | 21 | Chicago Black Hawks | NHL | 3 | 2 | 0 | 2 | 0 |
| 1945–46 | 25 | Chicago Black Hawks | NHL | 4 | 1 | 0 | 1 | 4 |
| 1947–48 | 27 | Toronto Maple Leafs | NHL | 9 | 4 | 7 | 11 | 0 |
| 1948–49 | 28 | Toronto Maple Leafs | NHL | 9 | 4 | 3 | 7 | 2 |
| 1949–50 | 29 | Toronto Maple Leafs | NHL | 7 | 3 | 3 | 6 | 0 |
| 1950–51 | 30 | Toronto Maple Leafs | NHL | 11 | 2 | 11 | 13 | 4 |
| 1951–52 | 31 | Toronto Maple Leafs | NHL | 4 | 1 | 0 | 1 | 2 |
| NHL Career — 8 Seasons | | | | 51 | 18 | 27 | 45 | 14 |

## Frank Boucher — Profile: See page 80

### REGULAR SEASON

| SEASON | AGE | TEAM | LG | GP | G | A | PTS | PIM |
|---|---|---|---|---|---|---|---|---|
| 1921–22 | 20 | Ottawa Senators | NHL | 24 | 8 | 2 | 10 | 4 |
| 1922–23 | 21 | Vancouver Maroons | PCHA | 29 | 11 | 9 | 20 | 2 |
| 1923–24 | 22 | Vancouver Maroons | PCHA | 28 | 15 | 5 | 20 | 10 |
| 1924–25 | 23 | Vancouver Maroons | WCHL | 27 | 16 | 12 | 28 | 6 |
| 1925–26 | 24 | Vancouver Maroons | WHL | 29 | 15 | 7 | 22 | 14 |
| 1926–27 | 25 | New York Rangers | NHL | 44 | 13 | 15 | 28 | 17 |
| 1927–28 | 26 | New York Rangers | NHL | 44 | 23 | 12 | 35 | 12 |
| 1928–29 | 27 | New York Rangers | NHL | 44 | 10 | 16 | 26 | 8 |
| 1929–30 | 28 | New York Rangers | NHL | 42 | 26 | 36 | 62 | 16 |
| 1930–31 | 29 | New York Rangers | NHL | 44 | 12 | 27 | 39 | 18 |
| 1931–32 | 30 | New York Rangers | NHL | 48 | 12 | 24 | 36 | 14 |
| 1932–33 | 31 | New York Rangers | NHL | 46 | 7 | 28 | 35 | 4 |
| 1933–34 | 32 | New York Rangers | NHL | 48 | 14 | 30 | 44 | 4 |
| 1934–35 | 33 | New York Rangers | NHL | 48 | 13 | 32 | 45 | 2 |
| 1935–36 | 34 | New York Rangers | NHL | 48 | 11 | 18 | 29 | 2 |
| 1936–37 | 35 | New York Rangers | NHL | 44 | 7 | 13 | 20 | 5 |
| 1937–38 | 36 | New York Rangers | NHL | 18 | 0 | 1 | 1 | 2 |
| 1943–44 | 42 | New York Rangers | NHL | 15 | 4 | 10 | 14 | 2 |
| Career — 18 Seasons | | | | 670 | 217 | 297 | 514 | 142 |

### PLAYOFFS

| SEASON | AGE | TEAM | LG | GP | G | A | PTS | PIM |
|---|---|---|---|---|---|---|---|---|
| 1921–22 | 20 | Ottawa Senators | NHL | 1 | 0 | 0 | 0 | 0 |
| 1922–23 | 21 | Vancouver Maroons | PCHA | 2 | 0 | 1 | 1 | 2 |
| 1922–23 | 21 | Vancouver Maroons | St-Cup | 4 | 2 | 0 | 2 | 0 |
| 1923–24 | 22 | Vancouver Maroons | PCHA | 2 | 1 | 0 | 1 | 0 |
| 1923–24 | 22 | Vancouver Maroons | St-Cup | 2 | 1 | 1 | 2 | 2 |
| 1923–24 | 22 | Vancouver Millionaires | West-P | 3 | 1 | 0 | 1 | 0 |
| 1926–27 | 25 | New York Rangers | NHL | 2 | 0 | 0 | 0 | 4 |
| 1927–28 | 26 | New York Rangers | NHL | 9 | 7 | 3 | 10 | 2 |
| 1928–29 | 27 | New York Rangers | NHL | 6 | 1 | 0 | 1 | 0 |
| 1929–30 | 28 | New York Rangers | NHL | 3 | 1 | 1 | 2 | 0 |
| 1930–31 | 29 | New York Rangers | NHL | 4 | 0 | 2 | 2 | 0 |
| 1931–32 | 30 | New York Rangers | NHL | 7 | 3 | 6 | 9 | 0 |
| 1932–33 | 31 | New York Rangers | NHL | 8 | 2 | 2 | 4 | 6 |
| 1933–34 | 32 | New York Rangers | NHL | 2 | 0 | 0 | 0 | 0 |
| 1934–35 | 33 | New York Rangers | NHL | 4 | 0 | 3 | 3 | 0 |
| 1936–37 | 35 | New York Rangers | NHL | 9 | 2 | 3 | 5 | 0 |
| Career — 13 Seasons | | | | 68 | 21 | 22 | 43 | 16 |

## Billy Burch — Profile: See page 81

### REGULAR SEASON

| SEASON | AGE | TEAM | LG | GP | G | A | PTS | PIM |
|---|---|---|---|---|---|---|---|---|
| 1922–23 | 22 | Hamilton Tigers | NHL | 10 | 6 | 3 | 9 | 2 |
| 1923–24 | 23 | Hamilton Tigers | NHL | 24 | 16 | 6 | 22 | 6 |
| 1924–25 | 24 | Hamilton Tigers | NHL | 27 | 20 | 6 | 26 | 10 |
| 1925–26 | 25 | New York Americans | NHL | 36 | 22 | 3 | 24 | 33 |
| 1926–27 | 26 | New York Americans | NHL | 43 | 19 | 8 | 27 | 42 |
| 1927–28 | 27 | New York Americans | NHL | 32 | 10 | 2 | 12 | 34 |
| 1928–29 | 28 | New York Americans | NHL | 44 | 11 | 5 | 16 | 47 |
| 1929–30 | 29 | New York Americans | NHL | 35 | 7 | 3 | 10 | 24 |
| 1930–31 | 30 | New York Americans | NHL | 44 | 14 | 8 | 22 | 35 |

### REGULAR SEASON

| SEASON | AGE | TEAM | LG | GP | G | A | PTS | PIM |
|---|---|---|---|---|---|---|---|---|
| 1931–32 | 31 | New York Americans | NHL | 48 | 7 | 15 | 22 | 24 |
| 1932–33 | 32 | Boston Bruins | NHL | 25 | 3 | 1 | 4 | 4 |
| 1932–33 | 32 | Chicago Black Hawks | NHL | 22 | 2 | 0 | 2 | 2 |
| NHL Career — 11 Seasons | | | | 390 | 136 | 60 | 196 | 263 |

### PLAYOFFS

| SEASON | AGE | TEAM | LG | GP | G | A | PTS | PIM |
|---|---|---|---|---|---|---|---|---|
| 1928–29 | 28 | New York Americans | NHL | 2 | 0 | 0 | 0 | 0 |
| NHL Career — 1 Season | | | | 2 | 0 | 0 | 0 | 0 |

## Bobby Clarke — Profile: See page 82

### REGULAR SEASON

| SEASON | AGE | TEAM | LG | GP | G | A | PTS | +/- | PIM | ESG | PPG | SHG | GWG | SOG | S% |
|---|---|---|---|---|---|---|---|---|---|---|---|---|---|---|---|
| 1969–70 | 20 | Philadelphia Flyers | NHL | 76 | 15 | 31 | 46 | -1 | 68 | 9 | 5 | 1 | 0 | 214 | 7.0 |
| 1970–71 | 21 | Philadelphia Flyers | NHL | 77 | 27 | 36 | 63 | 9 | 78 | 16 | 10 | 1 | 5 | 185 | 14.6 |
| 1971–72 | 22 | Philadelphia Flyers | NHL | 78 | 35 | 46 | 81 | 24 | 87 | 23 | 11 | 1 | 3 | 225 | 15.6 |
| 1972–73 | 23 | Philadelphia Flyers | NHL | 78 | 37 | 67 | 104 | 32 | 80 | 25 | 10 | 2 | 4 | 231 | 16.0 |
| 1973–74 | 24 | Philadelphia Flyers | NHL | 77 | 35 | 52 | 87 | 35 | 113 | 20 | 10 | 5 | 5 | 221 | 15.8 |
| 1974–75 | 25 | Philadelphia Flyers | NHL | 80 | 27 | 89 | 116 | 79 | 125 | 14 | 10 | 3 | 4 | 195 | 13.8 |
| 1975–76 | 26 | Philadelphia Flyers | NHL | 76 | 30 | 89 | 119 | 83 | 136 | 16 | 10 | 4 | 2 | 194 | 15.5 |
| 1976–77 | 27 | Philadelphia Flyers | NHL | 80 | 27 | 63 | 90 | 40 | 71 | 15 | 6 | 6 | 3 | 158 | 17.1 |
| 1977–78 | 28 | Philadelphia Flyers | NHL | 71 | 21 | 68 | 89 | 47 | 83 | 14 | 5 | 2 | 1 | 126 | 16.7 |
| 1978–79 | 29 | Philadelphia Flyers | NHL | 80 | 16 | 57 | 73 | 12 | 68 | 10 | 5 | 1 | 1 | 143 | 11.2 |
| 1979–80 | 30 | Philadelphia Flyers | NHL | 76 | 12 | 57 | 69 | 42 | 65 | 9 | 1 | 2 | 2 | 139 | 8.6 |

## Bobby Clarke (continued)

**REGULAR SEASON**

| SEASON | AGE | TEAM | LG | GP | G | A | PTS | +/- | PIM | ESG | PPG | SHG | GWG | SOG | S% |
|---|---|---|---|---|---|---|---|---|---|---|---|---|---|---|---|
| 1980–81 | 31 | Philadelphia Flyers | NHL | 80 | 19 | 46 | 65 | 16 | 140 | 13 | 5 | 1 | 2 | 150 | 12.7 |
| 1981–82 | 32 | Philadelphia Flyers | NHL | 62 | 17 | 46 | 63 | 28 | 154 | 14 | 2 | 1 | 3 | 110 | 15.5 |
| 1982–83 | 33 | Philadelphia Flyers | NHL | 80 | 23 | 62 | 85 | 37 | 115 | 16 | 6 | 1 | 2 | 164 | 14.0 |
| 1983–84 | 34 | Philadelphia Flyers | NHL | 73 | 17 | 43 | 60 | 24 | 70 | 13 | 3 | 1 | 1 | 127 | 13.4 |
| NHL Career — 15 Seasons | | | | 1144 | 358 | 852 | 1210 | 507 | 1453 | 227 | 99 | 32 | 38 | 2582 | 13.9 |

**PLAYOFFS**

| SEASON | AGE | TEAM | LG | GP | G | A | PTS | +/- | PIM | ESG | PPG | SHG | GWG | SOG | S% |
|---|---|---|---|---|---|---|---|---|---|---|---|---|---|---|---|
| 1970–71 | 21 | Philadelphia Flyers | NHL | 4 | 0 | 0 | 0 | -3 | 2 | 0 | 0 | 0 | 0 | 7 | 0.0 |
| 1972–73 | 23 | Philadelphia Flyers | NHL | 11 | 2 | 6 | 8 | -1 | 6 | 0 | 2 | 0 | 1 | 28 | 7.1 |
| 1973–74 | 24 | Philadelphia Flyers | NHL | 17 | 5 | 11 | 16 | 1 | 42 | 3 | 2 | 0 | 2 | 46 | 10.9 |
| 1974–75 | 25 | Philadelphia Flyers | NHL | 17 | 4 | 12 | 16 | 6 | 16 | 1 | 2 | 1 | 2 | 39 | 10.3 |
| 1975–76 | 26 | Philadelphia Flyers | NHL | 16 | 2 | 14 | 16 | 11 | 28 | 1 | 1 | 0 | 0 | 29 | 6.9 |
| 1976–77 | 27 | Philadelphia Flyers | NHL | 10 | 5 | 5 | 10 | 0 | 8 | 3 | 2 | 0 | 0 | 20 | 25.0 |
| 1977–78 | 28 | Philadelphia Flyers | NHL | 12 | 4 | 7 | 11 | -5 | 8 | 3 | 1 | 0 | 0 | 18 | 22.2 |
| 1978–79 | 29 | Philadelphia Flyers | NHL | 8 | 2 | 4 | 6 | -8 | 10 | 1 | 1 | 0 | 0 | 21 | 9.5 |
| 1979–80 | 30 | Philadelphia Flyers | NHL | 19 | 8 | 12 | 20 | 10 | 16 | 5 | 3 | 0 | 2 | 41 | 19.5 |
| 1980–81 | 31 | Philadelphia Flyers | NHL | 12 | 3 | 3 | 6 | 3 | 6 | 2 | 0 | 1 | 0 | 19 | 15.8 |
| 1981–82 | 32 | Philadelphia Flyers | NHL | 4 | 4 | 2 | 6 | 3 | 4 | 2 | 1 | 1 | 0 | 7 | 57.1 |
| 1982–83 | 33 | Philadelphia Flyers | NHL | 3 | 1 | 0 | 1 | 1 | 2 | 1 | 0 | 0 | 0 | 3 | 33.3 |
| 1983–84 | 34 | Philadelphia Flyers | NHL | 3 | 2 | 1 | 3 | -1 | 6 | 2 | 0 | 0 | 0 | 8 | 25.0 |
| NHL Career — 13 Seasons | | | | 136 | 42 | 77 | 119 | 17 | 154 | 24 | 15 | 3 | 7 | 286 | 14.7 |

## Bill Cowley  Profile: See page 84

**REGULAR SEASON**

| SEASON | AGE | TEAM | LG | GP | G | A | PTS | PIM |
|---|---|---|---|---|---|---|---|---|
| 1934–35 | 22 | St. Louis Eagles | NHL | 41 | 5 | 7 | 12 | 10 |
| 1935–36 | 23 | Boston Bruins | NHL | 48 | 11 | 10 | 21 | 17 |
| 1936–37 | 24 | Boston Bruins | NHL | 46 | 13 | 22 | 34 | 4 |
| 1937–38 | 25 | Boston Bruins | NHL | 48 | 17 | 21 | 39 | 8 |
| 1938–39 | 26 | Boston Bruins | NHL | 34 | 8 | 34 | 42 | 2 |
| 1939–40 | 27 | Boston Bruins | NHL | 48 | 13 | 27 | 40 | 24 |
| 1940–41 | 28 | Boston Bruins | NHL | 46 | 17 | 47 | 64 | 16 |
| 1941–42 | 29 | Boston Bruins | NHL | 28 | 4 | 23 | 27 | 6 |
| 1942–43 | 30 | Boston Bruins | NHL | 48 | 27 | 45 | 72 | 10 |
| 1943–44 | 31 | Boston Bruins | NHL | 36 | 30 | 41 | 71 | 12 |
| 1944–45 | 32 | Boston Bruins | NHL | 49 | 25 | 40 | 65 | 12 |
| 1945–46 | 33 | Boston Bruins | NHL | 26 | 12 | 12 | 24 | 6 |
| 1946–47 | 34 | Boston Bruins | NHL | 51 | 13 | 25 | 38 | 16 |
| NHL Career — 13 Seasons | | | | 549 | 195 | 354 | 549 | 143 |

**PLAYOFFS**

| SEASON | AGE | TEAM | LG | GP | G | A | PTS | PIM |
|---|---|---|---|---|---|---|---|---|
| 1935–36 | 23 | Boston Bruins | NHL | 2 | 2 | 1 | 3 | 2 |
| 1936–37 | 24 | Boston Bruins | NHL | 3 | 0 | 3 | 3 | 0 |
| 1937–38 | 25 | Boston Bruins | NHL | 3 | 2 | 0 | 2 | 0 |
| 1938–39 | 26 | Boston Bruins | NHL | 12 | 3 | 11 | 14 | 2 |
| 1939–40 | 27 | Boston Bruins | NHL | 6 | 0 | 1 | 1 | 7 |
| 1940–41 | 28 | Boston Bruins | NHL | 2 | 0 | 0 | 0 | 0 |
| 1941–42 | 29 | Boston Bruins | NHL | 5 | 0 | 3 | 3 | 5 |
| 1942–43 | 30 | Boston Bruins | NHL | 9 | 1 | 7 | 8 | 4 |
| 1944–45 | 32 | Boston Bruins | NHL | 7 | 3 | 3 | 6 | 0 |
| 1945–46 | 33 | Boston Bruins | NHL | 10 | 1 | 3 | 4 | 2 |
| 1946–47 | 34 | Boston Bruins | NHL | 5 | 0 | 2 | 2 | 0 |
| NHL Career — 11 Seasons | | | | 64 | 12 | 34 | 46 | 22 |

## Marcel Dionne  Profile: See page 85

**REGULAR SEASON**

| SEASON | AGE | TEAM | LG | GP | G | A | PTS | +/- | PIM | ESG | PPG | SHG | GWG | SOG | S% |
|---|---|---|---|---|---|---|---|---|---|---|---|---|---|---|---|
| 1971–72 | 20 | Detroit Red Wings | NHL | 78 | 28 | 49 | 77 | 0 | 14 | 21 | 7 | 0 | 2 | 268 | 10.5 |
| 1972–73 | 21 | Detroit Red Wings | NHL | 77 | 40 | 50 | 90 | -4 | 21 | 30 | 10 | 0 | 6 | 282 | 14.2 |
| 1973–74 | 22 | Detroit Red Wings | NHL | 74 | 24 | 54 | 78 | -31 | 10 | 21 | 3 | 0 | 1 | 280 | 8.6 |
| 1974–75 | 23 | Detroit Red Wings | NHL | 80 | 47 | 74 | 121 | -15 | 14 | 22 | 15 | 10 | 1 | 378 | 12.4 |
| 1975–76 | 24 | Los Angeles Kings | NHL | 80 | 40 | 54 | 94 | 4 | 38 | 32 | 7 | 1 | 6 | 329 | 12.2 |
| 1976–77 | 25 | Los Angeles Kings | NHL | 80 | 53 | 69 | 122 | 11 | 12 | 38 | 14 | 1 | 5 | 378 | 14.1 |
| 1977–78 | 26 | Los Angeles Kings | NHL | 70 | 36 | 43 | 79 | -7 | 37 | 27 | 9 | 0 | 4 | 294 | 12.2 |
| 1978–79 | 27 | Los Angeles Kings | NHL | 80 | 59 | 71 | 130 | 22 | 30 | 40 | 19 | 0 | 7 | 362 | 16.3 |
| 1979–80 | 28 | Los Angeles Kings | NHL | 80 | 53 | 84 | 137 | 34 | 32 | 36 | 17 | 0 | 6 | 348 | 15.2 |
| 1980–81 | 29 | Los Angeles Kings | NHL | 80 | 58 | 77 | 135 | 54 | 70 | 31 | 23 | 4 | 9 | 342 | 17.0 |
| 1981–82 | 30 | Los Angeles Kings | NHL | 78 | 50 | 67 | 117 | -10 | 50 | 32 | 17 | 1 | 5 | 346 | 14.5 |
| 1982–83 | 31 | Los Angeles Kings | NHL | 80 | 56 | 51 | 107 | 10 | 22 | 38 | 17 | 1 | 7 | 346 | 16.2 |
| 1983–84 | 32 | Los Angeles Kings | NHL | 66 | 39 | 53 | 92 | 7 | 28 | 26 | 13 | 0 | 2 | 282 | 14.0 |
| 1984–85 | 33 | Los Angeles Kings | NHL | 80 | 46 | 80 | 126 | 11 | 46 | 29 | 16 | 1 | 2 | 316 | 13.8 |
| 1985–86 | 34 | Los Angeles Kings | NHL | 80 | 36 | 58 | 94 | -22 | 42 | 25 | 11 | 0 | 4 | 283 | 12.7 |
| 1986–87 | 35 | Los Angeles Kings | NHL | 67 | 24 | 50 | 74 | -9 | 54 | 15 | 9 | 0 | 2 | 224 | 10.7 |
| 1986–87 | 35 | New York Rangers | NHL | 14 | 4 | 6 | 10 | -8 | 6 | 3 | 1 | 0 | 0 | 48 | 8.3 |
| 1987–88 | 36 | New York Rangers | NHL | 67 | 31 | 34 | 65 | -14 | 54 | 9 | 22 | 0 | 4 | 184 | 16.9 |
| 1988–89 | 37 | New York Rangers | NHL | 37 | 7 | 16 | 23 | -6 | 20 | 3 | 4 | 0 | 0 | 74 | 9.5 |
| NHL Career — 18 Seasons | | | | 1348 | 731 | 1040 | 1771 | 27 | 600 | 478 | 234 | 19 | 73 | 5363 | 13.6 |

### Marcel Dionne (continued)

**PLAYOFFS**

| SEASON | AGE | TEAM | LG | GP | G | A | PTS | +/- | PIM | ESG | PPG | SHG | GWG | SOG | S% |
|--------|-----|------|----|----|---|---|-----|-----|-----|-----|-----|-----|-----|-----|-----|
| 1975-76 | 24 | Los Angeles Kings | NHL | 9 | 6 | 1 | 7 | 0 | 0 | 3 | 3 | 0 | 0 | 30 | 20.0 |
| 1976-77 | 25 | Los Angeles Kings | NHL | 9 | 5 | 9 | 14 | -4 | 2 | 4 | 1 | 0 | 1 | 38 | 13.2 |
| 1977-78 | 26 | Los Angeles Kings | NHL | 2 | 0 | 0 | 0 | -1 | 0 | 0 | 0 | 0 | 0 | 2 | 0.0 |
| 1978-79 | 27 | Los Angeles Kings | NHL | 2 | 0 | 1 | 1 | -5 | 0 | 0 | 0 | 0 | 0 | 14 | 0.0 |
| 1979-80 | 28 | Los Angeles Kings | NHL | 4 | 0 | 3 | 3 | -4 | 4 | 0 | 0 | 0 | 0 | 18 | 0.0 |
| 1980-81 | 29 | Los Angeles Kings | NHL | 4 | 1 | 3 | 4 | -6 | 7 | 0 | 1 | 0 | 0 | 13 | 7.7 |
| 1981-82 | 30 | Los Angeles Kings | NHL | 10 | 7 | 4 | 11 | -2 | 0 | 3 | 4 | 0 | 0 | 44 | 15.9 |
| 1984-85 | 33 | Los Angeles Kings | NHL | 3 | 1 | 2 | 3 | -1 | 2 | 0 | 1 | 0 | 0 | 13 | 7.7 |
| 1986-87 | 35 | New York Rangers | NHL | 6 | 1 | 1 | 2 | -4 | 2 | 1 | 0 | 0 | 0 | 15 | 6.7 |
| NHL Career — 9 Seasons | | | | 49 | 21 | 24 | 45 | -23 | 17 | 10 | 11 | 0 | 1 | 187 | 11.2 |

## Phil Esposito  Profile: See page 86

**REGULAR SEASON**

| SEASON | AGE | TEAM | LG | GP | G | A | PTS | +/- | PIM | ESG | PPG | SHG | GWG | SOG | S% |
|--------|-----|------|----|----|---|---|-----|-----|-----|-----|-----|-----|-----|-----|-----|
| 1963-64 | 21 | Chicago Black Hawks | NHL | 27 | 3 | 2 | 5 | 2 | 2 | 3 | 0 | 0 | 0 | 19 | 15.8 |
| 1964-65 | 22 | Chicago Black Hawks | NHL | 70 | 23 | 32 | 55 | 5 | 44 | 17 | 5 | 1 | 9 | 187 | 12.3 |
| 1965-66 | 23 | Chicago Black Hawks | NHL | 69 | 27 | 26 | 53 | 21 | 49 | 20 | 7 | 0 | 6 | 172 | 15.7 |
| 1966-67 | 24 | Chicago Black Hawks | NHL | 69 | 21 | 40 | 61 | 34 | 40 | 18 | 2 | 1 | 3 | 192 | 10.9 |
| 1967-68 | 25 | Boston Bruins | NHL | 74 | 35 | 49 | 84 | 18 | 21 | 26 | 8 | 1 | 3 | 284 | 12.3 |
| 1968-69 | 26 | Boston Bruins | NHL | 74 | 49 | 77 | 126 | 55 | 79 | 37 | 10 | 2 | 9 | 351 | 14.0 |
| 1969-70 | 27 | Boston Bruins | NHL | 76 | 43 | 56 | 99 | 26 | 50 | 24 | 18 | 1 | 5 | 405 | 10.6 |
| 1970-71 | 28 | Boston Bruins | NHL | 78 | 76 | 76 | 152 | 69 | 71 | 51 | 24 | 1 | 16 | 550 | 13.8 |
| 1971-72 | 29 | Boston Bruins | NHL | 76 | 66 | 67 | 133 | 54 | 76 | 37 | 27 | 2 | 16 | 426 | 15.5 |
| 1972-73 | 30 | Boston Bruins | NHL | 78 | 55 | 75 | 130 | 17 | 87 | 31 | 19 | 5 | 11 | 411 | 13.4 |
| 1973-74 | 31 | Boston Bruins | NHL | 78 | 68 | 77 | 145 | 51 | 58 | 50 | 14 | 4 | 9 | 393 | 17.3 |
| 1974-75 | 32 | Boston Bruins | NHL | 79 | 61 | 66 | 127 | 17 | 62 | 30 | 27 | 4 | 8 | 346 | 17.6 |
| 1975-76 | 33 | Boston Bruins | NHL | 12 | 6 | 10 | 16 | -1 | 8 | 3 | 3 | 0 | 0 | 57 | 10.5 |
| 1975-76 | 33 | New York Rangers | NHL | 62 | 29 | 38 | 67 | -38 | 28 | 12 | 16 | 1 | 2 | 217 | 13.4 |
| 1976-77 | 34 | New York Rangers | NHL | 80 | 34 | 46 | 80 | -27 | 52 | 19 | 15 | 0 | 4 | 344 | 9.9 |
| 1977-78 | 35 | New York Rangers | NHL | 79 | 38 | 43 | 81 | -21 | 53 | 17 | 21 | 0 | 5 | 261 | 14.6 |
| 1978-79 | 36 | New York Rangers | NHL | 80 | 42 | 36 | 78 | -1 | 37 | 28 | 14 | 0 | 7 | 215 | 19.5 |
| 1979-80 | 37 | New York Rangers | NHL | 80 | 34 | 44 | 78 | -14 | 73 | 21 | 13 | 0 | 5 | 245 | 13.9 |
| 1980-81 | 38 | New York Rangers | NHL | 41 | 7 | 13 | 20 | -15 | 20 | 4 | 3 | 0 | 0 | 91 | 7.7 |
| NHL Career — 18 Seasons | | | | 1282 | 717 | 873 | 1590 | 252 | 910 | 448 | 246 | 23 | 118 | 5166 | 13.9 |

**PLAYOFFS**

| SEASON | AGE | TEAM | LG | GP | G | A | PTS | +/- | PIM | ESG | PPG | SHG | GWG | SOG | S% |
|--------|-----|------|----|----|---|---|-----|-----|-----|-----|-----|-----|-----|-----|-----|
| 1963-64 | 21 | Chicago Black Hawks | NHL | 4 | 0 | 0 | 0 | -1 | 0 | 0 | 0 | 0 | 0 | 1 | 0.0 |
| 1964-65 | 22 | Chicago Black Hawks | NHL | 13 | 3 | 3 | 6 | 2 | 15 | 3 | 0 | 0 | 0 | 32 | 9.4 |
| 1965-66 | 23 | Chicago Black Hawks | NHL | 6 | 1 | 1 | 2 | 0 | 2 | 0 | 1 | 0 | 0 | 13 | 7.7 |
| 1966-67 | 24 | Chicago Black Hawks | NHL | 6 | 0 | 0 | 0 | -2 | 7 | 0 | 0 | 0 | 0 | 11 | 0.0 |
| 1967-68 | 25 | Boston Bruins | NHL | 4 | 0 | 3 | 3 | 0 | 0 | 0 | 0 | 0 | 0 | 17 | 0.0 |
| 1968-69 | 26 | Boston Bruins | NHL | 10 | 8 | 10 | 18 | 6 | 8 | 3 | 5 | 0 | 2 | 63 | 12.7 |
| 1969-70 | 27 | Boston Bruins | NHL | 14 | 13 | 14 | 27 | 12 | 16 | 9 | 4 | 0 | 2 | 72 | 18.1 |
| 1970-71 | 28 | Boston Bruins | NHL | 7 | 3 | 7 | 10 | 0 | 6 | 1 | 2 | 0 | 0 | 54 | 5.6 |
| 1971-72 | 29 | Boston Bruins | NHL | 15 | 9 | 15 | 24 | 16 | 24 | 7 | 2 | 0 | 3 | 101 | 8.9 |
| 1972-73 | 30 | Boston Bruins | NHL | 2 | 0 | 1 | 1 | -4 | 2 | 0 | 0 | 0 | 0 | 5 | 0.0 |
| 1973-74 | 31 | Boston Bruins | NHL | 16 | 9 | 5 | 14 | -2 | 25 | 5 | 4 | 0 | 2 | 73 | 12.3 |
| 1974-75 | 32 | Boston Bruins | NHL | 3 | 4 | 1 | 5 | 2 | 0 | 3 | 1 | 0 | 0 | 19 | 21.1 |
| 1977-78 | 35 | New York Rangers | NHL | 3 | 0 | 1 | 1 | -1 | 5 | 0 | 0 | 0 | 0 | 7 | 0.0 |
| 1978-79 | 36 | New York Rangers | NHL | 18 | 8 | 12 | 20 | -1 | 20 | 6 | 2 | 0 | 2 | 37 | 21.6 |
| 1979-80 | 37 | New York Rangers | NHL | 9 | 3 | 3 | 6 | -2 | 8 | 2 | 1 | 0 | 1 | 30 | 10.0 |
| NHL Career — 15 Seasons | | | | 130 | 61 | 76 | 137 | 25 | 138 | 39 | 22 | 0 | 12 | 535 | 11.4 |

## Bernie Federko  Profile: See page 88

**REGULAR SEASON**

| SEASON | AGE | TEAM | LG | GP | G | A | PTS | +/- | PIM | ESG | PPG | SHG | GWG | SOG | S% |
|--------|-----|------|----|----|---|---|-----|-----|-----|-----|-----|-----|-----|-----|-----|
| 1976-77 | 20 | St. Louis Blues | NHL | 31 | 14 | 9 | 23 | -6 | 15 | 8 | 6 | 0 | 3 | 67 | 20.9 |
| 1977-78 | 21 | St. Louis Blues | NHL | 72 | 17 | 24 | 41 | -34 | 27 | 13 | 4 | 0 | 1 | 128 | 13.3 |
| 1978-79 | 22 | St. Louis Blues | NHL | 74 | 31 | 64 | 95 | -15 | 14 | 24 | 7 | 0 | 1 | 156 | 19.9 |
| 1979-80 | 23 | St. Louis Blues | NHL | 79 | 38 | 56 | 94 | 3 | 24 | 31 | 7 | 0 | 4 | 183 | 20.8 |
| 1980-81 | 24 | St. Louis Blues | NHL | 78 | 31 | 73 | 104 | 9 | 47 | 20 | 9 | 2 | 4 | 170 | 18.2 |
| 1981-82 | 25 | St. Louis Blues | NHL | 74 | 30 | 62 | 92 | -11 | 70 | 18 | 12 | 0 | 6 | 177 | 17.0 |
| 1982-83 | 26 | St. Louis Blues | NHL | 75 | 24 | 60 | 84 | -9 | 24 | 15 | 9 | 0 | 1 | 184 | 13.0 |
| 1983-84 | 27 | St. Louis Blues | NHL | 79 | 41 | 66 | 107 | -2 | 43 | 27 | 14 | 0 | 4 | 196 | 20.9 |
| 1984-85 | 28 | St. Louis Blues | NHL | 76 | 30 | 73 | 103 | -10 | 27 | 24 | 6 | 0 | 3 | 175 | 17.1 |
| 1985-86 | 29 | St. Louis Blues | NHL | 80 | 34 | 68 | 102 | 11 | 34 | 18 | 16 | 0 | 2 | 166 | 20.5 |
| 1986-87 | 30 | St. Louis Blues | NHL | 64 | 20 | 52 | 72 | -27 | 32 | 11 | 9 | 0 | 3 | 130 | 15.4 |

## Bernie Federko (continued)

### REGULAR SEASON

| SEASON | AGE | TEAM | LG | GP | G | A | PTS | +/- | PIM | ESG | PPG | SHG | GWG | SOG | S% |
|--------|-----|------|----|----|----|----|-----|-----|-----|-----|-----|-----|-----|-----|-----|
| 1987-88 | 31 | St. Louis Blues | NHL | 79 | 20 | 69 | 89 | -12 | 52 | 11 | 9 | 0 | 2 | 119 | 16.8 |
| 1988-89 | 32 | St. Louis Blues | NHL | 66 | 22 | 45 | 67 | -20 | 54 | 13 | 9 | 0 | 6 | 115 | 19.1 |
| 1989-90 | 33 | Detroit Red Wings | NHL | 73 | 17 | 40 | 57 | -8 | 24 | 14 | 3 | 0 | 0 | 108 | 15.7 |
| NHL Career — 14 Seasons | | | | 1000 | 369 | 761 | 1130 | -131 | 487 | 247 | 120 | 2 | 40 | 2074 | 17.8 |

### PLAYOFFS

| SEASON | AGE | TEAM | LG | GP | G | A | PTS | +/- | PIM | ESG | PPG | SHG | GWG | SOG | S% |
|--------|-----|------|----|----|----|----|-----|-----|-----|-----|-----|-----|-----|-----|-----|
| 1976-77 | 20 | St. Louis Blues | NHL | 4 | 1 | 1 | 2 | -2 | 2 | 1 | 0 | 0 | 0 | 11 | 9.1 |
| 1979-80 | 23 | St. Louis Blues | NHL | 3 | 1 | 0 | 1 | -5 | 2 | 1 | 0 | 0 | 0 | 6 | 16.7 |
| 1980-81 | 24 | St. Louis Blues | NHL | 11 | 8 | 10 | 18 | -7 | 2 | 4 | 4 | 0 | 1 | 38 | 21.1 |
| 1981-82 | 25 | St. Louis Blues | NHL | 10 | 3 | 15 | 18 | 8 | 10 | 2 | 1 | 0 | 1 | 17 | 17.6 |
| 1982-83 | 26 | St. Louis Blues | NHL | 4 | 2 | 3 | 5 | -3 | 0 | 1 | 1 | 0 | 0 | 13 | 15.4 |
| 1983-84 | 27 | St. Louis Blues | NHL | 11 | 4 | 4 | 8 | -5 | 10 | 3 | 1 | 0 | 1 | 26 | 15.4 |
| 1984-85 | 28 | St. Louis Blues | NHL | 3 | 0 | 2 | 2 | 1 | 4 | 0 | 0 | 0 | 0 | 3 | 0.0 |
| 1985-86 | 29 | St. Louis Blues | NHL | 19 | 7 | 14 | 21 | 2 | 17 | 6 | 1 | 0 | 1 | 34 | 20.6 |
| 1986-87 | 30 | St. Louis Blues | NHL | 6 | 3 | 3 | 6 | -2 | 18 | 2 | 1 | 0 | 0 | 8 | 37.5 |
| 1987-88 | 31 | St. Louis Blues | NHL | 10 | 2 | 6 | 8 | -6 | 18 | 0 | 2 | 0 | 0 | 8 | 25.0 |
| 1988-89 | 32 | St. Louis Blues | NHL | 10 | 4 | 8 | 12 | -2 | 0 | 2 | 2 | 0 | 0 | 19 | 21.1 |
| NHL Career — 11 Seasons | | | | 91 | 35 | 66 | 101 | -21 | 83 | 22 | 13 | 0 | 4 | 183 | 19.1 |

## Sergei Fedorov   Profile: See page 89

### REGULAR SEASON

| SEASON | AGE | TEAM | LG | GP | G | A | PTS | +/- | PIM | ESG | PPG | SHG | GWG | SOG | S% |
|--------|-----|------|----|----|----|----|-----|-----|-----|-----|-----|-----|-----|-----|-----|
| 1990-91 | 21 | Detroit Red Wings | NHL | 77 | 31 | 48 | 79 | 11 | 66 | 17 | 11 | 3 | 5 | 259 | 12.0 |
| 1991-92 | 22 | Detroit Red Wings | NHL | 80 | 32 | 54 | 86 | 26 | 72 | 23 | 7 | 2 | 5 | 249 | 12.9 |
| 1992-93 | 23 | Detroit Red Wings | NHL | 73 | 34 | 53 | 87 | 33 | 72 | 17 | 13 | 4 | 3 | 217 | 15.7 |
| 1993-94 | 24 | Detroit Red Wings | NHL | 82 | 56 | 64 | 120 | 48 | 34 | 39 | 13 | 4 | 10 | 337 | 16.6 |
| 1994-95 | 25 | Detroit Red Wings | NHL | 42 | 20 | 30 | 50 | 6 | 24 | 10 | 7 | 3 | 5 | 147 | 13.6 |
| 1995-96 | 26 | Detroit Red Wings | NHL | 78 | 39 | 68 | 107 | 49 | 48 | 25 | 11 | 3 | 11 | 306 | 12.7 |
| 1996-97 | 27 | Detroit Red Wings | NHL | 74 | 30 | 33 | 63 | 29 | 30 | 19 | 9 | 2 | 4 | 273 | 11.0 |
| 1997-98 | 28 | Detroit Red Wings | NHL | 21 | 6 | 11 | 17 | 10 | 25 | 4 | 2 | 0 | 2 | 68 | 8.8 |
| 1998-99 | 29 | Detroit Red Wings | NHL | 77 | 26 | 37 | 63 | 9 | 66 | 18 | 6 | 2 | 3 | 224 | 11.6 |
| 1999-00 | 30 | Detroit Red Wings | NHL | 68 | 27 | 35 | 62 | 8 | 22 | 19 | 4 | 4 | 7 | 263 | 10.3 |
| 2000-01 | 31 | Detroit Red Wings | NHL | 75 | 32 | 37 | 69 | 12 | 40 | 16 | 14 | 2 | 7 | 268 | 11.9 |
| 2001-02 | 32 | Detroit Red Wings | NHL | 81 | 31 | 37 | 68 | 20 | 36 | 21 | 10 | 0 | 6 | 256 | 12.1 |
| 2002-03 | 33 | Detroit Red Wings | NHL | 80 | 36 | 47 | 83 | 15 | 52 | 24 | 10 | 2 | 11 | 281 | 12.8 |
| 2003-04 | 34 | Mighty Ducks of Anaheim | NHL | 80 | 31 | 34 | 65 | -5 | 42 | 20 | 9 | 2 | 6 | 268 | 11.6 |
| 2005-06 | 36 | Mighty Ducks of Anaheim | NHL | 5 | 0 | 1 | 1 | -1 | 2 | 0 | 0 | 0 | 0 | 18 | 0.0 |
| 2005-06 | 36 | Columbus Blue Jackets | NHL | 62 | 12 | 31 | 43 | -1 | 64 | 8 | 3 | 1 | 2 | 142 | 8.5 |
| 2006-07 | 37 | Columbus Blue Jackets | NHL | 73 | 18 | 24 | 42 | -7 | 56 | 9 | 7 | 2 | 2 | 163 | 11.0 |
| 2007-08 | 38 | Columbus Blue Jackets | NHL | 50 | 9 | 19 | 28 | -3 | 30 | 4 | 5 | 0 | 1 | 94 | 9.6 |
| 2007-08 | 38 | Washington Capitals | NHL | 18 | 2 | 11 | 13 | -2 | 8 | 1 | 1 | 0 | 1 | 34 | 5.9 |
| 2008-09 | 39 | Washington Capitals | NHL | 52 | 11 | 22 | 33 | 4 | 50 | 9 | 2 | 0 | 2 | 118 | 9.3 |
| NHL Career — 18 Seasons | | | | 1248 | 483 | 696 | 1179 | 261 | 839 | 303 | 144 | 36 | 93 | 3985 | 12.1 |

### PLAYOFFS

| SEASON | AGE | TEAM | LG | GP | G | A | PTS | +/- | PIM | ESG | PPG | SHG | GWG | SOG | S% |
|--------|-----|------|----|----|----|----|-----|-----|-----|-----|-----|-----|-----|-----|-----|
| 1990-91 | 21 | Detroit Red Wings | NHL | 7 | 1 | 5 | 6 | -1 | 4 | 1 | 0 | 0 | 1 | 22 | 4.5 |
| 1991-92 | 22 | Detroit Red Wings | NHL | 11 | 5 | 5 | 10 | 2 | 8 | 2 | 1 | 2 | 1 | 27 | 18.5 |
| 1992-93 | 23 | Detroit Red Wings | NHL | 7 | 3 | 6 | 9 | 4 | 23 | 1 | 1 | 1 | 0 | 26 | 11.5 |
| 1993-94 | 24 | Detroit Red Wings | NHL | 7 | 1 | 7 | 8 | -1 | 6 | 1 | 0 | 0 | 0 | 19 | 5.3 |
| 1994-95 | 25 | Detroit Red Wings | NHL | 17 | 7 | 17 | 24 | 13 | 6 | 4 | 3 | 0 | 0 | 53 | 13.2 |
| 1995-96 | 26 | Detroit Red Wings | NHL | 19 | 2 | 18 | 20 | 8 | 10 | 2 | 0 | 0 | 2 | 59 | 3.4 |
| 1996-97 | 27 | Detroit Red Wings | NHL | 20 | 8 | 12 | 20 | 5 | 12 | 5 | 3 | 0 | 4 | 79 | 10.1 |
| 1997-98 | 28 | Detroit Red Wings | NHL | 22 | 10 | 10 | 20 | 0 | 12 | 7 | 2 | 1 | 1 | 86 | 11.6 |
| 1998-99 | 29 | Detroit Red Wings | NHL | 10 | 1 | 8 | 9 | 3 | 8 | 1 | 0 | 0 | 0 | 38 | 2.6 |
| 1999-00 | 30 | Detroit Red Wings | NHL | 9 | 4 | 4 | 8 | 2 | 4 | 2 | 2 | 0 | 1 | 34 | 11.8 |
| 2000-01 | 31 | Detroit Red Wings | NHL | 6 | 2 | 5 | 7 | 0 | 0 | 1 | 1 | 0 | 1 | 16 | 12.5 |
| 2001-02 | 32 | Detroit Red Wings | NHL | 23 | 5 | 14 | 19 | 4 | 20 | 2 | 2 | 1 | 0 | 88 | 5.7 |
| 2002-03 | 33 | Detroit Red Wings | NHL | 4 | 1 | 2 | 3 | -1 | 0 | 1 | 0 | 0 | 0 | 14 | 7.1 |
| 2007-08 | 38 | Washington Capitals | NHL | 7 | 1 | 4 | 5 | -1 | 8 | 1 | 0 | 0 | 0 | 18 | 5.6 |
| 2008-09 | 39 | Washington Capitals | NHL | 14 | 1 | 7 | 8 | 1 | 12 | 1 | 0 | 0 | 1 | 24 | 4.2 |
| NHL Career — 15 Seasons | | | | 183 | 52 | 124 | 176 | 38 | 133 | 32 | 15 | 5 | 12 | 603 | 8.6 |

# Peter Forsberg   Profile: See page 91

## REGULAR SEASON

| SEASON | AGE | TEAM | LG | GP | G | A | PTS | +/- | PIM | ESG | PPG | SHG | GWG | SOG | S% |
|---|---|---|---|---|---|---|---|---|---|---|---|---|---|---|---|
| 1994–95 | 21 | Quebec Nordiques | NHL | 47 | 15 | 35 | 50 | 17 | 16 | 12 | 3 | 0 | 3 | 86 | 17.4 |
| 1995–96 | 22 | Colorado Avalanche | NHL | 82 | 30 | 86 | 116 | 26 | 47 | 20 | 7 | 3 | 3 | 217 | 13.8 |
| 1996–97 | 23 | Colorado Avalanche | NHL | 65 | 28 | 58 | 86 | 31 | 73 | 19 | 5 | 4 | 4 | 188 | 14.9 |
| 1997–98 | 24 | Colorado Avalanche | NHL | 72 | 25 | 66 | 91 | 6 | 94 | 15 | 7 | 3 | 7 | 202 | 12.4 |
| 1998–99 | 25 | Colorado Avalanche | NHL | 78 | 30 | 67 | 97 | 27 | 108 | 19 | 9 | 2 | 7 | 217 | 13.8 |
| 1999–00 | 26 | Colorado Avalanche | NHL | 49 | 14 | 37 | 51 | 9 | 52 | 11 | 3 | 0 | 2 | 105 | 13.3 |
| 2000–01 | 27 | Colorado Avalanche | NHL | 73 | 27 | 62 | 89 | 23 | 54 | 13 | 12 | 2 | 5 | 178 | 15.2 |
| 2002–03 | 29 | Colorado Avalanche | NHL | 75 | 29 | 77 | 106 | 52 | 70 | 21 | 8 | 0 | 2 | 166 | 17.5 |
| 2003–04 | 30 | Colorado Avalanche | NHL | 39 | 18 | 37 | 55 | 16 | 30 | 14 | 3 | 1 | 5 | 85 | 21.2 |
| 2005–06 | 32 | Philadelphia Flyers | NHL | 60 | 19 | 56 | 75 | 21 | 46 | 10 | 8 | 1 | 2 | 132 | 14.4 |
| 2006–07 | 33 | Philadelphia Flyers | NHL | 40 | 11 | 29 | 40 | 2 | 72 | 6 | 5 | 0 | 2 | 63 | 17.5 |
| 2006–07 | 33 | Nashville Predators | NHL | 17 | 2 | 13 | 15 | 5 | 16 | 1 | 1 | 0 | 1 | 36 | 5.6 |
| 2007–08 | 34 | Colorado Avalanche | NHL | 9 | 1 | 13 | 14 | 7 | 8 | 1 | 0 | 0 | 0 | 15 | 6.7 |
| 2010–11 | 37 | Colorado Avalanche | NHL | 2 | 0 | 0 | 0 | -4 | 4 | 0 | 0 | 0 | 0 | 3 | 0.0 |
| NHL Career – 14 Seasons | | | | 708 | 249 | 636 | 885 | 238 | 690 | 162 | 71 | 16 | 43 | 1693 | 14.7 |

## PLAYOFFS

| SEASON | AGE | TEAM | LG | GP | G | A | PTS | +/- | PIM | ESG | PPG | SHG | GWG | SOG | S% |
|---|---|---|---|---|---|---|---|---|---|---|---|---|---|---|---|
| 1994–95 | 21 | Quebec Nordiques | NHL | 6 | 2 | 4 | 6 | 2 | 4 | 1 | 1 | 0 | 0 | 13 | 15.4 |
| 1995–96 | 22 | Colorado Avalanche | NHL | 22 | 10 | 11 | 21 | 10 | 18 | 7 | 3 | 0 | 1 | 50 | 20.0 |
| 1996–97 | 23 | Colorado Avalanche | NHL | 14 | 5 | 12 | 17 | -6 | 10 | 2 | 3 | 0 | 0 | 35 | 14.3 |
| 1997–98 | 24 | Colorado Avalanche | NHL | 7 | 6 | 5 | 11 | 3 | 12 | 4t | 2 | 0 | 0 | 18 | 33.3 |
| 1998–99 | 25 | Colorado Avalanche | NHL | 19 | 8 | 16 | 24 | 7 | 31 | 6 | 1 | 1 | 0 | 54 | 14.8 |
| 1999–00 | 26 | Colorado Avalanche | NHL | 16 | 7 | 8 | 15 | 9 | 12 | 4 | 2 | 1 | 4 | 54 | 13.0 |
| 2000–01 | 27 | Colorado Avalanche | NHL | 11 | 4 | 10 | 14 | 5 | 6 | 3 | 1 | 0 | 2 | 23 | 17.4 |
| 2001–02 | 28 | Colorado Avalanche | NHL | 20 | 9 | 18 | 27 | 8 | 20 | 9 | 0 | 0 | 4 | 35 | 25.7 |
| 2002–03 | 29 | Colorado Avalanche | NHL | 7 | 2 | 6 | 8 | 3 | 6 | 1 | 1 | 0 | 0 | 23 | 8.7 |
| 2003–04 | 30 | Colorado Avalanche | NHL | 11 | 4 | 7 | 11 | 6 | 12 | 3 | 1 | 0 | 1 | 16 | 25.0 |
| 2005–06 | 32 | Philadelphia Flyers | NHL | 6 | 4 | 4 | 8 | 2 | 6 | 3 | 1 | 0 | 2 | 12 | 33.3 |
| 2006–07 | 33 | Nashville Predators | NHL | 5 | 2 | 2 | 4 | 2 | 12 | 2 | 0 | 0 | 0 | 7 | 28.6 |
| 2007–08 | 34 | Colorado Avalanche | NHL | 7 | 1 | 4 | 5 | 3 | 14 | 1 | 0 | 0 | 0 | 13 | 7.7 |
| NHL Career – 13 Seasons | | | | 151 | 64 | 107 | 171 | 54 | 163 | 46 | 16 | 2 | 14 | 353 | 18.1 |

# Frank Foyston   Profile: See page 92

## REGULAR SEASON

| SEASON | AGE | TEAM | LG | GP | G | A | PTS | PIM |
|---|---|---|---|---|---|---|---|---|
| 1912–13 | 21 | Toronto Blueshirts | NHA | 16 | 8 | 0 | 8 | 8 |
| 1913–14 | 22 | Toronto Blueshirts | NHA | 19 | 16 | 2 | 18 | 8 |
| 1914–15 | 23 | Toronto Blueshirts | NHA | 20 | 13 | 9 | 22 | 11 |
| 1915–16 | 24 | Toronto Blueshirts | NHA | 1 | 0 | 0 | 0 | 0 |
| 1915–16 | 24 | Seattle Metropolitans | PCHA | 18 | 9 | 4 | 13 | 6 |
| 1916–17 | 25 | Seattle Metropolitans | PCHA | 24 | 36 | 12 | 48 | 51 |
| 1917–18 | 26 | Seattle Metropolitans | PCHA | 13 | 9 | 5 | 14 | 9 |
| 1918–19 | 27 | Seattle Metropolitans | PCHA | 18 | 15 | 4 | 19 | 0 |
| 1919–20 | 28 | Seattle Metropolitans | PCHA | 22 | 26 | 3 | 29 | 3 |
| 1920–21 | 29 | Seattle Metropolitans | PCHA | 23 | 26 | 4 | 30 | 10 |
| 1921–22 | 30 | Seattle Metropolitans | PCHA | 24 | 16 | 7 | 23 | 25 |
| 1922–23 | 31 | Seattle Metropolitans | PCHA | 30 | 20 | 8 | 28 | 21 |
| 1923–24 | 32 | Seattle Metropolitans | PCHA | 30 | 17 | 6 | 23 | 8 |
| 1924–25 | 33 | Victoria Cougars | WCHL | 27 | 6 | 5 | 11 | 6 |
| 1925–26 | 34 | Victoria Cougars | WHL | 12 | 6 | 3 | 9 | 8 |
| 1926–27 | 35 | Detroit Cougars | NHL | 41 | 10 | 5 | 15 | 16 |
| 1927–28 | 36 | Detroit Cougars | NHL | 23 | 7 | 2 | 9 | 14 |
| Career – 16 Seasons | | | | 361 | 240 | 79 | 319 | 204 |

## PLAYOFFS

| SEASON | AGE | TEAM | LG | GP | G | A | PTS | PIM |
|---|---|---|---|---|---|---|---|---|
| 1913–14 | 22 | Toronto Blueshirts | NHA | 2 | 1 | 0 | 1 | 0 |
| 1913–14 | 22 | Toronto Blueshirts | St-Cup | 3 | 2 | 0 | 2 | 3 |
| 1916–17 | 25 | Seattle Metropolitans | St-Cup | 4 | 7 | 3 | 10 | 3 |
| 1917–18 | 26 | Seattle Metropolitans | PCHA | 2 | 0 | 0 | 0 | 3 |
| 1918–19 | 27 | Seattle Metropolitans | PCHA | 2 | 3 | 0 | 3 | 0 |
| 1918–19 | 27 | Seattle Metropolitans | St-Cup | 5 | 9 | 1 | 10 | 0 |
| 1919–20 | 28 | Seattle Metropolitans | PCHA | 2 | 3 | 1 | 4 | 0 |
| 1919–20 | 28 | Seattle Metropolitans | St-Cup | 5 | 6 | 1 | 7 | 7 |
| 1920–21 | 29 | Seattle Metropolitans | PCHA | 2 | 1 | 0 | 1 | 0 |
| 1921–22 | 30 | Seattle Metropolitans | PCHA | 2 | 0 | 0 | 0 | 3 |
| 1923–24 | 32 | Seattle Metropolitans | PCHA | 2 | 1 | 0 | 1 | 0 |
| 1924–25 | 33 | Victoria Cougars | St-Cup | 4 | 1 | 0 | 1 | 0 |
| 1924–25 | 33 | Victoria Cougars | WCHL | 4 | 1 | 1 | 2 | 2 |
| 1925–26 | 34 | Victoria Cougars | St-Cup | 4 | 0 | 0 | 0 | 2 |
| 1925–26 | 34 | Victoria Cougars | WHL | 3 | 2 | 0 | 2 | 4 |
| Career – 10 Seasons | | | | 46 | 42 | 7 | 49 | 27 |

# Ron Francis   Profile: See page 93

## REGULAR SEASON

| SEASON | AGE | TEAM | LG | GP | G | A | PTS | +/- | PIM | ESG | PPG | SHG | GWG | SOG | S% |
|---|---|---|---|---|---|---|---|---|---|---|---|---|---|---|---|
| 1981-82 | 18 | Hartford Whalers | NHL | 59 | 25 | 43 | 68 | -15 | 51 | 13 | 12 | 0 | 1 | 163 | 15.3 |
| 1982-83 | 19 | Hartford Whalers | NHL | 79 | 31 | 59 | 90 | -26 | 60 | 25 | 4 | 2 | 4 | 210 | 14.8 |
| 1983-84 | 20 | Hartford Whalers | NHL | 72 | 23 | 60 | 83 | -12 | 45 | 18 | 5 | 0 | 5 | 202 | 11.4 |
| 1984-85 | 21 | Hartford Whalers | NHL | 80 | 24 | 57 | 81 | -24 | 64 | 20 | 4 | 0 | 1 | 199 | 12.1 |
| 1985-86 | 22 | Hartford Whalers | NHL | 53 | 24 | 53 | 77 | 5 | 24 | 16 | 7 | 1 | 4 | 120 | 20.0 |
| 1986-87 | 23 | Hartford Whalers | NHL | 75 | 30 | 63 | 93 | 11 | 45 | 23 | 7 | 0 | 7 | 189 | 15.9 |
| 1987-88 | 24 | Hartford Whalers | NHL | 80 | 25 | 50 | 75 | -8 | 87 | 13 | 11 | 1 | 3 | 172 | 14.5 |
| 1988-89 | 25 | Hartford Whalers | NHL | 69 | 29 | 48 | 77 | 4 | 36 | 21 | 8 | 0 | 4 | 156 | 18.6 |
| 1989-90 | 26 | Hartford Whalers | NHL | 80 | 32 | 69 | 101 | 13 | 73 | 16 | 15 | 1 | 5 | 170 | 18.8 |
| 1990-91 | 27 | Hartford Whalers | NHL | 67 | 21 | 55 | 76 | -2 | 51 | 10 | 10 | 1 | 6 | 149 | 14.1 |
| 1990-91 | 27 | Pittsburgh Penguins | NHL | 14 | 2 | 9 | 11 | 0 | 21 | 2 | 0 | 0 | 1 | 25 | 8.0 |
| 1991-92 | 28 | Pittsburgh Penguins | NHL | 70 | 21 | 33 | 54 | -7 | 30 | 15 | 5 | 1 | 2 | 121 | 17.4 |
| 1992-93 | 29 | Pittsburgh Penguins | NHL | 84 | 24 | 76 | 100 | 6 | 68 | 13 | 9 | 2 | 4 | 215 | 11.2 |
| 1993-94 | 30 | Pittsburgh Penguins | NHL | 82 | 27 | 66 | 93 | -3 | 62 | 19 | 8 | 0 | 2 | 216 | 12.5 |
| 1994-95 | 31 | Pittsburgh Penguins | NHL | 44 | 11 | 48 | 59 | 30 | 18 | 8 | 3 | 0 | 1 | 94 | 11.7 |
| 1995-96 | 32 | Pittsburgh Penguins | NHL | 77 | 27 | 92 | 119 | 25 | 56 | 14 | 12 | 1 | 4 | 158 | 17.1 |
| 1996-97 | 33 | Pittsburgh Penguins | NHL | 81 | 27 | 63 | 90 | 7 | 20 | 16 | 10 | 1 | 2 | 183 | 14.8 |
| 1997-98 | 34 | Pittsburgh Penguins | NHL | 81 | 25 | 62 | 87 | 12 | 20 | 18 | 7 | 0 | 5 | 189 | 13.2 |
| 1998-99 | 35 | Carolina Hurricanes | NHL | 82 | 21 | 31 | 52 | -2 | 34 | 13 | 8 | 0 | 2 | 133 | 15.8 |
| 1999-00 | 36 | Carolina Hurricanes | NHL | 78 | 23 | 50 | 73 | 10 | 18 | 16 | 7 | 0 | 4 | 150 | 15.3 |
| 2000-01 | 37 | Carolina Hurricanes | NHL | 82 | 15 | 50 | 65 | -15 | 32 | 8 | 7 | 0 | 4 | 130 | 11.5 |
| 2001-02 | 38 | Carolina Hurricanes | NHL | 80 | 27 | 50 | 77 | 4 | 18 | 13 | 14 | 0 | 5 | 165 | 16.4 |
| 2002-03 | 39 | Carolina Hurricanes | NHL | 82 | 22 | 35 | 57 | -22 | 30 | 13 | 8 | 1 | 1 | 156 | 14.1 |
| 2003-04 | 40 | Carolina Hurricanes | NHL | 68 | 10 | 20 | 30 | -12 | 14 | 5 | 5 | 0 | 1 | 79 | 12.7 |
| 2003-04 | 40 | Toronto Maple Leafs | NHL | 12 | 3 | 7 | 10 | 3 | 0 | 1 | 2 | 0 | 1 | 12 | 25.0 |
| NHL Career—23 Seasons | | | | 1731 | 549 | 1249 | 1798 | -18 | 979 | 349 | 188 | 12 | 79 | 3756 | 14.6 |

## PLAYOFFS

| SEASON | AGE | TEAM | LG | GP | G | A | PTS | +/- | PIM | ESG | PPG | SHG | GWG | SOG | S% |
|---|---|---|---|---|---|---|---|---|---|---|---|---|---|---|---|
| 1985-86 | 22 | Hartford Whalers | NHL | 10 | 1 | 2 | 3 | -1 | 4 | 1 | 0 | 0 | 0 | 27 | 3.7 |
| 1986-87 | 23 | Hartford Whalers | NHL | 6 | 2 | 2 | 4 | -1 | 6 | 1 | 1 | 0 | 0 | 15 | 13.3 |
| 1987-88 | 24 | Hartford Whalers | NHL | 6 | 2 | 5 | 7 | 5 | 2 | 1 | 1 | 0 | 0 | 8 | 25.0 |
| 1988-89 | 25 | Hartford Whalers | NHL | 4 | 0 | 2 | 2 | -2 | 0 | 0 | 0 | 0 | 0 | 10 | 0.0 |
| 1989-90 | 26 | Hartford Whalers | NHL | 7 | 3 | 3 | 6 | 2 | 8 | 2 | 1 | 0 | 0 | 21 | 14.3 |
| 1990-91 | 27 | Pittsburgh Penguins | NHL | 24 | 7 | 10 | 17 | 13 | 24 | 7 | 0 | 0 | 4 | 48 | 14.6 |
| 1991-92 | 28 | Pittsburgh Penguins | NHL | 21 | 8 | 19 | 27 | 8 | 6 | 6 | 2 | 0 | 2 | 58 | 13.8 |
| 1992-93 | 29 | Pittsburgh Penguins | NHL | 12 | 6 | 11 | 17 | 5 | 19 | 5 | 1 | 0 | 1 | 26 | 23.1 |
| 1993-94 | 30 | Pittsburgh Penguins | NHL | 6 | 0 | 2 | 2 | -2 | 6 | 0 | 0 | 0 | 0 | 9 | 0.0 |
| 1994-95 | 31 | Pittsburgh Penguins | NHL | 12 | 6 | 13 | 19 | 3 | 4 | 4 | 2 | 0 | 0 | 30 | 20.0 |
| 1995-96 | 32 | Pittsburgh Penguins | NHL | 11 | 3 | 6 | 9 | 3 | 4 | 1 | 2 | 0 | 1 | 23 | 13.0 |
| 1996-97 | 33 | Pittsburgh Penguins | NHL | 5 | 1 | 2 | 3 | -7 | 2 | 0 | 1 | 0 | 0 | 6 | 16.7 |
| 1997-98 | 34 | Pittsburgh Penguins | NHL | 6 | 1 | 5 | 6 | 5 | 2 | 1 | 0 | 0 | 0 | 19 | 5.3 |
| 1998-99 | 35 | Carolina Hurricanes | NHL | 3 | 0 | 1 | 1 | 1 | 0 | 0 | 0 | 0 | 0 | 4 | 0.0 |
| 2000-01 | 37 | Carolina Hurricanes | NHL | 3 | 0 | 0 | 0 | -2 | 0 | 0 | 0 | 0 | 0 | 5 | 0.0 |
| 2001-02 | 38 | Carolina Hurricanes | NHL | 23 | 6 | 10 | 16 | -2 | 6 | 2 | 4 | 0 | 3 | 51 | 11.8 |
| 2003-04 | 40 | Toronto Maple Leafs | NHL | 12 | 0 | 4 | 4 | 0 | 2 | 0 | 0 | 0 | 0 | 14 | 0.0 |
| NHL Career—17 Seasons | | | | 171 | 46 | 97 | 143 | 28 | 95 | 31 | 15 | 0 | 11 | 374 | 12.3 |

# Frank Fredrickson   Profile: See page 94

## REGULAR SEASON

| SEASON | AGE | TEAM | LG | GP | G | A | PTS | PIM |
|---|---|---|---|---|---|---|---|---|
| 1920-21 | 25 | Victoria Aristocrats | PCHA | 21 | 20 | 12 | 32 | 3 |
| 1921-22 | 26 | Victoria Aristocrats | PCHA | 24 | 15 | 10 | 25 | 26 |
| 1922-23 | 27 | Victoria Cougars | PCHA | 30 | 39 | 16 | 55 | 26 |
| 1923-24 | 28 | Victoria Cougars | PCHA | 30 | 19 | 8 | 27 | 28 |
| 1924-25 | 29 | Victoria Cougars | WCHL | 28 | 22 | 8 | 30 | 43 |
| 1925-26 | 30 | Victoria Cougars | WHL | 30 | 16 | 8 | 24 | 89 |
| 1926-27 | 31 | Detroit Cougars | NHL | 17 | 4 | 6 | 10 | 18 |
| 1926-27 | 31 | Boston Bruins | NHL | 27 | 14 | 7 | 21 | 32 |
| 1927-28 | 32 | Boston Bruins | NHL | 41 | 10 | 4 | 14 | 85 |
| 1928-29 | 33 | Boston Bruins | NHL | 12 | 3 | 1 | 4 | 24 |
| 1928-29 | 33 | Pittsburgh Pirates | NHL | 31 | 3 | 7 | 10 | 26 |
| 1929-30 | 34 | Pittsburgh Pirates | NHL | 9 | 4 | 7 | 11 | 20 |
| 1930-31 | 35 | Detroit Falcons | NHL | 24 | 1 | 2 | 3 | 6 |
| Career—11 Seasons | | | | 324 | 170 | 96 | 266 | 426 |

## PLAYOFFS

| SEASON | AGE | TEAM | LG | GP | G | A | PTS | PIM |
|---|---|---|---|---|---|---|---|---|
| 1922-23 | 27 | Victoria Cougars | PCHA | 2 | 2 | 0 | 2 | 4 |
| 1924-25 | 29 | Victoria Cougars | St-Cup | 4 | 3 | 2 | 5 | 6 |
| 1924-25 | 29 | Victoria Cougars | WCHL | 4 | 3 | 1 | 4 | 2 |
| 1925-26 | 30 | Victoria Cougars | St-Cup | 4 | 1 | 1 | 2 | 10 |
| 1925-26 | 30 | Victoria Cougars | WHL | 4 | 2 | 1 | 3 | 6 |
| 1926-27 | 31 | Boston Bruins | NHL | 8 | 2 | 2 | 4 | 20 |
| 1927-28 | 32 | Boston Bruins | NHL | 2 | 0 | 1 | 1 | 4 |
| Career—5 Seasons | | | | 28 | 13 | 8 | 21 | 52 |

# Doug Gilmour   Profile: See page 96

## REGULAR SEASON

| SEASON | AGE | TEAM | LG | GP | G | A | PTS | +/- | PIM | ESG | PPG | SHG | GWG | SOG | S% |
|---|---|---|---|---|---|---|---|---|---|---|---|---|---|---|---|
| 1983–84 | 20 | St. Louis Blues | NHL | 80 | 25 | 28 | 53 | 6 | 57 | 21 | 3 | 1 | 1 | 157 | 15.9 |
| 1984–85 | 21 | St. Louis Blues | NHL | 78 | 21 | 36 | 57 | 3 | 49 | 17 | 3 | 1 | 3 | 162 | 13.0 |
| 1985–86 | 22 | St. Louis Blues | NHL | 74 | 25 | 28 | 53 | -4 | 41 | 22 | 2 | 1 | 5 | 183 | 13.7 |
| 1986–87 | 23 | St. Louis Blues | NHL | 80 | 42 | 63 | 105 | -4 | 58 | 24 | 17 | 1 | 2 | 208 | 20.2 |
| 1987–88 | 24 | St. Louis Blues | NHL | 72 | 36 | 50 | 86 | -13 | 59 | 15 | 19 | 2 | 4 | 163 | 22.1 |
| 1988–89 | 25 | Calgary Flames | NHL | 72 | 26 | 59 | 85 | 45 | 44 | 15 | 11 | 0 | 5 | 161 | 16.1 |
| 1989–90 | 26 | Calgary Flames | NHL | 78 | 24 | 67 | 91 | 20 | 54 | 11 | 12 | 1 | 3 | 152 | 15.8 |
| 1990–91 | 27 | Calgary Flames | NHL | 78 | 20 | 61 | 81 | 27 | 144 | 16 | 2 | 2 | 5 | 135 | 14.8 |
| 1991–92 | 28 | Calgary Flames | NHL | 38 | 11 | 27 | 38 | 12 | 46 | 6 | 4 | 1 | 1 | 64 | 17.2 |
| 1991–92 | 28 | Toronto Maple Leafs | NHL | 40 | 15 | 34 | 49 | 13 | 32 | 9 | 6 | 0 | 3 | 104 | 14.4 |
| 1992–93 | 29 | Toronto Maple Leafs | NHL | 83 | 32 | 95 | 127 | 32 | 100 | 14 | 15 | 3 | 2 | 211 | 15.2 |
| 1993–94 | 30 | Toronto Maple Leafs | NHL | 83 | 27 | 84 | 111 | 25 | 105 | 16 | 10 | 1 | 3 | 167 | 16.2 |
| 1994–95 | 31 | Toronto Maple Leafs | NHL | 44 | 10 | 23 | 33 | -5 | 26 | 7 | 3 | 0 | 1 | 73 | 13.7 |
| 1995–96 | 32 | Toronto Maple Leafs | NHL | 81 | 32 | 40 | 72 | -5 | 77 | 20 | 10 | 2 | 3 | 180 | 17.8 |
| 1996–97 | 33 | Toronto Maple Leafs | NHL | 61 | 15 | 45 | 60 | -5 | 46 | 12 | 2 | 1 | 1 | 103 | 14.6 |
| 1996–97 | 33 | New Jersey Devils | NHL | 20 | 7 | 15 | 22 | 7 | 22 | 5 | 2 | 0 | 0 | 40 | 17.5 |
| 1997–98 | 34 | New Jersey Devils | NHL | 63 | 13 | 40 | 53 | 10 | 68 | 10 | 3 | 0 | 5 | 94 | 13.8 |
| 1998–99 | 35 | Chicago Blackhawks | NHL | 72 | 16 | 40 | 56 | -16 | 56 | 8 | 7 | 1 | 4 | 110 | 14.5 |
| 1999–00 | 36 | Chicago Blackhawks | NHL | 63 | 22 | 34 | 56 | -12 | 51 | 14 | 8 | 0 | 3 | 100 | 22.0 |
| 1999–00 | 36 | Buffalo Sabres | NHL | 11 | 3 | 14 | 17 | 3 | 12 | 1 | 2 | 0 | 0 | 13 | 23.1 |
| 2000–01 | 37 | Buffalo Sabres | NHL | 71 | 7 | 31 | 38 | 3 | 70 | 3 | 4 | 0 | 0 | 91 | 7.7 |
| 2001–02 | 38 | Montreal Canadiens | NHL | 70 | 10 | 31 | 41 | -7 | 48 | 5 | 5 | 0 | 2 | 78 | 12.8 |
| 2002–03 | 39 | Montreal Canadiens | NHL | 61 | 11 | 19 | 30 | -6 | 36 | 8 | 3 | 0 | 0 | 85 | 12.9 |
| 2002–03 | 39 | Toronto Maple Leafs | NHL | 1 | 0 | 0 | 0 | 0 | 0 | 0 | 0 | 0 | 0 | 0 | 0.0 |
| NHL Career — 20 Seasons | | | | 1474 | 450 | 964 | 1414 | 129 | 1301 | 279 | 153 | 18 | 56 | 2834 | 15.9 |

## PLAYOFFS

| SEASON | AGE | TEAM | LG | GP | G | A | PTS | +/- | PIM | ESG | PPG | SHG | GWG | SOG | S% |
|---|---|---|---|---|---|---|---|---|---|---|---|---|---|---|---|
| 1983–84 | 20 | St. Louis Blues | NHL | 11 | 2 | 9 | 11 | 2 | 10 | 1 | 1 | 0 | 1 | 20 | 10.0 |
| 1984–85 | 21 | St. Louis Blues | NHL | 3 | 1 | 1 | 2 | -4 | 2 | 1 | 0 | 0 | 0 | 13 | 7.7 |
| 1985–86 | 22 | St. Louis Blues | NHL | 19 | 9 | 12 | 21 | 3 | 25 | 6 | 1 | 2 | 2 | 55 | 16.4 |
| 1986–87 | 23 | St. Louis Blues | NHL | 6 | 2 | 2 | 4 | 1 | 16 | 1 | 1 | 0 | 1 | 14 | 14.3 |
| 1987–88 | 24 | St. Louis Blues | NHL | 10 | 3 | 14 | 17 | 3 | 18 | 2 | 1 | 0 | 1 | 18 | 16.7 |
| 1988–89 | 25 | Calgary Flames | NHL | 22 | 11 | 11 | 22 | 12 | 20 | 8 | 3 | 0 | 3 | 49 | 22.4 |
| 1989–90 | 26 | Calgary Flames | NHL | 6 | 3 | 1 | 4 | -6 | 8 | 3 | 0 | 0 | 1 | 12 | 25.0 |
| 1990–91 | 27 | Calgary Flames | NHL | 7 | 1 | 1 | 2 | 1 | 0 | 1 | 0 | 0 | 1 | 11 | 9.1 |
| 1992–93 | 29 | Toronto Maple Leafs | NHL | 21 | 10 | 25 | 35 | 16 | 30 | 6 | 4 | 0 | 1 | 51 | 19.6 |
| 1993–94 | 30 | Toronto Maple Leafs | NHL | 18 | 6 | 22 | 28 | 3 | 42 | 1 | 5 | 0 | 1 | 31 | 19.4 |
| 1994–95 | 31 | Toronto Maple Leafs | NHL | 7 | 0 | 6 | 6 | 2 | 6 | 0 | 0 | 0 | 0 | 8 | 0.0 |
| 1995–96 | 32 | Toronto Maple Leafs | NHL | 6 | 1 | 7 | 8 | -4 | 12 | 0 | 1 | 0 | 0 | 15 | 6.7 |
| 1996–97 | 33 | New Jersey Devils | NHL | 10 | 0 | 4 | 4 | -2 | 14 | 0 | 0 | 0 | 0 | 21 | 0.0 |
| 1997–98 | 34 | New Jersey Devils | NHL | 6 | 5 | 2 | 7 | 4 | 4 | 4 | 1 | 0 | 1 | 12 | 41.7 |
| 1999–00 | 36 | Buffalo Sabres | NHL | 5 | 0 | 1 | 1 | -1 | 0 | 0 | 0 | 0 | 0 | 3 | 0.0 |
| 2000–01 | 37 | Buffalo Sabres | NHL | 13 | 2 | 4 | 6 | -1 | 12 | 1 | 1 | 0 | 1 | 17 | 11.8 |
| 2001–02 | 38 | Montreal Canadiens | NHL | 12 | 4 | 6 | 10 | -2 | 16 | 3 | 1 | 0 | 0 | 17 | 23.5 |
| NHL Career — 17 Seasons | | | | 182 | 60 | 128 | 188 | 27 | 235 | 38 | 20 | 2 | 13 | 367 | 16.3 |

# Cammi Granato   Profile: See page 98

## REGULAR SEASON

| SEASON | AGE | TEAM | LG | GP | G | A | PTS | PIM |
|---|---|---|---|---|---|---|---|---|
| 1989–90 | 18 | Providence College | ECAC | 24 | 24 | 22 | 46 | |
| 1989–90 | 18 | U.S. National Team | WWC | 5 | 9 | 5 | 14 | 4 |
| 1990–91 | 19 | Providence College | ECAC | 22 | 26 | 20 | 46 | |
| 1991–92 | 20 | Providence College | ECAC | 25 | 48 | 32 | 80 | |
| 1991–92 | 20 | U.S. National Team | WWC | 5 | 8 | 2 | 10 | 2 |
| 1992–93 | 21 | Providence College | ECAC | 28 | 41 | 43 | 84 | |
| 1993–94 | 22 | U.S. National Team | WWC | 5 | 5 | 7 | 12 | 6 |
| 1994–95 | 23 | U.S. National Team | Pacific Rim | 5 | 4 | 7 | 11 | 4 |
| 1995–96 | 24 | Concordia Stingers | QSSF | | | | | |
| 1995–96 | 24 | U.S. National Team | Pacific Rim | 5 | 5 | 3 | 8 | 0 |
| 1996–97 | 25 | Concordia Stingers | QSSF | | | | | |
| 1996–97 | 25 | U.S. National Team | WWC | 5 | 5 | 3 | 8 | 4 |
| 1997–98 | 26 | U.S. National Team | Nat-Team | 33 | 14 | 19 | 33 | |
| 1997–98 | 26 | U.S. National Team | Olympics | 6 | 4 | 4 | 8 | 4 |
| 1998–99 | 27 | U.S. National Team | WWC | 5 | 3 | 5 | 8 | 0 |
| 1999–00 | 28 | U.S. National Team | Nat-Team | 20 | 17 | 25 | 42 | |
| 1999–00 | 28 | U.S. National Team | WWC | 5 | 7 | 6 | 13 | 0 |
| 2000–01 | 29 | U.S. National Team | Nat-Team | 38 | 36 | 32 | 68 | |

## Cammi Granato (continued)

### REGULAR SEASON

| SEASON | AGE | TEAM | LG | GP | G | A | PTS | PIM |
|--------|-----|------|-----|-----|-----|-----|-----|-----|
| 2001–02 | 30 | U.S. National Team | Nat-Team | 25 | 27 | 21 | 48 | |
| 2001–02 | 30 | U.S. National Team | Olympics | 5 | 6 | 4 | 10 | 0 |
| 2002–03 | 31 | Vancouver Griffins | NWHL | 16 | 18 | 14 | 32 | 6 |
| 2003–04 | 32 | U.S. National Team | WWC | 3 | 0 | 2 | 2 | 0 |
| 2004–05 | 33 | B.C. Breakers | NWHL | 21 | 8 | 11 | 19 | 30 |
| 2004–05 | 33 | U.S. National Team | WWC | 5 | 1 | 3 | 4 | 2 |
| Career – 16 Seasons | | | | 306 | 323 | 287 | 610 | 62 |

### PLAYOFFS

| SEASON | AGE | TEAM | LG | GP | G | A | PTS | PIM |
|--------|-----|------|-----|-----|-----|-----|-----|-----|
| 2002–03 | 31 | Vancouver Griffins | NWHL | 1 | 0 | 1 | 1 | 0 |
| Career – 1 Season | | | | 1 | 0 | 1 | 1 | 0 |

# Wayne Gretzky  Profile: See page 100

### REGULAR SEASON

| SEASON | AGE | TEAM | LG | GP | G | A | PTS | +/- | PIM | ESG | PPG | SHG | GWG | SOG | S% |
|--------|-----|------|-----|-----|-----|-----|-----|-----|-----|-----|-----|-----|-----|-----|-----|
| 1978–79 | 18 | Indianapolis Racers | WHA | 8 | 3 | 3 | 6 | -3 | 0 | 3 | 0 | 0 | | 17 | 17.6 |
| 1978–79 | 18 | Edmonton Oilers | WHA | 72 | 43 | 61 | 104 | 23 | 19 | 34 | 9 | 0 | | 253 | 17.0 |
| 1979–80 | 19 | Edmonton Oilers | NHL | 79 | 51 | 86 | 137 | 14 | 21 | 37 | 13 | 1 | 6 | 284 | 18.0 |
| 1980–81 | 20 | Edmonton Oilers | NHL | 80 | 55 | 109 | 164 | 41 | 28 | 36 | 15 | 4 | 3 | 261 | 21.1 |
| 1981–82 | 21 | Edmonton Oilers | NHL | 80 | 92 | 120 | 212 | 80 | 26 | 68 | 18 | 6 | 12 | 370 | 24.9 |
| 1982–83 | 22 | Edmonton Oilers | NHL | 80 | 71 | 125 | 196 | 61 | 59 | 47 | 18 | 6 | 9 | 348 | 20.4 |
| 1983–84 | 23 | Edmonton Oilers | NHL | 74 | 87 | 118 | 205 | 78 | 39 | 55 | 20 | 12 | 11 | 326 | 26.7 |
| 1984–85 | 24 | Edmonton Oilers | NHL | 80 | 73 | 135 | 208 | 100 | 52 | 54 | 8 | 11 | 7 | 354 | 20.6 |
| 1985–86 | 25 | Edmonton Oilers | NHL | 80 | 52 | 163 | 215 | 71 | 46 | 38 | 11 | 3 | 6 | 350 | 14.9 |
| 1986–87 | 26 | Edmonton Oilers | NHL | 79 | 62 | 121 | 183 | 69 | 28 | 42 | 13 | 7 | 4 | 288 | 21.5 |
| 1987–88 | 27 | Edmonton Oilers | NHL | 64 | 40 | 109 | 149 | 39 | 24 | 26 | 9 | 5 | 3 | 211 | 19.0 |
| 1988–89 | 28 | Los Angeles Kings | NHL | 78 | 54 | 114 | 168 | 15 | 26 | 38 | 11 | 5 | 5 | 303 | 17.8 |
| 1989–90 | 29 | Los Angeles Kings | NHL | 73 | 40 | 102 | 142 | 8 | 42 | 26 | 10 | 4 | 4 | 236 | 16.9 |
| 1990–91 | 30 | Los Angeles Kings | NHL | 78 | 41 | 122 | 163 | 30 | 16 | 33 | 8 | 0 | 5 | 212 | 19.3 |
| 1991–92 | 31 | Los Angeles Kings | NHL | 74 | 31 | 90 | 121 | -12 | 34 | 17 | 12 | 2 | 2 | 215 | 14.4 |
| 1992–93 | 32 | Los Angeles Kings | NHL | 45 | 16 | 49 | 65 | 6 | 6 | 14 | 0 | 2 | 1 | 141 | 11.3 |
| 1993–94 | 33 | Los Angeles Kings | NHL | 81 | 38 | 92 | 130 | -25 | 20 | 20 | 14 | 4 | 0 | 233 | 16.3 |
| 1994–95 | 34 | Los Angeles Kings | NHL | 48 | 11 | 37 | 48 | -20 | 6 | 8 | 3 | 0 | 1 | 142 | 7.7 |
| 1995–96 | 35 | Los Angeles Kings | NHL | 62 | 15 | 66 | 81 | -7 | 32 | 10 | 5 | 0 | 2 | 144 | 10.4 |
| 1995–96 | 35 | St. Louis Blues | NHL | 18 | 8 | 13 | 21 | -6 | 2 | 6 | 1 | 1 | 1 | 51 | 15.7 |
| 1996–97 | 36 | New York Rangers | NHL | 82 | 25 | 72 | 97 | 12 | 28 | 19 | 6 | 0 | 2 | 286 | 8.7 |
| 1997–98 | 37 | New York Rangers | NHL | 82 | 23 | 67 | 90 | -11 | 28 | 17 | 6 | 0 | 4 | 201 | 11.4 |
| 1998–99 | 38 | New York Rangers | NHL | 70 | 9 | 53 | 62 | -23 | 14 | 6 | 3 | 0 | 3 | 132 | 6.8 |
| Career – 21 Seasons | | | | 1567 | 940 | 2027 | 2967 | 540 | 596 | 654 | 213 | 73 | 91 | 5358 | 17.5 |

### PLAYOFFS

| SEASON | AGE | TEAM | LG | GP | G | A | PTS | +/- | PIM | ESG | PPG | SHG | GWG | SOG | S% |
|--------|-----|------|-----|-----|-----|-----|-----|-----|-----|-----|-----|-----|-----|-----|-----|
| 1978–79 | 18 | Edmonton Oilers | WHA | 13 | 10 | 10 | 20 | 6 | 2 | | | | 1 | | |
| 1979–80 | 19 | Edmonton Oilers | NHL | 3 | 2 | 1 | 3 | -3 | 0 | 2 | 0 | 0 | 0 | 8 | 25.0 |
| 1980–81 | 20 | Edmonton Oilers | NHL | 9 | 7 | 14 | 21 | 10 | 4 | 4 | 2 | 1 | 1 | 39 | 18.0 |
| 1981–82 | 21 | Edmonton Oilers | NHL | 5 | 5 | 7 | 12 | -1 | 8 | 2 | 2 | 1 | 1 | 27 | 18.5 |
| 1982–83 | 22 | Edmonton Oilers | NHL | 16 | 12 | 26 | 38 | 20 | 4 | 7 | 2 | 3 | 3 | 76 | 15.8 |
| 1983–84 | 23 | Edmonton Oilers | NHL | 19 | 13 | 22 | 35 | 18 | 12 | 10 | 2 | 1 | 3 | 87 | 15.0 |
| 1984–85 | 24 | Edmonton Oilers | NHL | 18 | 17 | 30 | 47 | 27 | 4 | 11 | 4 | 2 | 3 | 67 | 25.4 |
| 1985–86 | 25 | Edmonton Oilers | NHL | 10 | 8 | 11 | 19 | -1 | 2 | 3 | 4 | 1 | 2 | 41 | 19.5 |
| 1986–87 | 26 | Edmonton Oilers | NHL | 21 | 5 | 29 | 34 | 10 | 6 | 3 | 2 | 0 | 0 | 55 | 9.1 |
| 1987–88 | 27 | Edmonton Oilers | NHL | 19 | 12 | 31 | 43 | 9 | 16 | 6 | 5 | 1 | 3 | 62 | 19.4 |
| 1988–89 | 28 | Los Angeles Kings | NHL | 11 | 5 | 17 | 22 | -4 | 0 | 3 | 1 | 1 | 0 | 42 | 11.9 |
| 1989–90 | 29 | Los Angeles Kings | NHL | 7 | 3 | 7 | 10 | -4 | 0 | 2 | 1 | 0 | 0 | 13 | 23.1 |
| 1990–91 | 30 | Los Angeles Kings | NHL | 12 | 4 | 11 | 15 | 0 | 2 | 3 | 1 | 0 | 2 | 26 | 15.4 |
| 1991–92 | 31 | Los Angeles Kings | NHL | 6 | 2 | 5 | 7 | -3 | 2 | 1 | 1 | 0 | 0 | 11 | 18.2 |
| 1992–93 | 32 | Los Angeles Kings | NHL | 24 | 15 | 25 | 40 | 6 | 4 | 10 | 4 | 1 | 3 | 76 | 19.7 |
| 1995–96 | 35 | St. Louis Blues | NHL | 13 | 2 | 14 | 16 | 2 | 0 | 1 | 1 | 0 | 1 | 25 | 8.0 |
| 1996–97 | 36 | New York Rangers | NHL | 15 | 10 | 10 | 20 | 5 | 2 | 7 | 3 | 0 | 2 | 44 | 22.7 |
| Career – 17 Seasons | | | | 221 | 132 | 270 | 402 | 97 | 68 | 75 | 35 | 12 | 25 | 699 | 17.5 |

# Dale Hawerchuk  Profile: See page 102

## REGULAR SEASON

| SEASON | AGE | TEAM | LG | GP | G | A | PTS | +/- | PIM | ESG | PPG | SHG | GWG | SOG | S% |
|---|---|---|---|---|---|---|---|---|---|---|---|---|---|---|---|
| 1981–82 | 18 | Winnipeg Jets | NHL | 80 | 45 | 58 | 103 | -7 | 47 | 33 | 12 | 0 | 2 | 339 | 13.3 |
| 1982–83 | 19 | Winnipeg Jets | NHL | 79 | 40 | 51 | 91 | -17 | 31 | 27 | 13 | 0 | 3 | 297 | 13.5 |
| 1983–84 | 20 | Winnipeg Jets | NHL | 80 | 37 | 65 | 102 | -14 | 73 | 27 | 10 | 0 | 4 | 256 | 14.5 |
| 1984–85 | 21 | Winnipeg Jets | NHL | 80 | 53 | 77 | 130 | 20 | 74 | 33 | 17 | 3 | 4 | 280 | 18.9 |
| 1985–86 | 22 | Winnipeg Jets | NHL | 80 | 46 | 59 | 105 | -27 | 44 | 26 | 18 | 2 | 2 | 313 | 14.7 |
| 1986–87 | 23 | Winnipeg Jets | NHL | 80 | 47 | 53 | 100 | 2 | 52 | 37 | 10 | 0 | 4 | 267 | 17.6 |
| 1987–88 | 24 | Winnipeg Jets | NHL | 80 | 44 | 77 | 121 | -9 | 59 | 21 | 20 | 3 | 4 | 292 | 15.1 |
| 1988–89 | 25 | Winnipeg Jets | NHL | 75 | 41 | 55 | 96 | -30 | 28 | 24 | 14 | 3 | 4 | 239 | 17.2 |
| 1989–90 | 26 | Winnipeg Jets | NHL | 79 | 26 | 55 | 81 | -11 | 70 | 18 | 8 | 0 | 2 | 211 | 12.3 |
| 1990–91 | 27 | Buffalo Sabres | NHL | 80 | 31 | 58 | 89 | 2 | 32 | 19 | 12 | 0 | 1 | 194 | 16.0 |
| 1991–92 | 28 | Buffalo Sabres | NHL | 77 | 23 | 75 | 98 | -22 | 27 | 10 | 13 | 0 | 4 | 242 | 9.5 |
| 1992–93 | 29 | Buffalo Sabres | NHL | 81 | 16 | 80 | 96 | -17 | 52 | 8 | 8 | 0 | 2 | 259 | 6.2 |
| 1993–94 | 30 | Buffalo Sabres | NHL | 81 | 35 | 51 | 86 | 10 | 91 | 21 | 13 | 1 | 7 | 227 | 15.4 |
| 1994–95 | 31 | Buffalo Sabres | NHL | 23 | 5 | 11 | 16 | -2 | 2 | 3 | 2 | 0 | 2 | 56 | 8.9 |
| 1995–96 | 32 | St. Louis Blues | NHL | 66 | 13 | 28 | 41 | 5 | 22 | 8 | 5 | 0 | 1 | 136 | 9.6 |
| 1995–96 | 32 | Philadelphia Flyers | NHL | 16 | 4 | 16 | 20 | 10 | 4 | 3 | 1 | 0 | 1 | 44 | 9.1 |
| 1996–97 | 33 | Philadelphia Flyers | NHL | 51 | 12 | 22 | 34 | 9 | 32 | 6 | 6 | 0 | 2 | 102 | 11.8 |
| NHL Career—16 Seasons | | | | 1188 | 518 | 891 | 1409 | -98 | 740 | 324 | 182 | 12 | 49 | 3754 | 13.8 |

## PLAYOFFS

| SEASON | AGE | TEAM | LG | GP | G | A | PTS | +/- | PIM | ESG | PPG | SHG | GWG | SOG | S% |
|---|---|---|---|---|---|---|---|---|---|---|---|---|---|---|---|
| 1981–82 | 18 | Winnipeg Jets | NHL | 4 | 1 | 7 | 8 | -5 | 5 | 1 | 0 | 0 | 0 | 13 | 7.7 |
| 1982–83 | 19 | Winnipeg Jets | NHL | 3 | 1 | 4 | 5 | -2 | 6 | 0 | 1 | 0 | 0 | 12 | 8.3 |
| 1983–84 | 20 | Winnipeg Jets | NHL | 3 | 1 | 1 | 2 | -6 | 0 | 0 | 1 | 0 | 0 | 15 | 6.7 |
| 1984–85 | 21 | Winnipeg Jets | NHL | 3 | 2 | 1 | 3 | 1 | 4 | 1 | 1 | 0 | 0 | 8 | 25.0 |
| 1985–86 | 22 | Winnipeg Jets | NHL | 3 | 0 | 3 | 3 | -2 | 0 | 0 | 0 | 0 | 0 | 10 | 0.0 |
| 1986–87 | 23 | Winnipeg Jets | NHL | 10 | 5 | 8 | 13 | -4 | 4 | 2 | 3 | 0 | 0 | 38 | 13.2 |
| 1987–88 | 24 | Winnipeg Jets | NHL | 5 | 3 | 4 | 7 | -4 | 16 | 1 | 2 | 0 | 0 | 16 | 18.8 |
| 1989–90 | 26 | Winnipeg Jets | NHL | 7 | 3 | 5 | 8 | 5 | 2 | 3 | 0 | 0 | 1 | 21 | 14.3 |
| 1990–91 | 27 | Buffalo Sabres | NHL | 6 | 2 | 4 | 6 | -3 | 10 | 1 | 1 | 0 | 0 | 19 | 10.5 |
| 1991–92 | 28 | Buffalo Sabres | NHL | 7 | 2 | 5 | 7 | 3 | 0 | 2 | 0 | 0 | 0 | 24 | 8.3 |
| 1992–93 | 29 | Buffalo Sabres | NHL | 8 | 5 | 9 | 14 | 0 | 2 | 2 | 3 | 0 | 0 | 31 | 16.1 |
| 1993–94 | 30 | Buffalo Sabres | NHL | 7 | 0 | 7 | 7 | -1 | 4 | 0 | 0 | 0 | 0 | 16 | 0.0 |
| 1994–95 | 31 | Buffalo Sabres | NHL | 2 | 0 | 0 | 0 | -1 | 0 | 0 | 0 | 0 | 0 | 3 | 0.0 |
| 1995–96 | 32 | Philadelphia Flyers | NHL | 12 | 3 | 6 | 9 | 0 | 12 | 2 | 1 | 0 | 0 | 48 | 6.3 |
| 1996–97 | 33 | Philadelphia Flyers | NHL | 17 | 2 | 5 | 7 | -2 | 0 | 1 | 1 | 0 | 1 | 24 | 8.3 |
| NHL Career—15 Seasons | | | | 97 | 30 | 69 | 99 | -21 | 65 | 16 | 14 | 0 | 2 | 298 | 10.1 |

# Dick Irvin  Profile: See page 103

## REGULAR SEASON

| SEASON | AGE | TEAM | LG | GP | G | A | PTS | PIM |
|---|---|---|---|---|---|---|---|---|
| 1916–17 | 24 | Portland Rosebuds | PCHA | 23 | 35 | 10 | 45 | 24 |
| 1917–18 | 25 | Winnipeg Ypres | MHL-Sr. | 9 | 29 | 8 | 37 | 26 |
| 1919–20 | 27 | Regina Victorias | SSHL | 12 | 32 | 4 | 36 | 22 |
| 1920–21 | 28 | Regina Victorias | SSHL | 11 | 19 | 5 | 24 | 12 |
| 1921–22 | 29 | Regina Capitals | WCHL | 20 | 21 | 7 | 28 | 17 |
| 1922–23 | 30 | Regina Capitals | WCHL | 25 | 9 | 4 | 13 | 12 |
| 1923–24 | 31 | Regina Capitals | WCHL | 29 | 15 | 8 | 23 | 33 |
| 1924–25 | 32 | Regina Capitals | WCHL | 28 | 13 | 5 | 18 | 38 |
| 1925–26 | 33 | Portland Rosebuds | WHL | 30 | 31 | 5 | 36 | 29 |
| 1926–27 | 34 | Chicago Black Hawks | NHL | 44 | 18 | 18 | 36 | 34 |
| 1927–28 | 35 | Chicago Black Hawks | NHL | 12 | 5 | 4 | 9 | 14 |
| 1928–29 | 36 | Chicago Black Hawks | NHL | 39 | 6 | 1 | 7 | 36 |
| Career—12 Seasons | | | | 282 | 233 | 79 | 312 | 297 |

## PLAYOFFS

| SEASON | AGE | TEAM | LG | GP | G | A | PTS | PIM |
|---|---|---|---|---|---|---|---|---|
| 1919–20 | 27 | Regina Victorias | SSHL | 2 | 1 | 0 | 1 | 4 |
| 1920–21 | 28 | Regina Victorias | SSHL | 4 | 8 | 0 | 8 | 4 |
| 1921–22 | 29 | Regina Capitals | WCHL | 4 | 3 | 0 | 3 | 2 |
| 1921–22 | 29 | Regina Capitals | West-P | 2 | 1 | 0 | 1 | 0 |
| 1922–23 | 30 | Regina Capitals | WCHL | 2 | 1 | 0 | 1 | 0 |
| 1923–24 | 31 | Regina Capitals | WCHL | 2 | 0 | 0 | 0 | 4 |
| 1926–27 | 34 | Chicago Black Hawks | NHL | 2 | 2 | 0 | 2 | 4 |
| Career—6 Seasons | | | | 18 | 16 | 0 | 16 | 18 |

# Angela James  Profile: See page 104

## REGULAR SEASON

| SEASON | AGE | TEAM | LG | GP | G | A | PTS | PIM |
|---|---|---|---|---|---|---|---|---|
| 1982–83 | 18 | Seneca College | OCAA | 8 | 15 | 10 | 25 | |
| 1983–84 | 19 | Seneca College | OCAA | 10 | 15 | 15 | 30 | |
| 1984–85 | 20 | Seneca College | OCAA | 14 | 50 | 23 | 73 | |
| 1989–90 | 25 | Canada | WWC | 5 | 11 | 2 | 13 | 10 |
| 1991–92 | 27 | Canada | WWC | 5 | 5 | 2 | 7 | 2 |
| 1992–93 | 28 | Toronto Aeros | COWHL | 23 | 16 | 18 | 34 | 67 |
| 1993–94 | 29 | Canada | WWC | 5 | 4 | 5 | 9 | 2 |
| 1993–94 | 29 | Toronto Aeros | COWHL | 28 | 30 | 40 | 70 | 41 |
| 1995–96 | 31 | Canada | Pacific Rim | 5 | 3 | 4 | 7 | 2 |

## Angela James (continued)

### REGULAR SEASON

| SEASON | AGE | TEAM | LG | GP | G | A | PTS | PIM |
|--------|-----|------|-----|-----|-----|-----|-----|-----|
| 1995–96 | 31 | Canada | 3 Nations Cup | 5 | 1 | 2 | 3 | 2 |
| 1995–96 | 31 | Toronto Red Wings | COWHL | 29 | 35 | 35 | 70 | 37 |
| 1996–97 | 32 | Newtonbrook Panthers | COWHL | 28 | 29 | 29 | 58 | 57 |
| 1996–97 | 32 | Canada | WWC | 5 | 2 | 3 | 5 | 2 |
| 1997–98 | 33 | Toronto Aeros | COWHL | 9 | 6 | 3 | 9 | 19 |
| 1997–98 | 33 | Canada | Nat-Team | 15 | 7 | 1 | 8 | 4 |
| 1998–99 | 34 | North York/Beatrice Aeros | NWHL | 31 | 36 | 19 | 55 | 30 |
| 1998–99 | 34 | Canada | 3 Nations Cup | 3 | 0 | 2 | 2 | 0 |
| 1999–00 | 35 | Canada | 3 Nations Cup | 2 | 0 | 0 | 0 | 0 |
| 1999–00 | 35 | North York/Beatrice Aeros | NWHL | 27 | 22 | 22 | 44 | 10 |
| Career — 12 Seasons | | | | 257 | 281 | 235 | 516 | 285 |

## Duke Keats   Profile: See page 106

### REGULAR SEASON

| SEASON | AGE | TEAM | LG | GP | G | A | PTS | PIM |
|--------|-----|------|-----|-----|-----|-----|-----|-----|
| 1915–16 | 20 | Toronto Blueshirts | NHA | 24 | 22 | 7 | 29 | 112 |
| 1916–17 | 21 | Toronto Blueshirts | NHA | 13 | 15 | 3 | 18 | 54 |
| 1919–20 | 24 | Edmonton Eskimos | Big-4 | 12 | 18 | 14 | 32 | 41 |
| 1920–21 | 25 | Edmonton Eskimos | Big-4 | 15 | 23 | 6 | 29 | 36 |
| 1921–22 | 26 | Edmonton Eskimos | WCHL | 25 | 31 | 24 | 55 | 47 |
| 1922–23 | 27 | Edmonton Eskimos | WCHL | 25 | 24 | 13 | 37 | 72 |
| 1923–24 | 28 | Edmonton Eskimos | WCHL | 29 | 19 | 12 | 31 | 41 |
| 1924–25 | 29 | Edmonton Eskimos | WCHL | 28 | 23 | 9 | 32 | 63 |
| 1925–26 | 30 | Edmonton Eskimos | WHL | 30 | 20 | 9 | 29 | 134 |
| 1926–27 | 31 | Boston Bruins | NHL | 17 | 4 | 4 | 8 | 20 |
| 1926–27 | 31 | Detroit Cougars | NHL | 25 | 11 | 4 | 15 | 36 |

### REGULAR SEASON

| SEASON | AGE | TEAM | LG | GP | G | A | PTS | PIM |
|--------|-----|------|-----|-----|-----|-----|-----|-----|
| 1927–28 | 32 | Detroit Cougars | NHL | 4 | 0 | 2 | 2 | 6 |
| 1927–28 | 32 | Chicago Black Hawks | NHL | 33 | 14 | 8 | 22 | 52 |
| 1928–29 | 33 | Chicago Black Hawks | NHL | 3 | 0 | 1 | 1 | 0 |
| Career — 12 Seasons | | | | 303 | 232 | 123 | 355 | 858 |

### PLAYOFFS

| SEASON | AGE | TEAM | LG | GP | G | A | PTS | PIM |
|--------|-----|------|-----|-----|-----|-----|-----|-----|
| 1919–20 | 24 | Edmonton Eskimos | Big-4 | 2 | 2 | 2 | 4 | 2 |
| 1921–22 | 26 | Edmonton Eskimos | WCHL | 2 | 0 | 1 | 1 | 6 |
| 1922–23 | 27 | Edmonton Eskimos | WCHL | 2 | 2 | 2 | 4 | 0 |
| 1925–26 | 30 | Edmoton Eskimos | WHL | 2 | 0 | 0 | 0 | 28 |
| Careers — 4 Seasons | | | | 8 | 4 | 5 | 9 | 36 |

## Ted Kennedy   Profile: See page 107

### REGULAR SEASON

| SEASON | AGE | TEAM | LG | GP | G | A | PTS | PIM |
|--------|-----|------|-----|-----|-----|-----|-----|-----|
| 1942–43 | 17 | Toronto Maple Leafs | NHL | 2 | 0 | 1 | 1 | 0 |
| 1943–44 | 18 | Toronto Maple Leafs | NHL | 49 | 25 | 24 | 49 | 2 |
| 1944–45 | 19 | Toronto Maple Leafs | NHL | 49 | 29 | 25 | 54 | 14 |
| 1945–46 | 20 | Toronto Maple Leafs | NHL | 21 | 3 | 2 | 5 | 4 |
| 1946–47 | 21 | Toronto Maple Leafs | NHL | 60 | 28 | 32 | 60 | 27 |
| 1947–48 | 22 | Toronto Maple Leafs | NHL | 60 | 25 | 21 | 46 | 32 |
| 1948–49 | 23 | Toronto Maple Leafs | NHL | 59 | 18 | 21 | 39 | 25 |
| 1949–50 | 24 | Toronto Maple Leafs | NHL | 53 | 20 | 24 | 44 | 34 |
| 1950–51 | 25 | Toronto Maple Leafs | NHL | 63 | 18 | 43 | 61 | 32 |
| 1951–52 | 26 | Toronto Maple Leafs | NHL | 70 | 19 | 33 | 52 | 33 |
| 1952–53 | 27 | Toronto Maple Leafs | NHL | 43 | 14 | 23 | 37 | 42 |
| 1953–54 | 28 | Toronto Maple Leafs | NHL | 67 | 15 | 23 | 38 | 78 |
| 1954–55 | 29 | Toronto Maple Leafs | NHL | 70 | 10 | 42 | 52 | 74 |
| 1956–57 | 31 | Toronto Maple Leafs | NHL | 30 | 6 | 16 | 22 | 35 |
| NHL Career — 14 Seasons | | | | 696 | 230 | 330 | 560 | 432 |

### PLAYOFFS

| SEASON | AGE | TEAM | LG | GP | G | A | PTS | PIM |
|--------|-----|------|-----|-----|-----|-----|-----|-----|
| 1943–44 | 18 | Toronto Maple Leafs | NHL | 5 | 1 | 1 | 2 | 4 |
| 1944–45 | 19 | Toronto Maple Leafs | NHL | 13 | 7 | 2 | 9 | 2 |
| 1946–47 | 21 | Toronto Maple Leafs | NHL | 11 | 4 | 5 | 9 | 4 |
| 1947–48 | 22 | Toronto Maple Leafs | NHL | 9 | 8 | 6 | 14 | 0 |
| 1948–49 | 23 | Toronto Maple Leafs | NHL | 9 | 2 | 6 | 8 | 2 |
| 1949–50 | 24 | Toronto Maple Leafs | NHL | 7 | 1 | 2 | 3 | 8 |
| 1950–51 | 25 | Toronto Maple Leafs | NHL | 11 | 4 | 5 | 9 | 6 |
| 1951–52 | 26 | Toronto Maple Leafs | NHL | 4 | 0 | 0 | 0 | 4 |
| 1953–54 | 28 | Toronto Maple Leafs | NHL | 5 | 1 | 1 | 2 | 2 |
| 1954–55 | 29 | Toronto Maple Leafs | NHL | 4 | 1 | 3 | 4 | 0 |
| NHL Career — 10 Seasons | | | | 78 | 29 | 31 | 60 | 32 |

## Dave Keon   Profile: See page 108

### REGULAR SEASON

| SEASON | AGE | TEAM | LG | GP | G | A | PTS | +/- | PIM | ESG | PPG | SHG | GWG | SOG | S% |
|--------|-----|------|-----|-----|-----|-----|-----|-----|-----|-----|-----|-----|-----|-----|-----|
| 1960–61 | 20 | Toronto Maple Leafs | NHL | 70 | 20 | 25 | 45 | 12 | 6 | 17 | 2 | 1 | 3 | 206 | 9.7 |
| 1961–62 | 21 | Toronto Maple Leafs | NHL | 64 | 26 | 35 | 61 | 40 | 2 | 21 | 3 | 2 | 6 | 252 | 10.3 |
| 1962–63 | 22 | Toronto Maple Leafs | NHL | 68 | 28 | 28 | 56 | 8 | 2 | 19 | 6 | 3 | 4 | 232 | 12.1 |
| 1963–64 | 23 | Toronto Maple Leafs | NHL | 70 | 23 | 37 | 60 | 2 | 6 | 16 | 7 | 0 | 2 | 240 | 9.6 |
| 1964–65 | 24 | Toronto Maple Leafs | NHL | 65 | 21 | 29 | 50 | 15 | 10 | 14 | 6 | 1 | 2 | 191 | 11.0 |
| 1965–66 | 25 | Toronto Maple Leafs | NHL | 69 | 24 | 30 | 54 | 6 | 4 | 18 | 6 | 0 | 6 | 246 | 9.8 |
| 1966–67 | 26 | Toronto Maple Leafs | NHL | 66 | 19 | 33 | 52 | -7 | 2 | 13 | 5 | 1 | 2 | 212 | 9.0 |
| 1967–68 | 27 | Toronto Maple Leafs | NHL | 67 | 11 | 37 | 48 | 15 | 4 | 10 | 1 | 0 | 3 | 196 | 5.6 |
| 1968–69 | 28 | Toronto Maple Leafs | NHL | 75 | 27 | 34 | 61 | 18 | 12 | 18 | 3 | 6 | 2 | 281 | 9.6 |
| 1969–70 | 29 | Toronto Maple Leafs | NHL | 72 | 32 | 30 | 62 | -15 | 6 | 21 | 9 | 2 | 4 | 284 | 11.3 |
| 1970–71 | 30 | Toronto Maple Leafs | NHL | 76 | 38 | 38 | 76 | 25 | 4 | 25 | 5 | 8 | 9 | 277 | 13.7 |
| 1971–72 | 31 | Toronto Maple Leafs | NHL | 72 | 18 | 30 | 48 | 1 | 4 | 14 | 2 | 2 | 5 | 265 | 6.8 |
| 1972–73 | 32 | Toronto Maple Leafs | NHL | 76 | 37 | 36 | 73 | 3 | 2 | 27 | 8 | 2 | 6 | 277 | 13.4 |
| 1973–74 | 33 | Toronto Maple Leafs | NHL | 74 | 25 | 28 | 53 | 13 | 7 | 22 | 1 | 2 | 3 | 244 | 10.3 |
| 1974–75 | 34 | Toronto Maple Leafs | NHL | 78 | 16 | 43 | 59 | 3 | 4 | 14 | 1 | 1 | 2 | 183 | 8.7 |
| 1975–76 | 35 | Minnesota Fighting Saints | WHA | 57 | 26 | 38 | 64 | 14 | 4 | 19 | 5 | 2 | 3 | 144 | 18.1 |
| 1975–76 | 35 | Indianapolis Racers | WHA | 12 | 3 | 7 | 10 | 2 | 2 | 2 | 1 | 0 | 0 | 40 | 7.5 |

## Dave Keon (continued)

### REGULAR SEASON

| SEASON | AGE | TEAM | LG | GP | G | A | PTS | +/- | PIM | ESG | PPG | SHG | GWG | SOG | S% |
|---|---|---|---|---|---|---|---|---|---|---|---|---|---|---|---|
| 1976–77 | 36 | Minnesota Fighting Saints | WHA | 42 | 13 | 38 | 51 | 25 | 2 | 11 | 1 | 1 | | 151 | 8.6 |
| 1976–77 | 36 | New England Whalers | WHA | 34 | 14 | 25 | 39 | 13 | 8 | 8 | 5 | 1 | | 107 | 13.1 |
| 1977–78 | 37 | New England Whalers | WHA | 77 | 24 | 38 | 62 | -4 | 2 | 18 | 1 | 5 | | 169 | 14.2 |
| 1978–79 | 38 | New England Whalers | WHA | 79 | 22 | 43 | 65 | 4 | 2 | 15 | 7 | 0 | | 189 | 11.6 |
| 1979–80 | 39 | Hartford Whalers | NHL | 76 | 10 | 52 | 62 | -13 | 10 | 10 | 0 | 0 | 0 | 146 | 6.8 |
| 1980–81 | 40 | Hartford Whalers | NHL | 80 | 13 | 34 | 47 | -33 | 26 | 11 | 2 | 0 | 1 | 130 | 10.0 |
| 1981–82 | 41 | Hartford Whalers | NHL | 78 | 8 | 11 | 19 | -32 | 6 | 7 | 0 | 1 | 1 | 84 | 9.5 |
| Career — 22 Seasons | | | | 1597 | 498 | 779 | 1277 | 105 | 137 | 370 | 87 | 41 | 68 | 4746 | 10.5 |

### PLAYOFFS

| SEASON | AGE | TEAM | LG | GP | G | A | PTS | +/- | PIM | ESG | PPG | SHG | GWG | SOG | S% |
|---|---|---|---|---|---|---|---|---|---|---|---|---|---|---|---|
| 1960–61 | 20 | Toronto Maple Leafs | NHL | 5 | 1 | 1 | 2 | -2 | 0 | 1 | 0 | 0 | 0 | 4 | 25.0 |
| 1961–62 | 21 | Toronto Maple Leafs | NHL | 12 | 5 | 3 | 8 | 6 | 0 | 3 | 2 | 0 | 0 | 47 | 10.6 |
| 1962–63 | 22 | Toronto Maple Leafs | NHL | 10 | 7 | 5 | 12 | 10 | 0 | 4 | 1 | 2 | 3 | 33 | 21.2 |
| 1963–64 | 23 | Toronto Maple Leafs | NHL | 14 | 7 | 2 | 9 | 5 | 2 | 5 | 1 | 1 | 1 | 52 | 13.5 |
| 1964–65 | 24 | Toronto Maple Leafs | NHL | 6 | 2 | 2 | 4 | 1 | 2 | 1 | 0 | 1 | 1 | 19 | 10.5 |
| 1965–66 | 25 | Toronto Maple Leafs | NHL | 4 | 0 | 2 | 2 | -1 | 0 | 0 | 0 | 0 | 0 | 9 | 0.0 |
| 1966–67 | 26 | Toronto Maple Leafs | NHL | 12 | 3 | 5 | 8 | 1 | 0 | 2 | 0 | 1 | 1 | 35 | 8.6 |
| 1968–69 | 28 | Toronto Maple Leafs | NHL | 4 | 1 | 3 | 4 | -2 | 2 | 0 | 0 | 1 | 0 | 15 | 6.7 |
| 1970–71 | 30 | Toronto Maple Leafs | NHL | 6 | 3 | 2 | 5 | 2 | 0 | 3 | 0 | 0 | 0 | 25 | 12.0 |
| 1971–72 | 31 | Toronto Maple Leafs | NHL | 5 | 2 | 3 | 5 | -2 | 0 | 2 | 0 | 0 | 0 | 16 | 12.5 |
| 1973–74 | 33 | Toronto Maple Leafs | NHL | 4 | 1 | 2 | 3 | -2 | 0 | 1 | 0 | 0 | 0 | 10 | 10.0 |
| 1974–75 | 34 | Toronto Maple Leafs | NHL | 7 | 0 | 5 | 5 | 0 | 0 | 0 | 0 | 0 | 0 | 13 | 0.0 |
| 1975–76 | 35 | Indianapolis Racers | WHA | 7 | 2 | 2 | 4 | 0 | 2 | | | | | | |
| 1976–77 | 36 | New England Whalers | WHA | 5 | 3 | 1 | 4 | 4 | 0 | | | | 0 | | |
| 1977–78 | 37 | New England Whalers | WHA | 14 | 5 | 11 | 16 | 2 | 4 | | | | 1 | | |
| 1978–79 | 38 | New England Whalers | WHA | 10 | 3 | 9 | 12 | 2 | 2 | | | | 1 | | |
| 1979–80 | 39 | Hartford Whalers | NHL | 3 | 0 | 1 | 1 | -3 | 0 | 0 | 0 | 0 | 0 | 6 | 0.0 |
| Career — 17 Seasons | | | | 128 | 45 | 59 | 104 | 21 | 14 | 22 | 4 | 6 | 8 | 284 | 11.3 |

## Elmer Lach   Profile: See page 110

### REGULAR SEASON

| SEASON | AGE | TEAM | LG | GP | G | A | PTS | PIM |
|---|---|---|---|---|---|---|---|---|
| 1940–41 | 23 | Montreal Canadiens | NHL | 43 | 7 | 14 | 21 | 16 |
| 1941–42 | 24 | Montreal Canadiens | NHL | 1 | 0 | 1 | 1 | 0 |
| 1942–43 | 25 | Montreal Canadiens | NHL | 45 | 18 | 40 | 58 | 14 |
| 1943–44 | 26 | Montreal Canadiens | NHL | 48 | 24 | 48 | 72 | 23 |
| 1944–45 | 27 | Montreal Canadiens | NHL | 50 | 26 | 54 | 80 | 37 |
| 1945–46 | 28 | Montreal Canadiens | NHL | 50 | 13 | 34 | 47 | 34 |
| 1946–47 | 29 | Montreal Canadiens | NHL | 31 | 14 | 16 | 30 | 22 |
| 1947–48 | 30 | Montreal Canadiens | NHL | 60 | 30 | 31 | 61 | 72 |
| 1948–49 | 31 | Montreal Canadiens | NHL | 36 | 11 | 18 | 29 | 59 |
| 1949–50 | 32 | Montreal Canadiens | NHL | 64 | 15 | 33 | 48 | 33 |
| 1950–51 | 33 | Montreal Canadiens | NHL | 65 | 21 | 24 | 45 | 48 |
| 1951–52 | 34 | Montreal Canadiens | NHL | 70 | 15 | 50 | 65 | 36 |
| 1952–53 | 35 | Montreal Canadiens | NHL | 53 | 16 | 25 | 41 | 56 |
| 1953–54 | 36 | Montreal Canadiens | NHL | 48 | 5 | 20 | 25 | 28 |
| NHL Career — 14 Seasons | | | | 664 | 215 | 408 | 623 | 478 |

### PLAYOFFS

| SEASON | AGE | TEAM | LG | GP | G | A | PTS | PIM |
|---|---|---|---|---|---|---|---|---|
| 1940–41 | 23 | Montreal Canadiens | NHL | 1 | 1 | 0 | 1 | 0 |
| 1942–43 | 25 | Montreal Canadiens | NHL | 5 | 2 | 4 | 6 | 6 |
| 1943–44 | 26 | Montreal Canadiens | NHL | 9 | 2 | 11 | 13 | 4 |
| 1944–45 | 27 | Montreal Canadiens | NHL | 6 | 4 | 4 | 8 | 2 |
| 1945–46 | 28 | Montreal Canadiens | NHL | 9 | 5 | 12 | 17 | 4 |
| 1948–49 | 31 | Montreal Canadiens | NHL | 1 | 0 | 0 | 0 | 4 |
| 1949–50 | 32 | Montreal Canadiens | NHL | 5 | 1 | 2 | 3 | 4 |
| 1950–51 | 33 | Montreal Canadiens | NHL | 11 | 2 | 2 | 4 | 2 |
| 1951–52 | 34 | Montreal Canadiens | NHL | 11 | 1 | 2 | 3 | 4 |
| 1952–53 | 35 | Montreal Canadiens | NHL | 12 | 1 | 6 | 7 | 6 |
| 1953–54 | 36 | Montreal Canadiens | NHL | 4 | 0 | 2 | 2 | 0 |
| NHL Career — 11 Seasons | | | | 74 | 19 | 45 | 64 | 36 |

## Pat LaFontaine   Profile: See page 111

### REGULAR SEASON

| SEASON | AGE | TEAM | LG | GP | G | A | PTS | +/- | PIM | ESG | PPG | SHG | GWG | SOG | S% |
|---|---|---|---|---|---|---|---|---|---|---|---|---|---|---|---|
| 1983–84 | 18 | New York Islanders | NHL | 15 | 13 | 6 | 19 | 9 | 6 | 12 | 1 | 0 | 0 | 35 | 37.1 |
| 1984–85 | 19 | New York Islanders | NHL | 67 | 19 | 35 | 54 | 7 | 32 | 18 | 1 | 0 | 1 | 172 | 11.1 |
| 1985–86 | 20 | New York Islanders | NHL | 65 | 30 | 23 | 53 | 15 | 43 | 28 | 2 | 0 | 4 | 172 | 17.4 |
| 1986–87 | 21 | New York Islanders | NHL | 80 | 38 | 32 | 70 | -9 | 70 | 18 | 19 | 1 | 6 | 219 | 17.4 |
| 1987–88 | 22 | New York Islanders | NHL | 75 | 47 | 45 | 92 | 12 | 52 | 32 | 15 | 0 | 7 | 242 | 19.4 |
| 1988–89 | 23 | New York Islanders | NHL | 79 | 45 | 43 | 88 | -8 | 26 | 29 | 16 | 0 | 4 | 288 | 15.6 |
| 1989–90 | 24 | New York Islanders | NHL | 74 | 54 | 51 | 105 | -13 | 38 | 39 | 13 | 2 | 8 | 286 | 18.9 |
| 1990–91 | 25 | New York Islanders | NHL | 75 | 41 | 44 | 85 | -6 | 42 | 27 | 12 | 2 | 5 | 225 | 18.2 |
| 1991–92 | 26 | Buffalo Sabres | NHL | 57 | 46 | 47 | 93 | 10 | 98 | 23 | 23 | 0 | 5 | 203 | 22.7 |
| 1992–93 | 27 | Buffalo Sabres | NHL | 84 | 53 | 95 | 148 | 11 | 63 | 31 | 20 | 2 | 7 | 306 | 17.3 |
| 1993–94 | 28 | Buffalo Sabres | NHL | 16 | 5 | 13 | 18 | -4 | 2 | 4 | 1 | 0 | 0 | 40 | 12.5 |
| 1994–95 | 29 | Buffalo Sabres | NHL | 22 | 12 | 15 | 27 | 2 | 4 | 5 | 6 | 1 | 3 | 54 | 22.2 |
| 1995–96 | 30 | Buffalo Sabres | NHL | 76 | 40 | 51 | 91 | -8 | 36 | 22 | 15 | 3 | 7 | 224 | 17.9 |
| 1996–97 | 31 | Buffalo Sabres | NHL | 13 | 2 | 6 | 8 | -8 | 4 | 1 | 1 | 0 | 0 | 38 | 5.3 |
| 1997–98 | 32 | New York Rangers | NHL | 67 | 23 | 39 | 62 | -16 | 36 | 12 | 11 | 0 | 2 | 160 | 14.4 |
| NHL Career — 15 Seasons | | | | 865 | 468 | 545 | 1013 | -6 | 552 | 301 | 156 | 11 | 59 | 2665 | 17.6 |

## Pat LaFontaine (continued)

### PLAYOFFS

| SEASON | AGE | TEAM | LG | GP | G | A | PTS | +/- | PIM | ESG | PPG | SHG | GWG | SOG | S% |
|---|---|---|---|---|---|---|---|---|---|---|---|---|---|---|---|
| 1983–84 | 18 | New York Islanders | NHL | 16 | 3 | 6 | 9 | -1 | 8 | 3 | 0 | 0 | 0 | 21 | 14.3 |
| 1984–85 | 19 | New York Islanders | NHL | 9 | 1 | 2 | 3 | -3 | 4 | 1 | 0 | 0 | 0 | 7 | 14.3 |
| 1985–86 | 20 | New York Islanders | NHL | 3 | 1 | 0 | 1 | -2 | 0 | 0 | 1 | 0 | 0 | 7 | 14.3 |
| 1986–87 | 21 | New York Islanders | NHL | 14 | 5 | 8 | 13 | -6 | 10 | 4 | 1 | 0 | 2 | 39 | 12.8 |
| 1987–88 | 22 | New York Islanders | NHL | 6 | 4 | 5 | 9 | 2 | 8 | 3 | 1 | 0 | 1 | 16 | 25.0 |
| 1989–90 | 24 | New York Islanders | NHL | 2 | 0 | 1 | 1 | -1 | 0 | 0 | 0 | 0 | 0 | 5 | 0.0 |
| 1991–92 | 26 | Buffalo Sabres | NHL | 7 | 8 | 3 | 11 | 0 | 4 | 2 | 5 | 1 | 1 | 27 | 29.6 |
| 1992–93 | 27 | Buffalo Sabres | NHL | 7 | 2 | 10 | 12 | 0 | 0 | 1 | 1 | 0 | 0 | 13 | 15.4 |
| 1994–95 | 29 | Buffalo Sabres | NHL | 5 | 2 | 2 | 4 | -2 | 2 | 1 | 1 | 0 | 0 | 11 | 18.2 |
| NHL Career — 9 Seasons | | | | 69 | 26 | 37 | 63 | -13 | 36 | 15 | 10 | 1 | 4 | 146 | 17.8 |

## Newsy Lalonde   Profile: See page 112

### REGULAR SEASON

| SEASON | AGE | TEAM | LG | GP | G | A | PTS | PIM |
|---|---|---|---|---|---|---|---|---|
| 1906–07 | 18 | Canadian Soo | IHL | 18 | 29 | 4 | 33 | 27 |
| 1907–08 | 19 | Portage la Prairie | MHL-Pro | 1 | 0 | 0 | 0 | 0 |
| 1907–08 | 19 | Toronto Professionals | OPHL | 9 | 32 | 0 | 32 | 37 |
| 1908–09 | 20 | Toronto Professionals | OPHL | 11 | 29 | 0 | 29 | 79 |
| 1909–10 | 21 | Les Canadiens (Montreal) | NHA | 1 | 2 | 0 | 2 | 3 |
| 1909–10 | 21 | Les Canadiens (Montreal) | NHA | 6 | 16 | 0 | 16 | 40 |
| 1909–10 | 21 | Renfrew Hockey Club | NHA | 5 | 22 | 0 | 22 | 16 |
| 1910–11 | 22 | Montreal Canadiens | NHA | 16 | 19 | 0 | 19 | 54 |
| 1911–12 | 23 | Vancouver Millionaires | PCHA | 15 | 27 | 0 | 27 | 60 |
| 1912–13 | 24 | Montreal Canadiens | NHA | 13 | 9 | 5 | 14 | 52 |
| 1913–14 | 25 | Montreal Canadiens | NHA | 14 | 22 | 5 | 27 | 34 |
| 1914–15 | 26 | Montreal Canadiens | NHA | 7 | 4 | 3 | 7 | 17 |
| 1915–16 | 27 | Montreal Canadiens | NHA | 24 | 28 | 6 | 34 | 78 |
| 1916–17 | 28 | Montreal Canadiens | NHA | 18 | 28 | 7 | 35 | 61 |
| 1917–18 | 29 | Montreal Canadiens | NHL | 14 | 23 | 7 | 30 | 51 |
| 1918–19 | 30 | Montreal Canadiens | NHL | 17 | 23 | 9 | 32 | 42 |
| 1919–20 | 31 | Montreal Canadiens | NHL | 23 | 37 | 10 | 47 | 34 |
| 1920–21 | 32 | Montreal Canadiens | NHL | 24 | 33 | 10 | 43 | 36 |
| 1921–22 | 33 | Montreal Canadiens | NHL | 20 | 9 | 6 | 15 | 20 |

### REGULAR SEASON

| SEASON | AGE | TEAM | LG | GP | G | A | PTS | PIM |
|---|---|---|---|---|---|---|---|---|
| 1922–23 | 34 | Saskatoon Sheiks | WCHL | 29 | 30 | 4 | 34 | 44 |
| 1923–24 | 35 | Saskatoon Crescents | WCHL | 21 | 10 | 10 | 20 | 24 |
| 1924–25 | 36 | Saskatoon Crescents | WCHL | 22 | 8 | 6 | 14 | 42 |
| 1925–26 | 37 | Saskatoon Crescents | WHL | 3 | 0 | 0 | 0 | 2 |
| 1926–27 | 38 | New York Americans | NHL | 1 | 0 | 0 | 0 | 2 |
| Career — 21 Seasons | | | | 332 | 440 | 92 | 532 | 851 |

### PLAYOFFS

| SEASON | AGE | TEAM | LG | GP | G | A | PTS | PIM |
|---|---|---|---|---|---|---|---|---|
| 1907–08 | 19 | Toronto Professionals | St-Cup | 1 | 2 | 0 | 2 | 0 |
| 1907–08 | 19 | Haileybury Hockey Club | TPHL | 1 | 3 | 0 | 3 | 0 |
| 1913–14 | 25 | Montreal Canadiens | NHA | 1 | 0 | 0 | 0 | 2 |
| 1915–16 | 27 | Montreal Canadiens | St-Cup | 4 | 3 | 0 | 3 | 41 |
| 1916–17 | 28 | Montreal Canadiens | NHA | 1 | 1 | 0 | 1 | 23 |
| 1916–17 | 28 | Montreal Canadiens | St-Cup | 4 | 1 | 0 | 1 | 24 |
| 1917–18 | 29 | Montreal Canadiens | NHL | 2 | 4 | 2 | 6 | 17 |
| 1918–19 | 30 | Montreal Canadiens | NHL | 5 | 11 | 2 | 13 | 15 |
| 1918–19 | 31 | Montreal Canadiens | St-Cup | 5 | 6 | 0 | 6 | 3 |
| 1924–25 | 36 | Saskatoon Crescents | WCHL | 2 | 0 | 0 | 0 | 4 |
| 1925–26 | 37 | Saskatoon Crescents | WHL | 2 | 0 | 0 | 0 | 2 |
| Career — 8 Seasons | | | | 28 | 31 | 4 | 35 | 131 |

## Edgar Laprade   Profile: See page 113

### REGULAR SEASON

| SEASON | AGE | TEAM | LG | GP | G | A | PTS | PIM |
|---|---|---|---|---|---|---|---|---|
| 1945–46 | 26 | New York Rangers | NHL | 49 | 15 | 19 | 34 | 0 |
| 1946–47 | 27 | New York Rangers | NHL | 58 | 15 | 25 | 40 | 9 |
| 1947–48 | 28 | New York Rangers | NHL | 59 | 13 | 34 | 47 | 7 |
| 1948–49 | 29 | New York Rangers | NHL | 56 | 18 | 12 | 30 | 12 |
| 1949–50 | 30 | New York Rangers | NHL | 60 | 22 | 22 | 44 | 2 |
| 1950–51 | 31 | New York Rangers | NHL | 42 | 10 | 13 | 23 | 0 |
| 1951–52 | 32 | New York Rangers | NHL | 70 | 9 | 29 | 38 | 8 |
| 1952–53 | 33 | New York Rangers | NHL | 11 | 2 | 1 | 3 | 2 |

### REGULAR SEASON

| SEASON | AGE | TEAM | LG | GP | G | A | PTS | PIM |
|---|---|---|---|---|---|---|---|---|
| 1953–54 | 34 | New York Rangers | NHL | 35 | 1 | 6 | 7 | 2 |
| 1954–55 | 35 | New York Rangers | NHL | 60 | 3 | 11 | 14 | 0 |
| NHL Career — 10 Seasons | | | | 500 | 108 | 172 | 280 | 42 |

### PLAYOFFS

| SEASON | AGE | TEAM | LG | GP | G | A | PTS | PIM |
|---|---|---|---|---|---|---|---|---|
| 1947–48 | 28 | New York Rangers | NHL | 6 | 1 | 4 | 5 | 0 |
| 1949–50 | 30 | New York Rangers | NHL | 12 | 3 | 5 | 8 | 4 |
| NHL Career — 2 Seasons | | | | 18 | 4 | 9 | 13 | 4 |

## Igor Larionov   Profile: See page 114

### REGULAR SEASON

| SEASON | AGE | TEAM | LG | GP | G | A | PTS | +/- | PIM | ESG | PPG | SHG | GWG | SOG | S% |
|---|---|---|---|---|---|---|---|---|---|---|---|---|---|---|---|
| 1989–90 | 29 | Vancouver Canucks | NHL | 74 | 17 | 27 | 44 | -5 | 20 | 9 | 8 | 0 | 2 | 118 | 14.4 |
| 1990–91 | 30 | Vancouver Canucks | NHL | 64 | 13 | 21 | 34 | -3 | 14 | 11 | 1 | 1 | 0 | 66 | 19.7 |
| 1991–92 | 31 | Vancouver Canucks | NHL | 72 | 21 | 44 | 65 | 7 | 54 | 8 | 10 | 3 | 4 | 97 | 21.6 |
| 1993–94 | 33 | San Jose Sharks | NHL | 60 | 18 | 38 | 56 | 20 | 40 | 13 | 3 | 2 | 2 | 72 | 25.0 |
| 1994–95 | 34 | San Jose Sharks | NHL | 33 | 4 | 20 | 24 | -3 | 14 | 4 | 0 | 0 | 1 | 69 | 5.8 |
| 1995–96 | 35 | San Jose Sharks | NHL | 4 | 1 | 1 | 2 | -6 | 0 | 0 | 1 | 0 | 0 | 5 | 20.0 |
| 1995–96 | 35 | Detroit Red Wings | NHL | 69 | 21 | 50 | 71 | 37 | 34 | 11 | 9 | 1 | 5 | 108 | 19.4 |
| 1996–97 | 36 | Detroit Red Wings | NHL | 64 | 12 | 42 | 54 | 31 | 26 | 9 | 2 | 1 | 4 | 95 | 12.6 |
| 1997–98 | 37 | Detroit Red Wings | NHL | 69 | 8 | 39 | 47 | 14 | 40 | 5 | 3 | 0 | 2 | 93 | 8.6 |
| 1998–99 | 38 | Detroit Red Wings | NHL | 75 | 14 | 49 | 63 | 13 | 48 | 8 | 4 | 2 | 2 | 83 | 16.9 |
| 1999–00 | 39 | Detroit Red Wings | NHL | 79 | 9 | 38 | 47 | 13 | 28 | 6 | 3 | 0 | 4 | 69 | 13.0 |
| 2000–01 | 40 | Florida Panthers | NHL | 26 | 5 | 6 | 11 | -11 | 10 | 3 | 2 | 0 | 0 | 15 | 33.3 |
| 2000–01 | 40 | Detroit Red Wings | NHL | 39 | 4 | 25 | 29 | 6 | 28 | 2 | 2 | 0 | 1 | 31 | 12.9 |
| 2001–02 | 41 | Detroit Red Wings | NHL | 70 | 11 | 32 | 43 | -5 | 50 | 7 | 4 | 0 | 1 | 50 | 22.0 |
| 2002–03 | 42 | Detroit Red Wings | NHL | 74 | 10 | 33 | 43 | -7 | 48 | 5 | 5 | 0 | 3 | 50 | 20.0 |

## Igor Larionov (continued)

### REGULAR SEASON

| SEASON | AGE | TEAM | LG | GP | G | A | PTS | +/- | PIM | ESG | PPG | SHG | GWG | SOG | S% |
|---|---|---|---|---|---|---|---|---|---|---|---|---|---|---|---|
| 2003–04 | 43 | New Jersey Devils | NHL | 49 | 1 | 10 | 11 | 3 | 20 | 1 | 0 | 0 | 0 | 25 | 4.0 |
| NHL Career — 14 Seasons | | | | 921 | 169 | 475 | 644 | 104 | 474 | 102 | 57 | 10 | 31 | 1046 | 16.2 |

### PLAYOFFS

| SEASON | AGE | TEAM | LG | GP | G | A | PTS | +/- | PIM | ESG | PPG | SHG | GWG | SOG | S% |
|---|---|---|---|---|---|---|---|---|---|---|---|---|---|---|---|
| 1990–91 | 30 | Vancouver Canucks | NHL | 6 | 1 | 0 | 1 | -5 | 6 | 1 | 0 | 0 | 0 | 8 | 12.5 |
| 1991–92 | 31 | Vancouver Canucks | NHL | 13 | 3 | 7 | 10 | 1 | 4 | 2 | 1 | 0 | 0 | 12 | 25.0 |
| 1993–94 | 33 | San Jose Sharks | NHL | 14 | 5 | 13 | 18 | -1 | 10 | 5 | 0 | 0 | 0 | 27 | 18.5 |
| 1994–95 | 34 | San Jose Sharks | NHL | 11 | 1 | 8 | 9 | -4 | 2 | 1 | 0 | 0 | 0 | 19 | 5.3 |
| 1995–96 | 35 | Detroit Red Wings | NHL | 19 | 6 | 7 | 13 | 5 | 6 | 3 | 3 | 0 | 2 | 46 | 13.0 |
| 1996–97 | 36 | Detroit Red Wings | NHL | 20 | 4 | 8 | 12 | 8 | 8 | 1 | 3 | 0 | 1 | 29 | 13.8 |
| 1997–98 | 37 | Detroit Red Wings | NHL | 22 | 3 | 10 | 13 | 5 | 12 | 3 | 0 | 0 | 0 | 27 | 11.1 |
| 1998–99 | 38 | Detroit Red Wings | NHL | 7 | 0 | 2 | 2 | -1 | 0 | 0 | 0 | 0 | 0 | 3 | 0.0 |
| 1999–00 | 39 | Detroit Red Wings | NHL | 9 | 1 | 2 | 3 | -2 | 6 | 0 | 1 | 0 | 0 | 5 | 20.0 |
| 2000–01 | 40 | Detroit Red Wings | NHL | 6 | 1 | 3 | 4 | -2 | 2 | 0 | 1 | 0 | 0 | 7 | 14.3 |
| 2001–02 | 41 | Detroit Red Wings | NHL | 18 | 5 | 6 | 11 | 5 | 4 | 5 | 0 | 0 | 1 | 24 | 20.8 |
| 2002–03 | 42 | Detroit Red Wings | NHL | 4 | 0 | 1 | 1 | 1 | 0 | 0 | 0 | 0 | 0 | 6 | 0.0 |
| 2003–04 | 43 | New Jersey Devils | NHL | 1 | 0 | 0 | 0 | -1 | 0 | 0 | 0 | 0 | 0 | 0 | 0.0 |
| NHL Career — 13 Seasons | | | | 150 | 30 | 67 | 97 | 9 | 60 | 21 | 9 | 0 | 4 | 213 | 14.1 |

## Jacques Lemaire  Profile: See page 115

### REGULAR SEASON

| SEASON | AGE | TEAM | LG | GP | G | A | PTS | +/- | PIM | ESG | PPG | SHG | GWG | SOG | S% |
|---|---|---|---|---|---|---|---|---|---|---|---|---|---|---|---|
| 1967–68 | 22 | Montreal Canadiens | NHL | 69 | 22 | 20 | 42 | 15 | 16 | 18 | 3 | 1 | 3 | 182 | 12.1 |
| 1968–69 | 23 | Montreal Canadiens | NHL | 75 | 29 | 34 | 63 | 29 | 29 | 24 | 5 | 0 | 4 | 330 | 8.8 |
| 1969–70 | 24 | Montreal Canadiens | NHL | 69 | 32 | 28 | 60 | 19 | 17 | 20 | 12 | 0 | 5 | 237 | 13.5 |
| 1970–71 | 25 | Montreal Canadiens | NHL | 78 | 28 | 28 | 56 | -1 | 18 | 22 | 6 | 0 | 3 | 252 | 11.1 |
| 1971–72 | 26 | Montreal Canadiens | NHL | 77 | 32 | 49 | 81 | 37 | 26 | 24 | 8 | 0 | 7 | 266 | 12.0 |
| 1972–73 | 27 | Montreal Canadiens | NHL | 77 | 44 | 51 | 95 | 59 | 16 | 35 | 9 | 0 | 5 | 294 | 15.0 |
| 1973–74 | 28 | Montreal Canadiens | NHL | 66 | 29 | 38 | 67 | 4 | 10 | 19 | 10 | 0 | 7 | 219 | 13.2 |
| 1974–75 | 29 | Montreal Canadiens | NHL | 80 | 36 | 56 | 92 | 25 | 20 | 24 | 12 | 0 | 8 | 260 | 13.9 |
| 1975–76 | 30 | Montreal Canadiens | NHL | 61 | 20 | 32 | 52 | 27 | 20 | 14 | 6 | 0 | 3 | 226 | 8.9 |
| 1976–77 | 31 | Montreal Canadiens | NHL | 75 | 34 | 41 | 75 | 69 | 22 | 27 | 5 | 2 | 4 | 272 | 12.5 |
| 1977–78 | 32 | Montreal Canadiens | NHL | 76 | 36 | 61 | 97 | 54 | 14 | 30 | 6 | 0 | 5 | 310 | 11.6 |
| 1978–79 | 33 | Montreal Canadiens | NHL | 50 | 24 | 31 | 55 | 9 | 10 | 17 | 6 | 1 | 4 | 204 | 11.8 |
| NHL Career — 12 Seasons | | | | 853 | 366 | 469 | 835 | 344 | 217 | 274 | 88 | 4 | 58 | 3052 | 12.0 |

### PLAYOFFS

| SEASON | AGE | TEAM | LG | GP | G | A | PTS | +/- | PIM | ESG | PPG | SHG | GWG | SOG | S% |
|---|---|---|---|---|---|---|---|---|---|---|---|---|---|---|---|
| 1967–68 | 22 | Montreal Canadiens | NHL | 13 | 7 | 6 | 13 | 5 | 8 | 5 | 2 | 0 | 2 | 49 | 14.3 |
| 1968–69 | 23 | Montreal Canadiens | NHL | 14 | 4 | 2 | 6 | -1 | 6 | 3 | 1 | 0 | 0 | 39 | 10.3 |
| 1970–71 | 25 | Montreal Canadiens | NHL | 20 | 9 | 10 | 19 | 8 | 17 | 5 | 4 | 0 | 1 | 69 | 13.0 |
| 1971–72 | 26 | Montreal Canadiens | NHL | 6 | 2 | 1 | 3 | -3 | 2 | 2 | 0 | 0 | 0 | 32 | 6.3 |
| 1972–73 | 27 | Montreal Canadiens | NHL | 17 | 7 | 13 | 20 | 10 | 2 | 4 | 3 | 0 | 1 | 71 | 9.9 |
| 1973–74 | 28 | Montreal Canadiens | NHL | 6 | 0 | 4 | 4 | 0 | 2 | 0 | 0 | 0 | 0 | 20 | 0.0 |
| 1974–75 | 29 | Montreal Canadiens | NHL | 11 | 5 | 7 | 12 | 2 | 4 | 4 | 1 | 0 | 0 | 42 | 11.9 |
| 1975–76 | 30 | Montreal Canadiens | NHL | 13 | 3 | 3 | 6 | 5 | 2 | 1 | 1 | 1 | 1 | 36 | 8.3 |
| 1976–77 | 31 | Montreal Canadiens | NHL | 14 | 7 | 12 | 19 | 12 | 6 | 6 | 1 | 0 | 3 | 38 | 18.4 |
| 1977–78 | 32 | Montreal Canadiens | NHL | 15 | 6 | 8 | 14 | 13 | 10 | 6 | 0 | 0 | 1 | 66 | 9.1 |
| 1978–79 | 33 | Montreal Canadiens | NHL | 16 | 11 | 12 | 23 | 3 | 6 | 5 | 6 | 0 | 2 | 59 | 18.6 |
| NHL Career — 11 Seasons | | | | 145 | 61 | 78 | 139 | 54 | 65 | 41 | 19 | 1 | 11 | 521 | 11.7 |

# Mario Lemieux   Profile: See page 116

## REGULAR SEASON

| SEASON | AGE | TEAM | LG | GP | G | A | PTS | +/- | PIM | ESG | PPG | SHG | GWG | SOG | S% |
|---|---|---|---|---|---|---|---|---|---|---|---|---|---|---|---|
| 1984-85 | 19 | Pittsburgh Penguins | NHL | 73 | 43 | 57 | 100 | -33 | 54 | 32 | 11 | 0 | 2 | 209 | 20.6 |
| 1985-86 | 20 | Pittsburgh Penguins | NHL | 79 | 48 | 93 | 141 | -8 | 43 | 31 | 17 | 0 | 4 | 276 | 17.4 |
| 1986-87 | 21 | Pittsburgh Penguins | NHL | 63 | 54 | 53 | 107 | 12 | 57 | 35 | 19 | 0 | 4 | 267 | 20.2 |
| 1987-88 | 22 | Pittsburgh Penguins | NHL | 77 | 70 | 98 | 168 | 23 | 92 | 38 | 22 | 10 | 7 | 382 | 18.3 |
| 1988-89 | 23 | Pittsburgh Penguins | NHL | 76 | 85 | 114 | 199 | 41 | 100 | 41 | 31 | 13 | 8 | 313 | 27.2 |
| 1989-90 | 24 | Pittsburgh Penguins | NHL | 59 | 45 | 78 | 123 | -18 | 78 | 28 | 14 | 3 | 4 | 226 | 19.9 |
| 1990-91 | 25 | Pittsburgh Penguins | NHL | 26 | 19 | 26 | 45 | 8 | 30 | 12 | 6 | 1 | 2 | 89 | 21.3 |
| 1991-92 | 26 | Pittsburgh Penguins | NHL | 64 | 44 | 87 | 131 | 27 | 94 | 28 | 12 | 4 | 5 | 249 | 17.7 |
| 1992-93 | 27 | Pittsburgh Penguins | NHL | 60 | 69 | 91 | 160 | 55 | 38 | 47 | 16 | 6 | 10 | 286 | 24.1 |
| 1993-94 | 28 | Pittsburgh Penguins | NHL | 22 | 17 | 20 | 37 | -2 | 32 | 10 | 7 | 0 | 4 | 92 | 18.5 |
| 1995-96 | 30 | Pittsburgh Penguins | NHL | 70 | 69 | 92 | 161 | 10 | 54 | 30 | 31 | 8 | 8 | 338 | 20.4 |
| 1996-97 | 31 | Pittsburgh Penguins | NHL | 76 | 50 | 72 | 122 | 27 | 65 | 32 | 15 | 3 | 7 | 327 | 15.3 |
| 2000-01 | 35 | Pittsburgh Penguins | NHL | 43 | 35 | 41 | 76 | 15 | 18 | 18 | 16 | 1 | 5 | 171 | 20.5 |
| 2001-02 | 36 | Pittsburgh Penguins | NHL | 24 | 6 | 25 | 31 | 0 | 14 | 4 | 2 | 0 | 0 | 75 | 8.0 |
| 2002-03 | 37 | Pittsburgh Penguins | NHL | 67 | 28 | 63 | 91 | -25 | 43 | 14 | 14 | 0 | 4 | 235 | 11.9 |
| 2003-04 | 38 | Pittsburgh Penguins | NHL | 10 | 1 | 8 | 9 | -2 | 6 | 1 | 0 | 0 | 0 | 21 | 4.8 |
| 2005-06 | 40 | Pittsburgh Penguins | NHL | 26 | 7 | 15 | 22 | -16 | 16 | 4 | 3 | 0 | 0 | 77 | 9.1 |
| NHL Career — 17 Seasons | | | | 915 | 690 | 1033 | 1723 | 114 | 834 | 405 | 236 | 49 | 74 | 3633 | 19.0 |

## PLAYOFFS

| SEASON | AGE | TEAM | LG | GP | G | A | PTS | +/- | PIM | ESG | PPG | SHG | GWG | SOG | S% |
|---|---|---|---|---|---|---|---|---|---|---|---|---|---|---|---|
| 1988-89 | 23 | Pittsburgh Penguins | NHL | 11 | 12 | 7 | 19 | -1 | 16 | 4 | 7 | 1 | 0 | 41 | 29.3 |
| 1990-91 | 25 | Pittsburgh Penguins | NHL | 23 | 16 | 28 | 44 | 14 | 16 | 8 | 6 | 2 | 0 | 93 | 17.2 |
| 1991-92 | 26 | Pittsburgh Penguins | NHL | 15 | 16 | 18 | 34 | 6 | 2 | 6 | 8 | 2 | 5 | 69 | 23.2 |
| 1992-93 | 27 | Pittsburgh Penguins | NHL | 11 | 8 | 10 | 18 | 2 | 10 | 4 | 3 | 1 | 1 | 40 | 20.0 |
| 1993-94 | 28 | Pittsburgh Penguins | NHL | 6 | 4 | 3 | 7 | -4 | 2 | 3 | 1 | 0 | 0 | 23 | 17.4 |
| 1995-96 | 30 | Pittsburgh Penguins | NHL | 18 | 11 | 16 | 27 | 3 | 33 | 7 | 3 | 1 | 2 | 78 | 14.1 |
| 1996-97 | 31 | Pittsburgh Penguins | NHL | 5 | 3 | 3 | 6 | -4 | 4 | 3 | 0 | 0 | 0 | 19 | 15.8 |
| 2000-01 | 35 | Pittsburgh Penguins | NHL | 18 | 6 | 11 | 17 | 4 | 4 | 5 | 1 | 0 | 3 | 39 | 15.4 |
| NHL Career — 8 Seasons | | | | 107 | 76 | 96 | 172 | 20 | 87 | 40 | 29 | 7 | 11 | 402 | 18.9 |

# Eric Lindros   Profile: See page 118

## REGULAR SEASON

| SEASON | AGE | TEAM | LG | GP | G | A | PTS | +/- | PIM | ESG | PPG | SHG | GWG | SOG | S% |
|---|---|---|---|---|---|---|---|---|---|---|---|---|---|---|---|
| 1992-93 | 19 | Philadelphia Flyers | NHL | 61 | 41 | 34 | 75 | 28 | 147 | 32 | 8 | 1 | 5 | 180 | 22.8 |
| 1993-94 | 20 | Philadelphia Flyers | NHL | 65 | 44 | 53 | 97 | 16 | 103 | 29 | 13 | 2 | 9 | 197 | 22.3 |
| 1994-95 | 21 | Philadelphia Flyers | NHL | 46 | 29 | 41 | 70 | 27 | 60 | 22 | 7 | 0 | 4 | 144 | 20.1 |
| 1995-96 | 22 | Philadelphia Flyers | NHL | 73 | 47 | 68 | 115 | 26 | 163 | 32 | 15 | 0 | 4 | 294 | 16.0 |
| 1996-97 | 23 | Philadelphia Flyers | NHL | 52 | 32 | 47 | 79 | 31 | 136 | 23 | 9 | 0 | 7 | 198 | 16.2 |
| 1997-98 | 24 | Philadelphia Flyers | NHL | 63 | 30 | 41 | 71 | 14 | 134 | 19 | 10 | 1 | 4 | 202 | 14.9 |
| 1998-99 | 25 | Philadelphia Flyers | NHL | 71 | 40 | 53 | 93 | 35 | 120 | 29 | 10 | 1 | 2 | 242 | 16.5 |
| 1999-00 | 26 | Philadelphia Flyers | NHL | 55 | 27 | 32 | 59 | 11 | 83 | 16 | 10 | 1 | 2 | 187 | 14.4 |
| 2001-02 | 28 | New York Rangers | NHL | 72 | 37 | 36 | 73 | 19 | 138 | 24 | 12 | 1 | 4 | 196 | 18.9 |
| 2002-03 | 29 | New York Rangers | NHL | 81 | 19 | 34 | 53 | 5 | 141 | 10 | 9 | 0 | 3 | 235 | 8.1 |
| 2003-04 | 30 | New York Rangers | NHL | 39 | 10 | 22 | 32 | 7 | 60 | 7 | 3 | 0 | 0 | 83 | 12.0 |
| 2005-06 | 32 | Toronto Maple Leafs | NHL | 33 | 11 | 11 | 22 | -3 | 43 | 7 | 4 | 0 | 2 | 59 | 18.6 |
| 2006-07 | 33 | Dallas Stars | NHL | 49 | 5 | 21 | 26 | -1 | 70 | 4 | 1 | 0 | 0 | 95 | 5.3 |
| NHL Career — 13 Seasons | | | | 760 | 372 | 493 | 865 | 215 | 1398 | 254 | 111 | 7 | 46 | 2312 | 16.1 |

## PLAYOFFS

| SEASON | AGE | TEAM | LG | GP | G | A | PTS | +/- | PIM | ESG | PPG | SHG | GWG | SOG | S% |
|---|---|---|---|---|---|---|---|---|---|---|---|---|---|---|---|
| 1994-95 | 21 | Philadelphia Flyers | NHL | 12 | 4 | 11 | 15 | 7 | 18 | 4 | 0 | 0 | 1 | 28 | 14.3 |
| 1995-96 | 22 | Philadelphia Flyers | NHL | 12 | 6 | 6 | 12 | -1 | 43 | 3 | 3 | 0 | 2 | 46 | 13.0 |
| 1996-97 | 23 | Philadelphia Flyers | NHL | 19 | 12 | 14 | 26 | 7 | 40 | 8 | 4 | 0 | 1 | 71 | 16.9 |
| 1997-98 | 24 | Philadelphia Flyers | NHL | 5 | 1 | 2 | 3 | -3 | 17 | 1 | 0 | 0 | 0 | 13 | 7.7 |
| 1999-00 | 26 | Philadelphia Flyers | NHL | 2 | 1 | 0 | 1 | 0 | 0 | 1 | 0 | 0 | 0 | 3 | 33.3 |
| 2006-07 | 33 | Dallas Stars | NHL | 3 | 0 | 0 | 0 | -2 | 4 | 0 | 0 | 0 | 0 | 3 | 0.0 |
| NHL Career — 6 Seasons | | | | 53 | 24 | 33 | 57 | 8 | 122 | 17 | 7 | 0 | 4 | 164 | 14.6 |

## Mickey MacKay   Profile: See page 119

**REGULAR SEASON**

| SEASON | AGE | TEAM | LG | GP | G | A | PTS | PIM |
|---|---|---|---|---|---|---|---|---|
| 1914–15 | 20 | Vancouver Millionaires | PCHA | 17 | 33 | 11 | 44 | 9 |
| 1915–16 | 21 | Vancouver Millionaires | PCHA | 14 | 12 | 7 | 19 | 32 |
| 1916–17 | 22 | Vancouver Millionaires | PCHA | 23 | 22 | 11 | 33 | 37 |
| 1917–18 | 23 | Vancouver Millionaires | PCHA | 18 | 10 | 8 | 18 | 31 |
| 1918–19 | 24 | Vancouver Millionaires | PCHA | 17 | 9 | 9 | 18 | 9 |
| 1919–20 | 25 | Calgary Columbus Club | Big-4 | 11 | 4 | 6 | 10 | 14 |
| 1920–21 | 26 | Vancouver Millionaires | PCHA | 21 | 10 | 8 | 18 | 15 |
| 1921–22 | 27 | Vancouver Millionaires | PCHA | 24 | 14 | 12 | 26 | 20 |
| 1922–23 | 28 | Vancouver Maroons | PCHA | 30 | 28 | 12 | 40 | 38 |
| 1923–24 | 29 | Vancouver Maroons | PCHA | 28 | 21 | 4 | 25 | 2 |
| 1924–25 | 30 | Vancouver Maroons | WCHL | 28 | 27 | 6 | 33 | 17 |
| 1925–26 | 31 | Vancouver Maroons | WHL | 27 | 12 | 4 | 16 | 24 |
| 1926–27 | 32 | Chicago Black Hawks | NHL | 34 | 14 | 8 | 22 | 23 |
| 1927–28 | 33 | Chicago Black Hawks | NHL | 36 | 17 | 4 | 21 | 23 |
| 1928–29 | 34 | Pittsburgh Pirates | NHL | 12 | 1 | 0 | 1 | 2 |
| 1928–29 | 34 | Boston Bruins | NHL | 28 | 8 | 2 | 10 | 18 |
| 1929–30 | 35 | Boston Bruins | NHL | 37 | 4 | 5 | 9 | 13 |
| Career — 16 Seasons | | | | 405 | 246 | 117 | 363 | 327 |

**PLAYOFFS**

| SEASON | AGE | TEAM | LG | GP | G | A | PTS | PIM |
|---|---|---|---|---|---|---|---|---|
| 1914–15 | 20 | Vancouver Millionaires | St-Cup | 3 | 4 | 2 | 6 | 9 |
| 1917–18 | 23 | Vancouver Millionaires | PCHA | 2 | 2 | 1 | 3 | 0 |
| 1917–18 | 23 | Vancouver Millionaires | St-Cup | 5 | 5 | 5 | 10 | 12 |
| 1920–21 | 26 | Vancouver Millionaires | PCHA | 2 | 0 | 3 | 3 | 0 |
| 1920–21 | 26 | Vancouver Millionaires | St-Cup | 5 | 0 | 1 | 1 | 0 |
| 1921–22 | 27 | Vancouver Millionaires | PCHA | 2 | 0 | 0 | 0 | 0 |
| 1921–22 | 27 | Vancouver Millionaires | West-P | 2 | 0 | 0 | 0 | 0 |
| 1921–22 | 27 | Vancouver Millionaires | St-Cup | 5 | 1 | 0 | 1 | 6 |
| 1922–23 | 28 | Vancouver Maroons | PCHA | 2 | 2 | 0 | 2 | 12 |
| 1922–23 | 28 | Vancouver Maroons | St-Cup | 4 | 1 | 0 | 1 | 4 |
| 1923–24 | 29 | Vancouver Maroons | PCHA | 2 | 1 | 0 | 1 | 0 |
| 1923–24 | 29 | Vancouver Millionaires | West-P | 3 | 2 | 0 | 2 | 2 |
| 1923–24 | 29 | Vancouver Millionaires | St-Cup | 2 | 0 | 0 | 0 | 0 |
| 1926–27 | 32 | Chicago Black Hawks | NHL | 2 | 0 | 0 | 0 | 0 |
| 1928–29 | 34 | Boston Bruins | NHL | 3 | 0 | 0 | 0 | 2 |
| 1929–30 | 35 | Boston Bruins | NHL | 6 | 0 | 0 | 0 | 4 |
| Career — 9 Seasons | | | | 50 | 18 | 12 | 30 | 51 |

## Joe Malone   Profile: See page 120

**REGULAR SEASON**

| SEASON | AGE | TEAM | LG | GP | G | A | PTS | PIM |
|---|---|---|---|---|---|---|---|---|
| 1909–10 | 19 | Quebec Bulldogs | CHA | 3 | 5 | 0 | 5 | 2 |
| 1909–10 | 19 | Waterloo Colts | OPHL | 12 | 10 | 0 | 10 | 16 |
| 1910–11 | 20 | Quebec Bulldogs | NHA | 13 | 9 | 0 | 9 | 3 |
| 1911–12 | 21 | Quebec Bulldogs | NHA | 18 | 21 | 0 | 21 | 0 |
| 1912–13 | 22 | Quebec Bulldogs | NHA | 20 | 43 | 0 | 43 | 34 |
| 1913–14 | 23 | Quebec Bulldogs | NHA | 17 | 24 | 4 | 28 | 20 |
| 1914–15 | 24 | Quebec Bulldogs | NHA | 12 | 16 | 5 | 21 | 21 |
| 1915–16 | 25 | Quebec Bulldogs | NHA | 24 | 25 | 10 | 35 | 21 |
| 1916–17 | 26 | Quebec Bulldogs | NHA | 19 | 41 | 8 | 49 | 15 |
| 1917–18 | 27 | Montreal Canadiens | NHL | 20 | 44 | 4 | 48 | 30 |
| 1918–19 | 28 | Montreal Canadiens | NHL | 8 | 7 | 2 | 9 | 3 |
| 1919–20 | 29 | Quebec Bulldogs | NHL | 24 | 39 | 10 | 49 | 12 |
| 1920–21 | 30 | Hamilton Tigers | NHL | 20 | 28 | 9 | 37 | 6 |

**REGULAR SEASON**

| SEASON | AGE | TEAM | LG | GP | G | A | PTS | PIM |
|---|---|---|---|---|---|---|---|---|
| 1921–22 | 31 | Hamilton Tigers | NHL | 24 | 24 | 7 | 31 | 4 |
| 1922–23 | 32 | Montreal Canadiens | NHL | 20 | 1 | 0 | 1 | 2 |
| 1923–24 | 33 | Montreal Canadiens | NHL | 10 | 0 | 1 | 1 | 0 |
| Career — 15 Seasons | | | | 264 | 337 | 60 | 397 | 189 |

**PLAYOFFS**

| SEASON | AGE | TEAM | LG | GP | G | A | PTS | PIM |
|---|---|---|---|---|---|---|---|---|
| 1911–12 | 21 | Quebec Bulldogs | St-Cup | 2 | 5 | 0 | 5 | 0 |
| 1912–13 | 22 | Quebec Bulldogs | St-Cup | 1 | 9 | 0 | 9 | 0 |
| 1917–18 | 27 | Montreal Canadiens | NHL | 2 | 1 | 0 | 1 | 3 |
| 1918–19 | 28 | Montreal Canadiens | NHL | 5 | 5 | 2 | 7 | 3 |
| 1922–23 | 32 | Montreal Canadiens | NHL | 2 | 0 | 0 | 0 | 0 |
| Career — 5 Seasons | | | | 12 | 20 | 2 | 22 | 6 |

## Frank McGee   Profile: See page 122

**REGULAR SEASON**

| SEASON | AGE | TEAM | LG | GP | G | A | PTS | PIM |
|---|---|---|---|---|---|---|---|---|
| 1899–00 | 19 | Ottawa Seconds | CAIHL | | | | | |
| 1900–01 | 20 | Ottawa Aberdeens | OCJHL | | | | | |
| 1901–02 | 21 | Ottawa Aberdeens | CAIHL | | | | | |
| 1902–03 | 22 | Ottawa Silver Seven | CAHL | 6 | 14 | 0 | 14 | 9 |
| 1903–04 | 23 | Ottawa Silver Seven | CAHL | 4 | 12 | 0 | 12 | 9 |
| 1904–05 | 24 | Ottawa Silver Seven | FAHL | 6 | 17 | 0 | 17 | 14 |
| 1905–06 | 25 | Ottawa Silver Seven | ECAHA | 7 | 28 | 0 | 28 | 18 |
| Career — 7 Seasons | | | | 23 | 71 | 0 | 71 | 50 |

**PLAYOFFS**

| SEASON | AGE | TEAM | LG | GP | G | A | PTS | PIM |
|---|---|---|---|---|---|---|---|---|
| 1902–03 | 22 | Ottawa Silver Seven | CAHL | 2 | 3 | 0 | 3 | 3 |
| 1902–03 | 22 | Ottawa Silver Seven | St-Cup | 2 | 4 | 0 | 4 | |
| 1903–04 | 23 | Ottawa Silver Seven | St-Cup | 8 | 21 | 0 | 21 | |
| 1904–05 | 24 | Ottawa Silver Seven | St-Cup | 2 | 18 | 0 | 18 | |
| 1905–06 | 25 | Ottawa Silver Seven | ECAHA | 2 | 2 | 0 | 2 | 9 |
| 1905–06 | 25 | Ottawa Silver Seven | St-Cup | 4 | 16 | 0 | 16 | 6 |
| Career — 4 Seasons | | | | 22 | 64 | 0 | 64 | 18 |

## Billy McGimsie   Profile: See page 123

**REGULAR SEASON**

| SEASON | AGE | TEAM | LG | GP | G | A | PTS | PIM |
|---|---|---|---|---|---|---|---|---|
| 1901–02 | 21 | Rat Portage Thistles | MNWHA-Int | 4 | 8 | 0 | 8 | 0 |
| 1902–03 | 22 | Rat Portage Thistles | MNWHA | 4 | 10 | 0 | 10 | |
| 1903–04 | 23 | Rat Portage Thistles | MNWHA | 11 | 14 | 2 | 16 | |
| 1904–05 | 24 | Rat Portage Thistles | MHL | 8 | 28 | 0 | 28 | 3 |
| 1905–06 | 25 | Kenora Thistles | MHL | 9 | 21 | 0 | 21 | |
| 1906–07 | 26 | Kenora Thistles | MHL-Pro | 2 | 2 | 0 | 2 | |
| Career — 6 Seasons | | | | 38 | 83 | 2 | 85 | 3 |

**PLAYOFFS**

| SEASON | AGE | TEAM | LG | GP | G | A | PTS | PIM |
|---|---|---|---|---|---|---|---|---|
| 1902–03 | 22 | Rat Portage Thistles | St-Cup | 2 | 3 | 0 | 3 | |
| 1904–05 | 24 | Rat Portage Thistles | St-Cup | 3 | 0 | 0 | 0 | |
| 1906–07 | 26 | Kenora Thistles | St-Cup | 2 | 1 | 0 | 1 | 8 |
| Career — 3 Seasons | | | | 7 | 4 | 0 | 4 | 8 |

# Mark Messier Profile: See page 124

**REGULAR SEASON**

| SEASON | AGE | TEAM | LG | GP | G | A | PTS | +/- | PIM | ESG | PPG | SHG | GWG | SOG | S% |
|--------|-----|------|----|----|---|---|-----|-----|-----|-----|-----|-----|-----|-----|----|
| 1978-79 | 18 | Indianapolis Racers | WHA | 5 | 0 | 0 | 0 | -4 | 0 | 0 | 0 | 0 | | 7 | 0.0 |
| 1978-79 | 18 | Cincinnati Stingers | WHA | 47 | 1 | 10 | 11 | -6 | 58 | 1 | 0 | 0 | | 55 | 1.8 |
| 1979-80 | 19 | Edmonton Oilers | NHL | 75 | 12 | 21 | 33 | -9 | 120 | 10 | 1 | 1 | 1 | 113 | 10.6 |
| 1980-81 | 20 | Edmonton Oilers | NHL | 72 | 23 | 40 | 63 | -12 | 102 | 19 | 4 | 0 | 1 | 179 | 12.9 |
| 1981-82 | 21 | Edmonton Oilers | NHL | 78 | 50 | 38 | 88 | 20 | 119 | 40 | 10 | 0 | 3 | 235 | 21.3 |
| 1982-83 | 22 | Edmonton Oilers | NHL | 77 | 48 | 58 | 106 | 18 | 72 | 35 | 12 | 1 | 2 | 237 | 20.3 |
| 1983-84 | 23 | Edmonton Oilers | NHL | 73 | 37 | 64 | 101 | 40 | 165 | 26 | 7 | 4 | 7 | 220 | 16.8 |
| 1984-85 | 24 | Edmonton Oilers | NHL | 55 | 23 | 31 | 54 | 10 | 57 | 14 | 4 | 5 | 1 | 138 | 16.7 |
| 1985-86 | 25 | Edmonton Oilers | NHL | 63 | 35 | 49 | 84 | 35 | 68 | 20 | 10 | 5 | 7 | 198 | 17.7 |
| 1986-87 | 26 | Edmonton Oilers | NHL | 77 | 37 | 70 | 107 | 22 | 73 | 26 | 7 | 4 | 5 | 210 | 17.6 |
| 1987-88 | 27 | Edmonton Oilers | NHL | 77 | 37 | 74 | 111 | 21 | 103 | 22 | 12 | 3 | 7 | 182 | 20.3 |
| 1988-89 | 28 | Edmonton Oilers | NHL | 72 | 33 | 61 | 94 | -5 | 130 | 21 | 6 | 6 | 4 | 164 | 20.1 |
| 1989-90 | 29 | Edmonton Oilers | NHL | 79 | 45 | 84 | 129 | 19 | 79 | 26 | 13 | 6 | 3 | 211 | 21.3 |
| 1990-91 | 30 | Edmonton Oilers | NHL | 53 | 12 | 52 | 64 | 15 | 34 | 8 | 3 | 1 | 2 | 109 | 11.0 |
| 1991-92 | 31 | New York Rangers | NHL | 79 | 35 | 72 | 107 | 31 | 76 | 19 | 12 | 4 | 6 | 212 | 16.5 |
| 1992-93 | 32 | New York Rangers | NHL | 75 | 25 | 66 | 91 | -6 | 72 | 16 | 7 | 2 | 2 | 215 | 11.6 |
| 1993-94 | 33 | New York Rangers | NHL | 76 | 26 | 58 | 84 | 25 | 76 | 18 | 6 | 2 | 5 | 216 | 12.0 |
| 1994-95 | 34 | New York Rangers | NHL | 46 | 14 | 39 | 53 | 8 | 40 | 8 | 3 | 3 | 2 | 126 | 11.1 |
| 1995-96 | 35 | New York Rangers | NHL | 74 | 47 | 52 | 99 | 29 | 122 | 32 | 14 | 1 | 5 | 241 | 19.5 |
| 1996-97 | 36 | New York Rangers | NHL | 71 | 36 | 48 | 84 | 12 | 88 | 24 | 7 | 5 | 9 | 227 | 15.9 |
| 1997-98 | 37 | Vancouver Canucks | NHL | 82 | 22 | 38 | 60 | -10 | 58 | 12 | 8 | 2 | 2 | 139 | 15.8 |
| 1998-99 | 38 | Vancouver Canucks | NHL | 59 | 13 | 35 | 48 | -12 | 33 | 7 | 4 | 2 | 2 | 97 | 13.4 |
| 1999-00 | 39 | Vancouver Canucks | NHL | 66 | 17 | 37 | 54 | -15 | 30 | 11 | 6 | 0 | 4 | 131 | 13.0 |
| 2000-01 | 40 | New York Rangers | NHL | 82 | 24 | 43 | 67 | -25 | 89 | 9 | 12 | 3 | 2 | 131 | 18.3 |
| 2001-02 | 41 | New York Rangers | NHL | 41 | 7 | 16 | 23 | -1 | 32 | 5 | 2 | 0 | 2 | 69 | 10.1 |
| 2002-03 | 42 | New York Rangers | NHL | 78 | 18 | 22 | 40 | -2 | 30 | 9 | 8 | 1 | 5 | 117 | 15.4 |
| 2003-04 | 43 | New York Rangers | NHL | 76 | 18 | 25 | 43 | 3 | 42 | 15 | 1 | 2 | 3 | 104 | 17.3 |
| Career — 26 Seasons | | | | 1808 | 695 | 1203 | 1898 | 201 | 1970 | 453 | 179 | 63 | 92 | 4283 | 16.2 |

**PLAYOFFS**

| SEASON | AGE | TEAM | LG | GP | G | A | PTS | +/- | PIM | ESG | PPG | SHG | GWG | SOG | S% |
|--------|-----|------|----|----|---|---|-----|-----|-----|-----|-----|-----|-----|-----|----|
| 1979-80 | 19 | Edmonton Oilers | NHL | 3 | 1 | 2 | 3 | 2 | 2 | 0 | 0 | 1 | 0 | 11 | 9.1 |
| 1980-81 | 20 | Edmonton Oilers | NHL | 9 | 2 | 5 | 7 | 1 | 13 | 2 | 0 | 0 | 0 | 24 | 8.3 |
| 1981-82 | 21 | Edmonton Oilers | NHL | 5 | 1 | 2 | 3 | -4 | 8 | 1 | 0 | 0 | 0 | 17 | 5.9 |
| 1982-83 | 22 | Edmonton Oilers | NHL | 15 | 15 | 6 | 21 | 11 | 14 | 9 | 4 | 2 | 2 | 50 | 30.0 |
| 1983-84 | 23 | Edmonton Oilers | NHL | 19 | 8 | 18 | 26 | 9 | 19 | 6 | 1 | 1 | 2 | 63 | 12.7 |
| 1984-85 | 24 | Edmonton Oilers | NHL | 18 | 12 | 13 | 25 | 14 | 12 | 10 | 1 | 1 | 1 | 56 | 21.4 |
| 1985-86 | 25 | Edmonton Oilers | NHL | 10 | 4 | 6 | 10 | 0 | 18 | 2 | 0 | 2 | 0 | 23 | 17.4 |
| 1986-87 | 26 | Edmonton Oilers | NHL | 21 | 12 | 16 | 28 | 13 | 16 | 9 | 1 | 2 | 1 | 62 | 19.4 |
| 1987-88 | 27 | Edmonton Oilers | NHL | 19 | 11 | 23 | 34 | 9 | 29 | 3 | 7 | 1 | 0 | 42 | 26.2 |
| 1988-89 | 28 | Edmonton Oilers | NHL | 7 | 1 | 11 | 12 | -1 | 8 | 1 | 0 | 0 | 0 | 23 | 4.3 |
| 1989-90 | 29 | Edmonton Oilers | NHL | 22 | 9 | 22 | 31 | 5 | 20 | 7 | 1 | 1 | 1 | 47 | 19.1 |
| 1990-91 | 30 | Edmonton Oilers | NHL | 18 | 4 | 11 | 15 | 2 | 16 | 3 | 1 | 0 | 0 | 41 | 9.8 |
| 1991-92 | 31 | New York Rangers | NHL | 11 | 7 | 7 | 14 | -4 | 6 | 3 | 2 | 2 | 0 | 27 | 25.9 |
| 1993-94 | 33 | New York Rangers | NHL | 23 | 12 | 18 | 30 | 14 | 33 | 9 | 2 | 1 | 4 | 75 | 16.0 |
| 1994-95 | 34 | New York Rangers | NHL | 10 | 3 | 10 | 13 | -11 | 8 | 1 | 2 | 0 | 1 | 26 | 11.5 |
| 1995-96 | 35 | New York Rangers | NHL | 11 | 4 | 7 | 11 | -10 | 16 | 2 | 2 | 0 | 1 | 41 | 9.8 |
| 1996-97 | 36 | New York Rangers | NHL | 15 | 3 | 9 | 12 | 2 | 6 | 3 | 0 | 0 | 1 | 43 | 7.0 |
| Career — 17 Seasons | | | | 236 | 109 | 186 | 295 | 52 | 244 | 71 | 24 | 14 | 14 | 671 | 16.2 |

# Stan Mikita Profile: See page 126

**REGULAR SEASON**

| SEASON | AGE | TEAM | LG | GP | G | A | PTS | +/- | PIM | ESG | PPG | SHG | GWG | SOG | S% |
|--------|-----|------|----|----|---|---|-----|-----|-----|-----|-----|-----|-----|-----|----|
| 1958-59 | 18 | Chicago Black Hawks | NHL | 3 | 0 | 1 | 1 | | 4 | 0 | 0 | 0 | | | |
| 1959-60 | 19 | Chicago Black Hawks | NHL | 67 | 8 | 18 | 26 | 13 | 119 | 8 | 0 | 0 | 1 | 127 | 6.3 |
| 1960-61 | 20 | Chicago Black Hawks | NHL | 68 | 19 | 34 | 53 | 27 | 94 | 15 | 4 | 0 | 5 | 205 | 9.3 |
| 1961-62 | 21 | Chicago Black Hawks | NHL | 70 | 25 | 52 | 77 | 12 | 97 | 16 | 9 | 0 | 5 | 208 | 12.0 |
| 1962-63 | 22 | Chicago Black Hawks | NHL | 65 | 31 | 45 | 76 | 26 | 69 | 22 | 9 | 0 | 6 | 235 | 13.2 |
| 1963-64 | 23 | Chicago Black Hawks | NHL | 70 | 39 | 50 | 89 | 21 | 146 | 24 | 14 | 1 | 7 | 305 | 12.8 |
| 1964-65 | 24 | Chicago Black Hawks | NHL | 70 | 28 | 59 | 87 | 29 | 154 | 20 | 8 | 0 | 6 | 256 | 10.9 |
| 1965-66 | 25 | Chicago Black Hawks | NHL | 68 | 30 | 48 | 78 | 6 | 58 | 18 | 11 | 1 | 1 | 244 | 12.3 |
| 1966-67 | 26 | Chicago Black Hawks | NHL | 70 | 35 | 62 | 97 | 40 | 12 | 26 | 8 | 1 | 5 | 279 | 12.5 |
| 1967-68 | 27 | Chicago Black Hawks | NHL | 72 | 40 | 47 | 87 | 0 | 14 | 25 | 13 | 2 | 8 | 303 | 13.2 |
| 1968-69 | 28 | Chicago Black Hawks | NHL | 74 | 30 | 67 | 97 | 14 | 52 | 20 | 7 | 3 | 2 | 299 | 10.0 |
| 1969-70 | 29 | Chicago Black Hawks | NHL | 76 | 39 | 47 | 86 | 27 | 50 | 32 | 7 | 0 | 8 | 352 | 11.1 |
| 1970-71 | 30 | Chicago Black Hawks | NHL | 74 | 24 | 48 | 72 | 20 | 85 | 17 | 7 | 0 | 4 | 220 | 10.9 |
| 1971-72 | 31 | Chicago Black Hawks | NHL | 74 | 26 | 39 | 65 | 16 | 46 | 21 | 5 | 0 | 6 | 185 | 14.1 |
| 1972-73 | 32 | Chicago Black Hawks | NHL | 57 | 27 | 56 | 83 | 31 | 32 | 19 | 7 | 1 | 5 | 177 | 15.3 |
| 1973-74 | 33 | Chicago Black Hawks | NHL | 76 | 30 | 50 | 80 | 24 | 46 | 22 | 6 | 2 | 1 | 171 | 17.5 |

## Stan Mikita (continued)

### REGULAR SEASON

| SEASON | AGE | TEAM | LG | GP | G | A | PTS | +/- | PIM | ESG | PPG | SHG | GWG | SOG | S% |
|---|---|---|---|---|---|---|---|---|---|---|---|---|---|---|---|
| 1974–75 | 34 | Chicago Black Hawks | NHL | 79 | 36 | 50 | 86 | 14 | 48 | 24 | 12 | 0 | 6 | 253 | 14.2 |
| 1975–76 | 35 | Chicago Black Hawks | NHL | 48 | 16 | 41 | 57 | -4 | 37 | 10 | 6 | 0 | 1 | 159 | 10.1 |
| 1976–77 | 36 | Chicago Black Hawks | NHL | 57 | 19 | 30 | 49 | -9 | 20 | 12 | 6 | 1 | 4 | 128 | 14.8 |
| 1977–78 | 37 | Chicago Black Hawks | NHL | 76 | 18 | 41 | 59 | 17 | 35 | 12 | 6 | 0 | 2 | 201 | 8.9 |
| 1978–79 | 38 | Chicago Black Hawks | NHL | 65 | 19 | 36 | 55 | 3 | 34 | 15 | 4 | 0 | 1 | 147 | 12.9 |
| 1979–80 | 39 | Chicago Black Hawks | NHL | 17 | 2 | 5 | 7 | 2 | 12 | 2 | 0 | 0 | 0 | 28 | 7.1 |
| NHL Career – 22 Seasons | | | | 1396 | 541 | 926 | 1467 | 329 | 1264 | 379 | 150 | 12 | 84 | 4482 | 12.1 |

### PLAYOFFS

| SEASON | AGE | TEAM | LG | GP | G | A | PTS | +/- | PIM | ESG | PPG | SHG | GWG | SOG | S% |
|---|---|---|---|---|---|---|---|---|---|---|---|---|---|---|---|
| 1959–60 | 19 | Chicago Black Hawks | NHL | 3 | 0 | 1 | 1 | -2 | 2 | 0 | 0 | 0 | 0 | 6 | 0.0 |
| 1960–61 | 20 | Chicago Black Hawks | NHL | 12 | 6 | 5 | 11 | 5 | 21 | 4 | 2 | 0 | 1 | 32 | 18.8 |
| 1961–62 | 21 | Chicago Black Hawks | NHL | 12 | 6 | 15 | 21 | 9 | 19 | 5 | 0 | 1 | 2 | 44 | 13.6 |
| 1962–63 | 22 | Chicago Black Hawks | NHL | 6 | 3 | 2 | 5 | 0 | 2 | 1 | 2 | 0 | 0 | 18 | 16.7 |
| 1963–64 | 23 | Chicago Black Hawks | NHL | 7 | 3 | 6 | 9 | -1 | 8 | 2 | 1 | 0 | 1 | 34 | 8.8 |
| 1964–65 | 24 | Chicago Black Hawks | NHL | 14 | 3 | 7 | 10 | 3 | 53 | 3 | 0 | 0 | 1 | 32 | 9.4 |
| 1965–66 | 25 | Chicago Black Hawks | NHL | 6 | 1 | 2 | 3 | -5 | 2 | 0 | 1 | 0 | 0 | 16 | 6.3 |
| 1966–67 | 26 | Chicago Black Hawks | NHL | 6 | 2 | 2 | 4 | -1 | 2 | 2 | 0 | 0 | 0 | 30 | 6.7 |
| 1967–68 | 27 | Chicago Black Hawks | NHL | 11 | 5 | 7 | 12 | -2 | 6 | 2 | 3 | 0 | 0 | 60 | 8.3 |
| 1969–70 | 29 | Chicago Black Hawks | NHL | 8 | 4 | 6 | 10 | -2 | 2 | 1 | 3 | 0 | 1 | 33 | 12.1 |
| 1970–71 | 30 | Chicago Black Hawks | NHL | 18 | 5 | 13 | 18 | 7 | 16 | 4 | 1 | 0 | 1 | 58 | 8.6 |
| 1971–72 | 31 | Chicago Black Hawks | NHL | 8 | 3 | 1 | 4 | -7 | 4 | 3 | 0 | 0 | 0 | 26 | 11.5 |
| 1972–73 | 32 | Chicago Black Hawks | NHL | 15 | 7 | 13 | 20 | -3 | 8 | 5 | 1 | 1 | 2 | 45 | 15.6 |
| 1973–74 | 33 | Chicago Black Hawks | NHL | 11 | 5 | 6 | 11 | 1 | 8 | 4 | 1 | 0 | 1 | 29 | 17.2 |
| 1974–75 | 34 | Chicago Black Hawks | NHL | 8 | 3 | 4 | 7 | -1 | 12 | 2 | 1 | 0 | 1 | 14 | 21.4 |
| 1975–76 | 35 | Chicago Black Hawks | NHL | 4 | 0 | 0 | 0 | -2 | 4 | 0 | 0 | 0 | 0 | 7 | 0.0 |
| 1976–77 | 36 | Chicago Black Hawks | NHL | 2 | 0 | 1 | 1 | -2 | 0 | 0 | 0 | 0 | 0 | 5 | 0.0 |
| 1977–78 | 37 | Chicago Black Hawks | NHL | 4 | 3 | 0 | 3 | -5 | 0 | 1 | 2 | 0 | 0 | 7 | 42.9 |
| NHL Career – 18 Seasons | | | | 155 | 59 | 91 | 150 | -8 | 169 | 39 | 18 | 2 | 11 | 496 | 11.9 |

## Mike Modano   Profile: See page 128

### REGULAR SEASON

| SEASON | AGE | TEAM | LG | GP | G | A | PTS | +/- | PIM | ESG | PPG | SHG | GWG | SOG | S% |
|---|---|---|---|---|---|---|---|---|---|---|---|---|---|---|---|
| 1989–90 | 19 | Minnesota North Stars | NHL | 80 | 29 | 46 | 75 | -7 | 63 | 17 | 12 | 0 | 2 | 172 | 16.9 |
| 1990–91 | 20 | Minnesota North Stars | NHL | 79 | 28 | 36 | 64 | 2 | 61 | 19 | 9 | 0 | 2 | 232 | 12.1 |
| 1991–92 | 21 | Minnesota North Stars | NHL | 76 | 33 | 44 | 77 | -9 | 46 | 28 | 5 | 0 | 8 | 256 | 12.9 |
| 1992–93 | 22 | Minnesota North Stars | NHL | 82 | 33 | 60 | 93 | -7 | 83 | 24 | 9 | 0 | 7 | 307 | 10.7 |
| 1993–94 | 23 | Dallas Stars | NHL | 76 | 50 | 43 | 93 | -8 | 54 | 32 | 18 | 0 | 4 | 281 | 17.8 |
| 1994–95 | 24 | Dallas Stars | NHL | 30 | 12 | 17 | 29 | 7 | 8 | 7 | 4 | 1 | 0 | 100 | 12.0 |
| 1995–96 | 25 | Dallas Stars | NHL | 78 | 36 | 45 | 81 | -12 | 63 | 24 | 8 | 4 | 4 | 320 | 11.3 |
| 1996–97 | 26 | Dallas Stars | NHL | 80 | 35 | 48 | 83 | 43 | 42 | 21 | 9 | 5 | 9 | 291 | 12.0 |
| 1997–98 | 27 | Dallas Stars | NHL | 52 | 21 | 38 | 59 | 25 | 32 | 9 | 7 | 5 | 2 | 191 | 11.0 |
| 1998–99 | 28 | Dallas Stars | NHL | 77 | 34 | 47 | 81 | 29 | 44 | 24 | 6 | 4 | 7 | 224 | 15.2 |
| 1999–00 | 29 | Dallas Stars | NHL | 77 | 38 | 43 | 81 | 0 | 48 | 26 | 11 | 1 | 8 | 188 | 20.2 |
| 2000–01 | 30 | Dallas Stars | NHL | 81 | 33 | 51 | 84 | 26 | 52 | 22 | 8 | 3 | 7 | 208 | 15.9 |
| 2001–02 | 31 | Dallas Stars | NHL | 78 | 34 | 43 | 77 | 14 | 38 | 26 | 6 | 2 | 5 | 219 | 15.5 |
| 2002–03 | 32 | Dallas Stars | NHL | 79 | 28 | 57 | 85 | 34 | 30 | 21 | 5 | 2 | 6 | 193 | 14.5 |
| 2003–04 | 33 | Dallas Stars | NHL | 76 | 14 | 30 | 44 | -21 | 46 | 8 | 6 | 0 | 0 | 152 | 9.2 |
| 2005–06 | 35 | Dallas Stars | NHL | 78 | 27 | 50 | 77 | 23 | 58 | 14 | 12 | 1 | 4 | 207 | 13.0 |
| 2006–07 | 36 | Dallas Stars | NHL | 59 | 22 | 21 | 43 | 9 | 34 | 13 | 9 | 0 | 7 | 141 | 15.6 |
| 2007–08 | 37 | Dallas Stars | NHL | 82 | 21 | 36 | 57 | -11 | 48 | 15 | 5 | 1 | 4 | 200 | 10.5 |
| 2008–09 | 38 | Dallas Stars | NHL | 80 | 15 | 31 | 46 | -13 | 46 | 11 | 4 | 0 | 4 | 197 | 7.6 |
| 2009–10 | 39 | Dallas Stars | NHL | 59 | 14 | 16 | 30 | -6 | 22 | 11 | 3 | 0 | 2 | 115 | 12.2 |
| 2010–11 | 40 | Detroit Red Wings | NHL | 40 | 4 | 11 | 15 | -4 | 8 | 3 | 1 | 0 | 0 | 79 | 5.1 |
| NHL Career – 21 Seasons | | | | 1499 | 561 | 813 | 1374 | 114 | 926 | 375 | 157 | 29 | 92 | 4273 | 13.1 |

### PLAYOFFS

| SEASON | AGE | TEAM | LG | GP | G | A | PTS | +/- | PIM | ESG | PPG | SHG | GWG | SOG | S% |
|---|---|---|---|---|---|---|---|---|---|---|---|---|---|---|---|
| 1988–89 | 18 | Minnesota North Stars | NHL | 2 | 0 | 0 | 0 | -2 | 0 | 0 | 0 | 0 | 0 | 0 | 0.0 |
| 1989–90 | 19 | Minnesota North Stars | NHL | 7 | 1 | 1 | 2 | -3 | 12 | 1 | 0 | 0 | 0 | 17 | 5.9 |
| 1990–91 | 20 | Minnesota North Stars | NHL | 23 | 8 | 12 | 20 | -3 | 16 | 5 | 3 | 0 | 1 | 59 | 13.6 |
| 1991–92 | 21 | Minnesota North Stars | NHL | 7 | 3 | 2 | 5 | -2 | 4 | 2 | 1 | 0 | 0 | 19 | 15.8 |
| 1993–94 | 23 | Dallas Stars | NHL | 9 | 7 | 3 | 10 | -2 | 16 | 5 | 2 | 0 | 2 | 48 | 14.6 |
| 1996–97 | 26 | Dallas Stars | NHL | 7 | 4 | 1 | 5 | 2 | 0 | 2 | 1 | 1 | 2 | 27 | 14.8 |

## Mike Modano (continued)

**PLAYOFFS**

| SEASON | AGE | TEAM | LG | GP | G | A | PTS | +/- | PIM | ESG | PPG | SHG | GWG | SOG | S% |
|---|---|---|---|---|---|---|---|---|---|---|---|---|---|---|---|
| 1997-98 | 27 | Dallas Stars | NHL | 17 | 4 | 10 | 14 | 4 | 12 | 3 | 1 | 0 | 1 | 49 | 8.2 |
| 1998-99 | 28 | Dallas Stars | NHL | 23 | 5 | 18 | 23 | 6 | 16 | 3 | 1 | 1 | 1 | 83 | 6.0 |
| 1999-00 | 29 | Dallas Stars | NHL | 23 | 10 | 13 | 23 | 3 | 10 | 6 | 4 | 0 | 2 | 67 | 14.9 |
| 2000-01 | 30 | Dallas Stars | NHL | 9 | 3 | 4 | 7 | 1 | 0 | 1 | 2 | 0 | 0 | 23 | 13.0 |
| 2002-03 | 32 | Dallas Stars | NHL | 12 | 5 | 10 | 15 | 2 | 4 | 4 | 1 | 0 | 2 | 30 | 16.7 |
| 2003-04 | 33 | Dallas Stars | NHL | 5 | 1 | 2 | 3 | -4 | 8 | 0 | 1 | 0 | 0 | 12 | 8.3 |
| 2005-06 | 35 | Dallas Stars | NHL | 5 | 1 | 3 | 4 | 0 | 4 | 0 | 1 | 0 | 0 | 12 | 8.3 |
| 2006-07 | 36 | Dallas Stars | NHL | 7 | 1 | 1 | 2 | 0 | 4 | 0 | 1 | 0 | 1 | 19 | 5.3 |
| 2007-08 | 37 | Dallas Stars | NHL | 18 | 5 | 7 | 12 | -3 | 22 | 0 | 5 | 0 | 3 | 37 | 13.5 |
| 2010-11 | 40 | Detroit Red Wings | NHL | 2 | 0 | 1 | 1 | 1 | 0 | 0 | 0 | 0 | 0 | 5 | 0.0 |
| NHL Career — 16 Seasons | | | | 176 | 58 | 88 | 146 | 0 | 128 | 32 | 24 | 2 | 15 | 507 | 11.4 |

## Howie Morenz   Profile: See page 130

**REGULAR SEASON**

| SEASON | AGE | TEAM | LG | GP | G | A | PTS | PIM |
|---|---|---|---|---|---|---|---|---|
| 1923-24 | 21 | Montreal Canadiens | NHL | 24 | 13 | 3 | 16 | 32 |
| 1924-25 | 22 | Montreal Canadiens | NHL | 30 | 27 | 12 | 39 | 46 |
| 1925-26 | 23 | Montreal Canadiens | NHL | 31 | 23 | 3 | 26 | 41 |
| 1926-27 | 24 | Montreal Canadiens | NHL | 44 | 25 | 7 | 32 | 51 |
| 1927-28 | 25 | Montreal Canadiens | NHL | 43 | 33 | 18 | 51 | 66 |
| 1928-29 | 26 | Montreal Canadiens | NHL | 42 | 17 | 10 | 27 | 47 |
| 1929-30 | 27 | Montreal Canadiens | NHL | 44 | 40 | 13 | 53 | 72 |
| 1930-31 | 28 | Montreal Canadiens | NHL | 39 | 28 | 23 | 51 | 49 |
| 1931-32 | 29 | Montreal Canadiens | NHL | 48 | 24 | 25 | 49 | 46 |
| 1932-33 | 30 | Montreal Canadiens | NHL | 46 | 14 | 22 | 36 | 32 |
| 1933-34 | 31 | Montreal Canadiens | NHL | 39 | 9 | 12 | 21 | 21 |
| 1934-35 | 32 | Chicago Black Hawks | NHL | 48 | 8 | 26 | 34 | 21 |
| 1935-36 | 33 | Chicago Black Hawks | NHL | 24 | 4 | 10 | 14 | 20 |
| 1935-36 | 33 | New York Rangers | NHL | 18 | 2 | 5 | 7 | 6 |
| 1936-37 | 34 | Montreal Canadiens | NHL | 30 | 4 | 16 | 20 | 12 |
| Career — 14 Seasons | | | | 550 | 271 | 205 | 476 | 562 |

**PLAYOFFS**

| SEASON | AGE | TEAM | LG | GP | G | A | PTS | PIM |
|---|---|---|---|---|---|---|---|---|
| 1923-24 | 21 | Montreal Canadiens | NHL | 2 | 3 | 1 | 4 | 6 |
| 1923-24 | 21 | Montreal Canadiens | St-Cup | 4 | 4 | 2 | 6 | 4 |
| 1924-25 | 22 | Montreal Canadiens | NHL | 2 | 3 | 0 | 3 | 4 |
| 1924-25 | 22 | Montreal Canadiens | St-Cup | 4 | 4 | 1 | 5 | 4 |
| 1926-27 | 24 | Montreal Canadiens | NHL | 4 | 1 | 0 | 1 | 4 |
| 1927-28 | 25 | Montreal Canadiens | NHL | 2 | 0 | 0 | 0 | 12 |
| 1928-29 | 26 | Montreal Canadiens | NHL | 3 | 0 | 0 | 0 | 6 |
| 1929-30 | 27 | Montreal Canadiens | NHL | 6 | 3 | 0 | 3 | 10 |
| 1930-31 | 28 | Montreal Canadiens | NHL | 10 | 1 | 4 | 5 | 10 |
| 1931-32 | 29 | Montreal Canadiens | NHL | 4 | 1 | 0 | 1 | 4 |
| 1932-33 | 30 | Montreal Canadiens | NHL | 2 | 0 | 3 | 3 | 2 |
| 1933-34 | 31 | Montreal Canadiens | NHL | 2 | 1 | 1 | 2 | 0 |
| 1934-35 | 32 | Chicago Black Hawks | NHL | 2 | 0 | 0 | 0 | 0 |
| Career — 11 Seasons | | | | 47 | 21 | 12 | 33 | 66 |

## Joe Nieuwendyk   Profile: See page 132

**REGULAR SEASON**

| SEASON | AGE | TEAM | LG | GP | G | A | PTS | +/- | PIM | ESG | PPG | SHG | GWG | SOG | S% |
|---|---|---|---|---|---|---|---|---|---|---|---|---|---|---|---|
| 1986-87 | 20 | Calgary Flames | NHL | 9 | 5 | 1 | 6 | 0 | 0 | 3 | 2 | 0 | 1 | 16 | 31.3 |
| 1987-88 | 21 | Calgary Flames | NHL | 75 | 51 | 41 | 92 | 20 | 23 | 17 | 31 | 3 | 8 | 212 | 24.1 |
| 1988-89 | 22 | Calgary Flames | NHL | 77 | 51 | 31 | 82 | 26 | 40 | 29 | 19 | 3 | 11 | 215 | 23.7 |
| 1989-90 | 23 | Calgary Flames | NHL | 79 | 45 | 50 | 95 | 32 | 40 | 27 | 18 | 0 | 3 | 226 | 19.9 |
| 1990-91 | 24 | Calgary Flames | NHL | 79 | 45 | 40 | 85 | 19 | 36 | 19 | 22 | 4 | 1 | 222 | 20.3 |
| 1991-92 | 25 | Calgary Flames | NHL | 69 | 22 | 34 | 56 | -1 | 55 | 15 | 7 | 0 | 2 | 137 | 16.1 |
| 1992-93 | 26 | Calgary Flames | NHL | 79 | 38 | 37 | 75 | 9 | 52 | 24 | 14 | 0 | 6 | 208 | 18.3 |
| 1993-94 | 27 | Calgary Flames | NHL | 64 | 36 | 39 | 75 | 19 | 51 | 21 | 14 | 1 | 7 | 191 | 18.8 |
| 1994-95 | 28 | Calgary Flames | NHL | 46 | 21 | 29 | 50 | 11 | 33 | 18 | 3 | 0 | 4 | 122 | 17.2 |
| 1995-96 | 29 | Dallas Stars | NHL | 52 | 14 | 18 | 32 | -17 | 41 | 6 | 8 | 0 | 3 | 138 | 10.1 |
| 1996-97 | 30 | Dallas Stars | NHL | 66 | 30 | 21 | 51 | -5 | 32 | 22 | 8 | 0 | 2 | 173 | 17.3 |
| 1997-98 | 31 | Dallas Stars | NHL | 73 | 39 | 30 | 69 | 16 | 30 | 25 | 14 | 0 | 11 | 203 | 19.2 |
| 1998-99 | 32 | Dallas Stars | NHL | 67 | 28 | 27 | 55 | 11 | 34 | 20 | 8 | 0 | 8 | 157 | 17.8 |
| 1999-00 | 33 | Dallas Stars | NHL | 48 | 15 | 19 | 34 | -1 | 26 | 8 | 7 | 0 | 2 | 110 | 13.6 |
| 2000-01 | 34 | Dallas Stars | NHL | 69 | 29 | 23 | 52 | 5 | 30 | 17 | 12 | 0 | 4 | 166 | 17.5 |
| 2001-02 | 35 | Dallas Stars | NHL | 67 | 23 | 24 | 47 | -2 | 18 | 17 | 6 | 0 | 5 | 157 | 14.6 |
| 2001-02 | 35 | New Jersey Devils | NHL | 14 | 2 | 9 | 11 | 2 | 4 | 2 | 0 | 0 | 1 | 32 | 6.3 |
| 2002-03 | 36 | New Jersey Devils | NHL | 80 | 17 | 28 | 45 | 10 | 56 | 14 | 3 | 0 | 4 | 201 | 8.5 |
| 2003-04 | 37 | Toronto Maple Leafs | NHL | 64 | 22 | 28 | 50 | 7 | 26 | 11 | 10 | 1 | 5 | 131 | 16.8 |
| 2005-06 | 39 | Florida Panthers | NHL | 65 | 26 | 30 | 56 | -2 | 46 | 19 | 7 | 0 | 3 | 195 | 13.3 |
| 2006-07 | 40 | Florida Panthers | NHL | 15 | 5 | 3 | 8 | -4 | 4 | 3 | 2 | 0 | 2 | 30 | 16.7 |
| NHL Career — 20 Seasons | | | | 1257 | 564 | 562 | 1126 | 155 | 677 | 337 | 215 | 12 | 93 | 3242 | 17.4 |

**PLAYOFFS**

| SEASON | AGE | TEAM | LG | GP | G | A | PTS | +/- | PIM | ESG | PPG | SHG | GWG | SOG | S% |
|---|---|---|---|---|---|---|---|---|---|---|---|---|---|---|---|
| 1986-87 | 20 | Calgary Flames | NHL | 6 | 2 | 2 | 4 | -2 | 0 | 2 | 0 | 0 | 0 | 8 | 25.0 |
| 1987-88 | 21 | Calgary Flames | NHL | 8 | 3 | 4 | 7 | 0 | 2 | 2 | 1 | 0 | 0 | 21 | 14.3 |
| 1988-89 | 22 | Calgary Flames | NHL | 22 | 10 | 4 | 14 | 0 | 10 | 4 | 6 | 0 | 1 | 57 | 17.5 |
| 1989-90 | 23 | Calgary Flames | NHL | 6 | 4 | 6 | 10 | 6 | 4 | 3 | 1 | 0 | 1 | 19 | 21.1 |
| 1990-91 | 24 | Calgary Flames | NHL | 7 | 4 | 1 | 5 | -4 | 10 | 2 | 2 | 0 | 0 | 27 | 14.8 |
| 1992-93 | 26 | Calgary Flames | NHL | 6 | 3 | 6 | 9 | -4 | 10 | 2 | 1 | 0 | 0 | 21 | 14.3 |
| 1993-94 | 27 | Calgary Flames | NHL | 6 | 2 | 2 | 4 | 0 | 0 | 1 | 1 | 0 | 0 | 8 | 25.0 |
| 1994-95 | 28 | Calgary Flames | NHL | 5 | 4 | 3 | 7 | 0 | 0 | 2 | 2 | 0 | 1 | 21 | 19.0 |

### Joe Nieuwendyk (continued)

| PLAYOFFS | | | | | | | | | | | | | | |
|---|---|---|---|---|---|---|---|---|---|---|---|---|---|---|
| SEASON | AGE | TEAM | LG | GP | G | A | PTS | +/- | PIM | ESG | PPG | SHG | GWG | SOG | S% |
| 1996–97 | 30 | Dallas Stars | NHL | 7 | 2 | 2 | 4 | -1 | 6 | 2 | 0 | 0 | 0 | 21 | 9.5 |
| 1997–98 | 31 | Dallas Stars | NHL | 1 | 1 | 0 | 1 | 1 | 0 | 1 | 0 | 0 | 0 | 1 | 100.0 |
| 1998–99 | 32 | Dallas Stars | NHL | 23 | 11 | 10 | 21 | 7 | 19 | 8 | 3 | 0 | 6 | 72 | 15.3 |
| 1999–00 | 33 | Dallas Stars | NHL | 23 | 7 | 3 | 10 | -2 | 18 | 4 | 3 | 0 | 2 | 45 | 15.6 |
| 2000–01 | 34 | Dallas Stars | NHL | 7 | 4 | 0 | 4 | -2 | 4 | 3 | 1 | 0 | 1 | 18 | 22.2 |
| 2001–02 | 35 | New Jersey Devils | NHL | 5 | 0 | 1 | 1 | -2 | 0 | 0 | 0 | 0 | 0 | 8 | 0.0 |
| 2002–03 | 36 | New Jersey Devils | NHL | 17 | 3 | 6 | 9 | -2 | 4 | 2 | 1 | 0 | 0 | 24 | 12.5 |
| 2003–04 | 37 | Toronto Maple Leafs | NHL | 9 | 6 | 0 | 6 | 0 | 4 | 5 | 1 | 0 | 2 | 23 | 26.1 |
| NHL Career — 16 Seasons | | | | 158 | 66 | 50 | 116 | -5 | 91 | 43 | 23 | 0 | 14 | 394 | 16.8 |

## Frank Nighbor    Profile: See page 134

| REGULAR SEASON | | | | | | | | |
|---|---|---|---|---|---|---|---|---|
| SEASON | AGE | TEAM | LG | GP | G | A | PTS | PIM |
| 1912–13 | 20 | Toronto Blueshirts | NHA | 19 | 25 | 0 | 25 | 9 |
| 1913–14 | 21 | Vancouver Millionaires | PCHA | 11 | 10 | 5 | 15 | 6 |
| 1914–15 | 22 | Vancouver Millionaires | PCHA | 17 | 23 | 7 | 30 | 12 |
| 1915–16 | 23 | Ottawa Senators | NHA | 23 | 19 | 5 | 24 | 26 |
| 1916–17 | 24 | Ottawa Senators | NHA | 19 | 41 | 10 | 51 | 24 |
| 1917–18 | 25 | Ottawa Senators | NHL | 10 | 11 | 8 | 19 | 6 |
| 1918–19 | 26 | Ottawa Senators | NHL | 18 | 19 | 9 | 28 | 30 |
| 1919–20 | 27 | Ottawa Senators | NHL | 23 | 26 | 16 | 42 | 20 |
| 1920–21 | 28 | Ottawa Senators | NHL | 24 | 19 | 10 | 29 | 10 |
| 1921–22 | 29 | Ottawa Senators | NHL | 20 | 8 | 10 | 18 | 4 |
| 1922–23 | 30 | Ottawa Senators | NHL | 22 | 11 | 7 | 18 | 14 |
| 1923–24 | 31 | Ottawa Senators | NHL | 20 | 11 | 6 | 17 | 16 |
| 1924–25 | 32 | Ottawa Senators | NHL | 26 | 5 | 5 | 10 | 18 |
| 1925–26 | 33 | Ottawa Senators | NHL | 35 | 12 | 14 | 26 | 40 |
| 1926–27 | 34 | Ottawa Senators | NHL | 38 | 6 | 6 | 12 | 28 |
| 1927–28 | 35 | Ottawa Senators | NHL | 42 | 8 | 5 | 13 | 48 |
| 1928–29 | 36 | Ottawa Senators | NHL | 30 | 1 | 4 | 5 | 22 |
| 1929–30 | 37 | Ottawa Senators | NHL | 18 | 0 | 0 | 0 | 8 |
| 1929–30 | 37 | Toronto Maple Leafs | NHL | 23 | 2 | 0 | 2 | 2 |
| Career — 18 Seasons | | | | 438 | 257 | 127 | 384 | 343 |

| PLAYOFFS | | | | | | | | |
|---|---|---|---|---|---|---|---|---|
| SEASON | AGE | TEAM | LG | GP | G | A | PTS | PIM |
| 1914–15 | 22 | Vancouver Millionaires | St-Cup | 3 | 4 | 6 | 10 | 6 |
| 1916–17 | 24 | Ottawa Senators | NHA | 2 | 1 | 1 | 2 | 6 |
| 1918–19 | 26 | Ottawa Senators | NHL | 2 | 0 | 2 | 2 | 3 |
| 1919–20 | 27 | Ottawa Senators | St-Cup | 5 | 6 | 1 | 7 | 2 |
| 1920–21 | 28 | Ottawa Senators | NHL | 2 | 1 | 3 | 4 | 2 |
| 1920–21 | 28 | Ottawa Senators | St-Cup | 5 | 0 | 1 | 1 | 0 |
| 1921–22 | 29 | Ottawa Senators | NHL | 2 | 2 | 1 | 3 | 4 |
| 1922–23 | 30 | Ottawa Senators | NHL | 2 | 0 | 1 | 1 | 0 |
| 1922–23 | 30 | Ottawa Senators | St-Cup | 6 | 1 | 1 | 2 | 10 |
| 1923–24 | 31 | Ottawa Senators | NHL | 2 | 0 | 1 | 1 | 0 |
| 1925–26 | 33 | Ottawa Senators | NHL | 2 | 0 | 0 | 0 | 2 |
| 1926–27 | 34 | Ottawa Senators | NHL | 6 | 1 | 1 | 2 | 0 |
| 1927–28 | 35 | Ottawa Senators | NHL | 2 | 0 | 0 | 0 | 2 |
| Career — 11 Seasons | | | | 41 | 16 | 19 | 35 | 37 |

## Reg Noble    Profile: See page 136

| REGULAR SEASON | | | | | | | | |
|---|---|---|---|---|---|---|---|---|
| SEASON | AGE | TEAM | LG | GP | G | A | PTS | PIM |
| 1916–17 | 19 | Toronto Blueshirts | NHA | 14 | 7 | 5 | 12 | 41 |
| 1916–17 | 20 | Montreal Canadiens | NHA | 6 | 4 | 0 | 4 | 15 |
| 1917–18 | 21 | Toronto Arenas | NHL | 20 | 29 | 10 | 39 | 35 |
| 1918–19 | 22 | Toronto Arenas | NHL | 17 | 10 | 4 | 14 | 43 |
| 1919–20 | 23 | Toronto St. Patricks | NHL | 24 | 24 | 7 | 31 | 49 |
| 1920–21 | 24 | Toronto St. Patricks | NHL | 24 | 19 | 8 | 27 | 54 |
| 1921–22 | 25 | Toronto St. Patricks | NHL | 24 | 17 | 11 | 28 | 19 |
| 1922–23 | 26 | Toronto St. Patricks | NHL | 24 | 12 | 12 | 24 | 46 |
| 1923–24 | 27 | Toronto St. Patricks | NHL | 24 | 12 | 5 | 17 | 79 |
| 1924–25 | 28 | Toronto St. Patricks | NHL | 3 | 1 | 0 | 1 | 8 |
| 1924–25 | 28 | Montreal Maroons | NHL | 27 | 8 | 12 | 20 | 54 |
| 1925–26 | 29 | Montreal Maroons | NHL | 33 | 9 | 9 | 18 | 98 |
| 1926–27 | 30 | Montreal Maroons | NHL | 43 | 3 | 3 | 6 | 110 |
| 1927–28 | 31 | Detroit Cougars | NHL | 44 | 6 | 9 | 15 | 62 |
| 1928–29 | 32 | Detroit Cougars | NHL | 43 | 6 | 4 | 10 | 54 |
| 1929–30 | 33 | Detroit Cougars | NHL | 43 | 6 | 4 | 10 | 72 |
| 1930–31 | 34 | Detroit Falcons | NHL | 44 | 2 | 5 | 7 | 46 |
| 1931–32 | 35 | Detroit Falcons | NHL | 48 | 3 | 3 | 6 | 74 |
| 1932–33 | 36 | Detroit Red Wings | NHL | 4 | 0 | 0 | 0 | 6 |
| 1932–33 | 36 | Montreal Maroons | NHL | 21 | 0 | 0 | 0 | 16 |
| Career — 17 Seasons | | | | 530 | 178 | 111 | 289 | 981 |

| PLAYOFFS | | | | | | | | |
|---|---|---|---|---|---|---|---|---|
| SEASON | AGE | TEAM | LG | GP | G | A | PTS | PIM |
| 1916–17 | 20 | Montreal Canadiens | NHA | 2 | 0 | 1 | 1 | 3 |
| 1917–18 | 21 | Toronto Arenas | NHL | 2 | 1 | 1 | 2 | 9 |
| 1917–18 | 21 | Toronto Arenas | St-Cup | 5 | 2 | 1 | 3 | 12 |
| 1920–21 | 24 | Toronto St. Patricks | NHL | 2 | 0 | 0 | 0 | 0 |
| 1921–22 | 25 | Toronto St. Patricks | NHL | 2 | 0 | 0 | 0 | 12 |
| 1921–22 | 25 | Toronto St. Patricks | St-Cup | 5 | 0 | 1 | 1 | 6 |
| 1925–26 | 29 | Montreal Maroons | NHL | 4 | 1 | 1 | 2 | 6 |
| 1925–26 | 29 | Montreal Maroons | St-Cup | 4 | 0 | 0 | 0 | 4 |
| 1926–27 | 30 | Montreal Maroons | NHL | 2 | 0 | 0 | 0 | 2 |
| 1928–29 | 32 | Detroit Cougars | NHL | 2 | 0 | 0 | 0 | 0 |
| 1931–32 | 35 | Detroit Falcons | NHL | 2 | 0 | 0 | 0 | 0 |
| 1932–33 | 36 | Montreal Maroons | NHL | 2 | 0 | 0 | 0 | 2 |
| Career — 9 Seasons | | | | 34 | 4 | 5 | 9 | 58 |

# Buddy O'Connor  Profile: See page 137

**REGULAR SEASON**

| SEASON | AGE | TEAM | LG | GP | G | A | PTS | PIM |
|---|---|---|---|---|---|---|---|---|
| 1941–42 | 25 | Montreal Canadiens | NHL | 36 | 9 | 16 | 25 | 4 |
| 1942–43 | 26 | Montreal Canadiens | NHL | 50 | 15 | 43 | 58 | 2 |
| 1943–44 | 27 | Montreal Canadiens | NHL | 44 | 12 | 42 | 54 | 6 |
| 1944–45 | 28 | Montreal Canadiens | NHL | 50 | 21 | 23 | 44 | 2 |
| 1945–46 | 29 | Montreal Canadiens | NHL | 45 | 11 | 11 | 22 | 2 |
| 1946–47 | 30 | Montreal Canadiens | NHL | 46 | 10 | 20 | 30 | 6 |
| 1947–48 | 31 | New York Rangers | NHL | 60 | 24 | 36 | 60 | 8 |
| 1948–49 | 32 | New York Rangers | NHL | 46 | 11 | 24 | 35 | 0 |
| 1949–50 | 33 | New York Rangers | NHL | 66 | 11 | 22 | 33 | 4 |
| 1950–51 | 34 | New York Rangers | NHL | 66 | 16 | 20 | 36 | 0 |
| NHL Career — 10 Seasons | | | | 509 | 140 | 257 | 397 | 34 |

**PLAYOFFS**

| SEASON | AGE | TEAM | LG | GP | G | A | PTS | PIM |
|---|---|---|---|---|---|---|---|---|
| 1941–42 | 25 | Montreal Canadiens | NHL | 3 | 0 | 1 | 1 | 0 |
| 1942–43 | 26 | Montreal Canadiens | NHL | 5 | 4 | 5 | 9 | 0 |
| 1943–44 | 27 | Montreal Canadiens | NHL | 8 | 1 | 2 | 3 | 2 |
| 1944–45 | 28 | Montreal Canadiens | NHL | 2 | 0 | 0 | 0 | 0 |
| 1945–46 | 29 | Montreal Canadiens | NHL | 9 | 2 | 3 | 5 | 0 |
| 1946–47 | 30 | Montreal Canadiens | NHL | 8 | 3 | 4 | 7 | 0 |
| 1947–48 | 31 | New York Rangers | NHL | 6 | 1 | 4 | 5 | 0 |
| 1949–50 | 33 | New York Rangers | NHL | 12 | 4 | 2 | 6 | 4 |
| NHL Career — 8 Seasons | | | | 53 | 15 | 21 | 36 | 6 |

# Adam Oates  Profile: See page 138

**REGULAR SEASON**

| SEASON | AGE | TEAM | LG | GP | G | A | PTS | +/- | PIM | ESG | PPG | SHG | GWG | SOG | S% |
|---|---|---|---|---|---|---|---|---|---|---|---|---|---|---|---|
| 1985–86 | 23 | Detroit Red Wings | NHL | 38 | 9 | 11 | 20 | -25 | 10 | 8 | 1 | 0 | 1 | 49 | 18.4 |
| 1986–87 | 24 | Detroit Red Wings | NHL | 76 | 15 | 32 | 47 | -1 | 21 | 11 | 4 | 0 | 1 | 138 | 10.9 |
| 1987–88 | 25 | Detroit Red Wings | NHL | 63 | 14 | 40 | 54 | 16 | 20 | 11 | 3 | 0 | 3 | 111 | 12.6 |
| 1988–89 | 26 | Detroit Red Wings | NHL | 69 | 16 | 62 | 78 | -1 | 14 | 14 | 2 | 0 | 1 | 127 | 12.6 |
| 1989–90 | 27 | St. Louis Blues | NHL | 80 | 23 | 79 | 102 | 9 | 30 | 15 | 6 | 2 | 3 | 168 | 13.7 |
| 1990–91 | 28 | St. Louis Blues | NHL | 61 | 25 | 90 | 115 | 15 | 29 | 21 | 3 | 1 | 3 | 139 | 18.0 |
| 1991–92 | 29 | St. Louis Blues | NHL | 54 | 10 | 59 | 69 | -4 | 12 | 7 | 3 | 0 | 3 | 118 | 8.5 |
| 1991–92 | 29 | Boston Bruins | NHL | 26 | 10 | 20 | 30 | -5 | 10 | 7 | 3 | 0 | 1 | 73 | 13.7 |
| 1992–93 | 30 | Boston Bruins | NHL | 84 | 45 | 97 | 142 | 15 | 32 | 20 | 24 | 1 | 11 | 254 | 17.7 |
| 1993–94 | 31 | Boston Bruins | NHL | 77 | 32 | 80 | 112 | 10 | 45 | 14 | 16 | 2 | 3 | 197 | 16.2 |
| 1994–95 | 32 | Boston Bruins | NHL | 48 | 12 | 41 | 53 | -11 | 8 | 7 | 4 | 1 | 2 | 109 | 11.0 |
| 1995–96 | 33 | Boston Bruins | NHL | 70 | 25 | 67 | 92 | 16 | 18 | 17 | 7 | 1 | 2 | 183 | 13.7 |
| 1996–97 | 34 | Boston Bruins | NHL | 63 | 18 | 52 | 70 | -3 | 10 | 14 | 2 | 2 | 4 | 138 | 13.0 |
| 1996–97 | 34 | Washington Capitals | NHL | 17 | 4 | 8 | 12 | -2 | 4 | 3 | 1 | 0 | 1 | 22 | 18.2 |
| 1997–98 | 35 | Washington Capitals | NHL | 82 | 18 | 58 | 76 | 6 | 36 | 13 | 3 | 2 | 3 | 121 | 14.9 |
| 1998–99 | 36 | Washington Capitals | NHL | 59 | 12 | 42 | 54 | -1 | 22 | 9 | 3 | 0 | 0 | 79 | 15.2 |
| 1999–00 | 37 | Washington Capitals | NHL | 82 | 15 | 56 | 71 | 13 | 14 | 10 | 5 | 0 | 6 | 93 | 16.1 |
| 2000–01 | 38 | Washington Capitals | NHL | 81 | 13 | 69 | 82 | -9 | 28 | 8 | 5 | 0 | 4 | 72 | 18.1 |
| 2001–02 | 39 | Washington Capitals | NHL | 66 | 11 | 57 | 68 | -2 | 22 | 8 | 3 | 0 | 1 | 85 | 12.9 |
| 2001–02 | 39 | Philadelphia Flyers | NHL | 14 | 3 | 7 | 10 | -2 | 6 | 3 | 0 | 0 | 0 | 17 | 17.6 |
| 2002–03 | 40 | Mighty Ducks of Anaheim | NHL | 67 | 9 | 36 | 45 | -1 | 16 | 5 | 4 | 0 | 2 | 67 | 13.4 |
| 2003–04 | 41 | Edmonton Oilers | NHL | 60 | 2 | 16 | 18 | 0 | 8 | 1 | 1 | 0 | 1 | 32 | 6.3 |
| NHL Career — 19 Seasons | | | | 1337 | 341 | 1079 | 1420 | 33 | 415 | 226 | 103 | 12 | 56 | 2392 | 14.3 |

**PLAYOFFS**

| SEASON | AGE | TEAM | LG | GP | G | A | PTS | +/- | PIM | ESG | PPG | SHG | GWG | SOG | S% |
|---|---|---|---|---|---|---|---|---|---|---|---|---|---|---|---|
| 1986–87 | 24 | Detroit Red Wings | NHL | 16 | 4 | 7 | 11 | 7 | 6 | 4 | 0 | 0 | 1 | 32 | 12.5 |
| 1987–88 | 25 | Detroit Red Wings | NHL | 16 | 8 | 12 | 20 | -2 | 6 | 4 | 4 | 0 | 1 | 33 | 24.2 |
| 1988–89 | 26 | Detroit Red Wings | NHL | 6 | 0 | 8 | 8 | -1 | 2 | 0 | 0 | 0 | 0 | 11 | 0.0 |
| 1989–90 | 27 | St. Louis Blues | NHL | 12 | 2 | 12 | 14 | -10 | 4 | 1 | 1 | 0 | 0 | 27 | 7.4 |
| 1990–91 | 28 | St. Louis Blues | NHL | 13 | 7 | 13 | 20 | 7 | 10 | 5 | 2 | 0 | 1 | 39 | 17.9 |
| 1991–92 | 29 | Boston Bruins | NHL | 15 | 5 | 14 | 19 | -6 | 4 | 2 | 3 | 0 | 2 | 35 | 14.3 |
| 1992–93 | 30 | Boston Bruins | NHL | 4 | 0 | 9 | 9 | 0 | 4 | 0 | 0 | 0 | 0 | 11 | 0.0 |
| 1993–94 | 31 | Boston Bruins | NHL | 13 | 3 | 9 | 12 | -3 | 8 | 1 | 2 | 0 | 0 | 42 | 7.1 |
| 1994–95 | 32 | Boston Bruins | NHL | 5 | 1 | 0 | 1 | -6 | 2 | 0 | 1 | 0 | 0 | 7 | 14.3 |
| 1995–96 | 33 | Boston Bruins | NHL | 5 | 2 | 5 | 7 | -3 | 2 | 1 | 0 | 1 | 0 | 13 | 15.4 |
| 1997–98 | 35 | Washington Capitals | NHL | 21 | 6 | 11 | 17 | 8 | 8 | 4 | 1 | 1 | 1 | 31 | 19.4 |
| 1999–00 | 37 | Washington Capitals | NHL | 5 | 0 | 3 | 3 | 0 | 4 | 0 | 0 | 0 | 0 | 3 | 0.0 |
| 2000–01 | 38 | Washington Capitals | NHL | 6 | 0 | 0 | 0 | -4 | 0 | 0 | 0 | 0 | 0 | 6 | 0.0 |
| 2001–02 | 39 | Philadelphia Flyers | NHL | 5 | 0 | 2 | 2 | -1 | 0 | 0 | 0 | 0 | 0 | 4 | 0.0 |
| 2002–03 | 40 | Mighty Ducks of Anaheim | NHL | 21 | 4 | 9 | 13 | 2 | 6 | 1 | 3 | 0 | 1 | 18 | 22.2 |
| NHL Career — 15 Seasons | | | | 163 | 42 | 114 | 156 | -12 | 66 | 23 | 17 | 2 | 7 | 312 | 13.5 |

# Gilbert Perreault  Profile: See page 139

**REGULAR SEASON**

| SEASON | AGE | TEAM | LG | GP | G | A | PTS | +/- | PIM | ESG | PPG | SHG | GWG | SOG | S% |
|---|---|---|---|---|---|---|---|---|---|---|---|---|---|---|---|
| 1970–71 | 20 | Buffalo Sabres | NHL | 78 | 38 | 34 | 72 | -38 | 19 | 24 | 14 | 0 | 5 | 210 | 18.1 |
| 1971–72 | 21 | Buffalo Sabres | NHL | 76 | 26 | 48 | 74 | -41 | 24 | 15 | 11 | 0 | 1 | 218 | 11.9 |
| 1972–73 | 22 | Buffalo Sabres | NHL | 78 | 28 | 60 | 88 | 11 | 10 | 20 | 8 | 0 | 7 | 234 | 12.0 |
| 1973–74 | 23 | Buffalo Sabres | NHL | 55 | 18 | 33 | 51 | -8 | 10 | 12 | 6 | 0 | 7 | 163 | 11.0 |
| 1974–75 | 24 | Buffalo Sabres | NHL | 68 | 39 | 57 | 96 | 1 | 36 | 27 | 12 | 0 | 8 | 243 | 16.1 |
| 1975–76 | 25 | Buffalo Sabres | NHL | 80 | 44 | 69 | 113 | 17 | 36 | 30 | 14 | 0 | 4 | 237 | 18.6 |

## Gilbert Perreault (continued)

### REGULAR SEASON

| SEASON | AGE | TEAM | LG | GP | G | A | PTS | +/- | PIM | ESG | PPG | SHG | GWG | SOG | S% |
|--------|-----|------|----|----|---|---|-----|-----|-----|-----|-----|-----|-----|-----|-----|
| 1976–77 | 26 | Buffalo Sabres | NHL | 80 | 39 | 56 | 95 | 9 | 30 | 30 | 7 | 2 | 9 | 195 | 20.0 |
| 1977–78 | 27 | Buffalo Sabres | NHL | 79 | 41 | 48 | 89 | 18 | 20 | 34 | 7 | 0 | 7 | 192 | 21.4 |
| 1978–79 | 28 | Buffalo Sabres | NHL | 79 | 27 | 58 | 85 | 12 | 20 | 21 | 6 | 0 | 4 | 172 | 15.7 |
| 1979–80 | 29 | Buffalo Sabres | NHL | 80 | 40 | 66 | 106 | 33 | 57 | 30 | 10 | 0 | 5 | 180 | 22.2 |
| 1980–81 | 30 | Buffalo Sabres | NHL | 56 | 20 | 39 | 59 | 2 | 56 | 15 | 5 | 0 | 3 | 150 | 13.3 |
| 1981–82 | 31 | Buffalo Sabres | NHL | 62 | 31 | 42 | 73 | 19 | 40 | 29 | 2 | 0 | 4 | 155 | 20.0 |
| 1982–83 | 32 | Buffalo Sabres | NHL | 77 | 30 | 46 | 76 | -9 | 34 | 20 | 8 | 2 | 5 | 192 | 15.6 |
| 1983–84 | 33 | Buffalo Sabres | NHL | 73 | 31 | 59 | 90 | 19 | 32 | 21 | 8 | 2 | 7 | 165 | 18.8 |
| 1984–85 | 34 | Buffalo Sabres | NHL | 78 | 30 | 53 | 83 | 8 | 42 | 19 | 10 | 1 | 1 | 172 | 17.4 |
| 1985–86 | 35 | Buffalo Sabres | NHL | 72 | 21 | 39 | 60 | -10 | 28 | 15 | 5 | 1 | 3 | 164 | 12.8 |
| 1986–87 | 36 | Buffalo Sabres | NHL | 20 | 9 | 7 | 16 | -2 | 6 | 8 | 1 | 0 | 1 | 35 | 25.7 |
| NHL Career – 17 Seasons | | | | 1191 | 512 | 814 | 1326 | 41 | 500 | 370 | 134 | 8 | 81 | 3077 | 16.6 |

### PLAYOFFS

| SEASON | AGE | TEAM | LG | GP | G | A | PTS | +/- | PIM | ESG | PPG | SHG | GWG | SOG | S% |
|--------|-----|------|----|----|---|---|-----|-----|-----|-----|-----|-----|-----|-----|-----|
| 1972–73 | 22 | Buffalo Sabres | NHL | 6 | 3 | 7 | 10 | 2 | 2 | 2 | 1 | 0 | 1 | 22 | 13.6 |
| 1974–75 | 24 | Buffalo Sabres | NHL | 17 | 6 | 9 | 15 | -3 | 10 | 2 | 4 | 0 | 1 | 66 | 9.1 |
| 1975–76 | 25 | Buffalo Sabres | NHL | 9 | 4 | 4 | 8 | -2 | 4 | 4 | 0 | 0 | 0 | 24 | 16.7 |
| 1976–77 | 26 | Buffalo Sabres | NHL | 6 | 1 | 8 | 9 | -4 | 4 | 1 | 0 | 0 | 0 | 18 | 5.6 |
| 1977–78 | 27 | Buffalo Sabres | NHL | 8 | 3 | 2 | 5 | -1 | 0 | 3 | 0 | 0 | 1 | 23 | 13.0 |
| 1978–79 | 28 | Buffalo Sabres | NHL | 3 | 1 | 0 | 1 | -2 | 2 | 0 | 1 | 0 | 0 | 11 | 9.1 |
| 1979–80 | 29 | Buffalo Sabres | NHL | 14 | 10 | 11 | 21 | 3 | 8 | 7 | 3 | 0 | 2 | 48 | 20.8 |
| 1980–81 | 30 | Buffalo Sabres | NHL | 8 | 2 | 10 | 12 | -7 | 2 | 2 | 0 | 0 | 0 | 21 | 9.5 |
| 1981–82 | 31 | Buffalo Sabres | NHL | 4 | 0 | 7 | 7 | -1 | 0 | 0 | 0 | 0 | 0 | 10 | 0.0 |
| 1982–83 | 32 | Buffalo Sabres | NHL | 10 | 0 | 7 | 7 | -7 | 8 | 0 | 0 | 0 | 0 | 19 | 0.0 |
| 1984–85 | 34 | Buffalo Sabres | NHL | 5 | 3 | 5 | 8 | 1 | 4 | 2 | 1 | 0 | 0 | 10 | 30.0 |
| NHL Career – 11 Seasons | | | | 90 | 33 | 70 | 103 | -21 | 44 | 23 | 10 | 0 | 5 | 272 | 12.1 |

## Joe Primeau   Profile: See page 140

### REGULAR SEASON

| SEASON | AGE | TEAM | LG | GP | G | A | PTS | PIM |
|--------|-----|------|----|----|---|---|-----|-----|
| 1927–28 | 22 | Toronto Maple Leafs | NHL | 2 | 0 | 0 | 0 | 0 |
| 1928–29 | 23 | Toronto Maple Leafs | NHL | 6 | 0 | 1 | 1 | 2 |
| 1929–30 | 24 | Toronto Maple Leafs | NHL | 43 | 5 | 21 | 26 | 22 |
| 1930–31 | 25 | Toronto Maple Leafs | NHL | 38 | 9 | 32 | 41 | 18 |
| 1931–32 | 26 | Toronto Maple Leafs | NHL | 46 | 13 | 37 | 50 | 25 |
| 1932–33 | 27 | Toronto Maple Leafs | NHL | 48 | 11 | 21 | 32 | 4 |
| 1933–34 | 28 | Toronto Maple Leafs | NHL | 45 | 14 | 32 | 46 | 8 |
| 1934–35 | 29 | Toronto Maple Leafs | NHL | 37 | 10 | 20 | 30 | 16 |
| 1935–36 | 30 | Toronto Maple Leafs | NHL | 45 | 4 | 13 | 17 | 10 |
| NHL Career – 9 Seasons | | | | 310 | 66 | 177 | 243 | 105 |

### PLAYOFFS

| SEASON | AGE | TEAM | LG | GP | G | A | PTS | PIM |
|--------|-----|------|----|----|---|---|-----|-----|
| 1930–31 | 25 | Toronto Maple Leafs | NHL | 2 | 0 | 0 | 0 | 0 |
| 1931–32 | 26 | Toronto Maple Leafs | NHL | 7 | 0 | 6 | 6 | 2 |
| 1932–33 | 27 | Toronto Maple Leafs | NHL | 8 | 0 | 1 | 1 | 4 |
| 1933–34 | 28 | Toronto Maple Leafs | NHL | 5 | 2 | 4 | 6 | 6 |
| 1934–35 | 29 | Toronto Maple Leafs | NHL | 7 | 0 | 3 | 3 | 0 |
| 1935–36 | 30 | Toronto Maple Leafs | NHL | 9 | 3 | 4 | 7 | 0 |
| NHL Career – 6 Seasons | | | | 38 | 5 | 18 | 23 | 12 |

## Jean Ratelle   Profile: See page 141

### REGULAR SEASON

| SEASON | AGE | TEAM | LG | GP | G | A | PTS | +/- | PIM | ESG | PPG | SHG | GWG | SOG | S% |
|--------|-----|------|----|----|---|---|-----|-----|-----|-----|-----|-----|-----|-----|-----|
| 1960–61 | 20 | New York Rangers | NHL | 3 | 2 | 1 | 3 | 1 | 0 | 2 | 0 | 0 | 0 | 7 | 28.6 |
| 1961–62 | 21 | New York Rangers | NHL | 31 | 4 | 8 | 12 | -8 | 4 | 4 | 0 | 0 | 1 | 43 | 9.3 |
| 1962–63 | 22 | New York Rangers | NHL | 47 | 11 | 9 | 20 | -10 | 8 | 11 | 0 | 0 | 3 | 55 | 20.0 |
| 1963–64 | 23 | New York Rangers | NHL | 15 | 0 | 7 | 7 | -3 | 6 | 0 | 0 | 0 | 0 | 22 | 0.0 |
| 1964–65 | 24 | New York Rangers | NHL | 54 | 14 | 21 | 35 | -20 | 14 | 12 | 2 | 0 | 1 | 104 | 13.5 |
| 1965–66 | 25 | New York Rangers | NHL | 67 | 21 | 30 | 51 | -11 | 10 | 17 | 4 | 0 | 2 | 156 | 13.5 |
| 1966–67 | 26 | New York Rangers | NHL | 41 | 6 | 5 | 11 | -8 | 4 | 4 | 2 | 0 | 1 | 51 | 11.8 |
| 1967–68 | 27 | New York Rangers | NHL | 74 | 32 | 46 | 78 | 23 | 18 | 22 | 10 | 0 | 5 | 180 | 17.8 |
| 1968–69 | 28 | New York Rangers | NHL | 75 | 32 | 46 | 78 | 16 | 26 | 24 | 8 | 0 | 4 | 204 | 15.7 |
| 1969–70 | 29 | New York Rangers | NHL | 75 | 32 | 42 | 74 | 7 | 28 | 22 | 10 | 0 | 6 | 198 | 16.2 |
| 1970–71 | 30 | New York Rangers | NHL | 78 | 26 | 46 | 72 | 27 | 14 | 19 | 6 | 1 | 3 | 203 | 12.8 |
| 1971–72 | 31 | New York Rangers | NHL | 63 | 46 | 63 | 109 | 61 | 4 | 40 | 5 | 1 | 6 | 183 | 25.1 |
| 1972–73 | 32 | New York Rangers | NHL | 78 | 41 | 53 | 94 | 24 | 12 | 30 | 11 | 0 | 4 | 241 | 17.0 |
| 1973–74 | 33 | New York Rangers | NHL | 68 | 28 | 39 | 67 | 5 | 16 | 22 | 6 | 0 | 3 | 165 | 17.0 |
| 1974–75 | 34 | New York Rangers | NHL | 79 | 36 | 55 | 91 | 1 | 26 | 20 | 16 | 0 | 6 | 205 | 17.6 |
| 1975–76 | 35 | New York Rangers | NHL | 13 | 5 | 10 | 15 | 3 | 2 | 3 | 2 | 0 | 1 | 28 | 17.9 |
| 1975–76 | 35 | Boston Bruins | NHL | 67 | 31 | 59 | 90 | 17 | 16 | 15 | 15 | 1 | 3 | 186 | 16.7 |
| 1976–77 | 36 | Boston Bruins | NHL | 78 | 33 | 61 | 94 | 18 | 22 | 24 | 8 | 1 | 6 | 185 | 17.8 |
| 1977–78 | 37 | Boston Bruins | NHL | 80 | 25 | 59 | 84 | 48 | 10 | 22 | 3 | 0 | 5 | 156 | 16.0 |
| 1978–79 | 38 | Boston Bruins | NHL | 80 | 27 | 45 | 72 | 17 | 12 | 16 | 11 | 0 | 5 | 137 | 19.7 |
| 1979–80 | 39 | Boston Bruins | NHL | 67 | 28 | 45 | 73 | 10 | 8 | 14 | 14 | 0 | 1 | 145 | 19.3 |
| 1980–81 | 40 | Boston Bruins | NHL | 47 | 11 | 26 | 37 | 18 | 16 | 7 | 4 | 0 | 2 | 62 | 17.7 |
| NHL Career – 21 Seasons | | | | 1280 | 491 | 776 | 1267 | 236 | 276 | 350 | 137 | 4 | 68 | 2916 | 16.8 |

## Jean Ratelle (continued)

### PLAYOFFS

| SEASON | AGE | TEAM | LG | GP | G | A | PTS | +/- | PIM | ESG | PPG | SHG | GWG | SOG | S% |
|---|---|---|---|---|---|---|---|---|---|---|---|---|---|---|---|
| 1966–67 | 26 | New York Rangers | NHL | 4 | 0 | 0 | 0 | -1 | 0 | 0 | 0 | 0 | 0 | 2 | 0.0 |
| 1967–68 | 27 | New York Rangers | NHL | 6 | 0 | 4 | 4 | 2 | 2 | 0 | 0 | 0 | 0 | 8 | 0.0 |
| 1968–69 | 28 | New York Rangers | NHL | 4 | 1 | 0 | 1 | -3 | 0 | 0 | 1 | 0 | 0 | 10 | 10.0 |
| 1969–70 | 29 | New York Rangers | NHL | 6 | 1 | 3 | 4 | -6 | 0 | 1 | 0 | 0 | 0 | 11 | 9.1 |
| 1970–71 | 30 | New York Rangers | NHL | 13 | 2 | 9 | 11 | 3 | 8 | 2 | 0 | 0 | 0 | 19 | 10.5 |
| 1971–72 | 31 | New York Rangers | NHL | 6 | 0 | 1 | 1 | -3 | 0 | 0 | 0 | 0 | 0 | 7 | 0.0 |
| 1972–73 | 32 | New York Rangers | NHL | 10 | 2 | 7 | 9 | 6 | 0 | 1 | 1 | 0 | 0 | 22 | 9.1 |
| 1973–74 | 33 | New York Rangers | NHL | 13 | 2 | 4 | 6 | -7 | 0 | 2 | 0 | 0 | 1 | 29 | 6.9 |
| 1974–75 | 34 | New York Rangers | NHL | 3 | 1 | 5 | 6 | 3 | 2 | 0 | 1 | 0 | 0 | 12 | 8.3 |
| 1975–76 | 35 | Boston Bruins | NHL | 12 | 8 | 8 | 16 | 2 | 4 | 3 | 5 | 0 | 1 | 33 | 24.2 |
| 1976–77 | 36 | Boston Bruins | NHL | 14 | 5 | 12 | 17 | 12 | 4 | 4 | 1 | 0 | 1 | 34 | 14.7 |
| 1977–78 | 37 | Boston Bruins | NHL | 15 | 3 | 7 | 10 | 6 | 0 | 3 | 0 | 0 | 0 | 22 | 13.6 |
| 1978–79 | 38 | Boston Bruins | NHL | 11 | 7 | 6 | 13 | 5 | 2 | 5 | 2 | 0 | 2 | 22 | 31.8 |
| 1979–80 | 39 | Boston Bruins | NHL | 3 | 0 | 0 | 0 | -1 | 0 | 0 | 0 | 0 | 0 | 4 | 0.0 |
| 1980–81 | 40 | Boston Bruins | NHL | 3 | 0 | 0 | 0 | -3 | 0 | 0 | 0 | 0 | 0 | 1 | 0.0 |
| NHL Career — 15 Seasons | | | | 123 | 32 | 66 | 98 | 15 | 22 | 21 | 11 | 0 | 5 | 236 | 13.6 |

## Henri Richard   Profile: See page 142

### REGULAR SEASON

| SEASON | AGE | TEAM | LG | GP | G | A | PTS | +/- | PIM | ESG | PPG | SHG | GWG | SOG | S% |
|---|---|---|---|---|---|---|---|---|---|---|---|---|---|---|---|
| 1955–56 | 19 | Montreal Canadiens | NHL | 64 | 19 | 21 | 40 | | 46 | 17 | 2 | 0 | 5 | | |
| 1956–57 | 20 | Montreal Canadiens | NHL | 63 | 18 | 36 | 54 | | 71 | 15 | 3 | 0 | 2 | | |
| 1957–58 | 21 | Montreal Canadiens | NHL | 67 | 28 | 52 | 80 | | 58 | 22 | 6 | 0 | 3 | | |
| 1958–59 | 22 | Montreal Canadiens | NHL | 63 | 21 | 30 | 51 | | 33 | 19 | 2 | 0 | 1 | | |
| 1959–60 | 23 | Montreal Canadiens | NHL | 70 | 30 | 43 | 73 | 21 | 66 | 24 | 6 | 0 | 3 | 223 | 13.5 |
| 1960–61 | 24 | Montreal Canadiens | NHL | 70 | 24 | 44 | 68 | 18 | 91 | 20 | 4 | 0 | 4 | 274 | 8.8 |
| 1961–62 | 25 | Montreal Canadiens | NHL | 53 | 21 | 29 | 50 | 21 | 48 | 18 | 3 | 0 | 5 | 191 | 11.0 |
| 1962–63 | 26 | Montreal Canadiens | NHL | 67 | 23 | 50 | 73 | 24 | 57 | 21 | 2 | 0 | 2 | 289 | 8.0 |
| 1963–64 | 27 | Montreal Canadiens | NHL | 66 | 14 | 39 | 53 | 10 | 73 | 13 | 1 | 0 | 1 | 258 | 5.4 |
| 1964–65 | 28 | Montreal Canadiens | NHL | 53 | 23 | 29 | 52 | 16 | 43 | 18 | 5 | 0 | 5 | 199 | 11.6 |
| 1965–66 | 29 | Montreal Canadiens | NHL | 62 | 22 | 39 | 61 | 6 | 47 | 19 | 3 | 0 | 7 | 240 | 9.2 |
| 1966–67 | 30 | Montreal Canadiens | NHL | 65 | 21 | 34 | 55 | 2 | 28 | 19 | 2 | 0 | 1 | 247 | 8.5 |
| 1967–68 | 31 | Montreal Canadiens | NHL | 54 | 9 | 19 | 28 | 4 | 16 | 7 | 2 | 0 | 3 | 123 | 7.3 |
| 1968–69 | 32 | Montreal Canadiens | NHL | 64 | 15 | 37 | 52 | 24 | 47 | 13 | 2 | 0 | 0 | 210 | 7.1 |
| 1969–70 | 33 | Montreal Canadiens | NHL | 62 | 16 | 36 | 52 | 25 | 61 | 14 | 2 | 0 | 4 | 204 | 7.8 |
| 1970–71 | 34 | Montreal Canadiens | NHL | 75 | 12 | 37 | 49 | 13 | 46 | 11 | 1 | 0 | 1 | 226 | 5.3 |
| 1971–72 | 35 | Montreal Canadiens | NHL | 78 | 12 | 32 | 44 | 10 | 48 | 12 | 0 | 0 | 1 | 175 | 6.9 |
| 1972–73 | 36 | Montreal Canadiens | NHL | 71 | 8 | 35 | 43 | 34 | 21 | 8 | 0 | 0 | 2 | 133 | 6.0 |
| 1973–74 | 37 | Montreal Canadiens | NHL | 75 | 19 | 36 | 55 | 7 | 28 | 18 | 1 | 0 | 3 | 175 | 10.9 |
| 1974–75 | 38 | Montreal Canadiens | NHL | 16 | 3 | 10 | 13 | 9 | 4 | 3 | 0 | 0 | 0 | 32 | 9.4 |
| NHL Career — 20 Seasons | | | | 1258 | 358 | 688 | 1046 | 243 | 932 | 311 | 47 | 0 | 53 | 3199 | 8.5 |

### PLAYOFFS

| SEASON | AGE | TEAM | LG | GP | G | A | PTS | +/- | PIM | ESG | PPG | SHG | GWG | SOG | S% |
|---|---|---|---|---|---|---|---|---|---|---|---|---|---|---|---|
| 1955–56 | 19 | Montreal Canadiens | NHL | 10 | 4 | 4 | 8 | | 21 | 4 | 0 | 0 | 1 | | |
| 1956–57 | 20 | Montreal Canadiens | NHL | 10 | 2 | 6 | 8 | | 10 | 2 | 0 | 0 | 1 | | |
| 1957–58 | 21 | Montreal Canadiens | NHL | 10 | 1 | 7 | 8 | | 11 | 1 | 0 | 0 | 0 | | |
| 1958–59 | 22 | Montreal Canadiens | NHL | 11 | 3 | 8 | 11 | | 13 | 3 | 0 | 0 | 0 | | |
| 1959–60 | 23 | Montreal Canadiens | NHL | 8 | 3 | 9 | 12 | 6 | 9 | 3 | 0 | 0 | 0 | 26 | 11.5 |
| 1960–61 | 24 | Montreal Canadiens | NHL | 6 | 2 | 4 | 6 | 2 | 22 | 1 | 1 | 0 | 0 | 18 | 11.1 |
| 1962–63 | 26 | Montreal Canadiens | NHL | 5 | 1 | 1 | 2 | 0 | 2 | 1 | 0 | 0 | 0 | 18 | 5.6 |
| 1963–64 | 27 | Montreal Canadiens | NHL | 7 | 1 | 1 | 2 | -1 | 9 | 1 | 0 | 0 | 0 | 23 | 4.3 |
| 1964–65 | 28 | Montreal Canadiens | NHL | 13 | 7 | 4 | 11 | -5 | 24 | 3 | 4 | 0 | 0 | 49 | 14.3 |
| 1965–66 | 29 | Montreal Canadiens | NHL | 8 | 1 | 4 | 5 | 3 | 2 | 1 | 0 | 0 | 1 | 18 | 5.6 |
| 1966–67 | 30 | Montreal Canadiens | NHL | 10 | 4 | 6 | 10 | 4 | 2 | 4 | 0 | 0 | 0 | 48 | 4.3 |
| 1967–68 | 31 | Montreal Canadiens | NHL | 13 | 4 | 4 | 8 | 5 | 4 | 3 | 1 | 0 | 0 | 28 | 14.3 |
| 1968–69 | 32 | Montreal Canadiens | NHL | 14 | 2 | 4 | 6 | 0 | 8 | 2 | 0 | 0 | 0 | 37 | 5.4 |
| 1970–71 | 34 | Montreal Canadiens | NHL | 20 | 5 | 7 | 12 | 4 | 20 | 5 | 0 | 0 | 1 | 41 | 12.2 |
| 1971–72 | 35 | Montreal Canadiens | NHL | 6 | 0 | 3 | 3 | 2 | 4 | 0 | 0 | 0 | 0 | 9 | 0.0 |
| 1972–73 | 36 | Montreal Canadiens | NHL | 17 | 6 | 4 | 10 | 2 | 14 | 6 | 0 | 0 | 2 | 49 | 12.2 |
| 1973–74 | 37 | Montreal Canadiens | NHL | 6 | 2 | 2 | 4 | 2 | 2 | 2 | 0 | 0 | 0 | 15 | 13.3 |
| 1974–75 | 38 | Montreal Canadiens | NHL | 6 | 1 | 2 | 3 | -3 | 4 | 1 | 0 | 0 | 0 | 9 | 11.1 |
| NHL Career — 18 Seasons | | | | 180 | 49 | 80 | 129 | 21 | 181 | 43 | 6 | 0 | 9 | 388 | 10.1 |

## Joe Sakic  Profile: See page 144

### REGULAR SEASON

| SEASON | AGE | TEAM | LG | GP | G | A | PTS | +/- | PIM | ESG | PPG | SHG | GWG | SOG | S% |
|---|---|---|---|---|---|---|---|---|---|---|---|---|---|---|---|
| 1988–89 | 19 | Quebec Nordiques | NHL | 70 | 23 | 39 | 62 | -36 | 24 | 13 | 10 | 0 | 2 | 148 | 15.5 |
| 1989–90 | 20 | Quebec Nordiques | NHL | 80 | 39 | 63 | 102 | -40 | 27 | 30 | 8 | 1 | 2 | 234 | 16.7 |
| 1990–91 | 21 | Quebec Nordiques | NHL | 80 | 48 | 61 | 109 | -26 | 24 | 33 | 12 | 3 | 7 | 245 | 19.6 |
| 1991–92 | 22 | Quebec Nordiques | NHL | 69 | 29 | 65 | 94 | 5 | 20 | 20 | 6 | 3 | 1 | 217 | 13.4 |
| 1992–93 | 23 | Quebec Nordiques | NHL | 78 | 48 | 57 | 105 | -3 | 40 | 26 | 20 | 2 | 4 | 264 | 18.2 |
| 1993–94 | 24 | Quebec Nordiques | NHL | 84 | 28 | 64 | 92 | -8 | 18 | 17 | 10 | 1 | 9 | 279 | 10.0 |
| 1994–95 | 25 | Quebec Nordiques | NHL | 47 | 19 | 43 | 62 | 7 | 30 | 14 | 3 | 2 | 5 | 157 | 12.1 |
| 1995–96 | 26 | Colorado Avalanche | NHL | 82 | 51 | 69 | 120 | 14 | 44 | 28 | 17 | 6 | 7 | 339 | 15.0 |
| 1996–97 | 27 | Colorado Avalanche | NHL | 65 | 22 | 52 | 74 | -10 | 34 | 10 | 10 | 2 | 5 | 261 | 8.4 |
| 1997–98 | 28 | Colorado Avalanche | NHL | 64 | 27 | 36 | 63 | 0 | 50 | 14 | 12 | 1 | 2 | 254 | 10.6 |
| 1998–99 | 29 | Colorado Avalanche | NHL | 73 | 41 | 55 | 96 | 23 | 29 | 24 | 12 | 5 | 6 | 255 | 16.1 |
| 1999–00 | 30 | Colorado Avalanche | NHL | 60 | 28 | 53 | 81 | 30 | 28 | 22 | 5 | 1 | 5 | 242 | 11.6 |
| 2000–01 | 31 | Colorado Avalanche | NHL | 82 | 54 | 64 | 118 | 45 | 30 | 32 | 19 | 3 | 12 | 332 | 16.3 |
| 2001–02 | 32 | Colorado Avalanche | NHL | 82 | 26 | 53 | 79 | 12 | 18 | 16 | 9 | 1 | 4 | 260 | 10.0 |
| 2002–03 | 33 | Colorado Avalanche | NHL | 58 | 26 | 32 | 58 | 4 | 24 | 18 | 8 | 0 | 1 | 190 | 13.7 |
| 2003–04 | 34 | Colorado Avalanche | NHL | 81 | 33 | 54 | 87 | 11 | 42 | 19 | 13 | 1 | 3 | 253 | 13.0 |
| 2005–06 | 36 | Colorado Avalanche | NHL | 82 | 32 | 55 | 87 | 10 | 60 | 22 | 10 | 0 | 6 | 263 | 12.2 |
| 2006–07 | 37 | Colorado Avalanche | NHL | 82 | 36 | 64 | 100 | 2 | 46 | 20 | 16 | 0 | 4 | 258 | 14.0 |
| 2007–08 | 38 | Colorado Avalanche | NHL | 44 | 13 | 27 | 40 | -4 | 20 | 8 | 5 | 0 | 1 | 124 | 10.5 |
| 2008–09 | 39 | Colorado Avalanche | NHL | 15 | 2 | 10 | 12 | -6 | 6 | 2 | 0 | 0 | 0 | 46 | 4.3 |
| NHL Career — 20 Seasons | | | | 1378 | 625 | 1016 | 1641 | 30 | 614 | 388 | 205 | 32 | 86 | 4621 | 13.5 |

### PLAYOFFS

| SEASON | AGE | TEAM | LG | GP | G | A | PTS | +/- | PIM | ESG | PPG | SHG | GWG | SOG | S% |
|---|---|---|---|---|---|---|---|---|---|---|---|---|---|---|---|
| 1992–93 | 23 | Quebec Nordiques | NHL | 6 | 3 | 3 | 6 | -3 | 2 | 2 | 1 | 0 | 0 | 24 | 12.5 |
| 1994–95 | 25 | Quebec Nordiques | NHL | 6 | 4 | 1 | 5 | -4 | 0 | 2 | 1 | 1 | 1 | 15 | 26.7 |
| 1995–96 | 26 | Colorado Avalanche | NHL | 22 | 18 | 16 | 34 | 10 | 14 | 12 | 6 | 0 | 6 | 98 | 18.4 |
| 1996–97 | 27 | Colorado Avalanche | NHL | 17 | 8 | 17 | 25 | 5 | 14 | 5 | 3 | 0 | 0 | 50 | 16.0 |
| 1997–98 | 28 | Colorado Avalanche | NHL | 6 | 2 | 3 | 5 | 0 | 6 | 1 | 0 | 1 | 2 | 24 | 8.3 |
| 1998–99 | 29 | Colorado Avalanche | NHL | 19 | 6 | 13 | 19 | -2 | 8 | 4 | 1 | 1 | 1 | 56 | 10.7 |
| 1999–00 | 30 | Colorado Avalanche | NHL | 17 | 2 | 7 | 9 | -5 | 8 | 0 | 2 | 0 | 0 | 48 | 4.2 |
| 2000–01 | 31 | Colorado Avalanche | NHL | 21 | 13 | 13 | 26 | 6 | 6 | 8 | 5 | 0 | 3 | 79 | 16.5 |
| 2001–02 | 32 | Colorado Avalanche | NHL | 21 | 9 | 10 | 19 | -2 | 4 | 5 | 4 | 0 | 1 | 76 | 11.8 |
| 2002–03 | 33 | Colorado Avalanche | NHL | 7 | 6 | 3 | 9 | 1 | 2 | 4 | 2 | 0 | 1 | 26 | 23.1 |
| 2003–04 | 34 | Colorado Avalanche | NHL | 11 | 7 | 5 | 12 | 0 | 8 | 5 | 1 | 1 | 2 | 35 | 20.0 |
| 2005–06 | 36 | Colorado Avalanche | NHL | 9 | 4 | 5 | 9 | -1 | 6 | 3 | 1 | 0 | 1 | 21 | 19.0 |
| 2007–08 | 38 | Colorado Avalanche | NHL | 10 | 2 | 8 | 10 | -7 | 0 | 2 | 0 | 0 | 1 | 30 | 6.7 |
| NHL Career — 13 Seasons | | | | 172 | 84 | 104 | 188 | -2 | 78 | 53 | 27 | 4 | 19 | 582 | 14.4 |

## Denis Savard  Profile: See page 146

### REGULAR SEASON

| SEASON | AGE | TEAM | LG | GP | G | A | PTS | +/- | PIM | ESG | PPG | SHG | GWG | SOG | S% |
|---|---|---|---|---|---|---|---|---|---|---|---|---|---|---|---|
| 1980–81 | 19 | Chicago Black Hawks | NHL | 76 | 28 | 47 | 75 | 27 | 47 | 24 | 4 | 0 | 3 | 159 | 17.6 |
| 1981–82 | 20 | Chicago Black Hawks | NHL | 80 | 32 | 87 | 119 | 0 | 82 | 24 | 8 | 0 | 4 | 231 | 13.9 |
| 1982–83 | 21 | Chicago Black Hawks | NHL | 78 | 35 | 86 | 121 | 26 | 99 | 22 | 13 | 0 | 4 | 212 | 16.5 |
| 1983–84 | 22 | Chicago Black Hawks | NHL | 75 | 37 | 57 | 94 | -12 | 71 | 25 | 12 | 0 | 5 | 211 | 17.5 |
| 1984–85 | 23 | Chicago Black Hawks | NHL | 79 | 38 | 67 | 105 | 16 | 56 | 31 | 7 | 0 | 1 | 265 | 14.3 |
| 1985–86 | 24 | Chicago Blackhawks | NHL | 80 | 47 | 69 | 116 | 10 | 111 | 32 | 14 | 1 | 8 | 281 | 16.7 |
| 1986–87 | 25 | Chicago Blackhawks | NHL | 70 | 40 | 50 | 90 | 17 | 108 | 33 | 7 | 0 | 7 | 235 | 17.0 |
| 1987–88 | 26 | Chicago Blackhawks | NHL | 80 | 44 | 87 | 131 | 4 | 95 | 23 | 14 | 7 | 6 | 270 | 16.3 |
| 1988–89 | 27 | Chicago Blackhawks | NHL | 58 | 23 | 59 | 82 | -5 | 110 | 11 | 7 | 5 | 1 | 182 | 12.6 |
| 1989–90 | 28 | Chicago Blackhawks | NHL | 60 | 27 | 53 | 80 | 8 | 56 | 15 | 10 | 2 | 4 | 181 | 14.9 |
| 1990–91 | 29 | Montreal Canadiens | NHL | 70 | 28 | 31 | 59 | -1 | 52 | 19 | 7 | 2 | 0 | 187 | 15.0 |
| 1991–92 | 30 | Montreal Canadiens | NHL | 77 | 28 | 42 | 70 | 6 | 73 | 15 | 12 | 1 | 5 | 174 | 16.1 |
| 1992–93 | 31 | Montreal Canadiens | NHL | 63 | 16 | 34 | 50 | 1 | 90 | 11 | 4 | 1 | 2 | 99 | 16.2 |
| 1993–94 | 32 | Tampa Bay Lightning | NHL | 74 | 18 | 28 | 46 | -1 | 106 | 15 | 1 | 2 | 2 | 181 | 9.9 |
| 1994–95 | 33 | Tampa Bay Lightning | NHL | 31 | 6 | 11 | 17 | -6 | 10 | 5 | 1 | 0 | 1 | 56 | 10.7 |
| 1994–95 | 33 | Chicago Blackhawks | NHL | 12 | 4 | 4 | 8 | 3 | 8 | 3 | 1 | 0 | 0 | 26 | 15.4 |
| 1995–96 | 34 | Chicago Blackhawks | NHL | 69 | 13 | 35 | 48 | 20 | 102 | 11 | 2 | 0 | 1 | 110 | 11.8 |
| 1996–97 | 35 | Chicago Blackhawks | NHL | 64 | 9 | 18 | 27 | -10 | 60 | 7 | 2 | 0 | 2 | 82 | 11.0 |
| NHL Career — 17 Seasons | | | | 1196 | 473 | 865 | 1338 | 103 | 1336 | 326 | 127 | 20 | 56 | 3142 | 15.1 |

### PLAYOFFS

| SEASON | AGE | TEAM | LG | GP | G | A | PTS | +/- | PIM | ESG | PPG | SHG | GWG | SOG | S% |
|---|---|---|---|---|---|---|---|---|---|---|---|---|---|---|---|
| 1980–81 | 19 | Chicago Black Hawks | NHL | 3 | 0 | 0 | 0 | -4 | 0 | 0 | 0 | 0 | 0 | 6 | 0.0 |
| 1981–82 | 20 | Chicago Black Hawks | NHL | 15 | 11 | 7 | 18 | -2 | 52 | 6 | 5 | 0 | 2 | 57 | 19.3 |
| 1982–83 | 21 | Chicago Black Hawks | NHL | 13 | 8 | 9 | 17 | 3 | 22 | 5 | 3 | 0 | 1 | 47 | 17.0 |
| 1983–84 | 22 | Chicago Black Hawks | NHL | 5 | 1 | 3 | 4 | 3 | 9 | 1 | 0 | 0 | 0 | 8 | 12.5 |
| 1984–85 | 23 | Chicago Black Hawks | NHL | 15 | 9 | 20 | 29 | 4 | 20 | 6 | 3 | 0 | 0 | 49 | 18.4 |

## Denis Savard (continued)

**PLAYOFFS**

| SEASON | AGE | TEAM | LG | GP | G | A | PTS | +/- | PIM | ESG | PPG | SHG | GWG | SOG | S% |
|---|---|---|---|---|---|---|---|---|---|---|---|---|---|---|---|
| 1985–86 | 24 | Chicago Black Hawks | NHL | 3 | 4 | 1 | 5 | -1 | 6 | 2 | 2 | 0 | 0 | 16 | 25.0 |
| 1986–87 | 25 | Chicago Blackhawks | NHL | 4 | 1 | 0 | 1 | -3 | 10 | 1 | 0 | 0 | 0 | 8 | 12.5 |
| 1987–88 | 26 | Chicago Blackhawks | NHL | 5 | 4 | 3 | 7 | 3 | 17 | 3 | 0 | 1 | 1 | 13 | 30.8 |
| 1988–89 | 27 | Chicago Blackhawks | NHL | 16 | 8 | 11 | 19 | 8 | 10 | 5 | 2 | 1 | 1 | 68 | 11.8 |
| 1989–90 | 28 | Chicago Blackhawks | NHL | 20 | 7 | 15 | 22 | 0 | 41 | 3 | 4 | 0 | 1 | 69 | 10.1 |
| 1990–91 | 29 | Montreal Canadiens | NHL | 13 | 2 | 11 | 13 | -1 | 35 | 1 | 1 | 0 | 0 | 33 | 6.1 |
| 1991–92 | 30 | Montreal Canadiens | NHL | 11 | 3 | 9 | 12 | 1 | 8 | 2 | 1 | 0 | 0 | 33 | 9.1 |
| 1992–93 | 31 | Montreal Canadiens | NHL | 14 | 0 | 5 | 5 | -3 | 4 | 0 | 0 | 0 | 0 | 15 | 0.0 |
| 1994–95 | 33 | Chicago Blackhawks | NHL | 16 | 7 | 11 | 18 | 12 | 10 | 4 | 3 | 0 | 0 | 39 | 17.9 |
| 1995–96 | 34 | Chicago Blackhawks | NHL | 10 | 1 | 2 | 3 | 0 | 8 | 1 | 0 | 0 | 0 | 12 | 8.3 |
| 1996–97 | 35 | Chicago Blackhawks | NHL | 6 | 0 | 2 | 2 | -3 | 2 | 0 | 0 | 0 | 0 | 14 | 0.0 |
| NHL Career – 16 Seasons | | | | 169 | 66 | 109 | 175 | 17 | 254 | 40 | 24 | 2 | 6 | 487 | 13.6 |

## Milt Schmidt   Profile: See page 147

**REGULAR SEASON**

| SEASON | AGE | TEAM | LG | GP | G | A | PTS | PIM |
|---|---|---|---|---|---|---|---|---|
| 1936–37 | 18 | Boston Bruins | NHL | 26 | 2 | 8 | 10 | 15 |
| 1937–38 | 19 | Boston Bruins | NHL | 44 | 13 | 14 | 27 | 15 |
| 1938–39 | 20 | Boston Bruins | NHL | 41 | 15 | 17 | 32 | 13 |
| 1939–40 | 21 | Boston Bruins | NHL | 48 | 22 | 30 | 52 | 37 |
| 1940–41 | 22 | Boston Bruins | NHL | 45 | 13 | 25 | 38 | 23 |
| 1941–42 | 23 | Boston Bruins | NHL | 36 | 14 | 21 | 35 | 34 |
| 1945–46 | 27 | Boston Bruins | NHL | 48 | 13 | 18 | 31 | 21 |
| 1946–47 | 28 | Boston Bruins | NHL | 59 | 27 | 35 | 62 | 40 |
| 1947–48 | 29 | Boston Bruins | NHL | 33 | 9 | 17 | 26 | 28 |
| 1948–49 | 30 | Boston Bruins | NHL | 44 | 10 | 22 | 32 | 25 |
| 1949–50 | 31 | Boston Bruins | NHL | 68 | 19 | 22 | 41 | 41 |
| 1950–51 | 32 | Boston Bruins | NHL | 62 | 22 | 39 | 61 | 33 |
| 1951–52 | 33 | Boston Bruins | NHL | 69 | 21 | 29 | 50 | 57 |
| 1952–53 | 34 | Boston Bruins | NHL | 68 | 11 | 23 | 34 | 30 |
| 1953–54 | 35 | Boston Bruins | NHL | 62 | 14 | 18 | 32 | 28 |
| 1954–55 | 36 | Boston Bruins | NHL | 23 | 4 | 8 | 12 | 26 |
| NHL Career – 16 Seasons | | | | 776 | 229 | 346 | 575 | 466 |

**PLAYOFFS**

| SEASON | AGE | TEAM | LG | GP | G | A | PTS | PIM |
|---|---|---|---|---|---|---|---|---|
| 1936–37 | 18 | Boston Bruins | NHL | 3 | 0 | 0 | 0 | 0 |
| 1937–38 | 19 | Boston Bruins | NHL | 3 | 0 | 0 | 0 | 0 |
| 1938–39 | 20 | Boston Bruins | NHL | 12 | 3 | 3 | 6 | 2 |
| 1939–40 | 21 | Boston Bruins | NHL | 6 | 0 | 0 | 0 | 4 |
| 1940–41 | 22 | Boston Bruins | NHL | 11 | 5 | 6 | 11 | 9 |
| 1945–46 | 27 | Boston Bruins | NHL | 10 | 3 | 5 | 8 | 2 |
| 1946–47 | 28 | Boston Bruins | NHL | 5 | 3 | 1 | 4 | 4 |
| 1947–48 | 29 | Boston Bruins | NHL | 5 | 2 | 5 | 7 | 2 |
| 1948–49 | 30 | Boston Bruins | NHL | 4 | 0 | 2 | 2 | 8 |
| 1950–51 | 32 | Boston Bruins | NHL | 6 | 0 | 1 | 1 | 7 |
| 1951–52 | 33 | Boston Bruins | NHL | 7 | 2 | 1 | 3 | 0 |
| 1952–53 | 34 | Boston Bruins | NHL | 10 | 5 | 1 | 6 | 6 |
| 1953–54 | 35 | Boston Bruins | NHL | 4 | 1 | 0 | 1 | 20 |
| NHL Career – 13 Seasons | | | | 86 | 24 | 25 | 49 | 64 |

## Oliver Seibert   Profile: See page 148

**REGULAR SEASON**

| SEASON | AGE | TEAM | LG | GP | G | A | PTS |
|---|---|---|---|---|---|---|---|
| 1899–00 | 18 | Berlin Hockey Club | WOHA | 8 | 10 | 0 | 10 |
| 1900–01 | 19 | Berlin Hockey Club | WOHA | 6 | 13 | 0 | 13 |
| 1901–02 | 20 | Berlin Hockey Club | WOHA | 8 | 17 | 0 | 17 |
| 1902–03 | 21 | Guelph OAC | OHA-Sr | | | | |

**REGULAR SEASON**

| SEASON | AGE | TEAM | LG | GP | G | A | PTS |
|---|---|---|---|---|---|---|---|
| 1903–04 | 22 | Berlin Hockey Club | WOHA | | | | |
| 1904–05 | 23 | Canadian Soo | IHL | 1 | 0 | 0 | 0 |
| Career – 6 Seasons | | | | 23 | 40 | 0 | 40 |

## Darryl Sittler   Profile: See page 149

**REGULAR SEASON**

| SEASON | AGE | TEAM | LG | GP | G | A | PTS | +/- | PIM | ESG | PPG | SHG | GWG | SOG | S% |
|---|---|---|---|---|---|---|---|---|---|---|---|---|---|---|---|
| 1970–71 | 20 | Toronto Maple Leafs | NHL | 49 | 10 | 8 | 18 | 2 | 37 | 7 | 2 | 0 | 3 | 131 | 7.6 |
| 1971–72 | 21 | Toronto Maple Leafs | NHL | 74 | 15 | 17 | 32 | -1 | 44 | 14 | 1 | 0 | 4 | 174 | 8.6 |
| 1972–73 | 22 | Toronto Maple Leafs | NHL | 78 | 29 | 48 | 77 | -12 | 69 | 21 | 8 | 0 | 1 | 331 | 8.8 |
| 1973–74 | 23 | Toronto Maple Leafs | NHL | 78 | 38 | 46 | 84 | 12 | 55 | 27 | 11 | 0 | 6 | 270 | 14.1 |
| 1974–75 | 24 | Toronto Maple Leafs | NHL | 72 | 36 | 44 | 80 | -10 | 47 | 23 | 12 | 1 | 2 | 273 | 13.2 |
| 1975–76 | 25 | Toronto Maple Leafs | NHL | 79 | 41 | 59 | 100 | 12 | 90 | 29 | 11 | 1 | 2 | 346 | 11.9 |
| 1976–77 | 26 | Toronto Maple Leafs | NHL | 73 | 38 | 52 | 90 | 7 | 89 | 25 | 12 | 1 | 5 | 307 | 12.4 |
| 1977–78 | 27 | Toronto Maple Leafs | NHL | 80 | 45 | 72 | 117 | 34 | 100 | 31 | 14 | 0 | 8 | 311 | 14.5 |
| 1978–79 | 28 | Toronto Maple Leafs | NHL | 70 | 36 | 51 | 87 | 9 | 69 | 24 | 12 | 0 | 4 | 290 | 12.4 |
| 1979–80 | 29 | Toronto Maple Leafs | NHL | 73 | 40 | 57 | 97 | 3 | 62 | 22 | 17 | 1 | 5 | 315 | 12.7 |
| 1980–81 | 30 | Toronto Maple Leafs | NHL | 80 | 43 | 53 | 96 | -8 | 77 | 27 | 14 | 2 | 2 | 267 | 16.1 |
| 1981–82 | 31 | Toronto Maple Leafs | NHL | 38 | 18 | 20 | 38 | -13 | 24 | 11 | 5 | 2 | 0 | 127 | 14.2 |
| 1981–82 | 31 | Philadelphia Flyers | NHL | 35 | 14 | 18 | 32 | -1 | 50 | 8 | 5 | 1 | 2 | 114 | 12.3 |
| 1982–83 | 32 | Philadelphia Flyers | NHL | 80 | 43 | 40 | 83 | 17 | 60 | 33 | 10 | 0 | 8 | 231 | 18.6 |
| 1983–84 | 33 | Philadelphia Flyers | NHL | 76 | 27 | 36 | 63 | 13 | 38 | 15 | 11 | 1 | 3 | 213 | 12.7 |
| 1984–85 | 34 | Detroit Red Wings | NHL | 61 | 11 | 16 | 27 | -7 | 37 | 7 | 4 | 0 | 2 | 115 | 9.6 |
| NHL Career – 15 Seasons | | | | 1096 | 484 | 637 | 1121 | 57 | 948 | 324 | 150 | 10 | 57 | 3815 | 12.7 |

### Darryl Sittler (continued)

**PLAYOFFS**

| SEASON | AGE | TEAM | LG | GP | G | A | PTS | +/- | PIM | ESG | PPG | SHG | GWG | SOG | S% |
|---|---|---|---|---|---|---|---|---|---|---|---|---|---|---|---|
| 1970–71 | 20 | Toronto Maple Leafs | NHL | 6 | 2 | 1 | 3 | -2 | 31 | 1 | 1 | 0 | 0 | 12 | 16.7 |
| 1971–72 | 21 | Toronto Maple Leafs | NHL | 3 | 0 | 0 | 0 | -1 | 2 | 0 | 0 | 0 | 0 | 3 | 0.0 |
| 1973–74 | 23 | Toronto Maple Leafs | NHL | 4 | 2 | 1 | 3 | -1 | 6 | 1 | 1 | 0 | 0 | 15 | 13.3 |
| 1974–75 | 24 | Toronto Maple Leafs | NHL | 7 | 2 | 1 | 3 | -2 | 15 | 1 | 1 | 0 | 0 | 20 | 10.0 |
| 1975–76 | 25 | Toronto Maple Leafs | NHL | 10 | 5 | 7 | 12 | -4 | 19 | 3 | 2 | 0 | 1 | 42 | 11.9 |
| 1976–77 | 26 | Toronto Maple Leafs | NHL | 9 | 5 | 16 | 21 | -1 | 4 | 2 | 3 | 0 | 0 | 34 | 14.7 |
| 1977–78 | 27 | Toronto Maple Leafs | NHL | 13 | 3 | 8 | 11 | -3 | 12 | 1 | 2 | 0 | 0 | 53 | 5.7 |
| 1978–79 | 28 | Toronto Maple Leafs | NHL | 6 | 5 | 4 | 9 | 3 | 17 | 3 | 2 | 0 | 0 | 23 | 21.7 |
| 1979–80 | 29 | Toronto Maple Leafs | NHL | 3 | 1 | 2 | 3 | -1 | 10 | 0 | 1 | 0 | 0 | 14 | 7.1 |
| 1980–81 | 30 | Toronto Maple Leafs | NHL | 3 | 0 | 0 | 0 | -2 | 4 | 0 | 0 | 0 | 0 | 6 | 0.0 |
| 1981–82 | 31 | Philadelphia Flyers | NHL | 4 | 3 | 1 | 4 | -2 | 6 | 2 | 1 | 0 | 0 | 11 | 27.3 |
| 1982–83 | 32 | Philadelphia Flyers | NHL | 3 | 1 | 0 | 1 | -4 | 4 | 1 | 0 | 0 | 0 | 11 | 9.1 |
| 1983–84 | 33 | Philadelphia Flyers | NHL | 3 | 0 | 2 | 2 | -1 | 7 | 0 | 0 | 0 | 0 | 6 | 0.0 |
| 1984–85 | 34 | Detroit Red Wings | NHL | 2 | 0 | 2 | 2 | 0 | 0 | 0 | 0 | 0 | 0 | 2 | 0.0 |
| NHL Career—14 Seasons | | | | 76 | 29 | 45 | 74 | -21 | 137 | 15 | 14 | 0 | 1 | 252 | 11.5 |

## Clint Smith   Profile: See page 150

**REGULAR SEASON**

| SEASON | AGE | TEAM | LG | GP | G | A | PTS | PIM |
|---|---|---|---|---|---|---|---|---|
| 1936–37 | 23 | New York Rangers | NHL | 2 | 1 | 0 | 1 | 0 |
| 1937–38 | 24 | New York Rangers | NHL | 48 | 14 | 23 | 37 | 0 |
| 1938–39 | 25 | New York Rangers | NHL | 48 | 21 | 20 | 41 | 2 |
| 1939–40 | 26 | New York Rangers | NHL | 41 | 8 | 16 | 24 | 2 |
| 1940–41 | 27 | New York Rangers | NHL | 48 | 14 | 11 | 25 | 0 |
| 1941–42 | 28 | New York Rangers | NHL | 47 | 10 | 25 | 35 | 4 |
| 1942–43 | 29 | New York Rangers | NHL | 47 | 12 | 21 | 33 | 4 |
| 1943–44 | 30 | Chicago Black Hawks | NHL | 50 | 23 | 49 | 72 | 4 |
| 1944–45 | 31 | Chicago Black Hawks | NHL | 50 | 23 | 31 | 54 | 0 |
| 1945–46 | 32 | Chicago Black Hawks | NHL | 50 | 26 | 24 | 50 | 2 |
| 1946–47 | 33 | Chicago Black Hawks | NHL | 52 | 9 | 17 | 26 | 6 |
| NHL Career—11 Seasons | | | | 483 | 161 | 236 | 398 | 24 |

**PLAYOFFS**

| SEASON | AGE | TEAM | LG | GP | G | A | PTS | PIM |
|---|---|---|---|---|---|---|---|---|
| 1937–38 | 24 | New York Rangers | NHL | 3 | 2 | 0 | 2 | 0 |
| 1938–39 | 25 | New York Rangers | NHL | 7 | 1 | 2 | 3 | 0 |
| 1939–40 | 26 | New York Rangers | NHL | 11 | 1 | 3 | 4 | 2 |
| 1940–41 | 27 | New York Rangers | NHL | 3 | 0 | 0 | 0 | 0 |
| 1941–42 | 28 | New York Rangers | NHL | 5 | 0 | 0 | 0 | 0 |
| 1943–44 | 30 | Chicago Black Hawks | NHL | 9 | 4 | 8 | 12 | 0 |
| 1945–46 | 32 | Chicago Black Hawks | NHL | 4 | 2 | 1 | 3 | 0 |
| NHL Career—7 Seasons | | | | 42 | 10 | 14 | 24 | 2 |

## Hooley Smith   Profile: See page 151

**REGULAR SEASON**

| SEASON | AGE | TEAM | LG | GP | G | A | PTS | PIM |
|---|---|---|---|---|---|---|---|---|
| 1924–25 | 22 | Ottawa Senators | NHL | 30 | 10 | 14 | 24 | 87 |
| 1925–26 | 23 | Ottawa Senators | NHL | 28 | 16 | 9 | 25 | 58 |
| 1926–27 | 24 | Ottawa Senators | NHL | 43 | 9 | 6 | 15 | 135 |
| 1927–28 | 25 | Montreal Maroons | NHL | 34 | 14 | 5 | 19 | 74 |
| 1928–29 | 26 | Montreal Maroons | NHL | 41 | 10 | 9 | 19 | 124 |
| 1929–30 | 27 | Montreal Maroons | NHL | 42 | 21 | 9 | 30 | 87 |
| 1930–31 | 28 | Montreal Maroons | NHL | 40 | 12 | 14 | 26 | 68 |
| 1931–32 | 29 | Montreal Maroons | NHL | 43 | 11 | 33 | 44 | 57 |
| 1932–33 | 30 | Montreal Maroons | NHL | 48 | 20 | 21 | 41 | 66 |
| 1933–34 | 31 | Montreal Maroons | NHL | 47 | 18 | 19 | 37 | 58 |
| 1934–35 | 32 | Montreal Maroons | NHL | 46 | 5 | 22 | 27 | 44 |
| 1935–36 | 33 | Montreal Maroons | NHL | 47 | 19 | 19 | 38 | 75 |
| 1936–37 | 34 | Boston Bruins | NHL | 44 | 8 | 10 | 18 | 36 |
| 1937–38 | 35 | New York Americans | NHL | 47 | 10 | 10 | 20 | 23 |
| 1938–39 | 36 | New York Americans | NHL | 48 | 8 | 11 | 19 | 18 |
| 1939–40 | 37 | New York Americans | NHL | 48 | 7 | 8 | 15 | 51 |
| 1940–41 | 38 | New York Americans | NHL | 41 | 2 | 7 | 9 | 4 |
| NHL Career—17 Seasons | | | | 717 | 200 | 226 | 426 | 1062 |

**PLAYOFFS**

| SEASON | AGE | TEAM | LG | GP | G | A | PTS | PIM |
|---|---|---|---|---|---|---|---|---|
| 1925–26 | 23 | Ottawa Senators | NHL | 2 | 0 | 0 | 0 | 14 |
| 1926–27 | 24 | Ottawa Senators | NHL | 6 | 1 | 1 | 2 | 16 |
| 1927–28 | 25 | Montreal Maroons | NHL | 9 | 2 | 1 | 3 | 23 |
| 1929–30 | 27 | Montreal Maroons | NHL | 4 | 1 | 1 | 2 | 14 |
| 1931–32 | 29 | Montreal Maroons | NHL | 4 | 2 | 1 | 3 | 2 |
| 1932–33 | 30 | Montreal Maroons | NHL | 2 | 0 | 2 | 2 | 2 |
| 1933–34 | 31 | Montreal Maroons | NHL | 4 | 0 | 1 | 1 | 6 |
| 1934–35 | 32 | Montreal Maroons | NHL | 6 | 0 | 0 | 0 | 14 |
| 1935–36 | 33 | Montreal Maroons | NHL | 3 | 0 | 0 | 0 | 2 |
| 1936–37 | 34 | Boston Bruins | NHL | 3 | 0 | 0 | 0 | 0 |
| 1937–38 | 35 | New York Americans | NHL | 6 | 0 | 3 | 3 | 0 |
| 1938–39 | 36 | New York Americans | NHL | 2 | 0 | 0 | 0 | 14 |
| 1939–40 | 37 | New York Americans | NHL | 3 | 3 | 1 | 4 | 2 |
| NHL Career—13 Seasons | | | | 54 | 11 | 9 | 20 | 109 |

## Tommy Smith   Profile: See page 152

**REGULAR SEASON**

| SEASON | AGE | TEAM | LG | GP | G | A | PTS | PIM |
|---|---|---|---|---|---|---|---|---|
| 1905–06 | 19 | Ottawa Vics | FAHL | 8 | 12 | 0 | 12 | |
| 1905–06 | 19 | Ottawa Silver Seven | ECAHA | 3 | 6 | 0 | 6 | 12 |
| 1906–07 | 20 | Pittsburgh Professionals | IHL | 23 | 31 | 13 | 44 | 47 |
| 1907–08 | 21 | Pittsburgh Lyceum | WPHL | 16 | 33 | 0 | 33 | |
| 1908–09 | 22 | Brantford Professionals | OPHL | 13 | 40 | 0 | 40 | 30 |
| 1908–09 | 22 | Pittsburgh Lyceum | WPHL | 10 | 15 | 0 | 15 | |
| 1908–09 | 22 | Haileybury Hockey Club | TPHL | 1 | 3 | 0 | 3 | 2 |
| 1909–10 | 23 | Brantford Redmen | OPHL | 2 | 1 | 0 | 1 | 3 |
| 1910–11 | 24 | Galt Professionals | OPHL | 18 | 22 | 0 | 22 | |

**REGULAR SEASON**

| SEASON | AGE | TEAM | LG | GP | G | A | PTS | PIM |
|---|---|---|---|---|---|---|---|---|
| 1911–12 | 25 | Moncton Victorias | MPHL | 18 | 53 | 0 | 53 | 48 |
| 1912–13 | 26 | Quebec Bulldogs | NHA | 18 | 39 | 0 | 39 | 30 |
| 1913–14 | 27 | Quebec Bulldogs | NHA | 20 | 39 | 6 | 45 | 35 |
| 1914–15 | 28 | Toronto Shamrocks | NHA | 10 | 17 | 2 | 19 | 14 |
| 1914–15 | 28 | Quebec Bulldogs | NHA | 9 | 23 | 2 | 25 | 29 |
| 1915–16 | 29 | Quebec Bulldogs | NHA | 22 | 16 | 3 | 19 | 39 |
| 1916–17 | 30 | Montreal Canadiens | NHA | 14 | 7 | 4 | 11 | 32 |
| 1919–20 | 33 | Quebec Bulldogs | NHL | 10 | 0 | 1 | 1 | 11 |
| Career—13 Seasons | | | | 200 | 357 | 31 | 388 | 323 |

## Tommy Smith (continued)

| PLAYOFFS | | | | | | | | |
|---|---|---|---|---|---|---|---|---|
| SEASON | AGE | TEAM | LG | GP | G | A | PTS | PIM |
| 1905–06 | 19 | Ottawa Silver Seven | St-Cup | 1 | 0 | 0 | 0 | 9 |
| 1907–08 | 21 | Pittsburgh Lyceum | WPHL | 1 | 2 | 0 | 2 | |
| 1908–09 | 22 | Haileybury Hockey Club | TPHL | 2 | 3 | 0 | 3 | 0 |
| 1908–09 | 22 | Pittsburgh Bankers | WPHL | 3 | 3 | 0 | 3 | 3 |
| 1910–11 | 24 | Galt Professionals | OPHL | 3 | 10 | 0 | 10 | 0 |
| 1910–11 | 24 | Galt Professionals | St-Cup | 1 | 1 | 0 | 1 | 0 |

| PLAYOFFS | | | | | | | | |
|---|---|---|---|---|---|---|---|---|
| SEASON | AGE | TEAM | LG | GP | G | A | PTS | PIM |
| 1911–12 | 25 | Moncton Victorias | St-Cup | 2 | 2 | 0 | 2 | 3 |
| 1912–13 | 26 | Quebec Bulldogs | St-Cup | 2 | 4 | 0 | 4 | 0 |
| 1916–17 | 30 | Montreal Canadiens | NHA | 2 | 2 | 0 | 2 | 11 |
| 1916–17 | 30 | Montreal Canadiens | St-Cup | 4 | 2 | 0 | 2 | 3 |
| Career — 7 Seasons | | | | 21 | 29 | 0 | 29 | 29 |

## Peter Stastny   Profile: See page 153

| REGULAR SEASON | | | | | | | | | | | | | | | |
|---|---|---|---|---|---|---|---|---|---|---|---|---|---|---|---|
| SEASON | AGE | TEAM | LG | GP | G | A | PTS | +/- | PIM | ESG | PPG | SHG | GWG | SOG | S% |
| 1980–81 | 24 | Quebec Nordiques | NHL | 77 | 39 | 70 | 109 | 10 | 37 | 26 | 11 | 2 | 4 | 232 | 16.8 |
| 1981–82 | 25 | Quebec Nordiques | NHL | 80 | 46 | 93 | 139 | -10 | 91 | 27 | 16 | 3 | 3 | 227 | 20.3 |
| 1982–83 | 26 | Quebec Nordiques | NHL | 75 | 47 | 77 | 124 | 29 | 78 | 42 | 5 | 0 | 4 | 201 | 23.4 |
| 1983–84 | 27 | Quebec Nordiques | NHL | 80 | 46 | 73 | 119 | 22 | 73 | 35 | 11 | 0 | 4 | 189 | 24.3 |
| 1984–85 | 28 | Quebec Nordiques | NHL | 75 | 32 | 68 | 100 | 21 | 95 | 24 | 7 | 1 | 9 | 207 | 15.5 |
| 1985–86 | 29 | Quebec Nordiques | NHL | 76 | 41 | 81 | 122 | 2 | 60 | 26 | 15 | 0 | 8 | 207 | 19.8 |
| 1986–87 | 30 | Quebec Nordiques | NHL | 64 | 24 | 53 | 77 | -22 | 43 | 12 | 12 | 0 | 4 | 157 | 15.3 |
| 1987–88 | 31 | Quebec Nordiques | NHL | 76 | 46 | 65 | 111 | 2 | 69 | 26 | 20 | 0 | 2 | 199 | 23.1 |
| 1988–89 | 32 | Quebec Nordiques | NHL | 72 | 35 | 50 | 85 | -23 | 117 | 22 | 13 | 0 | 5 | 195 | 17.9 |
| 1989–90 | 33 | Quebec Nordiques | NHL | 62 | 24 | 38 | 62 | -45 | 24 | 14 | 10 | 0 | 0 | 131 | 18.3 |
| 1989–90 | 33 | New Jersey Devils | NHL | 12 | 5 | 6 | 11 | -1 | 16 | 3 | 2 | 0 | 1 | 25 | 20.0 |
| 1990–91 | 34 | New Jersey Devils | NHL | 77 | 18 | 42 | 60 | 0 | 53 | 14 | 4 | 0 | 3 | 117 | 15.4 |
| 1991–92 | 35 | New Jersey Devils | NHL | 66 | 24 | 38 | 62 | 6 | 42 | 13 | 10 | 1 | 3 | 142 | 16.9 |
| 1992–93 | 36 | New Jersey Devils | NHL | 62 | 17 | 23 | 40 | -5 | 22 | 10 | 7 | 0 | 3 | 106 | 16.0 |
| 1993–94 | 37 | St. Louis Blues | NHL | 17 | 5 | 11 | 16 | -2 | 4 | 3 | 2 | 0 | 1 | 30 | 16.7 |
| 1994–95 | 38 | St. Louis Blues | NHL | 6 | 1 | 1 | 2 | 1 | 0 | 1 | 0 | 0 | 0 | 9 | 11.1 |
| NHL Career — 15 Seasons | | | | 977 | 450 | 789 | 1239 | -15 | 824 | 298 | 145 | 7 | 54 | 2374 | 19.0 |

| PLAYOFFS | | | | | | | | | | | | | | | |
|---|---|---|---|---|---|---|---|---|---|---|---|---|---|---|---|
| SEASON | AGE | TEAM | LG | GP | G | A | PTS | +/- | PIM | ESG | PPG | SHG | GWG | SOG | S% |
| 1980–81 | 24 | Quebec Nordiques | NHL | 5 | 2 | 8 | 10 | -3 | 7 | 1 | 1 | 0 | 0 | 4 | 50.0 |
| 1981–82 | 25 | Quebec Nordiques | NHL | 12 | 7 | 11 | 18 | 1 | 10 | 3 | 4 | 0 | 1 | 26 | 26.9 |
| 1982–83 | 26 | Quebec Nordiques | NHL | 4 | 3 | 2 | 5 | 2 | 10 | 2 | 1 | 0 | 0 | 9 | 33.3 |
| 1983–84 | 27 | Quebec Nordiques | NHL | 9 | 2 | 7 | 9 | 3 | 31 | 0 | 2 | 0 | 0 | 18 | 11.1 |
| 1984–85 | 28 | Quebec Nordiques | NHL | 18 | 4 | 19 | 23 | 2 | 24 | 3 | 1 | 0 | 2 | 27 | 14.8 |
| 1985–86 | 29 | Quebec Nordiques | NHL | 3 | 0 | 1 | 1 | -5 | 2 | 0 | 0 | 0 | 0 | 10 | 0.0 |
| 1986–87 | 30 | Quebec Nordiques | NHL | 13 | 6 | 9 | 15 | 3 | 12 | 3 | 2 | 1 | 2 | 24 | 25.0 |
| 1989–90 | 33 | New Jersey Devils | NHL | 6 | 3 | 2 | 5 | -1 | 4 | 2 | 1 | 0 | 1 | 9 | 33.3 |
| 1990–91 | 34 | New Jersey Devils | NHL | 7 | 3 | 4 | 7 | -2 | 2 | 2 | 1 | 0 | 2 | 7 | 42.9 |
| 1991–92 | 35 | New Jersey Devils | NHL | 7 | 3 | 7 | 10 | 1 | 19 | 3 | 0 | 0 | 0 | 12 | 25.0 |
| 1992–93 | 36 | New Jersey Devils | NHL | 5 | 0 | 2 | 2 | 0 | 2 | 0 | 0 | 0 | 0 | 3 | 0.0 |
| 1993–94 | 37 | St. Louis Blues | NHL | 4 | 0 | 0 | 0 | -4 | 2 | 0 | 0 | 0 | 0 | 3 | 0.0 |
| NHL Career — 12 Seasons | | | | 93 | 33 | 72 | 105 | -3 | 125 | 19 | 13 | 1 | 8 | 152 | 21.7 |

## Nels Stewart   Profile: See page 154

| REGULAR SEASON | | | | | | | | |
|---|---|---|---|---|---|---|---|---|
| SEASON | AGE | TEAM | LG | GP | G | A | PTS | PIM |
| 1925–26 | 23 | Montreal Maroons | NHL | 36 | 34 | 8 | 42 | 121 |
| 1926–27 | 24 | Montreal Maroons | NHL | 43 | 17 | 4 | 21 | 129 |
| 1927–28 | 25 | Montreal Maroons | NHL | 41 | 27 | 7 | 34 | 106 |
| 1928–29 | 26 | Montreal Maroons | NHL | 44 | 21 | 8 | 29 | 74 |
| 1929–30 | 27 | Montreal Maroons | NHL | 44 | 39 | 16 | 55 | 85 |
| 1930–31 | 28 | Montreal Maroons | NHL | 42 | 25 | 14 | 39 | 75 |
| 1931–32 | 29 | Montreal Maroons | NHL | 38 | 22 | 11 | 33 | 61 |
| 1932–33 | 30 | Boston Bruins | NHL | 47 | 18 | 18 | 36 | 62 |
| 1933–34 | 31 | Boston Bruins | NHL | 48 | 22 | 17 | 39 | 68 |
| 1934–35 | 32 | Boston Bruins | NHL | 47 | 21 | 18 | 39 | 45 |
| 1935–36 | 33 | New York Americans | NHL | 48 | 14 | 15 | 29 | 16 |
| 1936–37 | 34 | Boston Bruins | NHL | 11 | 3 | 2 | 5 | 6 |
| 1936–37 | 34 | New York Americans | NHL | 32 | 20 | 10 | 30 | 31 |
| 1937–38 | 35 | New York Americans | NHL | 48 | 19 | 17 | 36 | 29 |
| 1938–39 | 36 | New York Americans | NHL | 46 | 16 | 19 | 35 | 43 |
| 1939–40 | 37 | New York Americans | NHL | 35 | 6 | 7 | 13 | 6 |
| NHL Career — 15 Seasons | | | | 650 | 324 | 191 | 515 | 955 |

| PLAYOFFS | | | | | | | | |
|---|---|---|---|---|---|---|---|---|
| SEASON | AGE | TEAM | LG | GP | G | A | PTS | PIM |
| 1925–26 | 23 | Montreal Maroons | NHL | 4 | 0 | 2 | 2 | 10 |
| 1925–26 | 23 | Montreal Maroons | St-Cup NHL | 4 | 6 | 1 | 7 | 16 |
| 1926–27 | 24 | Montreal Maroons | NHL | 2 | 0 | 0 | 0 | 4 |
| 1927–28 | 25 | Montreal Maroons | NHL | 9 | 2 | 2 | 4 | 13 |
| 1929–30 | 27 | Montreal Maroons | NHL | 4 | 1 | 1 | 2 | 2 |
| 1930–31 | 28 | Montreal Maroons | NHL | 2 | 1 | 0 | 1 | 6 |
| 1931–32 | 29 | Montreal Maroons | NHL | 4 | 0 | 1 | 1 | 2 |
| 1932–33 | 30 | Boston Bruins | NHL | 5 | 2 | 0 | 2 | 4 |
| 1934–35 | 32 | Boston Bruins | NHL | 4 | 0 | 1 | 1 | 0 |
| 1935–36 | 33 | New York Americans | NHL | 5 | 1 | 2 | 3 | 4 |
| 1937–38 | 35 | New York Americans | NHL | 6 | 2 | 3 | 5 | 2 |
| 1938–39 | 36 | New York Americans | NHL | 2 | 0 | 0 | 0 | 0 |
| 1939–40 | 37 | New York Americans | NHL | 3 | 0 | 0 | 0 | 0 |
| NHL Career — 12 Seasons | | | | 54 | 15 | 13 | 28 | 63 |

# Mats Sundin  Profile: See page 156

## REGULAR SEASON

| SEASON | AGE | TEAM | LG | GP | G | A | PTS | +/- | PIM | ESG | PPG | SHG | GWG | SOG | S% |
|---|---|---|---|---|---|---|---|---|---|---|---|---|---|---|---|
| 1990–91 | 19 | Quebec Nordiques | NHL | 80 | 23 | 36 | 59 | -24 | 58 | 19 | 4 | 0 | 0 | 155 | 14.8 |
| 1991–92 | 20 | Quebec Nordiques | NHL | 80 | 33 | 43 | 76 | -19 | 103 | 23 | 8 | 2 | 2 | 231 | 14.3 |
| 1992–93 | 21 | Quebec Nordiques | NHL | 80 | 47 | 67 | 114 | 21 | 96 | 30 | 13 | 4 | 9 | 215 | 21.9 |
| 1993–94 | 22 | Quebec Nordiques | NHL | 84 | 32 | 53 | 85 | 1 | 60 | 24 | 6 | 2 | 4 | 226 | 14.2 |
| 1994–95 | 23 | Toronto Maple Leafs | NHL | 47 | 23 | 24 | 47 | -5 | 14 | 14 | 9 | 0 | 4 | 173 | 13.3 |
| 1995–96 | 24 | Toronto Maple Leafs | NHL | 76 | 33 | 50 | 83 | 8 | 46 | 20 | 7 | 6 | 7 | 301 | 11.0 |
| 1996–97 | 25 | Toronto Maple Leafs | NHL | 82 | 41 | 53 | 94 | 6 | 59 | 30 | 7 | 4 | 8 | 281 | 14.6 |
| 1997–98 | 26 | Toronto Maple Leafs | NHL | 82 | 33 | 41 | 74 | -3 | 49 | 23 | 9 | 1 | 5 | 219 | 15.1 |
| 1998–99 | 27 | Toronto Maple Leafs | NHL | 82 | 31 | 52 | 83 | 22 | 58 | 27 | 4 | 0 | 6 | 209 | 14.8 |
| 1999–00 | 28 | Toronto Maple Leafs | NHL | 73 | 32 | 41 | 73 | 16 | 46 | 20 | 10 | 2 | 7 | 184 | 17.4 |
| 2000–01 | 29 | Toronto Maple Leafs | NHL | 82 | 28 | 46 | 74 | 15 | 76 | 19 | 9 | 0 | 6 | 226 | 12.4 |
| 2001–02 | 30 | Toronto Maple Leafs | NHL | 82 | 41 | 39 | 80 | 6 | 94 | 29 | 10 | 2 | 9 | 262 | 15.6 |
| 2002–03 | 31 | Toronto Maple Leafs | NHL | 75 | 37 | 35 | 72 | 1 | 58 | 18 | 16 | 3 | 8 | 223 | 16.6 |
| 2003–04 | 32 | Toronto Maple Leafs | NHL | 81 | 31 | 44 | 75 | 11 | 52 | 19 | 11 | 1 | 10 | 226 | 13.7 |
| 2005–06 | 34 | Toronto Maple Leafs | NHL | 70 | 31 | 47 | 78 | 7 | 58 | 13 | 16 | 2 | 2 | 220 | 14.1 |
| 2006–07 | 35 | Toronto Maple Leafs | NHL | 75 | 27 | 49 | 76 | -2 | 62 | 20 | 6 | 1 | 3 | 321 | 8.4 |
| 2007–08 | 36 | Toronto Maple Leafs | NHL | 74 | 32 | 46 | 78 | 17 | 76 | 21 | 10 | 1 | 4 | 259 | 12.4 |
| 2008–09 | 37 | Vancouver Canucks | NHL | 41 | 9 | 19 | 28 | -5 | 28 | 4 | 5 | 0 | 2 | 84 | 10.7 |
| NHL Career—18 Seasons | | | | 1346 | 564 | 785 | 1349 | 73 | 1093 | 373 | 160 | 31 | 96 | 4015 | 14.0 |

## PLAYOFFS

| SEASON | AGE | TEAM | LG | GP | G | A | PTS | +/- | PIM | ESG | PPG | SHG | GWG | SOG | S% |
|---|---|---|---|---|---|---|---|---|---|---|---|---|---|---|---|
| 1992–93 | 21 | Quebec Nordiques | NHL | 6 | 3 | 1 | 4 | -4 | 6 | 2 | 1 | 0 | 0 | 19 | 15.8 |
| 1994–95 | 23 | Toronto Maple Leafs | NHL | 7 | 5 | 4 | 9 | -2 | 4 | 3 | 2 | 0 | 1 | 27 | 18.5 |
| 1995–96 | 24 | Toronto Maple Leafs | NHL | 6 | 3 | 1 | 4 | -8 | 4 | 1 | 2 | 0 | 1 | 23 | 13.0 |
| 1998–99 | 27 | Toronto Maple Leafs | NHL | 17 | 8 | 8 | 16 | 2 | 16 | 5 | 3 | 0 | 2 | 44 | 18.2 |
| 1999–00 | 28 | Toronto Maple Leafs | NHL | 12 | 3 | 5 | 8 | 8 | 10 | 3 | 0 | 0 | 1 | 20 | 15.0 |
| 2000–01 | 29 | Toronto Maple Leafs | NHL | 11 | 6 | 7 | 13 | 5 | 14 | 3 | 2 | 1 | 1 | 42 | 14.3 |
| 2001–02 | 30 | Toronto Maple Leafs | NHL | 8 | 2 | 5 | 7 | 5 | 4 | 2 | 0 | 0 | 0 | 21 | 9.5 |
| 2002–03 | 31 | Toronto Maple Leafs | NHL | 7 | 1 | 3 | 4 | -1 | 6 | 0 | 1 | 0 | 0 | 16 | 6.3 |
| 2003–04 | 32 | Toronto Maple Leafs | NHL | 9 | 4 | 5 | 9 | -2 | 8 | 4 | 0 | 0 | 1 | 19 | 21.1 |
| 2008–09 | 37 | Vancouver Canucks | NHL | 8 | 3 | 5 | 8 | -1 | 2 | 3 | 0 | 0 | 1 | 15 | 20.0 |
| NHL Career—10 Seasons | | | | 91 | 38 | 44 | 82 | 2 | 74 | 26 | 11 | 1 | 8 | 246 | 15.4 |

# Harry Trihey  Profile: See page 157

## REGULAR SEASON

| SEASON | AGE | TEAM | LG | GP | G | A | PTS | PIM |
|---|---|---|---|---|---|---|---|---|
| 1895–96 | 18 | Montreal Orioles | QAHA | | | | | |
| 1896–97 | 19 | Montreal Shamrocks | QAHA | | | | | |
| 1896–97 | 19 | Montreal Shamrocks | MCSHL | 1 | 0 | 0 | 0 | |
| 1897–98 | 20 | Montreal Shamrocks | CAHL | 8 | 3 | 0 | 3 | |
| 1898–99 | 21 | Montreal Shamrocks | CAHL | 7 | 19 | 0 | 19 | |
| 1899–00 | 22 | Montreal Shamrocks | CAHL | 7 | 17 | 0 | 17 | |
| 1900–01 | 23 | Montreal Shamrocks | CAHL | 7 | 7 | 0 | 7 | |
| Career—6 Seasons | | | | 30 | 46 | 0 | 46 | |

## PLAYOFFS

| SEASON | AGE | TEAM | LG | GP | G | A | PTS | PIM |
|---|---|---|---|---|---|---|---|---|
| 1898–99 | 21 | Montreal Shamrocks | St-Cup | 1 | 3 | 0 | 3 | |
| 1899–00 | 22 | Montreal Shamrocks | St-Cup | 5 | 12 | 0 | 12 | |
| 1900–01 | 23 | Montreal Shamrocks | St-Cup | 2 | 1 | 0 | 1 | |
| Career—3 Seasons | | | | 8 | 16 | 0 | 16 | |

# Bryan Trottier  Profile: See page 158

## REGULAR SEASON

| SEASON | AGE | TEAM | LG | GP | G | A | PTS | +/- | PIM | ESG | PPG | SHG | GWG | SOG | S% |
|---|---|---|---|---|---|---|---|---|---|---|---|---|---|---|---|
| 1975–76 | 19 | New York Islanders | NHL | 80 | 32 | 63 | 95 | 27 | 21 | 20 | 11 | 1 | 5 | 178 | 18.0 |
| 1976–77 | 20 | New York Islanders | NHL | 76 | 30 | 42 | 72 | 28 | 34 | 18 | 11 | 1 | 6 | 175 | 17.1 |
| 1977–78 | 21 | New York Islanders | NHL | 77 | 46 | 77 | 123 | 52 | 46 | 31 | 13 | 2 | 6 | 193 | 23.8 |
| 1978–79 | 22 | New York Islanders | NHL | 76 | 47 | 87 | 134 | 76 | 50 | 32 | 15 | 0 | 8 | 187 | 25.1 |
| 1979–80 | 23 | New York Islanders | NHL | 78 | 42 | 62 | 104 | 31 | 68 | 27 | 15 | 0 | 7 | 186 | 22.6 |
| 1980–81 | 24 | New York Islanders | NHL | 73 | 31 | 72 | 103 | 50 | 74 | 20 | 9 | 2 | 5 | 156 | 19.9 |
| 1981–82 | 25 | New York Islanders | NHL | 80 | 50 | 79 | 129 | 70 | 88 | 30 | 18 | 2 | 10 | 217 | 23.0 |
| 1982–83 | 26 | New York Islanders | NHL | 80 | 34 | 55 | 89 | 36 | 68 | 21 | 13 | 0 | 5 | 179 | 19.0 |
| 1983–84 | 27 | New York Islanders | NHL | 68 | 40 | 71 | 111 | 68 | 59 | 30 | 7 | 3 | 4 | 194 | 20.6 |
| 1984–85 | 28 | New York Islanders | NHL | 68 | 28 | 31 | 59 | 3 | 47 | 19 | 4 | 5 | 3 | 158 | 17.7 |
| 1985–86 | 29 | New York Islanders | NHL | 78 | 37 | 59 | 96 | 30 | 72 | 31 | 5 | 1 | 3 | 185 | 20.0 |
| 1986–87 | 30 | New York Islanders | NHL | 80 | 23 | 64 | 87 | 4 | 50 | 10 | 13 | 0 | 1 | 195 | 11.8 |
| 1987–88 | 31 | New York Islanders | NHL | 77 | 30 | 52 | 82 | 10 | 48 | 15 | 15 | 0 | 3 | 176 | 17.1 |
| 1988–89 | 32 | New York Islanders | NHL | 73 | 17 | 28 | 45 | -7 | 44 | 12 | 5 | 0 | 3 | 163 | 10.4 |
| 1989–90 | 33 | New York Islanders | NHL | 59 | 13 | 11 | 24 | -11 | 29 | 9 | 4 | 0 | 0 | 84 | 15.5 |
| 1990–91 | 34 | Pittsburgh Penguins | NHL | 52 | 9 | 19 | 28 | 5 | 24 | 8 | 0 | 1 | 0 | 68 | 13.2 |
| 1991–92 | 35 | Pittsburgh Penguins | NHL | 63 | 11 | 18 | 29 | -11 | 54 | 7 | 3 | 1 | 0 | 102 | 10.8 |
| 1993–94 | 37 | Pittsburgh Penguins | NHL | 41 | 4 | 11 | 15 | -12 | 36 | 4 | 0 | 0 | 0 | 45 | 8.9 |
| NHL Career—18 Seasons | | | | 1279 | 524 | 901 | 1425 | 449 | 912 | 344 | 161 | 19 | 69 | 2841 | 18.4 |

## Bryan Trottier (continued)

### PLAYOFFS

| SEASON | AGE | TEAM | LG | GP | G | A | PTS | +/- | PIM | ESG | PPG | SHG | GWG | SOG | S% |
|---|---|---|---|---|---|---|---|---|---|---|---|---|---|---|---|
| 1975–76 | 19 | New York Islanders | NHL | 13 | 1 | 7 | 8 | -2 | 8 | 1 | 0 | 0 | 0 | 27 | 3.7 |
| 1976–77 | 20 | New York Islanders | NHL | 12 | 2 | 8 | 10 | 4 | 2 | 2 | 0 | 0 | 0 | 26 | 7.7 |
| 1977–78 | 21 | New York Islanders | NHL | 7 | 0 | 3 | 3 | 0 | 4 | 0 | 0 | 0 | 0 | 18 | 0.0 |
| 1978–79 | 22 | New York Islanders | NHL | 10 | 2 | 4 | 6 | 3 | 13 | 2 | 0 | 0 | 1 | 18 | 11.1 |
| 1979–80 | 23 | New York Islanders | NHL | 21 | 12 | 17 | 29 | 8 | 16 | 6 | 4 | 2 | 2 | 53 | 22.6 |
| 1980–81 | 24 | New York Islanders | NHL | 18 | 11 | 18 | 29 | 18 | 34 | 5 | 4 | 2 | 1 | 49 | 22.4 |
| 1981–82 | 25 | New York Islanders | NHL | 19 | 6 | 23 | 29 | 9 | 40 | 4 | 2 | 0 | 2 | 52 | 11.5 |
| 1982–83 | 26 | New York Islanders | NHL | 17 | 8 | 12 | 20 | 8 | 18 | 5 | 3 | 0 | 1 | 44 | 18.2 |
| 1983–84 | 27 | New York Islanders | NHL | 21 | 8 | 6 | 14 | 4 | 49 | 7 | 1 | 0 | 0 | 39 | 20.5 |
| 1984–85 | 28 | New York Islanders | NHL | 10 | 4 | 2 | 6 | 0 | 8 | 3 | 1 | 0 | 1 | 25 | 16.0 |
| 1985–86 | 29 | New York Islanders | NHL | 3 | 1 | 1 | 2 | -1 | 2 | 1 | 0 | 0 | 0 | 10 | 10.0 |
| 1986–87 | 30 | New York Islanders | NHL | 14 | 8 | 4 | 12 | -6 | 12 | 5 | 3 | 0 | 2 | 46 | 17.4 |
| 1987–88 | 31 | New York Islanders | NHL | 6 | 0 | 0 | 0 | -9 | 10 | 0 | 0 | 0 | 0 | 11 | 0.0 |
| 1989–90 | 33 | New York Islanders | NHL | 4 | 1 | 0 | 1 | -4 | 4 | 1 | 0 | 0 | 0 | 7 | 14.3 |
| 1990–91 | 34 | Pittsburgh Penguins | NHL | 23 | 3 | 4 | 7 | -1 | 49 | 3 | 0 | 0 | 2 | 16 | 18.8 |
| 1991–92 | 35 | Pittsburgh Penguins | NHL | 21 | 4 | 3 | 7 | 0 | 8 | 4 | 0 | 0 | 0 | 30 | 13.3 |
| 1993–94 | 37 | Pittsburgh Penguins | NHL | 2 | 0 | 0 | 0 | 0 | 0 | 0 | 0 | 0 | 0 | 1 | 0.0 |
| NHL Career — 17 Seasons | | | | 221 | 71 | 112 | 183 | 31 | 277 | 49 | 18 | 4 | 12 | 472 | 15.0 |

## Norm Ullman    Profile: See page 160

### REGULAR SEASON

| SEASON | AGE | TEAM | LG | GP | G | A | PTS | +/- | PIM | ESG | PPG | SHG | GWG | SOG | S% |
|---|---|---|---|---|---|---|---|---|---|---|---|---|---|---|---|
| 1955–56 | 20 | Detroit Red Wings | NHL | 66 | 9 | 9 | 18 | | 26 | 9 | 9 | 0 | 1 | | |
| 1956–57 | 21 | Detroit Red Wings | NHL | 64 | 16 | 36 | 52 | | 47 | 10 | 10 | 0 | 0 | | |
| 1957–58 | 22 | Detroit Red Wings | NHL | 69 | 23 | 28 | 51 | | 38 | 15 | 15 | 0 | 3 | | |
| 1958–59 | 23 | Detroit Red Wings | NHL | 69 | 22 | 36 | 58 | | 42 | 17 | 17 | 0 | 5 | | |
| 1959–60 | 24 | Detroit Red Wings | NHL | 70 | 24 | 34 | 58 | -19 | 46 | 20 | 20 | 1 | 2 | 226 | 10.6 |
| 1960–61 | 25 | Detroit Red Wings | NHL | 70 | 28 | 42 | 70 | 13 | 34 | 23 | 23 | 0 | 5 | 205 | 13.7 |
| 1961–62 | 26 | Detroit Red Wings | NHL | 70 | 26 | 38 | 64 | -20 | 54 | 20 | 20 | 0 | 6 | 200 | 13.0 |
| 1962–63 | 27 | Detroit Red Wings | NHL | 70 | 26 | 30 | 56 | -5 | 53 | 20 | 20 | 2 | 3 | 248 | 10.5 |
| 1963–64 | 28 | Detroit Red Wings | NHL | 61 | 21 | 30 | 51 | -14 | 55 | 17 | 3 | 1 | 5 | 213 | 9.9 |
| 1964–65 | 29 | Detroit Red Wings | NHL | 70 | 42 | 41 | 83 | 15 | 70 | 29 | 10 | 1 | 10 | 251 | 16.7 |
| 1965–66 | 30 | Detroit Red Wings | NHL | 70 | 31 | 41 | 72 | 2 | 35 | 24 | 7 | 0 | 2 | 259 | 12.0 |
| 1966–67 | 31 | Detroit Red Wings | NHL | 68 | 26 | 44 | 70 | -8 | 26 | 20 | 5 | 1 | 3 | 243 | 10.7 |
| 1967–68 | 32 | Detroit Red Wings | NHL | 58 | 30 | 25 | 55 | 0 | 26 | 23 | 7 | 0 | 4 | 189 | 15.9 |
| 1967–68 | 32 | Toronto Maple Leafs | NHL | 13 | 5 | 12 | 17 | 12 | 2 | 4 | 1 | 0 | 0 | 39 | 12.8 |
| 1968–69 | 33 | Toronto Maple Leafs | NHL | 75 | 35 | 42 | 77 | 20 | 39 | 22 | 13 | 0 | 2 | 247 | 14.2 |
| 1969–70 | 34 | Toronto Maple Leafs | NHL | 74 | 18 | 42 | 60 | 19 | 37 | 12 | 5 | 1 | 0 | 207 | 8.7 |
| 1970–71 | 35 | Toronto Maple Leafs | NHL | 73 | 34 | 51 | 85 | 14 | 24 | 22 | 11 | 1 | 4 | 226 | 15.0 |
| 1971–72 | 36 | Toronto Maple Leafs | NHL | 77 | 23 | 50 | 73 | 7 | 26 | 14 | 9 | 0 | 1 | 204 | 11.3 |
| 1972–73 | 37 | Toronto Maple Leafs | NHL | 65 | 20 | 35 | 55 | -16 | 10 | 17 | 3 | 0 | 1 | 174 | 11.5 |
| 1973–74 | 38 | Toronto Maple Leafs | NHL | 78 | 22 | 47 | 69 | 11 | 12 | 18 | 4 | 0 | 2 | 178 | 12.4 |
| 1974–75 | 39 | Toronto Maple Leafs | NHL | 80 | 9 | 26 | 35 | -12 | 8 | 8 | 1 | 0 | 0 | 117 | 7.7 |
| 1975–76 | 40 | Edmonton Oilers | WHA | 77 | 31 | 56 | 87 | -21 | 12 | 17 | 13 | 1 | 1 | 158 | 19.6 |
| 1976–77 | 41 | Edmonton Oilers | WHA | 67 | 16 | 27 | 43 | -23 | 28 | 12 | 4 | 0 | | 107 | 15.0 |
| Career — 22 Seasons | | | | 1554 | 537 | 822 | 1359 | 37 | 750 | 395 | 133 | 9 | 60 | 3691 | 14.5 |

### PLAYOFFS

| SEASON | AGE | TEAM | LG | GP | G | A | PTS | +/- | PIM | ESG | PPG | SHG | GWG | SOG | S% |
|---|---|---|---|---|---|---|---|---|---|---|---|---|---|---|---|
| 1955–56 | 20 | Detroit Red Wings | NHL | 10 | 1 | 3 | 4 | | 13 | 1 | 0 | 0 | 0 | | |
| 1956–57 | 21 | Detroit Red Wings | NHL | 5 | 1 | 1 | 2 | | 8 | 1 | 0 | 0 | 0 | | |
| 1957–58 | 22 | Detroit Red Wings | NHL | 4 | 0 | 2 | 2 | | 4 | 0 | 0 | 0 | 0 | | |
| 1959–60 | 24 | Detroit Red Wings | NHL | 6 | 2 | 2 | 4 | -4 | 0 | 0 | 2 | 0 | 0 | 28 | 7.1 |
| 1960–61 | 25 | Detroit Red Wings | NHL | 11 | 0 | 4 | 4 | -2 | 4 | 0 | 0 | 0 | 0 | 27 | 0.0 |
| 1962–63 | 27 | Detroit Red Wings | NHL | 11 | 4 | 12 | 16 | -1 | 14 | 1 | 3 | 0 | 0 | 41 | 9.8 |
| 1963–64 | 28 | Detroit Red Wings | NHL | 14 | 7 | 10 | 17 | 1 | 6 | 4 | 2 | 1 | 1 | 46 | 15.2 |
| 1964–65 | 29 | Detroit Red Wings | NHL | 7 | 6 | 4 | 10 | -3 | 2 | 4 | 2 | 0 | 2 | 31 | 19.4 |
| 1965–66 | 30 | Detroit Red Wings | NHL | 12 | 6 | 9 | 15 | 0 | 12 | 5 | 1 | 0 | 0 | 48 | 12.5 |
| 1968–69 | 33 | Toronto Maple Leafs | NHL | 4 | 1 | 0 | 1 | -2 | 0 | 1 | 0 | 0 | 0 | 10 | 10.0 |
| 1970–71 | 35 | Toronto Maple Leafs | NHL | 6 | 0 | 2 | 2 | -1 | 2 | 0 | 0 | 0 | 0 | 17 | 0.0 |
| 1971–72 | 36 | Toronto Maple Leafs | NHL | 5 | 1 | 3 | 4 | -6 | 2 | 1 | 0 | 0 | 0 | 14 | 7.1 |
| 1973–74 | 38 | Toronto Maple Leafs | NHL | 4 | 1 | 1 | 2 | -2 | 0 | 1 | 0 | 0 | 0 | 7 | 14.3 |
| 1974–75 | 39 | Toronto Maple Leafs | NHL | 7 | 0 | 0 | 0 | -2 | 2 | 0 | 0 | 0 | 0 | 5 | 0.0 |
| 1975–76 | 40 | Edmonton Oilers | WHA | 4 | 1 | 3 | 4 | 3 | 2 | | | | | | |
| 1976–77 | 41 | Edmonton Oilers | WHA | 5 | 0 | 3 | 3 | -2 | 0 | 0 | 0 | 0 | 0 | | |
| Career — 16 Seasons | | | | 115 | 31 | 59 | 90 | -21 | 71 | 19 | 10 | 1 | 3 | 274 | 10.2 |

## Jack Walker   Profile: See page 161

### REGULAR SEASON

| SEASON | AGE | TEAM | LG | GP | G | A | PTS | PIM |
|---|---|---|---|---|---|---|---|---|
| 1910–11 | 22 | Port Arthur Lake City | NOHL | 14 | 30 | 0 | 30 | |
| 1911–12 | 23 | Port Arthur Lake City | NOHL | 13 | 17 | 0 | 17 | 0 |
| 1912–13 | 24 | Toronto Blueshirts | NHA | 1 | 0 | 0 | 0 | 0 |
| 1912–13 | 24 | Moncton Victorias | MPHL | 15 | 21 | 0 | 21 | 9 |
| 1913–14 | 25 | Toronto Blueshirts | NHA | 20 | 20 | 16 | 36 | 17 |
| 1914–15 | 26 | Toronto Blueshirts | NHA | 19 | 12 | 7 | 19 | 11 |
| 1915–16 | 27 | Seattle Metropolitans | PCHA | 18 | 13 | 6 | 19 | 6 |
| 1916–17 | 28 | Seattle Metropolitans | PCHA | 24 | 11 | 15 | 26 | 3 |
| 1917–18 | 29 | Seattle Metropolitans | PCHA | 1 | 0 | 0 | 0 | 0 |
| 1918–19 | 30 | Seattle Metropolitans | PCHA | 20 | 9 | 6 | 15 | 9 |
| 1919–20 | 31 | Seattle Metropolitans | PCHA | 22 | 4 | 8 | 12 | 3 |
| 1920–21 | 32 | Seattle Metropolitans | PCHA | 23 | 6 | 4 | 10 | 6 |
| 1921–22 | 33 | Seattle Metropolitans | PCHA | 20 | 8 | 4 | 12 | 0 |
| 1922–23 | 34 | Seattle Metropolitans | PCHA | 29 | 13 | 10 | 23 | 4 |
| 1923–24 | 35 | Seattle Metropolitans | PCHA | 29 | 18 | 5 | 23 | 0 |
| 1924–25 | 36 | Victoria Cougars | WCHL | 28 | 7 | 7 | 14 | 6 |
| 1925–26 | 37 | Victoria Cougars | WHL | 30 | 9 | 8 | 17 | 16 |
| 1926–27 | 38 | Detroit Cougars | NHL | 41 | 3 | 4 | 7 | 6 |
| 1927–28 | 39 | Detroit Cougars | NHL | 43 | 2 | 4 | 6 | 10 |
| Career — 18 Seasons | | | | 410 | 203 | 104 | 307 | 106 |

### PLAYOFFS

| SEASON | AGE | TEAM | LG | GP | G | A | PTS | PIM |
|---|---|---|---|---|---|---|---|---|
| 1910–11 | 22 | Port Arthur Lake City | NOHL | 2 | 2 | 0 | 2 | 0 |
| 1910–11 | 22 | Port Arthur Lake City | St-Cup | 1 | 1 | 0 | 1 | 0 |
| 1911–12 | 23 | Port Arthur Lake City | NOHL | 2 | 3 | 0 | 3 | 0 |
| 1913–14 | 25 | Toronto Blueshirts | NHA | 2 | 3 | 0 | 3 | 2 |
| 1913–14 | 25 | Toronto Blueshirts | St-Cup | 3 | 1 | 0 | 1 | 3 |
| 1916–17 | 28 | Seattle Metropolitans | St-Cup | 4 | 1 | 2 | 3 | 0 |
| 1918–19 | 30 | Seattle Metropolitans | PCHA | 2 | 0 | 2 | 2 | 0 |
| 1918–19 | 30 | Seattle Metropolitans | St-Cup | 5 | 3 | 0 | 3 | 9 |
| 1919–20 | 31 | Seattle Metropolitans | PCHA | 2 | 1 | 1 | 2 | 0 |
| 1919–20 | 31 | Seattle Metropolitans | St-Cup | 5 | 1 | 3 | 4 | 0 |
| 1920–21 | 32 | Seattle Metropolitans | PCHA | 2 | 0 | 0 | 0 | 0 |
| 1921–22 | 33 | Seattle Metropolitans | PCHA | 2 | 0 | 0 | 0 | 0 |
| 1923–24 | 35 | Seattle Metropolitans | PCHA | 2 | 0 | 1 | 1 | 0 |
| 1924–25 | 36 | Victoria Cougars | St-Cup | 4 | 4 | 2 | 6 | 0 |
| 1924–25 | 36 | Victoria Cougars | WCHL | 4 | 2 | 0 | 2 | 0 |
| 1925–26 | 37 | Victoria Cougars | WHL | 4 | 0 | 0 | 0 | 2 |
| Career — 11 Seasons | | | | 46 | 24 | 11 | 35 | 16 |

## Marty Walsh   Profile: See page 162

### REGULAR SEASON

| SEASON | AGE | TEAM | LG | GP | G | A | PTS | PIM |
|---|---|---|---|---|---|---|---|---|
| 1902–03 | 18 | Queen's University | CIHU | | | | | |
| 1903–04 | 19 | Queen's University | CIHU | 4 | 9 | 0 | 9 | 30 |
| 1903–04 | 19 | Kingston A.C. | OHA-Int. | | | | | |
| 1904–05 | 20 | Queen's University | CIHU | 4 | 9 | 0 | 9 | 15 |
| 1905–06 | 21 | Queen's University | CIHU | 4 | 15 | 0 | 15 | 12 |
| 1906–07 | 22 | Canadian Soo | IHL | 7 | 4 | 5 | 9 | 0 |
| 1907–08 | 23 | Ottawa Senators | ECAHA | 9 | 27 | 0 | 27 | 30 |
| 1908–09 | 24 | Ottawa Senators | ECHA | 12 | 42 | 0 | 42 | 41 |
| 1909–10 | 25 | Ottawa Senators | CHA | 2 | 9 | 0 | 9 | 18 |
| 1909–10 | 25 | Ottawa Senators | NHA | 11 | 19 | 0 | 19 | 44 |

### REGULAR SEASON

| SEASON | AGE | TEAM | LG | GP | G | A | PTS | PIM |
|---|---|---|---|---|---|---|---|---|
| 1910–11 | 26 | Ottawa Senators | NHA | 16 | 35 | 0 | 35 | 51 |
| 1911–12 | 27 | Ottawa Senators | NHA | 12 | 9 | 0 | 9 | 0 |
| Career — 10 Seasons | | | | 81 | 178 | 5 | 183 | 249 |

### PLAYOFFS

| SEASON | AGE | TEAM | LG | GP | G | A | PTS | PIM |
|---|---|---|---|---|---|---|---|---|
| 1905–06 | 21 | Queen's University | St-Cup | 2 | 4 | 0 | 4 | 3 |
| 1909–10 | 25 | Ottawa Senators | St-Cup | 4 | 8 | 0 | 8 | 12 |
| 1910–11 | 26 | Ottawa Senators | St-Cup | 2 | 13 | 0 | 13 | 0 |
| Career — 3 Seasons | | | | 8 | 25 | 0 | 25 | 15 |

## Cooney Weiland   Profile: See page 163

### REGULAR SEASON

| SEASON | AGE | TEAM | LG | GP | G | A | PTS | PIM |
|---|---|---|---|---|---|---|---|---|
| 1928–29 | 24 | Boston Bruins | NHL | 42 | 11 | 7 | 18 | 14 |
| 1929–30 | 25 | Boston Bruins | NHL | 44 | 43 | 30 | 73 | 29 |
| 1930–31 | 26 | Boston Bruins | NHL | 44 | 25 | 13 | 38 | 14 |
| 1931–32 | 27 | Boston Bruins | NHL | 46 | 14 | 13 | 27 | 24 |
| 1932–33 | 28 | Ottawa Senators | NHL | 48 | 16 | 11 | 27 | 4 |
| 1933–34 | 29 | Ottawa Senators | NHL | 8 | 2 | 0 | 2 | 4 |
| 1933–34 | 29 | Detroit Red Wings | NHL | 40 | 11 | 19 | 30 | 6 |
| 1934–35 | 30 | Detroit Red Wings | NHL | 48 | 13 | 25 | 38 | 10 |
| 1935–36 | 31 | Boston Bruins | NHL | 48 | 14 | 14 | 28 | 15 |
| 1936–37 | 32 | Boston Bruins | NHL | 48 | 6 | 9 | 15 | 6 |
| 1937–38 | 33 | Boston Bruins | NHL | 48 | 11 | 12 | 23 | 16 |
| 1938–39 | 34 | Boston Bruins | NHL | 45 | 7 | 9 | 16 | 7 |
| NHL Career — 11 Seasons | | | | 509 | 173 | 162 | 335 | 149 |

### PLAYOFFS

| SEASON | AGE | TEAM | LG | GP | G | A | PTS | PIM |
|---|---|---|---|---|---|---|---|---|
| 1928–29 | 24 | Boston Bruins | NHL | 5 | 2 | 0 | 2 | 2 |
| 1929–30 | 25 | Boston Bruins | NHL | 6 | 1 | 5 | 6 | 2 |
| 1930–31 | 26 | Boston Bruins | NHL | 5 | 6 | 3 | 9 | 2 |
| 1933–34 | 29 | Detroit Red Wings | NHL | 9 | 2 | 2 | 4 | 6 |
| 1935–36 | 31 | Boston Bruins | NHL | 2 | 1 | 0 | 1 | 2 |
| 1936–37 | 32 | Boston Bruins | NHL | 3 | 0 | 0 | 0 | 0 |
| 1937–38 | 33 | Boston Bruins | NHL | 3 | 0 | 0 | 0 | 0 |
| 1938–39 | 34 | Boston Bruins | NHL | 12 | 0 | 0 | 0 | 0 |
| NHL Career — 8 Seasons | | | | 45 | 12 | 10 | 22 | 14 |

# Steve Yzerman   Profile: See page 164

## REGULAR SEASON

| SEASON | AGE | TEAM | LG | GP | G | A | PTS | +/- | PIM | ESG | PPG | SHG | GWG | SOG | S% |
|---|---|---|---|---|---|---|---|---|---|---|---|---|---|---|---|
| 1983–84 | 18 | Detroit Red Wings | NHL | 80 | 39 | 48 | 87 | -19 | 33 | 26 | 13 | 0 | 2 | 177 | 22.0 |
| 1984–85 | 19 | Detroit Red Wings | NHL | 80 | 30 | 59 | 89 | -17 | 58 | 21 | 9 | 0 | 3 | 231 | 13.0 |
| 1985–86 | 20 | Detroit Red Wings | NHL | 51 | 14 | 28 | 42 | -22 | 16 | 11 | 3 | 0 | 3 | 132 | 10.6 |
| 1986–87 | 21 | Detroit Red Wings | NHL | 80 | 31 | 59 | 90 | -2 | 43 | 21 | 9 | 1 | 2 | 217 | 14.3 |
| 1987–88 | 22 | Detroit Red Wings | NHL | 64 | 50 | 52 | 102 | 30 | 44 | 34 | 10 | 6 | 6 | 242 | 20.7 |
| 1988–89 | 23 | Detroit Red Wings | NHL | 80 | 65 | 90 | 155 | 17 | 61 | 45 | 17 | 3 | 7 | 388 | 16.8 |
| 1989–90 | 24 | Detroit Red Wings | NHL | 79 | 62 | 65 | 127 | -6 | 79 | 39 | 16 | 7 | 8 | 332 | 18.7 |
| 1990–91 | 25 | Detroit Red Wings | NHL | 80 | 51 | 57 | 108 | -2 | 34 | 33 | 12 | 6 | 4 | 326 | 15.6 |
| 1991–92 | 26 | Detroit Red Wings | NHL | 79 | 45 | 58 | 103 | 26 | 64 | 28 | 9 | 8 | 9 | 295 | 15.3 |
| 1992–93 | 27 | Detroit Red Wings | NHL | 84 | 58 | 79 | 137 | 33 | 44 | 38 | 13 | 7 | 6 | 307 | 18.9 |
| 1993–94 | 28 | Detroit Red Wings | NHL | 58 | 24 | 58 | 82 | 11 | 36 | 14 | 7 | 3 | 3 | 217 | 11.1 |
| 1994–95 | 29 | Detroit Red Wings | NHL | 47 | 12 | 26 | 38 | 6 | 40 | 8 | 4 | 0 | 1 | 134 | 9.0 |
| 1995–96 | 30 | Detroit Red Wings | NHL | 80 | 36 | 59 | 95 | 29 | 64 | 18 | 16 | 2 | 8 | 220 | 16.4 |
| 1996–97 | 31 | Detroit Red Wings | NHL | 81 | 22 | 63 | 85 | 22 | 78 | 14 | 8 | 0 | 3 | 232 | 9.5 |
| 1997–98 | 32 | Detroit Red Wings | NHL | 75 | 24 | 45 | 69 | 3 | 46 | 16 | 6 | 2 | 0 | 188 | 12.8 |
| 1998–99 | 33 | Detroit Red Wings | NHL | 80 | 29 | 45 | 74 | 8 | 42 | 14 | 13 | 2 | 4 | 231 | 12.6 |
| 1999–00 | 34 | Detroit Red Wings | NHL | 78 | 35 | 44 | 79 | 28 | 34 | 18 | 15 | 2 | 6 | 234 | 15.0 |
| 2000–01 | 35 | Detroit Red Wings | NHL | 54 | 18 | 34 | 52 | 4 | 18 | 13 | 5 | 0 | 7 | 155 | 11.6 |
| 2001–02 | 36 | Detroit Red Wings | NHL | 52 | 13 | 35 | 48 | 11 | 18 | 7 | 5 | 1 | 5 | 104 | 12.5 |
| 2002–03 | 37 | Detroit Red Wings | NHL | 16 | 2 | 6 | 8 | 6 | 8 | 1 | 1 | 0 | 1 | 13 | 15.4 |
| 2003–04 | 38 | Detroit Red Wings | NHL | 75 | 18 | 33 | 51 | 10 | 46 | 11 | 7 | 0 | 3 | 141 | 12.8 |
| 2005–06 | 40 | Detroit Red Wings | NHL | 61 | 14 | 20 | 34 | 8 | 18 | 10 | 4 | 0 | 3 | 86 | 16.3 |
| NHL Career – 22 Seasons | | | | 1514 | 692 | 1063 | 1755 | 184 | 924 | 440 | 202 | 50 | 94 | 4602 | 15.0 |

## PLAYOFFS

| SEASON | AGE | TEAM | LG | GP | G | A | PTS | +/- | PIM | ESG | PPG | SHG | GWG | SOG | S% |
|---|---|---|---|---|---|---|---|---|---|---|---|---|---|---|---|
| 1983–84 | 18 | Detroit Red Wings | NHL | 4 | 3 | 3 | 6 | 1 | 0 | 2 | 1 | 0 | 1 | 9 | 33.3 |
| 1984–85 | 19 | Detroit Red Wings | NHL | 3 | 2 | 1 | 3 | -5 | 2 | 1 | 1 | 0 | 0 | 11 | 18.2 |
| 1986–87 | 21 | Detroit Red Wings | NHL | 16 | 5 | 13 | 18 | -2 | 8 | 4 | 1 | 0 | 0 | 40 | 12.5 |
| 1987–88 | 22 | Detroit Red Wings | NHL | 3 | 1 | 3 | 4 | -3 | 6 | 1 | 0 | 0 | 0 | 12 | 8.3 |
| 1988–89 | 23 | Detroit Red Wings | NHL | 6 | 5 | 5 | 10 | -7 | 2 | 3 | 2 | 0 | 0 | 35 | 14.3 |
| 1990–91 | 25 | Detroit Red Wings | NHL | 7 | 3 | 3 | 6 | -1 | 4 | 2 | 1 | 0 | 0 | 27 | 11.1 |
| 1991–92 | 26 | Detroit Red Wings | NHL | 11 | 3 | 5 | 8 | -3 | 12 | 2 | 0 | 1 | 1 | 48 | 6.3 |
| 1992–93 | 27 | Detroit Red Wings | NHL | 7 | 4 | 3 | 7 | -4 | 4 | 2 | 1 | 1 | 1 | 24 | 16.7 |
| 1993–94 | 28 | Detroit Red Wings | NHL | 3 | 1 | 3 | 4 | 4 | 0 | 1 | 0 | 0 | 0 | 8 | 12.5 |
| 1994–95 | 29 | Detroit Red Wings | NHL | 15 | 4 | 8 | 12 | -2 | 0 | 2 | 2 | 0 | 1 | 37 | 10.8 |
| 1995–96 | 30 | Detroit Red Wings | NHL | 18 | 8 | 12 | 20 | -1 | 4 | 4 | 4 | 0 | 0 | 52 | 15.4 |
| 1996–97 | 31 | Detroit Red Wings | NHL | 20 | 7 | 6 | 13 | 3 | 4 | 4 | 3 | 0 | 2 | 65 | 10.8 |
| 1997–98 | 32 | Detroit Red Wings | NHL | 22 | 6 | 18 | 24 | 10 | 22 | 2 | 3 | 1 | 0 | 65 | 9.2 |
| 1998–99 | 33 | Detroit Red Wings | NHL | 10 | 9 | 4 | 13 | 2 | 0 | 5 | 4 | 0 | 2 | 41 | 22.0 |
| 1999–00 | 34 | Detroit Red Wings | NHL | 8 | 0 | 4 | 4 | -4 | 0 | 0 | 0 | 0 | 0 | 20 | 0.0 |
| 2000–01 | 35 | Detroit Red Wings | NHL | 1 | 0 | 0 | 0 | 0 | 0 | 0 | 0 | 0 | 0 | 0 | 0.0 |
| 2001–02 | 36 | Detroit Red Wings | NHL | 23 | 6 | 17 | 23 | 4 | 10 | 2 | 4 | 0 | 2 | 52 | 11.5 |
| 2002–03 | 37 | Detroit Red Wings | NHL | 4 | 0 | 1 | 1 | 0 | 2 | 0 | 0 | 0 | 0 | 10 | 0.0 |
| 2003–04 | 38 | Detroit Red Wings | NHL | 11 | 3 | 2 | 5 | -1 | 0 | 3 | 0 | 0 | 1 | 18 | 16.7 |
| 2005–06 | 40 | Detroit Red Wings | NHL | 4 | 0 | 4 | 4 | -2 | 4 | 0 | 0 | 0 | 0 | 10 | 0.0 |
| NHL Career – 20 Seasons | | | | 196 | 70 | 115 | 185 | -11 | 84 | 40 | 27 | 3 | 12 | 584 | 12.0 |

## Glenn Anderson   Profile: See page 168

### REGULAR SEASON

| SEASON | AGE | TEAM | LG | GP | G | A | PTS | +/- | PIM | ESG | PPG | SHG | GWG | SOG | S% |
|--------|-----|------|-----|-----|-----|-----|------|-----|------|-----|-----|-----|-----|------|------|
| 1980–81 | 20 | Edmonton Oilers | NHL | 58 | 30 | 23 | 53 | 4 | 24 | 17 | 10 | 3 | 5 | 161 | 18.6 |
| 1981–82 | 21 | Edmonton Oilers | NHL | 80 | 38 | 67 | 105 | 45 | 71 | 29 | 9 | 0 | 8 | 252 | 15.1 |
| 1982–83 | 22 | Edmonton Oilers | NHL | 72 | 48 | 56 | 104 | 40 | 70 | 37 | 11 | 0 | 10 | 243 | 19.8 |
| 1983–84 | 23 | Edmonton Oilers | NHL | 80 | 54 | 45 | 99 | 41 | 65 | 39 | 11 | 4 | 11 | 277 | 19.5 |
| 1984–85 | 24 | Edmonton Oilers | NHL | 80 | 42 | 39 | 81 | 26 | 69 | 29 | 12 | 1 | 6 | 258 | 16.3 |
| 1985–86 | 25 | Edmonton Oilers | NHL | 72 | 54 | 48 | 102 | 38 | 90 | 34 | 18 | 2 | 9 | 242 | 22.3 |
| 1986–87 | 26 | Edmonton Oilers | NHL | 80 | 35 | 38 | 73 | 27 | 65 | 27 | 7 | 1 | 5 | 189 | 18.5 |
| 1987–88 | 27 | Edmonton Oilers | NHL | 80 | 38 | 50 | 88 | 5 | 58 | 21 | 16 | 1 | 3 | 255 | 14.9 |
| 1988–89 | 28 | Edmonton Oilers | NHL | 79 | 16 | 48 | 64 | -16 | 93 | 9 | 7 | 0 | 3 | 212 | 7.5 |
| 1989–90 | 29 | Edmonton Oilers | NHL | 73 | 34 | 38 | 72 | -1 | 107 | 16 | 17 | 1 | 7 | 204 | 16.7 |
| 1990–91 | 30 | Edmonton Oilers | NHL | 74 | 24 | 31 | 55 | -7 | 59 | 16 | 8 | 0 | 4 | 193 | 12.4 |
| 1991–92 | 31 | Toronto Maple Leafs | NHL | 72 | 24 | 33 | 57 | -13 | 100 | 19 | 5 | 0 | 4 | 188 | 12.8 |
| 1992–93 | 32 | Toronto Maple Leafs | NHL | 76 | 22 | 43 | 65 | 19 | 117 | 11 | 11 | 0 | 3 | 161 | 13.7 |
| 1993–94 | 33 | Toronto Maple Leafs | NHL | 73 | 17 | 18 | 35 | -6 | 50 | 12 | 5 | 0 | 3 | 127 | 13.4 |
| 1993–94 | 33 | New York Rangers | NHL | 12 | 4 | 2 | 6 | 1 | 12 | 2 | 2 | 0 | 0 | 22 | 18.2 |
| 1994–95 | 34 | St. Louis Blues | NHL | 36 | 12 | 14 | 26 | 9 | 37 | 12 | 0 | 0 | 3 | 54 | 22.2 |
| 1995–96 | 35 | Edmonton Oilers | NHL | 17 | 4 | 6 | 10 | 0 | 27 | 4 | 0 | 0 | 1 | 36 | 11.1 |
| 1995–96 | 35 | St. Louis Blues | NHL | 15 | 2 | 2 | 4 | -11 | 6 | 0 | 2 | 0 | 0 | 35 | 5.7 |
| NHL Career – 16 Seasons | | | | 1129 | 498 | 601 | 1099 | 201 | 1120 | 334 | 151 | 13 | 85 | 3109 | 16.0 |

### PLAYOFFS

| SEASON | AGE | TEAM | LG | GP | G | A | PTS | +/- | PIM | ESG | PPG | SHG | GWG | SOG | S% |
|--------|-----|------|-----|-----|-----|-----|------|-----|------|-----|-----|-----|-----|------|------|
| 1980–81 | 20 | Edmonton Oilers | NHL | 9 | 5 | 7 | 12 | -3 | 12 | 2 | 3 | 0 | 0 | 20 | 25.0 |
| 1981–82 | 21 | Edmonton Oilers | NHL | 5 | 2 | 5 | 7 | -2 | 8 | 2 | 0 | 0 | 1 | 23 | 8.7 |
| 1982–83 | 22 | Edmonton Oilers | NHL | 16 | 10 | 10 | 20 | 5 | 32 | 9 | 1 | 0 | 2 | 49 | 20.4 |
| 1983–84 | 23 | Edmonton Oilers | NHL | 19 | 6 | 11 | 17 | 6 | 33 | 5 | 1 | 0 | 1 | 68 | 8.8 |
| 1984–85 | 24 | Edmonton Oilers | NHL | 18 | 10 | 16 | 26 | 11 | 38 | 8 | 2 | 0 | 1 | 46 | 21.7 |
| 1985–86 | 25 | Edmonton Oilers | NHL | 10 | 8 | 3 | 11 | 2 | 14 | 7 | 1 | 0 | 2 | 38 | 21.1 |
| 1986–87 | 26 | Edmonton Oilers | NHL | 21 | 14 | 13 | 27 | 13 | 59 | 10 | 4 | 0 | 2 | 62 | 22.6 |
| 1987–88 | 27 | Edmonton Oilers | NHL | 19 | 9 | 16 | 25 | 5 | 49 | 5 | 4 | 0 | 1 | 43 | 20.9 |
| 1988–89 | 28 | Edmonton Oilers | NHL | 7 | 1 | 2 | 3 | -1 | 8 | 0 | 1 | 0 | 0 | 16 | 6.3 |
| 1989–90 | 29 | Edmonton Oilers | NHL | 22 | 10 | 12 | 22 | 12 | 20 | 8 | 2 | 0 | 2 | 46 | 21.7 |
| 1990–91 | 30 | Edmonton Oilers | NHL | 18 | 6 | 7 | 13 | -2 | 41 | 3 | 3 | 0 | 0 | 43 | 14.0 |
| 1992–93 | 32 | Toronto Maple Leafs | NHL | 21 | 7 | 11 | 18 | 7 | 31 | 7 | 0 | 0 | 2 | 46 | 15.2 |
| 1993–94 | 33 | New York Rangers | NHL | 23 | 3 | 3 | 6 | 5 | 42 | 2 | 0 | 1 | 2 | 31 | 9.7 |
| 1994–95 | 34 | St. Louis Blues | NHL | 6 | 1 | 1 | 2 | 0 | 49 | 1 | 0 | 0 | 0 | 3 | 33.3 |
| 1995–96 | 35 | St. Louis Blues | NHL | 11 | 1 | 4 | 5 | 5 | 6 | 1 | 0 | 0 | 1 | 20 | 5.0 |
| NHL Career – 15 Seasons | | | | 225 | 93 | 121 | 214 | 63 | 442 | 70 | 22 | 1 | 17 | 554 | 16.8 |

## George Armstrong   Profile: See page 169

### REGULAR SEASON

| SEASON | AGE | TEAM | LG | GP | G | A | PTS | +/- | PIM | ESG | PPG | SHG | GWG | SOG | S% |
|--------|-----|------|-----|-----|-----|-----|------|-----|------|-----|-----|-----|-----|------|------|
| 1949–50 | 19 | Toronto Maple Leafs | NHL | 2 | 0 | 0 | 0 | | 0 | 0 | 0 | 0 | 0 | | |
| 1951–52 | 21 | Toronto Maple Leafs | NHL | 20 | 3 | 3 | 6 | | 30 | 2 | 1 | 0 | 1 | | |
| 1952–53 | 22 | Toronto Maple Leafs | NHL | 52 | 14 | 11 | 25 | | 54 | 11 | 3 | 0 | 2 | | |
| 1953–54 | 23 | Toronto Maple Leafs | NHL | 63 | 17 | 15 | 32 | | 60 | 12 | 5 | 0 | 4 | | |
| 1954–55 | 24 | Toronto Maple Leafs | NHL | 66 | 10 | 18 | 28 | | 80 | 6 | 4 | 0 | 0 | | |
| 1955–56 | 25 | Toronto Maple Leafs | NHL | 67 | 16 | 32 | 48 | | 97 | 14 | 2 | 0 | 3 | | |
| 1956–57 | 26 | Toronto Maple Leafs | NHL | 54 | 18 | 26 | 44 | | 40 | 10 | 8 | 0 | 2 | | |
| 1957–58 | 27 | Toronto Maple Leafs | NHL | 59 | 17 | 25 | 42 | | 93 | 13 | 4 | 0 | 1 | | |
| 1958–59 | 28 | Toronto Maple Leafs | NHL | 59 | 20 | 16 | 36 | | 37 | 16 | 3 | 1 | 3 | | |
| 1959–60 | 29 | Toronto Maple Leafs | NHL | 70 | 23 | 28 | 51 | -4 | 62 | 19 | 3 | 1 | 2 | 183 | 12.6 |
| 1960–61 | 30 | Toronto Maple Leafs | NHL | 47 | 14 | 19 | 33 | 19 | 21 | 10 | 4 | 0 | 3 | 114 | 12.3 |
| 1961–62 | 31 | Toronto Maple Leafs | NHL | 70 | 21 | 32 | 53 | 48 | 27 | 18 | 3 | 0 | 2 | 187 | 11.2 |
| 1962–63 | 32 | Toronto Maple Leafs | NHL | 70 | 19 | 24 | 43 | 5 | 27 | 13 | 3 | 3 | 1 | 204 | 9.3 |
| 1963–64 | 33 | Toronto Maple Leafs | NHL | 67 | 20 | 17 | 37 | -3 | 14 | 13 | 7 | 0 | 3 | 170 | 11.8 |
| 1964–65 | 34 | Toronto Maple Leafs | NHL | 59 | 15 | 22 | 37 | 12 | 14 | 12 | 3 | 0 | 3 | 135 | 11.1 |
| 1965–66 | 35 | Toronto Maple Leafs | NHL | 70 | 16 | 35 | 51 | 11 | 12 | 11 | 3 | 2 | 3 | 186 | 8.6 |
| 1966–67 | 36 | Toronto Maple Leafs | NHL | 70 | 9 | 24 | 33 | -2 | 26 | 6 | 3 | 0 | 3 | 155 | 5.8 |
| 1967–68 | 37 | Toronto Maple Leafs | NHL | 62 | 13 | 21 | 34 | 8 | 4 | 11 | 2 | 0 | 2 | 125 | 10.4 |
| 1968–69 | 38 | Toronto Maple Leafs | NHL | 53 | 11 | 16 | 27 | -8 | 10 | 9 | 1 | 1 | 1 | 103 | 10.7 |
| 1969–70 | 39 | Toronto Maple Leafs | NHL | 49 | 13 | 15 | 28 | 8 | 12 | 11 | 2 | 0 | 3 | 93 | 14.0 |
| 1970–71 | 40 | Toronto Maple Leafs | NHL | 59 | 7 | 18 | 25 | 7 | 6 | 7 | 0 | 0 | 1 | 93 | 7.5 |
| NHL Career – 21 Seasons | | | | 1188 | 296 | 417 | 713 | 101 | 726 | 224 | 64 | 8 | 43 | 1748 | 10.4 |

## George Armstrong (continued)

### PLAYOFFS

| SEASON | AGE | TEAM | LG | GP | G | A | PTS | +/- | PIM | ESG | PPG | SHG | GWG | SOG | S% |
|---|---|---|---|---|---|---|---|---|---|---|---|---|---|---|---|
| 1951-52 | 21 | Toronto Maple Leafs | NHL | 4 | 0 | 0 | 0 | | 2 | 0 | 0 | 0 | 0 | | |
| 1953-54 | 23 | Toronto Maple Leafs | NHL | 5 | 1 | 0 | 1 | | 2 | 1 | 0 | 0 | 0 | | |
| 1954-55 | 24 | Toronto Maple Leafs | NHL | 4 | 1 | 0 | 1 | | 4 | 1 | 0 | 0 | 0 | | |
| 1955-56 | 25 | Toronto Maple Leafs | NHL | 5 | 4 | 2 | 6 | | 0 | 2 | 2 | 0 | 0 | | |
| 1958-59 | 28 | Toronto Maple Leafs | NHL | 12 | 0 | 4 | 4 | | 10 | 0 | 0 | 0 | 0 | | |
| 1959-60 | 29 | Toronto Maple Leafs | NHL | 10 | 1 | 4 | 5 | 0 | 4 | 1 | 0 | 0 | 0 | 26 | 3.8 |
| 1960-61 | 30 | Toronto Maple Leafs | NHL | 5 | 1 | 1 | 2 | 1 | 0 | 1 | 0 | 0 | 1 | 4 | 25.0 |
| 1961-62 | 31 | Toronto Maple Leafs | NHL | 12 | 7 | 5 | 12 | 6 | 2 | 6 | 1 | 0 | 1 | 37 | 18.9 |
| 1962-63 | 32 | Toronto Maple Leafs | NHL | 10 | 3 | 6 | 9 | 10 | 4 | 2 | 1 | 0 | 0 | 29 | 10.3 |
| 1963-64 | 33 | Toronto Maple Leafs | NHL | 14 | 5 | 8 | 13 | 7 | 10 | 2 | 3 | 0 | 0 | 37 | 13.5 |
| 1964-65 | 34 | Toronto Maple Leafs | NHL | 6 | 1 | 0 | 1 | -1 | 4 | 1 | 0 | 0 | 1 | 17 | 5.9 |
| 1965-66 | 35 | Toronto Maple Leafs | NHL | 4 | 0 | 1 | 1 | -1 | 4 | 0 | 0 | 0 | 0 | 10 | 0.0 |
| 1966-67 | 36 | Toronto Maple Leafs | NHL | 9 | 2 | 1 | 3 | 2 | 6 | 1 | -1 | 0 | 0 | 13 | 15.4 |
| 1968-69 | 38 | Toronto Maple Leafs | NHL | 4 | 0 | 0 | 0 | -5 | 0 | 0 | 0 | 0 | 0 | 10 | 0.0 |
| 1970-71 | 40 | Toronto Maple Leafs | NHL | 6 | 0 | 2 | 2 | -3 | 0 | 0 | 0 | 0 | 0 | 10 | 0.0 |
| NHL Career — 15 Seasons | | | | 110 | 26 | 34 | 60 | 16 | 52 | 18 | 8 | 0 | 3 | 193 | 10.4 |

# Ace Bailey    Profile: See page 170

### REGULAR SEASON

| SEASON | AGE | TEAM | LG | GP | G | A | PTS | PIM |
|---|---|---|---|---|---|---|---|---|
| 1926-27 | 23 | Toronto St. Pats/Maple Leafs | NHL | 42 | 15 | 13 | 28 | 80 |
| 1927-28 | 24 | Toronto Maple Leafs | NHL | 43 | 9 | 2 | 11 | 72 |
| 1928-29 | 25 | Toronto Maple Leafs | NHL | 44 | 22 | 10 | 32 | 80 |
| 1929-30 | 26 | Toronto Maple Leafs | NHL | 43 | 22 | 21 | 43 | 69 |
| 1930-31 | 27 | Toronto Maple Leafs | NHL | 40 | 23 | 19 | 42 | 48 |
| 1931-32 | 28 | Toronto Maple Leafs | NHL | 44 | 8 | 5 | 13 | 76 |
| 1932-33 | 29 | Toronto Maple Leafs | NHL | 47 | 10 | 8 | 18 | 52 |
| 1933-34 | 30 | Toronto Maple Leafs | NHL | 13 | 2 | 3 | 5 | 11 |
| NHL Career — 8 Seasons | | | | 316 | 111 | 81 | 192 | 488 |

### PLAYOFFS

| SEASON | AGE | TEAM | LG | GP | G | A | PTS | PIM |
|---|---|---|---|---|---|---|---|---|
| 1928-29 | 25 | Toronto Maple Leafs | NHL | 4 | 1 | 2 | 3 | 4 |
| 1930-31 | 27 | Toronto Maple Leafs | NHL | 2 | 1 | 1 | 2 | 0 |
| 1931-32 | 28 | Toronto Maple Leafs | NHL | 7 | 1 | 1 | 2 | 4 |
| 1932-33 | 29 | Toronto Maple Leafs | NHL | 7 | 0 | 1 | 1 | 4 |
| NHL Career — 4 Seasons | | | | 20 | 3 | 5 | 8 | 12 |

# Andy Bathgate    Profile: See page 172

### REGULAR SEASON

| SEASON | AGE | TEAM | LG | GP | G | A | PTS | +/- | PIM | ESG | PPG | SHG | GWG | SOG | S% |
|---|---|---|---|---|---|---|---|---|---|---|---|---|---|---|---|
| 1952-53 | 20 | New York Rangers | NHL | 18 | 0 | 1 | 1 | | 6 | 0 | 0 | 0 | 0 | | |
| 1953-54 | 21 | New York Rangers | NHL | 20 | 2 | 2 | 4 | | 18 | 1 | 1 | 0 | 0 | | |
| 1954-55 | 22 | New York Rangers | NHL | 70 | 20 | 20 | 40 | | 37 | 12 | 8 | 0 | 1 | | |
| 1955-56 | 23 | New York Rangers | NHL | 70 | 19 | 47 | 66 | | 59 | 12 | 6 | 1 | 2 | | |
| 1956-57 | 24 | New York Rangers | NHL | 70 | 27 | 50 | 77 | | 60 | 19 | 6 | 2 | 1 | | |
| 1957-58 | 25 | New York Rangers | NHL | 65 | 30 | 48 | 78 | | 42 | 23 | 6 | 1 | 0 | | |
| 1958-59 | 26 | New York Rangers | NHL | 70 | 40 | 48 | 88 | | 48 | 30 | 9 | 1 | 1 | | |
| 1959-60 | 27 | New York Rangers | NHL | 70 | 26 | 48 | 74 | 4 | 28 | 23 | 3 | 0 | 0 | 275 | 9.5 |
| 1960-61 | 28 | New York Rangers | NHL | 70 | 29 | 48 | 77 | -12 | 22 | 22 | 6 | 1 | 0 | 304 | 9.5 |
| 1961-62 | 29 | New York Rangers | NHL | 70 | 28 | 56 | 84 | 3 | 44 | 24 | 4 | 0 | 0 | 305 | 9.2 |
| 1962-63 | 30 | New York Rangers | NHL | 70 | 35 | 46 | 81 | -5 | 54 | 30 | 5 | 0 | 0 | 268 | 13.1 |
| 1963-64 | 31 | New York Rangers | NHL | 56 | 16 | 43 | 59 | -18 | 26 | 16 | 5 | 0 | 1 | 52 | 5.8 |
| 1963-64 | 31 | Toronto Maple Leafs | NHL | 15 | 3 | 15 | 18 | 6 | 8 | 3 | 0 | 0 | 0 | 232 | 6.9 |
| 1964-65 | 32 | Toronto Maple Leafs | NHL | 55 | 16 | 29 | 45 | 5 | 34 | 10 | 6 | 0 | 1 | 151 | 10.6 |
| 1965-66 | 33 | Detroit Red Wings | NHL | 70 | 15 | 32 | 47 | -5 | 25 | 11 | 4 | 0 | 0 | 216 | 6.9 |
| 1966-67 | 34 | Detroit Red Wings | NHL | 60 | 8 | 23 | 31 | -15 | 24 | 8 | 0 | 0 | 1 | 157 | 5.1 |
| 1967-68 | 35 | Pittsburgh Penguins | NHL | 74 | 20 | 39 | 59 | -11 | 55 | 18 | 2 | 0 | 4 | 292 | 6.8 |
| 1970-71 | 38 | Pittsburgh Penguins | NHL | 76 | 15 | 29 | 44 | -12 | 34 | 8 | 7 | 0 | 3 | 209 | 7.2 |
| 1974-75 | 42 | Vancouver Blazers | WHA | 11 | 1 | 6 | 7 | | 2 | | | 0 | 0 | 12 | 8.3 |
| Career — 18 Seasons | | | | 1080 | 350 | 630 | 980 | 60 | 626 | 265 | 78 | 6 | 35 | 2473 | 14.2 |

### PLAYOFFS

| SEASON | AGE | TEAM | LG | GP | G | A | PTS | +/- | PIM | ESG | PPG | SHG | GWG | SOG | S% |
|---|---|---|---|---|---|---|---|---|---|---|---|---|---|---|---|
| 1955-56 | 23 | New York Rangers | NHL | 5 | 1 | 2 | 3 | | 2 | 1 | 0 | 0 | 0 | | |
| 1956-57 | 24 | New York Rangers | NHL | 5 | 2 | 0 | 2 | | 7 | 2 | 0 | 0 | 0 | | |
| 1957-58 | 25 | New York Rangers | NHL | 6 | 5 | 3 | 8 | | 6 | 2 | 2 | 1 | 0 | | |
| 1961-62 | 29 | New York Rangers | NHL | 6 | 1 | 2 | 3 | -5 | 4 | 1 | 0 | 0 | 0 | 24 | 4.2 |
| 1963-64 | 31 | Toronto Maple Leafs | NHL | 14 | 5 | 4 | 9 | -4 | 25 | 3 | 2 | 0 | 2 | 53 | 9.4 |
| 1964-65 | 32 | Toronto Maple Leafs | NHL | 6 | 1 | 0 | 1 | -1 | 6 | 0 | 1 | 0 | 0 | 11 | 9.1 |
| 1965-66 | 33 | Detroit Red Wings | NHL | 12 | 6 | 3 | 9 | 3 | 6 | 0 | 6 | 0 | 0 | 31 | 19.4 |
| Career — 7 Seasons | | | | 54 | 21 | 14 | 35 | -7 | 56 | 9 | 11 | 1 | 2 | 119 | 10.9 |

## Bobby Bauer   Profile: See page 173

**REGULAR SEASON**

| SEASON | AGE | TEAM | LG | GP | G | A | PTS | PIM |
|---|---|---|---|---|---|---|---|---|
| 1936–37 | 21 | Boston Bruins | NHL | 1 | 1 | 0 | 1 | 0 |
| 1937–38 | 22 | Boston Bruins | NHL | 48 | 20 | 13 | 33 | 9 |
| 1938–39 | 23 | Boston Bruins | NHL | 48 | 13 | 18 | 31 | 4 |
| 1939–40 | 24 | Boston Bruins | NHL | 48 | 17 | 26 | 43 | 4 |
| 1940–41 | 25 | Boston Bruins | NHL | 48 | 17 | 22 | 39 | 2 |
| 1941–42 | 26 | Boston Bruins | NHL | 36 | 13 | 22 | 35 | 11 |
| 1945–46 | 30 | Boston Bruins | NHL | 39 | 11 | 10 | 21 | 4 |
| 1946–47 | 31 | Boston Bruins | NHL | 58 | 30 | 24 | 54 | 4 |
| 1951–52 | 36 | Boston Bruins | NHL | 1 | 1 | 1 | 2 | 0 |
| NHL Career – 9 Seasons | | | | 327 | 123 | 136 | 259 | 38 |

**PLAYOFFS**

| SEASON | AGE | TEAM | LG | GP | G | A | PTS | PIM |
|---|---|---|---|---|---|---|---|---|
| 1936–37 | 21 | Boston Bruins | NHL | 1 | 0 | 0 | 0 | 0 |
| 1937–38 | 22 | Boston Bruins | NHL | 3 | 0 | 0 | 0 | 2 |
| 1938–39 | 23 | Boston Bruins | NHL | 12 | 3 | 2 | 5 | 0 |
| 1939–40 | 24 | Boston Bruins | NHL | 6 | 1 | 0 | 1 | 2 |
| 1940–41 | 25 | Boston Bruins | NHL | 11 | 2 | 2 | 4 | 0 |
| 1945–46 | 30 | Boston Bruins | NHL | 10 | 4 | 3 | 7 | 2 |
| 1946–47 | 31 | Boston Bruins | NHL | 5 | 1 | 1 | 2 | 0 |
| NHL Career – 7 Seasons | | | | 48 | 11 | 8 | 19 | 6 |

## Mike Bossy   Profile: See page 174

**REGULAR SEASON**

| SEASON | AGE | TEAM | LG | GP | G | A | PTS | +/– | PIM | ESG | PPG | SHG | GWG | SOG | S% |
|---|---|---|---|---|---|---|---|---|---|---|---|---|---|---|---|
| 1977–78 | 21 | New York Islanders | NHL | 73 | 53 | 38 | 91 | 31 | 6 | 28 | 25 | 0 | 4 | 235 | 22.6 |
| 1978–79 | 22 | New York Islanders | NHL | 80 | 69 | 57 | 126 | 63 | 25 | 42 | 27 | 0 | 9 | 279 | 24.7 |
| 1979–80 | 23 | New York Islanders | NHL | 75 | 51 | 41 | 92 | 28 | 12 | 36 | 15 | 0 | 8 | 246 | 20.7 |
| 1980–81 | 24 | New York Islanders | NHL | 79 | 68 | 51 | 119 | 38 | 32 | 38 | 28 | 2 | 10 | 315 | 21.6 |
| 1981–82 | 25 | New York Islanders | NHL | 80 | 64 | 83 | 147 | 69 | 22 | 47 | 17 | 0 | 10 | 301 | 21.3 |
| 1982–83 | 26 | New York Islanders | NHL | 79 | 60 | 58 | 118 | 27 | 20 | 41 | 19 | 0 | 7 | 274 | 22.9 |
| 1983–84 | 27 | New York Islanders | NHL | 67 | 51 | 67 | 118 | 65 | 8 | 45 | 6 | 0 | 11 | 246 | 20.7 |
| 1984–85 | 28 | New York Islanders | NHL | 76 | 58 | 59 | 117 | 37 | 38 | 40 | 14 | 4 | 7 | 285 | 20.4 |
| 1985–86 | 29 | New York Islanders | NHL | 80 | 61 | 62 | 123 | 30 | 14 | 39 | 21 | 1 | 9 | 302 | 20.2 |
| 1986–87 | 30 | New York Islanders | NHL | 63 | 38 | 37 | 75 | -8 | 33 | 29 | 8 | 1 | 5 | 226 | 16.8 |
| NHL Career – 10 Seasons | | | | 752 | 573 | 553 | 1126 | 380 | 210 | 385 | 180 | 8 | 80 | 2709 | 21.2 |

**PLAYOFFS**

| SEASON | AGE | TEAM | LG | GP | G | A | PTS | +/– | PIM | ESG | PPG | SHG | GWG | SOG | S% |
|---|---|---|---|---|---|---|---|---|---|---|---|---|---|---|---|
| 1977–78 | 21 | New York Islanders | NHL | 7 | 2 | 2 | 4 | 3 | 2 | 2 | 0 | 0 | 1 | 29 | 6.9 |
| 1978–79 | 22 | New York Islanders | NHL | 10 | 6 | 2 | 8 | 5 | 2 | 4 | 2 | 0 | 1 | 25 | 24.0 |
| 1979–80 | 23 | New York Islanders | NHL | 16 | 10 | 13 | 23 | -4 | 8 | 4 | 6 | 0 | 1 | 55 | 18.2 |
| 1980–81 | 24 | New York Islanders | NHL | 18 | 17 | 18 | 35 | 14 | 4 | 8 | 9 | 0 | 3 | 69 | 24.6 |
| 1981–82 | 25 | New York Islanders | NHL | 19 | 17 | 10 | 27 | 7 | 0 | 11 | 6 | 0 | 3 | 62 | 27.4 |
| 1982–83 | 26 | New York Islanders | NHL | 19 | 17 | 9 | 26 | 7 | 10 | 11 | 6 | 0 | 5 | 78 | 21.8 |
| 1983–84 | 27 | New York Islanders | NHL | 21 | 8 | 10 | 18 | 5 | 4 | 6 | 2 | 0 | 3 | 62 | 12.9 |
| 1984–85 | 28 | New York Islanders | NHL | 10 | 5 | 6 | 11 | 1 | 4 | 3 | 2 | 0 | 0 | 32 | 15.6 |
| 1985–86 | 29 | New York Islanders | NHL | 3 | 1 | 2 | 3 | -2 | 4 | 1 | 0 | 0 | 0 | 14 | 7.1 |
| 1986–87 | 30 | New York Islanders | NHL | 6 | 2 | 3 | 5 | -2 | 0 | 0 | 2 | 0 | 0 | 10 | 20.0 |
| NHL Career – 10 Seasons | | | | 129 | 85 | 75 | 160 | 34 | 38 | 50 | 35 | 0 | 17 | 436 | 19.5 |

## Punch Broadbent   Profile: See page 176

**REGULAR SEASON**

| SEASON | AGE | TEAM | LG | GP | G | A | PTS | PIM |
|---|---|---|---|---|---|---|---|---|
| 1912–13 | 20 | Ottawa Senators | NHA | 20 | 20 | 0 | 20 | 15 |
| 1913–14 | 21 | Ottawa Senators | NHA | 17 | 6 | 7 | 13 | 61 |
| 1914–15 | 22 | Ottawa Senators | NHA | 20 | 24 | 3 | 27 | 115 |
| 1918–19 | 26 | Ottawa Senators | NHL | 8 | 4 | 3 | 7 | 12 |
| 1919–20 | 27 | Ottawa Senators | NHL | 21 | 19 | 6 | 25 | 38 |
| 1920–21 | 28 | Ottawa Senators | NHL | 9 | 4 | 1 | 5 | 10 |
| 1921–22 | 29 | Ottawa Senators | NHL | 24 | 31 | 14 | 45 | 24 |
| 1922–23 | 30 | Ottawa Senators | NHL | 24 | 14 | 0 | 14 | 32 |
| 1923–24 | 31 | Ottawa Senators | NHL | 22 | 9 | 5 | 14 | 48 |
| 1924–25 | 32 | Montreal Maroons | NHL | 30 | 14 | 6 | 20 | 83 |
| 1925–26 | 33 | Montreal Maroons | NHL | 36 | 12 | 6 | 18 | 116 |
| 1926–27 | 34 | Montreal Maroons | NHL | 42 | 9 | 6 | 14 | 86 |
| 1927–28 | 35 | Ottawa Senators | NHL | 43 | 3 | 2 | 5 | 62 |
| 1928–29 | 36 | New York Americans | NHL | 44 | 1 | 4 | 5 | 61 |
| Career – 14 Seasons | | | | 360 | 170 | 62 | 232 | 767 |

**PLAYOFFS**

| SEASON | AGE | TEAM | LG | GP | G | A | PTS | PIM |
|---|---|---|---|---|---|---|---|---|
| 1914–15 | 22 | Ottawa Senators | NHA | 5 | 3 | 0 | 3 | 26 |
| 1918–19 | 26 | Ottawa Senators | NHL | 5 | 2 | 2 | 4 | 28 |
| 1919–20 | 27 | Ottawa Senators | St-Cup | 4 | 0 | 0 | 0 | 2 |
| 1920–21 | 28 | Ottawa Senators | NHL | 2 | 0 | 2 | 2 | 4 |
| 1920–21 | 28 | Ottawa Senators | St-Cup | 4 | 2 | 0 | 2 | 0 |
| 1921–22 | 29 | Ottawa Senators | NHL | 2 | 0 | 1 | 1 | 8 |
| 1922–23 | 30 | Ottawa Senators | NHL | 2 | 0 | 0 | 0 | 2 |
| 1922–23 | 30 | Ottawa Senators | St-Cup | 6 | 6 | 1 | 7 | 10 |
| 1923–24 | 31 | Ottawa Senators | NHL | 2 | 0 | 0 | 0 | 2 |
| 1925–26 | 33 | Montreal Maroons | NHL | 4 | 2 | 1 | 3 | 14 |
| 1925–26 | 33 | Montreal Maroons | St-Cup | 4 | 1 | 0 | 1 | 22 |
| 1926–27 | 34 | Montreal Maroons | NHL | 2 | 0 | 0 | 0 | 0 |
| 1927–28 | 35 | Ottawa Senators | NHL | 2 | 0 | 0 | 0 | 0 |
| 1928–29 | 36 | New York Americans | NHL | 2 | 0 | 0 | 0 | 2 |
| Career – 11 Seasons | | | | 46 | 16 | 7 | 23 | 120 |

## Pavel Bure  Profile: See page 177

### REGULAR SEASON

| SEASON | AGE | TEAM | LG | GP | G | A | PTS | +/- | PIM | ESG | PPG | SHG | GWG | SOG | S% |
|---|---|---|---|---|---|---|---|---|---|---|---|---|---|---|---|
| 1991–92 | 20 | Vancouver Canucks | NHL | 65 | 34 | 26 | 60 | 0 | 30 | 24 | 7 | 3 | 6 | 268 | 12.7 |
| 1992–93 | 21 | Vancouver Canucks | NHL | 83 | 60 | 50 | 110 | 35 | 69 | 40 | 13 | 7 | 9 | 407 | 14.7 |
| 1993–94 | 22 | Vancouver Canucks | NHL | 76 | 60 | 47 | 107 | 1 | 86 | 31 | 25 | 4 | 9 | 374 | 16.0 |
| 1994–95 | 23 | Vancouver Canucks | NHL | 44 | 20 | 23 | 43 | -8 | 47 | 12 | 6 | 2 | 2 | 198 | 10.1 |
| 1995–96 | 24 | Vancouver Canucks | NHL | 15 | 6 | 7 | 13 | -2 | 8 | 4 | 1 | 1 | 0 | 78 | 7.7 |
| 1996–97 | 25 | Vancouver Canucks | NHL | 63 | 23 | 32 | 55 | -14 | 40 | 18 | 4 | 1 | 2 | 265 | 8.7 |
| 1997–98 | 26 | Vancouver Canucks | NHL | 82 | 51 | 39 | 90 | 5 | 48 | 32 | 13 | 6 | 4 | 329 | 15.5 |
| 1998–99 | 27 | Florida Panthers | NHL | 11 | 13 | 3 | 16 | 3 | 4 | 7 | 5 | 1 | 0 | 44 | 29.5 |
| 1999–00 | 28 | Florida Panthers | NHL | 74 | 58 | 36 | 94 | 25 | 16 | 45 | 11 | 2 | 14 | 360 | 16.1 |
| 2000–01 | 29 | Florida Panthers | NHL | 82 | 59 | 33 | 92 | -2 | 58 | 35 | 19 | 5 | 8 | 384 | 15.4 |
| 2001–02 | 30 | Florida Panthers | NHL | 56 | 22 | 27 | 49 | -14 | 56 | 12 | 9 | 1 | 1 | 238 | 9.2 |
| 2001–02 | 30 | New York Rangers | NHL | 12 | 12 | 8 | 20 | 9 | 6 | 9 | 3 | 0 | 1 | 49 | 24.5 |
| 2002–03 | 31 | New York Rangers | NHL | 39 | 19 | 11 | 30 | 4 | 16 | 13 | 5 | 1 | 3 | 136 | 14.0 |
| NHL Career — 12 Seasons | | | | 702 | 437 | 342 | 779 | 42 | 484 | 282 | 121 | 34 | 59 | 3130 | 14.0 |

### PLAYOFFS

| SEASON | AGE | TEAM | LG | GP | G | A | PTS | +/- | PIM | ESG | PPG | SHG | GWG | SOG | S% |
|---|---|---|---|---|---|---|---|---|---|---|---|---|---|---|---|
| 1991–92 | 20 | Vancouver Canucks | NHL | 13 | 6 | 4 | 10 | 4 | 14 | 6 | 0 | 0 | 0 | 50 | 12.0 |
| 1992–93 | 21 | Vancouver Canucks | NHL | 12 | 5 | 7 | 12 | 0 | 8 | 5 | 0 | 0 | 1 | 47 | 10.6 |
| 1993–94 | 22 | Vancouver Canucks | NHL | 24 | 16 | 15 | 31 | 8 | 40 | 13 | 3 | 0 | 2 | 101 | 15.8 |
| 1994–95 | 23 | Vancouver Canucks | NHL | 11 | 7 | 6 | 13 | -1 | 10 | 3 | 2 | 2 | 0 | 39 | 17.9 |
| 1999–00 | 28 | Florida Panthers | NHL | 4 | 1 | 3 | 4 | -3 | 2 | 0 | 1 | 0 | 0 | 15 | 6.7 |
| NHL Career — 5 Seasons | | | | 64 | 35 | 35 | 70 | 8 | 74 | 27 | 6 | 2 | 3 | 252 | 13.9 |

## Dino Ciccarelli  Profile: See page 178

### REGULAR SEASON

| SEASON | AGE | TEAM | LG | GP | G | A | PTS | +/- | PIM | ESG | PPG | SHG | GWG | SOG | S% |
|---|---|---|---|---|---|---|---|---|---|---|---|---|---|---|---|
| 1980–81 | 20 | Minnesota North Stars | NHL | 32 | 18 | 12 | 30 | 2 | 29 | 10 | 8 | 0 | 0 | 126 | 14.3 |
| 1981–82 | 21 | Minnesota North Stars | NHL | 76 | 55 | 51 | 106 | 14 | 138 | 35 | 20 | 0 | 4 | 289 | 19.0 |
| 1982–83 | 22 | Minnesota North Stars | NHL | 77 | 37 | 38 | 75 | 15 | 94 | 23 | 14 | 0 | 4 | 210 | 17.6 |
| 1983–84 | 23 | Minnesota North Stars | NHL | 79 | 38 | 33 | 71 | 1 | 58 | 22 | 16 | 0 | 2 | 211 | 18.0 |
| 1984–85 | 24 | Minnesota North Stars | NHL | 51 | 15 | 17 | 32 | -12 | 41 | 10 | 5 | 0 | 0 | 133 | 11.3 |
| 1985–86 | 25 | Minnesota North Stars | NHL | 75 | 44 | 45 | 89 | 12 | 51 | 25 | 19 | 0 | 5 | 262 | 16.8 |
| 1986–87 | 26 | Minnesota North Stars | NHL | 80 | 52 | 51 | 103 | 11 | 88 | 30 | 22 | 0 | 5 | 255 | 20.4 |
| 1987–88 | 27 | Minnesota North Stars | NHL | 67 | 41 | 45 | 86 | -29 | 79 | 27 | 13 | 1 | 2 | 262 | 15.6 |
| 1988–89 | 28 | Minnesota North Stars | NHL | 65 | 32 | 27 | 59 | -16 | 64 | 19 | 13 | 0 | 5 | 208 | 15.4 |
| 1988–89 | 28 | Washington Capitals | NHL | 11 | 12 | 3 | 15 | 10 | 12 | 9 | 3 | 0 | 3 | 39 | 30.8 |
| 1989–90 | 29 | Washington Capitals | NHL | 80 | 41 | 38 | 79 | -5 | 122 | 31 | 10 | 0 | 6 | 267 | 15.4 |
| 1990–91 | 30 | Washington Capitals | NHL | 54 | 21 | 18 | 39 | -17 | 66 | 19 | 2 | 0 | 2 | 186 | 11.3 |
| 1991–92 | 31 | Washington Capitals | NHL | 78 | 38 | 38 | 76 | -10 | 78 | 25 | 13 | 0 | 7 | 279 | 13.6 |
| 1992–93 | 32 | Detroit Red Wings | NHL | 82 | 41 | 56 | 97 | 12 | 81 | 20 | 21 | 0 | 8 | 200 | 20.5 |
| 1993–94 | 33 | Detroit Red Wings | NHL | 66 | 28 | 29 | 57 | 10 | 73 | 16 | 12 | 0 | 1 | 153 | 18.3 |
| 1994–95 | 34 | Detroit Red Wings | NHL | 42 | 16 | 27 | 43 | 12 | 39 | 10 | 6 | 0 | 3 | 106 | 15.1 |
| 1995–96 | 35 | Detroit Red Wings | NHL | 64 | 22 | 21 | 43 | 14 | 99 | 9 | 13 | 0 | 5 | 107 | 20.6 |
| 1996–97 | 36 | Tampa Bay Lightning | NHL | 77 | 35 | 25 | 60 | -11 | 116 | 23 | 12 | 0 | 6 | 229 | 15.3 |
| 1997–98 | 37 | Tampa Bay Lightning | NHL | 34 | 11 | 6 | 17 | -14 | 42 | 8 | 3 | 0 | 3 | 104 | 10.6 |
| 1997–98 | 37 | Florida Panthers | NHL | 28 | 5 | 11 | 16 | -2 | 28 | 3 | 2 | 0 | 1 | 57 | 8.8 |
| 1998–99 | 38 | Florida Panthers | NHL | 14 | 6 | 1 | 7 | -1 | 27 | 1 | 5 | 0 | 1 | 23 | 26.1 |
| NHL Career – 19 Seasons | | | | 1232 | 608 | 592 | 1200 | -4 | 1425 | 375 | 232 | 1 | 73 | 3706 | 16.4 |

### PLAYOFFS

| SEASON | AGE | TEAM | LG | GP | G | A | PTS | +/- | PIM | ESG | PPG | SHG | GWG | SOG | S% |
|---|---|---|---|---|---|---|---|---|---|---|---|---|---|---|---|
| 1980–81 | 20 | Minnesota North Stars | NHL | 19 | 14 | 7 | 21 | -2 | 25 | 9 | 5 | 0 | 3 | 70 | 20.0 |
| 1981–82 | 21 | Minnesota North Stars | NHL | 4 | 3 | 1 | 4 | -2 | 2 | 1 | 2 | 0 | 1 | 14 | 21.4 |
| 1982–83 | 22 | Minnesota North Stars | NHL | 9 | 4 | 6 | 10 | 0 | 11 | 3 | 1 | 0 | 2 | 22 | 18.2 |
| 1983–84 | 23 | Minnesota North Stars | NHL | 16 | 4 | 5 | 9 | -6 | 27 | 3 | 1 | 0 | 1 | 38 | 10.5 |
| 1984–85 | 24 | Minnesota North Stars | NHL | 9 | 3 | 3 | 6 | -4 | 8 | 2 | 1 | 0 | 0 | 36 | 8.3 |
| 1985–86 | 25 | Minnesota North Stars | NHL | 5 | 0 | 1 | 1 | -6 | 6 | 0 | 0 | 0 | 0 | 8 | 0.0 |
| 1988–89 | 28 | Washington Capitals | NHL | 6 | 3 | 3 | 6 | -2 | 12 | 0 | 3 | 0 | 0 | 16 | 18.8 |
| 1989–90 | 29 | Washington Capitals | NHL | 8 | 8 | 3 | 11 | 0 | 6 | 7 | 1 | 0 | 1 | 28 | 28.6 |
| 1990–91 | 30 | Washington Capitals | NHL | 11 | 5 | 4 | 9 | -3 | 22 | 4 | 1 | 0 | 2 | 44 | 11.4 |
| 1991–92 | 31 | Washington Capitals | NHL | 7 | 5 | 4 | 9 | -1 | 14 | 4 | 1 | 0 | 0 | 12 | 41.7 |
| 1992–93 | 32 | Detroit Red Wings | NHL | 7 | 4 | 2 | 6 | -6 | 16 | 1 | 3 | 0 | 0 | 17 | 23.5 |
| 1993–94 | 33 | Detroit Red Wings | NHL | 7 | 5 | 2 | 7 | 1 | 14 | 4 | 1 | 0 | 0 | 22 | 22.7 |
| 1994–95 | 34 | Detroit Red Wings | NHL | 16 | 9 | 2 | 11 | -4 | 22 | 3 | 6 | 0 | 2 | 49 | 18.4 |
| 1995–96 | 35 | Detroit Red Wings | NHL | 17 | 6 | 2 | 8 | -6 | 26 | 0 | 6 | 0 | 1 | 36 | 16.7 |
| NHL Career – 14 Seasons | | | | 141 | 73 | 45 | 118 | -41 | 211 | 39 | 34 | 0 | 13 | 412 | 17.7 |

## Charlie Conacher  Profile: See page 179

### REGULAR SEASON

| SEASON | AGE | TEAM | LG | GP | G | A | PTS | PIM |
|---|---|---|---|---|---|---|---|---|
| 1929–30 | 20 | Toronto Maple Leafs | NHL | 39 | 20 | 9 | 29 | 46 |
| 1930–31 | 21 | Toronto Maple Leafs | NHL | 38 | 31 | 12 | 43 | 80 |
| 1931–32 | 22 | Toronto Maple Leafs | NHL | 44 | 34 | 14 | 48 | 66 |
| 1932–33 | 23 | Toronto Maple Leafs | NHL | 40 | 14 | 19 | 33 | 64 |
| 1933–34 | 24 | Toronto Maple Leafs | NHL | 42 | 32 | 20 | 52 | 38 |
| 1934–35 | 25 | Toronto Maple Leafs | NHL | 47 | 36 | 21 | 57 | 24 |
| 1935–36 | 26 | Toronto Maple Leafs | NHL | 44 | 23 | 15 | 38 | 74 |
| 1936–37 | 27 | Toronto Maple Leafs | NHL | 15 | 3 | 5 | 8 | 13 |
| 1937–38 | 28 | Toronto Maple Leafs | NHL | 19 | 7 | 9 | 16 | 6 |
| 1938–39 | 29 | Detroit Red Wings | NHL | 40 | 7 | 15 | 22 | 39 |
| 1939–40 | 30 | New York Americans | NHL | 47 | 10 | 18 | 28 | 41 |
| 1940–41 | 31 | New York Americans | NHL | 46 | 7 | 15 | 22 | 32 |
| NHL Career—12 Seasons | | | | 461 | 224 | 172 | 396 | 523 |

### PLAYOFFS

| SEASON | AGE | TEAM | LG | GP | G | A | PTS | PIM |
|---|---|---|---|---|---|---|---|---|
| 1930–31 | 21 | Toronto Maple Leafs | NHL | 2 | 0 | 1 | 1 | 0 |
| 1931–32 | 22 | Toronto Maple Leafs | NHL | 7 | 6 | 2 | 8 | 6 |
| 1932–33 | 23 | Toronto Maple Leafs | NHL | 9 | 1 | 1 | 2 | 10 |
| 1933–34 | 24 | Toronto Maple Leafs | NHL | 5 | 3 | 2 | 5 | 0 |
| 1934–35 | 25 | Toronto Maple Leafs | NHL | 7 | 1 | 4 | 5 | 6 |
| 1935–36 | 26 | Toronto Maple Leafs | NHL | 9 | 3 | 2 | 5 | 12 |
| 1936–37 | 27 | Toronto Maple Leafs | NHL | 2 | 0 | 0 | 0 | 7 |
| 1938–39 | 29 | Detroit Red Wings | NHL | 5 | 2 | 5 | 7 | 2 |
| 1939–40 | 30 | New York Americans | NHL | 3 | 1 | 1 | 2 | 8 |
| NHL Career—9 Seasons | | | | 49 | 17 | 18 | 35 | 51 |

## Bill Cook  Profile: See page 180

### REGULAR SEASON

| SEASON | AGE | TEAM | LG | GP | G | A | PTS | PIM |
|---|---|---|---|---|---|---|---|---|
| 1922–23 | 26 | Saskatoon Sheiks | WCHL | 30 | 9 | 16 | 25 | 19 |
| 1923–24 | 27 | Saskatoon Crescents | WCHL | 30 | 26 | 14 | 40 | 20 |
| 1924–25 | 28 | Saskatoon Crescents | WCHL | 27 | 22 | 10 | 32 | 79 |
| 1925–26 | 29 | Saskatoon Crescents | WHL | 30 | 31 | 13 | 44 | 26 |
| 1926–27 | 30 | New York Rangers | NHL | 44 | 33 | 4 | 37 | 56 |
| 1927–28 | 31 | New York Rangers | NHL | 43 | 18 | 6 | 24 | 42 |
| 1928–29 | 32 | New York Rangers | NHL | 43 | 15 | 8 | 23 | 47 |
| 1929–30 | 33 | New York Rangers | NHL | 44 | 29 | 30 | 59 | 56 |
| 1930–31 | 34 | New York Rangers | NHL | 44 | 30 | 12 | 42 | 39 |
| 1931–32 | 35 | New York Rangers | NHL | 48 | 33 | 14 | 47 | 33 |
| 1932–33 | 36 | New York Rangers | NHL | 48 | 28 | 22 | 50 | 51 |
| 1933–34 | 37 | New York Rangers | NHL | 48 | 13 | 13 | 26 | 21 |
| 1934–35 | 38 | New York Rangers | NHL | 48 | 21 | 15 | 36 | 23 |
| 1935–36 | 39 | New York Rangers | NHL | 44 | 7 | 10 | 17 | 16 |
| 1936–37 | 40 | New York Rangers | NHL | 21 | 1 | 4 | 5 | 2 |
| Career—15 Seasons | | | | 592 | 316 | 191 | 508 | 530 |

### PLAYOFFS

| SEASON | AGE | TEAM | LG | GP | G | A | PTS | PIM |
|---|---|---|---|---|---|---|---|---|
| 1924–25 | 28 | Saskatoon Crescents | WCHL | 2 | 0 | 0 | 0 | 4 |
| 1925–26 | 29 | Saskatoon Crescents | WHL | 2 | 2 | 0 | 2 | 26 |
| 1926–27 | 30 | New York Rangers | NHL | 2 | 1 | 0 | 1 | 10 |
| 1927–28 | 31 | New York Rangers | NHL | 9 | 2 | 3 | 5 | 26 |
| 1928–29 | 32 | New York Rangers | NHL | 6 | 0 | 0 | 0 | 6 |
| 1929–30 | 33 | New York Rangers | NHL | 4 | 0 | 1 | 1 | 11 |
| 1930–31 | 34 | New York Rangers | NHL | 4 | 3 | 0 | 3 | 4 |
| 1931–32 | 35 | New York Rangers | NHL | 7 | 3 | 3 | 6 | 2 |
| 1932–33 | 36 | New York Rangers | NHL | 8 | 3 | 2 | 5 | 2 |
| 1933–34 | 37 | New York Rangers | NHL | 2 | 0 | 0 | 0 | 2 |
| 1934–35 | 38 | New York Rangers | NHL | 4 | 1 | 2 | 3 | 7 |
| Career—11 Seasons | | | | 50 | 15 | 11 | 26 | 100 |

## Yvan Cournoyer  Profile: See page 181

### REGULAR SEASON

| SEASON | AGE | TEAM | LG | GP | G | A | PTS | +/- | PIM | ESG | PPG | SHG | GWG | SOG | S% |
|---|---|---|---|---|---|---|---|---|---|---|---|---|---|---|---|
| 1963–64 | 20 | Montreal Canadiens | NHL | 5 | 4 | 0 | 4 | 1 | 0 | 3 | 1 | 0 | 0 | 15 | 26.7 |
| 1964–65 | 21 | Montreal Canadiens | NHL | 55 | 7 | 10 | 17 | -4 | 4 | 3 | 4 | 0 | 0 | 101 | 6.9 |
| 1965–66 | 22 | Montreal Canadiens | NHL | 65 | 18 | 11 | 29 | -2 | 2 | 16 | 0 | 0 | 89 | 20.2 |
| 1966–67 | 23 | Montreal Canadiens | NHL | 69 | 25 | 15 | 40 | -11 | 4 | 5 | 20 | 0 | 7 | 130 | 19.2 |
| 1967–68 | 24 | Montreal Canadiens | NHL | 64 | 28 | 32 | 60 | 19 | 23 | 20 | 7 | 1 | 4 | 221 | 12.7 |
| 1968–69 | 25 | Montreal Canadiens | NHL | 76 | 43 | 44 | 87 | 18 | 31 | 29 | 14 | 0 | 8 | 245 | 17.6 |
| 1969–70 | 26 | Montreal Canadiens | NHL | 72 | 27 | 36 | 63 | 1 | 23 | 17 | 10 | 0 | 4 | 233 | 11.6 |
| 1970–71 | 27 | Montreal Canadiens | NHL | 65 | 37 | 36 | 73 | 18 | 21 | 19 | 18 | 0 | 5 | 197 | 18.8 |
| 1971–72 | 28 | Montreal Canadiens | NHL | 73 | 47 | 36 | 83 | 24 | 15 | 30 | 17 | 0 | 5 | 208 | 22.6 |
| 1972–73 | 29 | Montreal Canadiens | NHL | 67 | 40 | 39 | 79 | 50 | 18 | 34 | 6 | 0 | 4 | 194 | 20.6 |
| 1973–74 | 30 | Montreal Canadiens | NHL | 67 | 40 | 33 | 73 | 16 | 18 | 30 | 10 | 0 | 9 | 187 | 21.4 |
| 1974–75 | 31 | Montreal Canadiens | NHL | 76 | 29 | 45 | 74 | 17 | 32 | 18 | 11 | 0 | 2 | 175 | 16.5 |
| 1975–76 | 32 | Montreal Canadiens | NHL | 71 | 32 | 36 | 68 | 38 | 20 | 24 | 8 | 0 | 12 | 163 | 19.6 |
| 1976–77 | 33 | Montreal Canadiens | NHL | 60 | 25 | 28 | 53 | 25 | 8 | 19 | 6 | 0 | 2 | 121 | 20.5 |
| 1977–78 | 34 | Montreal Canadiens | NHL | 68 | 24 | 29 | 53 | 39 | 12 | 20 | 4 | 0 | 6 | 125 | 19.2 |
| 1978–79 | 35 | Montreal Canadiens | NHL | 15 | 2 | 5 | 7 | 5 | 2 | 2 | 0 | 0 | 0 | 23 | 8.7 |
| NHL Career—16 Seasons | | | | 968 | 428 | 435 | 863 | 254 | 233 | 275 | 152 | 1 | 68 | 2427 | 17.6 |

### PLAYOFFS

| SEASON | AGE | TEAM | LG | GP | G | A | PTS | +/- | PIM | ESG | PPG | SHG | GWG | SOG | S% |
|---|---|---|---|---|---|---|---|---|---|---|---|---|---|---|---|
| 1964–65 | 21 | Montreal Canadiens | NHL | 12 | 3 | 1 | 4 | -2 | 0 | 0 | 3 | 0 | 1 | 19 | 15.8 |
| 1965–66 | 22 | Montreal Canadiens | NHL | 10 | 2 | 3 | 5 | 1 | 2 | 1 | 1 | 0 | 1 | 20 | 10.0 |
| 1966–67 | 23 | Montreal Canadiens | NHL | 10 | 2 | 3 | 5 | -1 | 6 | 0 | 2 | 0 | 1 | 38 | 5.3 |
| 1967–68 | 24 | Montreal Canadiens | NHL | 13 | 6 | 8 | 14 | 5 | 4 | 3 | 3 | 0 | 1 | 42 | 14.3 |
| 1968–69 | 25 | Montreal Canadiens | NHL | 14 | 4 | 7 | 11 | 2 | 5 | 2 | 2 | 0 | 2 | 50 | 8.0 |
| 1970–71 | 27 | Montreal Canadiens | NHL | 20 | 10 | 12 | 22 | 14 | 6 | 8 | 2 | 0 | 1 | 60 | 16.7 |
| 1971–72 | 28 | Montreal Canadiens | NHL | 6 | 2 | 1 | 3 | 0 | 2 | 2 | 0 | 0 | 0 | 11 | 18.2 |
| 1972–73 | 29 | Montreal Canadiens | NHL | 17 | 15 | 10 | 25 | 6 | 2 | 12 | 3 | 0 | 3 | 49 | 30.6 |
| 1973–74 | 30 | Montreal Canadiens | NHL | 6 | 5 | 2 | 7 | -1 | 2 | 5 | 0 | 0 | 2 | 17 | 29.4 |
| 1974–75 | 31 | Montreal Canadiens | NHL | 11 | 5 | 6 | 11 | 5 | 4 | 3 | 2 | 0 | 0 | 28 | 17.9 |
| 1975–76 | 32 | Montreal Canadiens | NHL | 13 | 3 | 6 | 9 | 1 | 4 | 1 | 2 | 0 | 1 | 27 | 11.1 |

## Yvan Cournoyer (continued)

**PLAYOFFS**

| SEASON | AGE | TEAM | LG | GP | G | A | PTS | +/- | PIM | ESG | PPG | SHG | GWG | SOG | S% |
|--------|-----|------|----|----|----|----|-----|-----|-----|-----|-----|-----|-----|-----|-----|
| 1977–78 | 34 | Montreal Canadiens | NHL | 15 | 7 | 4 | 11 | 7 | 10 | 7 | 0 | 0 | 2 | 26 | 26.9 |
| NHL Career – 12 Seasons | | | | 147 | 64 | 63 | 127 | 37 | 47 | 44 | 20 | 0 | 15 | 387 | 16.5 |

## Jack Darragh  Profile: See page 182

**REGULAR SEASON**

| SEASON | AGE | TEAM | LG | GP | G | A | PTS | PIM |
|--------|-----|------|----|----|----|----|-----|-----|
| 1910–11 | 20 | Ottawa Senators | NHA | 16 | 18 | 0 | 18 | 36 |
| 1911–12 | 21 | Ottawa Senators | NHA | 17 | 15 | 0 | 15 | 10 |
| 1912–13 | 22 | Ottawa Senators | NHA | 20 | 15 | 0 | 15 | 16 |
| 1913–14 | 23 | Ottawa Senators | NHA | 20 | 23 | 5 | 28 | 69 |
| 1914–15 | 24 | Ottawa Senators | NHA | 18 | 11 | 2 | 13 | 32 |
| 1915–16 | 25 | Ottawa Senators | NHA | 21 | 16 | 5 | 21 | 41 |
| 1916–17 | 26 | Ottawa Senators | NHA | 20 | 24 | 4 | 28 | 17 |
| 1917–18 | 27 | Ottawa Senators | NHL | 18 | 14 | 5 | 19 | 23 |
| 1918–19 | 28 | Ottawa Senators | NHL | 14 | 11 | 4 | 15 | 30 |
| 1919–20 | 29 | Ottawa Senators | NHL | 23 | 23 | 14 | 37 | 22 |
| 1920–21 | 30 | Ottawa Senators | NHL | 24 | 11 | 14 | 25 | 20 |
| 1922–23 | 32 | Ottawa Senators | NHL | 24 | 7 | 12 | 19 | 10 |
| 1923–24 | 33 | Ottawa Senators | NHL | 18 | 2 | 0 | 2 | 2 |
| Career – 13 Seasons | | | | 253 | 190 | 65 | 255 | 228 |

**PLAYOFFS**

| SEASON | AGE | TEAM | LG | GP | G | A | PTS | PIM |
|--------|-----|------|----|----|----|----|-----|-----|
| 1910–11 | 20 | Ottawa Senators | St-Cup | 2 | 0 | 0 | 0 | 6 |
| 1914–15 | 24 | Ottawa Senators | NHA | 5 | 4 | 0 | 4 | 9 |
| 1916–17 | 26 | Ottawa Senators | NHA | 2 | 2 | 0 | 2 | 3 |
| 1918–19 | 28 | Ottawa Senators | NHL | 5 | 2 | 0 | 2 | 3 |
| 1919–20 | 29 | Ottawa Senators | St-Cup | 5 | 5 | 2 | 7 | 2 |
| 1920–21 | 30 | Ottawa Senators | NHL | 2 | 0 | 0 | 0 | 2 |
| 1920–21 | 30 | Ottawa Senators | St-Cup | 5 | 5 | 0 | 5 | 12 |
| 1922–23 | 32 | Ottawa Senators | NHL | 2 | 1 | 0 | 1 | 2 |
| 1923–24 | 33 | Ottawa Senators | NHL | 2 | 0 | 0 | 0 | 2 |
| Career – 8 Seasons | | | | 30 | 19 | 2 | 21 | 41 |

## Scotty Davidson  Profile: See page 183

**REGULAR SEASON**

| SEASON | AGE | TEAM | LG | GP | G | A | PTS | PIM |
|--------|-----|------|----|----|----|----|-----|-----|
| 1908–09 | 17 | Kingston 14th Regiment | OHA-Sr. | 4 | 8 | 0 | 8 | 11 |
| 1909–10 | 18 | Kingston Frontenacs | OHA-Jr. | | | | | |
| 1910–11 | 19 | Kingston Frontenacs | OHA-Jr. | | | | | |
| 1911–12 | 20 | Calgary Athletics | S-ASHL | 4 | 3 | 0 | 3 | |
| 1912–13 | 21 | Toronto Blueshirts | NHA | 20 | 19 | 0 | 19 | 69 |
| 1912–13 | 21 | Toronto Tecumsehs | Exhib. | 2 | 0 | 0 | 0 | 0 |
| 1913–14 | 22 | Toronto Blueshirts | NHA | 20 | 23 | 13 | 36 | 64 |
| Career – 6 Seasons | | | | 50 | 53 | 13 | 66 | 210 |

**PLAYOFFS**

| SEASON | AGE | TEAM | LG | GP | G | A | PTS | PIM |
|--------|-----|------|----|----|----|----|-----|-----|
| 1908–09 | 17 | Kingston 14th Regiment | OHA-Sr. | 4 | 4 | 0 | 4 | 6 |
| 1911–12 | 20 | Calgary Athletics | S-ASHL | 3 | 3 | 0 | 3 | 6 |
| 1913–14 | 22 | Toronto Blueshirts | NHA | 2 | 2 | 0 | 2 | 11 |
| 1913–14 | 22 | Toronto Blueshirts | St-Cup | 2 | 1 | 0 | 1 | 7 |
| Career – 3 Seasons | | | | 11 | 10 | 0 | 10 | 30 |

## Gordie Drillon  Profile: See page 184

**REGULAR SEASON**

| SEASON | AGE | TEAM | LG | GP | G | A | PTS | PIM |
|--------|-----|------|----|----|----|----|-----|-----|
| 1936–37 | 23 | Toronto Maple Leafs | NHL | 41 | 16 | 17 | 33 | 2 |
| 1937–38 | 24 | Toronto Maple Leafs | NHL | 48 | 26 | 26 | 52 | 4 |
| 1938–39 | 25 | Toronto Maple Leafs | NHL | 40 | 18 | 16 | 34 | 15 |
| 1939–40 | 26 | Toronto Maple Leafs | NHL | 44 | 21 | 20 | 41 | 13 |
| 1940–41 | 27 | Toronto Maple Leafs | NHL | 42 | 23 | 21 | 44 | 2 |
| 1941–42 | 28 | Toronto Maple Leafs | NHL | 48 | 23 | 18 | 41 | 6 |
| 1942–43 | 29 | Montreal Canadiens | NHL | 49 | 28 | 22 | 50 | 14 |
| NHL Career – 7 Seasons | | | | 312 | 155 | 140 | 295 | 56 |

**PLAYOFFS**

| SEASON | AGE | TEAM | LG | GP | G | A | PTS | PIM |
|--------|-----|------|----|----|----|----|-----|-----|
| 1936–37 | 23 | Toronto Maple Leafs | NHL | 2 | 0 | 0 | 0 | 0 |
| 1937–38 | 24 | Toronto Maple Leafs | NHL | 7 | 7 | 1 | 8 | 2 |
| 1938–39 | 25 | Toronto Maple Leafs | NHL | 10 | 7 | 6 | 13 | 4 |
| 1939–40 | 26 | Toronto Maple Leafs | NHL | 10 | 3 | 1 | 4 | 0 |
| 1940–41 | 27 | Toronto Maple Leafs | NHL | 7 | 3 | 2 | 5 | 2 |
| 1941–42 | 28 | Toronto Maple Leafs | NHL | 9 | 2 | 3 | 5 | 2 |
| 1942–43 | 29 | Montreal Canadiens | NHL | 5 | 4 | 2 | 6 | 0 |
| NHL Career – 7 Seasons | | | | 50 | 26 | 15 | 41 | 10 |

## Babe Dye  Profile: See page 185

**REGULAR SEASON**

| SEASON | AGE | TEAM | LG | GP | G | A | PTS | PIM |
|--------|-----|------|----|----|----|----|-----|-----|
| 1919–20 | 21 | Toronto St. Patricks | NHL | 23 | 11 | 2 | 13 | 10 |
| 1920–21 | 22 | Hamilton Tigers | NHL | 1 | 2 | 0 | 2 | 0 |
| 1920–21 | 22 | Toronto St. Patricks | NHL | 23 | 33 | 5 | 38 | 32 |
| 1921–22 | 23 | Toronto St. Patricks | NHL | 24 | 31 | 7 | 38 | 39 |
| 1922–23 | 24 | Toronto St. Patricks | NHL | 22 | 27 | 13 | 40 | 21 |
| 1923–24 | 25 | Toronto St. Patricks | NHL | 19 | 17 | 4 | 21 | 23 |
| 1924–25 | 26 | Toronto St. Patricks | NHL | 29 | 38 | 8 | 46 | 38 |
| 1925–26 | 27 | Toronto St. Patricks | NHL | 31 | 18 | 6 | 24 | 26 |
| 1926–27 | 28 | Chicago Black Hawks | NHL | 41 | 25 | 5 | 30 | 14 |
| 1927–28 | 29 | Chicago Black Hawks | NHL | 11 | 0 | 0 | 0 | 0 |
| 1928–29 | 30 | New York Americans | NHL | 42 | 1 | 0 | 1 | 17 |
| 1930–31 | 32 | Toronto Maple Leafs | NHL | 6 | 0 | 0 | 0 | 0 |
| Career – 11 Seasons | | | | 272 | 203 | 50 | 253 | 220 |

**PLAYOFFS**

| SEASON | AGE | TEAM | LG | GP | G | A | PTS | PIM |
|--------|-----|------|----|----|----|----|-----|-----|
| 1920–21 | 22 | Toronto St. Patricks | NHL | 2 | 0 | 0 | 0 | 7 |
| 1921–22 | 23 | Toronto St. Patricks | NHL | 2 | 2 | 0 | 2 | 2 |
| 1921–22 | 23 | Toronto St. Patricks | St-Cup | 5 | 9 | 1 | 10 | 2 |
| 1924–25 | 26 | Toronto St. Patricks | NHL | 2 | 0 | 0 | 0 | 0 |
| 1926–27 | 28 | Chicago Black Hawks | NHL | 2 | 0 | 0 | 0 | 2 |
| Career – 4 Seasons | | | | 13 | 11 | 1 | 12 | 13 |

# Mike Gartner   Profile: See page 186

## REGULAR SEASON

| SEASON | AGE | TEAM | LG | GP | G | A | PTS | +/- | PIM | ESG | PPG | SHG | GWG | SOG | S% |
|---|---|---|---|---|---|---|---|---|---|---|---|---|---|---|---|
| 1978-79 | 19 | Cincinnati Stingers | WHA | 78 | 27 | 25 | 52 | -18 | 123 | 18 | 9 | 0 | | 227 | 11.9 |
| 1979-80 | 20 | Washington Capitals | NHL | 77 | 36 | 32 | 68 | 16 | 66 | 32 | 4 | 0 | 3 | 226 | 15.9 |
| 1980-81 | 21 | Washington Capitals | NHL | 80 | 48 | 46 | 94 | -4 | 100 | 35 | 13 | 0 | 3 | 326 | 14.7 |
| 1981-82 | 22 | Washington Capitals | NHL | 80 | 35 | 45 | 80 | -12 | 121 | 28 | 5 | 2 | 5 | 301 | 11.6 |
| 1982-83 | 23 | Washington Capitals | NHL | 73 | 38 | 38 | 76 | -3 | 54 | 27 | 10 | 1 | 3 | 269 | 14.1 |
| 1983-84 | 24 | Washington Capitals | NHL | 80 | 40 | 45 | 85 | 23 | 90 | 32 | 8 | 0 | 7 | 286 | 14.0 |
| 1984-85 | 25 | Washington Capitals | NHL | 80 | 50 | 52 | 102 | 16 | 71 | 33 | 17 | 0 | 11 | 331 | 15.1 |
| 1985-86 | 26 | Washington Capitals | NHL | 74 | 35 | 40 | 75 | -5 | 63 | 22 | 11 | 2 | 4 | 279 | 12.5 |
| 1986-87 | 27 | Washington Capitals | NHL | 78 | 41 | 32 | 73 | 2 | 61 | 29 | 5 | 7 | 10 | 317 | 12.9 |
| 1987-88 | 28 | Washington Capitals | NHL | 80 | 48 | 33 | 81 | 20 | 73 | 29 | 19 | 0 | 7 | 316 | 15.2 |
| 1988-89 | 29 | Washington Capitals | NHL | 56 | 26 | 29 | 55 | 8 | 71 | 20 | 6 | 0 | 1 | 190 | 13.7 |
| 1988-89 | 29 | Minnesota North Stars | NHL | 13 | 7 | 7 | 14 | 3 | 2 | 4 | 3 | 0 | 0 | 33 | 21.2 |
| 1989-90 | 30 | Minnesota North Stars | NHL | 67 | 34 | 36 | 70 | -8 | 32 | 15 | 15 | 4 | 2 | 240 | 14.2 |
| 1989-90 | 30 | New York Rangers | NHL | 12 | 11 | 5 | 16 | 4 | 6 | 5 | 6 | 0 | 3 | 48 | 22.9 |
| 1990-91 | 31 | New York Rangers | NHL | 79 | 49 | 20 | 69 | -9 | 53 | 26 | 22 | 1 | 4 | 262 | 18.7 |
| 1991-92 | 32 | New York Rangers | NHL | 76 | 40 | 41 | 81 | 11 | 55 | 25 | 15 | 0 | 6 | 286 | 14.0 |
| 1992-93 | 33 | New York Rangers | NHL | 84 | 45 | 23 | 68 | -4 | 59 | 32 | 13 | 0 | 3 | 323 | 13.9 |
| 1993-94 | 34 | New York Rangers | NHL | 71 | 28 | 24 | 52 | 11 | 58 | 13 | 10 | 5 | 4 | 245 | 11.4 |
| 1993-94 | 34 | Toronto Maple Leafs | NHL | 10 | 6 | 6 | 12 | 9 | 4 | 5 | 1 | 0 | 0 | 30 | 20.0 |
| 1994-95 | 35 | Toronto Maple Leafs | NHL | 38 | 12 | 8 | 20 | 0 | 6 | 9 | 2 | 1 | 1 | 91 | 13.2 |
| 1995-96 | 36 | Toronto Maple Leafs | NHL | 82 | 35 | 19 | 54 | 5 | 52 | 20 | 15 | 0 | 4 | 275 | 12.7 |
| 1996-97 | 37 | Phoenix Coyotes | NHL | 82 | 32 | 31 | 63 | -11 | 38 | 18 | 13 | 1 | 7 | 271 | 11.8 |
| 1997-98 | 38 | Phoenix Coyotes | NHL | 60 | 12 | 15 | 27 | -4 | 24 | 8 | 4 | 0 | 2 | 145 | 8.3 |
| Career – 20 Seasons | | | | 1510 | 735 | 652 | 1387 | 50 | 1282 | 485 | 226 | 24 | 90 | 5316 | 13.8 |

## PLAYOFFS

| SEASON | AGE | TEAM | LG | GP | G | A | PTS | +/- | PIM | ESG | PPG | SHG | GWG | SOG | S% |
|---|---|---|---|---|---|---|---|---|---|---|---|---|---|---|---|
| 1978-79 | 19 | Cincinnati Stingers | WHA | 3 | 0 | 0 | 0 | -2 | 2 | | | | 0 | | |
| 1982-83 | 23 | Washington Capitals | NHL | 4 | 0 | 0 | 0 | -5 | 4 | 0 | 0 | 0 | 0 | 17 | 0.0 |
| 1983-84 | 24 | Washington Capitals | NHL | 8 | 3 | 7 | 10 | -1 | 16 | 1 | 2 | 0 | 0 | 30 | 10.0 |
| 1984-85 | 25 | Washington Capitals | NHL | 5 | 4 | 3 | 7 | 3 | 9 | 3 | 1 | 0 | 1 | 23 | 17.4 |
| 1985-86 | 26 | Washington Capitals | NHL | 9 | 2 | 10 | 12 | 6 | 4 | 2 | 0 | 0 | 0 | 26 | 7.7 |
| 1986-87 | 27 | Washington Capitals | NHL | 7 | 4 | 3 | 7 | 0 | 14 | 4 | 0 | 0 | 0 | 33 | 12.1 |
| 1987-88 | 28 | Washington Capitals | NHL | 14 | 3 | 4 | 7 | -7 | 14 | 2 | 1 | 0 | 0 | 45 | 6.7 |
| 1988-89 | 29 | MinnesotaNorthStars | NHL | 5 | 0 | 0 | 0 | -4 | 6 | 0 | 0 | 0 | 0 | 14 | 0.0 |
| 1989-90 | 30 | New York Rangers | NHL | 10 | 5 | 3 | 8 | 0 | 12 | 1 | 4 | 0 | 1 | 26 | 19.2 |
| 1990-91 | 31 | New York Rangers | NHL | 6 | 1 | 1 | 2 | -4 | 0 | 0 | 1 | 0 | 0 | 22 | 4.5 |
| 1991-92 | 32 | New York Rangers | NHL | 13 | 8 | 8 | 16 | 3 | 4 | 5 | 3 | 0 | 1 | 66 | 12.1 |
| 1993-94 | 34 | Toronto Maple Leafs | NHL | 18 | 5 | 6 | 11 | 3 | 14 | 4 | 1 | 0 | 3 | 53 | 9.4 |
| 1994-95 | 35 | Toronto Maple Leafs | NHL | 5 | 2 | 2 | 4 | 4 | 2 | 2 | 0 | 0 | 1 | 10 | 20.0 |
| 1995-96 | 36 | Toronto Maple Leafs | NHL | 6 | 4 | 1 | 5 | -5 | 4 | 2 | 2 | 0 | 1 | 18 | 22.2 |
| 1996-97 | 37 | Phoenix Coyotes | NHL | 7 | 1 | 2 | 3 | -1 | 4 | 1 | 0 | 0 | 0 | 17 | 5.9 |
| 1997-98 | 38 | Phoenix Coyotes | NHL | 5 | 1 | 0 | 1 | -2 | 18 | 0 | 1 | 0 | 0 | 11 | 9.1 |
| Career – 16 Seasons | | | | 125 | 43 | 50 | 93 | -12 | 127 | 27 | 16 | 0 | 7 | 411 | 10.5 |

# Bernie Geoffrion   Profile: See page 188

## REGULAR SEASON

| SEASON | AGE | TEAM | LG | GP | G | A | PTS | +/- | PIM | ESG | PPG | SHG | GWG | SOG | S% |
|---|---|---|---|---|---|---|---|---|---|---|---|---|---|---|---|
| 1950-51 | 19 | Montreal Canadiens | NHL | 18 | 8 | 6 | 14 | | 9 | 8 | 0 | 0 | 2 | | |
| 1951-52 | 20 | Montreal Canadiens | NHL | 67 | 30 | 24 | 54 | | 66 | 19 | 10 | 1 | 7 | | |
| 1952-53 | 21 | Montreal Canadiens | NHL | 65 | 22 | 17 | 39 | | 37 | 18 | 4 | 0 | 3 | | |
| 1953-54 | 22 | Montreal Canadiens | NHL | 54 | 29 | 25 | 54 | | 87 | 20 | 9 | 0 | 7 | | |
| 1954-55 | 23 | Montreal Canadiens | NHL | 70 | 38 | 37 | 75 | | 57 | 25 | 13 | 0 | 8 | | |
| 1955-56 | 24 | Montreal Canadiens | NHL | 59 | 29 | 33 | 62 | | 66 | 17 | 12 | 0 | 8 | | |
| 1956-57 | 25 | Montreal Canadiens | NHL | 41 | 19 | 21 | 40 | | 16 | 15 | 4 | 0 | 3 | | |
| 1957-58 | 26 | Montreal Canadiens | NHL | 42 | 27 | 23 | 50 | | 51 | 17 | 10 | 0 | 1 | | |
| 1958-59 | 27 | Montreal Canadiens | NHL | 59 | 22 | 44 | 66 | | 30 | 15 | 7 | 0 | 3 | | |
| 1959-60 | 28 | Montreal Canadiens | NHL | 59 | 30 | 41 | 71 | 8 | 36 | 23 | 6 | 1 | 5 | 267 | 11.2 |
| 1960-61 | 29 | Montreal Canadiens | NHL | 64 | 50 | 45 | 95 | 29 | 27 | 34 | 16 | 0 | 12 | 316 | 15.8 |
| 1961-62 | 30 | Montreal Canadiens | NHL | 62 | 23 | 36 | 59 | 17 | 36 | 15 | 8 | 0 | 1 | 240 | 9.6 |
| 1962-63 | 31 | Montreal Canadiens | NHL | 51 | 23 | 18 | 41 | 5 | 71 | 16 | 7 | 0 | 4 | 172 | 13.4 |
| 1963-64 | 32 | Montreal Canadiens | NHL | 55 | 21 | 18 | 39 | 7 | 41 | 16 | 5 | 0 | 9 | 170 | 12.4 |
| 1966-67 | 35 | New York Rangers | NHL | 58 | 17 | 25 | 42 | -2 | 42 | 12 | 5 | 0 | 2 | 155 | 11.0 |
| 1967-68 | 36 | New York Rangers | NHL | 59 | 5 | 16 | 21 | 1 | 11 | 1 | 4 | 0 | 0 | 84 | 6.0 |
| NHL Career – 16 Seasons | | | | 883 | 393 | 429 | 822 | 39 | 683 | 271 | 120 | 2 | 75 | 1404 | 12.0 |

## Bernie Geoffrion (continued)

**PLAYOFFS**

| SEASON | AGE | TEAM | LG | GP | G | A | PTS | +/- | PIM | ESG | PPG | SHG | GWG | SOG | S% |
|---|---|---|---|---|---|---|---|---|---|---|---|---|---|---|---|
| 1950–51 | 19 | Montreal Canadiens | NHL | 11 | 1 | 1 | 2 | | 6 | 1 | 0 | 0 | 1 | | |
| 1951–52 | 20 | Montreal Canadiens | NHL | 11 | 3 | 1 | 4 | | 6 | 2 | 1 | 0 | 0 | | |
| 1952–53 | 21 | Montreal Canadiens | NHL | 12 | 6 | 4 | 10 | | 12 | 4 | 2 | 0 | 2 | | |
| 1953–54 | 22 | Montreal Canadiens | NHL | 11 | 6 | 5 | 11 | | 18 | 5 | 1 | 0 | 1 | | |
| 1954–55 | 23 | Montreal Canadiens | NHL | 12 | 8 | 5 | 13 | | 8 | 4 | 4 | 0 | 3 | | |
| 1955–56 | 24 | Montreal Canadiens | NHL | 10 | 5 | 9 | 14 | | 6 | 4 | 1 | 0 | 0 | | |
| 1956–57 | 25 | Montreal Canadiens | NHL | 10 | 11 | 7 | 18 | | 2 | 8 | 3 | 0 | 2 | | |
| 1957–58 | 26 | Montreal Canadiens | NHL | 10 | 6 | 5 | 11 | | 2 | 3 | 3 | 0 | 1 | | |
| 1958–59 | 27 | Montreal Canadiens | NHL | 11 | 5 | 8 | 13 | | 10 | 2 | 3 | 0 | 2 | | |
| 1959–60 | 28 | Montreal Canadiens | NHL | 8 | 2 | 10 | 12 | 9 | 4 | 2 | 0 | 0 | 1 | 32 | 6.3 |
| 1960–61 | 29 | Montreal Canadiens | NHL | 4 | 2 | 1 | 3 | 3 | 0 | 2 | 0 | 0 | 0 | 1 | 200.0 |
| 1961–62 | 30 | Montreal Canadiens | NHL | 5 | 0 | 1 | 1 | -2 | 6 | 0 | 0 | 0 | 0 | 8 | 0.0 |
| 1962–63 | 31 | Montreal Canadiens | NHL | 5 | 0 | 1 | 1 | -2 | 4 | 0 | 0 | 0 | 0 | 12 | 0.0 |
| 1963–64 | 32 | Montreal Canadiens | NHL | 7 | 1 | 1 | 2 | -4 | 4 | 1 | 0 | 0 | 1 | 14 | 7.1 |
| 1966–67 | 35 | New York Rangers | NHL | 4 | 2 | 0 | 2 | -1 | 0 | 0 | 0 | 0 | 0 | 8 | 25.0 |
| 1967–68 | 36 | New York Rangers | NHL | 1 | 0 | 1 | 1 | 0 | 0 | 0 | 0 | 0 | 0 | 0 | |
| NHL Career — 16 Seasons | | | | 132 | 58 | 60 | 118 | 3 | 88 | 38 | 20 | 0 | 14 | 75 | 9.3 |

## Rod Gilbert Profile: See page 190

**REGULAR SEASON**

| SEASON | AGE | TEAM | LG | GP | G | A | PTS | +/- | PIM | ESG | PPG | SHG | GWG | SOG | S% |
|---|---|---|---|---|---|---|---|---|---|---|---|---|---|---|---|
| 1960–61 | 19 | New York Rangers | NHL | 1 | 0 | 1 | 1 | 1 | 2 | 0 | 0 | 0 | 0 | 3 | 0 |
| 1961–62 | 20 | New York Rangers | NHL | 1 | 0 | 0 | 0 | 0 | 0 | 0 | 0 | 0 | 0 | 0 | |
| 1962–63 | 21 | New York Rangers | NHL | 70 | 11 | 20 | 31 | -11 | 20 | 11 | 0 | 0 | 2 | 123 | 8.9 |
| 1963–64 | 22 | New York Rangers | NHL | 70 | 24 | 40 | 64 | -5 | 62 | 17 | 7 | 0 | 0 | 185 | 13.0 |
| 1964–65 | 23 | New York Rangers | NHL | 70 | 25 | 36 | 61 | -23 | 54 | 15 | 10 | 0 | 3 | 238 | 10.5 |
| 1965–66 | 24 | New York Rangers | NHL | 34 | 10 | 15 | 25 | -11 | 20 | 7 | 3 | 0 | 2 | 127 | 7.9 |
| 1966–67 | 25 | New York Rangers | NHL | 64 | 28 | 18 | 46 | -2 | 12 | 23 | 5 | 0 | 5 | 168 | 16.7 |
| 1967–68 | 26 | New York Rangers | NHL | 73 | 29 | 48 | 77 | 17 | 12 | 21 | 8 | 0 | 6 | 282 | 10.3 |
| 1968–69 | 27 | New York Rangers | NHL | 66 | 28 | 49 | 77 | 13 | 22 | 20 | 8 | 0 | 5 | 301 | 9.3 |
| 1969–70 | 28 | New York Rangers | NHL | 72 | 16 | 37 | 53 | 0 | 22 | 13 | 3 | 0 | 1 | 230 | 7.0 |
| 1970–71 | 29 | New York Rangers | NHL | 78 | 30 | 31 | 61 | 20 | 65 | 22 | 8 | 0 | 5 | 226 | 13.3 |
| 1971–72 | 30 | New York Rangers | NHL | 73 | 43 | 54 | 97 | 50 | 64 | 37 | 6 | 0 | 4 | 238 | 18.1 |
| 1972–73 | 31 | New York Rangers | NHL | 76 | 25 | 59 | 84 | 12 | 25 | 19 | 6 | 0 | 4 | 183 | 13.7 |
| 1973–74 | 32 | New York Rangers | NHL | 75 | 36 | 41 | 77 | 11 | 20 | 20 | 16 | 0 | 8 | 171 | 21.1 |
| 1974–75 | 33 | New York Rangers | NHL | 76 | 36 | 61 | 97 | 1 | 22 | 25 | 11 | 0 | 1 | 243 | 14.8 |
| 1975–76 | 34 | New York Rangers | NHL | 70 | 36 | 50 | 86 | -8 | 32 | 27 | 9 | 0 | 4 | 211 | 17.1 |
| 1976–77 | 35 | New York Rangers | NHL | 77 | 27 | 48 | 75 | -17 | 50 | 20 | 7 | 0 | 2 | 186 | 14.5 |
| 1977–78 | 36 | New York Rangers | NHL | 19 | 2 | 7 | 9 | -10 | 6 | 1 | 1 | 0 | 0 | 27 | 7.4 |
| NHL Career — 18 Seasons | | | | 1065 | 406 | 615 | 1021 | 38 | 508 | 298 | 108 | 0 | 52 | 3142 | 12.9 |

**PLAYOFFS**

| SEASON | AGE | TEAM | LG | GP | G | A | PTS | +/- | PIM | ESG | PPG | SHG | GWG | SOG | S% |
|---|---|---|---|---|---|---|---|---|---|---|---|---|---|---|---|
| 1961–62 | 20 | New York Rangers | NHL | 4 | 2 | 3 | 5 | 2 | 4 | 2 | 0 | 0 | 0 | 10 | 20.0 |
| 1966–67 | 25 | New York Rangers | NHL | 4 | 2 | 2 | 4 | -2 | 6 | 0 | 2 | 0 | 0 | 15 | 13.3 |
| 1967–68 | 26 | New York Rangers | NHL | 6 | 5 | 0 | 5 | 3 | 4 | 5 | 0 | 0 | 0 | 18 | 27.8 |
| 1968–69 | 27 | New York Rangers | NHL | 4 | 1 | 0 | 1 | 0 | 2 | 1 | 0 | 0 | 0 | 9 | 11.1 |
| 1969–70 | 28 | New York Rangers | NHL | 6 | 4 | 5 | 9 | -4 | 0 | 1 | 3 | 0 | 0 | 26 | 15.4 |
| 1970–71 | 29 | New York Rangers | NHL | 13 | 4 | 6 | 10 | 4 | 8 | 3 | 1 | 0 | 1 | 28 | 14.3 |
| 1971–72 | 30 | New York Rangers | NHL | 16 | 7 | 8 | 15 | 2 | 11 | 3 | 4 | 0 | 2 | 33 | 21.2 |
| 1972–73 | 31 | New York Rangers | NHL | 10 | 5 | 1 | 6 | 4 | 2 | 5 | 0 | 0 | 1 | 19 | 26.3 |
| 1973–74 | 32 | New York Rangers | NHL | 13 | 3 | 5 | 8 | -4 | 4 | 2 | 1 | 0 | 1 | 36 | 8.3 |
| 1974–75 | 33 | New York Rangers | NHL | 3 | 1 | 3 | 4 | 3 | 2 | 1 | 0 | 0 | 0 | 13 | 7.7 |
| NHL Career — 10 Seasons | | | | 79 | 34 | 33 | 67 | 8 | 43 | 23 | 11 | 0 | 5 | 207 | 16.4 |

## Billy Gilmour Profile: See page 191

**REGULAR SEASON**

| SEASON | AGE | TEAM | LG | GP | G | A | PTS | PIM |
|---|---|---|---|---|---|---|---|---|
| 1902–03 | 21 | Ottawa Silver Seven | CAHL | 7 | 10 | 0 | 10 | 3 |
| 1903–04 | 22 | McGill Redmen | MCHL | 4 | 5 | 0 | 5 | 12 |
| 1904–05 | 23 | McGill Redmen | MCHL | 4 | 5 | 0 | 5 | 12 |
| 1904–05 | 23 | Ottawa Silver Seven | FAHL | 1 | 0 | 0 | 0 | 0 |
| 1905–06 | 24 | Ottawa Silver Seven | ECAHA | 1 | 0 | 0 | 0 | 0 |
| 1905–06 | 24 | McGill Redmen | MCHL | 4 | 5 | 0 | 5 | 21 |
| 1906–07 | 25 | McGill Redmen | MCHL | 3 | 2 | 0 | 2 | 8 |
| 1907–08 | 26 | Montreal Victorias | ECAHA | 10 | 5 | 0 | 5 | 33 |
| 1908–09 | 27 | Ottawa Senators | ECHA | 11 | 9 | 0 | 9 | 74 |

**REGULAR SEASON**

| SEASON | AGE | TEAM | LG | GP | G | A | PTS | PIM |
|---|---|---|---|---|---|---|---|---|
| 1915–16 | 34 | Ottawa Senators | NHA | 2 | 1 | 0 | 1 | 0 |
| Career — 8 Seasons | | | | 47 | 42 | 0 | 42 | 163 |

**PLAYOFFS**

| SEASON | AGE | TEAM | LG | GP | G | A | PTS | PIM |
|---|---|---|---|---|---|---|---|---|
| 1902–03 | 21 | Ottawa Silver Seven | CAHL | 2 | 1 | 0 | 1 | |
| 1902–03 | 21 | Ottawa Silver Seven | St-Cup | 2 | 4 | 0 | 4 | 3 |
| 1903–04 | 22 | Ottawa Silver Seven | St-Cup | 3 | 1 | 0 | 1 | 0 |
| 1904–05 | 23 | Ottawa Silver Seven | St-Cup | 2 | 1 | 0 | 1 | 8 |
| Career — 3 Seasons | | | | 9 | 7 | 0 | 7 | 11 |

## Shorty Green  Profile: See page 192

### REGULAR SEASON

| SEASON | AGE | TEAM | LG | GP | G | A | PTS | PIM |
|---|---|---|---|---|---|---|---|---|
| 1918–19 | 22 | Hamilton Tigers | OHA-Sr | 8 | 12 | 13 | 15 | |
| 1919–20 | 23 | Sudbury Wolves | NOHA | 6 | 23 | 4 | 27 | 16 |
| 1920–21 | 24 | Sudbury Wolves | NOHA | 4 | 4 | 2 | 6 | 7 |
| 1921–22 | 25 | Sudbury Wolves | NOHA | 9 | 5 | 4 | 9 | 9 |
| 1922–23 | 26 | Sudbury Wolves | NOHA | 7 | 3 | 1 | 4 | 16 |
| 1923–24 | 27 | Hamilton Tigers | NHL | 22 | 7 | 7 | 14 | 33 |
| 1924–25 | 28 | Hamilton Tigers | NHL | 28 | 18 | 9 | 27 | 73 |
| 1925–26 | 29 | New York Americans | NHL | 32 | 7 | 5 | 12 | 44 |
| 1926–27 | 30 | New York Americans | NHL | 21 | 2 | 1 | 3 | 17 |
| Career — 9 Seasons | | | | 137 | 81 | 36 | 117 | 215 |

### PLAYOFFS

| SEASON | AGE | TEAM | LG | GP | G | A | PTS | PIM |
|---|---|---|---|---|---|---|---|---|
| 1918–19 | 22 | Hamilton Tigers | OHA-Sr | 4 | 5 | 3 | 8 | |
| 1919–20 | 23 | Sudbury Wolves | NOHA | 7 | 13 | 4 | 17 | 8 |
| 1922–23 | 26 | Sudbury Wolves | NOHA | 1 | 0 | 1 | 1 | 2 |
| Career — 3 Seasons | | | | 12 | 18 | 8 | 26 | 10 |

## Bryan Hextall  Profile: See page 193

### REGULAR SEASON

| SEASON | AGE | TEAM | LG | GP | G | A | PTS | PIM |
|---|---|---|---|---|---|---|---|---|
| 1936–37 | 23 | New York Rangers | NHL | 3 | 0 | 1 | 1 | 0 |
| 1937–38 | 24 | New York Rangers | NHL | 48 | 17 | 4 | 21 | 6 |
| 1938–39 | 25 | New York Rangers | NHL | 48 | 20 | 16 | 36 | 18 |
| 1939–40 | 26 | New York Rangers | NHL | 48 | 24 | 16 | 40 | 52 |
| 1940–41 | 27 | New York Rangers | NHL | 48 | 26 | 21 | 47 | 16 |
| 1941–42 | 28 | New York Rangers | NHL | 48 | 24 | 32 | 56 | 30 |
| 1942–43 | 29 | New York Rangers | NHL | 50 | 27 | 32 | 59 | 28 |
| 1943–44 | 30 | New York Rangers | NHL | 50 | 21 | 33 | 54 | 41 |
| 1945–46 | 32 | New York Rangers | NHL | 3 | 0 | 1 | 1 | 0 |
| 1946–47 | 33 | New York Rangers | NHL | 60 | 20 | 10 | 30 | 18 |
| 1947–48 | 34 | New York Rangers | NHL | 43 | 8 | 14 | 22 | 18 |
| NHL Career — 11 Seasons | | | | 449 | 187 | 180 | 367 | 227 |

### PLAYOFFS

| SEASON | AGE | TEAM | LG | GP | G | A | PTS | PIM |
|---|---|---|---|---|---|---|---|---|
| 1937–38 | 24 | New York Rangers | NHL | 3 | 2 | 0 | 2 | 0 |
| 1938–39 | 25 | New York Rangers | NHL | 7 | 0 | 1 | 1 | 4 |
| 1939–40 | 26 | New York Rangers | NHL | 12 | 4 | 3 | 7 | 11 |
| 1940–41 | 27 | New York Rangers | NHL | 3 | 0 | 1 | 1 | 0 |
| 1941–42 | 28 | New York Rangers | NHL | 6 | 1 | 1 | 2 | 4 |
| 1947–48 | 34 | New York Rangers | NHL | 6 | 1 | 3 | 4 | 0 |
| NHL Career — 6 Seasons | | | | 37 | 8 | 9 | 17 | 19 |

## Gordie Howe  Profile: See page 194

### REGULAR SEASON

| SEASON | AGE | TEAM | LG | GP | G | A | PTS | PIM |
|---|---|---|---|---|---|---|---|---|
| 1946–47 | 18 | Detroit Red Wings | NHL | 58 | 7 | 15 | 22 | 52 |
| 1947–48 | 19 | Detroit Red Wings | NHL | 60 | 16 | 28 | 44 | 63 |
| 1948–49 | 20 | Detroit Red Wings | NHL | 40 | 12 | 25 | 37 | 57 |
| 1949–50 | 21 | Detroit Red Wings | NHL | 70 | 35 | 33 | 68 | 69 |
| 1950–51 | 22 | Detroit Red Wings | NHL | 70 | 43 | 43 | 86 | 74 |
| 1951–52 | 23 | Detroit Red Wings | NHL | 70 | 47 | 39 | 86 | 78 |
| 1952–53 | 24 | Detroit Red Wings | NHL | 70 | 49 | 46 | 95 | 57 |
| 1953–54 | 25 | Detroit Red Wings | NHL | 70 | 33 | 48 | 81 | 109 |
| 1954–55 | 26 | Detroit Red Wings | NHL | 64 | 29 | 33 | 62 | 68 |
| 1955–56 | 27 | Detroit Red Wings | NHL | 70 | 38 | 41 | 79 | 100 |
| 1956–57 | 28 | Detroit Red Wings | NHL | 70 | 44 | 45 | 89 | 74 |
| 1957–58 | 29 | Detroit Red Wings | NHL | 64 | 33 | 44 | 77 | 38 |
| 1958–59 | 30 | Detroit Red Wings | NHL | 70 | 32 | 46 | 78 | 57 |
| 1959–60 | 31 | Detroit Red Wings | NHL | 70 | 28 | 45 | 73 | 46 |
| 1960–61 | 32 | Detroit Red Wings | NHL | 64 | 23 | 49 | 72 | 30 |
| 1961–62 | 33 | Detroit Red Wings | NHL | 70 | 33 | 44 | 77 | 54 |
| 1962–63 | 34 | Detroit Red Wings | NHL | 70 | 38 | 48 | 86 | 100 |
| 1963–64 | 35 | Detroit Red Wings | NHL | 69 | 26 | 47 | 73 | 70 |
| 1964–65 | 36 | Detroit Red Wings | NHL | 70 | 29 | 47 | 76 | 104 |
| 1965–66 | 37 | Detroit Red Wings | NHL | 70 | 29 | 46 | 75 | 83 |
| 1966–67 | 38 | Detroit Red Wings | NHL | 69 | 25 | 40 | 65 | 53 |
| 1967–68 | 39 | Detroit Red Wings | NHL | 74 | 39 | 43 | 82 | 53 |
| 1968–69 | 40 | Detroit Red Wings | NHL | 76 | 44 | 59 | 103 | 58 |
| 1969–70 | 41 | Detroit Red Wings | NHL | 76 | 31 | 40 | 71 | 58 |
| 1970–71 | 42 | Detroit Red Wings | NHL | 63 | 23 | 29 | 52 | 38 |
| 1973–74 | 45 | Houston Aeros | WHA | 70 | 31 | 69 | 100 | 46 |
| 1974–75 | 46 | Houston Aeros | WHA | 75 | 34 | 65 | 99 | 84 |
| 1975–76 | 47 | Houston Aeros | WHA | 78 | 32 | 70 | 102 | 76 |
| 1976–77 | 48 | Houston Aeros | WHA | 62 | 24 | 44 | 68 | 57 |
| 1977–78 | 49 | New England Whalers | WHA | 76 | 34 | 62 | 96 | 85 |
| 1978–79 | 50 | New England Whalers | WHA | 58 | 19 | 24 | 43 | 51 |
| 1979–80 | 51 | Hartford Whalers | NHL | 80 | 15 | 26 | 41 | 42 |
| Career — 32 Seasons | | | | 2186 | 975 | 1383 | 2358 | 2084 |

### PLAYOFFS

| SEASON | AGE | TEAM | LG | GP | G | A | PTS | PIM |
|---|---|---|---|---|---|---|---|---|
| 1946–47 | 18 | Detroit Red Wings | NHL | 5 | 0 | 0 | 0 | 18 |
| 1947–48 | 19 | Detroit Red Wings | NHL | 10 | 1 | 1 | 2 | 11 |
| 1948–49 | 20 | Detroit Red Wings | NHL | 11 | 8 | 3 | 11 | 19 |
| 1949–50 | 21 | Detroit Red Wings | NHL | 1 | 0 | 0 | 0 | 7 |
| 1950–51 | 22 | Detroit Red Wings | NHL | 6 | 4 | 3 | 7 | 4 |
| 1951–52 | 23 | Detroit Red Wings | NHL | 8 | 2 | 5 | 7 | 2 |
| 1952–53 | 24 | Detroit Red Wings | NHL | 6 | 2 | 5 | 7 | 2 |
| 1953–54 | 25 | Detroit Red Wings | NHL | 12 | 4 | 5 | 9 | 31 |
| 1954–55 | 26 | Detroit Red Wings | NHL | 11 | 9 | 11 | 20 | 24 |
| 1955–56 | 27 | Detroit Red Wings | NHL | 10 | 3 | 9 | 12 | 8 |
| 1956–57 | 28 | Detroit Red Wings | NHL | 5 | 2 | 5 | 7 | 6 |
| 1957–58 | 29 | Detroit Red Wings | NHL | 4 | 1 | 1 | 2 | 0 |
| 1959–60 | 31 | Detroit Red Wings | NHL | 6 | 1 | 5 | 6 | 4 |
| 1960–61 | 32 | Detroit Red Wings | NHL | 11 | 4 | 11 | 15 | 10 |
| 1962–63 | 34 | Detroit Red Wings | NHL | 11 | 7 | 9 | 16 | 22 |
| 1963–64 | 35 | Detroit Red Wings | NHL | 14 | 9 | 10 | 19 | 16 |
| 1964–65 | 36 | Detroit Red Wings | NHL | 7 | 4 | 2 | 6 | 20 |
| 1965–66 | 37 | Detroit Red Wings | NHL | 12 | 4 | 6 | 10 | 12 |
| 1969–70 | 41 | Detroit Red Wings | NHL | 4 | 2 | 0 | 2 | 2 |
| 1973–74 | 45 | Houston Aeros | WHA | 13 | 3 | 14 | 17 | 34 |
| 1974–75 | 46 | Houston Aeros | WHA | 13 | 8 | 12 | 20 | 20 |
| 1975–76 | 47 | Houston Aeros | WHA | 17 | 4 | 8 | 12 | 31 |
| 1976–77 | 48 | Houston Aeros | WHA | 11 | 5 | 3 | 8 | 11 |
| 1977–78 | 49 | New England Whalers | WHA | 14 | 5 | 5 | 10 | 15 |
| 1978–79 | 50 | New England Whalers | WHA | 10 | 3 | 1 | 4 | 4 |
| 1979–80 | 51 | Hartford Whalers | NHL | 3 | 1 | 1 | 2 | 2 |
| Career — 26 Seasons | | | | 235 | 96 | 135 | 231 | 335 |

# Brett Hull   Profile: See page 196

## REGULAR SEASON

| SEASON | AGE | TEAM | LG | GP | G | A | PTS | +/- | PIM | ESG | PPG | SHG | GWG | SOG | S% |
|---|---|---|---|---|---|---|---|---|---|---|---|---|---|---|---|
| 1986-87 | 22 | Calgary Flames | NHL | 5 | 1 | 0 | 1 | -1 | 0 | 1 | 0 | 0 | 1 | 5 | 20.0 |
| 1987-88 | 23 | Calgary Flames | NHL | 52 | 26 | 24 | 50 | 10 | 12 | 22 | 4 | 0 | 3 | 153 | 17.0 |
| 1987-88 | 23 | St. Louis Blues | NHL | 13 | 6 | 8 | 14 | 4 | 4 | 4 | 2 | 0 | 0 | 58 | 10.3 |
| 1988-89 | 24 | St. Louis Blues | NHL | 78 | 41 | 43 | 84 | -17 | 33 | 25 | 16 | 0 | 6 | 305 | 13.4 |
| 1989-90 | 25 | St. Louis Blues | NHL | 80 | 72 | 41 | 113 | -1 | 24 | 45 | 27 | 0 | 12 | 385 | 18.7 |
| 1990-91 | 26 | St. Louis Blues | NHL | 78 | 86 | 45 | 131 | 23 | 22 | 57 | 29 | 0 | 11 | 389 | 22.1 |
| 1991-92 | 27 | St. Louis Blues | NHL | 73 | 70 | 39 | 109 | -2 | 48 | 45 | 20 | 5 | 9 | 408 | 17.2 |
| 1992-93 | 28 | St. Louis Blues | NHL | 80 | 54 | 47 | 101 | -27 | 41 | 25 | 29 | 0 | 2 | 390 | 13.8 |
| 1993-94 | 29 | St. Louis Blues | NHL | 81 | 57 | 40 | 97 | -3 | 38 | 29 | 25 | 3 | 6 | 392 | 14.5 |
| 1994-95 | 30 | St. Louis Blues | NHL | 48 | 29 | 21 | 50 | 13 | 10 | 17 | 9 | 3 | 6 | 200 | 14.5 |
| 1995-96 | 31 | St. Louis Blues | NHL | 70 | 43 | 40 | 83 | 4 | 30 | 22 | 16 | 5 | 6 | 327 | 13.1 |
| 1996-97 | 32 | St. Louis Blues | NHL | 77 | 42 | 40 | 82 | -9 | 10 | 28 | 12 | 2 | 6 | 302 | 13.9 |
| 1997-98 | 33 | St. Louis Blues | NHL | 66 | 27 | 45 | 72 | -1 | 26 | 17 | 10 | 0 | 6 | 211 | 12.8 |
| 1998-99 | 34 | Dallas Stars | NHL | 60 | 32 | 26 | 58 | 19 | 30 | 17 | 15 | 0 | 11 | 192 | 16.7 |
| 1999-00 | 35 | Dallas Stars | NHL | 79 | 24 | 35 | 59 | -21 | 43 | 13 | 11 | 0 | 3 | 223 | 10.8 |
| 2000-01 | 36 | Dallas Stars | NHL | 79 | 39 | 40 | 79 | 10 | 18 | 28 | 11 | 0 | 8 | 219 | 17.8 |
| 2001-02 | 37 | Detroit Red Wings | NHL | 82 | 30 | 33 | 63 | 18 | 35 | 22 | 7 | 1 | 4 | 247 | 12.1 |
| 2002-03 | 38 | Detroit Red Wings | NHL | 82 | 37 | 39 | 76 | 11 | 22 | 24 | 12 | 1 | 4 | 262 | 14.1 |
| 2003-04 | 39 | Detroit Red Wings | NHL | 81 | 25 | 43 | 68 | -4 | 12 | 15 | 10 | 0 | 6 | 200 | 12.5 |
| 2005-06 | 41 | Phoenix Coyotes | NHL | 5 | 0 | 1 | 1 | -3 | 0 | 0 | 0 | 0 | 0 | 8 | 0.0 |
| NHL Career — 19 Seasons | | | | 1269 | 741 | 650 | 1391 | 23 | 458 | 456 | 265 | 20 | 110 | 4876 | 15.2 |

## PLAYOFFS

| SEASON | AGE | TEAM | LG | GP | G | A | PTS | +/- | PIM | ESG | PPG | SHG | GWG | SOG | S% |
|---|---|---|---|---|---|---|---|---|---|---|---|---|---|---|---|
| 1985-86 | 21 | Calgary Flames | NHL | 2 | 0 | 0 | 0 | 0 | 0 | 0 | 0 | 0 | 0 | 1 | 0.0 |
| 1986-87 | 22 | Calgary Flames | NHL | 4 | 2 | 1 | 3 | 4 | 0 | 2 | 0 | 0 | 0 | 18 | 11.1 |
| 1987-88 | 23 | St. Louis Blues | NHL | 10 | 7 | 2 | 9 | 1 | 4 | 3 | 4 | 0 | 3 | 39 | 17.9 |
| 1988-89 | 24 | St. Louis Blues | NHL | 10 | 5 | 5 | 10 | -4 | 6 | 4 | 1 | 0 | 2 | 43 | 11.6 |
| 1989-90 | 25 | St. Louis Blues | NHL | 12 | 13 | 8 | 21 | 1 | 17 | 6 | 7 | 0 | 3 | 68 | 19.1 |
| 1990-91 | 26 | St. Louis Blues | NHL | 13 | 11 | 8 | 19 | 5 | 4 | 8 | 3 | 0 | 2 | 58 | 19.0 |
| 1991-92 | 27 | St. Louis Blues | NHL | 6 | 4 | 4 | 8 | 2 | 4 | 2 | 1 | 1 | 1 | 38 | 10.5 |
| 1992-93 | 28 | St. Louis Blues | NHL | 11 | 8 | 5 | 13 | -2 | 2 | 3 | 5 | 0 | 2 | 52 | 15.4 |
| 1993-94 | 29 | St. Louis Blues | NHL | 4 | 2 | 1 | 3 | 1 | 0 | 1 | 1 | 0 | 0 | 22 | 9.1 |
| 1994-95 | 30 | St. Louis Blues | NHL | 7 | 6 | 2 | 8 | 0 | 0 | 4 | 2 | 0 | 0 | 34 | 17.6 |
| 1995-96 | 31 | St. Louis Blues | NHL | 13 | 6 | 5 | 11 | 2 | 10 | 3 | 2 | 1 | 1 | 52 | 11.5 |
| 1996-97 | 32 | St. Louis Blues | NHL | 6 | 2 | 7 | 9 | 4 | 2 | 2 | 0 | 0 | 0 | 25 | 8.0 |
| 1997-98 | 33 | St. Louis Blues | NHL | 10 | 3 | 3 | 6 | -3 | 2 | 2 | 1 | 0 | 1 | 32 | 9.4 |
| 1998-99 | 34 | Dallas Stars | NHL | 22 | 8 | 7 | 15 | 3 | 4 | 5 | 3 | 0 | 2 | 86 | 9.3 |
| 1999-00 | 35 | Dallas Stars | NHL | 23 | 11 | 13 | 24 | 3 | 4 | 8 | 3 | 0 | 4 | 79 | 13.9 |
| 2000-01 | 36 | Dallas Stars | NHL | 10 | 2 | 5 | 7 | -1 | 6 | 1 | 1 | 0 | 0 | 41 | 4.9 |
| 2001-02 | 37 | Detroit Red Wings | NHL | 23 | 10 | 8 | 18 | 1 | 4 | 5 | 3 | 2 | 2 | 61 | 16.4 |
| 2002-03 | 38 | Detroit Red Wings | NHL | 4 | 0 | 1 | 1 | -4 | 0 | 0 | 0 | 0 | 0 | 15 | 0.0 |
| 2003-04 | 39 | Detroit Red Wings | NHL | 12 | 3 | 2 | 5 | 0 | 4 | 2 | 1 | 0 | 1 | 39 | 7.7 |
| NHL Career — 19 Seasons | | | | 202 | 103 | 87 | 190 | 13 | 73 | 61 | 38 | 4 | 24 | 803 | 12.8 |

# Harry Hyland   Profile: See page 198

## REGULAR SEASON

| SEASON | AGE | TEAM | LG | GP | G | A | PTS | PIM |
|---|---|---|---|---|---|---|---|---|
| 1908-09 | 20 | Montreal Shamrocks | ECHA | 11 | 19 | 0 | 19 | 36 |
| 1909-10 | 21 | Montreal Wanderers | NHA | 12 | 24 | 0 | 24 | 23 |
| 1910-11 | 22 | Montreal Wanderers | NHA | 15 | 14 | 0 | 14 | 43 |
| 1911-12 | 23 | New Westminster Royals | PCHA | 15 | 26 | 0 | 26 | 44 |
| 1912-13 | 24 | Montreal Wanderers | NHA | 20 | 27 | 0 | 27 | 38 |
| 1913-14 | 25 | Montreal Wanderers | NHA | 18 | 30 | 12 | 42 | 18 |
| 1914-15 | 26 | Montreal Wanderers | NHA | 19 | 23 | 6 | 29 | 49 |
| 1915-16 | 27 | Montreal Wanderers | NHA | 20 | 14 | 0 | 14 | 69 |
| 1916-17 | 28 | Montreal Wanderers | NHA | 13 | 12 | 2 | 14 | 21 |
| 1917-18 | 29 | Montreal Wanderers | NHL | 4 | 6 | 1 | 7 | 6 |
| 1917-18 | 29 | Ottawa Senators | NHL | 13 | 8 | 1 | 9 | 59 |
| Career — 10 Seasons | | | | 160 | 203 | 22 | 225 | 414 |

## PLAYOFFS

| SEASON | AGE | TEAM | LG | GP | G | A | PTS | PIM |
|---|---|---|---|---|---|---|---|---|
| 1909-10 | 21 | Montreal Wanderers | St-Cup | 1 | 3 | 0 | 3 | 3 |
| 1914-15 | 26 | Montreal Wanderers | NHA | 2 | 0 | 0 | 0 | 26 |
| Career — 2 Seasons | | | | 3 | 3 | 0 | 3 | 29 |

## Jari Kurri  Profile: See page 199

### REGULAR SEASON

| SEASON | AGE | TEAM | LG | GP | G | A | PTS | +/- | PIM | ESG | PPG | SHG | GWG | SOG | S% |
|---|---|---|---|---|---|---|---|---|---|---|---|---|---|---|---|
| 1980–81 | 20 | Edmonton Oilers | NHL | 75 | 32 | 43 | 75 | 27 | 40 | 23 | 9 | 0 | 1 | 202 | 15.8 |
| 1981–82 | 21 | Edmonton Oilers | NHL | 71 | 32 | 54 | 86 | 39 | 32 | 25 | 6 | 1 | 5 | 211 | 15.2 |
| 1982–83 | 22 | Edmonton Oilers | NHL | 80 | 45 | 59 | 104 | 48 | 22 | 34 | 10 | 1 | 3 | 218 | 20.6 |
| 1983–84 | 23 | Edmonton Oilers | NHL | 64 | 52 | 61 | 113 | 39 | 14 | 37 | 10 | 5 | 4 | 195 | 26.7 |
| 1984–85 | 24 | Edmonton Oilers | NHL | 73 | 71 | 64 | 135 | 78 | 30 | 54 | 14 | 3 | 13 | 267 | 26.6 |
| 1985–86 | 25 | Edmonton Oilers | NHL | 78 | 68 | 63 | 131 | 45 | 22 | 46 | 16 | 6 | 9 | 236 | 28.8 |
| 1986–87 | 26 | Edmonton Oilers | NHL | 79 | 54 | 54 | 108 | 35 | 41 | 37 | 12 | 5 | 10 | 211 | 25.6 |
| 1987–88 | 27 | Edmonton Oilers | NHL | 80 | 43 | 53 | 96 | 25 | 30 | 30 | 10 | 3 | 5 | 207 | 20.8 |
| 1988–89 | 28 | Edmonton Oilers | NHL | 76 | 44 | 58 | 102 | 19 | 69 | 29 | 10 | 5 | 8 | 214 | 20.6 |
| 1989–90 | 29 | Edmonton Oilers | NHL | 78 | 33 | 60 | 93 | 18 | 48 | 21 | 10 | 2 | 2 | 201 | 16.4 |
| 1991–92 | 31 | Los Angeles Kings | NHL | 73 | 23 | 37 | 60 | -24 | 24 | 12 | 10 | 1 | 3 | 167 | 13.8 |
| 1992–93 | 32 | Los Angeles Kings | NHL | 82 | 27 | 60 | 87 | 19 | 38 | 13 | 12 | 2 | 3 | 210 | 12.9 |
| 1993–94 | 33 | Los Angeles Kings | NHL | 81 | 31 | 46 | 77 | -24 | 48 | 13 | 14 | 4 | 3 | 198 | 15.7 |
| 1994–95 | 34 | Los Angeles Kings | NHL | 38 | 10 | 19 | 29 | -17 | 24 | 8 | 2 | 0 | 0 | 84 | 11.9 |
| 1995–96 | 35 | Los Angeles Kings | NHL | 57 | 17 | 23 | 40 | -12 | 37 | 11 | 5 | 1 | 0 | 131 | 13.0 |
| 1995–96 | 35 | New York Rangers | NHL | 14 | 1 | 4 | 5 | -4 | 2 | 1 | 0 | 0 | 0 | 27 | 3.7 |
| 1996–97 | 36 | Mighty Ducks of Anaheim | NHL | 82 | 13 | 22 | 35 | -13 | 12 | 10 | 3 | 0 | 3 | 109 | 11.9 |
| 1997–98 | 37 | Colorado Avalanche | NHL | 70 | 5 | 17 | 22 | 6 | 12 | 3 | 2 | 0 | 0 | 61 | 8.2 |
| NHL Career — 17 Seasons | | | | 1251 | 601 | 797 | 1398 | 304 | 545 | 407 | 155 | 39 | 72 | 3149 | 19.1 |

### PLAYOFFS

| SEASON | AGE | TEAM | LG | GP | G | A | PTS | +/- | PIM | ESG | PPG | SHG | GWG | SOG | S% |
|---|---|---|---|---|---|---|---|---|---|---|---|---|---|---|---|
| 1980–81 | 20 | Edmonton Oilers | NHL | 9 | 5 | 7 | 12 | 12 | 4 | 5 | 0 | 0 | 0 | 14 | 35.7 |
| 1981–82 | 21 | Edmonton Oilers | NHL | 5 | 2 | 5 | 7 | 2 | 10 | 2 | 0 | 0 | 0 | 10 | 20.0 |
| 1982–83 | 22 | Edmonton Oilers | NHL | 16 | 8 | 15 | 23 | 16 | 8 | 4 | 2 | 2 | 0 | 31 | 25.8 |
| 1983–84 | 23 | Edmonton Oilers | NHL | 19 | 14 | 14 | 28 | 9 | 13 | 10 | 4 | 0 | 0 | 60 | 23.3 |
| 1984–85 | 24 | Edmonton Oilers | NHL | 18 | 19 | 12 | 31 | 23 | 6 | 16 | 1 | 2 | 2 | 91 | 20.9 |
| 1985–86 | 25 | Edmonton Oilers | NHL | 10 | 2 | 10 | 12 | 0 | 4 | 1 | 0 | 1 | 0 | 26 | 7.7 |
| 1986–87 | 26 | Edmonton Oilers | NHL | 21 | 15 | 10 | 25 | 11 | 20 | 10 | 4 | 1 | 5 | 52 | 28.9 |
| 1987–88 | 27 | Edmonton Oilers | NHL | 19 | 14 | 17 | 31 | 15 | 12 | 9 | 5 | 0 | 3 | 57 | 24.6 |
| 1988–89 | 28 | Edmonton Oilers | NHL | 7 | 3 | 5 | 8 | -2 | 6 | 2 | 0 | 1 | 0 | 17 | 17.6 |
| 1989–90 | 29 | Edmonton Oilers | NHL | 22 | 10 | 15 | 25 | 13 | 18 | 4 | 6 | 0 | 3 | 58 | 17.2 |
| 1991–92 | 31 | Los Angeles Kings | NHL | 4 | 1 | 2 | 3 | 1 | 4 | 0 | 1 | 0 | 0 | 10 | 10.0 |
| 1992–93 | 32 | Los Angeles Kings | NHL | 24 | 9 | 8 | 17 | 2 | 12 | 5 | 2 | 2 | 0 | 50 | 18.0 |
| 1995–96 | 35 | New York Rangers | NHL | 11 | 3 | 5 | 8 | -2 | 2 | 2 | 0 | 1 | 1 | 31 | 9.7 |
| 1996–97 | 36 | Mighty Ducks of Anaheim | NHL | 11 | 1 | 2 | 3 | 2 | 4 | 1 | 0 | 0 | 0 | 18 | 5.6 |
| 1997–98 | 37 | Colorado Avalanche | NHL | 4 | 0 | 0 | 0 | -1 | 0 | 0 | 0 | 0 | 0 | 2 | 0.0 |
| NHL Career — 15 Seasons | | | | 200 | 106 | 127 | 233 | 101 | 123 | 71 | 25 | 10 | 14 | 527 | 20.1 |

## Guy Lafleur  Profile: See page 200

### REGULAR SEASON

| SEASON | AGE | TEAM | LG | GP | G | A | PTS | +/- | PIM | ESG | PPG | SHG | GWG | SOG | S% |
|---|---|---|---|---|---|---|---|---|---|---|---|---|---|---|---|
| 1971–72 | 20 | Montreal Canadiens | NHL | 73 | 29 | 35 | 64 | 27 | 48 | 24 | 5 | 0 | 5 | 187 | 15.5 |
| 1972–73 | 21 | Montreal Canadiens | NHL | 69 | 28 | 27 | 55 | 15 | 51 | 19 | 9 | 0 | 7 | 176 | 15.9 |
| 1973–74 | 22 | Montreal Canadiens | NHL | 73 | 21 | 35 | 56 | 9 | 29 | 17 | 3 | 1 | 2 | 167 | 12.6 |
| 1974–75 | 23 | Montreal Canadiens | NHL | 70 | 53 | 66 | 119 | 53 | 37 | 36 | 15 | 2 | 11 | 260 | 20.4 |
| 1975–76 | 24 | Montreal Canadiens | NHL | 80 | 56 | 69 | 125 | 67 | 36 | 38 | 18 | 0 | 12 | 303 | 18.5 |
| 1976–77 | 25 | Montreal Canadiens | NHL | 80 | 56 | 80 | 136 | 89 | 20 | 42 | 14 | 0 | 8 | 290 | 19.3 |
| 1977–78 | 26 | Montreal Canadiens | NHL | 78 | 60 | 72 | 132 | 73 | 26 | 45 | 15 | 0 | 12 | 305 | 19.7 |
| 1978–79 | 27 | Montreal Canadiens | NHL | 80 | 52 | 77 | 129 | 55 | 28 | 39 | 13 | 0 | 13 | 342 | 15.2 |
| 1979–80 | 28 | Montreal Canadiens | NHL | 74 | 50 | 75 | 125 | 40 | 12 | 35 | 15 | 0 | 7 | 323 | 15.5 |
| 1980–81 | 29 | Montreal Canadiens | NHL | 51 | 27 | 43 | 70 | 24 | 29 | 20 | 7 | 0 | 7 | 191 | 14.1 |
| 1981–82 | 30 | Montreal Canadiens | NHL | 66 | 27 | 57 | 84 | 33 | 24 | 18 | 9 | 0 | 3 | 233 | 11.6 |
| 1982–83 | 31 | Montreal Canadiens | NHL | 68 | 27 | 49 | 76 | 5 | 12 | 18 | 9 | 0 | 1 | 176 | 15.3 |
| 1983–84 | 32 | Montreal Canadiens | NHL | 80 | 30 | 40 | 70 | -16 | 19 | 23 | 7 | 0 | 6 | 217 | 13.8 |
| 1984–85 | 33 | Montreal Canadiens | NHL | 19 | 2 | 3 | 5 | -3 | 10 | 2 | 0 | 0 | 0 | 34 | 5.9 |
| 1988–89 | 37 | New York Rangers | NHL | 67 | 18 | 27 | 45 | 1 | 12 | 12 | 6 | 0 | 2 | 122 | 14.8 |
| 1989–90 | 38 | Quebec Nordiques | NHL | 39 | 12 | 22 | 34 | -15 | 4 | 6 | 6 | 0 | 2 | 100 | 12.0 |
| 1990–91 | 39 | Quebec Nordiques | NHL | 59 | 12 | 16 | 28 | -10 | 2 | 9 | 3 | 0 | 0 | 90 | 13.3 |
| NHL Career — 17 Seasons | | | | 1126 | 560 | 793 | 1353 | 446 | 399 | 403 | 154 | 3 | 98 | 3516 | 15.9 |

### PLAYOFFS

| SEASON | AGE | TEAM | LG | GP | G | A | PTS | +/- | PIM | ESG | PPG | SHG | GWG | SOG | S% |
|---|---|---|---|---|---|---|---|---|---|---|---|---|---|---|---|
| 1971–72 | 20 | Montreal Canadiens | NHL | 6 | 1 | 4 | 5 | -1 | 2 | 1 | 0 | 0 | 0 | 11 | 9.1 |
| 1972–73 | 21 | Montreal Canadiens | NHL | 17 | 3 | 5 | 8 | 2 | 9 | 1 | 2 | 0 | 1 | 25 | 12.0 |
| 1973–74 | 22 | Montreal Canadiens | NHL | 6 | 0 | 1 | 1 | -4 | 4 | 0 | 0 | 0 | 0 | 5 | 0.0 |
| 1974–75 | 23 | Montreal Canadiens | NHL | 11 | 12 | 7 | 19 | 6 | 15 | 8 | 4 | 0 | 4 | 44 | 27.3 |
| 1975–76 | 24 | Montreal Canadiens | NHL | 13 | 7 | 10 | 17 | 10 | 2 | 7 | 0 | 0 | 3 | 46 | 15.2 |
| 1976–77 | 25 | Montreal Canadiens | NHL | 14 | 9 | 17 | 26 | 20 | 6 | 8 | 1 | 0 | 2 | 57 | 15.8 |
| 1977–78 | 26 | Montreal Canadiens | NHL | 15 | 10 | 11 | 21 | 10 | 16 | 7 | 3 | 0 | 2 | 46 | 21.7 |

## Guy Lafleur (continued)

### PLAYOFFS

| SEASON | AGE | TEAM | LG | GP | G | A | PTS | +/- | PIM | ESG | PPG | SHG | GWG | SOG | S% |
|---|---|---|---|---|---|---|---|---|---|---|---|---|---|---|---|
| 1978–79 | 27 | Montreal Canadiens | NHL | 16 | 10 | 13 | 23 | 8 | 0 | 8 | 2 | 0 | 2 | 73 | 13.7 |
| 1979–80 | 28 | Montreal Canadiens | NHL | 3 | 3 | 1 | 4 | 4 | 0 | 3 | 0 | 0 | 0 | 7 | 42.9 |
| 1980–81 | 29 | Montreal Canadiens | NHL | 3 | 0 | 1 | 1 | -3 | 2 | 0 | 0 | 0 | 0 | 7 | 0.0 |
| 1981–82 | 30 | Montreal Canadiens | NHL | 5 | 2 | 1 | 3 | -1 | 4 | 0 | 2 | 0 | 0 | 18 | 11.1 |
| 1982–83 | 31 | Montreal Canadiens | NHL | 3 | 0 | 2 | 2 | 0 | 2 | 0 | 0 | 0 | 0 | 5 | 0.0 |
| 1983–84 | 32 | Montreal Canadiens | NHL | 12 | 0 | 3 | 3 | 1 | 5 | 0 | 0 | 0 | 0 | 16 | 0.0 |
| 1988–89 | 37 | New York Rangers | NHL | 4 | 1 | 0 | 1 | -3 | 0 | 0 | 1 | 0 | 0 | 10 | 10.0 |
| NHL Career — 14 Seasons | | | | 128 | 58 | 76 | 134 | 50 | 67 | 43 | 15 | 0 | 14 | 370 | 15.7 |

## Sergei Makarov   Profile: See page 202

### REGULAR SEASON

| SEASON | AGE | TEAM | LG | GP | G | A | PTS | +/- | PIM | ESG | PPG | SHG | GWG | SOG | S% |
|---|---|---|---|---|---|---|---|---|---|---|---|---|---|---|---|
| 1989–90 | 31 | Calgary Flames | NHL | 80 | 24 | 62 | 86 | 33 | 55 | 18 | 6 | 0 | 4 | 118 | 20.3 |
| 1990–91 | 32 | Calgary Flames | NHL | 78 | 30 | 49 | 79 | 15 | 44 | 21 | 9 | 0 | 5 | 93 | 32.3 |
| 1991–92 | 33 | Calgary Flames | NHL | 68 | 22 | 48 | 70 | 14 | 60 | 16 | 6 | 0 | 2 | 83 | 26.5 |
| 1992–93 | 34 | Calgary Flames | NHL | 71 | 18 | 39 | 57 | 0 | 40 | 13 | 5 | 0 | 3 | 105 | 17.1 |
| 1993–94 | 35 | San Jose Sharks | NHL | 80 | 30 | 38 | 68 | 11 | 78 | 20 | 10 | 0 | 5 | 155 | 19.4 |
| 1994–95 | 36 | San Jose Sharks | NHL | 43 | 10 | 14 | 24 | -4 | 40 | 9 | 1 | 0 | 1 | 56 | 17.9 |
| 1996–97 | 38 | Dallas Stars | NHL | 4 | 0 | 0 | 0 | -2 | 0 | 0 | 0 | 0 | 0 | 0 | 0.0 |
| NHL Career — 7 Seasons | | | | 424 | 134 | 250 | 384 | 67 | 317 | 97 | 37 | 0 | 20 | 610 | 22.0 |

### PLAYOFFS

| SEASON | AGE | TEAM | LG | GP | G | A | PTS | +/- | PIM | ESG | PPG | SHG | GWG | SOG | S% |
|---|---|---|---|---|---|---|---|---|---|---|---|---|---|---|---|
| 1989–90 | 31 | Calgary Flames | NHL | 6 | 0 | 6 | 6 | 3 | 0 | 0 | 0 | 0 | 0 | 5 | 0.0 |
| 1990–91 | 32 | Calgary Flames | NHL | 3 | 1 | 0 | 1 | -1 | 0 | 1 | 0 | 0 | 0 | 2 | 50.0 |
| 1993–94 | 35 | San Jose Sharks | NHL | 14 | 8 | 2 | 10 | 2 | 4 | 5 | 3 | 0 | 2 | 26 | 30.8 |
| 1994–95 | 36 | San Jose Sharks | NHL | 11 | 3 | 3 | 6 | -3 | 4 | 3 | 0 | 0 | 0 | 8 | 37.5 |
| NHL Career — 4 Seasons | | | | 34 | 12 | 11 | 23 | 1 | 8 | 9 | 3 | 0 | 2 | 41 | 29.3 |

## Lanny McDonald   Profile: See page 204

### REGULAR SEASON

| SEASON | AGE | TEAM | LG | GP | G | A | PTS | +/- | PIM | ESG | PPG | SHG | GWG | SOG | S% |
|---|---|---|---|---|---|---|---|---|---|---|---|---|---|---|---|
| 1973–74 | 20 | Toronto Maple Leafs | NHL | 70 | 14 | 16 | 30 | 2 | 43 | 12 | 2 | 0 | 3 | 142 | 9.9 |
| 1974–75 | 21 | Toronto Maple Leafs | NHL | 64 | 17 | 27 | 44 | 6 | 86 | 14 | 2 | 1 | 1 | 165 | 10.3 |
| 1975–76 | 22 | Toronto Maple Leafs | NHL | 75 | 37 | 56 | 93 | 24 | 70 | 26 | 6 | 5 | 4 | 270 | 13.7 |
| 1976–77 | 23 | Toronto Maple Leafs | NHL | 80 | 46 | 44 | 90 | 12 | 77 | 26 | 16 | 4 | 5 | 293 | 15.7 |
| 1977–78 | 24 | Toronto Maple Leafs | NHL | 74 | 47 | 40 | 87 | 35 | 54 | 36 | 11 | 0 | 5 | 241 | 19.5 |
| 1978–79 | 25 | Toronto Maple Leafs | NHL | 79 | 43 | 42 | 85 | 11 | 32 | 27 | 16 | 0 | 2 | 314 | 13.7 |
| 1979–80 | 26 | Toronto Maple Leafs | NHL | 35 | 15 | 15 | 30 | -2 | 10 | 9 | 6 | 0 | 3 | 140 | 10.7 |
| 1979–80 | 26 | Colorado Rockies | NHL | 46 | 25 | 20 | 45 | -15 | 43 | 17 | 8 | 0 | 3 | 194 | 12.9 |
| 1980–81 | 27 | Colorado Rockies | NHL | 80 | 35 | 46 | 81 | -28 | 56 | 24 | 11 | 0 | 2 | 298 | 11.7 |
| 1981–82 | 28 | Colorado Rockies | NHL | 16 | 6 | 9 | 15 | -3 | 20 | 6 | 0 | 0 | 1 | 65 | 9.2 |
| 1981–82 | 28 | Calgary Flames | NHL | 55 | 34 | 33 | 67 | 22 | 37 | 23 | 10 | 1 | 3 | 178 | 19.1 |
| 1982–83 | 29 | Calgary Flames | NHL | 80 | 66 | 32 | 98 | -1 | 90 | 49 | 17 | 0 | 8 | 275 | 24.0 |
| 1983–84 | 30 | Calgary Flames | NHL | 65 | 33 | 33 | 66 | -16 | 64 | 23 | 10 | 0 | 1 | 246 | 13.4 |
| 1984–85 | 31 | Calgary Flames | NHL | 43 | 19 | 18 | 37 | -4 | 36 | 10 | 9 | 0 | 2 | 117 | 16.2 |
| 1985–86 | 32 | Calgary Flames | NHL | 80 | 28 | 43 | 71 | -2 | 44 | 17 | 11 | 0 | 3 | 227 | 12.3 |
| 1986–87 | 33 | Calgary Flames | NHL | 58 | 14 | 12 | 26 | -3 | 54 | 10 | 4 | 0 | 3 | 129 | 10.9 |
| 1987–88 | 34 | Calgary Flames | NHL | 60 | 10 | 13 | 23 | 2 | 57 | 10 | 0 | 0 | 2 | 79 | 12.7 |
| 1988–89 | 35 | Calgary Flames | NHL | 51 | 11 | 7 | 18 | -1 | 26 | 11 | 0 | 0 | 3 | 72 | 15.3 |
| NHL Career — 16 Seasons | | | | 1111 | 500 | 506 | 1006 | 39 | 899 | 350 | 139 | 11 | 54 | 3445 | 14.5 |

### PLAYOFFS

| SEASON | AGE | TEAM | LG | GP | G | A | PTS | +/- | PIM | ESG | PPG | SHG | GWG | SOG | S% |
|---|---|---|---|---|---|---|---|---|---|---|---|---|---|---|---|
| 1974–75 | 21 | Toronto Maple Leafs | NHL | 7 | 0 | 0 | 0 | -4 | 2 | 0 | 0 | 0 | 0 | 15 | 0.0 |
| 1975–76 | 22 | Toronto Maple Leafs | NHL | 10 | 4 | 4 | 8 | -6 | 4 | 2 | 2 | 0 | 1 | 33 | 12.1 |
| 1976–77 | 23 | Toronto Maple Leafs | NHL | 9 | 10 | 7 | 17 | 0 | 6 | 7 | 3 | 0 | 1 | 33 | 30.3 |
| 1977–78 | 24 | Toronto Maple Leafs | NHL | 13 | 3 | 4 | 7 | -5 | 10 | 2 | 1 | 0 | 2 | 36 | 8.3 |
| 1978–79 | 25 | Toronto Maple Leafs | NHL | 6 | 3 | 2 | 5 | 1 | 0 | 3 | 0 | 0 | 0 | 11 | 27.3 |
| 1981–82 | 28 | Calgary Flames | NHL | 3 | 0 | 1 | 1 | -3 | 6 | 0 | 0 | 0 | 0 | 13 | 0.0 |
| 1982–83 | 29 | Calgary Flames | NHL | 7 | 3 | 4 | 7 | -4 | 19 | 2 | 1 | 0 | 0 | 19 | 15.8 |
| 1983–84 | 30 | Calgary Flames | NHL | 11 | 6 | 7 | 13 | 2 | 6 | 3 | 3 | 0 | 1 | 29 | 20.7 |
| 1984–85 | 31 | Calgary Flames | NHL | 1 | 0 | 0 | 0 | 0 | 0 | 0 | 0 | 0 | 0 | 1 | 0.0 |
| 1985–86 | 32 | Calgary Flames | NHL | 22 | 11 | 7 | 18 | 5 | 30 | 7 | 4 | 0 | 2 | 71 | 15.5 |
| 1986–87 | 33 | Calgary Flames | NHL | 5 | 0 | 0 | 0 | -3 | 2 | 0 | 0 | 0 | 0 | 7 | 0.0 |
| 1987–88 | 34 | Calgary Flames | NHL | 9 | 3 | 1 | 4 | 3 | 6 | 3 | 0 | 0 | 0 | 17 | 17.6 |
| 1988–89 | 35 | Calgary Flames | NHL | 14 | 1 | 3 | 4 | 2 | 29 | 1 | 0 | 0 | 0 | 13 | 7.7 |
| NHL Career — 13 Seasons | | | | 117 | 44 | 40 | 84 | -12 | 120 | 30 | 14 | 0 | 7 | 298 | 14.8 |

## Bill Mosienko  Profile: See page 206

### REGULAR SEASON

| SEASON | AGE | TEAM | LG | GP | G | A | PTS | PIM |
|---|---|---|---|---|---|---|---|---|
| 1941–42 | 20 | Chicago Black Hawks | NHL | 12 | 6 | 8 | 14 | 4 |
| 1942–43 | 21 | Chicago Black Hawks | NHL | 2 | 2 | 0 | 2 | 0 |
| 1943–44 | 22 | Chicago Black Hawks | NHL | 50 | 32 | 38 | 70 | 10 |
| 1944–45 | 23 | Chicago Black Hawks | NHL | 50 | 28 | 26 | 54 | 0 |
| 1945–46 | 24 | Chicago Black Hawks | NHL | 40 | 18 | 30 | 48 | 12 |
| 1946–47 | 25 | Chicago Black Hawks | NHL | 59 | 25 | 27 | 52 | 2 |
| 1947–48 | 26 | Chicago Black Hawks | NHL | 40 | 16 | 9 | 25 | 0 |
| 1948–49 | 27 | Chicago Black Hawks | NHL | 60 | 17 | 25 | 42 | 6 |
| 1949–50 | 28 | Chicago Black Hawks | NHL | 69 | 18 | 28 | 46 | 10 |
| 1950–51 | 29 | Chicago Black Hawks | NHL | 65 | 21 | 15 | 36 | 18 |
| 1951–52 | 30 | Chicago Black Hawks | NHL | 70 | 31 | 22 | 53 | 20 |
| 1952–53 | 31 | Chicago Black Hawks | NHL | 65 | 17 | 20 | 37 | 8 |
| 1953–54 | 32 | Chicago Black Hawks | NHL | 65 | 15 | 19 | 34 | 17 |
| 1954–55 | 33 | Chicago Black Hawks | NHL | 64 | 12 | 15 | 27 | 24 |
| NHL Career – 14 Seasons | | | | 711 | 258 | 282 | 540 | 133 |

### PLAYOFFS

| SEASON | AGE | TEAM | LG | GP | G | A | PTS | PIM |
|---|---|---|---|---|---|---|---|---|
| 1941–42 | 20 | Chicago Black Hawks | NHL | 3 | 2 | 0 | 2 | 0 |
| 1942–44 | 22 | Chicago Black Hawks | NHL | 8 | 2 | 2 | 4 | 6 |
| 1945–46 | 24 | Chicago Black Hawks | NHL | 4 | 2 | 0 | 2 | 2 |
| 1952–53 | 31 | Chicago Black Hawks | NHL | 7 | 4 | 2 | 6 | 7 |
| NHL Career – 4 Seasons | | | | 22 | 10 | 4 | 14 | 15 |

## Joseph Mullen  Profile: See page 207

### REGULAR SEASON

| SEASON | AGE | TEAM | LG | GP | G | A | PTS | +/- | PIM | ESG | PPG | SHG | GWG | SOG | S% |
|---|---|---|---|---|---|---|---|---|---|---|---|---|---|---|---|
| 1981–82 | 24 | St. Louis Blues | NHL | 45 | 25 | 34 | 59 | 11 | 4 | 15 | 10 | 0 | 3 | 141 | 17.7 |
| 1982–83 | 25 | St. Louis Blues | NHL | 49 | 17 | 30 | 47 | -7 | 6 | 12 | 5 | 0 | 0 | 128 | 13.3 |
| 1983–84 | 26 | St. Louis Blues | NHL | 80 | 41 | 44 | 85 | -9 | 19 | 28 | 13 | 0 | 6 | 228 | 18.0 |
| 1984–85 | 27 | St. Louis Blues | NHL | 79 | 40 | 52 | 92 | 7 | 6 | 27 | 13 | 0 | 4 | 253 | 15.8 |
| 1985–86 | 28 | St. Louis Blues | NHL | 48 | 28 | 24 | 52 | -3 | 10 | 19 | 9 | 0 | 4 | 141 | 19.9 |
| 1985–86 | 28 | Calgary Flames | NHL | 29 | 16 | 22 | 38 | 2 | 11 | 11 | 5 | 0 | 4 | 61 | 26.2 |
| 1986–87 | 29 | Calgary Flames | NHL | 79 | 47 | 40 | 87 | 19 | 14 | 32 | 15 | 0 | 12 | 206 | 22.8 |
| 1987–88 | 30 | Calgary Flames | NHL | 80 | 40 | 44 | 84 | 28 | 30 | 28 | 12 | 0 | 5 | 205 | 19.5 |
| 1988–89 | 31 | Calgary Flames | NHL | 79 | 51 | 59 | 110 | 51 | 16 | 37 | 13 | 1 | 7 | 270 | 18.9 |
| 1989–90 | 32 | Calgary Flames | NHL | 78 | 36 | 33 | 69 | 6 | 24 | 25 | 8 | 3 | 5 | 236 | 15.3 |
| 1990–91 | 33 | Pittsburgh Penguins | NHL | 47 | 17 | 22 | 39 | 9 | 6 | 9 | 8 | 0 | 2 | 85 | 20.0 |
| 1991–92 | 34 | Pittsburgh Penguins | NHL | 77 | 42 | 45 | 87 | 12 | 30 | 28 | 14 | 0 | 4 | 226 | 18.6 |
| 1992–93 | 35 | Pittsburgh Penguins | NHL | 72 | 33 | 37 | 70 | 19 | 14 | 21 | 9 | 3 | 3 | 175 | 18.9 |
| 1993–94 | 36 | Pittsburgh Penguins | NHL | 84 | 38 | 32 | 70 | 9 | 41 | 30 | 6 | 2 | 9 | 231 | 16.5 |
| 1994–95 | 37 | Pittsburgh Penguins | NHL | 45 | 16 | 21 | 37 | 15 | 6 | 9 | 5 | 2 | 3 | 78 | 20.5 |
| 1995–96 | 38 | Boston Bruins | NHL | 37 | 8 | 7 | 15 | -2 | 0 | 4 | 4 | 0 | 1 | 60 | 13.3 |
| 1996–97 | 39 | Pittsburgh Penguins | NHL | 54 | 7 | 15 | 22 | 0 | 4 | 6 | 1 | 0 | 1 | 63 | 11.1 |
| NHL Career – 16 Seasons | | | | 1062 | 502 | 561 | 1063 | 167 | 241 | 341 | 150 | 11 | 73 | 2787 | 18.0 |

### PLAYOFFS

| SEASON | AGE | TEAM | LG | GP | G | A | PTS | +/- | PIM | ESG | PPG | SHG | GWG | SOG | S% |
|---|---|---|---|---|---|---|---|---|---|---|---|---|---|---|---|
| 1979–80 | 22 | St. Louis Blues | NHL | 1 | 0 | 0 | 0 | -1 | 0 | 0 | 0 | 0 | 0 | 0 | |
| 1981–82 | 24 | St. Louis Blues | NHL | 10 | 7 | 11 | 18 | 7 | 4 | 6 | 1 | 0 | 0 | 35 | 20.0 |
| 1983–84 | 26 | St. Louis Blues | NHL | 6 | 2 | 0 | 2 | 0 | 0 | 2 | 0 | 0 | 0 | 21 | 9.5 |
| 1984–85 | 27 | St. Louis Blues | NHL | 3 | 0 | 0 | 0 | 1 | 0 | 0 | 0 | 0 | 0 | 10 | 0.0 |
| 1985–86 | 28 | Calgary Flames | NHL | 21 | 12 | 7 | 19 | -3 | 4 | 8 | 4 | 0 | 2 | 53 | 22.6 |
| 1986–87 | 29 | Calgary Flames | NHL | 6 | 2 | 1 | 3 | -4 | 0 | 1 | 1 | 0 | 1 | 12 | 16.7 |
| 1987–88 | 30 | Calgary Flames | NHL | 7 | 2 | 4 | 6 | 0 | 10 | 2 | 0 | 0 | 0 | 21 | 9.5 |
| 1988–89 | 31 | Calgary Flames | NHL | 21 | 16 | 8 | 24 | 8 | 4 | 10 | 6 | 0 | 1 | 91 | 17.6 |
| 1989–90 | 32 | Calgary Flames | NHL | 6 | 3 | 0 | 3 | -4 | 0 | 2 | 0 | 1 | 0 | 12 | 25.0 |
| 1990–91 | 33 | Pittsburgh Penguins | NHL | 22 | 8 | 9 | 17 | 9 | 4 | 7 | 1 | 0 | 1 | 44 | 18.2 |
| 1991–92 | 34 | Pittsburgh Penguins | NHL | 9 | 3 | 1 | 4 | -4 | 4 | 2 | 1 | 0 | 0 | 21 | 14.3 |
| 1992–93 | 35 | Pittsburgh Penguins | NHL | 12 | 4 | 2 | 6 | 4 | 6 | 3 | 0 | 1 | 1 | 32 | 12.5 |
| 1993–94 | 36 | Pittsburgh Penguins | NHL | 6 | 1 | 0 | 1 | -1 | 2 | 1 | 0 | 0 | 0 | 6 | 16.7 |
| 1994–95 | 37 | Pittsburgh Penguins | NHL | 12 | 0 | 3 | 3 | -5 | 4 | 0 | 0 | 0 | 0 | 12 | 0.0 |
| 1996–97 | 39 | Pittsburgh Penguins | NHL | 1 | 0 | 0 | 0 | 0 | 0 | 0 | 0 | 0 | 0 | 0 | 0.0 |
| NHL Career – 15 Seasons | | | | 143 | 60 | 46 | 106 | 15 | 42 | 44 | 14 | 2 | 6 | 370 | 16.2 |

## Cam Neely  Profile: See page 208

### REGULAR SEASON

| SEASON | AGE | TEAM | LG | GP | G | A | PTS | +/- | PIM | ESG | PPG | SHG | GWG | SOG | S% |
|---|---|---|---|---|---|---|---|---|---|---|---|---|---|---|---|
| 1983–84 | 18 | Vancouver Canucks | NHL | 56 | 16 | 15 | 31 | 1 | 57 | 13 | 3 | 0 | 1 | 87 | 18.4 |
| 1984–85 | 19 | Vancouver Canucks | NHL | 72 | 21 | 18 | 39 | -26 | 137 | 17 | 4 | 0 | 1 | 140 | 15.0 |
| 1985–86 | 20 | Vancouver Canucks | NHL | 73 | 14 | 20 | 34 | -29 | 126 | 8 | 6 | 0 | 3 | 113 | 12.4 |
| 1986–87 | 21 | Boston Bruins | NHL | 75 | 36 | 36 | 72 | 22 | 143 | 29 | 7 | 0 | 3 | 206 | 17.5 |
| 1987–88 | 22 | Boston Bruins | NHL | 69 | 42 | 27 | 69 | 30 | 175 | 31 | 11 | 0 | 3 | 207 | 20.3 |
| 1988–89 | 23 | Boston Bruins | NHL | 74 | 37 | 38 | 75 | 14 | 190 | 19 | 18 | 0 | 6 | 235 | 15.7 |
| 1989–90 | 24 | Boston Bruins | NHL | 76 | 55 | 37 | 92 | 10 | 117 | 30 | 25 | 0 | 12 | 271 | 20.3 |
| 1990–91 | 25 | Boston Bruins | NHL | 69 | 51 | 40 | 91 | 26 | 98 | 32 | 18 | 1 | 8 | 262 | 19.5 |
| 1991–92 | 26 | Boston Bruins | NHL | 9 | 9 | 3 | 12 | 9 | 16 | 8 | 1 | 0 | 2 | 30 | 30.0 |
| 1992–93 | 27 | Boston Bruins | NHL | 13 | 11 | 7 | 18 | 4 | 25 | 5 | 6 | 0 | 1 | 45 | 24.4 |
| 1993–94 | 28 | Boston Bruins | NHL | 49 | 50 | 24 | 74 | 12 | 54 | 30 | 20 | 0 | 13 | 185 | 27.0 |

## Cam Neely (continued)

### REGULAR SEASON

| SEASON | AGE | TEAM | LG | GP | G | A | PTS | +/- | PIM | ESG | PPG | SHG | GWG | SOG | S% |
|---|---|---|---|---|---|---|---|---|---|---|---|---|---|---|---|
| 1994-95 | 29 | Boston Bruins | NHL | 42 | 27 | 14 | 41 | 7 | 72 | 11 | 16 | 0 | 5 | 178 | 15.2 |
| 1995-96 | 30 | Boston Bruins | NHL | 49 | 26 | 20 | 46 | 3 | 31 | 19 | 7 | 0 | 3 | 191 | 13.6 |
| NHL Career—13 Seasons | | | | 726 | 395 | 299 | 694 | 82 | 1241 | 252 | 142 | 1 | 61 | 2148 | 18.4 |

### PLAYOFFS

| SEASON | AGE | TEAM | LG | GP | G | A | PTS | +/- | PIM | ESG | PPG | SHG | GWG | SOG | S% |
|---|---|---|---|---|---|---|---|---|---|---|---|---|---|---|---|
| 1983-84 | 18 | Vancouver Canucks | NHL | 4 | 2 | 0 | 2 | -4 | 2 | 1 | 1 | 0 | 0 | 4 | 50.0 |
| 1985-86 | 20 | Vancouver Canucks | NHL | 3 | 0 | 0 | 0 | -3 | 6 | 0 | 0 | 0 | 0 | 4 | 0.0 |
| 1986-87 | 21 | Boston Bruins | NHL | 4 | 5 | 1 | 6 | -2 | 8 | 2 | 3 | 0 | 0 | 19 | 26.3 |
| 1987-88 | 22 | Boston Bruins | NHL | 23 | 9 | 8 | 17 | 1 | 51 | 7 | 2 | 0 | 2 | 71 | 12.7 |
| 1988-89 | 23 | Boston Bruins | NHL | 10 | 7 | 2 | 9 | -2 | 8 | 3 | 4 | 0 | 2 | 24 | 29.2 |
| 1989-90 | 24 | Boston Bruins | NHL | 21 | 12 | 16 | 28 | 7 | 51 | 7 | 4 | 1 | 2 | 65 | 18.5 |
| 1990-91 | 25 | Boston Bruins | NHL | 19 | 16 | 4 | 20 | -3 | 36 | 7 | 9 | 0 | 4 | 72 | 22.2 |
| 1992-93 | 27 | Boston Bruins | NHL | 4 | 4 | 1 | 5 | 0 | 4 | 3 | 1 | 0 | 0 | 16 | 25.0 |
| 1994-95 | 29 | Boston Bruins | NHL | 5 | 2 | 0 | 2 | -4 | 2 | 1 | 1 | 0 | 1 | 13 | 15.4 |
| NHL Career—9 Seasons | | | | 93 | 57 | 32 | 89 | -10 | 168 | 31 | 25 | 1 | 11 | 288 | 19.8 |

## Harry Oliver   Profile: See page 209

### REGULAR SEASON

| SEASON | AGE | TEAM | LG | GP | G | A | PTS | PIM |
|---|---|---|---|---|---|---|---|---|
| 1921-22 | 23 | Calgary Tigers | WCHL | 20 | 10 | 4 | 14 | 7 |
| 1922-23 | 24 | Calgary Tigers | WCHL | 29 | 25 | 7 | 32 | 10 |
| 1923-24 | 25 | Calgary Tigers | WCHL | 27 | 22 | 12 | 34 | 14 |
| 1924-25 | 26 | Calgary Tigers | WCHL | 24 | 20 | 13 | 33 | 23 |
| 1925-26 | 27 | Calgary Tigers | WHL | 30 | 13 | 12 | 25 | 14 |
| 1926-27 | 28 | Boston Bruins | NHL | 43 | 18 | 6 | 24 | 17 |
| 1927-28 | 29 | Boston Bruins | NHL | 43 | 13 | 5 | 18 | 20 |
| 1928-29 | 30 | Boston Bruins | NHL | 43 | 17 | 6 | 23 | 26 |
| 1929-30 | 31 | Boston Bruins | NHL | 41 | 16 | 5 | 21 | 12 |
| 1930-31 | 32 | Boston Bruins | NHL | 44 | 16 | 14 | 30 | 20 |
| 1931-32 | 33 | Boston Bruins | NHL | 44 | 13 | 7 | 20 | 18 |
| 1932-33 | 34 | Boston Bruins | NHL | 47 | 11 | 7 | 18 | 10 |
| 1933-34 | 35 | Boston Bruins | NHL | 48 | 5 | 9 | 14 | 6 |
| 1934-35 | 36 | New York Americans | NHL | 47 | 7 | 9 | 16 | 4 |
| 1935-36 | 37 | New York Americans | NHL | 45 | 9 | 16 | 25 | 12 |
| 1936-37 | 38 | New York Americans | NHL | 20 | 2 | 1 | 3 | 2 |
| Career—16 Seasons | | | | 595 | 217 | 133 | 350 | 215 |

### PLAYOFFS

| SEASON | AGE | TEAM | LG | GP | G | A | PTS | PIM |
|---|---|---|---|---|---|---|---|---|
| 1921-22 | 23 | Calgary Tigers | WCHL | 2 | 1 | 0 | 1 | 0 |
| 1923-24 | 25 | Calgary Tigers | St-Cup | 2 | 0 | 0 | 0 | 0 |
| 1923-24 | 25 | Calgary Tigers | WCHL | 2 | 0 | 1 | 1 | 2 |
| 1923-24 | 25 | Calgary Tigers | West-P | 3 | 2 | 1 | 3 | 2 |
| 1924-25 | 26 | Calgary Tigers | WCHL | 2 | 0 | 0 | 0 | 2 |
| 1926-27 | 28 | Boston Bruins | NHL | 8 | 4 | 2 | 6 | 4 |
| 1927-28 | 29 | Boston Bruins | NHL | 2 | 2 | 0 | 2 | 4 |
| 1928-29 | 30 | Boston Bruins | NHL | 5 | 1 | 1 | 2 | 8 |
| 1929-30 | 31 | Boston Bruins | NHL | 6 | 2 | 1 | 3 | 6 |
| 1930-31 | 32 | Boston Bruins | NHL | 5 | 0 | 0 | 0 | 2 |
| 1932-33 | 34 | Boston Bruins | NHL | 5 | 0 | 0 | 0 | 0 |
| 1935-36 | 37 | New York Americans | NHL | 5 | 1 | 2 | 3 | 0 |
| Career—10 Seasons | | | | 47 | 13 | 8 | 21 | 30 |

## Didier Pitre   Profile: See page 210

### REGULAR SEASON

| SEASON | AGE | TEAM | LG | GP | G | A | PTS | PIM |
|---|---|---|---|---|---|---|---|---|
| 1903-04 | 20 | Montreal Nationals | FAHL | 2 | 1 | 0 | 1 | 0 |
| 1904-05 | 21 | Montreal Nationals | CAHL | 2 | 0 | 0 | 0 | 0 |
| 1904-05 | 21 | American Soo Indians | IHL | 13 | 11 | 0 | 11 | 6 |
| 1905-06 | 22 | American Soo Indians | IHL | 22 | 41 | 0 | 41 | 29 |
| 1906-07 | 23 | American Soo Indians | IHL | 23 | 25 | 11 | 36 | 28 |
| 1907-08 | 24 | Montreal Shamrocks | ECAHA | 10 | 3 | 0 | 3 | 15 |
| 1908-09 | 25 | Renfrew Creamery Kings | FAHL | 5 | 5 | 0 | 5 | 16 |
| 1909-10 | 26 | Les Canadiens (Montreal) | NHA | 13 | 11 | 0 | 11 | 11 |
| 1910-11 | 27 | Montreal Canadiens | NHA | 16 | 19 | 0 | 19 | 22 |
| 1911-12 | 28 | Montreal Canadiens | NHA | 18 | 27 | 0 | 27 | 40 |
| 1912-13 | 29 | Montreal Canadiens | NHA | 17 | 24 | 0 | 24 | 80 |
| 1913-14 | 30 | Vancouver Millionaires | PCHA | 16 | 14 | 2 | 16 | 12 |
| 1914-15 | 31 | Montreal Canadiens | NHA | 20 | 30 | 4 | 34 | 15 |
| 1915-16 | 32 | Montreal Canadiens | NHA | 24 | 24 | 15 | 39 | 42 |
| 1916-17 | 33 | Montreal Canadiens | NHA | 20 | 21 | 6 | 27 | 50 |
| 1917-18 | 34 | Montreal Canadiens | NHL | 20 | 17 | 8 | 25 | 29 |

### REGULAR SEASON

| SEASON | AGE | TEAM | LG | GP | G | A | PTS | PIM |
|---|---|---|---|---|---|---|---|---|
| 1918-19 | 35 | Montreal Canadiens | NHL | 17 | 14 | 4 | 18 | 15 |
| 1919-20 | 36 | Montreal Canadiens | NHL | 22 | 14 | 12 | 26 | 6 |
| 1920-21 | 37 | Montreal Canadiens | NHL | 23 | 16 | 5 | 21 | 25 |
| 1921-22 | 38 | Montreal Canadiens | NHL | 23 | 2 | 4 | 6 | 12 |
| 1922-23 | 39 | Montreal Canadiens | NHL | 22 | 1 | 2 | 3 | 0 |
| Career—19 Seasons | | | | 348 | 320 | 73 | 393 | 453 |

### PLAYOFFS

| SEASON | AGE | TEAM | LG | GP | G | A | PTS | PIM |
|---|---|---|---|---|---|---|---|---|
| 1908-09 | 25 | Edmonton Professionals | St-Cup | 2 | 0 | 0 | 0 | 11 |
| 1915-16 | 32 | Montreal Canadiens | St-Cup | 5 | 4 | 0 | 4 | 18 |
| 1916-17 | 33 | Montreal Canadiens | NHA | 2 | 2 | 2 | 4 | 32 |
| 1916-17 | 33 | Montreal Canadiens | St-Cup | 4 | 5 | 0 | 5 | 6 |
| 1917-18 | 34 | Montreal Canadiens | NHL | 2 | 0 | 1 | 1 | 13 |
| 1918-19 | 35 | Montreal Canadiens | NHL | 5 | 2 | 3 | 5 | 6 |
| 1918-19 | 35 | Montreal Canadiens | St-Cup | 5 | 0 | 3 | 3 | 0 |
| 1922-23 | 39 | Montreal Canadiens | NHL | 2 | 0 | 0 | 0 | 0 |
| Career—6 Seasons | | | | 27 | 13 | 9 | 22 | 86 |

## Mark Recchi   Profile: See page 211

### REGULAR SEASON

| SEASON | AGE | TEAM | LG | GP | G | A | PTS | +/- | PIM | ESG | PPG | SHG | GWG | SOG | S% |
|---|---|---|---|---|---|---|---|---|---|---|---|---|---|---|---|
| 1988–89 | 20 | Pittsburgh Penguins | NHL | 15 | 1 | 1 | 2 | -2 | 0 | 1 | 0 | 0 | 0 | 11 | 9.1 |
| 1989–90 | 21 | Pittsburgh Penguins | NHL | 74 | 30 | 37 | 67 | 6 | 44 | 22 | 6 | 2 | 4 | 143 | 21.0 |
| 1990–91 | 22 | Pittsburgh Penguins | NHL | 78 | 40 | 73 | 113 | 0 | 48 | 28 | 12 | 0 | 9 | 184 | 21.7 |
| 1991–92 | 23 | Pittsburgh Penguins | NHL | 58 | 33 | 37 | 70 | -16 | 78 | 16 | 16 | 1 | 4 | 156 | 21.2 |
| 1991–92 | 23 | Philadelphia Flyers | NHL | 22 | 10 | 17 | 27 | -5 | 18 | 6 | 4 | 0 | 1 | 54 | 18.5 |
| 1992–93 | 24 | Philadelphia Flyers | NHL | 84 | 53 | 70 | 123 | 1 | 95 | 34 | 15 | 4 | 6 | 274 | 19.3 |
| 1993–94 | 25 | Philadelphia Flyers | NHL | 84 | 40 | 67 | 107 | -2 | 46 | 29 | 11 | 0 | 5 | 217 | 18.4 |
| 1994–95 | 26 | Philadelphia Flyers | NHL | 10 | 2 | 3 | 5 | -6 | 12 | 1 | 1 | 0 | 2 | 17 | 11.8 |
| 1994–95 | 26 | Montreal Canadiens | NHL | 39 | 14 | 29 | 43 | -3 | 16 | 6 | 8 | 0 | 1 | 104 | 13.5 |
| 1995–96 | 27 | Montreal Canadiens | NHL | 82 | 28 | 50 | 78 | 20 | 69 | 15 | 11 | 2 | 6 | 191 | 14.7 |
| 1996–97 | 28 | Montreal Canadiens | NHL | 82 | 34 | 46 | 80 | -1 | 58 | 25 | 7 | 2 | 3 | 202 | 16.8 |
| 1997–98 | 29 | Montreal Canadiens | NHL | 82 | 32 | 42 | 74 | 11 | 51 | 22 | 9 | 1 | 6 | 216 | 14.8 |
| 1998–99 | 30 | Montreal Canadiens | NHL | 61 | 12 | 35 | 47 | -4 | 28 | 9 | 3 | 0 | 2 | 152 | 7.9 |
| 1998–99 | 30 | Philadelphia Flyers | NHL | 10 | 4 | 2 | 6 | -3 | 6 | 4 | 0 | 0 | 0 | 19 | 21.1 |
| 1999–00 | 31 | Philadelphia Flyers | NHL | 82 | 28 | 63 | 91 | 20 | 50 | 20 | 7 | 1 | 5 | 223 | 12.6 |
| 2000–01 | 32 | Philadelphia Flyers | NHL | 69 | 27 | 50 | 77 | 15 | 33 | 19 | 7 | 1 | 8 | 191 | 14.1 |
| 2001–02 | 33 | Philadelphia Flyers | NHL | 80 | 22 | 42 | 64 | 5 | 46 | 13 | 7 | 2 | 4 | 205 | 10.7 |
| 2002–03 | 34 | Philadelphia Flyers | NHL | 79 | 20 | 32 | 52 | 0 | 35 | 11 | 8 | 1 | 3 | 171 | 11.7 |
| 2003–04 | 35 | Philadelphia Flyers | NHL | 82 | 26 | 49 | 75 | 18 | 47 | 11 | 14 | 1 | 5 | 167 | 15.6 |
| 2005–06 | 37 | Pittsburgh Penguins | NHL | 63 | 24 | 33 | 57 | -28 | 56 | 13 | 11 | 0 | 2 | 164 | 14.6 |
| 2005–06 | 37 | Carolina Hurricanes | NHL | 20 | 4 | 3 | 7 | -8 | 12 | 2 | 2 | 0 | 1 | 35 | 11.4 |
| 2006–07 | 38 | Pittsburgh Penguins | NHL | 82 | 24 | 44 | 68 | 1 | 62 | 10 | 14 | 0 | 3 | 190 | 12.6 |
| 2007–08 | 39 | Pittsburgh Penguins | NHL | 19 | 2 | 6 | 8 | -2 | 12 | 0 | 2 | 0 | 0 | 36 | 5.6 |
| 2007–08 | 39 | Atlanta Thrashers | NHL | 53 | 12 | 28 | 40 | -16 | 20 | 7 | 5 | 0 | 1 | 85 | 14.1 |
| 2008–09 | 40 | Tampa Bay Lightning | NHL | 62 | 13 | 32 | 45 | -15 | 20 | 11 | 2 | 0 | 1 | 97 | 13.4 |
| 2008–09 | 40 | Boston Bruins | NHL | 18 | 10 | 6 | 16 | -3 | 2 | 6 | 4 | 0 | 2 | 32 | 31.3 |
| 2009–10 | 41 | Boston Bruins | NHL | 81 | 18 | 25 | 43 | 4 | 34 | 10 | 8 | 0 | 2 | 152 | 11.8 |
| 2010–11 | 42 | Boston Bruins | NHL | 81 | 14 | 34 | 48 | 13 | 35 | 8 | 6 | 0 | 6 | 132 | 10.6 |
| NHL Career — 22 Seasons | | | | 1652 | 577 | 956 | 1533 | 0 | 1033 | 359 | 200 | 18 | 91 | 3820 | 15.1 |

### PLAYOFFS

| SEASON | AGE | TEAM | LG | GP | G | A | PTS | +/- | PIM | ESG | PPG | SHG | GWG | SOG | S% |
|---|---|---|---|---|---|---|---|---|---|---|---|---|---|---|---|
| 1990–91 | 22 | Pittsburgh Penguins | NHL | 24 | 10 | 24 | 34 | 6 | 33 | 5 | 5 | 0 | 2 | 60 | 16.7 |
| 1995–96 | 27 | Montreal Canadiens | NHL | 6 | 3 | 3 | 6 | 1 | 0 | 0 | 3 | 0 | 0 | 13 | 23.1 |
| 1996–97 | 28 | Montreal Canadiens | NHL | 5 | 4 | 2 | 6 | 2 | 2 | 4 | 0 | 0 | 0 | 18 | 22.2 |
| 1997–98 | 29 | Montreal Canadiens | NHL | 10 | 4 | 8 | 12 | 2 | 6 | 4 | 0 | 0 | 2 | 22 | 18.2 |
| 1998–99 | 30 | Philadelphia Flyers | NHL | 6 | 0 | 1 | 1 | -1 | 2 | 0 | 0 | 0 | 0 | 18 | 0.0 |
| 1999–00 | 31 | Philadelphia Flyers | NHL | 18 | 6 | 12 | 18 | 3 | 6 | 4 | 2 | 0 | 1 | 53 | 11.3 |
| 2000–01 | 32 | Philadelphia Flyers | NHL | 6 | 2 | 2 | 4 | -3 | 2 | 1 | 1 | 0 | 1 | 18 | 11.1 |
| 2001–02 | 33 | Philadelphia Flyers | NHL | 4 | 0 | 0 | 0 | -1 | 2 | 0 | 0 | 0 | 0 | 5 | 0.0 |
| 2002–03 | 34 | Philadelphia Flyers | NHL | 13 | 7 | 3 | 10 | 4 | 2 | 6 | 1 | 0 | 1 | 29 | 24.1 |
| 2003–04 | 35 | Philadelphia Flyers | NHL | 18 | 4 | 2 | 6 | -3 | 4 | 2 | 2 | 0 | 0 | 33 | 12.1 |
| 2005–06 | 37 | Carolina Hurricanes | NHL | 25 | 7 | 9 | 16 | -5 | 18 | 5 | 2 | 0 | 2 | 45 | 15.6 |
| 2006–07 | 38 | Pittsburgh Penguins | NHL | 5 | 0 | 4 | 4 | -3 | 0 | 0 | 0 | 0 | 0 | 11 | 0.0 |
| 2008–09 | 40 | Boston Bruins | NHL | 11 | 3 | 3 | 6 | 0 | 2 | 2 | 1 | 0 | 1 | 19 | 15.8 |
| 2009–10 | 41 | Boston Bruins | NHL | 13 | 6 | 4 | 10 | 0 | 6 | 3 | 3 | 0 | 0 | 26 | 23.1 |
| 2010–11 | 42 | Boston Bruins | NHL | 25 | 5 | 9 | 14 | 7 | 8 | 3 | 2 | 0 | 1 | 40 | 12.5 |
| NHL Career — 15 Seasons | | | | 189 | 61 | 86 | 147 | 9 | 93 | 39 | 22 | 0 | 11 | 410 | 14.9 |

# Maurice Richard  Profile: See page 212

## REGULAR SEASON

| SEASON | AGE | TEAM | LG | GP | G | A | PTS | PIM |
|---|---|---|---|---|---|---|---|---|
| 1942–43 | 21 | Montreal Canadiens | NHL | 16 | 5 | 6 | 11 | 4 |
| 1943–44 | 22 | Montreal Canadiens | NHL | 46 | 32 | 22 | 54 | 45 |
| 1944–45 | 23 | Montreal Canadiens | NHL | 50 | 50 | 23 | 73 | 46 |
| 1945–46 | 24 | Montreal Canadiens | NHL | 50 | 27 | 22 | 49 | 50 |
| 1946–47 | 25 | Montreal Canadiens | NHL | 60 | 45 | 26 | 71 | 69 |
| 1947–48 | 26 | Montreal Canadiens | NHL | 53 | 28 | 25 | 53 | 91 |
| 1948–49 | 27 | Montreal Canadiens | NHL | 59 | 20 | 18 | 38 | 110 |
| 1949–50 | 28 | Montreal Canadiens | NHL | 70 | 43 | 22 | 65 | 114 |
| 1950–51 | 29 | Montreal Canadiens | NHL | 65 | 42 | 24 | 66 | 97 |
| 1951–52 | 30 | Montreal Canadiens | NHL | 48 | 27 | 17 | 44 | 44 |
| 1952–53 | 31 | Montreal Canadiens | NHL | 70 | 28 | 33 | 61 | 112 |
| 1953–54 | 32 | Montreal Canadiens | NHL | 70 | 37 | 30 | 67 | 112 |
| 1954–55 | 33 | Montreal Canadiens | NHL | 67 | 38 | 36 | 74 | 125 |
| 1955–56 | 34 | Montreal Canadiens | NHL | 70 | 38 | 33 | 71 | 89 |
| 1956–57 | 35 | Montreal Canadiens | NHL | 63 | 33 | 29 | 62 | 74 |
| 1957–58 | 36 | Montreal Canadiens | NHL | 28 | 15 | 19 | 34 | 28 |
| 1958–59 | 37 | Montreal Canadiens | NHL | 42 | 17 | 21 | 38 | 27 |
| 1959–60 | 38 | Montreal Canadiens | NHL | 51 | 19 | 16 | 35 | 50 |
| NHL Career – 18 Seasons | | | | 978 | 544 | 422 | 966 | 1287 |

## PLAYOFFS

| SEASON | AGE | TEAM | LG | GP | G | A | PTS | PIM |
|---|---|---|---|---|---|---|---|---|
| 1943–44 | 22 | Montreal Canadiens | NHL | 9 | 12 | 5 | 17 | 10 |
| 1944–45 | 23 | Montreal Canadiens | NHL | 6 | 6 | 2 | 8 | 10 |
| 1945–46 | 24 | Montreal Canadiens | NHL | 9 | 7 | 4 | 11 | 15 |
| 1946–47 | 25 | Montreal Canadiens | NHL | 10 | 6 | 5 | 11 | 64 |
| 1948–49 | 27 | Montreal Canadiens | NHL | 7 | 2 | 1 | 3 | 14 |
| 1949–50 | 28 | Montreal Canadiens | NHL | 5 | 1 | 1 | 2 | 6 |
| 1950–51 | 29 | Montreal Canadiens | NHL | 11 | 9 | 4 | 13 | 13 |
| 1951–52 | 30 | Montreal Canadiens | NHL | 11 | 4 | 2 | 6 | 6 |
| 1952–53 | 31 | Montreal Canadiens | NHL | 12 | 7 | 1 | 8 | 2 |
| 1953–54 | 32 | Montreal Canadiens | NHL | 11 | 3 | 0 | 3 | 22 |
| 1955–56 | 34 | Montreal Canadiens | NHL | 10 | 5 | 9 | 14 | 24 |
| 1956–57 | 35 | Montreal Canadiens | NHL | 10 | 8 | 3 | 11 | 8 |
| 1957–58 | 36 | Montreal Canadiens | NHL | 10 | 11 | 4 | 15 | 10 |
| 1958–59 | 37 | Montreal Canadiens | NHL | 3 | 0 | 0 | 0 | 2 |
| 1959–60 | 38 | Montreal Canadiens | NHL | 8 | 1 | 3 | 4 | 2 |
| NHL Career – 15 Seasons | | | | 132 | 82 | 44 | 126 | 208 |

# Teemu Selanne  Profile: See page 214

## REGULAR SEASON

| SEASON | AGE | TEAM | LG | GP | G | A | PTS | +/- | PIM | ESG | PPG | SHG | GWG | SOG | S% |
|---|---|---|---|---|---|---|---|---|---|---|---|---|---|---|---|
| 1992–93 | 22 | Winnipeg Jets | NHL | 84 | 76 | 56 | 132 | 8 | 45 | 52 | 24 | 0 | 7 | 387 | 19.6 |
| 1993–94 | 23 | Winnipeg Jets | NHL | 51 | 25 | 29 | 54 | -23 | 22 | 14 | 11 | 0 | 2 | 191 | 13.1 |
| 1994–95 | 24 | Winnipeg Jets | NHL | 45 | 22 | 26 | 48 | 1 | 2 | 12 | 8 | 2 | 1 | 167 | 13.2 |
| 1995–96 | 25 | Winnipeg Jets | NHL | 51 | 24 | 48 | 72 | 3 | 18 | 17 | 6 | 1 | 4 | 163 | 14.7 |
| 1995–96 | 25 | Mighty Ducks of Anaheim | NHL | 28 | 16 | 20 | 36 | 2 | 4 | 13 | 3 | 0 | 1 | 104 | 15.4 |
| 1996–97 | 26 | Mighty Ducks of Anaheim | NHL | 78 | 51 | 58 | 109 | 28 | 34 | 39 | 11 | 1 | 8 | 273 | 18.7 |
| 1997–98 | 27 | Mighty Ducks of Anaheim | NHL | 73 | 52 | 34 | 86 | 12 | 30 | 41 | 10 | 1 | 10 | 268 | 19.4 |
| 1998–99 | 28 | Mighty Ducks of Anaheim | NHL | 75 | 47 | 60 | 107 | 18 | 30 | 22 | 25 | 0 | 7 | 281 | 16.7 |
| 1999–00 | 29 | Mighty Ducks of Anaheim | NHL | 79 | 33 | 52 | 85 | 6 | 12 | 25 | 8 | 0 | 6 | 236 | 14.0 |
| 2000–01 | 30 | Mighty Ducks of Anaheim | NHL | 61 | 26 | 33 | 59 | -8 | 36 | 16 | 10 | 0 | 5 | 202 | 12.9 |
| 2000–01 | 30 | San Jose Sharks | NHL | 12 | 7 | 6 | 13 | 1 | 0 | 5 | 2 | 0 | 2 | 31 | 22.6 |
| 2001–02 | 31 | San Jose Sharks | NHL | 82 | 29 | 25 | 54 | -11 | 40 | 19 | 9 | 1 | 8 | 202 | 14.4 |
| 2002–03 | 32 | San Jose Sharks | NHL | 82 | 28 | 36 | 64 | -6 | 30 | 21 | 7 | 0 | 5 | 253 | 11.1 |
| 2003–04 | 33 | Colorado Avalanche | NHL | 78 | 16 | 16 | 32 | 2 | 32 | 9 | 6 | 1 | 4 | 182 | 8.8 |
| 2005–06 | 35 | Mighty Ducks of Anaheim | NHL | 80 | 40 | 50 | 90 | 28 | 44 | 22 | 18 | 0 | 5 | 267 | 15.0 |
| 2006–07 | 36 | Anaheim Ducks | NHL | 82 | 48 | 46 | 94 | 26 | 82 | 23 | 25 | 0 | 10 | 257 | 18.7 |
| 2007–08 | 37 | Anaheim Ducks | NHL | 26 | 12 | 11 | 23 | 5 | 8 | 5 | 7 | 0 | 2 | 87 | 13.8 |
| 2008–09 | 38 | Anaheim Ducks | NHL | 65 | 27 | 27 | 54 | -3 | 36 | 11 | 16 | 0 | 5 | 186 | 14.5 |
| 2009–10 | 39 | Anaheim Ducks | NHL | 54 | 27 | 21 | 48 | 3 | 16 | 13 | 14 | 0 | 5 | 173 | 15.6 |
| 2010–11 | 40 | Anaheim Ducks | NHL | 73 | 31 | 49 | 80 | 6 | 49 | 15 | 16 | 0 | 5 | 213 | 14.6 |
| 2011–12 | 41 | Anaheim Ducks | NHL | 82 | 26 | 40 | 66 | -1 | 50 | 14 | 12 | 0 | 4 | 210 | 12.4 |
| 2012–13 | 42 | Anaheim Ducks | NHL | 46 | 12 | 12 | 24 | -10 | 28 | 9 | 3 | 0 | 1 | 96 | 12.5 |
| 2013–14 | 43 | Anaheim Ducks | NHL | 64 | 9 | 18 | 27 | 8 | 12 | 5 | 4 | 0 | 3 | 111 | 8.1 |
| NHL Career – 21 seasons | | | | 1451 | 684 | 773 | 1457 | 95 | 660 | 422 | 255 | 7 | 10 | 4540 | 15.1 |

## PLAYOFFS

| SEASON | AGE | TEAM | LG | GP | G | A | PTS | +/- | PIM | ESG | PPG | SHG | GWG | SOG | S% |
|---|---|---|---|---|---|---|---|---|---|---|---|---|---|---|---|
| 1992–93 | 22 | Winnipeg Jets | NHL | 6 | 4 | 2 | 6 | -3 | 2 | 2 | 2 | 0 | 2 | 27 | 14.8 |
| 1996–97 | 26 | Mighty Ducks of Anaheim | NHL | 11 | 7 | 3 | 10 | -3 | 4 | 4 | 3 | 0 | 1 | 38 | 18.4 |
| 1998–99 | 28 | Mighty Ducks of Anaheim | NHL | 4 | 2 | 2 | 4 | -1 | 2 | 1 | 1 | 0 | 0 | 7 | 28.6 |
| 2000–01 | 30 | San Jose Sharks | NHL | 6 | 0 | 2 | 2 | 2 | 2 | 0 | 0 | 0 | 0 | 5 | 0.0 |
| 2001–02 | 31 | San Jose Sharks | NHL | 12 | 5 | 3 | 8 | -3 | 2 | 3 | 2 | 0 | 1 | 35 | 14.3 |
| 2003–04 | 33 | Colorado Avalanche | NHL | 10 | 0 | 3 | 3 | -2 | 2 | 0 | 0 | 0 | 0 | 9 | 0.0 |
| 2005–06 | 35 | Mighty Ducks of Anaheim | NHL | 16 | 6 | 8 | 14 | 0 | 6 | 5 | 1 | 0 | 2 | 53 | 11.3 |
| 2006–07 | 36 | Anaheim Ducks | NHL | 21 | 5 | 10 | 15 | 1 | 10 | 5 | 0 | 0 | 2 | 60 | 8.3 |
| 2007–08 | 37 | Anaheim Ducks | NHL | 6 | 2 | 2 | 4 | -1 | 6 | 0 | 2 | 0 | 1 | 20 | 10.0 |
| 2008–09 | 38 | Anaheim Ducks | NHL | 13 | 4 | 2 | 6 | -2 | 4 | 2 | 2 | 0 | 1 | 31 | 12.9 |
| 2010–11 | 40 | Anaheim Ducks | NHL | 6 | 6 | 1 | 7 | -3 | 6 | 2 | 4 | 0 | 0 | 25 | 24 |
| 2012–13 | 42 | Anaheim Ducks | NHL | 7 | 1 | 2 | 3 | 1 | 6 | 0 | 1 | 0 | 1 | 16 | 6.3 |
| 2013–14 | 43 | Anaheim Ducks | NHL | 12 | 2 | 4 | 6 | -2 | 4 | 1 | 1 | 0 | 0 | 24 | 8.3 |
| NHL Career – 13 Seasons | | | | 130 | 44 | 44 | 88 | -16 | 62 | 25 | 19 | 0 | 11 | 350 | 12.6 |

## Alf Smith  Profile: See page 216

REGULAR SEASON

| SEASON | AGE | TEAM | LG | GP | G | A | PTS | PIM |
|---|---|---|---|---|---|---|---|---|
| 1894–95 | 21 | Ottawa Hockey Club | AHAC | 8 | 5 | 0 | 5 | |
| 1895–96 | 22 | Ottawa Hockey Club | AHAC | 8 | 7 | 0 | 7 | |
| 1896–97 | 23 | Ottawa Hockey Club | AHAC | 8 | 12 | 0 | 12 | |
| 1899–00 | 26 | Ottawa Capitals | AHA-Sr. | | | | | |
| 1901–02 | 28 | Pittsburgh PAC | WPHL | 14 | 11 | 9 | 20 | 17 |
| 1902–03 | 29 | Ottawa Silver Seven | CAHL | | | | | |
| 1903–04 | 30 | Ottawa Silver Seven | CAHL | 4 | 8 | 0 | 8 | 6 |
| 1904–05 | 31 | Ottawa Silver Seven | FAHL | 8 | 13 | 0 | 13 | 30 |
| 1905–06 | 32 | Ottawa Silver Seven | ECAHA | 10 | 13 | 0 | 13 | 36 |
| 1906–07 | 33 | Ottawa Senators | ECAHA | 9 | 17 | 0 | 17 | 19 |
| 1906–07 | 33 | Kenora Thistles | MHL-Pro | 1 | 2 | 0 | 2 | |
| 1907–08 | 34 | Ottawa Senators | ECAHA | 9 | 12 | 0 | 12 | 20 |

REGULAR SEASON

| SEASON | AGE | TEAM | LG | GP | G | A | PTS | PIM |
|---|---|---|---|---|---|---|---|---|
| 1908–09 | 35 | Pittsburgh Duquesne | WPHL | 2 | 3 | 0 | 3 | |
| 1908–09 | 35 | Pittsburgh Bankers | WPHL | 3 | 2 | 0 | 2 | |
| 1908–09 | 35 | Ottawa Senators | FAHL | 1 | 1 | 0 | 1 | 0 |
| Career – 12 Seasons | | | | 85 | 106 | 9 | 115 | 128 |

PLAYOFFS

| SEASON | AGE | TEAM | LG | GP | G | A | PTS | PIM |
|---|---|---|---|---|---|---|---|---|
| 1903–04 | 30 | Ottawa Silver Seven | St-Cup | 7 | 13 | 0 | 13 | 20 |
| 1904–05 | 31 | Ottawa Silver Seven | St-Cup | 5 | 11 | 0 | 11 | 9 |
| 1905–06 | 32 | Ottawa Silver Seven | St-Cup | 6 | 6 | 0 | 8 | 6 |
| 1906–07 | 33 | Kenora Thistles | MHL-Pro | 2 | 1 | 0 | 1 | 3 |
| 1906–07 | 33 | Kenora Thistles | St-Cup | 2 | 2 | 0 | 2 | 3 |
| Career – 4 Seasons | | | | 22 | 35 | 0 | 35 | 41 |

## Barney Stanley  Profile: See page 217

REGULAR SEASON

| SEASON | AGE | TEAM | LG | GP | G | A | PTS | PIM |
|---|---|---|---|---|---|---|---|---|
| 1914–15 | 22 | Vancouver Millionaires | PCHA | 5 | 7 | 1 | 8 | 0 |
| 1915–16 | 23 | Vancouver Millionaires | PCHA | 14 | 6 | 6 | 12 | 9 |
| 1916–17 | 24 | Vancouver Millionaires | PCHA | 23 | 28 | 18 | 46 | 9 |
| 1917–18 | 25 | Vancouver Millionaires | PCHA | 18 | 11 | 6 | 17 | 9 |
| 1918–19 | 26 | Vancouver Millionaires | PCHA | 20 | 10 | 6 | 16 | 19 |
| 1919–20 | 27 | Edmonton Eskimos | Big-4 | 12 | 10 | 12 | 22 | 20 |
| 1920–21 | 28 | Calgary Tigers | Big-4 | 15 | 11 | 10 | 21 | 5 |
| 1921–22 | 29 | Calgary Tigers | WCHL | 24 | 26 | 5 | 31 | 17 |
| 1922–23 | 30 | Regina Capitals | WCHL | 29 | 14 | 7 | 21 | 10 |
| 1923–24 | 31 | Regina Capitals | WCHL | 30 | 15 | 11 | 26 | 27 |
| 1924–25 | 32 | Edmonton Eskimos | WCHL | 25 | 12 | 5 | 17 | 36 |
| 1925–26 | 33 | Edmonton Eskimos | WHL | 29 | 14 | 8 | 22 | 47 |
| 1926–27 | 34 | Winnipeg Maroons | AHA | 35 | 8 | 8 | 16 | 78 |
| 1927–28 | 35 | Chicago Black Hawks | NHL | 1 | 0 | 0 | 0 | 0 |
| Career – 14 Seasons | | | | 280 | 172 | 103 | 275 | 286 |

PLAYOFFS

| SEASON | AGE | TEAM | LG | GP | G | A | PTS | PIM |
|---|---|---|---|---|---|---|---|---|
| 1914–15 | 22 | Vancouver Millionaires | St-Cup | 3 | 5 | 1 | 6 | 0 |
| 1917–18 | 25 | Vancouver Millionaires | PCHA | 2 | 1 | 0 | 1 | 3 |
| 1917–18 | 25 | Vancouver Millionaires | St-Cup | 5 | 2 | 0 | 2 | 6 |
| 1918–19 | 26 | Vancouver Millionaires | PCHA | 2 | 0 | 0 | 0 | 0 |
| 1919–20 | 27 | Edmonton Eskimos | Big-4 | 2 | 0 | 1 | 1 | 5 |
| 1921–22 | 29 | Calgary Tigers | WCHL | 2 | 0 | 0 | 0 | 0 |
| 1922–23 | 30 | Regina Capitals | WCHL | 2 | 1 | 0 | 1 | 2 |
| 1923–24 | 31 | Regina Capitals | WCHL | 2 | 1 | 0 | 1 | 2 |
| 1925–26 | 33 | Edmonton Eskimos | WHL | 2 | 1 | 0 | 1 | 0 |
| Career – 8 Seasons | | | | 29 | 12 | 2 | 14 | 22 |

# Rob Blake  Profile: See page 220

## REGULAR SEASON

| SEASON | AGE | TEAM | LG | GP | G | A | PTS | +/- | PIM | ESG | PPG | SHG | GWG | SOG | S% |
|--------|-----|------|----|----|---|---|-----|-----|-----|-----|-----|-----|-----|-----|----|
| 1989–90 | 20 | Los Angeles Kings | NHL | 4 | 0 | 0 | 0 | 0 | 4 | 0 | 0 | 0 | 0 | 3 | 0.0 |
| 1990–91 | 21 | Los Angeles Kings | NHL | 75 | 12 | 34 | 46 | 3 | 125 | 3 | 9 | 0 | 2 | 150 | 8.0 |
| 1991–92 | 22 | Los Angeles Kings | NHL | 57 | 7 | 13 | 20 | -5 | 102 | 2 | 5 | 0 | 0 | 131 | 5.3 |
| 1992–93 | 23 | Los Angeles Kings | NHL | 76 | 16 | 43 | 59 | 18 | 152 | 6 | 10 | 0 | 4 | 243 | 6.6 |
| 1993–94 | 24 | Los Angeles Kings | NHL | 84 | 20 | 48 | 68 | -7 | 137 | 13 | 7 | 0 | 6 | 304 | 6.6 |
| 1994–95 | 25 | Los Angeles Kings | NHL | 24 | 4 | 7 | 11 | -16 | 38 | 0 | 4 | 0 | 1 | 76 | 5.3 |
| 1995–96 | 26 | Los Angeles Kings | NHL | 6 | 1 | 2 | 3 | 0 | 8 | 1 | 0 | 0 | 0 | 13 | 7.7 |
| 1996–97 | 27 | Los Angeles Kings | NHL | 62 | 8 | 23 | 31 | -28 | 82 | 4 | 4 | 0 | 1 | 169 | 4.7 |
| 1997–98 | 28 | Los Angeles Kings | NHL | 81 | 23 | 27 | 50 | -3 | 94 | 12 | 11 | 0 | 4 | 261 | 8.8 |
| 1998–99 | 29 | Los Angeles Kings | NHL | 62 | 12 | 23 | 35 | -7 | 128 | 6 | 5 | 1 | 2 | 216 | 5.6 |
| 1999–00 | 30 | Los Angeles Kings | NHL | 77 | 18 | 39 | 57 | 10 | 112 | 6 | 12 | 0 | 5 | 327 | 5.5 |
| 2000–01 | 31 | Los Angeles Kings | NHL | 54 | 17 | 32 | 49 | -8 | 69 | 8 | 9 | 0 | 1 | 223 | 7.6 |
| 2000–01 | 31 | Colorado Avalanche | NHL | 13 | 2 | 8 | 10 | 11 | 8 | 1 | 1 | 0 | 1 | 44 | 4.5 |
| 2001–02 | 32 | Colorado Avalanche | NHL | 75 | 16 | 40 | 56 | 16 | 58 | 6 | 10 | 0 | 2 | 229 | 7.0 |
| 2002–03 | 33 | Colorado Avalanche | NHL | 79 | 17 | 28 | 45 | 20 | 57 | 7 | 8 | 2 | 3 | 269 | 6.3 |
| 2003–04 | 34 | Colorado Avalanche | NHL | 74 | 13 | 33 | 46 | 6 | 61 | 5 | 8 | 0 | 3 | 242 | 5.4 |
| 2005–06 | 36 | Colorado Avalanche | NHL | 81 | 14 | 37 | 51 | 2 | 94 | 6 | 7 | 1 | 1 | 264 | 5.3 |
| 2006–07 | 37 | Los Angeles Kings | NHL | 72 | 14 | 20 | 34 | -26 | 82 | 3 | 11 | 0 | 1 | 208 | 6.7 |
| 2007–08 | 38 | Los Angeles Kings | NHL | 71 | 9 | 22 | 31 | -19 | 98 | 4 | 5 | 0 | 2 | 144 | 6.3 |
| 2008–09 | 39 | San Jose Sharks | NHL | 73 | 10 | 35 | 45 | 15 | 110 | 4 | 6 | 0 | 1 | 198 | 5.1 |
| 2009–10 | 40 | San Jose Sharks | NHL | 70 | 7 | 23 | 30 | 14 | 60 | 3 | 4 | 0 | 1 | 182 | 3.8 |
| NHL Career – 20 Seasons | | | | 1270 | 240 | 537 | 777 | -4 | 1679 | 100 | 136 | 4 | 41 | 3896 | 6.2 |

## PLAYOFFS

| SEASON | AGE | TEAM | LG | GP | G | A | PTS | +/- | PIM | ESG | PPG | SHG | GWG | SOG | S% |
|--------|-----|------|----|----|---|---|-----|-----|-----|-----|-----|-----|-----|-----|----|
| 1989–90 | 20 | Los Angeles Kings | NHL | 8 | 1 | 3 | 4 | -4 | 4 | 0 | 1 | 0 | 0 | 11 | 9.1 |
| 1990–91 | 21 | Los Angeles Kings | NHL | 12 | 1 | 4 | 5 | -1 | 26 | 0 | 1 | 0 | 0 | 19 | 5.3 |
| 1991–92 | 22 | Los Angeles Kings | NHL | 6 | 2 | 1 | 3 | 2 | 12 | 2 | 0 | 0 | 0 | 12 | 16.7 |
| 1992–93 | 23 | Los Angeles Kings | NHL | 23 | 4 | 6 | 10 | 3 | 46 | 2 | 1 | 1 | 0 | 60 | 6.7 |
| 1997–98 | 28 | Los Angeles Kings | NHL | 4 | 0 | 0 | 0 | -4 | 6 | 0 | 0 | 0 | 0 | 15 | 0.0 |
| 1999–00 | 30 | Los Angeles Kings | NHL | 4 | 0 | 2 | 2 | 1 | 4 | 0 | 0 | 0 | 0 | 19 | 0.0 |
| 2000–01 | 31 | Colorado Avalanche | NHL | 23 | 6 | 13 | 19 | 6 | 16 | 3 | 3 | 0 | 0 | 83 | 7.2 |
| 2001–02 | 32 | Colorado Avalanche | NHL | 20 | 6 | 6 | 12 | -1 | 16 | 5 | 1 | 0 | 0 | 67 | 9.0 |
| 2002–03 | 33 | Colorado Avalanche | NHL | 7 | 1 | 2 | 3 | 2 | 8 | 1 | 0 | 0 | 0 | 27 | 3.7 |
| 2003–04 | 34 | Colorado Avalanche | NHL | 9 | 0 | 5 | 5 | 0 | 6 | 0 | 0 | 0 | 0 | 17 | 0.0 |
| 2005–06 | 36 | Colorado Avalanche | NHL | 9 | 3 | 1 | 4 | 1 | 8 | 1 | 2 | 0 | 1 | 42 | 7.1 |
| 2008–09 | 39 | San Jose Sharks | NHL | 6 | 1 | 3 | 4 | -5 | 4 | 1 | 0 | 0 | 0 | 26 | 3.8 |
| 2009–10 | 40 | San Jose Sharks | NHL | 15 | 1 | 1 | 2 | 0 | 10 | 1 | 0 | 0 | 0 | 38 | 2.6 |
| NHL Career – 16 Seasons | | | | 146 | 26 | 47 | 73 | 0 | 166 | 16 | 9 | 1 | 1 | 436 | 6.0 |

# Leo Boivin  Profile: See page 221

## REGULAR SEASON

| SEASON | AGE | TEAM | LG | GP | G | A | PTS | +/- | PIM | ESG | PPG | SHG | GWG | SOG | S% |
|--------|-----|------|----|----|---|---|-----|-----|-----|-----|-----|-----|-----|-----|----|
| 1951–52 | 19 | Toronto Maple Leafs | NHL | 2 | 0 | 1 | 1 | | 0 | 0 | 0 | 0 | 0 | | |
| 1952–53 | 20 | Toronto Maple Leafs | NHL | 70 | 2 | 13 | 15 | | 97 | 1 | 0 | 1 | 0 | | |
| 1953–54 | 21 | Toronto Maple Leafs | NHL | 58 | 1 | 6 | 7 | | 83 | 1 | 0 | 0 | 0 | | |
| 1954–55 | 22 | Toronto Maple Leafs | NHL | 7 | 0 | 0 | 0 | | 8 | 0 | 0 | 0 | 0 | | |
| 1954–55 | 22 | Boston Bruins | NHL | 59 | 6 | 11 | 17 | | 105 | 6 | 2 | 0 | 0 | | |
| 1955–56 | 23 | Boston Bruins | NHL | 68 | 4 | 16 | 20 | | 80 | 3 | 0 | 1 | 1 | | |
| 1956–57 | 24 | Boston Bruins | NHL | 55 | 2 | 8 | 10 | | 55 | 2 | 0 | 0 | 1 | | |
| 1957–58 | 25 | Boston Bruins | NHL | 33 | 0 | 4 | 4 | | 54 | 0 | 0 | 0 | 0 | | |
| 1958–59 | 26 | Boston Bruins | NHL | 70 | 5 | 16 | 21 | | 94 | 5 | 0 | 0 | 0 | | |
| 1959–60 | 27 | Boston Bruins | NHL | 70 | 4 | 21 | 25 | -7 | 66 | 4 | 0 | 0 | 0 | 132 | 3.0 |
| 1960–61 | 28 | Boston Bruins | NHL | 57 | 6 | 17 | 23 | -18 | 50 | 6 | 0 | 0 | 1 | 110 | 5.5 |
| 1961–62 | 29 | Boston Bruins | NHL | 65 | 5 | 18 | 23 | -46 | 70 | 4 | 0 | 1 | 0 | 123 | 4.1 |
| 1962–63 | 30 | Boston Bruins | NHL | 62 | 2 | 24 | 26 | -26 | 50 | 1 | 0 | 1 | 0 | 103 | 1.9 |
| 1963–64 | 31 | Boston Bruins | NHL | 65 | 10 | 14 | 24 | 1 | 42 | 8 | 1 | 1 | 0 | 140 | 7.1 |
| 1964–65 | 32 | Boston Bruins | NHL | 67 | 3 | 10 | 13 | -17 | 68 | 3 | 0 | 0 | 1 | 122 | 2.5 |
| 1965–66 | 33 | Boston Bruins | NHL | 46 | 0 | 5 | 5 | -26 | 34 | 0 | 0 | 0 | 0 | 55 | 0.0 |
| 1965–66 | 33 | Detroit Red Wings | NHL | 16 | 0 | 5 | 5 | -11 | 16 | 0 | 0 | 0 | 0 | 29 | 0.0 |
| 1966–67 | 34 | Detroit Red Wings | NHL | 69 | 4 | 17 | 21 | -19 | 78 | 4 | 0 | 0 | 1 | 134 | 3.0 |
| 1967–68 | 35 | Pittsburgh Penguins | NHL | 73 | 9 | 13 | 22 | -16 | 74 | 5 | 4 | 0 | 1 | 163 | 5.5 |
| 1968–69 | 36 | Pittsburgh Penguins | NHL | 41 | 5 | 13 | 18 | -6 | 26 | 3 | 2 | 0 | 1 | 74 | 6.8 |
| 1968–69 | 36 | Minnesota North Stars | NHL | 28 | 1 | 6 | 7 | -19 | 16 | 0 | 1 | 0 | 0 | 64 | 1.6 |

### Leo Boivin (continued)

**REGULAR SEASON**

| SEASON | AGE | TEAM | LG | GP | G | A | PTS | +/- | PIM | ESG | PPG | SHG | GWG | SOG | S% |
|---|---|---|---|---|---|---|---|---|---|---|---|---|---|---|---|
| 1969-70 | 37 | Minnesota North Stars | NHL | 69 | 3 | 12 | 15 | -2 | 30 | 3 | 0 | 0 | 0 | 95 | 3.2 |
| NHL Career — 19 Seasons | | | | 1150 | 72 | 250 | 322 | -212 | 1196 | 57 | 10 | 5 | 7 | 1344 | 3.9 |

**PLAYOFFS**

| SEASON | AGE | TEAM | LG | GP | G | A | PTS | +/- | PIM | ESG | PPG | SHG | GWG | SOG | S% |
|---|---|---|---|---|---|---|---|---|---|---|---|---|---|---|---|
| 1953-54 | 21 | Toronto Maple Leafs | NHL | 5 | 0 | 0 | 0 | | 2 | 0 | 0 | 0 | 0 | | |
| 1954-55 | 22 | Boston Bruins | NHL | 5 | 0 | 1 | 1 | | 4 | 0 | 0 | 0 | 0 | | |
| 1956-57 | 24 | Boston Bruins | NHL | 10 | 2 | 3 | 5 | | 12 | 2 | 0 | 0 | 0 | | |
| 1957-58 | 25 | Boston Bruins | NHL | 12 | 0 | 3 | 3 | | 21 | 0 | 0 | 0 | 0 | | |
| 1958-59 | 26 | Boston Bruins | NHL | 7 | 1 | 2 | 3 | | 4 | 1 | 0 | 0 | 0 | | |
| 1965-66 | 33 | Detroit Red Wings | NHL | 12 | 0 | 1 | 1 | 2 | 16 | 0 | 0 | 0 | 0 | 17 | 0.0 |
| 1969-70 | 37 | Minnesota North Stars | NHL | 3 | 0 | 0 | 0 | 0 | 0 | 0 | 0 | 0 | 0 | 5 | 0.0 |
| NHL Career — 7 Seasons | | | | 54 | 3 | 10 | 13 | 2 | 59 | 3 | 0 | 0 | 0 | 22 | 0.0 |

## Dickie Boon  Profile: See page 222

**REGULAR SEASON**

| SEASON | AGE | TEAM | LG | GP | G | A | PTS | PIM |
|---|---|---|---|---|---|---|---|---|
| 1899-00 | 22 | Montreal AAA | CAHL | 8 | 2 | 0 | 2 | |
| 1900-01 | 23 | Montreal AAA | CAHL | 7 | 3 | 0 | 3 | |
| 1901-02 | 24 | Montreal AAA | CAHL | 8 | 2 | 0 | 2 | 6 |
| 1902-03 | 25 | Montreal AAA | CAHL | 7 | 3 | 0 | 3 | 6 |
| 1903-04 | 26 | Montreal Wanderers | FAHL | 4 | 0 | 0 | 0 | |
| 1904-05 | 27 | Montreal Wanderers | FAHL | 8 | 0 | 0 | 0 | 6 |
| Career — 6 Seasons | | | | 42 | 10 | 0 | 10 | 18 |

**PLAYOFFS**

| SEASON | AGE | TEAM | LG | GP | G | A | PTS | PIM |
|---|---|---|---|---|---|---|---|---|
| 1901-02 | 24 | Montreal AAA | St-Cup | 3 | 0 | 0 | 0 | 3 |
| 1902-03 | 25 | Montreal AAA | St-Cup | 4 | 0 | 0 | 0 | 10 |
| Career — 2 Seasons | | | | 7 | 0 | 0 | 0 | 13 |

## Butch Bouchard  Profile: See page 223

**REGULAR SEASON**

| SEASON | AGE | TEAM | LG | GP | G | A | PTS | PIM |
|---|---|---|---|---|---|---|---|---|
| 1941-42 | 22 | Montreal Canadiens | NHL | 44 | 0 | 6 | 6 | 38 |
| 1942-43 | 23 | Montreal Canadiens | NHL | 45 | 2 | 16 | 18 | 47 |
| 1943-44 | 24 | Montreal Canadiens | NHL | 39 | 5 | 14 | 19 | 52 |
| 1944-45 | 25 | Montreal Canadiens | NHL | 50 | 11 | 23 | 34 | 34 |
| 1945-46 | 26 | Montreal Canadiens | NHL | 46 | 7 | 9 | 16 | 52 |
| 1946-47 | 27 | Montreal Canadiens | NHL | 60 | 5 | 7 | 12 | 60 |
| 1947-48 | 28 | Montreal Canadiens | NHL | 60 | 4 | 6 | 10 | 78 |
| 1948-49 | 29 | Montreal Canadiens | NHL | 27 | 3 | 3 | 6 | 42 |
| 1949-50 | 30 | Montreal Canadiens | NHL | 69 | 1 | 7 | 8 | 88 |
| 1950-51 | 31 | Montreal Canadiens | NHL | 52 | 3 | 10 | 13 | 80 |
| 1951-52 | 32 | Montreal Canadiens | NHL | 60 | 3 | 9 | 12 | 45 |
| 1952-53 | 33 | Montreal Canadiens | NHL | 58 | 2 | 8 | 10 | 55 |
| 1953-54 | 34 | Montreal Canadiens | NHL | 70 | 1 | 10 | 11 | 89 |
| 1954-55 | 35 | Montreal Canadiens | NHL | 70 | 2 | 16 | 18 | 83 |
| 1955-56 | 36 | Montreal Canadiens | NHL | 36 | 0 | 0 | 0 | 22 |
| NHL Career — 15 Seasons | | | | 786 | 49 | 144 | 193 | 865 |

**PLAYOFFS**

| SEASON | AGE | TEAM | LG | GP | G | A | PTS | PIM |
|---|---|---|---|---|---|---|---|---|
| 1941-42 | 22 | Montreal Canadiens | NHL | 3 | 1 | 1 | 2 | 0 |
| 1942-43 | 23 | Montreal Canadiens | NHL | 5 | 0 | 1 | 1 | 4 |
| 1943-44 | 24 | Montreal Canadiens | NHL | 9 | 1 | 3 | 4 | 4 |
| 1944-45 | 25 | Montreal Canadiens | NHL | 6 | 3 | 4 | 7 | 4 |
| 1945-46 | 26 | Montreal Canadiens | NHL | 9 | 2 | 1 | 3 | 17 |
| 1946-47 | 27 | Montreal Canadiens | NHL | 11 | 0 | 3 | 3 | 21 |
| 1948-49 | 29 | Montreal Canadiens | NHL | 7 | 0 | 0 | 0 | 6 |
| 1949-50 | 30 | Montreal Canadiens | NHL | 5 | 0 | 2 | 2 | 2 |
| 1950-51 | 31 | Montreal Canadiens | NHL | 11 | 1 | 1 | 2 | 2 |
| 1951-52 | 32 | Montreal Canadiens | NHL | 11 | 0 | 2 | 2 | 14 |
| 1952-53 | 33 | Montreal Canadiens | NHL | 12 | 1 | 1 | 2 | 6 |
| 1953-54 | 34 | Montreal Canadiens | NHL | 11 | 2 | 1 | 3 | 4 |
| 1954-55 | 35 | Montreal Canadiens | NHL | 12 | 0 | 1 | 1 | 37 |
| 1955-56 | 36 | Montreal Canadiens | NHL | 2 | 0 | 0 | 0 | 0 |
| NHL Career — 14 Seasons | | | | 114 | 11 | 21 | 32 | 121 |

## George Boucher  Profile: See page 224

**REGULAR SEASON**

| SEASON | AGE | TEAM | LG | GP | G | A | PTS | PIM |
|---|---|---|---|---|---|---|---|---|
| 1915-16 | 19 | Ottawa Senators | NHA | 19 | 9 | 1 | 10 | 62 |
| 1916-17 | 20 | Ottawa Senators | NHA | 18 | 10 | 5 | 15 | 27 |
| 1917-18 | 21 | Ottawa Senators | NHL | 21 | 9 | 8 | 16 | 46 |
| 1918-19 | 22 | Ottawa Senators | NHL | 17 | 3 | 2 | 5 | 29 |
| 1919-20 | 23 | Ottawa Senators | NHL | 22 | 9 | 7 | 16 | 55 |
| 1920-21 | 24 | Ottawa Senators | NHL | 23 | 11 | 7 | 18 | 53 |
| 1921-22 | 25 | Ottawa Senators | NHL | 23 | 13 | 12 | 25 | 12 |
| 1922-23 | 26 | Ottawa Senators | NHL | 24 | 15 | 10 | 25 | 60 |
| 1923-24 | 27 | Ottawa Senators | NHL | 21 | 13 | 9 | 22 | 42 |
| 1924-25 | 28 | Ottawa Senators | NHL | 28 | 15 | 6 | 21 | 90 |
| 1925-26 | 29 | Ottawa Senators | NHL | 36 | 8 | 4 | 12 | 66 |
| 1926-27 | 30 | Ottawa Senators | NHL | 40 | 8 | 4 | 12 | 115 |
| 1927-28 | 31 | Ottawa Senators | NHL | 44 | 7 | 5 | 12 | 80 |
| 1928-29 | 32 | Ottawa Senators | NHL | 31 | 3 | 1 | 4 | 60 |
| 1928-29 | 32 | Montreal Maroons | NHL | 10 | 1 | 1 | 2 | 12 |
| 1929-30 | 33 | Montreal Maroons | NHL | 37 | 2 | 6 | 8 | 46 |
| 1930-31 | 34 | Montreal Maroons | NHL | 30 | 0 | 0 | 0 | 25 |
| 1931-32 | 35 | Chicago Black Hawks | NHL | 43 | 1 | 5 | 6 | 54 |
| Career — 17 Seasons | | | | 487 | 137 | 93 | 230 | 934 |

**PLAYOFFS**

| SEASON | AGE | TEAM | LG | GP | G | A | PTS | PIM |
|---|---|---|---|---|---|---|---|---|
| 1916-17 | 20 | Ottawa Senators | NHA | 2 | 1 | 0 | 1 | 8 |
| 1918-19 | 22 | Ottawa Senators | NHL | 5 | 2 | 0 | 2 | 9 |
| 1919-20 | 23 | Ottawa Senators | St-Cup | 5 | 2 | 0 | 2 | 2 |
| 1920-21 | 24 | Ottawa Senators | NHL | 2 | 3 | 0 | 3 | 10 |
| 1920-21 | 24 | Ottawa Senators | St-Cup | 5 | 2 | 0 | 2 | 6 |
| 1921-22 | 25 | Ottawa Senators | NHL | 2 | 0 | 0 | 0 | 4 |
| 1922-23 | 26 | Ottawa Senators | NHL | 2 | 0 | 1 | 1 | 2 |
| 1922-23 | 26 | Ottawa Senators | St-Cup | 6 | 2 | 1 | 3 | 6 |
| 1923-24 | 27 | Ottawa Senators | NHL | 2 | 0 | 1 | 1 | 4 |
| 1925-26 | 29 | Ottawa Senators | NHL | 2 | 0 | 0 | 0 | 10 |
| 1926-27 | 30 | Ottawa Senators | NHL | 6 | 0 | 0 | 0 | 38 |
| 1927-28 | 31 | Ottawa Senators | NHL | 2 | 0 | 0 | 0 | 4 |
| 1929-30 | 33 | Montreal Maroons | NHL | 3 | 0 | 0 | 0 | 2 |
| 1931-32 | 35 | Chicago Black Hawks | NHL | 2 | 0 | 1 | 1 | 0 |
| Career — 12 Seasons | | | | 46 | 12 | 4 | 16 | 105 |

# Ray Bourque   Profile: See page 225

## REGULAR SEASON

| SEASON | AGE | TEAM | LG | GP | G | A | PTS | +/- | PIM | ESG | PPG | SHG | GWG | SOG | S% |
|---|---|---|---|---|---|---|---|---|---|---|---|---|---|---|---|
| 1979–80 | 19 | Boston Bruins | NHL | 80 | 17 | 48 | 65 | 52 | 73 | 12 | 3 | 2 | 1 | 185 | 9.2 |
| 1980–81 | 20 | Boston Bruins | NHL | 67 | 27 | 29 | 56 | 29 | 96 | 17 | 9 | 1 | 6 | 207 | 13.0 |
| 1981–82 | 21 | Boston Bruins | NHL | 65 | 17 | 49 | 66 | 21 | 51 | 13 | 4 | 0 | 2 | 211 | 8.1 |
| 1982–83 | 22 | Boston Bruins | NHL | 65 | 22 | 51 | 73 | 49 | 20 | 15 | 7 | 0 | 5 | 205 | 10.7 |
| 1983–84 | 23 | Boston Bruins | NHL | 78 | 31 | 65 | 96 | 51 | 57 | 18 | 12 | 1 | 5 | 343 | 9.0 |
| 1984–85 | 24 | Boston Bruins | NHL | 73 | 20 | 66 | 86 | 30 | 53 | 9 | 10 | 1 | 1 | 333 | 6.0 |
| 1985–86 | 25 | Boston Bruins | NHL | 74 | 19 | 58 | 77 | 17 | 68 | 8 | 11 | 0 | 3 | 289 | 6.6 |
| 1986–87 | 26 | Boston Bruins | NHL | 78 | 23 | 72 | 95 | 44 | 36 | 16 | 6 | 1 | 3 | 334 | 6.9 |
| 1987–88 | 27 | Boston Bruins | NHL | 78 | 17 | 64 | 81 | 34 | 72 | 9 | 7 | 1 | 5 | 344 | 4.9 |
| 1988–89 | 28 | Boston Bruins | NHL | 60 | 18 | 43 | 61 | 20 | 52 | 12 | 6 | 0 | 0 | 243 | 7.4 |
| 1989–90 | 29 | Boston Bruins | NHL | 76 | 19 | 65 | 84 | 31 | 50 | 11 | 8 | 0 | 3 | 310 | 6.1 |
| 1990–91 | 30 | Boston Bruins | NHL | 76 | 21 | 73 | 94 | 33 | 75 | 14 | 7 | 0 | 3 | 323 | 6.5 |
| 1991–92 | 31 | Boston Bruins | NHL | 80 | 21 | 60 | 81 | 11 | 56 | 13 | 7 | 1 | 2 | 334 | 6.3 |
| 1992–93 | 32 | Boston Bruins | NHL | 78 | 19 | 63 | 82 | 38 | 40 | 11 | 8 | 0 | 7 | 330 | 5.8 |
| 1993–94 | 33 | Boston Bruins | NHL | 72 | 20 | 71 | 91 | 26 | 58 | 7 | 10 | 3 | 1 | 386 | 5.2 |
| 1994–95 | 34 | Boston Bruins | NHL | 46 | 12 | 31 | 43 | 3 | 20 | 3 | 9 | 0 | 2 | 210 | 5.7 |
| 1995–96 | 35 | Boston Bruins | NHL | 82 | 20 | 62 | 82 | 31 | 58 | 9 | 9 | 2 | 2 | 390 | 5.1 |
| 1996–97 | 36 | Boston Bruins | NHL | 62 | 19 | 31 | 50 | -11 | 18 | 10 | 8 | 1 | 3 | 230 | 8.3 |
| 1997–98 | 37 | Boston Bruins | NHL | 82 | 13 | 35 | 48 | 2 | 80 | 4 | 9 | 0 | 3 | 264 | 4.9 |
| 1998–99 | 38 | Boston Bruins | NHL | 81 | 10 | 47 | 57 | -7 | 34 | 2 | 8 | 0 | 3 | 262 | 3.8 |
| 1999–00 | 39 | Boston Bruins | NHL | 65 | 10 | 28 | 38 | -11 | 20 | 4 | 6 | 0 | 0 | 217 | 4.6 |
| 1999–00 | 39 | Colorado Avalanche | NHL | 14 | 8 | 6 | 14 | 9 | 6 | 1 | 7 | 0 | 0 | 43 | 18.6 |
| 2000–01 | 40 | Colorado Avalanche | NHL | 80 | 7 | 52 | 59 | 25 | 48 | 3 | 2 | 2 | 0 | 216 | 3.2 |
| NHL Career – 22 Seasons | | | | 1612 | 410 | 1169 | 1579 | 527 | 1141 | 221 | 173 | 16 | 60 | 6209 | 6.6 |

## PLAYOFFS

| SEASON | AGE | TEAM | LG | GP | G | A | PTS | +/- | PIM | ESG | PPG | SHG | GWG | SOG | S% |
|---|---|---|---|---|---|---|---|---|---|---|---|---|---|---|---|
| 1979–80 | 19 | Boston Bruins | NHL | 10 | 2 | 9 | 11 | 4 | 27 | 2 | 0 | 0 | 0 | 45 | 4.4 |
| 1980–81 | 20 | Boston Bruins | NHL | 3 | 0 | 1 | 1 | -2 | 2 | 0 | 0 | 0 | 0 | 11 | 0.0 |
| 1981–82 | 21 | Boston Bruins | NHL | 9 | 1 | 5 | 6 | 5 | 16 | 1 | 0 | 0 | 1 | 31 | 3.2 |
| 1982–83 | 22 | Boston Bruins | NHL | 17 | 8 | 15 | 23 | 15 | 10 | 6 | 2 | 0 | 1 | 79 | 10.1 |
| 1983–84 | 23 | Boston Bruins | NHL | 3 | 0 | 2 | 2 | -3 | 0 | 0 | 0 | 0 | 0 | 10 | 0.0 |
| 1984–85 | 24 | Boston Bruins | NHL | 5 | 0 | 3 | 3 | 1 | 4 | 0 | 0 | 0 | 0 | 15 | 0.0 |
| 1985–86 | 25 | Boston Bruins | NHL | 3 | 0 | 0 | 0 | 0 | 0 | 0 | 0 | 0 | 0 | 7 | 0.0 |
| 1986–87 | 26 | Boston Bruins | NHL | 4 | 1 | 2 | 3 | -1 | 0 | 1 | 0 | 0 | 0 | 22 | 4.6 |
| 1987–88 | 27 | Boston Bruins | NHL | 23 | 3 | 18 | 21 | 16 | 26 | 3 | 0 | 0 | 1 | 65 | 4.6 |
| 1988–89 | 28 | Boston Bruins | NHL | 10 | 0 | 4 | 4 | -1 | 6 | 0 | 0 | 0 | 0 | 40 | 0.0 |
| 1989–90 | 29 | Boston Bruins | NHL | 17 | 5 | 12 | 17 | 11 | 16 | 4 | 1 | 0 | 0 | 64 | 7.8 |
| 1990–91 | 30 | Boston Bruins | NHL | 19 | 7 | 18 | 25 | -4 | 12 | 4 | 3 | 0 | 0 | 84 | 8.3 |
| 1991–92 | 31 | Boston Bruins | NHL | 12 | 3 | 6 | 9 | -10 | 12 | 1 | 2 | 0 | 0 | 51 | 5.9 |
| 1992–93 | 32 | Boston Bruins | NHL | 4 | 1 | 0 | 1 | -2 | 2 | 0 | 1 | 0 | 0 | 20 | 5.0 |
| 1993–94 | 33 | Boston Bruins | NHL | 13 | 2 | 8 | 10 | -5 | 0 | 1 | 1 | 0 | 0 | 64 | 3.1 |
| 1994–95 | 34 | Boston Bruins | NHL | 5 | 0 | 3 | 3 | -5 | 0 | 0 | 0 | 0 | 0 | 15 | 0.0 |
| 1995–96 | 35 | Boston Bruins | NHL | 5 | 1 | 6 | 7 | -4 | 2 | 0 | 1 | 0 | 0 | 28 | 3.6 |
| 1997–98 | 37 | Boston Bruins | NHL | 6 | 1 | 4 | 5 | -2 | 2 | 0 | 1 | 0 | 0 | 42 | 2.4 |
| 1998–99 | 38 | Boston Bruins | NHL | 12 | 1 | 9 | 10 | 1 | 14 | 1 | 0 | 0 | 0 | 44 | 2.3 |
| 1999–00 | 39 | Boston Bruins | NHL | 13 | 1 | 8 | 9 | 4 | 8 | 1 | 0 | 0 | 0 | 28 | 3.6 |
| 2000–01 | 40 | Boston Bruins | NHL | 21 | 4 | 6 | 10 | 9 | 12 | 1 | 3 | 0 | 1 | 49 | 8.2 |
| NHL Career – 21 Seasons | | | | 214 | 41 | 139 | 180 | 27 | 171 | 26 | 15 | 0 | 4 | 812 | 5.0 |

# Harry Cameron   Profile: See page 227

## REGULAR SEASON

| SEASON | AGE | TEAM | LG | GP | G | A | PTS | PIM |
|---|---|---|---|---|---|---|---|---|
| 1912–13 | 22 | Toronto Blueshirts | NHA | 20 | 9 | 0 | 9 | 20 |
| 1913–14 | 23 | Toronto Blueshirts | NHA | 19 | 15 | 4 | 19 | 22 |
| 1914–15 | 24 | Toronto Blueshirts | NHA | 17 | 12 | 8 | 20 | 43 |
| 1915–16 | 25 | Toronto Blueshirts | NHA | 24 | 8 | 3 | 11 | 70 |
| 1916–17 | 26 | Toronto Blueshirts | NHA | 14 | 8 | 4 | 12 | 20 |
| 1916–17 | 26 | Montreal Wanderers | NHA | 6 | 1 | 1 | 2 | 12 |
| 1917–18 | 27 | Toronto Arenas | NHL | 21 | 17 | 10 | 27 | 28 |
| 1918–19 | 28 | Toronto Arenas | NHL | 7 | 6 | 4 | 10 | 12 |
| 1918–19 | 28 | Ottawa Senators | NHL | 7 | 5 | 1 | 6 | 23 |
| 1919–20 | 29 | Toronto St. Patricks | NHL | 7 | 3 | 0 | 3 | 6 |
| 1919–20 | 29 | Montreal Canadiens | NHL | 16 | 12 | 6 | 18 | 29 |
| 1920–21 | 30 | Toronto St. Patricks | NHL | 24 | 18 | 9 | 27 | 35 |
| 1921–22 | 31 | Toronto St. Patricks | NHL | 24 | 18 | 17 | 35 | 22 |
| 1922–23 | 32 | Toronto St. Patricks | NHL | 23 | 9 | 7 | 16 | 25 |
| 1923–24 | 33 | Saskatoon Crescents | WCHL | 29 | 10 | 10 | 20 | 16 |

## REGULAR SEASON

| SEASON | AGE | TEAM | LG | GP | G | A | PTS | PIM |
|---|---|---|---|---|---|---|---|---|
| 1924–25 | 34 | Saskatoon Crescents | WCHL | 28 | 13 | 7 | 20 | 21 |
| 1925–26 | 35 | Saskatoon Crescents | WHL | 30 | 9 | 3 | 12 | 12 |
| Career – 14 Seasons | | | | 316 | 173 | 94 | 267 | 413 |

## PLAYOFFS

| SEASON | AGE | TEAM | LG | GP | G | A | PTS | PIM |
|---|---|---|---|---|---|---|---|---|
| 1913–14 | 23 | Toronto Blueshirts | NHA | 2 | 0 | 2 | 2 | 6 |
| 1913–14 | 23 | Toronto Blueshirts | St-Cup | 3 | 1 | 0 | 1 | 4 |
| 1917–18 | 27 | Toronto Arenas | NHL | 2 | 1 | 2 | 3 | 0 |
| 1917–18 | 27 | Toronto Arenas | St-Cup | 5 | 3 | 1 | 4 | 12 |
| 1918–19 | 28 | Ottawa Senators | NHL | 5 | 4 | 0 | 4 | 6 |
| 1920–21 | 30 | Toronto St. Patricks | NHL | 2 | 0 | 0 | 0 | 2 |
| 1921–22 | 31 | Toronto St. Patricks | NHL | 2 | 0 | 2 | 2 | 8 |
| 1921–22 | 31 | Toronto St. Patricks | St-Cup | 4 | 0 | 2 | 2 | 12 |
| 1924–25 | 34 | Saskatoon Crescents | WCHL | 2 | 1 | 0 | 1 | 0 |
| 1925–26 | 35 | Saskatoon Crescents | WHL | 2 | 0 | 0 | 0 | 0 |
| Career – 7 Seasons | | | | 29 | 10 | 9 | 19 | 50 |

# Chris Chelios  Profile: See page 228

## REGULAR SEASON

| SEASON | AGE | TEAM | LG | GP | G | A | PTS | +/- | PIM | ESG | PPG | SHG | GWG | SOG | S% |
|--------|-----|------|----|----|----|----|-----|-----|-----|-----|-----|-----|-----|-----|-----|
| 1983–84 | 22 | Montreal Canadiens | NHL | 12 | 0 | 2 | 2 | -5 | 12 | 0 | 0 | 0 | 0 | 23 | 0.0 |
| 1984–85 | 23 | Montreal Canadiens | NHL | 74 | 9 | 55 | 64 | 10 | 87 | 6 | 2 | 1 | 0 | 200 | 4.5 |
| 1985–86 | 24 | Montreal Canadiens | NHL | 41 | 8 | 26 | 34 | 6 | 67 | 6 | 2 | 0 | 0 | 101 | 7.9 |
| 1986–87 | 25 | Montreal Canadiens | NHL | 71 | 11 | 33 | 44 | -5 | 124 | 5 | 6 | 0 | 2 | 141 | 7.8 |
| 1987–88 | 26 | Montreal Canadiens | NHL | 71 | 20 | 41 | 61 | 14 | 172 | 9 | 10 | 1 | 5 | 199 | 10.1 |
| 1988–89 | 27 | Montreal Canadiens | NHL | 80 | 15 | 58 | 73 | 35 | 185 | 7 | 8 | 0 | 6 | 206 | 7.3 |
| 1989–90 | 28 | Montreal Canadiens | NHL | 53 | 9 | 22 | 31 | 20 | 136 | 6 | 1 | 2 | 1 | 123 | 7.3 |
| 1990–91 | 29 | Chicago Blackhawks | NHL | 77 | 12 | 52 | 64 | 23 | 192 | 5 | 5 | 2 | 2 | 187 | 6.4 |
| 1991–92 | 30 | Chicago Blackhawks | NHL | 80 | 9 | 47 | 56 | 24 | 245 | 5 | 2 | 2 | 2 | 239 | 3.8 |
| 1992–93 | 31 | Chicago Blackhawks | NHL | 84 | 15 | 58 | 73 | 14 | 282 | 7 | 8 | 0 | 2 | 290 | 5.2 |
| 1993–94 | 32 | Chicago Blackhawks | NHL | 76 | 16 | 44 | 60 | 12 | 212 | 8 | 7 | 1 | 2 | 219 | 7.3 |
| 1994–95 | 33 | Chicago Blackhawks | NHL | 48 | 5 | 33 | 38 | 17 | 72 | 1 | 3 | 1 | 0 | 166 | 3.0 |
| 1995–96 | 34 | Chicago Blackhawks | NHL | 81 | 14 | 58 | 72 | 25 | 140 | 7 | 7 | 0 | 3 | 219 | 6.4 |
| 1996–97 | 35 | Chicago Blackhawks | NHL | 72 | 10 | 38 | 48 | 16 | 112 | 8 | 2 | 0 | 2 | 194 | 5.2 |
| 1997–98 | 36 | Chicago Blackhawks | NHL | 81 | 3 | 39 | 42 | -7 | 151 | 2 | 1 | 0 | 0 | 205 | 1.5 |
| 1998–99 | 37 | Chicago Blackhawks | NHL | 65 | 8 | 26 | 34 | -4 | 89 | 5 | 2 | 1 | 0 | 172 | 4.7 |
| 1998–99 | 37 | Detroit Red Wings | NHL | 10 | 1 | 1 | 2 | 5 | 4 | 0 | 1 | 0 | 1 | 15 | 6.7 |
| 1999–00 | 38 | Detroit Red Wings | NHL | 81 | 3 | 31 | 34 | 48 | 103 | 3 | 0 | 0 | 0 | 135 | 2.2 |
| 2000–01 | 39 | Detroit Red Wings | NHL | 24 | 0 | 3 | 3 | 4 | 45 | 0 | 0 | 0 | 0 | 26 | 0.0 |
| 2001–02 | 40 | Detroit Red Wings | NHL | 79 | 6 | 33 | 39 | 40 | 126 | 5 | 1 | 0 | 1 | 128 | 4.7 |
| 2002–03 | 41 | Detroit Red Wings | NHL | 66 | 2 | 17 | 19 | 4 | 78 | 1 | 0 | 1 | 1 | 92 | 2.2 |
| 2003–04 | 42 | Detroit Red Wings | NHL | 69 | 2 | 19 | 21 | 12 | 61 | 2 | 0 | 0 | 0 | 113 | 1.8 |
| 2005–06 | 44 | Detroit Red Wings | NHL | 81 | 4 | 7 | 11 | 22 | 108 | 2 | 1 | 1 | 0 | 83 | 4.8 |
| 2006–07 | 45 | Detroit Red Wings | NHL | 71 | 0 | 11 | 11 | 11 | 34 | 0 | 0 | 0 | 0 | 72 | 0.0 |
| 2007–08 | 46 | Detroit Red Wings | NHL | 69 | 3 | 9 | 12 | 11 | 36 | 3 | 0 | 0 | 1 | 60 | 5.0 |
| 2008–09 | 47 | Detroit Red Wings | NHL | 28 | 0 | 0 | 0 | 1 | 18 | 0 | 0 | 0 | 0 | 14 | 0.0 |
| 2009–10 | 48 | Atlanta Thrashers | NHL | 7 | 0 | 0 | 0 | -2 | 0 | 0 | 0 | 0 | 0 | 5 | 0.0 |
| NHL Career — 26 Seasons | | | | 1651 | 185 | 763 | 948 | 351 | 2891 | 103 | 69 | 13 | 31 | 3627 | 5.1 |

## PLAYOFFS

| SEASON | AGE | TEAM | LG | GP | G | A | PTS | +/- | PIM | ESG | PPG | SHG | GWG | SOG | S% |
|--------|-----|------|----|----|----|----|-----|-----|-----|-----|-----|-----|-----|-----|-----|
| 1983–84 | 22 | Montreal Canadiens | NHL | 15 | 1 | 9 | 10 | 3 | 17 | 0 | 1 | 0 | 0 | 25 | 4.0 |
| 1984–85 | 23 | Montreal Canadiens | NHL | 9 | 2 | 8 | 10 | 2 | 17 | 0 | 2 | 0 | 0 | 19 | 10.5 |
| 1985–86 | 24 | Montreal Canadiens | NHL | 20 | 2 | 9 | 11 | 3 | 49 | 1 | 1 | 0 | 0 | 57 | 3.5 |
| 1986–87 | 25 | Montreal Canadiens | NHL | 17 | 4 | 9 | 13 | -1 | 38 | 1 | 2 | 1 | 0 | 49 | 8.2 |
| 1987–88 | 26 | Montreal Canadiens | NHL | 11 | 3 | 1 | 4 | 3 | 29 | 2 | 1 | 0 | 0 | 39 | 7.7 |
| 1988–89 | 27 | Montreal Canadiens | NHL | 21 | 4 | 15 | 19 | 2 | 28 | 3 | 1 | 0 | 2 | 53 | 7.5 |
| 1989–90 | 28 | Montreal Canadiens | NHL | 5 | 0 | 1 | 1 | -4 | 8 | 0 | 0 | 0 | 0 | 6 | 0.0 |
| 1990–91 | 29 | Chicago Blackhawks | NHL | 6 | 1 | 7 | 8 | 2 | 46 | 0 | 1 | 0 | 0 | 11 | 9.1 |
| 1991–92 | 30 | Chicago Blackhawks | NHL | 18 | 6 | 15 | 21 | 19 | 37 | 3 | 3 | 0 | 1 | 54 | 11.1 |
| 1992–93 | 31 | Chicago Blackhawks | NHL | 4 | 0 | 2 | 2 | -1 | 14 | 0 | 0 | 0 | 0 | 18 | 0.0 |
| 1993–94 | 32 | Chicago Blackhawks | NHL | 6 | 1 | 1 | 2 | 0 | 8 | 0 | 1 | 0 | 0 | 29 | 3.4 |
| 1994–95 | 33 | Chicago Blackhawks | NHL | 16 | 4 | 7 | 11 | 6 | 12 | 3 | 0 | 1 | 3 | 49 | 8.2 |
| 1995–96 | 34 | Chicago Blackhawks | NHL | 9 | 0 | 3 | 3 | 2 | 8 | 0 | 0 | 0 | 0 | 28 | 0.0 |
| 1996–97 | 35 | Chicago Blackhawks | NHL | 6 | 0 | 1 | 1 | -2 | 8 | 0 | 0 | 0 | 0 | 18 | 0.0 |
| 1998–99 | 37 | Detroit Red Wings | NHL | 10 | 0 | 4 | 4 | -6 | 14 | 0 | 0 | 0 | 0 | 21 | 0.0 |
| 1999–00 | 38 | Detroit Red Wings | NHL | 9 | 0 | 1 | 1 | -3 | 8 | 0 | 0 | 0 | 0 | 11 | 0.0 |
| 2000–01 | 39 | Detroit Red Wings | NHL | 5 | 1 | 0 | 1 | -1 | 2 | 1 | 0 | 0 | 0 | 9 | 11.1 |
| 2001–02 | 40 | Detroit Red Wings | NHL | 23 | 1 | 13 | 14 | 15 | 44 | 0 | 1 | 0 | 0 | 28 | 3.6 |
| 2002–03 | 41 | Detroit Red Wings | NHL | 4 | 0 | 0 | 0 | -3 | 2 | 0 | 0 | 0 | 0 | 4 | 0.0 |
| 2003–04 | 42 | Detroit Red Wings | NHL | 8 | 0 | 1 | 1 | 1 | 4 | 0 | 0 | 0 | 0 | 14 | 0.0 |
| 2005–06 | 44 | Detroit Red Wings | NHL | 6 | 0 | 0 | 0 | 2 | 6 | 0 | 0 | 0 | 0 | 3 | 0.0 |
| 2006–07 | 45 | Detroit Red Wings | NHL | 18 | 1 | 6 | 7 | 7 | 12 | 0 | 0 | 1 | 0 | 27 | 3.7 |
| 2007–08 | 46 | Detroit Red Wings | NHL | 14 | 0 | 0 | 0 | 2 | 10 | 0 | 0 | 0 | 0 | 11 | 0.0 |
| 2008–09 | 47 | Detroit Red Wings | NHL | 6 | 0 | 0 | 0 | 0 | 2 | 0 | 0 | 0 | 0 | 4 | 0.0 |
| NHL Career — 24 Seasons | | | | 266 | 31 | 113 | 144 | 48 | 423 | 14 | 14 | 3 | 6 | 587 | 5.3 |

## King Clancy  Profile: See page 229

| REGULAR SEASON | | | | | | | | |
|---|---|---|---|---|---|---|---|---|
| SEASON | AGE | TEAM | LG | GP | G | A | PTS | PIM |
| 1921–22 | 18 | Ottawa Senators | NHL | 24 | 4 | 6 | 10 | 21 |
| 1922–23 | 19 | Ottawa Senators | NHL | 24 | 3 | 2 | 5 | 20 |
| 1923–24 | 20 | Ottawa Senators | NHL | 24 | 8 | 10 | 18 | 18 |
| 1924–25 | 21 | Ottawa Senators | NHL | 29 | 14 | 8 | 22 | 63 |
| 1925–26 | 22 | Ottawa Senators | NHL | 35 | 8 | 4 | 12 | 82 |
| 1926–27 | 23 | Ottawa Senators | NHL | 43 | 10 | 10 | 20 | 78 |
| 1927–28 | 24 | Ottawa Senators | NHL | 39 | 8 | 7 | 15 | 73 |
| 1928–29 | 25 | Ottawa Senators | NHL | 44 | 13 | 2 | 15 | 95 |
| 1929–30 | 26 | Ottawa Senators | NHL | 44 | 17 | 23 | 40 | 83 |
| 1930–31 | 27 | Toronto Maple Leafs | NHL | 44 | 7 | 14 | 21 | 63 |
| 1931–32 | 28 | Toronto Maple Leafs | NHL | 48 | 10 | 9 | 19 | 59 |
| 1932–33 | 29 | Toronto Maple Leafs | NHL | 48 | 13 | 12 | 25 | 79 |
| 1933–34 | 30 | Toronto Maple Leafs | NHL | 46 | 11 | 17 | 28 | 62 |
| 1934–35 | 31 | Toronto Maple Leafs | NHL | 47 | 5 | 16 | 21 | 53 |
| 1935–36 | 32 | Toronto Maple Leafs | NHL | 47 | 5 | 10 | 15 | 61 |
| 1936–37 | 33 | Toronto Maple Leafs | NHL | 6 | 1 | 0 | 1 | 4 |
| Career – 16 Seasons | | | | 592 | 137 | 150 | 287 | 914 |

| PLAYOFFS | | | | | | | | |
|---|---|---|---|---|---|---|---|---|
| SEASON | AGE | TEAM | LG | GP | G | A | PTS | PIM |
| 1921–22 | 18 | Ottawa Senators | NHL | 2 | 0 | 0 | 0 | 2 |
| 1922–23 | 19 | Ottawa Senators | NHL | 2 | 0 | 0 | 0 | 0 |
| 1922–23 | 19 | Ottawa Senators | St-Cup | 6 | 1 | 0 | 1 | 4 |
| 1923–24 | 20 | Ottawa Senators | NHL | 2 | 0 | 0 | 0 | 6 |
| 1925–26 | 22 | Ottawa Senators | NHL | 2 | 1 | 0 | 1 | 4 |
| 1926–27 | 23 | Ottawa Senators | NHL | 6 | 1 | 1 | 2 | 14 |
| 1927–28 | 24 | Ottawa Senators | NHL | 2 | 0 | 0 | 0 | 6 |
| 1929–30 | 26 | Ottawa Senators | NHL | 2 | 0 | 1 | 1 | 2 |
| 1930–31 | 27 | Toronto Maple Leafs | NHL | 2 | 1 | 0 | 1 | 2 |
| 1931–32 | 28 | Toronto Maple Leafs | NHL | 7 | 2 | 1 | 3 | 14 |
| 1932–33 | 29 | Toronto Maple Leafs | NHL | 9 | 0 | 3 | 3 | 14 |
| 1933–34 | 30 | Toronto Maple Leafs | NHL | 3 | 0 | 0 | 0 | 8 |
| 1934–35 | 31 | Toronto Maple Leafs | NHL | 7 | 1 | 0 | 1 | 8 |
| 1935–36 | 32 | Toronto Maple Leafs | NHL | 9 | 2 | 2 | 4 | 10 |
| Career – 13 Seasons | | | | 61 | 9 | 8 | 17 | 94 |

## Dit Clapper  Profile: See page 230

| REGULAR SEASON | | | | | | | | |
|---|---|---|---|---|---|---|---|---|
| SEASON | AGE | TEAM | LG | GP | G | A | PTS | PIM |
| 1927–28 | 20 | Boston Bruins | NHL | 42 | 4 | 2 | 6 | 18 |
| 1928–29 | 21 | Boston Bruins | NHL | 40 | 9 | 2 | 11 | 48 |
| 1929–30 | 22 | Boston Bruins | NHL | 44 | 41 | 20 | 61 | 38 |
| 1930–31 | 23 | Boston Bruins | NHL | 43 | 22 | 8 | 30 | 50 |
| 1931–32 | 24 | Boston Bruins | NHL | 48 | 17 | 22 | 39 | 23 |
| 1932–33 | 25 | Boston Bruins | NHL | 48 | 14 | 14 | 28 | 42 |
| 1933–34 | 26 | Boston Bruins | NHL | 48 | 10 | 12 | 22 | 6 |
| 1934–35 | 27 | Boston Bruins | NHL | 48 | 22 | 16 | 38 | 21 |
| 1935–36 | 28 | Boston Bruins | NHL | 44 | 12 | 13 | 25 | 14 |
| 1936–37 | 29 | Boston Bruins | NHL | 48 | 17 | 8 | 25 | 25 |
| 1937–38 | 30 | Boston Bruins | NHL | 46 | 6 | 9 | 15 | 24 |
| 1938–39 | 31 | Boston Bruins | NHL | 42 | 13 | 13 | 26 | 22 |
| 1939–40 | 32 | Boston Bruins | NHL | 44 | 10 | 18 | 28 | 25 |
| 1940–41 | 33 | Boston Bruins | NHL | 48 | 8 | 18 | 26 | 24 |
| 1941–42 | 34 | Boston Bruins | NHL | 32 | 3 | 12 | 15 | 31 |
| 1942–43 | 35 | Boston Bruins | NHL | 38 | 5 | 18 | 23 | 12 |
| 1943–44 | 36 | Boston Bruins | NHL | 50 | 6 | 25 | 31 | 13 |
| 1944–45 | 37 | Boston Bruins | NHL | 46 | 8 | 15 | 23 | 16 |
| 1945–46 | 38 | Boston Bruins | NHL | 30 | 2 | 3 | 5 | 0 |
| 1946–47 | 39 | Boston Bruins | NHL | 6 | 0 | 0 | 0 | 0 |
| NHL Career – 20 Seasons | | | | 835 | 229 | 248 | 477 | 452 |

| PLAYOFFS | | | | | | | | |
|---|---|---|---|---|---|---|---|---|
| SEASON | AGE | TEAM | LG | GP | G | A | PTS | PIM |
| 1927–28 | 20 | Boston Bruins | NHL | 2 | 0 | 0 | 0 | 2 |
| 1928–29 | 21 | Boston Bruins | NHL | 5 | 1 | 0 | 1 | 0 |
| 1929–30 | 22 | Boston Bruins | NHL | 6 | 4 | 0 | 4 | 4 |
| 1930–31 | 23 | Boston Bruins | NHL | 5 | 2 | 4 | 6 | 4 |
| 1932–33 | 25 | Boston Bruins | NHL | 5 | 1 | 1 | 2 | 2 |
| 1934–35 | 27 | Boston Bruins | NHL | 3 | 1 | 0 | 1 | 0 |
| 1935–36 | 28 | Boston Bruins | NHL | 2 | 0 | 1 | 1 | 0 |
| 1936–37 | 29 | Boston Bruins | NHL | 3 | 2 | 0 | 2 | 5 |
| 1937–38 | 30 | Boston Bruins | NHL | 3 | 0 | 0 | 0 | 12 |
| 1938–39 | 31 | Boston Bruins | NHL | 12 | 0 | 1 | 1 | 6 |
| 1939–40 | 32 | Boston Bruins | NHL | 5 | 0 | 2 | 2 | 2 |
| 1940–41 | 33 | Boston Bruins | NHL | 11 | 0 | 5 | 5 | 4 |
| 1942–43 | 35 | Boston Bruins | NHL | 9 | 2 | 2 | 4 | 9 |
| 1944–45 | 37 | Boston Bruins | NHL | 7 | 0 | 0 | 0 | 0 |
| 1945–46 | 38 | Boston Bruins | NHL | 4 | 0 | 0 | 0 | 0 |
| NHL Career – 15 Seasons | | | | 82 | 13 | 16 | 29 | 50 |

## Sprague Cleghorn  Profile: See page 231

| REGULAR SEASON | | | | | | | | |
|---|---|---|---|---|---|---|---|---|
| SEASON | AGE | TEAM | LG | GP | G | A | PTS | PIM |
| 1910–11 | 20 | Renfrew Hockey Club | NHA | 12 | 5 | 0 | 5 | 27 |
| 1911–12 | 21 | Montreal Wanderers | NHA | 18 | 9 | 0 | 9 | 40 |
| 1912–13 | 22 | Montreal Wanderers | NHA | 19 | 12 | 0 | 12 | 46 |
| 1913–14 | 23 | Montreal Wanderers | NHA | 20 | 12 | 8 | 20 | 17 |
| 1914–15 | 24 | Montreal Wanderers | NHA | 19 | 21 | 12 | 33 | 51 |
| 1915–16 | 25 | Montreal Wanderers | NHA | 8 | 9 | 4 | 13 | 22 |
| 1916–17 | 26 | Montreal Wanderers | NHA | 19 | 16 | 9 | 25 | 62 |
| 1918–19 | 28 | Ottawa Senators | NHL | 18 | 7 | 8 | 15 | 27 |
| 1919–20 | 29 | Ottawa Senators | NHL | 21 | 16 | 5 | 21 | 83 |
| 1919–20 | 30 | Ottawa Senators | NHL | 3 | 2 | 3 | 5 | 9 |
| 1920–21 | 30 | Toronto St. Patricks | NHL | 13 | 3 | 5 | 8 | 31 |
| 1921–22 | 31 | Montreal Canadiens | NHL | 24 | 17 | 9 | 26 | 80 |
| 1922–23 | 32 | Montreal Canadiens | NHL | 24 | 9 | 8 | 17 | 34 |
| 1923–24 | 33 | Montreal Canadiens | NHL | 23 | 8 | 4 | 12 | 47 |
| 1924–25 | 34 | Montreal Canadiens | NHL | 27 | 8 | 10 | 18 | 87 |
| 1925–26 | 35 | Boston Bruins | NHL | 28 | 6 | 8 | 14 | 59 |
| 1926–27 | 36 | Boston Bruins | NHL | 44 | 7 | 1 | 8 | 78 |
| 1927–28 | 37 | Boston Bruins | NHL | 37 | 2 | 2 | 4 | 14 |
| Career – 17 Seasons | | | | 374 | 167 | 96 | 265 | 814 |

| PLAYOFFS | | | | | | | | |
|---|---|---|---|---|---|---|---|---|
| SEASON | AGE | TEAM | LG | GP | G | A | PTS | PIM |
| 1914–15 | 24 | Montreal Wanderers | NHA | 2 | 0 | 0 | 0 | 17 |
| 1918–19 | 28 | Ottawa Senators | NHL | 5 | 2 | 1 | 3 | 9 |
| 1919–20 | 29 | Ottawa Senators | St-Cup | 5 | 0 | 1 | 1 | 4 |
| 1920–21 | 30 | Toronto St. Patricks | NHL | 1 | 0 | 0 | 0 | 0 |
| 1920–21 | 30 | Ottawa Senators | St-Cup | 5 | 1 | 2 | 3 | 34 |
| 1922–23 | 32 | Montreal Canadiens | NHL | 1 | 0 | 0 | 0 | 7 |
| 1923–24 | 33 | Montreal Canadiens | NHL | 2 | 0 | 0 | 0 | 0 |
| 1923–24 | 33 | Montreal Canadiens | St-Cup | 4 | 2 | 1 | 3 | 2 |
| 1924–25 | 34 | Montreal Canadiens | NHL | 2 | 1 | 2 | 3 | 2 |
| 1924–25 | 34 | Montreal Canadiens | St-Cup | 4 | 0 | 0 | 0 | 2 |
| 1926–27 | 36 | Boston Bruins | NHL | 8 | 1 | 0 | 1 | 8 |
| 1927–28 | 37 | Boston Bruins | NHL | 2 | 0 | 0 | 0 | 0 |
| Career – 9 Seasons | | | | 41 | 7 | 7 | 14 | 85 |

## Paul Coffey  Profile: See page 232

### REGULAR SEASON

| SEASON | AGE | TEAM | LG | GP | G | A | PTS | +/- | PIM | ESG | PPG | SHG | GWG | SOG | S% |
|---|---|---|---|---|---|---|---|---|---|---|---|---|---|---|---|
| 1980–81 | 19 | Edmonton Oilers | NHL | 74 | 9 | 23 | 32 | 5 | 130 | 7 | 2 | 0 | 0 | 113 | 8.0 |
| 1981–82 | 20 | Edmonton Oilers | NHL | 80 | 29 | 60 | 89 | 35 | 106 | 16 | 13 | 0 | 1 | 234 | 12.4 |
| 1982–83 | 21 | Edmonton Oilers | NHL | 80 | 29 | 67 | 96 | 52 | 87 | 19 | 9 | 1 | 2 | 260 | 11.2 |
| 1983–84 | 22 | Edmonton Oilers | NHL | 80 | 40 | 86 | 126 | 52 | 104 | 25 | 14 | 1 | 4 | 259 | 15.4 |
| 1984–85 | 23 | Edmonton Oilers | NHL | 80 | 37 | 84 | 121 | 57 | 97 | 23 | 12 | 2 | 6 | 285 | 13.0 |
| 1985–86 | 24 | Edmonton Oilers | NHL | 79 | 48 | 90 | 138 | 61 | 120 | 30 | 9 | 9 | 2 | 308 | 15.6 |
| 1986–87 | 25 | Edmonton Oilers | NHL | 59 | 17 | 50 | 67 | 13 | 49 | 5 | 10 | 2 | 3 | 165 | 10.3 |
| 1987–88 | 26 | Pittsburgh Penguins | NHL | 46 | 15 | 52 | 67 | -1 | 93 | 7 | 6 | 2 | 2 | 193 | 7.8 |
| 1988–89 | 27 | Pittsburgh Penguins | NHL | 75 | 30 | 83 | 113 | -10 | 195 | 19 | 11 | 0 | 2 | 342 | 8.8 |
| 1989–90 | 28 | Pittsburgh Penguins | NHL | 80 | 29 | 74 | 103 | -25 | 95 | 19 | 10 | 0 | 3 | 324 | 9.0 |
| 1990–91 | 29 | Pittsburgh Penguins | NHL | 76 | 24 | 69 | 93 | -18 | 128 | 16 | 8 | 0 | 3 | 240 | 10.0 |
| 1991–92 | 30 | Pittsburgh Penguins | NHL | 54 | 10 | 54 | 64 | 4 | 62 | 5 | 5 | 0 | 1 | 207 | 4.8 |
| 1991–92 | 30 | Los Angeles Kings | NHL | 10 | 1 | 4 | 5 | -3 | 25 | 1 | 0 | 0 | 0 | 25 | 4.0 |
| 1992–93 | 31 | Los Angeles Kings | NHL | 50 | 8 | 49 | 57 | 9 | 50 | 6 | 2 | 0 | 0 | 182 | 4.4 |
| 1992–93 | 31 | Detroit Red Wings | NHL | 30 | 4 | 26 | 30 | 7 | 27 | 1 | 3 | 0 | 0 | 72 | 5.6 |
| 1993–94 | 32 | Detroit Red Wings | NHL | 80 | 14 | 63 | 77 | 28 | 106 | 9 | 5 | 0 | 3 | 278 | 5.0 |
| 1994–95 | 33 | Detroit Red Wings | NHL | 45 | 14 | 44 | 58 | 18 | 72 | 9 | 4 | 1 | 2 | 181 | 7.7 |
| 1995–96 | 34 | Detroit Red Wings | NHL | 76 | 14 | 60 | 74 | 19 | 90 | 10 | 3 | 1 | 3 | 234 | 6.0 |
| 1996–97 | 35 | Hartford Whalers | NHL | 20 | 3 | 5 | 8 | 0 | 18 | 2 | 1 | 0 | 1 | 39 | 7.7 |
| 1996–97 | 35 | Philadelphia Flyers | NHL | 37 | 6 | 20 | 26 | 11 | 20 | 5 | 0 | 1 | 1 | 71 | 8.5 |
| 1997–98 | 36 | Philadelphia Flyers | NHL | 57 | 2 | 27 | 29 | 3 | 30 | 1 | 1 | 0 | 1 | 107 | 1.9 |
| 1998–99 | 37 | Chicago Blackhawks | NHL | 10 | 0 | 4 | 4 | -6 | 0 | 0 | 0 | 0 | 0 | 8 | 0.0 |
| 1998–99 | 37 | Carolina Hurricanes | NHL | 44 | 2 | 8 | 10 | -1 | 28 | 1 | 1 | 0 | 0 | 79 | 2.5 |
| 1999–00 | 38 | Carolina Hurricanes | NHL | 69 | 11 | 29 | 40 | -6 | 40 | 5 | 6 | 0 | 3 | 155 | 7.1 |
| 2000–01 | 39 | Boston Bruins | NHL | 18 | 0 | 4 | 4 | -6 | 30 | 0 | 0 | 0 | 0 | 28 | 0.0 |
| NHL Career — 21 Seasons | | | | 1409 | 396 | 1135 | 1531 | 298 | 1802 | 241 | 135 | 20 | 43 | 4389 | 9.0 |

### PLAYOFFS

| SEASON | AGE | TEAM | LG | GP | G | A | PTS | +/- | PIM | ESG | PPG | SHG | GWG | SOG | S% |
|---|---|---|---|---|---|---|---|---|---|---|---|---|---|---|---|
| 1980–81 | 19 | Edmonton Oilers | NHL | 9 | 4 | 3 | 7 | 5 | 22 | 3 | 1 | 0 | 0 | 26 | 15.4 |
| 1981–82 | 20 | Edmonton Oilers | NHL | 5 | 1 | 1 | 2 | -3 | 6 | 0 | 1 | 0 | 0 | 9 | 11.1 |
| 1982–83 | 21 | Edmonton Oilers | NHL | 16 | 7 | 7 | 14 | 15 | 14 | 3 | 2 | 2 | 0 | 42 | 16.7 |
| 1983–84 | 22 | Edmonton Oilers | NHL | 19 | 8 | 14 | 22 | 18 | 21 | 6 | 2 | 0 | 1 | 66 | 12.1 |
| 1984–85 | 23 | Edmonton Oilers | NHL | 18 | 12 | 25 | 37 | 23 | 44 | 8 | 3 | 1 | 4 | 67 | 17.9 |
| 1985–86 | 24 | Edmonton Oilers | NHL | 10 | 1 | 9 | 10 | 0 | 30 | 0 | 1 | 0 | 0 | 33 | 3.0 |
| 1986–87 | 25 | Edmonton Oilers | NHL | 17 | 3 | 8 | 11 | 7 | 30 | 2 | 1 | 0 | 1 | 45 | 6.7 |
| 1988–89 | 27 | Pittsburgh Penguins | NHL | 11 | 2 | 13 | 15 | -7 | 31 | 0 | 2 | 0 | 1 | 48 | 4.2 |
| 1990–91 | 29 | Pittsburgh Penguins | NHL | 12 | 2 | 9 | 11 | -1 | 6 | 2 | 0 | 0 | 0 | 37 | 5.4 |
| 1991–92 | 30 | Los Angeles Kings | NHL | 6 | 4 | 3 | 7 | -5 | 2 | 1 | 3 | 0 | 0 | 28 | 14.3 |
| 1992–93 | 31 | Detroit Red Wings | NHL | 7 | 2 | 9 | 11 | -3 | 2 | 2 | 0 | 0 | 0 | 24 | 8.3 |
| 1993–94 | 32 | Detroit Red Wings | NHL | 7 | 1 | 6 | 7 | 6 | 8 | 1 | 0 | 0 | 0 | 23 | 4.3 |
| 1994–95 | 33 | Detroit Red Wings | NHL | 18 | 6 | 12 | 18 | 4 | 10 | 3 | 2 | 1 | 0 | 74 | 8.1 |
| 1995–96 | 34 | Detroit Red Wings | NHL | 17 | 5 | 9 | 14 | -3 | 30 | 0 | 3 | 2 | 1 | 49 | 10.2 |
| 1996–97 | 35 | Philadelphia Flyers | NHL | 17 | 1 | 8 | 9 | -3 | 6 | 1 | 0 | 0 | 0 | 37 | 2.7 |
| 1998–99 | 37 | Carolina Hurricanes | NHL | 5 | 0 | 1 | 1 | 0 | 2 | 0 | 0 | 0 | 0 | 8 | 0.0 |
| NHL Career — 16 Seasons | | | | 194 | 59 | 137 | 196 | 53 | 264 | 32 | 21 | 6 | 8 | 616 | 9.6 |

## Neil Colville  Profile: See page 233

### REGULAR SEASON

| SEASON | AGE | TEAM | LG | GP | G | A | PTS | PIM |
|---|---|---|---|---|---|---|---|---|
| 1935–36 | 21 | New York Rangers | NHL | 1 | 0 | 0 | 0 | 0 |
| 1936–37 | 22 | New York Rangers | NHL | 45 | 10 | 18 | 28 | 33 |
| 1937–38 | 23 | New York Rangers | NHL | 45 | 18 | 19 | 37 | 11 |
| 1938–39 | 24 | New York Rangers | NHL | 47 | 18 | 20 | 38 | 12 |
| 1939–40 | 25 | New York Rangers | NHL | 48 | 19 | 18 | 37 | 22 |
| 1940–41 | 26 | New York Rangers | NHL | 48 | 14 | 28 | 42 | 28 |
| 1941–42 | 27 | New York Rangers | NHL | 48 | 8 | 25 | 33 | 37 |
| 1944–45 | 30 | New York Rangers | NHL | 4 | 0 | 1 | 1 | 2 |
| 1945–46 | 31 | New York Rangers | NHL | 49 | 5 | 4 | 9 | 25 |
| 1946–47 | 32 | New York Rangers | NHL | 60 | 4 | 16 | 20 | 16 |
| 1947–48 | 33 | New York Rangers | NHL | 55 | 4 | 12 | 16 | 25 |
| 1948–49 | 34 | New York Rangers | NHL | 14 | 0 | 5 | 5 | 2 |
| NHL Career — 12 Seasons | | | | 464 | 100 | 166 | 266 | 213 |

### PLAYOFFS

| SEASON | AGE | TEAM | LG | GP | G | A | PTS | PIM |
|---|---|---|---|---|---|---|---|---|
| 1936–37 | 22 | New York Rangers | NHL | 9 | 3 | 3 | 6 | 0 |
| 1937–38 | 23 | New York Rangers | NHL | 2 | 0 | 1 | 1 | 0 |
| 1938–39 | 24 | New York Rangers | NHL | 7 | 0 | 2 | 2 | 2 |
| 1939–40 | 25 | New York Rangers | NHL | 12 | 2 | 7 | 9 | 18 |
| 1940–41 | 26 | New York Rangers | NHL | 3 | 1 | 1 | 2 | 0 |
| 1941–42 | 27 | New York Rangers | NHL | 6 | 0 | 5 | 5 | 6 |
| 1947–48 | 33 | New York Rangers | NHL | 6 | 1 | 0 | 1 | 6 |
| NHL Career — 7 Seasons | | | | 45 | 7 | 19 | 26 | 32 |

## Lionel Conacher    Profile: See page 234

### REGULAR SEASON

| SEASON | AGE | TEAM | LG | GP | G | A | PTS | PIM |
|---|---|---|---|---|---|---|---|---|
| 1925–26 | 24 | Pittsburgh Pirates | NHL | 33 | 9 | 6 | 15 | 66 |
| 1926–27 | 25 | Pittsburgh Pirates | NHL | 8 | 0 | 1 | 1 | 12 |
| 1926–27 | 25 | New York Americans | NHL | 31 | 7 | 8 | 15 | 63 |
| 1927–28 | 26 | New York Americans | NHL | 35 | 11 | 6 | 17 | 82 |
| 1928–29 | 27 | New York Americans | NHL | 44 | 5 | 2 | 7 | 136 |
| 1929–30 | 28 | New York Americans | NHL | 40 | 4 | 6 | 10 | 75 |
| 1930–31 | 29 | Montreal Maroons | NHL | 36 | 4 | 3 | 7 | 55 |
| 1931–32 | 30 | Montreal Maroons | NHL | 45 | 7 | 9 | 16 | 60 |
| 1932–33 | 31 | Montreal Maroons | NHL | 47 | 7 | 21 | 28 | 61 |
| 1933–34 | 32 | Chicago Black Hawks | NHL | 48 | 9 | 14 | 23 | 87 |
| 1934–35 | 33 | Montreal Maroons | NHL | 38 | 2 | 6 | 8 | 64 |
| 1935–36 | 34 | Montreal Maroons | NHL | 46 | 7 | 7 | 14 | 65 |
| 1936–37 | 35 | Montreal Maroons | NHL | 47 | 6 | 19 | 25 | 64 |
| NHL Career — 12 Seasons | | | | 498 | 78 | 108 | 186 | 890 |

### PLAYOFFS

| SEASON | AGE | TEAM | LG | GP | G | A | PTS | PIM |
|---|---|---|---|---|---|---|---|---|
| 1925–26 | 24 | Pittsburgh Pirates | NHL | 2 | 0 | 0 | 0 | 0 |
| 1928–29 | 27 | New York Americans | NHL | 2 | 0 | 0 | 0 | 10 |
| 1930–31 | 29 | Montreal Maroons | NHL | 2 | 0 | 0 | 0 | 2 |
| 1931–32 | 30 | Montreal Maroons | NHL | 4 | 0 | 0 | 0 | 8 |
| 1932–33 | 31 | Montreal Maroons | NHL | 2 | 0 | 1 | 1 | 0 |
| 1933–34 | 32 | Chicago Black Hawks | NHL | 8 | 2 | 0 | 2 | 4 |
| 1934–35 | 33 | Montreal Maroons | NHL | 7 | 0 | 0 | 0 | 14 |
| 1935–36 | 34 | Montreal Maroons | NHL | 3 | 0 | 0 | 0 | 0 |
| 1936–37 | 35 | Montreal Maroons | NHL | 5 | 0 | 1 | 1 | 2 |
| NHL Career — 9 Seasons | | | | 35 | 2 | 2 | 4 | 40 |

## Art Coulter    Profile: See page 236

### REGULAR SEASON

| SEASON | AGE | TEAM | LG | GP | G | A | PTS | PIM |
|---|---|---|---|---|---|---|---|---|
| 1931–32 | 22 | Chicago Black Hawks | NHL | 13 | 0 | 1 | 1 | 26 |
| 1932–33 | 23 | Chicago Black Hawks | NHL | 46 | 3 | 2 | 5 | 53 |
| 1933–34 | 24 | Chicago Black Hawks | NHL | 41 | 5 | 2 | 7 | 39 |
| 1934–35 | 25 | Chicago Black Hawks | NHL | 48 | 5 | 8 | 13 | 68 |
| 1935–36 | 26 | Chicago Black Hawks | NHL | 22 | 0 | 1 | 1 | 18 |
| 1935–36 | 26 | New York Rangers | NHL | 23 | 1 | 6 | 7 | 26 |
| 1936–37 | 27 | New York Rangers | NHL | 47 | 1 | 5 | 6 | 27 |
| 1937–38 | 28 | New York Rangers | NHL | 43 | 5 | 10 | 15 | 90 |
| 1938–39 | 29 | New York Rangers | NHL | 44 | 4 | 8 | 12 | 58 |
| 1939–40 | 30 | New York Rangers | NHL | 48 | 1 | 9 | 10 | 68 |
| 1940–41 | 31 | New York Rangers | NHL | 36 | 5 | 14 | 19 | 42 |
| 1941–42 | 32 | New York Rangers | NHL | 47 | 1 | 16 | 17 | 31 |
| NHL Career — 11 Seasons | | | | 458 | 31 | 82 | 113 | 546 |

### PLAYOFFS

| SEASON | AGE | TEAM | LG | GP | G | A | PTS | PIM |
|---|---|---|---|---|---|---|---|---|
| 1931–32 | 22 | Chicago Black Hawks | NHL | 2 | 1 | 0 | 1 | 0 |
| 1933–34 | 24 | Chicago Black Hawks | NHL | 8 | 1 | 0 | 1 | 10 |
| 1934–35 | 25 | Chicago Black Hawks | NHL | 2 | 0 | 0 | 0 | 2 |
| 1936–37 | 27 | New York Rangers | NHL | 9 | 0 | 3 | 3 | 15 |
| 1938–39 | 29 | New York Rangers | NHL | 7 | 1 | 1 | 2 | 6 |
| 1939–40 | 30 | New York Rangers | NHL | 12 | 1 | 0 | 1 | 21 |
| 1940–41 | 31 | New York Rangers | NHL | 3 | 0 | 0 | 0 | 0 |
| 1941–42 | 32 | New York Rangers | NHL | 6 | 0 | 1 | 1 | 4 |
| NHL Career — 8 Seasons | | | | 49 | 4 | 5 | 9 | 72 |

## Hap Day    Profile: See page 237

### REGULAR SEASON

| SEASON | AGE | TEAM | LG | GP | G | A | PTS | PIM |
|---|---|---|---|---|---|---|---|---|
| 1924–25 | 23 | Toronto St. Patricks | NHL | 26 | 10 | 17 | 27 | 29 |
| 1925–26 | 24 | Toronto St. Patricks | NHL | 36 | 14 | 2 | 16 | 30 |
| 1926–27 | 25 | Toronto St. Pats/ Maple Leafs | NHL | 44 | 11 | 5 | 16 | 48 |
| 1927–28 | 26 | Toronto Maple Leafs | NHL | 27 | 9 | 8 | 17 | 50 |
| 1928–29 | 27 | Toronto Maple Leafs | NHL | 44 | 6 | 6 | 12 | 85 |
| 1929–30 | 28 | Toronto Maple Leafs | NHL | 43 | 7 | 14 | 21 | 77 |
| 1930–31 | 29 | Toronto Maple Leafs | NHL | 44 | 1 | 13 | 14 | 56 |
| 1931–32 | 30 | Toronto Maple Leafs | NHL | 47 | 7 | 8 | 15 | 28 |
| 1932–33 | 31 | Toronto Maple Leafs | NHL | 47 | 6 | 14 | 20 | 46 |
| 1933–34 | 32 | Toronto Maple Leafs | NHL | 48 | 9 | 10 | 19 | 35 |
| 1934–35 | 33 | Toronto Maple Leafs | NHL | 45 | 2 | 4 | 6 | 38 |
| 1935–36 | 34 | Toronto Maple Leafs | NHL | 44 | 1 | 13 | 14 | 41 |
| 1926–37 | 35 | Toronto Maple Leafs | NHL | 48 | 3 | 4 | 7 | 20 |
| 1937–38 | 36 | New York Americans | NHL | 43 | 0 | 3 | 3 | 14 |
| NHL Career — 14 Seasons | | | | 586 | 86 | 121 | 207 | 597 |

### PLAYOFFS

| SEASON | AGE | TEAM | LG | GP | G | A | PTS | PIM |
|---|---|---|---|---|---|---|---|---|
| 1924–25 | 23 | Toronto St. Patricks | NHL | 2 | 0 | 0 | 0 | 0 |
| 1928–29 | 27 | Toronto Maple Leafs | NHL | 4 | 1 | 0 | 1 | 4 |
| 1930–31 | 29 | Toronto Maple Leafs | NHL | 2 | 0 | 3 | 3 | 7 |
| 1931–32 | 30 | Toronto Maple Leafs | NHL | 7 | 3 | 3 | 6 | 6 |
| 1932–33 | 31 | Toronto Maple Leafs | NHL | 9 | 0 | 1 | 1 | 21 |
| 1933–34 | 32 | Toronto Maple Leafs | NHL | 5 | 0 | 0 | 0 | 6 |
| 1934–35 | 33 | Toronto Maple Leafs | NHL | 7 | 0 | 0 | 0 | 4 |
| 1935–36 | 34 | Toronto Maple Leafs | NHL | 9 | 0 | 0 | 0 | 8 |
| 1936–37 | 35 | Toronto Maple Leafs | NHL | 2 | 0 | 0 | 0 | 0 |
| 1937–38 | 36 | New York Americans | NHL | 6 | 0 | 0 | 0 | 0 |
| NHL Career — 10 Seasons | | | | 53 | 4 | 7 | 11 | 56 |

## Red Dutton    Profile: See page 239

### REGULAR SEASON

| SEASON | AGE | TEAM | LG | GP | G | A | PTS | PIM |
|---|---|---|---|---|---|---|---|---|
| 1921–22 | 23 | Calgary Tigers | WCHL | 22 | 16 | 5 | 21 | 73 |
| 1922–23 | 24 | Calgary Tigers | WCHL | 18 | 2 | 4 | 6 | 24 |
| 1923–24 | 25 | Calgary Tigers | WCHL | 30 | 6 | 7 | 13 | 54 |
| 1924–25 | 26 | Calgary Tigers | WCHL | 23 | 8 | 4 | 12 | 72 |
| 1925–26 | 27 | Calgary Tigers | WHL | 30 | 10 | 5 | 15 | 87 |
| 1926–27 | 28 | Montreal Maroons | NHL | 44 | 4 | 4 | 8 | 108 |
| 1927–28 | 29 | Montreal Maroons | NHL | 42 | 7 | 6 | 13 | 97 |
| 1928–29 | 30 | Montreal Maroons | NHL | 44 | 1 | 3 | 4 | 141 |
| 1929–30 | 31 | Montreal Maroons | NHL | 43 | 3 | 13 | 16 | 102 |
| 1930–31 | 32 | New York Americans | NHL | 44 | 1 | 11 | 12 | 71 |
| 1931–32 | 33 | New York Americans | NHL | 47 | 2 | 5 | 7 | 111 |
| 1932–33 | 34 | New York Americans | NHL | 43 | 0 | 2 | 2 | 74 |
| 1933–34 | 35 | New York Americans | NHL | 48 | 2 | 9 | 11 | 65 |
| 1934–35 | 36 | New York Americans | NHL | 48 | 3 | 7 | 10 | 46 |
| 1935–36 | 37 | New York Americans | NHL | 46 | 5 | 8 | 13 | 69 |
| Career — 15 Seasons | | | | 572 | 70 | 93 | 163 | 1194 |

## Red Dutton (continued)

| PLAYOFFS | | | | | | | | | PLAYOFFS | | | | | | | | |
|---|---|---|---|---|---|---|---|---|---|---|---|---|---|---|---|---|---|
| SEASON | AGE | TEAM | LG | GP | G | A | PTS | PIM | SEASON | AGE | TEAM | LG | GP | G | A | PTS | PIM |
| 1921–22 | 23 | Calgary Tigers | WCHL | 2 | 0 | 0 | 0 | 2 | 1926–27 | 28 | Montreal Maroons | NHL | 2 | 0 | 0 | 0 | 4 |
| 1923–24 | 25 | Calgary Tigers | WCHL | 2 | 0 | 1 | 1 | 2 | 1927–28 | 29 | Montreal Maroons | NHL | 9 | 1 | 0 | 1 | 27 |
| 1923–24 | 25 | Calgary Tigers | West-P | 3 | 1 | 0 | 1 | 2 | 1929–30 | 31 | Montreal Maroons | NHL | 4 | 0 | 0 | 0 | 2 |
| 1923–24 | 25 | Calgary Tigers | St-Cup | 2 | 0 | 0 | 0 | 6 | 1935–36 | 37 | New York Americans | NHL | 3 | 0 | 0 | 0 | 0 |
| 1924–25 | 26 | Calgary Tigers | WCHL | 2 | 0 | 0 | 0 | 8 | Career—7 Seasons | | | | 29 | 2 | 1 | 3 | 53 |

# Viacheslav Fetisov   Profile: See page 240

### REGULAR SEASON

| SEASON | AGE | TEAM | LG | GP | G | A | PTS | +/- | PIM | ESG | PPG | SHG | GWG | SOG | S% |
|---|---|---|---|---|---|---|---|---|---|---|---|---|---|---|---|
| 1989–90 | 31 | New Jersey Devils | NHL | 72 | 8 | 34 | 42 | 9 | 52 | 6 | 2 | 0 | 0 | 108 | 7.4 |
| 1990–91 | 32 | New Jersey Devils | NHL | 67 | 3 | 16 | 19 | 5 | 62 | 2 | 1 | 0 | 0 | 71 | 4.2 |
| 1991–92 | 33 | New Jersey Devils | NHL | 70 | 3 | 23 | 26 | 11 | 108 | 3 | 0 | 0 | 1 | 70 | 4.3 |
| 1992–93 | 34 | New Jersey Devils | NHL | 76 | 4 | 23 | 27 | 7 | 158 | 2 | 1 | 1 | 0 | 63 | 6.3 |
| 1993–94 | 35 | New Jersey Devils | NHL | 52 | 1 | 14 | 15 | 14 | 30 | 1 | 0 | 0 | 0 | 36 | 2.8 |
| 1994–95 | 36 | New Jersey Devils | NHL | 4 | 0 | 1 | 1 | -2 | 0 | 0 | 0 | 0 | 0 | 1 | 0.0 |
| 1994–95 | 36 | Detroit Red Wings | NHL | 14 | 3 | 11 | 14 | 3 | 2 | 0 | 3 | 0 | 0 | 36 | 8.3 |
| 1995–96 | 37 | Detroit Red Wings | NHL | 69 | 7 | 35 | 42 | 37 | 96 | 5 | 1 | 1 | 1 | 127 | 5.5 |
| 1996–97 | 38 | Detroit Red Wings | NHL | 64 | 5 | 23 | 28 | 26 | 76 | 5 | 0 | 0 | 1 | 95 | 5.3 |
| 1997–98 | 39 | Detroit Red Wings | NHL | 58 | 2 | 12 | 14 | 4 | 72 | 2 | 0 | 0 | 1 | 55 | 3.6 |
| NHL Career—9 Seasons | | | | 546 | 36 | 192 | 228 | 114 | 656 | 26 | 8 | 2 | 4 | 662 | 5.4 |

### PLAYOFFS

| SEASON | AGE | TEAM | LG | GP | G | A | PTS | +/- | PIM | ESG | PPG | SHG | GWG | SOG | S% |
|---|---|---|---|---|---|---|---|---|---|---|---|---|---|---|---|
| 1989–90 | 31 | New Jersey Devils | NHL | 6 | 0 | 2 | 2 | -5 | 10 | 0 | 0 | 0 | 0 | 11 | 0.0 |
| 1990–91 | 32 | New Jersey Devils | NHL | 7 | 0 | 0 | 0 | -3 | 17 | 0 | 0 | 0 | 0 | 7 | 0.0 |
| 1991–92 | 33 | New Jersey Devils | NHL | 6 | 0 | 3 | 3 | 5 | 8 | 0 | 0 | 0 | 0 | 3 | 0.0 |
| 1992–93 | 34 | New Jersey Devils | NHL | 5 | 0 | 2 | 2 | -3 | 4 | 0 | 0 | 0 | 0 | 2 | 0.0 |
| 1993–94 | 35 | New Jersey Devils | NHL | 14 | 1 | 0 | 1 | -1 | 8 | 1 | 0 | 0 | 0 | 14 | 7.1 |
| 1994–95 | 36 | Detroit Red Wings | NHL | 18 | 0 | 8 | 8 | 1 | 14 | 0 | 0 | 0 | 0 | 31 | 0.0 |
| 1995–96 | 37 | Detroit Red Wings | NHL | 19 | 1 | 4 | 5 | 3 | 34 | 1 | 0 | 0 | 1 | 24 | 4.2 |
| 1996–97 | 38 | Detroit Red Wings | NHL | 20 | 0 | 4 | 4 | 2 | 42 | 0 | 0 | 0 | 0 | 27 | 0.0 |
| 1997–98 | 39 | Detroit Red Wings | NHL | 21 | 0 | 3 | 3 | 4 | 10 | 0 | 0 | 0 | 0 | 14 | 0.0 |
| NHL Career—9 Seasons | | | | 116 | 2 | 26 | 28 | 3 | 147 | 2 | 0 | 0 | 1 | 133 | 1.5 |

# Fernie Flaman   Profile: See page 242

### REGULAR SEASON

| SEASON | AGE | TEAM | LG | GP | G | A | PTS | PIM |
|---|---|---|---|---|---|---|---|---|
| 1944–45 | 18 | Boston Bruins | NHL | 1 | 0 | 0 | 0 | 0 |
| 1945–46 | 19 | Boston Bruins | NHL | 1 | 0 | 0 | 0 | 0 |
| 1946–47 | 20 | Boston Bruins | NHL | 24 | 1 | 4 | 5 | 41 |
| 1947–48 | 21 | Boston Bruins | NHL | 56 | 4 | 6 | 10 | 69 |
| 1948–49 | 22 | Boston Bruins | NHL | 60 | 4 | 12 | 16 | 62 |
| 1949–50 | 23 | Boston Bruins | NHL | 69 | 2 | 5 | 7 | 122 |
| 1950–51 | 23 | Boston Bruins | NHL | 14 | 1 | 1 | 2 | 37 |
| 1950–51 | 24 | Toronto Maple Leafs | NHL | 39 | 2 | 6 | 8 | 64 |
| 1951–52 | 25 | Toronto Maple Leafs | NHL | 61 | 0 | 7 | 7 | 110 |
| 1952–53 | 26 | Toronto Maple Leafs | NHL | 66 | 2 | 6 | 8 | 110 |
| 1953–54 | 27 | Toronto Maple Leafs | NHL | 62 | 0 | 8 | 8 | 84 |
| 1954–55 | 28 | Boston Bruins | NHL | 70 | 4 | 14 | 18 | 150 |
| 1955–56 | 29 | Boston Bruins | NHL | 62 | 4 | 17 | 21 | 70 |
| 1956–57 | 30 | Boston Bruins | NHL | 68 | 6 | 25 | 31 | 108 |
| 1957–58 | 31 | Boston Bruins | NHL | 66 | 0 | 15 | 15 | 73 |
| 1958–59 | 32 | Boston Bruins | NHL | 70 | 0 | 21 | 21 | 101 |

| SEASON | AGE | TEAM | LG | GP | G | A | PTS | PIM |
|---|---|---|---|---|---|---|---|---|
| 1959–60 | 33 | Boston Bruins | NHL | 60 | 2 | 18 | 20 | 112 |
| 1960–61 | 34 | Boston Bruins | NHL | 62 | 2 | 9 | 11 | 59 |
| NHL Career—17 Seasons | | | | 911 | 34 | 174 | 208 | 1372 |

### PLAYOFFS

| SEASON | AGE | TEAM | LG | GP | G | A | PTS | PIM |
|---|---|---|---|---|---|---|---|---|
| 1946–47 | 20 | Boston Bruins | NHL | 5 | 0 | 0 | 0 | 8 |
| 1947–48 | 21 | Boston Bruins | NHL | 5 | 0 | 0 | 0 | 12 |
| 1948–49 | 22 | Boston Bruins | NHL | 5 | 0 | 1 | 1 | 8 |
| 1950–51 | 24 | Toronto Maple Leafs | NHL | 9 | 1 | 0 | 1 | 8 |
| 1951–52 | 25 | Toronto Maple Leafs | NHL | 4 | 0 | 2 | 2 | 18 |
| 1953–54 | 27 | Toronto Maple Leafs | NHL | 2 | 0 | 0 | 0 | 0 |
| 1954–55 | 28 | Boston Bruins | NHL | 4 | 1 | 0 | 1 | 2 |
| 1956–57 | 30 | Boston Bruins | NHL | 10 | 0 | 3 | 3 | 19 |
| 1957–58 | 31 | Boston Bruins | NHL | 12 | 2 | 2 | 4 | 10 |
| 1958–59 | 32 | Boston Bruins | NHL | 7 | 0 | 0 | 0 | 8 |
| NHL Career—10 Seasons | | | | 63 | 4 | 8 | 12 | 93 |

# Bill Gadsby   Profile: See page 243

### REGULAR SEASON

| SEASON | AGE | TEAM | LG | GP | G | A | PTS | PIM | ESG | PPG | SHG | GWG |
|---|---|---|---|---|---|---|---|---|---|---|---|---|
| 1946–47 | 19 | Chicago Black Hawks | NHL | 48 | 8 | 10 | 18 | 31 | 6 | 2 | 0 | 2 |
| 1947–48 | 20 | Chicago Black Hawks | NHL | 60 | 6 | 10 | 16 | 66 | 4 | 2 | 0 | 1 |
| 1948–49 | 21 | Chicago Black Hawks | NHL | 50 | 3 | 10 | 13 | 85 | 3 | 0 | 0 | 0 |
| 1949–50 | 22 | Chicago Black Hawks | NHL | 70 | 10 | 25 | 35 | 138 | 9 | 1 | 0 | 1 |
| 1950–51 | 23 | Chicago Black Hawks | NHL | 25 | 3 | 7 | 10 | 32 | 2 | 1 | 0 | 0 |
| 1951–52 | 24 | Chicago Black Hawks | NHL | 59 | 7 | 15 | 22 | 87 | 6 | 1 | 0 | 1 |
| 1952–53 | 25 | Chicago Black Hawks | NHL | 68 | 2 | 20 | 22 | 84 | 2 | 0 | 0 | 1 |
| 1953–54 | 26 | Chicago Black Hawks | NHL | 70 | 12 | 29 | 41 | 108 | 7 | 4 | 1 | 1 |
| 1954–55 | 27 | Chicago Black Hawks | NHL | 18 | 3 | 6 | 9 | 19 | 3 | 0 | 1 | 1 |
| 1954–55 | 27 | New York Rangers | NHL | 52 | 8 | 7 | 15 | 42 | 2 | 8 | 0 | 1 |
| 1955–56 | 28 | New York Rangers | NHL | 70 | 9 | 42 | 51 | 84 | 3 | 6 | 0 | 2 |

## Bill Gadsby (continued)

### REGULAR SEASON

| SEASON | AGE | TEAM | LG | GP | G | A | PTS | PIM | ESG | PPG | SHG | GWG |
|--------|-----|------|-----|----|----|----|-----|-----|-----|-----|-----|-----|
| 1956–57 | 29 | New York Rangers | NHL | 70 | 4 | 37 | 41 | 72 | 3 | 0 | 1 | 0 |
| 1957–58 | 30 | New York Rangers | NHL | 65 | 14 | 32 | 46 | 48 | 5 | 8 | 1 | 1 |
| 1958–59 | 31 | New York Rangers | NHL | 70 | 5 | 46 | 51 | 56 | 3 | 1 | 1 | 0 |
| 1959–60 | 32 | New York Rangers | NHL | 65 | 9 | 22 | 31 | 60 | 3 | 6 | 0 | 0 |
| 1960–61 | 33 | New York Rangers | NHL | 65 | 9 | 26 | 35 | 49 | 8 | 1 | 0 | 1 |
| 1961–62 | 34 | Detroit Red Wings | NHL | 70 | 7 | 30 | 37 | 88 | 7 | 0 | 0 | 0 |
| 1962–63 | 35 | Detroit Red Wings | NHL | 70 | 4 | 24 | 28 | 116 | 3 | 0 | 1 | 1 |
| 1963–64 | 36 | Detroit Red Wings | NHL | 64 | 2 | 16 | 18 | 80 | 2 | 0 | 0 | 0 |
| 1964–65 | 37 | Detroit Red Wings | NHL | 61 | 0 | 12 | 12 | 122 | 0 | 0 | 0 | 0 |
| 1965–66 | 38 | Detroit Red Wings | NHL | 58 | 5 | 12 | 17 | 72 | 5 | 0 | 0 | 0 |
| NHL Career — 20 Seasons | | | | 1248 | 130 | 438 | 568 | 1539 | 92 | 6 | 32 | 14 |

### PLAYOFFS

| SEASON | AGE | TEAM | LG | GP | G | A | PTS | PIM | ESG | PPG | SHG | GWG |
|--------|-----|------|-----|----|----|----|-----|-----|-----|-----|-----|-----|
| 1952–53 | 25 | Chicago Black Hawks | NHL | 7 | 0 | 1 | 1 | 4 | 0 | 0 | 0 | 0 |
| 1955–56 | 28 | New York Rangers | NHL | 5 | 1 | 3 | 4 | 4 | 0 | 1 | 0 | 0 |
| 1956–57 | 29 | New York Rangers | NHL | 5 | 1 | 2 | 3 | 2 | 0 | 1 | 0 | 0 |
| 1957–58 | 30 | New York Rangers | NHL | 6 | 0 | 3 | 3 | 4 | 0 | 0 | 0 | 0 |
| 1962–63 | 35 | Detroit Red Wings | NHL | 11 | 1 | 4 | 5 | 36 | 1 | 0 | 0 | 0 |
| 1963–64 | 36 | Detroit Red Wings | NHL | 14 | 0 | 4 | 4 | 22 | 0 | 0 | 0 | 0 |
| 1964–65 | 37 | Detroit Red Wings | NHL | 7 | 0 | 3 | 3 | 8 | 0 | 0 | 0 | 0 |
| 1965–66 | 38 | Detroit Red Wings | NHL | 12 | 1 | 3 | 4 | 12 | 1 | 0 | 0 | 0 |
| NHL Career — 8 Seasons | | | | 67 | 4 | 23 | 27 | 92 | 2 | 2 | 0 | 0 |

## Herb Gardiner   Profile: See page 244

Profile: See page 244

### REGULAR SEASON

| SEASON | AGE | TEAM | LG | GP | G | A | PTS | PIM |
|--------|-----|------|-----|----|----|----|-----|-----|
| 1921–22 | 30 | Calgary Tigers | WCHL | 24 | 4 | 1 | 5 | 6 |
| 1922–23 | 31 | Calgary Tigers | WCHL | 29 | 9 | 3 | 12 | 9 |
| 1923–24 | 32 | Calgary Tigers | WCHL | 22 | 5 | 5 | 10 | 4 |
| 1924–25 | 33 | Calgary Tigers | WCHL | 28 | 12 | 8 | 20 | 18 |
| 1925–26 | 34 | Calgary Tigers | WHL | 27 | 3 | 1 | 4 | 10 |
| 1926–27 | 35 | Montreal Canadiens | NHL | 44 | 6 | 7 | 13 | 26 |
| 1927–28 | 36 | Montreal Canadiens | NHL | 44 | 4 | 3 | 7 | 22 |
| 1928–29 | 37 | Chicago Black Hawks | NHL | 4 | 0 | 0 | 0 | 0 |
| 1928–29 | 37 | Montreal Canadiens | NHL | 8 | 0 | 0 | 0 | 0 |
| Career — 8 Seasons | | | | 230 | 43 | 28 | 71 | 95 |

### PLAYOFFS

| SEASON | AGE | TEAM | LG | GP | G | A | PTS | PIM |
|--------|-----|------|-----|----|----|----|-----|-----|
| 1921–22 | 30 | Calgary Tigers | WCHL | 2 | 0 | 0 | 0 | 0 |
| 1923–24 | 32 | Calgary Tigers | WCHL | 2 | 1 | 0 | 1 | 0 |
| 1923–24 | 32 | Calgary Tigers | West-P | 3 | 1 | 1 | 2 | 0 |
| 1923–24 | 32 | Calgary Tigers | St-Cup | 2 | 1 | 0 | 1 | 0 |
| 1924–25 | 33 | Calgary Tigers | WCHL | 2 | 0 | 0 | 0 | 0 |
| 1926–27 | 35 | Montreal Canadiens | NHL | 4 | 0 | 0 | 0 | 10 |
| 1927–28 | 36 | Montreal Canadiens | NHL | 2 | 0 | 1 | 1 | 4 |
| 1928–29 | 37 | Montreal Canadiens | NHL | 3 | 0 | 0 | 0 | 2 |
| Career — 6 Seasons | | | | 20 | 3 | 2 | 5 | 16 |

## Eddie Gerard   Profile: See page 245

Profile: See page 245

### REGULAR SEASON

| SEASON | AGE | TEAM | LG | GP | G | A | PTS | PIM |
|--------|-----|------|-----|----|----|----|-----|-----|
| 1913–14 | 23 | Ottawa Senators | NHA | 11 | 6 | 7 | 13 | 34 |
| 1914–15 | 24 | Ottawa Senators | NHA | 20 | 9 | 10 | 19 | 39 |
| 1915–16 | 25 | Ottawa Senators | NHA | 24 | 13 | 5 | 18 | 57 |
| 1916–17 | 26 | Ottawa Senators | NHA | 19 | 18 | 16 | 34 | 48 |
| 1917–18 | 27 | Ottawa Senators | NHL | 20 | 13 | 8 | 21 | 26 |
| 1918–19 | 28 | Ottawa Senators | NHL | 18 | 4 | 9 | 13 | 17 |
| 1919–20 | 29 | Ottawa Senators | NHL | 22 | 9 | 8 | 17 | 19 |
| 1920–21 | 30 | Ottawa Senators | NHL | 24 | 11 | 4 | 15 | 18 |
| 1921–22 | 31 | Ottawa Senators | NHL | 21 | 7 | 11 | 18 | 16 |
| 1922–23 | 32 | Ottawa Senators | NHL | 23 | 6 | 11 | 17 | 30 |
| Career — 10 Seasons | | | | 202 | 96 | 89 | 182 | 304 |

### PLAYOFFS

| SEASON | AGE | TEAM | LG | GP | G | A | PTS | PIM |
|--------|-----|------|-----|----|----|----|-----|-----|
| 1914–15 | 24 | Ottawa Senators | NHA | 5 | 1 | 0 | 1 | 6 |
| 1916–17 | 26 | Ottawa Senators | NHA | 2 | 1 | 2 | 3 | 6 |
| 1918–19 | 28 | Ottawa Senators | NHL | 5 | 3 | 0 | 3 | 3 |
| 1919–20 | 29 | Ottawa Senators | St-Cup | 5 | 2 | 1 | 3 | 2 |
| 1920–21 | 30 | Ottawa Senators | NHL | 2 | 1 | 0 | 1 | 6 |
| 1920–21 | 30 | Ottawa Senators | St-Cup | 5 | 0 | 0 | 0 | 36 |
| 1921–22 | 31 | Ottawa Senators | NHL | 2 | 0 | 0 | 0 | 8 |
| 1921–22 | 31 | Toronto St. Patricks | St-Cup | 1 | 0 | 0 | 0 | 0 |
| 1922–23 | 32 | Ottawa Senators | NHL | 2 | 1 | 0 | 1 | 4 |
| 1922–23 | 32 | Ottawa Senators | St-Cup | 6 | 1 | 0 | 1 | 0 |
| Career — 7 Seasons | | | | 35 | 9 | 3 | 12 | 71 |

## Ebbie Goodfellow   Profile: See page 246

Profile: See page 246

### REGULAR SEASON

| SEASON | AGE | TEAM | LG | GP | G | A | PTS | PIM |
|--------|-----|------|-----|----|----|----|-----|-----|
| 1929–30 | 22 | Detroit Cougars | NHL | 44 | 17 | 17 | 34 | 54 |
| 1930–31 | 23 | Detroit Falcons | NHL | 44 | 25 | 23 | 48 | 32 |
| 1931–32 | 24 | Detroit Falcons | NHL | 48 | 14 | 16 | 30 | 56 |
| 1932–33 | 25 | Detroit Red Wings | NHL | 41 | 12 | 8 | 20 | 47 |
| 1933–34 | 26 | Detroit Red Wings | NHL | 48 | 13 | 13 | 26 | 45 |
| 1934–35 | 27 | Detroit Red Wings | NHL | 48 | 13 | 24 | 37 | 44 |
| 1935–36 | 28 | Detroit Red Wings | NHL | 48 | 5 | 18 | 23 | 69 |
| 1936–37 | 29 | Detroit Red Wings | NHL | 48 | 9 | 16 | 25 | 43 |

### REGULAR SEASON

| SEASON | AGE | TEAM | LG | GP | G | A | PTS | PIM |
|--------|-----|------|-----|----|----|----|-----|-----|
| 1937–38 | 30 | Detroit Red Wings | NHL | 30 | 0 | 7 | 7 | 13 |
| 1938–39 | 31 | Detroit Red Wings | NHL | 48 | 8 | 8 | 16 | 36 |
| 1939–40 | 32 | Detroit Red Wings | NHL | 43 | 11 | 18 | 29 | 31 |
| 1940–41 | 33 | Detroit Red Wings | NHL | 47 | 5 | 18 | 22 | 35 |
| 1941–42 | 34 | Detroit Red Wings | NHL | 9 | 2 | 2 | 4 | 2 |
| 1942–43 | 35 | Detroit Red Wings | NHL | 11 | 1 | 4 | 5 | 4 |
| NHL Career — 14 Seasons | | | | 557 | 135 | 191 | 326 | 511 |

### Ebbie Goodfellow (continued)

| PLAYOFFS | | | | | | | | |
|---|---|---|---|---|---|---|---|---|
| SEASON | AGE | TEAM | LG | GP | G | A | PTS | PIM |
| 1931–32 | 24 | Detroit Falcons | NHL | 2 | 0 | 0 | 0 | 0 |
| 1932–33 | 25 | Detroit Red Wings | NHL | 4 | 1 | 0 | 1 | 11 |
| 1933–34 | 26 | Detroit Red Wings | NHL | 9 | 4 | 3 | 7 | 12 |
| 1935–36 | 28 | Detroit Red Wings | NHL | 7 | 1 | 0 | 1 | 4 |
| 1936–37 | 29 | Detroit Red Wings | NHL | 9 | 2 | 2 | 4 | 14 |

| PLAYOFFS | | | | | | | | |
|---|---|---|---|---|---|---|---|---|
| SEASON | AGE | TEAM | LG | GP | G | A | PTS | PIM |
| 1938–39 | 31 | Detroit Red Wings | NHL | 6 | 0 | 0 | 0 | 8 |
| 1939–40 | 32 | Detroit Red Wings | NHL | 5 | 0 | 2 | 2 | 9 |
| 1940–41 | 33 | Detroit Red Wings | NHL | 3 | 0 | 1 | 1 | 9 |
| NHL Career — 9 Seasons | | | | 45 | 8 | 8 | 16 | 67 |

## Mike Grant  Profile: See page 247

| REGULAR SEASON | | | | | | | |
|---|---|---|---|---|---|---|---|
| SEASON | AGE | TEAM | LG | GP | G | A | PTS |
| 1893–94 | 20 | Montreal Maples | MCJHL | | | | |
| 1893–94 | 20 | Montreal Victorias | AHAC | 5 | 0 | 0 | 0 |
| 1894–95 | 21 | Montreal Victorias | AHAC | 8 | 1 | 0 | 1 |
| 1895–96 | 22 | Montreal Victorias | AHAC | 8 | 3 | 0 | 3 |
| 1896–97 | 23 | Montreal Victorias | AHAC | 8 | 3 | 0 | 3 |
| 1897–98 | 24 | Montreal Victorias | AHAC | 8 | 1 | 0 | 1 |
| 1898–99 | 25 | Montreal Victorias | CAHL | 7 | 2 | 0 | 2 |
| 1899–00 | 26 | Montreal Victorias | CAHL | 2 | 0 | 0 | 0 |
| 1900–01 | 27 | Montreal Shamrocks | CAHL | 2 | 0 | 0 | 0 |
| 1901–02 | 28 | Montreal Victorias | CAHL | 7 | 0 | 0 | 0 |
| Career — 9 Seasons | | | | 55 | 10 | 0 | 10 |

| PLAYOFFS | | | | | | | |
|---|---|---|---|---|---|---|---|
| SEASON | AGE | TEAM | LG | GP | G | A | PTS |
| 1893–94 | 20 | Montreal Victorias | AHAC | 1 | 0 | 0 | 0 |
| 1895–96 | 22 | Montreal Victorias | St-Cup | 2 | 0 | 0 | 0 |
| 1896–97 | 23 | Montreal Victorias | St-Cup | 1 | 0 | 0 | 0 |
| 1898–99 | 25 | Montreal Victorias | St-Cup | 2 | 0 | 0 | 0 |
| 1900–01 | 27 | Montreal Shamrocks | St-Cup | 2 | 0 | 0 | 0 |
| Career — 5 Seasons | | | | 8 | 0 | 0 | 0 |

## Si Griffis  Profile: See page 248

| REGULAR SEASON | | | | | | | | |
|---|---|---|---|---|---|---|---|---|
| SEASON | AGE | TEAM | LG | GP | G | A | PTS | PIM |
| 1902–03 | 19 | Rat Portage Thistles | MNWHA | 5 | 5 | 0 | 5 | |
| 1903–04 | 20 | Rat Portage Thistles | MNWHA | 12 | 12 | 2 | 14 | |
| 1904–05 | 21 | Rat Portage Thistles | MHL | 8 | 15 | 0 | 15 | 3 |
| 1905–06 | 22 | Kenora Thistles | MHL | 9 | 9 | 0 | 9 | |
| 1906–07 | 23 | Kenora Thistles | MHL-Pro | 6 | 5 | 0 | 5 | |
| 1911–12 | 28 | Vancouver Millionaires | PCHA | 15 | 8 | 0 | 8 | 18 |
| 1912–13 | 29 | Vancouver Millionaires | PCHA | 14 | 10 | 3 | 13 | 30 |
| 1913–14 | 30 | Vancouver Millionaires | PCHA | 13 | 2 | 3 | 5 | 21 |
| 1914–15 | 31 | Vancouver Millionaires | PCHA | 17 | 2 | 3 | 5 | 32 |
| 1915–16 | 32 | Vancouver Millionaires | PCHA | 18 | 7 | 5 | 12 | 12 |
| 1916–17 | 33 | Vancouver Millionaires | PCHA | 23 | 7 | 4 | 11 | 34 |

| REGULAR SEASON | | | | | | | | |
|---|---|---|---|---|---|---|---|---|
| SEASON | AGE | TEAM | LG | GP | G | A | PTS | PIM |
| 1917–18 | 34 | Vancouver Millionaires | PCHA | 8 | 2 | 6 | 8 | 0 |
| 1918–19 | 35 | Vancouver Millionaires | PCHA | 2 | 0 | 2 | 2 | 0 |
| Career — 13 Seasons | | | | 150 | 84 | 28 | 112 | 150 |

| PLAYOFFS | | | | | | | | |
|---|---|---|---|---|---|---|---|---|
| SEASON | AGE | TEAM | LG | GP | G | A | PTS | PIM |
| 1902–03 | 19 | Rat Portage Thistles | St-Cup | 2 | 0 | 0 | 0 | |
| 1904–05 | 21 | Rat Portage Thistles | St-Cup | 3 | 3 | 0 | 3 | 3 |
| 1906–07 | 23 | Kenora Thistles | St-Cup | 4 | 1 | 0 | 1 | 6 |
| 1917–18 | 34 | Vancouver Millionaires | PCHA | 2 | 0 | 0 | 0 | 0 |
| 1918–19 | 35 | Vancouver Millionaires | St-Cup | 5 | 1 | 0 | 1 | 9 |
| 1918–19 | 35 | Vancouver Millionaires | PCHA | 2 | 1 | 1 | 2 | 0 |
| Career — 5 Seasons | | | | 18 | 6 | 1 | 7 | 18 |

## Joe Hall  Profile: See page 249

| REGULAR SEASON | | | | | | | | |
|---|---|---|---|---|---|---|---|---|
| SEASON | AGE | TEAM | LG | GP | G | A | PTS | PIM |
| 1902–03 | 20 | Brandon Elks | MNWHA | 6 | 8 | 0 | 8 | |
| 1903–04 | 21 | Winnipeg Rowing Club | WCAHA | 6 | 6 | 3 | 9 | 10 |
| 1904–05 | 22 | Brandon Elks | MHL | 8 | 11 | 0 | 11 | |
| 1905–06 | 23 | Portage Lakes | IHL | 20 | 33 | 0 | 33 | 98 |
| 1906–07 | 24 | Brandon Elks | MHL-Pro | 9 | 14 | 0 | 14 | 32 |
| 1907–08 | 25 | Montreal AAA | ECAHA | 4 | 5 | 0 | 5 | 11 |
| 1907–08 | 25 | Montreal Shamrocks | ECAHA | 4 | 4 | 0 | 4 | 6 |
| 1908–09 | 26 | Edmonton Professionals | APHL | 1 | 8 | 0 | 8 | 6 |
| 1908–09 | 26 | Montreal Wanderers | ECHA | 5 | 10 | 0 | 10 | 18 |
| 1908–09 | 26 | Winnipeg Maple Leafs | MHL-Pro | 2 | 2 | 1 | 3 | 0 |
| 1909–10 | 27 | Montreal Shamrocks | CHA | 1 | 7 | 0 | 7 | 6 |
| 1909–10 | 27 | Montreal Shamrocks | NHA | 10 | 8 | 0 | 8 | 47 |
| 1910–11 | 28 | Quebec Bulldogs | NHA | 10 | 0 | 1 | 1 | 24 |
| 1911–12 | 29 | Quebec Bulldogs | NHA | 18 | 15 | 1 | 16 | 43 |
| 1912–13 | 30 | Quebec Bulldogs | NHA | 18 | 6 | 2 | 8 | 78 |
| 1913–14 | 31 | Quebec Bulldogs | NHA | 19 | 13 | 4 | 17 | 61 |
| 1914–15 | 32 | Quebec Bulldogs | NHA | 20 | 3 | 2 | 5 | 52 |
| 1915–16 | 33 | Quebec Bulldogs | NHA | 23 | 1 | 2 | 3 | 89 |
| 1916–17 | 34 | Quebec Bulldogs | NHA | 19 | 6 | 5 | 11 | 95 |
| 1917–18 | 35 | Montreal Canadiens | NHL | 21 | 8 | 7 | 15 | 100 |
| 1918–19 | 36 | Montreal Canadiens | NHL | 16 | 7 | 2 | 9 | 130 |
| Career — 17 Seasons | | | | 240 | 175 | 30 | 205 | 906 |

## Joe Hall (continued)

**PLAYOFFS**

| SEASON | AGE | TEAM | LG | GP | G | A | PTS | PIM |
|---|---|---|---|---|---|---|---|---|
| 1903–04 | 21 | Winnipeg Rowing Club | St-Cup | 3 | 1 | 0 | 1 | |
| 1906–07 | 24 | Brandon Elks | MHL-Pro | 2 | 5 | 0 | 5 | 5 |
| 1908–09 | 26 | Winnipeg Maple Leafs | MHL-Pro | 2 | 2 | 1 | 3 | 9 |
| 1911–12 | 29 | Quebec Bulldogs | NHA | 2 | 2 | 0 | 2 | 0 |
| 1911–12 | 29 | Quebec Bulldogs | St-Cup | 2 | 2 | 0 | 2 | 2 |
| 1912–13 | 30 | Quebec Bulldogs | NHA | 2 | 3 | 0 | 3 | 0 |
| 1912–13 | 30 | Quebec Bulldogs | St-Cup | 2 | 3 | 0 | 3 | 0 |
| 1917–18 | 35 | Montreal Canadiens | NHL | 2 | 0 | 1 | 1 | 12 |
| 1918–19 | 36 | Montreal Canadiens | St-Cup | 5 | 0 | 0 | 0 | 6 |
| 1918–19 | 36 | Montreal Canadiens | NHL | 5 | 0 | 0 | 0 | 26 |
| Career — 7 Seasons | | | | 27 | 18 | 2 | 20 | 60 |

# Doug Harvey  Profile: See page 250

**REGULAR SEASON**

| SEASON | AGE | TEAM | LG | GP | G | A | PTS | +/- | PIM | ESG | PPG | SHG | GWG | SOG | S% |
|---|---|---|---|---|---|---|---|---|---|---|---|---|---|---|---|
| 1947–48 | 23 | Montreal Canadiens | NHL | 35 | 4 | 4 | 8 | | 32 | 2 | 0 | 2 | 0 | | |
| 1948–49 | 24 | Montreal Canadiens | NHL | 55 | 3 | 13 | 16 | | 87 | 2 | 0 | 1 | 0 | | |
| 1949–50 | 25 | Montreal Canadiens | NHL | 70 | 4 | 20 | 24 | | 76 | 2 | 2 | 0 | 0 | | |
| 1950–51 | 26 | Montreal Canadiens | NHL | 70 | 5 | 24 | 29 | | 91 | 4 | 1 | 0 | 0 | | |
| 1951–52 | 27 | Montreal Canadiens | NHL | 68 | 6 | 23 | 29 | | 82 | 6 | 0 | 0 | 1 | | |
| 1952–53 | 28 | Montreal Canadiens | NHL | 69 | 4 | 30 | 34 | | 67 | 2 | 2 | 0 | 0 | | |
| 1953–54 | 29 | Montreal Canadiens | NHL | 68 | 8 | 29 | 37 | | 110 | 6 | 2 | 0 | 2 | | |
| 1954–55 | 30 | Montreal Canadiens | NHL | 70 | 6 | 43 | 49 | | 58 | 3 | 3 | 0 | 1 | | |
| 1955–56 | 31 | Montreal Canadiens | NHL | 62 | 5 | 39 | 44 | | 60 | 3 | 2 | 0 | 1 | | |
| 1956–57 | 32 | Montreal Canadiens | NHL | 70 | 6 | 44 | 50 | | 100 | 4 | 2 | 0 | 2 | | |
| 1957–58 | 33 | Montreal Canadiens | NHL | 68 | 9 | 32 | 41 | | 131 | 5 | 4 | 0 | 5 | | |
| 1958–59 | 34 | Montreal Canadiens | NHL | 61 | 4 | 16 | 20 | | 64 | 3 | 1 | 0 | 1 | | |
| 1959–60 | 35 | Montreal Canadiens | NHL | 66 | 6 | 21 | 27 | 37 | 45 | 4 | 2 | 0 | 0 | 87 | 6.9 |
| 1960–61 | 36 | Montreal Canadiens | NHL | 58 | 6 | 33 | 39 | 16 | 48 | 5 | 1 | 0 | 0 | 63 | 9.5 |
| 1961–62 | 37 | New York Rangers | NHL | 69 | 6 | 24 | 30 | -9 | 42 | 2 | 3 | 1 | 3 | 77 | 7.8 |
| 1962–63 | 38 | New York Rangers | NHL | 68 | 4 | 35 | 39 | -1 | 92 | 3 | 0 | 1 | 1 | 65 | 6.2 |
| 1963–64 | 39 | New York Rangers | NHL | 14 | 0 | 2 | 2 | -7 | 10 | 0 | 0 | 0 | 0 | 12 | 0.0 |
| 1966–67 | 42 | Detroit Red Wings | NHL | 2 | 0 | 0 | 0 | -1 | 0 | 0 | 0 | 0 | 0 | 0 | |
| 1968–69 | 44 | St. Louis Blues | NHL | 70 | 2 | 20 | 22 | 11 | 30 | 1 | 1 | 0 | 0 | 46 | 4.4 |
| NHL Career — 19 Seasons | | | | 1113 | 88 | 452 | 540 | 46 | 1225 | 57 | 26 | 5 | 17 | 350 | 6.9 |

**PLAYOFFS**

| SEASON | AGE | TEAM | LG | GP | G | A | PTS | +/- | PIM | ESG | PPG | SHG | GWG | SOG | S% |
|---|---|---|---|---|---|---|---|---|---|---|---|---|---|---|---|
| 1948–49 | 24 | Montreal Canadiens | NHL | 7 | 0 | 1 | 1 | | 10 | 0 | 0 | 0 | 0 | | |
| 1949–50 | 25 | Montreal Canadiens | NHL | 5 | 0 | 2 | 2 | | 10 | 0 | 0 | 0 | 0 | | |
| 1950–51 | 26 | Montreal Canadiens | NHL | 11 | 0 | 5 | 5 | | 12 | 0 | 0 | 0 | 0 | | |
| 1951–52 | 27 | Montreal Canadiens | NHL | 11 | 0 | 3 | 3 | | 8 | 0 | 0 | 0 | 0 | | |
| 1952–53 | 28 | Montreal Canadiens | NHL | 12 | 0 | 5 | 5 | | 8 | 0 | 0 | 0 | 0 | | |
| 1953–54 | 29 | Montreal Canadiens | NHL | 10 | 0 | 2 | 2 | | 12 | 0 | 0 | 0 | 0 | | |
| 1954–55 | 30 | Montreal Canadiens | NHL | 12 | 0 | 8 | 8 | | 6 | 0 | 0 | 0 | 0 | | |
| 1955–56 | 31 | Montreal Canadiens | NHL | 10 | 2 | 5 | 7 | | 10 | 0 | 2 | 0 | 1 | | |
| 1956–57 | 32 | Montreal Canadiens | NHL | 10 | 0 | 7 | 7 | | 10 | 0 | 0 | 0 | 0 | | |
| 1957–58 | 33 | Montreal Canadiens | NHL | 10 | 2 | 9 | 11 | | 16 | 2 | 0 | 0 | 0 | | |
| 1958–59 | 34 | Montreal Canadiens | NHL | 11 | 1 | 11 | 12 | | 22 | 1 | 0 | 0 | 0 | | |
| 1959–60 | 35 | Montreal Canadiens | NHL | 8 | 3 | 0 | 3 | 13 | 6 | 3 | 0 | 0 | 1 | 10 | 30.0 |
| 1960–61 | 36 | Montreal Canadiens | NHL | 6 | 0 | 1 | 1 | -3 | 8 | 0 | 0 | 0 | 0 | 7 | 0.0 |
| 1961–62 | 37 | New York Rangers | NHL | 6 | 0 | 1 | 1 | 1 | 2 | 0 | 0 | 0 | 0 | 3 | 0.0 |
| 1967–68 | 43 | St. Louis Blues | NHL | 8 | 0 | 4 | 4 | -4 | 12 | 0 | 0 | 0 | 0 | 8 | 0.0 |
| NHL Career — 15 Seasons | | | | 137 | 8 | 64 | 72 | 7 | 152 | 6 | 2 | 0 | 2 | 28 | 10.7 |

# Geraldine Heaney   Profile: See page 252

## REGULAR SEASON

| SEASON | AGE | TEAM | LG | GP | G | A | PTS | PIM |
|---|---|---|---|---|---|---|---|---|
| 1986–87 | 19 | Seneca College | OCAA | 12 | 13 | 24 | 37 | |
| 1987–88 | 20 | Seneca College | OCAA | | | | | |
| 1988–89 | 21 | Toronto Aeros | COWHL | | | | | |
| 1989–90 | 22 | Canadian National Team | WWC | 5 | 2 | 6 | 8 | 4 |
| 1990–91 | 23 | Toronto Aeros | COWHL | | | | | |
| 1991–92 | 24 | Canadian National Team | WWC | 5 | 0 | 6 | 6 | 2 |
| 1992–93 | 25 | Toronto Aeros | COWHL | 21 | 8 | 12 | 20 | 14 |
| 1993–94 | 25 | Toronto Aeros | COWHL | 28 | 13 | 28 | 41 | 27 |
| 1993–94 | 25 | Canadian National Team | WWC | 5 | 1 | 6 | 7 | 8 |
| 1994–95 | 26 | Toronto Aeros | COWHL | | | | | |
| 1995–96 | 26 | North York Beatrice Aeros | COWHL | 29 | 21 | 28 | 49 | 20 |
| 1995–96 | 26 | Canadian National Team | Pacific Rim | 5 | 2 | 3 | 5 | 0 |
| 1995–96 | 26 | North York Beatrice Aeros | COWHL | 32 | 21 | 45 | 66 | 18 |
| 1996–97 | 27 | Canadian National Team | 3 Nations | 4 | 0 | 0 | 0 | 2 |
| 1996–97 | 27 | Canadian National Team | WWC | 5 | 1 | 4 | 5 | 0 |
| 1997–98 | 27 | Canadian National Team | Nat-Team Tour | 19 | 6 | 10 | 16 | 18 |
| 1997–98 | 27 | Canadian National Team | 3 Nations | 5 | 0 | 2 | 2 | 6 |
| 1997–98 | 27 | Canada | Olympics | 6 | 2 | 4 | 6 | 2 |
| 1998–99 | 28 | North York Beatrice Aeros | COWHL | 29 | 8 | 25 | 33 | 22 |
| 1998–99 | 28 | Canadian National Team | 3 Nations | 4 | 0 | 0 | 0 | 2 |
| 1998–99 | 28 | Canadian National Team | Nat-Team Tour | 4 | 1 | 0 | 1 | 0 |
| 1998–99 | 28 | Canadian National Team | Pre-WWC | 3 | 0 | 1 | 1 | 0 |
| 1998–99 | 28 | Canadian National Team | WWC | 5 | 3 | 0 | 3 | 4 |
| 1999–00 | 29 | Toronto Beatrice Aeros | NWHL | 29 | 8 | 25 | 33 | 22 |
| 1999–00 | 29 | Canadian National Team | Nat-Team Tour | 2 | 0 | 0 | 0 | 2 |
| 1999–00 | 29 | Canadian National Team | Pre-WWC | 2 | 1 | 5 | 6 | 0 |
| 1999–00 | 29 | Canadian National Team | WWC | 5 | 0 | 1 | 1 | 4 |
| 2000–01 | 30 | Toronto Beatrice Aeros | NWHL | 23 | 7 | 22 | 29 | 21 |
| 2000–01 | 30 | Canadian National Team | 4 Nations | 4 | 3 | 1 | 4 | 4 |
| 2000–01 | 30 | Canadian National Team | Nat-Team | 7 | 0 | 5 | 5 | 0 |
| 2000–01 | 30 | Canadian National Team | Pre-WWC | 2 | 0 | 1 | 1 | 0 |
| 2000–01 | 30 | Canadian National Team | WWC | 5 | 1 | 5 | 6 | 0 |
| 2001–02 | 31 | Toronto Beatrice Aeros | NWHL | 27 | 8 | 27 | 35 | 25 |
| 2001–02 | 31 | Canadian National Team | Nat-Team Tour | 14 | 4 | 2 | 6 | 2 |
| 2001–02 | 31 | Canadian National Team | 3 Nations | 4 | 0 | 2 | 2 | 2 |
| 2001–02 | 32 | Canada | Olympics | 5 | 0 | 2 | 2 | 0 |
| 2002–03 | 33 | Toronto Beatrice Aeros | NWHL | 19 | 10 | 21 | 31 | 18 |
| 2003–04 | 34 | Toronto Beatrice Aeros | NWHL | 28 | 6 | 17 | 23 | 30 |
| Career — 17 seasons | | | | 402 | 150 | 340 | 490 | 279 |

## PLAYOFFS

| SEASON | AGE | TEAM | LG | GP | G | A | PTS | PIM |
|---|---|---|---|---|---|---|---|---|
| 2003–04 | 34 | Toronto Beatrice Aeros | NWHL | 2 | 0 | 1 | 1 | 0 |
| Career — 1 season | | | | 2 | 0 | 1 | 1 | 0 |

# Red Horner   Profile: See page 254

## REGULAR SEASON

| SEASON | AGE | TEAM | LG | GP | G | A | PTS | PIM |
|---|---|---|---|---|---|---|---|---|
| 1928–29 | 19 | Toronto Maple Leafs | NHL | 22 | 0 | 0 | 0 | 30 |
| 1929–30 | 20 | Toronto Maple Leafs | NHL | 33 | 2 | 7 | 9 | 96 |
| 1930–31 | 21 | Toronto Maple Leafs | NHL | 42 | 1 | 11 | 12 | 73 |
| 1931–32 | 22 | Toronto Maple Leafs | NHL | 42 | 7 | 9 | 16 | 109 |
| 1932–33 | 23 | Toronto Maple Leafs | NHL | 48 | 3 | 8 | 11 | 144 |
| 1933–34 | 24 | Toronto Maple Leafs | NHL | 40 | 11 | 10 | 21 | 156 |
| 1934–35 | 25 | Toronto Maple Leafs | NHL | 46 | 4 | 8 | 12 | 125 |
| 1935–36 | 26 | Toronto Maple Leafs | NHL | 43 | 2 | 9 | 11 | 167 |
| 1936–37 | 27 | Toronto Maple Leafs | NHL | 48 | 3 | 9 | 12 | 134 |
| 1937–38 | 28 | Toronto Maple Leafs | NHL | 47 | 4 | 20 | 24 | 82 |
| 1938–39 | 29 | Toronto Maple Leafs | NHL | 48 | 4 | 10 | 14 | 85 |
| 1939–40 | 30 | Toronto Maple Leafs | NHL | 31 | 1 | 9 | 10 | 87 |
| NHL Career — 12 Seasons | | | | 490 | 42 | 110 | 152 | 1288 |

## PLAYOFFS

| SEASON | AGE | TEAM | LG | GP | G | A | PTS | PIM |
|---|---|---|---|---|---|---|---|---|
| 1928–29 | 19 | Toronto Maple Leafs | NHL | 4 | 1 | 0 | 1 | 2 |
| 1930–31 | 21 | Toronto Maple Leafs | NHL | 2 | 0 | 0 | 0 | 4 |
| 1931–32 | 22 | Toronto Maple Leafs | NHL | 7 | 2 | 2 | 4 | 20 |
| 1932–33 | 23 | Toronto Maple Leafs | NHL | 9 | 1 | 0 | 1 | 10 |
| 1933–34 | 24 | Toronto Maple Leafs | NHL | 5 | 1 | 0 | 1 | 6 |
| 1934–35 | 25 | Toronto Maple Leafs | NHL | 7 | 0 | 1 | 1 | 4 |
| 1935–36 | 26 | Toronto Maple Leafs | NHL | 9 | 1 | 2 | 3 | 22 |
| 1936–37 | 27 | Toronto Maple Leafs | NHL | 2 | 0 | 0 | 0 | 7 |
| 1937–38 | 28 | Toronto Maple Leafs | NHL | 7 | 0 | 1 | 1 | 14 |
| 1938–39 | 29 | Toronto Maple Leafs | NHL | 10 | 1 | 2 | 3 | 26 |
| 1939–40 | 30 | Toronto Maple Leafs | NHL | 9 | 0 | 2 | 2 | 55 |
| NHL Career — 11 Seasons | | | | 71 | 7 | 10 | 17 | 170 |

# Tim Horton  Profile: See page 255

## REGULAR SEASON

| SEASON | AGE | TEAM | LG | GP | G | A | PTS | +/- | PIM | ESG | PPG | SHG | GWG | SOG | S% |
|--------|-----|------|-----|------|-----|-----|-----|-----|------|-----|-----|-----|-----|------|-----|
| 1949-50 | 20 | Toronto Maple Leafs | NHL | 1 | 0 | 0 | 0 | | 2 | 0 | 0 | 0 | 0 | | |
| 1951-52 | 22 | Toronto Maple Leafs | NHL | 4 | 0 | 0 | 0 | | 8 | 0 | 0 | 0 | 0 | | |
| 1952-53 | 23 | Toronto Maple Leafs | NHL | 70 | 2 | 14 | 16 | | 85 | 2 | 0 | 0 | 0 | | |
| 1953-54 | 24 | Toronto Maple Leafs | NHL | 70 | 7 | 24 | 31 | | 94 | 5 | 2 | 0 | 2 | | |
| 1954-55 | 25 | Toronto Maple Leafs | NHL | 66 | 5 | 9 | 14 | | 84 | 5 | 0 | 0 | 1 | | |
| 1955-56 | 26 | Toronto Maple Leafs | NHL | 35 | 0 | 5 | 5 | | 36 | 0 | 0 | 0 | 0 | | |
| 1956-57 | 27 | Toronto Maple Leafs | NHL | 66 | 6 | 19 | 25 | | 72 | 5 | 1 | 0 | 0 | | |
| 1957-58 | 28 | Toronto Maple Leafs | NHL | 53 | 6 | 20 | 26 | | 39 | 6 | 0 | 0 | 0 | | |
| 1958-59 | 29 | Toronto Maple Leafs | NHL | 70 | 5 | 21 | 26 | | 76 | 5 | 0 | 0 | 2 | | |
| 1959-60 | 30 | Toronto Maple Leafs | NHL | 70 | 3 | 29 | 32 | -1 | 69 | 3 | 0 | 0 | 0 | 171 | 1.8 |
| 1960-61 | 31 | Toronto Maple Leafs | NHL | 57 | 6 | 15 | 21 | 31 | 75 | 5 | 1 | 0 | 1 | 89 | 6.7 |
| 1961-62 | 32 | Toronto Maple Leafs | NHL | 70 | 10 | 28 | 38 | 35 | 88 | 8 | 2 | 0 | 0 | 140 | 7.1 |
| 1962-63 | 33 | Toronto Maple Leafs | NHL | 70 | 6 | 19 | 25 | 1 | 69 | 5 | 0 | 1 | 0 | 147 | 4.1 |
| 1963-64 | 34 | Toronto Maple Leafs | NHL | 70 | 9 | 20 | 29 | 10 | 71 | 7 | 2 | 0 | 7 | 180 | 5.0 |
| 1964-65 | 35 | Toronto Maple Leafs | NHL | 70 | 12 | 16 | 28 | 8 | 97 | 8 | 3 | 1 | 2 | 156 | 7.7 |
| 1965-66 | 36 | Toronto Maple Leafs | NHL | 70 | 6 | 22 | 28 | 30 | 76 | 4 | 2 | 0 | 1 | 138 | 4.3 |
| 1966-67 | 37 | Toronto Maple Leafs | NHL | 70 | 8 | 17 | 25 | -2 | 70 | 5 | 3 | 0 | 1 | 113 | 7.1 |
| 1967-68 | 38 | Toronto Maple Leafs | NHL | 69 | 4 | 23 | 27 | 20 | 82 | 2 | 1 | 1 | 0 | 178 | 2.3 |
| 1968-69 | 39 | Toronto Maple Leafs | NHL | 74 | 11 | 29 | 40 | 14 | 107 | 8 | 3 | 0 | 1 | 169 | 6.5 |
| 1969-70 | 40 | Toronto Maple Leafs | NHL | 59 | 3 | 19 | 22 | 4 | 91 | 2 | 1 | 0 | 1 | 116 | 2.6 |
| 1969-70 | 40 | New York Rangers | NHL | 15 | 1 | 5 | 6 | -7 | 16 | 0 | 1 | 0 | 0 | 41 | 2.4 |
| 1970-71 | 41 | New York Rangers | NHL | 78 | 2 | 18 | 20 | 27 | 57 | 1 | 1 | 0 | 1 | 124 | 1.6 |
| 1971-72 | 42 | Pittsburgh Penguins | NHL | 44 | 2 | 9 | 11 | 5 | 40 | 2 | 0 | 0 | 1 | 84 | 2.4 |
| 1972-73 | 43 | Buffalo Sabres | NHL | 69 | 1 | 16 | 17 | 12 | 56 | 1 | 0 | 0 | 0 | 73 | 1.4 |
| 1973-74 | 44 | Buffalo Sabres | NHL | 55 | 0 | 6 | 6 | 4 | 53 | 0 | 0 | 0 | 0 | 59 | 0.0 |
| NHL Career – 24 Seasons | | | | 1445 | 115 | 403 | 518 | 191 | 1611 | 89 | 23 | 3 | 21 | 1978 | 4.2 |

## PLAYOFFS

| SEASON | AGE | TEAM | LG | GP | G | A | PTS | +/- | PIM | ESG | PPG | SHG | GWG | SOG | S% |
|--------|-----|------|-----|------|-----|-----|-----|-----|------|-----|-----|-----|-----|------|-----|
| 1949-50 | 20 | Toronto Maple Leafs | NHL | 1 | 0 | 0 | 0 | | 2 | 0 | 0 | 0 | 0 | | |
| 1953-54 | 24 | Toronto Maple Leafs | NHL | 5 | 1 | 1 | 2 | | 4 | 1 | 0 | 0 | 0 | | |
| 1955-56 | 26 | Toronto Maple Leafs | NHL | 2 | 0 | 0 | 0 | | 4 | 0 | 0 | 0 | 0 | | |
| 1958-59 | 29 | Toronto Maple Leafs | NHL | 12 | 0 | 3 | 3 | | 16 | 0 | 0 | 0 | 0 | | |
| 1959-60 | 30 | Toronto Maple Leafs | NHL | 10 | 0 | 1 | 1 | -5 | 6 | 0 | 0 | 0 | 0 | 17 | 0.0 |
| 1960-61 | 31 | Toronto Maple Leafs | NHL | 5 | 0 | 0 | 0 | -2 | 0 | 0 | 0 | 0 | 0 | 7 | 0.0 |
| 1961-62 | 32 | Toronto Maple Leafs | NHL | 12 | 3 | 13 | 16 | -2 | 16 | 1 | 1 | 1 | 1 | 39 | 7.7 |
| 1962-63 | 33 | Toronto Maple Leafs | NHL | 10 | 1 | 3 | 4 | 10 | 10 | 1 | 0 | 0 | 0 | 17 | 5.9 |
| 1963-64 | 34 | Toronto Maple Leafs | NHL | 14 | 0 | 4 | 4 | 2 | 20 | 0 | 0 | 0 | 0 | 25 | 0.0 |
| 1964-65 | 35 | Toronto Maple Leafs | NHL | 6 | 0 | 2 | 2 | 2 | 13 | 0 | 0 | 0 | 0 | 18 | 0.0 |
| 1965-66 | 36 | Toronto Maple Leafs | NHL | 4 | 1 | 0 | 1 | -2 | 12 | 1 | 0 | 0 | 0 | 12 | 8.3 |
| 1966-67 | 37 | Toronto Maple Leafs | NHL | 12 | 3 | 5 | 8 | -4 | 25 | 2 | 1 | 0 | 0 | 25 | 12.0 |
| 1968-69 | 39 | Toronto Maple Leafs | NHL | 4 | 0 | 0 | 0 | -6 | 7 | 0 | 0 | 0 | 0 | 10 | 0.0 |
| 1969-70 | 40 | New York Rangers | NHL | 6 | 1 | 1 | 2 | -3 | 28 | 1 | 0 | 0 | 0 | 13 | 7.7 |
| 1970-71 | 41 | New York Rangers | NHL | 13 | 1 | 4 | 5 | 1 | 14 | 1 | 0 | 0 | 0 | 15 | 6.7 |
| 1971-72 | 42 | Pittsburgh Penguins | NHL | 4 | 0 | 1 | 1 | 1 | 2 | 0 | 0 | 0 | 0 | 7 | 0.0 |
| 1972-73 | 43 | Buffalo Sabres | NHL | 6 | 0 | 1 | 1 | -4 | 4 | 0 | 0 | 0 | 0 | 5 | 0.0 |
| NHL Career – 17 Seasons | | | | 126 | 11 | 39 | 50 | -12 | 183 | 8 | 2 | 1 | 1 | 210 | 4.8 |

# Phil Housley  Profile: See page 256

## REGULAR SEASON

| SEASON | AGE | TEAM | LG | GP | G | A | PTS | +/- | PIM | ESG | PPG | SHG | GWG | SOG | S% |
|--------|-----|------|-----|------|-----|-----|-----|-----|------|-----|-----|-----|-----|------|-----|
| 1982-83 | 18 | Buffalo Sabres | NHL | 77 | 19 | 47 | 66 | -4 | 39 | 8 | 11 | 0 | 2 | 183 | 10.4 |
| 1983-84 | 19 | Buffalo Sabres | NHL | 75 | 31 | 46 | 77 | 1 | 33 | 16 | 13 | 2 | 6 | 235 | 13.2 |
| 1984-85 | 20 | Buffalo Sabres | NHL | 73 | 16 | 53 | 69 | 15 | 28 | 13 | 3 | 0 | 5 | 189 | 8.5 |
| 1985-86 | 21 | Buffalo Sabres | NHL | 79 | 15 | 47 | 62 | -10 | 54 | 8 | 7 | 0 | 2 | 180 | 8.3 |
| 1986-87 | 22 | Buffalo Sabres | NHL | 78 | 21 | 46 | 67 | -1 | 57 | 12 | 8 | 1 | 2 | 200 | 10.5 |
| 1987-88 | 23 | Buffalo Sabres | NHL | 74 | 29 | 37 | 66 | -17 | 96 | 23 | 6 | 0 | 1 | 231 | 12.6 |
| 1988-89 | 24 | Buffalo Sabres | NHL | 72 | 26 | 44 | 70 | 6 | 47 | 21 | 5 | 0 | 3 | 178 | 14.6 |
| 1989-90 | 25 | Buffalo Sabres | NHL | 80 | 21 | 60 | 81 | 11 | 32 | 12 | 8 | 1 | 4 | 201 | 10.4 |
| 1990-91 | 26 | Winnipeg Jets | NHL | 78 | 23 | 53 | 76 | -13 | 24 | 10 | 12 | 1 | 3 | 206 | 11.2 |
| 1991-92 | 27 | Winnipeg Jets | NHL | 74 | 23 | 63 | 86 | -5 | 92 | 12 | 11 | 0 | 4 | 234 | 9.8 |
| 1992-93 | 28 | Winnipeg Jets | NHL | 80 | 18 | 79 | 97 | -14 | 52 | 12 | 6 | 0 | 2 | 249 | 7.2 |
| 1993-94 | 29 | St. Louis Blues | NHL | 26 | 7 | 15 | 22 | -5 | 12 | 3 | 4 | 0 | 1 | 60 | 11.7 |
| 1994-95 | 30 | Calgary Flames | NHL | 43 | 8 | 35 | 43 | 17 | 18 | 5 | 3 | 0 | 0 | 135 | 5.9 |
| 1995-96 | 31 | Calgary Flames | NHL | 59 | 16 | 36 | 52 | -2 | 22 | 10 | 6 | 0 | 1 | 155 | 10.3 |

## Phil Housley (continued)

### REGULAR SEASON

| SEASON | AGE | TEAM | LG | GP | G | A | PTS | +/- | PIM | ESG | PPG | SHG | GWG | SOG | S% |
|---|---|---|---|---|---|---|---|---|---|---|---|---|---|---|---|
| 1995–96 | 31 | New Jersey Devils | NHL | 22 | 1 | 15 | 16 | –4 | 8 | 1 | 0 | 0 | 0 | 50 | 2.0 |
| 1996–97 | 32 | Washington Capitals | NHL | 77 | 11 | 29 | 40 | –10 | 24 | 7 | 3 | 1 | 2 | 167 | 6.6 |
| 1997–98 | 33 | Washington Capitals | NHL | 64 | 6 | 25 | 31 | –10 | 24 | 1 | 4 | 1 | 0 | 116 | 5.2 |
| 1998–99 | 34 | Calgary Flames | NHL | 79 | 11 | 43 | 54 | 14 | 52 | 7 | 4 | 0 | 1 | 193 | 5.7 |
| 1999–00 | 35 | Calgary Flames | NHL | 78 | 11 | 44 | 55 | –12 | 24 | 6 | 5 | 0 | 2 | 176 | 6.3 |
| 2000–01 | 36 | Calgary Flames | NHL | 69 | 4 | 30 | 34 | –15 | 24 | 4 | 0 | 0 | 0 | 115 | 3.5 |
| 2001–02 | 37 | Chicago Blackhawks | NHL | 80 | 15 | 24 | 39 | –3 | 34 | 7 | 8 | 0 | 6 | 218 | 6.9 |
| 2002–03 | 38 | Chicago Blackhawks | NHL | 57 | 6 | 23 | 29 | 7 | 24 | 4 | 2 | 0 | 2 | 134 | 4.5 |
| 2002–03 | 38 | Toronto Maple Leafs | NHL | 1 | 0 | 0 | 0 | –1 | 2 | 0 | 0 | 0 | 0 | 3 | 0.0 |
| NHL Career — 21 Seasons | | | | 1495 | 338 | 894 | 1232 | –53 | 822 | 202 | 129 | 7 | 48 | 3808 | 8.9 |

### PLAYOFFS

| SEASON | AGE | TEAM | LG | GP | G | A | PTS | +/- | PIM | ESG | PPG | SHG | GWG | SOG | S% |
|---|---|---|---|---|---|---|---|---|---|---|---|---|---|---|---|
| 1982–83 | 18 | Buffalo Sabres | NHL | 10 | 3 | 4 | 7 | –4 | 2 | 2 | 1 | 0 | 0 | 31 | 9.7 |
| 1983–84 | 19 | Buffalo Sabres | NHL | 3 | 0 | 0 | 0 | –1 | 6 | 0 | 0 | 0 | 0 | 11 | 0.0 |
| 1984–85 | 20 | Buffalo Sabres | NHL | 5 | 3 | 2 | 5 | 0 | 2 | 3 | 0 | 0 | 0 | 12 | 25.0 |
| 1987–88 | 23 | Buffalo Sabres | NHL | 6 | 2 | 4 | 6 | –5 | 6 | 1 | 1 | 0 | 0 | 20 | 10.0 |
| 1988–89 | 24 | Buffalo Sabres | NHL | 5 | 1 | 3 | 4 | 0 | 2 | 1 | 0 | 0 | 0 | 10 | 10.0 |
| 1989–90 | 25 | Buffalo Sabres | NHL | 6 | 1 | 4 | 5 | 0 | 4 | 0 | 1 | 0 | 0 | 16 | 6.3 |
| 1991–92 | 27 | Winnipeg Jets | NHL | 7 | 1 | 4 | 5 | –6 | 0 | 0 | 1 | 0 | 1 | 31 | 3.2 |
| 1992–93 | 28 | Winnipeg Jets | NHL | 6 | 0 | 7 | 7 | –3 | 2 | 0 | 0 | 0 | 0 | 10 | 0.0 |
| 1993–94 | 29 | St. Louis Blues | NHL | 4 | 2 | 1 | 3 | –3 | 4 | 0 | 2 | 0 | 0 | 10 | 20.0 |
| 1994–95 | 30 | Calgary Flames | NHL | 7 | 0 | 9 | 9 | 5 | 0 | 0 | 0 | 0 | 0 | 22 | 0.0 |
| 1997–98 | 33 | Washington Capitals | NHL | 18 | 0 | 4 | 4 | –2 | 4 | 0 | 0 | 0 | 0 | 27 | 0.0 |
| 2001–02 | 37 | Chicago Blackhawks | NHL | 5 | 0 | 1 | 1 | –1 | 4 | 0 | 0 | 0 | 0 | 13 | 0.0 |
| 2002–03 | 38 | Toronto Maple Leafs | NHL | 3 | 0 | 0 | 0 | –3 | 0 | 0 | 0 | 0 | 0 | 0 | 0.0 |
| NHL Career — 13 Seasons | | | | 85 | 13 | 43 | 56 | –23 | 36 | 7 | 6 | 0 | 1 | 213 | 6.1 |

## Mark Howe    Profile: See page 257

### REGULAR SEASON

| SEASON | AGE | TEAM | LG | GP | G | A | PTS | +/- | PIM | ESG | PPG | SHG | GWG | SOG | S% |
|---|---|---|---|---|---|---|---|---|---|---|---|---|---|---|---|
| 1973–74 | 18 | Houston Aeros | WHA | 76 | 38 | 41 | 79 | | 20 | 28 | 5 | 5 | 3 | | |
| 1974–75 | 19 | Houston Aeros | WHA | 74 | 36 | 40 | 76 | 40 | 30 | 25 | 7 | 4 | | 256 | 14.1 |
| 1975–76 | 20 | Houston Aeros | WHA | 72 | 39 | 37 | 76 | 29 | 38 | 20 | 13 | 6 | 8 | 270 | 14.4 |
| 1976–77 | 21 | Houston Aeros | WHA | 57 | 23 | 52 | 75 | 41 | 46 | 15 | 5 | 3 | 8 | 220 | 10.5 |
| 1977–78 | 22 | New England Whalers | WHA | 70 | 30 | 61 | 91 | 30 | 32 | 26 | 4 | 0 | | 220 | 13.6 |
| 1978–79 | 23 | New England Whalers | WHA | 77 | 42 | 65 | 107 | 14 | 32 | 23 | 13 | 6 | | 314 | 13.4 |
| 1979–80 | 24 | Hartford Whalers | NHL | 74 | 24 | 56 | 80 | 14 | 20 | 17 | 5 | 2 | 3 | 178 | 13.5 |
| 1980–81 | 25 | Hartford Whalers | NHL | 63 | 19 | 46 | 65 | 9 | 54 | 10 | 7 | 2 | 3 | 172 | 11.0 |
| 1981–82 | 26 | Hartford Whalers | NHL | 76 | 8 | 45 | 53 | –9 | 18 | 5 | 3 | 0 | 1 | 225 | 3.6 |
| 1982–83 | 27 | Philadelphia Flyers | NHL | 76 | 20 | 47 | 67 | 47 | 18 | 10 | 5 | 5 | 4 | 219 | 9.1 |
| 1983–84 | 28 | Philadelphia Flyers | NHL | 71 | 19 | 34 | 53 | 30 | 44 | 13 | 3 | 3 | 2 | 184 | 10.3 |
| 1984–85 | 29 | Philadelphia Flyers | NHL | 73 | 18 | 39 | 57 | 51 | 31 | 13 | 3 | 2 | 0 | 215 | 8.4 |
| 1985–86 | 30 | Philadelphia Flyers | NHL | 77 | 24 | 58 | 82 | 87 | 36 | 13 | 4 | 7 | 3 | 193 | 12.4 |
| 1986–87 | 31 | Philadelphia Flyers | NHL | 69 | 15 | 43 | 58 | 57 | 37 | 9 | 2 | 4 | 0 | 150 | 10.0 |
| 1987–88 | 32 | Philadelphia Flyers | NHL | 75 | 19 | 43 | 62 | 23 | 62 | 10 | 8 | 1 | 4 | 177 | 10.7 |
| 1988–89 | 33 | Philadelphia Flyers | NHL | 52 | 9 | 29 | 38 | 7 | 45 | 3 | 5 | 1 | 1 | 95 | 9.5 |
| 1989–90 | 34 | Philadelphia Flyers | NHL | 40 | 7 | 21 | 28 | 22 | 24 | 3 | 3 | 1 | 1 | 63 | 11.1 |
| 1990–91 | 35 | Philadelphia Flyers | NHL | 19 | 0 | 10 | 10 | 9 | 8 | 0 | 0 | 0 | 0 | 40 | 0.0 |
| 1991–92 | 36 | Philadelphia Flyers | NHL | 42 | 7 | 18 | 25 | 18 | 18 | 1 | 6 | 0 | 0 | 63 | 11.1 |
| 1992–93 | 37 | Detroit Red Wings | NHL | 60 | 3 | 31 | 34 | 22 | 22 | 0 | 3 | 0 | 0 | 72 | 4.2 |
| 1993–94 | 38 | Detroit Red Wings | NHL | 44 | 4 | 20 | 24 | 16 | 8 | 3 | 1 | 0 | 0 | 72 | 5.6 |
| 1994–95 | 39 | Detroit Red Wings | NHL | 18 | 1 | 5 | 6 | –3 | 10 | 1 | 0 | 0 | 1 | 14 | 7.1 |
| Career — 22 Seasons | | | | 1355 | 405 | 841 | 1246 | 556 | 653 | 248 | 105 | 52 | 42 | 3412 | 10.8 |

### PLAYOFFS

| SEASON | AGE | TEAM | LG | GP | G | A | PTS | +/- | PIM | ESG | PPG | SHG | GWG | SOG | S% |
|---|---|---|---|---|---|---|---|---|---|---|---|---|---|---|---|
| 1973–74 | 18 | Houston Aeros | WHA | 14 | 1 | 5 | 6 | | 31 | | | | 0 | | |
| 1974–75 | 19 | Houston Aeros | WHA | 11 | 0 | 2 | 2 | | 11 | 0 | 0 | 0 | 0 | | |
| 1975–76 | 20 | Houston Aeros | WHA | 16 | 4 | 4 | 8 | –1 | 12 | | | | 0 | | |
| 1976–77 | 21 | Houston Aeros | WHA | 11 | 3 | 1 | 4 | –3 | 10 | | | | 1 | | |
| 1977–78 | 22 | New England Whalers | WHA | 14 | 1 | 1 | 2 | –2 | 13 | | | | 1 | | |
| 1978–79 | 23 | New England Whalers | WHA | 9 | 0 | 1 | 1 | –3 | 8 | | | | 0 | | |
| 1979–80 | 24 | Hartford Whalers | NHL | 3 | 1 | 2 | 3 | | 2 | 1 | 0 | 0 | 0 | | |
| 1982–83 | 27 | Philadelphia Flyers | NHL | 3 | 0 | 2 | 2 | | 4 | 0 | 0 | 0 | 0 | | |
| 1983–84 | 28 | Philadelphia Flyers | NHL | 3 | 0 | 0 | 0 | 0 | 2 | 0 | 0 | 0 | 0 | 10 | 0.0 |
| 1984–85 | 29 | Philadelphia Flyers | NHL | 19 | 3 | 8 | 11 | 7 | 6 | 2 | 1 | 0 | 1 | 46 | 6.5 |
| 1985–86 | 30 | Philadelphia Flyers | NHL | 5 | 0 | 4 | 4 | 0 | 0 | 0 | 0 | 0 | 0 | 16 | 0.0 |
| 1986–87 | 31 | Philadelphia Flyers | NHL | 26 | 2 | 10 | 12 | 15 | 4 | 2 | 0 | 0 | 0 | 67 | 3.0 |

## Mark Howe (continued)

**PLAYOFFS**

| SEASON | AGE | TEAM | LG | GP | G | A | PTS | +/- | PIM | ESG | PPG | SHG | GWG | SOG | S% |
|---|---|---|---|---|---|---|---|---|---|---|---|---|---|---|---|
| 1987–88 | 32 | Philadelphia Flyers | NHL | 7 | 3 | 6 | 9 | 7 | 4 | 3 | 0 | 0 | 0 | 16 | 18.8 |
| 1988–89 | 33 | Philadelphia Flyers | NHL | 19 | 0 | 15 | 15 | 14 | 10 | 0 | 0 | 0 | 0 | 33 | 0.0 |
| 1992–93 | 37 | Detroit Red Wings | NHL | 7 | 1 | 3 | 4 | 6 | 2 | 1 | 0 | 0 | 0 | 8 | 12.5 |
| 1993–94 | 38 | Detroit Red Wings | NHL | 6 | 0 | 1 | 1 | 0 | 0 | 0 | 0 | 0 | 0 | 2 | 0.0 |
| 1994–95 | 39 | Detroit Red Wings | NHL | 3 | 0 | 0 | 0 | 2 | 0 | 0 | 0 | 0 | 0 | 1 | 0.0 |
| Career — 17 Seasons | | | | 176 | 19 | 65 | 84 | 42 | 119 | 9 | 1 | 0 | 3 | 199 | 4.5 |

# Harry Howell   Profile: See page 258

**REGULAR SEASON**

| SEASON | AGE | TEAM | LG | GP | G | A | PTS | +/- | PIM | ESG | PPG | SHG | GWG | SOG | S% |
|---|---|---|---|---|---|---|---|---|---|---|---|---|---|---|---|
| 1952–53 | 20 | New York Rangers | NHL | 67 | 3 | 8 | 11 | | 46 | 1 | 2 | 0 | 2 | | |
| 1953–54 | 21 | New York Rangers | NHL | 67 | 7 | 9 | 16 | | 58 | 7 | 0 | 0 | 1 | | |
| 1954–55 | 22 | New York Rangers | NHL | 70 | 2 | 14 | 16 | | 87 | 0 | 2 | 0 | 1 | | |
| 1955–56 | 23 | New York Rangers | NHL | 70 | 3 | 15 | 18 | | 77 | 3 | 0 | 0 | 0 | | |
| 1956–57 | 24 | New York Rangers | NHL | 65 | 2 | 10 | 12 | | 70 | 2 | 0 | 0 | 0 | | |
| 1957–58 | 25 | New York Rangers | NHL | 70 | 4 | 7 | 11 | | 62 | 3 | 0 | 1 | 1 | | |
| 1958–59 | 26 | New York Rangers | NHL | 70 | 4 | 10 | 14 | | 101 | 4 | 0 | 0 | 0 | | |
| 1959–60 | 27 | New York Rangers | NHL | 67 | 7 | 6 | 13 | -16 | 58 | 7 | 0 | 0 | 0 | 128 | 5.5 |
| 1960–61 | 28 | New York Rangers | NHL | 70 | 7 | 10 | 17 | -8 | 62 | 7 | 0 | 0 | 1 | 150 | 4.7 |
| 1961–62 | 29 | New York Rangers | NHL | 66 | 6 | 15 | 21 | -10 | 89 | 5 | 1 | 0 | 1 | 122 | 4.9 |
| 1962–63 | 30 | New York Rangers | NHL | 70 | 5 | 20 | 25 | -19 | 55 | 5 | 0 | 0 | 0 | 131 | 3.8 |
| 1963–64 | 31 | New York Rangers | NHL | 70 | 5 | 31 | 36 | -9 | 75 | 3 | 2 | 0 | 2 | 208 | 2.4 |
| 1964–65 | 32 | New York Rangers | NHL | 68 | 2 | 20 | 22 | -13 | 63 | 2 | 0 | 0 | 0 | 222 | 0.9 |
| 1965–66 | 33 | New York Rangers | NHL | 70 | 4 | 29 | 33 | -20 | 92 | 3 | 1 | 0 | 0 | 181 | 2.2 |
| 1966–67 | 34 | New York Rangers | NHL | 70 | 12 | 28 | 40 | 4 | 54 | 10 | 2 | 0 | 0 | 200 | 6.0 |
| 1967–68 | 35 | New York Rangers | NHL | 74 | 5 | 24 | 29 | 11 | 62 | 4 | 1 | 0 | 2 | 219 | 2.3 |
| 1968–69 | 36 | New York Rangers | NHL | 56 | 4 | 7 | 11 | 3 | 36 | 3 | 1 | 0 | 1 | 140 | 2.9 |
| 1969–70 | 37 | Oakland Seals | NHL | 55 | 4 | 16 | 20 | -16 | 52 | 1 | 3 | 0 | 3 | 147 | 2.7 |
| 1970–71 | 38 | California Golden Seals | NHL | 28 | 0 | 9 | 9 | -20 | 14 | 0 | 0 | 0 | 0 | 51 | 0.0 |
| 1970–71 | 38 | Los Angeles Kings | NHL | 18 | 3 | 8 | 11 | 1 | 4 | 2 | 1 | 0 | 0 | 33 | 9.1 |
| 1971–72 | 39 | Los Angeles Kings | NHL | 77 | 1 | 17 | 18 | -35 | 53 | 1 | 0 | 0 | 0 | 138 | 0.7 |
| 1972–73 | 40 | Los Angeles Kings | NHL | 73 | 4 | 11 | 15 | -5 | 28 | 4 | 0 | 0 | 0 | 97 | 4.1 |
| 1973–74 | 41 | New York Golden Blades/ New Jersey Knights | WHA | 65 | 3 | 23 | 26 | | 24 | 3 | 0 | 0 | 2 | | |
| 1974–75 | 42 | San Diego Mariners | WHA | 74 | 4 | 10 | 14 | 28 | 28 | 3 | 0 | 1 | | 78 | 5.1 |
| 1975–76 | 43 | Calgary Cowboys | WHA | 31 | 0 | 3 | 3 | 4 | 6 | 0 | 0 | 0 | 0 | 26 | 0.0 |
| Career — 24 Seasons | | | | 1581 | 101 | 360 | 461 | 120 | 1356 | 83 | 16 | 2 | 17 | 2271 | 3.3 |

**PLAYOFFS**

| SEASON | AGE | TEAM | LG | GP | G | A | PTS | +/- | PIM | ESG | PPG | SHG | GWG | SOG | S% |
|---|---|---|---|---|---|---|---|---|---|---|---|---|---|---|---|
| 1955–56 | 23 | New York Rangers | NHL | 5 | 0 | 1 | 1 | | 4 | 0 | 0 | 0 | 0 | | |
| 1956–57 | 24 | New York Rangers | NHL | 5 | 1 | 0 | 1 | | 6 | 1 | 0 | 0 | 0 | | |
| 1957–58 | 25 | New York Rangers | NHL | 6 | 1 | 0 | 1 | | 8 | 1 | 0 | 0 | 0 | | |
| 1961–62 | 29 | New York Rangers | NHL | 6 | 0 | 1 | 1 | -4 | 8 | 0 | 0 | 0 | 0 | 9 | 0.0 |
| 1966–67 | 34 | New York Rangers | NHL | 4 | 0 | 0 | 0 | -2 | 4 | 0 | 0 | 0 | 0 | 9 | 0.0 |
| 1967–68 | 35 | New York Rangers | NHL | 6 | 1 | 0 | 1 | -6 | 0 | 0 | 1 | 0 | 1 | 23 | 4.3 |
| 1968–69 | 36 | New York Rangers | NHL | 2 | 0 | 0 | 0 | -1 | 0 | 0 | 0 | 0 | 0 | 0 | |
| 1969–70 | 37 | Oakland Seals | NHL | 4 | 0 | 1 | 1 | -1 | 2 | 0 | 0 | 0 | 0 | 8 | 0.0 |
| 1974–75 | 42 | San Diego Mariners | WHA | 5 | 1 | 0 | 1 | | 10 | | | | 0 | | |
| 1975–76 | 43 | Calgary Cowboys | WHA | 2 | 0 | 0 | 0 | 1 | 2 | | | | | | |
| Career – 10 Seasons | | | | 45 | 4 | 3 | 7 | -13 | 44 | 2 | 1 | 0 | 1 | 49 | 2.0 |

# Ching Johnson   Profile: See page 259

**REGULAR SEASON**

| SEASON | AGE | TEAM | LG | GP | G | A | PTS | PIM |
|---|---|---|---|---|---|---|---|---|
| 1926–27 | 28 | New York Rangers | NHL | 27 | 3 | 2 | 5 | 68 |
| 1927–28 | 29 | New York Rangers | NHL | 42 | 10 | 6 | 16 | 146 |
| 1928–29 | 30 | New York Rangers | NHL | 8 | 0 | 0 | 0 | 18 |
| 1929–30 | 31 | New York Rangers | NHL | 30 | 3 | 3 | 6 | 84 |
| 1930–31 | 32 | New York Rangers | NHL | 44 | 2 | 6 | 8 | 79 |
| 1931–32 | 33 | New York Rangers | NHL | 47 | 3 | 10 | 13 | 106 |
| 1932–33 | 34 | New York Rangers | NHL | 48 | 8 | 9 | 17 | 127 |
| 1933–34 | 35 | New York Rangers | NHL | 48 | 2 | 6 | 8 | 86 |
| 1934–35 | 36 | New York Rangers | NHL | 29 | 2 | 3 | 5 | 34 |
| 1935–36 | 37 | New York Rangers | NHL | 47 | 5 | 3 | 8 | 58 |
| 1936–37 | 38 | New York Rangers | NHL | 35 | 0 | 0 | 0 | 20 |
| 1937–38 | 39 | New York Americans | NHL | 31 | 0 | 0 | 0 | 10 |
| NHL Career — 12 Seasons | | | | 436 | 38 | 48 | 86 | 836 |

**PLAYOFFS**

| SEASON | AGE | TEAM | LG | GP | G | A | PTS | PIM |
|---|---|---|---|---|---|---|---|---|
| 1926–27 | 28 | New York Rangers | NHL | 2 | 0 | 0 | 0 | 8 |
| 1927–28 | 29 | New York Rangers | NHL | 9 | 1 | 1 | 2 | 46 |
| 1928–29 | 30 | New York Rangers | NHL | 6 | 0 | 0 | 0 | 26 |
| 1929–30 | 31 | New York Rangers | NHL | 4 | 0 | 0 | 0 | 14 |
| 1930–31 | 32 | New York Rangers | NHL | 4 | 1 | 0 | 1 | 10 |
| 1931–32 | 33 | New York Rangers | NHL | 7 | 2 | 0 | 2 | 24 |
| 1932–33 | 34 | New York Rangers | NHL | 8 | 1 | 0 | 1 | 12 |
| 1933–34 | 35 | New York Rangers | NHL | 2 | 0 | 0 | 0 | 4 |
| 1934–35 | 36 | New York Rangers | NHL | 3 | 0 | 0 | 0 | 2 |
| 1936–37 | 38 | New York Rangers | NHL | 9 | 0 | 1 | 1 | 4 |
| 1937–38 | 39 | New York Americans | NHL | 6 | 0 | 0 | 0 | 2 |
| NHL Career — 11 Seasons | | | | 60 | 5 | 2 | 5 | 152 |

## Ernie Johnson   Profile: See page 260

**REGULAR SEASON**

| SEASON | AGE | TEAM | LG | GP | G | A | PTS | PIM |
|---|---|---|---|---|---|---|---|---|
| 1903–04 | 17 | Montreal AAA | CAHL | 2 | 1 | 0 | 1 | |
| 1904–05 | 18 | Montreal AAA | CAHL | 9 | 8 | 0 | 8 | 9 |
| 1905–06 | 19 | Montreal Wanderers | ECAHA | 10 | 12 | 0 | 12 | 44 |
| 1906–07 | 20 | Montreal Wanderers | ECAHA | 10 | 15 | 0 | 15 | 42 |
| 1907–08 | 21 | Montreal Wanderers | ECAHA | 10 | 9 | 0 | 9 | 33 |
| 1908–09 | 22 | Montreal Wanderers | ECHA | 10 | 10 | 0 | 10 | 34 |
| 1909–10 | 23 | Montreal Wanderers | NHA | 1 | 0 | 0 | 0 | 6 |
| 1909–10 | 23 | Montreal Wanderers | NHA | 13 | 7 | 0 | 7 | 47 |
| 1910–11 | 24 | Montreal Wanderers | NHA | 16 | 6 | 0 | 6 | 60 |
| 1911–12 | 25 | New Westminster Royals | PCHA | 14 | 9 | 0 | 9 | 13 |
| 1912–13 | 26 | New Westminster Royals | PCHA | 13 | 7 | 3 | 10 | 15 |
| 1913–14 | 27 | New Westminster Royals | PCHA | 16 | 3 | 5 | 8 | 27 |
| 1914–15 | 28 | Portland Rosebuds | PCHA | 18 | 6 | 4 | 10 | 21 |
| 1915–16 | 29 | Portland Rosebuds | PCHA | 18 | 6 | 3 | 9 | 62 |
| 1916–17 | 30 | Portland Rosebuds | PCHA | 24 | 12 | 9 | 21 | 54 |

**REGULAR SEASON**

| SEASON | AGE | TEAM | LG | GP | G | A | PTS | PIM |
|---|---|---|---|---|---|---|---|---|
| 1917–18 | 31 | Portland Rosebuds | PCHA | 15 | 3 | 2 | 5 | 3 |
| 1918–19 | 32 | Victoria Aristocrats | PCHA | 15 | 3 | 3 | 6 | 0 |
| 1919–20 | 33 | Victoria Aristocrats | PCHA | 21 | 0 | 5 | 5 | 22 |
| 1920–21 | 34 | Victoria Aristocrats | PCHA | 24 | 5 | 2 | 7 | 26 |
| 1921–22 | 35 | Victoria Cougars | PCHA | 13 | 1 | 1 | 2 | 12 |
| Career — 19 Seasons | | | | 272 | 123 | 37 | 160 | 530 |

**PLAYOFFS**

| SEASON | AGE | TEAM | LG | GP | G | A | PTS | PIM |
|---|---|---|---|---|---|---|---|---|
| 1905–06 | 19 | Montreal Wanderers | ECAHA | 2 | 1 | 0 | 1 | 3 |
| 1906–07 | 20 | Montreal Wanderers | St-Cup | 6 | 5 | 0 | 5 | 8 |
| 1907–08 | 21 | Montreal Wanderers | St-Cup | 5 | 11 | 0 | 11 | 28 |
| 1908–09 | 22 | Montreal Wanderers | St-Cup | 2 | 1 | 0 | 1 | 6 |
| 1909–10 | 23 | Montreal Wanderers | St-Cup | 1 | 0 | 0 | 0 | 9 |
| 1915–16 | 29 | Portland Rosebuds | St-Cup | 5 | 1 | 0 | 1 | 9 |
| Career — 6 Seasons | | | | 21 | 19 | 0 | 19 | 63 |

## Tom Johnson   Profile: See page 261

**REGULAR SEASON**

| SEASON | AGE | TEAM | LG | GP | G | A | PTS | PIM | ESG | PPG | SHG | GWG |
|---|---|---|---|---|---|---|---|---|---|---|---|---|
| 1947–48 | 19 | Montreal Canadiens | NHL | 1 | 0 | 0 | 0 | 0 | 0 | 0 | 0 | 0 |
| 1950–51 | 22 | Montreal Canadiens | NHL | 70 | 2 | 8 | 10 | 128 | 2 | 0 | 0 | 1 |
| 1951–52 | 23 | Montreal Canadiens | NHL | 68 | 0 | 7 | 7 | 76 | 0 | 0 | 0 | 0 |
| 1952–53 | 24 | Montreal Canadiens | NHL | 70 | 3 | 8 | 11 | 65 | 3 | 0 | 0 | 1 |
| 1953–54 | 25 | Montreal Canadiens | NHL | 70 | 7 | 11 | 18 | 85 | 5 | 2 | 0 | 2 |
| 1954–55 | 26 | Montreal Canadiens | NHL | 70 | 6 | 19 | 25 | 74 | 5 | 0 | 1 | 1 |
| 1955–56 | 27 | Montreal Canadiens | NHL | 64 | 3 | 10 | 13 | 75 | 2 | 1 | 0 | 0 |
| 1956–57 | 28 | Montreal Canadiens | NHL | 70 | 4 | 11 | 15 | 59 | 4 | 0 | 0 | 0 |
| 1957–58 | 29 | Montreal Canadiens | NHL | 66 | 3 | 18 | 21 | 75 | 3 | 0 | 0 | 0 |
| 1958–59 | 30 | Montreal Canadiens | NHL | 70 | 10 | 29 | 39 | 76 | 5 | 4 | 1 | 2 |
| 1959–60 | 31 | Montreal Canadiens | NHL | 64 | 4 | 25 | 29 | 59 | 2 | 2 | 0 | 2 |
| 1960–61 | 32 | Montreal Canadiens | NHL | 70 | 1 | 15 | 16 | 54 | 0 | 0 | 1 | 0 |
| 1961–62 | 33 | Montreal Canadiens | NHL | 62 | 1 | 17 | 18 | 43 | 1 | 0 | 0 | 0 |
| 1962–63 | 34 | Montreal Canadiens | NHL | 42 | 3 | 5 | 8 | 28 | 3 | 0 | 0 | 0 |
| 1963–64 | 35 | Boston Bruins | NHL | 70 | 4 | 21 | 25 | 33 | 4 | 0 | 0 | 1 |
| 1964–65 | 36 | Boston Bruins | NHL | 51 | 0 | 9 | 9 | 30 | 0 | 0 | 0 | 0 |
| NHL Career — 16 Seasons | | | | 978 | 51 | 213 | 264 | 960 | 39 | 9 | 3 | 10 |

**PLAYOFFS**

| SEASON | AGE | TEAM | LG | GP | G | A | PTS | PIM | ESG | PPG | SHG | GWG |
|---|---|---|---|---|---|---|---|---|---|---|---|---|
| 1949–50 | 21 | Montreal Canadiens | NHL | 1 | 0 | 0 | 0 | 0 | 0 | 0 | 0 | 0 |
| 1950–51 | 22 | Montreal Canadiens | NHL | 11 | 0 | 0 | 0 | 6 | 0 | 0 | 0 | 0 |
| 1951–52 | 23 | Montreal Canadiens | NHL | 11 | 1 | 0 | 1 | 2 | 1 | 0 | 0 | 0 |
| 1952–53 | 24 | Montreal Canadiens | NHL | 12 | 2 | 3 | 5 | 8 | 2 | 0 | 0 | 1 |
| 1953–54 | 25 | Montreal Canadiens | NHL | 11 | 1 | 2 | 3 | 30 | 0 | 0 | 1 | 0 |
| 1954–55 | 26 | Montreal Canadiens | NHL | 12 | 2 | 0 | 2 | 22 | 2 | 0 | 0 | 1 |
| 1955–56 | 27 | Montreal Canadiens | NHL | 10 | 0 | 2 | 2 | 8 | 0 | 0 | 0 | 0 |
| 1956–57 | 28 | Montreal Canadiens | NHL | 10 | 0 | 2 | 2 | 16 | 0 | 0 | 0 | 0 |
| 1957–58 | 29 | Montreal Canadiens | NHL | 2 | 0 | 0 | 0 | 0 | 0 | 0 | 0 | 0 |
| 1958–59 | 30 | Montreal Canadiens | NHL | 11 | 2 | 3 | 5 | 8 | 1 | 1 | 0 | 0 |
| 1959–60 | 31 | Montreal Canadiens | NHL | 8 | 0 | 1 | 1 | 4 | 0 | 0 | 0 | 0 |
| 1960–61 | 32 | Montreal Canadiens | NHL | 6 | 0 | 1 | 1 | 8 | 0 | 0 | 0 | 0 |
| 1961–62 | 33 | Montreal Canadiens | NHL | 6 | 0 | 1 | 1 | 0 | 0 | 0 | 0 | 0 |
| NHL Career — 13 Seasons | | | | 111 | 8 | 15 | 23 | 112 | 6 | 1 | 1 | 2 |

# Red Kelly Profile: See page 262

### REGULAR SEASON

| SEASON | AGE | TEAM | LG | GP | G | A | PTS | PIM | ESG | PPG | SHG | GWG |
|---|---|---|---|---|---|---|---|---|---|---|---|---|
| 1947–48 | 20 | Detroit Red Wings | NHL | 60 | 6 | 14 | 20 | 13 | 5 | 0 | 1 | 0 |
| 1948–49 | 21 | Detroit Red Wings | NHL | 59 | 5 | 11 | 16 | 10 | 4 | 0 | 1 | 2 |
| 1949–50 | 22 | Detroit Red Wings | NHL | 70 | 15 | 25 | 40 | 9 | 8 | 7 | 0 | 5 |
| 1950–51 | 23 | Detroit Red Wings | NHL | 70 | 17 | 37 | 54 | 24 | 13 | 4 | 0 | 3 |
| 1951–52 | 24 | Detroit Red Wings | NHL | 67 | 16 | 31 | 47 | 16 | 12 | 2 | 2 | 3 |
| 1952–53 | 25 | Detroit Red Wings | NHL | 70 | 19 | 27 | 46 | 8 | 15 | 4 | 0 | 1 |
| 1953–54 | 26 | Detroit Red Wings | NHL | 62 | 16 | 33 | 49 | 18 | 9 | 6 | 1 | 2 |
| 1954–55 | 27 | Detroit Red Wings | NHL | 70 | 15 | 30 | 45 | 28 | 6 | 6 | 3 | 3 |
| 1955–56 | 28 | Detroit Red Wings | NHL | 70 | 16 | 34 | 50 | 39 | 7 | 9 | 0 | 3 |
| 1956–57 | 29 | Detroit Red Wings | NHL | 70 | 10 | 25 | 35 | 18 | 4 | 6 | 0 | 1 |
| 1957–58 | 30 | Detroit Red Wings | NHL | 61 | 13 | 18 | 31 | 26 | 9 | 3 | 1 | 2 |
| 1958–59 | 31 | Detroit Red Wings | NHL | 67 | 8 | 13 | 21 | 34 | 5 | 1 | 2 | 1 |
| 1959–60 | 32 | Detroit Red Wings | NHL | 50 | 6 | 12 | 18 | 10 | 6 | 1 | 0 | 1 |
| 1959–60 | 32 | Toronto Maple Leafs | NHL | 18 | 6 | 5 | 11 | 8 | 6 | 0 | 0 | 3 |
| 1960–61 | 33 | Toronto Maple Leafs | NHL | 64 | 20 | 50 | 70 | 12 | 16 | 3 | 1 | 0 |
| 1961–62 | 34 | Toronto Maple Leafs | NHL | 58 | 22 | 27 | 49 | 6 | 17 | 4 | 1 | 2 |
| 1962–63 | 35 | Toronto Maple Leafs | NHL | 66 | 20 | 40 | 60 | 8 | 14 | 6 | 0 | 4 |
| 1963–64 | 36 | Toronto Maple Leafs | NHL | 70 | 11 | 34 | 45 | 16 | 10 | 1 | 0 | 2 |
| 1964–65 | 37 | Toronto Maple Leafs | NHL | 70 | 18 | 28 | 46 | 8 | 11 | 6 | 1 | 1 |
| 1965–66 | 38 | Toronto Maple Leafs | NHL | 63 | 8 | 24 | 32 | 12 | 8 | 0 | 0 | 2 |
| 1966–67 | 39 | Toronto Maple Leafs | NHL | 61 | 14 | 24 | 38 | 4 | 12 | 2 | 0 | 0 |
| NHL Career – 20 Seasons | | | | 1316 | 281 | 542 | 823 | 327 | 195 | 71 | 15 | 41 |

### PLAYOFFS

| SEASON | AGE | TEAM | LG | GP | G | A | PTS | PIM | ESG | PPG | SHG | GWG |
|---|---|---|---|---|---|---|---|---|---|---|---|---|
| 1947–48 | 20 | Detroit Red Wings | NHL | 10 | 3 | 2 | 5 | 2 | 1 | 2 | 0 | 0 |
| 1948–49 | 21 | Detroit Red Wings | NHL | 11 | 1 | 1 | 2 | 6 | 0 | 0 | 1 | 0 |
| 1949–50 | 22 | Detroit Red Wings | NHL | 14 | 1 | 3 | 4 | 2 | 0 | 1 | 0 | 0 |
| 1950–51 | 23 | Detroit Red Wings | NHL | 6 | 0 | 1 | 1 | 0 | 0 | 0 | 0 | 0 |
| 1951–52 | 24 | Detroit Red Wings | NHL | 5 | 1 | 0 | 1 | 0 | 1 | 0 | 0 | 1 |
| 1952–53 | 25 | Detroit Red Wings | NHL | 6 | 0 | 4 | 4 | 0 | 0 | 0 | 0 | 0 |
| 1953–54 | 26 | Detroit Red Wings | NHL | 12 | 5 | 1 | 6 | 4 | 3 | 1 | 1 | 1 |
| 1954–55 | 27 | Detroit Red Wings | NHL | 11 | 2 | 4 | 6 | 17 | 1 | 1 | 0 | 0 |
| 1955–56 | 28 | Detroit Red Wings | NHL | 10 | 2 | 4 | 6 | 2 | 1 | 1 | 0 | 0 |
| 1956–57 | 29 | Detroit Red Wings | NHL | 5 | 1 | 0 | 1 | 0 | 1 | 0 | 0 | 0 |
| 1957–58 | 30 | Detroit Red Wings | NHL | 4 | 0 | 1 | 1 | 2 | 0 | 0 | 0 | 0 |
| 1959–60 | 32 | Toronto Maple Leafs | NHL | 10 | 3 | 8 | 11 | 2 | 2 | 1 | 0 | 0 |
| 1960–61 | 33 | Toronto Maple Leafs | NHL | 2 | 1 | 0 | 1 | 0 | 0 | 1 | 0 | 0 |
| 1961–62 | 34 | Toronto Maple Leafs | NHL | 12 | 4 | 6 | 10 | 0 | 1 | 3 | 0 | 1 |
| 1962–63 | 35 | Toronto Maple Leafs | NHL | 10 | 2 | 6 | 8 | 6 | 1 | 1 | 0 | 0 |
| 1963–64 | 36 | Toronto Maple Leafs | NHL | 14 | 4 | 9 | 13 | 4 | 3 | 1 | 0 | 0 |
| 1964–65 | 37 | Toronto Maple Leafs | NHL | 6 | 3 | 2 | 5 | 2 | 1 | 1 | 1 | 0 |
| 1965–66 | 38 | Toronto Maple Leafs | NHL | 4 | 0 | 2 | 2 | 0 | 0 | 0 | 0 | 0 |
| 1966–67 | 39 | Toronto Maple Leafs | NHL | 12 | 0 | 5 | 5 | 2 | 0 | 0 | 0 | 0 |
| NHL Career – 19 Seasons | | | | 164 | 33 | 59 | 92 | 51 | 16 | 14 | 3 | 3 |

# Rod Langway Profile: See page 264

### REGULAR SEASON

| SEASON | AGE | TEAM | LG | GP | G | A | PTS | +/- | PIM | ESG | PPG | SHG | GWG | SOG | S% |
|---|---|---|---|---|---|---|---|---|---|---|---|---|---|---|---|
| 1977–78 | 20 | Birmingham Bulls | WHA | 52 | 3 | 18 | 21 | 10 | 52 | 3 | 0 | 0 | | 75 | 4.0 |
| 1978–79 | 21 | Montreal Canadiens | NHL | 45 | 3 | 4 | 7 | 6 | 30 | 3 | 0 | 0 | 0 | 48 | 6.3 |
| 1979–80 | 22 | Montreal Canadiens | NHL | 77 | 7 | 29 | 36 | 36 | 81 | 7 | 0 | 0 | 1 | 112 | 6.3 |
| 1980–81 | 23 | Montreal Canadiens | NHL | 80 | 11 | 34 | 45 | 52 | 120 | 5 | 5 | 1 | 2 | 165 | 6.7 |
| 1981–82 | 24 | Montreal Canadiens | NHL | 66 | 5 | 34 | 39 | 66 | 116 | 4 | 1 | 0 | 1 | 139 | 3.6 |
| 1982–83 | 25 | Washington Capitals | NHL | 80 | 3 | 29 | 32 | -2 | 75 | 2 | 1 | 0 | 0 | 125 | 2.4 |
| 1983–84 | 26 | Washington Capitals | NHL | 80 | 9 | 24 | 33 | 14 | 61 | 6 | 1 | 2 | 2 | 168 | 5.4 |
| 1984–95 | 27 | Washington Capitals | NHL | 79 | 4 | 22 | 26 | 36 | 54 | 4 | 0 | 0 | 1 | 102 | 3.9 |
| 1985–86 | 28 | Washington Capitals | NHL | 71 | 1 | 17 | 18 | 27 | 61 | 0 | 1 | 0 | 0 | 54 | 1.9 |
| 1986–87 | 29 | Washington Capitals | NHL | 78 | 2 | 25 | 27 | 11 | 53 | 2 | 0 | 0 | 1 | 79 | 2.5 |
| 1987–88 | 30 | Washington Capitals | NHL | 63 | 3 | 13 | 16 | 1 | 28 | 3 | 0 | 0 | 1 | 49 | 6.1 |
| 1988–89 | 31 | Washington Capitals | NHL | 76 | 2 | 19 | 21 | 12 | 67 | 2 | 0 | 0 | 0 | 80 | 2.5 |
| 1989–90 | 32 | Washington Capitals | NHL | 58 | 0 | 8 | 8 | 7 | 39 | 0 | 0 | 0 | 0 | 46 | 0.0 |
| 1990–91 | 33 | Washington Capitals | NHL | 56 | 1 | 7 | 8 | 12 | 24 | 1 | 0 | 0 | 0 | 32 | 3.1 |
| 1991–92 | 34 | Washington Capitals | NHL | 64 | 0 | 13 | 13 | 11 | 22 | 0 | 0 | 0 | 0 | 32 | 0.0 |
| 1992–93 | 35 | Washington Capitals | NHL | 21 | 0 | 0 | 0 | -13 | 20 | 0 | 0 | 0 | 0 | 6 | 0.0 |
| Career – 16 Seasons | | | | 1046 | 54 | 296 | 350 | 276 | 903 | 42 | 9 | 3 | 9 | 1312 | 4.1 |

## Rod Langway (continued)

**PLAYOFFS**

| SEASON | AGE | TEAM | LG | GP | G | A | PTS | +/- | PIM | ESG | PPG | SHG | GWG | SOG | S% |
|---|---|---|---|---|---|---|---|---|---|---|---|---|---|---|---|
| 1977–78 | 20 | Birmingham Bulls | WHA | 4 | 0 | 0 | 0 | -2 | 9 | | | | 0 | | |
| 1978–79 | 21 | Montreal Canadiens | NHL | 8 | 0 | 0 | 0 | -2 | 16 | 0 | 0 | 0 | 0 | 6 | 0.0 |
| 1979–80 | 22 | Montreal Canadiens | NHL | 10 | 3 | 3 | 6 | 6 | 2 | 2 | 1 | 0 | 0 | 26 | 11.5 |
| 1980–81 | 23 | Montreal Canadiens | NHL | 3 | 0 | 0 | 0 | 0 | 6 | 0 | 0 | 0 | 0 | 9 | 0.0 |
| 1981–82 | 24 | Montreal Canadiens | NHL | 5 | 0 | 3 | 3 | 2 | 18 | 0 | 0 | 0 | 0 | 12 | 0.0 |
| 1982–83 | 25 | Washington Capitals | NHL | 4 | 0 | 0 | 0 | -1 | 0 | 0 | 0 | 0 | 0 | 9 | 0.0 |
| 1983–84 | 26 | Washington Capitals | NHL | 8 | 0 | 5 | 5 | 0 | 7 | 0 | 0 | 0 | 0 | 16 | 0.0 |
| 1984–85 | 27 | Washington Capitals | NHL | 5 | 0 | 1 | 1 | -2 | 6 | 0 | 0 | 0 | 0 | 12 | 0.0 |
| 1985–86 | 28 | Washington Capitals | NHL | 9 | 1 | 2 | 3 | 4 | 6 | 0 | 1 | 0 | 0 | 17 | 5.9 |
| 1986–87 | 29 | Washington Capitals | NHL | 7 | 0 | 1 | 1 | 0 | 2 | 0 | 0 | 0 | 0 | 15 | 0.0 |
| 1987–88 | 30 | Washington Capitals | NHL | 6 | 0 | 0 | 0 | 2 | 8 | 0 | 0 | 0 | 0 | 7 | 0.0 |
| 1988–89 | 31 | Washington Capitals | NHL | 6 | 0 | 0 | 0 | -4 | 6 | 0 | 0 | 0 | 0 | 10 | 0.0 |
| 1989–90 | 32 | Washington Capitals | NHL | 15 | 1 | 4 | 5 | 0 | 12 | 1 | 0 | 0 | 1 | 17 | 5.9 |
| 1990–91 | 33 | Washington Capitals | NHL | 11 | 0 | 2 | 2 | 1 | 6 | 0 | 0 | 0 | 0 | 12 | 0.0 |
| 1991–92 | 34 | Washington Capitals | NHL | 7 | 0 | 1 | 1 | 0 | 2 | 0 | 0 | 0 | 0 | 2 | 0.0 |
| Career — 15 Seasons | | | | 108 | 5 | 22 | 27 | 4 | 106 | 3 | 2 | 0 | 1 | 170 | 2.9 |

# Jacques Laperriere   Profile: See page 265

**REGULAR SEASON**

| SEASON | AGE | TEAM | LG | GP | G | A | PTS | +/- | PIM | ESG | PPG | SHG | GWG | SOG | S% |
|---|---|---|---|---|---|---|---|---|---|---|---|---|---|---|---|
| 1962–63 | 21 | Montreal Canadiens | NHL | 6 | 0 | 2 | 2 | 0 | 2 | 0 | 0 | 0 | 0 | 8 | 0.0 |
| 1963–64 | 22 | Montreal Canadiens | NHL | 65 | 2 | 28 | 30 | 25 | 102 | 0 | 1 | 1 | 1 | 196 | 1.0 |
| 1964–65 | 23 | Montreal Canadiens | NHL | 67 | 5 | 22 | 27 | -2 | 92 | 5 | 0 | 0 | 0 | 127 | 3.9 |
| 1965–66 | 24 | Montreal Canadiens | NHL | 57 | 6 | 25 | 31 | 14 | 85 | 3 | 2 | 1 | 2 | 116 | 5.2 |
| 1966–67 | 25 | Montreal Canadiens | NHL | 61 | 0 | 20 | 20 | -17 | 48 | 0 | 0 | 0 | 0 | 109 | 0.0 |
| 1967–68 | 26 | Montreal Canadiens | NHL | 72 | 4 | 21 | 25 | 23 | 84 | 3 | 1 | 0 | 0 | 122 | 3.3 |
| 1968–69 | 27 | Montreal Canadiens | NHL | 69 | 5 | 26 | 31 | 37 | 45 | 5 | 0 | 0 | 1 | 166 | 3.0 |
| 1969–70 | 28 | Montreal Canadiens | NHL | 73 | 6 | 31 | 37 | 27 | 103 | 3 | 2 | 1 | 1 | 169 | 3.6 |
| 1970–71 | 29 | Montreal Canadiens | NHL | 49 | 0 | 16 | 16 | 24 | 20 | 0 | 0 | 0 | 0 | 65 | 0.0 |
| 1971–72 | 30 | Montreal Canadiens | NHL | 73 | 3 | 25 | 28 | 34 | 50 | 1 | 2 | 0 | 0 | 97 | 3.1 |
| 1972–73 | 31 | Montreal Canadiens | NHL | 58 | 7 | 16 | 23 | 77 | 34 | 5 | 2 | 0 | 0 | 89 | 7.9 |
| 1973–74 | 32 | Montreal Canadiens | NHL | 42 | 2 | 10 | 12 | 15 | 14 | 1 | 0 | 1 | 0 | 60 | 3.3 |
| NHL Career — 12 Seasons | | | | 692 | 40 | 242 | 282 | 256 | 679 | 26 | 10 | 4 | 5 | 1324 | 3.0 |

**PLAYOFFS**

| SEASON | AGE | TEAM | LG | GP | G | A | PTS | +/- | PIM | ESG | PPG | SHG | GWG | SOG | S% |
|---|---|---|---|---|---|---|---|---|---|---|---|---|---|---|---|
| 1962–63 | 21 | Montreal Canadiens | NHL | 5 | 0 | 1 | 1 | -4 | 4 | 0 | 0 | 0 | 0 | 13 | 0.0 |
| 1963–64 | 22 | Montreal Canadiens | NHL | 7 | 1 | 1 | 2 | 6 | 8 | 1 | 0 | 0 | 0 | 18 | 5.6 |
| 1964–65 | 23 | Montreal Canadiens | NHL | 6 | 1 | 1 | 2 | -3 | 16 | 0 | 1 | 0 | 0 | 11 | 9.1 |
| 1966–67 | 25 | Montreal Canadiens | NHL | 9 | 0 | 1 | 1 | 1 | 9 | 0 | 0 | 0 | 0 | 28 | 0.0 |
| 1967–68 | 26 | Montreal Canadiens | NHL | 13 | 1 | 3 | 4 | 7 | 20 | 1 | 0 | 0 | 0 | 46 | 2.2 |
| 1968–69 | 27 | Montreal Canadiens | NHL | 14 | 1 | 3 | 4 | 6 | 28 | 0 | 1 | 0 | 0 | 34 | 2.9 |
| 1970–71 | 29 | Montreal Canadiens | NHL | 20 | 4 | 9 | 13 | 11 | 12 | 3 | 1 | 0 | 1 | 25 | 16.0 |
| 1971–72 | 30 | Montreal Canadiens | NHL | 4 | 0 | 0 | 0 | -1 | 2 | 0 | 0 | 0 | 0 | 3 | 0.0 |
| 1972–73 | 31 | Montreal Canadiens | NHL | 10 | 1 | 3 | 4 | 2 | 2 | 1 | 0 | 0 | 0 | 10 | 10.0 |
| NHL Career — 9 Seasons | | | | 88 | 9 | 22 | 31 | 25 | 101 | 6 | 3 | 0 | 1 | 188 | 4.8 |

# Guy Lapointe   Profile: See page 266

**REGULAR SEASON**

| SEASON | AGE | TEAM | LG | GP | G | A | PTS | +/- | PIM | ESG | PPG | SHG | GWG | SOG | S% |
|---|---|---|---|---|---|---|---|---|---|---|---|---|---|---|---|
| 1968–69 | 20 | Montreal Canadiens | NHL | 1 | 0 | 0 | 0 | 0 | 2 | 0 | 0 | 0 | 0 | 0 | |
| 1969–70 | 21 | Montreal Canadiens | NHL | 5 | 0 | 0 | 0 | 4 | 4 | 0 | 0 | 0 | 0 | 0 | |
| 1970–71 | 22 | Montreal Canadiens | NHL | 78 | 15 | 29 | 44 | 27 | 107 | 10 | 5 | 0 | 1 | 228 | 6.6 |
| 1971–72 | 23 | Montreal Canadiens | NHL | 69 | 11 | 38 | 49 | 13 | 58 | 7 | 4 | 0 | 4 | 227 | 4.9 |
| 1972–73 | 24 | Montreal Canadiens | NHL | 76 | 19 | 35 | 54 | 52 | 117 | 16 | 3 | 0 | 2 | 196 | 9.7 |
| 1973–74 | 25 | Montreal Canadiens | NHL | 71 | 13 | 40 | 53 | 12 | 63 | 7 | 5 | 1 | 2 | 205 | 6.3 |
| 1974–75 | 26 | Montreal Canadiens | NHL | 80 | 28 | 47 | 75 | 46 | 88 | 16 | 11 | 1 | 0 | 220 | 12.7 |
| 1975–76 | 27 | Montreal Canadiens | NHL | 77 | 21 | 47 | 68 | 64 | 78 | 12 | 8 | 1 | 1 | 317 | 6.6 |
| 1976–77 | 28 | Montreal Canadiens | NHL | 77 | 25 | 51 | 76 | 70 | 53 | 15 | 10 | 0 | 6 | 287 | 8.7 |
| 1977–78 | 29 | Montreal Canadiens | NHL | 49 | 13 | 29 | 42 | 46 | 19 | 9 | 4 | 0 | 2 | 148 | 8.8 |
| 1978–79 | 30 | Montreal Canadiens | NHL | 69 | 13 | 42 | 55 | 27 | 43 | 7 | 6 | 0 | 1 | 204 | 6.4 |
| 1979–80 | 31 | Montreal Canadiens | NHL | 45 | 6 | 20 | 26 | -2 | 29 | 6 | 0 | 0 | 0 | 124 | 4.8 |
| 1980–81 | 32 | Montreal Canadiens | NHL | 33 | 1 | 9 | 10 | -6 | 79 | 0 | 1 | 0 | 1 | 47 | 2.1 |
| 1981–82 | 33 | Montreal Canadiens | NHL | 47 | 1 | 19 | 20 | -3 | 72 | 1 | 0 | 0 | 0 | 97 | 1.0 |
| 1981–82 | 33 | St. Louis Blues | NHL | 8 | 0 | 6 | 6 | -3 | 4 | 0 | 0 | 0 | 0 | 15 | 0.0 |
| 1982–83 | 34 | St. Louis Blues | NHL | 54 | 3 | 23 | 26 | -12 | 43 | 1 | 1 | 1 | 1 | 107 | 2.8 |
| 1983–84 | 35 | Boston Bruins | NHL | 45 | 2 | 16 | 18 | -2 | 34 | 1 | 1 | 0 | 1 | 57 | 3.5 |
| NHL Career — 16 Seasons | | | | 884 | 171 | 451 | 622 | 329 | 893 | 108 | 59 | 4 | 22 | 2479 | 6.9 |

## Guy Lapointe (continued)

### PLAYOFFS

| SEASON | AGE | TEAM | LG | GP | G | A | PTS | +/- | PIM | ESG | PPG | SHG | GWG | SOG | S% |
|---|---|---|---|---|---|---|---|---|---|---|---|---|---|---|---|
| 1970–71 | 22 | Montreal Canadiens | NHL | 20 | 4 | 5 | 9 | 7 | 34 | 3 | 1 | 0 | 2 | 55 | 7.3 |
| 1971–72 | 23 | Montreal Canadiens | NHL | 6 | 0 | 1 | 1 | -3 | 0 | 0 | 0 | 0 | 0 | 7 | 0.0 |
| 1972–73 | 24 | Montreal Canadiens | NHL | 17 | 6 | 7 | 13 | 14 | 20 | 4 | 2 | 0 | 1 | 54 | 11.1 |
| 1973–74 | 25 | Montreal Canadiens | NHL | 6 | 0 | 2 | 2 | 0 | 4 | 0 | 0 | 0 | 0 | 9 | 0.0 |
| 1974–75 | 26 | Montreal Canadiens | NHL | 11 | 6 | 4 | 10 | 7 | 4 | 2 | 3 | 1 | 0 | 36 | 16.7 |
| 1975–76 | 27 | Montreal Canadiens | NHL | 13 | 3 | 3 | 6 | 3 | 12 | 2 | 1 | 0 | 1 | 52 | 5.8 |
| 1976–77 | 28 | Montreal Canadiens | NHL | 12 | 3 | 9 | 12 | 8 | 4 | 2 | 1 | 0 | 0 | 48 | 6.3 |
| 1977–78 | 29 | Montreal Canadiens | NHL | 14 | 1 | 6 | 7 | -2 | 16 | 0 | 1 | 0 | 0 | 30 | 3.3 |
| 1978–79 | 30 | Montreal Canadiens | NHL | 10 | 2 | 6 | 8 | 5 | 10 | 1 | 1 | 0 | 0 | 25 | 8.0 |
| 1979–80 | 31 | Montreal Canadiens | NHL | 2 | 0 | 0 | 0 | 1 | 0 | 0 | 0 | 0 | 0 | 2 | 0.0 |
| 1980–81 | 32 | Montreal Canadiens | NHL | 1 | 0 | 0 | 0 | -1 | 17 | 0 | 0 | 0 | 0 | 0 | |
| 1981–82 | 33 | St. Louis Blues | NHL | 7 | 1 | 0 | 1 | 2 | 8 | 0 | 1 | 0 | 1 | 18 | 5.6 |
| 1982–83 | 34 | St. Louis Blues | NHL | 4 | 0 | 1 | 1 | -2 | 9 | 0 | 0 | 0 | 0 | 6 | 0.0 |
| NHL Career — 13 Seasons | | | | 123 | 26 | 44 | 70 | 39 | 138 | 14 | 11 | 1 | 5 | 342 | 7.6 |

## Jack Laviolette   Profile: See page 267

### REGULAR SEASON

| SEASON | AGE | TEAM | LG | GP | G | A | PTS | PIM |
|---|---|---|---|---|---|---|---|---|
| 1903–04 | 24 | Montreal Nationals | FAHL | 6 | 8 | 0 | 8 | |
| 1904–05 | 25 | Michigan Soo Indians | IHL | 24 | 15 | 0 | 15 | 24 |
| 1905–06 | 26 | Michigan Soo Indians | IHL | 17 | 15 | 0 | 15 | 28 |
| 1906–07 | 27 | Michigan Soo Indians | IHL | 19 | 10 | 7 | 17 | 34 |
| 1907–08 | 28 | Montreal Shamrocks | ECAHA | 6 | 1 | 0 | 1 | 36 |
| 1908–09 | 29 | Montreal Shamrocks | ECHA | 9 | 1 | 0 | 1 | 36 |
| 1909–10 | 30 | Les Canadiens (Montreal) | NHA | 12 | 4 | 0 | 4 | 41 |
| 1910–11 | 31 | Montreal Canadiens | NHA | 16 | 0 | 0 | 0 | 24 |
| 1911–12 | 32 | Montreal Canadiens | NHA | 17 | 7 | 0 | 7 | 10 |
| 1912–13 | 33 | Montreal Canadiens | NHA | 20 | 8 | 0 | 8 | 77 |
| 1913–14 | 34 | Montreal Canadiens | NHA | 20 | 7 | 9 | 16 | 30 |
| 1914–15 | 35 | Montreal Canadiens | NHA | 18 | 6 | 3 | 9 | 35 |

### REGULAR SEASON

| SEASON | AGE | TEAM | LG | GP | G | A | PTS | PIM |
|---|---|---|---|---|---|---|---|---|
| 1915–16 | 36 | Montreal Canadiens | NHA | 18 | 8 | 3 | 11 | 62 |
| 1916–17 | 37 | Montreal Canadiens | NHA | 17 | 7 | 3 | 10 | 24 |
| 1917–18 | 38 | Montreal Canadiens | NHL | 18 | 2 | 1 | 3 | 6 |
| Career — 15 Seasons | | | | 237 | 99 | 26 | 125 | 467 |

### PLAYOFFS

| SEASON | AGE | TEAM | LG | GP | G | A | PTS | PIM |
|---|---|---|---|---|---|---|---|---|
| 1913–14 | 34 | Montreal Canadiens | NHA | 2 | 0 | 1 | 1 | 0 |
| 1915–16 | 36 | Montreal Canadiens | St-Cup | 4 | 0 | 0 | 0 | 6 |
| 1916–17 | 37 | Montreal Canadiens | NHA | 2 | 0 | 0 | 0 | 0 |
| 1916–17 | 37 | Montreal Canadiens | St-Cup | 4 | 1 | 2 | 3 | 9 |
| 1917–18 | 38 | Montreal Canadiens | NHL | 2 | 0 | 0 | 0 | 0 |
| Career — 4 Seasons | | | | 14 | 1 | 3 | 4 | 15 |

## Brian Leetch   Profile: See page 268

### REGULAR SEASON

| SEASON | AGE | TEAM | LG | GP | G | A | PTS | +/- | PIM | ESG | PPG | SHG | GWG | SOG | S% |
|---|---|---|---|---|---|---|---|---|---|---|---|---|---|---|---|
| 1987–88 | 19 | New York Rangers | NHL | 17 | 2 | 12 | 14 | 5 | 0 | 1 | 1 | 0 | 1 | 40 | 5.0 |
| 1988–89 | 20 | New York Rangers | NHL | 68 | 23 | 48 | 71 | 8 | 50 | 12 | 8 | 3 | 1 | 268 | 8.6 |
| 1989–90 | 21 | New York Rangers | NHL | 72 | 11 | 45 | 56 | -18 | 26 | 6 | 5 | 0 | 2 | 222 | 5.0 |
| 1990–91 | 22 | New York Rangers | NHL | 80 | 16 | 72 | 88 | 2 | 42 | 10 | 6 | 0 | 4 | 206 | 7.8 |
| 1991–92 | 23 | New York Rangers | NHL | 80 | 22 | 80 | 102 | 25 | 26 | 11 | 10 | 1 | 3 | 245 | 9.0 |
| 1992–93 | 24 | New York Rangers | NHL | 36 | 6 | 30 | 36 | 2 | 26 | 3 | 2 | 1 | 1 | 150 | 4.0 |
| 1993–94 | 25 | New York Rangers | NHL | 84 | 23 | 56 | 79 | 28 | 67 | 5 | 17 | 1 | 4 | 328 | 7.0 |
| 1994–95 | 26 | New York Rangers | NHL | 48 | 9 | 32 | 41 | 0 | 18 | 6 | 3 | 0 | 2 | 182 | 4.9 |
| 1995–96 | 27 | New York Rangers | NHL | 82 | 15 | 70 | 85 | 12 | 30 | 8 | 7 | 0 | 3 | 276 | 5.4 |
| 1996–97 | 28 | New York Rangers | NHL | 82 | 20 | 58 | 78 | 31 | 40 | 11 | 9 | 0 | 2 | 256 | 7.8 |
| 1997–98 | 29 | New York Rangers | NHL | 76 | 17 | 33 | 50 | -36 | 32 | 6 | 11 | 0 | 2 | 230 | 7.4 |
| 1998–99 | 30 | New York Rangers | NHL | 82 | 13 | 42 | 55 | -7 | 42 | 9 | 4 | 0 | 1 | 184 | 7.1 |
| 1999–00 | 31 | New York Rangers | NHL | 50 | 7 | 19 | 26 | -16 | 20 | 4 | 3 | 0 | 2 | 124 | 5.6 |
| 2000–01 | 32 | New York Rangers | NHL | 82 | 21 | 58 | 79 | -18 | 34 | 10 | 10 | 1 | 3 | 241 | 8.7 |
| 2001–02 | 33 | New York Rangers | NHL | 82 | 10 | 45 | 55 | 14 | 28 | 9 | 1 | 0 | 3 | 202 | 5.0 |
| 2002–03 | 34 | New York Rangers | NHL | 51 | 12 | 18 | 30 | -3 | 20 | 7 | 5 | 0 | 2 | 150 | 8.0 |
| 2003–04 | 35 | New York Rangers | NHL | 57 | 13 | 23 | 36 | -5 | 24 | 8 | 4 | 1 | 1 | 165 | 7.9 |
| 2003–04 | 35 | Toronto Maple Leafs | NHL | 15 | 2 | 13 | 15 | 11 | 10 | 1 | 1 | 0 | 1 | 41 | 4.9 |
| 2005–06 | 37 | Boston Bruins | NHL | 61 | 5 | 27 | 32 | -10 | 36 | 1 | 4 | 0 | 0 | 130 | 3.8 |
| NHL Career — 18 Seasons | | | | 1205 | 247 | 781 | 1028 | 25 | 571 | 128 | 111 | 8 | 38 | 3640 | 6.8 |

### PLAYOFFS

| SEASON | AGE | TEAM | LG | GP | G | A | PTS | +/- | PIM | ESG | PPG | SHG | GWG | SOG | S% |
|---|---|---|---|---|---|---|---|---|---|---|---|---|---|---|---|
| 1988–89 | 20 | New York Rangers | NHL | 4 | 3 | 2 | 5 | -4 | 2 | 1 | 2 | 0 | 0 | 25 | 12.0 |
| 1990–91 | 22 | New York Rangers | NHL | 6 | 1 | 3 | 4 | -2 | 0 | 1 | 0 | 0 | 0 | 13 | 7.7 |
| 1991–92 | 23 | New York Rangers | NHL | 13 | 4 | 11 | 15 | -5 | 4 | 2 | 1 | 1 | 0 | 67 | 6.0 |
| 1993–94 | 25 | New York Rangers | NHL | 23 | 11 | 23 | 34 | 19 | 6 | 7 | 4 | 0 | 4 | 88 | 12.5 |
| 1994–95 | 26 | New York Rangers | NHL | 10 | 6 | 8 | 14 | -1 | 8 | 3 | 3 | 0 | 1 | 46 | 13.0 |
| 1995–96 | 27 | New York Rangers | NHL | 11 | 1 | 6 | 7 | -11 | 4 | 0 | 1 | 0 | 0 | 34 | 2.9 |
| 1996–97 | 28 | New York Rangers | NHL | 15 | 2 | 8 | 10 | 5 | 6 | 1 | 1 | 0 | 1 | 56 | 3.6 |
| 2003–04 | 35 | Toronto Maple Leafs | NHL | 13 | 0 | 8 | 8 | 1 | 6 | 0 | 0 | 0 | 0 | 23 | 0.0 |
| NHL Career — 8 Seasons | | | | 95 | 28 | 69 | 97 | 2 | 36 | 15 | 12 | 1 | 6 | 352 | 8.0 |

## Nicklas Lidstrom  Profile: See page 270

### REGULAR SEASON

| SEASON | AGE | TEAM | LG | GP | G | A | PTS | +/- | PIM | ESG | PPG | SHG | GWG | SOG | S% |
|---|---|---|---|---|---|---|---|---|---|---|---|---|---|---|---|
| 1991–92 | 21 | Detroit Red Wings | NHL | 80 | 11 | 49 | 60 | 36 | 22 | 6 | 5 | 0 | 1 | 168 | 6.5 |
| 1992–93 | 22 | Detroit Red Wings | NHL | 84 | 7 | 34 | 41 | 7 | 28 | 4 | 3 | 0 | 2 | 156 | 4.5 |
| 1993–94 | 23 | Detroit Red Wings | NHL | 84 | 10 | 46 | 56 | 43 | 26 | 6 | 4 | 0 | 3 | 200 | 5.0 |
| 1994–95 | 24 | Detroit Red Wings | NHL | 43 | 10 | 16 | 26 | 15 | 6 | 3 | 7 | 0 | 0 | 90 | 11.1 |
| 1995–96 | 25 | Detroit Red Wings | NHL | 81 | 17 | 50 | 67 | 29 | 20 | 8 | 8 | 1 | 1 | 211 | 8.1 |
| 1996–97 | 26 | Detroit Red Wings | NHL | 79 | 15 | 42 | 57 | 11 | 30 | 7 | 8 | 0 | 1 | 214 | 7.0 |
| 1997–98 | 27 | Detroit Red Wings | NHL | 80 | 17 | 42 | 59 | 22 | 18 | 9 | 7 | 1 | 1 | 205 | 8.3 |
| 1998–99 | 28 | Detroit Red Wings | NHL | 81 | 14 | 43 | 57 | 14 | 14 | 6 | 6 | 2 | 3 | 205 | 6.8 |
| 1999–00 | 29 | Detroit Red Wings | NHL | 81 | 20 | 53 | 73 | 19 | 18 | 7 | 9 | 4 | 3 | 218 | 9.2 |
| 2000–01 | 30 | Detroit Red Wings | NHL | 82 | 15 | 56 | 71 | 9 | 18 | 7 | 8 | 0 | 0 | 272 | 5.5 |
| 2001–02 | 31 | Detroit Red Wings | NHL | 78 | 9 | 50 | 59 | 13 | 20 | 3 | 6 | 0 | 0 | 215 | 4.2 |
| 2002–03 | 32 | Detroit Red Wings | NHL | 82 | 18 | 44 | 62 | 40 | 38 | 9 | 8 | 1 | 4 | 175 | 10.3 |
| 2003–04 | 33 | Detroit Red Wings | NHL | 81 | 10 | 28 | 38 | 19 | 18 | 6 | 3 | 1 | 3 | 194 | 5.2 |
| 2005–06 | 35 | Detroit Red Wings | NHL | 80 | 16 | 64 | 80 | 21 | 50 | 7 | 9 | 0 | 2 | 243 | 6.6 |
| 2006–07 | 36 | Detroit Red Wings | NHL | 80 | 13 | 49 | 62 | 40 | 46 | 3 | 10 | 0 | 1 | 224 | 5.8 |
| 2007–08 | 37 | Detroit Red Wings | NHL | 76 | 10 | 60 | 70 | 40 | 40 | 5 | 5 | 0 | 4 | 188 | 5.3 |
| 2008–09 | 38 | Detroit Red Wings | NHL | 78 | 16 | 43 | 59 | 31 | 30 | 6 | 10 | 0 | 4 | 180 | 8.9 |
| 2009–10 | 39 | Detroit Red Wings | NHL | 82 | 9 | 40 | 49 | 22 | 24 | 4 | 5 | 0 | 1 | 194 | 4.6 |
| 2010–11 | 40 | Detroit Red Wings | NHL | 82 | 16 | 46 | 62 | -2 | 20 | 9 | 7 | 0 | 1 | 175 | 9.1 |
| 2011–12 | 41 | Detroit Red Wings | NHL | 70 | 11 | 23 | 34 | 21 | 28 | 7 | 4 | 0 | 0 | 148 | 7.4 |
| NHL Career — 20 Seasons | | | | 1564 | 264 | 878 | 1142 | 450 | 514 | 122 | 132 | 10 | 35 | 3875 | 6.8 |

### PLAYOFFS

| SEASON | AGE | TEAM | LG | GP | G | A | PTS | +/- | PIM | ESG | PPG | SHG | GWG | SOG | S% |
|---|---|---|---|---|---|---|---|---|---|---|---|---|---|---|---|
| 1991–92 | 21 | Detroit Red Wings | NHL | 11 | 1 | 2 | 3 | -5 | 0 | 0 | 1 | 0 | 0 | 16 | 6.3 |
| 1992–93 | 22 | Detroit Red Wings | NHL | 7 | 1 | 0 | 1 | -2 | 0 | 0 | 1 | 0 | 0 | 8 | 12.5 |
| 1993–94 | 23 | Detroit Red Wings | NHL | 7 | 3 | 2 | 5 | 4 | 0 | 1 | 1 | 1 | 0 | 20 | 15.0 |
| 1994–95 | 24 | Detroit Red Wings | NHL | 18 | 4 | 12 | 16 | 4 | 8 | 1 | 3 | 0 | 2 | 37 | 10.8 |
| 1995–96 | 25 | Detroit Red Wings | NHL | 19 | 5 | 9 | 14 | 2 | 10 | 4 | 1 | 0 | 0 | 50 | 10.0 |
| 1996–97 | 26 | Detroit Red Wings | NHL | 20 | 2 | 6 | 8 | 12 | 2 | 2 | 0 | 0 | 0 | 79 | 2.5 |
| 1997–98 | 27 | Detroit Red Wings | NHL | 22 | 6 | 13 | 19 | 12 | 8 | 4 | 2 | 0 | 2 | 59 | 10.2 |
| 1998–99 | 28 | Detroit Red Wings | NHL | 10 | 2 | 9 | 11 | 0 | 4 | 0 | 2 | 0 | 0 | 29 | 6.9 |
| 1999–00 | 29 | Detroit Red Wings | NHL | 9 | 2 | 4 | 6 | -6 | 4 | 1 | 1 | 0 | 0 | 21 | 9.5 |
| 2000–01 | 30 | Detroit Red Wings | NHL | 6 | 1 | 7 | 8 | 1 | 0 | 1 | 0 | 0 | 0 | 15 | 6.7 |
| 2001–02 | 31 | Detroit Red Wings | NHL | 23 | 5 | 11 | 16 | 6 | 2 | 2 | 2 | 1 | 2 | 41 | 12.2 |
| 2002–03 | 32 | Detroit Red Wings | NHL | 4 | 0 | 2 | 2 | -1 | 0 | 0 | 0 | 0 | 0 | 15 | 0.0 |
| 2003–04 | 33 | Detroit Red Wings | NHL | 12 | 2 | 5 | 7 | 4 | 4 | 0 | 2 | 0 | 0 | 27 | 7.4 |
| 2005–06 | 35 | Detroit Red Wings | NHL | 6 | 1 | 1 | 2 | -4 | 2 | 0 | 1 | 0 | 1 | 21 | 4.8 |
| 2006–07 | 36 | Detroit Red Wings | NHL | 18 | 4 | 14 | 18 | 0 | 6 | 0 | 4 | 0 | 2 | 39 | 10.3 |
| 2007–08 | 37 | Detroit Red Wings | NHL | 22 | 3 | 10 | 13 | 8 | 14 | 1 | 1 | 1 | 1 | 41 | 7.3 |
| 2008–09 | 38 | Detroit Red Wings | NHL | 21 | 4 | 12 | 16 | 11 | 6 | 1 | 3 | 0 | 1 | 59 | 6.8 |
| 2009–10 | 39 | Detroit Red Wings | NHL | 12 | 4 | 6 | 10 | 7 | 2 | 1 | 3 | 0 | 0 | 39 | 10.3 |
| 2010–11 | 40 | Detroit Red Wings | NHL | 11 | 4 | 4 | 8 | 8 | 4 | 2 | 2 | 0 | 0 | 26 | 15.4 |
| 2011–12 | 41 | Detroit Red Wings | NHL | 5 | 0 | 0 | 0 | 0 | 0 | 0 | 0 | 0 | 0 | 14 | 0.0 |
| NHL Career — 20 Seasons | | | | 263 | 54 | 129 | 183 | 61 | 76 | 21 | 30 | 3 | 11 | 656 | 8.2 |

# Al MacInnis   Profile: See page 272

**REGULAR SEASON**

| SEASON | AGE | TEAM | LG | GP | G | A | PTS | +/- | PIM | ESG | PPG | SHG | GWG | SOG | S% |
|--------|-----|------|-----|-----|-----|-----|------|------|------|-----|-----|-----|-----|------|------|
| 1981–82 | 18 | Calgary Flames | NHL | 2 | 0 | 0 | 0 | 0 | 0 | 0 | 0 | 0 | 0 | 2 | 0.0 |
| 1982–83 | 19 | Calgary Flames | NHL | 14 | 1 | 3 | 4 | 0 | 9 | 1 | 0 | 0 | 0 | 7 | 14.3 |
| 1983–84 | 20 | Calgary Flames | NHL | 51 | 11 | 34 | 45 | -1 | 42 | 4 | 7 | 0 | 2 | 160 | 6.9 |
| 1984–85 | 21 | Calgary Flames | NHL | 67 | 14 | 52 | 66 | 7 | 75 | 6 | 8 | 0 | 0 | 259 | 5.4 |
| 1985–86 | 22 | Calgary Flames | NHL | 77 | 11 | 57 | 68 | 37 | 76 | 7 | 4 | 0 | 0 | 241 | 4.6 |
| 1986–87 | 23 | Calgary Flames | NHL | 79 | 20 | 56 | 76 | 20 | 97 | 13 | 7 | 0 | 2 | 262 | 7.6 |
| 1987–88 | 24 | Calgary Flames | NHL | 80 | 25 | 58 | 83 | 13 | 114 | 16 | 7 | 2 | 2 | 245 | 10.2 |
| 1988–89 | 25 | Calgary Flames | NHL | 79 | 16 | 58 | 74 | 38 | 136 | 8 | 8 | 0 | 3 | 277 | 5.8 |
| 1989–90 | 26 | Calgary Flames | NHL | 79 | 28 | 62 | 90 | 20 | 82 | 13 | 14 | 1 | 3 | 304 | 9.2 |
| 1990–91 | 27 | Calgary Flames | NHL | 78 | 28 | 75 | 103 | 42 | 90 | 11 | 17 | 0 | 1 | 305 | 9.2 |
| 1991–92 | 28 | Calgary Flames | NHL | 72 | 20 | 57 | 77 | 13 | 83 | 9 | 11 | 0 | 0 | 304 | 6.6 |
| 1992–93 | 29 | Calgary Flames | NHL | 50 | 11 | 43 | 54 | 15 | 61 | 4 | 7 | 0 | 4 | 201 | 5.5 |
| 1993–94 | 30 | Calgary Flames | NHL | 75 | 28 | 54 | 82 | 35 | 95 | 15 | 12 | 1 | 5 | 324 | 8.6 |
| 1994–95 | 31 | St. Louis Blues | NHL | 32 | 8 | 20 | 28 | 19 | 43 | 6 | 2 | 0 | 0 | 110 | 7.3 |
| 1995–96 | 32 | St. Louis Blues | NHL | 82 | 17 | 44 | 61 | 5 | 88 | 7 | 9 | 1 | 1 | 317 | 5.4 |
| 1996–97 | 33 | St. Louis Blues | NHL | 72 | 13 | 30 | 43 | 2 | 65 | 6 | 6 | 1 | 1 | 296 | 4.4 |
| 1997–98 | 34 | St. Louis Blues | NHL | 71 | 19 | 30 | 49 | 6 | 80 | 9 | 9 | 1 | 2 | 227 | 8.4 |
| 1998–99 | 35 | St. Louis Blues | NHL | 82 | 20 | 42 | 62 | 33 | 70 | 8 | 11 | 1 | 2 | 314 | 6.4 |
| 1999–00 | 36 | St. Louis Blues | NHL | 61 | 11 | 28 | 39 | 20 | 34 | 5 | 6 | 0 | 7 | 245 | 4.5 |
| 2000–01 | 37 | St. Louis Blues | NHL | 59 | 12 | 42 | 54 | 23 | 52 | 5 | 6 | 1 | 3 | 218 | 5.5 |
| 2001–02 | 38 | St. Louis Blues | NHL | 71 | 11 | 35 | 46 | 3 | 52 | 5 | 6 | 0 | 4 | 231 | 4.8 |
| 2002–03 | 39 | St. Louis Blues | NHL | 80 | 16 | 52 | 68 | 22 | 61 | 6 | 9 | 1 | 2 | 299 | 5.4 |
| 2003–04 | 40 | St. Louis Blues | NHL | 3 | 0 | 2 | 2 | -1 | 6 | 0 | 0 | 0 | 0 | 9 | 0.0 |
| NHL Career – 23 Seasons | | | | 1416 | 340 | 934 | 1274 | 371 | 1511 | 164 | 166 | 10 | 44 | 5157 | 6.6 |

**PLAYOFFS**

| SEASON | AGE | TEAM | LG | GP | G | A | PTS | +/- | PIM | ESG | PPG | SHG | GWG | SOG | S% |
|--------|-----|------|-----|-----|-----|-----|------|------|------|-----|-----|-----|-----|------|------|
| 1983–84 | 20 | Calgary Flames | NHL | 11 | 2 | 12 | 14 | -1 | 13 | 0 | 2 | 0 | 1 | 38 | 5.3 |
| 1984–85 | 21 | Calgary Flames | NHL | 4 | 1 | 2 | 3 | -1 | 8 | 0 | 1 | 0 | 0 | 13 | 7.7 |
| 1985–86 | 22 | Calgary Flames | NHL | 21 | 4 | 15 | 19 | 10 | 30 | 2 | 2 | 0 | 0 | 79 | 5.1 |
| 1986–87 | 23 | Calgary Flames | NHL | 4 | 1 | 0 | 1 | -1 | 0 | 0 | 1 | 0 | 0 | 10 | 10.0 |
| 1987–88 | 24 | Calgary Flames | NHL | 7 | 3 | 6 | 9 | 0 | 18 | 1 | 2 | 0 | 0 | 28 | 10.7 |
| 1988–89 | 25 | Calgary Flames | NHL | 22 | 7 | 24 | 31 | 6 | 46 | 2 | 5 | 0 | 4 | 69 | 10.1 |
| 1989–90 | 26 | Calgary Flames | NHL | 6 | 2 | 3 | 5 | 1 | 8 | 1 | 1 | 0 | 0 | 19 | 10.5 |
| 1990–91 | 27 | Calgary Flames | NHL | 7 | 2 | 3 | 5 | -5 | 8 | 0 | 2 | 0 | 0 | 25 | 8.0 |
| 1992–93 | 29 | Calgary Flames | NHL | 6 | 1 | 6 | 7 | -4 | 10 | 0 | 1 | 0 | 0 | 25 | 4.0 |
| 1993–94 | 30 | Calgary Flames | NHL | 7 | 2 | 6 | 8 | 5 | 12 | 1 | 1 | 0 | 0 | 32 | 6.3 |
| 1994–95 | 31 | St. Louis Blues | NHL | 7 | 1 | 5 | 6 | -3 | 10 | 1 | 0 | 0 | 0 | 22 | 4.5 |
| 1995–96 | 32 | St. Louis Blues | NHL | 13 | 3 | 4 | 7 | 2 | 20 | 2 | 1 | 0 | 0 | 48 | 6.3 |
| 1996–97 | 33 | St. Louis Blues | NHL | 6 | 1 | 2 | 3 | -1 | 4 | 0 | 1 | 0 | 0 | 22 | 4.5 |
| 1997–98 | 34 | St. Louis Blues | NHL | 8 | 2 | 6 | 8 | 1 | 12 | 1 | 1 | 0 | 0 | 27 | 7.4 |
| 1998–99 | 35 | St. Louis Blues | NHL | 13 | 4 | 8 | 12 | -2 | 20 | 2 | 2 | 0 | 0 | 66 | 6.1 |
| 1999–00 | 36 | St. Louis Blues | NHL | 7 | 1 | 3 | 4 | -1 | 14 | 0 | 1 | 0 | 0 | 40 | 2.5 |
| 2000–01 | 37 | St. Louis Blues | NHL | 15 | 2 | 8 | 10 | 2 | 18 | 0 | 2 | 0 | 0 | 67 | 3.0 |
| 2001–02 | 38 | St. Louis Blues | NHL | 10 | 0 | 7 | 7 | 3 | 4 | 0 | 0 | 0 | 0 | 30 | 0.0 |
| 2002–03 | 39 | St. Louis Blues | NHL | 3 | 0 | 1 | 1 | 0 | 0 | 0 | 0 | 0 | 0 | 3 | 0.0 |
| NHL Career – 19 Seasons | | | | 177 | 39 | 121 | 160 | 11 | 255 | 13 | 26 | 0 | 5 | 663 | 5.9 |

# Sylvio Mantha   Profile: See page 274

**REGULAR SEASON**

| SEASON | AGE | TEAM | LG | GP | G | A | PTS | PIM |
|--------|-----|------|-----|-----|-----|-----|------|------|
| 1923–24 | 21 | Montreal Canadiens | NHL | 24 | 1 | 1 | 2 | 11 |
| 1924–25 | 22 | Montreal Canadiens | NHL | 30 | 2 | 3 | 5 | 18 |
| 1925–26 | 23 | Montreal Canadiens | NHL | 34 | 2 | 2 | 4 | 68 |
| 1926–27 | 24 | Montreal Canadiens | NHL | 43 | 10 | 5 | 15 | 77 |
| 1927–28 | 25 | Montreal Canadiens | NHL | 43 | 4 | 11 | 15 | 63 |
| 1928–29 | 26 | Montreal Canadiens | NHL | 44 | 9 | 4 | 13 | 58 |
| 1929–30 | 27 | Montreal Canadiens | NHL | 44 | 13 | 11 | 24 | 108 |
| 1930–31 | 28 | Montreal Canadiens | NHL | 44 | 4 | 7 | 11 | 73 |
| 1931–32 | 29 | Montreal Canadiens | NHL | 47 | 5 | 5 | 10 | 62 |
| 1932–33 | 30 | Montreal Canadiens | NHL | 48 | 4 | 7 | 11 | 50 |
| 1933–34 | 31 | Montreal Canadiens | NHL | 48 | 4 | 6 | 10 | 24 |
| 1934–35 | 32 | Montreal Canadiens | NHL | 47 | 3 | 11 | 14 | 36 |
| 1935–36 | 33 | Montreal Canadiens | NHL | 42 | 2 | 4 | 6 | 25 |
| 1936–37 | 34 | Boston Bruins | NHL | 4 | 0 | 0 | 0 | 2 |
| Career – 14 Seasons | | | | 542 | 63 | 77 | 140 | 675 |

**PLAYOFFS**

| SEASON | AGE | TEAM | LG | GP | G | A | PTS | PIM |
|--------|-----|------|-----|-----|-----|-----|------|------|
| 1923–24 | 21 | Montreal Canadiens | NHL | 2 | 0 | 0 | 0 | 0 |
| 1923–24 | 21 | Montreal Canadiens | St-Cup | 4 | 0 | 0 | 0 | 0 |
| 1924–25 | 22 | Montreal Canadiens | NHL | 2 | 0 | 1 | 1 | 0 |
| 1924–25 | 22 | Montreal Canadiens | St-Cup | 4 | 0 | 0 | 0 | 2 |
| 1926–27 | 24 | Montreal Canadiens | NHL | 4 | 1 | 0 | 1 | 0 |
| 1927–28 | 25 | Montreal Canadiens | NHL | 2 | 0 | 0 | 0 | 6 |
| 1928–29 | 26 | Montreal Canadiens | NHL | 3 | 0 | 0 | 0 | 0 |
| 1929–30 | 27 | Montreal Canadiens | NHL | 6 | 2 | 1 | 3 | 18 |
| 1930–31 | 28 | Montreal Canadiens | NHL | 10 | 2 | 1 | 3 | 26 |
| 1931–32 | 29 | Montreal Canadiens | NHL | 4 | 0 | 1 | 1 | 8 |
| 1932–33 | 30 | Montreal Canadiens | NHL | 2 | 0 | 1 | 1 | 2 |
| 1933–34 | 31 | Montreal Canadiens | NHL | 2 | 0 | 0 | 0 | 2 |
| 1934–35 | 32 | Montreal Canadiens | NHL | 2 | 0 | 0 | 0 | 2 |
| Career – 11 Seasons | | | | 47 | 5 | 5 | 10 | 66 |

## Jack Marshall   Profile: See page 275

### REGULAR SEASON

| SEASON | AGE | TEAM | LG | GP | G | A | PTS | PIM |
|---|---|---|---|---|---|---|---|---|
| 1900–01 | 23 | Winnipeg Victorias | WSrHL | 2 | 2 | 0 | 2 | |
| 1901–02 | 24 | Montreal AAA | CAHL | 8 | 11 | 0 | 11 | 8 |
| 1902–03 | 25 | Montreal AAA | CAHL | 2 | 8 | 0 | 8 | 3 |
| 1903–04 | 26 | Montreal Wanderers | FAHL | 4 | 11 | 0 | 11 | 6 |
| 1904–05 | 27 | Montreal Wanderers | FAHL | 8 | 17 | 0 | 17 | 9 |
| 1906–07 | 29 | Ottawa Montagnards | FAHL | 3 | 6 | 0 | 6 | |
| 1906–07 | 29 | Montreal Wanderers | ECAHA | 3 | 6 | 0 | 6 | 0 |
| 1907–08 | 30 | Montreal Shamrocks | ECAHA | 9 | 20 | 0 | 20 | 13 |
| 1908–09 | 31 | Montreal Shamrocks | ECHA | 12 | 10 | 0 | 10 | 14 |
| 1909–10 | 32 | Montreal Wanderers | NHA | 12 | 2 | 0 | 2 | 8 |
| 1910–11 | 33 | Montreal Wanderers | NHA | 5 | 1 | 0 | 1 | 2 |
| 1911–12 | 34 | Montreal Wanderers | NHA | 3 | 0 | 0 | 0 | 0 |
| 1912–13 | 35 | Toronto Blueshirts | NHA | 13 | 3 | 0 | 3 | 8 |
| 1913–14 | 36 | Toronto Blueshirts | NHA | 20 | 3 | 3 | 6 | 16 |
| 1914–15 | 37 | Toronto Blueshirts | NHA | 4 | 0 | 1 | 1 | 8 |
| 1915–16 | 38 | Montreal Wanderers | NHA | 15 | 1 | 0 | 1 | 2 |
| 1916–17 | 39 | Montreal Wanderers | NHA | 8 | 0 | 0 | 0 | 3 |
| Career — 16 Seasons | | | | 131 | 101 | 4 | 105 | 102 |

### PLAYOFFS

| SEASON | AGE | TEAM | LG | GP | G | A | PTS | PIM |
|---|---|---|---|---|---|---|---|---|
| 1900–01 | 23 | Winnipeg Victorias | St-Cup | 2 | 0 | 0 | 0 | |
| 1901–02 | 24 | Montreal AAA | St-Cup | 3 | 2 | 0 | 2 | 8 |
| 1902–03 | 25 | Montreal AAA | St-Cup | 4 | 7 | 0 | 7 | 2 |
| 1903–04 | 26 | Montreal Wanderers | St-Cup | 1 | 1 | 0 | 1 | 0 |
| 1906–07 | 29 | Montreal Wanderers | St-Cup | 1 | 1 | 0 | 1 | 0 |
| 1909–10 | 32 | Montreal Wanderers | St-Cup | 1 | 0 | 0 | 0 | 0 |
| 1913–14 | 36 | Toronto Blueshirts | NHA | 2 | 0 | 0 | 0 | 0 |
| 1913–14 | 36 | Toronto Blueshirts | St-Cup | 3 | 1 | 0 | 1 | 2 |
| Career — 7 Seasons | | | | 17 | 12 | 0 | 12 | 12 |

## George McNamara   Profile: See page 276

### REGULAR SEASON

| SEASON | AGE | TEAM | LG | GP | G | A | PTS | PIM |
|---|---|---|---|---|---|---|---|---|
| 1906–07 | 20 | Canadian Soo | IHL | 3 | 0 | 0 | 0 | 0 |
| 1907–08 | 21 | Montreal Shamrocks | ECAHA | 10 | 3 | 0 | 3 | 34 |
| 1908–09 | 22 | Montreal Shamrocks | ECHA | 12 | 4 | 0 | 4 | 60 |
| 1910–11 | 24 | Waterloo Colts | OPHL | 16 | 15 | 0 | 15 | |
| 1911–12 | 25 | Halifax Crescents | MPHL | 10 | 2 | 0 | 2 | 24 |
| 1912–13 | 26 | Toronto Tecumsehs | NHA | 20 | 4 | 0 | 4 | 23 |
| 1913–14 | 27 | Toronto Ontarios | NHA | 9 | 0 | 1 | 1 | 0 |
| 1913–14 | 27 | Toronto Blueshirts | NHA | 9 | 0 | 1 | 1 | 2 |
| 1915–16 | 29 | Toronto Blueshirts | NHA | 23 | 5 | 2 | 7 | 74 |
| 1916–17 | 30 | Toronto 228th Battalion | NHA | 11 | 2 | 1 | 3 | 15 |
| Career — 10 Seasons | | | | 141 | 39 | 13 | 52 | 299 |

### PLAYOFFS

| SEASON | AGE | TEAM | LG | GP | G | A | PTS | PIM |
|---|---|---|---|---|---|---|---|---|
| 1910–11 | 24 | Waterloo Colts | OPHL | 1 | 0 | 0 | 0 | 0 |
| 1913–14 | 27 | Toronto Blueshirts | St-Cup | 3 | 2 | 0 | 2 | 0 |
| Career — 2 Seasons | | | | 4 | 2 | 0 | 2 | 0 |

## Larry Murphy   Profile: See page 277

### REGULAR SEASON

| SEASON | AGE | TEAM | LG | GP | G | A | PTS | +/- | PIM | ESG | PPG | SHG | GWG | SOG | S% |
|---|---|---|---|---|---|---|---|---|---|---|---|---|---|---|---|
| 1980–81 | 19 | Los Angeles Kings | NHL | 80 | 16 | 60 | 76 | 16 | 79 | 10 | 5 | 1 | 0 | 153 | 10.5 |
| 1981–82 | 20 | Los Angeles Kings | NHL | 79 | 22 | 44 | 66 | -12 | 95 | 13 | 8 | 1 | 2 | 191 | 11.5 |
| 1982–83 | 21 | Los Angeles Kings | NHL | 77 | 14 | 48 | 62 | 1 | 81 | 5 | 9 | 0 | 2 | 172 | 8.1 |
| 1983–84 | 22 | Los Angeles Kings | NHL | 6 | 0 | 3 | 3 | -5 | 0 | 0 | 0 | 0 | 0 | 11 | 0.0 |
| 1983–84 | 22 | Washington Capitals | NHL | 72 | 13 | 33 | 46 | 11 | 50 | 11 | 2 | 0 | 2 | 138 | 9.4 |
| 1984–85 | 23 | Washington Capitals | NHL | 79 | 14 | 42 | 56 | 21 | 51 | 11 | 3 | 0 | 0 | 153 | 8.5 |
| 1985–86 | 24 | Washington Capitals | NHL | 78 | 21 | 44 | 65 | 2 | 50 | 12 | 8 | 1 | 2 | 180 | 11.7 |
| 1986–87 | 25 | Washington Capitals | NHL | 80 | 23 | 58 | 81 | 25 | 39 | 15 | 8 | 0 | 4 | 224 | 10.3 |
| 1987–88 | 26 | Washington Capitals | NHL | 79 | 8 | 53 | 61 | 2 | 72 | 1 | 7 | 0 | 1 | 201 | 4.0 |
| 1988–89 | 27 | Washington Capitals | NHL | 65 | 7 | 29 | 36 | -5 | 70 | 4 | 3 | 0 | 0 | 129 | 5.4 |
| 1988–89 | 27 | Minnesota North Stars | NHL | 13 | 4 | 6 | 10 | 5 | 12 | 1 | 3 | 0 | 1 | 31 | 12.9 |
| 1989–90 | 28 | Minnesota North Stars | NHL | 77 | 10 | 58 | 68 | -13 | 44 | 6 | 4 | 0 | 1 | 173 | 5.8 |
| 1990–91 | 29 | Minnesota North Stars | NHL | 31 | 4 | 11 | 15 | -8 | 38 | 3 | 1 | 0 | 2 | 103 | 3.9 |
| 1990–91 | 29 | Pittsburgh Penguins | NHL | 44 | 5 | 23 | 28 | 2 | 30 | 3 | 2 | 0 | 0 | 85 | 5.9 |
| 1991–92 | 30 | Pittsburgh Penguins | NHL | 77 | 21 | 56 | 77 | 33 | 48 | 12 | 7 | 2 | 3 | 206 | 10.2 |
| 1992–93 | 31 | Pittsburgh Penguins | NHL | 83 | 22 | 63 | 85 | 45 | 73 | 14 | 6 | 2 | 2 | 230 | 9.6 |
| 1993–94 | 32 | Pittsburgh Penguins | NHL | 84 | 17 | 56 | 73 | 10 | 44 | 10 | 7 | 0 | 4 | 236 | 7.2 |
| 1994–95 | 33 | Pittsburgh Penguins | NHL | 48 | 13 | 25 | 38 | 12 | 18 | 9 | 4 | 0 | 3 | 124 | 10.5 |
| 1995–96 | 34 | Toronto Maple Leafs | NHL | 82 | 12 | 49 | 61 | -2 | 34 | 4 | 8 | 0 | 1 | 182 | 6.6 |
| 1996–97 | 35 | Toronto Maple Leafs | NHL | 69 | 7 | 32 | 39 | 1 | 20 | 3 | 4 | 0 | 0 | 137 | 5.1 |
| 1996–97 | 35 | Detroit Red Wings | NHL | 12 | 2 | 4 | 6 | 2 | 0 | 1 | 1 | 0 | 1 | 21 | 9.5 |
| 1997–98 | 36 | Detroit Red Wings | NHL | 82 | 11 | 41 | 52 | 35 | 37 | 8 | 2 | 1 | 2 | 129 | 8.5 |
| 1998–99 | 37 | Detroit Red Wings | NHL | 80 | 10 | 42 | 52 | 21 | 42 | 4 | 5 | 1 | 2 | 168 | 6.0 |
| 1999–00 | 38 | Detroit Red Wings | NHL | 81 | 10 | 30 | 40 | 4 | 45 | 3 | 7 | 0 | 0 | 146 | 6.8 |
| 2000–01 | 39 | Detroit Red Wings | NHL | 57 | 2 | 19 | 21 | -6 | 12 | 2 | 0 | 0 | 1 | 81 | 2.5 |
| NHL Career — 21 Seasons | | | | 1615 | 288 | 929 | 1217 | 197 | 1084 | 165 | 114 | 9 | 36 | 3604 | 8.0 |

### PLAYOFFS

| SEASON | AGE | TEAM | LG | GP | G | A | PTS | +/- | PIM | ESG | PPG | SHG | GWG | SOG | S% |
|---|---|---|---|---|---|---|---|---|---|---|---|---|---|---|---|
| 1980–81 | 19 | Los Angeles Kings | NHL | 4 | 3 | 0 | 3 | -2 | 2 | 2 | 1 | 0 | 0 | 8 | 37.5 |
| 1981–82 | 20 | Los Angeles Kings | NHL | 10 | 2 | 8 | 10 | 3 | 12 | 1 | 1 | 0 | 0 | 28 | 7.1 |
| 1983–84 | 22 | Washington Capitals | NHL | 8 | 0 | 3 | 3 | 2 | 6 | 0 | 0 | 0 | 0 | 20 | 0.0 |
| 1984–85 | 23 | Washington Capitals | NHL | 5 | 2 | 3 | 5 | -3 | 0 | 0 | 2 | 0 | 0 | 17 | 11.8 |
| 1985–86 | 24 | Washington Capitals | NHL | 9 | 1 | 5 | 6 | 1 | 6 | 0 | 1 | 0 | 0 | 21 | 4.8 |
| 1986–87 | 25 | Washington Capitals | NHL | 7 | 2 | 2 | 4 | 3 | 6 | 2 | 2 | 0 | 1 | 25 | 8.0 |
| 1987–88 | 26 | Washington Capitals | NHL | 13 | 4 | 4 | 8 | 0 | 33 | 2 | 2 | 0 | 0 | 21 | 19.0 |
| 1988–89 | 27 | Minnesota North Stars | NHL | 5 | 0 | 2 | 2 | -5 | 8 | 0 | 0 | 0 | 0 | 9 | 0.0 |

## Larry Murphy (continued)

**PLAYOFFS**

| SEASON | AGE | TEAM | LG | GP | G | A | PTS | +/- | PIM | ESG | PPG | SHG | GWG | SOG | S% |
|--------|-----|------|----|----|---|---|-----|-----|-----|-----|-----|-----|-----|-----|-----|
| 1989–90 | 28 | Minnesota North Stars | NHL | 7 | 1 | 2 | 3 | -4 | 31 | 1 | 0 | 0 | 1 | 16 | 6.3 |
| 1990–91 | 29 | Pittsburgh Penguins | NHL | 23 | 5 | 18 | 23 | 17 | 44 | 1 | 4 | 0 | 0 | 66 | 1.6 |
| 1991–92 | 30 | Pittsburgh Penguins | NHL | 21 | 6 | 10 | 16 | -4 | 19 | 3 | 3 | 0 | 1 | 59 | 10.2 |
| 1992–93 | 31 | Pittsburgh Penguins | NHL | 12 | 2 | 11 | 13 | 2 | 10 | 0 | 2 | 0 | 1 | 26 | 7.7 |
| 1993–94 | 32 | Pittsburgh Penguins | NHL | 6 | 0 | 5 | 5 | -6 | 0 | 0 | 0 | 0 | 0 | 13 | 0.0 |
| 1994–95 | 33 | Pittsburgh Penguins | NHL | 12 | 2 | 13 | 15 | 3 | 0 | 1 | 1 | 0 | 0 | 35 | 5.7 |
| 1995–96 | 34 | Toronto Maple Leafs | NHL | 6 | 0 | 2 | 2 | -8 | 4 | 0 | 0 | 0 | 0 | 16 | 0.0 |
| 1996–97 | 35 | Detroit Red Wings | NHL | 20 | 2 | 9 | 11 | 16 | 8 | 1 | 1 | 0 | 1 | 51 | 3.9 |
| 1997–98 | 36 | Detroit Red Wings | NHL | 22 | 3 | 12 | 15 | 12 | 2 | 0 | 1 | 2 | 1 | 36 | 8.3 |
| 1998–99 | 37 | Detroit Red Wings | NHL | 10 | 0 | 2 | 2 | 2 | 8 | 0 | 0 | 0 | 0 | 14 | 0.0 |
| 1999–00 | 38 | Detroit Red Wings | NHL | 9 | 2 | 3 | 5 | 1 | 2 | 0 | 1 | 1 | 0 | 16 | 12.5 |
| 2000–01 | 39 | Detroit Red Wings | NHL | 6 | 0 | 1 | 1 | 2 | 0 | 0 | 0 | 0 | 0 | 7 | 0.0 |
| NHL Career — 20 Seasons | | | | 215 | 37 | 115 | 152 | 32 | 201 | 14 | 20 | 3 | 7 | 504 | 7.3 |

# Scott Niedermayer   Profile: See page 278

**REGULAR SEASON**

| SEASON | AGE | TEAM | LG | GP | G | A | PTS | +/- | PIM | ESG | PPG | SHG | GWG | SOG | S% |
|--------|-----|------|----|----|---|---|-----|-----|-----|-----|-----|-----|-----|-----|-----|
| 1991–92 | 18 | New Jersey Devils | NHL | 4 | 0 | 1 | 1 | 1 | 2 | 0 | 0 | 0 | 0 | 4 | 0.0 |
| 1992–93 | 19 | New Jersey Devils | NHL | 80 | 11 | 29 | 40 | 8 | 47 | 6 | 5 | 0 | 0 | 131 | 8.4 |
| 1993–94 | 20 | New Jersey Devils | NHL | 81 | 10 | 36 | 46 | 34 | 42 | 5 | 5 | 0 | 2 | 135 | 7.4 |
| 1994–95 | 21 | New Jersey Devils | NHL | 48 | 4 | 15 | 19 | 19 | 18 | 0 | 4 | 0 | 0 | 52 | 7.7 |
| 1995–96 | 22 | New Jersey Devils | NHL | 79 | 8 | 25 | 33 | 5 | 46 | 2 | 6 | 0 | 0 | 179 | 4.5 |
| 1996–97 | 23 | New Jersey Devils | NHL | 81 | 5 | 30 | 35 | -4 | 64 | 2 | 3 | 0 | 3 | 159 | 3.1 |
| 1997–98 | 24 | New Jersey Devils | NHL | 81 | 14 | 43 | 57 | 5 | 27 | 3 | 11 | 0 | 1 | 175 | 8.0 |
| 1998–99 | 25 | New Jersey Devils | NHL | 72 | 11 | 35 | 46 | 16 | 26 | 9 | 1 | 1 | 3 | 161 | 6.8 |
| 1999–00 | 26 | New Jersey Devils | NHL | 71 | 7 | 31 | 38 | 19 | 48 | 6 | 1 | 0 | 0 | 109 | 6.4 |
| 2000–01 | 27 | New Jersey Devils | NHL | 57 | 6 | 29 | 35 | 14 | 22 | 5 | 1 | 0 | 5 | 87 | 6.9 |
| 2001–02 | 28 | New Jersey Devils | NHL | 76 | 11 | 22 | 33 | 12 | 30 | 9 | 2 | 0 | 6 | 129 | 8.5 |
| 2002–03 | 29 | New Jersey Devils | NHL | 81 | 11 | 28 | 39 | 23 | 62 | 8 | 3 | 0 | 3 | 164 | 6.7 |
| 2003–04 | 30 | New Jersey Devils | NHL | 81 | 14 | 40 | 54 | 20 | 44 | 5 | 9 | 0 | 3 | 165 | 8.5 |
| 2005–06 | 32 | Mighty Ducks of Anaheim | NHL | 82 | 13 | 50 | 63 | 8 | 96 | 4 | 9 | 0 | 3 | 181 | 7.2 |
| 2006–07 | 33 | Anaheim Ducks | NHL | 79 | 15 | 54 | 69 | 6 | 86 | 6 | 9 | 0 | 3 | 172 | 8.7 |
| 2007–08 | 34 | Anaheim Ducks | NHL | 48 | 8 | 17 | 25 | -2 | 16 | 1 | 7 | 0 | 3 | 87 | 9.2 |
| 2008–09 | 35 | Anaheim Ducks | NHL | 82 | 14 | 45 | 59 | -8 | 70 | 5 | 9 | 0 | 2 | 178 | 7.9 |
| 2009–10 | 36 | Anaheim Ducks | NHL | 80 | 10 | 38 | 48 | -9 | 38 | 5 | 5 | 0 | 2 | 168 | 6.0 |
| NHL Career — 18 Seasons | | | | 1263 | 172 | 568 | 740 | 167 | 784 | 81 | 90 | 1 | 39 | 2436 | 7.1 |

**PLAYOFFS**

| SEASON | AGE | TEAM | LG | GP | G | A | PTS | +/- | PIM | ESG | PPG | SHG | GWG | SOG | S% |
|--------|-----|------|----|----|---|---|-----|-----|-----|-----|-----|-----|-----|-----|-----|
| 1992–93 | 19 | New Jersey Devils | NHL | 5 | 0 | 3 | 3 | -3 | 2 | 0 | 0 | 0 | 0 | 11 | 0.0 |
| 1993–94 | 20 | New Jersey Devils | NHL | 20 | 2 | 2 | 4 | -1 | 8 | 1 | 1 | 0 | 0 | 29 | 6.9 |
| 1994–95 | 21 | New Jersey Devils | NHL | 20 | 4 | 7 | 11 | 11 | 10 | 2 | 2 | 0 | 1 | 53 | 7.5 |
| 1996–97 | 23 | New Jersey Devils | NHL | 10 | 2 | 4 | 6 | 0 | 6 | 0 | 2 | 0 | 1 | 34 | 5.9 |
| 1997–98 | 24 | New Jersey Devils | NHL | 6 | 0 | 2 | 2 | 0 | 4 | 0 | 0 | 0 | 0 | 15 | 0.0 |
| 1998–99 | 25 | New Jersey Devils | NHL | 7 | 1 | 3 | 4 | -5 | 18 | 0 | 1 | 0 | 0 | 13 | 7.7 |
| 1999–00 | 26 | New Jersey Devils | NHL | 22 | 5 | 2 | 7 | 5 | 10 | 3 | 0 | 2 | 1 | 40 | 12.5 |
| 2000–01 | 27 | New Jersey Devils | NHL | 21 | 0 | 6 | 6 | 7 | 14 | 0 | 0 | 0 | 0 | 29 | 0.0 |
| 2001–02 | 28 | New Jersey Devils | NHL | 6 | 0 | 2 | 2 | -1 | 6 | 0 | 0 | 0 | 0 | 6 | 0.0 |
| 2002–03 | 29 | New Jersey Devils | NHL | 24 | 2 | 16 | 18 | 11 | 16 | 1 | 1 | 0 | 0 | 40 | 5.0 |
| 2003–04 | 30 | New Jersey Devils | NHL | 5 | 1 | 0 | 1 | -5 | 6 | 1 | 0 | 0 | 0 | 12 | 8.3 |
| 2005–06 | 32 | Mighty Ducks of Anaheim | NHL | 16 | 2 | 9 | 11 | 1 | 14 | 0 | 1 | 1 | 1 | 48 | 4.2 |
| 2006–07 | 33 | Anaheim Ducks | NHL | 21 | 3 | 8 | 11 | 2 | 26 | 2 | 1 | 0 | 2 | 42 | 7.1 |
| 2007–08 | 34 | Anaheim Ducks | NHL | 6 | 0 | 2 | 2 | -2 | 4 | 0 | 0 | 0 | 0 | 7 | 0.0 |
| 2008–09 | 35 | Anaheim Ducks | NHL | 13 | 3 | 7 | 10 | 0 | 11 | 0 | 3 | 0 | 2 | 32 | 9.4 |
| NHL Career — 15 Seasons | | | | 202 | 25 | 73 | 98 | 20 | 155 | 10 | 12 | 3 | 8 | 411 | 6.1 |

## Bobby Orr   Profile: See page 280

### REGULAR SEASON

| SEASON | AGE | TEAM | LG | GP | G | A | PTS | +/- | PIM | ESG | PPG | SHG | GWG | SOG | S% |
|---|---|---|---|---|---|---|---|---|---|---|---|---|---|---|---|
| 1966–67 | 18 | Boston Bruins | NHL | 61 | 13 | 28 | 41 | 1 | 102 | 9 | 3 | 1 | 0 | 262 | 5.0 |
| 1967–68 | 19 | Boston Bruins | NHL | 46 | 11 | 20 | 31 | 28 | 53 | 8 | 3 | 0 | 1 | 173 | 6.4 |
| 1968–69 | 20 | Boston Bruins | NHL | 67 | 21 | 43 | 64 | 55 | 133 | 17 | 4 | 0 | 2 | 285 | 7.4 |
| 1969–70 | 21 | Boston Bruins | NHL | 76 | 33 | 87 | 120 | 54 | 125 | 18 | 11 | 4 | 3 | 413 | 8.0 |
| 1970–71 | 22 | Boston Bruins | NHL | 78 | 37 | 102 | 139 | 124 | 91 | 29 | 5 | 3 | 5 | 392 | 9.4 |
| 1971–72 | 23 | Boston Bruins | NHL | 76 | 37 | 80 | 117 | 83 | 106 | 22 | 11 | 4 | 4 | 353 | 10.5 |
| 1972–73 | 24 | Boston Bruins | NHL | 63 | 29 | 72 | 101 | 55 | 99 | 21 | 7 | 1 | 3 | 282 | 10.3 |
| 1973–74 | 25 | Boston Bruins | NHL | 74 | 32 | 90 | 122 | 84 | 82 | 21 | 11 | 0 | 4 | 384 | 8.3 |
| 1974–75 | 26 | Boston Bruins | NHL | 80 | 46 | 89 | 135 | 80 | 101 | 28 | 16 | 2 | 4 | 384 | 12.0 |
| 1975–76 | 27 | Boston Bruins | NHL | 10 | 5 | 13 | 18 | 10 | 22 | 1 | 3 | 1 | 0 | 57 | 8.8 |
| 1976–77 | 28 | Chicago Black Hawks | NHL | 20 | 4 | 19 | 23 | 6 | 25 | 2 | 2 | 0 | 0 | 55 | 7.3 |
| 1978–79 | 30 | Chicago Black Hawks | NHL | 6 | 2 | 2 | 4 | 2 | 4 | 2 | 0 | 0 | 0 | 18 | 11.1 |
| NHL Career—12 Seasons | | | | 657 | 270 | 645 | 915 | 582 | 953 | 178 | 76 | 16 | 26 | 3058 | 8.8 |

### PLAYOFFS

| SEASON | AGE | TEAM | LG | GP | G | A | PTS | +/- | PIM | ESG | PPG | SHG | GWG | SOG | S% |
|---|---|---|---|---|---|---|---|---|---|---|---|---|---|---|---|
| 1967–68 | 19 | Boston Bruins | NHL | 4 | 0 | 2 | 2 | -1 | 2 | 0 | 0 | 0 | 0 | 16 | 0.0 |
| 1968–69 | 20 | Boston Bruins | NHL | 10 | 1 | 7 | 8 | 9 | 10 | 1 | 0 | 0 | 1 | 32 | 3.1 |
| 1969–70 | 21 | Boston Bruins | NHL | 14 | 9 | 11 | 20 | 24 | 14 | 5 | 3 | 1 | 2 | 78 | 11.5 |
| 1970–71 | 22 | Boston Bruins | NHL | 7 | 5 | 7 | 12 | -2 | 25 | 3 | 1 | 1 | 1 | 38 | 13.2 |
| 1971–72 | 23 | Boston Bruins | NHL | 15 | 5 | 19 | 24 | 20 | 19 | 2 | 3 | 0 | 1 | 61 | 8.2 |
| 1972–73 | 24 | Boston Bruins | NHL | 5 | 1 | 1 | 2 | -4 | 7 | 1 | 0 | 0 | 0 | 20 | 5.0 |
| 1973–74 | 25 | Boston Bruins | NHL | 16 | 4 | 14 | 18 | 7 | 28 | 3 | 1 | 0 | 2 | 96 | 4.2 |
| 1974–75 | 26 | Boston Bruins | NHL | 3 | 1 | 5 | 6 | 7 | 2 | 0 | 0 | 1 | 0 | 17 | 5.9 |
| NHL Career—8 Seasons | | | | 74 | 26 | 66 | 92 | 60 | 107 | 15 | 8 | 3 | 7 | 358 | 7.3 |

## Brad Park   Profile: See page 282

### REGULAR SEASON

| SEASON | AGE | TEAM | LG | GP | G | A | PTS | +/- | PIM | ESG | PPG | SHG | GWG | SOG | S% |
|---|---|---|---|---|---|---|---|---|---|---|---|---|---|---|---|
| 1968–69 | 20 | New York Rangers | NHL | 54 | 3 | 23 | 26 | 11 | 70 | 1 | 2 | 0 | 0 | 103 | 2.9 |
| 1969–70 | 21 | New York Rangers | NHL | 60 | 11 | 26 | 37 | 24 | 98 | 4 | 6 | 1 | 2 | 161 | 6.8 |
| 1970–71 | 22 | New York Rangers | NHL | 68 | 7 | 37 | 44 | 26 | 114 | 4 | 3 | 0 | 0 | 199 | 3.5 |
| 1971–72 | 23 | New York Rangers | NHL | 75 | 24 | 49 | 73 | 63 | 130 | 14 | 8 | 2 | 4 | 263 | 9.1 |
| 1972–73 | 24 | New York Rangers | NHL | 52 | 10 | 43 | 53 | 30 | 51 | 6 | 4 | 0 | 1 | 142 | 7.0 |
| 1973–74 | 25 | New York Rangers | NHL | 78 | 25 | 57 | 82 | 23 | 148 | 21 | 4 | 0 | 4 | 234 | 10.7 |
| 1974–75 | 26 | New York Rangers | NHL | 65 | 13 | 44 | 57 | 5 | 104 | 6 | 7 | 0 | 2 | 190 | 6.9 |
| 1975–76 | 27 | New York Rangers | NHL | 13 | 2 | 4 | 6 | -4 | 23 | 2 | 0 | 0 | 1 | 28 | 7.1 |
| 1975–76 | 27 | Boston Bruins | NHL | 43 | 16 | 37 | 53 | 23 | 95 | 8 | 7 | 1 | 2 | 163 | 9.8 |
| 1976–77 | 28 | Boston Bruins | NHL | 77 | 12 | 55 | 67 | 49 | 67 | 7 | 4 | 1 | 4 | 234 | 5.1 |
| 1977–78 | 29 | Boston Bruins | NHL | 80 | 22 | 57 | 79 | 69 | 79 | 13 | 9 | 0 | 3 | 222 | 9.9 |
| 1978–79 | 30 | Boston Bruins | NHL | 40 | 7 | 32 | 39 | 28 | 10 | 4 | 3 | 0 | 0 | 96 | 7.3 |
| 1979–80 | 31 | Boston Bruins | NHL | 32 | 5 | 16 | 21 | 11 | 27 | 3 | 2 | 0 | 2 | 67 | 7.5 |
| 1980–81 | 32 | Boston Bruins | NHL | 78 | 14 | 52 | 66 | 21 | 111 | 4 | 10 | 0 | 2 | 201 | 7.0 |
| 1981–82 | 33 | Boston Bruins | NHL | 75 | 14 | 42 | 56 | 11 | 82 | 6 | 8 | 0 | 1 | 159 | 8.8 |
| 1982–83 | 34 | Boston Bruins | NHL | 76 | 10 | 26 | 36 | 20 | 82 | 5 | 5 | 0 | 0 | 130 | 7.7 |
| 1983–84 | 35 | Detroit Red Wings | NHL | 80 | 5 | 53 | 58 | -31 | 85 | 1 | 4 | 0 | 0 | 141 | 3.6 |
| 1984–85 | 36 | Detroit Red Wings | NHL | 67 | 13 | 30 | 43 | -17 | 53 | 7 | 6 | 0 | 0 | 94 | 13.8 |
| NHL Career—17 Seasons | | | | 1113 | 213 | 683 | 896 | 363 | 1429 | 116 | 92 | 5 | 28 | 2827 | 7.5 |

### PLAYOFFS

| SEASON | AGE | TEAM | LG | GP | G | A | PTS | +/- | PIM | ESG | PPG | SHG | GWG | SOG | S% |
|---|---|---|---|---|---|---|---|---|---|---|---|---|---|---|---|
| 1968–69 | 20 | New York Rangers | NHL | 4 | 0 | 2 | 2 | -3 | 7 | 0 | 0 | 0 | 0 | 5 | 0.0 |
| 1969–70 | 21 | New York Rangers | NHL | 5 | 1 | 2 | 3 | -1 | 11 | 0 | 1 | 0 | 0 | 11 | 9.1 |
| 1970–71 | 22 | New York Rangers | NHL | 13 | 0 | 4 | 4 | 0 | 42 | 0 | 0 | 0 | 0 | 41 | 0.0 |
| 1971–72 | 23 | New York Rangers | NHL | 16 | 4 | 7 | 11 | 5 | 21 | 2 | 2 | 0 | 1 | 37 | 10.8 |
| 1972–73 | 24 | New York Rangers | NHL | 10 | 2 | 5 | 7 | 3 | 8 | 1 | 1 | 0 | 1 | 24 | 8.3 |
| 1973–74 | 25 | New York Rangers | NHL | 13 | 4 | 8 | 12 | 0 | 38 | 2 | 2 | 0 | 1 | 30 | 13.3 |
| 1974–75 | 26 | New York Rangers | NHL | 3 | 1 | 4 | 5 | 4 | 2 | 1 | 0 | 0 | 0 | 10 | 10.0 |
| 1975–76 | 27 | Boston Bruins | NHL | 11 | 3 | 8 | 11 | -3 | 14 | 1 | 1 | 1 | 0 | 33 | 9.1 |
| 1976–77 | 28 | Boston Bruins | NHL | 14 | 2 | 10 | 12 | 0 | 4 | 2 | 0 | 0 | 0 | 45 | 4.4 |
| 1977–78 | 29 | Boston Bruins | NHL | 15 | 9 | 11 | 20 | 13 | 14 | 5 | 4 | 0 | 0 | 32 | 28.1 |
| 1978–79 | 30 | Boston Bruins | NHL | 11 | 1 | 4 | 5 | 3 | 8 | 1 | 0 | 0 | 1 | 22 | 4.6 |
| 1979–80 | 31 | Boston Bruins | NHL | 10 | 3 | 6 | 9 | 1 | 4 | 3 | 0 | 0 | 0 | 30 | 10.0 |
| 1980–81 | 32 | Boston Bruins | NHL | 3 | 1 | 3 | 4 | -1 | 11 | 0 | 1 | 0 | 0 | 8 | 12.5 |
| 1981–82 | 33 | Boston Bruins | NHL | 11 | 1 | 4 | 5 | 2 | 4 | 1 | 0 | 0 | 1 | 17 | 5.9 |
| 1982–83 | 34 | Boston Bruins | NHL | 16 | 3 | 9 | 12 | 9 | 18 | 2 | 1 | 0 | 1 | 28 | 10.7 |
| 1983–84 | 35 | Detroit Red Wings | NHL | 3 | 0 | 3 | 3 | 0 | 0 | 0 | 0 | 0 | 0 | 5 | 0.0 |
| 1984–85 | 36 | Detroit Red Wings | NHL | 3 | 0 | 0 | 0 | -8 | 11 | 0 | 0 | 0 | 0 | 5 | 0.0 |
| NHL Career—17 Seasons | | | | 161 | 35 | 90 | 125 | 24 | 217 | 21 | 13 | 1 | 6 | 383 | 9.1 |

## Lester Patrick   Profile: See page 284

### REGULAR SEASON

| SEASON | AGE | TEAM | LG | GP | G | A | PTS | PIM |
|---|---|---|---|---|---|---|---|---|
| 1903–04 | 20 | Brandon Hockey Club | MNWHA | 12 | 4 | 2 | 6 | |
| 1904–05 | 21 | Westmount Hockey Club | CAHL | 8 | 4 | 0 | 4 | |
| 1905–06 | 22 | Montreal Wanderers | ECAHA | 9 | 17 | 0 | 17 | 26 |
| 1906–07 | 23 | Montreal Wanderers | ECAHA | 9 | 11 | 0 | 11 | 11 |
| 1907–08 | 24 | Nelson HC | BCBHL | 3 | 3 | 0 | 3 | |
| 1908–09 | 25 | Nelson HC | BCBHL | 22 | 6 | 0 | 6 | |
| 1909–10 | 26 | Renfrew Hockey Club | NHA | 12 | 24 | 0 | 24 | 25 |
| 1910–11 | 27 | Nelson HC | BCBHL | 11 | 5 | 0 | 5 | |
| 1911–12 | 28 | Victoria Aristocrats | PCHA | 16 | 10 | 0 | 10 | 9 |
| 1912-13 | 29 | Victoria Aristocrats | PCHA | 15 | 14 | 5 | 19 | 12 |
| 1913–14 | 30 | Victoria Aristocrats | PCHA | 9 | 5 | 5 | 10 | 0 |
| 1914–15 | 31 | Victoria Aristocrats | PCHA | 17 | 12 | 5 | 17 | 15 |
| 1915–16 | 32 | Victoria Aristocrats | PCHA | 18 | 13 | 11 | 24 | 27 |
| 1916–17 | 33 | Spokane Canaries | PCHA | 23 | 10 | 11 | 21 | 15 |
| 1917–18 | 34 | Seattle Metropolitans | PCHA | 17 | 2 | 8 | 10 | 15 |
| 1918–19 | 35 | Victoria Aristocrats | PCHA | 9 | 2 | 5 | 7 | 0 |
| 1919–20 | 36 | Victoria Aristocrats | PCHA | 11 | 2 | 2 | 4 | 3 |

### REGULAR SEASON

| SEASON | AGE | TEAM | LG | GP | G | A | PTS | PIM |
|---|---|---|---|---|---|---|---|---|
| 1920–21 | 37 | Victoria Aristocrats | PCHA | 5 | 2 | 3 | 5 | 13 |
| 1921–22 | 38 | Victoria Aristocrats | PCHA | 2 | 0 | 0 | 0 | 0 |
| 1925–26 | 42 | Victoria Cougars | WHL | 23 | 5 | 8 | 13 | 20 |
| 1926–27 | 43 | New York Rangers | NHL | 1 | 0 | 0 | 0 | 2 |
| Career — 18 Seasons | | | | 252 | 151 | 65 | 403 | 213 |

### PLAYOFFS

| SEASON | AGE | TEAM | LG | GP | G | A | PTS | PIM |
|---|---|---|---|---|---|---|---|---|
| 1903–04 | 20 | Brandon Hockey Club | St-Cup | 2 | 0 | 0 | 0 | 0 |
| 1905–06 | 22 | Montreal Wanderers | ECAHA | 2 | 3 | 0 | 3 | 3 |
| 1906–07 | 23 | Montreal Wanderers | St-Cup | 6 | 10 | 0 | 10 | 32 |
| 1907–08 | 24 | Nelson Seniors | BCHL | 2 | 1 | 0 | 1 | |
| 1908–09 | 25 | Edmonton Professionals | St-Cup | 2 | 1 | 1 | 2 | 3 |
| 1913–14 | 30 | Victoria Aristocrats | St-Cup | 3 | 2 | 0 | 2 | 0 |
| 1917–18 | 34 | Seattle Metropolitans | PCHA | 2 | 0 | 1 | 1 | 0 |
| 1925–26 | 42 | Victoria Cougars | WHL | 2 | 0 | 0 | 0 | 2 |
| 1927–28 | 44 | New York Rangers | NHL | 1 | 0 | 0 | 0 | 0 |
| Career — 9 Seasons | | | | 22 | 17 | 2 | 19 | 40 |

## Pierre Pilote   Profile: See page 286

### REGULAR SEASON

| SEASON | AGE | TEAM | LG | GP | G | A | PTS | +/- | PIM | ESG | PPG | SHG | GWG | SOG | S% |
|---|---|---|---|---|---|---|---|---|---|---|---|---|---|---|---|
| 1955–56 | 24 | Chicago Black Hawks | NHL | 20 | 3 | 5 | 8 | | 34 | 2 | 1 | 0 | 0 | | |
| 1956–57 | 25 | Chicago Black Hawks | NHL | 70 | 3 | 14 | 17 | | 119 | 3 | 0 | 0 | 2 | | |
| 1957–58 | 26 | Chicago Black Hawks | NHL | 70 | 6 | 24 | 30 | | 91 | 5 | 1 | 0 | 0 | | |
| 1958–59 | 27 | Chicago Black Hawks | NHL | 70 | 7 | 30 | 37 | | 79 | 3 | 4 | 0 | 2 | | |
| 1959–60 | 28 | Chicago Black Hawks | NHL | 70 | 7 | 38 | 45 | 20 | 100 | 2 | 5 | 0 | 1 | 89 | 7.9 |
| 1960–61 | 29 | Chicago Black Hawks | NHL | 70 | 6 | 29 | 35 | 29 | 169 | 3 | 3 | 0 | 2 | 68 | 8.8 |
| 1961–62 | 30 | Chicago Black Hawks | NHL | 59 | 7 | 35 | 42 | 14 | 97 | 3 | 3 | 1 | 2 | 99 | 7.1 |
| 1962–63 | 31 | Chicago Black Hawks | NHL | 59 | 8 | 18 | 26 | -4 | 57 | 3 | 5 | 0 | 2 | 89 | 9.0 |
| 1963–64 | 32 | Chicago Black Hawks | NHL | 70 | 7 | 46 | 53 | 31 | 84 | 7 | 0 | 0 | 2 | 104 | 6.7 |
| 1964–65 | 33 | Chicago Black Hawks | NHL | 68 | 14 | 45 | 59 | 25 | 162 | 6 | 7 | 1 | 2 | 109 | 12.8 |
| 1965–66 | 34 | Chicago Black Hawks | NHL | 51 | 2 | 34 | 36 | 23 | 60 | 1 | 1 | 0 | 0 | 47 | 4.3 |
| 1966–67 | 35 | Chicago Black Hawks | NHL | 70 | 6 | 46 | 52 | 54 | 90 | 2 | 4 | 0 | 2 | 70 | 8.6 |
| 1967–68 | 36 | Chicago Black Hawks | NHL | 74 | 1 | 36 | 37 | -10 | 69 | 1 | 0 | 0 | 0 | 68 | 1.5 |
| 1968–69 | 37 | Toronto Maple Leafs | NHL | 69 | 3 | 18 | 21 | 5 | 46 | 2 | 1 | 0 | 0 | 48 | 6.3 |
| NHL Career — 14 Seasons | | | | 890 | 80 | 418 | 498 | 187 | 1257 | 43 | 35 | 2 | 17 | 791 | 7.7 |

### PLAYOFFS

| SEASON | AGE | TEAM | LG | GP | G | A | PTS | +/- | PIM | ESG | PPG | SHG | GWG | SOG | S% |
|---|---|---|---|---|---|---|---|---|---|---|---|---|---|---|---|
| 1958–59 | 27 | Chicago Black Hawks | NHL | 6 | 0 | 2 | 2 | | 10 | 0 | 0 | 0 | 0 | | |
| 1959–60 | 28 | Chicago Black Hawks | NHL | 4 | 0 | 1 | 1 | -3 | 8 | 0 | 0 | 0 | 0 | 3 | 0.0 |
| 1960–61 | 29 | Chicago Black Hawks | NHL | 12 | 3 | 12 | 15 | 11 | 8 | 2 | 1 | 0 | 0 | 15 | 20.0 |
| 1961–62 | 30 | Chicago Black Hawks | NHL | 12 | 0 | 7 | 7 | 3 | 8 | 0 | 0 | 0 | 0 | 17 | 0.0 |
| 1962–63 | 31 | Chicago Black Hawks | NHL | 6 | 0 | 8 | 8 | -3 | 8 | 0 | 0 | 0 | 0 | 7 | 0.0 |
| 1963–64 | 32 | Chicago Black Hawks | NHL | 7 | 2 | 6 | 8 | 0 | 6 | 2 | 0 | 0 | 1 | 11 | 18.2 |
| 1964–65 | 33 | Chicago Black Hawks | NHL | 12 | 0 | 7 | 7 | 4 | 22 | 0 | 0 | 0 | 0 | 16 | 0.0 |
| 1965–66 | 34 | Chicago Black Hawks | NHL | 6 | 0 | 2 | 2 | -5 | 10 | 0 | 0 | 0 | 0 | 6 | 0.0 |
| 1966–67 | 35 | Chicago Black Hawks | NHL | 6 | 2 | 4 | 6 | 1 | 6 | 2 | 0 | 0 | 0 | 10 | 20.0 |
| 1967–68 | 36 | Chicago Black Hawks | NHL | 11 | 1 | 3 | 4 | 0 | 12 | 0 | 1 | 0 | 0 | 7 | 14.3 |
| 1968–69 | 37 | Toronto Maple Leafs | NHL | 4 | 0 | 1 | 1 | -1 | 4 | 0 | 0 | 0 | 0 | 2 | 0.0 |
| NHL Career — 11 Seasons | | | | 86 | 8 | 53 | 61 | 7 | 102 | 6 | 2 | 0 | 1 | 94 | 8.5 |

## Denis Potvin   Profile: See page 288

### REGULAR SEASON

| SEASON | AGE | TEAM | LG | GP | G | A | PTS | +/- | PIM | ESG | PPG | SHG | GWG | SOG | S% |
|---|---|---|---|---|---|---|---|---|---|---|---|---|---|---|---|
| 1973–74 | 20 | New York Islanders | NHL | 77 | 17 | 37 | 54 | -17 | 175 | 11 | 6 | 0 | 3 | 209 | 8.1 |
| 1974–75 | 21 | New York Islanders | NHL | 79 | 21 | 55 | 76 | 28 | 105 | 14 | 5 | 2 | 4 | 211 | 10.0 |
| 1975–76 | 22 | New York Islanders | NHL | 78 | 31 | 67 | 98 | 12 | 100 | 13 | 18 | 0 | 4 | 256 | 12.1 |
| 1976–77 | 23 | New York Islanders | NHL | 80 | 25 | 55 | 80 | 42 | 103 | 17 | 7 | 1 | 4 | 238 | 10.5 |
| 1977–78 | 24 | New York Islanders | NHL | 80 | 30 | 64 | 94 | 57 | 81 | 21 | 9 | 0 | 6 | 287 | 10.5 |
| 1978–79 | 25 | New York Islanders | NHL | 73 | 31 | 70 | 101 | 71 | 58 | 16 | 12 | 3 | 2 | 237 | 13.1 |
| 1979–80 | 26 | New York Islanders | NHL | 31 | 8 | 33 | 41 | 13 | 44 | 4 | 4 | 0 | 0 | 98 | 8.2 |
| 1980–81 | 27 | New York Islanders | NHL | 74 | 20 | 56 | 76 | 39 | 104 | 11 | 9 | 0 | 4 | 206 | 9.7 |
| 1981–82 | 28 | New York Islanders | NHL | 60 | 24 | 37 | 61 | 39 | 83 | 12 | 11 | 1 | 4 | 169 | 14.2 |
| 1982–83 | 29 | New York Islanders | NHL | 69 | 12 | 54 | 66 | 33 | 60 | 7 | 4 | 1 | 1 | 190 | 6.3 |
| 1983–84 | 30 | New York Islanders | NHL | 78 | 22 | 63 | 85 | 54 | 87 | 10 | 11 | 1 | 3 | 247 | 8.9 |
| 1984–85 | 31 | New York Islanders | NHL | 77 | 17 | 51 | 68 | 32 | 96 | 11 | 6 | 0 | 1 | 199 | 8.6 |

## Denis Potvin (continued)

### REGULAR SEASON

| SEASON | AGE | TEAM | LG | GP | G | A | PTS | +/- | PIM | ESG | PPG | SHG | GWG | SOG | S% |
|---|---|---|---|---|---|---|---|---|---|---|---|---|---|---|---|
| 1985-86 | 32 | New York Islanders | NHL | 74 | 21 | 38 | 59 | 34 | 78 | 12 | 8 | 1 | 4 | 168 | 12.5 |
| 1986-87 | 33 | New York Islanders | NHL | 58 | 12 | 30 | 42 | -6 | 70 | 4 | 8 | 0 | 1 | 147 | 8.2 |
| 1987-88 | 34 | New York Islanders | NHL | 72 | 19 | 32 | 51 | 26 | 112 | 10 | 9 | 0 | 3 | 188 | 10.1 |
| NHL Career—15 Seasons | | | | 1060 | 310 | 742 | 1052 | 456 | 1356 | 173 | 127 | 10 | 44 | 3050 | 10.2 |

### PLAYOFFS

| SEASON | AGE | TEAM | LG | GP | G | A | PTS | +/- | PIM | ESG | PPG | SHG | GWG | SOG | S% |
|---|---|---|---|---|---|---|---|---|---|---|---|---|---|---|---|
| 1974-75 | 21 | New York Islanders | NHL | 17 | 5 | 9 | 14 | -5 | 30 | 1 | 3 | 1 | 0 | 55 | 9.1 |
| 1975-76 | 22 | New York Islanders | NHL | 13 | 5 | 14 | 19 | 9 | 32 | 3 | 2 | 0 | 1 | 42 | 11.9 |
| 1976-77 | 23 | New York Islanders | NHL | 12 | 6 | 4 | 10 | 12 | 20 | 4 | 2 | 0 | 0 | 37 | 16.2 |
| 1977-78 | 24 | New York Islanders | NHL | 7 | 2 | 2 | 4 | 1 | 6 | 2 | 0 | 0 | 0 | 32 | 6.3 |
| 1978-79 | 25 | New York Islanders | NHL | 10 | 4 | 7 | 11 | 6 | 8 | 4 | 0 | 0 | 1 | 40 | 10.0 |
| 1979-80 | 26 | New York Islanders | NHL | 21 | 6 | 13 | 19 | 10 | 24 | 2 | 4 | 0 | 1 | 85 | 7.1 |
| 1980-81 | 27 | New York Islanders | NHL | 18 | 8 | 17 | 25 | 18 | 16 | 1 | 6 | 1 | 2 | 44 | 18.2 |
| 1981-82 | 28 | New York Islanders | NHL | 19 | 5 | 16 | 21 | 9 | 30 | 2 | 3 | 0 | 0 | 56 | 8.9 |
| 1982-83 | 29 | New York Islanders | NHL | 20 | 8 | 12 | 20 | 20 | 22 | 4 | 4 | 0 | 1 | 68 | 11.8 |
| 1983-84 | 30 | New York Islanders | NHL | 20 | 1 | 5 | 6 | -4 | 28 | 0 | 1 | 0 | 0 | 56 | 1.8 |
| 1984-85 | 31 | New York Islanders | NHL | 10 | 3 | 2 | 5 | 0 | 10 | 2 | 1 | 0 | 1 | 22 | 13.6 |
| 1985-86 | 32 | New York Islanders | NHL | 3 | 0 | 1 | 1 | -2 | 0 | 0 | 0 | 0 | 0 | 4 | 0.0 |
| 1986-87 | 33 | New York Islanders | NHL | 10 | 2 | 2 | 4 | -7 | 21 | 1 | 1 | 0 | 0 | 22 | 9.1 |
| 1987-88 | 34 | New York Islanders | NHL | 5 | 1 | 4 | 5 | -3 | 6 | 0 | 1 | 0 | 0 | 15 | 6.7 |
| NHL Career—14 Seasons | | | | 185 | 56 | 108 | 164 | 64 | 253 | 26 | 28 | 2 | 7 | 578 | 9.7 |

## Babe Pratt   Profile: See page 290

### REGULAR SEASON

| SEASON | AGE | TEAM | LG | GP | G | A | PTS | PIM |
|---|---|---|---|---|---|---|---|---|
| 1935-36 | 20 | New York Rangers | NHL | 17 | 1 | 1 | 2 | 16 |
| 1936-37 | 21 | New York Rangers | NHL | 47 | 8 | 7 | 15 | 23 |
| 1937-38 | 22 | New York Rangers | NHL | 47 | 5 | 14 | 19 | 56 |
| 1938-39 | 23 | New York Rangers | NHL | 48 | 2 | 19 | 21 | 20 |
| 1939-40 | 24 | New York Rangers | NHL | 48 | 4 | 13 | 17 | 61 |
| 1940-41 | 25 | New York Rangers | NHL | 48 | 3 | 17 | 20 | 52 |
| 1941-42 | 26 | New York Rangers | NHL | 47 | 4 | 24 | 28 | 65 |
| 1942-43 | 27 | New York Rangers | NHL | 6 | 0 | 2 | 2 | 6 |
| 1942-43 | 27 | Toronto Maple Leafs | NHL | 38 | 12 | 25 | 37 | 44 |
| 1943-44 | 28 | Toronto Maple Leafs | NHL | 50 | 17 | 41 | 58 | 48 |
| 1944-45 | 29 | Toronto Maple Leafs | NHL | 50 | 18 | 23 | 41 | 39 |
| 1945-46 | 30 | Toronto Maple Leafs | NHL | 41 | 5 | 20 | 25 | 36 |
| 1946-47 | 31 | Boston Bruins | NHL | 31 | 4 | 4 | 8 | 25 |
| NHL Career—12 Seasons | | | | 518 | 83 | 210 | 293 | 491 |

### PLAYOFFS

| SEASON | AGE | TEAM | LG | GP | G | A | PTS | PIM |
|---|---|---|---|---|---|---|---|---|
| 1936-37 | 21 | New York Rangers | NHL | 9 | 3 | 1 | 4 | 11 |
| 1937-38 | 22 | New York Rangers | NHL | 2 | 0 | 0 | 0 | 2 |
| 1938-39 | 23 | New York Rangers | NHL | 7 | 1 | 2 | 3 | 11 |
| 1939-40 | 24 | New York Rangers | NHL | 12 | 3 | 1 | 4 | 18 |
| 1940-41 | 25 | New York Rangers | NHL | 3 | 1 | 1 | 2 | 6 |
| 1941-42 | 26 | New York Rangers | NHL | 6 | 1 | 3 | 4 | 24 |
| 1942-43 | 27 | Toronto Maple Leafs | NHL | 6 | 1 | 2 | 3 | 8 |
| 1943-44 | 28 | Toronto Maple Leafs | NHL | 5 | 0 | 3 | 3 | 4 |
| 1944-45 | 29 | Toronto Maple Leafs | NHL | 13 | 2 | 4 | 6 | 8 |
| NHL Career—9 Seasons | | | | 63 | 12 | 17 | 29 | 92 |

## Chris Pronger   Profile: See page 292

### REGULAR SEASON

| SEASON | AGE | TEAM | LG | GP | G | A | PTS | +/- | PIM | ESG | PPG | SHG | GWG | SOG | S% |
|---|---|---|---|---|---|---|---|---|---|---|---|---|---|---|---|
| 1993-94 | 19 | Hartford Whalers | NHL | 81 | 5 | 25 | 30 | -3 | 113 | 3 | 2 | 0 | 0 | 174 | 2.9 |
| 1994-95 | 20 | Hartford Whalers | NHL | 43 | 5 | 9 | 14 | -12 | 54 | 2 | 3 | 0 | 1 | 94 | 5.3 |
| 1995-96 | 21 | St. Louis Blues | NHL | 78 | 7 | 18 | 25 | -18 | 110 | 3 | 3 | 1 | 1 | 138 | 5.1 |
| 1996-97 | 22 | St. Louis Blues | NHL | 79 | 11 | 24 | 35 | 15 | 143 | 7 | 4 | 0 | 0 | 147 | 7.5 |
| 1997-98 | 23 | St. Louis Blues | NHL | 81 | 9 | 27 | 36 | 47 | 180 | 8 | 1 | 0 | 2 | 145 | 6.2 |
| 1998-99 | 24 | St. Louis Blues | NHL | 67 | 13 | 33 | 46 | 3 | 113 | 5 | 8 | 0 | 0 | 172 | 7.6 |
| 1999-00 | 25 | St. Louis Blues | NHL | 79 | 14 | 48 | 62 | 52 | 92 | 6 | 8 | 0 | 3 | 192 | 7.3 |
| 2000-01 | 26 | St. Louis Blues | NHL | 51 | 8 | 39 | 47 | 21 | 75 | 4 | 4 | 0 | 0 | 121 | 6.6 |
| 2001-02 | 27 | St. Louis Blues | NHL | 78 | 7 | 40 | 47 | 23 | 120 | 2 | 4 | 1 | 3 | 204 | 3.4 |
| 2002-03 | 28 | St. Louis Blues | NHL | 5 | 1 | 3 | 4 | -2 | 10 | 1 | 0 | 0 | 0 | 11 | 9.1 |
| 2003-04 | 29 | St. Louis Blues | NHL | 80 | 14 | 40 | 54 | -1 | 88 | 7 | 7 | 0 | 3 | 203 | 6.9 |
| 2005-06 | 31 | Edmonton Oilers | NHL | 80 | 12 | 44 | 56 | 2 | 74 | 2 | 10 | 0 | 3 | 155 | 7.7 |
| 2006-07 | 32 | Anaheim Ducks | NHL | 66 | 13 | 46 | 59 | 27 | 69 | 5 | 8 | 0 | 2 | 166 | 7.8 |
| 2007-08 | 33 | Anaheim Ducks | NHL | 72 | 12 | 31 | 43 | -1 | 128 | 4 | 8 | 0 | 4 | 182 | 6.6 |
| 2008-09 | 34 | Anaheim Ducks | NHL | 82 | 11 | 37 | 48 | 0 | 88 | 7 | 4 | 0 | 2 | 196 | 5.6 |
| 2009-10 | 35 | Philadelphia Flyers | NHL | 82 | 10 | 45 | 55 | 22 | 79 | 5 | 5 | 0 | 2 | 175 | 5.7 |
| 2010-11 | 36 | Philadelphia Flyers | NHL | 50 | 4 | 21 | 25 | 7 | 44 | 1 | 3 | 0 | 1 | 112 | 3.6 |
| 2011-12 | 37 | Philadelphia Flyers | NHL | 13 | 1 | 11 | 12 | 1 | 10 | 0 | 1 | 0 | 0 | 23 | 4.3 |
| NHL Career—18 Seasons | | | | 1167 | 157 | 541 | 698 | 183 | 1590 | 72 | 83 | 2 | 27 | 2610 | 6.0 |

## Chris Pronger (continued)

**PLAYOFFS**

| SEASON | AGE | TEAM | LG | GP | G | A | PTS | +/- | PIM | ESG | PPG | SHG | GWG | SOG | S% |
|--------|-----|------|----|----|---|---|-----|-----|-----|-----|-----|-----|-----|-----|-----|
| 1995–96 | 21 | St. Louis Blues | NHL | 13 | 1 | 5 | 6 | 0 | 16 | 1 | 0 | 0 | 0 | 20 | 5.0 |
| 1996–97 | 22 | St. Louis Blues | NHL | 6 | 1 | 1 | 2 | 0 | 22 | 1 | 0 | 0 | 0 | 19 | 5.3 |
| 1997–98 | 23 | St. Louis Blues | NHL | 10 | 1 | 9 | 10 | -2 | 26 | 1 | 0 | 0 | 0 | 24 | 4.2 |
| 1998–99 | 24 | St. Louis Blues | NHL | 13 | 1 | 4 | 5 | -2 | 28 | 0 | 1 | 0 | 0 | 43 | 2.3 |
| 1999–00 | 25 | St. Louis Blues | NHL | 7 | 3 | 4 | 7 | 0 | 32 | 1 | 2 | 0 | 2 | 22 | 13.6 |
| 2000–01 | 26 | St. Louis Blues | NHL | 15 | 1 | 7 | 8 | 10 | 32 | 1 | 0 | 0 | 0 | 35 | 2.9 |
| 2001–02 | 27 | St. Louis Blues | NHL | 9 | 1 | 7 | 8 | 5 | 24 | 1 | 0 | 0 | 0 | 16 | 6.3 |
| 2002–03 | 28 | St. Louis Blues | NHL | 7 | 1 | 3 | 4 | 3 | 14 | 1 | 0 | 0 | 0 | 15 | 6.7 |
| 2003–04 | 29 | St. Louis Blues | NHL | 5 | 0 | 1 | 1 | 1 | 16 | 0 | 0 | 0 | 0 | 8 | 0.0 |
| 2005–06 | 31 | Edmonton Oilers | NHL | 24 | 5 | 16 | 21 | 10 | 26 | 2 | 3 | 0 | 0 | 61 | 8.2 |
| 2006–07 | 32 | Anaheim Ducks | NHL | 19 | 3 | 12 | 15 | 10 | 26 | 2 | 1 | 0 | 0 | 58 | 5.2 |
| 2007–08 | 33 | Anaheim Ducks | NHL | 6 | 2 | 3 | 5 | -1 | 12 | 0 | 2 | 0 | 1 | 12 | 16.7 |
| 2008–09 | 34 | Anaheim Ducks | NHL | 13 | 2 | 8 | 10 | 4 | 12 | 1 | 1 | 0 | 0 | 27 | 7.4 |
| 2009–10 | 35 | Philadelphia Flyers | NHL | 23 | 4 | 14 | 18 | 5 | 36 | 1 | 3 | 0 | 0 | 41 | 9.8 |
| 2010–11 | 36 | Philadelphia Flyers | NHL | 3 | 0 | 1 | 1 | -3 | 4 | 0 | 0 | 0 | 0 | 4 | 0.0 |
| **NHL Career — 15 Seasons** | | | | **173** | **26** | **95** | **121** | **40** | **326** | **13** | **13** | **0** | **3** | **405** | **6.4** |

# Marcel Pronovost  Profile: See page 293

**REGULAR SEASON**

| SEASON | AGE | TEAM | LG | GP | G | A | PTS | +/- | PIM | ESG | PPG | SHG | GWG | SOG | S% |
|--------|-----|------|----|----|---|---|-----|-----|-----|-----|-----|-----|-----|-----|-----|
| 1950–51 | 20 | Detroit Red Wings | NHL | 37 | 1 | 6 | 7 | | 20 | 1 | 0 | 0 | 0 | | |
| 1951–52 | 21 | Detroit Red Wings | NHL | 69 | 7 | 11 | 18 | | 50 | 6 | 1 | 0 | 1 | | |
| 1952–53 | 22 | Detroit Red Wings | NHL | 68 | 8 | 19 | 27 | | 72 | 5 | 3 | 0 | 2 | | |
| 1953–54 | 23 | Detroit Red Wings | NHL | 57 | 6 | 12 | 18 | | 50 | 4 | 1 | 1 | 3 | | |
| 1954–55 | 24 | Detroit Red Wings | NHL | 70 | 9 | 25 | 34 | | 88 | 8 | 1 | 0 | 2 | | |
| 1955–56 | 25 | Detroit Red Wings | NHL | 68 | 4 | 13 | 17 | | 46 | 2 | 0 | 2 | 0 | | |
| 1956–57 | 26 | Detroit Red Wings | NHL | 70 | 7 | 9 | 16 | | 36 | 7 | 0 | 0 | 1 | | |
| 1957–58 | 27 | Detroit Red Wings | NHL | 62 | 2 | 18 | 20 | | 52 | 2 | 0 | 0 | 0 | | |
| 1958–59 | 28 | Detroit Red Wings | NHL | 69 | 11 | 21 | 32 | | 44 | 10 | 1 | 0 | 0 | | |
| 1959–60 | 29 | Detroit Red Wings | NHL | 69 | 7 | 17 | 24 | 3 | 38 | 6 | 1 | 0 | 1 | 100 | 7 |
| 1960–61 | 30 | Detroit Red Wings | NHL | 70 | 6 | 11 | 17 | -15 | 44 | 4 | 1 | 1 | 0 | 110 | 5.5 |
| 1961–62 | 31 | Detroit Red Wings | NHL | 70 | 4 | 14 | 18 | -11 | 38 | 4 | 0 | 0 | 0 | 124 | 3.2 |
| 1962–63 | 32 | Detroit Red Wings | NHL | 69 | 4 | 9 | 13 | 10 | 48 | 3 | 0 | 1 | 0 | 92 | 4.4 |
| 1963–64 | 33 | Detroit Red Wings | NHL | 67 | 3 | 17 | 20 | 5 | 42 | 3 | 0 | 0 | 0 | 90 | 3.3 |
| 1964–65 | 34 | Detroit Red Wings | NHL | 68 | 1 | 15 | 16 | 24 | 45 | 1 | 0 | 0 | 1 | 98 | 1.0 |
| 1965–66 | 35 | Toronto Maple Leafs | NHL | 54 | 2 | 8 | 10 | -3 | 34 | 2 | 0 | 0 | 0 | 53 | 3.8 |
| 1966–67 | 36 | Toronto Maple Leafs | NHL | 58 | 2 | 12 | 14 | 23 | 28 | 2 | 0 | 0 | 0 | 41 | 4.9 |
| 1967–68 | 37 | Toronto Maple Leafs | NHL | 70 | 3 | 17 | 20 | 0 | 48 | 3 | 0 | 0 | 1 | 72 | 4.2 |
| 1968–69 | 38 | Toronto Maple Leafs | NHL | 34 | 1 | 2 | 3 | -2 | 20 | 1 | 0 | 0 | 0 | 18 | 5.6 |
| 1969–70 | 39 | Toronto Maple Leafs | NHL | 7 | 0 | 1 | 1 | 5 | 4 | 0 | 0 | 0 | 0 | 4 | 0.0 |
| **NHL Career — 20 Seasons** | | | | **1206** | **88** | **257** | **345** | **39** | **847** | **74** | **9** | **5** | **12** | **800** | **4.1** |

**PLAYOFFS**

| SEASON | AGE | TEAM | LG | GP | G | A | PTS | +/- | PIM | ESG | PPG | SHG | GWG | SOG | S% |
|--------|-----|------|----|----|---|---|-----|-----|-----|-----|-----|-----|-----|-----|-----|
| 1949–50 | 19 | Detroit Red Wings | NHL | 9 | 0 | 1 | 1 | | 10 | 0 | 0 | 0 | 0 | | |
| 1950–51 | 20 | Detroit Red Wings | NHL | 6 | 0 | 0 | 0 | | 0 | 0 | 0 | 0 | 0 | | |
| 1951–52 | 21 | Detroit Red Wings | NHL | 8 | 0 | 1 | 1 | | 10 | 0 | 0 | 0 | 0 | | |
| 1952–53 | 22 | Detroit Red Wings | NHL | 6 | 0 | 0 | 0 | | 6 | 0 | 0 | 0 | 0 | | |
| 1953–54 | 23 | Detroit Red Wings | NHL | 12 | 2 | 3 | 5 | | 12 | 1 | 1 | 0 | 0 | | |
| 1954–55 | 24 | Detroit Red Wings | NHL | 11 | 1 | 2 | 3 | | 6 | 0 | 0 | 1 | 0 | | |
| 1955–56 | 25 | Detroit Red Wings | NHL | 10 | 0 | 2 | 2 | | 8 | 0 | 0 | 0 | 0 | | |
| 1956–57 | 26 | Detroit Red Wings | NHL | 5 | 0 | 0 | 0 | | 6 | 0 | 0 | 0 | 0 | | |
| 1957–58 | 27 | Detroit Red Wings | NHL | 4 | 0 | 1 | 1 | | 4 | 0 | 0 | 0 | 0 | | |
| 1959–60 | 29 | Detroit Red Wings | NHL | 6 | 1 | 1 | 2 | 0 | 2 | 1 | 0 | 0 | 0 | 18 | 5.6 |
| 1960–61 | 30 | Detroit Red Wings | NHL | 9 | 2 | 3 | 5 | 3 | 0 | 2 | 0 | 0 | 0 | 11 | 18.2 |
| 1962–63 | 32 | Detroit Red Wings | NHL | 11 | 1 | 4 | 5 | -2 | 8 | 1 | 0 | 0 | 0 | 15 | 6.7 |
| 1963–64 | 33 | Detroit Red Wings | NHL | 14 | 0 | 2 | 2 | -3 | 14 | 0 | 0 | 0 | 0 | 18 | 0.0 |
| 1964–65 | 34 | Detroit Red Wings | NHL | 7 | 0 | 3 | 3 | -2 | 4 | 0 | 0 | 0 | 0 | 8 | 0.0 |
| 1965–66 | 35 | Toronto Maple Leafs | NHL | 4 | 0 | 0 | 0 | 6 | 0 | 0 | 0 | 0 | 0 | 3 | 0.0 |
| 1966–67 | 36 | Toronto Maple Leafs | NHL | 12 | 1 | 0 | 1 | 3 | 8 | 0 | 0 | 1 | 0 | 13 | 7.7 |
| **NHL Career — 16 Seasons** | | | | **134** | **8** | **23** | **31** | **-1** | **104** | **5** | **1** | **2** | **0** | **86** | **5.8** |

# Harvey Pulford  Profile: See page 294

| REGULAR SEASON | | | | | | | | |
|---|---|---|---|---|---|---|---|---|
| SEASON | AGE | TEAM | LG | GP | G | A | PTS | PIM |
| 1893–94 | 18 | Ottawa Hockey Club | AHAC | 6 | 0 | 0 | 0 | |
| 1894–95 | 19 | Ottawa Hockey Club | AHAC | 7 | 0 | 0 | 0 | |
| 1895–96 | 20 | Ottawa Hockey Club | AHAC | 8 | 0 | 0 | 0 | |
| 1896–97 | 21 | Ottawa Hockey Club | AHAC | 8 | 0 | 0 | 0 | |
| 1897–98 | 22 | Ottawa Hockey Club | AHAC | 7 | 0 | 0 | 0 | |
| 1898–99 | 23 | Ottawa Hockey Club | AHAC | 5 | 0 | 0 | 0 | |
| 1899–00 | 24 | Ottawa Hockey Club | CAHL | 6 | 1 | 0 | 1 | |
| 1899–00 | 24 | Ottawa Aberdeens | CAIHL | 5 | 1 | 0 | 1 | |
| 1900–01 | 25 | Ottawa Hockey Club | CAHL | 5 | 0 | 0 | 0 | |
| 1901–02 | 26 | Ottawa Hockey Club | CAHL | 5 | 0 | 0 | 0 | |
| 1902–03 | 27 | Ottawa Silver Seven | CAHL | 7 | 0 | 0 | 0 | 15 |
| 1903–04 | 28 | Ottawa Silver Seven | CAHL | 2 | 0 | 0 | 0 | 3 |
| 1904–05 | 29 | Ottawa Silver Seven | FAHL | 6 | 1 | 0 | 1 | 6 |
| 1905–06 | 30 | Ottawa Silver Seven | ECAHA | 10 | 3 | 0 | 3 | 27 |
| 1906–07 | 31 | Ottawa Senators | ECAHA | 10 | 0 | 0 | 0 | 31 |
| 1907–08 | 32 | Ottawa Senators | ECAHA | 9 | 1 | 0 | 1 | 32 |
| Career — 15 Seasons | | | | 106 | 7 | 0 | 7 | 114 |

| PLAYOFFS | | | | | | | | |
|---|---|---|---|---|---|---|---|---|
| SEASON | AGE | TEAM | LG | GP | G | A | PTS | PIM |
| 1893–94 | 18 | Ottawa Hockey Club | AHAC | 1 | 0 | 0 | 0 | 0 |
| 1902–03 | 27 | Ottawa Silver Seven | CAHL | 2 | 0 | 0 | 0 | 6 |
| 1902–03 | 27 | Ottawa Silver Seven | St-Cup | 2 | 0 | 0 | 0 | 3 |
| 1903–04 | 28 | Ottawa Silver Seven | St-Cup | 7 | 1 | 0 | 1 | 12 |
| 1904–05 | 29 | Ottawa Silver Seven | St-Cup | 4 | 0 | 0 | 0 | 6 |
| 1905–06 | 30 | Ottawa Silver Seven | ECAHA | 2 | 0 | 0 | 0 | 12 |
| 1905–06 | 30 | Ottawa Silver Seven | St-Cup | 4 | 1 | 0 | 1 | 24 |
| Career — 5 Seasons | | | | 22 | 2 | 0 | 2 | 63 |

# Bill Quackenbush  Profile: See page 295

| REGULAR SEASON | | | | | | | | |
|---|---|---|---|---|---|---|---|---|
| SEASON | AGE | TEAM | LG | GP | G | A | PTS | PIM |
| 1942–43 | 20 | Detroit Red Wings | NHL | 10 | 1 | 1 | 2 | 4 |
| 1943–44 | 21 | Detroit Red Wings | NHL | 43 | 4 | 14 | 18 | 6 |
| 1944–45 | 22 | Detroit Red Wings | NHL | 50 | 7 | 14 | 21 | 10 |
| 1945–46 | 23 | Detroit Red Wings | NHL | 49 | 11 | 11 | 22 | 6 |
| 1946–47 | 24 | Detroit Red Wings | NHL | 44 | 5 | 17 | 22 | 6 |
| 1947–48 | 25 | Detroit Red Wings | NHL | 58 | 6 | 16 | 22 | 17 |
| 1948–49 | 26 | Detroit Red Wings | NHL | 60 | 6 | 17 | 23 | 0 |
| 1949–50 | 27 | Boston Bruins | NHL | 70 | 8 | 17 | 25 | 4 |
| 1950–51 | 28 | Boston Bruins | NHL | 70 | 5 | 24 | 29 | 12 |
| 1951–52 | 29 | Boston Bruins | NHL | 69 | 2 | 17 | 19 | 6 |
| 1952–53 | 30 | Boston Bruins | NHL | 69 | 2 | 16 | 18 | 6 |
| 1953–54 | 31 | Boston Bruins | NHL | 45 | 0 | 17 | 17 | 6 |
| 1954–55 | 32 | Boston Bruins | NHL | 68 | 2 | 20 | 22 | 6 |
| 1955–56 | 33 | Boston Bruins | NHL | 70 | 3 | 22 | 25 | 4 |
| NHL Career — 14 Seasons | | | | 775 | 62 | 223 | 285 | 95 |

| PLAYOFFS | | | | | | | | |
|---|---|---|---|---|---|---|---|---|
| SEASON | AGE | TEAM | LG | GP | G | A | PTS | PIM |
| 1943–44 | 21 | Detroit Red Wings | NHL | 2 | 1 | 0 | 1 | 0 |
| 1944–45 | 22 | Detroit Red Wings | NHL | 14 | 0 | 2 | 2 | 2 |
| 1945–46 | 23 | Detroit Red Wings | NHL | 5 | 0 | 1 | 1 | 0 |
| 1946–47 | 24 | Detroit Red Wings | NHL | 5 | 0 | 0 | 0 | 2 |
| 1947–48 | 25 | Detroit Red Wings | NHL | 10 | 0 | 2 | 2 | 0 |
| 1948–49 | 26 | Detroit Red Wings | NHL | 11 | 1 | 1 | 2 | 0 |
| 1950–51 | 28 | Boston Bruins | NHL | 6 | 0 | 1 | 1 | 0 |
| 1951–52 | 29 | Boston Bruins | NHL | 7 | 0 | 3 | 3 | 0 |
| 1952–53 | 30 | Boston Bruins | NHL | 11 | 0 | 4 | 4 | 4 |
| 1953–54 | 31 | Boston Bruins | NHL | 4 | 0 | 0 | 0 | 0 |
| 1954–55 | 32 | Boston Bruins | NHL | 5 | 0 | 5 | 5 | 0 |
| NHL Career — 11 Seasons | | | | 80 | 2 | 19 | 21 | 8 |

# Kenny Reardon  Profile: See page 296

| REGULAR SEASON | | | | | | | | |
|---|---|---|---|---|---|---|---|---|
| SEASON | AGE | TEAM | LG | GP | G | A | PTS | PIM |
| 1940–41 | 19 | Montreal Canadiens | NHL | 46 | 2 | 8 | 10 | 41 |
| 1941–42 | 20 | Montreal Canadiens | NHL | 41 | 3 | 12 | 15 | 93 |
| 1945–46 | 24 | Montreal Canadiens | NHL | 43 | 5 | 4 | 9 | 45 |
| 1946–47 | 25 | Montreal Canadiens | NHL | 52 | 5 | 17 | 22 | 84 |
| 1947–48 | 26 | Montreal Canadiens | NHL | 58 | 7 | 15 | 22 | 129 |
| 1948–49 | 27 | Montreal Canadiens | NHL | 46 | 3 | 13 | 16 | 103 |
| 1949–50 | 28 | Montreal Canadiens | NHL | 67 | 1 | 27 | 28 | 109 |
| NHL Career — 7 Seasons | | | | 353 | 26 | 96 | 122 | 604 |

| PLAYOFFS | | | | | | | | |
|---|---|---|---|---|---|---|---|---|
| SEASON | AGE | TEAM | LG | GP | G | A | PTS | PIM |
| 1940–41 | 19 | Montreal Canadiens | NHL | 2 | 0 | 0 | 0 | 4 |
| 1941–42 | 20 | Montreal Canadiens | NHL | 3 | 0 | 0 | 0 | 4 |
| 1945–46 | 24 | Montreal Canadiens | NHL | 9 | 1 | 1 | 2 | 4 |
| 1946–47 | 25 | Montreal Canadiens | NHL | 7 | 1 | 2 | 3 | 20 |
| 1948–49 | 27 | Montreal Canadiens | NHL | 7 | 0 | 0 | 0 | 18 |
| 1949–50 | 28 | Montreal Canadiens | NHL | 2 | 0 | 2 | 2 | 12 |
| NHL Career — 6 Seasons | | | | 30 | 2 | 5 | 7 | 62 |

# Larry Robinson  Profile: See page 297

| REGULAR SEASON | | | | | | | | | | | | | | | |
|---|---|---|---|---|---|---|---|---|---|---|---|---|---|---|---|
| SEASON | AGE | TEAM | LG | GP | G | A | PTS | +/- | PIM | ESG | PPG | SHG | GWG | SOG | S% |
| 1972–73 | 21 | Montreal Canadiens | NHL | 36 | 2 | 4 | 6 | 3 | 20 | 2 | 0 | 0 | 1 | 36 | 5.6 |
| 1973–74 | 22 | Montreal Canadiens | NHL | 78 | 6 | 20 | 26 | 32 | 66 | 6 | 0 | 0 | 1 | 98 | 6.1 |
| 1974–75 | 23 | Montreal Canadiens | NHL | 80 | 14 | 47 | 61 | 60 | 76 | 13 | 1 | 0 | 2 | 101 | 13.9 |
| 1975–76 | 24 | Montreal Canadiens | NHL | 80 | 10 | 30 | 40 | 50 | 59 | 8 | 2 | 0 | 0 | 130 | 7.7 |
| 1976–77 | 25 | Montreal Canadiens | NHL | 77 | 19 | 66 | 85 | 120 | 45 | 16 | 3 | 0 | 3 | 196 | 9.7 |
| 1977–78 | 26 | Montreal Canadiens | NHL | 80 | 13 | 52 | 65 | 71 | 39 | 8 | 3 | 2 | 5 | 154 | 8.4 |
| 1978–79 | 27 | Montreal Canadiens | NHL | 67 | 16 | 45 | 61 | 49 | 33 | 12 | 4 | 0 | 1 | 146 | 11.0 |
| 1979–80 | 28 | Montreal Canadiens | NHL | 72 | 14 | 61 | 75 | 38 | 39 | 8 | 6 | 0 | 3 | 133 | 10.5 |
| 1980–81 | 29 | Montreal Canadiens | NHL | 65 | 12 | 38 | 50 | 47 | 37 | 5 | 7 | 0 | 2 | 130 | 9.2 |
| 1981–82 | 30 | Montreal Canadiens | NHL | 71 | 12 | 47 | 59 | 56 | 41 | 6 | 5 | 1 | 0 | 141 | 8.5 |
| 1982–83 | 31 | Montreal Canadiens | NHL | 71 | 14 | 49 | 63 | 32 | 33 | 8 | 6 | 0 | 1 | 146 | 9.6 |
| 1983–84 | 32 | Montreal Canadiens | NHL | 74 | 9 | 34 | 43 | 3 | 39 | 5 | 4 | 0 | 1 | 141 | 6.4 |
| 1984–85 | 33 | Montreal Canadiens | NHL | 76 | 14 | 33 | 47 | 33 | 44 | 8 | 6 | 0 | 3 | 120 | 11.7 |
| 1985–86 | 34 | Montreal Canadiens | NHL | 78 | 19 | 63 | 82 | 25 | 39 | 9 | 10 | 0 | 1 | 167 | 11.4 |

## Larry Robinson (continued)

### REGULAR SEASON

| SEASON | AGE | TEAM | LG | GP | G | A | PTS | +/- | PIM | ESG | PPG | SHG | GWG | SOG | S% |
|---|---|---|---|---|---|---|---|---|---|---|---|---|---|---|---|
| 1986-87 | 35 | Montreal Canadiens | NHL | 70 | 13 | 37 | 50 | 24 | 44 | 7 | 6 | 0 | 3 | 122 | 10.7 |
| 1987-88 | 36 | Montreal Canadiens | NHL | 53 | 6 | 34 | 40 | 26 | 30 | 4 | 2 | 0 | 1 | 96 | 6.3 |
| 1988-89 | 37 | Montreal Canadiens | NHL | 74 | 4 | 26 | 30 | 23 | 22 | 4 | 0 | 0 | 0 | 79 | 5.1 |
| 1989-90 | 38 | Los Angeles Kings | NHL | 64 | 7 | 32 | 39 | 7 | 34 | 6 | 1 | 0 | 1 | 80 | 8.8 |
| 1990-91 | 39 | Los Angeles Kings | NHL | 62 | 1 | 22 | 23 | 22 | 16 | 1 | 0 | 0 | 0 | 70 | 1.4 |
| 1991-92 | 40 | Los Angeles Kings | NHL | 56 | 3 | 10 | 13 | 1 | 37 | 3 | 0 | 0 | 0 | 46 | 6.5 |
| NHL Career — 20 Seasons | | | | 1384 | 208 | 750 | 958 | 722 | 793 | 139 | 66 | 3 | 29 | 2332 | 8.9 |

### PLAYOFFS

| SEASON | AGE | TEAM | LG | GP | G | A | PTS | +/- | PIM | ESG | PPG | SHG | GWG | SOG | S% |
|---|---|---|---|---|---|---|---|---|---|---|---|---|---|---|---|
| 1972-73 | 21 | Montreal Canadiens | NHL | 11 | 1 | 4 | 5 | 6 | 9 | 1 | 0 | 0 | 1 | 14 | 7.1 |
| 1973-74 | 22 | Montreal Canadiens | NHL | 6 | 0 | 1 | 1 | -1 | 26 | 0 | 0 | 0 | 0 | 7 | 0.0 |
| 1974-75 | 23 | Montreal Canadiens | NHL | 11 | 0 | 4 | 4 | 3 | 27 | 0 | 0 | 0 | 0 | 24 | 0.0 |
| 1975-76 | 24 | Montreal Canadiens | NHL | 13 | 3 | 3 | 6 | 11 | 10 | 3 | 0 | 0 | 1 | 21 | 14.3 |
| 1976-77 | 25 | Montreal Canadiens | NHL | 14 | 2 | 10 | 12 | 14 | 12 | 1 | 1 | 0 | 0 | 42 | 4.8 |
| 1977-78 | 26 | Montreal Canadiens | NHL | 15 | 4 | 17 | 21 | 21 | 6 | 2 | 2 | 0 | 0 | 41 | 9.8 |
| 1978-79 | 27 | Montreal Canadiens | NHL | 16 | 6 | 9 | 15 | 16 | 8 | 5 | 1 | 0 | 1 | 36 | 16.7 |
| 1979-80 | 28 | Montreal Canadiens | NHL | 10 | 0 | 4 | 4 | 9 | 2 | 0 | 0 | 0 | 0 | 27 | 0.0 |
| 1980-81 | 29 | Montreal Canadiens | NHL | 3 | 0 | 1 | 1 | -9 | 2 | 0 | 0 | 0 | 0 | 8 | 0.0 |
| 1981-82 | 30 | Montreal Canadiens | NHL | 5 | 0 | 1 | 1 | 3 | 8 | 0 | 0 | 0 | 0 | 6 | 0.0 |
| 1982-83 | 31 | Montreal Canadiens | NHL | 3 | 0 | 0 | 0 | -1 | 2 | 0 | 0 | 0 | 0 | 9 | 0.0 |
| 1983-84 | 32 | Montreal Canadiens | NHL | 15 | 0 | 5 | 5 | 7 | 22 | 0 | 0 | 0 | 0 | 27 | 0.0 |
| 1984-85 | 33 | Montreal Canadiens | NHL | 12 | 3 | 8 | 11 | 0 | 8 | 2 | 1 | 0 | 0 | 20 | 15.0 |
| 1985-86 | 34 | Montreal Canadiens | NHL | 20 | 0 | 13 | 13 | 4 | 22 | 0 | 0 | 0 | 0 | 42 | 0.0 |
| 1986-87 | 35 | Montreal Canadiens | NHL | 17 | 3 | 17 | 20 | 4 | 6 | 1 | 2 | 0 | 0 | 40 | 7.5 |
| 1987-88 | 36 | Montreal Canadiens | NHL | 11 | 1 | 4 | 5 | -3 | 4 | 1 | 0 | 0 | 0 | 10 | 10.0 |
| 1988-89 | 37 | Montreal Canadiens | NHL | 21 | 2 | 8 | 10 | 9 | 12 | 2 | 0 | 0 | 0 | 15 | 13.3 |
| 1989-90 | 38 | Los Angeles Kings | NHL | 10 | 2 | 3 | 5 | 2 | 10 | 2 | 0 | 0 | 0 | 12 | 16.7 |
| 1990-91 | 39 | Los Angeles Kings | NHL | 12 | 1 | 4 | 5 | 7 | 15 | 1 | 0 | 0 | 0 | 15 | 6.7 |
| 1991-92 | 40 | Los Angeles Kings | NHL | 2 | 0 | 0 | 0 | -2 | 0 | 0 | 0 | 0 | 0 | 1 | 0.0 |
| NHL Career — 20 Seasons | | | | 227 | 28 | 116 | 144 | 100 | 211 | 21 | 7 | 0 | 3 | 417 | 6.7 |

## Art Ross   Profile: See page 298

### REGULAR SEASON

| SEASON | AGE | TEAM | LG | GP | G | A | PTS | PIM |
|---|---|---|---|---|---|---|---|---|
| 1904-05 | 19 | Westmount Hockey Club | CAHL | 8 | 10 | 0 | 10 | |
| 1905-06 | 20 | Brandon Elks | MHL | 7 | 6 | 0 | 6 | |
| 1906-07 | 21 | Brandon Elks | MHL-Pro | 10 | 6 | 3 | 9 | 11 |
| 1907-08 | 22 | Montreal Wanderers | ECAHA | 10 | 8 | 0 | 8 | 27 |
| 1907-08 | 22 | Pembroke Lumber Kings | UOHVL | 1 | 5 | 0 | 5 | |
| 1908-09 | 23 | Montreal Wanderers | ECHA | 9 | 2 | 0 | 2 | 30 |
| 1909-10 | 24 | All-Montreal | CHA | 4 | 4 | 0 | 4 | 3 |
| 1909-10 | 24 | Haileybury Comets | NHA | 12 | 6 | 0 | 6 | 25 |
| 1910-11 | 25 | Montreal Wanderers | NHA | 11 | 4 | 0 | 4 | 24 |
| 1911-12 | 26 | Montreal Wanderers | NHA | 18 | 16 | 0 | 16 | 35 |
| 1912-13 | 27 | Montreal Wanderers | NHA | 19 | 11 | 0 | 11 | 58 |
| 1913-14 | 28 | Montreal Wanderers | NHA | 18 | 4 | 5 | 9 | 74 |
| 1914-15 | 29 | Ottawa Senators | NHA | 16 | 3 | 1 | 4 | 55 |

### REGULAR SEASON

| SEASON | AGE | TEAM | LG | GP | G | A | PTS | PIM |
|---|---|---|---|---|---|---|---|---|
| 1915-16 | 30 | Ottawa Senators | NHA | 21 | 8 | 8 | 16 | 69 |
| 1916-17 | 31 | Montreal Wanderers | NHA | 16 | 6 | 2 | 8 | 66 |
| 1917-18 | 32 | Montreal Wanderers | NHL | 3 | 1 | 0 | 1 | 12 |
| Career — 14 Seasons | | | | 183 | 100 | 19 | 119 | 492 |

### PLAYOFFS

| SEASON | AGE | TEAM | LG | GP | G | A | PTS | PIM |
|---|---|---|---|---|---|---|---|---|
| 1906-07 | 21 | Brandon Elks | MHL-Pro | 2 | 1 | 0 | 1 | 3 |
| 1906-07 | 21 | Kenora Thistles | St-Cup | 2 | 0 | 0 | 0 | 10 |
| 1907-08 | 22 | Montreal Wanderers | St-Cup | 5 | 3 | 0 | 3 | 23 |
| 1908-09 | 23 | Montreal Wanderers | St-Cup | 2 | 0 | 0 | 0 | 13 |
| 1908-09 | 23 | Cobalt Silver Kings | TPHL | 2 | 1 | 0 | 1 | 0 |
| 1914-15 | 29 | Ottawa Senators | NHA | 5 | 2 | 0 | 2 | 0 |
| Career — 4 Seasons | | | | 18 | 7 | 0 | 7 | 49 |

## Angela Ruggiero   Profile: See page 300

### REGULAR SEASON

| SEASON | AGE | TEAM | LG | GP | G | A | PTS | PIM |
|---|---|---|---|---|---|---|---|---|
| 1996-97 | 16 | U.S. National Team | Nat-Team | 5 | 2 | 1 | 3 | 0 |
| 1996-97 | 16 | U.S. National Team | WWC | 5 | 0 | 1 | 1 | 4 |
| 1997-98 | 17 | U.S. National Team | Nat-Team | 31 | 5 | 12 | 17 | 0 |
| 1997-98 | 17 | U.S. National Team | Olympics | 6 | 0 | 0 | 0 | 18 |
| 1998-99 | 18 | Harvard University Crimson | ECAC | 32 | 21 | 40 | 61 | 74 |
| 1998-99 | 18 | U.S. National Team | WWC | 5 | 1 | 1 | 2 | 2 |
| 1999-00 | 19 | U.S. National Team | Nat-Team | 2 | 0 | 0 | 0 | 0 |
| 1999-00 | 19 | Harvard University Crimson | ECAC | 29 | 21 | 33 | 54 | 38 |
| 1999-00 | 19 | U.S. National Team | WWC | 5 | 1 | 6 | 7 | 20 |
| 2000-01 | 20 | U.S. National Team | Nat-Team | 39 | 15 | 28 | 43 | 0 |
| 2000-01 | 20 | U.S. National Team | WWC | 5 | 2 | 4 | 6 | 2 |

### REGULAR SEASON

| SEASON | AGE | TEAM | LG | GP | G | A | PTS | PIM |
|---|---|---|---|---|---|---|---|---|
| 2001-02 | 21 | U.S. National Team | Nat-Team | 31 | 12 | 23 | 35 | 22 |
| 2001-02 | 21 | U.S. National Team | Olympics | 5 | 1 | 3 | 4 | 8 |
| 2002-03 | 22 | Harvard University Crimson | ECAC | 34 | 29 | 54 | 83 | 60 |
| 2002-03 | 22 | U.S. National Team | EEC | 0 | 0 | 0 | 0 | 0 |
| 2003-04 | 23 | U.S. National Team | Nat-Team | 4 | 0 | 4 | 4 | 0 |
| 2003-04 | 23 | Harvard University Crimson | ECAC | 32 | 25 | 30 | 55 | 80 |
| 2003-04 | 23 | U.S. National Team | WWC | 5 | 2 | 5 | 7 | 2 |
| 2004-05 | 24 | Tulsa Oilers | CHL | 1 | 0 | 1 | 1 | 0 |
| 2004-05 | 24 | U.S. National Team | Nat-Team | 4 | 1 | 1 | 2 | |
| 2004-05 | 24 | Montreal Axion | NWHL | 10 | 2 | 9 | 11 | 12 |
| 2004-05 | 24 | U.S. National Team | WWC | 5 | 3 | 3 | 6 | 10 |

## Angela Ruggiero (continued)

**REGULAR SEASON**

| SEASON | AGE | TEAM | LG | GP | G | A | PTS | PIM |
|--------|-----|------|----|----|----|----|-----|-----|
| 2005–06 | 25 | U.S. National Team | Nat-Team | 18 | 6 | 8 | 14 | 12 |
| 2005–06 | 25 | U.S. National Team | Olympics | 5 | 2 | 4 | 6 | 6 |
| 2006–07 | 26 | U.S. National Team | WWC | 5 | 1 | 3 | 4 | 8 |
| 2007–08 | 27 | Minnesota Whitecaps | WWHL | 15 | 8 | 10 | 18 | |
| 2007–08 | 27 | U.S. National Team | WWC | 5 | 0 | 5 | 5 | 2 |
| 2008–09 | 28 | Minnesota Whitecaps | WWHL | 12 | 7 | 8 | 15 | 14 |
| 2008–09 | 28 | U.S. National Team | WWC | 5 | 1 | 1 | 2 | 6 |
| 2009–10 | 29 | U.S. National Team | Nat-Team | 24 | 3 | 5 | 8 | 38 |

**REGULAR SEASON**

| SEASON | AGE | TEAM | LG | GP | G | A | PTS | PIM |
|--------|-----|------|----|----|----|----|-----|-----|
| 2009–10 | 29 | U.S. National Team | Olympics | 5 | 3 | 2 | 5 | 6 |
| 2010–11 | 30 | Boston Blades | CWHL | 22 | 11 | 15 | 26 | 38 |
| 2010–11 | 30 | U.S. National Team | WWC | 5 | 2 | 1 | 3 | 0 |
| Career — 15 Seasons | | | | 345 | 168 | 282 | 450 | 388 |

**PLAYOFFS**

| SEASON | AGE | TEAM | LG | GP | G | A | PTS | PIM |
|--------|-----|------|----|----|----|----|-----|-----|
| 2004–05 | 24 | Montreal Axion | NWHL | 3 | 1 | 4 | 5 | 0 |
| 2008–09 | 28 | Minnesota Whitecaps | WWHL | 2 | 0 | 1 | 1 | 0 |
| Career — 2 Seasons | | | | 5 | 1 | 5 | 6 | 0 |

## Jack Ruttan  Profile: See page 301

**REGULAR SEASON**

| SEASON | AGE | TEAM | LG | GP | G | A | PTS | PIM |
|--------|-----|------|----|----|----|----|-----|-----|
| 1905–06 | 16 | St. John's College | MAHA | | | | | |
| 1906–07 | 17 | St. John's College | MAHA | | | | | |
| 1907–08 | 18 | St. John's College | MAHA | | | | | |
| 1908–09 | 19 | University of Manitoba | WSrHL | 7 | 10 | 0 | 10 | |
| 1909–10 | 20 | University of Manitoba | WSrHL | 1 | 0 | 0 | 0 | 0 |
| 1910–11 | 21 | U. of Manitoba Varsity | MHL-Sr. | 4 | 2 | 0 | 2 | |
| 1911–12 | 22 | University of Manitoba | WSrHL | 8 | 4 | 0 | 4 | |
| 1912–13 | 23 | Winnipeg Winnipegs | MHL-Sr. | 6 | 4 | 0 | 4 | |
| 1917–18 | 28 | Winnipeg Somme | WNDHL | 1 | 0 | 0 | 0 | 2 |
| Career — 9 Seasons | | | | 27 | 20 | 0 | 20 | 2 |

**PLAYOFFS**

| SEASON | AGE | TEAM | LG | GP | G | A | PTS | PIM |
|--------|-----|------|----|----|----|----|-----|-----|
| 1912–13 | 23 | Winnipeg Winnipegs | Al-Cup | 4 | 2 | 0 | 2 | |
| 1913–14 | 24 | Winnipeg Winnipegs | MHL-Sr. | 1 | 0 | 0 | 0 | 4 |
| Career — 2 Seasons | | | | 5 | 2 | 0 | 2 | 4 |

## Borje Salming  Profile: See page 302

**REGULAR SEASON**

| SEASON | AGE | TEAM | LG | GP | G | A | PTS | +/- | PIM | ESG | PPG | SHG | GWG | SOG | S% |
|--------|-----|------|----|----|----|----|-----|-----|-----|-----|-----|-----|-----|-----|----|
| 1973–74 | 22 | Toronto Maple Leafs | NHL | 76 | 5 | 34 | 39 | 38 | 48 | 2 | 3 | 0 | 0 | 130 | 3.9 |
| 1974–75 | 23 | Toronto Maple Leafs | NHL | 60 | 12 | 25 | 37 | 4 | 34 | 7 | 4 | 1 | 1 | 136 | 8.8 |
| 1975–76 | 24 | Toronto Maple Leafs | NHL | 78 | 16 | 41 | 57 | 31 | 70 | 8 | 8 | 0 | 1 | 194 | 8.3 |
| 1976–77 | 25 | Toronto Maple Leafs | NHL | 76 | 12 | 66 | 78 | 45 | 46 | 11 | 1 | 0 | 0 | 186 | 6.5 |
| 1977–78 | 26 | Toronto Maple Leafs | NHL | 80 | 16 | 60 | 76 | 30 | 70 | 10 | 6 | 0 | 5 | 256 | 6.3 |
| 1978–79 | 27 | Toronto Maple Leafs | NHL | 78 | 17 | 56 | 73 | 31 | 76 | 13 | 4 | 0 | 2 | 230 | 7.4 |
| 1979–80 | 28 | Toronto Maple Leafs | NHL | 74 | 19 | 52 | 71 | 3 | 94 | 15 | 4 | 0 | 1 | 222 | 8.6 |
| 1980–81 | 29 | Toronto Maple Leafs | NHL | 72 | 5 | 61 | 66 | 0 | 154 | 3 | 1 | 1 | 1 | 210 | 2.4 |
| 1981–82 | 30 | Toronto Maple Leafs | NHL | 69 | 12 | 44 | 56 | 3 | 170 | 10 | 2 | 0 | 0 | 175 | 6.9 |
| 1982–83 | 31 | Toronto Maple Leafs | NHL | 69 | 7 | 38 | 45 | -5 | 104 | 4 | 2 | 1 | 0 | 111 | 6.3 |
| 1983–84 | 32 | Toronto Maple Leafs | NHL | 68 | 5 | 38 | 43 | -32 | 92 | 2 | 2 | 1 | 0 | 160 | 3.1 |
| 1984–85 | 33 | Toronto Maple Leafs | NHL | 73 | 6 | 33 | 39 | -23 | 76 | 3 | 3 | 0 | 0 | 184 | 3.3 |
| 1985–86 | 34 | Toronto Maple Leafs | NHL | 41 | 7 | 15 | 22 | -6 | 48 | 3 | 3 | 1 | 1 | 71 | 9.7 |
| 1986–87 | 35 | Toronto Maple Leafs | NHL | 56 | 4 | 16 | 20 | 17 | 42 | 3 | 0 | 1 | 1 | 72 | 5.6 |
| 1987–88 | 36 | Toronto Maple Leafs | NHL | 66 | 2 | 24 | 26 | 7 | 82 | 1 | 1 | 0 | 0 | 92 | 2.2 |
| 1988–89 | 37 | Toronto Maple Leafs | NHL | 63 | 3 | 17 | 20 | 7 | 86 | 2 | 1 | 0 | 0 | 58 | 5.2 |
| 1989–90 | 38 | Detroit Red Wings | NHL | 49 | 2 | 17 | 19 | 20 | 52 | 0 | 2 | 0 | 0 | 52 | 3.8 |
| NHL Career — 17 Seasons | | | | 1148 | 150 | 637 | 787 | 170 | 1344 | 97 | 47 | 6 | 13 | 2539 | 5.9 |

**PLAYOFFS**

| SEASON | AGE | TEAM | LG | GP | G | A | PTS | +/- | PIM | ESG | PPG | SHG | GWG | SOG | S% |
|--------|-----|------|----|----|----|----|-----|-----|-----|-----|-----|-----|-----|-----|----|
| 1973–74 | 22 | Toronto Maple Leafs | NHL | 4 | 0 | 1 | 1 | -2 | 4 | 0 | 0 | 0 | 0 | 8 | 0.0 |
| 1974–75 | 23 | Toronto Maple Leafs | NHL | 7 | 0 | 4 | 4 | 0 | 6 | 0 | 0 | 0 | 0 | 17 | 0.0 |
| 1975–76 | 24 | Toronto Maple Leafs | NHL | 10 | 3 | 4 | 7 | -2 | 9 | 2 | 1 | 0 | 0 | 32 | 9.4 |
| 1976–77 | 25 | Toronto Maple Leafs | NHL | 9 | 3 | 6 | 9 | -3 | 6 | 1 | 2 | 0 | 0 | 24 | 12.5 |
| 1977–78 | 26 | Toronto Maple Leafs | NHL | 6 | 2 | 2 | 4 | 3 | 6 | 2 | 0 | 0 | 1 | 25 | 8.0 |
| 1978–79 | 27 | Toronto Maple Leafs | NHL | 6 | 0 | 1 | 1 | -2 | 8 | 0 | 0 | 0 | 0 | 17 | 0.0 |
| 1979–80 | 28 | Toronto Maple Leafs | NHL | 3 | 1 | 1 | 2 | -5 | 2 | 0 | 1 | 0 | 0 | 7 | 14.3 |
| 1980–81 | 29 | Toronto Maple Leafs | NHL | 3 | 0 | 2 | 2 | -8 | 4 | 0 | 0 | 0 | 0 | 11 | 0.0 |
| 1982–83 | 31 | Toronto Maple Leafs | NHL | 4 | 1 | 4 | 5 | -5 | 10 | 0 | 1 | 0 | 0 | 20 | 5.0 |
| 1985–86 | 34 | Toronto Maple Leafs | NHL | 10 | 1 | 6 | 7 | 13 | 14 | 1 | 0 | 0 | 0 | 23 | 4.4 |
| 1986–87 | 35 | Toronto Maple Leafs | NHL | 13 | 0 | 3 | 3 | -1 | 14 | 0 | 0 | 0 | 0 | 20 | 0.0 |
| 1987–88 | 36 | Toronto Maple Leafs | NHL | 6 | 1 | 3 | 4 | 1 | 8 | 1 | 0 | 0 | 0 | 16 | 6.3 |
| NHL Career — 12 Seasons | | | | 81 | 12 | 37 | 49 | -11 | 91 | 7 | 5 | 0 | 1 | 220 | 5.5 |

# Serge Savard   Profile: See page 304

## REGULAR SEASON

| SEASON | AGE | TEAM | LG | GP | G | A | PTS | +/- | PIM | ESG | PPG | SHG | GWG | SOG | S% |
|---|---|---|---|---|---|---|---|---|---|---|---|---|---|---|---|
| 1966-67 | 21 | Montreal Canadiens | NHL | 2 | 0 | 0 | 0 | 0 | 0 | 0 | 0 | 0 | 0 | 0 | |
| 1967-68 | 22 | Montreal Canadiens | NHL | 67 | 2 | 13 | 15 | 15 | 34 | 1 | 1 | 0 | 0 | 59 | 3.4 |
| 1968-69 | 23 | Montreal Canadiens | NHL | 74 | 8 | 23 | 31 | 35 | 73 | 8 | 0 | 0 | 2 | 98 | 8.2 |
| 1969-70 | 24 | Montreal Canadiens | NHL | 64 | 12 | 19 | 31 | 4 | 38 | 4 | 5 | 3 | 2 | 151 | 8.0 |
| 1970-71 | 25 | Montreal Canadiens | NHL | 37 | 5 | 10 | 15 | 10 | 30 | 4 | 0 | 1 | 1 | 55 | 9.1 |
| 1971-72 | 26 | Montreal Canadiens | NHL | 23 | 1 | 8 | 9 | 21 | 16 | 1 | 0 | 0 | 0 | 45 | 2.2 |
| 1972-73 | 27 | Montreal Canadiens | NHL | 74 | 7 | 32 | 39 | 70 | 58 | 4 | 2 | 1 | 0 | 106 | 6.6 |
| 1973-74 | 28 | Montreal Canadiens | NHL | 67 | 4 | 14 | 18 | 20 | 49 | 3 | 1 | 0 | 1 | 98 | 4.1 |
| 1974-75 | 29 | Montreal Canadiens | NHL | 80 | 20 | 40 | 60 | 72 | 64 | 11 | 8 | 1 | 2 | 164 | 12.2 |
| 1975-76 | 30 | Montreal Canadiens | NHL | 71 | 8 | 39 | 47 | 52 | 38 | 6 | 1 | 1 | 1 | 112 | 7.1 |
| 1976-77 | 31 | Montreal Canadiens | NHL | 78 | 9 | 33 | 42 | 79 | 35 | 9 | 0 | 0 | 1 | 118 | 7.6 |
| 1977-78 | 32 | Montreal Canadiens | NHL | 77 | 8 | 34 | 42 | 62 | 24 | 4 | 4 | 0 | 1 | 102 | 7.8 |
| 1978-79 | 33 | Montreal Canadiens | NHL | 80 | 7 | 26 | 33 | 47 | 30 | 4 | 1 | 2 | 0 | 82 | 8.5 |
| 1979-80 | 34 | Montreal Canadiens | NHL | 46 | 5 | 8 | 13 | -2 | 18 | 5 | 0 | 0 | 1 | 45 | 11.1 |
| 1980-81 | 35 | Montreal Canadiens | NHL | 77 | 4 | 13 | 17 | 12 | 30 | 4 | 0 | 0 | 1 | 63 | 6.4 |
| 1981-82 | 36 | Winnipeg Jets | NHL | 47 | 2 | 5 | 7 | -9 | 26 | 2 | 0 | 0 | 1 | 41 | 4.9 |
| 1982-83 | 37 | Winnipeg Jets | NHL | 76 | 4 | 16 | 20 | -26 | 27 | 4 | 0 | 0 | 0 | 51 | 7.8 |
| NHL Career – 17 Seasons | | | | 1040 | 106 | 333 | 439 | 462 | 590 | 74 | 23 | 9 | 14 | 1390 | 7.6 |

## PLAYOFFS

| SEASON | AGE | TEAM | LG | GP | G | A | PTS | +/- | PIM | ESG | PPG | SHG | GWG | SOG | S% |
|---|---|---|---|---|---|---|---|---|---|---|---|---|---|---|---|
| 1967-68 | 22 | Montreal Canadiens | NHL | 6 | 2 | 0 | 2 | 3 | 0 | 0 | 0 | 2 | 1 | 6 | 33.3 |
| 1968-69 | 23 | Montreal Canadiens | NHL | 14 | 4 | 6 | 10 | 2 | 24 | 3 | 1 | 0 | 1 | 21 | 19.1 |
| 1971-72 | 26 | Montreal Canadiens | NHL | 6 | 0 | 0 | 0 | 0 | 10 | 0 | 0 | 0 | 0 | 4 | 0.0 |
| 1972-73 | 27 | Montreal Canadiens | NHL | 17 | 3 | 8 | 11 | 4 | 24 | 3 | 0 | 0 | 0 | 44 | 6.8 |
| 1973-74 | 28 | Montreal Canadiens | NHL | 6 | 1 | 1 | 2 | -5 | 4 | 1 | 0 | 0 | 0 | 4 | 25.0 |
| 1974-75 | 29 | Montreal Canadiens | NHL | 11 | 1 | 7 | 8 | 2 | 2 | 1 | 0 | 0 | 0 | 23 | 4.4 |
| 1975-76 | 30 | Montreal Canadiens | NHL | 13 | 3 | 6 | 9 | 15 | 6 | 1 | 1 | 1 | 2 | 23 | 13.0 |
| 1976-77 | 31 | Montreal Canadiens | NHL | 14 | 2 | 7 | 9 | 11 | 2 | 1 | 1 | 0 | 1 | 23 | 8.7 |
| 1977-78 | 32 | Montreal Canadiens | NHL | 15 | 1 | 7 | 8 | 21 | 8 | 1 | 0 | 0 | 0 | 22 | 4.6 |
| 1978-79 | 33 | Montreal Canadiens | NHL | 16 | 2 | 7 | 9 | 8 | 6 | 1 | 1 | 0 | 1 | 17 | 11.8 |
| 1979-80 | 34 | Montreal Canadiens | NHL | 2 | 0 | 0 | 0 | -1 | 0 | 0 | 0 | 0 | 0 | 0 | |
| 1980-81 | 35 | Montreal Canadiens | NHL | 3 | 0 | 0 | 0 | -7 | 0 | 0 | 0 | 0 | 0 | 4 | 0.0 |
| 1981-82 | 36 | Winnipeg Jets | NHL | 4 | 0 | 0 | 0 | -3 | 2 | 0 | 0 | 0 | 0 | 5 | 0.0 |
| 1982-83 | 37 | Winnipeg Jets | NHL | 3 | 0 | 0 | 0 | -3 | 2 | 0 | 0 | 0 | 0 | 2 | 0.0 |
| NHL Career – 14 Seasons | | | | 130 | 19 | 49 | 68 | 47 | 90 | 12 | 4 | 3 | 6 | 198 | 9.6 |

# Earl Seibert   Profile: See page 305

## REGULAR SEASON

| SEASON | AGE | TEAM | LG | GP | G | A | PTS | PIM |
|---|---|---|---|---|---|---|---|---|
| 1931-32 | 20 | New York Rangers | NHL | 46 | 4 | 6 | 10 | 88 |
| 1932-33 | 21 | New York Rangers | NHL | 45 | 2 | 3 | 5 | 92 |
| 1933-34 | 22 | New York Rangers | NHL | 48 | 13 | 10 | 23 | 66 |
| 1934-35 | 23 | New York Rangers | NHL | 48 | 6 | 19 | 25 | 86 |
| 1935-36 | 24 | New York Rangers | NHL | 17 | 2 | 3 | 5 | 6 |
| 1935-36 | 24 | Chicago Black Hawks | NHL | 26 | 3 | 6 | 9 | 19 |
| 1936-37 | 25 | Chicago Black Hawks | NHL | 43 | 9 | 6 | 15 | 46 |
| 1937-38 | 26 | Chicago Black Hawks | NHL | 48 | 8 | 13 | 21 | 38 |
| 1938-39 | 27 | Chicago Black Hawks | NHL | 48 | 4 | 11 | 15 | 57 |
| 1939-40 | 28 | Chicago Black Hawks | NHL | 37 | 3 | 7 | 10 | 35 |
| 1940-41 | 29 | Chicago Black Hawks | NHL | 46 | 3 | 17 | 20 | 52 |
| 1941-42 | 30 | Chicago Black Hawks | NHL | 46 | 7 | 14 | 21 | 52 |
| 1942-43 | 31 | Chicago Black Hawks | NHL | 44 | 5 | 27 | 32 | 48 |
| 1943-44 | 32 | Chicago Black Hawks | NHL | 50 | 8 | 25 | 33 | 40 |
| 1944-45 | 33 | Chicago Black Hawks | NHL | 22 | 7 | 8 | 15 | 13 |
| 1944-45 | 33 | Detroit Red Wings | NHL | 25 | 5 | 9 | 14 | 10 |
| 1945-46 | 34 | Detroit Red Wings | NHL | 18 | 0 | 3 | 3 | 18 |
| NHL Career – 15 Seasons | | | | 657 | 89 | 187 | 276 | 766 |

## PLAYOFFS

| SEASON | AGE | TEAM | LG | GP | G | A | PTS | PIM |
|---|---|---|---|---|---|---|---|---|
| 1931-32 | 20 | New York Rangers | NHL | 7 | 1 | 2 | 3 | 14 |
| 1932-33 | 21 | New York Rangers | NHL | 8 | 1 | 0 | 1 | 16 |
| 1933-34 | 22 | New York Rangers | NHL | 2 | 0 | 0 | 0 | 4 |
| 1934-35 | 23 | New York Rangers | NHL | 4 | 0 | 0 | 0 | 6 |
| 1935-36 | 24 | Chicago Black Hawks | NHL | 2 | 2 | 0 | 2 | 0 |
| 1937-38 | 26 | Chicago Black Hawks | NHL | 10 | 5 | 2 | 7 | 12 |
| 1939-40 | 28 | Chicago Black Hawks | NHL | 2 | 0 | 1 | 1 | 8 |
| 1940-41 | 29 | Chicago Black Hawks | NHL | 5 | 0 | 0 | 0 | 12 |
| 1941-42 | 30 | Chicago Black Hawks | NHL | 3 | 0 | 0 | 0 | 0 |
| 1943-44 | 32 | Chicago Black Hawks | NHL | 9 | 0 | 2 | 2 | 2 |
| 1944-45 | 33 | Detroit Red Wings | NHL | 14 | 2 | 1 | 3 | 4 |
| NHL Career – 11 Seasons | | | | 66 | 11 | 8 | 19 | 78 |

# Eddie Shore   Profile: See page 306

## REGULAR SEASON

| SEASON | AGE | TEAM | LG | GP | G | A | PTS | PIM |
|---|---|---|---|---|---|---|---|---|
| 1924-25 | 22 | Regina Capitals | WCHL | 24 | 6 | 0 | 6 | 75 |
| 1925-26 | 23 | Edmonton Eskimos | WHL | 30 | 12 | 2 | 14 | 86 |
| 1926-27 | 24 | Boston Bruins | NHL | 41 | 12 | 6 | 18 | 130 |
| 1927-28 | 25 | Boston Bruins | NHL | 43 | 11 | 6 | 17 | 165 |
| 1928-29 | 26 | Boston Bruins | NHL | 39 | 12 | 7 | 19 | 98 |
| 1929-30 | 27 | Boston Bruins | NHL | 42 | 12 | 19 | 31 | 109 |
| 1930-31 | 28 | Boston Bruins | NHL | 44 | 15 | 16 | 31 | 107 |
| 1931-32 | 29 | Boston Bruins | NHL | 45 | 9 | 13 | 22 | 80 |
| 1932-33 | 30 | Boston Bruins | NHL | 48 | 8 | 27 | 35 | 112 |
| 1933-34 | 31 | Boston Bruins | NHL | 30 | 2 | 10 | 12 | 67 |
| 1934-35 | 32 | Boston Bruins | NHL | 48 | 7 | 26 | 33 | 32 |
| 1935-36 | 33 | Boston Bruins | NHL | 45 | 3 | 16 | 19 | 61 |
| 1936-37 | 34 | Boston Bruins | NHL | 20 | 3 | 1 | 4 | 12 |
| 1937-38 | 35 | Boston Bruins | NHL | 48 | 3 | 14 | 17 | 42 |
| 1938-39 | 36 | Boston Bruins | NHL | 44 | 4 | 14 | 18 | 47 |
| 1939-40 | 37 | Boston Bruins | NHL | 4 | 2 | 1 | 3 | 4 |

## Eddie Shore (continued)

**REGULAR SEASON**

| SEASON | AGE | TEAM | LG | GP | G | A | PTS | PIM |
|---|---|---|---|---|---|---|---|---|
| 1939–40 | 37 | New York Americans | NHL | 10 | 2 | 3 | 5 | 9 |
| Career — 16 Seasons | | | | 605 | 123 | 181 | 304 | 1260 |

**PLAYOFFS**

| SEASON | AGE | TEAM | LG | GP | G | A | PTS | PIM |
|---|---|---|---|---|---|---|---|---|
| 1925–26 | 23 | Edmonton Eskimos | WHL | 2 | 0 | 0 | 0 | 8 |
| 1926–27 | 24 | Boston Bruins | NHL | 8 | 1 | 1 | 2 | 46 |
| 1927–28 | 25 | Boston Bruins | NHL | 2 | 0 | 0 | 0 | 8 |
| 1928–29 | 26 | Boston Bruins | NHL | 5 | 1 | 1 | 2 | 28 |
| 1929–30 | 27 | Boston Bruins | NHL | 6 | 1 | 0 | 1 | 26 |

**PLAYOFFS**

| SEASON | AGE | TEAM | LG | GP | G | A | PTS | PIM |
|---|---|---|---|---|---|---|---|---|
| 1930–31 | 28 | Boston Bruins | NHL | 5 | 2 | 1 | 3 | 22 |
| 1932–33 | 30 | Boston Bruins | NHL | 5 | 1 | 1 | 2 | 14 |
| 1934–35 | 32 | Boston Bruins | NHL | 4 | 0 | 1 | 1 | 2 |
| 1935–36 | 33 | Boston Bruins | NHL | 2 | 1 | 1 | 2 | 12 |
| 1937–38 | 35 | Boston Bruins | NHL | 3 | 0 | 1 | 1 | 6 |
| 1938–39 | 36 | Boston Bruins | NHL | 12 | 0 | 4 | 4 | 19 |
| 1939–40 | 37 | New York Americans | NHL | 3 | 0 | 2 | 2 | 2 |
| Career — 12 Seasons | | | | 57 | 7 | 13 | 23 | 193 |

## Joe Simpson   Profile: See page 308

**REGULAR SEASON**

| SEASON | AGE | TEAM | LG | GP | G | A | PTS | PIM |
|---|---|---|---|---|---|---|---|---|
| 1921–22 | 28 | Edmonton Eskimos | WCHL | 25 | 21 | 12 | 33 | 15 |
| 1922–23 | 29 | Edmonton Eskimos | WCHL | 30 | 15 | 14 | 29 | 6 |
| 1923–24 | 30 | Edmonton Eskimos | WCHL | 30 | 10 | 4 | 14 | 6 |
| 1924–25 | 31 | Edmonton Eskimos | WCHL | 28 | 11 | 12 | 23 | 16 |
| 1925–26 | 32 | New York Americans | NHL | 32 | 2 | 2 | 4 | 20 |
| 1926–27 | 33 | New York Americans | NHL | 43 | 4 | 2 | 6 | 39 |
| 1927–28 | 34 | New York Americans | NHL | 24 | 2 | 0 | 2 | 30 |
| 1928–29 | 35 | New York Americans | NHL | 43 | 3 | 2 | 5 | 29 |
| 1929–30 | 36 | New York Americans | NHL | 44 | 8 | 13 | 21 | 41 |

**REGULAR SEASON**

| SEASON | AGE | TEAM | LG | GP | G | A | PTS | PIM |
|---|---|---|---|---|---|---|---|---|
| 1930–31 | 37 | New York Americans | NHL | 42 | 2 | 0 | 2 | 13 |
| Career — 10 Seasons | | | | 341 | 78 | 61 | 139 | 215 |

**PLAYOFFS**

| SEASON | AGE | TEAM | LG | GP | G | A | PTS | PIM |
|---|---|---|---|---|---|---|---|---|
| 1921–22 | 28 | Edmonton Eskimos | WCHL | 2 | 1 | 0 | 1 | 2 |
| 1922–23 | 29 | Edmonton Eskimos | St-Cup | 2 | 0 | 1 | 1 | 0 |
| 1922–23 | 29 | Edmonton Eskimos | WCHL | 2 | 0 | 0 | 0 | 0 |
| 1928–29 | 35 | New York Americans | NHL | 2 | 0 | 0 | 0 | 0 |
| Career — 3 Seasons | | | | 8 | 1 | 1 | 2 | 2 |

## Allan Stanley   Profile: See page 309

**REGULAR SEASON**

| SEASON | AGE | TEAM | LG | GP | G | A | PTS | +/- | PIM | ESG | PPG | SHG | GWG | SOG | S% |
|---|---|---|---|---|---|---|---|---|---|---|---|---|---|---|---|
| 1948–49 | 22 | New York Rangers | NHL | 40 | 2 | 8 | 10 | | 22 | 1 | 1 | 0 | 1 | | |
| 1949–50 | 23 | New York Rangers | NHL | 55 | 4 | 4 | 8 | | 58 | 3 | 1 | 0 | 0 | | |
| 1950–51 | 24 | New York Rangers | NHL | 70 | 7 | 14 | 21 | | 75 | 6 | 0 | 1 | 1 | | |
| 1951–52 | 25 | New York Rangers | NHL | 50 | 5 | 14 | 19 | | 75 | 5 | 0 | 0 | 0 | | |
| 1952–53 | 26 | New York Rangers | NHL | 70 | 5 | 12 | 17 | | 52 | 4 | 1 | 0 | 1 | | |
| 1953–54 | 27 | New York Rangers | NHL | 10 | 0 | 2 | 2 | | 11 | 0 | 0 | 0 | 0 | | |
| 1954–55 | 28 | New York Rangers | NHL | 12 | 0 | 2 | 2 | | 2 | 0 | 0 | 0 | 0 | | |
| 1954–55 | 28 | Chicago Black Hawks | NHL | 52 | 10 | 14 | 24 | | 22 | 10 | 2 | 0 | 0 | | |
| 1955–56 | 29 | Chicago Black Hawks | NHL | 59 | 4 | 14 | 18 | | 70 | 3 | 1 | 0 | 0 | | |
| 1956–57 | 30 | Boston Bruins | NHL | 60 | 6 | 25 | 31 | | 45 | 3 | 3 | 0 | 1 | | |
| 1957–58 | 31 | Boston Bruins | NHL | 69 | 6 | 25 | 31 | | 37 | 5 | 0 | 1 | 1 | | |
| 1958–59 | 32 | Toronto Maple Leafs | NHL | 70 | 1 | 22 | 23 | | 47 | 1 | 0 | 0 | 0 | | |
| 1959–60 | 33 | Toronto Maple Leafs | NHL | 64 | 10 | 23 | 33 | -1 | 22 | 7 | 3 | 0 | 2 | 97 | 10.3 |
| 1960–61 | 34 | Toronto Maple Leafs | NHL | 68 | 9 | 25 | 34 | 24 | 42 | 7 | 2 | 0 | 2 | 101 | 8.9 |
| 1961–62 | 35 | Toronto Maple Leafs | NHL | 60 | 9 | 26 | 35 | 25 | 24 | 5 | 4 | 0 | 1 | 87 | 10.3 |
| 1962–63 | 36 | Toronto Maple Leafs | NHL | 61 | 4 | 15 | 19 | 2 | 22 | 3 | 0 | 1 | 1 | 61 | 6.6 |
| 1963–64 | 37 | Toronto Maple Leafs | NHL | 70 | 6 | 21 | 27 | 15 | 60 | 5 | 1 | 0 | 1 | 121 | 5.0 |
| 1964–65 | 38 | Toronto Maple Leafs | NHL | 64 | 2 | 15 | 17 | 4 | 30 | 2 | 0 | 0 | 0 | 65 | 3.1 |
| 1965–66 | 39 | Toronto Maple Leafs | NHL | 59 | 4 | 14 | 18 | 30 | 35 | 3 | 1 | 0 | 0 | 86 | 4.7 |
| 1966–67 | 40 | Toronto Maple Leafs | NHL | 53 | 1 | 12 | 13 | 7 | 20 | 1 | 0 | 0 | 0 | 36 | 2.8 |
| 1967–68 | 41 | Toronto Maple Leafs | NHL | 64 | 1 | 13 | 14 | 16 | 16 | 1 | 0 | 0 | 0 | 61 | 1.6 |
| 1968–69 | 42 | Philadelphia Flyers | NHL | 64 | 4 | 13 | 17 | -5 | 28 | 2 | 2 | 0 | 0 | 75 | 5.3 |
| NHL Career — 21 Seasons | | | | 1244 | 100 | 333 | 433 | 117 | 792 | 75 | 22 | 3 | 12 | 715 | 6.4 |

**PLAYOFFS**

| SEASON | AGE | TEAM | LG | GP | G | A | PTS | +/- | PIM | ESG | PPG | SHG | GWG | SOG | S% |
|---|---|---|---|---|---|---|---|---|---|---|---|---|---|---|---|
| 1949–50 | 23 | New York Rangers | NHL | 12 | 2 | 5 | 7 | | 10 | 1 | 1 | 0 | 0 | | |
| 1957–58 | 31 | Boston Bruins | NHL | 12 | 1 | 3 | 4 | | 6 | 0 | 1 | 0 | 0 | | |
| 1958–59 | 32 | Toronto Maple Leafs | NHL | 12 | 0 | 3 | 3 | | 2 | 0 | 0 | 0 | 0 | | |
| 1959–60 | 33 | Toronto Maple Leafs | NHL | 10 | 2 | 3 | 5 | -6 | 2 | 1 | 1 | 0 | 0 | 17 | 11.8 |
| 1960–61 | 34 | Toronto Maple Leafs | NHL | 5 | 0 | 3 | 3 | -2 | 0 | 0 | 0 | 0 | 0 | 4 | 0.0 |
| 1961–62 | 35 | Toronto Maple Leafs | NHL | 12 | 0 | 3 | 3 | -1 | 6 | 0 | 0 | 0 | 0 | 17 | 0.0 |
| 1962–63 | 36 | Toronto Maple Leafs | NHL | 10 | 1 | 6 | 7 | 9 | 8 | 1 | 0 | 0 | 0 | 13 | 7.7 |
| 1963–64 | 37 | Toronto Maple Leafs | NHL | 14 | 1 | 6 | 7 | 2 | 20 | 1 | 0 | 0 | 0 | 17 | 5.9 |
| 1964–65 | 38 | Toronto Maple Leafs | NHL | 6 | 0 | 1 | 1 | -1 | 12 | 0 | 0 | 0 | 0 | 6 | 0.0 |
| 1965–66 | 39 | Toronto Maple Leafs | NHL | 1 | 0 | 0 | 0 | | 0 | 0 | 0 | 0 | 0 | | |
| 1966–67 | 40 | Toronto Maple Leafs | NHL | 12 | 0 | 2 | 2 | 1 | 10 | 0 | 0 | 0 | 0 | 5 | 0.0 |
| 1968–69 | 42 | Philadelphia Flyers | NHL | 3 | 0 | 1 | 1 | 0 | 4 | 0 | 0 | 0 | 0 | 6 | 0.0 |
| NHL Career — 12 Seasons | | | | 109 | 7 | 36 | 43 | 2 | 80 | 4 | 3 | 0 | 0 | 85 | 4.7 |

# Scott Stevens  Profile: See page 310

## REGULAR SEASON

| SEASON | AGE | TEAM | LG | GP | G | A | PTS | +/- | PIM | ESG | PPG | SHG | GWG | SOG | S% |
|--------|-----|------|----|----|----|----|-----|-----|-----|-----|-----|-----|-----|-----|-----|
| 1982-83 | 18 | Washington Capitals | NHL | 77 | 9 | 16 | 25 | 15 | 195 | 9 | 0 | 0 | 0 | 121 | 7.4 |
| 1983-84 | 19 | Washington Capitals | NHL | 78 | 13 | 32 | 45 | 25 | 201 | 6 | 7 | 0 | 2 | 155 | 8.4 |
| 1984-85 | 20 | Washington Capitals | NHL | 80 | 21 | 44 | 65 | 19 | 221 | 5 | 16 | 0 | 5 | 170 | 12.4 |
| 1985-86 | 21 | Washington Capitals | NHL | 73 | 15 | 38 | 53 | 0 | 165 | 12 | 3 | 0 | 2 | 121 | 12.4 |
| 1986-87 | 22 | Washington Capitals | NHL | 77 | 10 | 51 | 61 | 15 | 283 | 8 | 2 | 0 | 0 | 163 | 6.1 |
| 1987-88 | 23 | Washington Capitals | NHL | 80 | 12 | 60 | 72 | 14 | 184 | 6 | 5 | 1 | 2 | 231 | 5.2 |
| 1988-89 | 24 | Washington Capitals | NHL | 80 | 7 | 61 | 68 | 1 | 225 | 1 | 6 | 0 | 3 | 195 | 3.6 |
| 1989-90 | 25 | Washington Capitals | NHL | 56 | 11 | 29 | 40 | 1 | 154 | 4 | 7 | 0 | 0 | 143 | 7.7 |
| 1990-91 | 26 | St. Louis Blues | NHL | 78 | 5 | 44 | 49 | 23 | 150 | 4 | 1 | 0 | 1 | 160 | 3.1 |
| 1991-92 | 27 | New Jersey Devils | NHL | 68 | 17 | 42 | 59 | 24 | 124 | 9 | 7 | 1 | 2 | 156 | 10.9 |
| 1992-93 | 28 | New Jersey Devils | NHL | 81 | 12 | 45 | 57 | 14 | 120 | 4 | 8 | 0 | 1 | 146 | 8.2 |
| 1993-94 | 29 | New Jersey Devils | NHL | 83 | 18 | 60 | 78 | 53 | 112 | 12 | 5 | 1 | 4 | 215 | 8.4 |
| 1994-95 | 30 | New Jersey Devils | NHL | 48 | 2 | 20 | 22 | 4 | 56 | 1 | 1 | 0 | 1 | 111 | 1.8 |
| 1995-96 | 31 | New Jersey Devils | NHL | 82 | 5 | 23 | 28 | 7 | 100 | 2 | 2 | 1 | 1 | 174 | 2.9 |
| 1996-97 | 32 | New Jersey Devils | NHL | 79 | 5 | 19 | 24 | 26 | 70 | 5 | 0 | 0 | 1 | 166 | 3.0 |
| 1997-98 | 33 | New Jersey Devils | NHL | 80 | 4 | 22 | 26 | 19 | 80 | 3 | 1 | 0 | 1 | 94 | 4.3 |
| 1998-99 | 34 | New Jersey Devils | NHL | 75 | 5 | 22 | 27 | 29 | 64 | 5 | 0 | 0 | 1 | 111 | 4.5 |
| 1999-00 | 35 | New Jersey Devils | NHL | 78 | 8 | 21 | 29 | 30 | 103 | 7 | 0 | 1 | 1 | 133 | 6.0 |
| 2000-01 | 36 | New Jersey Devils | NHL | 81 | 9 | 22 | 31 | 40 | 71 | 6 | 3 | 0 | 2 | 171 | 5.3 |
| 2001-02 | 37 | New Jersey Devils | NHL | 82 | 1 | 16 | 17 | 15 | 44 | 1 | 0 | 0 | 1 | 121 | 0.8 |
| 2002-03 | 38 | New Jersey Devils | NHL | 81 | 4 | 16 | 20 | 18 | 41 | 4 | 0 | 0 | 2 | 113 | 3.5 |
| 2003-04 | 39 | New Jersey Devils | NHL | 38 | 3 | 9 | 12 | 3 | 22 | 2 | 1 | 0 | 1 | 68 | 4.4 |
| **NHL Career – 22 Seasons** | | | | 1635 | 196 | 712 | 908 | 395 | 2785 | 116 | 75 | 5 | 34 | 3238 | 6.1 |

## PLAYOFFS

| SEASON | AGE | TEAM | LG | GP | G | A | PTS | +/- | PIM | ESG | PPG | SHG | GWG | SOG | S% |
|--------|-----|------|----|----|----|----|-----|-----|-----|-----|-----|-----|-----|-----|-----|
| 1982-83 | 18 | Washington Capitals | NHL | 4 | 1 | 0 | 1 | -2 | 26 | 1 | 0 | 0 | 0 | 8 | 12.5 |
| 1983-84 | 19 | Washington Capitals | NHL | 8 | 1 | 8 | 9 | 1 | 21 | 0 | 1 | 0 | 0 | 21 | 4.8 |
| 1984-85 | 20 | Washington Capitals | NHL | 5 | 0 | 1 | 1 | -4 | 20 | 0 | 0 | 0 | 0 | 11 | 0.0 |
| 1985-86 | 21 | Washington Capitals | NHL | 9 | 3 | 8 | 11 | 8 | 12 | 1 | 2 | 0 | 2 | 17 | 17.7 |
| 1986-87 | 22 | Washington Capitals | NHL | 7 | 0 | 5 | 5 | 4 | 19 | 0 | 0 | 0 | 0 | 19 | 0.0 |
| 1987-88 | 23 | Washington Capitals | NHL | 13 | 1 | 11 | 12 | -1 | 46 | 1 | 0 | 0 | 0 | 42 | 2.4 |
| 1988-89 | 24 | Washington Capitals | NHL | 6 | 1 | 4 | 5 | -2 | 11 | 1 | 0 | 0 | 0 | 16 | 6.3 |
| 1989-90 | 25 | Washington Capitals | NHL | 15 | 2 | 7 | 9 | -1 | 25 | 1 | 1 | 0 | 0 | 35 | 5.7 |
| 1990-91 | 26 | St. Louis Blues | NHL | 13 | 0 | 3 | 3 | 8 | 36 | 0 | 0 | 0 | 0 | 17 | 0.0 |
| 1991-92 | 27 | New Jersey Devils | NHL | 7 | 2 | 1 | 3 | -5 | 29 | 0 | 2 | 0 | 1 | 9 | 22.2 |
| 1992-93 | 28 | New Jersey Devils | NHL | 5 | 2 | 2 | 4 | -2 | 10 | 1 | 1 | 0 | 0 | 21 | 9.5 |
| 1993-94 | 29 | New Jersey Devils | NHL | 20 | 2 | 9 | 11 | -1 | 42 | 0 | 2 | 0 | 1 | 56 | 3.6 |
| 1994-95 | 30 | New Jersey Devils | NHL | 20 | 1 | 7 | 8 | 10 | 24 | 1 | 0 | 0 | 1 | 54 | 1.9 |
| 1996-97 | 32 | New Jersey Devils | NHL | 10 | 0 | 4 | 4 | -2 | 2 | 0 | 0 | 0 | 0 | 27 | 0.0 |
| 1997-98 | 33 | New Jersey Devils | NHL | 6 | 1 | 0 | 1 | 4 | 8 | 1 | 0 | 0 | 0 | 11 | 9.1 |
| 1998-99 | 34 | New Jersey Devils | NHL | 7 | 2 | 1 | 3 | -2 | 10 | 0 | 2 | 0 | 0 | 14 | 14.3 |
| 1999-00 | 35 | New Jersey Devils | NHL | 23 | 3 | 8 | 11 | 9 | 6 | 3 | 0 | 0 | 2 | 29 | 10.3 |
| 2000-01 | 36 | New Jersey Devils | NHL | 25 | 1 | 7 | 8 | 3 | 37 | 1 | 0 | 0 | 0 | 34 | 2.9 |
| 2001-02 | 37 | New Jersey Devils | NHL | 6 | 0 | 0 | 0 | 5 | 4 | 0 | 0 | 0 | 0 | 7 | 0.0 |
| 2002-03 | 38 | New Jersey Devils | NHL | 24 | 3 | 6 | 9 | 14 | 14 | 2 | 1 | 0 | 1 | 33 | 9.1 |
| **NHL Career – 20 Seasons** | | | | 233 | 26 | 92 | 118 | 44 | 402 | 14 | 12 | 0 | 8 | 481 | 5.4 |

# Jack Stewart  Profile: See page 311

## REGULAR SEASON

| SEASON | AGE | TEAM | LG | GP | G | A | PTS | PIM |
|--------|-----|------|----|----|----|----|-----|-----|
| 1938-39 | 21 | Detroit Red Wings | NHL | 32 | 0 | 1 | 1 | 18 |
| 1939-40 | 22 | Detroit Red Wings | NHL | 48 | 1 | 0 | 1 | 40 |
| 1940-41 | 23 | Detroit Red Wings | NHL | 47 | 2 | 5 | 7 | 56 |
| 1941-42 | 24 | Detroit Red Wings | NHL | 44 | 4 | 7 | 11 | 93 |
| 1942-43 | 25 | Detroit Red Wings | NHL | 44 | 2 | 9 | 11 | 68 |
| 1945-46 | 28 | Detroit Red Wings | NHL | 47 | 4 | 11 | 15 | 73 |
| 1946-47 | 29 | Detroit Red Wings | NHL | 55 | 5 | 9 | 14 | 83 |
| 1947-48 | 30 | Detroit Red Wings | NHL | 60 | 5 | 14 | 19 | 91 |
| 1948-49 | 31 | Detroit Red Wings | NHL | 60 | 4 | 11 | 15 | 96 |
| 1949-50 | 32 | Detroit Red Wings | NHL | 65 | 3 | 11 | 14 | 86 |
| 1950-51 | 33 | Chicago Black Hawks | NHL | 26 | 0 | 2 | 2 | 49 |
| 1951-52 | 34 | Chicago Black Hawks | NHL | 37 | 1 | 3 | 4 | 12 |
| **NHL Career – 12 Seasons** | | | | 565 | 31 | 83 | 114 | 765 |

## PLAYOFFS

| SEASON | AGE | TEAM | LG | GP | G | A | PTS | PIM |
|--------|-----|------|----|----|----|----|-----|-----|
| 1939-40 | 22 | Detroit Red Wings | NHL | 5 | 0 | 0 | 0 | 4 |
| 1940-41 | 23 | Detroit Red Wings | NHL | 9 | 1 | 2 | 3 | 8 |
| 1941-42 | 24 | Detroit Red Wings | NHL | 12 | 0 | 1 | 1 | 12 |
| 1942-43 | 25 | Detroit Red Wings | NHL | 10 | 1 | 2 | 3 | 35 |
| 1945-46 | 28 | Detroit Red Wings | NHL | 5 | 0 | 0 | 0 | 14 |
| 1946-47 | 29 | Detroit Red Wings | NHL | 5 | 0 | 1 | 1 | 12 |
| 1947-48 | 30 | Detroit Red Wings | NHL | 9 | 1 | 3 | 4 | 6 |
| 1948-49 | 31 | Detroit Red Wings | NHL | 11 | 1 | 1 | 2 | 32 |
| 1949-50 | 32 | Detroit Red Wings | NHL | 14 | 1 | 4 | 5 | 20 |
| **NHL Career – 9 Seasons** | | | | 80 | 5 | 14 | 19 | 143 |

# Hod Stuart  Profile: See page 312

**REGULAR SEASON**

| SEASON | AGE | TEAM | LG | GP | G | A | PTS | PIM |
|---|---|---|---|---|---|---|---|---|
| 1898–99 | 19 | Ottawa Hockey Club | CAHL | 3 | 1 | 0 | 1 | |
| 1899–00 | 20 | Ottawa Hockey Club | CAHL | 7 | 5 | 0 | 5 | |
| 1900–01 | 21 | Quebec Bulldogs | CAHL | 7 | 2 | 0 | 2 | |
| 1901–02 | 22 | Quebec Bulldogs | CAHL | 8 | 5 | 0 | 5 | |
| 1902–03 | 23 | Pittsburgh Bankers | WPHL | 13 | 7 | 8 | 15 | 29 |
| 1903–04 | 24 | Portage Lakes | Exhib. | 14 | 13 | 0 | 13 | 23 |
| 1904–05 | 25 | Calumet Miners | IHL | 22 | 18 | 0 | 18 | 19 |
| 1905–06 | 26 | Pittsburgh Professionals | IHL | 20 | 11 | 0 | 11 | 50 |
| 1905–06 | 26 | Calumet Miners | IHL | 1 | 0 | 0 | 0 | 0 |

**REGULAR SEASON**

| SEASON | AGE | TEAM | LG | GP | G | A | PTS | PIM |
|---|---|---|---|---|---|---|---|---|
| 1906–07 | 27 | Pittsburgh Professionals | IHL | 4 | 1 | 3 | 4 | 19 |
| 1906–07 | 27 | Montreal Wanderers | ECAHA | 8 | 3 | 0 | 3 | 21 |
| Career — 9 Seasons | | | | 107 | 66 | 11 | 77 | 161 |

**PLAYOFFS**

| SEASON | AGE | TEAM | LG | GP | G | A | PTS | PIM |
|---|---|---|---|---|---|---|---|---|
| 1902–03 | 23 | Pittsburgh Bankers | WPHL | 4 | 1 | 2 | 3 | 2 |
| 1903–04 | 24 | Portage Lakes | Exhib. | 9 | 4 | 0 | 4 | 12 |
| 1906–07 | 27 | Montreal Wanderers | St-Cup | 4 | 0 | 0 | 0 | 8 |
| Career — 3 Seasons | | | | 17 | 5 | 2 | 7 | 22 |

# Phat Wilson  Profile: See page 313

**REGULAR SEASON**

| SEASON | AGE | TEAM | LG | GP | G | A | PTS | PIM |
|---|---|---|---|---|---|---|---|---|
| 1915–16 | 20 | Port Arthur Shuniahs | TBSHL | 8 | 2 | 0 | 2 | 23 |
| 1916–17 | 21 | Port Arthur 141st Battalion | TBSHL | 1 | 0 | 0 | 0 | 0 |
| 1918–19 | 23 | Port Arthur Columbus Club | TBSHL | 13 | 8 | 2 | 10 | 42 |
| 1919–20 | 24 | Port Arthur War Vets | TBSHL | 11 | 9 | 0 | 9 | 10 |
| 1920–21 | 25 | Port Arthur Hockey Club | TBSHL | 15 | 11 | 5 | 16 | |
| 1921–22 | 26 | Iroquois Falls Flyers | NOHA | | | | | |
| 1922–23 | 27 | Port Arthur Hockey Club | MHL-Sr. | 16 | 5 | 6 | 11 | 32 |
| 1923–24 | 28 | Port Arthur Hockey Club | MHL-Sr. | 15 | 6 | 5 | 11 | 19 |
| 1924–25 | 29 | Port Arthur Hockey Club | MHL-Sr. | 19 | 7 | 1 | 8 | |
| 1925–26 | 30 | Port Arthur Hockey Club | TBSHL | 19 | 8 | 5 | 13 | 22 |
| 1926–27 | 31 | Port Arthur Ports | TBSHL | 20 | 11 | 5 | 16 | 24 |
| 1927–28 | 32 | Port Arthur Ports | MTBHL | 17 | 7 | 6 | 13 | 19 |
| 1928–29 | 33 | Port Arthur Hockey Club | MTBHL | 20 | 12 | 9 | 21 | 25 |
| 1929–30 | 34 | Port Arthur Hockey Club | TBSHL | 19 | 9 | 8 | 17 | 22 |
| 1930–31 | 35 | Port Arthur Hockey Club | TBSHL | 21 | 9 | 8 | 17 | 32 |
| 1931–32 | 36 | Port Arthur Ports | TBSHL | 15 | 5 | 2 | 7 | 26 |
| Career — 16 Seasons | | | | 229 | 109 | 62 | 171 | 296 |

**PLAYOFFS**

| SEASON | AGE | TEAM | LG | GP | G | A | PTS | PIM |
|---|---|---|---|---|---|---|---|---|
| 1918–19 | 23 | Port Arthur Columbus Club | Al-Cup | 1 | 0 | 0 | 0 | 0 |
| 1920–21 | 25 | Port Arthur Hockey Club | TBSHL | 2 | 1 | 0 | 1 | 5 |
| 1920–21 | 25 | Port Arthur Hockey Club | Al-Cup | 4 | 4 | 1 | 5 | 0 |
| 1922–23 | 27 | Port Arthur Hockey Club | MHL-Sr. | 2 | 0 | 0 | 0 | 2 |
| 1923–24 | 28 | Port Arthur Hockey Club | MHL-Sr. | 2 | 1 | 1 | 2 | 4 |
| 1924–25 | 29 | Port Arthur Hockey Club | MHL-Sr. | 10 | 9 | 3 | 12 | 24 |
| 1924–25 | 29 | Port Arthur Hockey Club | Al-Cup | 6 | 0 | 2 | 2 | 18 |
| 1925–26 | 30 | Port Arthur Hockey Club | TBSHL | 3 | 0 | 0 | 0 | 10 |
| 1925–26 | 30 | Port Arthur Hockey Club | Al-Cup | 6 | 0 | 2 | 2 | 18 |
| 1926–27 | 31 | Port Arthur Ports | TBSHL | 2 | 0 | 0 | 0 | 4 |
| 1928–29 | 33 | Port Arthur Hockey Club | MTBHL | 2 | 0 | 0 | 0 | 6 |
| 1928–29 | 33 | Port Arthur Hockey Club | Al-Cup | 7 | 3 | 1 | 4 | 20 |
| 1929–30 | 34 | Port Arthur Hockey Club | TBSHL | 4 | 4 | 1 | 5 | 11 |
| 1929–30 | 34 | Port Arthur Hockey Club | Al-Cup | 6 | 1 | 1 | 2 | 7 |
| 1930–31 | 35 | Port Arthur Hockey Club | TBSHL | 2 | 0 | 0 | 0 | 2 |
| 1931–32 | 36 | Port Arthur Ports | TBSHL | 2 | 1 | 1 | 2 | 10 |
| Career — 11 Seasons | | | | 61 | 24 | 13 | 37 | 141 |

# Ed Belfour   Profile: See page 316

## REGULAR SEASON

| SEASON | AGE | TEAM | LG | GP | W | L | T | SO | GA | GAA | G | A | PTS | PIM |
|---|---|---|---|---|---|---|---|---|---|---|---|---|---|---|
| 1988–89 | 23 | Chicago Blackhawks | NHL | 23 | 4 | 12 | 3 | 0 | 74 | 3.87 | 0 | 1 | 1 | 6 |
| 1990–91 | 25 | Chicago Blackhawks | NHL | 74 | 43 | 19 | 7 | 4 | 170 | 2.47 | 0 | 3 | 3 | 34 |
| 1991–92 | 26 | Chicago Blackhawks | NHL | 52 | 21 | 18 | 10 | 5 | 132 | 2.71 | 0 | 2 | 2 | 38 |
| 1992–93 | 27 | Chicago Blackhawks | NHL | 71 | 41 | 18 | 11 | 7 | 177 | 2.59 | 0 | 3 | 3 | 28 |
| 1993–94 | 28 | Chicago Blackhawks | NHL | 70 | 37 | 24 | 6 | 7 | 178 | 2.67 | 0 | 4 | 4 | 61 |
| 1994–95 | 29 | Chicago Blackhawks | NHL | 42 | 22 | 15 | 3 | 5 | 93 | 2.28 | 0 | 3 | 3 | 11 |
| 1995–96 | 30 | Chicago Blackhawks | NHL | 50 | 22 | 17 | 10 | 1 | 135 | 2.74 | 0 | 2 | 2 | 36 |
| 1996–97 | 31 | Chicago Blackhawks | NHL | 33 | 11 | 15 | 6 | 1 | 88 | 2.69 | 0 | 0 | 0 | 26 |
| 1996–97 | 31 | San Jose Sharks | NHL | 13 | 3 | 9 | 0 | 1 | 43 | 3.41 | 0 | 0 | 0 | 8 |
| 1997–98 | 32 | Dallas Stars | NHL | 61 | 37 | 12 | 10 | 9 | 112 | 1.88 | 0 | 0 | 0 | 18 |
| 1998–99 | 33 | Dallas Stars | NHL | 61 | 35 | 15 | 9 | 5 | 117 | 1.99 | 0 | 0 | 0 | 26 |
| 1999–00 | 34 | Dallas Stars | NHL | 62 | 32 | 21 | 7 | 4 | 127 | 2.10 | 0 | 3 | 3 | 10 |
| 2000–01 | 35 | Dallas Stars | NHL | 63 | 35 | 20 | 7 | 8 | 144 | 2.34 | 0 | 1 | 1 | 4 |
| 2001–02 | 36 | Dallas Stars | NHL | 60 | 21 | 27 | 11 | 1 | 153 | 2.65 | 0 | 5 | 5 | 12 |
| 2002–03 | 37 | Toronto Maple Leafs | NHL | 62 | 37 | 20 | 5 | 7 | 141 | 2.26 | 0 | 2 | 2 | 24 |
| 2003–04 | 38 | Toronto Maple Leafs | NHL | 59 | 34 | 19 | 6 | 10 | 122 | 2.13 | 0 | 2 | 2 | 16 |
| 2005–06 | 40 | Toronto Maple Leafs | NHL | 49 | 22 | 22 | 4 | 0 | 159 | 3.29 | 0 | 1 | 1 | 12 |
| 2006–07 | 41 | Florida Panthers | NHL | 58 | 27 | 17 | 10 | 1 | 152 | 2.77 | 0 | 2 | 2 | 10 |
| NHL Career — 17 Seasons | | | NHL | 963 | 484 | 320 | 125 | 76 | 2317 | 2.50 | 0 | 34 | 34 | 380 |

## PLAYOFFS

| SEASON | AGE | TEAM | LG | GP | W | L | T | SO | GA | GAA | G | A | PTS | PIM |
|---|---|---|---|---|---|---|---|---|---|---|---|---|---|---|
| 1989–90 | 24 | Chicago Blackhawks | NHL | 9 | 4 | 2 | | 0 | 17 | 2.49 | 1 | 1 | 0 | 6 |
| 1990–91 | 25 | Chicago Blackhawks | NHL | 6 | 2 | 4 | | 0 | 20 | 4.07 | 0 | 0 | 0 | 6 |
| 1991–92 | 26 | Chicago Blackhawks | NHL | 18 | 12 | 4 | | 1 | 39 | 2.47 | 0 | 0 | 4 | 0 |
| 1992–93 | 27 | Chicago Blackhawks | NHL | 4 | 0 | 4 | | 0 | 13 | 3.13 | 0 | 0 | 2 | 2 |
| 1993–94 | 28 | Chicago Blackhawks | NHL | 6 | 2 | 4 | | 0 | 15 | 2.50 | 0 | 0 | 0 | 2 |
| 1994–95 | 29 | Chicago Blackhawks | NHL | 16 | 9 | 7 | | 1 | 37 | 2.19 | 0 | 0 | 2 | 6 |
| 1995–96 | 30 | Chicago Blackhawks | NHL | 9 | 6 | 3 | | 1 | 23 | 2.07 | 0 | 0 | 6 | 4 |
| 1997–98 | 32 | Dallas Stars | NHL | 17 | 10 | 7 | | 1 | 31 | 1.79 | 0 | 0 | 0 | 18 |
| 1998–99 | 33 | Dallas Stars | NHL | 23 | 16 | 7 | | 3 | 43 | 1.67 | 0 | 0 | 2 | 4 |
| 1999–00 | 34 | Dallas Stars | NHL | 23 | 14 | 9 | | 4 | 45 | 1.87 | 0 | 0 | 2 | 8 |
| 2000–01 | 35 | Dallas Stars | NHL | 10 | 4 | 6 | | 0 | 25 | 2.23 | 0 | 0 | 0 | 6 |
| 2002–03 | 37 | Toronto Maple Leafs | NHL | 7 | 3 | 4 | | 0 | 24 | 2.71 | 0 | 0 | 4 | 4 |
| 2003–04 | 38 | Toronto Maple Leafs | NHL | 13 | 6 | 7 | | 3 | 27 | 2.09 | 0 | 0 | 2 | 8 |
| NHL Career — 13 Seasons | | | NHL | 161 | 88 | 68 | | 14 | 359 | 2.17 | 1 | 1 | 2 | 74 |

# Clint Benedict   Profile: See page 318

## REGULAR SEASON

| SEASON | AGE | TEAM | LG | GP | W | L | T | SO | GA | GAA | G | A | PTS | PIM |
|---|---|---|---|---|---|---|---|---|---|---|---|---|---|---|
| 1912–13 | 20 | Ottawa Senators | NHA | 10 | 7 | 2 | 1 | 1 | 16 | 3.49 | | | | |
| 1913–14 | 21 | Ottawa Senators | NHA | 9 | 5 | 3 | 0 | 0 | 29 | 3.67 | | | | |
| 1914–15 | 22 | Ottawa Senators | NHA | 20 | 14 | 6 | 0 | 0 | 65 | 3.14 | | | | |
| 1915–16 | 23 | Ottawa Senators | NHA | 24 | 13 | 11 | 0 | 1 | 72 | 2.99 | | | | |
| 1916–17 | 24 | Ottawa Senators | NHA | 18 | 14 | 4 | 0 | 1 | 50 | 2.72 | | | | |
| 1917–18 | 25 | Ottawa Senators | NHL | 22 | 9 | 13 | 0 | 1 | 114 | 5.11 | 0 | 0 | 0 | 0 |
| 1918–19 | 26 | Ottawa Senators | NHL | 18 | 12 | 6 | 0 | 2 | 53 | 2.85 | 0 | 0 | 0 | 3 |
| 1919–20 | 27 | Ottawa Senators | NHL | 24 | 19 | 5 | 0 | 5 | 64 | 2.66 | 0 | 0 | 0 | 0 |
| 1920–21 | 28 | Ottawa Senators | NHL | 24 | 14 | 10 | 0 | 2 | 75 | 3.08 | 0 | 0 | 0 | 0 |
| 1921–22 | 29 | Ottawa Senators | NHL | 24 | 14 | 8 | 2 | 2 | 84 | 3.34 | 0 | 0 | 0 | 0 |
| 1922–23 | 30 | Ottawa Senators | NHL | 24 | 14 | 9 | 1 | 4 | 54 | 2.18 | 0 | 0 | 0 | 2 |
| 1923–24 | 31 | Ottawa Senators | NHL | 22 | 15 | 7 | 0 | 3 | 45 | 1.99 | 0 | 0 | 0 | 0 |
| 1924–25 | 32 | Montreal Maroons | NHL | 30 | 9 | 19 | 2 | 2 | 65 | 2.12 | 0 | 0 | 0 | 2 |
| 1925–26 | 33 | Montreal Maroons | NHL | 36 | 20 | 11 | 5 | 6 | 73 | 1.92 | 0 | 0 | 0 | 0 |
| 1926–27 | 34 | Montreal Maroons | NHL | 43 | 20 | 19 | 4 | 13 | 65 | 1.42 | 0 | 0 | 0 | 0 |
| 1927–28 | 35 | Montreal Maroons | NHL | 44 | 24 | 14 | 6 | 6 | 76 | 1.70 | 0 | 0 | 0 | 0 |
| 1928–29 | 36 | Montreal Maroons | NHL | 37 | 14 | 16 | 7 | 11 | 57 | 1.49 | 0 | 0 | 0 | 0 |
| 1929–30 | 37 | Montreal Maroons | NHL | 14 | 5 | 5 | 1 | 0 | 35 | 2.95 | 0 | 0 | 0 | 0 |
| Career — 18 Seasons | | | | 443 | 242 | 168 | 29 | 60 | 1092 | 2.47 | 0 | 0 | 0 | 7 |

## PLAYOFFS

| SEASON | AGE | TEAM | LG | GP | W | L | T | SO | GA | GAA | G | A | PTS | PIM |
|---|---|---|---|---|---|---|---|---|---|---|---|---|---|---|
| 1914–15 | 22 | Ottawa Senators | NHA | 2 | 1 | 1 | 0 | 1 | 2 | 1.00 | | | | |
| 1914–15 | 22 | Ottawa Senators | St-Cup | 3 | 0 | 3 | 0 | 0 | 26 | 8.67 | | | | |
| 1916–17 | 24 | Ottawa Senators | NHA | 2 | 1 | 1 | 0 | 0 | 7 | 3.50 | | | | |
| 1918–19 | 26 | Ottawa Senators | NHL | 5 | 1 | 4 | 0 | 0 | 26 | 5.20 | 0 | 0 | 0 | 0 |
| 1919–20 | 27 | Ottawa Senators | St-Cup | 5 | 3 | 2 | 0 | 2 | 11 | 2.20 | | | | |
| 1920–21 | 28 | Ottawa Senators | NHL | 2 | 2 | 0 | 0 | 2 | 0 | 0.00 | 0 | 0 | 0 | 0 |

## Clint Benedict (continued)

### PLAYOFFS

| SEASON | AGE | TEAM | LG | GP | W | L | T | SO | GA | GAA | G | A | PTS | PIM |
|---|---|---|---|---|---|---|---|---|---|---|---|---|---|---|
| 1920–21 | 28 | Ottawa Senators | St-Cup | 5 | 3 | 2 | 0 | 0 | 12 | 2.40 | | | | |
| 1921–22 | 29 | Ottawa Senators | NHL | 2 | 0 | 1 | 1 | 1 | 5 | 2.50 | 0 | 0 | 0 | 0 |
| 1922–23 | 30 | Ottawa Senators | NHL | 2 | 1 | 1 | 0 | 1 | 2 | 1.00 | 0 | 0 | 0 | 0 |
| 1922–23 | 30 | Ottawa Senators | St-Cup | 6 | 5 | 1 | 0 | 1 | 8 | 1.33 | 0 | 0 | 0 | 0 |
| 1923–24 | 31 | Ottawa Senators | NHL | 2 | 0 | 2 | 0 | 0 | 5 | 2.50 | 0 | 0 | 0 | 0 |
| 1925–26 | 33 | Montreal Maroons | NHL | 4 | 2 | 0 | 2 | 1 | 5 | 1.25 | 0 | 0 | 0 | 0 |
| 1925–26 | 33 | Montreal Maroons | St-Cup | 4 | 3 | 1 | 0 | 3 | 3 | 0.75 | 0 | 0 | 0 | 0 |
| 1926–27 | 34 | Montreal Maroons | NHL | 2 | 0 | 1 | 1 | 0 | 2 | 0.91 | 0 | 0 | 0 | 0 |
| 1927–28 | 35 | Montreal Maroons | NHL | 9 | 5 | 3 | 1 | 4 | 8 | 0.86 | 0 | 0 | 0 | 0 |
| Career — 11 Seasons | | | | 55 | 27 | 23 | 5 | 15 | 122 | 2.22 | 0 | 0 | 0 | 0 |

## Johnny Bower   Profile: See page 320

### REGULAR SEASON

| SEASON | AGE | TEAM | LG | GP | W | L | T | SO | GA | GAA | G | A | PTS | PIM |
|---|---|---|---|---|---|---|---|---|---|---|---|---|---|---|
| 1953–54 | 29 | New York Rangers | NHL | 70 | 29 | 31 | 10 | 5 | 178 | 2.54 | 0 | 0 | 0 | 0 |
| 1954–55 | 30 | New York Rangers | NHL | 5 | 2 | 2 | 1 | 0 | 13 | 2.60 | 0 | 0 | 0 | 0 |
| 1956–57 | 32 | New York Rangers | NHL | 2 | 0 | 2 | 0 | 0 | 6 | 3.01 | 0 | 0 | 0 | 0 |
| 1958–59 | 34 | Toronto Maple Leafs | NHL | 39 | 15 | 17 | 7 | 3 | 106 | 2.72 | 0 | 0 | 0 | 2 |
| 1959–60 | 35 | Toronto Maple Leafs | NHL | 66 | 34 | 24 | 8 | 5 | 177 | 2.69 | 0 | 0 | 0 | 4 |
| 1960–61 | 36 | Toronto Maple Leafs | NHL | 58 | 33 | 15 | 10 | 2 | 145 | 2.50 | 0 | 0 | 0 | 0 |
| 1961–62 | 37 | Toronto Maple Leafs | NHL | 59 | 31 | 18 | 10 | 2 | 151 | 2.56 | 0 | 1 | 1 | 4 |
| 1962–63 | 38 | Toronto Maple Leafs | NHL | 42 | 20 | 15 | 7 | 1 | 109 | 2.60 | 0 | 0 | 0 | 2 |
| 1963–64 | 39 | Toronto Maple Leafs | NHL | 51 | 24 | 15 | 11 | 5 | 106 | 2.11 | 0 | 0 | 0 | 4 |
| 1964–65 | 40 | Toronto Maple Leafs | NHL | 34 | 14 | 13 | 7 | 3 | 81 | 2.38 | 0 | 0 | 0 | 6 |
| 1965–66 | 41 | Toronto Maple Leafs | NHL | 35 | 18 | 10 | 5 | 3 | 75 | 2.26 | 0 | 1 | 1 | 0 |
| 1966–67 | 42 | Toronto Maple Leafs | NHL | 27 | 11 | 8 | 3 | 2 | 63 | 2.65 | 0 | 0 | 0 | 0 |
| 1967–68 | 43 | Toronto Maple Leafs | NHL | 43 | 13 | 17 | 8 | 4 | 84 | 2.26 | 0 | 1 | 1 | 14 |
| 1968–69 | 44 | Toronto Maple Leafs | NHL | 20 | 6 | 4 | 3 | 2 | 37 | 2.86 | 0 | 0 | 0 | 0 |
| 1969–70 | 45 | Toronto Maple Leafs | NHL | 1 | 0 | 1 | 0 | 0 | 5 | 5.00 | 0 | 0 | 0 | 0 |
| NHL Career — 15 Seasons | | | | 552 | 250 | 192 | 90 | 37 | 1336 | 2.51 | 0 | 3 | 3 | 36 |

### PLAYOFFS

| SEASON | AGE | TEAM | LG | GP | W | L | T | SO | GA | GAA | G | A | PTS | PIM |
|---|---|---|---|---|---|---|---|---|---|---|---|---|---|---|
| 1958–59 | 34 | Toronto Maple Leafs | NHL | 12 | 5 | 7 | | 0 | 38 | 3.05 | 0 | 0 | 0 | 0 |
| 1959–60 | 35 | Toronto Maple Leafs | NHL | 10 | 4 | 6 | | 0 | 31 | 2.88 | 0 | 0 | 0 | 0 |
| 1960–61 | 36 | Toronto Maple Leafs | NHL | 3 | 0 | 3 | | 0 | 8 | 2.67 | 0 | 0 | 0 | 2 |
| 1961–62 | 37 | Toronto Maple Leafs | NHL | 10 | 6 | 3 | | 0 | 20 | 2.07 | 0 | 0 | 0 | 0 |
| 1962–63 | 38 | Toronto Maple Leafs | NHL | 10 | 8 | 2 | | 2 | 16 | 1.60 | 0 | 1 | 1 | 0 |
| 1963–64 | 39 | Toronto Maple Leafs | NHL | 14 | 8 | 6 | | 2 | 30 | 2.12 | 0 | 0 | 0 | 0 |
| 1964–65 | 40 | Toronto Maple Leafs | NHL | 5 | 2 | 3 | | 0 | 13 | 2.43 | 0 | 0 | 0 | 0 |
| 1965–66 | 41 | Toronto Maple Leafs | NHL | 2 | 0 | 2 | | 0 | 8 | 4.03 | 0 | 0 | 0 | 0 |
| 1966–67 | 42 | Toronto Maple Leafs | NHL | 4 | 2 | 0 | | 1 | 5 | 1.63 | 0 | 0 | 0 | 2 |
| 1968–69 | 44 | Toronto Maple Leafs | NHL | 4 | 0 | 2 | | 0 | 11 | 4.33 | 0 | 0 | 0 | 0 |
| NHL Career — 10 Seasons | | | | 74 | 35 | 34 | | 5 | 180 | 2.47 | 0 | 1 | 1 | 4 |

## Frank Brimsek   Profile: See page 322

### REGULAR SEASON

| SEASON | AGE | TEAM | LG | GP | W | L | T | SO | GA | GAA | G | A | PTS | PIM |
|---|---|---|---|---|---|---|---|---|---|---|---|---|---|---|
| 1938–39 | 23 | Boston Bruins | NHL | 43 | 33 | 9 | 1 | 10 | 68 | 1.56 | 0 | 0 | 0 | 0 |
| 1939–40 | 24 | Boston Bruins | NHL | 48 | 31 | 12 | 5 | 6 | 97 | 1.97 | 0 | 0 | 0 | 0 |
| 1940–41 | 25 | Boston Bruins | NHL | 48 | 27 | 8 | 13 | 6 | 102 | 2.01 | 0 | 0 | 0 | 0 |
| 1941–42 | 26 | Boston Bruins | NHL | 47 | 24 | 17 | 6 | 3 | 115 | 2.35 | 0 | 0 | 0 | 0 |
| 1942–43 | 27 | Boston Bruins | NHL | 50 | 24 | 17 | 9 | 1 | 176 | 3.52 | 0 | 0 | 0 | 0 |
| 1945–46 | 30 | Boston Bruins | NHL | 34 | 16 | 14 | 4 | 2 | 111 | 3.26 | 0 | 0 | 0 | 0 |
| 1946–47 | 31 | Boston Bruins | NHL | 60 | 26 | 23 | 11 | 3 | 175 | 2.92 | 0 | 0 | 0 | 2 |
| 1947–48 | 32 | Boston Bruins | NHL | 60 | 23 | 24 | 13 | 3 | 168 | 2.80 | 0 | 0 | 0 | 2 |
| 1948–49 | 33 | Boston Bruins | NHL | 54 | 26 | 20 | 8 | 1 | 147 | 2.72 | 0 | 0 | 0 | 2 |
| 1949–50 | 34 | Chicago Blackhawks | NHL | 70 | 22 | 38 | 10 | 5 | 244 | 3.49 | 0 | 0 | 0 | 0 |
| NHL Career — 10 Seasons | | | | 514 | 252 | 182 | 80 | 40 | 1403 | 2.70 | 0 | 0 | 0 | 6 |

### PLAYOFFS

| SEASON | AGE | TEAM | LG | GP | W | L | T | SO | GA | GAA | G | A | PTS | PIM |
|---|---|---|---|---|---|---|---|---|---|---|---|---|---|---|
| 1938–39 | 23 | Boston Bruins | NHL | 12 | 8 | 4 | | 1 | 18 | 1.25 | 0 | 0 | 0 | 0 |
| 1939–40 | 24 | Boston Bruins | NHL | 6 | 2 | 4 | | 0 | 15 | 2.50 | 0 | 0 | 0 | 0 |
| 1940–41 | 25 | Boston Bruins | NHL | 11 | 8 | 3 | | 1 | 23 | 2.04 | 0 | 0 | 0 | 0 |
| 1941–42 | 26 | Boston Bruins | NHL | 5 | 2 | 3 | | 0 | 16 | 3.13 | 0 | 0 | 0 | 0 |
| 1942–43 | 27 | Boston Bruins | NHL | 9 | 4 | 5 | | 0 | 33 | 3.54 | 0 | 0 | 0 | 0 |
| 1945–46 | 30 | Boston Bruins | NHL | 10 | 5 | 5 | | 0 | 29 | 2.67 | 0 | 0 | 0 | 0 |
| 1946–47 | 31 | Boston Bruins | NHL | 5 | 1 | 4 | | 0 | 16 | 2.80 | 0 | 0 | 0 | 0 |

### Frank Brimsek (continued)

**PLAYOFFS**

| SEASON | AGE | TEAM | LG | GP | W | L | T | SO | GA | GAA | G | A | PTS | PIM |
|--------|-----|------|----|----|----|----|----|----|----|----|----|----|----|----|
| 1947–48 | 32 | Boston Bruins | NHL | 5 | 1 | 4 | | 0 | 20 | 3.79 | 0 | 0 | 0 | 0 |
| 1948–49 | 33 | Boston Bruins | NHL | 5 | 1 | 4 | | 0 | 16 | 3.04 | 0 | 0 | 0 | 0 |
| NHL Career — 9 Seasons | | | | 68 | 32 | 36 | | 2 | 186 | 2.54 | 0 | 0 | 0 | 0 |

## Turk Broda   Profile: See page 323

**REGULAR SEASON**

| SEASON | AGE | TEAM | LG | GP | W | L | T | SO | GA | GAA | G | A | PTS | PIM |
|--------|-----|------|----|----|----|----|----|----|----|----|----|----|----|----|
| 1936–37 | 22 | Toronto Maple Leafs | NHL | 45 | 22 | 19 | 4 | 3 | 106 | 2.29 | 0 | 0 | 0 | 0 |
| 1937–38 | 23 | Toronto Maple Leafs | NHL | 48 | 24 | 15 | 9 | 6 | 127 | 2.56 | 0 | 0 | 0 | 0 |
| 1938–39 | 24 | Toronto Maple Leafs | NHL | 48 | 19 | 20 | 9 | 8 | 107 | 2.15 | 0 | 0 | 0 | 0 |
| 1939–40 | 25 | Toronto Maple Leafs | NHL | 47 | 25 | 17 | 5 | 4 | 108 | 2.23 | 0 | 0 | 0 | 0 |
| 1940–41 | 26 | Toronto Maple Leafs | NHL | 48 | 28 | 14 | 6 | 5 | 99 | 2.00 | 0 | 0 | 0 | 0 |
| 1941–42 | 27 | Toronto Maple Leafs | NHL | 48 | 27 | 18 | 3 | 6 | 136 | 2.76 | 0 | 0 | 0 | 0 |
| 1942–43 | 28 | Toronto Maple Leafs | NHL | 50 | 22 | 19 | 9 | 1 | 159 | 3.18 | 0 | 0 | 0 | 0 |
| 1945–46 | 31 | Toronto Maple Leafs | NHL | 15 | 7 | 5 | 3 | 0 | 53 | 3.53 | 0 | 0 | 0 | 0 |
| 1946–47 | 32 | Toronto Maple Leafs | NHL | 60 | 31 | 19 | 10 | 4 | 172 | 2.87 | 0 | 0 | 0 | 0 |
| 1947–48 | 33 | Toronto Maple Leafs | NHL | 60 | 32 | 15 | 13 | 5 | 143 | 2.38 | 0 | 0 | 0 | 2 |
| 1948–49 | 34 | Toronto Maple Leafs | NHL | 60 | 22 | 25 | 13 | 5 | 161 | 2.68 | 0 | 0 | 0 | 0 |
| 1949–50 | 35 | Toronto Maple Leafs | NHL | 68 | 30 | 25 | 12 | 9 | 166 | 2.47 | 0 | 0 | 0 | 2 |
| 1950–51 | 36 | Toronto Maple Leafs | NHL | 31 | 15 | 10 | 6 | 5 | 68 | 2.23 | 0 | 0 | 0 | 4 |
| 1951–52 | 37 | Toronto Maple Leafs | NHL | 1 | 0 | 1 | 0 | 0 | 3 | 6.00 | 0 | 0 | 0 | 0 |
| NHL Career — 14 Seasons | | | | 629 | 304 | 222 | 102 | 62 | 1608 | 2.53 | 0 | 0 | 0 | 8 |

**PLAYOFFS**

| SEASON | AGE | TEAM | LG | GP | W | L | T | SO | GA | GAA | G | A | PTS | PIM |
|--------|-----|------|----|----|----|----|----|----|----|----|----|----|----|----|
| 1936–37 | 22 | Toronto Maple Leafs | NHL | 2 | 0 | 2 | | 0 | 5 | 2.25 | 0 | 0 | 0 | 0 |
| 1937–38 | 23 | Toronto Maple Leafs | NHL | 7 | 4 | 3 | | 1 | 13 | 1.73 | 0 | 0 | 0 | 0 |
| 1938–39 | 24 | Toronto Maple Leafs | NHL | 10 | 5 | 5 | | 2 | 20 | 1.95 | 0 | 0 | 0 | 0 |
| 1939–40 | 25 | Toronto Maple Leafs | NHL | 10 | 6 | 4 | | 1 | 19 | 1.74 | 0 | 0 | 0 | 0 |
| 1940–41 | 26 | Toronto Maple Leafs | NHL | 7 | 3 | 4 | | 0 | 15 | 2.06 | 0 | 0 | 0 | 0 |
| 1941–42 | 27 | Toronto Maple Leafs | NHL | 13 | 8 | 5 | | 1 | 31 | 2.38 | 0 | 0 | 0 | 0 |
| 1942–43 | 28 | Toronto Maple Leafs | NHL | 6 | 2 | 4 | | 0 | 20 | 2.73 | 0 | 0 | 0 | 0 |
| 1946–47 | 32 | Toronto Maple Leafs | NHL | 11 | 8 | 3 | | 1 | 27 | 2.38 | 0 | 0 | 0 | 0 |
| 1947–48 | 33 | Toronto Maple Leafs | NHL | 9 | 8 | 1 | | 1 | 20 | 2.15 | 0 | 0 | 0 | 10 |
| 1948–49 | 34 | Toronto Maple Leafs | NHL | 9 | 8 | 1 | | 1 | 15 | 1.57 | 0 | 0 | 0 | 2 |
| 1949–50 | 35 | Toronto Maple Leafs | NHL | 7 | 3 | 4 | | 3 | 10 | 1.34 | 0 | 0 | 0 | 0 |
| 1950–51 | 36 | Toronto Maple Leafs | NHL | 8 | 5 | 1 | | 2 | 9 | 1.10 | 0 | 0 | 0 | 0 |
| 1951–52 | 37 | Toronto Maple Leafs | NHL | 2 | 0 | 2 | | 0 | 7 | 3.50 | 0 | 0 | 0 | 0 |
| NHL Career — 13 Seasons | | | | 101 | 60 | 39 | | 13 | 211 | 1.98 | 0 | 0 | 0 | 12 |

## Gerry Cheevers   Profile: See page 324

**REGULAR SEASON**

| SEASON | AGE | TEAM | LG | GP | W | L | T | SO | GA | GAA | G | A | PTS | PIM |
|--------|-----|------|----|----|----|----|----|----|----|----|----|----|----|----|
| 1961–62 | 21 | Toronto Maple Leafs | NHL | 2 | 1 | 1 | 0 | 0 | 6 | 3.00 | 0 | 0 | 0 | 0 |
| 1965–66 | 25 | Boston Bruins | NHL | 7 | 0 | 4 | 1 | 0 | 34 | 6.00 | 0 | 0 | 0 | 0 |
| 1966–67 | 26 | Boston Bruins | NHL | 22 | 5 | 10 | 6 | 1 | 72 | 3.33 | 0 | 0 | 0 | 12 |
| 1967–68 | 27 | Boston Bruins | NHL | 47 | 21 | 19 | 6 | 3 | 125 | 2.84 | 0 | 2 | 2 | 8 |
| 1968–69 | 28 | Boston Bruins | NHL | 52 | 27 | 12 | 13 | 3 | 145 | 2.80 | 0 | 0 | 0 | 14 |
| 1969–70 | 29 | Boston Bruins | NHL | 41 | 24 | 8 | 8 | 4 | 108 | 2.72 | 0 | 0 | 0 | 4 |
| 1970–71 | 30 | Boston Bruins | NHL | 40 | 27 | 8 | 5 | 3 | 109 | 2.73 | 0 | 0 | 0 | 4 |
| 1971–72 | 31 | Boston Bruins | NHL | 41 | 27 | 5 | 8 | 2 | 101 | 2.50 | 0 | 2 | 2 | 25 |
| 1972–73 | 32 | Cleveland Crusaders | WHA | 52 | 32 | 20 | 0 | 5 | 149 | 2.84 | 0 | 1 | 1 | 30 |
| 1973–74 | 33 | Cleveland Crusaders | WHA | 59 | 30 | 20 | 6 | 4 | 180 | 3.03 | 0 | 0 | 0 | 30 |
| 1974–75 | 34 | Cleveland Crusaders | WHA | 52 | 26 | 24 | 2 | 4 | 167 | 3.26 | 0 | 1 | 1 | 59 |
| 1975–76 | 35 | Cleveland Crusaders | WHA | 28 | 11 | 14 | 1 | 1 | 95 | 3.63 | 0 | 0 | 0 | 15 |
| 1975–76 | 35 | Boston Bruins | NHL | 15 | 8 | 2 | 5 | 1 | 41 | 2.74 | 0 | 0 | 0 | 2 |
| 1976–77 | 36 | Boston Bruins | NHL | 45 | 30 | 10 | 5 | 3 | 137 | 3.05 | 0 | 4 | 4 | 46 |
| 1977–78 | 37 | Boston Bruins | NHL | 21 | 10 | 5 | 2 | 1 | 48 | 2.66 | 0 | 1 | 1 | 14 |
| 1978–79 | 38 | Boston Bruins | NHL | 43 | 23 | 9 | 10 | 1 | 132 | 3.16 | 0 | 2 | 2 | 23 |
| 1979–80 | 39 | Boston Bruins | NHL | 42 | 24 | 11 | 7 | 4 | 116 | 2.81 | 0 | 0 | 0 | 62 |
| Career — 17 Seasons | | | | 609 | 326 | 182 | 85 | 40 | 1765 | 2.90 | 0 | 13 | 13 | 348 |

**PLAYOFFS**

| SEASON | AGE | TEAM | LG | GP | W | L | T | SO | GA | GAA | G | A | PTS | PIM |
|--------|-----|------|----|----|----|----|----|----|----|----|----|----|----|----|
| 1967–68 | 27 | Boston Bruins | NHL | 4 | 0 | 4 | | 0 | 15 | 3.77 | 0 | 0 | 0 | 4 |
| 1968–69 | 28 | Boston Bruins | NHL | 9 | 6 | 3 | | 3 | 16 | 1.68 | 0 | 0 | 0 | 17 |
| 1969–70 | 29 | Boston Bruins | NHL | 13 | 12 | 1 | | 0 | 29 | 2.23 | 0 | 1 | 1 | 2 |
| 1970–71 | 30 | Boston Bruins | NHL | 6 | 3 | 3 | | 0 | 21 | 3.51 | 0 | 0 | 0 | 4 |
| 1971–72 | 31 | Boston Bruins | NHL | 8 | 6 | 2 | | 2 | 21 | 2.61 | 0 | 0 | 0 | 0 |
| 1972–73 | 32 | Cleveland Crusaders | WHA | 9 | 5 | 4 | | 0 | 22 | 2.41 | 0 | 0 | 0 | 4 |

## Gerry Cheevers (continued)

### PLAYOFFS

| SEASON | AGE | TEAM | LG | GP | W | L | T | SO | GA | GAA | G | A | PTS | PIM |
|--------|-----|------|-----|----|----|----|----|----|----|------|----|----|-----|-----|
| 1973–74 | 33 | Cleveland Crusaders | WHA | 5 | 1 | 4 | | 0 | 18 | 3.56 | 0 | 0 | 0 | 6 |
| 1974–75 | 34 | Cleveland Crusaders | WHA | 5 | 1 | 4 | | 0 | 23 | 4.60 | 0 | 0 | 0 | 0 |
| 1975–76 | 35 | Boston Bruins | NHL | 6 | 2 | 4 | | 1 | 14 | 2.14 | 0 | 0 | 0 | 0 |
| 1976–77 | 36 | Boston Bruins | NHL | 14 | 8 | 5 | | 1 | 44 | 3.08 | 0 | 0 | 0 | 4 |
| 1977–78 | 37 | Boston Bruins | NHL | 12 | 8 | 4 | | 1 | 35 | 2.87 | 0 | 0 | 0 | 6 |
| 1978–79 | 38 | Boston Bruins | NHL | 6 | 4 | 2 | | 0 | 15 | 2.50 | 0 | 0 | 0 | 0 |
| 1979–80 | 39 | Boston Bruins | NHL | 10 | 4 | 6 | | 0 | 32 | 3.11 | 0 | 0 | 0 | 0 |
| Career — 13 Seasons | | | | 107 | 60 | 46 | | 8 | 305 | 2.85 | 0 | 1 | 1 | 47 |

## Alex Connell    Profile: See page 325

### REGULAR SEASON

| SEASON | AGE | TEAM | LG | GP | W | L | T | SO | GA | GAA | G | A | PTS | PIM |
|--------|-----|------|-----|----|----|----|----|----|----|------|----|----|-----|-----|
| 1924–25 | 22 | Ottawa Senators | NHL | 30 | 17 | 12 | 1 | 7 | 66 | 2.14 | 0 | 0 | 0 | 2 |
| 1925–26 | 23 | Ottawa Senators | NHL | 36 | 24 | 8 | 4 | 15 | 42 | 1.12 | 0 | 0 | 0 | 0 |
| 1926–27 | 24 | Ottawa Senators | NHL | 44 | 30 | 10 | 4 | 13 | 69 | 1.49 | 0 | 0 | 0 | 2 |
| 1927–28 | 25 | Ottawa Senators | NHL | 44 | 20 | 14 | 10 | 15 | 57 | 1.24 | 0 | 0 | 0 | 0 |
| 1928–29 | 26 | Ottawa Senators | NHL | 44 | 14 | 17 | 13 | 7 | 67 | 1.43 | 0 | 0 | 0 | 0 |
| 1929–30 | 27 | Ottawa Senators | NHL | 44 | 21 | 15 | 8 | 3 | 118 | 2.55 | 0 | 0 | 0 | 0 |
| 1930–31 | 28 | Ottawa Senators | NHL | 36 | 10 | 22 | 4 | 3 | 110 | 3.01 | 0 | 0 | 0 | 0 |
| 1931–32 | 29 | Detroit Falcons | NHL | 48 | 18 | 20 | 10 | 6 | 108 | 2.13 | 0 | 0 | 0 | 0 |
| 1932–33 | 30 | Ottawa Senators | NHL | 16 | 4 | 8 | 3 | 1 | 42 | 2.58 | 0 | 0 | 0 | 0 |
| 1933–34 | 31 | New York Americans | NHL | 1 | 1 | 0 | 0 | 0 | 2 | 3.00 | 0 | 0 | 0 | 0 |
| 1934–35 | 32 | Montreal Maroons | NHL | 48 | 24 | 19 | 5 | 9 | 92 | 1.86 | 0 | 0 | 0 | 0 |
| 1936–37 | 34 | Montreal Maroons | NHL | 27 | 10 | 11 | 6 | 2 | 63 | 2.21 | 0 | 0 | 0 | 0 |
| NHL Career — 12 Seasons | | | | 418 | 193 | 156 | 68 | 81 | 836 | 1.92 | 0 | 0 | 0 | 4 |

### PLAYOFFS

| SEASON | AGE | TEAM | LG | GP | W | L | T | SO | GA | GAA | G | A | PTS | PIM |
|--------|-----|------|-----|----|----|----|----|----|----|------|----|----|-----|-----|
| 1925–26 | 23 | Ottawa Senators | NHL | 2 | 0 | 1 | 1 | 0 | 2 | 1.00 | 0 | 0 | 0 | 0 |
| 1926–27 | 24 | Ottawa Senators | NHL | 6 | 3 | 0 | 3 | 2 | 4 | 0.60 | 0 | 0 | 0 | 0 |
| 1927–28 | 25 | Ottawa Senators | NHL | 2 | 0 | 2 | 0 | 0 | 3 | 1.50 | 0 | 0 | 0 | 0 |
| 1929–30 | 27 | Ottawa Senators | NHL | 2 | 0 | 1 | 1 | 0 | 6 | 3.00 | 0 | 0 | 0 | 0 |
| 1931–32 | 29 | Detroit Falcons | NHL | 2 | 0 | 1 | 1 | 0 | 3 | 1.50 | 0 | 0 | 0 | 0 |
| 1934–35 | 32 | Montreal Maroons | NHL | 7 | 5 | 0 | 2 | 2 | 8 | 1.12 | 0 | 0 | 0 | 0 |
| NHL Career — 6 Seasons | | | | 21 | 8 | 5 | 8 | 4 | 26 | 1.19 | 0 | 0 | 0 | 0 |

## Ken Dryden    Profile: See page 326

### REGULAR SEASON

| SEASON | AGE | TEAM | LG | GP | W | L | T | SO | GA | GAA | G | A | PTS | PIM |
|--------|-----|------|-----|----|----|----|----|----|----|------|----|----|-----|-----|
| 1970–71 | 23 | Montreal Canadiens | NHL | 6 | 6 | 0 | 0 | 0 | 9 | 1.65 | 0 | 0 | 0 | 0 |
| 1971–72 | 24 | Montreal Canadiens | NHL | 64 | 39 | 8 | 15 | 8 | 142 | 2.24 | 0 | 3 | 3 | 4 |
| 1972–73 | 25 | Montreal Canadiens | NHL | 54 | 33 | 7 | 13 | 6 | 119 | 2.26 | 0 | 4 | 4 | 2 |
| 1974–75 | 27 | Montreal Canadiens | NHL | 56 | 30 | 9 | 16 | 4 | 149 | 2.70 | 0 | 3 | 3 | 2 |
| 1975–76 | 28 | Montreal Canadiens | NHL | 62 | 42 | 10 | 8 | 8 | 121 | 2.03 | 0 | 2 | 2 | 0 |
| 1976–77 | 29 | Montreal Canadiens | NHL | 56 | 41 | 6 | 8 | 10 | 117 | 2.14 | 0 | 2 | 2 | 0 |
| 1977–78 | 30 | Montreal Canadiens | NHL | 52 | 37 | 7 | 7 | 5 | 105 | 2.05 | 0 | 2 | 2 | 0 |
| 1978–79 | 31 | Montreal Canadiens | NHL | 47 | 30 | 10 | 7 | 5 | 108 | 2.30 | 0 | 3 | 3 | 4 |
| NHL Career — 8 Seasons | | | | 397 | 258 | 57 | 74 | 46 | 870 | 2.24 | 0 | 19 | 19 | 12 |

### PLAYOFFS

| SEASON | AGE | TEAM | LG | GP | W | L | T | SO | GA | GAA | G | A | PTS | PIM |
|--------|-----|------|-----|----|----|----|----|----|----|------|----|----|-----|-----|
| 1970–71 | 23 | Montreal Canadiens | NHL | 20 | 12 | 8 | | 0 | 61 | 3.01 | 0 | 1 | 1 | 0 |
| 1971–72 | 24 | Montreal Canadiens | NHL | 6 | 2 | 4 | | 0 | 17 | 2.85 | 0 | 0 | 0 | 0 |
| 1972–73 | 25 | Montreal Canadiens | NHL | 17 | 12 | 5 | | 1 | 50 | 2.90 | 0 | 0 | 0 | 2 |
| 1974–75 | 27 | Montreal Canadiens | NHL | 11 | 6 | 5 | | 2 | 29 | 2.54 | 0 | 0 | 0 | 0 |
| 1975–76 | 28 | Montreal Canadiens | NHL | 13 | 12 | 1 | | 1 | 25 | 1.92 | 0 | 0 | 0 | 0 |
| 1976–77 | 29 | Montreal Canadiens | NHL | 14 | 12 | 2 | | 4 | 22 | 1.56 | 0 | 0 | 0 | 0 |
| 1977–78 | 30 | Montreal Canadiens | NHL | 15 | 12 | 3 | | 2 | 29 | 1.90 | 0 | 0 | 0 | 0 |
| 1978–79 | 31 | Montreal Canadiens | NHL | 16 | 12 | 4 | | 0 | 41 | 2.50 | 0 | 3 | 3 | 2 |
| NHL Career — 8 Seasons | | | | 112 | 80 | 32 | | 10 | 274 | 2.41 | 0 | 4 | 4 | 4 |

## Bill Durnan  Profile: See page 328

### REGULAR SEASON

| SEASON | AGE | TEAM | LG | GP | W | L | T | SO | GA | GAA | G | A | PTS | PIM |
|---|---|---|---|---|---|---|---|---|---|---|---|---|---|---|
| 1943–44 | 28 | Montreal Canadiens | NHL | 50 | 38 | 5 | 7 | 2 | 109 | 2.18 | 0 | 0 | 0 | 0 |
| 1944–45 | 29 | Montreal Canadiens | NHL | 50 | 38 | 8 | 4 | 1 | 121 | 2.42 | 0 | 0 | 0 | 0 |
| 1945–46 | 30 | Montreal Canadiens | NHL | 40 | 24 | 11 | 5 | 4 | 104 | 2.60 | 0 | 0 | 0 | 0 |
| 1946–47 | 31 | Montreal Canadiens | NHL | 60 | 34 | 16 | 10 | 4 | 138 | 2.30 | 0 | 0 | 0 | 0 |
| 1947–48 | 32 | Montreal Canadiens | NHL | 59 | 20 | 28 | 10 | 5 | 162 | 2.77 | 0 | 0 | 0 | 5 |
| 1948–49 | 33 | Montreal Canadiens | NHL | 60 | 28 | 23 | 9 | 10 | 126 | 2.10 | 0 | 0 | 0 | 0 |
| 1949–50 | 34 | Montreal Canadiens | NHL | 64 | 26 | 21 | 17 | 8 | 141 | 2.20 | 0 | 1 | 1 | 2 |
| NHL Career – 7 Seasons | | | | 383 | 208 | 112 | 62 | 34 | 901 | 2.36 | 0 | 1 | 1 | 7 |

### PLAYOFFS

| SEASON | AGE | TEAM | LG | GP | W | L | T | SO | GA | GAA | G | A | PTS | PIM |
|---|---|---|---|---|---|---|---|---|---|---|---|---|---|---|
| 1943–44 | 28 | Montreal Canadiens | NHL | 9 | 8 | 1 | | 1 | 14 | 1.53 | 0 | 0 | 0 | 0 |
| 1944–45 | 29 | Montreal Canadiens | NHL | 6 | 2 | 4 | | 0 | 15 | 2.41 | 0 | 0 | 0 | 0 |
| 1945–46 | 30 | Montreal Canadiens | NHL | 9 | 8 | 1 | | 0 | 20 | 2.07 | 0 | 0 | 0 | 0 |
| 1946–47 | 31 | Montreal Canadiens | NHL | 11 | 6 | 5 | | 1 | 23 | 1.92 | 0 | 0 | 0 | 0 |
| 1948–49 | 33 | Montreal Canadiens | NHL | 7 | 3 | 4 | | 0 | 17 | 2.18 | 0 | 0 | 0 | 0 |
| 1949–50 | 34 | Montreal Canadiens | NHL | 3 | 0 | 3 | | 0 | 10 | 3.33 | 0 | 0 | 0 | 0 |
| NHL Career – 6 Seasons | | | | 45 | 27 | 18 | | 2 | 99 | 2.07 | 0 | 0 | 0 | 0 |

## Tony Esposito  Profile: See page 330

### REGULAR SEASON

| SEASON | AGE | TEAM | LG | GP | W | L | T | SO | GA | GAA | G | A | PTS | PIM |
|---|---|---|---|---|---|---|---|---|---|---|---|---|---|---|
| 1968–69 | 25 | Montreal Canadiens | NHL | 13 | 5 | 4 | 4 | 2 | 34 | 2.75 | 0 | 0 | 0 | 0 |
| 1969–70 | 26 | Chicago Black Hawks | NHL | 63 | 38 | 17 | 8 | 15 | 136 | 2.17 | 0 | 2 | 2 | 2 |
| 1970–71 | 27 | Chicago Black Hawks | NHL | 57 | 35 | 14 | 7 | 6 | 126 | 2.27 | 0 | 1 | 1 | 4 |
| 1971–72 | 28 | Chicago Black Hawks | NHL | 48 | 31 | 10 | 6 | 9 | 82 | 1.77 | 0 | 1 | 1 | 2 |
| 1972–73 | 29 | Chicago Black Hawks | NHL | 56 | 32 | 17 | 7 | 4 | 140 | 2.52 | 0 | 2 | 2 | 0 |
| 1973–74 | 30 | Chicago Black Hawks | NHL | 70 | 34 | 14 | 21 | 10 | 141 | 2.05 | 0 | 1 | 1 | 0 |
| 1974–75 | 31 | Chicago Black Hawks | NHL | 71 | 34 | 30 | 7 | 6 | 193 | 2.75 | 0 | 1 | 1 | 11 |
| 1975–76 | 32 | Chicago Black Hawks | NHL | 68 | 30 | 23 | 13 | 4 | 198 | 2.98 | 0 | 1 | 1 | 2 |
| 1976–77 | 33 | Chicago Black Hawks | NHL | 69 | 25 | 36 | 8 | 2 | 234 | 3.46 | 0 | 2 | 2 | 6 |
| 1977–78 | 34 | Chicago Black Hawks | NHL | 64 | 28 | 22 | 14 | 5 | 168 | 2.63 | 0 | 4 | 4 | 0 |
| 1978–79 | 35 | Chicago Black Hawks | NHL | 63 | 24 | 28 | 11 | 4 | 206 | 2.38 | 0 | 1 | 1 | 2 |
| 1979–80 | 36 | Chicago Black Hawks | NHL | 69 | 31 | 22 | 16 | 6 | 205 | 2.98 | 0 | 1 | 1 | 2 |
| 1980–81 | 37 | Chicago Black Hawks | NHL | 66 | 29 | 23 | 14 | 0 | 246 | 3.76 | 0 | 3 | 3 | 0 |
| 1981–82 | 38 | Chicago Black Hawks | NHL | 52 | 19 | 25 | 8 | 1 | 231 | 4.53 | 0 | 2 | 2 | 0 |
| 1982–83 | 39 | Chicago Black Hawks | NHL | 39 | 23 | 11 | 5 | 1 | 135 | 3.47 | 0 | 0 | 0 | 0 |
| 1983–84 | 40 | Chicago Black Hawks | NHL | 18 | 5 | 10 | 3 | 1 | 88 | 4.84 | 0 | 3 | 3 | 0 |
| NHL Career – 16 Seasons | | | | 886 | 423 | 306 | 152 | 76 | 2563 | 2.93 | 0 | 25 | 25 | 31 |

### PLAYOFFS

| SEASON | AGE | TEAM | LG | GP | W | L | T | SO | GA | GAA | G | A | PTS | PIM |
|---|---|---|---|---|---|---|---|---|---|---|---|---|---|---|
| 1969–70 | 26 | Chicago Black Hawks | NHL | 8 | 4 | 4 | | 0 | 27 | 3.39 | 0 | 0 | 0 | 0 |
| 1970–71 | 27 | Chicago Black Hawks | NHL | 18 | 11 | 7 | | 2 | 42 | 2.20 | 0 | 0 | 0 | 0 |
| 1971–72 | 28 | Chicago Black Hawks | NHL | 5 | 2 | 3 | | 0 | 16 | 3.22 | 0 | 0 | 0 | 0 |
| 1972–73 | 29 | Chicago Black Hawks | NHL | 15 | 10 | 5 | | 1 | 46 | 3.09 | 0 | 0 | 0 | 0 |
| 1973–74 | 30 | Chicago Black Hawks | NHL | 10 | 6 | 4 | | 2 | 28 | 2.90 | 0 | 0 | 0 | 0 |
| 1974–75 | 31 | Chicago Black Hawks | NHL | 8 | 3 | 5 | | 0 | 34 | 4.33 | 0 | 0 | 0 | 0 |
| 1975–76 | 32 | Chicago Black Hawks | NHL | 4 | 0 | 4 | | 0 | 13 | 3.27 | 0 | 0 | 0 | 0 |
| 1976–77 | 33 | Chicago Black Hawks | NHL | 2 | 0 | 2 | | 0 | 6 | 3.03 | 0 | 0 | 0 | 0 |
| 1977–78 | 34 | Chicago Black Hawks | NHL | 4 | 0 | 4 | | 0 | 19 | 4.53 | 0 | 0 | 0 | 0 |
| 1978–79 | 35 | Chicago Black Hawks | NHL | 4 | 0 | 4 | | 0 | 14 | 3.52 | 0 | 0 | 0 | 0 |
| 1979–80 | 36 | Chicago Black Hawks | NHL | 6 | 3 | 3 | | 0 | 14 | 2.27 | 0 | 0 | 0 | 0 |
| 1980–81 | 37 | Chicago Black Hawks | NHL | 3 | 0 | 3 | | 0 | 15 | 4.19 | 0 | 0 | 0 | 0 |
| 1981–82 | 38 | Chicago Black Hawks | NHL | 7 | 3 | 3 | | 1 | 16 | 2.54 | 0 | 0 | 0 | 0 |
| 1982–83 | 39 | Chicago Black Hawks | NHL | 5 | 3 | 2 | | 0 | 18 | 3.49 | 0 | 0 | 0 | 0 |
| NHL Career – 14 Seasons | | | | 99 | 45 | 53 | | 6 | 308 | 3.09 | 0 | 0 | 0 | 0 |

## Grant Fuhr  Profile: See page 332

### REGULAR SEASON

| SEASON | AGE | TEAM | LG | GP | W | L | T | SO | GA | GAA | G | A | PTS | PIM |
|---|---|---|---|---|---|---|---|---|---|---|---|---|---|---|
| 1981–82 | 19 | Edmonton Oilers | NHL | 48 | 28 | 5 | 14 | 0 | 157 | 3.31 | 0 | 0 | 0 | 0 |
| 1982–83 | 20 | Edmonton Oilers | NHL | 32 | 13 | 12 | 5 | 0 | 129 | 4.30 | 0 | 0 | 0 | 6 |
| 1983–84 | 21 | Edmonton Oilers | NHL | 45 | 30 | 10 | 4 | 1 | 171 | 3.91 | 0 | 14 | 14 | 6 |
| 1984–85 | 22 | Edmonton Oilers | NHL | 46 | 26 | 8 | 7 | 1 | 165 | 3.87 | 0 | 3 | 3 | 6 |
| 1985–86 | 23 | Edmonton Oilers | NHL | 40 | 29 | 8 | 0 | 0 | 143 | 3.93 | 0 | 2 | 2 | 0 |
| 1986–87 | 24 | Edmonton Oilers | NHL | 44 | 22 | 13 | 3 | 0 | 137 | 3.44 | 0 | 2 | 2 | 6 |
| 1987–88 | 25 | Edmonton Oilers | NHL | 75 | 40 | 24 | 9 | 4 | 246 | 3.43 | 0 | 8 | 8 | 16 |
| 1988–89 | 26 | Edmonton Oilers | NHL | 59 | 23 | 26 | 6 | 1 | 213 | 3.83 | 0 | 1 | 1 | 6 |

## Grant Fuhr (continued)

### REGULAR SEASON

| SEASON | AGE | TEAM | LG | GP | W | L | T | SO | GA | GAA | G | A | PTS | PIM |
|--------|-----|------|-----|-----|-----|-----|-----|-----|-----|------|-----|-----|-----|-----|
| 1989–90 | 27 | Edmonton Oilers | NHL | 21 | 9 | 7 | 3 | 1 | 70 | 3.89 | 0 | 0 | 0 | 2 |
| 1990–91 | 28 | Edmonton Oilers | NHL | 13 | 6 | 4 | 3 | 1 | 39 | 3.01 | 0 | 0 | 0 | 0 |
| 1991–92 | 29 | Toronto Maple Leafs | NHL | 66 | 25 | 33 | 5 | 2 | 230 | 3.66 | 0 | 1 | 1 | 4 |
| 1992–93 | 30 | Toronto Maple Leafs | NHL | 29 | 13 | 9 | 4 | 1 | 87 | 3.13 | 0 | 0 | 0 | 0 |
| 1992–93 | 30 | Buffalo Sabres | NHL | 29 | 11 | 15 | 2 | 0 | 98 | 3.47 | 0 | 0 | 0 | 10 |
| 1993–94 | 31 | Buffalo Sabres | NHL | 32 | 13 | 12 | 3 | 2 | 106 | 3.69 | 0 | 4 | 4 | 16 |
| 1994–95 | 32 | Buffalo Sabres | NHL | 3 | 1 | 2 | 0 | 0 | 12 | 4.00 | 0 | 0 | 0 | 0 |
| 1994–95 | 32 | Los Angeles Kings | NHL | 14 | 1 | 7 | 3 | 0 | 47 | 4.04 | 0 | 0 | 0 | 2 |
| 1995–96 | 33 | St. Louis Blues | NHL | 79 | 30 | 28 | 16 | 3 | 209 | 2.87 | 0 | 1 | 1 | 8 |
| 1996–97 | 34 | St. Louis Blues | NHL | 73 | 33 | 27 | 11 | 3 | 193 | 2.72 | 0 | 2 | 2 | 6 |
| 1997–98 | 35 | St. Louis Blues | NHL | 58 | 29 | 21 | 6 | 3 | 138 | 2.53 | 0 | 2 | 2 | 6 |
| 1998–99 | 36 | St. Louis Blues | NHL | 39 | 16 | 11 | 8 | 2 | 89 | 2.43 | 0 | 0 | 0 | 12 |
| 1999–00 | 37 | Calgary Flames | NHL | 23 | 5 | 13 | 2 | 0 | 77 | 3.83 | 0 | 0 | 0 | 2 |
| NHL Career — 19 Seasons | | | | 868 | 403 | 295 | 114 | 25 | 2756 | 3.38 | 0 | 40 | 40 | 114 |

### PLAYOFFS

| SEASON | AGE | TEAM | LG | GP | W | L | T | SO | GA | GAA | G | A | PTS | PIM |
|--------|-----|------|-----|-----|-----|-----|-----|-----|-----|------|-----|-----|-----|-----|
| 1981–82 | 19 | Edmonton Oilers | NHL | 5 | 2 | 3 | | 0 | 26 | 5.05 | 0 | 1 | 1 | 0 |
| 1982–83 | 20 | Edmonton Oilers | NHL | 1 | 0 | 0 | | 0 | 0 | 0.00 | 0 | 0 | 0 | 0 |
| 1983–84 | 21 | Edmonton Oilers | NHL | 16 | 11 | 4 | | 1 | 44 | 2.99 | 0 | 3 | 3 | 4 |
| 1984–85 | 22 | Edmonton Oilers | NHL | 18 | 15 | 3 | | 0 | 55 | 3.10 | 0 | 3 | 3 | 2 |
| 1985–86 | 23 | Edmonton Oilers | NHL | 9 | 5 | 4 | | 0 | 28 | 3.12 | 0 | 1 | 1 | 0 |
| 1986–87 | 24 | Edmonton Oilers | NHL | 19 | 14 | 5 | | 0 | 47 | 2.47 | 0 | 1 | 1 | 0 |
| 1987–88 | 25 | Edmonton Oilers | NHL | 19 | 16 | 2 | | 0 | 55 | 2.91 | 0 | 1 | 1 | 6 |
| 1988–89 | 26 | Edmonton Oilers | NHL | 7 | 3 | 4 | | 1 | 24 | 3.45 | 0 | 0 | 0 | 0 |
| 1990–91 | 28 | Edmonton Oilers | NHL | 17 | 8 | 7 | | 0 | 51 | 3.00 | 0 | 2 | 2 | 2 |
| 1992–93 | 30 | Buffalo Sabres | NHL | 8 | 3 | 4 | | 1 | 27 | 3.42 | 0 | 0 | 0 | 2 |
| 1995–96 | 33 | St. Louis Blues | NHL | 2 | 1 | 0 | | 0 | 1 | 0.87 | 0 | 0 | 0 | 0 |
| 1996–97 | 34 | St. Louis Blues | NHL | 6 | 2 | 4 | | 2 | 13 | 2.18 | 0 | 0 | 0 | 4 |
| 1997–98 | 35 | St. Louis Blues | NHL | 10 | 6 | 4 | | 0 | 28 | 2.73 | 0 | 1 | 1 | 2 |
| 1998–99 | 36 | St. Louis Blues | NHL | 13 | 6 | 6 | | 1 | 31 | 2.35 | 0 | 1 | 1 | 2 |
| NHL Career — 14 Seasons | | | | 150 | 92 | 50 | | 6 | 430 | 2.91 | 0 | 14 | 14 | 24 |

## Chuck Gardiner  Profile: See page 334

### REGULAR SEASON

| SEASON | AGE | TEAM | LG | GP | W | L | T | SO | GA | GAA | G | A | PTS | PIM |
|--------|-----|------|-----|-----|-----|-----|-----|-----|-----|------|-----|-----|-----|-----|
| 1927–28 | 23 | Chicago Black Hawks | NHL | 40 | 6 | 32 | 2 | 3 | 114 | 2.83 | 0 | 0 | 0 | 0 |
| 1928–29 | 24 | Chicago Black Hawks | NHL | 44 | 7 | 29 | 8 | 5 | 85 | 1.85 | 0 | 0 | 0 | 0 |
| 1929–30 | 25 | Chicago Black Hawks | NHL | 44 | 21 | 18 | 5 | 3 | 111 | 2.42 | 0 | 0 | 0 | 0 |
| 1930–31 | 26 | Chicago Black Hawks | NHL | 44 | 24 | 17 | 3 | 12 | 78 | 1.73 | 0 | 0 | 0 | 0 |
| 1931–32 | 27 | Chicago Black Hawks | NHL | 48 | 18 | 18 | 11 | 4 | 92 | 1.85 | 0 | 0 | 0 | 0 |
| 1932–33 | 28 | Chicago Black Hawks | NHL | 48 | 16 | 20 | 12 | 5 | 101 | 2.01 | 0 | 0 | 0 | 0 |
| 1933–34 | 29 | Chicago Black Hawks | NHL | 48 | 20 | 17 | 11 | 10 | 83 | 1.63 | 0 | 0 | 0 | 0 |
| NHL Career — 7 Seasons | | | | 316 | 112 | 151 | 52 | 42 | 664 | 2.02 | 0 | 0 | 0 | 0 |

### PLAYOFFS

| SEASON | AGE | TEAM | LG | GP | W | L | T | SO | GA | GAA | G | A | PTS | PIM |
|--------|-----|------|-----|-----|-----|-----|-----|-----|-----|------|-----|-----|-----|-----|
| 1929–30 | 25 | Chicago Black Hawks | NHL | 2 | 0 | 1 | 1 | 0 | 3 | 1.05 | 0 | 0 | 0 | 0 |
| 1930–31 | 26 | Chicago Black Hawks | NHL | 9 | 5 | 3 | 1 | 2 | 14 | 1.32 | 0 | 0 | 0 | 0 |
| 1931–32 | 27 | Chicago Black Hawks | NHL | 2 | 1 | 1 | 0 | 1 | 6 | 3.00 | 0 | 0 | 0 | 0 |
| 1933–34 | 29 | Chicago Black Hawks | NHL | 8 | 6 | 1 | 1 | 2 | 12 | 1.33 | 0 | 0 | 0 | 0 |
| NHL Career — 4 Seasons | | | | 21 | 12 | 6 | 3 | 5 | 35 | 1.43 | 0 | 0 | 0 | 0 |

## Eddie Giacomin  Profile: See page 336

### REGULAR SEASON

| SEASON | AGE | TEAM | LG | GP | W | L | T | SO | GA | GAA | G | A | PTS | PIM |
|--------|-----|------|-----|-----|-----|-----|-----|-----|-----|------|-----|-----|-----|-----|
| 1965–66 | 26 | New York Rangers | NHL | 36 | 8 | 20 | 6 | 0 | 125 | 3.69 | 0 | 0 | 0 | 8 |
| 1966–67 | 27 | New York Rangers | NHL | 68 | 30 | 27 | 11 | 9 | 173 | 2.61 | 0 | 0 | 0 | 8 |
| 1967–68 | 28 | New York Rangers | NHL | 66 | 36 | 20 | 10 | 8 | 160 | 2.44 | 0 | 0 | 0 | 4 |
| 1968–69 | 29 | New York Rangers | NHL | 70 | 38 | 23 | 7 | 7 | 175 | 2.56 | 0 | 0 | 0 | 2 |
| 1969–70 | 30 | New York Rangers | NHL | 70 | 35 | 21 | 14 | 6 | 163 | 2.36 | 0 | 2 | 2 | 4 |
| 1970–71 | 31 | New York Rangers | NHL | 45 | 27 | 10 | 7 | 8 | 95 | 2.16 | 0 | 0 | 0 | 4 |
| 1971–72 | 32 | New York Rangers | NHL | 44 | 24 | 10 | 9 | 1 | 115 | 2.71 | 0 | 3 | 3 | 4 |
| 1972–73 | 33 | New York Rangers | NHL | 43 | 26 | 11 | 6 | 4 | 125 | 2.91 | 0 | 2 | 2 | 6 |
| 1973–74 | 34 | New York Rangers | NHL | 56 | 30 | 15 | 10 | 5 | 168 | 3.07 | 0 | 1 | 1 | 4 |
| 1974–75 | 35 | New York Rangers | NHL | 37 | 13 | 12 | 8 | 1 | 120 | 3.49 | 0 | 0 | 0 | 20 |
| 1975–76 | 36 | New York Rangers | NHL | 4 | 0 | 3 | 1 | 0 | 19 | 4.75 | 0 | 0 | 0 | 0 |
| 1975–76 | 36 | Detroit Red Wings | NHL | 29 | 12 | 14 | 3 | 2 | 100 | 3.46 | 0 | 0 | 0 | 0 |
| 1976–77 | 37 | Detroit Red Wings | NHL | 33 | 8 | 18 | 3 | 3 | 107 | 3.59 | 0 | 1 | 1 | 4 |

## Eddie Giacomin (continued)

### REGULAR SEASON

| SEASON | AGE | TEAM | LG | GP | W | L | T | SO | GA | GAA | G | A | PTS | PIM |
|---|---|---|---|---|---|---|---|---|---|---|---|---|---|---|
| 1977–78 | 38 | Detroit Red Wings | NHL | 9 | 3 | 5 | 1 | 0 | 27 | 3.14 | 0 | 0 | 0 | 0 |
| NHL Career — 13 Seasons | | | | 610 | 290 | 209 | 96 | 54 | 1672 | 2.82 | 0 | 9 | 9 | 66 |

### PLAYOFFS

| SEASON | AGE | TEAM | LG | GP | W | L | T | SO | GA | GAA | G | A | PTS | PIM |
|---|---|---|---|---|---|---|---|---|---|---|---|---|---|---|
| 1966–67 | 27 | New York Rangers | NHL | 4 | 0 | 4 | | 0 | 14 | 3.43 | 0 | 0 | 0 | 0 |
| 1967–68 | 28 | New York Rangers | NHL | 6 | 2 | 4 | | 0 | 18 | 3.02 | 0 | 0 | 0 | 0 |
| 1968–69 | 29 | New York Rangers | NHL | 3 | 0 | 3 | | 0 | 10 | 3.35 | 0 | 0 | 0 | 5 |
| 1969–70 | 30 | New York Rangers | NHL | 5 | 2 | 3 | | 0 | 19 | 4.15 | 0 | 0 | 0 | 2 |
| 1970–71 | 31 | New York Rangers | NHL | 12 | 7 | 5 | | 0 | 28 | 2.22 | 0 | 0 | 0 | 2 |
| 1971–72 | 32 | New York Rangers | NHL | 10 | 6 | 4 | | 0 | 27 | 2.72 | 0 | 0 | 0 | 2 |
| 1972–73 | 33 | New York Rangers | NHL | 10 | 5 | 4 | 1 | 0 | 23 | 2.57 | 0 | 0 | 0 | 4 |
| 1973–74 | 34 | New York Rangers | NHL | 13 | 7 | 6 | | 0 | 37 | 2.83 | 0 | 0 | 0 | 6 |
| 1974–75 | 35 | New York Rangers | NHL | 2 | 0 | 2 | | 0 | 4 | 2.82 | 0 | 0 | 0 | 4 |
| NHL Career — 9 Seasons | | | | 65 | 29 | 35 | 1 | 0 | 180 | 2.83 | 0 | 0 | 0 | 23 |

## George Hainsworth  Profile: See page 337

### REGULAR SEASON

| SEASON | AGE | TEAM | LG | GP | W | L | T | SO | GA | GAA | G | A | PTS | PIM |
|---|---|---|---|---|---|---|---|---|---|---|---|---|---|---|
| 1923–24 | 28 | Saskatoon Crescents | WCHL | 30 | 15 | 12 | 3 | 4 | 73 | 2.34 | | | | |
| 1924–25 | 29 | Saskatoon Crescents | WCHL | 28 | 16 | 11 | 1 | 2 | 75 | 2.65 | | | | |
| 1925–26 | 30 | Saskatoon Crescents | WHL | 30 | 18 | 11 | 1 | 4 | 64 | 2.12 | | | | |
| 1926–27 | 31 | Montreal Canadiens | NHL | 44 | 28 | 14 | 2 | 14 | 67 | 1.47 | 0 | 0 | 0 | 0 |
| 1927–28 | 32 | Montreal Canadiens | NHL | 44 | 26 | 11 | 7 | 13 | 48 | 1.05 | 0 | 0 | 0 | 0 |
| 1928–29 | 33 | Montreal Canadiens | NHL | 44 | 22 | 7 | 15 | 22 | 43 | 0.92 | 0 | 0 | 0 | 0 |
| 1929–30 | 34 | Montreal Canadiens | NHL | 42 | 20 | 13 | 9 | 4 | 108 | 2.42 | 0 | 0 | 0 | 0 |
| 1930–31 | 35 | Montreal Canadiens | NHL | 44 | 26 | 10 | 8 | 8 | 89 | 1.95 | 0 | 0 | 0 | 0 |
| 1931–32 | 36 | Montreal Canadiens | NHL | 48 | 25 | 15 | 7 | 6 | 110 | 2.19 | 0 | 0 | 0 | 2 |
| 1932–33 | 37 | Montreal Canadiens | NHL | 48 | 18 | 25 | 5 | 8 | 115 | 2.32 | 0 | 0 | 0 | 0 |
| 1933–34 | 38 | Toronto Maple Leafs | NHL | 48 | 26 | 13 | 9 | 3 | 119 | 2.37 | 0 | 0 | 0 | 0 |
| 1934–35 | 39 | Toronto Maple Leafs | NHL | 48 | 30 | 14 | 4 | 8 | 111 | 2.25 | 0 | 0 | 0 | 0 |
| 1935–36 | 40 | Toronto Maple Leafs | NHL | 48 | 23 | 19 | 6 | 8 | 106 | 2.12 | 0 | 0 | 0 | 0 |
| 1936–37 | 41 | Toronto Maple Leafs | NHL | 3 | 0 | 2 | 1 | 0 | 9 | 2.84 | 0 | 0 | 0 | 0 |
| 1936–37 | 41 | Montreal Canadiens | NHL | 4 | 2 | 1 | 1 | 0 | 12 | 2.67 | 0 | 0 | 0 | 0 |
| Career — 14 Seasons | | | | 553 | 295 | 178 | 79 | 104 | 1149 | 2.08 | 0 | 0 | 0 | 2 |

### PLAYOFFS

| SEASON | AGE | TEAM | LG | GP | W | L | T | SO | GA | GAA | G | A | PTS | PIM |
|---|---|---|---|---|---|---|---|---|---|---|---|---|---|---|
| 1924–25 | 29 | Saskatoon Crescents | WCHL | 2 | 0 | 1 | 1 | 0 | 6 | 3.00 | | | | |
| 1925–26 | 30 | Saskatoon Crescents | WHL | 2 | 0 | 1 | 1 | 0 | 4 | 1.86 | | | | |
| 1926–27 | 31 | Montreal Canadiens | NHL | 4 | 1 | 1 | 2 | 1 | 6 | 1.43 | 0 | 0 | 0 | 0 |
| 1927–28 | 32 | Montreal Canadiens | NHL | 2 | 0 | 1 | 1 | 0 | 3 | 1.40 | 0 | 0 | 0 | 0 |
| 1928–29 | 33 | Montreal Canadiens | NHL | 3 | 0 | 3 | 0 | 0 | 5 | 1.67 | 0 | 0 | 0 | 0 |
| 1929–30 | 34 | Montreal Canadiens | NHL | 6 | 5 | 0 | 1 | 3 | 6 | 0.75 | 0 | 0 | 0 | 0 |
| 1930–31 | 35 | Montreal Canadiens | NHL | 10 | 6 | 4 | 0 | 2 | 21 | 1.75 | 0 | 0 | 0 | 0 |
| 1931–32 | 36 | Montreal Canadiens | NHL | 4 | 1 | 3 | 0 | 0 | 13 | 2.60 | 0 | 0 | 0 | 0 |
| 1932–33 | 37 | Montreal Canadiens | NHL | 2 | 0 | 1 | 1 | 0 | 8 | 4.00 | 0 | 0 | 0 | 0 |
| 1933–34 | 38 | Toronto Maple Leafs | NHL | 5 | 2 | 3 | 0 | 0 | 11 | 2.19 | 0 | 0 | 0 | 0 |
| 1934–35 | 39 | Toronto Maple Leafs | NHL | 7 | 3 | 4 | 0 | 2 | 12 | 1.56 | 0 | 0 | 0 | 0 |
| 1935–36 | 40 | Toronto Maple Leafs | NHL | 9 | 4 | 5 | 0 | 0 | 27 | 3.00 | 0 | 0 | 0 | 0 |
| Career — 12 Seasons | | | | 56 | 22 | 27 | 7 | 8 | 122 | 2.18 | 0 | 0 | 0 | 0 |

## Glenn Hall  Profile: See page 338

### REGULAR SEASON

| SEASON | AGE | TEAM | LG | GP | W | L | T | SO | GA | GAA | G | A | PTS | PIM |
|---|---|---|---|---|---|---|---|---|---|---|---|---|---|---|
| 1952–53 | 21 | Detroit Red Wings | NHL | 6 | 4 | 1 | 1 | 1 | 10 | 1.67 | 0 | 0 | 0 | 0 |
| 1954–55 | 23 | Detroit Red Wings | NHL | 2 | 2 | 0 | 0 | 0 | 2 | 1.00 | 0 | 0 | 0 | 0 |
| 1955–56 | 24 | Detroit Red Wings | NHL | 70 | 30 | 24 | 16 | 12 | 147 | 2.10 | 0 | 0 | 0 | 14 |
| 1956–57 | 25 | Detroit Red Wings | NHL | 70 | 38 | 20 | 12 | 4 | 155 | 2.22 | 0 | 0 | 0 | 2 |
| 1957–58 | 26 | Chicago Black Hawks | NHL | 70 | 24 | 39 | 7 | 7 | 200 | 2.86 | 0 | 0 | 0 | 10 |
| 1958–59 | 27 | Chicago Black Hawks | NHL | 70 | 28 | 29 | 13 | 1 | 208 | 2.97 | 0 | 0 | 0 | 0 |
| 1959–60 | 28 | Chicago Black Hawks | NHL | 70 | 28 | 29 | 13 | 6 | 179 | 2.56 | 0 | 1 | 1 | 2 |
| 1960–61 | 29 | Chicago Black Hawks | NHL | 70 | 29 | 24 | 17 | 6 | 179 | 2.53 | 0 | 1 | 1 | 0 |
| 1961–62 | 30 | Chicago Black Hawks | NHL | 70 | 31 | 26 | 13 | 9 | 184 | 2.63 | 0 | 0 | 0 | 12 |
| 1962–63 | 31 | Chicago Black Hawks | NHL | 66 | 30 | 20 | 15 | 5 | 161 | 2.47 | 0 | 0 | 0 | 0 |
| 1963–64 | 32 | Chicago Black Hawks | NHL | 65 | 34 | 19 | 11 | 7 | 148 | 2.30 | 0 | 2 | 2 | 2 |
| 1964–65 | 33 | Chicago Black Hawks | NHL | 41 | 19 | 16 | 5 | 4 | 99 | 2.44 | 0 | 0 | 0 | 2 |
| 1965–66 | 34 | Chicago Black Hawks | NHL | 64 | 34 | 22 | 8 | 4 | 164 | 2.63 | 0 | 2 | 2 | 14 |
| 1966–67 | 35 | Chicago Black Hawks | NHL | 32 | 19 | 5 | 5 | 5 | 66 | 2.38 | 0 | 0 | 0 | 10 |
| 1967–68 | 36 | St. Louis Blues | NHL | 49 | 18 | 21 | 9 | 5 | 118 | 2.48 | 0 | 0 | 0 | 0 |

## Glenn Hall (continued)

### REGULAR SEASON

| SEASON | AGE | TEAM | LG | GP | W | L | T | SO | GA | GAA | G | A | PTS | PIM |
|---|---|---|---|---|---|---|---|---|---|---|---|---|---|---|
| 1968–69 | 37 | St. Louis Blues | NHL | 41 | 19 | 12 | 8 | 8 | 85 | 2.17 | 0 | 2 | 2 | 20 |
| 1969–70 | 38 | St. Louis Blues | NHL | 18 | 7 | 8 | 3 | 1 | 49 | 2.91 | 0 | 0 | 0 | 0 |
| 1970–71 | 39 | St. Louis Blues | NHL | 32 | 13 | 11 | 8 | 2 | 71 | 2.42 | 0 | 1 | 1 | 0 |
| NHL Career—18 Seasons | | | | 906 | 407 | 326 | 164 | 84 | 2222 | 2.50 | 0 | 9 | 9 | 88 |

### PLAYOFFS

| SEASON | AGE | TEAM | LG | GP | W | L | T | SO | GA | GAA | G | A | PTS | PIM |
|---|---|---|---|---|---|---|---|---|---|---|---|---|---|---|
| 1955–56 | 24 | Detroit Red Wings | NHL | 10 | 5 | 5 | | 0 | 28 | 2.78 | 0 | 0 | 0 | 0 |
| 1956–57 | 25 | Detroit Red Wings | NHL | 5 | 1 | 4 | | 0 | 15 | 3.00 | 0 | 0 | 0 | 10 |
| 1958–59 | 27 | Chicago Black Hawks | NHL | 6 | 2 | 4 | | 0 | 21 | 3.50 | 0 | 0 | 0 | 0 |
| 1959–60 | 28 | Chicago Black Hawks | NHL | 4 | 0 | 4 | | 0 | 14 | 3.39 | 0 | 0 | 0 | 0 |
| 1960–61 | 29 | Chicago Black Hawks | NHL | 12 | 8 | 4 | | 2 | 26 | 2.02 | 0 | 0 | 0 | 0 |
| 1961–62 | 30 | Chicago Black Hawks | NHL | 12 | 6 | 6 | | 2 | 31 | 2.58 | 0 | 0 | 0 | 0 |
| 1962–63 | 31 | Chicago Black Hawks | NHL | 6 | 2 | 4 | | 0 | 25 | 4.17 | 0 | 0 | 0 | 0 |
| 1963–64 | 32 | Chicago Black Hawks | NHL | 7 | 3 | 4 | | 0 | 22 | 3.23 | 0 | 0 | 0 | 0 |
| 1964–65 | 33 | Chicago Black Hawks | NHL | 13 | 7 | 6 | | 1 | 28 | 2.21 | 0 | 0 | 0 | 0 |
| 1965–66 | 34 | Chicago Black Hawks | NHL | 6 | 2 | 4 | | 0 | 22 | 3.78 | 0 | 0 | 0 | 0 |
| 1966–67 | 35 | Chicago Black Hawks | NHL | 3 | 1 | 2 | | 0 | 8 | 2.74 | 0 | 0 | 0 | 0 |
| 1967–68 | 36 | St. Louis Blues | NHL | 18 | 8 | 10 | | 1 | 45 | 2.44 | 0 | 0 | 0 | 0 |
| 1968–69 | 37 | St. Louis Blues | NHL | 3 | 0 | 2 | | 0 | 5 | 2.32 | 0 | 0 | 0 | 0 |
| 1969–70 | 38 | St. Louis Blues | NHL | 7 | 4 | 3 | | 0 | 21 | 3.00 | 0 | 0 | 0 | 0 |
| 1970–71 | 39 | St. Louis Blues | NHL | 3 | 0 | 3 | | 0 | 9 | 3.05 | 0 | 0 | 0 | 0 |
| NHL Career—15 Seasons | | | | 115 | 49 | 65 | | 6 | 320 | 2.79 | 0 | 0 | 0 | 10 |

## Dominik Hasek   Profile: See page 340

### REGULAR SEASON

| SEASON | AGE | TEAM | LG | GP | W | L | T | SO | GA | GAA | G | A | PTS | PIM |
|---|---|---|---|---|---|---|---|---|---|---|---|---|---|---|
| 1990–91 | 26 | Chicago Blackhawks | NHL | 5 | 3 | 0 | 1 | 0 | 8 | 2.46 | 0 | 0 | 0 | 0 |
| 1991–92 | 27 | Chicago Blackhawks | NHL | 20 | 10 | 4 | 1 | 1 | 44 | 2.60 | 0 | 0 | 0 | 8 |
| 1992–93 | 28 | Buffalo Sabres | NHL | 28 | 11 | 10 | 4 | 0 | 75 | 3.15 | 0 | 0 | 0 | 0 |
| 1993–94 | 29 | Buffalo Sabres | NHL | 58 | 30 | 20 | 6 | 7 | 109 | 1.95 | 0 | 3 | 3 | 6 |
| 1994–95 | 30 | Buffalo Sabres | NHL | 41 | 19 | 14 | 7 | 5 | 85 | 2.11 | 0 | 0 | 0 | 2 |
| 1995–96 | 31 | Buffalo Sabres | NHL | 59 | 22 | 30 | 6 | 2 | 161 | 2.83 | 0 | 1 | 1 | 6 |
| 1996–97 | 32 | Buffalo Sabres | NHL | 67 | 37 | 20 | 10 | 5 | 153 | 2.27 | 0 | 3 | 3 | 30 |
| 1997–98 | 33 | Buffalo Sabres | NHL | 72 | 33 | 23 | 13 | 13 | 147 | 2.09 | 0 | 2 | 2 | 12 |
| 1998–99 | 34 | Buffalo Sabres | NHL | 64 | 30 | 18 | 14 | 9 | 119 | 1.87 | 0 | 0 | 0 | 14 |
| 1999–00 | 35 | Buffalo Sabres | NHL | 35 | 15 | 11 | 6 | 3 | 76 | 2.21 | 0 | 1 | 1 | 12 |
| 2000–01 | 36 | Buffalo Sabres | NHL | 67 | 37 | 24 | 4 | 11 | 137 | 2.11 | 0 | 3 | 3 | 22 |
| 2001–02 | 37 | Detroit Red Wings | NHL | 65 | 41 | 15 | 8 | 5 | 140 | 2.17 | 0 | 1 | 1 | 8 |
| 2003–04 | 39 | Detroit Red Wings | NHL | 14 | 8 | 3 | 2 | 2 | 30 | 2.20 | 0 | 2 | 2 | 2 |
| 2005–06 | 41 | Ottawa Senators | NHL | 43 | 28 | 10 | 4 | 5 | 90 | 2.09 | 0 | 0 | 0 | 16 |
| 2006–07 | 42 | Detroit Red Wings | NHL | 56 | 38 | 11 | 6 | 8 | 114 | 2.05 | 0 | 2 | 2 | 20 |
| 2007–08 | 43 | Detroit Red Wings | NHL | 41 | 27 | 10 | 3 | 5 | 84 | 2.14 | 0 | 1 | 1 | 12 |
| NHL Career—16 Seasons | | | | 735 | 389 | 223 | 95 | 81 | 1572 | 2.20 | 0 | 19 | 19 | 170 |

### PLAYOFFS

| SEASON | AGE | TEAM | LG | GP | W | L | T | SO | GA | GAA | G | A | PTS | PIM |
|---|---|---|---|---|---|---|---|---|---|---|---|---|---|---|
| 1990–91 | 26 | Chicago Blackhawks | NHL | 3 | 0 | 0 | 0 | 0 | 3 | 2.62 | 0 | 1 | 1 | 0 |
| 1991–92 | 27 | Chicago Blackhawks | NHL | 3 | 0 | 2 | 0 | 0 | 8 | 3.05 | 0 | 0 | 0 | 0 |
| 1992–93 | 28 | Buffalo Sabres | NHL | 1 | 1 | 0 | 0 | 0 | 1 | 1.34 | 0 | 0 | 0 | 0 |
| 1993–94 | 29 | Buffalo Sabres | NHL | 7 | 3 | 4 | 0 | 2 | 13 | 1.61 | 0 | 0 | 0 | 2 |
| 1994–95 | 30 | Buffalo Sabres | NHL | 5 | 1 | 4 | 0 | 0 | 18 | 3.49 | 0 | 0 | 0 | 0 |
| 1996–97 | 32 | Buffalo Sabres | NHL | 3 | 1 | 1 | 0 | 0 | 5 | 1.96 | 0 | 0 | 0 | 2 |
| 1997–98 | 33 | Buffalo Sabres | NHL | 15 | 10 | 5 | 0 | 1 | 32 | 2.03 | 0 | 0 | 0 | 4 |
| 1998–99 | 34 | Buffalo Sabres | NHL | 19 | 13 | 6 | 0 | 2 | 36 | 1.77 | 0 | 1 | 1 | 8 |
| 1999–00 | 35 | Buffalo Sabres | NHL | 5 | 1 | 4 | 0 | 0 | 12 | 2.39 | 0 | 0 | 0 | 2 |
| 2000–01 | 36 | Buffalo Sabres | NHL | 13 | 7 | 6 | 0 | 1 | 29 | 2.09 | 0 | 0 | 0 | 14 |
| 2001–02 | 37 | Detroit Red Wings | NHL | 23 | 16 | 7 | 0 | 6 | 45 | 1.86 | 0 | 1 | 1 | 8 |
| 2006–07 | 42 | Detroit Red Wings | NHL | 18 | 10 | 8 | 0 | 2 | 34 | 1.79 | 0 | 0 | 0 | 2 |
| 2007–08 | 43 | Detroit Red Wings | NHL | 4 | 2 | 2 | 0 | 0 | 10 | 2.91 | 0 | 0 | 0 | 2 |
| Career—13 Seasons | | | | 119 | 65 | 49 | 0 | 14 | 246 | 2.02 | 0 | 3 | 3 | 44 |

# Riley Hern   Profile: See page 342

**REGULAR SEASON**

| SEASON | AGE | TEAM | LG | GP | W | L | T | SO | GA | GAA |
|---|---|---|---|---|---|---|---|---|---|---|
| 1901–02 | 23 | Pittsburgh Keystones | WPHL | 19 | 14 | 5 | 0 | 2 | 40 | 3.08 |
| 1902–03 | 24 | Pittsburgh Keystones | WPHL | 12 | 1 | 10 | 0 | 0 | 61 | 7.96 |
| 1903–04 | 25 | Portage Lakes | Exhib. | 14 | 13 | 1 | 0 | 4 | 21 | 1.50 |
| 1904–05 | 26 | Portage Lakes | IHL | 24 | 15 | 7 | 2 | 2 | 81 | 3.54 |
| 1905–06 | 27 | Portage Lakes | IHL | 20 | 15 | 5 | 0 | 1 | 70 | 3.46 |
| 1906–07 | 28 | Montreal Wanderers | ECAHA | 10 | 10 | 0 | 0 | 0 | 39 | 3.84 |
| 1907–08 | 29 | Montreal Wanderers | ECAHA | 10 | 8 | 2 | 0 | 0 | 52 | 5.11 |
| 1908–09 | 30 | Montreal Wanderers | ECHA | 12 | 9 | 3 | 0 | 0 | 61 | 5.03 |
| 1909–10 | 31 | Montreal Wanderers | NHA | 13 | 12 | 1 | 0 | 1 | 47 | 3.62 |
| 1910–11 | 32 | Montreal Wanderers | NHA | 16 | 7 | 9 | 0 | 0 | 88 | 5.43 |
| Career — 10 Seasons | | | | 150 | 104 | 43 | 2 | 10 | 560 | 3.73 |

**PLAYOFFS**

| SEASON | AGE | TEAM | LG | GP | W | L | T | SO | GA | GAA |
|---|---|---|---|---|---|---|---|---|---|---|
| 1901–02 | 23 | Pittsburgh Keystones | WPHL | 1 | 1 | 0 | 0 | 1 | 1 | 1.50 |
| 1906–07 | 28 | Montreal Wanderers | St-Cup | 6 | 3 | 3 | 0 | 0 | 25 | 4.17 |
| 1907–08 | 29 | Montreal Wanderers | St-Cup | 5 | 5 | 0 | 0 | 0 | 16 | 3.20 |
| 1908–09 | 30 | Montreal Wanderers | St-Cup | 2 | 1 | 1 | 0 | 0 | 10 | 5.00 |
| 1909–10 | 31 | Montreal Wanderers | St-Cup | 1 | 1 | 0 | 0 | 0 | 3 | 3.00 |
| Career — 5 Seasons | | | | 15 | 11 | 4 | 0 | 1 | 55 | 3.92 |

# Hap Holmes   Profile: See page 343

**REGULAR SEASON**

| SEASON | AGE | TEAM | LG | GP | W | L | T | SO | GA | GAA | G | A | PTS | PIM |
|---|---|---|---|---|---|---|---|---|---|---|---|---|---|---|
| 1912–13 | 24 | Toronto Blueshirts | NHA | 15 | 6 | 7 | 0 | 1 | 58 | 4.47 | | | | |
| 1913–14 | 25 | Toronto Blueshirts | NHA | 20 | 13 | 7 | 0 | 1 | 65 | 3.24 | | | | |
| 1914–15 | 26 | Toronto Blueshirts | NHA | 20 | 8 | 12 | 0 | 0 | 84 | 4.18 | | | | |
| 1915–16 | 27 | Seattle Metropolitans | PCHA | 18 | 9 | 9 | 0 | 0 | 66 | 3.67 | | | | |
| 1916–17 | 28 | Seattle Metropolitans | PCHA | 24 | 16 | 8 | 0 | 2 | 80 | 3.28 | | | | |
| 1917–18 | 29 | Toronto Arenas | NHL | 16 | 9 | 7 | 0 | 0 | 76 | 4.73 | 0 | 0 | 0 | 0 |
| 1918–19 | 30 | Toronto Arenas | NHL | 2 | 0 | 2 | 0 | 0 | 9 | 4.50 | 0 | 0 | 0 | 0 |
| 1918–19 | 30 | Seattle Metropolitans | PCHA | 20 | 11 | 9 | 0 | 0 | 46 | 2.25 | | | | |
| 1919–20 | 31 | Seattle Metropolitans | PCHA | 22 | 12 | 10 | 0 | 4 | 55 | 2.46 | | | | |
| 1920–21 | 32 | Seattle Metropolitans | PCHA | 24 | 12 | 11 | 1 | 0 | 68 | 2.63 | | | | |
| 1921–22 | 33 | Seattle Metropolitans | PCHA | 24 | 12 | 11 | 1 | 4 | 64 | 2.60 | | | | |
| 1922–23 | 34 | Seattle Metropolitans | PCHA | 30 | 15 | 15 | 0 | 2 | 106 | 3.45 | | | | |
| 1923–24 | 35 | Seattle Metropolitans | PCHA | 30 | 14 | 16 | 0 | 2 | 99 | 3.26 | | | | |
| 1924–25 | 36 | Victoria Cougars | WCHL | 28 | 16 | 12 | 0 | 3 | 63 | 2.25 | | | | |
| 1925–26 | 37 | Victoria Cougars | WHL | 30 | 15 | 11 | 4 | 4 | 53 | 1.68 | | | | |
| 1926–27 | 38 | Detroit Cougars | NHL | 41 | 11 | 26 | 4 | 6 | 100 | 2.32 | 0 | 0 | 0 | 0 |
| 1927–28 | 39 | Detroit Cougars | NHL | 44 | 19 | 19 | 6 | 11 | 79 | 1.73 | 0 | 0 | 0 | 0 |
| Career — 16 Seasons | | | | 408 | 198 | 192 | 16 | 40 | 1170 | 2.88 | 0 | 0 | 0 | 0 |

**PLAYOFFS**

| SEASON | AGE | TEAM | LG | GP | W | L | T | SO | GA | GAA | | | | |
|---|---|---|---|---|---|---|---|---|---|---|---|---|---|---|
| 1913–14 | 25 | Toronto Blueshirts | NHA | 2 | 1 | 1 | 0 | 1 | 2 | 1.00 | | | | |
| 1913–14 | 25 | Toronto Blueshirts | St-Cup | 3 | 3 | 0 | 0 | 0 | 8 | 2.46 | | | | |
| 1916–17 | 28 | Seattle Metropolitans | St-Cup | 4 | 3 | 1 | 0 | 0 | 11 | 2.75 | | | | |
| 1917–18 | 29 | Toronto Arenas | NHA | 2 | 1 | 1 | 0 | 0 | 7 | 3.50 | 0 | 0 | 0 | 0 |
| 1917–18 | 29 | Toronto Arenas | St-Cup | 5 | 3 | 2 | | 0 | 21 | 4.20 | | | | |
| 1918–19 | 30 | Seattle Metropolitans | PCHA | 2 | 1 | 1 | 0 | 0 | 5 | 2.50 | | | | |
| 1918–19 | 30 | Seattle Metropolitans | St-Cup | 5 | 2 | 2 | 1 | 2 | 10 | 1.79 | | | | |
| 1919–20 | 31 | Seattle Metropolitans | PCHA | 2 | 1 | 1 | 0 | 1 | 3 | 1.50 | | | | |
| 1919–20 | 31 | Seattle Metropolitans | St-Cup | 5 | 2 | 3 | 0 | 0 | 15 | 3.00 | | | | |
| 1920–21 | 32 | Seattle Metropolitans | PCHA | 2 | 0 | 2 | 0 | 0 | 13 | 6.50 | | | | |
| 1921–22 | 33 | Seattle Metropolitans | PCHA | 2 | 0 | 2 | 0 | 0 | 2 | 1.00 | | | | |
| 1923–24 | 35 | Seattle Metropolitans | PCHA | 2 | 0 | 1 | 1 | 0 | 4 | 1.79 | | | | |
| 1924–25 | 36 | Victoria Cougars | WCHL | 4 | 2 | 0 | 2 | 1 | 5 | 1.25 | | | | |
| 1924–25 | 36 | Victoria Cougars | St-Cup | 4 | 3 | 1 | 0 | 0 | 8 | 2.00 | | | | |
| 1925–26 | 37 | Victoria Cougars | WHL | 4 | 2 | 0 | 2 | 1 | 6 | 1.45 | | | | |
| 1925–26 | 37 | Victoria Cougars | St-Cup | 4 | 1 | 3 | 0 | 0 | 10 | 2.50 | | | | |
| Career — 10 Seasons | | | | 52 | 25 | 21 | 7 | 6 | 139 | 2.67 | 0 | 0 | 0 | 0 |

# Bouse Hutton  Profile: See page 344

## REGULAR SEASON

| SEASON | AGE | TEAM | LG | GP | W | L | T | SO | GA | GAA |
|--------|-----|------|----|----|----|----|----|----|----|-----|
| 1898–99 | 21 | Ottawa Hockey Club | CAHL | 2 | 1 | 1 | 0 | 0 | 11 | 5.50 |
| 1899–00 | 22 | Ottawa Hockey Club | CAHL | 7 | 4 | 3 | 0 | 0 | 19 | 2.71 |
| 1900–01 | 23 | Ottawa Hockey Club | CAHL | 7 | 7 | 0 | 0 | 0 | 20 | 2.50 |
| 1901–02 | 24 | Ottawa Hockey Club | CAHL | 8 | 5 | 3 | 0 | 2 | 15 | 1.88 |
| 1902–03 | 25 | Ottawa Silver Seven | CAHL | 8 | 6 | 2 | 0 | 0 | 26 | 3.25 |
| 1903–04 | 26 | Ottawa Silver Seven | CAHL | 4 | 4 | 0 | 0 | 0 | 15 | 3.75 |
| 1908–09 | 31 | Ottawa Senators | FAHL | 5 | 3 | 2 | 0 | 1 | 26 | 5.20 |
| Career — 7 Seasons | | | | 41 | 30 | 11 | 0 | 3 | 132 | 3.14 |

## PLAYOFFS

| SEASON | AGE | TEAM | LG | GP | W | L | T | SO | GA | GAA |
|--------|-----|------|----|----|----|----|----|----|----|-----|
| 1902–03 | 25 | Ottawa Silver Seven | CAHL | 2 | 1 | 0 | 1 | 1 | 1 | 0.50 |
| 1902–03 | 25 | Ottawa Silver Seven | St-Cup | 2 | 2 | 0 | 0 | 0 | 4 | 2.00 |
| 1903–04 | 26 | Ottawa Silver Seven | St-Cup | 8 | 6 | 1 | 1 | 1 | 23 | 2.87 |
| Career — 2 Seasons | | | | 12 | 9 | 1 | 2 | 2 | 28 | 2.33 |

# Hugh Lehman  Profile: See page 345

## REGULAR SEASON

| SEASON | AGE | TEAM | LG | GP | W | L | T | SO | GA | GAA |
|--------|-----|------|----|----|----|----|----|----|----|-----|
| 1906–07 | 21 | Canadian Soo | IHL | 24 | 13 | 11 | 0 | 0 | 123 | 5.12 |
| 1907–08 | 22 | Pembroke Lumber Kings | OVHL | 4 | 2 | 2 | 0 | 0 | 22 | 5.50 |
| 1908–09 | 23 | Berlin Professionals | OPHL | 15 | 9 | 6 | 0 | 0 | 72 | 4.85 |
| 1909–10 | 24 | Berlin Professionals | OPHL | 23 | 17 | 6 | 0 | 3 | 93 | 4.12 |
| 1910–11 | 25 | Berlin Professionals | OPHL | 15 | 7 | 8 | 0 | 0 | 87 | 5.80 |
| 1911–12 | 26 | New Westminster Royals | PCHA | 15 | 9 | 6 | 0 | 0 | 77 | 5.07 |
| 1912–13 | 27 | New Westminster Royals | PCHA | 12 | 4 | 8 | 0 | 0 | 51 | 4.14 |
| 1913–14 | 28 | New Westminster Royals | PCHA | 16 | 7 | 9 | 0 | 0 | 81 | 4.87 |
| 1914–15 | 29 | Vancouver Millionaires | PCHA | 17 | 13 | 4 | 0 | 1 | 71 | 4.08 |
| 1915–16 | 30 | Vancouver Millionaires | PCHA | 18 | 9 | 9 | 0 | 0 | 69 | 3.79 |
| 1916–17 | 31 | Vancouver Millionaires | PCHA | 23 | 14 | 9 | 0 | 0 | 124 | 5.30 |
| 1917–18 | 32 | Vancouver Millionaires | PCHA | 18 | 9 | 9 | 0 | 1 | 60 | 3.05 |
| 1918–19 | 33 | Vancouver Millionaires | PCHA | 20 | 12 | 8 | 0 | 1 | 55 | 2.58 |
| 1919–20 | 34 | Vancouver Millionaires | PCHA | 22 | 11 | 11 | 1 | 0 | 65 | 2.92 |
| 1920–21 | 35 | Vancouver Millionaires | PCHA | 24 | 13 | 11 | 0 | 3 | 78 | 3.23 |
| 1921–22 | 36 | Vancouver Millionaires | PCHA | 22 | 12 | 10 | 0 | 4 | 62 | 2.82 |
| 1922–23 | 37 | Vancouver Maroons | PCHA | 25 | 16 | 8 | 1 | 5 | 61 | 2.33 |
| 1923–24 | 38 | Vancouver Maroons | PCHA | 30 | 13 | 16 | 1 | 1 | 80 | 2.60 |
| 1924–25 | 39 | Vancouver Maroons | WCHL | 11 | 7 | 4 | 0 | 0 | 29 | 2.62 |
| 1925–26 | 40 | Vancouver Maroons | WHL | 30 | 10 | 18 | 2 | 3 | 90 | 2.94 |
| 1926–27 | 41 | Chicago Black Hawks | NHL | 44 | 19 | 22 | 3 | 5 | 116 | 2.49 |
| 1927–28 | 42 | Chicago Black Hawks | NHL | 4 | 1 | 2 | 1 | 1 | 20 | 4.80 |
| Career — 22 Seasons | | | | 432 | 227 | 196 | 9 | 28 | 1586 | 3.67 |

## PLAYOFFS

| SEASON | AGE | TEAM | LG | GP | W | L | T | SO | GA | GAA |
|--------|-----|------|----|----|----|----|----|----|----|-----|
| 1909–10 | 24 | Galt Professionals | St-Cup | 2 | 0 | 2 | 0 | 0 | 15 | 7.50 |
| 1909–10 | 24 | Berlin Professionals | St-Cup | 1 | 0 | 1 | 0 | 0 | 7 | 7.00 |
| 1914–15 | 29 | Vancouver Millionaires | St-Cup | 3 | 3 | 0 | 0 | 0 | 8 | 2.67 |
| 1917–18 | 32 | Vancouver Millionaires | PCHA | 2 | 1 | 0 | 1 | 1 | 2 | 1.00 |
| 1917–18 | 32 | Vancouver Millionaires | St-Cup | 5 | 2 | 3 | 0 | 0 | 18 | 3.60 |
| 1918–19 | 33 | Vancouver Millionaires | PCHA | 2 | 1 | 1 | 0 | 0 | 7 | 3.50 |
| 1919–20 | 34 | Vancouver Millionaires | PCHA | 2 | 1 | 1 | 0 | 0 | 7 | 3.50 |
| 1920–21 | 35 | Vancouver Millionaires | PCHA | 2 | 2 | 0 | 0 | 1 | 2 | 1.00 |
| 1920–21 | 35 | Vancouver Millionaires | St-Cup | 5 | 2 | 3 | 0 | 0 | 12 | 2.40 |
| 1921–22 | 36 | Vancouver Millionaires | PCHA | 2 | 2 | 0 | 0 | 2 | 0 | 0.00 |
| 1921–22 | 36 | Vancouver Millionaires | West-P | 2 | 1 | 1 | 0 | 1 | 2 | 1.00 |
| 1921–22 | 36 | Vancouver Millionaires | St-Cup | 5 | 2 | 3 | 0 | 1 | 16 | 3.15 |
| 1922–23 | 37 | Vancouver Maroons | PCHA | 2 | 1 | 1 | 0 | 1 | 3 | 1.50 |
| 1922–23 | 37 | Vancouver Maroons | St-Cup | 4 | 1 | 3 | 0 | 0 | 10 | 2.50 |
| 1923–24 | 38 | Vancouver Maroons | PCHA | 2 | 1 | 1 | 0 | 0 | 3 | 1.34 |
| 1923–24 | 38 | Vancouver Maroons | West-P | 3 | 1 | 2 | 0 | 0 | 10 | 3.33 |
| 1923–24 | 38 | Vancouver Maroons | St-Cup | 2 | 0 | 2 | 0 | 0 | 5 | 2.50 |
| 1926–27 | 41 | Chicago Black Hawks | NHL | 2 | 0 | 1 | 1 | 0 | 10 | 5.00 |
| Career — 10 Seasons | | | | 48 | 21 | 25 | 2 | 7 | 137 | 2.85 |

## Percy LeSueur  Profile: See page 346

**REGULAR SEASON**

| SEASON | AGE | TEAM | LG | GP | W | L | T | SO | GA | GAA |
|---|---|---|---|---|---|---|---|---|---|---|
| 1903–04 | 22 | Smiths Falls Seniors | OHA-Sr. | 6 | 3 | 3 | 0 | 2 | 13 | 2.11 |
| 1904–05 | 23 | Smiths Falls Seniors | OHA-Sr. | | | | | | | |
| 1905–06 | 24 | Smiths Falls Seniors | FAHL | 7 | 7 | 0 | 0 | 1 | 16 | 2.30 |
| 1906–07 | 25 | Ottawa Senators | ECAHA | 10 | 7 | 3 | 0 | 0 | 54 | 5.38 |
| 1907–08 | 26 | Ottawa Senators | ECAHA | 10 | 7 | 3 | 0 | 0 | 51 | 4.86 |
| 1908–09 | 27 | Ottawa Senators | ECHA | 12 | 10 | 2 | 0 | 0 | 63 | 5.19 |
| 1909–10 | 28 | Ottawa Senators | CHA | 2 | 2 | 0 | 0 | 0 | 9 | 4.50 |
| 1909–10 | 28 | Ottawa Senators | NHA | 12 | 9 | 3 | 0 | 0 | 66 | 5.42 |
| 1910–11 | 29 | Ottawa Senators | NHA | 16 | 13 | 3 | 0 | 1 | 69 | 4.18 |
| 1911–12 | 30 | Ottawa Senators | NHA | 18 | 9 | 9 | 0 | 0 | 91 | 4.85 |
| 1912–13 | 31 | Ottawa Senators | NHA | 18 | 7 | 10 | 0 | 0 | 65 | 4.18 |
| 1913–14 | 32 | Ottawa Senators | NHA | 13 | 6 | 6 | 0 | 1 | 42 | 3.26 |
| 1914–15 | 33 | Toronto Shamrocks | NHA | 19 | 8 | 11 | 0 | 0 | 96 | 5.03 |
| 1915–16 | 34 | Toronto Blueshirts | NHA | 23 | 9 | 13 | 0 | 1 | 92 | 3.90 |
| Career – 13 Seasons | | | | 166 | 97 | 66 | 0 | 6 | 729 | 4.39 |

**PLAYOFFS**

| SEASON | AGE | TEAM | LG | GP | W | L | T | SO | GA | GAA |
|---|---|---|---|---|---|---|---|---|---|---|
| 1905–06 | 24 | Smiths Falls Seniors | St-Cup | 2 | 0 | 2 | 0 | 0 | 14 | 7.00 |
| 1905–06 | 24 | Ottawa Silver Seven | St-Cup | 1 | 1 | 0 | 0 | 0 | 3 | 3.00 |
| 1909–10 | 28 | Ottawa Senators | St-Cup | 4 | 4 | 0 | 0 | 0 | 15 | 3.75 |
| 1910–11 | 29 | Ottawa Senators | St-Cup | 2 | 2 | 0 | 0 | 0 | 8 | 4.00 |
| Career – 3 Seasons | | | | 9 | 7 | 2 | 0 | 0 | 40 | 4.44 |

## Harry Lumley  Profile: See page 348

**REGULAR SEASON**

| SEASON | AGE | TEAM | LG | GP | W | L | T | SO | GA | GAA | G | A | PTS | PIM |
|---|---|---|---|---|---|---|---|---|---|---|---|---|---|---|
| 1943–44 | 17 | Detroit Red Wings | NHL | 2 | 0 | 2 | 0 | 0 | 13 | 6.50 | 0 | 0 | 0 | 0 |
| 1943–44 | 17 | New York Rangers | NHL | 1 | 0 | 0 | 0 | 0 | 0 | 0.00 | 0 | 0 | 0 | 0 |
| 1944–45 | 18 | Detroit Red Wings | NHL | 37 | 24 | 10 | 3 | 1 | 119 | 3.22 | 0 | 0 | 0 | 0 |
| 1945–46 | 19 | Detroit Red Wings | NHL | 50 | 20 | 20 | 10 | 2 | 159 | 3.18 | 0 | 0 | 0 | 6 |
| 1946–47 | 20 | Detroit Red Wings | NHL | 52 | 22 | 20 | 10 | 3 | 159 | 3.06 | 0 | 0 | 0 | 4 |
| 1947–48 | 21 | Detroit Red Wings | NHL | 60 | 30 | 18 | 12 | 7 | 147 | 2.46 | 0 | 0 | 0 | 8 |
| 1948–49 | 22 | Detroit Red Wings | NHL | 60 | 34 | 19 | 7 | 6 | 145 | 2.42 | 0 | 0 | 0 | 12 |
| 1949–50 | 23 | Detroit Red Wings | NHL | 63 | 33 | 16 | 14 | 7 | 148 | 2.35 | 0 | 0 | 0 | 10 |
| 1950–51 | 24 | Chicago Black Hawks | NHL | 64 | 12 | 41 | 10 | 3 | 245 | 3.88 | 0 | 0 | 0 | 4 |
| 1951–52 | 25 | Chicago Black Hawks | NHL | 70 | 17 | 44 | 9 | 2 | 237 | 3.40 | 0 | 0 | 0 | 2 |
| 1952–53 | 26 | Toronto Maple Leafs | NHL | 70 | 27 | 30 | 13 | 10 | 164 | 2.34 | 0 | 0 | 0 | 18 |
| 1953–54 | 27 | Toronto Maple Leafs | NHL | 69 | 32 | 24 | 13 | 13 | 128 | 1.86 | 0 | 0 | 0 | 6 |
| 1954–55 | 28 | Toronto Maple Leafs | NHL | 69 | 23 | 24 | 22 | 8 | 132 | 1.91 | 0 | 0 | 0 | 9 |
| 1955–56 | 29 | Toronto Maple Leafs | NHL | 59 | 21 | 28 | 10 | 3 | 157 | 2.67 | 0 | 0 | 0 | 2 |
| 1957–58 | 31 | Boston Bruins | NHL | 24 | 11 | 10 | 3 | 3 | 70 | 2.92 | 0 | 0 | 0 | 2 |
| 1958–59 | 32 | Boston Bruins | NHL | 11 | 8 | 2 | 1 | 1 | 27 | 2.45 | 0 | 0 | 0 | 0 |
| 1959–60 | 33 | Boston Bruins | NHL | 42 | 16 | 21 | 5 | 2 | 146 | 3.48 | 0 | 0 | 0 | 12 |
| NHL Career – 16 Seasons | | | | 803 | 330 | 329 | 142 | 71 | 2196 | 2.74 | 0 | 0 | 0 | 95 |

**PLAYOFFS**

| SEASON | AGE | TEAM | LG | GP | W | L | T | SO | GA | GAA | G | A | PTS | PIM |
|---|---|---|---|---|---|---|---|---|---|---|---|---|---|---|
| 1944–45 | 18 | Detroit Red Wings | NHL | 14 | 7 | 7 | | 2 | 31 | 2.13 | 0 | 0 | 0 | 0 |
| 1945–46 | 19 | Detroit Red Wings | NHL | 5 | 1 | 4 | | 1 | 16 | 3.10 | 0 | 0 | 0 | 0 |
| 1947–48 | 21 | Detroit Red Wings | NHL | 10 | 4 | 6 | | 0 | 30 | 3.00 | 0 | 0 | 0 | 10 |
| 1948–49 | 22 | Detroit Red Wings | NHL | 11 | 4 | 7 | | 0 | 26 | 2.15 | 0 | 0 | 0 | 2 |
| 1949–50 | 23 | Detroit Red Wings | NHL | 14 | 8 | 6 | | 3 | 28 | 1.85 | 0 | 0 | 0 | 0 |
| 1953–54 | 27 | Toronto Maple Leafs | NHL | 5 | 1 | 4 | | 0 | 14 | 2.62 | 0 | 0 | 0 | 0 |
| 1954–55 | 28 | Toronto Maple Leafs | NHL | 4 | 0 | 4 | | 0 | 13 | 3.26 | 0 | 0 | 0 | 0 |
| 1955–56 | 29 | Toronto Maple Leafs | NHL | 5 | 1 | 4 | | 1 | 13 | 2.57 | 0 | 0 | 0 | 2 |
| 1957–58 | 31 | Boston Bruins | NHL | 1 | 0 | 1 | | 0 | 5 | 5.00 | 0 | 0 | 0 | 0 |
| 1958–59 | 32 | Boston Bruins | NHL | 7 | 3 | 4 | | 0 | 20 | 2.75 | 0 | 0 | 0 | 4 |
| NHL Career – 10 Seasons | | | | 76 | 29 | 47 | | 7 | 196 | 2.46 | 0 | 0 | 0 | 18 |

## Paddy Moran   Profile: See page 349

### REGULAR SEASON

| SEASON | AGE | TEAM | LEAGUE | GP | W | L | T | SO | GA | GAA |
|---|---|---|---|---|---|---|---|---|---|---|
| 1901–02 | 24 | Quebec Athletics | CAHL | 8 | 4 | 4 | 0 | 0 | 34 | 4.25 |
| 1902–03 | 25 | Quebec Athletics | CAHL | 7 | 3 | 4 | 0 | 0 | 46 | 6.57 |
| 1903–04 | 26 | Quebec Athletics | CAHL | 6 | 5 | 1 | 0 | 0 | 37 | 6.17 |
| 1904–05 | 27 | Quebec Athletics | CAHL | 9 | 7 | 2 | 0 | 0 | 45 | 5.00 |
| 1905–06 | 28 | Quebec Bulldogs | ECAHA | 10 | 3 | 7 | 0 | 0 | 70 | 6.79 |
| 1906–07 | 29 | Quebec Bulldogs | ECAHA | 6 | 0 | 6 | 0 | 0 | 58 | 9.61 |
| 1907–08 | 30 | Quebec Bulldogs | ECAHA | 10 | 5 | 5 | 0 | 0 | 74 | 7.38 |
| 1908–09 | 31 | Quebec Bulldogs | ECHA | 12 | 3 | 9 | 0 | 0 | 106 | 8.83 |
| 1909–10 | 32 | All-Montreal | CHA | 4 | 2 | 2 | 0 | 0 | 24 | 6.00 |
| 1909–10 | 32 | Haileybury Comets | NHA | 11 | 3 | 8 | 0 | 0 | 80 | 7.22 |
| 1910–11 | 33 | Quebec Bulldogs | NHA | 16 | 4 | 12 | 0 | 0 | 97 | 5.92 |
| 1911–12 | 34 | Quebec Bulldogs | NHA | 18 | 10 | 8 | 0 | 0 | 78 | 4.26 |
| 1912–13 | 35 | Quebec Bulldogs | NHA | 20 | 16 | 4 | 0 | 1 | 75 | 3.70 |
| 1913–14 | 36 | Quebec Bulldogs | NHA | 20 | 12 | 8 | 0 | 1 | 73 | 3.58 |
| 1914–15 | 37 | Quebec Bulldogs | NHA | 20 | 11 | 9 | 0 | 0 | 85 | 3.91 |
| 1915–16 | 38 | Quebec Bulldogs | NHA | 22 | 10 | 10 | 0 | 0 | 82 | 3.54 |
| 1916–17 | 39 | Quebec Bulldogs | NHA | 7 | 1 | 5 | 0 | 0 | 35 | 6.84 |
| Career — 16 Seasons | | | | 206 | 99 | 104 | 0 | 2 | 1099 | 5.33 |

### PLAYOFFS

| SEASON | AGE | TEAM | LEAGUE | GP | W | L | T | SO | GA | GAA |
|---|---|---|---|---|---|---|---|---|---|---|
| 1911–12 | 34 | Quebec Bulldogs | St-Cup | 2 | 2 | 0 | 0 | 1 | 3 | 1.50 |
| 1912–13 | 35 | Quebec Bulldogs | St-Cup | 2 | 2 | 0 | 0 | 0 | 5 | 2.50 |
| Career — 2 Seasons | | | | 4 | 4 | 0 | 0 | 1 | 8 | 2.00 |

## Bernie Parent   Profile: See page 350

### REGULAR SEASON

| SEASON | AGE | TEAM | LG | GP | W | L | T | SO | GA | GAA | G | A | PTS | PIM |
|---|---|---|---|---|---|---|---|---|---|---|---|---|---|---|
| 1965–66 | 20 | Boston Bruins | NHL | 39 | 12 | 20 | 3 | 1 | 128 | 3.69 | 0 | 0 | 0 | 4 |
| 1966–67 | 21 | Boston Bruins | NHL | 18 | 4 | 12 | 2 | 0 | 62 | 3.65 | 0 | 0 | 0 | 2 |
| 1967–68 | 22 | Philadelphia Flyers | NHL | 38 | 15 | 17 | 5 | 4 | 93 | 2.49 | 0 | 1 | 1 | 23 |
| 1968–69 | 23 | Philadelphia Flyers | NHL | 58 | 17 | 23 | 16 | 1 | 151 | 2.70 | 0 | 0 | 0 | 4 |
| 1969–70 | 24 | Philadelphia Flyers | NHL | 62 | 13 | 29 | 20 | 3 | 171 | 2.80 | 0 | 3 | 3 | 14 |
| 1970–71 | 25 | Philadelphia Flyers | NHL | 30 | 9 | 12 | 6 | 2 | 73 | 2.77 | 0 | 2 | 2 | 5 |
| 1970–71 | 25 | Toronto Maple Leafs | NHL | 18 | 7 | 7 | 3 | 0 | 46 | 2.66 | 0 | 0 | 0 | 0 |
| 1971–72 | 26 | Toronto Maple Leafs | NHL | 47 | 17 | 18 | 9 | 3 | 116 | 2.57 | 0 | 1 | 1 | 6 |
| 1972–73 | 27 | Philadelphia Blazers | WHA | 63 | 33 | 28 | 0 | 2 | 220 | 3.61 | 0 | 1 | 1 | 36 |
| 1973–74 | 28 | Philadelphia Flyers | NHL | 73 | 47 | 13 | 12 | 12 | 136 | 1.89 | 0 | 3 | 3 | 24 |
| 1974–75 | 29 | Philadelphia Flyers | NHL | 68 | 44 | 14 | 9 | 12 | 137 | 2.04 | 0 | 0 | 0 | 16 |
| 1975–76 | 30 | Philadelphia Flyers | NHL | 11 | 6 | 2 | 2 | 0 | 24 | 2.35 | 0 | 0 | 0 | 2 |
| 1976–77 | 31 | Philadelphia Flyers | NHL | 61 | 35 | 13 | 12 | 5 | 159 | 2.71 | 0 | 0 | 0 | 0 |
| 1977–78 | 32 | Philadelphia Flyers | NHL | 49 | 29 | 6 | 13 | 7 | 108 | 2.22 | 0 | 0 | 0 | 4 |
| 1978–79 | 33 | Philadelphia Flyers | NHL | 36 | 16 | 12 | 7 | 4 | 89 | 2.71 | 0 | 2 | 2 | 8 |
| Career — 14 Seasons | | | | 671 | 304 | 226 | 119 | 56 | 1713 | 2.55 | 0 | 13 | 13 | 148 |

### PLAYOFFS

| SEASON | AGE | TEAM | LG | GP | W | L | T | SO | GA | GAA | G | A | PTS | PIM |
|---|---|---|---|---|---|---|---|---|---|---|---|---|---|---|
| 1967–68 | 22 | Philadelphia Flyers | NHL | 5 | 2 | 3 | | 0 | 8 | 1.36 | 0 | 0 | 0 | 0 |
| 1968–69 | 23 | Philadelphia Flyers | NHL | 3 | 0 | 3 | | 0 | 12 | 4.01 | 0 | 0 | 0 | 0 |
| 1970–71 | 25 | Toronto Maple Leafs | NHL | 4 | 2 | 2 | | 0 | 9 | 2.31 | 0 | 0 | 0 | 0 |
| 1971–72 | 26 | Toronto Maple Leafs | NHL | 4 | 1 | 3 | | 0 | 13 | 3.25 | 0 | 0 | 0 | 0 |
| 1972–73 | 27 | Philadelphia Blazers | WHA | 1 | 0 | 1 | | 0 | 3 | 2.57 | 0 | 0 | 0 | 0 |
| 1973–74 | 27 | Philadelphia Flyers | NHL | 17 | 12 | 5 | | 2 | 35 | 2.02 | 0 | 0 | 0 | 4 |
| 1974–75 | 29 | Philadelphia Flyers | NHL | 15 | 10 | 5 | | 4 | 29 | 1.89 | 0 | 0 | 0 | 0 |
| 1975–76 | 30 | Philadelphia Flyers | NHL | 8 | 4 | 4 | | 0 | 27 | 3.40 | 0 | 0 | 0 | 0 |
| 1976–77 | 31 | Philadelphia Flyers | NHL | 3 | 0 | 3 | | 0 | 8 | 3.95 | 0 | 0 | 0 | 0 |
| 1977–78 | 32 | Philadelphia Flyers | NHL | 12 | 7 | 5 | | 0 | 33 | 2.75 | 0 | 0 | 0 | 0 |
| Career — 10 Seasons | | | | 72 | 38 | 34 | | 6 | 177 | 2.46 | 0 | 0 | 0 | 4 |

# Jacques Plante   Profile: See page 352

## REGULAR SEASON

| SEASON | AGE | TEAM | LG | GP | W | L | T | SO | GA | GAA | G | A | PTS | PIM |
|---|---|---|---|---|---|---|---|---|---|---|---|---|---|---|
| 1952–53 | 24 | Montreal Canadiens | NHL | 3 | 2 | 0 | 1 | 0 | 4 | 1.33 | 0 | 0 | 0 | 0 |
| 1953–54 | 25 | Montreal Canadiens | NHL | 17 | 7 | 5 | 5 | 5 | 24 | 1.41 | 0 | 0 | 0 | 0 |
| 1954–55 | 26 | Montreal Canadiens | NHL | 52 | 33 | 12 | 7 | 5 | 109 | 2.12 | 0 | 0 | 0 | 2 |
| 1955–56 | 27 | Montreal Canadiens | NHL | 64 | 42 | 12 | 10 | 7 | 119 | 1.86 | 0 | 0 | 0 | 10 |
| 1956–57 | 28 | Montreal Canadiens | NHL | 61 | 31 | 18 | 12 | 9 | 122 | 2.00 | 0 | 0 | 0 | 16 |
| 1957–58 | 29 | Montreal Canadiens | NHL | 57 | 34 | 14 | 8 | 9 | 119 | 2.11 | 0 | 0 | 0 | 13 |
| 1958–59 | 30 | Montreal Canadiens | NHL | 67 | 38 | 16 | 13 | 9 | 144 | 2.16 | 0 | 1 | 1 | 11 |
| 1959–60 | 31 | Montreal Canadiens | NHL | 69 | 40 | 17 | 12 | 3 | 175 | 2.54 | 0 | 0 | 0 | 2 |
| 1960–61 | 32 | Montreal Canadiens | NHL | 40 | 23 | 11 | 6 | 2 | 112 | 2.80 | 0 | 0 | 0 | 2 |
| 1961–62 | 33 | Montreal Canadiens | NHL | 70 | 42 | 14 | 14 | 4 | 166 | 2.37 | 0 | 0 | 0 | 14 |
| 1962–63 | 34 | Montreal Canadiens | NHL | 56 | 22 | 14 | 19 | 5 | 138 | 2.49 | 0 | 1 | 1 | 2 |
| 1963–64 | 35 | New York Rangers | NHL | 65 | 22 | 36 | 7 | 3 | 220 | 3.39 | 0 | 1 | 1 | 6 |
| 1964–65 | 36 | New York Rangers | NHL | 33 | 10 | 17 | 5 | 2 | 109 | 3.38 | 0 | 1 | 1 | 6 |
| 1968–69 | 40 | St. Louis Blues | NHL | 37 | 18 | 12 | 6 | 5 | 70 | 1.96 | 0 | 0 | 0 | 2 |
| 1969–70 | 41 | St. Louis Blues | NHL | 32 | 18 | 9 | 5 | 5 | 67 | 2.19 | 0 | 2 | 2 | 0 |
| 1970–71 | 42 | Toronto Maple Leafs | NHL | 40 | 24 | 11 | 4 | 4 | 73 | 1.89 | 0 | 0 | 0 | 2 |
| 1971–72 | 43 | Toronto Maple Leafs | NHL | 34 | 16 | 13 | 5 | 2 | 86 | 2.63 | 0 | 0 | 0 | 2 |
| 1972–73 | 44 | Toronto Maple Leafs | NHL | 32 | 8 | 14 | 6 | 1 | 87 | 3.05 | 0 | 0 | 0 | 0 |
| 1972–73 | 44 | Boston Bruins | NHL | 8 | 7 | 1 | 0 | 2 | 16 | 2.00 | 0 | 2 | 2 | 2 |
| 1974–75 | 46 | Edmonton Oilers | WHA | 31 | 15 | 14 | 1 | 1 | 88 | 3.32 | 0 | 1 | 1 | 2 |
| Career – 19 Seasons | | | | 868 | 452 | 260 | 146 | 83 | 2048 | 2.38 | 0 | 9 | 9 | 94 |

## PLAYOFFS

| SEASON | AGE | TEAM | LG | GP | W | L | T | SO | GA | GAA | G | A | PTS | PIM |
|---|---|---|---|---|---|---|---|---|---|---|---|---|---|---|
| 1952–53 | 24 | Montreal Canadiens | NHL | 4 | 3 | 1 | | 1 | 7 | 1.75 | 0 | 0 | 0 | 0 |
| 1953–54 | 25 | Montreal Canadiens | NHL | 8 | 5 | 3 | | 2 | 14 | 1.75 | 0 | 0 | 0 | 0 |
| 1954–55 | 26 | Montreal Canadiens | NHL | 12 | 6 | 3 | | 0 | 29 | 2.72 | 0 | 0 | 0 | 0 |
| 1955–56 | 27 | Montreal Canadiens | NHL | 10 | 8 | 2 | | 2 | 18 | 1.80 | 0 | 0 | 0 | 2 |
| 1956–57 | 28 | Montreal Canadiens | NHL | 10 | 8 | 2 | | 1 | 17 | 1.66 | 0 | 0 | 0 | 4 |
| 1957–58 | 29 | Montreal Canadiens | NHL | 10 | 8 | 2 | | 1 | 20 | 1.94 | 0 | 0 | 0 | 2 |
| 1958–59 | 30 | Montreal Canadiens | NHL | 11 | 8 | 3 | | 0 | 26 | 2.33 | 0 | 0 | 0 | 0 |
| 1959–60 | 31 | Montreal Canadiens | NHL | 8 | 8 | 0 | | 3 | 11 | 1.35 | 0 | 0 | 0 | 0 |
| 1960–61 | 32 | Montreal Canadiens | NHL | 6 | 2 | 4 | | 0 | 16 | 2.33 | 0 | 0 | 0 | 2 |
| 1961–62 | 33 | Montreal Canadiens | NHL | 6 | 2 | 4 | | 0 | 19 | 3.17 | 0 | 0 | 0 | 0 |
| 1962–63 | 34 | Montreal Canadiens | NHL | 5 | 1 | 4 | | 0 | 14 | 2.80 | 0 | 0 | 0 | 0 |
| 1968–69 | 40 | St. Louis Blues | NHL | 10 | 8 | 2 | | 3 | 14 | 1.43 | 0 | 1 | 1 | 0 |
| 1969–70 | 41 | St. Louis Blues | NHL | 6 | 4 | 1 | | 1 | 8 | 1.49 | 0 | 0 | 0 | 2 |
| 1970–71 | 42 | Toronto Maple Leafs | NHL | 3 | 0 | 2 | | 0 | 7 | 3.16 | 0 | 0 | 0 | 0 |
| 1971–72 | 43 | Toronto Maple Leafs | NHL | 1 | 0 | 1 | | 0 | 5 | 5.00 | 0 | 0 | 0 | 0 |
| 1972–73 | 44 | Boston Bruins | NHL | 2 | 0 | 2 | | 0 | 10 | 5.00 | 0 | 0 | 0 | 0 |
| Career – 16 Seasons | | | | 112 | 71 | 36 | | 14 | 235 | 2.12 | 0 | 1 | 1 | 12 |

# Chuck Rayner   Profile: See page 354

## REGULAR SEASON

| SEASON | AGE | TEAM | LG | GP | W | L | T | SO | GA | GAA | G | A | PTS | PIM |
|---|---|---|---|---|---|---|---|---|---|---|---|---|---|---|
| 1940–41 | 20 | New York Americans | NHL | 12 | 2 | 7 | 3 | 0 | 44 | 3.42 | 0 | 0 | 0 | 0 |
| 1941–42 | 21 | Brooklyn Americans | NHL | 36 | 13 | 21 | 2 | 1 | 129 | 3.47 | 0 | 0 | 0 | 0 |
| 1945–46 | 25 | New York Rangers | NHL | 41 | 12 | 21 | 7 | 1 | 151 | 3.72 | 0 | 0 | 0 | 6 |
| 1946–47 | 26 | New York Rangers | NHL | 58 | 22 | 30 | 6 | 5 | 177 | 3.05 | 0 | 0 | 0 | 0 |
| 1947–48 | 27 | New York Rangers | NHL | 12 | 4 | 7 | 0 | 0 | 42 | 3.65 | 0 | 0 | 0 | 0 |
| 1948–49 | 28 | New York Rangers | NHL | 58 | 16 | 31 | 11 | 7 | 168 | 2.90 | 0 | 0 | 0 | 2 |
| 1949–50 | 29 | New York Rangers | NHL | 69 | 28 | 30 | 11 | 6 | 181 | 2.62 | 0 | 0 | 0 | 6 |
| 1950–51 | 30 | New York Rangers | NHL | 66 | 19 | 27 | 20 | 2 | 185 | 2.82 | 0 | 0 | 0 | 6 |
| 1951–52 | 31 | New York Rangers | NHL | 53 | 18 | 25 | 10 | 2 | 156 | 2.94 | 0 | 0 | 0 | 4 |
| 1952–53 | 32 | New York Rangers | NHL | 20 | 4 | 8 | 8 | 1 | 58 | 2.90 | 0 | 0 | 0 | 2 |
| NHL Career – 10 Seasons | | | | 425 | 138 | 207 | 78 | 25 | 1291 | 3.03 | 0 | 0 | 0 | 26 |

## PLAYOFFS

| SEASON | AGE | TEAM | LG | GP | W | L | T | SO | GA | GAA | G | A | PTS | PIM |
|---|---|---|---|---|---|---|---|---|---|---|---|---|---|---|
| 1947–48 | 27 | New York Rangers | NHL | 6 | 2 | 4 | | 0 | 17 | 2.83 | 0 | 0 | 0 | 0 |
| 1949–50 | 29 | New York Rangers | NHL | 12 | 7 | 5 | | 1 | 29 | 2.25 | 0 | 0 | 0 | 0 |
| NHL Career – 2 Seasons | | | | 18 | 9 | 9 | | 1 | 46 | 2.43 | 0 | 0 | 0 | 0 |

# Patrick Roy   Profile: See page 356

## REGULAR SEASON

| SEASON | AGE | TEAM | LG | GP | W | L | T | SO | GA | GAA | G | A | PTS | PIM |
|--------|-----|------|----|----|---|---|---|----|----|-----|---|---|-----|-----|
| 1984–85 | 19 | Montreal Canadiens | NHL | 1 | 1 | 0 | 0 | 0 | 0 | 0.00 | 0 | 0 | 0 | 0 |
| 1985–86 | 20 | Montreal Canadiens | NHL | 47 | 23 | 18 | 3 | 1 | 148 | 3.36 | 0 | 3 | 3 | 4 |
| 1986–87 | 21 | Montreal Canadiens | NHL | 46 | 22 | 16 | 6 | 1 | 131 | 2.94 | 0 | 1 | 1 | 8 |
| 1987–88 | 22 | Montreal Canadiens | NHL | 45 | 23 | 12 | 9 | 3 | 125 | 2.90 | 0 | 2 | 2 | 14 |
| 1988–89 | 23 | Montreal Canadiens | NHL | 48 | 33 | 5 | 6 | 4 | 113 | 2.47 | 0 | 6 | 6 | 2 |
| 1989–90 | 24 | Montreal Canadiens | NHL | 54 | 31 | 16 | 5 | 3 | 134 | 2.53 | 0 | 5 | 5 | 0 |
| 1990–91 | 25 | Montreal Canadiens | NHL | 48 | 25 | 15 | 6 | 1 | 128 | 2.71 | 0 | 2 | 2 | 6 |
| 1991–92 | 26 | Montreal Canadiens | NHL | 67 | 36 | 22 | 8 | 5 | 155 | 2.36 | 0 | 5 | 5 | 4 |
| 1992–93 | 27 | Montreal Canadiens | NHL | 62 | 31 | 25 | 5 | 2 | 192 | 3.20 | 0 | 2 | 2 | 16 |
| 1993–94 | 28 | Montreal Canadiens | NHL | 68 | 35 | 17 | 11 | 7 | 161 | 2.50 | 0 | 1 | 1 | 30 |
| 1994–95 | 29 | Montreal Canadiens | NHL | 43 | 17 | 20 | 6 | 1 | 127 | 2.97 | 0 | 1 | 1 | 20 |
| 1995–96 | 30 | Montreal Canadiens | NHL | 22 | 12 | 9 | 1 | 1 | 62 | 2.95 | 0 | 0 | 0 | 6 |
| 1995–96 | 30 | Colorado Avalanche | NHL | 39 | 22 | 15 | 1 | 1 | 103 | 2.68 | 0 | 0 | 0 | 4 |
| 1996–97 | 31 | Colorado Avalanche | NHL | 62 | 38 | 15 | 7 | 7 | 143 | 2.32 | 0 | 1 | 1 | 15 |
| 1997–98 | 32 | Colorado Avalanche | NHL | 65 | 31 | 19 | 13 | 4 | 153 | 2.39 | 0 | 3 | 3 | 39 |
| 1998–99 | 33 | Colorado Avalanche | NHL | 61 | 32 | 19 | 8 | 5 | 139 | 2.29 | 0 | 2 | 2 | 28 |
| 1999–00 | 34 | Colorado Avalanche | NHL | 63 | 32 | 21 | 8 | 2 | 141 | 2.28 | 0 | 3 | 3 | 10 |
| 2000–01 | 35 | Colorado Avalanche | NHL | 62 | 40 | 13 | 7 | 4 | 132 | 2.21 | 0 | 5 | 5 | 10 |
| 2001–02 | 36 | Colorado Avalanche | NHL | 63 | 32 | 23 | 8 | 9 | 122 | 1.94 | 0 | 3 | 3 | 26 |
| 2002–03 | 37 | Colorado Avalanche | NHL | 63 | 35 | 15 | 13 | 5 | 137 | 2.18 | 0 | 0 | 0 | 20 |
| NHL Career — 19 Seasons | | | | 1029 | 551 | 315 | 131 | 66 | 2546 | 2.54 | 0 | 45 | 45 | 262 |

## PLAYOFFS

| SEASON | AGE | TEAM | LG | GP | W | L | T | SO | GA | GAA | G | A | PTS | PIM |
|--------|-----|------|----|----|---|---|---|----|----|-----|---|---|-----|-----|
| 1985–86 | 20 | Montreal Canadiens | NHL | 20 | 15 | 5 | | 1 | 39 | 1.93 | 0 | 0 | 0 | 10 |
| 1986–87 | 21 | Montreal Canadiens | NHL | 6 | 4 | 2 | | 0 | 22 | 4.00 | 0 | 0 | 0 | 0 |
| 1987–88 | 22 | Montreal Canadiens | NHL | 8 | 3 | 4 | | 0 | 24 | 3.36 | 0 | 0 | 0 | 0 |
| 1988–89 | 23 | Montreal Canadiens | NHL | 19 | 13 | 6 | | 2 | 42 | 2.09 | 0 | 2 | 2 | 16 |
| 1989–90 | 24 | Montreal Canadiens | NHL | 11 | 5 | 6 | | 1 | 26 | 2.43 | 0 | 1 | 1 | 0 |
| 1990–91 | 25 | Montreal Canadiens | NHL | 13 | 7 | 5 | | 0 | 40 | 3.06 | 0 | 0 | 0 | 2 |
| 1991–92 | 26 | Montreal Canadiens | NHL | 11 | 4 | 7 | | 1 | 30 | 2.63 | 0 | 0 | 0 | 2 |
| 1992–93 | 27 | Montreal Canadiens | NHL | 20 | 16 | 4 | | 0 | 46 | 2.13 | 0 | 1 | 1 | 4 |
| 1993–94 | 28 | Montreal Canadiens | NHL | 6 | 3 | 3 | | 0 | 16 | 2.56 | 0 | 0 | 0 | 0 |
| 1995–96 | 30 | Colorado Avalanche | NHL | 22 | 16 | 6 | | 3 | 51 | 2.10 | 0 | 0 | 0 | 0 |
| 1996–97 | 31 | Colorado Avalanche | NHL | 17 | 10 | 7 | | 3 | 38 | 2.21 | 0 | 0 | 0 | 12 |
| 1997–98 | 32 | Colorado Avalanche | NHL | 7 | 3 | 4 | | 0 | 18 | 2.51 | 0 | 1 | 1 | 0 |
| 1998–99 | 33 | Colorado Avalanche | NHL | 19 | 11 | 8 | | 1 | 52 | 2.66 | 0 | 2 | 2 | 4 |
| 1999–00 | 34 | Colorado Avalanche | NHL | 17 | 11 | 6 | | 3 | 31 | 1.79 | 0 | 1 | 1 | 4 |
| 2000–01 | 35 | Colorado Avalanche | NHL | 23 | 16 | 7 | | 4 | 41 | 1.70 | 0 | 1 | 1 | 0 |
| 2001–02 | 36 | Colorado Avalanche | NHL | 21 | 11 | 10 | | 3 | 52 | 2.51 | 0 | 2 | 2 | 0 |
| 2002–03 | 37 | Colorado Avalanche | NHL | 7 | 3 | 4 | | 1 | 16 | 2.27 | 0 | 0 | 0 | 0 |
| NHL Career — 17 Seasons | | | | 247 | 151 | 94 | | 23 | 584 | 2.30 | 0 | 11 | 11 | 54 |

# Terry Sawchuk   Profile: See page 358

## REGULAR SEASON

| SEASON | AGE | TEAM | LG | GP | W | L | T | SO | GA | GAA | G | A | PTS | PIM |
|--------|-----|------|----|----|---|---|---|----|----|-----|---|---|-----|-----|
| 1949–50 | 20 | Detroit Red Wings | NHL | 7 | 4 | 3 | 0 | 1 | 16 | 2.29 | 0 | 0 | 0 | 2 |
| 1950–51 | 21 | Detroit Red Wings | NHL | 70 | 44 | 13 | 13 | 11 | 138 | 1.97 | 0 | 0 | 0 | 2 |
| 1951–52 | 22 | Detroit Red Wings | NHL | 70 | 44 | 14 | 12 | 12 | 133 | 1.90 | 0 | 0 | 0 | 2 |
| 1952–53 | 23 | Detroit Red Wings | NHL | 63 | 32 | 15 | 16 | 9 | 119 | 1.89 | 0 | 0 | 0 | 5 |
| 1953–54 | 24 | Detroit Red Wings | NHL | 67 | 35 | 19 | 13 | 12 | 129 | 1.93 | 0 | 1 | 1 | 31 |
| 1954–55 | 25 | Detroit Red Wings | NHL | 68 | 40 | 17 | 11 | 12 | 132 | 1.96 | 0 | 1 | 1 | 10 |
| 1955–56 | 26 | Boston Bruins | NHL | 68 | 22 | 33 | 13 | 9 | 177 | 2.60 | 0 | 0 | 0 | 20 |
| 1956–57 | 27 | Boston Bruins | NHL | 34 | 18 | 10 | 6 | 2 | 81 | 2.38 | 0 | 0 | 0 | 14 |
| 1957–58 | 28 | Detroit Red Wings | NHL | 70 | 29 | 29 | 12 | 3 | 206 | 2.94 | 0 | 0 | 0 | 39 |
| 1958–59 | 29 | Detroit Red Wings | NHL | 67 | 23 | 36 | 8 | 5 | 207 | 3.09 | 0 | 0 | 0 | 12 |
| 1959–60 | 30 | Detroit Red Wings | NHL | 58 | 24 | 20 | 14 | 5 | 154 | 2.66 | 0 | 0 | 0 | 22 |
| 1960–61 | 31 | Detroit Red Wings | NHL | 37 | 11 | 17 | 8 | 2 | 112 | 3.13 | 0 | 1 | 1 | 8 |
| 1961–62 | 32 | Detroit Red Wings | NHL | 43 | 14 | 21 | 8 | 5 | 141 | 3.28 | 0 | 0 | 0 | 12 |
| 1962–63 | 33 | Detroit Red Wings | NHL | 48 | 21 | 16 | 7 | 3 | 117 | 2.54 | 0 | 0 | 0 | 14 |
| 1963–64 | 34 | Detroit Red Wings | NHL | 53 | 25 | 20 | 7 | 5 | 138 | 2.64 | 0 | 0 | 0 | 0 |
| 1964–65 | 35 | Toronto Maple Leafs | NHL | 36 | 16 | 13 | 7 | 1 | 92 | 2.56 | 0 | 2 | 2 | 24 |
| 1965–66 | 36 | Toronto Maple Leafs | NHL | 27 | 10 | 11 | 3 | 1 | 80 | 3.16 | 0 | 1 | 1 | 12 |
| 1966–67 | 37 | Toronto Maple Leafs | NHL | 28 | 16 | 6 | 3 | 2 | 66 | 2.81 | 0 | 0 | 0 | 0 |
| 1967–68 | 38 | Los Angeles Kings | NHL | 36 | 10 | 17 | 5 | 2 | 99 | 3.07 | 0 | 0 | 0 | 0 |
| 1968–69 | 39 | Detroit Red Wings | NHL | 13 | 4 | 5 | 3 | 0 | 28 | 2.62 | 0 | 0 | 0 | 0 |
| 1969–70 | 40 | New York Rangers | NHL | 8 | 3 | 1 | 2 | 1 | 20 | 2.63 | 0 | 1 | 1 | 0 |
| NHL Career — 21 Seasons | | | | 971 | 445 | 336 | 171 | 103 | 2385 | 2.50 | 0 | 7 | 7 | 229 |

## Terry Sawchuk (continued)

### PLAYOFFS

| SEASON | AGE | TEAM | LG | GP | W | L | T | SO | GA | GAA | G | A | PTS | PIM |
|---|---|---|---|---|---|---|---|---|---|---|---|---|---|---|
| 1950–51 | 21 | Detroit Red Wings | NHL | 6 | 2 | 4 | | 1 | 13 | 1.68 | 0 | 0 | 0 | 0 |
| 1951–52 | 22 | Detroit Red Wings | NHL | 8 | 8 | 0 | | 4 | 5 | 0.63 | 0 | 0 | 0 | 0 |
| 1952–53 | 23 | Detroit Red Wings | NHL | 6 | 2 | 4 | | 1 | 21 | 3.38 | 0 | 0 | 0 | 10 |
| 1953–54 | 24 | Detroit Red Wings | NHL | 12 | 8 | 4 | | 2 | 20 | 1.60 | 0 | 0 | 0 | 2 |
| 1954–55 | 25 | Detroit Red Wings | NHL | 11 | 8 | 3 | | 1 | 26 | 2.36 | 0 | 0 | 0 | 12 |
| 1957–58 | 28 | Detroit Red Wings | NHL | 4 | 0 | 4 | | 0 | 19 | 4.53 | 0 | 0 | 0 | 0 |
| 1959–60 | 30 | Detroit Red Wings | NHL | 6 | 2 | 4 | | 0 | 19 | 2.82 | 0 | 0 | 0 | 0 |
| 1960–61 | 31 | Detroit Red Wings | NHL | 8 | 5 | 3 | | 1 | 18 | 2.32 | 0 | 0 | 0 | 0 |
| 1962–63 | 33 | Detroit Red Wings | NHL | 11 | 5 | 6 | | 0 | 35 | 3.18 | 0 | 0 | 0 | 0 |
| 1963–64 | 34 | Detroit Red Wings | NHL | 13 | 6 | 5 | | 1 | 31 | 2.75 | 0 | 0 | 0 | 2 |
| 1964–65 | 35 | Toronto Maple Leafs | NHL | 1 | 0 | 1 | | 0 | 3 | 3.00 | 0 | 0 | 0 | 0 |
| 1965–66 | 36 | Toronto Maple Leafs | NHL | 2 | 0 | 2 | | 0 | 6 | 3.00 | 0 | 0 | 0 | 0 |
| 1966–67 | 37 | Toronto Maple Leafs | NHL | 10 | 6 | 4 | | 0 | 25 | 2.66 | 0 | 0 | 0 | 0 |
| 1967–68 | 38 | Los Angeles Kings | NHL | 5 | 2 | 3 | | 1 | 18 | 3.86 | 0 | 0 | 0 | 0 |
| 1969–70 | 40 | New York Rangers | NHL | 3 | 0 | 1 | | 0 | 6 | 4.51 | 0 | 0 | 0 | 0 |
| NHL Career – 15 Seasons | | | | 106 | 54 | 48 | | 12 | 265 | 2.53 | 0 | 0 | 0 | 26 |

## Billy Smith   Profile: See page 360

### REGULAR SEASON

| SEASON | AGE | TEAM | LG | GP | W | L | T | SO | GA | GAA | G | A | PTS | PIM |
|---|---|---|---|---|---|---|---|---|---|---|---|---|---|---|
| 1971–72 | 21 | Los Angeles Kings | NHL | 5 | 1 | 3 | 1 | 0 | 23 | 4.60 | 0 | 0 | 0 | 5 |
| 1972–73 | 22 | New York Islanders | NHL | 37 | 7 | 24 | 3 | 0 | 147 | 4.16 | 0 | 0 | 0 | 42 |
| 1973–74 | 23 | New York Islanders | NHL | 46 | 9 | 23 | 12 | 0 | 134 | 3.08 | 0 | 0 | 0 | 11 |
| 1974–75 | 24 | New York Islanders | NHL | 58 | 21 | 18 | 17 | 3 | 156 | 2.78 | 0 | 0 | 0 | 21 |
| 1975–76 | 25 | New York Islanders | NHL | 39 | 19 | 10 | 9 | 3 | 98 | 2.62 | 0 | 1 | 1 | 10 |
| 1976–77 | 26 | New York Islanders | NHL | 36 | 21 | 8 | 6 | 2 | 87 | 2.50 | 0 | 1 | 1 | 12 |
| 1977–78 | 27 | New York Islanders | NHL | 38 | 20 | 8 | 8 | 2 | 95 | 2.65 | 0 | 0 | 0 | 35 |
| 1978–79 | 28 | New York Islanders | NHL | 39 | 25 | 8 | 4 | 1 | 108 | 2.87 | 0 | 2 | 2 | 54 |
| 1979–80 | 29 | New York Islanders | NHL | 38 | 15 | 14 | 7 | 2 | 104 | 2.96 | 1 | 0 | 1 | 39 |
| 1980–81 | 30 | New York Islanders | NHL | 41 | 22 | 10 | 8 | 2 | 129 | 3.28 | 0 | 0 | 0 | 33 |
| 1981–82 | 31 | New York Islanders | NHL | 46 | 32 | 9 | 4 | 0 | 133 | 2.97 | 0 | 1 | 1 | 24 |
| 1982–83 | 32 | New York Islanders | NHL | 41 | 18 | 14 | 7 | 1 | 112 | 2.87 | 0 | 0 | 0 | 41 |
| 1983–84 | 33 | New York Islanders | NHL | 42 | 23 | 13 | 2 | 2 | 130 | 3.43 | 0 | 2 | 2 | 23 |
| 1984–85 | 34 | New York Islanders | NHL | 37 | 18 | 14 | 3 | 0 | 133 | 3.83 | 0 | 0 | 0 | 25 |
| 1985–86 | 35 | New York Islanders | NHL | 41 | 20 | 14 | 4 | 1 | 143 | 3.73 | 0 | 3 | 3 | 49 |
| 1986–87 | 36 | New York Islanders | NHL | 40 | 14 | 18 | 5 | 1 | 132 | 3.53 | 0 | 2 | 2 | 37 |
| 1987–88 | 37 | New York Islanders | NHL | 38 | 17 | 14 | 5 | 2 | 113 | 3.22 | 0 | 0 | 0 | 20 |
| 1988–89 | 38 | New York Islanders | NHL | 17 | 3 | 11 | 0 | 0 | 54 | 4.44 | 0 | 0 | 0 | 8 |
| NHL Career – 18 Seasons | | | | 679 | 305 | 233 | 105 | 22 | 2031 | 3.18 | 1 | 12 | 13 | 489 |

### PLAYOFFS

| SEASON | AGE | TEAM | LG | GP | W | L | T | SO | GA | GAA | G | A | PTS | PIM |
|---|---|---|---|---|---|---|---|---|---|---|---|---|---|---|
| 1974–75 | 24 | New York Islanders | NHL | 6 | 1 | 4 | | 0 | 23 | 4.16 | 0 | 0 | 0 | 6 |
| 1975–76 | 25 | New York Islanders | NHL | 8 | 4 | 3 | | 0 | 21 | 2.89 | 0 | 0 | 0 | 11 |
| 1976–77 | 26 | New York Islanders | NHL | 10 | 7 | 3 | | 0 | 27 | 2.80 | 0 | 0 | 0 | 8 |
| 1977–78 | 27 | New York Islanders | NHL | 1 | 0 | 0 | | 0 | 1 | 1.27 | 0 | 0 | 0 | 9 |
| 1978–79 | 28 | New York Islanders | NHL | 5 | 4 | 1 | | 1 | 10 | 1.93 | 0 | 0 | 0 | 4 |
| 1979–80 | 29 | New York Islanders | NHL | 20 | 15 | 4 | | 1 | 54 | 2.70 | 0 | 0 | 0 | 11 |
| 1980–81 | 30 | New York Islanders | NHL | 17 | 14 | 3 | | 0 | 42 | 2.54 | 0 | 1 | 1 | 2 |
| 1981–82 | 31 | New York Islanders | NHL | 18 | 15 | 3 | | 1 | 47 | 2.51 | 0 | 0 | 0 | 6 |
| 1982–83 | 32 | New York Islanders | NHL | 17 | 13 | 3 | | 2 | 43 | 2.69 | 0 | 1 | 1 | 9 |
| 1983–84 | 33 | New York Islanders | NHL | 21 | 12 | 8 | | 0 | 54 | 2.73 | 0 | 0 | 0 | 17 |
| 1984–85 | 34 | New York Islanders | NHL | 6 | 3 | 3 | | 0 | 19 | 3.33 | 0 | 0 | 0 | 6 |
| 1985–86 | 35 | New York Islanders | NHL | 1 | 0 | 1 | | 0 | 4 | 4.06 | 0 | 0 | 0 | 0 |
| 1986–87 | 36 | New York Islanders | NHL | 2 | 0 | 0 | | 0 | 1 | 0.90 | 0 | 0 | 0 | 0 |
| NHL Career – 13 Seasons | | | | 132 | 88 | 36 | | 5 | 346 | 2.72 | 0 | 2 | 2 | 89 |

# Tiny Thompson   Profile: See page 361

## REGULAR SEASON

| SEASON | AGE | TEAM | LG | GP | W | L | T | SO | GA | GAA | G | A | PTS | PIM |
|---|---|---|---|---|---|---|---|---|---|---|---|---|---|---|
| 1928–29 | 25 | Boston Bruins | NHL | 44 | 26 | 13 | 5 | 12 | 52 | 1.15 | 0 | 0 | 0 | 0 |
| 1929–30 | 26 | Boston Bruins | NHL | 44 | 38 | 5 | 1 | 3 | 98 | 2.19 | 0 | 0 | 0 | 0 |
| 1930–31 | 27 | Boston Bruins | NHL | 44 | 28 | 10 | 6 | 3 | 90 | 1.98 | 0 | 0 | 0 | 0 |
| 1931–32 | 28 | Boston Bruins | NHL | 43 | 13 | 19 | 11 | 9 | 103 | 2.29 | 0 | 0 | 0 | 0 |
| 1932–33 | 29 | Boston Bruins | NHL | 48 | 25 | 15 | 8 | 11 | 88 | 1.76 | 0 | 0 | 0 | 0 |
| 1933–34 | 30 | Boston Bruins | NHL | 48 | 18 | 25 | 5 | 5 | 128 | 2.58 | 0 | 0 | 0 | 0 |
| 1934–35 | 31 | Boston Bruins | NHL | 48 | 26 | 16 | 6 | 8 | 112 | 2.26 | 0 | 0 | 0 | 0 |
| 1935–36 | 32 | Boston Bruins | NHL | 48 | 22 | 20 | 6 | 10 | 82 | 1.68 | 0 | 1 | 1 | 0 |
| 1936–37 | 33 | Boston Bruins | NHL | 48 | 23 | 18 | 7 | 6 | 110 | 2.22 | 0 | 0 | 0 | 0 |
| 1937–38 | 34 | Boston Bruins | NHL | 48 | 30 | 11 | 7 | 7 | 89 | 1.80 | 0 | 0 | 0 | 0 |
| 1938–39 | 35 | Boston Bruins | NHL | 5 | 3 | 1 | 1 | 0 | 8 | 1.55 | 0 | 0 | 0 | 0 |
| 1938–39 | 35 | Detroit Red Wings | NHL | 39 | 16 | 17 | 6 | 4 | 100 | 2.50 | 0 | 0 | 0 | 0 |
| 1939–40 | 36 | Detroit Red Wings | NHL | 46 | 16 | 24 | 6 | 3 | 120 | 2.54 | 0 | 0 | 0 | 0 |
| NHL Career—12 Seasons | | | | 553 | 284 | 194 | 75 | 81 | 1180 | 2.07 | 0 | 1 | 1 | 0 |

## PLAYOFFS

| SEASON | AGE | TEAM | LG | GP | W | L | T | SO | GA | GAA | G | A | PTS | PIM |
|---|---|---|---|---|---|---|---|---|---|---|---|---|---|---|
| 1928–29 | 25 | Boston Bruins | NHL | 5 | 5 | 0 | 0 | 3 | 3 | 0.60 | 0 | 0 | 0 | 0 |
| 1929–30 | 26 | Boston Bruins | NHL | 6 | 3 | 3 | 0 | 0 | 12 | 1.67 | 0 | 0 | 0 | 0 |
| 1930–31 | 27 | Boston Bruins | NHL | 5 | 2 | 3 | 0 | 0 | 13 | 2.27 | 0 | 0 | 0 | 0 |
| 1932–33 | 29 | Boston Bruins | NHL | 5 | 2 | 3 | 0 | 0 | 9 | 1.23 | 0 | 0 | 0 | 0 |
| 1934–35 | 31 | Boston Bruins | NHL | 4 | 1 | 3 | 0 | 1 | 7 | 1.53 | 0 | 0 | 0 | 0 |
| 1935–36 | 32 | Boston Bruins | NHL | 2 | 1 | 1 | 0 | 1 | 8 | 4.00 | 0 | 0 | 0 | 0 |
| 1936–37 | 33 | Boston Bruins | NHL | 3 | 1 | 2 | | 1 | 8 | 2.67 | 0 | 0 | 0 | 0 |
| 1937–38 | 34 | Boston Bruins | NHL | 3 | 0 | 3 | | 0 | 6 | 1.70 | 0 | 0 | 0 | 0 |
| 1938–39 | 35 | Detroit Red Wings | NHL | 6 | 3 | 3 | | 1 | 15 | 2.41 | 0 | 0 | 0 | 0 |
| 1939–40 | 36 | Detroit Red Wings | NHL | 5 | 2 | 3 | | 0 | 12 | 2.40 | 0 | 0 | 0 | 0 |
| NHL Career—10 Seasons | | | | 44 | 20 | 24 | 0 | 7 | 93 | 1.88 | 0 | 0 | 0 | 0 |

# Vladislav Tretiak   Profile: See page 362

## REGULAR SEASON

| SEASON | AGE | TEAM | LG | GP | W | L | T | SO | GA | GAA |
|---|---|---|---|---|---|---|---|---|---|---|
| 1968–69 | 16 | CSKA Moscow | USSR | 3 | | | | | 2 | 0.67 |
| 1969–70 | 17 | CSKA Moscow | USSR | 34 | | | | | 76 | 2.24 |
| 1970–71 | 18 | CSKA Moscow | USSR | 40 | | | | | 81 | 2.03 |
| 1971–72 | 19 | CSKA Moscow | USSR | 30 | | | | | 78 | 2.60 |
| 1972–73 | 20 | CSKA Moscow | USSR | 30 | | | | | 80 | 2.67 |
| 1973–74 | 21 | CSKA Moscow | USSR | 27 | | | | | 94 | 3.48 |
| 1974–75 | 22 | CSKA Moscow | USSR | 35 | | | | | 104 | 2.97 |
| 1975–76 | 23 | CSKA Moscow | USSR | 33 | | | | | 100 | 3.03 |
| 1976–77 | 24 | CSKA Moscow | USSR | 35 | | | | | 98 | 2.80 |
| 1977–78 | 25 | CSKA Moscow | USSR | 29 | | | | | 72 | 2.48 |
| 1978–79 | 26 | CSKA Moscow | USSR | 40 | | | | | 111 | 2.78 |
| 1979–80 | 27 | CSKA Moscow | USSR | 36 | | | | | 85 | 2.36 |
| 1980–81 | 28 | CSKA Moscow | USSR | 18 | | | | | 32 | 1.78 |
| 1981–82 | 29 | CSKA Moscow | USSR | 41 | 34 | 4 | 3 | 6 | 65 | 1.59 |
| 1982–83 | 30 | CSKA Moscow | USSR | 29 | 25 | 3 | 1 | 6 | 40 | 1.38 |
| 1983–84 | 31 | CSKA Moscow | USSR | 22 | 22 | 0 | 0 | 4 | 40 | 1.82 |
| Career—16 Seasons | | | | 482 | 81 | 7 | 4 | 16 | 1158 | 2.40 |

## Rogie Vachon   Profile: See page 364

### REGULAR SEASON

| SEASON | AGE | TEAM | LG | GP | W | L | T | SO | GA | GAA | G | A | PTS | PIM |
|---|---|---|---|---|---|---|---|---|---|---|---|---|---|---|
| 1966–67 | 21 | Montreal Canadiens | NHL | 19 | 11 | 3 | 5 | 1 | 47 | 2.48 | 0 | 1 | 1 | 0 |
| 1967–68 | 22 | Montreal Canadiens | NHL | 39 | 21 | 15 | 2 | 4 | 92 | 2.48 | 0 | 0 | 0 | 2 |
| 1968–69 | 23 | Montreal Canadiens | NHL | 36 | 22 | 9 | 3 | 2 | 98 | 2.87 | 0 | 0 | 0 | 2 |
| 1969–70 | 24 | Montreal Canadiens | NHL | 64 | 31 | 18 | 12 | 4 | 162 | 2.64 | 0 | 0 | 0 | 0 |
| 1970–71 | 25 | Montreal Canadiens | NHL | 47 | 23 | 12 | 9 | 2 | 118 | 2.65 | 0 | 0 | 0 | 0 |
| 1971–72 | 26 | Montreal Canadiens | NHL | 1 | 0 | 1 | 0 | 0 | 4 | 12.00 | 0 | 0 | 0 | 0 |
| 1971–72 | 26 | Los Angeles Kings | NHL | 28 | 6 | 18 | 3 | 0 | 107 | 4.05 | 0 | 0 | 0 | 0 |
| 1972–73 | 27 | Los Angeles Kings | NHL | 53 | 22 | 20 | 10 | 4 | 148 | 2.85 | 0 | 1 | 1 | 2 |
| 1973–74 | 28 | Los Angeles Kings | NHL | 65 | 28 | 26 | 10 | 5 | 175 | 2.81 | 0 | 0 | 0 | 6 |
| 1974–75 | 29 | Los Angeles Kings | NHL | 54 | 27 | 14 | 13 | 6 | 121 | 2.24 | 0 | 1 | 1 | 2 |
| 1975–76 | 30 | Los Angeles Kings | NHL | 51 | 26 | 20 | 5 | 5 | 160 | 3.15 | 0 | 0 | 0 | 0 |
| 1976–77 | 31 | Los Angeles Kings | NHL | 68 | 33 | 23 | 12 | 8 | 184 | 2.73 | 0 | 1 | 1 | 2 |
| 1977–78 | 32 | Los Angeles Kings | NHL | 70 | 29 | 27 | 13 | 4 | 196 | 2.87 | 0 | 0 | 0 | 2 |
| 1978–79 | 33 | Detroit Red Wings | NHL | 50 | 10 | 27 | 11 | 0 | 189 | 3.91 | 0 | 1 | 1 | 21 |
| 1979–80 | 34 | Detroit Red Wings | NHL | 59 | 20 | 30 | 8 | 4 | 209 | 3.62 | 0 | 3 | 3 | 2 |
| 1980–81 | 35 | Boston Bruins | NHL | 53 | 25 | 19 | 6 | 1 | 168 | 3.34 | 0 | 1 | 1 | 6 |
| 1981–82 | 36 | Boston Bruins | NHL | 38 | 19 | 11 | 6 | 1 | 132 | 3.66 | 0 | 1 | 1 | 0 |
| Career – 16 Seasons | | | | 795 | 353 | 293 | 128 | 51 | 2310 | 3.00 | 0 | 10 | 10 | 47 |

### PLAYOFFS

| SEASON | AGE | TEAM | LG | GP | W | L | T | SO | GA | GAA | G | A | PTS | PIM |
|---|---|---|---|---|---|---|---|---|---|---|---|---|---|---|
| 1966–67 | 21 | Montreal Canadiens | NHL | 9 | 6 | 3 | | 0 | 22 | 2.38 | 0 | 0 | 0 | 0 |
| 1967–68 | 22 | Montreal Canadiens | NHL | 2 | 1 | 1 | | 0 | 4 | 2.12 | 0 | 0 | 0 | 0 |
| 1968–69 | 23 | Montreal Canadiens | NHL | 8 | 7 | 1 | | 1 | 12 | 1.42 | 0 | 0 | 0 | 2 |
| 1973–74 | 28 | Los Angeles Kings | NHL | 4 | 0 | 4 | | 0 | 7 | 1.77 | 0 | 0 | 0 | 0 |
| 1974–75 | 29 | Los Angeles Kings | NHL | 3 | 1 | 2 | | 0 | 7 | 2.12 | 0 | 0 | 0 | 0 |
| 1975–76 | 30 | Los Angeles Kings | NHL | 7 | 4 | 3 | | 1 | 17 | 2.33 | 0 | 0 | 0 | 0 |
| 1976–77 | 31 | Los Angeles Kings | NHL | 9 | 4 | 5 | | 0 | 36 | 4.17 | 0 | 0 | 0 | 0 |
| 1977–78 | 32 | Los Angeles Kings | NHL | 2 | 0 | 2 | | 0 | 11 | 5.50 | 0 | 0 | 0 | 2 |
| 1980–81 | 35 | Boston Bruins | NHL | 3 | 0 | 2 | | 0 | 16 | 5.88 | 0 | 0 | 0 | 0 |
| 1981–82 | 36 | Boston Bruins | NHL | 1 | 0 | 0 | | 0 | 1 | 3.00 | 0 | 0 | 0 | 0 |
| Career – 8 Seasons | | | | 48 | 23 | 23 | | 2 | 133 | 2.78 | 0 | 0 | 0 | 4 |

## Georges Vezina   Profile: See page 366

### REGULAR SEASON

| SEASON | AGE | TEAM | LG | GP | W | L | T | SO | GA | GAA | G | A | PTS | PIM |
|---|---|---|---|---|---|---|---|---|---|---|---|---|---|---|
| 1910–11 | 24 | Montreal Canadiens | NHA | 16 | 8 | 8 | 0 | 0 | 62 | 3.80 | | | | |
| 1911–12 | 25 | Montreal Canadiens | NHA | 18 | 8 | 10 | 0 | 0 | 66 | 3.57 | | | | |
| 1912–13 | 26 | Montreal Canadiens | NHA | 20 | 11 | 9 | 0 | 1 | 81 | 3.99 | | | | |
| 1913–14 | 27 | Montreal Canadiens | NHA | 20 | 13 | 7 | 0 | 1 | 64 | 3.14 | | | | |
| 1914–15 | 28 | Montreal Canadiens | NHA | 20 | 6 | 14 | 0 | 0 | 81 | 3.87 | | | | |
| 1915–16 | 29 | Montreal Canadiens | NHA | 24 | 16 | 7 | 1 | 0 | 76 | 3.08 | | | | |
| 1916–17 | 30 | Montreal Canadiens | NHA | 20 | 10 | 10 | 0 | 0 | 80 | 3.94 | | | | |
| 1917–18 | 31 | Montreal Canadiens | NHL | 21 | 12 | 9 | 0 | 1 | 84 | 3.93 | 0 | 0 | 0 | 0 |
| 1918–19 | 32 | Montreal Canadiens | NHL | 18 | 10 | 8 | 0 | 1 | 78 | 4.27 | 0 | 1 | 1 | 0 |
| 1919–20 | 33 | Montreal Canadiens | NHL | 24 | 13 | 11 | 0 | 0 | 113 | 4.66 | 0 | 0 | 0 | 0 |
| 1920–21 | 34 | Montreal Canadiens | NHL | 24 | 13 | 11 | 0 | 1 | 99 | 4.12 | 0 | 0 | 0 | 0 |
| 1921–22 | 35 | Montreal Canadiens | NHL | 24 | 12 | 11 | 1 | 0 | 94 | 3.84 | 0 | 0 | 0 | 2 |
| 1922–23 | 36 | Montreal Canadiens | NHL | 24 | 13 | 9 | 2 | 2 | 61 | 2.46 | 0 | 0 | 0 | 0 |
| 1923–24 | 37 | Montreal Canadiens | NHL | 24 | 13 | 11 | 0 | 3 | 48 | 1.97 | 0 | 0 | 0 | 0 |
| 1924–25 | 38 | Montreal Canadiens | NHL | 30 | 17 | 11 | 2 | 5 | 56 | 1.81 | 0 | 0 | 0 | 0 |
| 1925–26 | 39 | Montreal Canadiens | NHL | 1 | 0 | 0 | 0 | 0 | 0 | 0.00 | 0 | 0 | 0 | 0 |
| Career – 16 Seasons | | | | 328 | 175 | 146 | 6 | 15 | 1143 | 3.48 | 0 | 1 | 1 | 2 |

### PLAYOFFS

| SEASON | AGE | TEAM | LG | GP | W | L | T | SO | GA | GAA | G | A | PTS | PIM |
|---|---|---|---|---|---|---|---|---|---|---|---|---|---|---|
| 1913–14 | 27 | Montreal Canadiens | NHA | 2 | 1 | 1 | 0 | 1 | 6 | 3.00 | | | | |
| 1915–16 | 29 | Montreal Canadiens | St-Cup | 5 | 3 | 2 | 0 | 0 | 13 | 2.60 | | | | |
| 1916–17 | 30 | Montreal Canadiens | NHA | 2 | 1 | 1 | 0 | 0 | 6 | 3.00 | | | | |
| 1916–17 | 30 | Montreal Canadiens | St-Cup | 4 | 1 | 3 | 0 | 0 | 23 | 5.75 | | | | |
| 1917–18 | 31 | Montreal Canadiens | NHL | 2 | 1 | 1 | 0 | 0 | 10 | 5.00 | 0 | 0 | 0 | 0 |
| 1918–19 | 32 | Montreal Canadiens | NHL | 5 | 2 | 2 | 1 | 1 | 19 | 3.39 | | | | |
| 1918–19 | 32 | Montreal Canadiens | St-Cup | 5 | 4 | 1 | 0 | 0 | 18 | 3.60 | 0 | 0 | 0 | 0 |
| 1922–23 | 36 | Montreal Canadiens | NHL | 2 | 1 | 1 | 0 | 0 | 3 | 1.50 | 0 | 0 | 0 | 0 |
| 1923–24 | 37 | Montreal Canadiens | St-Cup | 4 | 4 | 0 | 0 | 1 | 4 | 1.00 | | | | |
| 1923–24 | 37 | Montreal Canadiens | NHL | 2 | 2 | 0 | 0 | 1 | 2 | 1.00 | 0 | 0 | 0 | 0 |
| 1924–25 | 38 | Montreal Canadiens | St-Cup | 4 | 1 | 3 | 0 | 0 | 16 | 4.00 | | | | |
| 1924–25 | 38 | Montreal Canadiens | NHL | 2 | 2 | 0 | 0 | 1 | 2 | 1.00 | 0 | 0 | 0 | 0 |
| Career – 8 Seasons | | | | 39 | 23 | 15 | 1 | 5 | 122 | 3.13 | 0 | 0 | 0 | 0 |

# Gump Worsley  Profile: See page 368

## REGULAR SEASON

| SEASON | AGE | TEAM | LG | GP | W | L | T | SO | GA | GAA | G | A | PTS | PIM |
|---|---|---|---|---|---|---|---|---|---|---|---|---|---|---|
| 1952–53 | 23 | New York Rangers | NHL | 50 | 13 | 29 | 8 | 2 | 151 | 3.02 | 0 | 0 | 0 | 2 |
| 1954–55 | 25 | New York Rangers | NHL | 65 | 15 | 33 | 17 | 4 | 195 | 3.00 | 0 | 0 | 0 | 2 |
| 1955–56 | 26 | New York Rangers | NHL | 70 | 32 | 28 | 10 | 4 | 198 | 2.83 | 0 | 0 | 0 | 2 |
| 1956–57 | 27 | New York Rangers | NHL | 68 | 26 | 28 | 14 | 3 | 216 | 3.18 | 0 | 0 | 0 | 19 |
| 1957–58 | 28 | New York Rangers | NHL | 37 | 21 | 10 | 6 | 4 | 86 | 2.32 | 0 | 0 | 0 | 10 |
| 1958–59 | 29 | New York Rangers | NHL | 66 | 26 | 29 | 11 | 2 | 193 | 2.94 | 0 | 0 | 0 | 10 |
| 1959–60 | 30 | New York Rangers | NHL | 39 | 7 | 23 | 8 | 0 | 135 | 3.52 | 0 | 0 | 0 | 12 |
| 1960–61 | 31 | New York Rangers | NHL | 59 | 20 | 29 | 8 | 1 | 190 | 3.29 | 0 | 0 | 0 | 10 |
| 1961–62 | 32 | New York Rangers | NHL | 60 | 22 | 27 | 9 | 2 | 172 | 2.92 | 0 | 0 | 0 | 12 |
| 1962–63 | 33 | New York Rangers | NHL | 67 | 22 | 34 | 10 | 2 | 217 | 3.27 | 0 | 0 | 0 | 14 |
| 1963–64 | 34 | Montreal Canadiens | NHL | 8 | 3 | 2 | 2 | 1 | 22 | 2.98 | 0 | 0 | 0 | 0 |
| 1964–65 | 35 | Montreal Canadiens | NHL | 19 | 10 | 7 | 1 | 1 | 50 | 2.78 | 0 | 0 | 0 | 0 |
| 1965–66 | 36 | Montreal Canadiens | NHL | 51 | 28 | 13 | 6 | 2 | 114 | 2.36 | 0 | 1 | 1 | 4 |
| 1966–67 | 37 | Montreal Canadiens | NHL | 18 | 6 | 6 | 1 | 1 | 47 | 3.18 | 0 | 0 | 0 | 4 |
| 1967–68 | 38 | Montreal Canadiens | NHL | 40 | 21 | 7 | 8 | 6 | 73 | 1.98 | 0 | 0 | 0 | 10 |
| 1968–69 | 39 | Montreal Canadiens | NHL | 30 | 19 | 5 | 4 | 5 | 64 | 2.26 | 0 | 0 | 0 | 0 |
| 1969–70 | 40 | Montreal Canadiens | NHL | 6 | 3 | 1 | 2 | 0 | 14 | 2.33 | 0 | 0 | 0 | 0 |
| 1969–70 | 40 | Minnesota North Stars | NHL | 8 | 5 | 1 | 1 | 1 | 20 | 2.65 | 0 | 0 | 0 | 0 |
| 1970–71 | 41 | Minnesota North Stars | NHL | 24 | 4 | 10 | 8 | 0 | 57 | 2.50 | 0 | 0 | 0 | 10 |
| 1971–72 | 42 | Minnesota North Stars | NHL | 34 | 16 | 10 | 7 | 2 | 68 | 2.12 | 0 | 1 | 1 | 2 |
| 1972–73 | 43 | Minnesota North Stars | NHL | 12 | 6 | 2 | 3 | 0 | 30 | 2.88 | 0 | 1 | 1 | 22 |
| 1973–74 | 44 | Minnesota North Stars | NHL | 29 | 8 | 14 | 5 | 0 | 86 | 3.22 | 0 | 0 | 0 | 0 |
| NHL Career — 21 Seasons | | | | 860 | 333 | 348 | 149 | 43 | 2398 | 2.87 | 0 | 3 | 3 | 145 |

## PLAYOFFS

| SEASON | AGE | TEAM | LG | GP | W | L | T | SO | GA | GAA | G | A | PTS | PIM |
|---|---|---|---|---|---|---|---|---|---|---|---|---|---|---|
| 1955–56 | 26 | New York Rangers | NHL | 3 | 1 | 3 | | 0 | 14 | 4.67 | 0 | 0 | 0 | 2 |
| 1956–57 | 27 | New York Rangers | NHL | 5 | 1 | 4 | | 0 | 21 | 4.01 | 0 | 0 | 0 | 0 |
| 1957–58 | 28 | New York Rangers | NHL | 6 | 2 | 4 | | 0 | 28 | 4.61 | 0 | 0 | 0 | 0 |
| 1961–62 | 32 | New York Rangers | NHL | 6 | 2 | 4 | | 0 | 21 | 3.28 | 0 | 0 | 0 | 0 |
| 1964–65 | 35 | Montreal Canadiens | NHL | 8 | 5 | 3 | | 2 | 14 | 1.68 | 0 | 0 | 0 | 0 |
| 1965–66 | 36 | Montreal Canadiens | NHL | 10 | 8 | 2 | | 1 | 20 | 1.99 | 0 | 0 | 0 | 0 |
| 1966–67 | 37 | Montreal Canadiens | NHL | 2 | 0 | 1 | | 0 | 2 | 1.50 | 0 | 0 | 0 | 0 |
| 1967–68 | 38 | Montreal Canadiens | NHL | 12 | 11 | 0 | | 1 | 21 | 1.88 | 0 | 0 | 0 | 10 |
| 1968–69 | 39 | Montreal Canadiens | NHL | 7 | 5 | 1 | | 0 | 14 | 2.27 | 0 | 0 | 0 | 5 |
| 1969–70 | 40 | Minnesota North Stars | NHL | 3 | 1 | 2 | | 0 | 14 | 4.67 | 0 | 0 | 0 | 0 |
| 1970–71 | 41 | Minnesota North Stars | NHL | 4 | 3 | 1 | | 0 | 13 | 3.25 | 0 | 0 | 0 | 0 |
| 1971–72 | 42 | Minnesota North Stars | NHL | 4 | 2 | 1 | | 1 | 7 | 2.16 | 0 | 0 | 0 | 0 |
| NHL Career — 12 Seasons | | | | 70 | 40 | 26 | | 5 | 189 | 2.78 | 0 | 0 | 0 | 17 |

# Roy Worters  Profile: See page 369

## REGULAR SEASON

| SEASON | AGE | TEAM | LG | GP | W | L | T | SO | GA | GAA | G | A | PTS | PIM |
|---|---|---|---|---|---|---|---|---|---|---|---|---|---|---|
| 1925–26 | 25 | Pittsburgh Pirates | NHL | 35 | 18 | 16 | 1 | 7 | 68 | 1.90 | 0 | 0 | 0 | 0 |
| 1926–27 | 26 | Pittsburgh Pirates | NHL | 44 | 15 | 26 | 3 | 4 | 108 | 2.39 | 0 | 0 | 0 | 0 |
| 1927–28 | 27 | Pittsburgh Pirates | NHL | 44 | 19 | 17 | 8 | 11 | 76 | 1.66 | 0 | 0 | 0 | 0 |
| 1928–29 | 28 | New York Americans | NHL | 38 | 16 | 12 | 10 | 13 | 46 | 1.15 | 0 | 0 | 0 | 0 |
| 1929–30 | 29 | New York Americans | NHL | 36 | 11 | 21 | 4 | 2 | 135 | 3.57 | 0 | 0 | 0 | 0 |
| 1929–30 | 29 | Montreal Canadiens | NHL | 1 | 1 | 0 | 0 | 0 | 2 | 2.00 | 0 | 0 | 0 | 0 |
| 1930–31 | 30 | New York Americans | NHL | 44 | 18 | 16 | 10 | 8 | 74 | 1.61 | 0 | 0 | 0 | 0 |
| 1931–32 | 31 | New York Americans | NHL | 40 | 12 | 20 | 8 | 5 | 110 | 2.68 | 0 | 0 | 0 | 0 |
| 1932–33 | 32 | New York Americans | NHL | 47 | 15 | 22 | 10 | 5 | 116 | 2.34 | 0 | 0 | 0 | 0 |
| 1933–34 | 33 | New York Americans | NHL | 36 | 12 | 14 | 9 | 4 | 75 | 2.01 | 0 | 0 | 0 | 0 |
| 1934–35 | 34 | New York Americans | NHL | 48 | 12 | 27 | 9 | 3 | 142 | 2.84 | 0 | 0 | 0 | 0 |
| 1935–36 | 35 | New York Americans | NHL | 48 | 16 | 25 | 7 | 3 | 122 | 2.44 | 0 | 0 | 0 | 0 |
| 1936–37 | 36 | New York Americans | NHL | 23 | 6 | 14 | 3 | 2 | 69 | 2.90 | 0 | 0 | 0 | 0 |
| NHL Career — 12 Seasons | | | | 484 | 171 | 230 | 82 | 67 | 1143 | 2.27 | 0 | 0 | 0 | 0 |

## PLAYOFFS

| SEASON | AGE | TEAM | LG | GP | W | L | T | SO | GA | GAA | G | A | PTS | PIM |
|---|---|---|---|---|---|---|---|---|---|---|---|---|---|---|
| 1925–26 | 25 | Pittsburgh Pirates | NHL | 2 | 0 | 1 | 1 | 0 | 6 | 3.00 | 0 | 0 | 0 | 0 |
| 1927–28 | 27 | Pittsburgh Pirates | NHL | 2 | 1 | 1 | 0 | 0 | 6 | 3.00 | 0 | 0 | 0 | 0 |
| 1928–29 | 28 | New York Americans | NHL | 2 | 0 | 1 | 1 | 1 | 1 | 0.40 | 0 | 0 | 0 | 0 |
| 1925–36 | 35 | New York Americans | NHL | 5 | 2 | 3 | 0 | 2 | 11 | 2.20 | 0 | 0 | 0 | 0 |
| NHL Career — 4 Seasons | | | | 11 | 3 | 6 | 2 | 3 | 24 | 2.09 | 0 | 0 | 0 | 0 |

## Hobey Baker  Profile: See page 372

REGULAR SEASON

| SEASON | AGE | TEAM | LG | GP | G | A | PTS | PIM |
|---|---|---|---|---|---|---|---|---|
| 1906–07 | 15 | St. Paul's School | High-NH | | | | | |
| 1907–08 | 16 | St. Paul's School | High-NH | | | | | |
| 1908–09 | 17 | St. Paul's School | High-NH | | | | | |
| 1909–10 | 18 | St. Paul's School | High-NH | | | | | |
| 1910–11 | 19 | Princeton University Tigers | Ivy | | | | | |
| 1911–12 | 20 | Princeton University Tigers | Ivy | | | | | |
| 1912–13 | 21 | Princeton University Tigers | Ivy | | | | | |
| 1913–14 | 22 | Princeton University Tigers | Ivy | 11 | 12 | 0 | 12 | 2 |

REGULAR SEASON

| SEASON | AGE | TEAM | LG | GP | G | A | PTS | PIM |
|---|---|---|---|---|---|---|---|---|
| 1914–15 | 23 | New York St. Nicholas | AAHL | 8 | 17 | 0 | 17 | |
| 1915–16 | 24 | New York St. Nicholas | AAHL | 7 | 9 | 0 | 9 | |
| Career — 10 Seasons | | | | 26 | 38 | 0 | 38 | 2 |

PLAYOFFS

| SEASON | AGE | TEAM | LG | GP | G | A | PTS | PIM |
|---|---|---|---|---|---|---|---|---|
| 1915–16 | 24 | New York St. Nicholas | AAHL | 3 | 1 | 0 | 1 | |
| Career — 1 Season | | | | 3 | 1 | 0 | 1 | |

## Dubbie Bowie  Profile: See page 374

REGULAR SEASON

| SEASON | AGE | TEAM | LG | GP | G | A | PTS | PIM |
|---|---|---|---|---|---|---|---|---|
| 1898–99 | 18 | Montreal Victorias | CAHL | 7 | 11 | 0 | 11 | |
| 1899–00 | 19 | Montreal Victorias | CAHL | 7 | 15 | 0 | 15 | |
| 1900–01 | 20 | Montreal Victorias | CAHL | 7 | 24 | 0 | 24 | |
| 1901–02 | 21 | Montreal Victorias | CAHL | 7 | 13 | 0 | 13 | |
| 1902–03 | 22 | Montreal Victorias | CAHL | 7 | 22 | 0 | 22 | |
| 1903–04 | 23 | Montreal Victorias | CAHL | 8 | 27 | 0 | 27 | |
| 1904–05 | 24 | Montreal Victorias | CAHL | 8 | 27 | 0 | 27 | 9 |
| 1905–06 | 25 | Montreal Victorias | ECAHA | 9 | 30 | 0 | 30 | 8 |
| 1906–07 | 26 | Montreal Victorias | ECAHA | 10 | 39 | 0 | 39 | 13 |
| 1907–08 | 27 | Montreal Victorias | ECAHA | 10 | 31 | 0 | 31 | 19 |

REGULAR SEASON

| SEASON | AGE | TEAM | LG | GP | G | A | PTS | PIM |
|---|---|---|---|---|---|---|---|---|
| 1908–09 | 28 | Montreal Victorias | IPAHU | 5 | 21 | 0 | 21 | 19 |
| 1909–10 | 29 | Montreal Victorias | IPAHU | 3 | 6 | 0 | 6 | 0 |
| Career — 12 Seasons | | | | 88 | 266 | 0 | 266 | 68 |

PLAYOFFS

| SEASON | AGE | TEAM | LG | GP | G | A | PTS | PIM |
|---|---|---|---|---|---|---|---|---|
| 1898–99 | 18 | Montreal Victorias | St-Cup | 2 | 1 | 0 | 1 | |
| 1902–03 | 22 | Montreal Victorias | CAHL | 2 | 0 | 0 | 0 | 3 |
| 1909–10 | 29 | Montreal Victorias | IPAHU | 2 | 5 | 0 | 5 | 8 |
| Career — 3 Seasons | | | | 6 | 6 | 0 | 6 | 11 |

## Graham Drinkwater  Profile: See page 376

REGULAR SEASON

| SEASON | AGE | TEAM | LG | GP | G | A | PTS |
|---|---|---|---|---|---|---|---|
| 1892–93 | 17 | Montreal Victorias | AHAC | 3 | 1 | 0 | 1 |
| 1894–95 | 19 | Montreal Victorias | AHAC | 8 | 9 | 0 | 9 |
| 1895–96 | 20 | Montreal Victorias | AHAC | 8 | 7 | 0 | 7 |
| 1896–97 | 21 | Montreal Victorias | AHAC | 4 | 3 | 0 | 3 |
| 1897–98 | 22 | Montreal Victorias | AHAC | 8 | 10 | 0 | 10 |
| 1898–99 | 23 | Montreal Victorias | CAHL | 6 | 0 | 0 | 0 |
| Career — 6 Seasons | | | | 37 | 30 | 0 | 30 |

PLAYOFFS

| SEASON | AGE | TEAM | LG | GP | G | A | PTS |
|---|---|---|---|---|---|---|---|
| 1895–96 | 20 | Montreal Victorias | St-Cup | 1 | 1 | 0 | 1 |
| 1896–97 | 21 | Montreal Victorias | St-Cup | 1 | 0 | 0 | 0 |
| 1898–99 | 23 | Montreal Victorias | St-Cup | 2 | 1 | 0 | 1 |
| Career — 3 Seasons | | | | 4 | 2 | 0 | 2 |

## Tommy Dunderdale  Profile: See page 377

REGULAR SEASON

| SEASON | AGE | TEAM | LG | GP | G | A | PTS | PIM |
|---|---|---|---|---|---|---|---|---|
| 1906–07 | 19 | Winnipeg Strathconas | MHL-Pro | 10 | 8 | 0 | 8 | |
| 1907–08 | 20 | Winnipeg Maple Leafs | MHL-Pro | 3 | 1 | 0 | 1 | 3 |
| 1907–08 | 20 | Strathcona-Alberta | MHL-Pro | 5 | 11 | 1 | 12 | 17 |
| 1908–09 | 21 | Winnipeg Shamrocks | MHL-Pro | 9 | 17 | 7 | 24 | 9 |
| 1909–10 | 22 | Montreal Shamrocks | CHA | 3 | 7 | 0 | 7 | 5 |
| 1909–10 | 22 | Montreal Shamrocks | NHA | 12 | 14 | 0 | 14 | 19 |
| 1910–11 | 23 | Quebec Bulldogs | NHA | 9 | 13 | 0 | 13 | 25 |
| 1911–12 | 24 | Victoria Aristocrats | PCHA | 16 | 24 | 0 | 24 | 25 |
| 1912–13 | 25 | Victoria Aristocrats | PCHA | 15 | 24 | 5 | 29 | 36 |
| 1913–14 | 26 | Victoria Aristocrats | PCHA | 16 | 24 | 4 | 28 | 34 |
| 1914–15 | 27 | Victoria Aristocrats | PCHA | 17 | 17 | 10 | 27 | 22 |
| 1915–16 | 28 | Portland Rosebuds | PCHA | 18 | 14 | 3 | 17 | 45 |
| 1916–17 | 29 | Portland Rosebuds | PCHA | 24 | 22 | 4 | 26 | 141 |
| 1917–18 | 30 | Portland Rosebuds | PCHA | 18 | 14 | 6 | 20 | 57 |
| 1918–19 | 31 | Victoria Aristocrats | PCHA | 20 | 5 | 4 | 9 | 28 |

REGULAR SEASON

| SEASON | AGE | TEAM | LG | GP | G | A | PTS | PIM |
|---|---|---|---|---|---|---|---|---|
| 1919–20 | 32 | Victoria Aristocrats | PCHA | 22 | 26 | 7 | 33 | 35 |
| 1920–21 | 33 | Victoria Aristocrats | PCHA | 24 | 9 | 11 | 20 | 18 |
| 1921–22 | 34 | Victoria Cougars | PCHA | 24 | 13 | 6 | 19 | 37 |
| 1922–23 | 35 | Victoria Cougars | PCHA | 27 | 2 | 0 | 2 | 16 |
| 1923–24 | 36 | Saskatoon Crescents | WCHL | 6 | 1 | 0 | 1 | 4 |
| 1923–24 | 36 | Edmonton Eskimos | WCHL | 11 | 1 | 1 | 2 | 5 |
| Career — 18 Seasons | | | | 314 | 249 | 69 | 318 | 581 |

PLAYOFFS

| SEASON | | TEAM | LG | GP | G | A | PTS | PIM |
|---|---|---|---|---|---|---|---|---|
| 1907–08 | | Strathcona-Alberta | MHL-Pro | 3 | 6 | 1 | 7 | 3 |
| 1908–09 | | Winnipeg Shamrocks | MHL-Pro | 3 | 3 | 0 | 3 | 6 |
| 1913–14 | | Victoria Aristocrats | St-Cup | 3 | 2 | 0 | 2 | 11 |
| 1915–16 | | Portland Rosebuds | St-Cup | 5 | 1 | 1 | 2 | 9 |
| 1922–23 | | Victoria Cougars | PCHA | 2 | 0 | 1 | 1 | 0 |
| Career — 3 Seasons | | | | 16 | 12 | 3 | 15 | 29 |

## Arthur Farrell  Profile: See page 378

REGULAR SEASON

| SEASON | AGE | TEAM | LG | GP | G | A | PTS | PIM |
|---|---|---|---|---|---|---|---|---|
| 1896–97 | 19 | Montreal Shamrocks | AHAC | 2 | 2 | 0 | 2 | |
| 1897–98 | 20 | Berlin Hockey Club | OHA | 2 | 6 | 0 | 6 | |
| 1898–99 | 21 | Montreal Shamrocks | CAHL | 8 | 8 | 0 | 8 | |
| 1899–00 | 22 | Montreal Shamrocks | CAHL | 7 | 13 | 0 | 13 | |
| 1900–01 | 23 | Montreal Shamrocks | CAHL | 8 | 10 | 0 | 10 | |
| Career — 5 Seasons | | | | 27 | 39 | 0 | 39 | |

PLAYOFFS

| SEASON | AGE | TEAM | LG | GP | G | A | PTS | PIM |
|---|---|---|---|---|---|---|---|---|
| 1898–99 | 21 | Montreal Shamrocks | St-Cup | 1 | 2 | 0 | 2 | 0 |
| 1899–00 | 22 | Montreal Shamrocks | St-Cup | 5 | 10 | 0 | 10 | 0 |
| 1900–01 | 23 | Montreal Shamrocks | St-Cup | 2 | 1 | 0 | 1 | 0 |
| Career — 3 Seasons | | | | 8 | 13 | 0 | 13 | |

# Tom Hooper  Profile: See page 379

### REGULAR SEASON

| SEASON | AGE | TEAM | LG | GP | G | A | PTS | PIM |
|---|---|---|---|---|---|---|---|---|
| 1901–02 | 18 | Rat Portage Thistles | MNWHA-Int | 8 | 9 | 0 | 9 | 17 |
| 1902–03 | 19 | Rat Portage Thistles | MNWHA | 5 | 5 | 1 | 6 | |
| 1903–04 | 20 | Rat Portage Thistles | MNWHA | 10 | 2 | 1 | 3 | |
| 1904–05 | 21 | Rat Portage Thistles | MHL | 8 | 9 | 0 | 9 | |
| 1905–06 | 22 | Kenora Thistles | MHL | 9 | 4 | 0 | 4 | |
| 1906–07 | 23 | Kenora Thistles | MHL-Pro | 3 | 4 | 0 | 4 | |
| 1907–08 | 24 | Montreal AAA | ECAHA | 7 | 9 | 0 | 9 | 5 |
| 1907–08 | 24 | Pembroke Lumber Kings | UOVHL | 1 | 0 | 0 | 0 | 0 |
| 1907–08 | 24 | Montreal Wanderers | ECAHA | 2 | 1 | 0 | 1 | 0 |
| Career – 7 Seasons | | | | 53 | 43 | 2 | 45 | 22 |

### PLAYOFFS

| SEASON | AGE | TEAM | LG | GP | G | A | PTS | PIM |
|---|---|---|---|---|---|---|---|---|
| 1902–03 | 19 | Rat Portage Thistles | St-Cup | 2 | 0 | 0 | 0 | 0 |
| 1904–05 | 21 | Rat Portage Thistles | St-Cup | 3 | 2 | 0 | 2 | 12 |
| 1906–07 | 23 | Kenora Thistles | MHL-Pro | 2 | 0 | 0 | 0 | 11 |
| 1906–07 | 23 | Kenora Thistles | St-Cup | 3 | 3 | 0 | 3 | 0 |
| 1907–08 | 24 | Montreal Wanderers | St-Cup | 2 | 0 | 0 | 0 | 3 |
| Career – 4 Seasons | | | | 12 | 5 | 0 | 5 | 26 |

# Fred Maxwell  Profile: See page 380

### REGULAR SEASON

| SEASON | AGE | TEAM | LG | GP | G | A | PTS | PIM |
|---|---|---|---|---|---|---|---|---|
| 1909–10 | 19 | Winnipeg Winnipegs | MHL-Sr. | 1 | 0 | 0 | 0 | 0 |
| 1910–11 | 20 | Winnipeg Monarchs | MHL-Sr. | 5 | 6 | 0 | 6 | |
| 1911–12 | 21 | Winnipeg Monarchs | MHL-Sr. | 8 | 7 | 0 | 7 | |
| 1912–13 | 22 | Winnipeg Monarchs | MHL-Sr. | 8 | 2 | 0 | 2 | |
| 1913–14 | 23 | Winnipeg Monarchs | MHL-Sr. | 8 | 3 | 2 | 5 | 6 |
| 1914–15 | 24 | Winnipeg Monarchs | WSrHL | 7 | 3 | 2 | 5 | 22 |
| Career – 6 Seasons | | | | 37 | 21 | 4 | 25 | 28 |

### PLAYOFFS

| SEASON | AGE | TEAM | LG | GP | G | A | PTS | PIM |
|---|---|---|---|---|---|---|---|---|
| 1913–14 | 23 | Winnipeg Monarchs | Al-Cup | 2 | 1 | 0 | 1 | 6 |
| 1914–15 | 24 | Winnipeg Monarchs | WSrHL | 1 | 1 | 0 | 1 | 6 |
| Career – 2 Seasons | | | | 3 | 2 | 0 | 2 | 12 |

# Frank Rankin  Profile: See page 381

### REGULAR SEASON

| SEASON | AGE | TEAM | LG | GP | G | A | PTS | PIM |
|---|---|---|---|---|---|---|---|---|
| 1904–05 | 13 | Stratford Hockey Club | OHA-Sr | | | | | |
| 1905–06 | 14 | Stratford Hockey Club | OHA-Sr | | | | | |
| 1906–07 | 15 | Stratford Hockey Club | OHA-Sr | | | | | |
| 1907–08 | 16 | Stratford Hockey Club | OHA-Sr | | | | | |
| 1908–09 | 17 | Stratford Hockey Club | OHA-Sr | | | | | |
| 1909–10 | 18 | Stratford Hockey Club | Exhib. | 2 | 4 | 0 | 4 | |
| 1910–11 | 19 | Toronto Eaton's | OHA-Sr. | 4 | 15 | 0 | 15 | |
| 1911–12 | 20 | Toronto Eaton's | OHA-Sr. | 6 | 6 | 0 | 6 | |
| 1912–13 | 21 | Toronto St. Michael's | OHA-Sr. | 5 | 22 | 0 | 22 | |

| SEASON | AGE | TEAM | LG | GP | G | A | PTS | PIM |
|---|---|---|---|---|---|---|---|---|
| 1913–14 | 22 | Toronto St. Michael's | OHA-Sr. | 2 | 10 | 0 | 10 | |
| Career – 10 Seasons | | | | 19 | 57 | 0 | 57 | |

### PLAYOFFS

| SEASON | AGE | TEAM | LG | GP | G | A | PTS | PIM |
|---|---|---|---|---|---|---|---|---|
| 1910–11 | 19 | Toronto Eaton's | OHA-Sr. | 2 | 4 | 0 | 4 | |
| 1911–12 | 20 | Toronto Eaton's | OHA-Sr. | 4 | 3 | 0 | 3 | 12 |
| 1912–13 | 21 | Toronto St. Michael's | OHA-Sr. | 4 | 4 | 0 | 4 | |
| 1913–14 | 22 | Toronto St. Michael's | OHA-Sr. | 2 | 3 | 0 | 3 | |
| Career – 4 Seasons | | | | 12 | 14 | 0 | 14 | 12 |

# Ernie Russell  Profile: See page 382

### REGULAR SEASON

| SEASON | AGE | TEAM | LG | GP | G | A | PTS | PIM |
|---|---|---|---|---|---|---|---|---|
| 1904–05 | 21 | Montreal AAA | CAHL | 8 | 11 | 0 | 11 | |
| 1905–06 | 22 | Montreal Wanderers | ECAHA | 6 | 21 | 0 | 21 | 13 |
| 1906–07 | 23 | Montreal Wanderers | ECAHA | 9 | 43 | 0 | 43 | 26 |
| 1907–08 | 24 | Montreal Wanderers | ECHA | 9 | 20 | 0 | 20 | 37 |
| 1909–10 | 26 | Montreal Wanderers | NHA | 13 | 35 | 0 | 35 | 57 |
| 1910–11 | 27 | Montreal Wanderers | NHA | 11 | 18 | 0 | 18 | 56 |
| 1911–12 | 28 | Montreal Wanderers | NHA | 18 | 27 | 0 | 27 | 110 |
| 1912–13 | 29 | Montreal Wanderers | NHA | 15 | 7 | 0 | 7 | 48 |
| 1913–14 | 30 | Montreal Wanderers | NHA | 12 | 2 | 4 | 6 | 21 |
| Careers – 9 Seasons | | | | 101 | 184 | 4 | 188 | 368 |

### PLAYOFFS

| SEASON | AGE | TEAM | LG | GP | G | A | PTS | PIM |
|---|---|---|---|---|---|---|---|---|
| 1905–06 | 22 | Montreal Wanderers | St-Cup | 2 | 4 | 0 | 4 | 6 |
| 1906–07 | 23 | Montreal Wanderers | St-Cup | 5 | 12 | 0 | 12 | 35 |
| 1907–08 | 24 | Montreal Wanderers | St-Cup | 3 | 11 | 0 | 11 | 7 |
| 1909–10 | 26 | Montreal Wanderers | St-Cup | 1 | 4 | 0 | 4 | 3 |
| Career – 4 Seasons | | | | 11 | 31 | 0 | 31 | 51 |

## Bruce Stuart  Profile: See page 383

### REGULAR SEASON

| SEASON | AGE | TEAM | LG | GP | G | A | PTS | PIM |
|---|---|---|---|---|---|---|---|---|
| 1898–99 | 17 | Ottawa Hockey Club | CAHL | 1 | 1 | 0 | 1 | |
| 1899–00 | 18 | Ottawa Hockey Club | CAHL | 5 | 11 | 0 | 11 | |
| 1900–01 | 19 | Quebec Bulldogs | CAHL | 6 | 5 | 0 | 5 | |
| 1901–02 | 20 | Ottawa Hockey Club | CAHL | 8 | 9 | 0 | 9 | |
| 1902–03 | 21 | Pittsburgh Victorias | WPHL | 10 | 16 | 6 | 22 | 20 |
| 1903–04 | 22 | Portage Lakes | Exhib. | 14 | 44 | 0 | 44 | 6 |
| 1904–05 | 23 | Portage Lakes | IHL | 22 | 33 | 0 | 33 | 59 |
| 1905–06 | 24 | Portage Lakes | IHL | 20 | 15 | 0 | 15 | 22 |
| 1906–07 | 25 | Portage Lakes | IHL | 23 | 20 | 9 | 29 | 81 |
| 1907–08 | 26 | Montreal Wanderers | ECAHA | 3 | 3 | 0 | 3 | 18 |
| 1908–09 | 27 | Ottawa Senators | ECHA | 11 | 22 | 0 | 22 | 30 |

### REGULAR SEASON

| SEASON | AGE | TEAM | LG | GP | G | A | PTS | PIM |
|---|---|---|---|---|---|---|---|---|
| 1909–10 | 28 | Ottawa Senators | CHA | 2 | 4 | 0 | 4 | 0 |
| 1909–10 | 28 | Ottawa Senators | NHA | 7 | 14 | 0 | 14 | 17 |
| 1910–11 | 29 | Ottawa Senators | NHA | 3 | 0 | 0 | 0 | 0 |
| Career – 13 Seasons | | | | 135 | 197 | 15 | 212 | 253 |

### PLAYOFFS

| SEASON | AGE | TEAM | LG | GP | G | A | PTS | PIM |
|---|---|---|---|---|---|---|---|---|
| 1903–04 | 22 | Portage Lakes | Exhib. | 9 | 28 | 0 | 28 | 13 |
| 1907–08 | 26 | Montreal Wanderers | St-Cup | 3 | 8 | 0 | 8 | 18 |
| 1909–10 | 28 | Ottawa Senators | St-Cup | 4 | 10 | 0 | 10 | 6 |
| Career – 3 Seasons | | | | 16 | 46 | 0 | 46 | 37 |

## Cyclone Taylor  Profile: See page 384

### REGULAR SEASON

| SEASON | AGE | TEAM | LG | GP | G | A | PTS | PIM |
|---|---|---|---|---|---|---|---|---|
| 1905–06 | 21 | Portage la Prairie | MHL | 4 | 3 | 1 | 4 | |
| 1905–06 | 21 | Portage Lakes | IHL | 6 | 11 | 0 | 11 | 4 |
| 1906–07 | 22 | Portage Lakes | IHL | 23 | 18 | 7 | 25 | 31 |
| 1907–08 | 23 | Ottawa Senators | ECAHA | 10 | 9 | 0 | 9 | 40 |
| 1908–09 | 24 | Pittsburgh Professionals | WPHL | 3 | 0 | 0 | 0 | |
| 1908–09 | 24 | Ottawa Senators | ECHA | 11 | 9 | 0 | 9 | 28 |
| 1909–10 | 25 | Renfrew Hockey Club | NHA | 13 | 10 | 0 | 10 | 19 |
| 1910–11 | 26 | Renfrew Hockey Club | NHA | 16 | 12 | 0 | 12 | 21 |
| 1911–12 | 27 | Ottawa Senators | NHA | 1 | 0 | 0 | 0 | 0 |
| 1912–13 | 28 | Vancouver Millionaires | PCHA | 14 | 10 | 8 | 18 | 5 |
| 1913–14 | 29 | Vancouver Millionaires | PCHA | 16 | 24 | 15 | 39 | 18 |
| 1914–15 | 30 | Vancouver Millionaires | PCHA | 16 | 23 | 22 | 45 | 9 |
| 1915–16 | 31 | Vancouver Millionaires | PCHA | 18 | 22 | 13 | 35 | 9 |
| 1916–17 | 32 | Vancouver Millionaires | PCHA | 11 | 14 | 15 | 29 | 12 |
| 1917–18 | 33 | Vancouver Millionaires | PCHA | 18 | 32 | 11 | 43 | 0 |

### REGULAR SEASON

| SEASON | AGE | TEAM | LG | GP | G | A | PTS | PIM |
|---|---|---|---|---|---|---|---|---|
| 1918–19 | 34 | Vancouver Millionaires | PCHA | 20 | 23 | 13 | 36 | 12 |
| 1919–20 | 35 | Vancouver Millionaires | PCHA | 10 | 6 | 6 | 12 | 0 |
| 1920–21 | 36 | Vancouver Millionaires | PCHA | 6 | 5 | 1 | 6 | 0 |
| 1922–23 | 38 | Vancouver Maroons | PCHA | 1 | 0 | 0 | 0 | 0 |
| Career – 17 Seasons | | | | 217 | 231 | 112 | 343 | 208 |

### PLAYOFFS

| SEASON | AGE | TEAM | LG | GP | G | A | PTS | PIM |
|---|---|---|---|---|---|---|---|---|
| 1914–15 | 30 | Vancouver Millionaires | St-Cup | 3 | 8 | 2 | 10 | 3 |
| 1917–18 | 33 | Vancouver Millionaires | PCHA | 2 | 0 | 1 | 1 | 0 |
| 1917–18 | 33 | Vancouver Millionaires | St-Cup | 5 | 9 | 0 | 9 | 15 |
| 1918–19 | 34 | Vancouver Millionaires | PCHA | 2 | 1 | 0 | 1 | 0 |
| 1919–20 | 35 | Vancouver Millionaires | PCHA | 2 | 0 | 0 | 0 | 0 |
| 1920–21 | 36 | Vancouver Millionaires | PCHA | 2 | 0 | 0 | 0 | 0 |
| 1920–21 | 36 | Vancouver Millionaires | St-Cup | 2 | 0 | 1 | 1 | 5 |
| Career – 5 Seasons | | | | 19 | 18 | 4 | 22 | 23 |

## Harry Westwick  Profile: See page 386

### REGULAR SEASON

| SEASON | AGE | TEAM | LG | GP | G | A | PTS | PIM |
|---|---|---|---|---|---|---|---|---|
| 1894–95 | 18 | Ottawa Hockey Club | AHAC | 5 | 1 | 0 | 1 | |
| 1895–96 | 19 | Ottawa Hockey Club | AHAC | 8 | 8 | 0 | 8 | |
| 1896–97 | 20 | Ottawa Hockey Club | AHAC | 8 | 6 | 0 | 6 | |
| 1897–98 | 21 | Ottawa Hockey Club | AHAC | 5 | 1 | 0 | 1 | |
| 1899–00 | 23 | Ottawa Capitals | OHA-Sr. | | | | | |
| 1900–01 | 24 | Ottawa Hockey Club | CAHL | 7 | 6 | 0 | 6 | |
| 1901–02 | 25 | Ottawa Hockey Club | CAHL | 8 | 11 | 0 | 11 | 6 |
| 1902–03 | 26 | Ottawa Silver Seven | CAHL | 6 | 6 | 0 | 6 | 9 |
| 1903–04 | 27 | Ottawa Silver Seven | CAHL | 2 | 5 | 0 | 5 | 0 |
| 1904–05 | 28 | Ottawa Silver Seven | FAHL | 8 | 15 | 0 | 15 | 9 |
| 1905–06 | 29 | Ottawa Silver Seven | ECAHA | 8 | 6 | 0 | 6 | 15 |
| 1906–07 | 30 | Ottawa Senators | ECAHA | 9 | 14 | 0 | 14 | 12 |
| 1906–07 | 30 | Kenora Thistles | MHL-Pro | 1 | 0 | 0 | 0 | 0 |

### REGULAR SEASON

| SEASON | AGE | TEAM | LG | GP | G | A | PTS | PIM |
|---|---|---|---|---|---|---|---|---|
| 1907–08 | 31 | Ottawa Senators | ECAHA | 10 | 10 | 0 | 10 | 20 |
| 1908–09 | 32 | Ottawa Senators | ECHA | 6 | 3 | 0 | 3 | 8 |
| Career – 14 Seasons | | | | 91 | 92 | 0 | 92 | 79 |

### PLAYOFFS

| SEASON | AGE | TEAM | LG | GP | G | A | PTS | PIM |
|---|---|---|---|---|---|---|---|---|
| 1902–03 | 26 | Ottawa Silver Seven | CAHL | 1 | 0 | 0 | 0 | 0 |
| 1903–04 | 27 | Ottawa Silver Seven | St-Cup | 8 | 6 | 0 | 6 | 6 |
| 1904–05 | 28 | Ottawa Silver Seven | St-Cup | 5 | 9 | 0 | 9 | 3 |
| 1905–06 | 29 | Ottawa Silver Seven | ECAHA | 2 | 1 | 0 | 1 | 0 |
| 1905–06 | 29 | Ottawa Silver Seven | St-Cup | 4 | 7 | 0 | 7 | 9 |
| 1906–07 | 30 | Kenora Thistles | MHL-Pro | 2 | 2 | 0 | 2 | 6 |
| 1906–07 | 30 | Kenora Thistles | St-Cup | 2 | 0 | 0 | 0 | 6 |
| Career – 5 Seasons | | | | 24 | 25 | 0 | 25 | 30 |

## Fred Whitcroft  Profile: See page 387

### REGULAR SEASON

| SEASON | AGE | TEAM | LG | GP | G | A | PTS | PIM |
|---|---|---|---|---|---|---|---|---|
| 1902–03 | 20 | Peterborough Colts | OHA-Int. | | | | | |
| 1903–04 | 21 | Peterborough Colts | OHA-Int. | | | | | |
| 1904–05 | 22 | Midland Hockey Club | OHA-Int. | | | | | |
| 1905–06 | 23 | Peterborough Colts | OHA-Int. | | | | | |
| 1906–07 | 24 | Peterborough Colts | OHA-Int. | 5 | 13 | 0 | 13 | 33 |
| 1906–07 | 24 | Kenora Thistles | MHL-Pro | 4 | 3 | 0 | 3 | |
| 1907–08 | 25 | Edmonton Professionals | APHL | 10 | 35 | 7 | 42 | 12 |
| 1908–09 | 26 | Edmonton Professionals | Exhib. | 10 | 27 | 0 | 27 | 12 |
| 1909–10 | 27 | Renfrew Hockey Club | NHA | 5 | 3 | 0 | 3 | 13 |
| Career – 8 Seasons | | | | 34 | 81 | 7 | 88 | 70 |

### PLAYOFFS

| SEASON | AGE | TEAM | LG | GP | G | A | PTS | PIM |
|---|---|---|---|---|---|---|---|---|
| 1906–07 | 24 | Kenora Thistles | MHL-Pro | 2 | 5 | 0 | 5 | 0 |
| 1906–07 | 24 | Kenora Thistles | St-Cup | 2 | 2 | 0 | 2 | 3 |
| 1907–08 | 25 | Edmonton Professionals | APHL | 8 | 24 | 7 | 31 | 12 |
| 1908–09 | 26 | Edmonton Professionals | Exhib. | 7 | 19 | 0 | 19 | 14 |
| 1908–09 | 27 | Edmonton Professionals | St-Cup | 2 | 2 | 0 | 2 | 18 |
| 1909–10 | 28 | Edmonton Professionals | St-Cup | 2 | 5 | 0 | 5 | 2 |
| Career – 4 Seasons | | | | 23 | 57 | 7 | 64 | 49 |

# Player Profile Index